THE
WRITE
HANDBOOK
2006

Barry Turner has worked on both sides of publishing, as an editor and marketing director and as an author. He started his career as a journalist with *The Observer* before moving on to television and radio. He has written over twenty books including *A Place in the Country,* which inspired a television series, and a best-selling biography of the actor Richard Burton.

His recent work includes *Countdown to Victory,* a book about the last months of World War II, a radio play, travel articles, serialising books for *The Times,* editing the magazine *Country* and writing a one-man show based on the life of the legendary theatre critic James Agate. Barry has been editor of *The Writer's Handbook* for nineteen years and editor of *The Statesman's Yearbook* for eight.

THE
WRITER'S
HANDBOOK
2006

EDITOR
BARRY TURNER

MACMILLAN

First published 2005 by Macmillan
an imprint of Pan Macmillan Ltd
Pan Macmillan, 20 New Wharf Road,
London N1 9RR
Basingstoke and Oxford
Associated companies throughout the world
www.panmacmillan.com

ISBN 1 4050 4154 4

Copyright © Macmillan Publishers Ltd 2005

The right of Barry Turner to be identified as the
editor of this work has been asserted by him in accordance
with the Copyright, Design and Patents Act 1988.

All rights reserved. No part of this publication may be
reproduced, stored in or introduced into a retrieval system, or
transmitted, in any form, or by any means (electronic, mechanical,
photocopying, recording or otherwise) without the prior written
permission of the publisher. Any person who does any unauthorized
act in relation to this publication may be liable to criminal
prosecution and civil claims for damages.

9 8 7 6 5 4 3 2 1

Inclusion in *The Writer's Handbook* is entirely at the editor's discretion. Macmillan Publishers
Ltd makes no recommendation whatsoever by the inclusion or omission of any agency,
publisher or organisation.

While every effort has been made to ensure all of the information contained in this
publication is correct and accurate, the publisher cannot accept any responsibility for any
omission or errors that may occur or for any consequences arising therefrom.

A CIP catalogue record for this book is available from
the British Library

Credits
Editor *Barry Turner*
Editorial Assistants *Jill Fenner, Kenneth Hadley, Kyra Williams*
Poetry Editor *Peter Finch*
Contributors *Craig McGill*
             Bob G. Ritchie
             Andrew S. Walsh
Tax and Finance Adviser *Ian Spring*

Typeset by Heronwood Press, Medstead, Hants
Printed and bound in Great Britain by Mackays of Chatham plc, Kent

This book is sold subject to the condition that it shall not, by way of trade
or otherwise, be lent, re-sold, hired out, or otherwise circulated without
the publisher's prior consent in any form of binding or cover other than
that in which it is published and without a similar condition including
this condition being imposed on the subsequent purchaser.

Contents

Spreading the Word

*Barry Turner suggests ways for non-fiction writers
to raise their earning power*

It takes more than writing to write non-fiction. In fact, putting the words on paper is a doddle compared to the time and effort that goes into researching what to say and the order in which to say it.

Consider, for example, the biography of a major historical figure, Nelson, say, or Wellington. Even assuming a fair amount of background knowledge, the reading of secondary sources alone can take months. Then there is the search for original material – the hitherto unpublished letters and diaries that can give the author that essential edge over the competition. Discounting the lucky break (a bundle of incriminating correspondence found in an old trunk), trawling through the archives for something new to say can be like trying to find a plumber in an emergency. It is when the search proves less than fruitful that pitiful screams can be heard from dark corners of subterranean vaults and heretical thoughts occur to the sufferer like, why didn't I apply for that job as a parking attendant?

Once recovered from the crisis of confidence and having acquired a line of filing cabinets containing new or newish information, enough anyway to give the book a revisionist slant, the real work begins. No, not the writing, not yet. Before the words can flow, there is the business of sorting the material into an order that makes sense to the writer and, hopefully, to the reader. This stage in the critical curve of non-fiction has the author sitting on the living-room floor surrounded by little heaps of paper which are shuffled about in an ever desperate cycle of incomprehension. Frustration is expressed in muttered expletives too obscene for a family publication.

Only now does the writing begin. With such agony of creativity it might come as a surprise to find that in nearly all categories of non-fiction, biography and popular history in particular, more titles are published than ever before. How so? This is where we get to the good news. While the ability to write a compelling story rests on a combination of native talent and hard slog (thus far there is no difference between fiction and non-fiction) the effort involved in researching hard facts has been lightened by the channels of communication opened up by the World Wide Web.

Fast rewind to the search for secondary sources. Time was when the writer made for the nearest city library. A thick notepad and an inexhaustible supply of biros were among the essential accessories. Books that were out on loan or in store could take an age to recover. When the Reading Room at the British Museum catered for researchers, a week or more could pass before requested titles arrived from a warehouse somewhere in the countryside. Today, however, the British Library near King's Cross (see pages 630–633), successor to the Reading Room, is a model of efficiency. To find out what is available, you do not even have to move from your home computer. An 'integrated catalogue' website gives access to over 12 million items. All this comes free of charge. By the time this article appears, reader pass holders will be able to log in to reserve books.

At the wonderful London Library in St James's Square (see page 643) where all books can be taken out on loan, it is the simplest matter to call up volumes by e-mail which are then set aside for collection for up to two weeks.

Most city and university libraries have websites offering a range of services. In Birmingham, for example, the online catalogue for books, journals and newspapers also gives access to catalogues of other libraries in the Midlands as well as a link to the UK public libraries page, which lists websites for public libraries throughout the country. It helps too that the libraries themselves have become more attractive places to work in, a sea change from the days when hard seats and rough desks might have come from a job lot in a monastery sale.

If overseas research is involved it is always worth checking what can be seen on screen. Authors who used to waste many valuable writing hours thirty thousand feet above ground, jetting from one information source to another, find they can save money and energy by first exploring the Internet.

Search engines, such as Google, help to supplement library services. Although there is no discrimination between genuine enlightenment and looney tunes or unadulterated propaganda, the sheer range of material available is staggering. Earlier in this article the names of Nelson and Wellington were invoked. The first has 325,000 references on the net; the second, more than 400,000. One way of the separating the good stuff from the rubbish is to use Google Scholar which covers papers, theses, books, pre-prints, abstracts and technical reports from all conceivable areas of research. Since many of these documents have e-mail addresses attached, the prospects open up of fruitful discussions or interviews that might otherwise have had to be conducted by letter or telephone.

Whatever the topic under investigation, there are always books that are so critical they have to be bought. Since the chances are that they are out of print, resort must be made to the second-hand market. This used to present problems. However much writers love to browse along the dusty shelves of antiquarian shops, relying on serendipity, the frustration of not finding the elusive volumes can be intense. Remember those book-search columns in the weekly journals with their lists of last-ditch appeals? 'If anyone has a copy of such and such, *please* contact …' They still exist but with a much reduced clientele, for today we have AbeBooks, Alibris and Amazon, all of which encompass an international network of dealers. In recent instances, I have had a title sent from Auckland and another from Copenhagen. It is hard to imagine how either would have been acquired but for the Internet.

What about the expense? Certainly, book buying on any scale can damage the bank balance but there is always the prospect of returning to the second-hand market, this time as a seller. It could even be that a collection on a particular subject will have added value.

Some labour savers have become so much part of a writer's life that it is easy to forget how short a time they have been around. The photocopier is a good example. Some twenty years ago, I wrote a script for a video for a management course in which two IT companies (though we did not call them that in those days) battled it out to be the first to produce a compact, affordable copier for the mass market. I was told by the people who were supposed to know about these things, that my creative imagination was out of control. Who could possibly believe such a fanciful concept? Well, here we are with copiers, if not in every home, at least in every office and within easy access for every writer. Secondary sources, in fact all sources, are so much easier to manage when you can reproduce the few relevant pages from a doorstop-sized volume. And there is no need to feel guilty about infringing copyright. The Authors' Licensing and Collecting Society (ALCS, see page 505) has a deal with libraries and academic institutions which allows for the collection and distribution to authors of licensing fees for photocopying.

But top of the list of time savers, and here technology is a secondary factor, are the researchers. It is one of the safe assumptions of non-fiction writing that the greater the fame of the author, the more reluctant they are to admit to employing researchers. But used they are and to good effect. Professional researchers do not come cheaply and I can hear the plaintive 'if only' cry from authors on small advances. But writing is a business like any other. Investment in skilled research can save precious hours that need to go into the next project which, building on success, will persuade the publisher to be more generous with up-front money. What the marketing director wants most is an author he can build into a bestseller. For that he needs a succession of titles at neatly paced intervals. Only then do the rewards justify the effort.

The truth is this. With the ever gathering pace of the IT revolution, professional writers, by which I mean those who earn a decent living, cannot afford to ignore the opportunities to improve their act. Those who do will be lucky to get published at all.

UK Publishers

AA Publishing
The Automobile Association, Fanum House, Basingstoke RG21 4EA
☎01256 491573   Fax 01256 491974
✉ simon.davies@theAA.com
www.theAA.com
Managing Director *Stephen Mesquita*
Manager, Publishing *Simon Davies*
Publishes maps, atlases and guidebooks, motoring, travel and leisure. Since 2005, also children's books. About 100 titles a year.

Abacus
See **Time Warner Books UK**

ABC-Clio
26 Beaumont Street, Oxford OX1 2NP
☎01865 517222   Fax 01865 517228
✉ salesuk@abc-clio.com
www.abc-clio.com
Formerly Clio Press Ltd. Publishes academic and general reference works, social sciences and humanities. Markets, outside North America, the Web and reference books of the American parent company.
ROYALTIES twice-yearly.

Absolute Press
Scarborough House, 29 James Street West, Bath BA1 2BT
☎01225 316013   Fax 01225 445836
✉ sales@absolutepress.demon.co.uk
www.absolutepress.demon.co.uk
Managing/Editorial Director *Jon Croft*
Founded 1979. Publishes food and wine-related subjects. About 15 titles a year. No unsolicited mss. Synopses and ideas for books welcome.
ROYALTIES twice-yearly.

Abson Books London
5 Sidney Square, London E1 2EY
☎020 7790 4737   Fax 020 7790 7346
✉ absonbooks@aol.com
www.absonbooks.co.uk
Publisher *M.J. Ellison*
Founded 1971 in Bristol. Publishes language glossaries and curiosities. TITLES *Prison Slang*;

Gay Slang. No unsolicited mss; synopses and ideas for books welcome.
ROYALTIES twice-yearly.

Academic Press
See **Elsevier Ltd**

Acair Ltd
Unit 7, 7 James Street, Stornoway, Isle of Lewis HS1 2QN
☎01851 703020   Fax 01851 703294
✉ info@acairbooks.com
www.acairbooks.com
Specialising in matters pertaining to the Gaidhealtachd, Acair publishes books in Gaelic and English on Scottish history, culture and the Gaelic language. 75% of their children's books are targeted at primary school usage and are published exclusively in Gaelic.
ROYALTIES twice-yearly.

Acumen Publishing Limited
15A Lewins Yard, East Street, Chesham HP5 1HQ
☎01494 794398   Fax 01494 784850
✉ steven.gerrard@acumenpublishing.co.uk
www.acumenpublishing.co.uk
Managing Director *Steven Gerrard*
Founded in 1998 as an independent publisher for the higher education market. Publishes academic books on philosophy, history and politics. 15 titles in 2004. No unsolicited mss. Synopses and ideas for books welcome; send written proposal as per Acumen guidelines.
ROYALTIES annually.

Addison Wesley
See **Pearson Education**

Adlard Coles Nautical
See **A.&C. Black Publishers Ltd**

African Books Collective
Unit 13, Kings Meadow, Ferry Hinksey Road, Oxford OX2 0DP
☎01865 726686   Fax 01865 793298
✉ abc@africanbookscollective.com
www.africanbookscollective.com
Founded 1990. Collectively owned by its 17

founder publishers. Exclusive distribution in North America, UK, Europe and Commonwealth countries outside Africa for 100 African participating publishers. Concentration is on scholarly/academic, literature and children's books. Mainly concerned with the promotion and dissemination of African-published material outside Africa. Supplies African-published books to African libraries and organisations, and publishes resource books on African publishing. TITLES *The African Writers' Handbook*; *African Publishers Networking Directory*; *The Electronic African Bookworm: A Web Navigator*; *Courage and Consequence: Women Publishing in Africa*.

Age Concern Books
1268 London Road, London SW16 4ER
☎020 8765 7200   Fax 020 8765 7211
✉ books@ace.org.uk
www.ageconcern.org.uk
Approx. Annual Turnover £400,000+

Publishing arm of Age Concern England. Publishes related non-fiction only. No fiction. About 18 titles a year. Synopses and ideas welcome for new practical handbooks.

Airlife Publishing
See **The Crowood Press Ltd**

Ian Allan Publishing Ltd
Riverdene Business Park, Molesey Road, Hersham KT12 4RG
☎01932 266600   Fax 01932 266601
✉ info@ianallanpub.co.uk
www.ianallanpublishing.com
Chairman *David Allan*
Managing Director *Tony Saunders*

Specialist transport publisher – atlases, maps, railway, aviation, road transport, military, maritime, reference. Manages distribution and sales for third party publishers. IMPRINTS **Midland Publishing** (see entry); **Classic Publications**; **OPC** Railway titles. About 120 titles a year. Send sample chapter and synopsis with s.a.e

J.A. Allen & Co.
An imprint of Robert Hale Ltd, Clerkenwell House, 45–47 Clerkenwell Green, London EC1R 0HT
☎020 7251 2661   Fax 020 7490 4958
✉ allen@halebooks.com
Publisher *Caroline Burt*
Approx. Annual Turnover £1 million

Founded 1926 as part of J.A. Allen & Co. (The Horseman's Bookshop) Ltd. Bought by **Robert**

Hale Ltd in 1999. Publishes equine and equestrian non-fiction. About 20 titles a year. Mostly commissioned but willing to consider unsolicited mss of technical/instructional material related to all aspects of horses and horsemanship.
ROYALTIES twice-yearly.

Allen Lane
See **Penguin Group (UK)**

Allison & Busby
Suite 111, Bon Marche Centre, 241 Ferndale Road, London SW9 8BJ
☎020 7738 7888   Fax 020 7733 4344
✉ all@allisonbusby.co.uk
www.allisonandbusby.com
Publishing Director *Susie Dunlop*
Approx. Annual Turnover £815,893

Founded 1967. Publishes literary fiction, crime fiction, biography and writers' guides. TITLES *The Best British Mysteries* ed. Maxim Jakubowski; *Bushwhacked: Life in George W. Bush's America* Molly Ivins; *Blue Angel* Francine Prose. About 40 titles a year. No unsolicited mss. No replies without s.a.e.

Authors' Rating 'A testament to the ability of smaller publishers to survive in the retail jungle' (*Publishing News*), A&B is putting its effort into promoting lead titles with crime at the top of the list.

Alpha Press
See **Sussex Academic Press**

Alton Douglas Books
See **Brewin Books Ltd**

Amber Lane Press Ltd
Cheorl House, Church Street, Charlbury OX7 3PR
☎01608 810024   Fax 01608 810024
✉ info@amberlanepress.co.uk
www.amberlanepress.co.uk
Chairman *Brian Clark*
Managing Director/Editorial Head *Judith Scott*

Founded 1979 to publish modern play texts. Publishes plays and books on the theatre. TITLES *Whose Life is it Anyway?* Brian Clark; *The Dresser* Ronald Harwood; *Once a Catholic* Mary O'Malley (play texts); *Strindberg and Love* Eivor Martinus. About 4 titles a year. 'Expressly *not* interested in poetry.' No unsolicited mss.
ROYALTIES twice-yearly.

Amsco
See **Omnibus Press**

Andersen Press Ltd

20 Vauxhall Bridge Road, London SW1V 2SA
☎020 7840 8703/8700   Fax 020 7233 6263
✉ andersenpress@randomhouse.co.uk
www.andersenpress.co.uk

Managing Director/Publisher *Klaus Flugge*
Editorial Director *Rona Selby*
Editor, Fiction *Audrey Adams*

Founded 1976 by Klaus Flugge and named after
Hans Christian Andersen. Publishes children's
high-quality picture books and fiction sold in
association with **Random House Children's
Books**. Seventy per cent of the books are sold
as co-productions abroad. TITLES *Elmer* David
McKee; *I Want My Potty* Tony Ross; *little.com*
Ralph Steadman; *Cat in the Manger* Michael
Foreman; *Preston Pig Books* Colin McNaughton;
Junk Melvin Burgess; *You* Sandra Glover; *I Love
You, Blue Kangaroo* Emma Chichester Clark.
Unsolicited mss welcome for picture books;
synopsis in the first instance for books for young
readers up to age 12. No poetry or short stories.
ROYALTIES twice-yearly.

Authors' Rating The secret of Andersen's success is publishing children's books that are loved
by adults. That and a wicked sense of fun that
has been known to upset the education establishment – and hooray for that.

Chris Andrews Publications

15 Curtis Yard, North Hinksey Lane, Oxford
OX2 0LX
☎01865 723404   Fax 01865 725294
✉ chris.andrews1@btclick.com
www.cap-ox.co.uk

Managing Director *Chris Andrews*

Founded 1982. Publishes coffee-table, scenic
travel guides. Also calendars, diaries, cards and
posters. TITLES *Romance of Oxford; Romance of
the Cotswolds; Romance of the Thames & Chilterns.*
Also owns the **Oxford Picture Library** (see
entry under *Picture Libraries*). Unsolicited synopses and ideas for travel/guide books in the
areas listed above will be considered; phone in
the first instance.

Andromeda Children's Books

See **Pinwheel Limited**

The Angels' Share

See **Neil Wilson Publishing Ltd**

Anness Publishing Ltd

Hermes House, 88–89 Blackfriars Road,
London SE1 8HA

☎020 7401 2077   Fax 020 7633 9499
✉ info@anness.com
www.aquamarinebooks.com
www.lorenzbooks.com
www.southwaterbooks.com

Chairman/Managing Director *Paul Anness*
Publisher/Partner *Joanna Lorenz*

Founded 1989. Publishes highly illustrated co-
edition titles: general non-fiction – cookery,
crafts, interior design, gardening, photography,
decorating, lifestyle and children's. IMPRINTS
**Lorenz Books; Aquamarine; Hermes
House; Peony Press; Southwater**. About 500
titles a year.

Anthem Press

See **Wimbledon Publishing Company**

Antique Collectors' Club

Sandy Lane, Old Martlesham, Woodbridge
IP12 4SD
☎01394 389950   Fax 01394 389999
✉ sales@antique-acc.com
www.antiquecollectorsclub.com

Managing Director *Diana Steel*
Sales Director *Mark Eastment*

Founded 1966. Publishes specialist books on
antiques and collecting, the decorative arts,
architecture and gardening. The price guide
series was introduced in 1968 with the first edition of *The Price Guide to Antique Furniture.*
Subject areas include furniture, silver and gold,
metalwork, jewellery, glass, textiles, art reference, ceramics, horology. TITLES *Biba. The Biba
Experience* Alwyn Turner; *Understanding Jewellery*
David Bennett and Daniela Mascetti; *Margaret
Mee's Amazon. Diaries of an Artist Explorer.* Also
publishes subscription-only magazine, *Antique
Collecting*, published 10 times a year. Unsolicited
synopses and ideas for books welcome; no mss.
ROYALTIES twice-yearly as a rule, but can
vary.

Anvil Press Poetry Ltd

Neptune House, 70 Royal Hill, London
SE10 8RF
☎020 8469 3033   Fax 020 8469 3363
✉ anvil@anvilpresspoetry.com
www.anvilpresspoetry.com

Editorial Director *Peter Jay*

Founded 1968. England's oldest independent
publishing house dedicated to poetry. Publishes
new poets and translated classics. Contemporary
list includes Ros Barber, Martina Evans, Michael
Hamburger, Dennis O'Driscoll, A.B. Jackson,

Stanley Moss and Greta Stoddart. The backlist includes translations of Apollinaire, Baudelaire, Celan, Dante, Hikmet, Neuda, Tagore and Verlaine. Preliminary enquiry required for translations. Unsolicited book-length collections of poems are welcome from writers whose work has appeared in poetry magazines or literary journals. Please enclose adequate return postage.

Authors' Rating With a little help from the Arts Council, Anvil has become one of the foremost publishers of living poets.

Apollos
See **Inter-Varsity Press**

Apple
See **Quarto Publishing** under *UK Packagers*

Appletree Press Ltd
The Old Potato Station, 14 Howard Street South, Belfast BT7 1AP
☎028 9024 3074   Fax 028 9024 6756
✉ reception@appletree.ie
www.appletree.ie
Managing Director *John Murphy*
Founded 1974. Publishes cookery and other small-format gift books, plus general non-fiction of Irish and Scottish interest. TITLES *Little Cookbook* series (about 40 titles); *Ireland: The Complete Guide*. No unsolicited mss; send initial letter or synopsis.
ROYALTIES twice-yearly in the first year, annually thereafter.

Aquamarine
See **Anness Publishing Ltd**

Arc Publications
Nanholme Mill, Shaw Wood Road, Todmorden OL14 6DA
☎01706 812338   Fax 01706 818948
✉ arc.publications@btconnect.com
www.arcpublications.co.uk
Editorial Director *Tony Ward*
Associate Editors *John Kinsella* (International), *Jo Shapcott* (UK), *Jean Boase-Beier* (Translations), *Angela Jarman* (Music)
Founded in 1969 to specialise in the publication of contemporary poetry from new and established writers both in the UK and abroad. AUTHORS John Kinsella and Alison Croggan (Australia), Tony Curtis (Ireland), Bejan Matur (Turkey), Inna Lisnianskaya (Russia), Alamgir Hashmi (Pakistan), Elizabeth Smither and C.K. Stead (New Zealand), Donald Atkinson, Jackie

Wills, Julia Darling and Ivor Cutler (UK). IMPRINT **Arc Music** specialises in profiles of contemporary composers (particularly where none have existed hitherto) and symposia which take a 'new approach' to well-visited territory. Commissioned work only. About 25 titles a year. Authors submitting material should ensure that it is compatible with the current list, include a history of published works and enclose an s.a.e. if they wish mss to be returned. Electronic submissions are not accepted.
ROYALTIES as per contracts.

Arcadia Books
15–16 Nassau Street, London W1W 7AB
☎020 7436 9898   Fax 020 7436 9898
✉ info@arcadiabooks.co.uk
www.arcadiabooks.co.uk
Managing Director *Gary Pulsifer*
Publishing Director *Daniela de Groote*
Small, independent publishing house, founded in 1996, specialising in translated fiction from around the world. Winner of the *Sunday Times* Small Publisher of the Year Award 2002–03. Publishes literary fiction, gay fiction, biography, autobiography, gender studies, travel writing. TITLE *The Nick of Time* Francis King (longlisted for the 2003 **Man Booker Prize**). IMPRINT **Bliss Books** TITLE *The Real Diana* Lady Colin Campbell. Does not welcome unsolicited material.
ROYALTIES twice-yearly.

Authors' Rating A quality publisher that has great success with translated fiction.

Arcane
See **Sanctuary Books**

Architectural Press
See **Elsevier Ltd**

Ardis
See **Gerald Duckworth & Co. Ltd**

Argentum
See **Aurum Press Ltd**

Aris & Phillips
See **Oxbow Books**

Armchair Traveller
See **Haus Publishers**

Arrow
See **The Random House Group Ltd**

Artech House

46 Gillingham Street, London SW1V 1AH
☎020 7596 8750   Fax 020 7630 0166
✉ jlancashire@artechhouse.co.uk
www.artech-uk@artechhouse.com

Managing Director (USA) *William M. Bazzy*
Commissioning Editor *Tina Ruonamaa*

Founded 1969. European office of Artech House Inc., Boston. Publishes biomedical engineering, bioinformatics, nanotechnology, microwaves, radar, antennas and propagation, electro-magnetic analysis, wireless communications, telecommunications, space applications, remote sensing, solid state technology and devices, technology management. 60–70 titles a year. Unsolicited mss and synopses in the specialised areas listed are considered.
ROYALTIES twice-yearly.

Ashgate Publishing Ltd

Gower House, Croft Road, Aldershot
GU11 3HR
☎01252 331551
Fax 01252 317446 (Ashgate)/344405 (Gower)/
020 7837 6322 (Lund Humphries)
✉ info@ashgatepublishing.com
www.ashgate.com
www.gowerpub.com
www.lundhumphries.com

Chairman *Nigel Farrow*

Founded 1967. Publishes business and professional titles under the Gower imprint and humanities, social sciences, law and legal studies under the Ashgate imprint. In December 1999 acquired Lund Humphries, publisher of art books and exhibition catalogues. DIVISIONS **Ashgate** *Sarah Davies* Social sciences; *John Smedley* History/Variorum collected studies; *Heidi May* Music; *Erika Gaffney* Literary studies; *Tom Gray* History; *Sarah Lloyd* Theology and religious studies; *Paul Coulam* Philosophy; *John Hindley* Aviation studies. **Gower** *Jo Burges, Jonathan Norman* Business, management and training; *John Irwin* Law and legal studies. **Lund Humphries** *Lucy Myers.* Access the websites for information on submission of material.

Ashgrove Publishing

27 John Street, London WC1N 2BX
☎020 7831 5013   Fax 020 7831 5011
✉ gmo73@dial.pipex.com
www.ashgrovepublishing.com

Chairman/Managing Director *Brad Thompson*

Acquired by Hollydata Publishers in 1999, Ashgrove has been publishing for over 20 years.

Publishes mind, body, spirit, health, cookery, sports. 3 titles in 2004. No unsolicited mss; approach with letter and outline in the first instance.
ROYALTIES twice-yearly.

Ashmolean Museum Publications

Ashmolean Museum, Beaumont Street,
Oxford OX1 2PH
☎01865 278010   Fax 01865 278018
✉ publications@ashmus.ox.ac.uk
www.ashmol.ox.ac.uk

Contact *Declan McCarthy*

The Ashmolean Museum, which is wholly owned by Oxford University, was founded in 1683. The first publication appeared in 1890 but publishing did not really start in earnest until the 1960s. Publishes European and Oriental fine and applied arts, European archaeology and ancient history, Egyptology and numismatics, for both adult and children's markets. No fiction, American/African art, ethnography, modern art or post-medieval history. Most publications are based on and illustrated from the Museum's collections. About 8 titles a year. No unsolicited mss.
ROYALTIES annually.

Atlantic Books

26–27 Boswell Street, London WC1N 3JZ
☎020 7269 1617   Fax 020 7430 0916
✉ enquiries@groveatlantic.co.uk
www.groveatlantic.co.uk

Chairman *Morgan Entrekin*
Managing Director/Publisher *Toby Mundy*

Founded 2000. A subsidiary of **Grove/Atlantic Inc.** (see entry under *US Publishers*), New York. Publishes literary fiction, history, current affairs, autobiography, biography, politics and reference books. IMPRINT **Guardian/Observer Books** Editorial Head *Alice Hunt* TITLES *Guardian Media Directory; Guardian University Guide* (both annual). 70 titles in 2004. No unsolicited material.
ROYALTIES twice-yearly.

Authors' Rating The offshoot of US Grove/Atlantic has a reputation for punching above its weight. Clever marketing has a lot to do with it but it is marketing based on an instinct for what sells - still not the most common attribute in trade publishing.

Atlantic Europe Publishing Co. Ltd

Greys Court Farm, Greys Court, Nr Henley
on Thames RG9 4PG
☎01491 628188   Fax 01491 628189
✉ writers@atlanticeurope.com

www.AtlanticEurope.com
www.curriculumVisions.com

Directors *Dr B.J. Knapp, D.L.R. McCrae*

Closely associated, since 1990, with Earthscape Editions packaging operation. Publishes full-colour, highly illustrated children's non-fiction in hardback for international co-editions and text books. Not interested in any other material. Main focus is on National Curriculum titles, especially in the fields of mathematics, science, technology, social history and geography. About 50 titles a year. Unsolicited synopses and ideas for non-fiction curriculum-based books welcome by e-mail only – does not accept material sent by post.
FEES paid.

Atom
See **Time Warner Books UK**

Aurum Press Ltd
25 Bedford Avenue, London WC1B 3AT
☎020 7637 3225   Fax 020 7580 2469
✉ editorial@aurumpress.co.uk
www.aurumpress.co.uk

Managing Director *Bill McCreadie*
Editorial Director *Piers Burnett*
Approx. Annual Turnover £4 million

Founded 1976. Acquired by the Quarto Group in August 2004. Committed to producing high-quality, illustrated/non-illustrated adult non-fiction in the areas of general human interest, art and craft, lifestyle, sport and travel. IMPRINTS **Argentum** Practical photography books; **Jacqui Small** High-quality lifestyle books. About 70 titles a year.
ROYALTIES twice-yearly.

Authentic Media
9 Holdom Avenue, Bletchley, Milton Keynes MK1 1QR
☎01908 364204   Fax 01908 277169
www.authenticmedia.co.uk

Publishing Director *Mark Finnie*
Approx. Annual Turnover £2 million

A division of STL Ltd. IMPRINTS **Paternoster Press** Founded 1935. Editorial Coordinator *Lucy Atherton* Publishes academic, religion and learned/church/life-related journals. TITLES *After Christendom; Relational Leadership.* **Authentic Lifestyle** Founded 1966. Editorial Coordinator *Charlotte Hubback* Publishes Christian books on evangelism, discipleship and mission for Evangelical Alliance, Keswick Ministries, Icthus, Youth Work. Over 50 titles a year. Unsolicited mss, synopses and ideas for books welcome. No poetry.
ROYALTIES twice-yearly.

AuthorHouse UK
PO Box 7295, Milton Keynes MK13 8YJ
☎0800 197 4150   Fax 0800 197 4151
✉ info@authorhouse.co.uk
www.authorhouse.co.uk

President *Bryan Williams*
Vice President *W. Herbert Senft II*

Founded 1997. Publishes fiction, biography and memoirs, current affairs, history, politics, humour, travel, health, spirituality, sports and academic. Provides a comprehensive range of publishing and promotional services including editorial, design, production, distribution and marketing paid for by the author who retains editorial and creative control. Services range from Standard Paperback Publishing (£525) to a UK Advanced Press Release Package (£940). Authors retain full ownership and copyright and, assuming royalties are paid, choose their own rate from 5–20% on retail sales and 10–50% on direct sales. In the US, AuthorHouse has over 20,000 books in print by over 18,500 authors and over 2 million books printed. In the UK, it has helped over 200 authors get published.
ROYALTIES quarterly.

AuthorsOnline
40 Castle Street, Hertford SG14 1HR
☎0870 7500544   Fax 01480 382343
✉ theeditor@authorsonline.co.uk
www.authorsonline.co.uk

Submissions: Wayside, Downs Road, East Studdal CT15 5BZ Freephone 0800 107 2423

Owner *AuthorsOnLine Ltd.*
Managing Director *Richard Ovenden*
Editor *Richard Fitt*
Submissions Editor *Mrs W.A. Lake*
Approx. Annual Turnover £250,000

Founded 1998. A service for authors wishing to self-publish. Publishes new and reverted rights work in both electronic format via their website and traditional hard-copy. All genres welcome. Submit mss by e-mail or post (disk or CD-ROM) to the Submissions Editor at the East Studdal address above.

Autumn Publishing Ltd
Appledram Barns, Birdham Road, Chichester PO20 7EQ
☎01243 531660   Fax 01243 774433
✉ autumn@autumnpublishing.co.uk
www.autumnpublishing.co.uk

Managing Director *Michael Herridge*
Editorial Director *Lyn Coutts*

Founded 1976, part of the Bonnier Group. Publishes baby and toddler books, children's activity, sticker and early learning books. About 200 titles a year. No responsibility accepted for the return of unsolicited mss.

Authors' Rating The leading small publisher (along with **Little Tiger Press**) of children's books.

Award Publications Limited

1st Floor, 27 Longford Street, London NW1 3DZ
☎020 7388 7800   Fax 020 7388 7887
✉ info@awardpublications.co.uk

Founded 1958. Publishes children's books, both fiction and reference. IMPRINT **Horus Editions**. No unsolicited mss, synopses or ideas.

Azure

See **Society for Promoting Christian Knowledge**

Baillière Tindall

See **Elsevier Ltd**

Duncan Baird Publishers

Castle House, 75–76 Wells Street, London W1T 3QH
☎020 7323 2229   Fax 020 7580 5692
✉ info@dbairdpub.co.uk

Managing Director *Duncan Baird*
Editorial Director *Bob Saxton*
Approx. Annual Turnover £6 million

Founded in 1992 to publish and package co-editions overseas and went on to launch its own publishing operation in 1998. Publishes illustrated cultural reference, world religions, health, mind, body and spirit, lifestyle, graphic design. 45 titles in 2004. No unsolicited mss. Synopses and ideas welcome; approach in writing in the first instance with s.a.e. No fiction or UK-only subjects.
ROYALTIES twice-yearly.

Bantam/Bantam Press

See **Transworld Publishers**

Barefoot Books Ltd

124 Walcot Street, Bath BA1 5BG
☎01225 322400   Fax 01225 322499
✉ sales@barefootbooks.com
www.barefootbooks.com

Publisher *Tessa Strickland*

Founded in 1993. Publishes high-quality children's picture books, particularly new and traditional stories from a wide range of cultures. No unsolicited mss. See website for submission guidelines.
ROYALTIES twice-yearly.

Authors' Rating Writers of children's books would do well to keep track of Barefoot which, from small beginnings, is building a quality list that must be the envy of bigger publishers.

Barrington Stoke

Sandeman House, Trunk's Close, 55 High Street, Edinburgh EH1 1SR
☎0131 557 2020   Fax 0131 557 6060
✉ info@barringtonstoke.co.uk
www.barringtonstoke.co.uk

Chairman *David Croom*
Managing Director *Sonia Raphael*
Editorial Head *Anna Gibbons*
Approx. Annual Turnover £600,000

Founded in 1998 to publish books for 'reluctant, disenchanted and under-confident' young readers. Produces a series of audio books and issues teachers' notes to acccompany teenage fiction titles. DIVISIONS **4u2read.OK** for children aged 8–13 with a reading age below 8; **Fiction** for 8–13-year olds TITLES *Living With Vampires; Tod in Biker City*. **Teenage Fiction** TITLES *Runaway Teacher; No Stone Unturned*. Books commissioned via literary agents only. *No* unsolicited material.
ROYALTIES twice-yearly.

B.T. Batsford

See **Chrysalis Books Group**

BBC Books

Room A3100, BBC Worldwide Ltd, 80 Wood Lane, London W12 0TT
☎020 8433 2000   Fax 020 8749 0538
www.bbcworldwide.com

Director *Stuart Biles*

Publishes TV and radio tie-in titles including books which, though linked with BBC television or radio, may not simply be the 'book of the series'. TITLES *Delia's Vegetarian Collection; Rick Stein's Food Heroes; A History of Britain* Simon Schama; *Grumpy Old Men The Official Handbook; British Isles A Natural History* as well as TV personality autobiographies such as Terry Wogan and David Attenborough. 50 titles a year. Unsolicited mss are not accepted. However, strong ideas well expressed will always be considered, and promising letters stand a chance of further scrutiny.

ROYALTIES twice-yearly.

Authors' Rating Having scaled down its operation to around 50 new titles a year, nearly all directly related to television and radio output, BBC Books is once again looking for a joint venture deal that would maximise sales. One of the problems for BBC Books is that some of the biggest names at the BBC choose to sign up with rival publishers. Then again, with an increasing share of BBC output going to independent companies, the hold over particular programmes is getting weaker. BBC Books remains the leader in gardening, food and drink which BBC Audio book has the lion's share of that business.

BBC Children's Books
See **Penguin Group (UK)**

Beautiful Books Ltd
117 Sugden Road, London SW11 5ED
☎020 7738 2428   Fax 020 7223 4841
✉ office@beautiful-books.co.uk
www.beautiful-books.co.uk

Managing Director *Simon Petherick*
Approx. Annual Turnover £500,000

Founded 2004. Publishes adult and children's non-fiction. DIVISION **The Young Travellers Club** TITLE *Bonjour France!* Unsolicited mss, synopses and ideas welcome. Approach by letter in the first instance with outline and synopsis plus biographical information. No fiction.

Bedford Square Press
See **NCVO Publications**

Beeline
See **Blackstaff Press Ltd**

Belair
See **Folens Limited**

Berg Publishers
1st Floor, Angel Court, 81 St Clements Street, Oxford OX4 1AW
☎01865 245104   Fax 01865 791165
✉ enquiry@bergpublishers.com
www.bergpublishers.com

Editorial & Managing Director *Kathryn Earle*
Production Manager *Ken Bruce*

Publishes scholarly books in the fields of fashion, cultural studies, social sciences, history and humanities. TITLES *Cinema* Jean-Luc

Godard; *Hitler's Bounty Hunters* Ad van Liempt; *City of Panic* Paul Virilio; *The Latin American Fashion Reader* Regina Root; *The Intelligence of Evil or the Lucidity Pact* Jean Baudrillard. IMPRINT **Oswald Wolff Books**. About 65 titles a year plus five journals, *Fashion Theory, Home Cultures, Textile: The Journal of Cloth and Culture, Cultural Politics* and *Material Religion*. No unsolicited mss. Synopses and ideas for books welcome.

ROYALTIES annually.

Berghahn Books
3 Newtec Place, Magdalen Road, Oxford OX4 1RE
☎01865 250011   Fax 01865 250056
✉ publisher@berghahnbooks.com
www.berghahnbooks.com

Chairman/Managing Director *Marion Berghahn*
Approx. Annual Turnover £700,000

Founded 1994. Academic publisher of books and journals. TITLES *Imperial Germany, 1871–1918; Children of Palestine; Critical Interventions.* OVERSEAS ASSOCIATE Berghahn Books Inc., New York. About 90 titles a year. No unsolicited mss; will consider synopses and ideas for books. Approach by e-mail in the first instance. No fiction or trade books.

ROYALTIES annually.

Berlitz Publishing
58 Borough High Stret, London SE1 1XF
☎020 7403 0284   Fax 020 7403 0290
✉ berlitz@apaguide.co.uk
www.berlitzpublishing.com

Managing Director *Jeremy Westwood*

Founded 1970. Acquired by the Langenscheidt Publishing Group in February 2002. Publishes travel and language-learning products only: visual travel guides, phrasebooks and language courses. SERIES *Pocket Guides; Berlitz Complete Guide to Cruising and Cruise Ships; Phrase Books; Pocket Dictionaries; Business Phrase Books; Self-teach: Rush Hour Commuter Cassettes; Think & Talk; Berlitz Kids.* No unsolicited mss.

BeWrite Books
See entry under *Electronic Publishing and Other Services*

BFI Publishing
British Film Institute, 21 Stephen Street, London W1T 1LN
☎020 7255 1444   Fax 020 7636 2516
www.bfi.org.uk
Approx. Annual Turnover £600,000

Founded 1980. Part of the **British Film Institute**. Publishes academic, schools and general film/television-related books and resources. TITLE *The Cinema Book*, revised edition, eds. Pam Cook and Mieke Bernink. SERIES *Film Classics; BFI Screen Guides; Modern Classics; World Directors*. About 30 titles a year. E-mail submissions preferred.

ROYALTIES annually.

BFP Books

Focus House, 497 Green Lanes, London N13 4BP

☎020 8882 3315   Fax 020 8886 5174

✉ mail@thebfp.com

Chief Executive *John Tracy*

Commissioning Editor *Stewart Gibson*

Founded 1982. The publishing arm of the Bureau of Freelance Photographers. Publishes illustrated books on photography, mainly aspects of freelancing and marketing pictures. No unsolicited mss but ideas welcome.

Clive Bingley Books

See **Facet Publishing**

Birkbeck Law Press

See **Cavendish Publishing Limited**

Birlinn Ltd

West Newington House, 10 Newington Road, Edinburgh EH9 1QS

☎0131 668 4371   Fax 0131 668 4466

✉ info@birlinn.co.uk

www.birlinn.co.uk

Managing Editor *Hugh Andrew*

Founded 1992. Acquired **John Donald Publishers** in 1999 (see entry). Publishes local and military history, Gaelic, humour, Highland history, adventure, Scottish reference, guidebooks and folklore. Acquired **Polygon** in 2002 (see entry). 90 titles in 2004. No unsolicited mss; synopses and ideas welcome.

ROYALTIES paid.

Black & White Publishing Ltd

99 Giles Street, Edinburgh EH6 6BZ

☎0131 625 4500   Fax 0131 625 4501

✉ mail@blackandwhitepublishing.com

www.blackandwhitepublishing.com

Director *Campbell Brown*

Founded 1990. Publishes general fiction and non-fiction, including memoirs, sport, cookery, humour and guidebooks. IMPRINTS **Itchy Coo** Scots language resources for use in schools;

Chroma Literary fiction. Text only submissions via website, or synopsis and sample chapter by post with s.a.e. or return postage.

ROYALTIES twice-yearly.

A.&C. Black Publishers Ltd

Alderman House, 37 Soho Square, London W1D 3QZ

☎020 7758 0200   Fax 020 7758 0222

✉ enquiries@acblack.com

www.acblack.com

Chairman *Nigel Newton*

Managing Director *Jill Coleman*

Deputy Managing Director *Jonathan Glasspool*

Approx. Annual Turnover £11 million

Publishes children's and educational books, including music, for 3–15-year-olds, arts and crafts, ceramics, fishing, ornithology, nautical, reference, sport and theatre. Acquisitions brought the Herbert Press' art, design and general books, Adlard Coles' and Thomas Reed's sailing lists, plus *Reeds Nautical Almanac*, Christopher Helm, Pica Press and T&AD Poyser's natural history and ornithology lists into A.&C. Black's stable. Bought by **Bloomsbury Publishing** in May 2000. Owns *Whitaker's Almanack* and children's publisher Andrew Brodie Publications. IMPRINTS **Adlard Coles Nautical; Christopher Helm; The Herbert Press; Andrew Brodie; Chameleons.** TITLES *New Mermaid* drama series; *Who's Who; Writers' & Artists' Yearbook; Know the Game* sports series; *Rockets* and *Black Cats* children's series. Initial enquiry appreciated before submission of mss.

PAYMENT varies according to contract.

Black Ace Books

PO Box 6557, Forfar DD8 2YS

☎01307 465096   Fax 01307 465494

www.blackacebooks.com

Managing Director *Hunter Steele*

Founded 1991. Publishes new fiction, Scottish and general; some non-fiction including biography, history, philosophy and psychology. IMPRINTS **Black Ace Books; Black Ace Paperbacks** TITLES *Succeeding at Sex and Scotland, Or the Case of Louis Morel* Hunter Steele; *La Tendresse* Ken Strauss MD; *Count Dracula (The Authorized Version)* Hagen Slawkberg; *Caryddwen's Cauldron* Paul Hilton; *The Sinister Cabaret* John Herdman. No children's, poetry, cookery, DIY, religion. 36 titles in print. 'No submissions at all, please, without first checking our website for details of current requirements and submission guidelines.'

ROYALTIES twice-yearly.

Black Lace
See **Virgin Books Ltd**

Black Spring Press Ltd
Curtain House, 134–146 Curtain Road,
London EC2A 3AR
☎020 7613 3066   Fax 020 7613 0028
✉ general@blackspringpress.co.uk
Directors *Robert Hastings, Alexander Hastings*
Founded 1986. Publishes fiction and non-fiction,
literary criticism, biography. TITLES *The Lost
Weekend* Charles Jackson; *The Big Brass Ring*
Orson Welles; *The Tenant* Roland Topor; *Julian
Maclaren-Ross Collected Memoirs*. About 5 titles a
year. No unsolicited mss.
ROYALTIES annually.

Black Swan
See **Transworld Publishers**

Blackstaff Press Ltd
4C Heron Wharf, Sydenham Business Park,
Belfast BT3 9LE
☎028 9045 5006   Fax 028 9046 6237
✉ info@blackstaffpress.com
www.blackstaffpress.com
Managing Editor *Patsy Horton*
Founded 1971. Publishes mainly, but not exclusively, Irish interest books, fiction, poetry, history, sport, cookery, politics, illustrated editions,
natural history and humour. IMPRINT **Beeline**
Lively popular fiction in small paperback format. About 20 titles a year. Unsolicited mss
considered, but preliminary submission of synopsis plus short sample of writing preferred.
Return postage *must* be enclosed.
ROYALTIES twice-yearly.

Authors' Rating Regional and proud of it, this
Belfast publisher is noted for bringing on
young talent and for 'wonderfully well-presented catalogues and promotional material'.

Blackwell Publishing
9600 Garsington Road, Oxford OX4 2DQ
☎01865 776868   Fax 01865 714591
www.blackwellpublishing.com

Also at: 108 Cowley Road, Oxford OX4 1JF
Tel 01865 791100 Fax 01865 791347
Chief Executive *René Olivieri*
President *Robert Campbell*
Chairman *Nigel Blackwell*

Blackwell Publishing was formed by merging
Blackwell Science (founded 1939) and Blackwell
Publishers (founded 1926). Publishes around 700
books a year and 674 journals in medicine, veterinary medicine, dentistry (IMPRINT **Blackwell
Munksgaard**), nursing and allied health, science
(particularly biology, chemistry and geology),
social sciences, business and humanities. Journals
are delivered online through Blackwell Synergy.
Acquired BMJ Books in 2004.
ROYALTIES annually.

John Blake Publishing Ltd
3 Bramber Court, 2 Bramber Road, London
W14 9PB
☎020 7381 0666   Fax 020 7381 6868
✉ words@blake.co.uk
Managing Director *John Blake*
Deputy Managing Director *Rosie Ries*

Founded 1991 and expanding rapidly. Bought
the assets of Smith Gryphon Ltd in 1997 and
acquired Metro Publishing in 2001. Publishes
mass-market non-fiction. No fiction, children's,
specialist or non-commercial. About 100 titles a
year. No unsolicited mss; synopses and ideas
welcome. Please enclose s.a.e.
ROYALTIES twice-yearly.

Authors' Rating One of the few publishers able
to crack the market for celebrity memoirs, John
Blake brings the tabloid touch to books. In the
latest Book Trade Awards, Blake was named
Small Publisher of the Year.

Blandford Press
See **Octopus Publishing Group**

Bliss Books
See **Arcadia Books**

Bloodaxe Books Ltd
Highgreen, Tarset NE48 1RP
☎01434 240500   Fax 01434 240505
✉ editor@bloodaxebooks.demon.co.uk
www.bloodaxebooks.com
Managing/Editorial Director *Neil Astley*

Publishes poetry, literature and criticism, and
related titles by British, Irish, European, Commonwealth and American writers. Ninety-five
per cent of the list is poetry. TITLES include six
major anthologies, *Staying Alive; real poems for
unreal times* and *Being Alive*, both edited by Neil
Astley; *The Bloodaxe Book of 20th Century Poetry*
ed. Edna Longley; *The New Poetry* eds. Hulse,
Kennedy and Morley; *Sixty Women Poets* ed.
Linda France; collected editions of Fleur
Adcock, David Constantine, Helen Dunmore,
Roy Fisher, Brendan Kennelly, J.H. Prynne,
Peter Reading, Carol Rumens, Ken Smith and
Anne Stevenson. About 40 titles a year.

Unsolicited poetry mss welcome; send a sample of no more than 10 poems with s.a.e., 'but if you don't read contemporary poetry, don't bother'. No e-mail submissions of any kind.

ROYALTIES annually.

Authors' Rating Assisted by regional Arts Council funding, Bloodaxe is one of the liveliest and most innovative of poetry publishers with a list that takes in some of the best of the younger poets.

Bloomsbury Publishing Plc

38 Soho Square, London W1D 3HB
☎020 7494 2111   Fax 020 7434 0151
www.bloomsburymagazine.com
Chairman/Chief Executive *Nigel Newton*
Publishing Directors *Alexandra Pringle,*
   Liz Calder, Kathy Rooney, Sarah Odedina,
   Arzu Tahsin
Approx. Annual Turnover £61 million+

Founded in 1986 by Nigel Newton, David Reynolds, Alan Wherry and Liz Calder. Many of its authors have gone on to win prestigious literary prizes, most recently J.K. Rowling's *Harry Potter and the Philosopher's Stone, Harry Potter and the Chamber of Secrets* and *Harry Potter and the Prisoner of Azkaban* won the **Nestlé Smarties Book Prize** in 1997, 1998 and 1999 respectively. Margaret Atwood's *The Blind Assassin* won the **Booker Prize** in 2000. Started Bloomsbury USA in 1998. Acquired **A.&C. Black Publishers Ltd** in May 2000 (see entry), Peter Collin Publishing Ltd in September 2002 and Berlin Verlag in 2003. Publishes literary fiction and non-fiction, including general reference; also audiobooks. AUTHORS include Margaret Atwood, T.C. Boyle, Sophie Dahl, Jeffrey Eugenides, Neil Gaiman, Daniel Goleman, David Guterson, Ethan Hawke, John Irving, Jay McInerney, Tim Pears, Celia Rees, J.K. Rowling, Will Self, Donna Tartt, Rupert Thomson, Barbara Trapido, Joanna Trollope and Benjamin Zephaniah. Unsolicited mss and synopses for adult titles only; no poetry.

ROYALTIES twice-yearly.

Authors' Rating It is not often that a publisher is seen to be driving the Stock Market but that is what happened when Bloomsbury announced the July launch of the latest Harry Potter – the sixth book in the series. The question now for Bloomsbury (and how other publishers would love to have this problem) is what to do with all the money. An investment programme in the US including a takeover of Walker Publishing suggests that authors with trans-Atlantic appeal will have the welcome mat put out for them. An expansion of children's books is also planned.

BMJ Books
See **Blackwell Publishing**

BMM
See **SportsBooks Limited**

Boatswain Press
See **Kenneth Mason Publications Ltd**

Bobcat
See **Omnibus Press**

Bodley Head Children's Books
See **The Random House Group Ltd**

Book Blocks
See **CRW Publishing Ltd**

The Book Guild Ltd
Temple House, 25 High Street, Lewes BN7 2LU
☎01273 472534   Fax 01273 476472
✉ info@bookguild.co.uk
www.bookguild.co.uk
Chairman *George M. Nissen, CBE*
Managing Director *Carol Biss*

Founded 1982. Publishes fiction, human interest, media, children's fiction, academic, natural history, naval and military, biography, art. Expanding mainstream list plus developing the human interest/media genre. **Current Affairs** TITLE *Dare We Trust Them? A New Vision for Europe.* **Human Interest** TITLE *At Home With the Homeless.* **Biography** TITLE *Over the Airways – My Life in Broadcasting.* **General Interest** TITLES *The Shaker of the Speare – The Francis Bacon Story; The Voice Doctor.* **Fiction** TITLES *Oops!; Games of Chance.* **Food and Drink** TITLE *Persian Sofreh – Heavenly Food Made Easy.* About 80 titles a year. Unsolicited mss, ideas and synopses welcome.

ROYALTIES twice-yearly.

Authors' Rating Sensitive to suggestions that it is any way a vanity press, The Book Guild is keen to stress that most of its activity is linked to conventional publishing. But some authors do receive a come-on letter which leaves it until the last paragraph to mention that they will be expected to cover the 'costs of the first edition'.

Book House
See **Salariya Book Company Ltd** under *UK Packagers*

Border Lines Biographies
See **Seren**

Boulevard Books & The Babel Guides
71 Lytton Road, Oxford OX4 3NY
☎01865 712931   Fax 01865 712931
✉ raybabel@dircon.co.uk
www.babelguides.com
Managing Director *Ray Keenoy*
Specialises in contemporary world fiction by young writers in English translation. Existing or forthcoming series of fiction from Brazil, Italy, Latin America, Low Countries, Greece, and elsewhere. The Babel Guides series of popular guides to fiction in translation started in 1995. DIVISONS **Latin American** *Ray Keenoy* TITLE *Hotel Atlantico* J.G. Noll. **Italian** *Fiorenza Conte* TITLE *The Toy Catalogue* Sandra Petrignani. **Brazil** *Dr David Treece* TITLE *The Jaguar*. **Low Countries** *Prof. Theo Hermans*. **Greece** *Marina Coriolano-Likourezos*. **Babel Guides to Fiction in Translation** Series Editor *Ray Keenoy* TITLES *Babel Guide to Italian Fiction in Translation*; *Babel Guide to the Fiction of Portugal, Brazil & Africa in Translation*; *Babel Guide to French Fiction in English Translation*; *Babel Guide to Jewish Fiction*; *Babel Guide to Scandinavian Fiction*. Suggestions and proposals for translations of contemporary fiction welcome. Also seeking contributors to forthcoming Babel Guides (all literatures).
ROYALTIES annually.

Bound Biographies Limited
Heyford Park House, Heyford Park, Bicester OX25 5HD
☎01869 232911   Fax 01869 232766
✉ boundbiographies@aol.com
www.boundbiographies.com
Managing Director *Michael Oke*
Editorial Head *Dr A.J. Gray*
Approx. Annual Turnover £150,000
Founded in 1992 to assist in the writing and production of low numbers of private life stories. Print-on-demand facilities to provide short runs of paper or hardback books to complement the Bound Biographies leather-bound range. Publishes autobiographies predominantly although novels, poetry and special interest books are considered. TITLES *Out of the Shadows* J.V. Moloney; *Message From the Colonel* David Spencer. 25 titles in 2004. Unsolicited material welcome; approach by post, telephone or e-mail.
ROYALTIES annually.

Bounty
See **Octopus Publishing Group**

Bowker (UK) Ltd
3rd Floor, Farringdon House, Wood Street, East Grinstead RH19 1UZ
☎01342 310450   Fax 01342 310486
✉ sales@bowker.co.uk
www.bowker.co.uk
Managing Director *Doug McMillan*
Publisher *Michael Cairns*
Part of the Cambridge Information Group (CIG), based in Maryland in the USA. Publishes library reference, bibliography, biography, business and professional directories. TITLES *Books In Print*; *Ulrich's Periodicals Directory*; *Children's Books in Print*; *Ulrich's Serials Analysis System*. Unsolicited material will not be read.
ROYALTIES annually.

Boxtree
See **Macmillan Publishers Ltd**

Marion Boyars Publishers Ltd
24 Lacy Road, London SW15 1NL
☎020 8788 9522   Fax 020 8789 8122
✉ rebecca@marionboyars.com
www.marionboyars.co.uk
Editor *Rebecca Gillieron*
Editor, Non-fiction *Claus von Bohlen*
Founded 1975, formerly Calder and Boyars. Publishes biography and autobiography, fiction, literature and criticism, music, philosophy, psychology, sociology and anthropology, theatre and drama, film and cinema, women's studies. AUTHORS include Georges Bataille, Ingmar Bergman, Heinrich Böll, Hortense Calisher, Jean Cocteau, Carlo Gébler, Julian Green, Ivan Illich, Pauline Kael, Ken Kesey, Toby Litt, Kenzaburo Oe, Hubert Selby, Igor Stravinsky, Frederic Tuten, Eudora Welty, Judith Williamson, Tom Wiseman, Hong Ying. About 30 titles a year. Unsolicited mss not welcome for fiction or poetry; submissions from agents only. Unsolicited synopses and ideas welcome for non-fiction. OVERSEAS ASSOCIATES Marion Boyars Publishers Inc.
ROYALTIES annually.

Bradt Travel Guides
19 High Street, Chalfont St Peter SL9 9QE
☎01753 893444   Fax 01753 892333
✉ info@bradtguides.com
www.bradtguides.com
Managing Director *Hilary Bradt*
Editorial Head *Tricia Hayne*

Approx. Annual Turnover £650,000

Founded in 1974 by Hilary Bradt. Specialises in travel guides to off-beat places. SERIES Country guides and island guides (Azores, Falklands, St Helena); wildlife guides (Galapagos, Arctic, Antarctica, Southern Africa); mini guides to cities (Kabul, Baghdad, Lille, Budapest) and the 'Eccentric' series (Britain, London, France, America, Oxford). 24 titles in 2004. No unsolicited mss; synopses and ideas for travel guidebooks (not travelogues) welcome.
ROYALTIES twice-yearly.

Brassey's
See **Chrysalis Books Group**

Nicholas Brealey Publishing
3–5 Spafield Street, London EC1R 4QB
☎020 7239 0360   Fax 020 7239 0370
✉ rights@nbrealey-books.com
www.nbrealey-books.com

Managing Director *Nicholas Brealey*

Founded 1992. Independent publishing group focusing on innovative trade/professional books covering business and finance, intelligent self-help, popular psychology and the increasingly active fields of crossing cultures and travel writing. The group has offices in Boston and includes Intercultural Press Inc. TITLES *It's All Greek to Me!*; *Almost French*; *Money for Nothing*; *Authentic Happiness*; *50 Self-Help Classics*. No fiction, poetry or leisure titles. 30 titles a year. No unsolicited mss; synopses and ideas welcome.
ROYALTIES twice-yearly.

Authors' Rating Looks to be succeeding in breaking away from the usual computer-speak business manuals to publish information and literate texts. Lead titles have a distinct trans-Atlantic feel.

The Breedon Books Publishing Co. Ltd
Breedon House, 3 Parker Centre, Derby DE21 4SZ
☎01332 384235   Fax 01332 292755
✉ susan.last@breedonpublishing.co.uk

Commissioning Editor *Susan Last*
Approx. Annual Turnover £1 million

Founded 1983. Publishes football and sport, local history, old photographs, heritage. About 50 titles a year. Unsolicited mss, synopses and ideas welcome if accompanied by s.a.e. No poetry or fiction.
ROYALTIES annually.

Breese Books Ltd
10 Hanover Crescent, Brighton BN2 9SB
☎01273 687 555
✉ MBreese999@aol.com
www.abracadabra.co.uk

Chairman/Managing Director *Martin Ranicar-Breese*

Founded in 1975 to produce specialist conjuring books. No unsolicited submissions.

Brewin Books Ltd
Doric House, 56 Alcester Road, Studley B80 7LG
☎01527 854228   Fax 01527 852746
✉ admin@brewinbooks.com
www.brewinbooks.com

Chairman/Managing Director *Alan Brewin*
Company Secretary *Julie Brewin*

Founded 1976. Publishes books on all aspects of Midland life and history including social, hospital, police, military, transport and family histories as well as biographies and contemporary fiction. TITLES *Byways of Warwickshire* Alan Tyers; *Britain's Traditional Tramways* David Gladwin; *The Other Notting Hill* Chris Holmes; *Passion for Change – A Guide to Good Health* Rob Blakeman. IMPRINTS **Alton Douglas Books**; **History Into Print**; **Brewin Books**. About 25 titles a year. Not interested in children's, poetry, short stories or novels. Approach by letter, but do not send full mss. Unsolicited synopses and ideas welcome with s.a.e.
ROYALTIES twice-yearly.

Bristol Classical Press
See **Gerald Duckworth & Co. Ltd**

Bristol Phoenix Press
See **University of Exeter Press**

British Academic Press
See **I.B. Tauris & Co. Ltd**

The British Academy
10 Carlton House Terrace, London SW1Y 5AH
☎020 7969 5200   Fax 020 7969 5300
✉ secretary@britac.ac.uk
www.britac.ac.uk

Publications Officer *James Rivington*
Assistant Publications Officer *Janet English*
Publications Assistant *Amrit Bangard*

Founded 1902. The primary body for promoting scholarship in the humanities and social sciences, the Academy publishes many series stemming from its own long-standing research projects, or series of lectures and conference proceedings. Main subjects include history, philosophy and archaeology. SERIES *Auctores Britannici Medii Aevi; Early English Church Music; Fontes Historiae Africanae; Records of Social and Economic History*. About 20 titles a year. Proposals for these series are welcome and are forwarded to the relevant project committees. The British Academy is a registered charity and does not publish for profit.

ROYALTIES only when titles have covered their costs.

The British Computer Society

1 Sanford Street, Swindon SN1 1HJ
☎01793 417417   Fax 01793 480270
✉ publishing@hq.bcs.org.uk
www.bcs.org.uk
Chief Executive *David Clarke*
Head of Publishing & Information Products
  Elaine Boyes
Approx. Annual Turnover £15 million
  (Society)

Founded 1957. BCS is the leading professional and learned society in the field of computers and information systems. Publishes books which support the professional, academic and practical needs of the IT community. TITLES *A Guide to Global Sourcing; The British Computer Society Review 2005; A Manager's Guide to IT Law*. 4 titles in 2004. Unsolicited material welcome; submissions form and guide on website page: www.bcs.org/author

ROYALTIES annually.

The British Library

96 Euston Road, London NW1 2DB
☎020 7412 7469   Fax 020 7412 7768
✉ blpublications@bl.uk
www.bl.uk
Publishing Manager *David Way*
Approx. Annual Turnover £950,000

Founded 1979 as the publishing arm of The British Library to publish works based on the historic collections and related subjects. Publishes bibliographical reference, manuscript studies, illustrated books based on the Library's collections, and book arts. TITLES *1000 Years of English Literature; The Books of Henry VIII and His Wives; Futurist Typography*. About 50 titles a year. Unsolicited mss, synopses and ideas welcome if related to the history of the book, book arts or bibliography. No fiction or general nonfiction.

ROYALTIES annually.

The British Museum Press

33 Russell Square, London WC1B 3QQ
☎020 7323 1234   Fax 020 7436 7315
www.britishmuseum.co.uk
Managing Director *Andrew Thatcher*
Director of Publishing *Rosemary Bradley*

The book publishing division of The British Museum Company Ltd. Founded 1973 as British Museum Publications Ltd; relaunched 1991 as British Museum Press. Publishes ancient history, archaeology, ethnography, art history, exhibition catalogues, guides, children's books, and all official publications of the British Museum. TITLES *5000 Years of Textiles; Hellenistic Art; Classical Love Poetry; Sudan: Ancient Treasures; The Story of Venus; The Tale of Peter Rabbit: Hieroglyph Edition*. About 50 titles a year. Synopses and ideas for books welcome.

ROYALTIES twice-yearly.

Brockhampton Press Ltd

See **Caxton Publishing Group**

Andrew Brodie

See **A.&C. Black Publishers Ltd**

John Brown Citrus Publishing

The New Boathouse, 136–142 Bramley Road, London W10 6SR
☎020 7565 3000   Fax 020 7565 3060
✉ john.brown@jbcp.co.uk
www.jbcp.co.uk
Chief Executive *Andrew Hirsch*
Managing Director *Dean Fitzpatrick*
Chief Operating Officer *Andrew Jarvis*

Founded 1987. Contract magazine publisher. TITLES include *Sky Magazine* and *Waitrose Food Illustrated*.

Brown Skin Books

PO Box 46504, London N1 3YA
☎020 7226 4789
✉ info@brownskinbooks.co.uk
www.brownskinbooks.co.uk
Chairman *Dr John Lake*
Managing Director *Vastiana Belfon*

Founded 2002. Publishes 'quality, intelligent erotic fiction by black women around the world'. TITLES *Body and Soul* Jade Williams; *Personal Business* Isabel Baptiste; *Scandalous* Angela Campion; *Playthings* Faith Graham; *Online Wildfire* Crystal Humphries. 4 titles in 2004. No unsolicited mss; synopses and ideas welcome. Send by e-mail or post. No poetry.

ROYALTIES annually.

Brown, Son & Ferguson, Ltd

4–10 Darnley Street, Glasgow G41 2SD
☎0141 429 1234   Fax 0141 420 1694
✉ info@skipper.co.uk
www.skipper.co.uk
Chairman/Joint Managing Director *T. Nigel Brown*

Founded 1850. Specialises in nautical textbooks, both technical and non-technical. Also Scottish one-act/three-act plays. Unsolicited mss, synopses and ideas for books welcome.
ROYALTIES annually.

Bryntirion Press

Bryntirion, Bridgend CF31 4DX
☎01656 655886   Fax 01656 665919
✉ office@emw.org.uk
Press Manager *Huw Kinsey*

Owned by the Evangelical Movement of Wales. Publishes Christian books in English and Welsh. No unsolicited mss; synopses and ideas welcome.
ROYALTIES annually.

Burns & Oates

See **The Continuum International Publishing Group Limited**

Business Education Publishers Ltd

The Teleport Doxford International,
Sunderland SR3 3XD
☎0191 525 2410
✉ info@bepl.com
www.bepl.com
Managing Director *Mrs A. Murphy*
Approx. Annual Turnover £400,000

Founded 1981. Publishes business education, economics and law for BTEC and GNVQ reading. Currently expanding into further and higher education, computing, IT, business, travel and tourism, occasional papers for institutions and local government administration. Unsolicited mss and synopses welcome.
ROYALTIES annually.

Buster Books

See **Michael O'Mara Books Ltd**

Butterworth Heinemann

See **Elsevier Ltd**

C&B (Collins & Brown)

See **Chrysalis Books Group**

Cadogan Guides

2nd Floor, 233 High Holborn, London
WC1V 7DN
☎020 7611 4660   Fax 020 7611 4665
✉ info@cadoganguides.co.uk
www.cadoganguides.com
Managing Director *Jenny Calcutt*
Managing Editor *Natalie Pomier*

Founded 1982. Travel publisher: country, regional and city guides; parent travel guides (*Take the Kids*); guides to living, working and buying property abroad. Also publishes some travel literature. Most titles are commissioned. No unsolicited material.

Calder Publications Ltd

51 The Cut, London SE1 8LF
☎020 7633 0599   Fax 020 7928 5930
✉ info@calderpublications.com
www.calderpublications.com
Chairman/Managing Director/Editorial Head
John Calder

Formerly John Calder (Publishers) Ltd. A company which has grown around the tastes and contacts of John Calder, the iconoclast of the literary establishment. The list has a reputation for controversial and opinion-forming publications; Samuel Beckett is perhaps the most prestigious name. The list includes all of Beckett's prose and poetry. Publishes autobiography, biography, drama, literary fiction, literary criticism, music, opera, poetry, politics, sociology, ENO opera guides. SERIES *Thought Bites* Short polemical texts on current political and social issues. AUTHORS Antonin Artaud, Marguerite Duras, Martin Esslin, Erich Fried, P.J. Kavanagh, Robert Menasse, Robert Pinget, Luigi Pirandello, Alain Robbe-Grillet, Nathalie Sarraute, L.F. Celine, Eva Figes, Claude Simon, Howard Barker (plays). No new material accepted.
ROYALTIES annually.

Authors' Rating Known for his patronage of eccentric talents, John Calder is one of the few publishers to carry the flag for the English language '... which is in great danger of disappearing under the American vernacular'.

California University Press

See **University Presses of California, Columbia & Princeton Ltd**

Cambridge University Press

The Edinburgh Building, Shaftesbury Road,
Cambridge CB2 2RU
☎01223 312393   Fax 01223 315052

www.cambridge.org

Chief Executive *Stephen R.R. Bourne*

The oldest printer and publisher in the world with long-established branches in the USA and Australia and more recently established branches in Spain, Africa, South America and East Asia, and offices and agents around the world. Cambridge's books are sold in more than 200 countries. Publishing includes major ELT courses; tertiary textbooks and monographs; scientific and medical reference; professional lists in law and management; educational coursebooks for the National Curriculum; and e-learning materials for schools via the Cambridge-Hitachi joint venture. Publishes academic/educational, ELT and reference books for markets worldwide, at all levels from primary school to postgraduate and professional. Also Bibles and some 180 academic journals. Around 25,000 authors in 116 countries and between 1500 and 2000 new titles a year.

PUBLISHING GROUPS
Bibles *C.J. Wright*; **ELT** *A.C. Gilfillan*; **Humanities and Social Sciences** *R.K. Fisher*; **STM** *R.W.A. Barling*; **Education** *J.G. Tuttle*; **Journals** *C. Guettler.* Synopses and ideas for books are welcome (and preferable to the submission of unsolicited mss). No fiction or poetry.
ROYALTIES twice-yearly.

Authors' Rating With its traditional strength in the academic market CUP is well placed to create such intellectual blockbusters as the three volume *Economic History of Modern Britain.* An increasing number of titles reach out to the general reader.

Camden Press Ltd
43 Camden Passage, London N1 8EA
☎020 7226 4673
Chairman *Bob Borzello*

Founded 1985. Publishes social issues; all books are launched in connection with major national conferences. DIVISION **Publishing for Change** *Bob Borzello* TITLE *Living with the Legacy of Abuse.* IMPRINT **Mindfield** TITLES *Hate Thy Neighbour: The Race Issue*; *Therapy on the Couch.* No unsolicited material. Approach by telephone in the first instance.
ROYALTIES annually.

Campbell Books
See **Macmillan Publishers Ltd**

Candle
See **Lion Hudson plc**

Canongate Books Ltd
14 High Street, Edinburgh EH1 1TE
☎0131 557 5111   Fax 0131 557 5211
✉ info@canongate.co.uk
www.canongate.net
Publisher *Jamie Byng*
Managing Director *David Graham*
Approx. Annual Turnover £6 million

Founded 1973. Won 'Publisher of the Year' (2002) at the British Book Awards. Publishes a wide range of literary fiction and non-fiction. Historically there is a strong Scottish slant to the list but its output is increasingly international and Canongate has a growing reputation for originating unusual projects (typified by the *Pocket Canons Bible* series). Key AUTHORS include Michel Faber, Anne Donovan, John Fante, Will Ferguson, Alasdair Gray, Yann Martel, Martin Strong. IMPRINTS **Canongate Classics** Adult paperback series dedicated solely to important works of Scottish literature; **Canongate International** Fiction in translation.
ROYALTIES twice-yearly.

Authors' Rating Esquire magazine has named publisher Jamie Byng as the most influential man under 40 in UK literature, quite a compliment in what is increasingly a youth driven industry. Canongate's steady growth based on an imaginative list would seem to support the *Esquire* verdict.

Canterbury Press
See **SCM – Canterbury Press Ltd**

Capall Bann Publishing
Auton Farm, Milverton TA4 1NE
☎01823 401528   Fax 01823 401529
✉ enquiries@capallbann.co.uk
www.capallbann.co.uk
Chairman *Julia Day*
Editorial Head *Jon Day*

Founded 1993 with three titles and now has well over 250 in print. Family-owned and run company which publishes British traditions, folklore, animals, alternative healing, environmental, Celtic lore, mind, body and spirit. TITLES *Tarot Therapy*; *How to Talk with Fairies*; *Spiritual Journey*; *Crystals Folklore & Healing*; *Return of Yesterday's People.* About 40 titles a year.

Unsolicited proposals for books welcome. No fiction or poetry.
ROYALTIES twice-yearly.

Jonathan Cape/Jonathan Cape Children's Books
See **The Random House Group Ltd**

Capstone Publishing
(a **Wiley** company)
John Wiley & Sons Ltd, The Atrium, Southern Gate, Chichester PO19 8SQ
☎01243 779777   Fax 01243 775878
✉ info@wiley-capstone.co.uk
www.wiley.com
Founded 1997. Part of **John Wiley & Sons Inc.** Publishes business, personal development, lifestyle and humour books.

Carcanet Press Ltd
4th Floor, Alliance House, 30 Cross Street, Manchester M2 7AQ
☎0161 834 8730   Fax 0161 832 0084
✉ pnr@carcanet.u-net.com
www.carcanet.co.uk
Chairman *Kate Gavron*
Managing Director/Editorial Director *Michael Schmidt*
In the last 30 years Carcanet has grown from an undergraduate hobby into a substantial venture. Robert Gavron bought the company in 1983 and it has established strong European, Commonwealth and American links. Winner of the **Sunday Times Small Publisher of the Year** award in 2000, it took over the Oxford Poets list from **Oxford University Press** in 1999, which it now publishes as a distinct imprint. Primarily a poetry publisher but also publishes academic, literary biography, fiction in translation and translations. AUTHORS Homero Aridjis, John Ashbery, Eavan Boland, Joseph Brodsky, Donald Davie, Natalia Ginzburg, Robert Graves, Elizabeth Jennings, Edwin Morgan, Les Murray, Frederic Raphael, Leonardo Sciascia, Iain Crichton Smith, Pedro Tamen, Charles Tomlinson. About 60 titles a year, including the *PN Review* (six issues yearly). Poetry submissions (hard copy only): 6–10 poems with covering letter and return postage if the material is to be sent back. Prospective writers should familiarise themselves with the Carcanet list.
ROYALTIES annually.

Authors' Rating Ever in the forefront of imaginative publishing, Carcanet has taken a step closer to the source of its literary creativity by setting up a postgraduate Writing School at Manchester Metropolitan University. (See entry under *Writers' Courses*.)

Cardiff Academic Press
St Fagans Road, Fairwater, Cardiff CF5 3AE
☎029 2056 0333   Fax 029 2055 4909
✉ cap@drakeed.com
www.drakeed.com/cap
Managing Director *R. G. Drake*
Academic publishers.

Carlton Publishing Group
20 Mortimer Street, London W1T 3JW
☎020 7612 0400   Fax 020 7612 0401
✉ enquiries@carltonbooks.co.uk
Managing Director *Jonathan Goodman*
Editorial Director *Piers Murray Hill*
Approx. Annual Turnover £11 million
Founded 1992. Carlton Publishing Group is an independent publishing house. It has three main divisions: **Carlton Books** Illustrated leisure and entertainment books aimed at the mass market. Subjects include history, sport, puzzles, health, popular science, music and design. **André Deutsch** Autobiography, biography, history, current affairs and the arts. **Prion Books** Humour, drink and classic literature. DIVISIONS **Carlton Books**; **André Deutsch; Prion Books; Manchester United Books**. No unsolicited mss; synopses and ideas welcome. No novels, science fiction, poetry or children's fiction.

Carroll & Brown Publishers Limited
20 Lonsdale Road, London NW6 6RD
☎020 7372 0900   Fax 020 7372 0460
✉ mail@carrollandbrown.co.uk
Managing Director *Amy Carroll*
Approx. Annual Turnover £4 million
Founded in 1989 as a packaging operation and commenced publishing in 2000. Publishes practical parenting, health, fitness, lifestyle, mind, body and spirit. TITLES *How Perfect is Your Partner?*; *Watch Me Grow*; *Your Pregnancy Bible*. Synopses and ideas for illustrated books welcome; approach in writing in the first instance. No fiction
PAYMENT Fees or royalties paid.

Cassell
See **The Orion Publishing Group Limited**

Cassell Illustrated
See **Octopus Publishing Group**

Castle Publications
See **Nottingham University Press**

Kyle Cathie Ltd
122 Arlington Road, London NW1 7HP
☎020 7692 7215   Fax 020 7692 7260
✉ general.enquiries@kyle-cathie.com
www.kylecathie.co.uk

Founded 1990 to publish and promote 'books we have personal enthusiasm for'. Publishes non-fiction: cookery, food and drink, health and beauty, mind, body & spirit, gardening, homes and interiors, reference and occasional books of classic poetry. TITLES *The Wagamama Cookbook* Hugo Arnold; *The Game Cookbook* Clarissa Dickson Wright and Johnny Scott; *The 21st Century Beauty Bible* Jo Farley and Sarah Stacey; *Thoughts on Garden Design* Marylyn Abbott. About 25 titles a year. No unsolicited mss. 'Synopses and ideas are considered in the fields in which we publish.'
ROYALTIES twice-yearly.

Catholic Truth Society (CTS)
40–46 Harleyford Road, London SE11 5AY
☎020 7640 0042   Fax 020 7640 0046
✉ f.martin@cts-online.org.uk
www.cts-online.org.uk
Chairman *Most Rev. Peter Smith*
General Secretary *Fergal Martin*

Founded originally in 1868 and re-founded in 1884. Publishes religious books – Roman Catholic; a variety of doctrinal, moral, biographical, devotional and liturgical publications, including a large body of Vatican documents and sources. Unsolicited mss, synopses and ideas welcome if appropriate to their list.
ROYALTIES annually.

Causeway Press
See **Pearson Education**

Cavendish Publishing Limited
The Glass House, Wharton Street, London WC1X 9PX
☎020 7278 8000   Fax 020 7278 8080
✉ info@cavendishpublishing.com
www.cavendishpublishing.com
Executive Chairman *Sonny Leong*

Founded 1990. Publishes academic law books. IMPRINTS **Glass House Press; Birkbeck Law Press; UCL Press.** OVERSEAS ASSOCIATE

Cavendish Publishing (Australia) Pty Ltd. 160 titles in 2004. No unsolicited mss; send synopsis accompanied by a letter in the first instance.
ROYALTIES twice-yearly.

Caxton Publishing Group
20 Bloomsbury Street, London WC1B 3JH
☎020 7636 7171   Fax 020 7636 1922
✉ office@caxtonpublishing.com
www.caxtonpublishing.com
Managing Director *John Maxwell*
Approx. Annual Turnover £4 million

Founded 1999. Specialises in reprinting out-of-print works for the 'value' market worldwide and commissioning new general non-fiction publications in reference, cookery, gardening and children's. DIVISIONS/IMPRINTS **Brockhampton Press Ltd** Children's fiction and non-fiction. **Caxton Editions Ltd** General non-fiction, reference and military. **Knight Paperbacks Ltd** Fiction. **Chaucer Press** Art, architecture and literature. **Mercury Books** Illustrated non-fiction. **Mercury Junior** Children's books, illustrated, educational, novelty. 200 titles a year. No unsolicited mss; synopses and ideas welcome; send letter in the first instance.
ROYALTIES twice-yearly.

CBA Publishing
St Mary's House, 66 Bootham, York YO30 7BZ
☎01904 671417   Fax 01904 671384
www.britarch.ac.uk
Publications Officer *Jane Thorniley-Walker*
British Archaeology Editor *Mike Pitts*
Young Archaeologists' Club Coordinator
   Alison Bodley
Approx. Annual Turnover £110,000

Publishing arm of the **Council for British Archaeology**. Publishes academic archaeology reports, practical handbooks, yearbook, *British Archaeology* (bi-monthly magazine), *Young Archaeologist* (Young Archaeologists' Club magazine), monographs, archaeology and education. TITLES *The Vernacular Workshop; Mountains and Orefields; Submarine Prehistoric Archaeology of the North Sea; Historic Landscape Analysis Practical Handbook*. Please contact by telephone before submitting mss and proposals.
ROYALTIES paid for hardback and commercial publications.

CBD Research Ltd
Chancery House, 15 Wickham Road, Beckenham BR3 5JS
☎020 8650 7745   Fax 020 8650 0768

✉ cbd@cbdresearch.com
www.cbdresearch.com
Managing Director *S.P.A. Henderson*
Approx. Annual Turnover £500,000
Founded 1961. Publishes directories and other reference guides to sources of information. No fiction. IMPRINT **Chancery House Press** Non-fiction of an esoteric/specialist nature for 'serious researchers and the dedicated hobbyist'. About 6 titles a year.
ROYALTIES quarterly.

Centaur Press
See **Open Gate Press**

Century
See **The Random House Group Ltd**

CF4K
See **Christian Focus Publications**

Chadwyck-Healey
See **ProQuest Information and Learning Ltd**

Chambers Harrap Publishers Ltd
7 Hopetoun Crescent, Edinburgh EH7 4AY
☎0131 556 5929   Fax 0131 556 5313
✉ admin@chambersharrap.co.uk
www.chambersharrap.co.uk
Managing Director *Wendy Rimmington*
Administrator *Vicky Aldus*
Publishes dictionaries and reference. The Chambers imprint was founded in the early 1800s to publish self-education books but soon diversified into dictionaries and other reference works. The current list covers a broad range of subject areas and includes crossword titles. The Harrap imprint dates from 1901 and is used for bilingual dictionaries and study aids. About 55 titles a year. Send synopsis with accompanying letter rather than completed mss.

Chameleons
See **A.&C. Black Publishers Ltd**

Chancery House Press
See **CBD Research Ltd**

Channel 4 Books
See **Transworld Publishers**

Paul Chapman Publishing Ltd
See **Sage Publications**

Chapman Publishing
4 Broughton Place, Edinburgh EH1 3RX
☎0131 557 2207   Fax 0131 556 9565
✉ chapman-pub@blueyonder.co.uk
www.chapman-pub.co.uk
Managing Editor *Joy Hendry*
A venture devoted to publishing works by the best of Scottish writers, both up-and-coming and established, published in *Chapman*, Scotland's leading literary magazine. Has expanded publishing activities considerably over the last three years and is now publishing a wider range of works though the broad policy stands. Publishes poetry, drama, short stories, books of contemporary importance in 20th-century Scotland. TITLES *Clan MacHine* Ian McDonough; *Wild Women Series – Wild Women of a Certain Age* Magi Gibson; *Ye Cannae Win* Janet Paisley; *Lure* Dilys Rose. About 4 titles a year. No unsolicited mss; synopses and ideas for books welcome.
ROYALTIES annually.

Charnwood
See **F.A. Thorpe (Publishing)**

Chartered Institute of Personnel and Development (CIPD)
151 The Broadway, London SW19 1JQ
☎020 8612 6200   Fax 020 8612 6201
✉ publishing@cipd.co.uk
www.cipd.co.uk/bookstore
Publishing Manager *Sarah Brown*
Part of CIPD Enterprises Limited. Publishes personnel and training plus some general management titles. A list of over 200 titles including looseleaf and online subscription products, student textbooks and professional books and resources. New product proposals welcome.
ROYALTIES annually or flat fees paid.

Chatto & Windus
See **The Random House Group Ltd**

Chaucer Press
See **Caxton Publishing Group**

Cherrytree Books
See **Evans Brothers Ltd**

Chicken House Publishing
2 Palmer Street, Frome BA11 1DS
☎01373 454488   Fax 01373 454499
✉ chickenhouse@doublecluck.com
Chairman/Managing Director *Barry Cunningham*

Children's publishing house founded in 2000. Acquired by Scholastic Inc. in May 2005. Publishes books 'that are aimed at real children' – fiction, original picture books, gift books and fun non-fiction. Aiming to publish about 25 titles a year. 'We are always on the lookout for new talent.' Unsolicited fiction and picture book material welcome; send letter with synopsis, three sample chapters and s.a.e. ROYALTIES twice-yearly.

Authors' Rating Set up as a 'small, creative company', Chicken House has made such rapid progress as to attract a successful bid from Scholastic. Editorial freedom is part of the deal 'with no rules about what to publish as long as it's good'.

Child's Play (International) Ltd
Ashworth Road, Bridgemead, Swindon SN5 7YD
☎01793 616286   Fax 01793 512795
✉ allday@childs-play.com
www.childs-play.com
Chief Executive *Neil Burden*
Founded in 1972, Child's Play is an independent publisher specialising in learning through play, whole child development, life-skills and values. Publishes books, games and A-V materials. TITLES *Big Hungry Bear; There Was an Old Lady; Our Cat Cuddles; Royston Knapper; Children of the Sun; Ten Beads Tall; Pocket Pals; Sliders; Roly Poly Books; Animal Lullabies; Monkey's Clever Tale; What's the Time, Mr Wolf?; Sign and Sing-Along; Arithmetic Lotto.* Unsolicited mss welcome. Send s.a.e. for return or response. Expect to wait two months for a reply.
ROYALTIES Outright or royalty payments are subject to negotiation.

Chimera
See **Pegasus Elliot Mackenzie Publishers Ltd**

Chivers
See **BBC Audiobooks Ltd** under *Audio Books*

Christian Focus Publications
Geanies House, Fearn, Tain IV20 1TW
☎01862 871011   Fax 01862 871699
✉ info@christianfocus.com
www.christianfocus.com
Chairman *R.W.M. Mackenzie*
Managing Director *William Mackenzie*
Editorial Manager *Willie Mackenzie*
Children's Editor *Catherine Mackenzie*
Founded 1979 to produce children's books for the co-edition market. Now a major producer of Christian books. Publishes adult and children's books, including some fiction for children but not adults. No poetry. Publishes for all English-speaking markets, as well as the UK. IMPRINTS **CF4K** Children's books; **Christian Focus** General books; **Mentor** Study books; **Christian Heritage** Classic reprints. About 90 titles a year. Unsolicited mss, synopses and ideas welcome from Christian writers. See website for submission criteria.
ROYALTIES annually.

Christian Heritage
See **Christian Focus Publications**

Chroma
See **Black & White Publishing Ltd**

Chrome Dreams
See entry under *Audio Books*

Chrysalis Books Group
The Chrysalis Building, Bramley Road, London W10 6SP
☎020 7314 1400
✉ firstinitialsurname@chrysalisbooks.co.uk
www.chrysalisbooks.co.uk
CEO *Robin Wood*
Director of Publications *Roger Huggins*
Director of Trade Division *Colin Ziegler*
Publishing Director, Trade Division *Polly Powell*
Approx. Annual Turnover £33.9 million
Chrysalis Books Group, owned by Chrysalis Group Plc, specialises in illustrated non-fiction, publishing under the IMPRINTS **B.T. Batsford**; **Brassey's**; **C&B (Collins & Brown)**; **Conway Maritime Press**; **Paper Tiger**; **Pavilion**; **Putnam Aeronautical Books**; **Robson Books**; **Salamander**.

IMPRINTS
B.T. Batsford Associate Publisher *Tina Persaud* Founded in 1843 as a bookseller, and began publishing in 1874. Acquired by Chrysalis in 1999. A world leader in books on chess, arts and craft. Publishes non-fiction, architecture, heritage, bridge and chess, film and entertainment, fashion, crafts and hobbies. About 100 titles a year. ROYALTIES twice in the first year, annually thereafter.

Brassey's Associate Publisher *John Lee* Acquired by Chrysalis in 1999. Publishes military history and technology. ROYALTIES annually.

C&B (Collins & Brown) Associate Publisher *Katie Cowan* Publishes a range of lifestyle categories especially in the areas of practical art, photography and needlecrafts.

Conway Maritime Press Associate Publisher *John Lee* Publishes naval history, maritime culture and ship modelling. ROYALTIES annually.

Paper Tiger Associate Publisher *Katie Cowan* Acquired by Chrysalis in 2001 (part of C&B). Publishes science fiction and fantasy art.

Pavilion Associate Publisher *Kate Oldfield* Acquired by Chrysalis in 2001. Publishes illustrated books in biography, cookery, gardening, humour, art, interiors, music, sport and travel. Unsolicited mss not welcome. Ideas and synopses for non-fiction titles considered. ROYALTIES twice-yearly.

Putnam Aeronautical Books Associate Publisher *John Lee* Publishes classic aeronautical histories, technical and reference.

Robson Books Associate Publisher *Iain MacGregor* Founded 1973. Acquired by Chrysalis in 1998. Publishes general non-fiction including biography, cookery, gardening, sport and travel. About 90 titles a year. Unsolicited synopses and ideas for books welcome (s.a.e. essential for reply). ROYALTIES twice-yearly.

Salamander Publisher *Jo Messham* Founded 1973. Publishes colour illustrated books on collecting, cookery, interiors, gardening, music, crafts, military, aviation, sport and transport. Also a wide range of books on American interest subjects. No unsolicited mss but synopses and ideas for the above subjects welcome. ROYALTIES Outright fee paid instead of royalties.

Authors' Rating Having grown rapidly by acquisitions, Chrysalis has had its problems in developing a cohesive publishing programme that impresses the market. US co-editions account for a large part of total output.

Chrysalis Children's Books

The Chrysalis Building, Bramley Road, London W10 6SP
☎020 7314 1400   Fax 020 7314 1594
✉ childrens@chrysalisbooks.co.uk
www.chrysalisbooks.co.uk

Publisher *Sarah Fabiny*

Part of the **Chrysalis Books Group**. Publishes all kinds of children's books from baby and picture books to illustrated classics and educational books. DIVISIONS **Education** Associate Publisher *Joyce Bentley* Children's non-fiction in all curriculum areas. TITLES *Speaking and Listening; Start*

Writing; A First Look at Art; World Issues. **Trade** Publisher *Sarah Fabiny* Children's picture, novelty and gift books for ages 0 to 10. Also innovative and interactive children's books. TITLES *The Story of Little Mole; War Boy; If Elephants Wore Trousers; The Lady Who Lived in a Car.* No unsolicited mss. Synopses and ideas for books welcome from experienced children's writers.

Authors' Rating As we go to press, Chrysalis Children's Books has been put up for sale.

Churchill Livingstone
See **Elsevier Ltd**

Churchwarden Publications Ltd
PO Box 420, Warminster BA12 9XB
☎01985 840189   Fax 01985 840243

Managing Director *John Stidolph*

Founded 1974. Publishes books and stationery for churchwardens and church administrators including *The Churchwarden's Yearbook.* About 2 titles a year. Unsolicited mss, synopses and ideas for books welcome.

ROYALTIES paid according to contract.

Cicerone Press
2 Police Square, Milnthorpe LA7 7PY
☎01539 562069   Fax 01539 563417
✉ info@cicerone.co.uk
www.cicerone.co.uk

Managing/Editorial Director *Jonathan Williams*

Founded 1969. Guidebook publisher for outdoor enthusiasts. No fiction or poetry. TITLES *Hillwalker's Guide to Mountaineering; Tour of Mont Blanc; Coast to Coast Trail.* SERIES include *Alpine Walking; International Walking; British Long-Distance Trails, Cycling* and *Winter Activities.* About 20 titles a year. No unsolicited mss; synopses and ideas considered.

ROYALTIES twice-yearly.

Cico Books
1st Floor, 32 Great Sutton Street, London EC1V 0NB
☎020 7253 7960   Fax 020 7253 7967
✉ mail@cicobooks.co.uk

Managing Director *Mark Collins*
Publisher *Cindy Richards*

Founded in 1999 by Mark Collins and Cindy Richards (both formerly with **Collins & Brown**) 'to offer flexibility by being small, selling co-edition rights to overseas publishers'. Publishes lifestyle and interiors, mind, body and

spirit. About 15 titles a year. No unsolicited mss, synopses or ideas.
ROYALTIES twice-yearly.

Clairview Books
See **Temple Lodge Publishing Ltd**

Clarion
See **Elliot Right Way Books**

T&T Clark International
See **The Continuum International Publishing Group Ltd**

James Clarke & Co.
PO Box 60, Cambridge CB1 2NT
☎01223 350865   Fax 01223 366951
✉ publishing@jamesclarke.co.uk
www.jamesclarke.co.uk
Managing Director *Adrian Brink*

Parent company of **The Lutterworth Press** (see entry). Publishes scholarly and academic works, mainly theological, directory and reference titles. TITLES *Libraries Directory* (book and CD-ROM versions); *Encyclopedia of the Middle Ages*; *Henry VIII's Bishops*; *Nonconformity*; *Enlightenment Prelate*; *Let It Go Among Our People*. Approach in writing with ideas in the first instance.

Classic Publications
See **Ian Allan Publishing Ltd**

Collector's Library
See **CRW Publishing Ltd**

Peter Collin Publishing Ltd
See **Bloomsbury Publishing Plc**

Collins
See **HarperCollins Publishers Ltd**

Collins & Brown
See **Chrysalis Books Group**

Colonsay Books
See **House of Lochar**

Colourpoint Books
Colourpoint House, Jubilee Business Park, 21 Jubilee Road, Newtownards BT23 4YH
☎028 9182 0505   Fax 028 9182 1900
✉ info@colourpoint.co.uk
www.colourpoint.co.uk
Partners *Sheila M. Johnston, Norman Johnston, Malcolm Johnston, Wesley Johnston*

Founded 1993. Publishes school textbooks and transport (covering the whole of the British Isles), plus books of Irish and general interest. No fiction. About 25 titles a year. Unsolicited material accepted but approach in writing in the first instance; include return postage, please.
ROYALTIES twice-yearly.

Columbia University Press
See **University Presses of California, Columbia & Princeton Ltd**

Compendium Publishing Ltd
43 Frith Street, London W1D 4SA
☎020 7287 4570   Fax 020 7494 0583
✉ alan.greene@compendiumpublishing.com
Managing Director *Alan Greene*
Editorial Director *Simon Forty*

Founded 1996. Publishes and packages for international publishing companies – general non-fiction: history, reference, hobbies, children's and educational transport and militaria. No unsolicited mss; synopses and ideas preferred.
ROYALTIES twice-yearly.

Condor
See **Souvenir Press Ltd**

Conran Octopus
See **Octopus Publishing Group**

Constable & Robinson Ltd
3 The Lanchesters, 162 Fulham Palace Road, London W6 9ER
☎020 8741 3663   Fax 020 8748 7562
✉ enquiries@constablerobinson.com
www.constablerobinson.com
Non-Executive Chairman *Benjamin Glazebrook*
Managing Director *Nick Robinson*
Directors *Jan Chamier, Nova Jayne Heath, Adrian Andrews*

Constable & Co founded in 1890 by Archibald Constable, a grandson of Walter Scott's publisher. Robinson Publishing Ltd founded in 1983 by Nick Robinson. In December 1999 Constable and Robinson combined their individual shareholdings into a single company, Constable & Robinson Ltd. IMPRINTS **Constable** (Hardbacks) Editorial Director *Carol O'Brien* Publishes biography and autobiography, crime fiction, general and military history, psychology, travel, climbing, landscape photography and outdoor pursuits guidebooks. **Robinson** (Paperbacks) Senior Commissioning Editor *Krystyna Green* Publishes crime, science fiction, *Daily Telegraph* health books, the Mammoth series, psychology, true crime, military history and *Smarties* children's books. Unsolicited sample chapters, synopses and ideas for books welcome. No mss; no e-mail submissions. Enclose return postage.

Authors' Rating With an excellent result from a Society of Authors' survey of author/publisher relations, Constable & Robinson is one of the three top small publishers for sales and revenue.

Consultants Bureau
See **Springer**

The Continuum International Publishing Group Limited
The Tower Building, 11 York Road, London SE1 7NX
☎020 7922 0880   Fax 020 7922 0881
www.continuumbooks.com
Chairman & Chief Executive *Philip Sturrock*
Approx. Annual Turnover £16 million

Founded in 1999 by a buy-out of the academic and religious publishing of Cassell and the acquisition of Continuum New York. Publishes academic, religious and general books. DIVISIONS **Academic Humanities** Publishing Director *Anthony Haynes* Education, social sciences, literature, film and music, philosophy (including the **Thoemmes** imprint), linguistics, biblical studies and theology printed under the **T&T Clark** imprint. TITLES *Getting the Buggers to Add Up*; *Teaching in Further Education*; *What Philosophy Is*; *The Guerrilla Film Makers Handbook*. **General Trade & Continuum Religion** Publishing Director *Robin Baird-Smith* Publishes under **Continuum Burns & Oates** (RC books); **Morehouse** (Anglican titles). TITLES *Seven Basic Plots*; *Seven Last Words* (Burns & Oates); *Known to the Senses* (Morehouse). IMPRINTS **Continuum**; **T&T Clark International**; **Thoemmes**; **Burns & Oates**; **Morehouse**. 500 titles in 2004. Unsolicited synopses and ideas within the subject areas listed above welcome; approach in writing in the first instance. OVERSEAS SUBSIDIARIES The Continuum International Publishing Group Inc., New York and Harrisburg, PA.
ROYALTIES twice-yearly.

Authors' Rating Expanding religious and academic list takes in controversial ideas and original thinking.

Conway Maritime Press
See **Chrysalis Books Group**

Thomas Cook Publishing
PO Box 227, Peterborough PE3 8SB
☎01733 417352   Fax 01733 416688
Head of Publishing *Chris Young*

Part of the Thomas Cook Group Ltd, publishing commenced in 1873 with the first issue of *Cook's Continental Timetable*. Publishes guidebooks, maps and timetables. About 20 titles a year. No unsolicited mss; synopses and ideas welcome as long as they are travel-related.
ROYALTIES annually.

Leo Cooper
See **Pen & Sword Books Ltd**

Corgi
See **Transworld Publishers**

Corgi Children's Books
See **The Random House Group Ltd**

Countryside Books
2 Highfield Avenue, Newbury RG14 5DS
☎01635 43816   Fax 01635 551004
✉ info@countrysidebooks.co.uk
www.countrysidebooks.co.uk
Publisher *Nicholas Battle*

Founded 1976. Publishes local interest paperbacks on regional subjects, generally by English county. Local history, dialects, genealogy, walking and photographic, aviation and military, some transport. Over 400 titles available. Unsolicited mss and synopses welcome but no fiction, poetry, natural history or personal memories.
ROYALTIES twice-yearly.

Crème de la Crime Ltd
PO Box 523, Chesterfield S40 9AT
☎01246 520835   Fax 01246 520835
✉ info@cremedelacrime.com
www.cremedelacrime.com
Managing Director *Iain Pattison*
Editorial Director *Lynne Patrick*
Approx. Annual Turnover £60,000

Founded in 2003 to discover and publish crime fiction by new authors. 3 titles in 2004. Authors are urged to purchase detailed guidelines; send £2.50 with A4 s.a.e. and two first-class stamps. Initial approach by e-mail; submissions by post with s.a.e. (a one-off administration fee of £15 is charged).
ROYALTIES annually.

Crescent Books
See **Mercat Press Ltd**

Cressrelles Publishing Co. Ltd
10 Station Road Industrial Estate, Colwall,
Malvern WR13 6RN
☎01684 540154   Fax 01684 540154
✉ simonsmith@cressrelles4drama.
fsbusiness.co.uk

Managing Director *Leslie Smith*

Publishes a range of local interest books and drama titles. IMPRINTS **J. Garnet Miller** Plays and theatre texts; **Kenyon-Deane** Plays and drama textbooks. Submissions welcome.

Crombie Jardine Publishing Limited
13 Nonsuch Walk, Cheam SM2 7LG
☎020 8393 5454
✉ catriona@crombiejardine.com
www.crombiejardine.com

Sales & Publishing Director *David Crombie*
Publishing Director *Catriona Jardine*

Founded in 2004. Specialises in fun, quirky and topical humour books only. TITLES *The Little Book of Chavs*; *The World's Funniest Proverbs*; *Shag Youself Slim*. 6 titles in 2004. Unsolicited mss, synopses and ideas welcome; send by post to the publishing director.

ROYALTIES twice-yearly.

Authors' Rating Having cut their teeth with **Michael O'Mara Books** on such dubious classics as *Shite's Unoriginal Miscellany* and *The Little Book of Farting*, the co-founders of Crombie Jardine are out to grab a share of the young adult humour market.

Crossway
See **Inter-Varsity Press**

The Crowood Press Ltd
The Stable Block, Crowood Lane, Ramsbury, Marlborough SN8 2HR
☎01672 520320   Fax 01672 520280
✉ enquiries@crowood.com
www.crowood.com

Chairman *John Dennis*
Managing Director *Ken Hathaway*

Publishes sport and leisure titles, including animal and land husbandry, climbing and walking, maritime, country sports, equestrian, fishing and shooting; also crafts, dogs, gardening, DIY, theatre, natural history, aviation, military history and motoring. IMPRINT **Airlife Publishing** Specialist aviation titles for pilots, historians and enthusiasts. About 70 titles a year. Preliminary letter preferred in all cases.

ROYALTIES annually.

CRW Publishing Ltd
69 Gloucester Crescent, London NW1 7EG
☎020 7485 5764   Fax 0870 751 7254
✉ marcus.clapham@crw-publishing.co.uk
www.crw-publishing.co.uk

Chairman *Ken Webb*
Editorial Director *Marcus Clapham*
Approx. Annual Turnover £2 million

Founded 2003. Publishes literary classics, gift, children's, philosophy, myth and legend, reference, boxed sets. IMPRINTS **Collector's Library**; **Book Blocks**; **Essential Thinkers**; **Poetry Library**; **Myth & Legend**; **Reference Library**. 50 titles in 2004. No unsolicited mss. Synopses and ideas are welcome; send by post to the editorial director.

ROYALTIES annually.

James Currey Publishers
73 Botley Road, Oxford OX2 0BS
☎01865 244111   Fax 01865 246454
✉ editorial@jamescurrey.co.uk
www.jamescurrey.co.uk

Chairman *James Currey*
Managing Director/Editorial Director *Douglas H. Johnson*

Founded 1985. A specialist publisher. Publishes academic paperback books on Africa and Third World: history, anthropology, economics, sociology, politics and literary criticism. Approach in writing by post with synopsis if material is 'relevant to our needs'.

ROYALTIES annually.

Custom Publishing
See **The Orion Publishing Group Limited**

D&B Publishing
PO Box 18, Hassocks BN6 9WR
☎01273 834680   Fax 01273 831629
✉ info@dandbpublishing.com
www.dandbpublishing.com

Joint Managing Directors *Dan Addelman, Byron Jacobs*

Founded 2002. Publishes games books, specialising in gambling primarily. 6 titles in 2004. Unsolicited mss, synopses and ideas welcome; approach by e-mail in the first instance.

ROYALTIES annually.

Dalesman Publishing Co. Ltd
The Water Mill, Broughton Hall, Skipton BD23 3AG
☎01756 701381   Fax 01756 701326

✉ editorial@dalesman.co.uk
www.dalesman.co.uk

Book Editor *Mark Whitley*

Publishers of *Countryman, Dalesman, Cumbria* and *The Yorkshire Journal* magazines, and regional books covering the North of England. Subjects include walking, guidebooks, history, humour and folklore. About 10 titles a year. Will consider mss on subjects listed above, relating to the North.

ROYALTIES annually.

Terence Dalton Ltd

Water Street, Lavenham, Sudbury CO10 9RN
☎01787 249291   Fax 01787 248267
www.terencedalton.com

Director/Editorial Head *Elisabeth Whitehair*

Founded 1967. Part of the Lavenham Group Plc, a family company. No unsolicited mss. Ideas welcome; telephone in the first instance. Non-fiction only.

ROYALTIES annually.

Darton, Longman & Todd Ltd

1 Spencer Court, 140–142 Wandsworth High Street, London SW18 4JJ
☎020 8875 0155   Fax 020 8875 0133
✉ tradesales@darton-longman-todd.co.uk
www.darton-longman-todd.co.uk

Editorial Director *Brendan Walsh*
Editor/Rights Officer *Elizabeth Piercy*
Approx. Annual Turnover £1 million

Founded 1959. In July 1990 DLT became a common ownership company, owned and run by staff members. A leading ecumenical, predominantly Christian, publisher, with a strong emphasis on spirituality, theology and the ministry and mission of the Church. TITLES *Jerusalem Bible; New Jerusalem Bible; The Return of the Prodigal Son; Resurrection.* About 50 titles a year. Sample material for books on theological or spiritual subjects considered.

ROYALTIES twice-yearly.

David & Charles Publishers

Brunel House, Forde Close, Newton Abbot TQ12 4PU
☎01626 323200   Fax 01626 323317
✉ mail@davidandcharles.co.uk
www.davidandcharles.co.uk

Publishing Director *Sara Domville*

Founded 1960, owned by F.&W. Publications. Publishes illustrated non-fiction for international markets, specialising in needlecraft, crafts, art techniques, practical photography, military history, equestrian and gardening. No fiction, poetry or memoirs. TITLES *Voices from the Home Front; Branchline Britain; Bra; The Knitter's Bible; Groundwork Training for your Horse.* About 200 titles a year. Unsolicited mss will be considered if return postage is included; synopses and ideas welcome for the subjects listed above.

ROYALTIES twice-yearly or flat fees.

Christopher Davies Publishers Ltd

PO Box 403, Swansea SA1 4YF
☎01792 648825   Fax 01792 648825
✉ chris@cdaviesbookswales.com

Managing Director/Editorial Head *Christopher T. Davies*
Approx. Annual Turnover £20,000

Founded 1949 to promote and expand Welsh-language publications. Publishes biography, cookery, history, sport and literature of Welsh interest. TITLES *An A–Z of Wales and the Welsh; Welsh Birthplaces; Carwyn: A Personal Memoir; Who's Who in Welsh History.* About 2 titles a year. No unsolicited mss. Synopses and ideas for books welcome.

ROYALTIES twice-yearly.

Authors' Rating A favourite for Celtic readers and writers.

Giles de la Mare Publishers Ltd

PO Box 25351, London NW5 1ZT
☎020 7485 2533   Fax 020 7485 2534
✉ gilesdelamare@dial.pipex.com
www.gilesdelamare.co.uk

Chairman/Managing Director *Giles de la Mare*
Approx. Annual Turnover £30,000

Founded 1995 and commenced publishing in April 1996. Publishes mainly non-fiction, especially art and architecture, biography, history, music. TITLES *Flint Architecture of East Anglia* Stephen Hart; *19th Century British Painting* Luke Herrmann; *Short Stories,* Vols I & II Walter de la Mare; *Handsworth Revolution* David Winkley; *The Life of Henry Moore* Roger Berthoud; *Becoming an Orchestral Musician* Richard Davis; *Romanesque Churches of France: A Traveller's Guide* Peter Strafford. Unsolicited mss, synopses and ideas welcome after initial telephone call.

ROYALTIES twice-yearly.

Debrett's Ltd

1A Hammersmith Broadway, London W6 1DL
☎020 8600 8222   Fax 020 8600 8322
✉ people@debretts.co.uk
www.debretts.co.uk

Managing Director *David C. Tennant*

Editor-in-Chief *Charles Mosley*

Biographical reference plus etiquette, correct form and other social guides; also magazines. Book TITLES include triennial *Debrett's Peerage & Baronetage* and annual *People of Today* (as book, CD-ROM and online). Glossy, quarterly lifestyle magazine, *Debrett's*, is now main periodical. Web-based consumer and social conundrum guides, humorous books and individual 'world of' biographies. Book and article proposals welcome. Send synopsis in both hard copy and Word 2000 format.

Dedalus Ltd

Langford Lodge, St Judith's Lane, Sawtry
PE28 5XE
☎01487 832382
✉ info@dedalusbooks.com
www.dedalusbooks.com
Chairman *Juri Gabriel*
Managing Director *Eric Lane*
Approx. Annual Turnover £200,000

Founded 1983. Publishes contemporary European fiction and classics and original literary fiction. TITLES *The Dedalus Book of the Occult; The Arabian Nightmare* Robert Irwin; *Memoirs of a Gnostic Dwarf* David Madsen; *The Double Life of Daniel Glick* Maurice Caldera; *Music in a Foreign Language* Andrew Crumey (winner of the Saltire Best First Book Award in 1994).

DIVISIONS/IMPRINTS
Contemporary European Fiction 1992–2004; **Dedalus European Classics**; **Original Fiction in Paperback**; **Literary Concept Books**. Welcomes submissions for original fiction and books suitable for its list but 'most people sending work in have no idea what kind of books Dedalus publishes and merely waste their efforts'. Author guidelines on website. Particularly interested in intellectually clever and unusual fiction. A letter about the author should always accompany any submission. No replies without s.a.e.
ROYALTIES annually.

Authors' Rating A small, quality publisher which actually recognises that good books can come from foreign language writers.

JM Dent
See **The Orion Publishing Group Ltd**

André Deutsch Ltd
See **Carlton Publishing Group**

Digital Octopus
See **Octopus Publishing Group**

Digital Press
See **Elsevier Ltd**

Dinas
See **Y Lolfa Cyf**

Diverse Publications Ltd

Unit 56, 3 Courthill House, 60 Water Lane, Wilmslow SK9 5AJ
☎0870 240 9998   Fax 01625 535616
✉ diversepublications@yahoo.co.uk
www.DiversePublications.co.uk
Managing Director *Robin Barratt*
Publishing Director *Inna Zabrodskaya*
Approx. Annual Turnover £100,000

Originally established in Moscow in 2003, Diverse Publications publishes books on erotic photography, art, poetry and prose. TITLES *The Best of Modern Italian Erotica*; *The Best of Russian Erotica*. 3 titles in 2004. Synopsis and ideas welcome; approch by letter in the first instance.
ROYALTIES twice-yearly.

John Donald Publishers Ltd

West Newington House, 10 Newington Road, Edinburgh EH9 1QS
☎0131 668 4371   Fax 0131 668 4466
✉ info@birlinn.co.uk
www.birlinn.co.uk
Managing Director *Hugh Andrew*

Bought by **Birlinn Ltd** in 1999. Publishes academic and scholarly, archaeology, architecture, textbooks, guidebooks, local, and social history. New books are published as an imprint of Birlinn Ltd. About 20 titles a year.
ROYALTIES annually.

Donhead Publishing Ltd

Lower Coombe, Donhead St Mary, Shaftesbury SP7 9LY
☎01747 828422   Fax 01747 828522
✉ jillpearce@donhead.com
www.donhead.com
Contact *Jill Pearce*

Founded 1990 to specialise in publishing how-to books for building practitioners; particularly interested in architectural conservation material. Publishes building, architecture and heritage only. TITLES *Preserving Post-War Heritage; Stone Cleaning; Architecture 1900; Encyclopaedia of Architectural Terms; Cleaning Historic Buildings; Brickwork; Practical Stone Masonry; Conservation of*

Timber Buildings; Surveying Historic Buildings; English Heritage Directory of Building Limes; Journal of Architectural Conservation (3 issues yearly). 6 titles a year. Unsolicited mss, synopses and ideas welcome.

Dorling Kindersley Ltd

Part of the Penguin Group, 80 Strand, London WC2R 0RL
☎020 7010 3000   Fax 020 7010 6060
www.dk.com

Chief Executive *Anthony Forbes Watson*
Managing Director *Andrew Welham*
Publisher *Christopher Davis*

Founded 1974. Packager and publisher of illustrated non-fiction: cookery, crafts, gardening, health, travel guides, atlases, natural history and children's information and fiction. Launched a US imprint in 1991 and an Australian imprint in 1997. Acquired Henderson Publishing in 1995 and was purchased by Pearson plc for £311 million in 2000.

DIVISIONS
Adult: **Travel/Reference** Publisher *Douglas Amrine*; **General/Lifestyle** Publisher *John Roberts*. Children's: **Reference** Publisher *Miriam Farby*; **PreSchool/Primary** Publisher *Sophie Mitchell*. IMPRINTS **Ladybird; Ladybird Audio; Funfax; Eyewitness Guides; Eyewitness Travel Guides**. TITLES *BMA Complete Family Health Encyclopedia*; *RHS A–Z Encyclopedia of Garden Plants*; *Children's Illustrated Encyclopedia*; *The Way Things Work*. Unsolicited synopses/ideas for books welcome.

Authors' Rating A much slimmed version of the old DK is heavily dependent on 'soft learning' products for education markets. The aim is to make Dorling Kindersley products distinctive against low priced rivals and retailers' own brand product, not to mention the Internet. Most titles are team efforts with writers and illustrators working closely with an in-house editor.

Doubleday

See **Transworld Publishers**

Doubleday Children's Books

See **The Random House Group Ltd**

Drake Educational Associates

St Fagans Road, Fairwater, Cardiff CF5 3AE
☎029 2056 0333   Fax 029 2956 0313

Managing Director *R. G. Drake*

Literacy, phonics and language development games and activities. Ideas and scripts in these fields welcome. Also resources for subject areas in the primary school and modern languages at KS2.

Dref Wen

28 Church Road, Whitchurch CF14 2EA
☎029 2061 7860   Fax 029 2061 0507
✉ gwilym@drefwen.com

Chairman *R. Boore*
Managing Director *G. Boore*

Founded 1970. Publishes Welsh language and bilingual children's books, Welsh and English educational books for Welsh learners.

ROYALTIES annually.

Gerald Duckworth & Co. Ltd

First Floor, 90–93 Cowcross Street, London EC1M 6BF
☎020 7490 7300   Fax 020 7490 0080
✉ info@duckworth-publishers.co.uk
www.ducknet.co.uk

Managing Director *Peter Mayer*
Publishing Director *Eleanor Birne*
Editorial Director (Academic) *Deborah Blake*
Approx. Annual Turnover £2 million

Founded 1898 by Gerald Duckworth. Original publishers of Virginia Woolf. Other early authors include Hilaire Belloc, John Galsworthy, D.H. Lawrence and George Orwell. Duckworth is a general trade publisher whose authors include John Bayley, Mary Warnock, Joan Bakewell and J.J. Connolly. In addition to its trade list, Duckworth has a strong academic division. Acquired by Peter Mayer in 2003. IMPRINTS/ DIVISIONS **Bristol Classical Press** Classical texts and modern languages; **Ardis** Russian literature; **Duckworth Academic**; **Duckworth General**. No unsolicited mss; synopses and sample chapters only. Enclose s.a.e. or return postage for response/return.

ROYALTIES twice-yearly at first, annually thereafter.

Authors' Rating Responding to the magic touch of veteran publisher Peter Mayer, Duckworth has emerged from the doldrums to publish titles 'that larger publishers overlook'.

Duncan Petersen Publishing Limited

31 Ceylon Road, London W14 0PY
☎020 7371 2356   Fax 020 7371 2507
✉ dp@macunlimited.net

Director *Andrew Duncan*

Founded 1986. Publisher and packager of childcare, business, antiques, birds, nature, atlases, walking and travel books. IMPRINT **Duncan Petersen** SERIES *Charming Small Hotel Guides*; *Charming Restaurant Guides*; *On Foot* (city walking guides). Unsolicited synopses and ideas for books welcome.
FEES paid.

Dunedin Academic Press Ltd
Hudson House, 8 Albany Street, Edinburgh EH1 3QB
☎0131 473 2397   Fax 01250 870920
✉ mail@dunedinacademicpress.co.uk
www.dunedinacademicpress.co.uk
Managing Director *Anthony Kinahan*
Founded 2001. Publishes academic and serious general non-fiction. Considerable experience in academic and professional publishing. 7 titles in 2004. Not interested in science (other than earth sciences), fiction or children's. No unsolicited mss. Synopses and ideas welcome. Approach first in writing outlining proposal and identifying market.
ROYALTIES annually.

Earthscan Publications
See **Kogan Page Ltd**

Ebury Press
See **The Random House Group Ltd**

Economist Books
See **Profile Books**

Eden
See **Transworld Publishers**

Edinburgh University Press
22 George Square, Edinburgh EH8 9LF
☎0131 650 4218   Fax 0131 662 0053
www.eup.ed.ac.uk
Chairman *Timothy Rix*
Chief Executive *Timothy Wright*
Deputy Chief Executive/Head of Publishing *Jackie Jones*
Senior Editor *Nicola Carr*
Publishes academic and scholarly books (and journals): gender studies, geography, history – ancient, classical, medieval and modern – Islamic studies, linguistics, literary criticism, media and cultural studies, sociology and social theory, philosophy, politics, Scottish studies, theology and religious studies. About 100 titles a year.
ROYALTIES annually.

Egmont Books Limited
239 Kensington High Street, London W8 6SA
☎020 7761 3500   Fax 020 7761 3510
www.egmont.co.uk
Vice President/UK General Manager *Robert McMenemy*
Director of Egmont Press *Cally Poplak*
Director of Egmont Publishing *David Riley*
Part of the Egmont Group (Copenhagen), Egmont Press publishes children's fiction and non-fiction series and picture books, while Egmont Publishing publishes classic and contemporary characters, learning and colour & activity. TITLES *Thomas the Tank Engine*; *Winnie the Pooh*; *A Series of Unfortunate Events*; *The Wind on Fire* trilogy. About 500 titles a year. Synopses and sample chapters welcome; approach in writing with s.a.e. marked for the attention of 'The Reader'. 'We regret that we are unable to return unsolicited material without s.a.e.'

Authors' Rating The fourth largest children's book publishing group in the UK, Egmont uses its famous characters like Postman Pat to good effect in supermarket and direct sales.

Eland Publishing Ltd
Third Floor, 61 Exmouth Market, London EC1R 4QL
☎020 7833 0762   Fax 020 7833 4434
✉ info@travelbooks.co.uk
www.travelbooks.co.uk
Directors *Rose Baring, John Hatt, Barnaby Rogerson*
Approx. Annual Turnover £250,000
Eland reprints classics of travel literature with a backlist of 60 titles, including *Naples '44* Norman Lewis; *Travels with Myself and Another* Martha Gelhorn; *Portrait of a Turkish Family* Irfan Orga; *Travels into the Interior of Africa* Mungo Park. No unsolicited mss. Postcards and e-mails welcome.
ROYALTIES annually.

Element
See **HarperCollins Publishers Ltd**

11:9
See **Neil Wilson Publishing Ltd**

Edward Elgar Publishing Ltd
Glensanda House, Montpellier Parade, Cheltenham GL50 1UA
☎01242 226934   Fax 01242 262111
✉ info@e-elgar.co.uk
www.e-elgar.com

Managing Director *Edward Elgar*

Founded 1986. International publisher in economics, the environment, public policy, business and management and law. TITLES *Who's Who in Economics* (3rd ed.); *Handbook of Environmental and Resource Economics*; *Who's Who in the Management Sciences*. 277 titles in 2004. No unsolicited mss; synopses and ideas in the subject areas listed above welcome. Approach by letter or e-mail; no telephone inquiries.

ROYALTIES annually.

Elliot Right Way Books

Kingswood Buildings, Lower Kingswood, Tadworth KT20 6TD

☎01737 832202   Fax 01737 830311

✉ info@right-way.co.uk

www.right-way.co.uk

Managing Directors *A. Clive Elliot, Malcolm G. Elliot*

Founded 1946 by Andrew G. Elliot. Publishes paperback how-to and educative titles on an unlimited variety of home reference, indoor and outdoor leisure hobbies and pursuits, careers and business. Subjects include cookery, wine, family financial and legal matters, public speaking, weddings, jokes, parenting, etiquette, English skills, driving, fishing, horse riding, drawing, music, puzzles, crosswords and quizzes, job seeking, running your own company. IMPRINTS **Right Way** Instructional paperbacks in B format for the most popular subjects; **Right Way Plus** Larger C format for more specialised subjects; **Clarion** B format for promotional/ultra low-price range. Unsolicited mss, synopses and ideas for books welcome.

ROYALTIES annually.

Elliott & Thompson

27 John Street, London WC1N 2BX

☎020 7831 5013   Fax 020 7831 5011

www.elliottthompson.com

Publishers *David Elliott, Brad Thompson*

Approx. Annual Turnover £92,000

Founded 2001. Publishes literary fiction, biography, belles lettres, reprints of classic male writers. 16 titles in 2004. New proposals welcome (send synopsis and sample pages initially) but s.a.e. essential.

Aidan Ellis Publishing

Whinfield, Herbert Road, Salcombe TQ8 8HN

☎01548 842755   Fax 01548 844356

✉ mail@aidanellispublishing.co.uk

www.aepub.demon.co.uk

Partners/Editorial Heads *Aidan Ellis, Lucinda Ellis*

Founded in 1971. Specialises in general trade books and non-fiction. TITLES *The Royal Gardens in Windsor Great Park* Charles Lyte; *Trees For Your Garden* Roy Lancaster; *Pesca* Ian B. Hart; *Presumed Dead* Eunice Chapman; *That's Rich!* Craig Rich; *The Bird Table Book* Tony Soper; *Seahorses* Plymouth Marine Aquarium. Ideas and synopses welcome (return postage, please).

ROYALTIES twice-yearly.

Elm Publications/Training

(wholly owned subsidiary of

Elm Consulting Ltd)

Seaton House, Kings Ripton, Huntingdon PE28 2NJ

☎01487 773254

✉ sritchie@elm-training.co.uk

www.elm-training.co.uk

Managing Director *Sheila Ritchie*

Founded 1977. Publishes textbooks, teaching aids, educational resources and educational software in the fields of business and management for adult learners. Books and teaching/training resources are generally commissioned to meet specific business, management and other syllabuses. 'We seek good training materials for business/management, especially tested and proven. About 30 titles a year. Ideas are welcome; initial approach by post or e-mail with outline, or by a brief telephone call.

ROYALTIES annually.

Elsevier Ltd

The Boulevard, Langford Lane, Kidlington, Oxford OX5 1GB

☎01865 843000   Fax 01865 843010

www.elsevier.com

Chief Operating Officer *Gavin Howe*

CEO, Science & Technology (Books & Journals) *Herman van Campenhout*

Parent company Reed Elsevier, Amsterdam. Now incorporates Pergamon Press and Harcourt Publishers International. Publishes academic and professional reference books, scientific, technical and medical books, journals, CD-ROMs and magazines. IMPRINTS **Academic Press**; **Architectural Press**; **Butterworth Heinemann**; **Digital Press**; **Elsevier**; **Elsevier Advanced Technology**; **Focal Press**; **Gulf Professional Press**; **JAI**; **Made Simple Books**; **Morgan Kauffman**; **Newnes**; **North-Holland**. DIVISION **Elsevier**

(Health Sciences) 32 Jamestown Road, London NW1 7BY ☎020 7424 4200 Fax 020 7483 2293 Website www.elsevier-health.com CEO Health Sciences (Books & Journals) *Brian Nairn*, Managing Director *Dominic Vaughan* Publishes scientific, technical, medical books and journals. IMPRINTS **Baillière Tindall**; **Churchill Livingstone**; **Mosby**; **Pergamon**; **Saunders**. No unsolicited mss, but synopses and project proposals welcome.

ROYALTIES annually.

Emissary Publishing
PO Box 33, Bicester OX26 4ZZ
☎01869 323447   Fax 01869 324096

Editorial Director *Val Miller*

Founded 1992. Publishes mainly humorous paperback books including the complete set of Peter Pook novels; no poetry or children's. No unsolicited mss or synopses.

ROYALTIES twice-yearly.

Emma Treehouse Ltd
2nd Floor, The Old Brewhouse, Lower Charlton Trading Estate, Shepton Mallet BA4 5QE
☎01749 330529   Fax 01749 330544
✉ richard.powell4@virgin.net
www.emmatreehouse.com

Co-Directors *Richard Powell, David Bailey*
Approx. Annual Turnover £1 million

Founded 1992. Publishes children's pre-school novelty books. No mss. Illustrations, synopses and ideas for books welcome; write in the first instance.

FEES paid; no royalties.

Empiricus Books
See **Janus Publishing Company Ltd**

English Heritage (Publishing)
Kemble Drive, Swindon SN2 2GZ
☎01793 414497   Fax 01793 414769
www.english-heritage.org.uk

English Heritage's publishing programme is divided into two streams: commercial (titles commissioned to generate revenue) and not-for-profit, reflecting the organisation's academic and specialist publishing. 'All titles relate directly to the work of the organisation, so we do not accept unsolicited material.'

Enitharmon Press
26B Caversham Road, London NW5 2DU
☎020 7482 5967   Fax 020 7284 1787
✉ books@enitharmon.co.uk
www.enitharmon.co.uk

Director *Stephen Stuart-Smith*

Founded 1967. An independent company with an enterprising editorial policy, Enitharmon has established itself as one of Britain's leading literary presses. Patron of 'the new and the neglected', Enitharmon also prides itself on the success of its collaborations between writers and artists, now published by its associate company, **Enitharmon Editions**. Publishes poetry, literary criticism, fiction, art and photography. TITLES *The Ancient Mariner* David Jones; *The Rope-Makers* Michael Longley; *Medley for Morin Khur* Paul Muldoon; *The Ship of Swallows* Edward Thomas. No unsolicited mss.

ROYALTIES according to contract.

Epworth Press
c/o Methodist Publishing House, 4 John Wesley Road, Werrington, Peterborough PE4 6ZP
☎01733 325002   Fax 01733 384180
✉ comm.editor@mph.org.uk
www.mph.org.uk

Chairman *The Revd. Michael Townsend*
Commissioning Editor *Dr Natalie K. Watson*

Publishes Christian books only: philosophy, theology, biblical studies, pastoralia, social concern and Methodist studies. No fiction, poetry or children's. About 12 titles a year. Unsolicited mss, synopses and ideas welcome; send sample chapter and contents with covering letter and s.a.e.

ROYALTIES annually.

The Erotic Print Society
17 Harwood Road, London SW6 4QP
☎020 7736 5800   Fax 020 7736 6330
✉ eros@eroticprints.org
www.eroticprints.org

Managing Director *Mr J. Maclean*

Publishes books of erotic art and photography and three magazines of erotic literature. Unsolicited material accepted but approach in writing in the first instance with a summary or first chapter.

Essential Thinkers
See **CRW Publishing Ltd**

Euromonitor
60–61 Britton Street, London EC1M 5UX
☎020 7251 8024   Fax 020 7608 3149
www.euromonitor.com

Chairman *R.N. Senior*

Managing Director *T.J. Fenwick*
Approx. Annual Turnover £20 million

Founded 1972. International business information publisher specialising in library and professional reference books, market reports, electronic databases, journals and CD-ROMs. Publishes business reference, market analysis and information directories only. DIVISIONS **Market Analysis** *A. Irwin*; **Reference Books & Directories** *S. Holmes*. TITLES *Credit & Charge Cards: The International Market*; *European Marketing Handbook*; *European Directory of Trade and Business Associations*; *World Retail Directory and Sourcebook*. About 1000 titles a year.
PAYMENT is generally by flat fee.

Evans Brothers Ltd

2A Portman Mansions, Chiltern Street, London W1U 6NR
☎020 7487 0920   Fax 020 7487 0921
✉ sales@evansbrothers.co.uk
www.evansbooks.co.uk

Managing Director *Stephen Pawley*
International Publishing Director *Brian Jones*
UK Publisher *Su Swallow*
Approx. Annual Turnover £4.5 million

Founded 1908 by Robert and Edward Evans. Originally published educational journals, books for primary schools and teacher education. After rapid expansion into popular fiction and drama, both were sacrificed to a major programme of educational books for schools in East and West Africa. A UK programme was launched in 1986 followed by the acquisition of Hamish Hamilton's non-fiction list for children in 1990. Acquired interests in Cherrytree Books and Zero to Ten in 1999. Publishes UK children's and educational books, and educational books for Africa, the Caribbean and Latin America. IMPRINTS **Cherrytree Books**; **Zero to Ten** trade under Zero to Ten Ltd at the Evans address above. OVERSEAS ASSOCIATES in Kenya, Cameroon, Sierra Leone; Evans Bros (Nigeria Publishers) Ltd. About 120 titles a year.
ROYALTIES annually.

Everyman

See **The Orion Publishing Group Ltd**

Everyman Chess

See **Gloucester Publishers Plc**

Everyman's Library

Northburgh House, 10 Northburgh Street, London EC1V 0AT
☎020 7566 6350   Fax 020 7490 3708

✉ books@everyman.uk.com
Publisher *David Campbell*
Approx. Annual Turnover £3.5 million

Founded 1906. Publishes hardback classics of world literature, pocket poetry anthologies, children's books and travel guides. Publishes no new titles apart from poetry anthologies; only classics (no new authors). AUTHORS include Bulgakov, Bellow, Borges, Heller, Marquez, Nabokov, Naipaul, Orwell, Rushdie, Updike, Waugh and Wodehouse. No unsolicited mss.
ROYALTIES annually.

University of Exeter Press

Reed Hall, Streatham Drive, Exeter EX4 4QR
☎01392 263066   Fax 01392 263064
✉ uep@exeterpress.co.uk
www.exeterpress.co.uk

Publisher *Simon Baker*

Founded 1956. Publishes academic books: archaeology, classical studies and ancient history, history, maritime studies, English literature (especially medieval), European studies, modern languages and literature, film history, performance studies, Arabic studies and books on Exeter and the South West. IMPRINT **Bristol Phoenix Press** Commissioning Editor *John Betts* Classics and ancient history. About 30 titles a year. Proposals welcomed in the above subject areas.
ROYALTIES annually.

Exley Publications Ltd

16 Chalk Hill, Watford WD19 4BG
☎01923 248328   Fax 01923 800440
✉ editorial@exleypublications.co.uk
www.helenexleygiftbooks.com

Editorial Director *Helen Exley*

Founded 1976. Independent family company. Publishes giftbooks, quotation anthologies and humour. No submissions, please.

Expert Books

See **Transworld Publishers**

Eyewitness Guides/ Eyewitness Travel Guides

See **Dorling Kindersley Ltd**

Faber & Faber Ltd

3 Queen Square, London WC1N 3AU
☎020 7465 0045   Fax 020 7465 0034
www.faber.co.uk

Chief Executive *Stephen Page*
Approx. Annual Turnover £13.5 million

Geoffrey Faber founded the company in the 1920s, with T.S. Eliot as an early recruit to the board. The original list was based on contemporary poetry and plays (the distinguished backlist includes Eliot, Auden and MacNeice). Publishes poetry and drama, children's, fiction, film, music, politics, biography.

DIVISIONS
Fiction Senior Fiction Editor *Lee Brackstone* Authors P.D. James, Peter Carey, Giles Foden, Michael Frayn, Tobias Hill, Kazuo Ishiguro, Barbara Kingsolver, Milan Kundera, Hanif Kureishi, John Lanchester, John McGahern, Rohinton Mistry, Lorrie Moore, Andrew O'Hagan, DBC Pierre, Jane Smiley; **Children's** *Suzy Jenvey, Julia Wells* AUTHORS Philip Ardagh, Terry Deary, Ricky Gervais, Russell Stannard, G.P. Taylor; **Film** *Walter Donohue* and **Plays** *Dinah Wood* AUTHORS Samuel Beckett, Alan Bennett, David Hare, Brian Friel, Patrick Marber, Harold Pinter, Tom Stoppard, Woody Allen, John Boorman, Joel and Ethan Coen, John Hodge, Martin Scorsese, Quentin Tarantino; **Music** *Belinda Matthews* AUTHORS Alfred Brendel, Humphrey Burton, Nicholas Kenyon, Richard Morrison, Harvey Sachs, Elizabeth Wilson; **Poetry** *Paul Keegan* Authors Simon Armitage, Douglas Dunn, Seamus Heaney, Ted Hughes, Paul Muldoon, Tom Paulin; **Non-fiction** *Neil Belton, Julian Loose* AUTHORS John Carey, Simon Garfield, John Gray, Jan Morris, Francis Spufford, Frances Stonor Saunders, Jenny Uglow.
ROYALTIES twice-yearly.

Authors' Rating Faber has experienced something of a rebirth with authors benefiting from more energetic and imaginative marketing. The children's books division, catering for the six to 16 age group, has done particularly well with turnover doubling in less than two years. Such is Faber's commitment to working closely with authors that Ricky Gervais, author of *Flanimals*, was given his own office in Queen Square.

Facet Publishing
7 Ridgmount Street, London WC1E 7AE
☎020 7255 0590/0505 (text phone)
Fax 020 7255 0591
✉ info@facetpublishing.co.uk
www.facetpublishing.co.uk
Managing Director *John Woolley*

Publishing arm of **CILIP: The Chartered Institute of Library and Information Professionals** (formerly the Library Association). Publishes library and information science, monographs, reference, IT training materials and bibliography aimed at library and information professionals. IMPRINTS **Library Association Publishing**; **Clive Bingley Books**; **Facet Publishing**. Over 200 titles in print, including *The New Walford* and *AACR2*. 25–30 titles a year. Unsolicited mss, synopses and ideas welcome provided material falls firmly within the company's specialist subject areas.
ROYALTIES annually.

Fernhurst Books
Duke's Path, High Street, Arundel BN18 9AJ
☎01903 882277   Fax 01903 882715
✉ sales@fernhurstbooks.co.uk
www.fernhurstbooks.co.uk
Chairman/Managing Director *Tim Davison*

Founded 1979. Books for people who love watersports. Publishes practical, highly-illustrated handbooks on sailing and watersports. TITLES *Laser Book*; *Rules in Practice*; *Wind Strategy*; *Weather at Sea*; *Simple Boat Maintenance*; *Electric Afloat*. No unsolicited mss; synopses and ideas welcome.
ROYALTIES twice-yearly.

David Fickling Books
See **The Random House Group Ltd**

Findhorn Press Ltd
305A The Park, Findhorn IV36 3TE
☎01309 690582   Fax 01309 690036
✉ info@findhornpress.com
www.findhornpress.com
Directors *Karin Bogliolo, Thierry Bogliolo*

Founded 1971. Publishes mind, body, spirit, New Age and healing. 24 titles in 2004. Unsolicited synopses and ideas welcome if they come within their subject areas. No children's books, fiction or poetry.
ROYALTIES twice-yearly.

Firefly Publishing
See **Helter Skelter Publishing**

First & Best in Education Ltd
Unit K, Earlstrees Court, Earlstrees Road, Corby NN17 4HH
☎01536 399005   Fax 01536 399012
✉ editorial@firstandbest.co.uk
www.firstandbest.co.uk
www.shop.firstandbest.co.uk
Publisher *Tony Attwood*
Editor *Anne Cockburn*

Publishers of over 1000 educational books of all types for all ages of children and for parents and teachers. All books are published as being suitable for photocopying and/or as electronic books. 'Looking for new authors of educational books all the time. No fiction, please.' TITLES *Raising Grades Through Study Skills*; *Business Sponsorship of Secondary Schools*; *Policy Documents for Day Nurseries and Nursery Units*. IMPRINT **School Improvement Reports**. In the first instance check the website or send s.a.e. for details of requirements and current projects to *Anne Cockburn*, Editorial Dept. at the address above.

ROYALTIES twice-yearly.

Fitzgerald Publishing

89 Ermine Road, Ladywell, London SE13 5JJ
☎020 8690 0597
✉ fitzgeraldbooks@yahoo.co.uk

Managing Editor *Tim Fitzgerald*
General Editor *Andrew Smith*

Founded 1974. Specialises in scientific studies of insects and spiders. TITLES *The Tarantula*; *Keeping Spiders and Insects in Captivity*; *Scorpions of Medical Importance* (books) and *Earth Tigers – Tarantulas of Borneo*; *Desert Tarantulas* (TV/video documentaries). 1–2 titles a year. Unsolicited mss, synopses and ideas for books welcome. Also considers video scripts for video documentaries.

Fitzjames Press

See **Motor Racing Publications**

Fitzwarren Publishing

51 Nicolson Drive, Leighton Buzzard
LU7 4HQ
☎01525 384433
✉ pen2paper@btopenworld.com

Contact *Julie Stretton*

Publishes two or three books a year, mainly layman's handbooks on legal matters. All books follow a rigid 128-page format. TITLES *The E-Commerce Handbook*; *Landlord & Tenants Handbook*; *The Election Handbook*; *Licensing Handbook*; *Employment Handbook*. Welcomes written approaches and synopses from prospective authors who, though not necessarily legally qualified, are expected to know their subject as well as a lawyer would. No unsolicited mss.

ROYALTIES twice-yearly.

Five Star

See **Serpent's Tail**

Floris Books

15 Harrison Gardens, Edinburgh EH11 1SH
☎0131 337 2372   Fax 0131 347 9919
✉ floris@florisbooks.co.uk
www.florisbooks.co.uk

Managing Director *Christian Maclean*
Editors *Christopher Moore, Gale Winskill*
Approx. Annual Turnover £350,000

Founded 1977. Publishes books related to the Steiner movement, including The Christian Community, as well as arts & crafts, children's (including fiction with a Scottish theme), history, religious, science, social questions and Celtic studies. No unsolicited mss. Synopses and ideas for books welcome, except for children's picture books (not accepted).

ROYALTIES annually.

Focal Press

See **Elsevier Ltd**

Fodors

See **The Random House Group Ltd**

Folens Limited

Apex Business Centre, Boscombe Road, Dunstable LU5 4RL
☎0870 609 1237   Fax 0870 609 1236
✉ folens@folens.com
www.folens.com

Chairman *Dirk Folens*
Managing Director *Malcolm Watson*

Founded 1987. Leading educational publisher. IMPRINTS **Folens**; **Belair**. About 150 titles a year. Unsolicited mss, synopses and ideas for educational books welcome.

ROYALTIES annually.

Format Publishing Limited

31 Cattle Market Street, Norwich NR1 3DY
☎01603 766544   Fax 01603 215116
✉ contact@formatpublishing.co.uk
www.formatpublishing.co.uk

Managing Director *Jane Chittenden*
Approx. Annual Turnover £207,000

Founded 1999. Part of Format Design Ltd. Publishes business, management and self-development books. SERIES **Decision Makers**. 4 titles in 2004. Unsolicited mss, synopses and ideas welcome; approach by e-mail or post.

ROYALTIES twice-yearly.

Foulsham Publishers

The Publishing House, Bennetts Close, Slough
SL1 5AP
☎01753 526769   Fax 01753 535003
✉ reception@foulsham.com
www.foulsham.com

Chairman/Managing Director *B.A.R. Belasco*

Approx. Annual Turnover £2.5 million

Founded 1819 and now one of the few remaining independent family companies to survive takeover. Publishes non-fiction on most subjects including lifestyle, travel guides, family reference, cookery, diet, health, DIY, business, self improvement, self development, astrology, dreams, MBS. No fiction. IMPRINT **Quantum** Mind, body and spirit titles. TITLES *Classic 1000 Cocktails*; *A Brit's Guide to Orlando and Walt Disney World 2006*; *Old Moore's Almanack*; *Raphael's Astrological Ephemeris*. Around 60 titles a year. Unsolicited mss, synopses and ideas welcome.

ROYALTIES twice-yearly.

Fountain Press

Newpro UK Ltd., Old Sawmills Road, Faringdon SN7 7DS
☎01367 242411   Fax 01367 241124
✉ sales@newprouk.co.uk

Publisher *C.J. Coleman*
Approx. Annual Turnover £800,000

Founded 1923 when it was part of the Rowntree Trust Social Service. Owned by the British Electric Traction Group until 1982 when it was bought out by H.M. Ricketts. Acquired by Newpro UK Ltd in July 2000. Publishes mainly photography and natural history. TITLES *Photography and Digital 'Workshop'*; *Antique and Collectable Cameras*; *Camera Manual* (series). About 4 titles a year. Unsolicited mss and synopses welcome.

ROYALTIES twice-yearly.

Authors' Rating Highly regarded for production values, Fountain has the reputation for involving authors in every stage of the publishing process.

Fourth Estate
See **HarperCollins Publishers Ltd**

Free Association Books Ltd

PO Box 37664, London NW7 2XU
☎020 8906 0396   Fax 020 8906 0006
✉ info@fabooks.com
www.fabooks.com

Managing Director/Publisher *T.E. Brown*

Publishes psychoanalysis and psychotherapy, psychology, cultural studies, sexuality and gender, women's studies, applied social sciences. TITLES *Drug Use and Cultural Context* eds. Ross Coomber and Nigel South; *Skin Disease* Ann Maguire; *Caring for the Dying at Home* Gill Pharoah; *A History of Group Study and*

Psychodynamic Organizations Amy L. Fraher. Always send a letter in the first instance accompanied by a book outline. OVERSEAS ASSOCIATES ISBS, USA; Astam, Australia.

ROYALTIES twice-yearly.

The Free Press
See **Simon & Schuster UK Ltd**

W.H. Freeman

Palgrave, Houndsmill, Basingstoke RG21 6XS
☎01256 329242   Fax 01256 330688
www.palgrave.com

President *Elizabeth Widdicombe* (New York)
Sales & Marketing Director *Margaret Hewinson*

Following integration into the BFW (Bedford, Freeman, Worth) College Group, USA, Freeman now publishes academic educational and textbooks in biochemistry, biology and zoology, chemistry, economics, mathematics and statistics, natural history, neuroscience, palaeontology, physics. Freeman's editorial office is in New York (Basingstoke is a sales and marketing office only) but unsolicited mss can go through Basingstoke. Those which are obviously unsuitable will be sifted out; the rest will be forwarded to New York.

ROYALTIES annually.

Samuel French Ltd

52 Fitzroy Street, London W1T 5JR
☎020 7387 9373   Fax 020 7387 2161
✉ theatre@samuelfrench-london.co.uk
www.samuelfrench-london.co.uk

Chairman *Charles R. Van Nostrand*
Managing Director *Vivien Goodwin*

Founded 1830 with the object of acquiring acting rights and publishing plays. Publishes plays only. About 50 titles a year. Unsolicited mss considered only after initial submission of synopsis and specimen scene. Such material should be addressed to the Performing Rights Department.

ROYALTIES twice-yearly for books; performing royalties monthly, subject to a minimum amount.

Authors' Rating Thrives on the amateur dramatic societies who are forever in need of play texts. Editorial advisers give serious attention to new material but a high proportion of the list is staged before it goes into print. New writers are advised to try one-act plays, much in demand by the amateur dramatic societies but rarely turned out by established playwrights.

David Fulton Publishers Ltd

The Chiswick Centre, 414 Chiswick High Road, London W4 5TF
☎020 8996 3610   Fax 020 8996 3622
✉ mail@fultonpublishers.co.uk
www.fultonpublishers.co.uk

Publishing Director *Christopher Glennie*
Publishers *Linda Evans, Tracey Alcock, Margaret Marriott*

Approx. Annual Turnover £2.4 million

Founded 1987. Publishes books for trainee and working teachers at all levels of the curriculum (foundation stage to post compulsory), with particular emphasis on special educational needs (SEN) and inclusion. Special educational needs books also published in collaboration with the National Association for Special Educational Needs (NASEN); some overlap into other areas of health and social care, therapy, educational psychology, and speech and language therapy. A growing list of books for pre-school and nursery staff. About 100 titles a year. No unsolicited mss; synopses and ideas for books welcome.

ROYALTIES twice-yearly.

Funfax

See **Dorling Kindersley Ltd**

Gaia Books

See **Octopus Publishing Group**

J. Garnet Miller

See **Cressrelles Publishing Co. Ltd**

Garnet Publishing Ltd

8 Southern Court, South Street, Reading RG1 4QS
☎0118 959 7847   Fax 0118 959 7356
✉ enquiries@garnetpublishing.co.uk
www.garnetpublishing.co.uk

Editorial Manager *Emma G. Hawker*

Founded 1992 and purchased Ithaca Press in the same year. Publishes art, architecture, photography, archive photography, cookery, travel classics, travel, comparative religion, Islamic culture and history, foreign fiction in translation. Core subjects are Middle Eastern but list is rapidly expanding to be more general.

IMPRINTS **Garnet Publishing** TITLES *Simply Lebanese; The Art and Architecture of Islamic Cairo.* **Ithaca Press** Specialises in post-graduate academic works on the Middle East, political science and international relations TITLES *The Making of the Modern Gulf States; The Palestinian Exodus; French Imperialism in Syria; Philby of Arabia.* About 20 titles a year. Unsolicited mss not welcome; write with outline and ideas first plus current c.v.

ROYALTIES twice-yearly.

Geddes & Grosset

David Dale House, New Lanark ML11 9DJ
☎01555 665000   Fax 01555 665694

Publishers *Ron Grosset, R. Michael Miller*

Approx. Annual Turnover £3 million

Founded 1989. Publisher of children's and reference books. Unsolicited mss, synopses and ideas welcome. No adult fiction.

The Geological Society Publishing House

Unit 7, Brassmill Enterprise Centre, Brassmill Lane, Bath BA1 3JN
☎01225 445046   Fax 01225 442836
✉ sales@geolsoc.org.uk *or* enquiries@geolsoc.org.uk
www.geolsoc.org.uk

Commissioning Editor *Angharad Hills*

Publishing arm of the Geological Society which was founded in 1807. Publishes postgraduate texts in the earth sciences. 30 titles a year. Unsolicited synopses and ideas welcome.

Stanley Gibbons Publications

7 Parkside, Christchurch Road, Ringwood BH24 3SH
☎01425 472363   Fax 01425 470247
www.stanleygibbons.com

Chairman *P. Fraser*
Editorial Head *H. Jefferies*

Long-established force in the philatelic world with almost 150 years in the business. Publishes philatelic reference catalogues and handbooks. Reference works relating to other areas of collecting may be considered. TITLES *Stanley Gibbons British Commonwealth Stamp Catalogue; Stamps of the World.* Foreign catalogues include Japan and Korea, Portugal and Spain, Germany, Middle East, Balkans, China. Monthly publication: *Gibbons Stamp Monthly* (see entry under *Magazines*). www.collectorcafe.com – Internet site covering full range of collectables – editorial input always considered. About 20 titles a year. Unsolicited mss, synopses and ideas welcome.

ROYALTIES by negotiation.

Robert Gibson and Sons (Glasgow)

See **Hodder Gibson**

Gibson Square
15 Gibson Square, London N1 0RD
☎020 7689 4790   Fax 020 7689 7395
✉ info@gibsonsquare.com
www.gibsonsquare.com
Chairman *Martin Rynja*
Founded 2001. Publishes exclusively non-fiction: biography, current affairs, politics, cultural criticism, psychology, history, travel, art history, philosophy. Books must have high publicity profile. IMPRINTS **Gibson Square** TITLES *House of Bush House of Saud* Craig Unger; *A Dictionary of Idiocy* Stephen Bayley; *More France Please* Helena Frith Powell. **New Editions** Reprints TITLES *The Art of Always Being Right* Schopenhauer; *Nancy Mitford* Harold Acton. Welcomes unsolicited mss, synopses and ideas. Send self-addressed, franked, return envelope. No fiction.
ROYALTIES twice-yearly.

Ginn & Co
See **Harcourt Education**

Glass House Press
See **Cavendish Publishing Limited**

Gloucester Publishers Plc
10 Northburgh Street, London EC1V 0AT
☎020 7253 7887   Fax 020 7490 3708
✉ markbicknell@everyman.uk.com
www.everymanchess.com
Managing Director *Mark Bicknell*
Approx. Annual Turnover £1 million
Publishes exclusively academic and leisure books relating to chess. IMPRINT **Everyman Chess** TITLES *Garry Kasparov: My Great Predecessors, Vols 1–4*; *Play Winning Chess* Yasser Seirawan; *Art of Attack in Chess* Vladimir Vukovich. 31 titles in 2004. No unsolicited material.
ROYALTIES annually.

Godsfield Press
See **Octopus Publishing Group**

Gollancz
See **The Orion Publishing Group Limited**

Gomer Press/Gwasg Gomer
Llandysul Enterprise Park, Llandysul SA44 4JL
☎01559 363090   Fax 01559 363758
✉ gwasg@gomer.co.uk
www.gomer.co.uk
Chairman/Managing Director *J.E. Lewis*

Publishing Director *Mairwen Prys Jones*
Founded 1892. Publishes adult fiction and non-fiction, children's fiction and educational material in English and Welsh. IMPRINTS **Gomer** *Bethan Mair, Bryan James* (adult books – Welsh), *Ceri Wyn Jones* (adult books – English), *Sioned Lleinau, Helen Evans, Morys Rhys* (children's books – Welsh). **Pont Books** *Viv Sayer* (children's books – English). No unsolicited mss.

The Good Web Guide Ltd
65 Bromfelde Road, London SW4 6PP
☎020 7720 8919   Fax 020 7738 5717
✉ marketing@thegoodwebguide.com
www.thegoodwebguide.com
Chairman *David Teale*
Managing Director *Sarah Mahaffy*
Marketing Director *Nicky Granville*
Founded 1999. Publishes guides to the best sites on the Internet, both as books and online. Subscription available giving full access to the website where reviews are updated and added to. 5 titles in 2004. No unsolicited mss; send synopsis/idea by post or e-mail. No fiction or children's books.
ROYALTIES twice-yearly.

Gower
See **Ashgate Publishing Ltd**

GPC Books
See **University of Wales Press**

Graham-Cameron Publishing & Illustration
The Studio, 23 Holt Road, Sheringham NR26 8NB
☎01263 821333   Fax 01263 821334
✉ firstname@graham-cameron-illustration.com
www.graham-cameron-illustration.com
Also at: 59 Redvers Road, Brighton BN2 4BF
☎01273 385890
Editorial Director *Mike Graham-Cameron*
Art Director *Helen Graham-Cameron*
Founded 1984 as a packaging operation. Publishes illustrated books for children and adults for institutions and business. TITLES *Up From the Country*; *In All Directions*; *The Holywell Story*; *Flashbacks*; *Let's Look at Dairying*. Has 37 contracted book illustrators concentrating on educational and children's books. *Absolutely no* unsolicited mss.
ROYALTIES annually.

Granta Books
2–3 Hanover Yard, Noel Road, London
N1 8BE
☎020 7704 9776   Fax 020 7354 3469
www.granta.com
Publisher *Gail Lynch*
Editorial Director *George Miller*
Founded 1979. Publishes general non-fiction
and some literary fiction. About 35 titles a year.
No unsolicited mss; synopses and sample chap-
ters welcome.
ROYALTIES twice-yearly.

W. Green (Scotland)
See **Sweet & Maxwell Group**

Green Books
Foxhole, Dartington, Totnes TQ9 6EB
☎01803 863260   Fax 01803 863843
✉ edit@greenbooks.co.uk
www.greenbooks.co.uk
Chairman *Satish Kumar*
Publisher *John Elford*
Approx. Annual Turnover £400,000
Founded in 1987 with the support of a number
of Green organisations. Closely associated with
Resurgence magazine. Publishes high-quality
books on a wide range of Green issues, including economics, politics and the practical application of Green thinking. No fiction or books
for children. TITLES *Forest Gardening* Robert A.
de J. Hart; *Eco-Renovation* Edward Harland; *The
Growth Illusion* Richard Douthwaite; *The Green
Lanes of England* Valerie Belsey; *The Organic
Directory* ed. Clive Litchfield. No unsolicited
mss. Synopses and ideas welcome but check
guidelines on the website in the first instance.
ROYALTIES twice-yearly.

Green Print
See **The Merlin Press Ltd**

**Greenhill Books/
Lionel Leventhal Ltd**
Park House, 1 Russell Gardens, London
NW11 9NN
☎020 8458 6314   Fax 020 8905 5245
✉ L.Leventhal@greenhillbooks.com
www.greenhillbooks.com
Director *Michael Leventhal*
Founded 1984 by Lionel Leventhal (ex-Arms
& Armour Press). Publishes aviation, military
and naval books. Synopses and ideas for books
welcome. No unsolicited mss.
ROYALTIES twice-yearly.

Gresham Books Ltd
46 Victoria Road, Summertown, Oxford
OX2 7QD
☎01865 513582   Fax 01865 512718
✉ info@gresham-books.co.uk
www.gresham-books.co.uk
Managing Director *Paul A. Lewis*
Approx. Annual Turnover £350,000
A small specialist publishing house. Publishes
hymn and service books for schools and
churches, school histories, also craftbound choir
and orchestral folders and Records of Achievement. TITLES include music and melody editions of *Hymns for Church and School; The School
Hymnal; Praise and Thanksgiving*. No unsolicited
material but ideas welcome.

Grisewood & Dempsey
See **Kingfisher Publications Plc**

Grub Street
4 Rainham Close, London SW11 6SS
☎020 7924 3966/7738 1008
Fax 020 7738 1009
✉ post@grubstreet.co.uk
www.grubstreet.co.uk
Managing Director *John Davies*
Founded 1982. Publishes cookery, food and
wine, health, military and aviation history
books. About 20 titles a year. Unsolicited mss
and synopses welcome in the above categories
but please enclose return postage.
ROYALTIES twice-yearly.

Guardian/Observer Books
See **Atlantic Books**

**Guild of Master Craftsman
Publications Ltd**
166 High Street, Lewes BN7 1XU
☎01273 477374   Fax 01273 478606
✉ pubs@thegmcgroup.com
Joint Managing Directors *J.A.J. Phillips, J.A.B.
Phillips*
Approx. Annual Turnover £2 million
Founded 1974. Part of G.M.C. Services Ltd.
Publishes woodworking, craft, photography and
gardening books, magazines and videos; also
books on dolls' houses and miniatures. IMPRINT
Photographers' Institute Press (PIP)
launched in 2004. 41 titles in 2004. Unsolicited
mss, synopses and ideas for books welcome. No
fiction.
ROYALTIES twice-yearly.

Guinness World Records Ltd

338 Euston Road, London NW1 3BD
☎020 7891 4567   Fax 020 7891 4501
✉ info@guinnessrecords.com
www.guinnessworldrecords.com

Chief Operations Officer *Alistair Richards*

Founded in 1954 to publish *The Guinness Book of Records*, published in 35 languages and the highest-selling copyright book in the world. The company's television shows have gained a global audience of more than 100 million and are broadcast in over 30 countries. In addition to *Guinness World Records* the company publishes the annual industry-standard volume *British Hit Singles & Albums*. In October 2002 Guinness World Records became part of HIT Entertainment Plc. Contact from prospective researchers, editors and designers welcome.

Gulf Professional Press

See **Elsevier Ltd**

Gullane Children's Books

See **Pinwheel Limited**

Gwasg Carreg Gwalch

12 Iard yr Orsaf, Llanrwst LL26 0EH
☎01492 642031   Fax 01492 641502
✉ books@carreg-gwalch.co.uk
www.carreg-gwalch.co.uk

Managing Editor *Myrddin ap Dafydd*

Founded in 1980. Publishes Welsh language; English books of Welsh interest – history, folklore, guides and walks. About 90 titles a year. Unsolicited mss, synopses and ideas welcome if of Welsh interest. ROYALTIES paid.

Gwasg Prifysgol Cymru

See **University of Wales Press**

Hachette Children's Books

338 Euston Road, London NW1 3BH
☎020 7873 6000
✉ gm@wattspub.co.uk

Managing Director *Marlene Johnson*

Formed by the combining of Watts Publishing Group with Hodder Children's Books in April 2005. Publishes children's non-fiction, reference, information, gift, fiction, picture and novelty books and audio books. IMPRINTS **Hodder Children's Books** *Anne McNeil* Fiction, picture books, novelty, general non-fiction and audio. **Orchard Books** *Ann-Janine Murtagh* Fiction, picture and novelty books. **Franklin Watts**

Rachel Cooke Non-fiction and information books. **Wayland** *Joyce Bentley* Non-fiction and information books. Unsolicited material is not considered other than by referral or recommendation. ROYALTIES twice-yearly.

Hachette-Livre

French publishing conglomerate which embraces **Hodder Headline**, **Orion Publishing Group**, **Octopus Publishing Group**. For further information, see entry under *European Publishers*.

Halban Publishers

22 Golden Square, London W1F 9JW
☎020 7437 9300   Fax 020 7437 9512
✉ books@halbanpublishers.com
www.halbanpublishers.com

Directors *Peter Halban, Martine Halban*

Founded 1986. Independent publisher. Publishes biography, autobiography and memoirs, history, philosophy, theology, politics, literature and criticism, Judaica and world affairs. 6–8 titles a year. No unsolicited material. Approach by letter in first instance.

ROYALTIES twice-yearly for first two years, thereafter annually in December.

Robert Hale Ltd

Clerkenwell House, 45–47 Clerkenwell Green, London EC1R 0HT
☎020 7251 2661   Fax 020 7490 4958
✉ enquire@halebooks.com

Chairman/Managing Director *John Hale*

Founded 1936. Family-owned company. Publishes adult fiction (but not interested in category romance or science fiction) and non-fiction. No specialist material (education, law, medical or scientific). Acquired **NAG Press Ltd** in 1993 with its list of horological, gemmological, jewellery and metalwork titles, and **J.A. Allen & Co.** in 1999 with its extensive list of horse and dog books (see entry). TITLES Non-fiction: *A Trout and Salmon Fisherman for 75 Years* Edward R. Hewitt; *Chronometer Makers of the World* Tony Mercer; *Mario Lanza: A Life in Pictures*; *English Village Architecture* R.J. Brown; *Witchcraft out of the Shadows* Leo Ruickbie. Fiction: *Virgin in the Gym and Other Stories* Wendy Perriam; *Death and the Visiting Fellow* Tim Heald; *Heat of Passion* Harold Robbins; *In this Skin* Simon Clarke. Over 250 titles a year. Unsolicited mss, synopses and ideas for books welcome.

ROYALTIES twice-yearly.

Authors' Rating Smiled upon in a Society of Authors survey on author relations, Robert Hale has carved out a profitable niche for popular non-fiction.

Halsgrove

Halsgrove House, Tiverton Business Park, Lower Moor Way, Tiverton EX16 6SS
☎01884 243242   Fax 01884 243325
✉ sales@halsgrove.com
www.halsgrove.com

Publisher *Simon Butler*

Founded in 1990 and now the region's largest publishing and distribution group, specialising in books, video and audio tapes. Core interests remain in the South but now publishes books of regional interest throughout the UK. Publishes local history (including the *Community History* series), cookery, biography and art, mainly in hardback. Also established a series of local interest magazines in southern England. No fiction or poetry. 150 titles in 2004. Unsolicited mss, synopses and ideas for books of regional interest welcome.
ROYALTIES annually.

Hambledon and London

102 Gloucester Avenue, London NW1 8HX
☎020 7586 0817   Fax 020 7586 9970
✉ office@hambledon.co.uk

Editorial Director *Martin Sheppard*
Commissioning Director *Tony Morris*

Founded 1980 as The Hambledon Press. Winner of the **Sunday Times Award for Small Publishers** in 2001. Publishes history and biography. TITLES *Churchill: A Study in Greatness* Geoffrey Best; *The Ambassadors' Secret* John North; *Brunel: the Life and Times of Isambard Kingdom Brunel* Angus Buchanan; *Family Names and Family History* David Hey. No unsolicited mss; send preliminary letter. Synopses and ideas welcome. OVERSEAS DISTRIBUTOR Palgrave-Macmillan (USA and Canada).
ROYALTIES twice-yearly.

Hamish Hamilton
See **Penguin Group (UK)**

Hamlyn Octopus
See **Octopus Publishing Group**

Harcourt Education

Halley Court, Jordan Hill, Oxford OX2 8EJ
☎01865 311366   Fax 01865 314641
www.harcourteducation.co.uk

President/CEO *Christopher Jones*

A member of the **Reed Elsevier Group plc**, Harcourt Education incorporates Heinemann Educational and Ginn in the UK; Greenwood Heinemann in the USA; Rigby Heinemann in Australia. **Heinemann Educational** Fax 01865 314140 Managing Director *Paul Shuter*, Primary *Kath Donovan*, Secondary *Linden Harris*. Textbooks, literature and other educational resources for primary and secondary school and further education. Mss, synopses and ideas welcome. **Ginn & Co** Fax 01865 314189 Managing Director *Paul Shuter*. Textbook and other educational resources for primary and secondary schools.

ROYALTIES twice-yearly/annually, according to contract in all divisions.

Harlequin Mills & Boon Ltd

Eton House, 18–24 Paradise Road, Richmond TW9 1SR
☎020 8288 2800   Fax 020 8288 2899
www.eharlequin.com
www.millsandboon.co.uk

Managing Director *Guy Hallowes*
Editorial Director *Karin Stoecker*
Approx. Annual Turnover £22 million

Founded 1908. Owned by the Canadian-based Torstar Group. Publishes a wide range of women's fiction including romantic novels. IMPRINTS **Mills & Boon Modern Romance** *Tessa Shapcott* (50–55,000 words) Alpha males and attractive women swept up in intense emotions set against a backdrop of international locations, luxury and wealth; passion is guaranteed. **Mills & Boon Sensual Romance** *Tessa Shapcott* (60,000 words) Delivers a feel-good experience, focusing on the kind of relationship that women aged 18 to 35 aspire to. Young characters in urban settings meet, flirt, share experiences, have great sex and fall in love, finally making a commitment that will bind them forever. Based around emotional issues, other concerns – e.g. jobs and friendships – are also touched upon and resolved in upbeat way. **Mills & Boon Tender Romance** *Bryony Green* (50–55,000 words) Contemporary upbeat and heroine-focused romance, driven by strongly emotional conflicts which are believable and relevant to today's women. Capturing the depth of emotion and sheer excitement of falling in love in a variety of international settings. **Mills & Boon Medical Romance** *Sheila Hodgson* (50–55,000 words) Modern medical practice provides a unique background to highly emotional contemporary romances. **Mills & Boon Historical Romance** *Linda Fildew* (80–95,000 words) Richly textured, emotionally intense historical novels covering a wide range of settings and periods from ancient civilisations up to and including the Second World War. Over 600 titles a year. Other submissions: also accepting submissions in all general women's fiction genres (contemporary and historical) for longer series and single title imprints. Tip sheets and guidelines are available from the Mills & Boon or eHarlequin websites (see above) or Harlequin Mills & Boon Editorial Dept. (telephone or write sending s.a.e.). Agented and unagented submissions accepted. Send query letter, synopsis and first three chapters in the first instance. ROYALTIES twice-yearly.

Authors' Rating Sex has overtaken romance at M&B where the latest imprints allow writers' erotic imagination to run riot. But the staple M&B romance is still going strong providing a good income for writers who can adapt to the clearly defined M&B formula. Just think, M&B has a network of 12,000 authors worldwide and every title scores six-figure sales. But be warned. M&B gets 2000 unsolicited manuscripts a year.

Harley Books
Martins, Great Horkesley, Colchester CO6 4AH
☎01206 271216   Fax 01206 271182
✉ harley@harleybooks.co.uk
www.harleybooks.com
Managing Director *Basil Harley*

Founded 1983. Natural history publishers specialising in entomological and botanical books. Mostly definitive, high-quality illustrated reference works. TITLES *The Moths and Butterflies of Great Britain and Ireland*; *Dragonflies of Europe*; *The Aurelian Legacy: British Butterflies and their Collectors*; *The Liverwort Flora of the British Isles*; *Maggots, Murder and Men: Memories and Reflections of a Forensic Entomologist; Freshwater Fishes in Britain*. ROYALTIES twice-yearly in the first year, annually thereafter.

HarperCollins Publishers Ltd
77–85 Fulham Palace Road, London W6 8JB
☎020 8741 7070   Fax 020 8307 4440
www.harpercollins.co.uk

Also at: Westerhill Road, Bishopbriggs, Glasgow G64 2QT
☎0141 772 3200 Fax 0141 306 3119
CEO/Publisher *Victoria Barnsley*

HarperCollins is one of the leading book publishers in the UK, with a wider range of books than any other publisher; from cutting-edge contemporary fiction to block-busting thrillers, from fantasy literature and children's stories to enduring classics. The wholly-owned division of News Corporation also publishes a wide selection of non-fiction including history, celebrity memoirs, biography, popular science, mind, body and spirit, dictionaries, maps and reference books. HarperCollins is also one of the largest education publishers in the UK. Authors include many award-winning and international bestsellers such as Isabel Allende, Paulo Coelho, Josephine Cox, Michael Crichton, Cathy Kelly, Judith Kerr, Doris Lessing, Frank McCourt, Tony Parsons, Nigel Slater and Diana Wynne Jones. Bestselling licensed properties include Dr Seuss and Noddy. About 1500 titles a year.

GENERAL BOOKS DIVISION
Managing Director *Amanda Ridout*
Harper Fiction Publisher *Lynne Drew* IMPRINTS **HarperCollins** Publishing Directors *Susan Watt, Julia Wisdom*; **Voyager** Fantasy/science fiction Publishing Director *Jane Johnson* General, historical fiction, crime and thrillers and women's fiction.
   HarperEntertainment Managing Director/Publisher *Trevor Dolby* IMPRINTS **HarperCollins** Publishing Director *Ben Dunn*; Publishing Director *David Brawn* (Agatha Christie, J.R.R. Tolkien, C.S. Lewis) Media-related books from film companions to celebrity autobiographies and TV tie-ins; **HarperSport** Publishing Director *Michael Doggart* Sporting biographies, guides and histories; **HarperCollins Audio** Publishing Director *Rosalie George* (see entry under *Audio Books*).
   HarperThorsons/Element (division & imprint) Managing Director *Belinda Budge*, Publishing Directors *Wanda Whiteley* (Health), *Carole Tonkinson* (Mind, Body & Spirit).
   HarperCollins Children's Books Managing Director *Sally Gritten* Quality picture books for under-7s; fiction for age 6 up to young adult; TV and film tie-ins and properties Publishing Directors *Gillie Russell* (Fiction), *Sue Buswell* (Picture Books).

THE FOURTH ESTATE GROUP
Managing Director *John Bond*
Publisher *Caroline Michel*
IMPRINTS **Fourth Estate** Publishing Director *Nick Pearson* Fiction, literary fiction, current affairs, popular science, biography, humour, travel; **HarperPress** Publishing Director

Michael Fishwick General trade non-fiction; **HarperPerennial** Paperback imprint.

COLLINS DIVISION
Managing Director *Thomas Webster*

Collins Reference Managing Director *Sarah Bailey* Guides and handbooks, Times World Atlases, Collins World Atlases, phrase books and manuals on popular reference, art instruction, illustrated, cookery and wine, crafts, DIY, gardening, military, natural history, pet care, pastimes Publishing Directors *Denise Bates* (Illustrated Reference), *Martin Toseland* (Text Reference), *Sheena Barclay* (World Atlases), Associate Publisher *Myles Archibald* (Natural History) IMPRINTS **Collins**; **Collins Gem**; **Times Books**; **Jane's**.

Collins Dictionaries/COBUILD (division & imprint) Managing Director *Lorna Knight* Bilingual and English dictionaries, English dictionaries for foreign learners. Publishing Directors *Helen Newstead* (Digital Development), *Michela Clari* (Editorial), *Elaine Higgleton* (Editorial).

Collins Education Managing Director *Jim Green* Books, CD-ROMs and online material for UK primary and secondary schools and colleges. Publishing Directors *Paul Cherry* (Educational), *Brenda Stones* (Home Learning).

Collins Maps and Road Atlases (division & imprint) General Manager *Mike Cottingham*, Publishing Director *Helen Gordon* Maps, atlases, street plans and leisure guides.

Authors' Rating An important shift of emphasis this year spotlights the growing demand for popular non-fiction titles. HarperCollins now has a new division, the Fourth Estate Group, to develop the sort of books that the new independent publishers have sold so well. 'We are determined to be the publisher of choice for new and established writers,' says Caroline Michel. On the sales side, HarperCollins is all for experimenting with price, format and marketing to 'break down traditional barriers' between publishers and readers. Could be exciting.

Harrap
See **Chambers Harrap Publishers Ltd**

Harvard University Press
Fitzroy House, 11 Chenies Street, London WC1E 7EY
☎020 7306 0603   Fax 020 7306 0604
✉ info@HUP-MITpress.co.uk
www.hup.harvard.edu

Director *William Sisler*
General Manager *Ann Sexsmith*

European office of **Harvard University Press**, USA. Publishes academic and scholarly works in history, politics, philosophy, economics, literary criticism, psychology, sociology, anthropology, women's studies, biological sciences, classics, history of science, art, music, film, reference. All mss go to the American office: 79 Garden Street, Cambridge, MA 02138 (see entry under *US Publishers*).

Harvill Secker
See **The Random House Group Ltd**

Haus Publishers
26 Cadogan Court, Draycott Avenue, London SW3 3BX
☎020 7584 6738   Fax 020 7584 9501
✉ haus@hauspublishing.com
www.hauspublishing.co.uk
Managing Director *Barbara Schwepcke*
Founded 2001. Publishes biographies and literary travel books. DIVISIONS/IMPRINTS **Life&Times** Non-academic biographies of well-known and lesser-known personalities TITLES *P.G. Wodehouse*; *Martin Luther King*; *Yourcenar*. **Armchair Traveller** Literary travel series TITLES *Mumbai to Mecca*; *Venice for Lovers*. **Hbooks** Hardcover biographies TITLES *Emma Hamilton*; *Vermeer*. 18 titles in 2004. Unsolicited mss, synopses and ideas within the subject areas above are welcome; approach by e-mail or post. No children's, fiction or poetry.
ROYALTIES twice-yearly.

Haynes Publishing
Sparkford, Near Yeovil BA22 7JJ
☎01963 440635   Fax 01963 440825
✉ info@haynes.co.uk
www.haynes.co.uk
Chairman *John H. Haynes, OBE*
Approx. Annual Turnover £39 million
Founded in 1960 by John H. Haynes. Listed public company with majority family ownership. The mainstay of its programme has been the *Owners' Workshop Manual*, first published in the mid 1960s and still running off the presses today. Indeed the company maintains a strong bias towards motoring and transport titles. Acquired Sutton Publishing Ltd in March 2000. Publishes DIY service and repair manuals for cars, motorbikes and leisure plus other related topics under the Haynes imprint and a broad range of general non-fiction under the Sutton imprint.

AUTOMOTIVE DIVISION IMPRINT **Haynes** Editorial Director *Matthew Minter* Service and repair manuals; Editorial Director *Mark Hughes* Motoring, motor sport, cars, motorcycles, home, DIY and leisure titles.

GENERAL PUBLISHING DIVISION IMPRINT **Sutton Publishing Ltd** (see entry). Unsolicited submissions welcome if they come within the subject areas covered. OVERSEAS SUBSIDIARIES Haynes Manuals Inc., California, USA, Editions Haynes S.A., France, Haynes Publishing Nordiska AB, Sweden.

ROYALTIES twice-yearly.

Hazleton Publishing

5th Floor, Mermaid House, Puddle Dock, London EC4V 3DS
☎020 7332 2000   Fax 020 7332 2001
✉ info@hazletonpublishing.com
www.hazletonpublishing.com

Publisher of the leading motorsport annuals: *Autocourse*; *Rallycourse*; *Motocourse* as well as Open Golf and Wimbledon Tennis annuals. About 8 titles a year. No unsolicited mss; synopses and ideas welcome. Interested in all motor sport titles.

ROYALTIES Payment varies.

Hbooks

See **Haus Publishers**

Headline

See **Hodder Headline Ltd**

William Heinemann

See **The Random House Group Ltd**

Heinemann Educational

See **Harcourt Education**

Helicon Publishing

RM plc, New Mill House, 183 Milton Park, Abingdon OX14 4SE
☎01235 826000   Fax 01235 823222
✉ helicon@rm.com
www.helicon.co.uk

General Manager *Caroline Dodds*

A division of Research Machines plc. Helicon is a general reference database publisher for the UK, US and Australian markets. Licenses quality reference content for online, print and CD-ROM publications. TITLES include the flagship single volume *Hutchinson 2005 Encyclopedia* published under license from **Hodder Headline**. CD-ROM TITLES include *The Hutchinson Encyclopedia*; *The Hutchinson Science Reference Suite*; *The Hutchinson History Reference Suite*; *The Hutchinson Music Reference Suite*.

Christopher Helm

See **A.&C. Black Publishers Ltd**

Helm Information Ltd

The Banks, Mountfield, Nr Robertsbridge TN32 5JY
☎01580 880561   Fax 01580 880541
✉ amandahelm@helm-information.co.uk
www.helm-information.co.uk

Directors *Amanda Helm, Christopher Helm*

Founded 1990. Publishes academic books for students and university libraries. SERIES *The Critical Assessments of Writers in English* (collected criticism); *Literary Sources & Documents* (primary source material on various themes/events/cultural/aesthetic movements ranging from the American Civil War to the Gothic Revival); *Sources & Documents in Art History* (literary sources of various movements in art); *The Dickens Companions*; and a new series, *Icons*, which exposes the processes by which a figure, historical or fictional, achieves iconic status, e.g. Faust, Robin Hood. Will consider ideas and proposals provided they are relevant to the series listed above.

ROYALTIES annually.

Help Yourself

See **Hodder Headline Ltd**

Helter Skelter Publishing

South Bank House, Black Prince Road, London SE1 7SJ
☎020 7463 2204   Fax 020 7463 2295
✉ info@helterskelterbooks.com
www.helterskelterbooks.com

Contact *Sean Body*

Founded 1995. Publishes music and film books only. IMPRINTS **Helter Skelter Publishing**; **Firefly Publishing**. 15 titles a year. Unsolicited mss, synopses and ideas welcome.

Henderson Publishing

See **Dorling Kindersley Ltd**

Ian Henry Publications Ltd

20 Park Drive, Romford RM1 4LH
☎01708 749119   Fax 01708 736213
Managing Director *Ian Wilkes*

Founded 1976. Publishes local history, humour, transport history and Sherlockian pastiches.

TITLES *Without Warning; London Rabbit; Marine Pilot.* 8–10 titles a year. No unsolicited mss. Synopses and ideas for books welcome. ROYALTIES twice-yearly.

The Herbert Press
See **A.&C. Black Publishers Ltd**

Hermes House
See **Anness Publishing Ltd**

Nick Hern Books
The Glasshouse, 49a Goldhawk Road, London W12 8QP
☎020 8749 4953   Fax 020 8735 0250
✉ info@nickhernbooks.demon.co.uk
www.nickhernbooks.co.uk
Chairman/Managing Director *Nick Hern*
Founded 1988. Fully independent since 1992. Publishes books on theatre and film: from how-to and biography to plays and screenplays. About 30 titles a year. No unsolicited playscripts. Synopses, ideas and proposals for other theatre material welcome. Not interested in material unrelated to the theatre or cinema.

University of Hertfordshire Press
Learning and Information Services, Hatfield Campus Learning Resources Centre, College Lane, Hatfield AL10 9AB
☎01707 284681   Fax 01707 284666
✉ UHPress@herts.ac.uk
www.herts.ac.uk/UHPress
Contact *Jane Housham*
Founded 1992. Publishes academic books on Gypsies, literature, regional and local history, parapsychology. IMPRINTS **University of Hertfordshire Press**; **Interface Collection**; **Hertfordshire Publications**. TITLES *We are the Romani People* Ian Hancock; *Off-Centre Stages: Fringe Theatre at the Open Space and the Round House 1968–1983* Jinnie Schiele; *Refiguring Mimesis: Representation in early modern literature* eds. Jonathan Holmes and Adrian Streete.

Hesperus Press Limited
4 Rickett Street, London SW6 1RU
☎020 7610 3331   Fax 020 7610 3217
www.hesperuspress.com
Managing Director/Publisher *Alessandro Gallenzi*
Founded 2001. Publishes lesser-known works by classical authors, both in English and in translation. TITLES *Carlyle's House* Virginia

Woolf; *The Rich Boy* Francis Scott Fitzgerald; *Arctic Summer* E.M. Forster; *Hadji Murat* Lev Tolstoy. *Modern Classics* series launched in 2005; literary fiction list in 2006. 40 titles in 2004, including 5 poetry titles. Does not accept unsolicited mss.
ROYALTIES annually.

High Stakes
See **Oldcastle Books Ltd**

Hippo
See **Scholastic Ltd**

History Into Print
See **Brewin Books Ltd**

HMSO
See **TSO**

Hobsons Plc
Challenger House, 42 Adler Street, London E1 1EE
☎020 7958 5000   Fax 020 7958 5001
www.hobsons.com
Chairman *Martin Morgan*
Group Managing Director *Christopher Letcher*
Founded 1974. Part of the Daily Mail & General Trust. Publishes course and career guides, under exclusive licence and royalty agreements for CRAC (Careers Research and Advisory Centre), directories and specialist titles for students and young professionals. TITLES *Hobson's Directory; Hobsons Diversity Handbook; Industry Casebooks* series; *Hobsons Guide for Women; Hobsons Guide for Ethnic Minorities; Careers in Europe Casebook; Hobsons Study Europe Guide; The Edexcel Students' Guide to International Study Opportunities; Hobsons Job Book* (with CD-ROM); *Which Degree?* series.

Hodder & Stoughton
See **Hodder Headline Ltd**

Hodder Gibson
2a Christie Street, Paisley PA1 1NB
☎0141 848 1609   Fax 0141 889 6315
✉ hoddergibson@hodder.co.uk
www.hoddereducation.co.uk
Managing Director *John Mitchell*
Part of the **Hodder Headline Group**. Publishes educational books specifically for Scotland. Combines the former Robert Gibson and Sons (Glasgow) with the Scottish branch of Hodder Murray (a merger of **John Murray** and **Hodder Stoughton Educational**).

About 50 titles a year. Synopses/ideas preferred to unsolicited mss.
ROYALTIES annually.

Hodder Headline Ltd

338 Euston Road, London NW1 3BH
☎020 7873 6000   Fax 020 7873 6024
www.hodderheadline.co.uk
Group Chief Executive *Tim Hely Hutchinson*
Approx. Annual Turnover £130 million

Formed in June 1993 through the merger of Headline Book Publishing and Hodder & Stoughton. Headline was founded in 1986 and had grown dramatically, whereas Hodder & Stoughton was 125 years old with a diverse range of publishing. The company was acquired by WHSmith plc in 1999 and subsequently by Hachette Livre S.A. in October 2004. Purchased **John Murray (Publishers) Ltd** in 2002. About 2000 titles a year.

DIVISIONS
Headline Book Publishing Managing Director *Martin Neild*, Deputy Managing Director *Kerr MacRae*, Director of Non-fiction *Val Hudson*, Director of Fiction *Jane Morpeth* Publishes commercial and literary fiction (hardback and paperback) and popular non-fiction including autobiography, biography, food and wine, gardening, history, popular science, sport and TV tie-ins. IMPRINTS **Headline**; **Review**. AUTHORS Kate Adie, Catherine Alliott, Lyn Andrews, Emily Barr, Colin Bateman, Martina Cole, Janet Evanovich, Sophie Grigson, Wendy Holden, Matthew Jukes, Faye and Jonathan Kellerman, Jill Mansell, Maggie O'Farrell, Sheila O'Flanagan, James Patterson, Pamela Stephenson.

Hodder & Stoughton General Managing Director *Jamie Hodder-Williams*; **Non-fiction** *Rowena Webb*; **Sceptre** *Carole Welch*; **Fiction** *Carolyn Mays*; **Audio** (See entry under *Audio Books*). Publishes commercial and literary fiction; biography, autobiography, history, self-help, humour, travel and other general interest non-fiction; audio. IMPRINTS **Hodder & Stoughton**; **Hodder Paperbacks**; **Sceptre**; **Mobius**. AUTHORS Melvyn Bragg, Bill Cullen, Jeffrey Deaver, Charles Frazier, Elizabeth George, Thomas Keneally, Stephen King, John le Carré, Andrew Miller, David Mitchell, Elizabeth Noble, Rosamunde Pilcher, Mary Stewart, Fiona Walker.

Hodder Children's Books (See **Hachette Children's Books**).

Hodder & Stoughton Religious Managing Director *Martin Mullen*, Publishing Director *Judith Longman*, Bibles & Hodder Christian Books *David Moloney*. Publishes NIV Bibles, Christian books, autobiography, TV-tie-ins, gift books, self-help. IMPRINTS **Hodder & Stoughton**; **Hodder Christian Books**; **Help Yourself**.

Hodder Education Managing Director *Philip Walters* Publishes in the following areas: **Schoolbooks** *Lis Tribe*; **Consumer Education** *Katie Roden*; **Further Education/Higher Education Textbooks**; **Health Sciences**; **Journals/Reference Books** *Mary Attree*. IMPRINTS **Hodder Murray**; **Teach Yourself**; **Hodder Arnold**; **Hodder Gibson** (see entry).

John Murray (Publishers) Ltd (see entry).

Authors' Rating These are exciting times at Hodder, formerly part of WHSmith but now, following a £223 million sale, a division of the French publishing group Lagardère, better known here by its subsidiary Hachette Livre. Since Hachette already owns Orion, Octopus, Watts and Chambers Harrap, the new conglomerate is well placed to take on Random for first place in the list of UK consumer book publishers. The impact on authors has yet to be seen but the Hachette policy of encouraging competition between imprints within the group suggests that the close relationship between authos and editors fostered by Hodder will not be sacrificed to economies of size.

Honeyglen Publishing Ltd

56 Durrels House, Warwick Gardens, London W14 8QB
☎020 7602 2876   Fax 020 7602 2876
Directors *N.S. Poderegin, J. Poderegin*

Founded 1983. A small publishing house whose output is 'extremely limited'. Publishes history, philosophy of history, biography and selective fiction. No children's or science fiction. TITLES *The Soul of China; The Soul of India; Woman and Power in History; Lost World – Tibet; A Child of the Century* all by Amaury de Riencourt; *With Duncan Grant in South Turkey* Paul Roche; *Vladimir, The Russian Viking* Vladimir Volkoff; *The Dawning* Milka Bajic-Poderegin; *Quicksand* Louise Hide. Unsolicited mss welcome.

Honno Welsh Women's Press

c/o Canolfan Merched y Wawr, Vulcan Street, Aberystwyth SY23 1JH
☎01970 623150   Fax 01970 623150
✉ post@honno.co.uk
www.honno.co.uk
Editor *Caroline Oakley*

Founded in 1986 by a group of women who

wanted to create more opportunities for women in publishing. A co-operative operation which publishes fiction with a Welsh connection. Also publishes short story and autobiographical anthologies. 7 titles a year. Welcomes mss and ideas for books from women only. All material must have a Welsh connection and be sent as hard copy, not by e-mail.
ROYALTIES annually.

Horus Editions
See **Award Publications Limited**

House of Lochar
Isle of Colonsay PA61 7YR
☎01951 200232   Fax 01951 200232
✉ Lochar@colonsay.org.uk
www.houseoflochar.com
Chairman *Kevin Byrne*
Managing Director *Georgina Hobhouse*
Approx. Annual Turnover £95,000

Founded 1995 on a tiny island, taking advantage of new technology and mains electricity and taking over some 20 titles from Thomas and Lochar. Publishes mostly Scottish – history, topography, transport and fiction. IMPRINTS **House of Lochar** TITLES *The Clyde in Pictures; Alexander III; Ancient Scotland; The Clyde Puffer.* AUTHORS Neil Munro, Neill Gunn, John McPhee, Marion Campbell, Ronald Williams. **Colonsay Books** TITLE *Summer in the Hebrides.* **West Highland Series** Mini walking guides. No poetry or books unrelated to Scotland or Celtic theme. About 10 titles a year. Unsolicited mss, synopses and ideas welcome if relevant to subjects covered.
ROYALTIES annually.

How To Books Ltd
3 Newtec Place, Magdalen Road, Oxford OX4 1RE
☎01865 793806   Fax 01865 248780
✉ info@howtobooks.co.uk
www.howtobooks.co.uk
Managing Director *Giles Lewis*
Commissioning Editorial Director *Nikki Read*

An independent publishing house, founded in 1991. Publishes non-fiction, self-help reference books. How To titles are practical, accessible books that enable their readers to achieve their goals in life and work. How To authors must have first-hand experience of the subject about which they are writing. Subjects covered include management, leisure learning, career choices and career development, living and working abroad, small business and self employ-

ment, study skills & student guides, creative writing and property.

Human Horizons
See **Souvenir Press Ltd**

Hunt & Thorpe
See **John Hunt Publishing Ltd**

John Hunt Publishing Ltd
The Bothy, Deershot Lodge, Park Lane, Ropley SO24 0BE
☎01962 773768   Fax 01962 773769
✉ office@johnhunt-publishing.com
www.o-books.net
Approx. Annual Turnover £1.5 million

Publishes children's and world religions as well as mind, body & spirit titles. IMPRINTS **Hunt & Thorpe**; **John Hunt Publishing**; **Arthur James**; **O Books**. About 50 titles a year. Unsolicited material welcome.

C. Hurst & Co.
41 Great Russell Street, London WC1B 3PL
☎020 7255 2201   Fax 020 7255 2204
✉ hurst@atlas.co.uk
www.hurstpub.co.uk
Chairman/Managing Director *Christopher Hurst*
Editorial Heads *Christopher Hurst, Michael Dwyer*

Founded 1967. An independent company concerned with literacy, detail and visual aspects. Publishes contemporary history, politics, religion (not theology) and sociology. TITLES *The Hungarians* Paul Lendvai; *Greece: The Modern Sequel; Serbia: the History Behind the Name; Iceland's 1100 Years; Inside Al Qaeda: Global Network of Terror.* About 25 titles a year. No unsolicited mss. Synopses and ideas welcome.
ROYALTIES annually.

Hutchinson/Hutchinson Children's Books
See **The Random House Group Ltd**

Hymns Ancient & Modern Ltd
St Mary's Works, St Mary's Plain, Norwich NR3 3BH
☎01603 612914   Fax 01603 624483
✉ admin@scm-canterburypress.co.uk
www.scm-canterburypress.co.uk
Chairman *Patrick Coldstream, CBE*
Chief Executive *Andrew Moore*
Publisher, SCM Press and Canterbury Press *Christine Smith*
Publisher, RMEP *Mary Mears*

Approx. Annual Turnover £4.4 million

Publishing subsidiary **SCM-Canterbury Press Ltd** (see entry) controls **SCM Press, Canterbury Press** and **RMEP** IMPRINTS which cover hymn books, liturgical material, academic and general religious books, and multi-faith religious and social education resources for pupils and teachers. Media subsidiary **G.J. Palmer & Sons Ltd** includes *Church Times* (see entry under *Magazines*); monthly magazine inserts *The Sign* and *Home Words* and *Crucible*, a quarterly magazine. Ideas for new titles welcome but no unsolicited mss.

ROYALTIES annually.

Icon Books Ltd

The Old Dairy, Brook Road, Thriplow, Cambridge SG8 7RG
☎01763 208008   Fax 01763 208080
✉ info@iconbooks.co.uk
www.iconbooks.co.uk

Managing Director *Peter Pugh*
Sales & Marketing Director *Simon Flynn*

Founded 1992. SERIES *Introducing* Graphic introductions to key figures and ideas in the history of science, philosophy, psychology, religion and the arts. TITLE *Introducing Quantum Theory*. Publishes 'provocative and intelligent' non-fiction in science, politics and philosophy. TITLE *Why do People Hate America?* IMPRINT **Wizard Books** Children's fiction and non-fiction including SERIES *Fighting Fantasy* (adventure gamebooks). Submit synopsis only. OVERSEAS ASSOCIATE Totem Books, USA, distributed by National Book Network.

ROYALTIES twice yearly.

I.M.P. Fiction Ltd

PO Box 69, Church Stretton SY6 6WZ
☎01694 720049   Fax 01694 720049
✉ info@impbooks.com
www.impbooks.com

Managing Director *Kaye Roach*

Founded 1998. Publishes 'quality new fiction'. No crime, science fiction, horror or fantasy. 2 titles in 2004. Mss only accepted from recognised agents; no unsolicited mss.

ROYALTIES twice-yearly.

The In Pinn

See **Neil Wilson Publishing Ltd**

Independent Music Press

PO Box 69, Church Stretton SY6 6WZ
☎01694 720049   Fax 01694 720049
✉ info@impbooks.com

www.impbooks.com

Managing Director *Martin Roach*

Founded 1992. Publishes music biography and youth culture. No jazz or classical. TITLES include biographies of Dave Grohl, Stereophonics, Oasis, Prodigy as well as subculture classics such as *Scooter Boys* and Ian Hunter's *Diary of a Rock 'n' Roll Star*. Approach by letter or e-mail, enclosing biography, synopsis, first three chapters and s.a.e. if return of work required. Material will not be returned if postage and packing not provided.

ROYALTIES twice-yearly.

Independent Voices

See **Souvenir Press Ltd**

Infinite Ideas

36 St Giles, Oxford OX1 3LD
☎01865 514888   Fax 01865 514777
✉ richard@infideas.com
www.infideas.com

Chairman *Jesse Norman*
Joint Managing Directors *David Grant, Richard Burton*
Approx. Annual Turnover £500,000

Founded 2004. Publishes inspirational self-help. SERIES **52 Brilliant Ideas** *Richard Burton* Subject areas cover health and relationships; careers, finance and personal development; sports, hobbies and games; leisure and lifestyle; art, literature and music. No fiction, illustrated or children's books. 40 titles in 2005. No unsolicited mss. Synopses and ideas welcome; initial contact by e-mail or letter.

Flat FEES paid.

Informa Law

Informa House, 30–32 Mortimer Street, London W1W 7RE
☎020 7017 4600

Managing Director *Fotini Liontou*
Publishing Director *Wendy Gill*

Part of LLP Professional Publishing, a trading division of Informa Publishing Group Ltd. Publishes a range of maritime law, commercial law, insurance law, banking law, intellectual property law publications including newsletters, law reports, books, journals and magazines aimed at senior management and professional practices.

Inspire

c/o mph, 4 John Wesley Road, Werrington, Peterborough PE4 6ZP
☎01733 325002   Fax 01733 384180
✉ comm.editor@mph.org.uk

www.mph.org.uk

Commissioning Editor *Dr Natalie K. Watson*

Publishes accessible Christian books for the wider ecumenical market. Spirituality, social concern, worship resources, mission and evangelism, discipleship, prayer. No fiction or children's. 12 titles a year. Unsolicited mss, synopses and ideas welcome; send two sample chapters and proposal with covering letter and s.a.e. for return of mss. ROYALTIES annually.

Inter-Varsity Press

38 De Montfort Street, Leicester LE1 7GP
☎0116 255 1754   Fax 0116 254 2044
✉ ivp@uccf.org.uk
www.ivpbooks.com

Chairman *Ralph Evershed*
Chief Executive *Brian Wilson*

Founded mid-1930s as the publishing arm of Universities and Colleges Christian Fellowship, it has expanded to wider Christian markets worldwide. Publishes Christian belief and lifestyle, reference and bible commentaries. No secular material or anything which fails to empathise with orthodox Protestant Christianity. IMPRINTS **IVP**; **Apollos**; **Crossway** TITLES *The Bible Speaks Today*; *Life's Big Questions* Vaughan Roberts; *New Testament Theology* Howard Marshall. About 50 titles a year. Synopses and ideas welcome.
ROYALTIES twice-yearly.

Interface Collection

See **University of Hertfordshire Press**

Isis Publishing

7 Centremead, Osney Mead OX2 0ES
☎01865 250333   Fax 01865 790358
www.isis-publishing.co.uk

Part of the Ulverscroft Group Ltd. Publishes large-print books – fiction and non-fiction – and unabridged audio books. Together with **Soundings** (see entry under *Audio Books*) produces around 4000 titles on audio tape and CD. AUTHORS Lee Child, Martina Cole, Terry Pratchett, Susan Sallis. No unsolicited mss as Isis undertakes no original publishing.
ROYALTIES twice-yearly.

Itchy Coo

See **Black & White Publishing Ltd**

Ithaca Press

See **Garnet Publishing Ltd**

IVP

See **Inter-Varsity Press**

Jacqui Small

See **Aurum Press Ltd**

JAI

See **Elsevier Ltd**

Arthur James

See **John Hunt Publishing Ltd**

Jane's Information Group

Sentinel House, 163 Brighton Road,
Coulsdon CR5 2YH
☎020 8700 3700   Fax 020 8763 1006
✉ info.uk@janes.com
www.janes.com

Managing Director *Alfred Rolington*

Founded 1898 by Fred T. Jane with the publication of *All The World's Fighting Ships*. Now part of the Woodbridge Company Limited. In recent years management has been focusing on growth opportunities in its core business and in enhancing the performance of initiatives like Jane's information available online and on in-depth intelligence centres. Publishes Web journals, magazines and yearbooks on defence, aerospace, security and transport topics, with details of equipment and systems; plus directories and strategic studies. Also *Jane's Defence Weekly* (see entry under *Magazines*).

DIVISIONS
Magazines Sean Howe TITLES *Jane's Defence Weekly*; *Jane's International Defence Review*; *Jane's Airport Review*; *Jane's Navy International*; *Jane's Islamic Affairs Analyst*; *Jane's Missiles and Rockets*. **Publishing for Defence, Aerospace, Transport** Ian Kay TITLES *Defence, Aerospace Yearbooks*. **Transport** TITLES *Transportation Yearbooks*. **Security** Michael Dell TITLES *Jane's Intelligence Review*; *Foreign Report*; *Jane's Sentinel* (regional security assessment); *Jane's Police Review*. CD-ROM and electronic development and publication. Unsolicited mss, synopses and ideas for reference/yearbooks welcome. OVERSEAS ASSOCIATES Jane's Information Group Inc., USA.
ROYALTIES twice-yearly.

Janus Publishing Company Ltd

105–107 Gloucester Place, London W1U 6BY
☎020 7580 7664   Fax 020 7636 5756
✉ publisher@januspublishing.co.uk

Managing Director *Sandy Leung*

Publishes fiction, human interest, memoirs,

philosophy, mind, body and spirit, religion and theology, social questions, popular science, history, spiritualism and the paranormal, poetry and young adults. IMPRINTS **Janus Books** Subsidy publishing; **Empiricus Books** Non-subsidy publishing. TITLES *The Anarchists in the Spanish Civil War; Nature of the Self; Politics and Human Nature; Napoleon 1813; King David; Chameleon Candidate; Love Emporium; Digby.* 'Two of our authors won the European Literary Award in 2002.' About 400 titles in print. Unsolicited mss welcome. Agents in the USA, Europe and Asia.
ROYALTIES twice-yearly.

Authors' Rating Authors may be asked to cover their own productions costs but Janus seems to be moving into conventional publishing with its Empiricus imprint.

Jarrold Publishing
Whitefriars, Norwich NR3 1JR
☎01603 763300   Fax 01603 662748
✉ info@jarrold-publishing.co.uk
www.jarrold-publishing.co.uk
Managing Director *Margot Russell-King*

Part of Jarrold & Sons Ltd, the printing and publishing company founded in 1770. Publishes UK tourism, travel, leisure, history and calendars. Material tends to be of a high pictorial content. IMPRINTS **Pitkin; Unichrome**. About 30 titles a year. Unsolicited mss, synopses and ideas welcome but before submitting anything, approach in writing to the editorial department.

Michael Joseph
See **Penguin Group (UK)**

Kahn & Averill
9 Harrington Road, London SW7 3ES
☎020 8743 3278   Fax 020 8743 3278
✉ kahn@averill23.freeserve.co.uk
Managing Director *Mr M. Kahn*

Founded 1967 to publish children's titles but now specialises in music titles. A small independent publishing house. No unsolicited mss; synopses and ideas for books considered.
ROYALTIES twice-yearly.

Karnak House
157 Dudden Hill Lane, London NW10 1AU
☎020 8830 8301   Fax 020 8830 8301
✉ karnakhouse@aol.com
Publisher/Commissioning Editor *Amon Saba Saakana*

Founded 1979. Specialises in African and Caribbean studies. Publishes anthropology, education, Egyptology, history, language and linguistics, literary criticism, music, prehistory. No poetry, humour or sport. About 7 titles a year. No unsolicited mss; send introduction or synopsis with one sample chapter. Synopses and ideas welcome. OVERSEAS SUBSIDIARIES The Intef Institute, and Karnak House, Illinois, USA.
ROYALTIES annually.

Kenilworth Press Ltd
Addington, Buckingham MK18 2JR
☎01296 715101   Fax 01296 715148
✉ editorial@kenilworthpress.co.uk
www.kenilworthpress.co.uk
Chairman/Managing Director *David Blunt*
Approx. Annual Turnover £500,000

Founded in 1989 with the acquisition of Threshhold Books. The UK's principal instructional equestrian publisher, producing the official books of the British Horse Society, the famous *Threshold Picture Guides* and a range of authoritative titles sold around the world. IMPRINT **Kenilworth Press** Titles *British Horse Society Manuals; Real Riding; Ride With Your Mind Essentials; Navicular Syndrome Explained; Threshold Picture Guides 1–48.* About 10 titles a year. Unsolicited mss, synopses and ideas welcome but only for titles concerned with the care or riding of horses or ponies.
ROYALTIES twice-yearly.

Kenyon-Deane
See **Cressrelles Publishing Co. Ltd**

Laurence King Publishing Ltd
71 Great Russell Street, London WC1B 3BP
☎020 7430 8850   Fax 020 7430 8880
✉ enquiries@laurenceking.co.uk
www.laurenceking.co.uk
Chairman *Nick Perren*
Managing Director *Laurence King*
Approx. Annual Turnover £6 million

Founded in 1976 as a book packager under the name Calmann & King Ltd, the Laurence King publishing division commenced operations in 1991. College and trade divisions were united in 2002 under Laurence King Publishing Ltd. Publishes illustrated books on art, architecture, graphic design, interior design, the decorative arts, film and religion. TITLES *Atlas of World Art; A World History of Art; History of Modern Design; The Design Encyclopedia; A History of Western*

Architecture; A History of Interior Design. About 40 titles a year. Unsolicited material welcome; send synopsis by post or e-mail.
ROYALTIES twice-yearly.

Kingfisher Publications Plc
New Penderel House, 283–288 High Holborn, London WC1V 7HZ
☎020 7903 9999   Fax 020 7242 4979
✉ sales@kingfisherpub.com
Managing Director *John Richards*
Formerly Larousse plc until 1997 when the company name changed to Kingfisher Publications Plc. Founded 1994 when owners, Groupe de la Cité (also publishers of the Larousse dictionaries in France), merged their UK operations of Grisewood & Dempsey and **Chambers Harrap Publishers Ltd** (see entry). In 2002, Kingfisher officially became an imprint of **Houghton Mifflin Company** (see entry under *US Publishers*). DIVISION **Kingfisher** Non-fiction Publishing Director *Sue Grabham*, Fiction Publishing Director *Anne Marie Ryan* Founded in 1973 by Grisewood & Dempsey Ltd. Publishes children's fiction and non-fiction in hardback and paperback: story books, rhymes and picture books, fiction and poetry anthologies, young non-fiction, activity books, general series and reference. No unsolicited mss accepted.
ROYALTIES twice-yearly where applicable.

Jessica Kingsley Publishers Ltd
116 Pentonville Road, London N1 9JB
☎020 7833 2307   Fax 020 7837 2917
✉ post@jkp.com
www.jkp.com
Managing Director and Publisher *Jessica Kingsley*
Senior Acquisitions Editor *Stephen Jones*
Founded 1987. Independent, international publisher of books for professionals, academics and the general reader on autism, disability, special education, arts therapies, child psychology, mental health, practical theology and social work. Over 100 titles a year. 'We are actively publishing and commissioning in all these areas. We welcome suggestions for books and proposals from prospective authors. Proposals should consist of an outline of the book, a contents list, assessment of the market and author's c.v., and should be addressed to *Jessica Kingsley* or *Stephen Jones*. Complete manuscript should not be sent.'
ROYALTIES twice-yearly.

Kluwer Academic/ Plenum Publishers
See **Springer**

Kluwer Law International
145 London Road, Kingston-upon-Thames KT2 6SR
☎020 8247 1694   Fax 020 8247 1607
Publisher *Sian O'Neill*
Founded 1995. Parent company: Wolters Kluwer Group. Publishes international law. About 200 titles a year, including online, CD-ROM, loose-leaf journals and monographs. Unsolicited synopses and ideas for books on law at an international level welcome.
ROYALTIES annually.

Knight Paperbacks Ltd
See **Caxton Publishing Group**

Kogan Page Ltd
120 Pentonville Road, London N1 9JN
☎020 7278 0433   Fax 020 7837 3768/6348
✉ kpinfo@kogan-page.co.uk
www.kogan-page.co.uk
Managing Director *Philip Kogan*
Approx. Annual Turnover £6 million
Founded 1967 by Philip Kogan to publish *The Industrial Training Yearbook*. In 1992 acquired Earthscan Publications. Publishes business and management reference books and monographs, careers, marketing, personal finance, personnel, small business, training and industrial relations, transport. Further expansion is planned, particularly in the finance and high-tech, EC publications areas, yearbooks and directories. Has initiated a number of electronic publishing projects and provision of EP content. DIVISIONS **Kogan Page** *Pauline Goodwin, Helen Kogan, Jon Finch*; **Kogan Page Science** Publishes hi-tech engineering science monographs. About 50 titles a year.
ROYALTIES twice-yearly.

Authors' Rating Resisting blandishments from larger rivals, Kogan Page remains an independent publisher, resolutely dedicated to books about and for business in all forms. The latest development is a link up with US publisher Bloomberg Press to distribute its financial and business titles.

Ladybird
See **Dorling Kindersley Ltd**

Landmark Publishing Ltd

Ashbourne Hall, Cokayne Avenue, Ashbourne DE6 1EJ
☎01335 347349   Fax 01335 347303
✉ landmark@clara.net
www.landmarkpublishing.co.uk
Chairman *Mr R. Cork*
Managing Director *Mr C.L.M. Porter*
Approx. Annual Turnover £450,000

Founded in 1996. Publishes itinerary-based travel guides, regional, industrial countryside and local history. 50 titles in 2004. No unsolicited mss; telephone in the first instance.
ROYALTIES annually.

Lawrence & Wishart Ltd

99A Wallis Road, London E9 5LN
☎020 8533 2506   Fax 020 8533 7369
✉ lw@lwbooks.co.uk
www.lwbooks.co.uk
Managing Director/Editor *Sally Davison*

Founded 1936. An independent publisher with a substantial backlist. Publishes current affairs, cultural politics, economics, history, politics and education. TITLES *A New Modernity; Liberty or Death; The Struggle for Democracy in Britain 1780–1830; Rosa Luxemburg: An Intimate Portrait.* 10 titles a year.
ROYALTIES annually, unless by arrangement.

The Learning Institute

Honeycombe House, Bagley, Wedmore BS28 4TD
☎01934 713563   Fax 01934 713492
✉ courses@inst.org
www.inst.org
Managing Director *Kit Sadgrove*

Founded 1994 to publish home-study courses in vocational subjects such as garden design, writing and computing. Publishes subjects that show the reader how to work from home, gain a new skill or enter a new career. Interests include self-improvement, interior design, hobbies, parenting, health, careers, music and investment. TITLES *Diploma in Interior Design; Become a Garden Designer.* Author's guidelines sent on receipt of s.a.e. No unsolicited mss; send synopses and ideas only.
ROYALTIES quarterly.

Lennard Associates Ltd

Windmill Cottage, Mackerye End, Harpenden AL5 5DR
☎01582 715866   Fax 01582 715866
✉ stephenson@lennardqap.co.uk
Chairman/Managing Director *Adrian Stephenson*

Founded 1979. Publisher of sporting yearbooks; sponsored and commissioned projects only. YEARBOOKS *The Cricketers' Who's Who; PFA Footballers' Who's Who; Wooden Spoon Rugby World.* IMPRINTS **Lennard Publishing; Queen Anne Press.** Acquired the latter and most of its assets in 1992. No unsolicited mss.
PAYMENT Both fees and royalties by arrangement.

Charles Letts

See **New Holland Publishers (UK) Ltd**

Lionel Leventhal Ltd

See **Greenhill Books**

Dewi Lewis Publishing

8 Broomfield Road, Heaton Moor, Stockport SK4 4ND
☎0161 442 9450   Fax 0161 442 9450
✉ mail@dewilewispublishing.com
www.dewilewispublishing.com
Contacts *Dewi Lewis, Caroline Warhurst*
Approx. Annual Turnover £260,000

Founded 1994. Publishes fiction, photography and visual arts. TITLES *Industry of Souls* Martin Booth (Booker Prize shortlist, 1998); *Wolfy and the Strudelbakers* Zvi Jagendorf (Booker Prize longlist, 2001; Sagittarius Prize, 2002); *Common Sense* Martin Parr; *New York 1954–5* William Klein. 19 titles in 2004. Submissions: check website.
ROYALTIES annually.

LexisNexis

See **Reed Elsevier Group plc**

John Libbey Publishing

PO Box 276, Eastleigh SO50 5YS
☎01342 315440   Fax 023 8065 0259
✉ johnlibbey@aol.com
www.johnlibbey.com
Publisher *John Libbey*

Founded 1979. Publishes books and journals on cinema, animation and media. Now the publisher of the media series from University of Luton Press. Synopses and ideas welcome. OVERSEAS SUBSIDIARY John Libbey Eurotext Ltd, France (medical publishers).

Librapharm Ltd

29 Venture West, New Greenham Park, Newbury RG19 6HX
☎01635 522651   Fax 01635 36294
www.librapharm.com

Chairman *Mr M.W. Frost*
Managing Director *Dr P.L. Clarke*
Approx. Annual Turnover £1.5 million

Founded 1995 as a partial buyout from Kluwer Academic Publishers (UK) academic list. Publishes medical and scientific periodicals. No book publishing.

Library Association Publishing
See **Facet Publishing**

Life&Times
See **Haus Publishers**

Frances Lincoln Ltd
4 Torriano Mews, Torriano Avenue, London NW5 2RZ
☎020 7284 4009   Fax 020 7267 5249
✉ firstname and initial of surname@franceslincoln.com
www.franceslincoln.com

Managing Director *John Nicoll*

Founded 1977. Publishes highly illustrated non-fiction: gardening, art and interiors, architecture, parenting, walking and climbing, children's picture and information books; and stationery. DIVISIONS **Adult Non-fiction** *Jo Christian* TITLES *Chatsworth* Duchess of Devonshire; *Grow Your Own Vegetables* Joy Larkcom; *Pictorial Guides to the Lakeland Fells* A. Wainwright; **Children's General Fiction and Non-fiction** *Janetta Otter-Barry* TITLE *The Wanderings of Odysseus* Rosemary Sutcliffe, illus. Alan Lee; **Stationery** *Anne Fraser* TITLES *RHS Diary and Address Book*; *British Library Diary*. About 75 titles a year. Synopses and ideas for books considered.
ROYALTIES twice-yearly.

Linden Press
See **Open Gate Press**

Linford Romance/Linford Mystery/Linford Western
See **F.A. Thorpe (Publishing)**

Lion Hudson plc
Mayfield House, 256 Banbury Road, Oxford OX2 7DH
☎01865 302750   Fax 01865 302757
✉ enquiries@lionhudson.com
www.lionhudson.com

Managing Director *Paul Clifford*
Approx. Annual Turnover £8.5 million

Founded 1971. A Christian book publisher, strong on illustrated books for a popular inter-national readership, with rights sold in over 150 languages worldwide. Publishes a diverse list with Christian viewpoint the common denominator. All ages, from board books for children to multi-contributor adult reference, educational, paperbacks and colour co-editions and gift books. IMPRINTS **Lion** and **Lion Children's** *Juliet Mozley*; **Candle** and **Monarch** *Caroline Nicholls* (see entry). About 175 titles a year. Unsolicited mss accepted provided they have a positive Christian viewpoint intended for a Christian or wide general and international readership.
ROYALTIES twice-yearly.

Little Tiger Press
An imprint of Magi Publications, 1 The Coda Centre, 189 Munster Road, London SW6 6AW
☎020 7385 6333   Fax 020 7385 7333
✉ info@littletiger.co.uk
www.littletigerpress.com

Publisher *Monty Bhatia*
Editors *Jude Evans, Laura Workman*
Approx. Annual Turnover £5 million

Publishes children's picture and novelty books for ages 0–7. No texts over 750 words. IMPRINT **Stripes** Fiction for the 6–12 age range. About 24 titles a year. Unsolicited mss, synopses and new ideas welcome. See website for submission guidelines.
ROYALTIES annually.

Authors' Rating A thriving small publisher that is now moving into fiction for the six to 12 age range.

Little, Brown
See **Time Warner Books UK**

Liverpool University Press
4 Cambridge Street, Liverpool L69 7ZU
☎0151 794 2233   Fax 0151 794 2235
✉ robblo@liv.ac.uk
www.liverpool-unipress.co.uk

Managing Director/Editorial Head *Robin Bloxsidge*

LUP's primary activity is the publication of academic and scholarly books and journals but it also has a limited number of trade titles. Its principal focus is on the arts and social sciences, in which it is active in a variety of disciplines. TITLES *The Cannibal Hymn*; *Excavations on St Patrick's Isle, Peel, Isle of Man*; *Urban Visions*; *Public Sculpture of Warwickshire*; *Public Sculpture of the City of London*; *The Long Road to Peace in Northern Ireland*; *Knowledge and Learning in the*

Andes; *Identity Parades: Northern Irish Culture and Dissident Subjects*; *HIV Stories*; *Breeding Superman*; *The Business of Music*; *Claude Simon: A Retrospective*. 30–40 titles a year. ROYALTIES annually.

Authors' Rating A once rather staid publisher has jumped up in the ratings with a 'vigorous and distinctive' new publishing programme for the humanities and social sciences. Commercial considerations will come before university politics.

Livewire Books for Teenagers
See **The Women's Press**

Lonely Planet Publications Ltd
72–82 Rosebery Avenue, London EC1R 4RW
☎020 7841 9000   Fax 020 7841 9001
✉ go@lonelyplanet.co.uk
www.lonelyplanet.com
Owner *Lonely Planet (Australia)*
Editorial Head *Katharine Leck*
Approx. Annual Turnover £40 million

Founded in 1973 by Tony and Maureen Wheeler to document a journey from London across Asia to Australia. Since then, Lonely Planet has grown into a global operation with headquarters in Melbourne and offices in California and London. Publishes travel guidebooks, phrasebooks, travel literature, pictorial books, city maps, diving and snorkelling, walking, cycling, wildlife, health, and How To guides. Also operates a commercial travel slide library called **Lonely Planet Images** (www.lonelyplanetimages.com). No unsolicited mss; synopses and ideas welcome.

Longman
See **Pearson Education**

Lorenz Books
See **Anness Publishing Ltd**

Lucky Duck Publishing
See **Sage Publications**

Lund Humphries
See **Ashgate Publishing Ltd**

The Lutterworth Press
PO Box 60, Cambridge CB1 2NT
☎01223 350865   Fax 01223 366951
✉ publishing@jamesclarke.co.uk
www.lutterworth.com
Managing Director *Adrian Brink*

The Lutterworth Press dates back to the 18th century when it was founded by the Religious Tract Society. In the 19th century it was best known for its children's books and magazines, both religious and secular, including *The Boys' Own Paper*. Since 1984 it has been an imprint of **James Clarke & Co** (see entry). Publishes religious books for adults and children, adult nonfiction, children's fiction and non-fiction. TITLES *Whatever Happened to Religious Education?*; *Burn, Holy Fire!*; *The Germans We Trusted*; *Joanna Southcott's Box of Sealed Prophecies*. Approach in writing with ideas in the first instance.
ROYALTIES annually.

Macdonald & Co.
See **Time Warner Books UK**

McGraw Hill Education
McGraw-Hill House, Shoppenhangers Road, Maidenhead SL6 2QL
☎01628 502500   Fax 01628 770224
www.mcgraw-hill.co.uk
Publishing Director *John Reed*

Owned by US parent company, founded in 1888. Began publishing in Maidenhead in 1965, having had an office in the UK since 1899. Publishes business, economics, finance, accounting, computing science, social sciences and engineering for the academic, student and professional markets. Acquired **Open University Press** in 2002 (see entry). Around 100 titles a year. See website for author's guide and how to submit new book proposals.
ROYALTIES twice-yearly.

Macmillan Publishers Ltd
The Macmillan Building, 4 Crinan Street, London N1 9XW
☎020 7833 4000   Fax 020 7843 4640
www.macmillan.com
Chief Executive *Richard Charkin*
Approx. Annual Turnover £300 million (Book Publishing Group)

Founded 1843. Macmillan is one of the largest publishing houses in Britain, publishing approximately 1400 titles a year. In 1995, Verlagsgruppe Georg von Holtzbrinck, a major German publisher, acquired a majority stake in the Macmillan Group and in 1999 purchased the remaining shares. In 1996, Macmillan bought Boxtree, the successful media tie-in publisher and, in 1997, it purchased the Heinemann English language teaching list from Reed Elsevier. In 2004 the educational publishing division was strengthened by the acquisition of the Mexican list, Ediciones

Castillo. No unsolicited material except for the **Macmillan New Writing** list (see Author's Rating).

DIVISIONS
Palgrave Macmillan
Brunel Road, Houndmills, Basingstoke, Hampshire RG21 6XS
☎01256 329242 Fax 01256 479476
Managing Director *Dominic Knight*
Frances Arnold (College)
Sam Burridge (Scholarly & Reference)
David Bull (Journals)

Publishes textbooks, monographs and journals in academic and professional subjects. Publications in both hard copy and electronic format.

Macmillan Education
Macmillan Oxford, 4 Between Towns Road, Oxford OX4 3PP
☎ 01865 405700 Fax 01865 405701
✉ info@ macmillan.com
Website www.macmillaneducation.com
Executive Chairman *Christopher Paterson*
Managing Director *Chris Harrison*
Publishing Directors *Sue Bale* (ELT), *Alison Hubert* (Education), *Ian Johnstone* (Internet).

Publishes a wide range of ELT titles and educational materials for the international education market from Oxford and through 30 subsidiaries worldwide.

Pan Macmillan
20 New Wharf Road, London N1 9RR
☎ 020 7014 6000 Fax 020 7014 6001
www.panmacmillan.com
Managing Director *David North.*

IMPRINTS **Macmillan, Pan, Picador, Sidgwick & Jackson, Boxtree, Macmillan Children's Books, Campbell Books, Young Picador.**

Macmillan (founded 1843) Publishing Director *Maria Rejt*, Editorial Director *Imogen Taylor* Publishes hardback commercial and literary fiction including genre fiction, romantic, crime and thrillers.

Tor (founded 2003) Editorial Director *Peter Lavery* Publishes science fiction, fantasy and thrillers. Non-Fiction: Publisher *Richard Milner*, Editorial Director *Georgina Morley* Publishes serious and general non-fiction: autobiography, biography, economics, history, philosophy, politics and world affairs, psychology, popular science, trade reference titles.

Pan (founded 1947) Paperback imprint for Pan Macmillan. **Picador** (founded 1972) Publisher *Andrew Kidd*, Senior Editorial Director *Ursula Doyle.* Publishes literary international fiction and non-fiction.

Sidgwick & Jackson (founded 1908) Publishes popular non-fiction in hardback and trade paperback with strong personality or marketable identity, from celebrity and show-business to music and sport. Also military history list.

Boxtree (founded 1986) Publishes brand and media tie-in titles, including TV, film, music and Internet, plus entertainment licences, pop culture, humour and event-related books. TITLES *Dilbert; James Bond; Purple Ronnie; Viz; Wallace & Gromit; The Onion; Crap Towns.*

Macmillan Children's Books (New Wharf Road address) Managing Director *Emma Hopkin*; Fiction, Non-Fiction and Poetry *Sarah Davies*; Picture Books and Gift Books *Suzanne Carnell*; **Campbell Books** *Camilla Reid*; **Young Picador** *Andrew Kidd* Publishes novels, board books, picture books, non-fiction (illustrated and non-illustrated), poetry and novelty books in paperback and hardback.

ROYALTIES annually or twice-yearly depending on contract.

Authors' Rating Pan Macmillan may have trimmed its list (the aim is to give more attention to potentially strong sellers) but elsewhere in the group the mood is expansionary. A new popular science list is touting for 'entertaining, authoritative books about the politics, history and implications of research and discovery'. No advances are offered but authors get 30% royalties on all editions, in all languages. If this is not radical enough, Macmillan has launched an innovative scheme for writers of novels for adults. The Macmillan New Writing list (✉ newwriting@macmillan.co.uk), currently attracting some 200 manuscripts a month, is based on a non-negotiable contract giving authors 20% royalties but no advance. MNW will not accept manuscripts which need heavy editing or rewriting. Predictably, some published authors have attacked 'the Ryanair of publishing' but Macmillan defends 'a streamlined cost-effective model' which may launch writers who might not otherwise get near the mainstream.

Made Simple Books
See **Elsevier Ltd**

Mainstream Publishing Co. (Edinburgh) Ltd
7 Albany Street, Edinburgh EH1 3UG
☎0131 557 2959   Fax 0131 556 8720
✉ editorial@mainstreampublishing.com
www.mainstreampublishing.com
Directors *Bill Campbell, Peter MacKenzie*

Approx. Annual Turnover £3 million

Publishes art, autobiography/biography, current affairs, health, sport, history, illustrated and fine editions, photography, politics and world affairs, popular paperbacks. TITLES *Soldier Five* Mike Coburn; *The Real Nureyev* Carolyn Soutar; *Woodward's England* Mick Collins. Over 80 titles a year. Ideas for books considered, but they should be preceded by a letter, synopsis and s.a.e. or return postage.

ROYALTIES twice-yearly.

Authors' Rating As we go to press, Random House has bought a 50% share of Mainstream, boosting the potential for international sales. Mainstream is keen on finding authors who 'can develop with us'.

Management Books 2000 Ltd

Forge House, Limes Road, Kemble, Cirencester GL7 6AD
☎01285 771441   Fax 01285 771055
✉ info@mb2000.com
www.mb2000.com

Publisher *James Alexander*
Approx. Annual Turnover £500,000

Founded 1993 to develop a range of books for executives and managers working in the modern world of business. 'Essentially, the books are working books for working managers, practical and effective.' Publishes business, management, self-development and allied topics as well as sponsored titles. Launched the *In Ninety Minutes* series of compact guide books for managers in 2004, offering advice, ideas and practical help across a range of highly relevant business topics in an hour and a half of study. New ideas for this series are welcome. About 30 titles a year. Unsolicited mss, synopses and ideas for books welcome.

Manchester United Books

See **Carlton Publishing Group**

Manchester University Press

Oxford Road, Manchester M13 9NR
☎0161 275 2310   Fax 0161 274 3346
✉ mup@manchester.ac.uk
www.manchesteruniversitypress.co.uk

Publisher/Chief Executive *David Rodgers*
Head of Editorial *Matthew Frost*
Approx. Annual Turnover £2 million

Founded 1904. MUP is Britain's third largest university press, with a list marketed and sold worldwide. Remit consists of occasional trade publications but mainly A-level and undergraduate textbooks and research monographs. Publishes in the areas of: literature, TV, film, theatre and media, history and history of art, design, politics, economics and international law. DIVISIONS **Humanities** *Matthew Frost*; **History/Art History** *Alison Welsby*; **Politics and Law** *Tony Mason*. About 120 titles a year. Unsolicited mss welcome.

ROYALTIES annually.

George Mann Books

PO Box 22, Maidstone ME14 1AH
☎01622 759591   Fax 01622 209193

Chairman/Managing Director *George Mann*

Founded 1972. Publishes original non-fiction and selected reprints. Not considering new fiction for publication. 'Will only consider and respond to authors who, in the present publishing climate, are prepared to support *some of the costs* of publication on a shared venture basis. Unsolicited material not accompanied by return postage will neither be read nor returned.'

ROYALTIES annually.

Manson Publishing Ltd

73 Corringham Road, London NW11 7DL
☎020 8905 5150   Fax 020 8201 9233
✉ manson@mansonpublishing.com
www.mansonpublishing.com

Chairman/Managing Director *Michael Manson*

Founded 1992. Publishes scientific, medical and veterinary. TITLES *Clinical Medicine of the Dog and Cat*; *Clinical Bacteriology*; *A Colour Handbook of Biological Control in Plant Protection*; *Evolution of Fossil Ecosystems*. About 10 titles a year. No unsolicited mss; synopses and ideas will be considered.

ROYALTIES twice-yearly.

Marston House

Marston House, Marston Magna, Yeovil BA22 8DH
☎01935 851331   Fax 01935 851372
✉ alphaimage@marstonhouse.ndo.co.uk
www.marstonhouse.ndo.co.uk

Managing Director/Editorial Head *Anthony Birks-Hay*

Founded 1989. Publishing imprint of book packager Alphabet & Image Ltd. Publishes horticulture, beekeeping, architecture, ceramics. 4 titles a year.

ROYALTIES twice-yearly, or flat fee in lieu of royalties.

Martin Books
See **Simon & Schuster UK Ltd**

Kenneth Mason Publications Ltd
The Book Barn, Westbourne, Emsworth
PO10 8RS
☎01243 377977   Fax 01243 379136
✉ info@whitechimney.com
www.researchdisclosure.com
Chairman *Kenneth Mason*
Managing Director *Piers Mason*

Founded 1958. Publishes diet, health, fitness, nutrition and nautical. No fiction. IMPRINTS **Boatswain Press**; **Research Disclosure**. About 15 titles a year. Initial approach by letter with synopsis only.
ROYALTIES twice-yearly in first year, annually thereafter.

Kevin Mayhew Publishers
Buxhall, Stowmarket IP14 3BW
☎01449 737978   Fax 01449 737834
✉ info@kevinmayhewltd.com
www.kevinmayhewltd.com
Chairman/Commissioning Editor *Kevin Mayhew*

Founded in 1976. One of the leading sacred music and Christian book publishers in the UK. Publishes religious titles – liturgy, sacramental, devotional, also children's books and school resources. IMPRINT **Palm Tree Press** Worldwide worship. Unsolicited synopses and mss welcome; telephone prior to sending material, please.
ROYALTIES annually.

Meadowside Children's Books
185 Fleet Street, London EC4A 2HS
☎020 7400 1087   Fax 020 7400 1037
✉ info@meadowsidebooks.com
www.meadowsidebooks.com
Chairman *Mark Battles*
Publisher *Simon Rosenheim*
Editorial Manager *Alison Maloney*
Approx. Annual Turnover £1.4 million

Founded in September 2003 by D.C. Thomson. Publishes pre-school picture, novelty and early learning books. Over 100 titles a year. Unsolicited mss, synopses and ideas welcome. Send to the Editorial Department by mail or e-mail.

Melrose Press Ltd
St Thomas Place, Ely CB7 4GG
☎01353 646600   Fax 01353 646601
✉ tradesales@melrosepress.co.uk
www.melrosepress.co.uk
Chairman *Richard A. Kay*
Managing Director *Nicholas S. Law*
Approx. Annual Turnover £2 million

Founded 1960. Took on its present name in 1969. Publishes biographical who's who reference only (not including *Who's Who*, which is published by **A.&C. Black**).

Mentor
See **Christian Focus Publications**

Mercat Press Ltd
10 Coates Crescent, Edinburgh EH3 7AL
☎0131 225 5324   Fax 0131 226 6632
✉ enquiries@mercatpress.com
www.mercatpress.com
Directors *Seán Costello, Tom Johnstone*

Established as a stand-alone company in 2002 in a management buy-out following the collapse of parent firm James Thin. The Press was founded in 1971 as an adjunct to the former Scottish bookselling chain. It began by publishing reprints of classic Scottish literature but now produces a wide range of new titles. In 1992 the company acquired the bulk of the stock of Aberdeen University Press and the backlist expanded greatly as a result. In 1999 it took over some 60 titles from the Stationery Office's Scottish heritage list. New titles are added regularly. Publishes fiction and non-fiction of Scottish interest. This includes walking guides and historical and literary books. IMPRINT **Crescent Books** Adult fiction. TITLES *Elements: The Landscape of Scotland* Craig McMaster; *Love Scenes* Ralph Storer; *West Highland Way, Official Guide* Bob Aitken and Roger Smith; *25 Walks* series; *Jessie's Journey: Autobiography of a Traveller Girl* Jess Smith; *Television and Me* John Logie Baird. Unsolicited synopses of Scottish interest books, preferably with sample chapters, are welcome. No new poetry.
ROYALTIES annually.

Mercury Books/Mercury Junior
See **Caxton Publishing Group**

The Merlin Press Ltd
PO Box 30705, London WC2E 8QD
☎020 7836 3020   Fax 020 7497 0309
✉ info@merlinpress.co.uk
www.merlinpress.co.uk

Managing Director *Anthony W. Zurbrugg*

Founded 1956. Publishes economics, history, philosophy, left-wing politics. No fiction. IMPRINTS **Merlin Press**; **Green Print**. TITLES *Socialist Register* (annual); *Ralph Miliband and the Politics of the New Left*; *Pit Women*. About 10 titles a year. ROYALTIES twice-yearly.

Merrell Publishers Ltd

Head office: 42 Southwark Street, London SE1 1UN

☎020 7403 2047   Fax 020 7407 1333

✉ mail@merrellpublishers.com

www.merrellpublishers.com

US office: 49 West 24th Street, 8th Floor, New York, NY 10010

☎001 212 929 8344 Fax 001 212 929 8346

Managing Director *Hugh Merrell*

Editorial Director *Julian Honer*

US Director *Joan Brookbank*

Approx. Annual Turnover £1.8 million

Founded 1993. Publishes art, architecture, design and photography. 32 titles in 2004. Unsolicited synopses and ideas for books welcome. Send c.v. and synopsis giving details of the book's target markets and funding of illustrations. ROYALTIES annually.

Methodist Publishing House

See **mph**

Methuen Publishing Ltd

11–12 Buckingham Gate, London SW1E 6LB

☎020 7798 1600   Fax 020 7233 9827

✉ name@methuen.co.uk

www.methuen.co.uk

Managing Director *Peter Tummons*

Publishing Consultant (Methuen) *Max Eilenberg*

Publishing Consultant (Politico's) *Sean Magee*

Founded 1889. Methuen was owned by Reed International until it was bought by Random House in 1997. Purchased by a management buy-out team in 1998. Acquired **Politico's Publishing** in 2003 (see entry). Publishes fiction and non-fiction; travel, sport, drama, film, performing arts, humour. DIVISIONS **General**; **Drama**; **Film**; **Theatre**; **Politics**; **Current Affairs**. No unsolicited mss; synopses and ideas welcome. Prefers to be approached via agents or a letter of inquiry. No first novels, cookery books, personal memoirs. ROYALTIES twice-yearly.

Metro Publishing

See **John Blake Publishing Ltd**

Michelin Travel Publications

Hannay House, 39 Clarendon Road, Watford WD17 1JA

☎01923 205240   Fax 01923 205241

www.Viamichelin.co.uk

Founded 1900 as a travel publisher. Publishes travel guides, maps and atlases. Travel-related synopses and ideas welcome; no mss.

Midland Publishing

An imprint of Ian Allan Publishing Ltd, 4 Watling Drive, Hinckley LE10 3EY

☎01455 255490   Fax 01455 255495

✉ midlandbooks@compuserve.com

Publisher *N.P. Lewis*

Publishes aviation, military and railways. No wartime memoirs. No unsolicited mss; synopses and ideas welcome. ROYALTIES quarterly.

Milet Publishing Limited

6 North End Parade, London W14 0SJ

✉ info@milet.com

www.milet.com

Managing Directors *Sedat Turhan, Patricia Billings*

Founded 1995. Publishes children's picture books in English and dual language; language books; and world literature for adults. DIVISIONS **Children's, English**; **Children's, Dual Language** *Patricia Billings* TITLES *Alphabet Poem*; *Pink Lemon*; *Welcome to Lizard Lounge*. **World Literature**; **Language Books** *Sedat Turhan* TITLES *Milet Picture Dictionary*; *Milet Mini Picture Dictionary*. Welcomes synopses and ideas for books. Queries may be made by e-mail but all submissions – proposal, outline or synopsis with sample text and/or artwork – by post only. 'Please review submission guidelines and existing titles on our website before submitting. We like bold, original stories and artwork, universal and/or multicultural.' ROYALTIES twice-yearly.

Miller's

See **Octopus Publishing Group**

Millivres Prowler Limited

Unit M, Spectrum House, 32–34 Gordon House Road, London NW5 1LP

☎020 7424 7400   Fax 020 7424 7401

www.millivres.co.uk

Publishes *Gay Times, Diva Magazine, The Pink Paper* and *The National Free Gay Newspaper.*

Authors' Rating No longer interested in books; the focus is entirely on journals.

Mills & Boon
See **Harlequin Mills & Boon Ltd**

Mindfield
See **Camden Press Ltd**

Mitchell Beazley
See **Octopus Publishing Group**

Mobius
See **Hodder Headline Ltd**

Monarch Books
Lion Hudson plc, Mayfield House, 256 Banbury Road, Oxford OX2 7DH
☎01865 302750   Fax 01865 302757
✉ monarch@lionhudson.com
Editorial Director *Tony Collins*

An imprint of **Lion Hudson plc**. Publishes an independent list of Christian books across a wide range of concerns. IMPRINT **Monarch** Upmarket paperback list with Christian basis and strong social concern agenda including psychology, future studies, politics, mission, theology, leadership and spirituality. About 35 titles a year. Unsolicited mss, synopses and ideas welcome.

Morehouse
See **The Continuum International Publishing Group Limited**

Morgan Kauffman
See **Elsevier Ltd**

Mosby
See **Elsevier Ltd**

Motor Racing Publications
PO Box 1318, Croydon CR9 5YP
☎020 8654 2711   Fax 020 8407 0339
✉ mrp.books@virgin.net
www.motorracingpublications.co.uk
Chairman/Editorial Head *John Blunsden*

Founded soon after the end of World War II to concentrate on motor-racing titles. Fairly dormant in the mid 1960s but was reactivated in 1968 by a new shareholding structure. John Blunsden later acquired a majority share and major expansion followed in the 1970s. Publishes motor-sport history, classic and performance car collection and restoration, race track and off-road driving and related subjects. IMPRINTS **Fitzjames Press**; **Motor Racing Publications**. About 4–6 titles a year. No unsolicited mss. Send synopses and ideas in specified subject areas in the first instance.
ROYALTIES twice-yearly.

mph
4 John Wesley Road, Werrington, Peterborough PE4 6ZP
☎01733 325002   Fax 01733 384180
www.mph.org.uk
Chair *Eric Jarvis*
Chief Executive *Martin Stone*
Commissioning Editor *Dr Natalie K. Watson*
Approx. Annual Turnover £2 million

Founded 1800. Owned by the Methodist Church. Publishes a wide range of books, magazines and resources which are sold in the UK and overseas. Also *Epworth Review* quarterly magazine. IMPRINTS **Epworth Press** (see entry); **Inspire** (see entry); **Methodist Publishing House**. Approx 30 titles a year. Unsolicited mss, synopses and ideas welcome; send sample chapter and contents with covering letter and s.a.e. for return of mss.
ROYALTIES annually.

Multi-Sensory Learning Ltd
Highgate House, Groom's Lane, Creaton NN6 8NN
☎01604 505000   Fax 01604 505001
✉ info@msl-online.net
www.msl-online.net
Senior Editor *Philippa Chudley*

Publishes materials and books related to dyslexia; the multi-sensory learning course for dyslexic pupils and adults needing literacy skills development, plus numerous other items on assessment, reading, maths, music, etc. for dyslexics. Keen to locate authors able to write materials for dyslexic people and for teachers of dyslexics.

Murdoch Books UK Ltd
Erico House, 6th Floor North, 93–99 Upper Richmond Road, London SW15 2TG
☎020 8785 5995   Fax 020 8785 5985
CEO *Juliet Rogers*
Publisher *Kay Scarlett*

Owned by Australian media group Murdoch Books Pty Ltd. Publishes full-colour non-fiction: homes and interiors, gardening, cookery, craft, cake decorating and DIY. About 50 titles a year.

John Murray (Publishers) Ltd
338 Euston Road, London NW1 3BH
☎020 7873 6000   Fax 020 7873 6446
www.madaboutbooks.com
Managing Director *Roland Philipps*
Founded 1768. Acquired by **Hodder Headline** in May 2002. Publishes general trade books. **Non-fiction** *Gordon Wise*; **Fiction** *Anya Serota*. No unsolicited material; send preliminary letter.
ROYALTIES twice-yearly.

Authors' Rating Benefiting from the administrative and marketing backup from its new owners, Murray remains loyal to the editorial policy of turning out quality general non-fiction.

Muse Publishing Limited
26 Mill Road, Salisbury SP2 7RZ
☎01722 414568
✉ info@musepublishing.com
www.musepublishing.com
Managing Director *Guy Nicholls*
Editorial Head *Paul Greatorex*
Founded 1998. Publishes fiction only: novels in English about the Far East and Africa. No unsolicited material; initial enquiry by telephone or e-mail.
ROYALTIES annually.

Myth & Legend
See **CRW Publishing Ltd**

NAG Press Ltd
See **Robert Hale Ltd**

The National Archives
Kew TW9 4DU
☎020 8392 5289   Fax 020 8487 1974
✉ catherine.bradley@nationalarchives.gov.uk
www.nationalarchives.gov.uk
Publishing Manager *Catherine Bradley*
Publishes books, guides and document packs relating to the thousand years of historical records held in The National Archives. Specialist areas: family history, military history and general history. TITLES *English Monarchs Series – Treasures from The National Archives* (including *Elizabeth I*; *Henry V; James II*); *The Genealogist's Internet* Peter Christian; *Lord Haw Haw* Peter Martland; *DNA and Family History* Chris Pomery; *The Women's Century* Mary Turner. Also publishes *Ancestors*, a full-colour family history magazine.

National Trust Publications
36 Queen Anne's Gate, London SW1H 9AS
☎020 7222 9251   Fax 020 7222 5097

www.nationaltrust.org.uk
Chairman *Sir William Proby*
Director-General *Fiona Reynolds*
Publisher *Margaret Willes*
Publishing arm of The National Trust, founded in 1895 by Robert Hunter, Octavia Hill and Hardwicke Rawnsley to protect and conserve places of historic interest and beauty. Publishes gardening, cookery, handbooks, social history, architecture, general interest and children's books. TITLES *Gardens of the National Trust*; *Household Secrets*; *Farmhouse Cookery*; *Passions and Pleasures*. No unsolicited material.
ROYALTIES twice-yearly.

Nautical Data Ltd
The Book Barn, Westbourne, Emsworth PO10 8RS
☎01243 389352   Fax 01243 379136
✉ info@nauticaldata.com
www.nauticaldata.com
Managing Director *Piers Mason*
Founded 1999. Publishes pilots and nautical reference. 23 titles in 2004. No unsolicited mss; synopses and ideas welcome. No fiction or non-nautical themes.
ROYALTIES twice-yearly.

NCVO Publications
Regent's Wharf, 8 All Saints Street, London N1 9RL
☎020 7713 6161   Fax 020 7713 6300
www.ncvo-vol.org.uk/publications
Publications and Promotions Coordinator *Josephine Finn*
Approx. Annual Turnover £140,000
Founded 1928. Publishing imprint of the National Council for Voluntary Organisations, embracing former Bedford Square Press titles and NCVO's many other publications. The list reflects NCVO's role as the representative body for the voluntary sector. Publishes directories, good practice information on management and trustee development, finance and employment titles and information of primary interest to the voluntary sector. TITLES *The Voluntary Agencies Directory*; *The Good Trustee Guide*; *The Good Campaigns Guide*; *The Good Financial Management Guide*; *The Good Employment Guide*; *The Good Management Guide*; *The Good Membership Guide*; *The UK Voluntary Sector Almanac*. No unsolicited mss as all projects are commissioned in-house.

Thomas Nelson & Sons Ltd
See **Nelson Thornes Limited**

Nelson Thornes Limited
Delta Place, 27 Bath Road, Cheltenham
GL53 7TH
☎01242 267100   Fax 01242 221914
✉ cservices@nelsonthornes.com
www.nelsonthornes.com

Managing Director *Fred Grainger*

Founded in 2000 following the merger of Stanley Thornes (Publishers) Ltd and Thomas Nelson & Sons Ltd. Part of the Wolters Kluwer Group of companies. Educational publisher of printed and electronic product, from pre-school to Higher Education. Unsolicited mss, synopses and ideas for books welcome if appropriate to specialised lists.

ROYALTIES annually.

Authors' Rating The second largest education publisher in the UK after Pearson, Nelson Thornes does best in health and science where it is helped by the dominant position in the market of its parent company, Wolters Kluwer.

New Beacon Books Ltd
76 Stroud Green Road, London N4 3EN
☎020 7272 4889   Fax 020 7281 4662
✉ newbeaconbooks@btconnect.com

Chairman *John La Rose*
Managing Director *Sarah White*
Approx. Annual Turnover £120,000

Founded 1966. Publishes fiction, history, politics, poetry and language, all concerning black people. No unsolicited material.

ROYALTIES annually.

New Editions
See **Gibson Square**

New Holland Publishers (UK) Ltd
Garfield House, 86–88 Edgware Road,
London W2 2EA
☎020 7724 7773   Fax 020 7258 1293
(editorial)
✉ postmaster@nhpub.co.uk
www.newhollandpublishers.com

Managing Director *John Beaufoy*
Publishing Managers *Rosemary Wilkinson, Jo Hemmings*
Approx. Annual Turnover £6 million

Founded 1956. Relaunched in 1987 as a publisher of illustrated books for the international market. In 1993, NH acquired Charles Letts Publishing Division list and four years later the then parent company (New Holland Struik Group, South Africa) acquired Southern Book Publishers, while their sister company (New Holland Australia) acquired the natural history and lifestyle divisions of Reed Australia. With its HQ in London, New Holland Publishers (UK) Ltd has now become the International Publishing Division of Johnnic Communications, one of Africa's leading publishing groups. NHP also has offices in Australia and New Zealand. Publishes non-fiction, practical and inspirational books in categories including humour, cookery and food, crafts, DIY, fishing, gardening, interior design, mind, body and spirit, natural history, indoor and outdoor sports, travel, travel guides and general books. TITLES *Men and Sheds*; *How to Mix and Use Colour*; *Top Adventure Treks*; *Container Topiary*; *Worst Album Covers in the World*; *The Dive Atlas*. No unsolicited mss; synopses and ideas welcome.

Newnes
See **Elsevier Ltd**

Nexus
See **Virgin Books Ltd**

nferNELSON
The Chiswick Centre, 414 Chiswick High Road, London W4 5TF
☎020 8996 8444   Fax 020 8996 3660
www.nfer-nelson.co.uk

Founded 1981. A division of Granada Learning Ltd. Publishes educational and psychological tests and training materials. Main interest is in educational, clinical and occupational assessment and training material.

Nia
See **The X Press**

Nielsen BookData
3rd Floor, Midas House, 62 Goldsworth Road, Woking GU21 6LQ
☎0870 777 8710   Fax 0870 777 8711
✉ info@nielsenbookdata.co.uk
www.nielsenbookdata.co.uk

Contact *Sales Department*

Provides a range of bibliographic services for the book trade on CD-ROM, online and via direct feed which enables booksellers and libraries worldwide to select and order new, in print and out-of-print titles. Publishes the *Nielsen BookData Red Book*: directory of publishers.

Nightingale Books
See **Pegasus Elliot Mackenzie Publishers Ltd**

NMS Enterprises Limited – Publishing

National Museums of Scotland, Chambers Street, Edinburgh EH1 1JF
☎0131 247 4026   Fax 0131 247 4012
✉ publishing@nms.ac.uk
www.nms.ac.uk

Director *Lesley A. Taylor*
Approx. Annual Turnover £150,000

Founded 1987 to publish non-fiction related to the National Museums of Scotland collections: academic and general; children's; archaeology, history, decorative arts worldwide, history of science, technology, natural history and geology, poetry. TITLES *Treasures from Tuscany: The Etruscan Legacy*; *Renaissance Decorative Painting in Scotland*; *Minerals of Scotland*; *Audubon in Edinburgh*; *The Thin Red Line: War, Empire and Visions of Scotland*; *Weights and Measures in Scotland: a European Perspective*. No unsolicited mss; only interested in synopses and ideas for books which are genuinely related to NMS collections and to Scotland in general.
ROYALTIES twice-yearly.

No Exit Press
See **Oldcastle Books Ltd**

North-Holland
See **Elsevier Ltd**

Northcote House Publishers Ltd

Horndon House, Horndon, Tavistock PL19 9NQ
☎01822 810066   Fax 01822 810034
✉ northcote.house@virgin.net
www.northcotehouse.co.uk

Managing Director *Brian Hulme*

Founded 1985. Publishes a series of literary critical studies, in association with the British Council, *Writers and their Work*; education management, literary criticism, educational dance and drama. 25 titles in 2005. 'Well-thought-out proposals, including contents and sample chapter(s), with strong marketing arguments welcome.'
ROYALTIES annually.

W.W. Norton & Company Ltd

Castle House, 75–76 Wells Street, London W1T 3QT
☎020 7323 1579   Fax 020 7436 4553
✉ office@wwnorton.co.uk

Managing Director *Alan Cameron*

Subsidiary of the US parent company founded in 1923. Publishes non-fiction and academic books.

Nottingham University Press

Manor Farm, Main Street, Thrumpton NG11 0AX
☎0115 983 1011   Fax 0115 983 1003
✉ editor@nup.com
www.nup.com

Managing Editor *Dr D.J.A. Cole*

Initially concentrated on agricultural and food sciences titles but has now branched into new areas including engineering, lifesciences, medicine and law. TITLES *The Alcohol Textbooks*; *The Mycotoxin Handbook*; *Emerging Equine Science*; *Writing and Presenting Scientific Papers*. **Castle Publications** TITLES *The Cricket Coach's Guide to Man Management*; *The Games Guide*.
ROYALTIES twice-yearly.

NWP
See **Neil Wilson Publishing Ltd**

O Books
See **John Hunt Publishing Ltd**

Oak
See **Omnibus Press**

Oberon Books

521 Caledonian Road, London N7 9RH
☎020 7607 3637   Fax 020 7607 3629
✉ oberonbooks@btinternet.com
www.oberonbooks.com

Publishing Director *James Hogan*
Managing Director *Charles D. Glanville*
Editor *Stephen Watson*

A leading theatre publisher, Oberon publishes play texts (usually in conjunction with a production), and books on theatre and dance. Specialises in contemporary plays and translations of European classics. IMPRINTS **Oberon Modern Plays**; **Oberon Classics**. Publishes for the National Theatre, the Royal Opera House, the Royal Court, English Touring Theatre, LAMDA, the Gate Theatre, the Bush Theatre, West Yorkshire Playhouse, Chichester Festival Theatre, Salisbury Playhouse and many other London and regional theatre companies. Publishes over 300 writers and translators including Rodney Ackland, Tariq Ali, Howard Barker, John Barton, Ranjit Bolt, Howard Brenton, Ken Campbell, Pam Gems, Sir Peter Hall, Christopher Hampton, Bernard Kops, Adrian Mitchell, Sir John Mortimer. An extensive classics list includes performance (edited) versions of Shakespeare including *King Lear*, *A Midsummer Night's Dream*; *Romeo and Juliet* and *Twelfth Night*, as well as new translations of plays by Chekhov, Molière, Strindberg and others. About 80 titles a year.

Authors' Rating Now the publisher for the Royal Opera and the Royal Ballet, Oberon is aiming for the top slot in its chosen niche.

Octagon Press Ltd

PO Box 227, London N6 4EW
☎020 8348 9392   Fax 020 8341 5971
✉ info@octagonpress.com
Managing Director *George R. Schrager*
Approx. Annual Turnover £100,000

Founded 1960. Publishes travel, biography, literature, folklore, psychology, philosophy with the focus on East-West studies. Also distributes research monographs published by The Institute for Cultural Research. 4–5 titles a year. Unsolicited mss not accepted. Enquiries in writing only. Welcomes book proposals of no more than a single page; e-mail to editor@octagonpress.com
ROYALTIES annually.

Octopus Publishing Group

2–4 Heron Quays, London E14 4JP
☎020 7531 8400   Fax 020 7531 8650
www.octopus-publishing.co.uk
Chief Executive *Derek Freeman*
Approx. Annual Turnover £45 million (Group)

Formed following a management buyout of Reed Consumer Books from Reed Elsevier plc in 1998. Bought by French publishers Hachette-Livre in 2001 and acquired Cassell Illustrated and the lists of Ward Lock and Blandford Press; also, Gaia Books acquired in 2004.

Conran Octopus Fax 020 7531 8627
✉ info-co@conran-octopus.co.uk
www. conran-octopus.co.uk
Managing Director *Jane Aspden* Quality illustrated lifestyle books, particularly interiors, design, cookery, gardening and crafts TITLES *The Essential House Book* Terence Conran; *Fork to Fork* Monty Don; *Passion for Seafood* Gordon Ramsay; *New Retail* Rasshied Din.

Hamlyn Octopus Fax 020 7531 8562
✉ info-ho@hamlyn.co.uk
www.hamlyn.co.uk
Managing Director *Alison Goff* Popular non-fiction, particularly cookery, gardening, craft, sport, health, film and music TITLES *Larousse Gastronomique*; *Hamlyn All Colour Cookbook*; *Hamlyn Book of Gardening*; *Hamlyn Book of DIY & Decorating*.

Mitchell Beazley/Miller's Fax 020 7537 0773
✉ info-mb@mitchell-beazley.co.uk
www. mitchell-beazley.co.uk
Publisher/ Managing Director *Jane Aspden* Quality illustrated reference books, particularly food and wine, gardening, interior design and architecture, antiques, general reference TITLES *Hugh Johnson's Pocket Wine Book*; *The New Joy of Sex*; *Miller's Antiques and Collectibles Price Guides*.

Philip's Fax 020 7531 8460
✉ george.philip@philips-maps.co.uk
www.philips- maps.co.uk
Managing Director *John Gaisford* World atlases, globes, astronomy, road atlases, encyclopaedias, thematic reference TITLES *Philip's Atlas of the World*; *Philip's Modern School Atlas*; *Philip's Guide to the Stars and Planets*; *Ordnance Survey Street Atlas*; *Philip's Millennium Encyclopaedia*; *Philip's Atlas of World History*.

Bounty Fax 020 7531 8607
✉ bountybooksinfo-bp@bountybooks.co.uk
Managing Director *Alison Goff* Bargain and promotional books. New, repackaged and re-issued titles.

Cassell Illustrated Fax 020 731 8624
Publishing Director *Gabrielle Mander* Serious non-fiction covering a wide range of topics from history and cookery to fitness and art.

Digital Octopus Fax 020 7531 8650
Contact *Derek Freeman* Digitally-formatted titles.

Octopus TV
Fax 020 7531 8650
Contact *Derek Freeman* Television programmes from Octopus publications.

Godsfield Press Fax 020 7531 8562
✉enquiries@godsfieldpress.com
Publisher/Managing Director *Alison Goff* Mind, body and spirit encompassing original psychology, health and gift books.

Gaia Books
Publisher/Managing Director *Alison Goff* Mind, body and spirit and natural/ eco titles.
    ROYALTIES twice-yearly/annually, according to contract in all divisions.

Oldcastle Books Ltd

PO Box 394, Harpenden AL5 1XJ
☎01582 761264   Fax 01582 761264
www.noexit.co.uk
www.pocketessentials.com
www.highstakespublishing.com
Managing Director *Ion Mills*

Founded 1985. Publishes crime/noir fiction, gambling non-fiction and 160pp mini-reference titles on film, ideas, history, music, etc. IMPRINTS **No Exit Press** TITLES *Villa Incognito* Tom Robbins; *In the Hand of Dante* Nick Tosches;

High Stakes TITLES *Fast Company* Jon Bradshaw; *Betting to Win* Prof. Leighton V. Williams; **Pocketessentials** TITLES *Alfred Hitchcock; Knights Templar, Conspiracy Theories. No unsolicited mss*. Send synopses and ideas. ROYALTIES annually.

Michael O'Mara Books Ltd

9 Lion Yard, Tremadoc Road, London SW4 7NQ
☎020 7720 8643   Fax 020 7627 8953
✉ firstname.lastname@michaelomarabooks. com *or* www.mombooks.com *or* www.busterpreviews.com

Chairman *Michael O'Mara*
Managing Director *Lesley O'Mara*
Editorial Director (Commissioning) *Lindsay Davies*
Approx. Annual Turnover £5 million

Founded 1985. Independent publisher. Publishes general non-fiction, humour, anthologies, history, royalty and celebrity biographies. TITLES *Diana: Her True Story* Andrew Morton; *The Timewaster Letters* Robin Cooper; *Eats, Shites & Leaves* Antal Parody. IMPRINT **Buster Books** Children's titles: board books, picture books, novelty books, humour and quirky non-fiction. Unsolicited mss, synopses and ideas for books welcome. ROYALTIES twice-yearly.

Authors' Rating Most of the creative work for bestselling humour titles is done in-house but strong ideas for the gift market may well attract interest.

Omnibus Press

Music Sales Ltd, 8–9 Frith Street, London W1D 3JB
☎020 7434 0066   Fax 020 7734 2246
✉ chris.charlesworth@musicsales.co.uk
www.omnibuspress.com

Editorial Head *Chris Charlesworth*

Founded 1971. Independent publisher of music books, rock and pop biographies, song sheets, educational tutors, cassettes, videos and software. A Division of the Music Sales Group of Companies. IMPRINTS **Amsco**; **Bobcat**; **Oak**; **Omnibus**; **Vision On**; **Wise Publications**. Unsolicited mss, synopses and ideas for music-related titles welcome. ROYALTIES twice-yearly.

Oneworld Publications

185 Banbury Road, Oxford OX2 7AR
☎01865 310597   Fax 01865 310598
✉ info@oneworld-publications.com
www.oneworld-publications.com

Editorial Director *Juliet Mabey*

Founded 1986. Publishes adult non-fiction across a range of subjects from world religions to psychology and philosophy, history and popular science. SERIES include short histories of countries and one on world religions (with authors such as Geoffrey Parrinder, Keith Ward, Klaus Klostermaier and John Hick); also concise encyclopedias on world religions. **Oneworld Philosophers** series was launched in 2001 and **Oneworld Beginners' Guides** in 2002. TITLES *God: A Guide for the Perplexed* Keith Ward; *Palestine-Israeli Conflict: A Beginner's Guide*. About 45 titles a year. No unsolicited mss; synopses and ideas welcome, but should be accompanied by s.a.e. for return of material and/or notification of receipt. No autobiographies, fiction, poetry or children's. ROYALTIES annually.

Onlywomen Press Ltd

40 St Lawrence Terrace, London W10 5ST
☎020 8354 0796   Fax 020 8960 2817
✉ onlywomenpress@aol.com
www.onlywomenpress.com

Editorial Director *Lilian Mohin*

Founded 1974. Publishes feminist lesbian literature: fiction, poetry, literary criticism and political theory. Unsolicited mss and proposals welcome. Submissions must be accompanied by s.a.e. and explanatory letter.

OPC

See **Ian Allan Publishing Ltd**

Open Gate Press (incorporating Centaur Press 1954)

51 Achilles Road, London NW6 1DZ
☎020 7431 4391   Fax 020 7431 5129
✉ books@opengatepress.co.uk

Managing Directors *Jeannie Cohen, Elisabeth Petersdorff*

Founded in 1989 to provide a forum for psychoanalytic social and cultural studies. Publishes psychoanalysis, philosophy, social sciences, politics, literature, religion, animal rights, environment. SERIES *Psychoanalysis and Society*. Also publishes a journal of psychoanalytic social studies, *New Analysis*. IMPRINTS **Open Gate Press**; **Centaur Press**; **Linden Press**. Since the acquisition of Centaur Press, Open Gate Press is continuing its work, in particular the *Kinship Library* – a series on the philosophy, politics and application of humane education. No unsolicited mss. ROYALTIES twice-yearly.

Open University Press
McGraw-Hill House, Shoppenhangers Road,
Maidenhead SL6 2QL
☎01628 502500   Fax 01628 770224
✉ enquiries@openup.co.uk
www.openup.co.uk
Managing Director *Simon Allen*

Founded 1977 as an imprint independent of the Open University's course materials. Acquired by **McGraw Hill Education** in 2002. Publishes academic and professional books in the fields of education, sociology, health, psychology, women's studies, counselling, Higher Education. No economics or anthropology. Not interested in anything outside the social sciences. About 100 titles a year. No unsolicited mss; enquiries/proposals only.
ROYALTIES annually.

Orbit
See **Time Warner Books UK**

Orchard Books
See **Hachette Children's Books**

The Orion Publishing Group Limited
Orion House, 5 Upper St Martin's Lane,
London WC2H 9EA
☎020 7240 3444   Fax 020 7240 4822
www.orionbooks.co.uk/pub/index.htm
Chairman *Arnaud Nourry*
Chief Executive *Peter Roche*
Deputy Chief Executive *Malcolm Edwards*
Approx. Annual Turnover £70 million

Founded 1992. Incorporates Weidenfeld & Nicolson, JM Dent, Gollancz and Cassell.
DIVISIONS
Orion Managing Director *Lisa Milton* IMPRINTS **Orion Fiction** Publishing Director *Jon Wood* Hardcover fiction; **Orion Media** Publishing Director *Ian Marshall* Hardcover non-fiction; **Orion Children's** Publisher *Fiona Kennedy* Children's fiction/non-fiction; **Gollancz** Editorial Directors *Simon Spanton, Jo Fletcher* Science fiction and fantasy.
    Weidenfeld & Nicolson Managing Director *Malcolm Edwards* IMPRINTS **Weidenfeld Illustrated** Editor-in-Chief *Michael Dover* Illustrated non-fiction; **Weidenfeld General** Publishing Director *Ian Drury* General non-fiction, history and military; **Weidenfeld Fiction** Publisher *Alan Samson* History; **Cassell Reference** Publishing Director *Richard Milbank*

General reference; **Custom Publishing** Managing Director *Alasdair MacLeod*.
    Paperback Division Managing Director *Susan Lamb* IMPRINTS **Orion**; **Phoenix**; **Everyman**.

Authors' Rating As the book trade's choice as Publisher of the Year, Orion backs strong titles with even stronger marketing.

Osprey Publishing Ltd
Midland House, West Way, Botley, Oxford
OX2 0PH
☎01865 727022
Fax 01865 727017/727019
✉ info@ospreypublishing.com
www.ospreypublishing.com
Managing Director *William Shepherd*
Business Development Manager *Simone Drinkwater*
Editorial Development Manager *Anita Baker*

Publishes military history and aviation from around the world. Founded 1969, Osprey became independent from **Reed Elsevier** in February 1998 and launched Osprey Publishing Inc. as a wholly owned subsidiary in North America in 2004. Major illustrated SERIES include *Men-at-Arms*; *Fortress*; *Campaign*; *Essential Histories*; *Warrior*; *Elite*; *New Vanguard*; *Osprey Modelling*; *Aircraft of the Aces*; *Aviation Elite Units*; *Combat Aircraft*. Non-series books are also considered. About 130 titles a year. No unsolicited mss; ideas and synopses welcome.
ROYALTIES twice-yearly.

Peter Owen Ltd
73 Kenway Road, London SW5 0RE
☎020 7373 5628/7370 6093
Fax 020 7373 6760
✉ admin@peterowen.com
www.peterowen.com
Chairman *Peter Owen*
Editorial Director *Antonia Owen*

Founded 1951. Publishes biography, general non-fiction, English-language literary fiction and translations, history, literary criticism, the arts. 'No genre or children's fiction; the company almost never takes on first novels.' AUTHORS Jane Bowles, Paul Bowles, Yuri Druznikov, Shusaku Endo, Anna Kavan, Jean Giono, Anaïs Nin, Jeremy Reed, Peter Vansittart. 30–40 titles a year. Unsolicited synopses welcome for non-fiction material; no highly illustrated books. Please call in advance to admit fiction. Mss should be preceded by a descriptive letter and synopsis with s.a.e. OVERSEAS ASSOCIATES worldwide. ROYALTIES twice-yearly.

Authors' Rating Peter Owen has been described as 'a publisher of the old and idiosyncratic school'. He has seven Nobel prizewinners on his list to prove it.

Oxbow Books

Park End Place, Oxford OX1 1HN
☎01865 241249 Fax 01865 794449
✉ clare@oxbowbooks.com
www.oxbowbooks.com

Editorial Director *Clare Litt*

Founded 1983. Publishes academic archaeology, Egyptology, ancient and medieval history. IMPRINT **Aris & Phillips** Greek, Latin and Hispanic texts and translations. About 60 titles a year.

Oxford University Press

Great Clarendon Street, Oxford OX2 6DP
☎01865 556767 Fax 01865 556646
✉ enquiry@oup.com
www.oup.com

Chief Executive *Henry Reece*
Approx. Annual Turnover £389 million

A department of Oxford University, OUP started as the university's printing business and developed into a major publishing operation in the 19th century. Publishes academic works in all formats (print and online): dictionaries, lexical and non-lexical reference, scholarly journals, student texts, schoolbooks, ELT materials, music, bibles, paperbacks, and children's books. Around 6000 titles a year.

DIVISIONS
Academic *T.M. Barton* Academic and higher education titles in major disciplines, dictionaries (acquired *The Grove Dictionary of Music* in 2003), non-lexical reference, journals and trade books. OUP welcomes first-class academic material in the form of proposals or accepted theses.

Education *K. Harris* National Curriculum courses and support materials as well as children's literature.

ELT *P.R.C. Marshall* ELT courses and dictionaries for all levels.

OVERSEAS BRANCHES/SUBSIDIARIES Sister company in USA with branches or subsidiaries in Argentina, Australia, Brazil, Canada, China, East Africa, India, Japan, Malaysia, Mexico, Pakistan, Southern Africa, Spain and Turkey. Offices in France, Greece, Italy, Poland, Taiwan, Thailand. ROYALTIES twice-yearly.

Authors' Rating Increased investment in new publishing includes the *New Dictionary of National Biography*, one of the biggest projects of its kind in contemporary publishing and, latterly, the *Grove Dictionary of Music* and the *Grove Dictionary of Art*, bought from Macmillan. Following the acquisition of Blackstone Press, OUP now rivals Butterworths and Sweet & Maxwell as a leading law book publisher.

Palgrave Macmillan
See **Macmillan Publishers Ltd**

Palm Tree Press
See **Kevin Mayhew Publishers**

G.J. Palmer & Sons Ltd
See **Hymns Ancient & Modern Ltd**

Pan
See **Macmillan Publishers Ltd**

Paper Tiger
See **Chrysalis Books Group**

Parthian

The Old Surgery, Napier Street, Aberteifi (Cardigan) SA43 1ED
☎01239 612059 Fax 01239 612059
✉ parthianbooks@yahoo.co.uk
www.parthianbooks.co.uk

Publisher *Richard Davies*
Fiction Editor *Gwen Davies*
Poetry Editor *Richard Gwyn*

Founded 1993. Publishes contemporary Welsh writing in English including novels, poetry and drama, also translations from Welsh. Its list includes many young writers. TITLES *In and Out of the Goldfish Bowl* Rachel Trezise (Winner of the Orange Futures Award); *Fire and Water* Hayley Long; *Window Dressing for Hermes* Rhian Sadaat; *Playing Mercy* Matthew Scott; *Welsh Boys Too* John Sam Jones (Winner of the American Library Association Gay and Lesbian Honor Book Award); *The Pterodactyl's Wing* (poetry anthology) ed. Richard Gwyn. A new non-fiction list is planned for 2006. 12 – 15 titles a year. Synopsis with first three sample chapters welcome. 'An idea of what we do is always an advantage.' ROYALTIES annually.

Paternoster Press
See **Authentic Media**

Pavilion
See **Chrysalis Books Group**

Pearson Education

Edinburgh Gate, Harlow CM20 2JE
☎01279 623623   Fax 01279 431059
www.pearsoned.com

The world's largest educational publisher was created by the merger of Addison Wesley Longman, Financial Times Management and **Simon & Schuster**'s educational list. Publishes across a wide range of curriculum subjects from primary students to professional practictioners. IMPRINTS **Longman; Causeway Press; Prentice Hall; Addison Wesley.** OVERSEAS ASSOCIATES worldwide. Unsolicited mss should be addressed to the appropriate department: **ELT** *Lyn Kitteridge;* **Schools** *Carol Hayward;* **University and Professional Level** *Lisa Reading.*
ROYALTIES twice-yearly.

Pegasus Elliot Mackenzie Publishers Ltd

Sheraton House, Castle Park, Cambridge CB3 0AX
☎01223 370012   Fax 01223 370040
✉ editors@pegasuspublishers.com
www.pegasuspublishers.com

Senior Editor *D.W. Stern*
Editor *R. Sabir*

Publishes fiction and non-fiction, general interest, biography, autobiography, children's, history, humour, science fiction, poetry, travel, war, memoirs, crime and erotica, also Internet and e-books. IMPRINTS **Vanguard Press; Nightingale Books; Chimera** TITLES *The Lads from the Ferry* Alex Mabon; *Bullying – What Have I Ever Done to You?* Robert Higgs; *Understanding English Spelling* Masha Bell. Unsolicited mss, synopses and ideas considered if accompanied by return postage.
ROYALTIES annually.

Authors' Rating Liable to ask authors to contribute to production costs.

Pen & Sword Books Ltd

47 Church Street, Barnsley S70 2AS
☎01226 734734   Fax 01226 734438
✉ editorial@pen-and-sword.co.uk
www.pen-and-sword.co.uk

Commissioning Editor, Aviation *Peter Coles*
Commissioning Editor, Military & Maritime
  Henry Wilson
Commissioning Editor, History & Local
  History *Rupert Harding*

One of the leading military history publishers in the UK. Publishes non-fiction only, special-ising in naval and aviation history, WW1, WW2, Napoleonic, autobiography and biography. Also publishes *Battleground* series for battlefield tourists. IMPRINTS **Leo Cooper; Pen & Sword Aviation; Pen & Sword Maritime; Pen & Sword Military; Wharncliffe Books** (see entry). About 200 titles a year. Unsolicited synopses and ideas welcome; no unsolicited mss.
ROYALTIES twice-yearly.

Penguin Group (UK)

A Pearson Company, 80 Strand, London WC2R 0RL
☎020 7010 3000   Fax 020 7010 6060
www.penguin.co.uk

Group Chairman & Chief Executive *John Makinson*
Managing Director: Penguin *Helen Fraser*
Approx. Annual Turnover £121 million

Owned by Pearson plc. The world's best known book brand and for more than 60 years a leading publisher whose adult and children's lists include fiction, non-fiction, poetry, drama, classics, reference and special interest areas. Reprints and new work.

DIVISIONS
Penguin General Books Managing Director *Tom Weldon* Adult fiction and non-fiction is published in hardback under Michael Joseph, Viking and Hamish Hamilton imprints. Paperbacks come under the Penguin imprint. IMPRINTS **Viking/Penguin** Publisher *Venetia Butterfield* Publishing Director *Tony Lacey;* **Hamish Hamilton** Publishing Director *Simon Prosser;* **Michael Joseph/Penguin** Publishing Director *Louise Moore* Does not accept unsolicited mss.
  Penguin Press Managing Director *Stefan McGrath* Publishing Directors *Stuart Proffitt, Simon Winder* Academic adult non-fiction, reference, specialist and classics. IMPRINTS **Allen Lane; Penguin Reference** Publishing Director *Nigel Wilcockson* No unsolicited mss.
  Dorling Kindersley Ltd (see entry).
  Frederick Warne Managing Director *Sally Floyer* Classic children's publishing and merchandising including *Beatrix Potter*™; *Flower Fairies; Orlando.* **Ventura** Publisher *Sally Floyer* Producer and packager of *Spot* titles by Eric Hill.
  Ladybird (see **Dorling Kindersley Ltd**).
  BBC Children's Books *Sally Floyer* Children's imprint launched in 2004.
  Puffin Managing Director *Francesca Dow* (poetry and picture books) Publisher *Rebecca*

McNally (fiction), Senior Editor *Fran Hammond* (media and popular non-fiction) Leading children's paperback list, publishing in virtually all fields including fiction, non-fiction, poetry, picture books, media-related titles. No unsolicited mss; synopsis and ideas welcome.

Penguin Audiobooks (see entry under *Audio Books*).

ePenguin Commissioning Editor *Jeremy Ettinghausen* e-books list launched in 2001. OVERSEAS ASSOCIATES worldwide.

ROYALTIES twice-yearly.

Authors' Rating Penguin has certainly had a testing year. It started with a crisis in book distribution after a state-of-the-art system turned out to be less than perfect. Such was the impact on the shops that the Society of Authors mounted a campaign (later abandoned) for compensation to disappointed authors. Then there were reports of a downturn in American sales (Penguin is the second biggest book publisher in the US) made worse by the weak dollar, the closure of the television division set up only the previous year to develop book potential across the media and the abrupt departure of UK chief executive, Anthony Forbes Watson. There was even talk of Pearson calling it a day by selling off Penguin. Now, however, a streamlined management led by John Makinson, CEO of Penguin worldwide, is intent on reversing the downward trend. Penguin is still the best known British publishing house with a leading position in non-fiction and children's books.

Peony Press
See **Anness Publishing Ltd**

Pergamon
See **Elsevier Ltd**

Persephone Books
59 Lamb's Conduit Street, London
WC1N 3NB
☎020 7242 9292   Fax 020 7242 9272
✉ sales@persephonebooks.co.uk
www.persephonebooks.co.uk

Managing Director *Nicola Beauman*

Founded 1999. Publishes reprint fiction and non-fiction, mostly 'by women, for women and about women'. TITLES *Miss Pettigrew Lives for a Day* Winifred Watson; *Kitchen Essays* Agnes Jekyll; *The Far Cry* Emma Smith; *The Priory* Dorothy Whipple. 8 titles a year. No unsolicited material.

ROYALTIES twice-yearly.

Phaidon Press Limited
Regent's Wharf, All Saints Street, London
N1 9PA
☎020 7843 1000   Fax 020 7843 1010
✉ name@phaidon.com
www.phaidon.com

Group Chairman & Publisher *Richard Schlagman*
Chairman *Andrew Price*
Managing Director *Christopher North*
Deputy Publisher *Amanda Renshaw*
Approx. Annual Turnover £17.5 million

Publishes quality books on the visual arts, including fine art, art history, architecture, design, photography, decorative arts, music and performing arts, cookery and children's books. Also produces videos. DIVISIONS/SERIES (with Editorial Heads) **Architecture and Design** *Emilia Terragni*; **Contemporary Art** *Gilda Williams*; **Photography** *Amanda Renshaw*; **Art and Academic** *David Anfan*. About 100 titles a year. Unsolicited mss welcome but 'only a small amount of unsolicited material gets published'.

ROYALTIES twice-yearly.

Authors' Rating A move into the children's market will focus on art and design. With French and German subsidiaries, Phaidon's European scope gives it added appeal here and in the US for titles that might not otherwise enter the English language market.

Philip's
See **Octopus Publishing Group**

Phillimore & Co. Ltd
Shopwyke Manor Barn, Chichester
PO20 2BG
☎01243 787636   Fax 01243 787639
✉ bookshop@phillimore.co.uk
www.phillimore.co.uk

Chairman *Philip Harris*
Managing Director *Noel Osborne*
Approx. Annual Turnover £1.3 million

Founded in 1897 by W.P.W. Phillimore, Victorian campaigner for local archive conservation in Chancery Lane, London. Became the country's leading publisher of historical source material and local histories. Somewhat dormant in the 1960s, it was revived by Philip Harris in 1968. Publishes British local and family history, including histories of institutions, buildings, villages, towns and counties, plus guides to research and writing in these fields. IMPRINT **Phillimore** *Noel Osborne* TITLES *Domesday Book*; *A History of Essex*; *Carlisle*; *The Haberdashers' Company*; *Channel Island Churches*;

Bolton Past; Warwickshire Country Houses. About 70 titles a year. No unsolicited mss; synopses/ ideas welcome for local or family histories.

ROYALTIES annually.

Phoenix
See **The Orion Publishing Group Limited**

Photographers' Institute Press (PIP)
See **Guild of Master Craftsman Publications Ltd**

Piatkus Books
5 Windmill Street, London W1T 2JA
☎020 7631 0710   Fax 020 7436 7137
✉ info@piatkus.co.uk
www.piatkus.co.uk

Managing Director *Judy Piatkus*
Approx. Annual Turnover £7 million

Founded 1979 by Judy Piatkus. The company is customer-led and is committed to publishing a wide range of non-fiction and fiction, both commercial and literary. Specialises in publishing books and authors 'who we feel enthusiastic and committed to as we like to build for long-term success as well as short-term.' Publishes fiction, biography and autobiography, history, popular culture, reference 'and other books that tempt us' under the Portrait imprint, while the Piatkus imprint publishes lifestyle, health, self-help, mind, body and spirit, popular psychology, business, literary and commercial fiction.

DIVISIONS
Non-fiction Publisher *Judy Piatkus*, Editorial Director *Gill Bailey* IMPRINTS **Portrait** TITLES *Strange Laws of Old England* Nigel Cawthorne; *Girl Next Door* Anne Diamond; *The Children's War* Juliet Gardiner. **Piatkus** TITLES *The New Optimum Nutrition Bible* Patrick Holford; *Women Who Think Too Much* Susan Nolan-Hoeksema. **Fiction** Publisher *Judy Piatkus*, Senior Commissioning Editor *Gillian Green* TITLES *Northern Lights* Nora Roberts; *Hubble Bubble* Christina Jones; *The Third Child* Marge Piercy. About 150 titles a year (70 of which are fiction). Piatkus is expanding its range of books and welcomes synopses togethe with first three chapters.

ROYALTIES twice-yearly.

Authors' Rating A thriving independent publisher takes a leap forward from its core mind, body and spirit and lifestyle range with Portrait, a new non-fiction list for 'popular culture, his-

tory, memoirs and sport'. Also strong on women's fiction.

Pica Press
See **A.&C. Black Publishers Ltd**

Picador/Young Picador
See **Macmillan Publishers Ltd**

Piccadilly Press
5 Castle Road, London NW1 8PR
☎020 7267 4492   Fax 020 7267 4493
✉ books@piccadillypress.co.uk
www.piccadillypress.co.uk

Publisher/Managing Director *Brenda Gardner*
Approx. Annual Turnover £1.4 million

Founded 1983. Independent publisher of children's and parental books. 28 titles in 2004. Welcomes approaches from authors 'but we would like them to know the sort of books we do. It is frustrating to get inappropriate material. They should check in their local libraries, bookshops or look at our website. We will send a catalogue (please enclose s.a.e.).' No adult or cartoon-type material.

ROYALTIES twice-yearly.

Pictorial Presentations
See **Souvenir Press Ltd**

Pimlico
See **The Random House Group Ltd**

Pinwheel Limited
Winchester House, 259–269 Old Marylebone Road, London NW1 5XJ
☎020 7616 7200   Fax 020 7616 7201

Managing Director *Andrew Flatt*

Children's non-fiction, picture books and novelty titles. IMPRINTS **Andromeda Children's Books** Publishing/Creative Director *Linda Cole* Illustrated non-fiction for children from 3–12 years; **Gullane Children's Books** Creative Director *Paula Burgess* Picture books for children from 0–8 years; **Pinwheel Children's Books** Publishing/ Creative Director *Linda Cole* Cloth and novelty books for children from 0–5 years. Unsolicited mss will not be returned.

Pitkin
See **Jarrold Publishing**

Pluto Press Ltd
345 Archway Road, London N6 5AA
☎020 8348 2724   Fax 020 8348 9133
✉ pluto@plutobooks.com

www.plutobooks.com

Chair *Roger Van Zwanenberg*
Managing Director/Publisher *Anne Beech*

Founded 1970. Has developed a reputation for innovatory publishing in the field of non-fiction. Publishes academic and scholarly books across a range of subjects including cultural studies, politics and world affairs and more general titles on key aspects of currrent affairs. About 70 titles a year. Prospective authors are encouraged to consult the website for guidelines on submitting proposals.

Pocket Books
See **Simon & Schuster UK Limited**

Pocketessentials
See **Oldcastle Books Ltd**

Poetry Library
See **CRW Publishing Ltd**

Point
See **Scholastic Ltd**

The Policy Press
Fourth Floor, Beacon House, Queen's Road, Bristol BS8 1QU
☎0117 331 4054   Fax 0117 331 4093
✉ tpp-info@bristol.ac.uk
www.policypress.org.uk

Managing Director *Alison Shaw*

Publishes social welfare and policy work for students, academics, practitioners, professionals and policy-makers.

Politico's Publishing
215 Vauxhall Bridge Road, London SW1V 1EJ
☎020 7798 1600   Fax 020 7828 2098
✉ publishing@politicos.co.uk
www.politicos.co.uk/publishing

Chairman/Managing Director *Peter Tummons*
Publishing Director *Sean Magee*
Approx. Annual Turnover £325,000

Founded 1998. Acquired by **Methuen Publishing Ltd** in April 2003. Publishes political books. TITLES *In My Own Time* Jeremy Thorpe; *Cherie Blair* Linda McDougall; *Brief Encounters* Gyles Brandreth. 30 titles in 2004. Unsolicited mss, synopses and ideas welcome; telephone in the first instance.
ROYALTIES annually.

Polity Press
65 Bridge Street, Cambridge CB2 1UR
☎01223 324315   Fax 01223 461385
www.polity.co.uk

Founded 1984. Publishes archaeology and anthropology, criminology, economics, feminism, general interest, history, human geography, literature, media and cultural studies, medicine and society, philosophy, politics, psychology, religion and theology, social and political theory, sociology. Unsolicited synopses and ideas for books welcome.
ROYALTIES annually.

Polygon
West Newington House, 10 Newington Road, Edinburgh EH9 1QS
☎0131 668 4371   Fax 0131 668 4466
✉ info@birlinn.co.uk
www.birlinn.co.uk

Managing Director *Hugh Andrew*

Bought by **Birlinn Ltd** in 2002. Publishes literary fiction and poetry. About 20 titles a year. Unsolicited mss, synopses and ideas welcome.

Pont Books
See **Gomer**

Pop Universal
See **Souvenir Press Ltd**

Portland Press Ltd
3rd Floor, Eagle House, 16 Procter Street, London WC1V 6NX
☎020 7280 4110   Fax 020 7280 4169
✉ editorial@portlandpress.com
www.portlandpress.com

Chairman *Professor A.J. Turner*
Managing Director *Rhonda Oliver*
Managing Editor *Pauline Starley*
Approx. Annual Turnover £2.5 million

Founded 1990 to expand the publishing activities of the Biochemical Society (1911). Publishes biochemisty and medicine for graduate, postgraduate and research students. Expanding the list to include schools and general readership. TITLES *The Nuclear Receptor Superfamily*; *Free Radicals: Enzymology, Signalling and Disease*. 3 titles in 2004. Unsolicited mss, synopses and ideas welcome. No fiction.
ROYALTIES twice-yearly.

Portobello Books
Eardley House, 4 Uxbridge Street, Notting Hill Gate, London W8 7SY
☎020 7908 9892   Fax 020 7908 9899

✉ mail@portobellobooks.com
www.portobellobooks.com

Managing Director/Publisher *Philip Gwyn Jones*
Co-Publishers *Sigrid Rausing, Eric Abraham*

Founded in 2005 by Philip Gwyn Jones, formerly publishing director of HarperCollins' literary imprint Flamingo. Publishes international literature and activist non-fiction. No unsolicited mss; synopses and ideas for books welcome. Approach by post in the first instance. No science fiction, romance or genre fiction of any kind, gardening, cookery, mind, body & spirit or reference.

Portrait
See **Piatkus Books**

T&AD Poyser
See **A.&C. Black Publishers Ltd**

Prentice Hall
See **Pearson Education**

Prestel Publishing Limited
4 Bloomsbury Place, London WC1A 2QA
☎020 7323 5004   Fax 020 7636 8004
✉ sales@prestel-uk.co.uk
www.prestel.com

Chairman *Jürgen Tesch*

Founded 1924. Publishes art, architecture, photography, children's and general illustrated books. No fiction. Unsolicited mss, synopses and ideas welcome. Approach by post or e-mail.

Princeton University Press
See **University Presses of California, Columbia & Princeton Ltd**

Prion Books
See **Carlton Publishing Group**

Profile Books
3A Exmouth House, Pine Street, Exmouth Market, London EC1R 0JH
☎020 7841 6300   Fax 020 7833 3969
✉ info@profilebooks.com
www.profilebooks.com

Managing Director *Andrew Franklin*
Approx. Annual Turnover £5.06 million

Founded 1996. Publishes interesting non-fiction including current affairs, history, politics, psychology, cultural criticism, business management and economics. Named Small Publisher of the Year in 2004 and published the No.1 Christmas

2003 bestseller, *Eats, Shoots and Leaves* by Lynne Truss. AUTHORS include Alan Bennett, J.M. Coetzee, Francis Fukuyama and Peter Nichols. IMPRINTS **Profile Books** *Andrew Franklin*; **Economist Books** *Stephen Brough*. No unsolicited mss.
ROYALTIES twice-yearly.

Authors' Rating A wonderfully imaginative non-fiction list including business books that cut the crap. Riding high on sales of *Eats, Shoots and Leaves*, Profile is on the lookout for other strong sellers.

ProQuest Information and Learning Ltd
The Quorum, Barnwell Road, Cambridge CB5 8SW
☎01223 215512   Fax 01223 215514
www.proquest.co.uk

Vice President, Technology/General Manager
    John Taylor

Collects, organises and publishes information for reseachers, faculty, and students in libraries and schools. Users access information through the ProQuest online information system, Chadwyck-Healey™ electronic and microform resources, UMI microform and print reference products, eLibrary and SIRS educational resources and XanEdu resources.

Psychology Press (An imprint of Taylor & Francis Group, the academic division of T&F Informa plc)
27 Church Road, Hove BN3 2FA
☎01273 207411   Fax 01273 205612
www.psypress.co.uk

Managing Director *Mike Forster*
Deputy Managing Director *Rohays Perry*

Publishes psychology textbooks, monographs, professional books, tests and numerous journals which are available in both printed and online formats. TITLE *Cognitive Neuropsychology*. Send detailed proposal plus c.v. and sample chapters. Proposal requirements and submission procedures available on the website. No poetry, fiction, travel or astrology.
ROYALTIES according to contract.

Publishing House
Trinity Place, Barnstaple EX32 9HJ
☎01271 328892   Fax 01271 328768
✉ publishinghouse@vernoncoleman.com
www.vernoncoleman.com

Managing Director *Vernon Coleman*
Publishing Director *Sue Ward*
Approx. Annual Turnover £750,000

Founded 1989. Self-publisher of fiction, health, humour, animals, politics. Over 90 books published. TITLES *Mrs Caldicot's Cabbage War*; *England our England*; *Bodypower*; *Bilbury Chronicles*; *Second Innings*; *It's Never Too Late*; *How to Publish Your Own Book*; *Alice's Diary*; *Rogue Nation*; *Food for Thought*, all by Vernon Coleman. No submissions.

Puffin
See **Penguin Group (UK)**

Pushkin Press Ltd
12 Chester Terrace, London NW1 4ND
☎01474 533424   Fax 01474 533424
✉ sasha@pushkinpress.com
www.pushkinpress.com
Chairman *Melissa Ulfane*
Editorial Head *Sasha Lillie*
Approx. Annual Turnover £250,000

Publishes novels and essays in translation drawn from the best of classic and contemporary European literature.
ROYALTIES annually.

Authors' Rating English language writers who are short on ideas might do worse than raid this select list of translated European works for something fresh to say. A bold and imaginative venture.

Putnam Aeronautical Books
See **Chrysalis Books Group**

QED Publishing
226 City Road, London EC1V 2TT
☎020 7812 8600   Fax 020 7253 4370
www.qed-publishing.co.uk
Chairman, Quarto Group *Laurence Orbach*
Publisher *Steve Evans*
Editorial Head *Jean Coppendale*
Approx. Annual Turnover £2 million

A new company established by the Quarto Group in 2003. Publishes children's: education, reference, literacy, numeracy, fiction, geography, history, picture books, non-fiction. TITLES *QED Start Series*; *QED Learn Computing*; *QED Animal Art*. 63 titles in 2004. No unsolicited material; initial approach by e-mail. No adult books. OVERSEAS SUBSIDIARY QED Publishing Inc., USA.
FEES paid.

Quadrille Publishing Ltd
Alhambra House, 27–31 Charing Cross Road, London WC2H 0LS
☎020 7839 7117   Fax 020 7839 7118
www.quadrille.co.uk
Chairman *Sir David Cooksey*
Managing Director *Alison Cathie*
Editorial Director *Jane O'Shea*

Founded in 1994 by four ex-directors of Conran Octopus, with a view to producing a small list of top-quality illustrated books. Publishes non-fiction, including cookery, gardening, interior design and decoration, craft, health. TITLES *Gordon Ramsay Easy*; *Antonio Carluccio's Italia*; *Home is Where the Heart Is* Ilse Crawford. 54 titles in 2005. Synopses and ideas for books welcome. No fiction or children's books.
ROYALTIES twice-yearly.

Authors' Rating The top publisher for cookbooks, Quadrille has achieved an enviable reputation for high production values.

Quantum
See **Foulsham Publishers**

Quartet Books
27 Goodge Street, London W1T 2LD
☎020 7636 3992   Fax 020 7637 1866
Chairman *Naim Attallah*
Managing Director *Jeremy Beale*
Publishing Director *Stella Kane*

Founded 1972. Independent publisher. Publishes contemporary literary fiction including translations, popular culture, biography, music, history, politics and some photographic books. Unsolicited sample chapters with return postage welcome; no poetry, romance or science fiction. Submissions by disk or e-mail are not accepted.
ROYALTIES twice-yearly.

Queen Anne Press
See **Lennard Associates Ltd**

Quiller Press
(An imprint of Quiller Publishing Ltd), Wykey House, Wykey, Shrewsbury SY4 1JA
☎01939 261616   Fax 01939 261606
✉ info@quillerbooks.com
Managing Director *Andrew Johnston*

Specialises in sponsored books and publications sold through non-book trade channels as well as bookshops. Publishes architecture, biography, business and industry, collecting, cookery, DIY, gardening, guidebooks, humour, reference, sports, travel, wine and spirits. About 10 titles a year.

Unsolicited mss only if the author sees some potential for sponsorship or guaranteed sales. ROYALTIES twice-yearly.

Radcliffe Press
See **I.B. Tauris & Co. Ltd**

Radcliffe Publishing Ltd
18 Marcham Road, Abingdon OX14 1AA
☎01235 528820   Fax 01235 528830
✉ contact.us@radcliffemed.com
www.radcliffe-oxford.com
Managing Director *Andrew Bax*
Editorial Director *Gillian Nineham*
Approx. Annual Turnover £2 million

Founded 1987. Medical publishers which began by specialising in books for general practice and health service management. Publishes clinical, management, health policy books, training materials and CD-ROMs. 90 titles in 2004. Unsolicited mss, synopses and ideas welcome. No non-medical or medical books aimed at lay audience.
ROYALTIES twice-yearly.

The Ramsay Head Press
16 West Savile Gardens, Edinburgh EH9 3AB
☎0131 662 1915
✉ conradkwilson@aol.com
Managing Director *Conrad Wilson*

Founded 1968 by Norman Wilson, OBE. A small independent family publisher. Publishes biography, cookery, Scottish fiction and non-fiction. TITLES *When It Works It Feels Like Play* Tessa Ransford. Synopses and ideas for books of Scottish interest welcome.
ROYALTIES twice-yearly.

The Random House Group Ltd
Random House, 20 Vauxhall Bridge Road, London SW1V 2SA
☎020 7840 8400   Fax 020 7233 6058
✉ enquiries@randomhouse.co.uk
www.randomhouse.co.uk
Chief Executive/Chairman *Gail Rebuck*
Deputy Chairman *Simon Master*
Group Managing Director *Ian Hudson*

The Random House Group is the UK's leading trade publisher comprising 31 diverse imprints in four separate substantially autonomous divisions: the Random House Division, Ebury Press, Transworld (see entry) and Random House Children's Books.

RANDOM HOUSE DIVISION
Managing Director *Richard Cable*

IMPRINTS **Jonathan Cape** ☎020 7840 8576 Fax 020 7233 6117 Publishing Director *Dan Franklin* Biography and memoirs, current affairs, fiction, history, photography, poetry, politics and travel.

Yellow Jersey Press ☎020 7840 8637 Fax 020 7223 6117 Editorial Director *Tristan Jones* Narrative sports books.

Harvill Secker ☎020 7840 8649 Fax 020 7233 6117 Publishing Director *Geoff Mulligan* Principally literary fiction with some non-fiction. Literature in translation, English literature, quality thrillers.

Chatto & Windus ☎020 7840 8522 Fax 020 7233 6117 Publishing Director *Alison Samuel* Memoirs, current affairs, essays, literary fiction, history, poetry, politics, philosophy and translations.

Pimlico ☎020 7840 8784 Fax 020 7233 6117 Publisher *Will Sulkin* Quality non-fiction paperbacks, specialising in history, biography, popular culture and the arts.

Vintage ☎020 7840 8573 Fax 020 7233 6117 Publisher *Rachel Cugnoni* Quality paperback fiction and non-fiction. Vintage (founded in 1990) has been described as one of the 'greatest literary success stories in recent British publishing'.

Century ☎020 7840 8554 Fax 020 7233 6127 Publishing Director *Mark Booth* General fiction and non-fiction including commercial fiction, autobiography, biography, history and self-help.

William Heinemann ☎020 7840 8400 Fax 020 7233 6127 Publishing Director *Ravi Mirchandani* General non-fiction and fiction, especially history, literary fiction, crime, science, thrillers and women's fiction.

Hutchinson ☎020 7840 8564 Fax 020 7233 7870 Publishing Director *Sue Freestone* General fiction and non-fiction including notably belles-lettres, current affairs, politics, travel and history.

Random House Business Books ☎020 7840 8550 Fax 020 7233 6127 Publisher *Clare Smith*.

Arrow ☎020 7840 8557 Fax 020 7840 6127 Publishing Director *Kate Elton* Mass-market paperback fiction and non-fiction.

EBURY PRESS PUBLISHING DIVISION
1 Stephen Street, London W1T 1AL
☎020 7840 8400 Fax 020 7840 8406)
Publisher *Fiona MacIntyre*

IMPRINTS **Ebury Press; Vermilion; Rider; Time Out Guides; Fodors** Narrative non-fiction; autobiography and biography, cookery, travel writing and guides, memoir, popular history, popular science, humour, sport, TV tie-ins, personal development, parenting, diet, health and fitness, spirituality, Buddhism, philosophy, paranormal.

RANDOM HOUSE CHILDREN'S BOOKS DIVISION Transworld Publishers, 61–63 Uxbridge Road, London W5 5SA
☎020 8231 6800 Fax 020 8231 6767)
Managing Director *Philippa Dickinson*, Publishing Director (Fiction) *Annie Eaton*, Publishing Director (Picture Books) *Caroline Roberts*, Publisher (Doubleday Picture Books) *Penny Walker*, Senior Commissioning Editor (Fiction) *Alex Antscherl*, Senior Commissioning Editor (Picture Books) *Natascha Biebow*, Commissioning Editor (Jonathan Cape Picture Books) *Helen Mackenzie-Smith*, Associate Publisher (Jonathan Cape Fiction) *Delia Huddy*, Publisher (Jonathan Cape) *Tom Maschler* Publishes picture books, fiction, poetry, non-fiction and audio cassettes. IMPRINTS **Bodley Head Children's Books; Corgi Children's Books; Doubleday Children's Books; Hutchinson Children's Books; Jonathan Cape Children's Books; Red Fox Children's Books.**

David Fickling Books (31 Beaumont Street, Oxford OX1 2NP ☎01491 613711 Fax 01491 613733 ✉ dfickling@ randomhouse.co.uk www. davidficklingbooks.co.uk Publisher *David Fickling*, Editor *Pella Pearson* Children's fiction and picture books. Unsolicited mss, synopses and ideas for books welcome.
ROYALTIES twice-yearly for the most part.

Authors' Rating Way out in front as the UK's leading trade publisher, Random has a reputation for promoting new talent. Author relations are good according to a Society of Authors' survey. Synopses and manuscripts may be passed on to freelance readers, but there is reasonable assurance that they are at least read.

Ransom Publishing Ltd

Rose Cottage, Howe Hill, Watlington OX49 5HB
☎01491 613711   Fax 01491 613733
✉ jenny@ransom.co.uk
www.ransom.co.uk
Managing Director *Jenny Ertle*

An early years and educational publisher, Ransom Publishing specialises in interactive software, reading books, teachers' handbooks and resource materials including games and posters. Principal subject areas include early learning, phonics, special needs, literacy, numeracy, science, geography and ICT. Occasionally considers new submissions in suitable areas but cannot guarantee a reply. Specifically interested in reading materials suitable for older children with special needs.

Reader's Digest Association Ltd

11 Westferry Circus, Canary Wharf, London E14 4HE
☎020 7715 8000   Fax 020 7715 8181
✉ gbeditorial@readersdigest.co.uk
www.readersdigest.co.uk
Managing Director *Andrew Lynam-Smith*
Editorial Director, Books *Cortina Butler*

Editorial office in the USA (see entry under *US Publishers*). Publishes gardening, natural history, cookery, history, DIY, travel and word books. About 20 titles a year.

Reaktion Books

79 Farringdon Road, London EC1M 3JU
☎020 7404 9930   Fax 020 7404 9931
✉ info@reaktionbooks.co.uk
www.reaktionbooks.co.uk
Managing Director *Michael R. Leaman*

Founded in Edinburgh in 1985 and moved to London in 1987. Publishes art history, architecture, Asian studies, cultural studies, design, film, geography, history, natural history, photography and travel writing (*not* travel guides). TITLES *Pablo Picasso* Mary Ann Caws; SERIES 'Animal': *Oyster* Rebecca Stott; *Rat* Jonathan Burt; *Bear* Robert E. Bieder; *Whale* Joe Roman. About 30 titles a year.
ROYALTIES twice-yearly.

Reardon Publishing

56 Upper Norwood Street, Leckhampton, Cheltenham GL53 0DU
☎01242 231800
✉ reardon@bigfoot.com
www.reardon.co.uk
www.cotswoldbookshop.com
www.antarcticbookshop.com
Managing Editor *Nicholas Reardon*

Founded in the mid-1970s. Family-run publishing house specialising in local interest and tourism in the Cotswold area and books on Antarctica. Member of the **Outdoor Writers Guild**. Publishes walking and driving guides, and family history for societies. TITLES *The Cotswold Way* (video); *The Cotswold Way Map; Cotswold Walkabout; Cotswold Driveabout; The Donnington Way; The Haunted Cotswolds.* Also distributes for

other publishers such as Ordnance Survey. 10 titles a year. Unsolicited mss, synopses and ideas welcome with return postage only.
ROYALTIES twice-yearly.

Red Fox Children's Books
See **The Random House Group Ltd**

Thomas Reed
See **A.&C. Black Publishers Ltd**

William Reed Directories
Broadfield Park, Crawley RH11 9RT
☎01293 613400   Fax 01293 610322
✉ directories@william-reed.co.uk
www.william-reed.co.uk
Head of Content *Daniel Verrells*

William Reed Directories, a division of William Reed Publishing, was established in 1990. Its portfolio includes 13 titles covering the food, drink, non-food, catering, retail and export industries, including European versions. The titles are produced as directories, market research reports, exhibition catalogues and electronic publishing.

Reed Elsevier Group plc
1–3 Strand, London WC2N 5JR
☎020 7930 7077
www.reedelsevier.com
Also at: 125 Park Avenue, 23rd Floor, New York, NY 10017, USA
☎001 212 309 5498 Fax 001 212 309 5480
Raderweg 28, 1043 NX Amsterdam,
The Netherlands
☎00 31 20 485 3911
Chief Executive Officer (UK) *Crispin Davis*

Reed Elsevier Group plc is a world-leading publisher and information provider, operating in four core segments: science and medical, legal, education, business. No trade books. DIVISIONS **Harcourt Education** (see entry); **Elsevier** (see entry); **LexisNexis** (formerly Butterworths) Halsbury House, 35 Chancery Lane, London WC2A 1EL ☎020 7400 2500 Fax 020 7400 2842 Publishes legal and accountancy textbooks, journals, law reports, CD-ROMs and online services; **Harcourt School Publishers** (see entry under *US Publishers*); **Reed Business** Quadrant House, The Quadrant, Sutton SM2 5AS ☎020 8652 3500. No unsolicited material.

Reference Library
See **CRW Publishing Ltd**

Regency House Publishing Limited
Niall House, 24–26 Boulton Road, Stevenage SG1 4QX
☎01438 314488   Fax 01438 311303
✉ regency-house@btconnect.com
Chairman *Brian Trodd*
Managing Director *Nicolette Trodd*

Founded 1991. Publisher and packager of mass-market non-fiction. No fiction. No unsolicited material.

Research Disclosure
See **Kenneth Mason Publications Ltd**

Review
See **Hodder Headline Ltd**

Richmond House Publishing Company Ltd
70–76 Bell Street, Marylebone, London NW1 6SP
☎020 7224 9666   Fax 020 7224 9688
✉ sales@rhpco.co.uk
www.rhpco.co.uk
Managing Directors *Gloria Gordon, Spencer Block*

Publishes directories for the theatre and entertainment industries. TITLES *British Theatre Directory*; *Artistes and Agents*; *London Seating Plan Guide*. Synopses and ideas welcome.

Rider
See **The Random House Group Ltd**

Right Way/Right Way Plus
See **Elliot Right Way Books**

RMEP
See **Hymns Ancient & Modern Ltd**

Robinson
See **Constable & Robinson Ltd**

Robson Books
See **Chrysalis Books Group**

RotoVision
Sheridan House, 112/116A Western Road, Hove BN3 1DD
☎01273 727268   Fax 01273 727269
www.rotovision.com
Managing Director *Ken Fund*
Publishing Manager *April Sankey*
Founded 1996. Rapidly-expanding visual arts

publishers with a strong emphasis on education and inspiration. Publishes graphic design, photography, web design, advertising, film, architecture, lighting design, interiors, product design, packaging design. TITLES *World's Top Photographers: Wildlife*; *What Is Graphic Design?*; *The Total Beauty of Sustainable Products*; *Materials for Inspirational Design: Plastic*; *The Designer and the Grid*; *Screencraft: Directing*; *Up Against the Wall: International Poster Design*; *Stretch: The Art of Panoramic Photography*. No unsolicited mss; written synopses and ideas welcome. No phone calls, please. No academic or fiction.

FLAT FEE paid.

Roundhouse Publishing Group

Millstone, Limers Lane, Northam EX39 2RG
☎01237 474474   Fax 01237 474774
✉ roundhouse.group@ukgateway.net

Editorial Head *Alan Goodworth*

Founded 1991. Publishes cinema and media-related titles. TITLES *The Bent Lens: A World Guide to Gay & Lesbian Films*; *Cinema of Oliver Stone*; *Cinema of Martin Scorsese*. Represents and distributes a broad range of non-fiction publishing houses throughout the UK and Europe. No unsolicited mss.

ROYALTIES twice-yearly.

Routledge (An imprint of **Taylor & Francis Group**, the academic division of **T&F Informa plc**)

2 Park Square, Milton Park, Abingdon OX14 4RN
☎020 7017 6000   Fax 020 7017 6699
www.routledge.com

CEO *Roger Horton*
Managing Director *Roger Horton*
Publishing Directors *Claire L'Enfant, Alan Jarvis*
Approx. Annual Turnover £40 million (Group)

Routledge is an international academic imprint publishing books primarily for university students, researchers, academics and professionals. Most Routledge authors are academics with specialist knowledge of their subject. Publishes everything from core text books to research monographs and journals in the following subject areas: humanities, including anthropology, archaeology, classical studies, communications and media studies, cultural studies, history, language and literature, music, philosophy, religious studies, theatre studies and sports studies; social sciences, including geography, politics, military and strategic studies, sociology and urban studies; business, management and eco-

nomics; education; Asian and Middle Eastern studies. Over 1000 titles a year. Send a detailed proposal plus c.v. and sample chapters. Proposal requirements and submission procedures can be found on the website. No poetry, fiction, travel or astrology.

ROYALTIES annually or twice-yearly, according to contract.

RYA (Royal Yachting Association)

RYA House, Ensign Way, Hamble, Southampton SO31 4YA
☎023 8060 4100   Fax 023 8060 4299
✉ phil.williamsellis@rya.org.uk
www.rya.org.uk

Chief Executive *Rod Carr*
Publications Manager *Phil Williams-Ellis*
Approx. Annual Turnover £10 million+

The Royal Yachting Association, the UK governing body representing sailing, windsurfing, motorboating, powerboat racing both at sea and on inland waters, was founded in 1875. Publishes sports instruction books relating to specific training courses, technical, legal and boating advice, all written by experts in their field. TITLES *RYA Weather Handbook*; *RYA Navigation Exercises*; *RYA Start Sailing*. 8 titles a year. No unsolicited mss; synopses and ideas for books welcome. Approach by e-mail or post in the first instance.

ROYALTIES annually.

Ryland Peters and Small Limited

20–21 Jockey's Fields, London WC1R 5BN
☎020 7025 2200   Fax 020 7025 2201
✉ info@rps.co.uk
www.rylandpeters.com

Managing Director *David Peters*
Publishing Director *Alison Starling*

Founded 1996. Publishes highly illustrated lifestyle books aimed at an international market, covering gardening, cookery, interior design and mind, body, spirit. No fiction. No unsolicited mss; synopses and ideas welcome.

ROYALTIES twice-yearly.

Sage Publications

1 Oliver's Yard, 55 City Road, London EC1Y 1SP
☎020 7324 8500   Fax 020 7324 8600
✉ info@sagepub.co.uk
www.sagepub.co.uk

Managing Director *Stephen Barr*
Editorial Director *Ziyad Marar*

Founded 1971. Publishes academic books and

journals in humanities and the social sciences. Bought academic and professional books publisher Paul Chapman Publishing Ltd in 1998 and Lucky Duck Publishing in 2004.
ROYALTIES twice-yearly.

Saint Andrew Press
Church of Scotland, 121 George Street, Edinburgh EH2 4YN
☎0131 225 5722   Fax 0131 220 3113
✉ standrewpress@cofscotland.org.uk
www.standrewpress.com
www.williambarclay.org
Head of Publishing *Ann Crawford*
Approx. Annual Turnover £225,000

Founded in 1954. Owned by the Church of Scotland. Publishes religious, general reference and children's books aimed at the Christian trade and retail market in the UK and internationally. Lead TITLES in 2004 included BBC Scotland's *The Scots at Sea, Silent Heroes* by John D. Mills and *Jesus and People Like Us* by Nick Baines. About 20 titles a year. 'Saint Andrew Press is expanding and is actively seeking high-quality writing that is thought-provoking and, above all, helps readers to wrestle with the complexities of life today.' No unsolicited mss but proposals very welcome in synopsis form; approach in writing.
ROYALTIES annually.

St Pauls Publishing
187 Battersea Bridge Road, London SW11 3AS
☎020 7978 4300   Fax 020 7978 4370
✉ editions@stpauls.org.uk
Publisher *Andrew Pudussery*

Publishing division of the Society of St Paul. Began publishing in 1914 but activities were fairly limited until around 1948. Publishes religious material mainly: theology, scripture, catechetics, prayer books and biography. About 30 titles a year. Unsolicited mss, synopses and ideas welcome.

Salamander Books
See **Chrysalis Books Group**

Sanctuary Books
Sanctuary House, 45–53 Sinclair Road, London W14 0NS
☎020 7602 6351   Fax 020 7300 1897
✉ info@sanctuarygroup.com
www.sanctuarypublishing.com
CEO *Aky Najeeb*

Managing Director *Michael Wilson*

Founded 1996. Part of Sanctuary Group plc, international developers of music intellectual property rights. Publishes popular culture, sport, humour, music and music tuition. DIVISION **Sanctuary Publishing plc** Editorial Head *Albert DePetrillo* TITLE *I Hate Myself and Want to Die: The 52 Most Depressing Songs You've Ever Heard* Tom Reynolds. IMPRINTS **Arcane** *Albert DePetrillo* TITLE *Queer Facts: The Greatest Gay and Lesbian Trivia Book Ever* Michelle Baker and Stephen Tropiano; **SMT** *Chris Harvey* TITLE *Crash Course: Electric Guitar* Jamie Humphries. 53 titles in 2004. No unsolicited mss; synopses and ideas for books welcome. Approach by post in the first instance. No fiction or photography books.
ROYALTIES twice-yearly.

Sangam Books Ltd
57 London Fruit Exchange, Brushfield Street, London E1 6EP
☎020 7377 6399   Fax 020 7375 1230
✉ sangambks@aol.com
Executive Director *Anthony de Souza*

Traditionally an educational publisher of school and college level textbooks. Also publishes art, India, medicine, science, technology, social sciences, religion, plus some fiction in paperback.

Saqi Books
26 Westbourne Grove, London W2 5RH
☎020 7221 9347   Fax 020 7229 7492
✉ enquiries@saqibooks.com
www.saqibooks.com
Chairman/Managing Director *André Gaspard*

Founded 1981, initially as a specialist publisher of books on the Middle East and Arab world but now includes Central Asia, South Asia and European fiction. Publishes fiction and non-fiction – academic and illustrated. About 20 titles a year. Welcomes unsolicited material; approach by post or e-mail.
ROYALTIES annually.

Authors' Rating A blunt warning from the managing editor that unsolicited manuscripts are not returned. Saqi is not alone in this. Authors should retain copies of everything they send out.

Saunders
See **Elsevier Ltd**

Savitri Books Ltd
See entry under **UK Packagers**

SB Publications

14 Bishopstone Road, Seaford BN25 2UB
☎01323 893498   Fax 01323 893860
✉ sbpublications@tiscali.co.uk
www.sbpublications.co.uk

Owner *Mrs Lindsay Woods*

Founded 1987. Specialises in local history, including themes illustrated by old picture postcards and photographs; also travel, guides (town, walking) and railways. TITLES *Dorset As She Was Spoke*; *The Neat and Nippy Guide to Brighton*; *Pre-Raphaelite Trail in Sussex*. Also provides marketing and distribution services for local authors. 20 titles a year.
ROYALTIES annually.

Sceptre

See **Hodder Headline Ltd**

Scholastic Ltd

Villiers House, Clarendon Avenue, Leamington Spa CV32 5PR
☎01926 887799   Fax 01926 883331
www.scholastic.co.uk

Chairman *M.R. Robinson*
Managing Director *Kate Wilson*
Approx. Annual Turnover £42 million

Founded 1964. Owned by US parent company, Scholastic Inc. Acquired **Chicken House Publishing** in May 2005. Publishes children's fiction and non-fiction and education for primary schools.

DIVISIONS
Scholastic Children's Books *Elaine McQuade* Commonwealth House, 1–19 New Oxford Street, London WC1A 1NU ☎020 7421 9000 Fax 020 7421 9001 IMPRINTS **Scholastic Press** (hardback); **Hippo** (paperback); **Point** (paperback) TITLES *Horrible Histories*; *Goosebumps*; *Point Horror*, *His Dark Materials* trilogy by Philip Pullman.

Educational Publishing *Max Adam* (Villiers House address) Professional books and classroom materials for primary teachers, plus magazines such as *Child Education, Junior Education, Junior Focus, Infant Projects, Nursery Education; Literacy Time*.

Scholastic Book Clubs *Miles Stevens Hoare* Windrush Park, Witney, Oxford OX29 0YT ☎01993 893456 Fax 01993 776813 SBC is the UK's number one Schools Book Club. Offering five age specific clubs, it provides 'the best books at great prices and supports teachers in the process'.

School Book Fairs *Miles Stevens-Hoare* The Book Fair Division sells directly to children, parents and teachers in schools through 27,000 week-long book events held in schools throughout the UK.
ROYALTIES twice-yearly.

Authors' Rating Another beneficiary of the Harry Potter phenomenon (via its children's book clubs), Scholastic continues to expand the children's market. Among the latest bright ideas is an extension of the Horrible Science series into partwork magazines. Scholastic is noted for its author-friendly skills.

SCM – Canterbury Press Ltd

9–17 St Albans Place, London N1 0NX
☎020 7359 8033   Fax 020 7359 0049
✉ admin@scm-canterburypress.co.uk
www.scm-canterburypress.co.uk

Publishing Director *Christine Smith*
Approx. Annual Turnover £1.3 million

Part of **Hymns Ancient & Modern Ltd** (see entry). Has two publishing imprints: **SCM Press** Text and reference books for the study of theology, philosophy of religion, ethics and religious studies; **Canterbury Press** Religious titles for the general market, liturgy, spirituality and church resources. AUTHORS include Rowan Williams, Ronald Blythe, Libby Purves. 80 titles a year. Refer to website for guidelines on submitting proposals.
ROYALTIES annually.

Authors' Rating Leading publisher of religious ideas with well-deserved reputation for fresh thinking. At SCM, 'questioning theology is the norm'.

Scottish Cultural Press/ Scottish Children's Press

Unit 6, Newbattle Abbey Business Park, Newbattle Road, Dalkeith EH22 3LJ
☎0131 660 6366   Fax 0131 660 4666
✉ info@scottishbooks.com
www.scottishbooks.com

Directors *Avril Gray, Brian Pugh*

Founded 1992. Publishes Scottish interest titles, including cultural literature, poetry, archaeology, local history. DIVISION **S.C.P. Children's Ltd** (trading as **Scottish Children's Press**) Children's fiction and non-fiction. Unsolicited mss, synopses and ideas accepted provided return postage is included, but *always* telephone before sending material, please. 'Mss sent without advance telephone call and return postage will be destroyed.'
ROYALTIES paid.

Scribner

See **Simon & Schuster UK Limited**

Seafarer Books

102 Redwald Road, Rendlesham, Woodbridge
IP12 2TE
☎01394 420789   Fax 01394 461314
✉ info@seafarerbooks.com
www.seafarerbooks.com

Sole Proprietor *Patricia M. Eve*

Founded 1968. Publishes sailing titles, with an emphasis on the traditional. AUTHORS Erskine Childers, Cecily Gould, Bjorn Larsson, John Leather, Jack London, Frank Mulville, Bob Roberts, Adrian Seligman. No unsolicited mss; preliminary letter essential before making any type of submission.
ROYALTIES twice-yearly.

SeaNeverDry Publishing

PO Box 37, London KT8 9XE
☎020 8892 3438   Fax 020 8892 3101
✉ orders@seaneverdry.com
www.seaneverdry.com

Chairman *B. de Vaatt*
Managing Director *D.R. Abbott*
Approx. Annual Turnover £125,000

Founded 2003. Publishes general fiction, erotica and humour. DIVISIONS **General Fiction** *B. Hayes* TITLES *Arise Sir Humphrey; Dropping in on Idi.* **Humour** *D.R. Abbott* TITLES *Fake Honesty; His/Her Words of Love.* 5 titles in 2004. Unsolicited mss, synopses and ideas for books welcome; approach by e-mail. No academic texts or science fiction.
ROYALTIES quarterly.

Authors' Rating Not to be confused with vanity publishing, SeaNeverDry Publishing offers advanced technology to produce a low cost, low volume print run to test the market. If the book takes off well, good luck; the author gets a higher than average royalty of 15%. But there is a long way between hope and realisation. It remains to be seen if marketing can live up to expectations.

Search Press Ltd

Wellwood, North Farm Road, Tunbridge Wells TN2 3DR
☎01892 510850   Fax 01892 515903
✉ searchpress@searchpress.com
www.searchpress.com

Managing Director *Martin de la Bédoyère*
Commissioning Editor *Rosalind Dace*

Founded 1970. Publishes full-colour art, craft, needlecrafts – papermaking and papercrafts, painting on silk, art techniques and embroidery. No unsolicited mss; synopsis with sample chapter welcome.
ROYALTIES annually.

Seren

First Floor, 38–40 Nolton Street, Bridgend CF31 3BN
☎01656 663018   Fax 01656 649226
✉ seren@seren-books.com
www.seren-books.com

Chairman *Cary Archard*
Managing Director *Mick Felton*
Approx. Annual Turnover £150,000

Founded 1981 as a specialist poetry publisher but has now moved into general literary publishing with an emphasis on Wales. Publishes poetry, fiction, literary criticism, drama, biography, art, history and translations of fiction.

DIVISIONS
Poetry *Amy Wack* AUTHORS Owen Sheers, Pascale Petit, Sheenagh Pugh, Kathryn Gray, Deryn Rees-Jones. **Drama** *Amy Wack* AUTHORS Edward Thomas, Charles Way, Lucinda Coxon. **Fiction** *Will Atkins* Authors Leonora Brito, Richard Collins, Lloyd Jones, Richard John Evans. **Art, Literary Criticism, History, Translations** *Mick Felton* IMPRINT **Border Lines Biographies** TITLES *Bruce Chatwin; Dennis Potter; Mary Webb; Wilfred Owen; Raymond Williams.* About 25 titles a year. Unsolicited mss, synopses and ideas for books welcome.
ROYALTIES twice yearly.

Serpent's Tail

4 Blackstock Mews, London N4 2BT
☎020 7354 1949   Fax 020 7704 6467
✉ info@serpentstail.com
www.serpentstail.com

Contact *Martin Worthington*
Approx. Annual Turnover £650,000

Founded 1986. Winner of the **Sunday Times Small Publisher of the Year Award** (1989) and the Ralph Lewis Award for new fiction (1992). Serpent's Tail has introduced to British audiences a number of major internationally known writers. Noted for its strong emphasis on design and an eye for the unusual. Publishes contemporary fiction, contemporary gay fiction and non-fiction, including works in translation, crime, popular culture and biography. No poetry, romance or fantasy.
IMPRINTS **Serpent's Tail** TITLES *Fearless Jones* Walter Mosley; *Whatever* Michel Houellebecq;

This is Serbia Calling Matthew Collin; *Pornocopia* Laurence O'Toole. **Five Star** TITLES *Nineteen Seventy Four* David Peace; *Always Outnumbered, Always Outgunned* Walter Mosley; *Beneath the Blonde* Stella Duffy. About 40 titles a year. Send preliminary letter outlining proposal with a sample chapter and s.a.e. No unsolicited mss. Prospective authors unfamiliar with Serpent's Tail are advised to study the list before submitting anything.
ROYALTIES annually.

Authors' Rating A publisher noted for originality which means doing what the conglomerates are unwilling or unable to do. An exciting fiction list much praised by its own and other publishers' authors.

Severn House Publishers
9–15 High Street, Sutton SM1 1DF
☎020 8770 3930   Fax 020 8770 3850
✉ info@severnhouse.com
www.severnhouse.com
Chairman *Edwin Buckhalter*
Editorial *Amanda Stewart*

Founded 1974. A leader in library fiction publishing. Publishes hardback fiction: romance, science fiction, horror, fantasy, crime. About 140 titles a year. No unsolicited material. Synopses/proposals preferred through *bona fide* literary agents only. OVERSEAS ASSOCIATE Severn House Publishers Inc., New York.
ROYALTIES twice-yearly.

Sheldon Press
See **Society for Promoting Christian Knowledge**

Sheldrake Press
188 Cavendish Road, London SW12 0DA
☎020 8675 1767   Fax 020 8675 7736
✉ enquiries@sheldrakepress.co.uk
www.sheldrakepress..co.uk
Publisher *Simon Rigge*

Founded in 1979 as a book packager and commenced publishing under its own imprint in 1991. Publishes illustrated non-fiction: history, travel, style, cookery and stationery. TITLES *The Victorian House Book; The Shorter Mrs Beeton; The Power of Steam; The Railway Heritage of Britain; Wild Britain; Wild France; Wild Spain; Wild Italy; Wild Ireland; Amsterdam: Portrait of a City* and Kate Greenaway stationery books. Synopses and ideas for books welcome, but not interested in fiction.

Shepheard-Walwyn (Publishers) Ltd
Suite 604, The Chandlery, 50 Westminster Bridge Road, London SE1 7QY
☎020 7721 7666   Fax 020 7721 7667
✉ books@shepheard-walwyn.co.uk
www.shepheard-walwyn.co.uk
Managing Director *Anthony Werner*
Approx. Annual Turnover £150,000

Founded 1972. 'We regard books as food for the mind and want to offer a wholesome diet of original ideas and fresh approaches to old subjects.' Publishes general non-fiction in three main areas: Scottish interest; gift books in calligraphy and/or illustrated; history, political economy, perennial philosophy. About 5 titles a year. Synopses and ideas for books welcome.
ROYALTIES twice-yearly.

The Shetland Times Ltd
Gremista, Lerwick ZE1 0PX
☎01595 693622   Fax 01595 694637
✉ publishing@shetland-times.co.uk
www.shetland-books.co.uk
Managing Director *June Wishart*
Publications Manager *Charlotte Black*

Founded 1872 as publishers of the local newspaper. Book publishing followed thereafter plus publication of monthly magazine, *Shetland Life*. Publishes anything with Shetland connections – local and natural history, music, crafts, maritime. Prefers material with a Shetland theme/connection.
ROYALTIES annually.

Shire Publications Ltd
Cromwell House, Church Street, Princes Risborough HP27 9AA
☎01844 344301   Fax 01844 347080
✉ shire@shirebooks.co.uk
www.shirebooks.co.uk
General Manager *Sue Ross*

Founded 1962. Publishes original non-fiction paperbacks. About 25 titles a year. No unsolicited material; send introductory letter with detailed outline of idea.
ROYALTIES annually.

Authors' Rating You don't have to live in the country to write books for Shire but it helps. With titles like *Church Fonts, Haunted Inns* and *Discovering Preserved Railways* there is a distinct rural feel to the list. Another way of putting it, to quote owner John Rotheroe, Shire specialises in 'small books on all manner of obscure subjects'.

Short Books

15 Highbury Terrace, London N5 1UP
☎020 7226 1607   Fax 020 7226 4169
✉ emily@shortbooks.com
www.shortbooks.co.uk

Editorial Directors *Rebecca Nicolson, Aurea Carpenter*

Founded 2001. Publishes general adult and children's non-fiction: biography, history and politics, humour and children's narrative history. No unsolicited mss.

Sidgwick & Jackson

See **Macmillan Publishers Ltd**

Sigma Press

5 Alton Road, Wilmslow SK9 5DY
☎01625 531035   Fax 01625 531035
✉ info@sigma.press
www.sigmapress.co.uk

Chairman/Managing Director *Graham Beech*

Founded in 1980 as a publisher of technical books, Sigma Press now publishes mainly in the leisure area. Publishes outdoor, local heritage, adventure and biography. DIVISION **Sigma Leisure** TITLES *Holiday Walks in the Loire Valley*; *Leap into Legend* (biography); *All-Terrain Pushchair Walks*; *Discovering Manchester*. 10 titles in 2004. No unsolicited mss; synopses and ideas welcome. No poetry or novels required.
ROYALTIES twice-yearly.

Simon & Schuster UK Limited

Africa House, 64–78 Kingsway, London
WC2B 6AH
☎020 7316 1900   Fax 020 7316 0331
www.simonsays.co.uk

CEO/Managing Director *Ian S. Chapman*
Publishing Director *Suzanne Baboneau*
Publishers, Non-fiction *Andrew Gordon* (also The Free Press), *Angela Herlihy*
Publishers, Fiction *Suzanne Baboneau, Ben Ball, Kate Lyall-Grant*
Scribner *Tim Binding, Ben Ball*
Approx. Annual Turnover £27.2 million

Founded 1986. Sister company of the leading American company. Publishes hardback (**Simon & Schuster**) and paperback (**Pocket Books**) commercial and literary fiction and non-fiction, including autobiography, biography, sport, mind, body & spirit, humour, travel and other general interest non-fiction. **The Free Press** publishes serious non-fiction, including popular science, politics, history and current business. Literary international fiction and non-fiction is published

under the **Scribner** imprint. DIVISIONS **Martin Books** Director *Janet Copleston* Specialises in bespoke publishing and branded editions, and the Simon & Schuster UK cookery list. **Simon & Schuster Children's Books** Publishing Director *Ingrid Selberg*, Editor (Fiction) *Venetia Gosling*, Editor (Picture Books) *Katherine Halligan* Media tie-ins, picture books and fiction titles. Venetia Gosling is launching a list of young fiction titles in 2006.
ROYALTIES twice-yearly.

Authors' Rating After a radical restructuring, Simon & Schuster is in fine form, a medium sized publisher with a talent for spotting strong sellers. The American parent company governs with a light touch.

Skoob Russell Square

10 Brunswick Centre, off Bernard Street,
London WC1N 1AE
☎020 7278 8760   Fax 020 7278 3137
✉ books@skoob.com
www.skoob.com

Editorial *M. Lovell*

Publishes literary guides, cultural studies, esoterica/occult, poetry, new writing from the Orient. TITLES *Skoob Directory of Secondhand Bookshops*; *Perspectives on Post-Colonial Literature* D.C.R.A. Goonetilleke; *The Space of City Trees* Arthur Yap. 'Our lists are now closed. We will not be taking in any further mss.'

Smith Gryphon Ltd

See **John Blake Publishing Ltd**

SMT

See **Sanctuary Books**

Colin Smythe Ltd

PO Box 6, Gerrards Cross SL9 8XA
☎01753 886000   Fax 01753 886469
✉ cs@colinsmythe.co.uk
www.colinsmythe.co.uk

Managing Director *Colin Smythe*
Approx. Annual Turnover £2.7 million

Founded 1966. Publishes Anglo-Irish literature, drama; criticism and Irish history. About 5 titles a year. No unsolicited mss. (Also acts as agent for Terry Pratchett.)
ROYALTIES annually/twice-yearly.

Snowbooks Ltd

120 Pentonville Road, London N1 9JN
☎020 7837 6482   Fax 020 7837 6348
✉ editor@snowbooks.com

www.snowbooks.com

Managing Director *Emma Cahill*
Approx. Annual Turnover £250,000

Founded 2003. Publishes mainly fiction and some non-fiction. 'Keen on promoting open, friendly, productive relationships with authors.' TITLES *Adept* Robert Finn; *Longing* J.D. Landis; *The Idle Thoughts of an Idle Fellow* J.K. Jerome; *The London Scene* Virginia Woolf. 6–10 titles a year. Unsolicited mss welcome, by e-mail only. Read the submission guidelines in the authors' section of the website first.

ROYALTIES vary according to contract 'but tend to be higher than the industry average'.

Society for Promoting Christian Knowledge (SPCK)

36 Causton Street, London SW1P 4ST
☎020 7592 3900   Fax 020 7592 3939
www.spck.org.uk

Director of Publishing *Simon Kingston*

Founded 1698, SPCK is the third oldest publisher in the country. IMPRINTS **SPCK** Editorial Director *Joanna Moriarty* Theology, academic, liturgy, prayer, spirituality, biblical studies, educational resources, mission, pastoral care, gospel and culture, worldwide. **Sheldon Press** Editor *Fiona Marshall* Popular medicine, health, self-help, psychology. **Azure** Senior Editor *Alison Barr* General spirituality.

ROYALTIES annually.

Authors' Rating Religion with a strong social edge.

Sophia Books
See **Rudolf Steiner Press**

Southwater
See **Anness Publishing Ltd**

Souvenir Press Ltd

43 Great Russell Street, London WC1B 3PA
☎020 7580 9307/8 & 7637 5711/2/3
Fax 020 7580 5064
✉ souvenirpress@ukonline.co.uk

Chairman/Managing Director *Ernest Hecht*

Independent publishing house. Founded 1951. Publishes academic and scholarly, animal care and breeding, antiques and collecting, archaeology, autobiography and biography, business and industry, children's, cookery, crafts and hobbies, crime, educational, fiction, gardening, health and beauty, history and antiquarian, humour, illustrated and fine editions, magic and

the occult, medical, military, music, natural history, philosophy, poetry, psychology, religious, sociology, sports, theatre and women's studies. Souvenir's Human Horizons series for the disabled and their carers is one of the most pre-eminent in its field and recently celebrated 29 years of publishing for the disabled.

IMPRINTS/SERIES   **Condor**;   **Human Horizons**; **Independent Voices**; **Pictorial Presentations**; **Pop Universal**; **The Story-Tellers**. TITLES *Venice, the Enchanted Mirror* Alain Buisine; *The Food Medicine Bible* Earl Mindell; *The Science of Middle Earth* Henry Gee; *Morning Tide* Neil M. Gunn; *The Sinking of the Titanic* Captain L.M. Collins; *The Gladiators* Fik Meijer. About 55 titles a year. Unsolicited mss considered but initial letter of enquiry and outline always required in the first instance.

ROYALTIES twice-yearly.

Authors' Rating An intriguing, some might say eccentric, mix of non-fiction that seems to be leaning more towards the mystical and spiritual.

SPCK
See **Society for Promoting Christian Knowledge**

Special Interest Model Books

Stanley House, 3 Fleets Lane, Poole BH15 3AJ
☎01202 649930   Fax 01202 649950
✉ chrlloyd@globalnet.co.uk
www.specialinterestmodelbooks.co.uk

Contact *Chris Lloyd*

Publishes aviation, engineering, leisure and hobbies, modelling, electronics, wine and beer making. Send synopses rather than completed mss.

ROYALTIES twice-yearly.

Speechmark Publishing Ltd

Telford Road, Bicester OX26 4LQ
☎01869 244644   Fax 01869 320040
✉ info@speechmark.net
www.speechmark.net

Chairman and Managing Director *Ian Franklin*
Publishing Director *Sarah Miles*
Approx. Annual Turnover £1.5 million

Founded 1979. Formerly known as Winslow Publishing, Speechmark publishes practical books and *ColorCards* for health, education and special needs practitioners and students. Unsolicited mss, synopses and ideas welcome. Approach by letter or e-mail.

ROYALTIES annually.

Spellmount Ltd

The Village Centre, Staplehurst TN12 0BJ
☎01580 893730   Fax 01580 893731
✉ enquiries@spellmount.com
www.spellmount.com

Managing Director *Jamie Wilson*
Approx. Annual Turnover £500,000

Founded 1983. Publishes history and military history. About 40 titles a year. Synopses/ideas for books in these specialist fields welcome but no personal memoirs. Enclose return postage.
ROYALTIES biannually for two years, then annually.

Spiro Press

17–19 Rochester Row, London SW1P 1LA
☎0870 165 8968   Fax 0870 165 8989
www.spiropress.com

Publisher *Susannah Lear*
Approx. Annual Turnover (Publishing Division) £1 million

Spiro Press, formerly The Industrial Society Publishing, is part of the Capita Group and has been publishing for over 20 years. Specialises in business, management and self-development – books, manuals and special reports. TITLES *The Heart Aroused*; *Business 2010*; *Why Innovation Fails*. SERIES *Your Personal Trainer*. Unsolicited mss, synopses and ideas welcome. No fiction or illustrated non-fiction.
ROYALTIES twice-yearly.

SportsBooks Limited

PO Box 422, Cheltenham GL50 2YN
☎0870 071 3965   Fax 0870 075 0888
✉ randall@sportsbooks.ltd.uk
www.sportsbooks.ltd.uk

Chairman & Managing Director *Randall Northam*
Approx. Annual Turnover £100,000

Founded 1995. Publishes sports books including biographies, statistical and practical. TITLES *Phil Tufnell's A to Z of Cricket*; *Raich Carter – The Biography*; *The Complete Record of the FA Cup*. IMPRINT **BMM** Editorial Head *Mark Jones*. 9 titles in 2005. No unsolicited mss. Synopses and ideas welcome. Approach by letter or e-mail.

The Sportsman's Press

(An imprint of Quiller Publishing Ltd), Wykey House, Wykey, Shrewsbury SY4 1JA
☎01939 261616   Fax 01939 261606
✉ info@quillerbooks.com

Managing Director *Andrew Johnston*

Specialises in books on all country subjects and general sports including fishing, fencing, shooting, equestrian, cookery, gunmaking and wildlife art. About 10 titles a year.
ROYALTIES twice-yearly.

Springer

Central London Office: 100 Borough High Street, London SE1 1LB
☎020 7863 3000   Fax 020 7863 3314
www.springer-sbm.com

Editorial Director (Chemistry) *Dr Ken Derham*
Senior Publishing Editor (Chemistry) *Emma Roberts*

Founded 1966. Formerly **Kluwer Academic/ Plenum Publishing**, now the central London office of Springer: Science & Business Media and an editorial base for the chemistry and Russian translation programmes. Publishes postgraduate, professional and research-level scientific, textbooks, monographs, conference proceedings and reference books. IMPRINTS **Springer**; **Consultants Bureau**. Proposals for new publications will be considered, and should be sent to the editor.
ROYALTIES annually.

Springer-Verlag London Ltd

Ashbourne House, The Guildway, Old Portsmouth Road, Guildford GU3 1LP
☎01483 734433   Fax 01483 734411
✉ postmaster@svl.co.uk
www.springeronline.com
www.springer-sbm.de

Editorial Director *Beverley Ford*
Approx. Annual Turnover £5 million

The UK subsidiary of Springer Science & Business Media. Publishes science, technical and medical books and journals. Specialises in computing, engineering, medicine, mathematics, statistics, astronomy. All UK published books are sold through Springer's German and US companies as well as in the UK. About 150 titles a year, plus journals. Not interested in social sciences, fiction or school books but academic and professional science and amateur astronomy mss or synopses welcome.
ROYALTIES annually.

Stainer & Bell Ltd

PO Box 110, 23 Gruneisen Road, London N3 1DZ
☎020 8343 3303   Fax 020 8343 3024
✉ post@stainer.co.uk
www.stainer.co.uk

Managing Directors *Carol Y. Wakefield*, *Keith M. Wakefield*

Publishing Director *Nicholas Williams*
Approx. Annual Turnover £830,000

Founded 1907 to publish sheet music. Publishes music and religious subjects related to hymnody. Unsolicited synopses/ideas for books welcome. Send letter enclosing brief précis. ROYALTIES annually.

The Stationery Office
See **TSO**

Rudolf Steiner Press
Hillside House, The Square, Forest Row RH18 5ES
☎01342 824433
✉ office@rudolfsteinerpress.com
www.rudolfsteinerpress.com
Chairman *Mr P. Martyn*
Manager *Mr S. Gulbekian*
Approx. Annual Turnover £150,000

Founded in 1925 to publish the work of Rudolf Steiner and related materials. Publishes non-fiction: spirituality and philosophy. IMPRINT **Sophia Books** *S. Gulbekian* TITLES *From Stress to Serenity; Homemaking as a Social Art*. 15 titles in 2004. No unsolicited material.
ROYALTIES annually.

The Story-Tellers
See **Souvenir Press Ltd**

Straightline Publishing Ltd
29 Main Street, Bothwell G71 8RD
☎01698 853000   Fax 01698 854208
Director *Patrick Bellew*
Editor *Colin Calder*

Founded 1989. Publishes magazines and directories – trade and technical – books of local interest. TITLES *Wired In; enterprisingglasgow; enterprisinglanarkshire*. No unsolicited material.
ROYALTIES annually.

Stripes
See **Little Tiger Press**

Studymates Publishing Limited
PO Box 2, Bishops Lydeard TA4 3YE
☎01823 432002   Fax 01823 430097
✉ info@studymates.co.uk
www.studymates.co.uk
Managing Editor *Graham Lawler, MA*

Publishes **Studymates** Academic books for the 16 to 21 age group, covering A Levels and undergraduate studies. Authors need to be practising or recently-retired teachers/lecturers.

Ideas in writing first; unsolicited mss will not be considered.

Summersdale Publishers Ltd
46 West Street, Chichester PO19 1RP
☎01243 771107   Fax 01243 786300
✉ submissions@summersdale.com
www.summersdale.com

Directors *Stewart Ferris, Alastair Williams*
Commissioning Editor *Jennifer Barclay*
Approx. Annual Turnover £1 million

Founded 1990. Publishes travel literature, martial arts, self-help, cookery, humour and gift books. TITLES *How to be a Writer; How to Get Published; Pint-Sized Ireland; Shape Shifter; Exam-Busting Tips*. 50–60 titles a year. No unsolicited mss; synopses and ideas welcome by e-mail.
ROYALTIES paid.

Sussex Academic Press
PO Box 2950, Brighton BN2 5SP
☎01273 699533   Fax 01273 621262
✉ edit@sussex-academic.co.uk
www.sussex-academic.co.uk
Managing Director *Anthony Grahame*
Approx. Annual Turnover £250,000

Founded 1994. Academic publisher. DIVISION/IMPRINT **Sussex Academic** TITLES *Art, Crime & Madness; Dugald Stewart – The Pride and Ornament of Scotland; Human Rights & Religion*. **Alpha Press** TITLE *First and Last Editions – England's Second-Hand Bookshops*. 40 titles in 2004. No unsolicited material; send letter of inquiry in the first instance.
ROYALTIES annually.

Sutton Publishing Ltd
Phoenix Mill, Thrupp, Stroud GL5 2BU
☎01453 731114   Fax 01453 731117
✉ publishing@sutton-publishing.co.uk
Managing Director *Jeremy Yates-Round*
Senior Commissioning Editors *Jaqueline Mitchell* (biography), *Christopher Feeney* (general history), *Jonathan Falconer* (military), *Simon Fletcher* (local history)

Founded 1978. Acquired by **Haynes Publishing** in March 2000. Publishes academic, archaeology, biography, countryside, history, military, aviation, regional interest, local history. About 200 titles a year. Send synopses rather than complete mss.
ROYALTIES twice-yearly.

Authors' Rating Having started as a regional publisher, Sutton has branched out into general non-fiction. Strong on popular history.

Swan Hill Press (An imprint of Quiller Publishing Ltd)
Wykey House, Wykey, Shrewsbury SY4 1JA
☎01939 261616   Fax 01939 261606
✉ info@quillerbooks.com
Managing Director *Andrew Johnston*
Specialises in practical books on all country and field sports activities. Publishes books on fishing, shooting, gundog training, falconry, equestrian, deer, cookery. About 15 titles a year. Unsolicited mss must include s.a.e.
ROYALTIES twice-yearly.

Sweet & Maxwell Group
100 Avenue Road, London NW3 3PF
☎020 7393 7000   Fax 020 7393 7010
✉ customerservices@sweetandmaxwell.co.uk
www.sweetandmaxwell.co.uk
Managing Director *Peter Lake*
Founded 1799. Part of the Thomson Corporation. Publishes materials in all media; looseleaf works, journals, law reports, CD-ROMs and online. Not interested in non-legal material. The legal and professional list is varied and contains academic titles as well as treatises and reference works in the legal and related professional fields. IMPRINTS **Sweet & Maxwell**; **W. Green (Scotland)**; **Thomson Round Hall (Ireland)**. Over 1100 products, including 180 looseleafs, 80 periodicals, more than 40 digital products and online information services and 200 new titles each year. Ideas welcome. Writers with legal/professional projects in mind are advised to contact the Legal Business Unit at the earliest possible stage in order to lay the groundwork for best design, production and marketing of a project.
ROYALTIES and fees according to contract.

Tango Books Ltd
PO Box 32595, London W4 5YD
☎020 8996 9970   Fax 020 8996 9977
✉ sales@tangobooks.co.uk
Directors *David Fielder, Sheri Safran*
Founded 1981. Children's books publisher with international co-edition potential: pop-ups, three-dimensional, novelty, picture and board books, 1000 words maximum. About 30 titles a year. Approach with preliminary letter, sample material and s.a.e. in the first instance.
FEES paid.

Taschen UK
13 Old Burlington Street, London W1S 3AJ
☎020 7437 4350   Fax 020 7437 4360
www.taschen.com

UK office of the German photographic, art and architecture publisher. Editorial office in Cologne (see entry under *European Publishers*).

I.B.Tauris & Co. Ltd
6 Salem Road, London W2 4BU
☎020 7243 1225   Fax 020 7243 1226
✉ mail@ibtauris.com
www.ibtauris.com
Chairman/Publisher *Iradj Bagherzade*
Managing Director *Jonathan McDonnell*
Founded 1984. Independent publisher. Publishes general non-fiction and academic in the fields of international relations, religion, current affairs, history, politics, cultural, media and film studies, Middle East studies. Distributes Philip Wilson Publishers, The Federal Trust and the Khalili Collections worldwide. IMPRINTS **Tauris Parke Books** Illustrated books on architecture, travel, design and culture. **Tauris Parke Paperbacks** Trade titles, including art, travel and biography. **British Academic Press** and **Tauris Academic Studies** Academic monographs. **Radcliffe Press** Colonial history and biography. Unsolicited synopses and book proposals welcome.
ROYALTIES twice-yearly.

Authors' Rating Imprint Radcliffe Press may require authors to contribute towards costs of publication.

Taylor & Francis (An imprint of Taylor & Francis Group, the academic division of T&F Informa plc)
2 Park Square, Milton Park, Abingdon OX14 4RN
☎020 7017 6000   Fax 020 7017 6699
www.tandf.co.uk
CEO *Roger Horton*
Managing Director *Jeremy North*
Publishing Directors (based in USA) *John Lavender, Maryanne Russell*
Approx. Annual Turnover £246.3 million
Specialises in scientific, technical and medical books for professionals, university students and academics in the following subjects: built environment, architecture, planning and civil engineering; biology, including genetics, plant science, molecular biology and biotechnology; medicine, including cardiology, dentistry, dermatology, neurology, oncology, psychiatry and urology; nursing. About 1100 titles a year. Send detailed proposal plus c.v. and sample chapters. Proposal requirements and submission proce-

dures can be found on the website. No poetry, fiction, travel or astrology.

ROYALTIES annually.

Authors' Rating One of those companies that barely registers with authors until they look at some of the famous imprints that are gathered under the corporate umbrella. Very much into higher education and reference, further expansion is predicted. Recent restructuring reflects the growing importance of the US market. Among recent deals is an agreement to be publisher for the International Institute of Strategic Studies.

Teach Yourself
See **Hodder Headline Ltd**

Telegraph Books
1 Canada Square, Canary Wharf, London E14 5DT
☎020 7538 6826   Fax 020 7538 6064
www.telegraphbooksdirect.co.uk
Owner *Telegraph Group Ltd*
Publisher *Morven Knowles*
Approx. Annual Turnover £3 million

Concentrates on Telegraph branded books in association/collaboration with other publishers. Also runs Telegraph Books Direct, a direct mail, phone-line bookselling service and off-the-page sales for other publishers' books. Publishes general non-fiction: reference, personal finance, health, gardening, guides, sport, humour, puzzles and games. Mainly interested in books if a Telegraph link exists. About 50 titles a year. No unsolicited material.

ROYALTIES twice-yearly.

Temple Lodge Publishing Ltd
Hillside House, The Square, Forest Row RH18 5ES
☎01342 824000
✉ office@templelodge.com
www.templelodge.com
www.clairviewbooks.com
Chairman *Mr R. Pauli*
Manager *Mr S. Gulbekian*
Approx. Annual Turnover £150,000

Founded in 1990 to develop the work of Rudolf Steiner (see also **Rudolf Steiner Press**). Publishes non-fiction: mind, body & spirit, current affairs, health and therapy. IMPRINT **Clairview Books** *Mr S. Gulbekian* General books challenging conventional thinking TITLES *Dreaming War* Gore Vidal; *Foodwise* Wendy Cook; *My Descent Into Death* Howard Storm. 15 titles in

2004. No unsolicited material; send initial letter of enquiry. No poetry or fiction.

ROYALTIES annually.

Texere
See **Thomson Learning**

Thames and Hudson Ltd
181A High Holborn, London WC1V 7QX
☎020 7845 5000   Fax 020 7845 5050
✉ mail@thameshudson.co.uk
www.thamesandhudson.com
Managing Director *Thomas Neurath*
Editorial Head *Jamie Camplin*
Approx. Annual Turnover £25 million

Publishes art, archaeology, architecture and design, biography, fashion, garden and landscape design, graphics, history, illustrated and fine editions, mythology, photography, popular culture, style, travel and topography. SERIES *World of Art*; *Hip Hotels*; *StyleCity*; *New Horizons*; *Most Beautiful Villages*; *Earth From the Air*. TITLES *Fashion Illustration Next*; *Hockney's Pictures*; *Sensation*; *The Shock of the New*; *The Book of Kells*; *Germaine Greer's The Boy*; *Graffiti World*; *The Way We Live*; *At Home in Greece*; *The Eco-Design Handbook*; *The Seventy Great Inventions of the Ancient World*; *The Complete World of Greek Mythology*; *The Human Past*. 200 titles a year. Send preliminary letter and outline before mss.

ROYALTIES twice-yearly.

Authors' Rating Quality illustrated books on art and design. The World of Art series, a huge range of modestly priced, scholarly books, is probably the best of its kind. Financial success rests on producing the sort of books that easily carry over to other languages. Forthcoming publications include an *Artist's Handbook* which bears an uncanny resemblance to a more famous title.

Third Millennium Publishing
Farringdon House, 105–107 Farringdon Road, London EC1R 3BU
☎020 7837 4004   Fax 020 7837 5005
✉ info@tmiltd.com
www.tmiltd.com
Chairman/Managing Director *Julian Platt*
Approx. Annual Turnover £500,000

Founded 1999 as a highly illustrated book publisher in the international museum, heritage and art gallery markets. Also some 'coffee-table' titles in association with various Oxbridge colleges, independent schools and military organisations.

10–15 titles annually. Unsolicited material welcome; approach in writing with c.v., book synopsis, target market and any supporting information. No fiction.

ROYALTIES annually.

Thoemmes
See **The Continuum International Publishing Group Limited**

Thomson Learning
High Holborn House, 50–51 Bedford Row, London WC1R 4LR
☎020 7067 2500   Fax 020 7067 2600
www.thomson.com
CEO (Worldwide) *Ron Schlosser*
CEO (Thomson Learning EMEA) *Charles Iossi*
Publishing Director (Thomson Learning EMEA) *John Yates*

Founded 1993. Formerly International Thomson Publishing, part of the Thomson Corporation and as such has offices worldwide with the UK office being reported to by Copenhagen (for Europe), Turkey (Middle East) and South Africa. Acquired Texere in 2003. Publishes education. TITLES *Management and Cost Accounting* Drury; *Strategy – Process, Content, Contact* DeWit and Meyer. Unsolicited material aimed at students is welcome but telephone in the first instance to check out the idea.

ROYALTIES vary according to contract.

Thomson Round Hall (Ireland)
See **Sweet & Maxwell Group**

Stanley Thornes (Publishers) Ltd
See **Nelson Thornes Ltd**

F.A. Thorpe (Publishing)
The Green, Bradgate Road, Anstey LE7 7FU
☎0116 236 4325   Fax 0116 234 0205
Group Chief Executive *Robert Thirlby*
Approx. Annual Turnover £6 million

Founded in 1964 to supply large print books to libraries. Part of the Ulverscroft Group Ltd. Publishes fiction and non-fiction large print books. No educational, gardening or books that would not be suitable for large print. DIVISIONS **Charnwood**; **Ulverscroft**. IMPRINTS **Linford Romance**; **Linford Mystery**; **Linford Western**. 456 titles in 2004. No unsolicited material.

Thorsons/Element
See **HarperCollins Publishers Ltd**

Time Out Guides
See **The Random House Group Ltd**

Time Warner Books UK
Brettenham House, Lancaster Place, London WC2E 7EN
☎020 7911 8000   Fax 020 7911 8100
✉ uk@twbg.co.uk
www.twbg.co.uk
Chief Executive/Publisher *Ursula Mackenzie*
Approx. Annual Turnover £40 million

Founded 1988 as Little, Brown & Co. (UK). Part of Time Warner. Began by importing its US parent company's titles and in 1990 launched its own illustrated non-fiction list. Two years later the company took over former Macdonald & Co. Publishes hardback and paperback fiction, literary fiction, crime, science fiction and fantasy; and general non-fiction including true crime, biography and autobiography, cinema, gardening, history, humour, popular science, travel, reference, cookery, wines and spirits.

IMPRINTS **Little, Brown** *Ursula Mackenzie, Richard Beswick, Tim Whiting, Antonia Hodgson, Hilary Hale* Hardback fiction and general non-fiction; **Abacus** *Richard Beswick* Literary fiction and non-fiction paperbacks; **Atom** *Darren Nash* Young adult/teen paperbacks; **Audio** *Sarah Shrubb* (see entry under **Audio Books**); **Orbit** *Tim Holman* Science fiction and fantasy; **Time Warner** *Joanne Coen, Barbara Daniel, Hilary Hale* Mass-market fiction and non-fiction hardbacks and paperbacks; **X Libris** *Sarah Shrubb* Women's erotica; **Virago Press** (see entry). Approach in writing in the first instance. No unsolicited mss.

ROYALTIES twice-yearly.

Authors' Rating A quality list is based on strong author publisher relations.

Times Books
See **HarperCollins Publishers Ltd**

Titan Books
144 Southwark Street, London SE1 0UP
☎020 7620 0200   Fax 020 7620 0032
✉ editorial@titanmail.com
www.titanbooks.com
Managing Director *Nick Landau*
Editorial Director *Katy Wild*

Founded 1981. Now a leader in the publication of graphic novels and film and television tie-ins. Publishes comic books/graphic novels, film and television titles. IMPRINT **Titan Books** TITLES *Batman*; *The Battlestar Galactica Companion*; *CSI:*

Crime Scene Investigation; Scooby-Doo; The Simpsons; Star Wars; Superman; Transformers; Wallace & Gromit. About 200 titles a year. No unsolicited fiction or children's books. Ideas for film and TV titles considered; send synopsis/outline with sample chapter. No e-mail submissions. Author guidelines available. ROYALTIES twice-yearly.

Tor
See **Macmillan Publishers Ltd**

Transita Ltd
3 Newtec Place, Magdalen Road, Oxford OX4 1RE
☎01865 204393   Fax 01862 248780
✉ info@transita.co.uk
www.transita.co.uk
Managing Director *Giles Lewis*
Editorial Director *Nikki Read*

New, independent publishing house founded in 2004 devoted to publishing contemporary fiction for women 45-plus. 'Transita are novels about women who are evolving, independent spirits with the confidence to accept imperfection, embrace contradictions and explore the truths and desires that propel their lives.' Synopsis and three chapters required.

Transworld Publishers, a division of the Random House Group Ltd
61–63 Uxbridge Road, London W5 5SA
☎020 8579 2652   Fax 020 8579 5479
✉ info@transworld-publishers.co.uk
www.booksattransworld.co.uk
Managing Director *Larry Finlay*
Publisher *Patrick Janson-Smith*
Deputy Publisher *Bill Scott-Kerr*
Senior Publishing Director *Francesca Liversidge*
Approx. Annual Turnover £72 million

Founded 1950. A subsidiary of **Random House, Inc.**, New York, which in turn is a wholly-owned subsidiary of **Bertelsmann AG**, Germany. Publishes general fiction and non-fiction, gardening, sports and leisure. IMPRINTS **Bantam** *Francesca Liversidge;* **Bantam Press** *Sally Gaminara;* **Corgi** & **Black Swan** *Bill Scott-Kerr;* **Doubleday** *Marianne Velmans;* **Channel 4 Books** *Doug Young;* **Eden** *Susanna Wadeson;* **Expert Books** *Gareth Pottle.* AUTHORS Monica Ali, Kate Atkinson, Charlotte Bingham, Dan Brown, Bill Bryson, Lee Child, Jilly Cooper, Ben Elton, Nicholas Evans, Frederick Forsyth, David Gemmell, Tess Gerritsen, Robert Goddard, Joanne Harris, Stephen Hawking, D.G. Hessayon, John Irving, Sophie Kinsella,

Anne McCaffrey, Paul McKenna, Andy McNab, John O'Farrell, Terry Pratchett, Patricia Scanlan, Gerald Seymour, Danielle Steel, Joanna Trollope. No unsolicited mss. OVERSEAS ASSOCIATES Random House Australia Pty Ltd; Random House New Zealand; Random House (Pty) Ltd (South Africa). ROYALTIES twice-yearly.

Authors' Rating Leading the annual paperback Fastseller list, Transworld shows it has much more going for it than the superselling *Da Vinci Code.*

Travel Publishing Ltd
7A Apollo House, Calleva Park, Aldermaston RG7 8TN
☎0118 981 7777   Fax 0118 982 0077
✉ info@travelpublishing.co.uk
www.travelpublishing.co.uk
Directors *Peter Robinson, Chris Day*

Founded in 1997 by two former directors of **Reed Elsevier plc.** Publishes travel guides covering places of interest, accommodation, food, drink and specialist shops in Britain and Ireland. SERIES *Hidden Places; Hidden Inns; Country Pubs; Country Living Rural Guides* (in conjunction with *Country Living* magazine); *Golfers Guides; Off the Motorway.* Over 40 titles in print. Welcomes unsolicited material; send letter in the first instance. ROYALTIES twice-yearly.

Trentham Books Ltd
Westview House, 734 London Road, Stoke-on-Trent ST4 5NP
☎01782 745567/844699   Fax 01782 745553
www.trentham-books.co.uk
Directors *Dr Gillian Klein, Barbara Wiggins*
Approx. Annual Turnover £1 million

Publishes education (nursery, school to higher), social sciences, intercultural studies, gender studies and law for professional readers *not* for children and parents. Also academic and professional journals. No fiction, biography or poetry. Over 30 titles a year. Unsolicited mss, synopses and ideas welcome if relevant to their interests. Material only returned if adequate s.a.e. sent. ROYALTIES annually.

Trident Press Ltd
Empire House, 175 Piccadilly, London W1J 9TB
☎020 7491 8770   Fax 020 7491 8664
✉ admin@tridentpress.com

www.tridentpress.com
Managing Director *Peter Vine*
Approx. Annual Turnover £550,000
Founded 1997. Publishes TV tie-ins, natural history, travel, geography, underwater/marine life, history, archaeology, culture and fiction. DIVISIONS **Fiction/General Publishing** *Paula Vine*, Natural History *Peter Vine*. TITLES *Red Sea Sharks*; *The Elysium Testament*; *BBC Wildlife Specials*; *UAE in Focus*. No unsolicited mss; synopses and ideas welcome, particularly TV tie-ins. Approach in writing or *brief* communications by e-mail, fax or telephone. ROYALTIES annually.

Trotman & Co. Ltd
2 The Green, Richmond TW9 1PL
☎020 8486 1150   Fax 020 8486 1161
www.trotman.co.uk
Managing Director *Toby Trotman*
Editorial Director *Mina Patria*
Approx. Annual Turnover £3 million

Publishes general careers books, higher education guides, teaching support material, employment and training resources. TITLES *Degree Course Offers*; *The Student Book*; *Trotman Green Guides*; *Students' Money Matters*; *CRAC Degree Course Guides*; *Real Life Guides*; *Real Life Issues*; *Newscheck* (journal for careers professionals); *Careers 2006*. About 60 titles a year. Unsolicited material welcome. ROYALTIES twice-yearly.

TSO (The Stationery Office)
St Crispins, Duke Street, Norwich NR3 1PD
☎01603 622211   Fax 01603 694313
(Editorial)
www.tso.co.uk
Chief Executive *Tim Hailstone*
Approx. Annual Turnover £250 million

Formerly HMSO, which was founded in 1786. Became part of the private sector in October 1996. Publisher of material sponsored by Parliament, government departments and other official bodies. Also commercial publishing in the following broad categories: business and professional, environment, transport, education and law. 11,000 new titles each year with 50,000 titles in print.

Twenty First Century Publishers Ltd
Braunton Barn, Kiln Lane, Isfield TN22 5UE
☎01892 522802
✉TFCP@btinternet.com

www.twentyfirstcenturypublishers.com
Chairman *Fred Piechoczek*
Founded 2002. Publishes general fiction, financial thrillers and crime. Welcomes submissions by e-mail: manuscripts@connectfree.co.uk (contact *Fred Piechoczek*). Send brief synopsis in the body of the e-mail with extracts from the book in a file attachment (two to three chapters from anywhere in the book). No non-fiction or children's. ROYALTIES twice-yearly.

20/20
See **The X Press**

UCL Press
See **Cavendish Publishing Limited**

Ulverscroft
See **F.A. Thorpe (Publishing)**

Unichrome
See **Jarrold Publishing**

University Presses of California, Columbia & Princeton Ltd
1 Oldlands Way, Bognor Regis PO22 9SA
☎01243 842165   Fax 01243 842167
✉lois@upccp.demon.co.uk

Publishes academic titles only. US-based editorial offices. Enquiries only. Over 200 titles a year.

Usborne Publishing Ltd
83–85 Saffron Hill, London EC1N 8RT
☎020 7430 2800   Fax 020 7430 1562
✉mail@usborne.co.uk
www.usborne.com
Managing Director *Peter Usborne*
Publishing Director *Jenny Tyler*
Approx. Annual Turnover £20 million

Founded 1973. Publishes non-fiction, fiction, art and activity books, puzzle books and music for children, young adults and pre-school. Some titles for parents. Up to 250 titles a year. Non-fiction books are written in-house to a specific format and therefore unsolicited mss are not normally welcome. Ideas which may be developed in-house are sometimes considered. Fiction for children will be considered. Keen to hear from new illustrators and designers. ROYALTIES twice-yearly.

Authors' Rating A children's publisher that finds favour with parents who can learn a thing or two from an imaginative non-fiction list. But fiction too is growing – up to 30 titles a year.

Vanguard Press
See **Pegasus Elliot Mackenzie Publishers Ltd**

Ventura
See **Penguin Group (UK)**

Vermilion
See **The Random House Group Ltd**

Verso
6 Meard Street, London W1V 3HR
☎020 7437 3546   Fax 020 7734 0059
www.versobooks.com
Managing Director *Guy Bentham*
Approx. Annual Turnover £2 million

Formerly New Left Books which grew out of the *New Left Review*. Publishes politics, history, sociology, economics, philosophy, cultural studies, feminism. TITLES *Wobblies! A Graphic History* eds. Paul Buhle and Nicole Schulman; *The Soviet Century* Moshe Lewin; *NHS plc: The Privatisation of our Health Care* Allyson M. Pollock; *Street-Fighting Years* Tariq Ali; *Planet of Slums* Mike Davis. No unsolicited mss; synopses and ideas for books welcome. OVERSEAS OFFICE in New York.
ROYALTIES annually.

Authors' Rating Dubbed by the *Bookseller* as 'one of the most successful small independent publishers'.

Viking
See **Penguin Group (UK)**

Vintage
See **The Random House Group Ltd**

Virago Press
Time Warner Book Group UK, Brettenham House, Lancaster Place, London WC2E 7EN
☎020 7911 8000   Fax 020 7911 8100
www.virago.co.uk
Publisher *Lennie Goodings*
Editorial Director *Antonia Hodgson*
Editor, Virago Modern Classics *Jill Foulston*

An imprint of **Time Warner Books UK**. Founded in 1973 by Carmen Callil, Virago publishes women's literature, both fiction and non-fiction. IMPRINTS **Virago Modern Classics** 19th and 20th-century fiction reprints by writers such as Daphne du Maurier, Angela Carter and Edith Wharton. Virago AUTHORS include Margaret Atwood, Maya Angelou, Jennifer Belle, Waris Dirie, Sarah Dunant, Germaine Greer, Michèle Roberts, Gillian

Slovo, Talitha Stevenson, Natasha Walter, Sarah Waters. 50 titles a year.
ROYALTIES twice-yearly.

Authors' Rating The first name in women's publishing has gained marketing strength from its association with Time Warner. A team of young editors favour young writers with something new to say.

Virgin Books Ltd
Thames Wharf Studios, Rainville Road, London W6 9HT
☎020 7386 3300   Fax 020 7386 3360
✉ info@virgin-books.co.uk
www.virgin.com/books
Managing Director *KT Forster*
Approx. Annual Turnover £10 million

The Virgin Group's book publishing company. Publishes non-fiction, reference and large-format illustrated books on lifestyle, health, music, sport, biography, crime, film, TV and current affairs. No poetry, short stories, individual novels, children's books. DIVISIONS **Non-fiction** IMPRINT **Virgin** Editorial Director *Carolyn Thorne*, Commissioning Editor/Scout (esp. music) *Stuart Slater*, Commissioning Editor *Kirstie Addis*. **Fiction** IMPRINTS **Virgin**; **Black Lace** Senior Editor *Kerri Sharp* Erotic fiction 'written by women for women'; **Nexus** Editor *Adam Nevill* Erotic fiction.
ROYALTIES twice-yearly.

Vision On
See **Omnibus Press**

The Vital Spark
See **Neil Wilson Publishing Ltd**

Voyager
See **HarperCollins Publishers Ltd**

University of Wales Press
10 Columbus Walk, Brigantine Place, Cardiff CF10 4UP
☎029 2049 6899   Fax 029 2049 6108
✉ press@press.wales.ac.uk
www.wales.ac.uk/press
Director *Ashley Drake*
Deputy Director *Richard Houdmont*
Approx. Annual Turnover £500,000

Founded 1922. Publishes academic and scholarly books in English and Welsh in four core areas: history, Welsh and Celtic Studies, European Studies, religion and philosophy. IMPRINTS **GPC Books**; **Gwasg Prifysgol Cymru**;

University of Wales Press TITLES *Princesses of Wales* Deborah Fisher; *In Defence of Multinational Citizenship* Siobhán Harty and Michael Murphy; *Medieval Blood* Bettna Bildhauer. Unsolicited mss considered but see website for further guidance.
ROYALTIES annually.

Walker Books Ltd
87 Vauxhall Walk, London SE11 5HJ
☎020 7793 0909   Fax 020 7587 1123
✉ editorial@walker.co.uk
www.walkerbooks.co.uk
Publisher *Jane Winterbotham*
Editorial Director *Gill Evans*
Editors *Deirdre McDermott* (picture books), *Caroline Royds* (fiction, non-fiction & gift books), *Denise Johnstone-Burt* (picture books, board & novelty), *Lorraine Taylor* (character, audio, stationery & merchandising)
Approx. Annual Turnover £34.6 million
Founded 1979. Publishes illustrated children's books, children's fiction and non-fiction. TITLES *Maisy* Lucy Cousins; *Where's Wally?* Martin Handford; *Five Minutes' Peace* Jill Murphy; *Can't You Sleep, Little Bear?* Martin Waddell and Barbara Firth; *Guess How Much I Love You* Sam McBratney and Anita Jeram; *Alex Rider* series. About 300 titles a year.
ROYALTIES twice-yearly.

Authors' Rating Even with a weak dollar hitting US income, Walker continues to advance on overseas sales which may help to account for the nice things authors say about the company.

Wallflower Press
4th Floor, 26 Shacklewell Lane, London E8 2EZ
☎020 7690 0115   Fax 020 7690 4333
✉ info@wallflowerpress.co.uk
www.wallflowerpress.co.uk
Editorial Director *Yoram Allon*
Chief Editor *Del Cullen*
Approx. Annual Turnover £150,000
Founded 1999. Publishes academic and popular film studies and related media and cultural studies. SERIES *Short Cuts* Introductory undergraduate books; *Director's Cuts* Studies on significant international film-makers; *24 Frames* Anthologies focusing on national and regional cinemas. Over 25 titles a year. Unsolicited mss, synopses and proposals welcome. No fiction or academic material not related to the moving image.
ROYALTIES annually.

Ward Lock
See **Octopus Publishing Group**

Ward Lock Educational Co. Ltd
BIC Ling Kee House, 1 Christopher Road, East Grinstead RH19 3BT
☎01342 318980   Fax 01342 410980
✉ wle@lingkee.com
www.wardlockeducational.com
Owner *Ling Kee (UK) Ltd*
Founded 1952. Publishes educational books (primary, middle, secondary, teaching manuals) for all subjects, specialising in maths, science, geography, reading and English and currently focusing on Key Stages 1 and 2.

Frederick Warne
See **Penguin Group (UK)**

Franklin Watts
See **Hachette Children's Books**

Watts Publishing Group
See **Hachette Children's Books**

Wayland
See **Hachette Children's Books**

Weidenfeld & Nicolson
See **The Orion Publishing Group Ltd**

West Highland Series
See **House of Lochar**

Wharncliffe Books
47 Church Street, Barnsley S70 2AS
☎01226 734222   Fax 01226 734438
✉ enquiries@wharncliffebooks.co.uk
www.wharncliffebooks.co.uk
Commissioning Editor *Rupert Harding*
An imprint of **Pen & Sword Books Ltd**. Wharncliffe is the book and magazine publishing arm of an old-established, independently owned newspaper publishing and printing house. Publishes local history throughout the UK, focusing on nostalgia and old photographs. SERIES *Foul Deeds; Local History Companions; Pals; Aspects.* No unsolicited mss; synopses and ideas welcome.
ROYALTIES twice-yearly.

Which? Books
2 Marylebone Road, London NW1 4DF
☎020 7770 6000   Fax 020 7770 7660
www.which.net

Editorial Director *Helen Parker*

Founded 1957. Publishing arm of the Consumers' Association, a registered charity. Publishes non-fiction: information and reference on food, health, consumer markets personal finance, property, technology, consumer law, careers and lifestage events. All titles offer direct value to the consumer. IMPRINT **Which? Books** TITLES *The Good Food Guide*; *The Good Skiing and Snowboarding Guide*; *The Which? Guide to Good Hotels*; *Which? Medicine*; *Wills and Probate*; *Be Your Own Financial Adviser*. 25–30 titles a year. No unsolicited mss; send synopses and ideas only.

ROYALTIES, if applicable, twice-yearly.

Whittet Books Ltd

Hill Farm, Stonham Road, Cotton,
Stowmarket IP14 4RQ
☎01449 781877   Fax 01449 781898
✉ annabel@whittet.dircon.co.uk
www.whittetbooks.com

Managing Director *Annabel Whittet*

Publishes natural history, pets, poultry, horses, domestic livestock, horticulture, rural interest. Unsolicited mss, synopses and ideas for books welcome.

ROYALTIES twice-yearly.

Whurr Publishers Ltd

19B Compton Terrace, London N1 2UN
☎020 7359 5979   Fax 020 7226 5290
✉ info@whurr.co.uk
www.whurr.co.uk

Chairman/Managing Director *Colin Whurr*
Approx. Annual Turnover £1 million

Founded in 1987. Acquired by John Wiley & Sons in April 2005. Publishes speech and language therapy, nursing, psychology, psychotherapy, audiology, special education including dyslexia, ADHD, autism and Downs syndrome. No fiction and general trade books. 60 titles in 2004. Unsolicited mss, synopses and ideas welcome within their specialist fields only. 'Whurr Publishers believes authors can be best served by a small, specialised company combining old-fashioned service with the latest publishing technology.'

ROYALTIES twice-yearly.

Whydown Books Limited

Sedlescombe TN33 0RN
☎01424 870875   Fax 01424 870083
✉ readerspost@whydownbooks.com
www.whydownbooks.com

Chairman *Dick Nesbitt-Dufort*

Managing & Finance Director *Chris Martin*
Editorial Head *Pamela Richards*

Founded 2002. Publishes biography, fiction, general interest with a slant towards writers with first-hand experience of distant places and profound events. TITLES *Spies and Lovers* Adrian Hill; *Black Lysander* John Nesbitt-Dufort; *The Apothecary's Gift* Bradley Bernarde; *Chinnery's Hotel* Jaysinh Birje. No academic, children's or poetry at present. No unsolicited mss. Synopses and ideas welcome. Approach by letter or e-mail with idea and writing history.

ROYALTIES twice-yearly.

Wild Goose Publications

Iona Community, 4th Floor, The Savoy Centre, 140 Sauchiehall Street, Glasgow G2 3DH
☎0141 332 6292   Fax 0141 332 1090
✉ admin@ionabooks.com
www.ionabooks.com

Editorial Head *Sandra Kramer*
Approx. Annual Turnover £200,000

The publishing house of the Iona Community, established in the Celtic Christian tradition of St Columba, publishes books, tapes and CDs on holistic spirituality, social justice, political and peace issues, healing, innovative approaches to worship, song and material for meditation and reflection.

Wiley Europe Ltd

The Atrium, Southern Gate, Chichester
PO19 8SQ
☎01243 779777   Fax 01243 775878
www.wiley.com

Managing Director *Dr John Jarvis*
Publishing Directors *Mike Davis, Stephen Smith*
Approx. Annual Turnover £88 million

Founded 1807. US parent company. Publishes professional, reference trade and text books, scientific, technical and biomedical.

DIVISIONS **Architecture, Higher Education Group** *Vivien Ward*; **Business, Computing, Finance, General Interest** *Sarah Stevens*; **Communications, Engineering, Statistics** *Ann-Marie Halligan*; **Health Sciences** *Deborah Dixon*; **Physical Sciences & Reference Publishing Group** *Ernest Kirkwood*.

ROYALTIES annually.

Authors' Rating With an ever growing list of scientific, technical and medical books, Wiley is among the top educational and professional publishers. Academic authors are attracted by the American connection. Online publishing is set to increase.

Wiley-Academy

John Wiley & Sons, 4th Floor, International House, 7 High Street, Ealing Broadway, London W5 5DB

☎020 8326 3800   Fax 020 8326 3801

Chairman *John Jarvis*
Commissioning Editor *Helen Castle*

Founded 1969. Became part of the **John Wiley & Sons, Inc.** group in 1997. Publishes architectural design. No unsolicited mss; synopses and ideas only.

ROYALTIES annually.

Neil Wilson Publishing Ltd

Suite 303, The Pentagon Centre, 36 Washington Street, Glasgow G3 8AZ

☎0141 221 1117   Fax 0141 221 5363

✉ info@nwp.co.uk
www.nwp.co.uk
www.11-9.co.uk

Managing Director/Editorial Director *Neil Wilson*
Editorial Administrator *Sallie Moffat*
Approx. Annual Turnover £250,000

Founded 1992. Publishes Scottish interest and history, biography, humour and hillwalking, whisky; also cookery. IMPRINTS **The In Pinn** Outdoor pursuits; **The Angels' Share** Whisky, drink and food-related subjects; **The Vital Spark** Humour; **NWP** History, biography, reference, true crime; **11:9** Scottish fiction. About 10–15 titles a year. Unsolicited mss, synopses and ideas welcome. No politics, academic or technical.

ROYALTIES twice-yearly.

Philip Wilson Publishers Ltd

109 Drysdale Street, The Timber Yard, London N1 6ND

☎020 7033 9900   Fax 020 7033 9922

✉ pwilson@philip-wilson.co.uk
www.philip-wilson.co.uk

Chairman *Philip Wilson*

Founded 1976. Publishes art, art history, antiques and collectibles. About 20 titles a year.

Wimbledon Publishing Company

75–76 Blackfriars Road, London SE1 8HA

☎020 7401 4200   Fax 020 7401 4201

✉ editor@wpcpress.com
www.wpcpress.com

Managing Director *Kamaljit Sood*
General Manager *Renu Sood*

Founded in 1992 as a publisher of school texts, going on to launch Anthem Press, an academic and general interest imprint focusing on history, politics, economics, international affairs, literature and culture. IMPRINTS **Anthem Press** *Paolo Cabrelli*; **WPC Education** *K. Sood*. Welcomes mss, synopses and ideas for books. PARTNER ORGANISATION Stylus Publishing LLC, Sterling, VA, US.

ROYALTIES annually.

Windhorse Publications

11 Park Road, Moseley B13 8AB

☎0121 449 9696   Fax 0121 449 9191

✉ jnanasiddhi@windhorsepublications.com
www.windhorsepublications.com

Chairman/Editorial Head *Jnanasiddhi*
Approx. Annual Turnover £250,000

Founded 1977. Publishes meditation and Buddhism. Associated with the FWBO, a worldwide Buddhist movement. Publishes across the Buddhist traditions. Unsolicited mss, synopses and ideas welcome; approach by letter or e-mail in the first instance.

ROYALTIES quarterly.

Wise Publications

See **Omnibus Press**

WIT Press

Ashurst Lodge, Ashurst, Southampton SO40 7AA

☎023 8029 3223   Fax 023 8029 2853

✉ marketing@witpress.com
www.witpress.com

Owner *Computational Mechanics International Ltd, Southampton*
Chairman/Managing Director/Editorial Head *Professor C.A. Brebbia*

Founded in 1980 as Computational Mechanics Publications to publish engineering analysis titles. Changed to WIT Press to reflect the increased range of publications. Publishes scientific and technical, mainly at postgraduate level and above, including architecture, environmental engineering, bioengineering. TITLES *The Sustainable City*; *Handling Missing Data*; *Human Exposure to Electromagnetic Fields*; *Computational Ballistics*. 50 titles in 2004. Unsolicited mss, synopses and ideas welcome; approach by post or e-mail. No non-scientific or technical material or lower level (school and college-level texts). OVERSEAS SUBSIDIARY Computational Mechanics, Inc., Billerica, USA.

ROYALTIES annually.

Wizard Books

See **Icon Books Ltd**

Oswald Wolff Books
See **Berg Publishers**

The Women's Press
27 Goodge Street, London W1T 2LD
☎020 7636 3992   Fax 020 7637 1866
www.the-womens-press.com
Managing Director *Stella Kane*
Approx. Annual Turnover £1 million

Part of the Namara Group. First title published in 1978. Publishes women only: quality fiction and non-fiction. Fiction usually has a female protagonist and a woman-centred theme. International writers and subject matter encouraged. Non-fiction: books for and about women generally; gender politics, race politics, disability, feminist theory, health and psychology, literary criticism. IMPRINTS **Women's Press Classics**; **Livewire Books for Teenagers** Fiction and non-fiction series for young adults. About 50 titles a year. Synopses and ideas for books welcome. No mss without previous letter, synopsis and sample material.
ROYALTIES twice-yearly.

Woodhead Publishing Ltd
Abington Hall, Abington, Cambridge CB1 6AH
☎01223 891358   Fax 01223 893694
✉ wp@woodhead-publishing.com
www.woodheadpublishing.com
Chairman *Alan Jessup*
Managing Director *Martin Woodhead*
Approx. Annual Turnover £1.5 million

Founded 1989. Publishes engineering, materials technology, textile technology, finance and investment, food technology, environmental science. TITLES *Welding International* (journal); *Reinforced Plastics Durability*; *Meat Science 6e*; *Base Metals Handbook*; *Foreign Exchange Options*. DIVISION **Woodhead Publishing** *Martin Woodhead*. About 50 titles a year. Unsolicited material welcome.
ROYALTIES annually.

Wordsworth Editions Ltd
8B East Street, Ware SG12 9HG
☎01920 465167   Fax 01920 462267
✉ enquiries@wordsworth-editions.com *or* dennis.hart@wordsworth-editions.com (editorial)
www.wordsworth-editions.co.uk
Directors *E. G. Trayler, D. R. Hart*
Approx. Annual Turnover £4 million

Founded 1987. Publishes classics of English and world literature, reference books, poetry, children's classics, military history and special editions. About 75 titles a year. No unsolicited mss.

WPC Education
See **Wimbledon Publishing Company**

X Libris
See **Time Warner Books UK**

The X Press
PO Box 25694, London N17 6FP
☎020 8801 2100   Fax 020 8885 1322
✉ vibes@xpress.co.uk
www.xpress.co.uk
Editorial Director *Dotun Adebayo*
Publisher *Steve Pope*

Launched in 1992 with the cult bestseller *Yardie*, The X Press is the leading publisher of Black-interest fiction in the UK. Also publishes general fiction and children's fiction. IMPRINTS **The X Press; Nia; 20/20**. About 26 titles a year. Send mss rather than synopses or ideas (enclose s.a.e.). No poetry.

Authors' Rating A small company that has done an inestimable service by introducing Black writers to the publishing mainstream. Popular fiction is the mainstay but the list also covers reprints of classic Black fiction.

Y Lolfa Cyf
Talybont, Ceredigion SY24 5AP
☎01970 832304   Fax 01970 832782
✉ ylolfa@ylolfa.com
www.ylolfa.com/
Managing Director *Garmon Gruffudd*
General Editor *Lefi Gruffudd*
Approx. Annual Turnover £800,000

Founded 1967. Small company which publishes mainly in Welsh; has its own four-colour printing and binding facilities. Publishes Welsh language publications; Celtic language tutors; English language books for the Welsh and Celtic tourist trade. Expanding slowly. TITLES *My Kingdom of Books* Richard Booth; *The Welsh Learner's Dictionary* Heini Gruffudd; *The Fight for Welsh Freedom* Gwynfor Evans; *Celtic Vision* John Merion Morris. IMPRINT **Dinas** Part-author-subsidised imprint for non-mainstream books of Welsh interest in English and Welsh. About 50 titles a year. Write first with synopses or ideas.
ROYALTIES twice-yearly.

Yale University Press (London)
47 Bedford Square, London WC1B 3DP
☎020 7079 4900   Fax 020 7079 4901
www.yalebooks.co.uk

Founded 1961. Owned by US parent company. Publishes academic and humanities. About 200 titles (worldwide) a year. Unsolicited mss and synopses welcome if within specialised subject areas.
ROYALTIES annually.

Authors' Rating A publisher with a marvellous talent for turning out scholarly books which appeal to the general reader. Academic writers who want to reach a wider audience take note.

Yellow Jersey Press
See **The Random House Group Ltd**

Zambezi Publishing Ltd
PO Box 221, Plymouth PL2 2YJ
☎01752 367300   Fax 01752 350453
✉ info@zampub.com
www.zampub.com

Chair *Sasha Fenton*
Managing Director *Jan Budkowski*

Founded 1999. Publishes non-fiction: mind, body and spirit, self-help, finance and business. IMPRINT **Zambezi Publishing** TITLES *Sun Signs Made Simple; The Last Bastion; Develop Your ESP; Fortune Telling With Playing Cards.* About 12 titles a year. Send synopsis and sample chapter by mail. Brief e-mail communication acceptable but *no* attachments, please.
ROYALTIES twice-yearly.

Zastrugi Books
PO Box 2963, Brighton BN1 6AW
☎01273 566369   Fax 01273 566369
Chairman *Ken Singleton*

Founded 1997. Publishes English-language teaching books only. No unsolicited mss; synopses and ideas for books welcome.
ROYALTIES twice-yearly.

Zed Books Ltd
7 Cynthia Street, London N1 9JF
☎020 7837 4014   Fax 020 7833 3960
✉ hosie@zedbooks.demon.co.uk
www.zedbooks.co.uk

Approx. Annual Turnover £1.4 million

Founded 1976. Publishes international and Third World affairs, development studies, women's studies, environmental studies, cultural studies, human rights and specific area studies. No fiction, children's or poetry. DIVISIONS **Development & Environment** *Robert Molteno, Dr Anna Hardman;* **Women's Studies, Cultural Studies.** TITLES *Rogue State: A Guide to the World's Only Superpower* William Blum; *Staying Alive* Vandana Shiva; *The Autobiography of Nawal* Nawal El Saadawi. About 60 titles a year. No unsolicited mss; synopses and ideas welcome though.
ROYALTIES annually.

Zero to Ten
See **Evans Brothers Ltd**

Irish Publishers

International Reply Coupons (IRCs) For return postage, IRCs are required (*not* UK postage stamps). These are available from post offices: letters, 60 pence; mss according to weight. For current postal rates from the Republic of Ireland to the UK go to www.letterpost.ie and click on 'Letterpost Services'.

An Gúm
27 Sr. Fhreidric Thuaidh, Baile Átha Cliath 1
☎00 353 1 889 2800   Fax 00 353 1 873 1140
✉ angum@forasnagaeilge.ie
www.gaeilge.ie
Senior Editor *Seosamh Ó Murchú*
Editors *Antain Mag Shamhráin*
Founded 1926. Formerly the Irish language publications branch of the Department of Education and Science. Has now become part of the North/South Language Body, Foras na Gaeilge. Publishes educational, children's, young adult, music, lexicography and general. Little adult fiction or poetry. About 50 titles a year. Unsolicited mss, synopses and ideas for books welcome. Also welcomes reading copies of first and second level school textbooks with a view to translating them into the Irish language.
ROYALTIES annually.

Anvil Books
45 Palmerston Road, Dublin 6
☎00 353 1 497 3628   Fax 00 353 1 496 8263
Managing Director *Rena Dardis*
Founded 1964 with emphasis on Irish history and biography. IMPRINT **The Children's Press**. Publishes Irish history, biography (particularly 1916–22), folklore and children's fiction. No adult fiction, poetry, fantasy, short stories or full-colour books for children. About 7 titles a year. 'Because of promotional requirements, only books by Irish-based authors considered and only books of Irish interest.' Send synopsis only with IRCs (no UK stamps); unsolicited mss not returned.
ROYALTIES annually.

Ashfield Press
30 Linden Grove, Blackrock, Co. Dublin
☎00 353 1 288 9808
✉ suswaine@gofree.indigo.ie
Directors *Susan Waine, John Davey, Gerry O'Connor*
Publishes Irish-interest non-fiction books. TITLES *Lady Icarus; The Weather is a Good Storyteller; Secret Sights II.* Unsolicited mss and synopses welcome. ASSOCIATE COMPANY Ashfield Press Publishing Services.
ROYALTIES twice-yearly.

Atrium
See **Cork University Press**

Attic Press
See **Cork University Press**

Blackhall Publishing
33 Carysfort Avenue, Blackrock, Co. Dublin
☎00 353 1 278 5090   Fax 00 353 1 278 4446
✉ blackhall@eircom.net
www.blackhallpublishing.com
Managing Director *Gerard O'Connor*
Commissioning Editor *Ruth Garvey*
Publishes business, management and living books. Main subject areas include accounting, finance, management, HRM and law books aimed at both students and professionals in the industry. TITLES *Managing Cross-Cultural Business Relations; Managing People in the Workplace; Talking the Talk; Law of Childcare; European Work Equipment Legislation; Bullying in the Workplace, Home and School; Parenting and Privilege.* Unsolicited mss and synopses welcome.
ROYALTIES annually.

Bradshaw Books
Tigh Fílí, Thompson House, MacCurtain Street, Cork
☎00 353 21 450 9274
Fax 00 353 21 455 1617
✉ admin@cwpc.ie
www.tighfili.com
Managing Director *Maire Bradshaw*
Founded 1985. Publishes poetry, women's issues, spiritual, children's books. Organisers of the annual Cork Literary Review poetry manuscript competition. SERIES *Cork Literary Review*.
ROYALTIES not generally paid.

Brandon/Mount Eagle

Dingle, Co. Kerry
☎00 353 66 915 1463
Fax 00 353 66 915 1234
www.brandonbooks.com
Publisher *Steve MacDonogh*
Approx. Annual Turnover €500,000

Founded in 1997. Publishes Irish fiction, biography, memoirs and other non-fiction. About 15 titles a year. Not seeking unsolicited mss.

Brookside

See **New Island**

Edmund Burke Publisher

Cloonagashel, 27 Priory Drive, Blackrock,
Co. Dublin
☎00 353 1 288 2159   Fax 00 353 1 283 4080
✉ deburca@indigo.ie
www.deburcararebooks.com
Managing Director *Eamonn De Búrca*
Publications Manager *Regina De Búrca-McAuley*
Approx. Annual Turnover €320,000

Small family-run business publishing historical and topographical and fine limited-edition books relating to Ireland. TITLES *The Great Book of Irish Genealogies*, 5 vols.; *The Annals of the Four Masters*, 7 vols; *Flowers of Mayo* (illus. Wendy Walsh); *O'Curry's Manners and Customs of the Ancient Irish*; *Joyce's Irish Names of Places*.Unsolicited mss welcome. No synopses or ideas.
ROYALTIES annually.

The Children's Press

See **Anvil Books**

Church of Ireland Publishing

Church of Ireland House, Church Avenue,
Rathmines, Dublin 6
☎00 353 1 492 3979   Fax 00 353 1 492 4770
✉ susan.hood@rcbdub.org
www.ireland.anglican.org
Chairman *Dr Kenneth Milne*
Publications Officer *Dr Susan Hood*

Founded 2004. Publishes official publications of the Church of Ireland: theological, historical and administrative, and facilitates publication for other church-related bodies. 2 titles in 2004.No unsolicited material.

Cló Iar-Chonnachta

Indreabhán, Connemara Galway
☎00 353 91 593307   Fax 00 353 91 593362
✉ cic@iol.ie
www.cic.ie

Chairman/Director *Micheál Ó Conghaile*
Approx. Annual Turnover €400,000

Founded 1985. Publishes fiction, poetry, plays, teenage fiction and children's, mostly in Irish, including translations.Also publishes cassettes of writers reading from their own works. TITLES *Máire Mhic Ghiolla Íosa: Beathaisnéis* Ray Mac Mánais; *Fardoras* Michael Davitt; *An Fear nach nDéanann Gáire* Micheál Ó Conghaile; *Ólann mo Mhiúil as an nGainséies* Gabriel Rosenstock; *Seal i Neipeal* Cathal Ó Searcaigh. 12 titles in 2004.
ROYALTIES annually.

The Columba Press

55A Spruce Avenue, Stillorgan Industrial Park,
Blackrock, Co. Dublin
☎00 353 1 294 2556
Fax 00 353 1 294 2564
✉ sean@columba.ie (editorial) *or*
info@columba.ie (general)
www.columba.ie
Chairman *Neil Kluepfel*
Managing Director *Seán O'Boyle*
Approx. Annual Turnover €1.02 million

Founded 1985. Small company committed to growth. Publishes religious and counselling titles. TITLES *Prism of Love* Donal O'Leary; *That Could Never Be* Kevin Dalton. IMPRINT **Currach Press** (see entry).35 titles in 2004. Backlist of 250 titles.Unsolicited ideas and synopses rather than full mss preferred.
ROYALTIES twice-yearly.

Cork University Press

Youngline Industrial Estate, Pouladuff Road,
Togher, Cork
☎00 353 21 490 2980
Fax 00 353 21 431 5329
✉ corkuniversitypress@ucc.ie
www.corkuniversitypress.com
Publications Director *Mike Collins*

Founded 1925. Relaunched in 1992, the Press publishes academic and some trade titles. TITLES *Staging the Easter Rising: 1916 as Theatre*; *Foreign Affections: Essays on Edmund Burke*; *The Honan Chapel: A Golden Vision*; *Landscape Design in 18th Century Ireland*.Also a biannual journal, *The Irish Review*, an interdisciplinary cultural review. No fiction. IMPRINTS **Attic Press**; **Atrium**.10 titles in 2004.Unsolicited synopses and ideas welcome for textbooks, academic monographs, belles lettres, illustrated histories and journals.
ROYALTIES annually.

Currach Press

55A Spruce Avenue, Stillorgan Industrial Park,
Blackrock, Co. Dublin
☎00 353 86 821 4842
Fax 00 353 1 294 2564
✉ brian@currach.ie
www.currach.ie
Publisher *Brian Lynch*

Founded 2002. An imprint of **The Columba Press**. Publishes non-fiction titles of Irish interest, including politics, history, biography, sport, music and criticism. TITLES *A Memoir* Terry de Valera; *The Harcourt Street Line* Brian Mac Aongusa; *Short Hands, Long Pockets* Eddie Hobbs. Unsolicited ideas welcome; synopses rather than full mss preferred.

A.&A. Farmar Ltd

78 Ranelagh Village, Dublin 6
☎00 353 1 496 3625
Fax 00 353 1 497 0107
✉ afarmar@iol.ie
www.farmarbooks.com
Managing Director *Anna Farmar*

Founded 1992. Publishes Irish social history, businss, food and wine.12 titles in 2004. No unsolicited mss. Synopses and ideas welcome; approach by letter or e-mail in the first instance.

Flyleaf Press

4 Spencer Villas, Glenageary, Co. Dublin
☎00 353 1 284 5906
✉ Flyleaf@indigo.ie
www.flyleaf.ie
Managing Director *Dr James Ryan*
Sales & Administration *Brian Smith*

Founded 1981. Concentrates on family history and Irish history as a background to family history. No fiction. TITLES *Irish Records*; *Longford and its People*; *Tracing Your Kerry Ancestors*; *Tracing Your Limerick Ancestors*. Unsolicited mss, synopses and ideas for books welcome.
ROYALTIES twice-yearly.

Four Courts Press Ltd

7 Malpas Street, Dublin 8
☎00 353 1 453 4668
Fax 00 353 1 453 4672
✉ info@four-courts-press.ie
www.four-courts-press.ie
Chairman/Managing Director *Michael Adams*
Director *Martin Healy*

Founded 1972. Publishes mainly scholarly books in the humanities. About 60 titles a year. Synopses and ideas for books welcome.
ROYALTIES annually.

Gill & Macmillan

10 Hume Avenue, Park West, Dublin 12
☎00 353 1 500 9500   Fax 00 353 1 500 9599
www.gillmacmillan.ie
Managing Director *M.H. Gill*
Approx. Annual Turnover €11.5 million

Founded 1968 when M.H. Gill & Son Ltd and Macmillan Ltd formed a jointly owned publishing company. Publishes biography/autobiography, history, current affairs, literary criticism (all mainly of Irish interest), guidebooks, cookery, popular fiction. Also educational textbooks for secondary and tertiary levels. Contacts: *Hubert Mahony* (educational); *Fergal Tobin* (general). IMPRINT **Tivoli** *Alison Walsh* Popular fiction. About 80 titles a year. Unsolicited synopses and ideas welcome.
ROYALTIES subject to contract.

Institute of Public Administration

57–61 Lansdowne Road, Dublin 4
☎00 353 1 240 3600   Fax 00 353 1 269 8644
✉ Sales@ipa.ie
www.ipa.ie
Director-General *John Cullen*
Publisher *Declan McDonagh*
Approx. Annual Turnover €1 million

Founded 1957 by a group of public servants, the Institute of Public Administration is the Irish public sector management development agency. The publishing arm of the organisation is one of its major activities. Publishes academic and professional books and periodicals: history, law, politics, economics and Irish public administration for students and practitioners. TITLES *Local Government in Ireland*; *E-Government and the Decentralisation of Service Delivery*; *Governance and Policy in Ireland*; *Cross-Departmental Challenges: A Whole of Government Approach for the 21st Century*. About 15 titles a year. No unsolicited mss; synopses and ideas welcome. No fiction or children's publishing.
ROYALTIES annually.

Irish Academic Press Ltd

44 Northumberland Road, Ballsbridge,
Dublin 4
☎00 353 1 668 8244   Fax 00 353 1 660 1610
✉ info@iap.ie
www.iap.ie
Chairman *Frank Cass* (London)
Managing Editor *Rachel Milotte*

Founded 1974. Publishes academic monographs and humanities. 17 titles in 2004. Unsolicited mss, synopses and ideas welcome.
ROYALTIES annually.

Irish Management Institute (IMI)

Sandyford Road, Dublin 16
☎00 353 1 207 8400   Fax 00 353 1 295 5150
✉ bill.carroll@imi.ie
www.imi.ie
Chief Executive *Dr Tom McCarthy*
Approx. Annual Turnover €13 million

Founded 1952. The IMI, owned by its members, corporate and individual, works to improve the practice of management. It offers a wide range of management development services. Publishes a quarterly newsletter *Management Focus*, distributed to members, featuring latest IMI research, case studies and management theory; also *Executive Salaries in Ireland*, an annual publication that reviews managerial salaries and fringe benefits. Mss, synopses and ideas relevant to Irish management practice welcome.
ROYALTIES annually.

The Liffey Press Ltd

Ashbrook House, 10 Main Street, Raheny, Dublin 5
☎00 353 1 851 1458
✉ info@theliffeypress.com
www.theliffeypress.com
Managing Director *David Givens*
Approx. Annual Turnover €380,000

Founded 2001. Publishes general interest, Irish-focused non-fiction.20 titles in 2004. No unsolicited mss. Synopses and ideas welcome; approach by letter or e-mail in the first instance. No fiction, children's or books not of interest to Irish readers.
ROYALTIES twice-yearly.

The Lilliput Press

62–63 Sitric Road, Arbour Hill, Dublin 7
☎00 353 1 671 1647   Fax 00 353 1 671 1233
✉ info@lilliputpress.ie
www.lilliputpress.ie
Chairman *Vincent Hurley*
Managing Director *Antony Farrell*
Approx. Annual Turnover €255,000

Founded 1984. Publishes non-fiction: literature, history, autobiography and biography, ecology, essays; criticism; fiction and poetry. TITLES *A Bloomsday Postcard*; *Vanishing Kingdoms: The Irish Chiefs and Their Families*; *Words, Words, Words*; *Shackleton: An Irishman in Antarctica*. About 20

titles a year. Unsolicited mss, synopses and ideas welcome. No children's or sport titles.
ROYALTIES annually.

Marino Books

See **Mercier Press Ltd**

Maverick House Publishers

Main Street, Dunshaughlin, Co. Meath
☎00 353 1 824 0077   Fax 00 353 1 824 1746
✉ info@maverickhouse.com
www.maverickhouse.com
Managing Director *Jean Harrington*

Founded 2001. Publishes biography and auto-biography, current affairs, non-fiction (mainly of Irish interest), politics. TITLES *The Irish Ballerina*; *Black Operations: A Secret History of the Real IRA*; *Rough Justice: Memoirs of a Gangster*. Unsolicited material welcome; send by post. No fiction, children's books or poetry.
ROYALTIES twice-yearly.

Mercier Press Ltd

Douglas Village, Cork
☎00 353 21 489 9858
Fax 00 353 21 489 9887
✉ books@mercierpress.ie
www.mercierpress.ie
Chairman *George Eaton*
CEO *Clodagh Feehan*

Founded 1944. One of Ireland's largest publishers with a list of approx 250 Irish interest titles. IMPRINTS **Mercier Press**; **Marino Books** Editorial Director *Mary Feehan* Children's, politics, history, folklore, biography, mind, body and spirit, current affairs, women's interest. TITLES *The Course of Irish History*; all of John B. Keane's works; *Beyond Prozac*; *It's a Long Way from Penny Apples*; *Ireland's Master Storyteller*. Unsolicited synopses and ideas welcome.
ROYALTIES annually.

Merlin Publishing

16 Upper Pembroke Street, Dublin 2
☎00 353 1 676 4373   Fax 00 353 1 676 4368
www.merlinwolfhound.com
Managing Director *Chenile Keogh*
Managing Editor *Aoife Barrett*

Founded 2000. Member of **Clé**. Publishes film, music, art, biography, general non-fiction, history, photography and gift books. IMPRINT **Wolfhound Press** Founded 1974. Non-fiction. TITLES *Famine*; *Eyewitness Bloody Sunday*; *Father Browne's Titanic Album*. About 20 titles a year (mainly Irish interest). Sample chapters of unsolicited mss (with synopses and s.a.e.) welcome but by post only. See Merlin website for submission guidelines and proposal form.

Mount Eagle
See **Brandon/Mount Eagle**

National Library of Ireland
Kildare Street, Dublin 2
☎00 353 1 603 0200   Fax 00 353 1 676 6690
✉ info@nli.ie
www.nli.ie
Founded 1877. Publishes books and booklets based on the library's collections; folders of historical documents; academic and specialist books; reproduction folders and CD-ROMs. TITLES *Ulysses Unbound: A Reader's Companion to James Joyce's Ulysses* Terence Killeen; *Cooper's Ireland: Drawings and Notes from an Eighteenth Century Gentleman* Peter Harbison; *Treasures from the National Library of Ireland* ed. Dr Noel Kissane. 19 titles in 2004.

New Island
2 Brookside, Dundrum Road, Dundrum, Dublin 14
☎00 353 1 298 9937/298 3411
Fax 00 353 1 298 7912
✉ fidelma.slattery@newisland.ie
www.newisland.ie
Managing Director/Editorial Head *Edwin Higel*
Editorial Manager *Deirdre Nolan*
Founded 1990. Publishes fiction, Irish non-fiction, poetry and drama. Branching out into popular fiction and memoirs. IMPRINT **Brookside**. About 25 titles a year. Unsolicited mss, synopses and ideas welcome. Send three chapters and synopsis by post.
ROYALTIES twice-yearly

The O'Brien Press Ltd
20 Victoria Road, Rathgar, Dublin 6
☎00 353 1 492 3333   Fax 00 353 1 492 2777
✉ books@obrien.ie
www.obrien.ie
Managing Director/Publisher *Michael O'Brien*
Editorial Director *Íde Ní Laoghaire*
Founded 1974. Publishes business, true crime, biography, music, travel, sport, Celtic subjects, food and drink, history, humour, politics, reference. Children's publishing – mainly fiction for every age from tiny tots to teenage. Illustrated fiction SERIES *Solos* (3 years+); *Pandas* (5 years+); *Flyers* (6 years+); *Red Flag* (8 years+). Novels (10 years+) – contemporary, historical,

fantasy. Some non-fiction – mainly historical, and art and craft, resource books for teachers. No poetry, adult fiction or academic. Unsolicited mss (sample chapters only), synopses and ideas for books welcome. No e-mail submissions. Submissions will not be returned.
ROYALTIES annually.

Oak Tree Press
19 Rutland Street, Cork
☎00 353 21 431 3855
Fax 00 353 21 431 3496
✉ info@oaktreepress.com
www.oaktreepress.com
Managing Director *Brian O'Kane*
Founded 1992. Specialist publisher of business and professional books with a focus on small business start-up and development. Unsolicited mss and synopses welcome; send to the managing director, at the address above.
ROYALTIES annually.

On Stream Publications Ltd
Currabaha, Cloghroe, Co. Cork
☎00 353 21 438 5798
✉ info@onstream.ie
www.onstream.ie
Chairman/Managing Director *Roz Crowley*
Founded 1992. Formerly Forum Publications. Publishes academic, cookery, wine, general health and fitness, local history, railways, photography and practical guides. TITLES *Keeping Resources Human – A Practical Guide to Retaining Staff; The Book of Scarves: 100 Ideas; Dealing With Chronic Pain; Stirmixmash – A Cookbook for Young People*. About 3 titles a year. Synopses and ideas welcome. No children's books.
ROYALTIES annually.

Penguin Ireland
25 St Stephen's Green, Dublin 2
☎00 353 1 661 7695   Fax 00 353 1 661 7696
✉ info@penguin.ie
www.penguin.ie
Managing Director *Michael McLoughlin*
Founded 2002. Part of the **Penguin Group UK**. DIVISIONS **Commercial fiction/non-fiction** Senior Editor *Patricia Deevy* TITLES *The Baby Trail* Sinéad Moriaty; *Nell* Nell McCafferty. **Literary fiction/non-fiction** *Brendan Barrington* TITLES *Sailing for Home* Theo Dorgan; *An Irish Solution* Cormac Millar. 9 titles in 2004. Unsolicited mss, synopses and ideas for books welcome; send by post.
ROYALTIES twice-yearly.

Poolbeg Press Ltd

123 Grange Hill, Baldoyle, Dublin 13
☎00 353 1 832 1477   Fax 00 353 1 832 1430
✉ poolbeg@poolbeg.com
www.poolbeg.com
Managing Director *Kieran Devlin*
Publisher *Paula Campbell*

Founded 1976 to publish the Irish short story and has since diversified to include all areas of fiction (literary and popular), children's fiction and non-fiction, and adult non-fiction: history, biography and topics of public interest. AUTHORS discovered and first published by Poolbeg include Marian Keyes, Sheila O'Flanagan, Cathy Kelly and Patricia Scanlan. 'Our slogan is Poolbeg.com – the Irish for Bestsellers!' IMPRINTS **Poolbeg** (paperback and hardback); **Poolbeg For Children**. About 70 titles a year. Unsolicited mss, synopses and ideas welcome (mss preferred). No drama.
ROYALTIES twice-yearly.

Royal Dublin Society

Science Section, Ballsbridge, Dublin 4
☎00 353 1 668 0866   Fax 00 353 1 660 4014
✉ ciaran.byrne@rds.ie
www.rds.ie

President *Dr Austin Mescal*

Founded 1731 for the promotion of agriculture, science and the arts, and throughout its history has published books and journals towards this end. Publishes conference proceedings, biology and the history of Irish science. TITLES *Agricultural Development for the 21st Century*; *The Right Trees in the Right Places*; *Agriculture & the Environment*; *Water of Life*; *Science, Technology & Realism*; *Science Centres for Ireland*; *Science Education in Crisis*; *Science in the Service of the Fishing Industry*; occasional papers in *Irish Science & Technology* series.
ROYALTIES not generally paid.

Royal Irish Academy

19 Dawson Street, Dublin 2
☎00 353 1 676 2570   Fax 00 353 1 676 2346
✉ editorial@ria.ie
www.ria.ie

Executive Secretary *Patrick Buckley*
Editor of Publications *Rachel McNicholl*

Founded in 1785, the Academy has been publishing since 1787. Core publications are journals but more books published in last 15 years. Publishes academic, Irish interest and Irish language. About 7 titles a year. Welcomes mss, synopses and ideas of an academic standard. Address correspondence to the managing editor of publications.

Simon & Schuster/Town House

See **Town House Dublin**

Sitric Books

62–63 Sitric Road, Arbour Hill, Dublin 7
☎00 353 1 671 1682
Fax 00 353 1 671 1233
www.sitric.com
Chair *Kathy Gilfillan*
Managing Director *Antony Farrell*

Founded 2000. Publishes current affairs, biography and fiction. TITLES *Mind Your Manners: A Guide to Good Behaviour*; *Revolutions*; *Eight Ball Boogie*; *The State of Grace*; *Overnight to Innsbruck*. About 5 titles a year. Unsolicited mss, synopses and ideas welcome. No children's or sports titles.
ROYALTIES annually.

Swordpoint Intercontinental Limited

'Solas Tobann', Ballyhillion, Malin Head, Co. Donegal
☎00 353 74 937 0278
Fax 00 353 74 937 0279
✉ writer@swordpoint.com
www.swordpoint.com
Chairman/Managing Director *Joseph A. Greenleaf*

Swordpoint was established in 1995 as a media company and branched out into books in 2003. Publishes fiction, children's, non-fiction, historical, travel, technical, Irish, poetry, plays, business, management, law, biography, fantasy, teenage fiction. Publication on cassettes and CDs as well as e-books. 15 titles in 2005. Unsolicited mss, synopses and ideas welcome by post with return postage.
ROYALTIES twice-yearly.

Tír Eolas

Newtownlynch, Doorus, Kinvara, Co. Galway
☎00 353 91 637452
Fax 00 353 91 637452
✉ info@tireolas.com
www.tireolas.com

Publisher/Managing Director *Anne Korff*

Founded 1987. Publishes books and guides on ecology, archaeology, folklore and culture. TITLES *The Book of the Burren*; *The Shores of Connemara*; *Not a Word of a Lie*; *The Book of Aran*; *Women of Ireland, A Biographic Dictionary*; *Kinvara, A Seaport Town on Galway Bay*; *A Burren Journal*; *Alive, Alive-O, The Shellfish and Shellfisheries of Ireland*. Unsolicited mss, synopses and ideas for books welcome. No specialist scientific and technical, fiction, plays, school textbooks or philosophy. ROYALTIES annually.

Tivoli
See **Gill & Macmillan**

Town House Dublin
Trinity House, Charleston Road, Ranelagh, Dublin 6
☎00 353 1 497 2399
Fax 00 353 1 497 0927
✉ books@townhouse.ie
Managing Director *Treasa Coady*
Founded 1980. Publishes commercial and literary fiction, art and archaeology, sport, biography and environment. TITLES *Full Time* Paul Kimmage; *Laptop Dancing and the Nanny Goat Mambo* Tom Humphries; *Irish Girls About Town* various authors; *Gardening the Soul* Sister Stan; *John McCormack The Great Irish Tenor* Gordon T. Ledbetter. IMPRINT **Simon & Schuster/ TownHouse** Founded 2001. Fiction and non-fiction. About 10–15 titles a year. Unsolicited mss, synopses and ideas welcome. No children's books.
ROYALTIES twice-yearly.

Veritas Publications
7–8 Lower Abbey Street, Dublin 1
☎00 353 1 878 8177   Fax 00 353 1 878 6507
✉ publications@veritas.ie
www.veritas.ie
Director *Maura Hyland*
Managing Editor *Helen Carr*
Founded 1969 to supply religious textbooks to schools and later introduced a wide-ranging general list. Part of the Catholic Communications Institute. Publishes books on religious, ethical, moral, societal and social issues. 30 titles a year. Unsolicited mss, synopses and ideas for books welcome.
ROYALTIES annually.

Wolfhound Press
See **Merlin Publishing**

Irish Literary Agents

The Book Bureau Literary Agency
7 Duncairn Avenue, Bray, Co. Wicklow
☎00 353 1 276 4996   Fax 00 353 1 276 4834
✉ thebookbureau@oceanfree.net
Contact *Ger Nichol*

Handles general and literary fiction. Special interest in women's fiction, crime and thrillers. Will suggest revision. Send preliminary letter, synopsis and first three chapters; return postage essential (IRCs only from UK and abroad). No reading fee. COMMISSION Home 10%; Overseas 20%. Works with foreign associates.

Marianne Gunn O'Connor Literary Agency
Morrison Chambers, Suite 17, 32 Nassau Street, Dublin 2
✉ mgoclitagency@eircom.net
Contact *Marianne Gunn O'Connor*

Founded 1996. Handles commercial and literary fiction, non-fiction: biography, health and children's fiction. CLIENTS include Niall Williams, Patrick McCabe, Morag Prunty, Claire Kilroy, Julie Dam, Cecelia Ahern, Paddy McMahon, Chris Binchy, Anita Notaro, Mike McCormack, Noelle Harrison, Claudia Carroll, Ken Bruen, John Lynch. Send preliminary letter plus half-page synopsis and first 50 pages. COMMISSION UK 15%; Overseas 20%; Film & TV 20%. Translation rights handled by Vicki Satlow Literary Agency, Milan.

The Lisa Richards Agency
46 Upper Baggot Street, Dublin 4
☎00 353 1 660 3534   Fax 00 353 1 660 3545
✉ faith@lisarichards.ie
Contact *Faith O'Grady*

Founded 1998. Handles fiction and general non-fiction. Approach with proposal and sample chapter for non-fiction, and 3–4 chapters and synopsis for fiction (s.a.e. essential). No reading fee. AUTHORS include June Considine, Judi Curtin, Denise Deegan, Christin Dwyer Hickey, Karen Gillece, Tara Heavey, Paul Howard (Ross O'Carroll-Kelly), Arlene Hunt, Roisin Ingle, Alison Jameson, Declan Lynch, Martin Malone, Roisin Meaney, Jennifer MacCann, Pauline McLynn, Sarah O'Brien (Helena Close and Trisha Rainsford), Damien Owens, Kevin Rafter. COMMISSION Home 10%; UK 15%; US & Translation 20%; Film & TV 15%. OVERSEAS ASSOCIATE **The Marsh Agency** for translation rights.

Jonathan Williams Literary Agency
Rosney Mews, Upper Glenageary Road, Glenageary, Co. Dublin
☎00 353 1 280 3482   Fax 00 353 1 280 3482
Contact *Jonathan Williams*

Founded 1980. Handles general trade books: fiction, auto/biography, travel, politics, history, music, literature and criticism, gardening, cookery, sport and leisure, humour, reference, social questions, photography. Some poetry, business and children's, but less of a speciality. No plays, science fiction, mind, body and spirit, computer books, theology, multimedia, motoring, aviation. No reading fee 'unless the author wants a very fast opinion'. Initial approach by phone or letter. COMMISSION Home 10%; US 20%; Translation 15%. OVERSEAS ASSOCIATES Piergiorgio Nicolazzini Literary Agency, Italy; Lora Fountain & Associates Agency, France; Linda Kohn, International Literature Bureau, Holland; Antonia Kerrigan Literary Agency, Spain; Tuttle-Mori Agency Inc., Japan.

Audio Books

Assembled Stories

PO Box 5212, Grantham NG33 5SR
☎0870 747 8070 Fax 01476 571333
✉ peter@assembledstories.com *or*
michael@assembledstories.com
www.assembledstories.com

Managing Directors *Peter Joyce, Michael Joyce*

Founded 1992. Publishes classic fiction on cassette and CD with all books read by Peter Joyce. TITLES *Idle Thoughts of an Idle Fellow* Jerome K. Jerome; *The Monkey's Paw* W.W. Jacobs; *The Beloved Vagabond* W.J. Locke; *Uncle Silas* J. Sheridan LeFanu; *The Sowers* H. Seton Merriman. 60 titles available; 12 titles on CD. Ideas for titles welcome.

AudioBooksForFree.Com Limited

25 Green Lane, Amersham HP6 6AS
☎01494 431119
✉ ToUs@AudioBooksForFree.Com
www.AudioBooksForFree.Com
www.DVDAudioBooks.com
www.MobileAudioBooks.com

Managing Director *Ruslan G. Fedorovsky*
CTO *Peter Morris*

Founded 2000. Publishes and sells MP3 and DVD audiobooks on- and offline. Genres: fiction, adventure, thrillers, crime, science fiction, children's, non-fiction, etc. AUTHORS include Michael Hartland, James Herlihy, Jon Schiller, Patrick Walsh, Jules Verne, Dumas. 200 titles in 2004.

Pays 100% royalties to 'contributors' (audiobook publishers, famous narrators or famous authors) for individual audiobook downloads.

BBC Audiobooks Ltd

St James House, The Square, Lower Bristol Road, Bath BA2 3BH
☎01225 335336 Fax 01225 310771
✉ bbcaudiobooks@bbc.co.uk
www.bbcshop.com

Managing Director *Paul Dempsey*
Publishing Director *Jan Paterson*

BBC Audiobooks Ltd was established in 2003 with the integration of BBC Radio Collection, Cover to Cover and Chivers Audio Books. Since then it has become a leading trade and library publisher in the UK, publishing a wide range of entertainment on a variety of formats including CD, cassette and MP3-CD.

DIVISIONS

Trade Titles range from original books and full-cast radio dramas through to abridged readings and full, unabridged recordings. TITLES *War and Peace; The Odyssey; Captain Corelli's Mandolin;* the complete Sherlock Holmes canon. IMPRINTS **BBC Audio – Children's** From pre-school nursery rhymes to modern classics. TITLES *The Chronicles of Narnia; His Dark Materials* trilogy. **BBC Audio – Radio Collection** Comedy classics from TV and radio. TITLES *The Goons; Hancock's Half Hour; Fawlty Towers; The News Quiz; Just a Minute.* **BBC Audio** Contemporary comedy. TITLES *Little Britain; Have I Got News For You; The League of Gentlemen.* **BBC Audio – Lifestyle** A range of titles to help the listener improve or learn. TITLES include the *Glenn Harrold's Ultimate Guide to ...* series. **BBC Audio – Radio 4** TITLES *This Sceptred Isle; Letter from America; A Suitable Boy.* **Science Fiction & Fantasy** TITLES *The Hitchhiker's Guide to the Galaxy; Doctor Who; Journey into Space; The Lord of the Rings.*

Library IMPRINTS **Chivers Audio Books; Chivers Children's Audio Books** Founded 1980. Publishes over 500 titles annually. Complete and unabridged books for adults and children are sold to libraries and to the public by direct mail through **The Audiobook Collection**. CDs and cassettes covering best-selling fiction and popular non-fiction.

Bloomsbury Publishing

See entry under *UK Publishers*

Bolinda Publishing Ltd

2 Ivanhoe Road, London SE5 8DH
☎020 7733 1088
✉ marisa@bolinda.com
www.bolinda.com

Publisher *Marisa McGreevy*

The London office of Bolinda Publishing Pty, Ltd, Australia became a company in its own right in the spring of 2004. Produces fiction titles (adult, children's and young adult); all genres. TITLES *Mates, Dates and Inflatable Bras* Cathy

Hopkins; *Troy* Adele Geras; *Mad Cows* Kathy Lette; *Contest* Matthew Reilly; *Dirt Music* Tim Winton. 36 titles in 2004.

Chivers Audio Books/
Chivers Children's Audio Books
See **BBC Audiobooks Ltd**

Chrome Dreams
12 Seaforth Avenue, New Malden KT3 6JP
☎020 8715 9781 Fax 020 8241 1426
✉ mail@chromedreams.co.uk
www.chromedreams.co.uk

Managing Director *Rob Johnstone*

A small record company and publisher founded 1998 to produce audio-biographies of current rock and pop artists and legendary performers on CD and, more recently, books on the same subjects. Ideas for biographies welcome.

Corgi Audio
Transworld Publishers, A division of the Random House Group Ltd, 61–63 Uxbridge Road, London W5 5SA
☎020 8579 2652

Managing Director *Larry Finlay*

Publishes fiction, autobiography and humour. TITLES *Discworld Series* Terry Pratchett; *Down Under* Bill Bryson and other travel writing; *High Society* and *Past Mortem* Ben Elton.

Cover to Cover
See **BBC Audiobooks Ltd**

CSA Word
6a Archway Mews, 241a Putney Bridge Road, London SW15 2PE
☎020 8871 0220 Fax 020 8877 0712
✉ info@csaword.co.uk
www.csaword.co.uk

Managing Director *Clive Stanhope*
Audio Director *Victoria Williams*

Founded 1989. Publishes fiction, children's, short stories, poetry, travel, biographies. Over 100 titles to-date on cassette and CD. Tends to favour quality/classic/nostalgic/timeless literature. TITLES *Carry on Jeeves* P.G. Wodehouse; *Alfie* Bill Naughton; *The Ordeal of Gilbert Penfold* Evelyn Waugh; *Just William – Home for the Holidays* Richmal Crompton; *Midwich Cuckoos* John Wyndham; *Lady Chatterley's Lover* D.H. Lawrence; *The Statement* Brian Moore; *Billy Bunter's Banknote* Frank Richards; *The Ragged Trousered Philanthropists* Robert Tressell; *Cautionary Verses* Hilaire Belloc.

CYP Children's Audio
The Fairway, Bush Fair, Harlow CM18 6LY
☎01279 444707 Fax 01279 445570
✉ enquiries@cypmusic.co.uk
www.kidsmusic.co.uk

Managing Director *Mike Kitson*

Founded 1978. Publishes music video and audiobooks for young children; educational, entertainment, licensed characters (*Mr Men*; *Little Miss*; *Wheels On the Bus*). TV music and soundtrack production.

Faber.Penguin Audiobooks
80 Strand, London WC2R 0RL
☎020 7010 3000 Fax 020 7010 6060
✉ audio@penguin.co.uk
www.penguin.co.uk
3 Queen Square, London WC1N 3AU
☎020 7465 0045 Fax 020 7465 0108

Head of Audio Publishing *Jeremy Ettinghausen*

A joint venture between **Penguin Books** and **Faber & Faber**. AUTHORS include Ted Hughes, Garrison Keillor, Sylvia Plath, T.S. Eliot, William Golding, Peter Carey, Alex Garland, D.B.C. Pierre, Philip Ardagh. Publishes up to 5 titles per year, drawing on the strength of Faber's authors.

57 Productions
See entry under **Organisations of Interest to Poets**

Hachette Children's Books
See entry under **UK Publishers**

Halsgrove
See entry under **UK Publishers**

HarperCollins AudioBooks
77–85 Fulham Palace Road, London W6 8JB
☎020 8741 7070 Fax 020 8307 4517
www.harpercollins.co.uk

Managing Director *Trevor Dolby*

The HarperCollins audio list was launched in 1990. ADULT Publisher *Rosalie George*. Publishes a wide range including popular and classic fiction, non-fiction, Shakespeare, poetry and self help (Thorsons' imprint) on cassette and CD. 50 titles in 2004. CHILDREN'S DIVISION Divisional Publishing Director *Sally Gritten*, Publisher *Rosalie George*. Publishes picture books/cassettes and story books/cassettes as well as single and double tapes and CDs for children aged 2–13 years. Fiction, songs, early learning, poetry, etc. 20 titles in 2004. AUTHORS C.S. Lewis, Roald Dahl, Dr Seuss, Lemony

Snicket, J.R.R. Tolkien, Enid Blyton, Robin Jarvis, Ian Whybrow, Nick Butterworth, Judith Kerr.

Hodder & Stoughton Audiobooks

338 Euston Road, London NW1 3BH
☎020 7873 6000 Fax 020 7873 6024
www.madaboutbooks.co.uk

Publisher *Rupert Lancaster*

Launched 1994. Publishes fiction and non-fiction. AUTHORS Pam Ayres, Tony Benn, Dickie Bird, Mevyn Bragg, John LeCarré, Alex Ferguson, Ranulph Fiennes, Elizabeth George, Joanne Harris, John Humphries, Stephen King, Ellis Peters, Rosamunde Pilcher, John Simpson. About 30 titles a year.

Isis Audio Books

See **Soundings**

Ladybird Audio

See **Dorling Kindersley Ltd** under *UK Publishers*

Laughing Stock Productions

81 Charlotte Street, London W1T 4PP
☎020 7637 7943 Fax 020 7436 1666
Managing Director *Colin Collino*

Founded 1991. Issues a wide range of comedy cassettes from family humour to alternative comedy. TITLES *Red Dwarf; Shirley Valentine* (read by Willy Russell); *Rory Bremner; Peter Cook Anthology; Sean Hughes; John Bird and John Fortune; Eddie Izzard.* 12–16 titles per year.

Macmillan Audio Books

20 New Wharf Road, London N1 9RR
☎020 7014 6040 Fax 020 7014 6141
✉ a.muirden@macmillan.co.uk
www.panmacmillan.co.uk

Owner *Macmillan Publishers Ltd*
Audio Publisher *Alison Muirden*

Founded 1995. Publishes adult fiction, non-fiction and autobiography, focusing mainly on lead book titles and releasing audio simultaneously with hard or paperback publication. Also publishes children's audio titles. Won Audio Publisher of the Year at the 2003 **Spoken Word Awards**.

Naxos AudioBooks

18 High Street, Welwyn AL6 9EQ
☎01438 717808 Fax 01438 717809
✉ naxos_audiobooks@compuserve.com

www.naxosaudiobooks.com
Owner *HNH International, Hong Kong/ Nicolas Soames*
Managing Director *Nicolas Soames*

Founded 1994. Part of Naxos, the classical budget CD company. Publisher of the Year in 2001 **Spoken Word Awards**. Publishes classic and modern fiction, non-fiction, children's and junior classics, drama and poetry. TITLES *Ulysses* Joyce; *King Lear* Shakespeare; *History of the Musical* Fawkes; *Just So Stories* Kipling.

Orion Audio Books (Division of the Orion Publishing Group Ltd)

Orion House, 5 Upper St Martin's Lane, London WC2H 9EA
☎020 7520 4425 Fax 020 7379 6518
✉ pandora.white@orionbooks.co.uk
www.orionbooks.co.uk

Publisher *Pandora White*

Orion Audio has released over 200 titles since it was founded in 1998. Publishes fiction, non-fiction, humour, children's, poetry, science, crime and thrillers. AUTHORS Penny Vincenzi, Maeve Binchy, Ian Rankin, Robert Crais, Michael Connelly, Francesca Simon (*Horrid Henry* series), Dan Brown, Kevin Crossley-Holland, Michelle Paver and Anita Shreve. Ideas for cassettes/CDs welcome.

Penguin Audiobooks

80 Strand, London WC2R 0RL
☎020 7010 3000 Fax 020 7010 6695
✉ audio@penguin.co.uk
www.penguin.co.uk

Head of Audio Publishing *Jeremy Ettinghausen*

Launched in November 1993 and has rapidly expanded since then to reflect the diversity of Penguin Books' list. Publishes mostly fiction, both classical and contemporary, non-fiction, autobiography and an increasing range of children's titles under the **Puffin Audiobooks** imprint. Contemporary AUTHORS include: Zadie Smith, Anne Fine, Eoin Colfer, John Mortimer, Roald Dahl, Sue Townsend, Nicci French, Michael Moore, Jonathan Coe. About 70 titles a year.

Puffin Audiobooks

See **Penguin Audiobooks**

Random House Audiobooks

20 Vauxhall Bridge Road, London SW1V 2SA
☎020 7840 8400 Fax 020 7233 6127
Owner *The Random House Group Ltd*

Publishing Director *Clare Smith*
Editor *Georgia Marnham*
Audiobooks Assistant *Louisa Gibbs*

The audiobooks division of Random House started early in 1991. Acquired the Reed Audio list in 1997. Publishes fiction, non-fiction and self help. AUTHORS include Sebastian Faulks, John Grisham, Mark Haddon, Robert Harris, Thomas Harris, Tony Hawks, Andy McNab, Alison Pearson, Ruth Rendell, Kathy Reichs, Chris Ryan.

Rickshaw Productions

Suite 125, 99 Warwick Street, Leamington Spa CV32 4RB
☎0780 3553214   Fax 01926 402490
✉ rickprod@aol.com
www.rickshawaudiobooks.co.uk

Executive Producer *Ms L.J. Fairgrieve*

Publishes adult fiction and non-fiction. Founded 1998, Rickshaw Productions' first audiobooks were English translations of Chinese stories. Other titles include a gothic fictional novella, four short stories and an anthology of music and poetry by Mark Yakes. TITLES *Chinese Classic Stories; Chinese Women's Stories; The Carved Pipe/The Tall Woman and Her Short Husband; The Halfway-House Hotel; Wednesdays and Other Stories; The Tailor of Salisbury; Poems and Music Vol I; The First Line of Defence – The Kent Castles; The Churchills and their Palace.* Will soon be publishing paperback editions. Submissions by snail-mail *only*; salacious material will not be accepted. Two sample chapters, one-page synopsis and s.a.e. to cover return by Recorded Delivery.

Simon & Schuster Audio

Africa House, 64–78 Kingsway, London WC2B 6AH
☎020 7316 1900   Fax 020 7316 0332
✉ sally.partington@simonandschuster.co.uk
www.simonsays.co.uk

Audio Manager *Sally Partington*

Simon & Schuster Audio began by distributing their American parent company's audio products. Moved on to repackaging products specifically for the UK market and in 1994 became more firmly established in this market with a huge rise in turnover. Publishes adult fiction, self help and business titles. TITLES *Rosie* Alan Titchmarsh; *The 7 Habits of Highly Effective People* Stephen R. Covey; *Chronicles* Bob Dylan; *Angels and Demons* and *Deception Point* Dan Brown; *Kate Remembered* A. Scott Berg.

SmartPass Ltd

15 Park Road, Rottingdean, Brighton BN2 7HL
☎01273 300742
✉ info@smartpass.co.uk
www.smartpass.co.uk

Managing Director *Phil Viner*

Founded 1999. Family-run business. Publishes audio education study guides, drama and analysis for English Literature set texts – novels, plays and poetry. TITLES include *A Kestrel for a Knave* Barry Hines; *An Inspector Calls* J.B. Priestley; *Pride and Prejudice* Jane Austen; *Great Expectations* Charles Dickens; *The Mayor of Casterbridge* Thomas Hardy; *Macbeth; Twelfth Night; Henry V; Shakespeare: the works; War Poetry; Classical Poetry.* IMPRINT **SPAudiobooks** Full-cast unabridged dramas. TITLE *The Antipope* Robert Rankin. Welcomes ideas from authors who are teachers and from agents who represent the authors of studied texts.

Smith/Doorstop Cassettes

The Poetry Business, The Studio, Byram Arcade, Huddersfield HD1 1ND
☎01484 434840   Fax 01484 426566
✉ edit@poetrybusiness.co.uk
www.poetrybusiness.co.uk

Co-directors *Peter Sansom, Janet Fisher*

Publishes poetry, read and introduced by the writer. AUTHORS Carol Ann Duffy, Simon Armitage, Les Murray, Ian McMillan, Sujata Bhatt.

Soundings

Isis House, Kings Drive, Whitley Bay NE26 2JT
☎0191 253 4155   Fax 0191 251 0662
www.isis-publishing.co.uk

Founded in 1982. Part of the Ulverscroft Group Ltd. Together with **Isis Publishing** publishes fiction and non-fiction; crime, romance. AUTHORS include Lyn Andrews, Rita Bradshaw, Lee Child, Catherine Cookson, Alexander Fullerton, Joanne Harris, Anna Jacobs, Robert Ludlum, Patrick O'Brian, Pamela Oldfield, Susan Sallis, Judith Saxton, Mary Jane Staples, Sally Worboyes. About 190 titles a year. Many also available on CD.

SPAudiobooks

See **SmartPass Ltd**

Time Warner Audiobooks

Brettenham House, Lancaster Place, London WC2E 7EN
☎020 7911 8044   Fax 020 7911 8109

✉ sarah.shrub@twbg.co.uk
www.twbg.co.uk

Managing Director *David Young*
Editor *Sarah Shrub*

Launched in 2003 with titles from Time Warner Books' bestselling authors Alexander McCall Smith, Mitch Albom and David Sedaris. Publishes fiction, humour and non-fiction. TITLES include new fiction from Anita Shreve and Peter Mayle, Mark Billingham's detective series featuring D.I. Tom Thorne and Ewan McGregor and Charley Boorman's account of their 20,000-mile odyssey by motorbike. 25 titles in 2004.

Poetry Stays Top Dog

Peter Finch

For the new millennium the poetry wars are taking a different shape. For decades it has been the avant garde in conflict with the centre, the innovators vs. the traditionalists, men suppressing women, and a white metropolitan middle class putting down anyone who came from anywhere else. But, barring a few residual skirmishes, those battles now seem to be over. Diversity rules. Innovative verse is as common in university literature departments as Hardy's traditional line. Women dominate the reading platforms. Years of government arts subsidy directed at broadening culture's base, improving access and letting anyone with a pencil have a go have borne fruit. Poetry has permeated all levels of our society. It is available in quantities like never before. A good thing? Not everyone is sure.

Advances in digital publishing have led to a rapid fall in the price of printing. Good quality Faber-clones are now within the financial reach of most operators. The number of writers self-publishing has shot up. Small poetry presses have at last found themselves able to take on the big boys, at least in the shape and look of their books. Production has increased enormously. Some of our small presses are now managing thirty new titles annually. Ten years ago they would have been lucky to afford seven. Decent, spine-bound, well-designed, slim volumes with glossy covers have become ubiquitous. It's so easy. Poets everywhere. But mostly ones you've never heard of. As a consequence, sales have suffered. Overpowered by a poorly-selling diverse range the bookshops have de-stocked giving over their valuable space to faster moving three-for-the-price-of-twos and similar promotions. Andy Warhol's fifteen seconds of fame may well be enjoyed by increasing numbers, but the actual value of having an individual *book* of your poetry published appears to have gone down.

Instead, the new battle arena is the anthology. In 2002 Bloodaxe's *Staying Alive: Real Poems for Unreal Times* developed the market pioneered by the BBC's anthologies of the *Nation's Favourite Poems* by selling 76,000 copies of fresh and worthy verse to those who'd previously never considered reading it. The commercial market realised that, after all these years, there was a way to make money from poetry. Dozens of similar anthologies appeared. Daisy Goodwin's *101 Poems That Could Save Your Life, Get You Through the Day, Keep You Sane, Help You Fall In Love, Help You Fix Your Bike* flooded the WH Smith bookshelves. Penguin published the Julia Watson edited *Poems for Weddings* and *Poems for Funerals*. The bastion of new generation verse, Picador, responded with *All the Poems You Need To Say Goodbye, All the Poems You Need To Say Hello* and *All the Poems You Need To Say I Do,* all edited by respectable literateurs: Peter Forbes, Kate Clanchy, Don Paterson. Elsewhere there were anthologies of poetry for parties, for Christmas, for disasters, for love, for death, for washing-machine repair, for political transcendation. Everyone was getting on board, the answer to declining slim-volume sales had been found, but it was not a panacea.

In an issue of Britain's longest-lived poetry magazine, *Poetry Review,* editors David Herd and Robert Potts suggest that 'nothing about these books encourages the general reader to a further engagement with poetry'. The new anthologies' content is all surface, gloss and sound bite. Poetry reduced to simple lyric statements of everyday life. Cheap as chips. Use it, then throw it away. True or not, what is certain is that the glut of accessible verse flooding the marketplace does not offer much chance for the newcomer. Most of these anthologies use work from the dead – out of copyright, free. And if it's from a living bard then it's more likely to be Roger McGough or Simon Armitage or Wendy Cope than a new young poet from Newcastle or a late-starter from Belfast. If that's you, then should you give up? No. Despite what's been said, the poetry world still booms. Forget the commercial marketplace and the occasional flash of verse you encounter on radio or TV. On the Internet, in the e-mags and the small mags and on the continually expanding circuit of poetry readings, workshops, discussions, hootenannies, performances, meetings, classes, slams and gatherings, poetry stays top dog.

Poets Laureate are appearing everywhere. Andrew Motion has been joined by Edwin Morgan in Scotland, Gwyneth Lewis in Wales, Gillian Clarke in Cardiff and Stewart Conn in Edinburgh. There's a national Children's Poet in Wales, a town poet at Newport, a poet laureate of the Internet and one for Birmingham. Official recognition at last. Attempts to stem the slide in sales of single volumes have seen a revival of 1994's New Generation Poets promotion with the selection of twenty new bards to be pushed as the Next Generation. Among them are Amanda Dalton, Nick Drake and Jacob Polley. Not household names. Not yet. Felix Dennis, the millionaire publisher and former *Oz* proprietor, took to composing rhyming couplets, self-published and toured the UK giving free readings accompanied by free wine. He flew by helicopter and sold thousands of books. If you have the money then anything is possible. But if, like most of us, you haven't, then worry not. Chances in poetry are still out there, available and waiting, by the thousand.

What should you read?

The way in is first to discover what poetry actually is. To do this means putting some time in. Be as open and catholic as you can in your selection. Ensure you check out the whole scene – the past, the present, mainstream English literature along with work in translation, the obvious poets you find you like as well as those you find difficult. Appreciation will not come without effort. Stay the course.

Start with a recent anthology of contemporary verse. You'll be spoilt for choice here, the new millennium has rushed a whole crop of century-definers into print. To get a broad view of what's going on, not only should you read Simon Armitage and Robert Crawford's *British and Irish Poetry Since the War* (Penguin);

Michael Schmidt's *The Harvill Book of Twentieth-Century Poetry in English* (Harvill), Andy Croft and Adrian Mitchell's *Red Sky at Night — Socialist Poetry* (Five Leaves), the latest annual *Forward Book of Poetry* (Faber) and Richard Caddel and Peter Quartermain's *Other: British and Irish Poetry since 1970* (Wesleyan), but also Keith Tuma's *Anthology of Twentieth-Century British & Irish Poetry* (OUP); Rod Mengham and John Kinsella's *Vanish Points — New Modernist Poems* (Salt), Neil Astley's *Staying Alive* and *Being Alive* (Bloodaxe), Jeni Couzyn's *The Bloodaxe Book of Contemporary Women Poets,* Jerome Rothenberg and Pierre Joris's two volume *Poems For the Millennium* (California) and Paul Hoover's *Postmodern American Poetry* (Norton). This last title might be harder to find but will be worth the effort. Fill in with a standard overview of poetry in English since Chaucer. John Gallas's *The Song Atlas: A Book of World Poetry* (Carcanet) is a good scattergun.

Progress to the literary magazine. Read the online journals. The Poetry Library offers a good list of e-magazines at www.poetrylibrary.org.uk/magazines/emagazines/ For traditional print, write to a number of the magazine addresses which follow this article and ask the price of sample copies. It is important that poets read not only to familiarise themselves with what is currently fashionable and to increase their own facility for self-criticism, but to help support the activity in which they wish to participate. Buy — this is vital for little mags, it is the only way in which they are going to survive.

Ok, I'm well read. What next?

Take a look at your own material. Are you personally convinced that it's ready? If you are uncertain, then most likely that will be the view of everyone else. Check your text for glips and blips. Rework it. Root out any clichés or archaic poetry expressions such as O, doeth, bewilld'd and the like. Drop any of what Peter Sansom calls 'spirit of the age' poetry words. Do without shards, lozenges, lambent patina, and stippled seagulls. Try and avoid shopping trolleys or tramps. If you work with rhyme avoid the obvious. Check that any meter you may be using actually works. Do not clank. If by this time your writing still sounds OK, then go ahead.

Internet

With the advent of cheap access, always-on, lightning-fast Broadband and complimentary Web space an increasing number of poetry enthusiasts, organisations and publishers have now established themselves on the Internet. The drift has been inexorable. Some have abandoned conventional print to operate solely online; others have launched without ever having known ink and paper. Cyberspace — the place where it all happens — is a mirror of the conventional world. The electronic replicates the real. Here are online books, magazines, historical and contemporary archives, reference works, creative tools, recordings, discussion forums and news round-ups. Many dedicate themselves entirely to poetry. Some of our national institutions, notably the BBC and the *Guardian*, have discovered that poetry makes for ideal Web content and dedicated significant sections of their sites to verse. On the Internet, poetry is a consumer staple.

Journals
Online magazines range from those which mirror their print-based cousins (and in some cases are simply direct copies) to completely innovative, interactive compilations which mix sound and action with the text. The Net is no static place. Some mags offer playable recordings of their poets performing, others give space for readers to add criticism. More and more run forums where readers can exchange views. The difference between online and print-based magazines becomes more apparent when you discover that what you get when you call them up is not simply an enhanced version of the current issue but access to the entire back catalogue. All searchable, storable and, for most of the poetry world, entirely free.

Geography dissolves online. America is no further and no more costly to access than Britain. One of the great mags, John Tranter's *Jacket,* is based in Australia. It's just as easy to read as George Simmers' UK *Snakeskin*, Ethan Paquan's US *Slope* or Rick Lupert's Los Angeles *Poetry Super Highway*. In fact, half the time, the user has no idea precisely where the site being accessed is physically based. Place ceases to matter, language takes over. Online journals can range from the terrible to the terrific. For my money, the aforementioned *Jacket, nthposition,* Joan Houlihan's *Perihelion,* Neil Rollinson's most professional UK *Boomerang,* Rupert Loydell's *Stride*, and Jennifer Ley's *Riding the Meridian* are some of the world's best.

How do you contribute? Read first. Will you fit in? If you think so then send your poems by e-mail. More than likely you'll get an instant answer. No more waiting around for six weeks before your poems return, rejected and dog-eared. Online can be lightening fast.

Cyberspace is huge. Some of the sites which list online journals, such as Peter Howard's Poetry Contacts, or Patrick Martin's Poetry Resource seem to go on for days. On the Web it is easy to put up more, so in terms of quality of content that often means less. As in the real world not everything is even. Check the site's design. If thought has gone into it then it's likely that consideration has been given to the content as well.

Personal sites
If you tire of contributing to the websites of others then why not start your own? A whole collection of verse online will present relatively little difficulty. Most Internet Service Providers (ISPs) offer an amount of free Web space to users. Building your own site is certainly not beyond anyone capable of using a word processor. Many ISPs also provide free page creation software. If you'd like to see the kind of thing that's possible have a look at the site of poets Matthew Francis and Attila the Stockbroker, or for something more graphically challenging, Tom

Leonard's site which includes his amazing reading of his poem 'The 6 O'clock News'. You might also care to look at my own, The Peter Finch Archive. If you are reticent, get a fan to set up a site devoted to your works. This has happened to David Gascoyne, to J.H. Prynne, Maya Angelou, Ivor Cutler, Benjamin Zephaniah and others. Most of us, however, seem to prefer the idea of self-build.

Hypertext

Naturally the Web has developed its own verse forms. Most of these straddle the boundaries between verse, sound and image, much in the way that concrete poetry did fifty years ago. Many critics dismiss the new work as simply moving graphic art but protagonists see the world very differently. The subject is large and at the real cutting edge. Check the Flash-driven examples on the BBC's poetry site as well as those created by poet and Web-watcher Peter Howard. Edward Picot's Hyperliterature Exchange offers an ever increasing number of links to new developments.

Groups

To reduce the poet's traditional feeling of isolation the Net presents a number of opportunities. E-mail provides one vehicle. Here, bands of poets circulate their work, their criticisms and their views of world literature. Join a group and you'll find a daily delivery of e-mails in your in-box. Some groups are moderated which means that contributions are filtered by a controlling individual although most are free-for-alls. Discussion can range from the moronic to the stimulating. The British and Irish Poets group and Poetryetc are two worth trying.

A variant on e-mail discussion groups are Usenet Newsgroups. Newsgroups are open to contributions from anyone anywhere. Articles are delivered to your browser for consumption. If you want to contribute then type it up and it's done. The principal poetry newsgroups, rec.arts.poems and alt.arts.poetry.comments, offer pretty varied fare. By their world-wide nature they tend to be American dominated and standards of contribution are not always that high. There are also masterclasses out there with established poets offering online advice. The BBC and the Poetry Society are some of the organisations which have offered virtual residencies with well-known bards.

Tools and resources

The Net offers a multitude of these. There are online spell-checkers (in many languages), thesauri, an anagram creator, Shakespeare concordances, a rhyming dictionary. Nottingham Trent University offers new media writing, creative online courses, incisive articles, innovative web design, and a broad range of resources, news, discussions and research at **TrAce**. You can learn online here. Peter Howard offers a course in animating poetry with Flash while Jane Draycott sticks to more conventional words. The archives of universities (particularly in America) offer the great poetry of the past in comprehensive quantity. Download facsimile editions of *The Germ* (the first ever poetry magazine from 1850), or hear

Seamus Heaney recite. Read the complete works of Blake, find out what powered the beat generation, discover how Hardy worked, check the roots of modern verse. See where it's all going at the Electronic Poetry Centre at Buffalo. Not only can you find the texts themselves but entire critical apparatuses, historical contexts, biographies, bibliographies, portraits, shoe sizes and names of lovers for most of the greats. You can access information on poetry readings locally and worldwide. Former UK journalist Martin Blyth offers a stimulating range of poetry reviews and opinion. Poet Martin Stannard has set up a poetry blog (an evolving diary) which encourages online comment and contribution. Bill Griffith's Lollipop tells you all you need to know about the small presses. Interested in a particular style? Haiku? Visual poetry? Traditional forms? They've all got their sites.

E-commerce

Shopping on the Net is now the preferred and often the only method for buying specialist material. The big Internet bookshop, Amazon, offers the hunter for that difficult to obtain poetry title searchable lists. Buying online is generally safe and swift although as with all mail order only as perfect as the van that brings the package to your door.

How to find it all

Use the search engine. The big ones – Google and Yahoo – can return enormous lists in response to keying in the word 'poetry'. I got 54,300,000 results out of Google, a fivefold increase on my results from a year ago, which does sound like verse is taking over the world. Much easier is to log onto a poetry resource site which runs clickable lists of relevant pages. The UK Poetry Society, the Poetry Library and Peter Howard's home page are worth consulting. Poetry Kit provides a large amount of poetry information, competition lists, and resources.

Some Web addresses for poets

Academi	www.academi.org
Attila The Stockbroker	www.attilathestockbroker.com
BBC	www.bbc.co.uk/arts/books
Martin Blyth	www.martinblyth.co.uk
Boomerang (magazine)	www.boomeranguk.com
British Poets e-mail list	www.jiscmail.ac.uk/lists/british-poets.html
Electronic Poetry Centre	wings.buffalo.edu/epc
Exultations & Difficulties (Martin Stannard's Blog	www.exultationsanddifficulties.blogspot.com
Matthew Francis	www.7greenhill.freeserve.co.uk
The Hyperliterature Exchange	hyperex.co.uk
Jacket (magazine)	www.jacketmagazine.com
Tom Leonard	www.tomleonard.co.uk

Lollipop (List of Little Press Publications)	www.indigogroup.co.uk/llpp
Patrick Martin's Poetry Resource	www.pmpoetry.com
Nth Position (magazine)	www.nthposition.com
Perihelion (magazine)	www.webdelsol.com/Perihelion
Peter Finch Archive	www.peterfinch.co.uk
Peter Howard's Poetry Page	www.hphoward.demon.co.uk/poetry
Poetry Super Highway (magazine)	poetrysuperhighway.com/PoetLinks.html
Poetry Kit (magazine)	www.poetrykit.org
The Poetry Library	www.poetrylibrary.org.uk
The Poetry Society (UK)	www.poetrysociety.org.uk
Poetryetc	www.jiscmail.ac.uk/lists/poetryetc.html
Riding the Meridian (magazine)	www.heelstone.com/meridian
Slope (magazine)	www.slope.org
Snakeskin (magazine)	homepages.nildram.co.uk/~simmers
Stride (magazine)	www.stridemagazine.co.uk
Trace	www.trace.ntu.ac.uk

Commercial publishers

It may come as a surprise to many but the number of commercial, stock-holding publishers who deal in poetry is actually extremely small. Despite the apparent acceptability of verse, profit is easier turned elsewhere. Where once there were a multitude of mainstream poetry imprints there are now only three or four. Poetry is a commercial risk and the bookshops generally don't welcome it. If it appears on a publisher's list then it's there for decoration.

The obvious exception to this approach is long-term market leader and envy of the whole business **Faber & Faber**. Here, editor Paul Keegan presides over a list which continues to be as important to the firm as when T.S. Eliot inaugurated it more than seventy years ago. This is the imprint most poets would like to join. The greats of the twentieth century are here – Pound, Eliot, Plath, Hughes, Larkin. Seamus Heaney sold half a million copies when he won the Nobel prize. The imprint is built on distinctively designed class reflected even in its anthologies (e.g. *The Thunder Mutters – 101 Poems for the Planet* – ed. Alice Oswald). Its roster of contemporary poets includes some of the best we have – Simon Armitage, Derek Walcott, Don Paterson, Andrew Motion, Christopher Logue, Alice Oswald, Hugo Williams, Paul Muldoon, Douglas Dunn. The press publishes forty or so poetry titles each year although new editions to the list are rare. If you fancy your chances then send a brief covering letter and a sample of your writing (6–10 poems) not forgetting s.a.e., if you think this is where you'll fit in.

A commercial editor with excellent taste is **Cape**'s Robin Robertson. His list is by no means all things to all people. Michael Longley, Sharon Olds, Peter Redgrove and John Burnside are typical. Roberston produces four or five titles annually including some selecteds (Burnside, Olds, Crawford) and new first volumes (Leonita Flynn, Helen Farish, James Sheard) – all books, no anthologies. Worth trying? Yes, but potential contributors should never waste anyone's time by not looking at the list first. Poetry at fellow Random House press, **Chatto & Windus**, is slightly lower than that at Cape and includes Bernard O'Donoghue, Ruth Padel and John Fuller. Anthologies are an increasing speciality. Worth trying? No, unless supported by a strong recommendation from an established fellow practitioner Chatto does not want to see unsolicited manuscripts.

Also at Random House, **The Harvill Press** hangs on with an interest in European translation and Paul Durcan. They also publish Michael Schmidt's fine anthology *The Harvill Book of Twentieth-Century Poetry in English*. Harvill will look at new manuscripts but chances are slim. New writers would be better off starting elsewhere. **Canongate** (along with its imprint **Payback Press**) recycles Robbie Burns and publishes new work from Lemn Sissay, Alan Spence, Gil Scott-Heron and Gillian Ferguson although its output appears to be on the decline. Among the other commercial houses activity appears to be limited to nominal titles, anthologies or back-list obligations. **HarperCollins** makes money from Daisy Goodwin's anthologies and its own version of Purple Ronnie, Edward Monkton. **Hutchinson** sticks with Dannie Abse. **Virgin** does Charles Bukowski and Spike Milligan. **Methuen** sells John Hegley and anthologies of cricket poetry and verse for everyday. **Allen Lane** does Patrick Kavanagh and anthologies from WW1. **Bloomsbury** has Michael Ondaatje, Lewis Carroll and anthologies edited by Roger McGough. **Cassell** anthologises the poems from the London Underground. **Hamish Hamilton** does John Updike. **John Murray** recycles Betjeman and prints anthologies of old chestnuts and travel verse. **Everyman** concentrates on work that's out of copyright, Dylan and R.S. Thomas. **W.W. Norton** mainly handles Americans and now has the legendary **New Directions** as one of its imprints. **Boxtree** keeps Purple Ronnie in the hands of those who don't like poetry. Some specialist interests are dealt with at **Lion** (Christian verse) and **Windhorse Publications** (Buddhist) – but it isn't a lot.

The smaller operators

Not all commercial publishing is vast and conglomerate. A few independents still exist and on their lists poetry occasionally occurs. Northern Ireland general publisher, the **Blackstaff Press**, brings out one or two poetry titles annually, including Patrick Crotty's groundbreaking *Modern Irish Poetry*. Welsh family firm **Gwasg Gomer** produces neat editions of Gillian Clarke, John Barnie, Nigel Jenkins and others. Check its site at www.gomer.co.uk **Polygon** (which is an imprint of **Birlinn Ltd**) continues to mix Gaelic with English. The press has at least half a dozen poets on the list including Roddy Gorman, Liz Lochhead and W.N. Herbert. At the **Onlywomen Press** editor Lilian Mohin publishes two poetry titles annually. Marilyn Hacker, Elana Dykewomon, Paula Jennings, and Suniti Namjoshi are typical. Check its anthology *Not for the Academy: Lesbian Poets*. Others in the field include **Frances Lincoln** and **Y Lolfa**.

Universities

With **OUP**'s contemporary list gone to Carcanet, interest among the UK's university presses is sparse. Reprints and literary studies at **Cambridge**, the same at **Manchester**. At the **University of Wales Press**, which publishes a splendid series of collected works from Welsh poets, you need to be dead. American university presses such as **Nebraska**, **Princetown**, **Louisiana**, **Wisconsin**, **Chicago**, **Harvard**, **Michigan**, North Carolina, **Washington**, **Alabama** and **California** do an increasing amount of verse but exclusively by Americans. King's College, London began **MPT Books** which publishes modern poetry in translation. Wolfgang Görtschacher's **Poetry Salzburg** is an independent Anglophone operation run from the University of Salzburg in Austria. It publishes six or so titles annually concentrating on translations from European minorities and collections from neglected English-language poets including a number from the UK. Its magazine is *Poetry Salzburg Review*. Its website is at www. poetrysalzburg.com

The mass-market paperback

The popular end is where many poets imagine the best starting place to be. Paperback houses were founded to publish inexpensive reprints of hard-covered originals and, despite years of innovation, to a large extent still fulfil this role. Being neither cheap nor (in sales terms) that popular, poetry does not really fit in. Among the carousels at airports you do not see it. Check the empires of **Arrow**, **Bantam**, **Corgi**, **Headline** and **Mills & Boon**. If you discount the inspirational, you won't find a book of verse between them. But there are exceptions. At **Penguin**, where things are always different, poetry has a significant role. With its unfailing commercial ear the company have correctly assessed the market for contemporary and traditional verse and filled it. Reprinting important volumes pioneered by less commercial poetry presses, originating historic and thematic anthologies, reviving classic authors and producing translations en route, Penguin continues to provide an almost unrivalled introduction to the world of verse. But appearances aside, this is most certainly no place for the beginner. 'We publish almost no new or unknown poets. In fact we publish very little new poetry beyond a small circle of established poets. We concentrate on selecteds and general anthologies,' publishing director Tony Lacey told me. The company focuses on sure sellers such as James Fenton, Michael Rosen, Geoffrey Hill, Tony Harrison and Roger McGough. The main thrust remains the re-packaging of Derek Mahon, Carol Ann Duffy and U.A. Fanthorpe, a good range of modern poets in translation along with larger collections from the likes of William Empson, Allen Ginsberg and Patrick Kavanagh. The company's poetry overview anthologies, the Simon Armitage and Robert Crawford edited *British and Irish Poetry Since the War*, Peter Forbes' *Scanning the Century* and Paul Keegan's *New Penguin Book of English Poetry* are musts. Despite these obvious winners Lacey sees the whole market for verse as small, despite the hype.

Penguin's nearest rival, **Picador**, the literary paperbacker from **Pan Macmillan**, has developed into one of the country's leading poetry publishers.

Under the commanding eye of successful and non-metropolitan poet Don Paterson it has moved into high gear putting out a stream of successful collections both from new poets such as Jacob Polley and Yusef Komunyaaka along with established names such as Kathleen Jamie, Peter Porter, Carol Ann Duffy, Kate Clanchy, Michael Donaghy, American poet laureate Billy Collins and Sean O'Brien. With its reliable content Picador is a UK reference point. Paterson will bring out at least six new titles annually as well as a range of bestselling anthologies. Recent examples include Kate Clanchy's *All the Poems You Need To Say Hello*, an anthology of poems to mark the birth of a baby. Worth trying here? 'Certainly: ten poems are better than a full-length ms, but establish some track record in the reputable journals first,' advises Paterson. The imprint reckons to receive around 700 book-length submissions annually and the rate of take-up from this slush pile is low.

The specialists

Despite a clear lack of success in the commercial marketplace, poetry still gets published in quantity. But by whom? By the specialist independents. These are the small army of semi-commercial operations scattered across the country. They are run by poetry enthusiasts whose prime concern starts not with money but with the furtherance of their art. Most (but not all) receive grant aid, without which their publishing programmes would be sunk. They are models of what poetry publishing should be – active, involving, alert and exciting. They promote their lists through readings, tours, websites and broadcasts and they involve their authors in the production and sales of their books. Never before have new poets been faced with so many publishing opportunities. Just how does the reader see through the flood? By reputation. Two specialists publishers have emerged well ahead of the pack – **Carcanet** and **Bloodaxe**. Along with Faber, Cape and Picador these two bring out and distribute more poetry books than any other British imprint. Distribution is a key here. The advent of print-on-demand technology has led to a considerable increase in the number of titles being published. But not all of these reach the shops.

Taking them alphabetically, Neil Astley's acclaimed **Bloodaxe Books** publishes at least thirty titles annually. Based in Northumberland and begun in Newcastle in the late1970s, the press is unhindered by a past catalogue of classical wonders or an overly regional concern. It relentlessly pursues the new. Astley presents the complete service from thematic anthologies, world greats and selecteds to slim volumes by total newcomers. The press has its own range of excellent handbooks to the scene including *Getting into Poetry* and *Writing Poems* along with an increasing range of critical volumes. Best poetry sellers are its anthologies: Neil Astley's own *Staying Alive* along with his *Being Alive* (both huge sellers), Edna Longley's *Bloodaxe Book of 20th Century Poetry* and its decade-framing anthology *The New Poetry*. Bloodaxe relishes the chance to publish work from outside the standard English mainstream – Ireland, Scotland and Wales are all well represented, as are more traditional UK outsiders such as J.H. Prynne. Bestsellers include Jackie Kay, Simon

Armitage, Benjamin Zephaniah, Tony Harrison and Brendan Kennelly. Bloodaxe will not go rusty with age. Check its website, one of the best poetry sites on the Web, at www.bloodaxe.com

The second, **Carcanet Press**, has been the consistent recipient of critical accolades. Publishing four Nobel Prize-winning authors and four Pulitzers helps. It is once again almost exclusively a publisher of verse, though some volumes of literary criticism, fiction and related titles also emanate from the house. Carcanet currently has over 900 titles in print, reps in forty-two countries and pursues a programme that brings out thirty-five or so poetry titles annually. Managing Director Michael Schmidt agrees with Auden's observation that most people who read verse read it for some reason other than for the poetry. He fights the tide with his own mainstream journal *PN Review*. Carcanet has a policy of serious quality. 'I am strongly aware of the anti-modernist slant in a lot of poetry publishing, and publish to balance this,' he comments. 'Most submissions we receive come from people ignorant of the list to which they are submitting. Nothing is more disheartening than to receive a telephone call asking whether Carcanet publishes poetry.' The press has a four-part editorial programme: to publish new writing, to dust down substantial but neglected figures of the last and earlier centuries, to encourage the translation of poetry, and to explore poets' prose and work relating to modern poetry. There is a bias against poetic nationalism and against Little Englandism. Typical of its list are John Ashbery, Sujata Bhatt, Eavan Boland, Alison Brackenbury, Gillian Clarke, Elaine Feinstein, Louise Gluck, Lorna Goodison, Jorie Graham, Sophie Hannah, Mimi Khalvati, Thomas Kinsella, Bill Manhire, Christopher Middleton, Edwin Morgan, Sinead Morrissey, Les Murray, John Peck, Tom Raworth, Peter Scupham, Charles Tomlinson and others. Carcanet has an air of purpose about it. 'We avoid the technicolour and pyrotechnic media razzmatazz,' says Schmidt. Have a look at its website – www. carcanet.co.uk New poets are welcome to submit. Send 6–10 pages of work and expect to wait six weeks for a reply. Carcanet's *New Poetries* and *Oxford Poets* series of anthologies give an idea where the taste of the press is going next.

There are other specialists with similar aims and style but perhaps with not quite the Carcanet/Bloodaxe reach.

Anvil Press Poetry, founded by Peter Jay in 1968, is England's longest-standing independent poetry publisher. They publish the best of English language poets: Ros Barber, Martina Evans, A.B. Jackson, Dennis O'Driscoll, Greta Stoddart and others. In addition, Anvil boasts a backlist containing four Nobel Prize Laureates and has a deserved reputation for the finest translations of the finest poets in the international canon (Apollinaire, Baudelaire, Bei Dao, Goethe, Hikmet, Lorca, Neruda, Seferis, Tagore, etc.). Output is steady at a dozen books a year and sales manager Jerry Whyte reports that sales are also steady, thanks largely to strong turnover Stateside. For those who wish to familiarise themselves with the flavour of the Anvil list, Jay's acclaimed anthology *The Spaces of Hope* gives a perfect starting point. Its informative website is at www.anvilpresspoetry. com **Enitharmon Press** cares about presentation and publishes fine quality literary editions with good bindings, quality paper and dust jackets. Enitharmon has little interest in fashion. The press is 'dedicated to a poetry of the human spirit in an age of rampant commercialism' (Anne Stevenson). Owner Stephen Stuart-Smith continues a policy of publishing new, established and unjustly neglected poets, with output now up to twenty volumes annually. Typical of the list are U.A. Fanthorpe, Anna Adams, Anthony Thwaite, Duncan Forbes, Isaac Rosenberg and Alan Brownjohn. The future looks bright and includes Paul Muldoon, Jane Duran and Seamus Heaney. Visit www.enitharmon.co.uk for more information and samples of some of its poets reading.

Tony Ward's **Arc Publications**, based in Lancashire, brings out around twenty-five poetry titles annually. 'We publish work that we believe important, innovative and of outstanding quality,' Ward told me. The imprint has Jean Boase-Beier, Jo Shapcott and John Kinsella on the board and maintains a backlist of in excess of 180 titles. Ivor Cutler, Julia Darling, Michael Haslam, Alamgir Hashmi (Pakistan) Bejan Matur (Turkey), Elizabeth Smither (New Zealand), Jackie Wills and the anthology *A Fine Line* are top sellers. Arc's policy is to publish the best in contemporary poetry and its list is particularly strong in translations in bilingual editions, authors from overseas whose first language/adopted tongue is English, and anthologies from Eastern and Central Europe specialising in translations from the minority languages. The Arc website is at www.arcpublications.co.uk Submissions from unpublished authors are not accepted. Poets should familiarise themselves with the list before sending anything and, unless accompanied by a publishing history and s.a.e. will not be considered. 'We do not wish to put writers off or dampen enthusiasm, but we have never yet accepted an unpublished author,' is the official line. You have been warned.

Ward has an excellent reputation as a printer to the poetry press community and over the years has done splendid job for David Tipton's **Redbeck Press**. Tipton, who came up the pamphlet route used by many a small press, drove Redbeck into the top echelon publishing everything from Argentinean poets to Michael Tolkien, Alexis Lykiard and the British beats. His star title of recent times has been Debjani Chatterjee's 200-page *Redbeck Anthology of British South Asian Poetry*. At the end of 2005 Redbeck ceased publishing new books and exists today only in order to sell its backlist. Non-centralist, politically incorrect and over. A great loss.

Seren Books is a Welsh-based literary house publishing novels, art books, short fiction, biographies and critical texts. The imprint has a solid interest in verse and publishes six to eight new single-author volumes annually. Poetry editor Amy Wack reads *everything* submitted but admits that she has only ever accepted one unsolicited manuscript in her entire tenure. Poets should read more, she says. Editions are quality productions with plenty of attention paid to design inside and out. Typical recent poets include Kathryn Gray, Christopher Meredith, Pascale Petit, Owen Sheers and Sheenagh Pugh. Its major bestseller is Dannie Abse's *Twentieth Century Anglo-Welsh Poetry*. A good press sampler is its anthology *Oxygen – New Poets from Wales*. Its website is www.serenbooks.com

Rupert Loydell's **Stride** has gathered a good reputation for catholic taste and running risks. After thirty-three issues in hard-copy his eponymous magazine is now available on the Web at www.stridemagazine.co.uk. This is an excellent sample of Stride's taste with an eclectic mix of verse, criticism and feature. Based in the southwest, output is six to ten titles annually. The back list now runs to more than 200 titles ranging from the totally unknown to the famous. Stride perfectly fills the gap between the avant-garde and the user-friendly. Recent successes include Peter Redgrove, Robert Lax, Rose Flint, Phil Bowen and Charles Wright. The future will see more American titles and a new anthology of lyrical verse. Visit its website at www.stridebooks.com for up to date information. Its anthology, *Ladder to the Next Floor,* offers a sampler of how the press got where it is.

Peterloo Poets, based in Cornwall, represents poetry without frills, without fuss, and most definitely without the avant-garde. Run by Harry Chambers, the press aims to publish quality work by new and neglected poets, some of them late starters, to co-publish with other reputable presses, and to establish a Peterloo list of succeeding volumes by a core of poets of proven worth. Heaney described Chambers as one of the 'great hearers and hearteners of the work being done in British and Irish Poetry'. Peterloo, which represents a stable centre for many people's idea of what poetry is, runs an active backlist of nearly 200 titles. Bestsellers include U.A. Fanthorpe, Dana Gioia, Elma Mitchell and M.R. Peakcoke. Poets central to the list are Ann Drysdale, John Mole, William Scammell, David Sutton and John Whitworth. Recent additions include R.V. Bailey, Brian Bartlett, Anne-Marie Fyfe, Kate Scott, Christine Webb and John Weston. Peterloo, now in its twenty-ninth year, runs its own poetry competition. The open section has a first prize of £1500 and thirteen other prizes. The 15–19 age group section has five prizes each of £100. Chambers insists that prospective contributors to the press have had at least six poems published in reputable magazines. Send a full ms accompanied by an s.a.e. large enough to carry your ms back to you. Chambers currently takes a couple of months to reply, and is full to the year 2007. Peterloo are at www.peterloopoets.com Peterloo has recently and unaccountably lost its Arts Council grant so its future is now uncertain.

John Kinsella and Chris Hamilton-Emery have established a Cambridge base for the international Australian-born **Salt**. Both the press and the journal of the same name have solid left-field leanings and an interest in contemporary poetics. Sales from its booming catalogue are rising. They stay alive by printing on-demand and command a large catalogue of substantial volumes. Salt has a contemporary modernist back list which includes Douglas Oliver, Jeff Nuttall, John Wilkinson, Allen Fisher, Annie Finch, Bill Griffiths, Peter Larkin and Drew Milne. Bestsellers include Todd Swift's *100 Poets Against the* War anthology, *Vanishing Points* – Rod Mengham and John Kinsella's modernist anthology, collections by Michael Hulse and John Tranter. Its excellent website, full of poetry news and reviews, is at www.saltpublishing.com – 'no boundaries, just great writing'. Critic Andrew Duncan's *The Failure of Conservatism in Modern British* Poetry is a roadmap. Expect more titles, more collections and more criticism. An innovator to watch.

There are other presses with less prodigious outputs but whose editions are still up there with the best of them. In Northumberland Margaret and Peter Lewis's **Flambard Press**, which also deals in northern fiction, publishes around four or five or so poetry titles annually in the Bloodaxe style. The press is interested in new and neglected poets especially from the North and the Borders. Wanda Barford, Desmond Graham, Gladys Mary Coles, Joolz and Amanda White are typical poets. Check www.flambardpress.co.uk Gladys Mary Coles has developed her **Headland Publications** into a regular Peterloo clone and is now producing an increasing number of fine books including an exciting range of anthologies. Her interest centres on north west England and Wales. Typical poets include John Barnie, Richard Poole, Brian Wake and Alison Chisholm. Ken Edwards' **Reality Street Editions** specialises in 'linguistically innovative writing by women and men on both sides of the Atlantic'. Publishing a small number of single-author volumes, translations and anthologies the press takes the new poetry seriously. Typical authors include Maggie O'Sullivan, Cris Cheek, Allen Fisher and Denise Riley. Reality Street discourages new submissions. Too much dross in the world already. Nicholas Johnson's **Etruscan Books** carries the flame for UK avant-garde poetry and performance with a series of readers, chapbooks and multi-contributor volumes along with a firstclass anthology of contemporary material, *Foil*. If anyone is pushing the edge out then Johnson is, and he's doing it with style. His poets include Bob Cobbing, Gael Turnbull, Stuart Montgomery, Harriet Tarlo, Ed Dorn, Maurice Scully, Wendy Mulford, Sean Rafferty, Carl Rakosi, Bill Griffiths and Tom Pickard. The press is on the Web at www. seaham.i12.com/ etruscan

Paul Beasley's poetry agency (see *Organisations of Interest to Poets*) **57 Productions**, represents performance poetry heartland and, realising that most of his material works better on audio, has concentrated on editions on cassette and CD. Recent releases include *Poetry in Performance Volume 1* and *Volume 2 (the Jukebox edition)*, Michael Rosen and Jean 'Binta' Breeze – with extant titles from R.S. Thomas, Christopher Logue and John Cooper Clarke. In Huddersfield Janet Fisher and Peter Sansom run **Smith/Doorstop** the poetry imprint of its enterprising **Poetry Business** (see *Organisations of Interest to Poets*). The press produces seven new titles annually. Michael Laskey, Andrew Wilson and Catherine Smith are recent authors. Smith/Doorstop also runs an annual poetry pamphlet competition as well as producing poetry on cassette. Its *Contemporary Poems* edited by Peter Sansom and Lesley Jeffries, offers a good critical introduction to the scene. Its magazine is *The North*. On the Web it is at www.poetrybusiness. co.uk With North American connections, Jessie Lendennie runs **Salmon Publishing** from the Cliffs of Moher, Co. Clare, in Ireland. The press has been in the business for twenty-four years and publishes some of the best-designed titles in the West. An Irish connection is pretty useful when trying here, although Salmon do look at material from further afield. Poets published include Adrienne Rich, Carol Ann Duffy, Ray Bradbury, James Liddy, Eamonn Wall, Rita Ann Higgins, Marvin Bell, James Simmons and Mary O'Malley. Salmon have an excellent website at www.salmonpoetry.com. which includes discussion, advice, events listings, sound files and a complete bookshop. And if the poetry is not flowing you can book into a Salmon Creative Writing Workshop. **Peepal Tree** is the largest independent publisher of Caribbean and black British poetry. Founded in 1986 they now produce about twelve poetry titles annually. Typical poets include Kwame Dawes, Dorothea Smartt, Raman Mundair, David Dabydeen and Anthony Kellman. Editor Jeremy Poynting reads over 1000 submissions annually and is not known for speedy responses. You can view the Peepal Tree catalogue at www.peepaltreepress.com

John Lucas's Nottingham-based **Shoestring Press** brings out established but unfashionable poets. Recent books include Nadine Brummer, Vernon Scannell, Alan Dent, Angela Leighton, Graham Holderness, J.C. Hall, Barbara Hardy, Evan Gwyn Williams and Ian Caws. *Take Five 04* is an introductory anthology. Check Shoestring's website at www.shoestringpress.co.uk Peter Fallon's **Gallery Press** in Co. Meath, after more than twenty-five years of publishing a veritable Irish institution, continues to produce substantial quality collections from the likes of Frank Orsmby, Paul Muldoon, Sean Dunne, Derek Mahon, Medbh McGuckian, Richard Murphy and everyone who is anyone on the Irish scene. Edinburgh's **Luath Press,** from the heart of Burns country, has spawned an increasing poetry roster which includes Alistair Findlay, Gerry Cambridge, Donald Smith and Angus Calder and Beth Junor's anthology of 2,000 years of war poetry. Its website is at www.luath.co.uk

In Wales **Parthian Books**, under poetry editor Richard Gwyn continues to publish poets who resist categorisation and challenge notions of what poetry might be. Typical poets include Lloyd Robson, David Greenslade, Rhian Saadat and Ifor Thomas. Its anthology *The Pterodactyl's Wing* collects the best of Welsh world poetry.

Now that technology, and in particular print on demand, has made life easier for publishers it's become harder and harder to draw the line between the poetry specialists and the classic small presses. The difference may simply be a matter of distribution although the new and much more stringent stocking policies adopted by chain booksellers may end up turning poetry into an entirely Amazon-sourced pursuit.

The regional anthologies

Running in parallel with the high-ground literary approach of much of the poetry world are empires largely unknown to the taste-makers and ignored by the critics. The biggest, Ian and Tracy Walton's **Forward Press** in Peterborough, now turns over 2.2 million pounds annually, has produced approximately 15,000 titles in print in fifteen years, and reckons to account for the highest proportion of all new verse published in the UK. Depressed with 'twenty years of not being able to enjoy poetry' because it was inevitably obscure, the couple moved from their back kitchen to a three-storey office-block in the service of 800,000 active British verse scribblers. Forward Press targets contributors who find much contemporary poetry 'over complex and difficult to understand'.

For over fifteen years Forward Press have enthusiastically promoted an 'accessible, sincere poetry which everyone can relate to'. Although they have printed the likes of Carol Ann Duffy and Simon Armitage the higher realms are not for them. Publishing under a number of imprints including Poetry Now, Anchor Books, Young Writers and Triumph House, the operation receives thousands of contributions annually. 'It is a bit like amateur dramatics,' Ian told me, 'anyone can take part.'

Forward Press' outstanding success is built on its approachability. The Walton's and their team of young editors include as many as one hundred and sixty to two hundred poems in each anthology. No entry fee is asked, nor are there purchase requirements. Submissions under thirty lines are preferred. Costs are kept down by using in-house printing equipment coupled to serviceable bindings. But if you want to own a copy of your work in print, and for most contributors this is the whole raison d'être for writing, then you have to buy a copy. However this is no traditional vanity operation. No one is actually being ripped off nor are the publishers raking in exorbitant profits. Page for page their titles are not much more expensive than those of Cape or Faber and are cheaper than the output of some little presses. All published poets are entered for free into the Top 100 Poets of the Year Award with an annual prize fund of £10,000. First prize is £3000. Critics claim that quality at Forward Press is being neglected in exchange for quantity. Dumb down your criteria for inclusion, cram the poems in, sell more copies. Undoubtedly the genuine literary achievement of appearing in one of Forward Press' books is questionable. In mitigation it must be said that for some writers this will be their much-needed beginning (check Angela Macnab and Sally Spedding), but for others the only success they are ever going to get.

In addition to its schools and regional collections Forward Press runs a bi-monthly journal, *Poetry Now Magazine*, which has been established for over twelve years; two young writer magazines, *Scribbler!* (7–11yrs) and *Wordsmith* (11–16 yrs); **New Fiction**, an imprint for short story writers; and **Spotlight Poets** – a joint publishing venture which showcases a dozen new poets a time. Its Writers' Bookshop imprint publishes a most useful series of reference books including subject and genre guides, directories and handbooks. Forward Press offers the complete poetry life. If *A Treasured Moment, Perceptions of Life, A Primrose Promise, In High Spirits, Message from Within* and *From A Distance* sound like your scene send for the group's information pack (Remus House, Peterborough, PE2 9JX), ring them on 01733 898105, fax them on 01733 313524, check the interactive website www.forwardpress.co.uk or e-mail your request to info@forwardpress. co.uk. You'll find no dubious accommodation address dealing here, but on the other hand, few literary giants either.

Envious of Forward's success at catching the hearts and minds of most of the

UK's poetry hobbyists a good number of rival empire builders have risen in its wake: regional poetry anthologies, Best of Britain collections, compendiums of English, Scottish, Irish and Welsh verse abound. Contributions are sourced through notices on library walls, local free-sheets, local radio and through direct mail. These operations vary from the glossy to a number of pathetically produced and, one hopes, short-lived incarnations based in the non-metropolitan sticks. No actual rip-off occurs and contributors tend to get in whether they purchase or not. But if you want to see your work then you must buy and the books can cost upwards of £30 pounds. Before agreeing to contribute, check the press's output. Do not submit blindly, research its back list. It is what Faber would demand of you. The rule applies to the whole poetry scene.

The small press and the little magazine

Small publishing ventures have been with us since the dawn of print. And today, from a technical point of view, things are easier to manage than ever. Costs are down. Technology scores. For the past decade small-press and little magazine publishing has seen a golden age, but there are signs of change. In the face of so-simple Internet, could print-only little mags be ending? Closures outnumber start-ups. Why bother with print? On the Web there are no distribution difficulties and size just doesn't matter. But the small mag isn't dead, not yet.

Statistically, the small presses and the little magazines have been the largest UK publishers of new poetry both in terms of range and circulation for decades, although there are signs that things are changing. They operate in a bewildering blur of shapes and sizes everywhere from Brighton to Birmingham and Aberystwyth to Aberdeen. For up to the moment data have a look at the address list maintained by the Poetry Library at www.poetrylibrary.org.uk/magazines

This country's best poetry magazines all began as classic littles. Between them *PN Review, Ambit, Orbis, Poetry Review*, Craig Raine's *Arete, The Rialto, Acumen, The North, Smiths Knoll* and *Envoi*, do not come up to even half the circulation of journals like *Shooting Times* and *All About Soap* – which says a lot about the way society values its poetry. Nonetheless, taken as a group, they will get to almost everyone who matters. They represent poetry as a whole. Read these and you will get some idea of where the cutting edge is. In the second division in terms of kudos lie the regional or genre specialists such as *Raw Edge* (new writing from the West Midlands), the *New Welsh Review, Poetry Wales, Poetry Ireland, Chapman* (Scotland's quality literary magazine), *Krax* (humorous verse), *Poetry Scotland, Mslexia* (for women who write), *Poetry Church, Borderlines* (Anglo-Welsh poets) and *Haiku Quarterly (HQ Magazine)*. All these magazines are well produced, sometimes with the help of grants, and all represent a specific point of view. In Wales there is *Barddas* for poets using strict meter and in Scotland *Lallans* for poets working in Lowland Scots. The vast majority of small magazines, however, owe no allegiance and range – from quality round-ups *Smoke, Tears in the*

Fence, Reach, Poetry Nottingham, former Rialto editor John Wakeman's splendid *SHOp,* Colin Shaddick's stapled occasional *Saw,* the Usk Valley's *Scintilla,* the enormously long-lived *Iota* (now managed by *Ragged Raven*) and Barry Tebb's notorious *Leeds Poetry Weekly,* to irregulars like the *Yellow Crane* (interesting new poems), *Rubies in the Darkness* (high-quality romantic), *Roundyhouse* (bards from both sides of the border), *Pulsar* (poems from the Ligden Poetry Society), *Moodswing* (Talking Pen's pocket broadsheet), *Other Poetry* (expresses the right to differ), *Quattrocento* (an independent journal), *Anon* (your work judged by what it says rather than your name), The *Interpreter's House* (the best prose and verse that the editor can get) and *Skald* (the innovative and experimental). Some like the *Penniless Press* are for the poor of pocket and the rich of mind, *Fire* goes for length and the otherwise unpublishable. If you can't find a magazine that suits you and your style then you can't be writing poetry. On the other hand, if you are really sure you are then start your own.

Among the small presses there is a similar range with increased production on all sides. Brian Wake and Tony Dash's enormously long-lived **Driftwood Publications** extends the Liverpool vision with Jim Mangnall, David Bateman and Henry Graham. Will Parfitt's **PS Avalon** publishes inspirational and contemplative poetry including Owen Ahrmanian and Keith Hackwood. Now that funding is flowing again David Perman's **Rockingham Press** is back in the heart of it. Recent collections from Ware poets Frances Wilson and Jane Evans plus Sally Carr, Jane Kirwan and Danielle Hope. The press has an online catalogue at www.rockpress.freeserve.co.uk/ The Leeds-based **Sixties Press** publishes Barry Tebb, Brenda Williams, Niall McGrath and an excellent anthology of Gregory Award-winners' work. Supplementing the magazine, **Rialto** brings out poetry scene stalwarts Julia Casterton, Andrew Waterhouse and others. **Feather Books** publishes Christian verse, Alan Halsey's **West House Books** publishes the innovative Geraldine Monk, David Annwn, Kelvin Corcoran, David Kennedy and others. **Five Leaves** anthologises British socialist poetry. **Katabasis** publishes Latin American poets. Andrea Brady and Keston Sutherland's **Barque Press** publishes post-language poets including John Tranter, Peter Manson, Andrew Duncan and Tom Jones. Janet Murch and Bob Mee's **Ragged Raven Press** looks to the middle path with Tony Petch, John Robinson, Chris Kinsey and others. Andy Croft's **Smokestack** magazine may no longer be with us but his new press of the same name has a list that includes Alison Fell, Sebastian Barker, John Goodby, Alan Dent, David Craig and Arnold Rattenbury. **Chapman New Writing** publishes the new generation from Scotland and includes Tom Bryan, Magi Gibson, Janet Paisley, Lydia Robb and Dilys Rose. With aid from Northern Arts, **Biscuit Publishing** publishes some excellent Tynesiders, as do fellow Independent Northern Publishers members **Arrowhead Books**, **Diamond Twig**, **Sand** and **Mudfog**. For the new writer these kinds of presses are the obvious place to try first. Indeed many have. Who put out T.S. Eliot's first? A small publisher. Dannie Abse, Peter Redgrove, James Fenton and Dylan Thomas, the same. R.S. Thomas, Ezra Pound and Edgar Allen Poe didn't even go that far – they published themselves.

Cash

Being a poet is not really much of an occupation. You get better wages delivering papers. There will be the odd £25 from the better-heeled magazine, perhaps even as much as £80 or so from those periodicals lucky enough to be in receipt of a grant, but generally it will be free copies of the issues concerned, thank you letters and little more. Those with collections published by a subsidised, specialist publisher can expect a couple of hundred pounds as an advance on royalties. Those using the small presses can look forward to complimentary copies. On the Internet published poets usually get nothing at all. The truth is that poetry itself is undervalued. You can earn money writing about it, reviewing it, lecturing on it, teaching it or, certainly, by giving public performances (£150 standard here, £1000 plus if you are Roger McGough, much more if you are Seamus Heaney). But at bottom, most things in the poetry business will earn better money than the verse itself. This isn't capitalism, this is art.

Readings

Since the great 1964 Beat Generation readings in the Albert Hall, there has been an ever-expanding phenomenon of poets on platforms, reading or reciting their stuff to an audience that can be anywhere between raptly attentive and fast asleep. Begin by attending and see how others manage. Watch out for local events advertised at your local library, ring your local arts council (in Wales look at www.academi.org). Poets with heavy reputations can often turn out to be lousy performers while many an amateur can really crack it. Don't expect to catch every image as you listen. Readings are not places for total comprehension but rather for glancing blows. Treat it as fun and it will be. If you are trying things yourself for the first time, make sure you've brought your books along to sell, stand upright, drop your shoulders, gaze at a spot at the back of the hall and blow.

Competitions and awards

Poetry competitions have been the vogue for decades with the most unlikely organisations sponsoring them. The notion here is that anonymity ensures fairness. Entries are made under pseudonyms so that if your name does happen to be Andrew Motion, then this won't help you much. Results seem to bear this out too. The big competitions, those run biennially by the **Arvon Foundation** with the help of commercial sponsors, the **Academi's** *Cardiff International* and the **Poetry Society's** *National* attract a large entry and usually throw up quite a number of complete unknowns among the winners. And why do people bother? Cash prizes can be large – thousands – but it costs at least a few pounds a poem to enter, and often much more than that. And there has been a trend for winners to come from places like Cape Girardeau, Missouri and Tibooburra, Australia. The odds are getting longer. Who won the last Arvon? I don't remember. But if you do fancy a try then it is a pretty innocent activity. You tie up a poem for a few months and you spend a little money. Winners' tips include reading the work of the judges to see how they do it, submitting non-controversial middle-of-the-road smiling things, and doing this just before the closing date so you won't have to wait too long. Try two or three of your best. Huge wodges are costly and will only convince the judges of your insecurity. Have a look at *The Ring of Words* (Sutton Publishing), an excellent historical anthology of Arvon contenders or the Arvon's own collections of its latest winners. For contests to enter watch the small mags, write to your local arts council, check out the *New Writer*, *Poetry London* or *Writer's News*, look on the notice board at your local library, or check the regularly updated list at **The Poetry Library** in London (see *Organisations of Interest to Poets*). And be wary of those that are free to enter. Before trying be sure it's not a vanity-press scam.

Poetry **Awards** are slightly different. These are usually made for published books and convention generally requires your publisher to make the nomination rather than yourself. These glittering prizes are increasing both in value and impact. Both the annual T.S. Eliot and Forward Prizes are now worth £10,000 a time with the poetry section of the Whitbread Book Award offering £5000. To win one of these your book needs to be pretty hot.

Radio and TV

Poetry on the broadcast media has never been much of a success. Verse is rarely visual. On TV, when it appears at all, it is usually great stuff read by actors whose over-trained voices relentlessly drive home the brightness, the melancholy or the laughter of their lines. Opportunities for the newcomer, even among the digital dross of Sky's outer reaches, are rare.

On radio, however, things can be different. In enlightened mode both Radio 3 and Radio 4 give over whole half-hours to verse and use a fair smattering of contemporary voices. What is usually important here are the poets themselves. Listen out for *Poetry Please*, for *The Verb*, for programmes produced by Sue Roberts, Sara Davies, Fiona Mclean, Julian May and others. The BBC's website (www.bbc.co.uk/arts/poetry/index.shtml) collects a great deal of information on the Corporation's poetry interests.

Poetry on radio is a large but difficult market. The BBC are pretty definite about having no remit to use 'unpublished or amateur verse'. Programme ideas should always be directed to a programme-making department at the BBC rather than to Radio 4 or Radio 3 themselves. If you are determined to put your verse on air then local and regional radio offer better possibilities. Try sending in self-produced readings on cassette (if you are any good at it) or topical poetry which regional magazine programmes could readily use. Don't expect to be paid much.

Starting up

Probably the best place will be locally. Find out through the library, your local arts council or check the Internet to find which writers' groups gather in your area and attend. There you will meet others of a like mind, encounter whatever locally produced magazines there might be and get a little direct feedback on your work. 'How am I doing?' is a big question for the emerging poet and although criticism is not all that hard to come by, do not expect it from all sources. Magazine editors, for example, will rarely have the time to offer advice. It is also reasonable to be suspicious of that offered by friends and relations – they will no doubt only be trying to please. Writers groups present the best chance for poets to engage in honest mutual criticism. But if you'd prefer a more detached, written analysis of your efforts and are willing to pay a small sum, then you could apply to *Prescription,* the service operated nationally by the Poetry Society (22 Betterton Street, London WC2H 9BU), to the service run by the Academi in Wales (see ***Organisations of Interest to Poets***) or to those run on an area basis by your regional arts council. There are also a number of non-subsidised critical services which you will find advertised in writers' magazines.

Read; if it's all a mystery to you, try Tony Curtis's *How to Study Modern Poetry* (Macmillan); Matthew Sweeney and John Hartley Williams' *Teach Yourself Writing Poetry* (Teach Yourself), John Whitworth's *Writing Poetry* (A&C Black) or my own *The Poetry Business* (Seren). How real poets actually work can be discovered by reading *Don't Ask Me What I Mean* (Picador), Don Paterson's collection of essays about modern British poets in their own words or *How Poets Work* (Seren). After all this, if you still think it's appropriate, try sending in.

How to do it

Increase your chances of acceptance by following simple, standard procedure:

- Type on a single side of the paper, A4 size, single-spacing with double between stanzas, exactly as you'd wish your poem to appear when published.
- Give the poem a title, clip multi-page works together, include your name and address at the foot of the final sheet. Avoid files, plastic covers, stiffeners and fancy clips of any sort.
- Keep a copy, make a record of what you send where and when, leave a space to note reaction.
- Send in small batches – six is a good number – with a brief covering letter saying who you are. Leave justification, apology and explanation for your writers group.
- Include a self-addressed, stamped envelope of sufficient size for reply and/or return of your work.
- Be prepared to wait some weeks for a response. Don't pester. Be patient. Most magazines will reply in the end.

- Never send the same poem to two places at the same time (and this includes e-zine vs. hard copy). If you've entered the poem for a competition then make sure you *never* simultaneously send it elsewhere.
- If you are thinking of sending your submission electronically *check* first. Some journals and publishers in the *Writer's Handbook* survey don't accept materials sent this way.
- Send your best. Work which fails to fully satisfy even the author is unlikely to impress anyone else.

Where?

Try the list which follows. This is by no means the whole UK small-press scene but only some of those where potential contributors might stand a chance. Even here do not expect unrelenting positive responses: magazines get overstocked, editors change, addresses shift, policy alters, operators run out of steam. Be prepared to hunt around, and for a lot of your work to come back. You can help improve things by buying copies. Send in an s.a.e. asking how much. The total market is vast and if you want to go further then you could consult the handout produced by *The Poetry Library* (see **Organisations of Interest to Poets**), *Light's List of Literary Magazines* which contains both UK and US addresses (John Light, Photon Press, The Lighthouse, 37 The Meadows, Berwick upon Tweed, Northumberland TD15 1NY) or Bill Griffiths' Internet list at *Lollipop* (www. indigogroup.co.uk/llpp/).

The next step

Once you have placed a few poems you may like to consider publishing a booklet. There are as many small presses around as there are magazines. Start with the upmarket professionals by all means but be prepared for compromise. The specialists and the small presses are swifter and more open to new work.

If all else fails you could do it yourself. Blake did, so did Walt Whitman. Technology puts the process within the reach of us all and if you can put up a shelf, there is a fair chance you will be able to produce a book to go on it. Read my *How to Publish Yourself* (Allison & Busby). Remember that publishing the book may be as hard as writing it but marketing and selling it is quite something else. Check Alison Baverstock's *Marketing Your Book: An Author's Guide* (A&C Black) if you really want to get ahead.

The listings

The list of addresses which follows is not exhaustive. Publishers come and go with amazing frequency. For up to the minute information check with some of the *Organisations of Interest to Poets* (see pages 158–162). Poetry has a huge market. It pays to keep your ear to the ground. The magazines and presses listed here have all been active during the past eighteen months and most (although be warned, *not all*) have indicated a willingness to look at new work. But do check before sending. Ask to see a catalogue or a sample copy. Good luck.

Poetry Presses

Abraxas Press
13 Copthall Gardens, Mill House, London
NW7 2NG

Agenda Editions
The Wheelwrights, Fletching Street, Mayfield
TN20 6TL
✉ agendapoetry@lycos.co.uk
Contact *Patricia McCarthy*
See also **Agenda** magazine.

Anvil Press Poetry Ltd
Neptune House, 70 Royal Hill, London
SE10 8RF
☎020 8469 3033   Fax 020 8469 3363
✉ anvil@anvilpresspoetry.com
www.anvilpresspoetry.com
Contact *Peter Jay*
Contemporary British poetry and poetry in
translation. See entry under *UK Publishers*.

Arc Publications
Nanholme Mill, Shaw Wood Road,
Todmorden OL14 6DA
☎01706 812338   Fax 01706 818948
✉ arc.publications@btconnect.com
www.arcpublications.co.uk
Contact *Tony Ward*
Contemporary poetry from new and established writers both in the UK and abroad. See
entry under *UK Publishers*.

Arrowhead Press
70 Clifton Road, Darlington DL1 5DX
✉ editor@arrowheadpress.co.uk
www.arrowheadpress.co.uk
Contact *Roger Collett*
Quality books and pamphlets of contemporary
poetry.

Astrapost
7 The Towers, Stevenage SG1 1HE
✉ octillion@ntlworld.com
Contact *Eric Ratcliffe*
Commissioned work only for non-profit, charity purposes, mainly.

Barque
13 Heathfield Park, Flat 2, London
NW2 5JE
✉ info@barquepress.com
www.barquepress.com
Contact *Andrea Brady*
See also **Quid** magazine.

BB Books
Spring Bank, Longsight Road, Copster Green,
Blackburn BB1 9EU
☎01254 249128
Contact *Dave Cunliffe*
Global Bohemia, post-Beat poetics and counter-
culture orientation. See also **Global Tapestry
Journal**.

Between the Lines
9 Woodstock Road, London N4 3ET
☎020 8374 5526   Fax 020 8374 5736
✉ btluk@aol.com
www.interviews-with-poets.com
Contact *Peter Dale & Others*
Interviews with leading contemporary poets.
See also **Waywiser Press**.

Beyond the Cloister Publications
74 Marina, St Leonards on Sea TN38 0BJ
☎01424 444072
Contact *Hugh Hellicar*
Anthologies of poetry and slim volumes to
launch poets. Themes of a multi-faith range welcome.

Big Little Poem Books
3 Park Avenue, Melton Mowbray LE13 0JB
Contact *Robert Richardson*
Effective contemporary approaches to the lyric
and epigram. See also **Door-To-Everywhere**
press.

Biscuit Publishing
Box 123, Washington, Newcastle upon Tyne
NE37 2YE
☎0191 431 1263
✉ brian@biscuitpublishing.com
www.biscuitpublishing.com

Contact *Brian Lister*

Publishers of fiction, non-fiction and poetry.

Black Arts Alliance
PO Box 86, Manchester M21 7BA
☎0161 832 7622   Fax 0161 832 2276
✉ baa@blackartists.org
www.blackartists.org.uk

Bloodaxe Books Ltd
Highgreen, Tarset NE48 1RP
☎01434 240500   Fax 01434 240505
✉ editor@bloodaxebooks.demon.co.uk
www.bloodaxebooks.com

Contact *Neil Astley*

Britain's leading publisher of new poetry. No submissions by e-mail attachments. See entry under **UK Publishers**.

The Boho Press
Bluechrome, PO Box 109, Portishead, Bristol BS20 7ZJ
✉ anthony@bluechrome.co.uk
www.bluechrome.co.uk

Contact *Anthony Delgrado*

See also **Reach** magazine.

Bucephalus Press
67 Hady Crescent, Chesterfield S41 0EB
☎01246 276532

Contact *David Holliday*

Founded in 2004 to publish small collections of poetry.

Canna Press
10 Severn Road, Canton, Cardiff CF11 9NB
✉ canna@care4free.net

Contact *Phil Maillard & Others*

Works of Chris Torrance.

Carcanet Press Ltd
4th Floor, Alliance House, 28–34 Cross Street, Manchester M2 7AQ
☎0161 834 8730   Fax 0161 832 0084
✉ info@carcanet.co.uk
www.carcanet.co.uk

Contact *Michael Schmidt*

Major poetry publisher. See entry under **UK Publishers**; also **PN Review** magazine.

Chanticleer Press
6/1 Jamaica Mews, Edinburgh EH3 6HN
☎0131 225 8883
✉ richard@livermore8304.freeserve.co.uk

Contact *Richard Livermore*

Poetry and ideas – not afraid to ask embarrassing questions and explore controversial issues. See also **Chanticleer Magazine**.

Chapman Publishing
4 Broughton Place, Edinburgh EH1 3RX
☎0131 557 2207   Fax 0131 556 9565
✉ chapman-pub@blueyonder.co.uk
www.chapman-pub.co.uk

Contact *Joy Hendry*

Scottish writing. See entry under **UK Publishers**.

Cinnamon Press
Meirion House, Glanyrafon, Tanygrisiau, Blaenau Festiniog LL4 3SU
☎01766 832112
✉ jan@coffeehousepoetry.co.uk
www.cinnamonpress.com

Contact *Dr Jan Fortune-Wood*

Contemporary poems of edge and depth from new voices and established writers. See also **Coffee House Poetry** magazine.

The Collective Press
c/o Penlanlas Farm, Llantilio Pertholey, Y-fenni NP7 7HN
☎01873 856350   Fax 01873 859559
✉ jj@jojowales.co.uk
www.welshwriters.com

Contact *John Jones & Frank Olding*

Non-profit promoter and publisher of contemporary poetry.

Cyhoeddiadau Barddas
Pen Rhiw, 71 Ffordd Pentrepoeth, Treforys, Swansea SA6 6AE
☎01792 792829

Contact *Alan Llwyd*

Barddoniaeth Gymreig – Welsh language poetry. See also **Barddas** magazine.

Day Dream Press
39 Exmouth Street, Swindon SN1 3PU
☎01793 523927

Contact *Kevin Bailey*

Diamond Twig
5 Bentinck Road, Newcastle upon Tyne NE4 6UT
☎0191 273 5326
✉ diamond.twig@virgin.net
www.diamondtwig.co.uk

Contact *Ellen Phethean & Others*

New writing by women in the north of England – no non-fiction or children's writing.

Diehard Publishers
3 Spittal Street, Edinburgh EH3 9DY
☎0131 229 7252
Contact *Ian W. King*

Poetry and drama, mainly Scottish. See also **Poetry Scotland** magazine.

Dionysia Press
20a Montgomery Street, Edinburgh EH7 5JS
☎0131 478 0680   Fax 0131 478 0680
Contact *Denise Smith*

Collections of poetry, words and translations. See also **Understanding Magazine**.

Doghouse Press
PO Box 312, Tralee GPO Co. Kerry, Republic of Ireland

Donut Press
46 Lothair RoadNorth, London N4 1EW
✉ donutcops@yahoo.co.uk
www.donutpress.co.uk

Door-To-Everywhere
3 Park Avenue, Melton Mowbray LE13 0JB
Contact *Robert Richardson*

Poem card series – imagination first! See also **Big Little Poem Books** press.

Driftwood Publications
5 Timms Lane, Formby L37 7DW
☎01704 833911   Fax 0151 524 0216
✉ janet.speedy@btinternet.com
Contact *Brian Wake*

New work by new and established poets more suited to the page than the stage.

Enitharmon Press
26B Caversham Road, London NW5 2DU
☎020 7482 5967   Fax 020 7284 1787
✉ books@enitharmon.co.uk
www.enitharmon.co.uk
Contact *Stephen Stuart-Smith*

Poetry and criticism. See entry under **UK Publishers**.

Erran Publishing
43 Willow Road, Carlton, Nottingham NG4 3BH
✉ erranpublishing@hotmail.com
www.poetichours.homestead.com

Contact *Nick Clark*

Non-profit supporter of Third World charities. See also **Poetic Hours** magazine.

Essence Press
8 Craiglea Drive, Edinburgh EH10 5PA
✉ jaj@essencepress.co.uk
www.essencepress.co.uk
Contact *Julie Johnstone*

Handbound editions of poetry, poetry postcards – interested in concrete poetry and nature. See also **Island** magazine.

Etruscan Books
28 Fowler's Court, Fore Street, Buckfastleigh TQ11 0AA
☎01364 643128   Fax 01364 643054
Contact *Nicholas Johnson*

Modernist, sound, visual poetry, US/UK poets.

Feather Books
PO Box 438, Shrewsbury SY3 0WN
☎01743 872177   Fax 01743 872177
✉ john@waddysweb.freeuk.com
www.waddysweb.freeuk.com
Contact *Rev. J. Waddington-Feather*

Christian poetry, drama, hymns, novels. See entry under **Small Presses**; also **The Poetry Church** magazine.

Feel Free Press
The Flat, Yew Tree Farm, Sealand Road, Chester CH1 6BS
☎07790 062317
✉ contact@openwidemagazine.co.uk
www.openwidemagazine.co.uk
Contact *James Quinton*

80 pages of punchy short fiction, poetry, reviews and interviews. See also **Open Wide** magazine.

57 Productions
57 Effingham Road, Lee Green, London SE12 8NT
☎020 8463 0866   Fax 020 8463 0866
✉ paul57prods@yahoo.co.uk
www.57productions.com
Contact *Paul Beasley*

Performance poetry on cassette and CD.

First Time Publications
The Snoring Cat, 16 Marianne Park, Dudley Road, Hastings TN35 5PU
☎01424 423105   Fax 01424 423105
✉ josephine.poetry@btopenworld.com

www.josephineaustin.co.uk
Contact *Josephine Austin*
See also **First Time** magazine.

Five Leaves Publications
PO Box 81, Nottingham NG5 4ER
☎0115 969 3597
✉ info@fiveleaves.co.uk
www.fiveleaves.co.uk
Contact *Ross Bradshaw*
Fiction, poetry, Jewish interest, social history.

Flambard
Stable Cottage, East Fourstones, Hexham
NE47 5DX
☎01434 674360   Fax 01434 674178
www.flambardpress.co.uk
Contact *Peter Elfed Lewis & Will Mackie*
Concentrates on poetry and literary fiction.

Flarestack Publishing
41 Buckley's Green, Alvechurch, Birmingham
B48 7NG
☎0121 445 2110
✉ flare.stack@virgin.net
Contact *Charles Johnson*
Considers first collections for A5 stapled pamphlet publication.

Forward Press
Remus House, Coltsfoot Drive, Woodston,
Peterborough PE2 9JX
☎01733 898105   Fax 01733 313524
✉ info@forwardpress.co.uk
www.forwardpress.co.uk
Contact *Kerrie Pateman*
General poetry and short fiction anthologies.
See also **Triumph House** press and **Poetry Now** magazine.

The Frogmore Press
18 Neville Road, Lewes BN7 1PF
☎07751 251689
www.frogmorepress.co.uk
Contact *Jeremy Page*
A forum for contemporary poetry, prose and artwork. See also **The Frogmore Papers** magazine.

The Gallery Press
Loughcrew, Oldcastle, Co. Meath, Republic of Ireland
☎00 353 49 854 1779
Fax 00 353 49 854 1779
✉ gallery@indigo.ie

www.gallerypress.com
Contact *Peter Fallon*
Poems, plays and prose by contemporary Irish writers.

Gomer Press/Gwasg Gomer
Llandysul Enterprise Park, Llandysul SA44 4JN
☎01559 363090   Fax 01559 363758
✉ gwasg@gomer.co.uk
www.gomer.co.uk
Contact *Ceri Wyn Jones*
Welsh interest. See entry under **UK Publishers**.

Green Arrow Publishing
2 Chambers Cottages, Underlyn Lane,
Marden, Tonbridge TN12 9BD
☎07967 315270
✉ mail@johndench.demon.co.uk
Contact *John Dench*
Collaborative publishing scheme and other services for writers. See also **Scriptor** magazine.

Gwasg Pantycelyn
Lôn Ddewi, Caernarfon LL55 1ER
☎01286 672018   Fax 01286 677823
✉ gwasgpantycelyn@ukonline.co.uk
Contact *R.M. Thomas*

Headland Publications
Ty Coch, Galltegfa, Ruthin LL15 2AR
☎0151 625 9128   Fax 0151 625 9128
Contact *Gladys Mary Coles*
Fine editions of poetry; anthologies.

Hearing Eye
Box 1, 99 Torriano Avenue, London NW5 2RX
www.torriano.org/hearing_eye
Contact *John Rety*
Poetry/literature publishers based in Kentish Town.

Hilltop Press
4 Nowell Place, Almondbury, Huddersfield
HD5 8PD
Contact *Steve Sneyd*
Specialist publisher of science fiction poetry and background material.

Hippopotamus Press
22 Whitewell Road, Frome BA11 4EL
☎01373 466653   Fax 01373 466653
✉ rjhippopress@aol.com
Contact *Roland John*

First collections of verse from those with a track record in the magazines. See also **Outposts** magazine.

Honno Welsh Women's Press

Canolfan Merched Y Wawr, Vulcan Street, Aberystwyth SY23 1JH
☎01970 623150   Fax 01970 623150
✉ post@honno.co.uk
www.honno.co.uk
Contact *Lindsay Ashford*

The Welsh women's press – novels, short stories, poetry and autobiographical anthologies. Must have a Welsh connection. See entry under **UK Publishers**.

I*D Books

Connah's Quay Library, Wepre Drive, Connah's Quay, Deeside
☎0161 226 3419

Poetry, short fiction, local history – mainly self-publishing by associated writers' group.

Iron Press

5 Marden Terrace, Cullercoats, North Shields NE30 4PD
☎0191 253 1901   Fax 0191 253 1901
✉ seaboy@freenetname.co.uk
www.ironpress.co.uk
Contact *Peter Mortimer*

Katabasis

10 St Martin's Close, London NW1 0HR
☎020 7485 3830
✉ katabasis@katabasis.co.uk
www.katabasis.co.uk
Contact *Dinah Livingstone*

Down-to-earth and Utopian poetry and prose from home an abroad – English and Latin American.

The King's England Press

Cambertown House, Commercial Road, Goldthorpe, Rotherham S63 9BL
☎01226 270258   Fax 01484 663790
✉ steve@kingsengland.com
www.kingsengland.com
Contact *Steve Rudd*

History, folklore, children's poetry. See also **The Potty Poets** press.

Kiss Production Limited

14 Carlisle Close, Colchester CO1 2NT
www.erotic-cafe.net

Ray Hollingsworth specialists.

KT Publications

16 Fane Close, Stamford PE9 1HG
☎01780 754193
Contact *Kevin Troop*

Always looking for new material of the highest standard. See also **Colours** and **The Third Half** magazines.

Landfill Press

17 Waldeck Road, Norwich NR4 7PG
www.landfillpress.co.uk
Contact *Jeremy Noel-Tod*

Laurel Books

282 The Common, Holt BA14 6QJ
☎01225 782874
✉ mail@laurelbooks.co.uk
www.laurelbooks.co.uk

Edward Thomas, Harold Monro and more.

Leafe Press

1 Leafe Close, Chilwell, Nottingham NG9 6NR
✉ leafepress@hotmail.com

Luath Press Ltd

543/2 Castlehill, The Royal Mile, Edinburgh EH1 2ND
☎0131 225 4326   Fax 0131 225 4324
✉ gavin.macdougall@luath.co.uk
www.luath.co.uk
Contact *Gavin MacDougall*

Fiction, poetry, history, travel, politics and much more.

Malfunction Press

Rose Cottage, 3 Tram Lane, Buckley CH7 3JB
✉ rosecot@presford.freeserve.co.uk
Contact *Peter E. Presford*

Mainly dedicated to science fiction, fantasy, light horror.

Mandrake

PO Box 250, Oxford OX1 1AP
☎01865 243671
✉ mandrake@mandrake.uk.net
Contact *Mogg Morgan*

New edge publishers specialising in magick and the occult – occasional poem used.

Mariscat Press

10 Bell Place, Edinburgh EH3 5HT
☎0131 343 1070
✉ hamish-whyte@virgin.net

Contact *Hamish Whyte & Diana Hendry*
Currently publishing poetry pamphlets only.

Masque Publishing
PO Box 3257, Littlehampton BN16 9AF
✉ masque_pub@tiscali.co.uk
myweb.tiscali.co.uk/masquepublishing
Contact *Lisa Stewart*
For self-publishers. See also **Decanto** magazine.

Morning Star Publications
Unit 6 (off Quay Building), Foundry Lane,
Byker, Newcastle upon Tyne NE6 1AF
✉ alexfinlay@yahoo.com
Contact *Alec Finlay*
Visual folios and pocketbooks.

Motet Press
17 Sea Road, Galway, Co. Galway, Republic of
Ireland

The Moving Finger
PO Box 4867, Birmingham B3 3HD
Contact *Dave Reeves*
See also **Raw Edge** magazine.

Mudfog Press
Arts Development, The Stables, Stewart Park,
The Grove, Marton, Middlesborough TS7 8AR
www.mudfog.co.uk
Contact *Andy Croft & Others*
The best new writers from Teesside.

New Departures/Poetry Olympics
PO Box 9819, London W11 2GQ
☎020 7229 7850   Fax 020 7729 7850
✉ bricolage92@hotmail.com
www.connectotel.com/PoetryOlympics
Contact *Michael Horovitz*

New Fountainhead Press
10 Frenchlands Hatch, Ockham Road South,
East Horsley KT24 6SJ
☎01483 285396
✉ stanley5@aol.com
Stanley Trevor writ large.

New Hope International
20 Werneth Avenue, Gee Cross, Hyde
SK14 5NL
✉ nhi@clara.net
www.nhi.clara.net/nhihome.htm
Contact *Gerald England*
Poetry booklet publisher. No longer considering unsolicited mss.

nthposition
38 Allcroft Road, London NW5 4NE
www.nthposition.com

The Old Stile Press
Catchmays Court, Llandogo, Nr Monmouth
NP25 4TN
☎01291 689226
✉ oldstile@dircon.co.uk
www.oldstilepress.com
Contact *Frances & Nicolas McDowall*
Fine, hand-printed books with text and images
– no unsolicited mss.

The Once Orange Badge Poetry Press
PO Box 184, South Ockenden RM15 5WT
☎01708 852827
✉ orangebadge@poetry.fsworld.co.uk
Contact *D.M. Heath*
A4 and A5 pamphlets – ideal for first collections. E-mail submissions preferred.

The One Time Press
Model Farm, Linstead Magna, Halesworth
IP19 0DT
☎01986 785422
www.onetimepress.com
Contact *Peter Wells*
Poetry of the forties in limited editions. Illus-
trated.

Orchard House
Criccieth LL52 0AH

Original Plus
Flat 3, 18 Oxford Grove, Ilfracombe
EX34 9HQ
☎01271 862708
✉ smithsssj@aol.com
members.aol.com/smithsssj/index.html
Contact *Sam Smith*
Requires something extra – another language
or markedly original. See also **The Journal**
magazine.

Othername Press
14 Rosebank, Rawtenstall, Rossendale
BB4 7RD
Poetry and surrealism.

Parthian Books
The Old Surgery, Napier Street, Cardigan
SA43 1ED

☎01239 612059   Fax 01239 612059
✉ parthianbooks@yahoo.co.uk
www.parthianbooks.co.uk
Contact *Richard Gwyn*
New Welsh writing.

Partners
289 Elmwood Avenue, Feltham TW13 7QB
✉ partners_writing_group@hotmail.com

Contact *Ian Deal*
Competitions and poetry pamphlets. See also **A Bard Hair Day**, **Imagenation** and **Poet Tree** magazines.

Peepal Tree Press Ltd
17 King's Avenue, Leeds LS1 1QS
☎0113 245 1703   Fax 0113 246 8368
✉ hannah@peepal.demon.co.uk
www.peepaltreepress.com
Contact *Jeremy Poynting*

Best in Caribbean and south Asian writing from around the world.

Peterloo Poets
The Old Chapel, Sand Lane, Calstock
PL18 9QX
☎01822 833473   Fax 01822 833989
✉ poets@peterloo.fsnet.co.uk
www.peterloopoets.co.uk
Contact *Harry Chambers*
Contemporary English poetry.

Pigasus Press
13 Hazely Combe, Arreton, Isle of Wight
PO30 3AJ
☎01983 865668
✉ mail@pigasuspress.co.uk
www.pigasus.press.co.uk
Contact *Tony Lee*
Publisher of science fiction magazine and genre poetry. See also **Scar Tissue** press.

Pighog Press
PO Box 145, Brighton BN1 6YU
✉ info@pighog.co.uk

Pikestaff Press
Ellon House, Harpford, Sidmouth
EX10 0NH
☎01395 568941
Contact *Robert Roberts*
Contemporary poetry belonging to the English tradition, mainly 24-page pamphlets.

Pipers' Ash Ltd
Pipers Ash, Church Road, Christian Malford,
Chippenham SN15 4BW
☎01249 720563   Fax 0870 056 8916
✉ pipersash@supamasu.com
www.supamasu.com
Contact *Mr A. Tyson*
Collections of 60 poems. See entry under **Small Presses**.

Planet
PO Box 44, Aberystwyth SY23 3ZZ
☎01970 611255   Fax 01970 611197
✉ planet.enquiries@planetmagazine.org.uk
www.planetmagazine.org.uk
Contact *John Barnie*

Fiction, poetry, current affairs, arts and environment. See also **Planet** magazine and entry under **Small Presses**.

Poems in the Waiting Room
PO Box 488, Richmond TW9 4SW
✉ pitwr@blueyonder.co.uk
Contact *Michael Lee*
Pamphlets for medical waiting rooms.

Poetry Monthly Press
39 Cavendish Road, Long Eaton, Nottingham
NG10 4HY
☎0115 946 1267
✉ martin.holroyd2@btinternet.com
Contact *Martin Holroyd*
See also **Poetry Monthly** magazine.

Poetry Now
Remus House, Coltsfoot Drive, Woodston,
Peterborough PE2 8JX
☎01733 8998101   Fax 01733 313524
✉ poetrynow@forwardpress.co.uk
www.forwardpress.co.uk
Contact *Kerrie Pateman*
Lively, personal and contemporary; also deals with womenswords. See also **Poetry Now** magazine.

Poetry Press Ltd
26 Park Grove, Edgware HA8 7SJ
☎020 8958 6499
✉ poetrypress@yahoo.co.uk
www.poetrypress.co.uk
Contact *Judy Carbritz*
Anthologies – rhyming poetry welcome.

Poetry Salzburg
Dept of English and American Studies,
University of Salzburg, Akademiestr. 24,
A–5020 Salzburg, Austria
✉ wolfgang.goertschacher@sbg.ac.at
www.poetrysalzburg.com
Contact *Wolfgang Görtschacher*
See also **Poetry Salzburg Review** magazine.

Poetry Wednesbury
25 Griffiths Road, West Bromwich B71 2EH
☎07950 591455
✉ ppatch66@hotmail.com
www.poetrywednesbury.co.uk
Contact *Geoff Stevens*
Occasional CDs, DVDs, leaflets and booklets.
See also **The Firing Squad** and **Purple Patch**
magazines.

Poets Anonymous
70 Aveling Close, Purley CR8 4DW
✉ poets@poetsanon.org.uk
www.poetsanon.org.uk
Contact *Peter L. Evans*
Anthologies and collections of predominantly
south London poets. See also **Poetic Licence**
magazine.

Poor Tom's Press
89a Winchester Avenue, Leicester LE3 1AY
☎0116 289 5400
✉ bfewster@gn.apc.org
Contact *Brian Fewster*

The Potty Poets
Cambertown House, Commercial Road,
Goldthorpe, Rotherham S63 9BL
☎01226 270258   Fax 01484 663790
✉ steve@kingsengland.com
www.kingsengland.com
Contact *Steve Rudd*
See also **The King's England Press**.

PS Avalon
Box 1865, Glastonbury BA6 8YR
✉ info@psavalon
www.psavalon.com
Contact *Will Parfitt*
Quality books of contemplative, inspirational
and ecstatic poetry.

QQ Press
York House, 15 Argyle Terrace, Rothesay, Isle
of Bute PA20 0BD

Contact *Alan Carter*
Collections of poetry plus poetry anthologies.
See also **Quantum Leap** magazine.

Ragged Raven Press
1 Lodge Farm, Snitterfield, Stratford upon
Avon CV37 0LR
☎01789 730358
✉ raggedravenpress@aol.com
www.raggedraven.co.uk
Contact *Bob Mee & Janet Murch*
Poetry. See also **Iota** magazine.

Raunchland Publications
18 Canon Lynch Court, Dunfermline
KY12 8AU
✉ raunchland@hotmail.com
www.raunchland.co.uk
Contact *John Mingay*
Limited edition poetry/graphics booklets and
online publications.

Reactions
School of Literature and Creative Writing,
University of East Anglia, Norwich NR4 7TJ
☎01603 592783
✉ sarah@penandinc.co.uk
www.impressbooks.co.uk/penandinc
Contact *Clare Pollard*
Annual poetry anthology – welcomes submis-
sions from poets at first collection stage. See also
Pretext magazine.

Reality Street Editions
63 All Saints Street, Hastings TN34 3BN
☎020 7639 7297
✉ reality.street@virgin.net
www.realitystreet.co.uk
Contact *Ken Edwards*
New poetry from Britain, Europe and America
– no unsolicited mss.

Red Candle Press
50 Manbey Grove, London E15 1EX
✉ rep@poetry7.fsnet.co.uk
www.members.tripod.com/redcandlepress
Contact *M.L. McCarthy*
Traditionalist press. See also **Candelabrum**
magazine.

Rialto Publications
PO Box 309, Aylsham, Norwich NR11 6LN
✉ mail@therialto.co.uk
www.therialto.co.uk

Contact *Michael Mackmin*

'We want to publish first collections by poets of promise.'

Rive Gauche Publishing
69 Lower Redland Road, Bristol BS6 6SP
☎0117 974 5106
✉ twinset1969@hotmail.com
Contact *PVT West*
Poetry by women writing and performing in Bristol.

Rockingham Press
11 Musley Lane, Ware SG12 7EN
☎01920 467868
✉ info@rockpress.freeserve.co.uk
www.rockingham-press.co.uk
Contact *David Perman*
New British poetry and poetry in translation.

Route Publishing
PO Box 167, Pontefract WF8 4WW
☎01977 797695
✉ info@route-online.com
www.route-online.com
Contact *Ian Daley*
Contemporary fiction and performance poetry – online magazine publishes downloadable books.

Rumney Publishing Co
10 South View Drive, Rumney, Cardiff CF3 3LY
✉ john.jones700@ntlworld.com
Contact *Graham Jones*

Salmon Poetry Ltd
Knockeven, Cliffs of Moher, Co Clare, Republic of Ireland
☎00 353 65 7081941
✉ siobhan@salmonpoetry.com
www.salmonpoetry.com
Contact *Jessie Lendennie*

Salt Publishing
PO Box 937, Great Wilbraham, Cambridge CB1 5JX
✉ cemery@saltpublishing.com
www.saltpublishing.com
Contact *Chris Hamilton-Emery*
International poetry and poetics.

Scar Tissue
13 Hazely Combe, Arreton, Isle of Wight PO30 3AJ

www.pigasuspress.co.uk
Contact *Tony Lee*
Horror and humour, fiction and poetry.

Seren
1st & 2nd Floors, 38–40 Nolton Street, Bridgend CF31 3BN
☎01656 663018   Fax 01656 649226
✉ seren@seren-books.com
www.seren-books.com
Contact *Mick Felton*
Poetry, fiction, lit crit, biography, essays. See entry under **UK Publishers**; also **Poetry Wales** magazine.

Shearsman Books
58 Velwell Road, Exeter EX4 4LD
☎01392 434511   Fax 01392 434511
✉ editor@shearsman.com
www.shearsman.com
Contact *Tony Frazer*
Publishes poetry almost exclusively. Contact editor before submitting. See also **Shearsman** magazine.

Shoestring Press
19 Devonshire Avenue, Beeston, Nottingham NG9 1BS
☎0115 925 1827   Fax 0115 925 1827
www.shoestringpress.co.uk
Contact *John Lucas*
Chapbooks and full collections of original poetry, Greek poetry in translation and some fiction – check before sending mss.

Sixties Press
89 Connaught Road, Sutton SM1 3RJ
☎020 8286 0419
Contact *Barry Tebb*
Small press concentrating on poetry and novellas. See also **Leeds Poetry Weekly** and **Literature and Psychoanalysis** magazines.

Smith/Doorstop Books
The Studio, Byram Arcade, Westgate, Huddersfield HD1 1ND
☎01484 434840   Fax 01484 426566
✉ edit@poetrybusiness.co.uk
www.poetrybusiness.co.uk
Contact *Peter Sansom & Janet Fisher*
Contemporary poetry books and pamphlets. See also **The North** magazine.

Spectacular Diseases
83b London Road, Peterborough PE2 9BS
Contact *Paul Green*
Innovative poetry and some prose. Translations of both.

Starborn Books
Glanrhydwilym, Llandissilio, Clunderwen SA66 7QH
☎01437 563562
✉ sales@starbornbooks.co.uk
www.starbornbooks.co.uk
Contact *Phil Forder*
Educational books, novels, poetry, biography with a Welsh slant.

Stride Publications
11 Sylvan Road, Exeter EX4 6EW
✉ editor@stridebooks.co.uk
www.stridebooks.co.uk
Contact *Rupert Loydell*
Innovative poetry, criticism and music, essays and interviews. See entry under **Small Presses**.

Tabor
2 Holyhead Road, Llanerchymedd, Ynys Mon LL71 7AB
Contact *M.A. Duxbury-Hibbert*
Poetry and prose booklets. No unsolicited mss, please.

Talking Pen
12 Derby Crescent, Moorside, Consett DH8 8DZ
☎01207 505724
Contact *Steve Urwin*
See also **Moodswing** magazine.

Triumph House
Remus House, Coltsfoot Drive, Woodston, Peterborough PE2 9JX
☎01733 898102   Fax 01733 313524
✉ triumphhouse@forwardpress.co.uk
www.forwardpress.co.uk
Contact *Kerrie Pateman*
A Christian poetry imprint publishing many anthologies annually. See also **Forward Press** and **Poetry Now** magazine.

Tuba Press
Tunley Cottage, Tunley, Near Cirencester GL7 6LW
☎01285 760424
Contact *Charles Graham*

Vane Women Press
31 Garthorne Avenue, Darlington DL3 9XL
☎01325 468464
www.vanewomen.co.uk
Contact *Margaret Rule*
Work by women of the North East.

Ver Poets
15 Brampton Road, St Albans AL1 4PP
☎01727 864898
Contact *Daphne Schiller*
Poetry society with local and postal members. See entry under **Writers' Circles and Workshops**.

Waterloo Press
51 Waterloo Street, Hove BN3 1AN
☎01273 202876
✉ dr.jenner@virgin.net
Contact *Simon Jenner*
Poetry and periodical publisher – please phone for submissions. See also **Eratica** magazine.

Waywiser Press
9 Woodstock Road, London N4 3ET
☎020 8374 5526   Fax 020 8374 5736
✉ waywiserpress@aol.com
www.waywiser-press.com
Contact *Philip Hoy*
Specialises in modern poetry in English. See entry under **Small Presses**.

Wendy Webb Books
9 Walnut Close, Tavernham, Norwich NR8 6YN
✉ tipsforwriters@yahoo.co.uk
www.webbw.freeserve.co.uk
Contact *Wendy Webb*
Poetry anthologies selected from competition entries. See also **Norfolk Poets and Writers** magazine.

West House Books
40 Crescent Road, Nether Edge, Sheffield S7 1HN
☎0114 258 6035
✉ alan@nethedge.demon.co.uk
Contact *Alan Halsey*
Contemporary poetry, poets' prose and related work.

Wild Honey Press
16a Ballyman Road, Bray, Co. Wicklow, Republic of Ireland

✉ healeymac@gofree.indigo.ie

Contact *Randolph Healey*

Worple Press

PO Box 328, Tonbridge TN9 1WR

☎01732 367466

✉ theworpleco@aol.com

Contact *Amanda Knight & Peter Carpenter*

Contemporary UK and international poetry, pamphlets, literary essays, arts titles.

Young Writers

Remus House, Coltsfoot Drive, Woodston, Peterborough PE2 9JX

☎01733 890066   Fax 01733 313524

✉ youngwriters@forwardpress.co.uk

www.youngwriters.co.uk

Contact *Steve Twelvetree*

Publishers of children's poetry. See also **Wordsmith** and **Scribbler!** magazines.

Poetry Magazines

Acorn
Acorn, South Scarle, Newark NG23 7JW
✉ acornmag@aol.com
Contact *Beth Rudkin*

Acumen
6 The Mount, Higher Furzeham, Brixham
TQ5 8QY
☎01803 851098   Fax 01803 851098
www.acumen-poetry.co.uk
Contact *Patricia Oxley*
Good poetry, intelligent articles and wide-ranging reviews.

Agenda
The Wheelwrights, Fletching Street, Mayfield
TN20 6TL
✉ agendapoetry@lycos.co.uk
Contact *Patricia McCarthy*
Quarterly poetry magazine, founded 1959.

Aireings
Dean Head Farm, Scotland Lane, Leeds
LS18 5HU
Contact *Jean Barker*
Poetry – 40 pages – published since 1980 – leans towards women's work.

Ambit
17 Priory Gardens, London N6 5QY
☎020 8340 3566
www.ambitmagazine.co.uk
Contact *Martin Bax*
Poetry, fiction, art, reviews – established and emerging writers.

The Amsterdam Review
Columbusplein 19-111, 1057 TT Amsterdam,
The Netherlands
www.amsterdamreview.nl
Contact *Duncan Bush & P.C. Evans*
Magazine for European literature.

Anon
67 Learmouth Grove, Edinburgh EH4 1BL
☎0131 332 2398
✉ mike@volta1.fsworld.co.uk

www.blanko.org.uk/anon
Contact *Mike Stocks*
Poems selected anonymously; for submission guidelines see website or send s.a.e.

Aquarius
Flat 4, Room B, 116 Sutherland Avenue,
London W9 2QP
☎020 7289 4338
www.geocities.com/eddielinden
Contact *Eddie S. Linden*
Literary magazine – prose and poetry.

Areopagus
48 Cornwood Road, Plympton, Plymouth
PL7 1AL
Fax 0870 134 6384
✉ areopagus@churchnet.org.uk
www.churchnet.org.uk/areopagus/index.html
Contact *Julian Barritt*
A Christian-based arena for creative writers.

Arete
8 New College Lane, Oxford OX1 3BN
☎01865 289193   Fax 01895 289194
✉ craig.raine@new.ox.ac.uk
www.aretemagazine.com
Contact *Craig Raine*
Fiction, poetry, reportage, reviews.

As Well As
69 Orchard Croft, Harlow CM20 3BG
Contact *John Steer*

Avocado
The Heaventree Press, PO Box 3342,
Coventry CV1 5YB
Contact *Jonathan Morley*

Awen
38 Pierrot Steps, 71 Kursaal Way, Southend on
Sea SS1 2UY
www.geocities.com/dj_tyrer/garbaj.html
Contact *David John Tyrer*
Poetry and vignette-length fiction of any style/genre. See also **Bard**, **Monomyth** and **Garbaj** magazines.

Banipal
PO Box 22300, London W13 8ZQ
☎020 8568 9747   Fax 020 8568 8509
✉ editor@banipal.co.uk
www.banipal.co.uk
Contact *Margaret Obank*

Contemporary Arab authors in English translation – poetry, fiction, interviews, reviews.

Bard
38 Pierrot Steps, 71 Kursal Way, Southend on Sea SS1 2UY
✉ atlanteanpublishing@hotmail.com
www.geocities.com/dj_tyrer/garbaj.html
Contact *David John Tyrer*

Short poetry – new/unpublished poets welcome. See also **Awen, Monomyth** and **Garbaj** magazines.

A Bard Hair Day
289 Elmwood Avenue, Feltham TW13 7QB
Contact *Ian Deal*

Contemporary poetry. See also **Partners** press, **Imagenation** and **Poet Tree** magazines.

Barddas
Pen Rhiw, 71 Fford Pentrepoeth, Treforys, Swansea SA6 6AE
☎01792 792829   Fax 01792 792829
✉ alanllwyd@barddas.freeserve.co.uk
Contact *Alan Llwyd*

A magazine dedicated to Welsh language poetry.

Blithe Spirit
38 Wayside Avenue, Hornchurch RM12 4LL
☎01547 528542   Fax 01547 520685
www.britishhaikusociety.org
Journal of the British Haiku Society – haiku and related forms.

Borderlines
Nant Y Brithyll, Llangynyw, Welshpool SY21 0JS
☎019388 810263
Open poetry mag with no axe to grind published by the Anglo-Welsh Poetry Society.

Braquemard
48 Clifton Street, Hull HU2 9AP
✉ braquemard@hotmail.com
www.braquemard.fsnet.co.uk
Contact *David Allenby*

Fifty-two pages of excellent poetry, prose and artwork.

Brittle Star
41 Whitton, 89 King Henry's Road, London NW3 3RE
☎020 8802 1507
✉ magazine@brittlestar.org.uk
www.brittlestar.org.uk
Contact *Jo Homan*

Poetry, short stories and articles on contemporary poetry.

Candelabrum Poetry Magazine
50 Manbey Grove, London E15 1EX
✉ rep@poetry7.fsnet.co.uk
www.members.tripod.com/redcandlepress
Contact *M.L. McCarthy*

Formalist poetry magazine for people who like poetry rhythmic and shapely. See also **Red Candle Press**.

Cannon's Mouth
22 Margaret Grove, Harborne, Birmingham B17 9JH
☎0121 426 6413
✉ cannonmouth@yahoo.co.uk
Contact *Greg Cox*

New poetry, criticism, articles, information.

Carillon
19 Godric Drive, Bainsworth, Rotherham S60 5NA
✉ editor@carillonmag.org.uk
www.carillonmag.org.uk
Contact *Graham Rippon*

Eclectic poetry and prose.

CFUK
105b Fidlas Road, Llanishen, Cardiff CF14 0LY
☎07786 988836
✉ CFUK@hotmail.co.uk
Contact *Dylan Moore*

Chanticleer Magazine
6/1 Jamaica Mews, Edinburgh EH3 6HN
☎0131 225 8883
✉ richard@livermore8304.freeserve.co.uk
Contact *Richad Livermore*

Ideas and poetry – not afraid to ask embarrassing quesions and explore controversial issues.

Chapman
4 Broughton Place, Edinburgh EH1 3RX
☎0131 557 2207   Fax 0131 556 9565
✉ chapman-pub@blueyonder.co.uk
www.chapman-pub.co.uk

Contact *Joy M. Hendry*

The best in Scottish and international writing, well-established writers and the up-and-coming. See entries under **UK Publishers** and **Magazines**.

Coffee House Poetry

Meirion House, Glanyrafon, Tanygrisiau, Blaenau Festiniog LL4 3SU

☎01766 832112

✉ jan@coffeehousepoetry.co.uk

www.coffeehousepoetry.co.uk

Contact *Dr Jan Fortune-Wood*

Contemporary poems of edge and depth from new voices and established writers. See also **Cinnamon Press**.

The Coffee House

Charnwood Arts, Loughborough Library, 31 Granby Street, Loughborough LE11 3DU

☎01509 822558   Fax 01509 822559

✉ charnwood-arts@ndirect.co.uk

www.charnwood-arts.org.uk

Contact *Deborah Tyler-Bennett*

A meeting place for the arts, poetry, prose and visual artwork.

Colours

16 Fane Close, Stamford PE9 1HG

☎01780 754193

Contact *Kevin Troop*

See also **KT Publications** press and **The Third Half** magazine.

Current Accounts

22 Longworth Road, Horwich, Bolton BL6 7BA

✉ bswscribe@aol.com

hometown.ao.co.uk/bswscribe/myhomepage/writing.html

Contact *Rod Riesco*

Poetry, short fiction, articles – magazine of the Bank Street Writers' Group.

Cyphers

3 Selskar Terrace, Ranelagh, Dublin 6, Republic of Ireland

Fax 00 353 1 497 8866

Contact *Eilean Ní Chuilleanain*

Irish literary magazine: poetry, prose, reviews.

Dandelion Arts Magazine

24 Frosty Hollow, East Hunsbury NN4 0SY

☎01604 701730   Fax 01604 701730

Contact *Jacqueline Gonzalez-Marina*

International arts magazine – modern poetry, articles, stories and interviews. See also **The Student Magazine**.

The David Jones Journal

The David Jones Society, 48 Sylvan Way, Sketty, Swansea SA2 9JB

☎01792 206144   Fax 01792 205305

✉ anne.price-owen@sihe.ac.uk

www.sihe.ac.uk/davidjones

Contact *Anne Price-Owen*

Articles, poetry, information, reviews and inspired works.

Decanto

PO Box 3257, Littlehampton BN16 9AF

✉ masque_pub@tiscali.co.uk

myweb.tiscali.co.uk/masquepublishing

Contact *Lisa Stewart*

Non-conformist poetry magazine – any style considered, not just contemporary. See also **Masque Publishing** press.

Dream Catcher

Flat 1, 25 Cross O Cliff Hill, Lincoln LN5 8PR

✉ paulsuther@hotmail.com

Contact *Paul Sutherland*

Poetry, prose, b&w photographs, from national & international contributors.

Earthlove

PO Box 11219, Paisley PA1 2WH

homepage.ntlworld.com/earth.love/earthlove.htm

Contact *Tracy Patrick*

Poetry magazine for the environment – proceeds to conservation charities.

Eastern Rainbow

17 Farrow Road, Whaplode Drove, Spalding PE12 0TS

✉ p_rance@yahoo.co.uk

uk.geocities.com/p_rance/pandf.htm

Contact *Paul Rance*

Focuses on 20th century culture via poetry, prose and art. See also **Peace and Freedom** magazine.

Echoes of Gilgamesh

18 Craighead Way, Barrhead, Glasgow G78 2RS

✉ paul@mcdonagh18.freeserve.co.uk

www.gilgamesh.fsworld.co.uk

Contact *Paul McDonagh*

Quarterly long poem magazine.

The Engine
3 Ardgreenan Drive, Belfast BT4 3FQ
☎028 9065 9866   Fax 028 9032 2767
✉ clitophon@yahoo.com
www.theengine.net
Contact *Paul Murphy*
Zine of poetry, reviews and short stories.

Envoi
44 Rudyard Road, Biddulph Moor, Stoke-on Trent ST8 7JN
☎01782 517892
Contact *Roger Elkin*
Poetry, sequences, features, reviews, letters pages, competitions.

Equinox
134b Joy Lane, Whitstable CT5 4ES
✉ dordi@baru.fsnet.co.uk
www.ctanaet.com/equinox
Contact *Barbara Dordi*
Twice-yearly journal of contemporary poetry.

Eratica
51 Waterloo Street, Hove BN3 1AN
☎01273 202876
✉ dr.jenner@virgin.net
Contact *Simon Jenner*
Biannual journal with colour plates – focus on poetry, strong on music and art. See also **Waterloo Press**.

Federation Magazine
Burslem School of Art, Queen Street, Stoke-on-Trent ST6 3EJ
☎01792 822327
✉ fedmag@tiscali.co.uk
www.thefwwcp.org.uk
Contact *Nick Pollard*
Articles, reviews, news for people working in community publishing.

Fire
Field Cottage, Old Whitehill, Tackley, Kidlington OX5 3AB
☎01869 331300
www.poetical.org
Contact *Jeremy Hilton*
Poetry: alternative, unfashionable, experimental, spiritual, demotic; occasional experimental prose.

The Firing Squad
25 Griffiths Road, West Bromwich B71 2EH
☎07950 591455

Contact *Geoff Stevens*
Protest poetry broadsheet. See also **Purple Patch** magazine and **Poetry Wednesbury** press.

First Offense
Syringa, The Street, Stodmarsh, Canterbury CT3 4BA
☎01227 721249
✉ tim@firstoffense.co.uk
www.firstoffense.co.uk
Contact *Tim Fletcher*
Magazine for contemporary poetry; not traditional but is received by most ground-breaking poets.

First Time
The Snoring Cat, 16 Marianne Park, Dudley Road, Hastings TN35 5PU
☎01424 423105   Fax 01424 428855
✉ josephine.poetry@btopenworld.com
www.josephineaustin.co.uk
Contact *Josephine Austin*
Biannual magazine designed to encourage first-time poets. See also **First Time Publications** press.

Flaming Arrows
Sligo-Leitrim Arts, V E C, Riverside, Sligo, Republic of Ireland
☎00 353 71 914 7304
Fax 00 353 71 914 3093
✉ leoregan@yahoo.ie
Contact *Leo Regan*
Poetry of the spirit: mystical, contemplative, metaphysical, grounded in the senses. Worldwide.

The Frogmore Papers
18 Nevill Road, Lewes BN7 1PF
www.frogmorepress.co.uk
Contact *Jeremy Page*
Biannual. Founded 1983. Biannual. Poetry, prose and artwork. See also **The Frogmore Press**.

Gabriel
27 Headingley Court, North Grange Road, Leeds LS6 2QU
Contact *Thelma Laycock*
Annual Christian poetry magazine.

Garbaj
38 Pierrot Steps, 71 Kursaal Way, Southend on Sea SS1 2UY
www.geocities.com/dj_tyrer/garbaj.html
Contact *David John Tyrer*

Humourous/non-pc poetry, vignette-length fiction, fake news, etc. See also **Awen**, **Bard** and **Monomyth** magazines.

Global Tapestry Journal
Spring Bank, Longsight Road, Copster Green, Blackburn BB1 9EU
☎01254 249128
Contact *Dave Cunliffe*
Global Bohemia, post-Beat and counterculture orientation. See also **BB Books** press.

The Green Door
The Dolls House, 103 Lincoln Street, Wakefield WF2 0ED
✉ r.masonharding@tiscali.co.uk
www.geocities.co.uk/masonharding
Contact *Rebecca Mason-Harding*

Green Queen
BM Box 5700, London WC1N 3XX
Contact *Elsa Wallace*
Occasional magazine, Green issues, lesbian & gay fiction, articles, poetry.

Handshake
5 Cross Farm, Station Road North, Fearnhead, Warrington WA2 0QG
Contact *John Francis Haines*
Newsletter of **The Eight Hand Gang**, an association of UK sci-fi poets.

Harlequin
PO Box 23392, Edinburgh EH7 5GL
✉ corvinewhite@yahoo.co.uk
www.harlequinmag.com
Contact *Jim Sinclair*
High quality poetry and artwork of intense beauty, mysticism and wisdom.

Imagenation
289 Elmwood Avenue, Feltham TW13 7QB
Contact *Ian Deal*
Poetry and artwork magazine. See also **Partners** press, **A Bard Hair Day** and **Poet Tree** magazines.

Inclement
White Rose House, 8 Newmarket Road, Fordham, Ely CB7 5LL
✉ inclement_poetry_magazine@hotmail.com
Contact *Michelle Foster*
All forms and styles of poetry – responses within a month.

The Interpreter's House
19 The Paddox, Squitchey Lane, Oxford OX2 7PN
Contact *Merryn Williams*
Poems and stories up to 2500 words; new and established writers.

Iota
1 Lodge Farm, Snitterfield, Stratford upon Avon CV37 0LR
☎01789 730358
✉ iotapoetry@aol.com
www.iotapoetry.co.uk
Contact *Bob Mee & Janet Murch*
Poetry, reviews; long and short poems welcome. No epics. See also **Ragged Raven Press**.

Irish Pages
The Linen Hall Library, 17 Donegall Square North, Belfast BT1 5GB
✉ irishpages@yahoo.co.uk
www.irishpages.org
Contact *Chris Agee*
Outstanding writing from Ireland and overseas: poetry, short fiction, essays, nature-writing, etc.

Island
8 Craiglea Drive, Edinburgh EH10 5PA
✉ jaj@essencepress.co.uk
www.essencepress.co.uk
Contact *Julie Johnstone*
A distinctive space for writing inspired by nature and exploring our place within the natural world. See also **Essence Press**.

The Journal
Flat 3, 18 Oxford Grove, Ilfracombe EX34 9HQ
☎01271 862708
✉ smithsssj@aol.com
Contact *Sam Smith*
Poems in translation alongside poetry written in English. See also **Original Plus** press.

Knightvision
4 Pedley Close, Westfield, Sheffield S20 8EY
Contact *Richard Middlebrook*
Sheffield's nationally acclaimed poetry and art magazine.

Krax
63 Dixon Lane, Wortley, Leeds LS12 4RR
Contact *Andy Robson*
Light-hearted, contemporary poetry, short fiction and graphics.

Lallans

Scots Language Society, A K Bell Library, York Place, Perth PH2 8AP
☎01738 440199
✉ johnmacphaillaw@aol.com
www.lallans.co.uk
Contact *John Law*

Scots language journalism and creative writing, twice-yearly.

Lamport Court

63 Lamport Court, Manchester M1 7EG
Contact *Adrian Slater*

Poetry, fiction, art.

Leeds Poetry Weekly

89 Connaught Road, Sutton SM1 3PJ
☎020 8286 0419
Contact *Barry Tebb*

New poems, reviews, articles on literary and psychoanalytic matters. See also **Sixties Press** and **Literature and Psychoanalysis** magazine.

Liar Republic

9 Moyle Terrace, Hobson, Burnopfield, Newcastle upon Tyne NE16 6EQ
☎0191 296 6787   Fax 0191 296 6787
✉ psummers@liarincltd.fsnet.co.uk
Contact *Paul Summers & Others*

State of the nation through fiction, journalism, poetry, visual art and reviews. Formerly *Billy Liar* magazine.

Linear B Publishing

PO Box 23614, 5/17 Saunders Street, Edinburgh EH3 6TT
☎0131 314 4471   Fax 0131 334 5353
✉ linearb26@hotmail.com
Contact *Jamie Kelly*

Poetry, literary fiction, short stories.

Linkway

The Shieling, The Links, Burry Port SA16 0HU
☎01554 834486   Fax 01554 834486
Contact *Fay C. Davies*

A publication for writers and friends – a general interest magazine for the whole family.

Literature and Psychoanalysis

89 Connaught Road, Sutton SM1 3PJ
☎020 8286 0419
Contact *Barry Tebb*

New poems, reviews, articles on literary and psychoanalytical matters. See also **Sixties Press** and **Leeds Poetry Weekly** magazine.

The London Magazine

32 Addison Grove, London W4 1ER
☎020 8400 5882   Fax 020 8994 1713
✉ editorial@londonmagazine.net
www.londonmagazine.net
Contact *Sebastian Barker*

A review of literature and the arts. See entry under *Magazines*.

Magma

43 Keslake Road, London NW6 6DH
✉ magmapoetry@aol.com
www.magmapoetry.com
Contact *David Boll*

New poetry plus poetry reviews and interviews.

Modern Poetry in Translation

The Queen's College, Oxford OX1 4AW
☎01865 244701
✉ helen-constantine@ip3.com
www.mptmagazine.com
Contact *David & Helen Constantine*

Publishes and promotes poetry in English translation.

Monkey Kettle

PO Box 4616, Kiln Farm, Milton Keynes MK12 6XZ
✉ monkeykettle@hotmail.com
www.monkeykettle.co.uk
Contact *Matthew Taylor*

Quarterly poetry, prose, photos, articles in Milton Keynes and further afield.

Monomyth

38 Pierrot Steps, 71 Kursaal Way, Southend on Sea SS1 2UY
www.geocities.com/dj_tyrer/monomyth.html
Contact *David John Tyrer*

Poetry, prose and articles; all genres, styles and lengths considered. New writers welcome. See also **Awen** and **Garbaj** magazines.

Moodswing

12 Derby Crescent, Moorside, Consett DH8 8DZ
☎01207 505724
Contact *Steve Urwin*

Short poems, short prose, light/dark psychologically charged. See also **Talking Pen** press.

Mslexia
PO Box 656, Newcastle upon Tyne
NE99 1PZ
☎0191 261 6656   Fax 0191 261 6636
✉ postbag@mslexia.demon.co.uk
www.mslexia.co.uk

Contact *Debbie Taylor*

National quarterly magazine for women who
write. Advice, inspiration, news, reviews, interviews, etc. See entry under *Magazines*.

Neon Highway
37 Grinshill Close, Liverpool L8 8LD
✉ poetshideout@yahoo.com
www.neonhighway.co.uk

Contact *Alice Lenkiewicz*

Innovative and experimental poetry/arts magazine.

Never Bury Poetry
Bracken Clock, Troutbeck Close, Hawkshaw,
Bury BL8 4LJ
☎01204 884080
✉ nbpoetry@zen.co.uk
www.nbpoetry.care4free.net

Contact *Jean Tarry*

Quarterly, founded 1989. International reputation. Each issue has a different theme.

The New Cauldron
19 The Sandhills, Wirral CH46 3ST
☎0151 678 1105   Fax 0151 678 1965
✉ luna.cantos@virgin.net
www.thenewcauldron.co.uk

Contact *Anita Luna-Cantos*

Short stories, articles, poetry, competitions,
letters, special features.

New Departures/Poetry Olympics
PO Box 9819, London W11 2GC
☎020 7229 7850   Fax 020 7229 7850

Contact *Mike Horovitz*

Poetry journal of the Poetry Olympics. See also
New Departures press.

New Welsh Review
PO Box 170, Aberystwyth SY23 1WZ
☎01970 626230
✉ admin@newwelshreview.com
www.newwelshreview.com

Contact *Francesca Rhydderch*

Vibrant literary which showcases the best new
writing from Wales – also includes features and
reviews. See entry under *Magazines*.

Norfolk Poets and Writers
9 Walnut Close, Taverham, Norwich NR8 6YN
☎0798 917 4076
✉ tipsforwriters@yahoo.co.uk
www.webbw.freeserve.co.uk

Contact *Wendy Webb*

Tips newsletter, quarterly mini comps, annual
davidian – rules of poetry forms. See also
Wendy Webb Books press.

The North
The Poetry Business, The Studio, Byram
Arcade, Westgate, Huddersfield HD1 1ND
☎01484 434840   Fax 01484 426566
✉ edit@poetrybusiness.co.uk
www.poetrybusiness.co.uk

Contact *Peter Sansom & Janet Fisher*

Contemporary poetry and articles, extensive
reviews.

The Once Orange Badge Poetry Supplement
PO Box 184, South Ockendon RM15 5WT
☎01708 852827
✉ onceorangebadge@poetry.fsworld.co.uk

Contact *D. Martyn Heath*

A4 poetry supplement for everyone whose life
has been touched by disability in some way.

Open Wide
The Flat, Yew Tree Farm, Sealand Road,
Chester CH1 6BS
☎07790 062317
✉ contact@openwidemagazine.co.uk
www.openwidemagazine.co.uk

Contact *James Quinton*

80 pages of punchy short fiction, poetry, reviews
and interviews. See also **Feel Free Press**.

Orbis
17 Greenhow Avenue, West Kirby CH48 5EL
☎0151 625 1446
✉ carolebaldock@hotmail.com

Contact *Carole Baldock*

An independent international quarterly of poetry
and prose with many reader-friendly features.

Other Poetry
29 Western Hill, Durham DH1 4RL
☎0191 386 4058
www.otherpoetry.com

Contact *Michael Standen & Others*

Thrice-yearly 60 – 70 poems per issue. Process of
selection involves all four editors. Token payment.

Outposts

22 Whitewell Road, Frome BA11 4EL
☎01373 466653   Fax 01373 466653
✉ rjhippopress@aol.com
Contact *Roland John*

Longest-surviving independent poetry magazine in the UK. See also **Hippopotamus Press**.

Peace and Freedom

17 Farrow Road, Whaplode Drove, Spalding PE12 0TS
☎01406 330242
✉ p_rance@yahoo.co.uk
uk.vgeocities.com/p_rance/pandf.htm
Contact *Paul Rance*

Poetry, prose, art mag – humanitarian, environmental, animal welfare. See also **Eastern Rainbow** magazine.

Peer Poetry International

26 (wh) Arlington House, Bath Street BA1 1QN
☎01225 445298
✉ peerpoetry@msn.com
www.publish-your-poetry.com
Contact *Paul Amphlett*

Biannual – 60 poets per issue.

The Penniless Press

100 Waterloo Road, Ashton, Preston PR2 1EP
☎01772 736421
Contact *Alan Dent*

Quarterly for the poor pocket and the rich mind. Poetry, fiction, essays, reviews.

Pennine Ink Magazine

The Gallery, Mid-Pennine Arts, Yorke Street, Burnley BB11 1HD
☎01282 703657
✉ sheridans@casanostra.p3online.net
Contact *Laura Sheridan*

Quality poetry reflecting traditional and modern trends.

Pennine Platform

Frizingley Hall, Frizinghall Road, Bradford BD9 4LD
☎01274 541015
www.pennineplatform.co.uk
Contact *Nicholas Bielby*

Poetry with reviews and critical articles.

Planet

PO Box 44, Aberystwyth SY23 3ZZ
☎01970 611255   Fax 01970 611197
✉ planet.enquiries@planetmagazine.org.uk
www.planetmagazine.org.uk
Contact *John Barnie*

The Welsh Internationalist – current affairs, arts, environment. See also **Planet** press.

PN Review

Carcanet Press, 4th Floor, Alliance House, 28–34 Cross Street, Manchester M2 7AQ
☎0161 834 8730   Fax 0161 832 0084
✉ info@carcanet.co.uk
www.carcanet.co.uk
Contact *Michael Schmidt*

Major poetry publisher. See **Carcanet Press Ltd** under *UK Publishers*.

Poet in the Round

18 Blackbridge Lane, Horsham RH12 1RP

Surrounded by talent.

Poet Tree

289 Elmwood Avenue, Feltham TW13 7QB
Contact *Ian Deal*

Contemporary poetry magazine. See also **Partners** press, **A Bard Hair Day** and **Imagenation** magazines.

Poetic Hours

43 Willow Road, Carlton, Nottingham NG4 3BH
✉ erranpublishing@hotmail.com
www.poetichours.homestead.com
Contact *Nick Clark*

Non-profit supporter of Third World charities. See also **Erran Publishing**.

Poetic Licence

70 Aveling Close, Purley CR8 4DW
✉ poets@poetsanon.org.uk
www.poetsanon.org.uk
Contact *Peter L. Evans*

Original unpublished poems and drawings. See also **Poets Anonymous** press.

The Poetry Church

Feather Books, PO Box 438, Shrewsbury SY3 0WN
☎01743 872177   Fax 01743 872177
✉ john@waddysweb.freeuk.com
www.waddysweb.freeuk.com
Contact *Rev. J. Waddington-Feather*

Quarterly magazine of Christian poetry and prayers. See **Feather Books** under *Small Presses*.

Poetry Combination Module (PCM)

PEF Productions, 196 High Road, London N22 8HH

✉ page84direct@yahoo.co.uk
www.alienonthenet.freehosting.net

Contact *Mr Page Eighty-Four*

Poetry, aphorism, graphics weirdly dressed on a wild bed of cuttings and bits of artwork. No unsolicited material.

Poetry Cornwall/ Bardhonyeth Kernow

1 Station Hill, Redruth TR15 2PP

✉ les.merton@tesco.net
www.poetrycornwall.freeserve.com

Contact *Les Merton*

Poetry from around the world, including poems in Kernewek and dialect.

Poetry Express

Diorama Arts Centre, 34 Osnaburgh Street, London NW1 3ND

☎ 020 7916 5317

✉ james@survivorspoetry.org.uk

Contact *James Ferguson*

Quarterly newsletter from **Survivors' Poetry** (see entry under *Organisations of Interest to Poets*).

Poetry Ireland News

120 St Stephen's Green, Dublin 2, Republic of Ireland

☎ 00 353 1 478 9974   Fax 00 353 1 478 0205

✉ publications@poetryireland.ie
www.poetryireland.ie

Contact *Paul Lenehan*

Bi-monthly newsletter. See also **Poetry Ireland Review** magazine.

Poetry Ireland Review/ Eigse Eireann

120 St Stephen's Green, Dublin 2, Republic of Ireland

☎ 00 353 1 478 9974   Fax 00 353 1 478 0205

✉ poetry@iol.ie
www.poetryireland.ie

Contact *Peter Sirr*

Quarterly journal of poetry and reviews. See also **Poetry Ireland News** magazine.

Poetry London

1a Jewel Road, London E17 4QU

✉ editors@poetrylondon.co.uk

www.poetrylondon.co.uk

Contact *Pascale Petit*

Poetry, listings, reviews, features and information.

Poetry Monthly

39 Cavendish Road, Long Eaton, Nottingham NG10 4HY

☎ 0115 946 1267

✉ martin.holroyd@btinternet.com

Contact *Martin Holroyd*

A gallery of contemporary poetry and graphics. See also **Poetry Monthly Press**.

Poetry Nottingham International

11 Orkney Close, Stenson Fields, Derby DE24 3LW

☎ 01322 270590

Contact *Adrian Buckner*

Poetry, articles, reviews, published quarterly.

Poetry Now

Remus House, Coltsfoot Drive, Woodston, Peterborough PE2 9JX

☎ 01733 898101   Fax 01733 313524

✉ poetrynow@forwardpress.co.uk
www.forwardpress.co.uk

Contact *Kerrie Pateman*

Incorporating *Rhyme Arrival* magazine – communicating across the barriers. See also **Foward Press**.

Poetry Review

Poetry Society, 22 Betterton Street, London WC2H 9BU

☎ 020 7420 9883   Fax 020 7240 4818

✉ poetryreview@poetrysoc.com
www.poetrysoc.com

Contact *Fiona Sampson*

A quarterly forum on the state of poetry.

Poetry Salzburg Review

Dept of English and American Studies, University of Salzburg, Akademiestr. 24, A–5020 Salzburg, Austria

✉ wolfgang.goertschacher@sbg.ac.uk
www.poetrysalzburg.com

Contact *Wolfgang Görtschacher*

Poetry magazine, formerly *The Poet's Voice*. Published with the University of Salzburg.

Poetry Scotland

3 Spittal Street, Edinburgh EH3 9DY

☎ 0131 229 7252

www.poetryscotland.co.uk

Contact *Sally Evans*

All-poetry broadsheet with Scottish emphasis. See also **Diehard Publishers** press.

Poetry Wales

1st & 2nd Floors, 38–40 Nolton Street, Bridgend CF31 3BN
☎01656 663018   Fax 01656 649226
✉ poetrywales@seren-books.com
www.poetrywales.co.uk

Contact *Robert Minhinnick*

An international magazine with a reputation for fine writing and criticism. See also **Seren Books** under *UK Publishers*.

Popularity Contest

Knoll House, Wadeford TA20 3AN
✉ lukekennard@hotmail.com

Contact *Luke Kennard*

Left-of-centre photocopied quarterly – inventive and exuberant poetry for intimacy and fighting.

Premonitions

13 Hazely Combe, Arreton, Isle of Wight PO30 3AJ
☎01983 865668
✉ mail@pigasus.press.co.uk
www.pigasuspress.co.uk

Contact *Tony Lee*

Magazine of science fiction and horror stories, with genre poetry and artwork. See also **Pigasus Press**.

Presence

12 Grovehall Avenue, Leeds LS11 7EX
✉ stuart_quine@hotmail.com
freespace.virgin.net/haiku.presence

Contact *Martin Lucas*

Haiku, senryu, tanka, renku and related poetry in English.

Pretext

School of Literature & Creative Writing, University of East Anglia, Norwich NR4 7TJ
☎01603 592783
✉ sarah@penandinc.co.uk
www.inpressbooks.co.uk/penandinc

Contact *Katri Skala*

New fiction and non-fiction. See also **Reactions** press.

Pulsar

34 Lineacre Close, Grange Park, Swindon SN5 6DA
☎01793 875941
✉ pulsar.ed@btopenworld.com
www.pulsarpoetry.com

Contact *David Pike*

Hard hitting/inspirational poetry – quarterly.

Purple Patch

25 Griffiths Road, West Bromwich B71 2EH
☎07950 591455
✉ ppatch66@hotmail.com
www.poetrywednesbury.co.uk

Contact *Geoff Stevens*

Poetry mag founded 1976 – includes reviews and gossip column. See also **The Firing Squad** magazine and **Poetry Wednesbury** press.

Quantum Leap

York House, 15 Argyle Terrace, Rothesay, Isle of Bute PA20 0BD

Contact *Alan Carter*

User-friendly magazine – encourages new writers – all types of poetry. See also **QQ Press**.

Quattrocento

Bodnant, 11 Llwynon Gardens, Llandudno LL30 2HP
✉ peter.barnes3@tesco.net

Contact *Malcolm Bradley*

An independent journal of the arts made in Wales.

Quid

13 Heathfield Park, Flat 2, London NW2 5JE
✉ info@barquepress.com
www.barquepress.com

Contact *Andrea Brady*

See also **Barque** press.

The Quiet Feather

St Mary's Cottage, Church Street, Dalton in Furness LA15 8BA
☎01229 468967
✉ editors@thequietfeather.co.uk
www.thequietfeather.co.uk

Contact *Dominic Hall & Taissa Csaky*

Lively and eclectic quarterly – short stories, poetry, travel, essays, cartoons, photographs, line drawings; all welcome.

Raw Edge

PO Box 4867, Birmingham B3 3HD

Contact *Dave Reeves*

New writing, free from outlets in ACE, West

Midlands area. Writers with a regional connection only. See also **The Moving Finger** press.

Reach
PO Box 109, Portishead, Bristol BS20 7ZJ
✉ anthony@bluechrome.co.uk
www.bluechrome.co.uk
Contact *Anthony Delgardo*
See also **The Boho Press**.

Read the Music
20 Wharfedale Street, Wednesbury
WS10 9AG
☎07970 441110
✉ mooncrow@tiscali.co.uk
www.poetrywednesbury.co.uk
Contact *Brendan Hawthorne*
Original poetry based on music and its influences.

The Reader
University of Liverpool, 19 Abercromby
Square, Liverpool L69 7ZG
✉ readers@liv.ac.uk
www.thereader.co.uk
Contact *Jane Davis*
Literary magazine, new fiction, poetry, essays, book recommendations and reviews. See entry under *Magazines*.

Red Poets - Y Beirdd Coch
26 Andrew's Close, Heolgerrig, Merthyr Tydfil
LL11 1QU
☎01685 376726
✉ m.v.jones@virgin.net
Contact *Mike Jenkins*
Radical Welsh poetry – socialists, republicans & anarchists welcome.

Reflections
PO Box 178, Sunderland SR1 1DU
Poetry by and for men and women of goodwill.

The Rialto
PO Box 309, Aylsham, Norwich NR11 6LN
✉ mail@therialto.co.uk
www.therialto.co.uk
Contact *Michael Mackmin*
Excellent poetry in a clear environment.

Roundyhouse
3 Crown Street, Port Talbot SA13 1BG
✉ srjones@alunbooks.co.uk

Contact *Sally R. Jones*
Poems and articles on poetry. Reviews. Eclectic approach.

Rubies In the Darkness
41 Grantham Road, Manor Park, London
E12 5LZ
Contact *Peter Geoffrey & Paul Thompson*
Romantic, lyrical, spiritual, inspirational and mystical poetry.

Sable
PO Box 33504, London E9 7YE
✉ info@sablelitmag.org
www.sablelitmag.org
Contact *Kadija Sesay*
Literary magazine of new writing for writers of colour.

Sand
PO Box 1091, Sunderland SR2 8DW
✉ sandpoems@aol.com
www.sandwriting.co.uk
Contact *Kevin Cadwallender*
Probably the most accessible literary magazine ever.

Saw
4 Masefield Avenue, Barnstaple EX31 1QJ
✉ sawpoems@btinternet.com
Contact *Colin Shaddick*
Poems that are radical, multicultural and international in outlook.

Scintilla
Little Wentwood Farm, Llantrisant, Usk
NP5 1ND
☎01291 673797
✉ anne.cluysenaar@virgin.net
www.cf.ac.uk/encap/scintilla
Contact *Anne Cluysenaar*
Explores connections between material and spiritual, imaginative and scientific – new poetry.

Scribbler!
Remus House, Coltsfoot Drive, Woodston,
Peterborough PE2 9JX
☎01733 890066   Fax 01733 313524
✉ youngwriters@forwardpress.co.uk
www.youngwriters.co.uk
Contact *Lynsey Hawkins*
Quarterly magazine for 7–11-year-olds – poetry, stories, guest authors, workshops, features.

Scriptor
2 Chambers Cottages, Underlyn Lane,
Marden, Tonbridge TN12 9BD
☎07967 315270
✉ mail@johndench.demon.co.uk
Contact *John Dench*
Poetry, short stories, essays from the UK – publishes biennally. See also **Green Arrow Publishing** press.

Second Light Publications
9 Greendale Close, London SE22 8TG
✉ dilyswood@tiscali.co.uk
Contact *Dilys Wood*

The Seventh Quarry
Dan-Y-Bryn, 74 Cwm Level Road,
Brynhyfryd, Swansea SA5 9DY
Fax 01792 774070
Contact *Peter Thabit Jones*
Poetry from Swansea and beyond.

Shearsman
58 Velwell Road, Exeter EX4 4LD
☎01392 434511   Fax 01392 434511
✉ editor@shearsman.com
www.shearsman.com
Contact *Tony Frazer*
Mainly poetry, some prose, some reviews. Poetry in the modernist tradition. No fiction. See also **Shearsman Books** press.

The ShOp: A Magazine Of Poetry
Skeagh, Schull, Co. Cork, Republic of Ireland
✉ wakeman@iol.ie (not for submissions)
Contact *John Wakeman*
International but with emphasis on Irish poetry.

Skald
2 Greenfield Terrace, Hill Street, Menai Bridge LL59 5AY
☎01248 716343
✉ editors@skald.co.uk
www.skald.co.uk
Contact *Zoe Skoulding*
Poetry and artwork, English and Welsh.

Smiths Knoll
Goldings, Goldings Lane, Leiston IP16 4EB
✉ royblackman@ukonline.co.uk
Contact *Joanna Cutts & Michael Laskey*
Honest, well-crafted poems.

Smoke
The Windows Project, 96 Bold Street,
Liverpool L1 4HY
☎0151 709 3688
✉ windows@windowsproject.demon.co.uk
www.windowsproject.demon.co.uk
Contact *Dave Ward*
Poetry, graphics, short prose – 24pp – biannual.

Smokestack Books
PO Box 408, Middlesbrough TS5 6WA
☎01642 813997
✉ info@smokestack-books.co.uk
Contact *Andy Croft*
Champions poets who are unconventional, unfashionable, radical or left-field.

Solo Survivors
37 Micklehill Drive, Shirley, Solihull B90 2PU
☎0121 745 4381
✉ johnalanhirst@ukonline.co.uk
www.johnalanhirst.com
Contact *John Hurst & Others*
A quarterly bound 60-pp poetry and art mag for sufferers but not expressly so.

South
PO Box 5369, Poole BH14 0XN
✉ south@martinblyth.co.uk
www.martinblyth.co.uk
Poetry magazine from the southern counties of England that welcomes poets from across the world.

Springboard
Corrimbla, Ballina, Co. Mayo, Republic of Ireland
✉ bobgroom@eircom.net
Contact *Robert Groom*
Short fiction, poetry and articles.

Stand
School of English, University of Leeds, Leeds LS2 9JT
☎0113 233 4794   Fax 0113 233 4791
✉ stand@leeds.ac.uk
www.people.vcu.edu~dlatane/stand.html
Contact *Jon Glover*
Quarterly magazine of poetry, fiction, reviews and cultural criticism.

Staple
74 Rangeley Road, Walkley, Sheffield S6 5DW
✉ e.barrett@shu.ac.uk

Contact *Elizabeth Barrett*
Poetry, short fiction, articles. Three issues a year.

The Stinging Fly
PO Box 6016, Dublin 8 Republic of Ireland
✉ stingingfly@hotmail.com
www.stingingfly.org
Contact *Declan Meade*

Dublin's literary magazine. New Irish and international writing. Poetry, short fiction, author interviews and book reviews.

The Student Magazine
Fern Publications, Casa Alba, 24 Frosty Hollow, East Hunsbury NN4 0SY
☎ 01604 701730   Fax 01604 701730
Contact *Jacqueline Gonzalez-Marina*

Sister magazine to **Dandelion Arts Magazine**. Articles, stories, poems, interviews and illustrations. New and established writes welcome.

Taliesin
Academi, 3rd Floor, Mount Stuart House, Mount Stuart Square, Cardiff CV10 5FQ
☎ 029 2047 2266   Fax 029 2049 2930
✉ taliesin@academi.org
www.academi.org
Contact *Manon Rhys & Christine James*

Wales' leading Welsh language literary journal.

Tears in the Fence
38 Hod View, Stourpaine, Nr Blandford Forum DT11 8TN
☎ 01258 456803   Fax 01258 454026
✉ esp@euphony.net
www.wanderingdog.co.uk
Contact *David Caddy*

A magazine looking for the unusual, perceptive, risk-taking, lived and visionary literature.

10th Muse
33 Hartington Road, Southampton SO14 0EW
✉ andyj@noplace.screaming.net
Contact *Andrew Jordan*

Poetry, prose and graphics – the main interest is innovative poetry and the poetries influenced by it.

The Third Half
16 Fane Close, Stamford PE9 1HG
☎ 01780 754193
Contact *Kevin Troop*

Searches for good poetry and fiction. See also **KT Publications** press and **Colours** magazine.

Timbuktu
13 Taliesin Street, Llandudno LL20 2YE
☎ 01492 872230
✉ bobtwice@hotmail.com
www.meetingpool.ik.com
Contact *Bob MacIntosh*

The international arts and literary journal made in Wales.

Understanding
20a Montgomery Street, Edinburgh EH7 5JS
☎ 0131 478 0680   Fax 0131 478 2572
Contact *Denise Smith*

Original poetry, short stories, parts of plays, reviews and articles. See also **Dionysia Press**.

The Unruly Sun
Rising Sun Arts Centre, 30 Silver Street, Reading RG1 2LT
✉ submissions@unrulysun.co.uk
www.unrulysun.co.uk
Contact *Jennifer Hoskins, Geoff Sawers, Kate Starling*

Contemporary poetry from the margins. 'We have no house-style – if we love it, we print it.'

Urthona
9a Auckland Road, Cambridge CB2 8DW
☎ 01223 309470
✉ urthona.mag@onetel.com
www.urthona.com
Contact *Ratnagabha*

The only Buddhist arts magazine – artists, poetry, essays, world culture from a Buddhist perspective.

Wasafiri
School of English, Queen Mary College, University of London, Mile End Road, London E1 4SN
☎ 020 7882 3120   Fax 020 7882 3120
✉ wasafiri@qmul.ac.uk
www.wasafiri.org
Contact *Susheila Nasta*

Literary journal of African, Asian, Caribbean and black British writing. See entry under *Magazines*.

Wordsmith
Remus House, Coltsfoot Drive, Woodston, Peterborough PE2 9JX
☎ 01733 890066   Fax 01733 313524
✉ youngwriters@forwardpress.co.uk

www.youngwriters.co.uk

Contact *Allison Dowse*

Poetry, stories, guest authors, features in a quarterly magazine for 11–18-year-olds. See also **Young Writers** press and **Scribbler!** magazine.

The Yellow Crane

20 Princes Court, The Walk, Roath, Cardiff CF23 3AU

Contact *J. Brookes*

Interesting new poems from S. Wales and beyond.

Organisations of Interest to Poets

A survey of some of the societies, groups and other bodies which may be of interest to practising poets. Organisations not listed should send details to the Editor for inclusion in future editions.

Academi – The Welsh National Literature Promotion Agency and Society for Writers

3rd Floor, Mount Stuart House, Mount Stuart Square, Cardiff Bay CF10 5FQ
☎029 2047 2266   Fax 029 2049 2930
✉ post@academi.org
www.academi.org

North Wales Office: Ty Newydd, Llanystumdwy, Cricieth, Gwynedd LL52 0LW

West Wales Office: Dylan Thomas Centre, Somerset Place, Swansea SA1 1RR Glyn Jones Centre: Wales Millennium Centre, Cardiff

Chief Executive *Peter Finch*

The writers' organisation of Wales with special responsibility for literary activity, writers' residencies, writers on tour, festivals, writers' groups, readings, tours, exchanges and other development work. Academi awards financial bursaries annually, runs a criticism service and organises the **Welsh Book of the Year Awards**. **Yr Academi Gymreig/The Welsh Academy** operates the Arts Council of Wales franchise for Wales-wide literature development. It has offices in Cardiff and fieldworkers elsewhere in Wales. Publisher of the lottery-funded *Encyclopedia of Wales*, the Welsh-medium literary magazine *Taliesin*, the *Academi English-Welsh Dictionary*, co-publisher of *The New Welsh Review* along with a number of other projects. The Academi sponsors a range of annual contests including the John Tripp Award For Spoken Poetry and the prestigious **Cardiff International Poetry Competition**. Publishes *A470*, a bi-monthly literary information magazine.

Apples & Snakes

Battersea Arts Centre, Lavender Hill, London SW11 5TN
☎020 7924 3410   Fax 020 7924 3763
✉ info@applesandsnakes.org
www.applesandsnakes.org

Director *Geraldine Collinge*

Set up in 1982 as a platform for poetry which would be popular, relevant, cross-cultural and accessible to the widest possible range of people, A&S aims to stretch the boundaries of Poetry in Education and performance. Currently undergoing an extensive programme of expansion, bringing performance poetry to new places and new audiences across England.

Arts Councils

See section on **Arts Councils and Regional Offices**, pages 556–557.

The Arvon Foundation

See entry under *UK Writers' Courses*

The British Haiku Society

38 Wayside Avenue, Hornchurch RM12 4LL
☎01772 251827
www.britishhaikusociety.org

General Secretary *Doreen King*

Formed in 1990. Promotes the appreciation and writing within the British Isles of haiku, senyru, tanka, haibun and renga by way of tutorials, workshops, exchange of poems, critical comment and information. The Society runs a haiku library and administers the annual James W. Hackett Award, the prestigious **Sasakawa** prize and the Nobuyuki Yuasa International Haibun in English Contest. Organises twice-yearly 'haiku gatherings'. Details from *Martin Lucas*, 90D Fishergate Hill, Preston PR1 8JD (✉ martin.lucas2@btinternet.com). Publishes *The Haiku Kit* teaching pack and the quarterly journal, *Blithe Spirit*.

The Eight Hand Gang

5 Cross Farm, Station Road North, Fearnhead, Warrington WA2 0QG
Secretary *John F. Haines*

An association of SF poets. Publishes *Handshake*, a single-sheet newsletter of SF poetry and information available free in exchange for an s.a.e.

57 Productions

57 Effingham Road, Lee Green, London SE12 8NT
☎020 8463 0866   Fax 020 8463 0866

✉ paul57prods@yahoo.co.uk
www.57productions.com

Contact *Paul Beasley*

Specialises in the promotion of poetry and its production through an agency service, a programme of events and a series of audio publications. Services are available to event promoters, festivals, education institutions and the media. Poets represented include Jean 'Binta' Breeze, Adrian Mitchell, John Cooper Clarke and Lemn Sissay. 57 Productions' series of audio cassettes, CDs and Poetry in Performance compilations offer access to some of the most exciting poets working in Britain today.

The Football Poets

4 The Retreat, Butterow, Stroud GL5 2LS
☎01453 757376
✉ editors@footballpoets.org
www.footballpoets.org

Performance *Crispin Thomas*
Co-Editors *Stuart Butler, Simon Williams*

The Football Poets exist to promote and encourage the writing and performing of football poetry. Formed in 1995, they appear regularly at festivals and venues around the country. They also provide comprehensive and entertaining football poetry workshops in schools and communities. Their website is a fast and entertaining mix of literature and soccer poetry from around the world. Anyone may contribute.

The Poetry Archive

Ball's Green House, Minchinhampton
GL6 9AR
☎01453 832090   Fax 01453 836450
✉ info@poetryarchive.org

Directors *Richard Carrington, Andrew Motion*

A permanent archive of audio recordings of work by poets who write in English. New 60-minute recordings will be made for the Archive by a wide-ranging list of poets. Extracts from those recordings will be made available on a website to be launched later in 2005 and will also contain educational and intepretative information. The full-length recordings will be sold by mail order on CDs. A registered charity, the Archive intends to ensure that all significant poets are recorded for posterity.

The Poetry Book Society

Fourth Floor, 2 Tavistock Place, London
WC1H 9RA
☎020 7833 9247   Fax 020 7833 5990
✉ info@poetrybooks.co.uk

www.poetrybooks.co.uk

Director *Chris Holifield*

For readers, writers, students and teachers of poetry. Founded in 1953 by T.S. Eliot and funded by the Arts Council, the PBS is a unique membership organisation and book club providing up-to-date and comprehensive information about poetry from publishers in the UK and Ireland. Members receive the quarterly *PBS Bulletin* packed with articles by poets, poems, news, listings and access to discounts of at least 25% off featured titles. These range from modern classics to contemporary works. The newly relaunched transactional website has a recruitment area and a closed section for members. PBS also has a website at www. poetrybookshoponline.com offering a range of over 30,000 poetry titles. There are three membership packages, two of which include a number of new books specially selected by the Society's panel of experts along with, at both primary and secondary levels, a special package for teachers. Subscriptions start at £10. The PBS also runs the annual **T.S. Eliot Prize** for the best collection of new poetry.

The Poetry Business

The Studio, Byram Arcade, Westgate, Huddersfield HD1 1ND
☎01484 434840   Fax 01484 426566
✉ edit@poetrybusiness.co.uk
www.poetrybusiness.co.uk

Directors *Peter Sansom, Janet Fisher*

Founded in 1986, the Business publishes *The North* magazine and books, pamphlets and cassettes under the **Smith/Doorstop** imprint. It runs an annual competition and organises monthly writing Saturdays. Send an s.a.e. for full details.

Poetry Can

Unit 11, 20–22 Hepburn Road, Bristol
BS2 8UD
☎0117 942 6976   Fax 0117 944 1478
✉ colin@poetrycan.demon.co.uk
www.poetrycan.demon.co.uk

Founded in 1995, Poetry Can is a poetry development agency working predominantly across the Bristol, Bath & North East Somerset and South Gloucestershire areas. It organises events such as the annual **Bristol Poetry Festival**, lifelong learning projects and provides information and advice concerning all aspects of poetry to individuals, agencies and organisations.

Poetry Ireland/Eigse Eireann

120 St Stephen's Green, Dublin 2, Republic of Ireland
☎00 353 1 478 9974
Fax 00 353 1 478 0205
✉ poetry@iol.ie
www.poetryireland.ie

Education ☎00 353 671 4216 Writers in Schools scheme ☎00 353 1 475 8601

Director *Joseph Woods*

The national organisation for poetry in Ireland, with its four core activities being readings, publications, education and an information and resource service. Organises readings by Irish and international poets countrywide. Through its website, telephone, post and public enquiries, Poetry Ireland operates as a clearing house for everything pertaining to poetry in Ireland. Operates the Writers in Schools scheme. Publishes *Poetry Ireland News*, a bi-monthly newsletter containing information on events, competitions and opportunities. *Poetry Ireland Review* appears quarterly and is the journal of record for poetry in Ireland; current editor: *Peter Sirr*.

The Poetry Library

Royal Festival Hall, Level 5, London SE1 8XX
☎020 7921 0943/0664   Fax 020 7921 0939
✉ info@poetrylibrary.org.uk
www.poetrylibrary.org.uk

Librarian *Simon Smith*

Founded by the Arts Council in 1953. A collection of 60,000 titles of modern poetry since 1912, from Georgian to Rap, representing all English-speaking countries and including translations into English by contemporary poets. Two copies of each title are held, one for loan and one for reference. A wide range of poetry magazines and ephemera from all over the world are kept along with casettes, records and videos for consultation, with many available for loan. There is a children's poetry section with teacher's resource collection.

An information service compiles lists of poetry magazines, competitions, publishers, groups and workshops which are available from the Library on receipt of a large s.a.e. or direct from the website. It also has a noticeboard for lost quotations through which it tries to identify lines or fragments of poetry which have been sent in by other readers.

General enquiry service available. Membership is free but proof of identity and address are essential to join. Open 11.00 am to 8.00 pm, Tuesday to Sunday. (The Library is closed as part

of the South Bank Transformation from April 2005 to January 2007.) The Library's website is one of the best poetry resources on the Net.

Next to the Library is *The Voice Box*, a performance space especially for literature. For details of current programme ring 020 7921 0971.

Poetry London

1A Jewel Road, London E17 4QU
✉ editors@poetrylondon.co.uk
www.poetrylondon.co.uk

Contacts *Kathryn Maris* (listings), *Pascale Petit* (poetry editor), *Scott Verner* (reviews)

Published three times a year, *Poetry London* includes poetry by new and established writers, reviews of recent collections and anthologies, articles on issues relating to poetry, and an encyclopædic listings section of virtually everything to do with poetry in the capital and elsewhere in the UK.

The Poetry School

1a Jewel Road, London E17 4QU
☎020 8223 0401   Fax 020 8223 0401
✉ programme@poetryschool.com
www.poetryschool.com

Administrator *Jacqueline Gabbitas*

Funded by London Arts, the School offers a wide range of courses and workshops on writing and reading poetry and is open to anyone regardless of experience or formal qualifications. Tutors include Graham Fawcett, Stephen Knight, Selima Hill, Carole Satyamurti, Myra Schneider and Mimi Khalvati. The School provides a forum for practitioners to share experiences, develop skills and extend appreciation of the traditional and innovative aspects of their art. There are masterclasses with visiting poets such as Marilyn Hacker, Jorie Graham, Galway Kinnell, Paul Muldoon and August Kleinzahler.

The Poetry Society

22 Betterton Street, London WC2H 9BX
☎020 7240 9881   Fax 020 7240 4818
✉ info@poetrysociety.org.uk
www.poetrysociety.org.uk

Director *Jules Mann*

Founded in 1909 which ought to make it venerable, the Society exists to help poets and poetry thrive in Britain. In the past decade it has undergone a renaissance, reaching out from its Covent Garden base to promote the national health of poetry in a range of imaginative ways. Membership costs £35 for individuals. *Poetry*

News membership is £15. Current activities include:

- Quarterly magazine of new verse, views and criticism, *Poetry Review*.
- Quarterly newsletter, *Poetry News*, with lively relevant articles for members.
- Promotions, events and cooperation with Britain's many literature festivals, poetry venues and poetry publishers.
- Competitions and awards, including the annual **National Poetry Competition** with a £5000 first prize.
- A manuscript diagnosis service, *The Poetry Prescription*, which gives detailed reports on submissions. Reduced rates for members.
- Provides information and advice, publishes books, posters and resources for schools and libraries. Education membership costs £50 (secondary) or £30 (primary) which includes free poetry anthologies, lesson plans and a subscription to Poems on the Underground. Publications include *The Poetry Book For Primary Schools* and *Jumpstart Poetry for the Secondary School*, colourful poetry posters for Keystages 1, 2, 3 and 4. Many of Britain's most popular poets – including Michael Rosen, Roger McGough and Jackie Kay – contribute, offering advice and inspiration.
- The Society's online poetry classroom is at www.poetryclass.net
- The Poetry Café serving snacks and drinks to members, friends and guests, part of The Poetry Place, a venue for many poetry activities – readings, workshops and poetry launches. This space is available for bookings (☎020 7420 9887).
- *Poetry Landmarks of Britain*, a free resource on the Society's website, packed with regional poetry places, publishers, venues and regular events.

Point

Ithaca, Apdo. 125, E–03590 Altea, Spain
☎00 34 96 584 2350   Fax 00 34 96 688 2767
✉ elpoeta@point-editions.com
www.point-editions.com
Also at: Schapenstraat 157, B–1750 Lennik, Belgium

Director *Germain Droogenbroodt*

Founded as POetry INTernational in 1984, Point is based in Spain and Belgium. A multilingual publisher of contemporary verse from *established* poets, the organisation has brought out more than 80 titles in at least eight languages, including English. Point Editions runs the original work alongside a verse translation

into Dutch made in cooperation with the poet. The organisation's website features the world's best-known and unknown poets in English, Spanish and Dutch. Point also co-organises an annual international poetry festival.

Scottish Poetry Library

5 Crichton's Close, Canongate, Edinburgh EH8 8DT
☎0131 557 2876
✉ inquiries@spl.org.uk
www.spl.org.uk

Director *Robyn Marsack*

A comprehensive reference and lending collection of work by Scottish poets in Gaelic, Scots and English, plus the work of British and international poets. Stock includes books, tapes, videos, news cuttings and magazines. Borrowing is free to all. Services include a postal lending scheme, for which there is a small fee; schools workshops throughout Scotland on application; exhibitions; bibliographies; publications; information and promotion in the field of poetry. Also available is an online catalogue and index to Scottish poetry periodicals. There is a Friends' scheme costing £20 annually. Friends receive a newsletter and other benefits and support the library.

Second Light

9 Greendale Close, London SE22 8TG
✉ dilyswood@tiscali.co.uk

Director *Dilys Wood*

A network of over 350 women poets, major names and less well-known. With its publishing arm, Second Light Publications, the network aims to develop and promote women's poetry. Issues a twice-yearly newsletter with poetry, articles and reviews; runs an annual poetry competition; holds residential workshops, readings; has published three anthologies of women's poetry.

Spiel Unlimited

20 Coxwell Street, Cirencester GL7 2BH
☎01285 640470   Fax 01285 640470
✉ spiel@arbury.freeserve.co.uk
www.author.co.uk/spiel

Directors *Marcus Moore, Sara-Jane Arbury*

'Spoken word, written word, anywhere, everywhere' with two writers who put a positive charge in live literature by organising quirky and original events such as Slam!Fests, Spontaneity Days and Living Room Poetry performances, hosting UK poetry slams and running *word*shops for schools and adults. Also produce *SPIEL*, a monthly e-mail newsletter. Specialists in breathing new life into literature.

Survivors' Poetry

Diorama Arts Centre, 34 Osnaburgh Street, London NW1 3ND
☎020 7916 5317   Fax 020 7916 0830
✉ survivor@survivorspoetry.org.uk *or* info@survivorspoetry.org.uk

London Outreach
maureen@survivorspoetry.org.uk

National Outreach
royb@survivorspoetry.org.uk

National Mentoring Scheme
alan@survivorspoetry.org.uk

A unique national literature organisation promoting poetry by survivors of mental distress through workshops, readings and performances to audiences all over the UK. It was founded in 1991 by four poets with first-hand experience of the mental health system. Survivors' community outreach work provides training and performance workshops and publishing projects. Survivors' Poetry National Mentoring Scheme continues to publish new survivor poets in solo pamphlets under the Survivors Press imprint until 2007. For the organisation's quarterly magazine, see *Poetry Express*. Survivors work with those who have survived mental distress and those who empathise with their experience.

Ty Newydd

Llanystumdwy, Cricieth LL52 0LW
☎01766 522811   Fax 01766 523095
✉ post@tynewydd.org
www.tynewydd.org
Director *Sally Baker*

Run by the Taliesin Trust, an independent, Arvon-style residential writers centre established in the one-time home of Lloyd George in North Wales. The programme (in both Welsh and English) has a regular poetry content. (See also *UK Writers' Courses*.) Fees from £350 inclusive. Among the many tutors to-date have been: Gillian Clarke, Owen Sheers, Robert Minhinnick, Olive Senior, Liz Lochhead, Ian Macmillan and Mervyn Morris. Send for the centre's descriptive leaflets and programme of courses.

The Virtual Writing School

Manchester Metropolitan University, Dept. of English, The Virtual Writing School, Geoffrey Manton Building, Rosamond Street West, Manchester M15 6LL
☎0161 247 1735
✉ h.beck@mmu.ac.uk
www.mmu.ac.uk/h-ss/eng

Contact *Heather Beck*

Manchester Metropolitan University's creative writing courses under Michael Schmidt (see also *UK Writers' Courses*) offer a virtual poetry strand with tutors Sophie Hannah, Michael Schmidt, Jeffrey Wainwright and others. The qualification is a MA/PgDip. Enquire early as places are strictly limited. The school also offers virtual novel writing.

Small Presses

Aard Press
c/o Aardverx, 31 Mountearl Gardens, London
SW16 2NL
Managing Editors *D. Jarvis, Dawn Redwood*
Founded 1971. Publishes artists' bookworks,
experimental/visual poetry and art theory,
topographics, ephemera and international mail-
art documentation. Very small editions. No
unsolicited material or proposals.
ROYALTIES not paid. No sale-or-return deals.

Accent Press
PO Box 50, Pembroke Dock SA72 6WY
☎01646 681389   Fax 0870 130 6934
✉ info@accentpress.co.uk
www.accentpress.co.uk
Managing Editor *Hazel Cushion*
Founded 2002. Publishes fiction, poetry, health,
humour and children's books. Unsolicited mss,
synopses and ideas welcome; send first three
chapters and synopsis. 11 titles in 2004.
ROYALTIES twice-yearly.

Akros Publications
33 Lady Nairn Avenue, Kirkcaldy KY1 2AW
☎01592 651522
Publisher *Duncan Glen*
Founded 1965. Publishes poetry collections,
pamphlets and anthologies; literary essays and
studies; local histories. Also publishes *Z20*
poetry magazine. About 10 titles a year. No
unsolicited mss. No fiction.
ROYALTIES twice-yearly.

Allardyce, Barnett, Publishers
14 Mount Street, Lewes BN7 1HL
☎01273 479393
www.abar.net
Publisher *Fiona Allardyce*
Managing Editor *Anthony Barnett*
Founded 1981. Publishes art, literature and
music. IMPRINT **Allardyce Book**. About 3
titles a year. Unsolicited mss and synopses cannot be considered.

Alphard Press
See **ignotus press**

Anglo-Saxon Books
Frithgarth, Thetford Forest Park, Hockwold
cum Wilton IP26 4NQ
☎01842 828430   Fax 01842 828332
✉ tony@asbooks.co.uk
www.asbooks.co.uk
Managing Editor *Tony Linsell*
Founded 1990 to promote a greater awareness
of and interest in early English history, language
and culture. Publishes Anglo-Saxon history,
culture, language. Please phone before sending
mss. About 5 titles a year.
ROYALTIES at standard rate.

Apex Publishing Ltd
PO Box 7445, Colchester CO4 9UA
☎001255 428500   Fax 0870 046 6536
✉ enquiry@apexpublishing.co.uk
www.apexpublishing.co.uk
Managing Editor *Susan Kidby*
Founded 2002. Subsidy publishing company
for unknown and established authors. Publishes
poetry, self-help, non-fiction, fiction, sci-fi, history, humour, fine art, art history, education and
textbooks, economics, crime, children's books,
biography, autobiography, academic, women's
interests, medical and philosophy. 42 titles in
print. Welcomes unsolicited mss, synopses and
ideas for books. Approach in writing to the
address above.
ROYALTIES annually.

Athelney
1 Providence Street, King's Lynn PE30 5ET
Fax 01842 828332
Managing Editor *John Cooper*
Founded 2000. Publishes nationalism in general;
English nationalism in particular. 'We are in-
terested in contemporary England and the Eng-
lish; e.g. culture, language, politics.' Unsolicited
outlines/contents page/first chapter welcome.
Please enclose return postage.
ROYALTIES at standard rate.

Authority Publishing
7 Coppice Hill, Bradford on Avon BA15 1JT
☎01225 863905
✉ authority@btinternet.com

www.authoritypublishing.co.uk
Managing Editors *Kerri Miles, David Littlefield*
Founded 2004. Self-publishing service offered by a team of published authors, designers and production professionals. Publishes across a wide range of categories, working with individual authors and commercial organisations. Phone or e-mail for a brochure and submission form.

M.&M. Baldwin
24 High Street, Cleobury Mortimer, Kidderminster DY14 8BY
☎01299 270110   Fax 01299 270110
✉ mb@mbaldwin.free-online.co.uk
Managing Editor *Dr Mark Baldwin*
Founded 1978. Publishes local interest/history, WW2 codebreaking and inland waterways books. Up to 5 titles a year. Unsolicited mss, synopses and ideas for books welcome (not general fiction).
ROYALTIES paid.

Barny Books
Hough on the Hill, near Grantham NG32 2BB
☎01400 250246/01522 790009
Fax 01400 251737
Managing Director/Editorial Head *Molly Burkett*
Business Manager *Jayne Thompson*
Founded with the aim of encouraging new writers and illustrators. Publishes mainly children's books but also adult fiction and non-fiction. Offers schools' projects where students help to produce books. Too small a concern to have the staff/resources to deal with unsolicited mss. Writers with strong ideas should approach Molly Burkett by letter in the first instance. Also runs a readership and advisory service for new writers (£15 fee for short stories or illustrations; £40 fee for full-length stories).
Division of profits 50/50.

BB Books
See entry under *Poetry Presses*

The Better Book Company Ltd
Warblington Lodge, The Gardens, Warblington, Havant PO9 2XH
☎023 9248 1160   Fax 023 9249 2819
✉ editors@better-book.co.uk
www.better-book.co.uk
Managing Editor *James Jude Garvey*
Book Progress Manager *John Littlefield*
Founded 1996. Offers a complete editorial, design, printing and marketing service to authors

wishing to self-publish their work in all genre. Marketing and distribution services available to all authors. Produces fiction, histories, memoirs, poetry, religious, scientific, company histories. A free booklet, *A Complete Guide to Self-Publishing*, is available on request. 90 titles in 2004.

Between the Lines
9 Woodstock Road, London N4 3ET
☎020 8374 5526   Fax 020 8374 5736
✉ btluk@aol.com
www.interviews-with-poets.com
Editorial Board *Peter Dale, Philip Hoy, J.D. McClatchy*
Founded 1998. Publishes in book form extended interviews with leading contemporary poets. Thirteen volumes currently in print, featuring Peter Dale, John Ashbery, Charles Simic, Ian Hamilton, Donald Justice, Seamus Heaney, Richard Wilbur, Thom Gunn, Donald Hall, Anthony Hecht, Anthony Thwaite, Michael Hamburger and W.D. Snodgrass. Each volume includes a career sketch, a comprehensive bibliography and a representative selection of quotations from the poets' critics and reviewers. More recent volumes include photographs as well as previously uncollected poems.

The Bewildered Publishing Company Ltd
Argoed Hall, Tregaron SY25 6JR
☎01974 298070
✉ john.wilson@virgin.net
Publisher *John Wilson*
Founded in 1999 'to provide a direct route to the book market for authors, with an unconventional approach to writing and publishing'. Publishes humorous paperbacks. No unsolicited material; initial inquiry by telephone, e-mail or letter.
ROYALTIES not paid.

Bitter Lemon Press
37 Arundel Gardens, London W11 2LW
☎020 7727 7927
✉ books@bitterlemonpress.com
www.bitterlemonpress.com
Managing Editor *Laurence Colchester*
Founded 2003. Publishes fiction only. 6 titles in 2004. No unsolicited mss; welcomes synopses and ideas for books. Approach by e-mail in the first instance.
ROYALTIES annually.

Black Cat Books
See **Neil Miller Publications**

The Book Castle

12 Church Street, Dunstable LU5 4RU
☎01582 605670   Fax 01582 662431
✉ bc@book-castle.co.uk
www.book-castle.co.uk

Managing Editor *Paul Bowes*

Founded 1986. Publishes non-fiction of local interest (Bedfordshire, Hertfordshire, Buckinghamshire, Oxfordshire, the Chilterns). About 100 titles in print. 12 titles a year. Unsolicited mss, synopses and ideas for books welcome. ROYALTIES paid.

Bookmarque Publishing

26 Cotswold Close, Minster Lovell OX29 0SX
☎01993 775179
✉ john@bookmarquepublishing.co.uk

Managing Editor *John Rose*

Founded 1987. Publishing business with aim of filling gaps in motoring history of which it is said 'there are still many'. Publishes motoring history, motor sport and some 'general' titles. All design and typesetting of books done in-house. About 8 titles a year. Unsolicited mss and synopses welcome on motoring, motor racing and specialist marque histories. S.a.e. required for reply or return of material or for advice on publishing your work. ROYALTIES paid.

Brilliant Publications

1 Church View, Sparrow Hall Farm, Edlesborough, Dunstable LU6 2ES
☎01525 229720   Fax 01525 229725
✉ sales@brilliantpublications.co.uk
www.brilliantpublications.co.uk

Publisher *Priscilla Hannaford*

Founded 1993. Publishes practical resource books for teachers, parents and others working with 0–13-year-olds. About 10–15 titles a year. Submit synopsis and sample pages in the first instance. All the books have black and white insides and many can be photocopied. Potential authors are strongly advised to look at the format of existing books before submitting synopses. 'We do not publish children's picture books.' ROYALTIES twice-yearly.

The Brodie Press

✉ thebrodiepress@hotmail.com
www.thebrodiepress.co.uk

Managing Editors *James Bainbridge, Rhiannon Davies, Hannah Sheppard, Tom Sperlinger*

Founded 2002. Publishes poetry and anthologies. SERIES *The Brodie Poets*, launched in 2003, including Julie-ann Rowell, Poetry Book Society Pamphlet Choice, Winter 2003. Send synopses and proposals by e-mail in the first instance.

Charlewood Press

7 Weavers Place, Chandlers Ford SO53 1TU
☎023 8026 1192
✉ gponting@clara.net
www.home.clara.net/gponting/
    index-page11.html

Managing Editors *Gerald Ponting, Anthony Light*

Founded 1987. Publishes local history books and walks booklets on Hampshire and adjacent counties, especially around the Fordingbridge area. Mss in this field considered.

Chrysalis Press

7 Lower Ladyes Hills, Kenilworth CV8 2GN
☎01926 855223
✉ editor@margaretbuckley.com
www.margaretbuckley.com

Managing Editor *Brian Boyd*

Founded 1994. Publishes fiction, literary criticism and biography. No unsolicited mss. ROYALTIES paid.

CNP Publications

See **Lyfrow Trelyspen**

Columbia Publishing Wales Limited

Glen More, 6 Cwrt y Camden, Brecon LD3 7RR
☎01874 625270   Fax 01874 625270
✉ dng@columbiawales.fsnet.co.uk
www.columbiapublishing.co.uk

Managing Editor *Dafydd Gittins*

Founded 2000. Publishes fiction and non-fiction – books, film and music (mainly pop and rock). Subjects suitable for film or television. 3 titles in 2004. No unsolicited mss. Synopses and ideas welcome; approach by letter or e-mail in the first instance. ROYALTIES paid.

Contact Publishing Ltd

Unit 346, 176 Finchley Road, London NW3 6BT
☎020 7794 1999   Fax 020 7794 1999
✉ info@contact-publishing.co.uk
www.contact-publishing.co.uk

Managing Director *Anne Kontoyannis*

Founded 2003. Publishes general fiction, non-fiction, self help and New Age. No children's,

political, sports or westerns. 2 titles in 2004.' Interested in seeing mss by new authors with original angles and new ideas.' See website for author guidelines. Send synopsis, three sample chapters and outline in the first instance.
ROYALTIES twice-yearly.

Copperfield Books

Hillbrook House, Lyncombe Vale Road, Bath BA2 4LS
☎01225 442835   Fax 01225 319755
✉ sales@www.darcybook.com
www.darcybook.com

Director *Jean Brushfield*

Publishes paperback fiction and general non-fiction. No unsolicited mss; 'we only commission books to our own specification'.

The Cosmic Elk

68 Elsham Crescent, Lincoln LN6 3YS
☎01522 820922
✉ cosmicelk@zoom.co.uk
www.cosmicelk.co.uk

Contact *Heather Hobden*

Founded 1988. Publishes easily updated books on science, history and the history of science. Websites designed and maintained, with or without associated printed books. 'Authors and books always welcome.' Check the website first for information and contacts.

Crescent Moon Publishing and Joe's Press

PO Box 393, Maidstone ME14 5XU
☎01622 729593
✉ cresmopub@yahoo.co.uk
www.crescentmoon.org.uk

Managing Editor *Jeremy Robinson*

Founded 1988 to publish critical studies of figures such as D.H. Lawrence, Thomas Hardy, André Gide, Walt Disney, Rilke, Leonardo da Vinci, Mark Rothko, C.P. Cavafy and Hélène Cixous. Publishes literature, criticism, media, art, feminism, painting, poetry, travel, guidebooks, cinema and some fiction. Literary magazine, *Passion*, launched February 1994 (quarterly). *Pagan America*, twice-yearly anthology of American poetry. About 15–20 titles per year. Unsolicited synopses and ideas welcome but approach in writing first and send an s.a.e. Do not send whole mss.
ROYALTIES negotiable.

Critical Vision

See **Headpress**

Crossbridge Books

345 Old Birmingham Road, Bromsgrove B60 1NX
☎0121 447 7897   Fax 0121 445 1063
✉ crossbridgebooks@btinternet.com
www.crossbridgebooks.com

Managing Director *Eileen Mohr*

Founded 1995. Publishes Christian books for adults and children. IMPRINT **Mohr Books**. 4–5 titles a year including Trevor Dearing's latest books. 'No new submissions for the foreseeable future.' No New Age or books not biblically Christian.
ROYALTIES twice-yearly.

Crown House Publishing

Crown Buildings, Bancyfelin, Carmarthen SA33 5ND
☎01267 211345   Fax 01267 211882
✉ books@crownhouse.co.uk
www.crownhouse.co.uk

Managing Director *David Bowman*

Founded 1998. Publishes titles in the areas of psychotherapy, education, business training and development, mind body spirit. The aim of the list is to both demystify the latest psychological advances, particularly in the fields of Accelerated Learning, Neuro-Linguistic Programming (NLP) and hypnosis. Crown House provides professional therapists, consultants and trainers with books detailing the latest cutting-edge developments in their field. About 40 titles a year.
ROYALTIES twice-yearly.

Culva House Publications

10 The Carrs, Sleights, Whitby YO21 1RR
☎01947 810819
✉ alan@culvahouse.co.uk
www.culvahouse.co.uk

Managing Editor *Alan Whitworth*

Founded in 1986 as a part-time self-publishing venture and grew into a full-time business in 2000. Publishes architecture and local history; biography. Unsolicited material welcome; approach by letter or e-mail.
ROYALTIES paid.

Day Books

Orchard Piece, Crawborough, Charlbury OX7 3TX
☎01608 811196   Fax 01608 811196
✉ diaries@day-books.com
www.day-books.com

Managing Editor *James Sanderson*

Founded in 1997 to publish a series of great

diaries from around the world. Unsolicited mss, synopses and ideas welcome. Include return postage if return of material is required.

Delancey Press Ltd
4 Delancey Passage, London NW1 7NN
☎020 7387 3544   Fax 020 7383 5314
✉ delanceypress@aol.com
www.delanceypress.com
Managing Editor *Tatiana von Saxe Wilson*

Founded 2000. Publishes fiction, children's and humour. Not interested in academic books. Overseas subsidiaries in association with **The Book Guild Ltd**. Accepts unsolicited mss sent by mail with s.a.e.
ROYALTIES twice-yearly.

Diagonal
See **Headpress**

Diggory Press
See **Meadow Books**

The Dragonby Press
15 High Street, Dragonby, Scunthorpe DN15 0BE
☎01724 840645
✉ rich@rah2williams.freeserve.co.uk
freespace.virgin.net/rah.williams
Managing Editor *Richard Williams*

Founded 1987 to publish affordable bibliography for reader, collector and dealer. About 3 titles a year. Unsolicited mss, synopses and ideas welcome for bibliographical projects only.
ROYALTIES paid.

Dramatic Lines
PO Box 201, Twickenham TW2 5RQ
☎020 8296 9502   Fax 020 8296 9503
✉ mail@dramaticlinespublishers.co.uk
www.dramaticlines.co.uk
Managing Editor *John Nicholas*

Founded to promote drama for all. Publications with a wide variety of theatrical applications including classroom use and school assemblies, drama examinations, auditions, festivals, theatre group performance, musicals and handbooks. Unsolicited drama-related mss, proposals and synopses welcome; enclose s.a.e.
ROYALTIES paid.

DreamStar Books
Lasyard House, Underhill Street, Bridgnorth WV16 4BB
☎0870 777 3339   Fax 01746 765354

✉ enquiries@dreamstarbooks.com
www.dreamstarbooks.com
Owner *Dreamstar Books*
Managing Director *Mark Horton-Oliver*

Founded 2002. Assists new and unpublished authors gain recognition for their work by offering low cost self-publishing/printing. 'No royalty tie-ins; authors are free to pursue traditional publishing deal.' Mss, synopses and ideas welcome.

Edgewell Publishing
42 Edgewell Grange, Prudhoe NE42 6RH
☎01661 833700   Fax 01661 833700
✉ kieth@tynedale-languages.co.uk
Editor *Keith Minton*

Founded 2005. Short story and poetry magazine (*Lively Tales*). Short stories, poems, articles on travel and languages, humour, anecdotes, and stories and poems for children.

Educational Heretics Press
113 Arundel Drive, Bramcote Hills, Nottingham NG9 3FQ
☎0115 925 7261   Fax 0115 925 7261
www.edheretics.gn.apc.org
Directors *Janet & Roland Meighan*

Non-profit venture which aims to question the dogmas of schooling in particular and education in general, and establish the logistics of the next learning system. No unsolicited material. Enquiries only.
ROYALTIES not paid but under review.

Enable Enterprises
PO Box 1974, Coventry CV3 1YF
☎0800 358 8484   Fax 0870 487 3483
✉ writers@enableenterprises.com
www.enableenterprises.com
Chief Executive *Simon Stevens*

Enable Enterprises provides a wide range of accessibilty and disability services including publications on relevant issues. It welcomes unsolicited material related to accessibility and disability issues.

Fand Music Press
The Barony, 16 Sandringham Road, Petersfield GU32 2AA
☎01730 267341   Fax 01730 267341
✉ Paul@fandmusic.com
www.fandmusic.com
Managing Editor *Peter Thompson*

Founded in 1989 as a sheet music publisher, Fand Music Press has expanded its range to include CD recordings and books on music. Recently started publishing poetry and short stories. 10 titles a year. No unsolicited mss. Write with ideas in the first instance.

Feather Books

PO Box 438, Shrewsbury SY3 0WN
☎01743 872177   Fax 01743 872177
✉ john@waddysweb.freeuk.com
www.waddysweb.freeuk.com

Managing Director *Rev. John Waddington-Feather*

Directors *David Grundy, Tony Reavill, Paul Evans*

Founded 1980 to publish writers' group work. All material has a strong Christian ethos. Publishes poetry (mainly, but not exclusively, religious); Christian mystery novels (the Revd. D.I. Blake Hartley series); Christian children's *Quill Hedgehog* novels; seasonal poetry collections and *The Poetry Church* quarterly magazine. Produces poetry, drama and hymn CD/cassettes. 20 titles a year. No unsolicited mss, synopses or ideas. All correspondence to include s.a.e., please.

Fern House

19 High Street, Haddenham, Ely CB6 3XA
☎01353 740222
✉ info@fernhouse.com
www.fernhouse.com

Proprietor *Rodney Dale*

Founded 1995 but now completing work in progress as the proprietor winds down. Backlist still available but no more submissions, please.

Five Leaves Publications

PO Box 81, Nottingham NG5 4ER
☎0115 969 3597
✉ info@fiveleaves.co.uk
www.fiveleaves.co.uk

Contact *Ross Bradshaw*

Founded 1995 (taking over the publishing programme of Mushroom Bookshop). Publishes fiction, poetry, social history, politics and Jewish interest. Titles normally commissioned. About 6–8 titles a year.
ROYALTIES paid.

Flambard

Stable Cottage, East Fourstones, Hexham NE47 5DX
☎01434 674360   Fax 01434 674178
www.flambardpress.co.uk
Also at: 43 Linskill Street, North Shields NE30 1DR
Managing Editor *Peter Lewis*

Founded 1990. Publishes poetry and literary fiction. 8 titles in 2004. Welcomes unsolicited mss but essential to send preliminary letter with details of author and either a sample of 10 poems or a synopsis plus 2–3 chapters and s.a.e.
ROYALTIES paid.

Forth Naturalist & Historian

University of Stirling, Stirling FK9 4LA
☎01259 215091   Fax 01786 464994
✉ lindsay.corbett@stir.ac.uk
www.fnh.stir.ac.uk
Also at: 30 Dunmar Drive, Alloa, Clackmannanshire FK10 2EH

Honorary Secretary *Lindsay Corbett*

Founded 1975 by the collaboration of Stirling University members and the Central Regional Council to promote interests and publications on central Scotland. Aims to provide a 'valuable local studies educational resource for mid-Scotland schools, libraries and people'. Runs an annual symposium: Man and the Landscape. Publishes naturalist, historical and environmental studies. Over 20 selected papers from the annual *The Forth Naturalist & Historian* (Vol. 27 in 2004) are published in pamphlet form. Welcomes papers, mss and ideas relevant to central Scotland.
ROYALTIES not paid.

Foxbury Press

15 St Michael's Road, Winchester SO23 9JE
☎01962 864037

Managing Editor *Robert Cross*

Founded 2000. 4 titles published.

Frontier Publishing

Windetts, Kirstead NR15 1EG
☎01508 558174
✉ frontier.pub@macunlimited.net
www.frontierpublishing.co.uk

Managing Editor *John Black*

Founded 1983. Publishes travel, photography, sculptural history and literature. 2–3 titles a year. No unsolicited mss; synopses and ideas welcome.
ROYALTIES paid.

Galactic Central Publications

Imladris, 25A Copgrove Road, Leeds LS8 2SP
✉ gcp@philsp.com
www.philsp.com

Managing Editor *Phil Stephensen-Payne*

Founded 1982 in the US. Publishes science fiction bibliographies. All new publications originate in the UK. About 4 titles a year. Unsolicited mss, synopses and ideas welcome.

GB Publishing Services
26 Percheron Drive, Spalding PE11 3GH
☎01775 768902
✉ garry.baker@btinternet.com
www.garrybaker.cjb.net
Managing Editor *Garry Baker*
Founded 2004. Publishes romance, fiction, non-fiction, history.Send first three chapters and synopsis (on A4 paper) with s.a.e.
ROYALTIES annually.

Glosa Education Organisation
PO Box 18, Richmond TW9 2GE
www.glosa.org
Managing Editor *Wendy Ashby*
Founded 1981. Publishes textbooks, dictionaries and translations for the teaching, speaking and promotion of Glosa (an international, auxiliary language); also a newsletter, *Plu Glosa Nota* and journal, *PGN*. Unsolicited mss and ideas for Glosa books welcome.

Godstow Press
60 Godstow Road, Wolvercote, Oxford OX2 8NY
☎01865 556215
✉ info@godstowpress.co.uk
www.godstowpress.co.uk
Managing Editors *Linda Smith, David Smith*
Founded in 2003 for the publication of creative work with a philosophical/spiritual content. 2–3 titles a year.Considers works self-published by the author for inclusion in the catalogue.The press works on a subscription scheme rather than through usual trade outlets. Synopses and ideas welcome but no unsolicited mss.

Grant Books
The Coach House, New Road, Cutnall Green, Droitwich WR9 0PQ
☎01299 851588   Fax 01299 851446
✉ golf@grantbooks.co.uk
www.grantbooks.co.uk
Managing Editor *H.R.J. Grant*
Founded 1978. Publishes golf-related titles only: course architecture, history, biography, etc., but not instructional, humour or fiction material. New titles and old, plus limited editions. About 6 titles a year. Mss, synopses and ideas welcome.
ROYALTIES paid.

Great Northern Publishing
PO Box 202, Scarborough YO11 3GE
☎01723 581329   Fax 01723 581329
✉ books@greatnorthernpublishing.co.uk
www.greatnorthernpublishing.co.uk
Production Manager *Mark Marsay*
Senior Editor *Diane Crowther*
Small, award-winning, family-owned company founded in 1999. Publishes books, magazines and journals: usually non-fiction (mainly military), adult erotic material and, occasionally, fiction. No romance, religious, political, feminist, New Age, medical or children's books. Publications include *The Great War (1914–1918)* magazine and *Jade – The Intenational Erotic Art and Literature Magazines* (see under *Magazines*). Also provides full book, magazine, print and internet production services to individuals, businesses, charities, museums and other small publishers and runs a mail-order and Internet-based bookshop stocking selected titles alongside its own. Website provides submission guidelines and current publishing requirements. No unsolicited mss; send letter or text-only e-mail in the first instance.
ROYALTIES twice-yearly.

Grevatt & Grevatt
9 Rectory Drive, Newcastle upon Tyne NE3 1XT
☎0191 285 8053
✉ grevatt@softhome.net
grevatt-grevatt.freeservers.com/index.htm
Chairman/Editorial Head *Dr Dermot Killingley*
Founded 1981. Alternative publisher of works not normally commercially viable. Three books have appeared with financial backing from professional bodies. Publishes academic titles, particularly language, linguistics and religious studies. Some poetry also. No unsolicited mss. Synopses and ideas should be accompanied by s.a.e.
ROYALTIES annually (after first 500 copies).

GSSE
11 Malford Grove, Gilwern, Abergavenny NP7 0RN
☎01873 830872
✉ GSSE@zoo.co.uk
www.gsse.org.uk
Owner/Manager *David P. Bosworth*
Publishes books and booklets describing classroom practice (at all levels of education and training). Ideas welcome – particularly from practising teachers, lecturers and trainers describing how they use technology in their teaching.
ROYALTIES by arrangement.

Happy House

3b Castledown Avenue, Hastings TN34 3RJ
☎01424 434778
✉ vibezone@excite.com
www.deadhappy.co.uk

Founded 1992 as a self-publishing venture for a Dave Arnold/Martin Honeysett collaboration of poetry and cartoons. Affiliated to indie record label, Dead Happy Records.

Haunted Library

Flat 1, 36 Hamilton Street, Hoole, Chester CH2 3JQ
☎01244 313685
✉ pardos@globalnet.co.uk
www.users.globalnet.co.uk/~pardos/GS.html

Managing Editor *Rosemary Pardoe*

Founded 1979. Publishes the *Ghosts and Scholars M.R. James Newsletter* two or three times a year, featuring articles, news and reviews (no fiction).
ROYALTIES not paid.

Headpress

40 Rossall Avenue, Radcliffe M26 1JD
☎0161 796 1935   Fax 0161 796 9703
✉ info.headpress@zen.co.uk
www.headpress.com

Managing Editor *David Kerekes*

Founded 1991. Publishes *Headpress* journal, devoted to the strange and esoteric, and *Creeping Flesh*, a journal devoted to horror and fantasy cinema. No fiction or poetry. IMPRINTS **Critical Vision**; **Diagonal**. Unsolicited material welcome; send letter and outline in the first instance.
ROYALTIES AND FLAT FEES vary.

Heart of Albion Press

2 Cross Hill Close, Wymeswold,
Loughborough LE12 6UJ
☎01509 880725   Fax 01509 881715
✉ albion@indigogroup.co.uk
www.hoap.co.uk

Managing Editor *R.N. Trubshaw*

Founded 1990 to publish local history. Publishes folklore, local history and mythology. Synopses relating to these subjects welcome.
ROYALTIES negotiable.

Hilmarton Manor Press

Calne SN11 8SB
☎01249 760208   Fax 01249 760379
✉ mailorder@hilmartonpress.co.uk

Chairman/Managing Director *Charles Baile de Laperriere*

Publisher of fine art dictionaries and art refer-ence only. Editor and publisher of *Who's Who In Art* (32nd edition).
ROYALTIES paid.

ignotus press

BCM-Writer, London WC1N 3XX
☎01530 831916   Fax 01530 831916
✉ ignotuspress@aol.com
www.ignotuspress.com

Publisher *Suzanne Ruthven*

Founded 1994. 'We are looking for positive, for-ward-looking material (fiction and non-fiction) on all aspects of British-based ritual magic, mys-teries, spiritual development, traditional and hereditary witchcraft and other paths which demonstrate the writer's grasp of both traditional and contemporary esoteric practice. No New Age idealism, fantasy, pseudo-spirituality or neo-Hammer House of Horror fiction.' IMPRINTS **Moonraker Books** (fiction); **Alphard Press** (self-help and lifestyle). 'We are looking to extend these areas with the addition of com-patible fiction and life-style titles).' About 20 titles a year. Send s.a.e. for authors' guidelines before submitting material for consideration.
ROYALTIES paid.

Immanion Press

8 Rowley Grove, Stafford ST17 9BJ
☎01785 613299
✉ info@immanionpress.wox.org
www.immanionpress.wox.org

Managing Editor *Storm Constantine*

Founded 2003. Publishes genre fiction (science fiction, fantasy, horror), slipstream fiction; eso-teric non-fiction. Submissions by e-mail or post (enclose s.a.e.). Website gives full submission details.
ROYALTIES paid.

Infinity Junction

PO Box 64, Neston DO CH64 0WB
✉ infin-info@infinityjunction.com
www.infinityjunction.com

Managing Editor *Neil Gee*

Established originally as a self-publishing, self-help organisation in 1991, Infinity Junction became a publisher in 2001. Currently offers a variety of services to authors, including advice, free web display space and full commercial publication. Authors are strongly advised to read the detailed information on the website before making contact. E-mail communication pre-ferred. 'We cannot undertake to read unso-licited whole mss.'

Inner Sanctum Publications

75 Greenleaf Gardens, Polegate BN26 6PQ
☎01323 484058
✉ innersanctum@clara.co.uk
www.innersanctumpublications.com

Managing Editor *Mary Hession*

Founded in 1999 to publish spiritual books. Unsolicited mss, synopses and ideas welcome; approach in writing in the first instance.
ROYALTIES not paid.

Iolo

38 Chaucer Road, Bedford MK40 2AJ
☎01234 301718/07909 934866
Fax 01234 301718
✉ newplays@dedwyddjones.screaming.net

Managing Director *Dedwydd Jones*

Publishes Welsh theatre-related material and campaigns for a Welsh National Theatre. Ideas on Welsh themes welcome; approach in writing.

Ivy Publications

72 Hyperion House, Somers Road, London SW2 1HZ
☎020 8671 6872
Proprietor *Ian Bruton-Simmonds*

Founded 1989. Publishes educational, science, fiction, philosophy, children's, travel, literary criticism, history, film scripts. No unsolicited mss; send two pages, one from the beginning and one from the body of the book, together with synopsis (one paragraph) and s.a.e. No cookery, gardening or science fiction.
ROYALTIES annually.

The Jupiter Press

The Coach House, Gatacre, Claverley, Nr Wolverhampton WV5 7AW
☎01746 710694   Fax 01746 710158
✉ gordon@jupiterpress.fsnet.co.uk
www.jupiter-press.com

Managing Editor *Gordon Thomas Drury*

Founded 1995. Looking for niche market and information publications, also quiz and game subjects. Interested in holistic, clairvoyance and esoteric subjects. Synopses and ideas for books welcome. Send idea and sample chapter. Unsolicited mss welcome 'but may request a reader's fee'. Currently seeking books for series entitled *How To Make Money At* ....
ROYALTIES paid.

Kinglake Publishing

61B Praed Street, London W2 1NS
✉ info@kinglakepublishing.co.uk
www.kinglakepublishing.co.uk

Contact *James Farrell*

Publishers of classic fiction. Authors include R.L. Stevenson, Joseph Conrad, Anthony Trollope and Charles Dickens.'Few opportunities for living authors but you could try your luck with an e-mail to James Farrell.'

Kittiwake

3 Glantwymyn Village Workshops, Glantwymyn, Nr Machynlleth SY20 8LY
☎01650 511314   Fax 01650 511314
✉ perrographics@btinternet.com
www.kittiwake-books.com

Managing Editor *David Perrott*

Founded 1986. Publishes guidebooks only, with an emphasis on careful design/production. Specialist research, writing, cartographic and electronic publishing services available. Unsolicited mss, synopses and ideas for guidebooks welcome.
ROYALTIES paid.

The Lindsey Press

Unitarian Headquarters, 1–6 Essex Street, Strand, London WC2R 3HY
☎020 7240 2384   Fax 020 7240 3089
✉ ga@unitarian.org.uk

Convenor *Kate Taylor*

Established at the end of the 18th century as a vehicle for disseminating liberal religion. Adopted the name of The Lindsey Press at the beginning of the 20th century (after Theophilus Lindsey, the great Unitarian Theologian). Publishes books reflecting liberal religious thought or Unitarian denominational history. Also worship material – hymn books, collections of prayers, etc. No unsolicited mss; synopses and ideas welcome.
ROYALTIES not paid.

Logaston Press

Logaston, Woonton, Almeley HR3 6QH
☎01544 327344
www.logastonpress.co.uk

Managing Editors *Andy Johnson, Ron Shoesmith*

Founded 1985. Publishes guides, archaeology, social history, rural issues and local history for Wales, the Welsh Border and West Midlands. 10–15 titles a year. Unsolicited mss, synopses and ideas welcome. Return postage appreciated.
ROYALTIES paid.

Luath Press Ltd

543/2 Castlehill, The Royal Mile, Edinburgh EH1 2ND
☎0131 225 4326   Fax 0131 225 4324

✉ gavin.macdougall@luath.co.uk
www.luath.co.uk
Managing Editor *G.H. MacDougall*
Founded 1981. Publishes mainly books with a Scottish connection. Current list includes fiction, poetry, guidebooks, walking and outdoor, history, folklore, politics and global issues, cartoons, biography, food and drink, environment, music and dance, sport and *On the Trail Of* and *The Quest For* SERIES. About 20–30 titles a year. Unsolicited mss, synopses and ideas welcome; 'committed to publishing well-written books worth reading'.
ROYALTIES paid.

Lyfrow Trelyspen
The Roseland Institute, Gorran, St Austell Cornwall
☎01726 843501 Fax 01726 843501
✉ trelispen@care4free.net
Managing Editor *Dr James Whetter*
Founded 1975. Publishes works on Cornish history, biography, essays, etc. Also **CNP Publications** which publishes the quarterly journal *The Cornish Banner/An Baner Kernewek*. 1–2 titles a year. Unsolicited mss, synopses and ideas welcome.
ROYALTIES not paid.

The Maia Press
82 Forest Road, London E8 3BH
☎020 7683 8181 Fax 020 7683 8181
✉ maggie@maiapress.com
www.maiapress.com
Contacts *Maggie Hamand, Jane Havell*
Founded 2002. Publishes fiction by known and new writers. 6 titles a year. No unsolicited mss, write with c.v. and synopsis only. S.a.e. essential.
ROYALTIES twice-yearly.

Maypole Editions
65 Mayfair Avenue, Ilford IG1 3DQ
☎020 8252 3937
www.maypoleeditions.co.uk
Contact *Barry Taylor*
Publisher of plays and poetry in the main. Catalogue available on the website.2–3 titles a year. Unsolicited mss welcome provided return postage is included. Poetry always welcome for collected anthologies and should be approximately 30 lines of tight verse, broadly covering social concerns, ethnic minority issues, feminist incident, romance generally, travel and lyric rhyming verse. No politics except evenly comparative. The biannual collected anthology is

designed as a small press platform for first-time poets who might not otherwise get into print, and a permanent showcase for those already published who want to break into the mainstream. Submissions must include A5 s.a.e. 'Please be patient when sending work because of the huge volume of submissions.' Exempt Charity Status.

Meadow Books
35 Stonefield Way, Burgess Hill RH15 8DW
☎01444 239044
✉ meadowbooks@hotmail.com
Managing Director *C. O'Neill*
Founded 1990. Publisher of nursing history books and nursing picture archive. IMPRINT **Diggory Press** Founded 2004. Mainly spiritual and folklore titles.Initial enquiries and submissions by e-mail only; no telephone calls.

Mercia Cinema Society
19 Pinder's Grove, Wakefield WF1 4AH
☎01924 372748
✉ mervyn.gould@virgin.net
Managing Editor *Paul Smith*
Founded 1980 to foster research into the history of picture houses. Publishes books and booklets on the subject, including cinema circuits and chains. Books are often tied in with specific geographical areas. Unsolicited mss, synopses and ideas.
ROYALTIES not paid.

Meridian Books
40 Hadzor Road, Oldbury B68 9LA
☎0121 429 4397
✉ meridian.books@btopenworld.com
Managing Editor *Peter Groves*
Founded 1985 as a small home-based enterprise following the acquisition of titles from Tetradon Publications Ltd. Publishes walking and regional guides. 4–5 titles a year. Unsolicited mss, synopses and ideas welcome if relevant. Send s.a.e. if mss to be returned.
ROYALTIES paid.

Merton Priory Press Ltd
67 Merthyr Road, Whitchurch, Cardiff CF14 1DD
☎029 2052 1956 Fax 029 2062 3599
✉ merton@dircon.co.uk
www.merton.dircon.co.uk
Managing Director *Philip Riden*
Founded 1993. Publishes academic and mid-

market history, especially local, industrial and transport history; also memoirs and autobiographies. Full catalogue available. About 6 titles a year.
ROYALTIES twice-yearly.

Neil Miller Publications

Ormonde House, 49 Ormonde Road, Hythe CT21 6DW
✉ millersbooks@bcbpublishers.wanadoo.co.uk
www.webspawner.com/users/neilmillerpubs

Also at: 4 Rue D'Equiire Bergueneuse, Pas de Calais, France 62134
Managing Editor *Neil Miller*
Founded 1994. Publishes novels and collections of short stories on any subject: adventure mystery, horror, detective, romance, fantasy, comedy and tales with a twist. IMPRINT **Black Cat Books** Non-fiction: war memoirs, true tales, biographies, history and comedy. Interested in working with new and published writers. Evaluation and critique service available. 'Send £7.75 for latest book/authors pack giving details on being published by us plus large s.a.e. No unrequested tales, please.'

Millers Dale Publications

7 Weavers Place, Chandlers Ford, Eastleigh SO53 1TU
☎023 8026 1192
✉ gponting@clara.net
www.home.clara.net/gponting/
index-page10.html
Managing Editor *Gerald Ponting*
Founded 1990. Publishes books on local history related to central Hampshire. Also books related to slide presentations by Gerald Ponting. Ideas for local history books on Hampshire considered.

Mohr Books

See **Crossbridge Books**

Moonraker Books

See **ignotus press**

Natzler Enterprises (Entertainments)

1 Wakeford Cottages, Selden Lane, Worthing BN11 2LQ
☎01903 211785   Fax 01903 211519
✉ natzler@btinternet.com
www.natzler.com
www.paulgordon.net

Managing Editor *Paul Gordon*
Founded 1993. Publishes magic (entertainment) books only. No unsolicited mss; send synopses and ideas by post.

Need2Know

Remus House, Coltsfoot Drive, Woodston PE2 9JX
☎01733 898105   Fax 01733 313524
✉ info@forwardpress.co.uk
www.n2kbooks.com

Founded 1995 'to fill a gap in the market for self-help books'. Need2Know is an imprint of **Forward Press** (see entry under *Poetry Presses*). Publishes contemporary health and lifestyle issues. No unsolicited mss. Call in the first instance.
ROYALTIES Advance plus 15% royalties.

Norvik Press Ltd

School of Language, Linguistics & Translation Studies, University of East Anglia, Norwich NR4 7TJ
☎01603 593356   Fax 01603 250599
✉ norvik.press@uea.ac.uk
www.uea.ac.uk/llt/norvik_press
Managing Editors *Janet Garton, Michael Robinson, C. Claire Thomson*
Small academic press. Publishes the journals *Scandinavica* and *Swedish Book Review* and books related to Scandinavian literature. About 6 titles a year. Interested in synopses and ideas for books within its *Literary History and Criticism* series. No unsolicited mss.
ROYALTIES paid.

The Nostalgia Collection

Silver Link Publishing Ltd, The Trundle, Ringstead Road, Great Addington, Kettering NN14 4BW
☎01536 330588   Fax 01536 330588
✉ sales@nostalgiacollection.com
www.nostalgiacollection.com
Managing Editor *Will Adams*
Founded 1985 in Lancashire, changed hands in 1990 and now based in Northamptonshire. Small independent company specialising in nostalgia titles including illustrated books on towns and cities, villages and rural life, rivers and inland waterways, industrial heritage, railways, trams, ships and other transport subjects. Publishes post-war nostalgia on all aspects of social history under the **Past and Present Publishing** imprint.
FEES paid.

Nyala Publishing

4 Christian Fields, London SW16 3JZ
☎020 8764 6292   Fax 020 8764 6292/0115
981 9418
✉ nyala.publish@geo-group.co.uk
www.geo-group.co.uk
Editorial Head *J.F.J. Douglas*

Founded 1996. Publishing arm of Geo Group. Publishes biography, travel and general non-fiction. Also offers a wide range of printing and publishing services. 'Quality low-cost printing a speciality.' No unsolicited mss; synopses and ideas considered.
ROYALTIES annually.

Orpheus Publishing House

4 Dunsborough Park, Ripley Green, Ripley, Guildford GU23 6AL
☎01483 225777   Fax 01483 225776
✉ orpheuspubl.ho@btinternet.com
Managing Editor *J.S. Gordon*

Founded 1996. Publishes 'well-researched and properly argued' books in the fields of occult science, esotericism and comparative philosophy/religion. 'Keen to encourage good (but sensible) new authors.' In the first instance, send maximum 3-page synopsis with s.a.e.
ROYALTIES by agreement.

Packard Publishing Limited

Forum House, Stirling Road, Chichester PO19 7DN
☎01243 537977   Fax 01243 537977
✉ info@packardpublishing.co.uk
www.packardpublishing.com
Chairman/Managing Director *Michael Packard*

Founded in 1977 to distribute overseas publishers' lists in biology, biochemistry and ecology. Publishes academic & professional: school/university interface, postgraduate – mainly in land management and applied ecology; agriculture, forestry, nature conservation, rural studies, landscape architecture and garden design; some languages (French, Arabic). SERIES Instructional books on garden and landscape design, and monographs or critical biographies in garden and landscape design and history. No unsolicited mss. Synopses and ideas in relevant areas welcome. Telephone first.
ROYALTIES twice-yearly in first year, then annually.

Palladour Books

23 Eldon Street, Southsea PO5 4BS
☎02392 826935   Fax 02392 826395
✉ palladour@powellj33.freeserve.co.uk
Managing Editors *Jeremy Powell, Anne Powell*

Founded 1986. Started with a twice-yearly issue of catalogues on the literature and poetry of World War I. Occasional catalogues on World War II poetry have also been issued. No unsolicited mss.
ROYALTIES not paid.

Panacea Press Limited

86 North Gate, Prince Albert Road, London NW8 7EJ
☎020 7722 8464   Fax 020 7586 8187
✉ ebrecher@panaceapress.net
Managing Editor *Erwin Brecher, PhD*

Founded as a self-publisher but now open for non-fiction from other authors. Material of academic value considered provided it commands a wide general market. No unsolicited mss; synopses and ideas welcome. Approach by fax or letter. No telephone calls.
ROYALTIES annually.

Paradise Press

80 College Road, Isleworth TW7 5DS
☎020 8568 3777
✉ prdsprss@netscape.net

Founded 1995. Considers only high quality lesbian and gay fiction workshopped through **Gay Authors Workshop**.

Parapress Ltd

The Basement, 9 Frant Road, Tunbridge Wells TN2 5SD
☎01892 512118   Fax 01892 512118
✉ office@parapress.eclipse.co.uk
www.parapress.co.uk
Managing Editor *Elizabeth Imlay*

Founded 1993. Publishes animals, autobiography, biography, history, literary criticism, military and naval, music, self-help. Some self-publishing. About 4 titles a year.

Past and Present Publishing

See **The Nostalgia Collection**

Paupers' Press

37 Quayside Close, Turney's Quay, Trent Bridge, Nottingham NG2 3BP
☎0115 986 3334   Fax 0115 986 3334
✉ books@pauperspress.com
www.pauperspress.com
Managing Editor *Colin Stanley*

Founded 1983. Publishes extended essays in

booklet form (about 15,000 words) on literary criticism and philosophy. 'Sometimes we stray from these criteria and produce full-length books, but only to accommodate an exceptional ms.' Limited hardback editions of bestselling titles. About 6 titles a year. No unsolicited mss but synopses and ideas for books welcome. ROYALTIES paid.

Peepal Tree Press
See entry under *Poetry Presses*

Pen Press Publishers Ltd
The Old School, 39 Chesham Road, Brighton BN2 1NB
☎0845 108 0530   Fax 01273 261434
✉ penpressltd@aol.com
www.penpress.net
Managing Director *Lynn Ashman*
Founded 1996. Publishing across a wide range of categories, Pen Press helps new authors to self-publish. Promotion and marketing included in self-publishing deal. Write, phone or e-mail for submission form and full details. Return form with full ms (digital or hard copy).
ROYALTIES 45%, payable twice-yearly.

Penniless Press
100 Waterloo Road, Ashton, Preston PR2 1EP
Managing Editor *Alan Dent*
Founded 1995. Publishes poetry, stories, essays, articles and reviews. 3 titles in 2004. Unsolicited mss welcome.

Pipers' Ash Ltd
'Pipers' Ash', Church Road, Christian Malford, Chippenham SN15 4BW
☎01249 720563   Fax 0870 0568916
✉ pipersash@supamasu.com
www.supamasu.com
Managing Editor *Mr A. Tyson*
Founded 1976. The company's publishing activities include individual collections of contemporary short stories, science fiction short stories, poetry, plays, short novels, local histories, children's fiction, philosophy, biographies, translations and general non-fiction. 12 titles a year. Synopses and ideas welcome; 'new authors with potential will be actively encouraged'. Offices in New Zealand and Australia.
ROYALTIES annually.

Planet
PO Box 44, Aberystwyth SY23 3ZZ
☎01970 611255   Fax 01970 611197
✉ planet.enquiries@planetmagazine.org.uk

www.planetmagazine.org.uk
Managing Editor *John Barnie*
Founded 1970 and relaunched in 1985 as publisher of the arts and current affairs magazine *Planet: The Welsh Internationalist* and branched out into book publishing in 1995. All books so far have been commissioned. Unsolicited synopses and ideas welcome.
ROYALTIES paid.

Playwrights Publishing Co.
70 Nottingham Road, Burton Joyce NG14 5AL
☎0115 931 3356
✉ playwrightspublishingco@yahoo.com
geocities.com/playwrightspublishingco
Managing Editors *Liz Breeze, Tony Breeze*
Founded 1990. Publishes one-act and full-length plays. Unsolicited scripts welcome. No synopses or ideas. Reading fees: £15 one act; £30 full length (waived if evidence of professional performance or if writer is unwaged).
ROYALTIES paid.

Pomegranate Press
Dolphin House, 51 St Nicholas Lane, Lewes BN7 2JZ
☎01273 470100   Fax 01273 470100
✉ pomegranatepress@aol.com
www.pomegranate-press.co.uk
Managing Editor *David Arscott*
Founded in 1992 by writer/broadcaster David Arscott, who also administers the **Sussex Book Club**. Specialises in books about Sussex. IMPRINT **Pomegranate Practicals** How-to books.
ROYALTIES twice-yearly.

Pond View
Remus House, Coltsfoot Drive, Woodston, Peterborough PE2 8JX
☎01733 898105   Fax 01733 313524
✉ info@forwardpress.co.uk
Pond View is an imprint of **Forward Press** (see entry under *Poetry Presses*). Publishes unrecorded biographies and novels, illustrated storybooks for children and educational titles.

David Porteous Editions
PO Box 5, Chudleigh, Newton Abbot TQ13 0YZ
☎01626 853310   Fax 01626 853663
✉ editorial@davidporteous.com
www.davidporteous.com
Publisher *David Porteous*

Founded 1992 to produce high quality colour illustrated books on hobbies and leisure for the UK and international markets. Publishes crafts, hobbies, art techniques and needlecrafts. No poetry or fiction. 3–4 titles a year. Unsolicited mss, synopses and ideas welcome if return postage included.
ROYALTIES twice-yearly.

Power Publications
1 Clayford Avenue, Ferndown BH22 9PQ
☎01202 875223   Fax 01202 875223
✉ powerpublications@hotmail.com
www.powerpublications.co.uk
Managing Editor *Mike Power*
Founded 1989. Publishes travel books: walking, cycling and local history; also pub guides.

Praxis Books
Crossways Cottage, Walterstone HR2 0DX
☎01873 890695
✉ author@rebeccatope.fsnet.co.uk
www.rebeccatope.com
Proprietor *Rebecca Smith*
Founded 1992. Publishes reissues of the works of Sabine Baring-Gould, memoirs, diaries and local interest. 20 titles to date. Unsolicited mss accepted with s.a.e. No fiction. Editing and advisory service available. Funding negotiable. 'I am most likely to accept work with a clearly identifiable market.'

Primrose Hill Press Ltd
Stratton Audley Park, Bicester OX27 9AB
☎01869 278000   Fax 01869 277820
✉ info@primrosehillpress.co.uk
www.primrosehillpress.co.uk
Managing Director *W.E. Butler*
Founded in 1997, having taken over the stock and projects in progress of Silent Books Ltd. Publishes general art titles, wood engraving, book studies, books on bookplates, bibliography, book design and books for the gift market, 'all high quality productions'. No fiction. About 12 titles a year. Unsolicited mss, synopses and ideas welcome.

Prospero Publishers
Peel House, 30 The Downs, Altrincham WA14 2PX
✉ editorial@prosperopublishers.co.uk
www.prosperopublishers.co.uk
Contacts *Nick Sayers, Charles Barrett*
Publishes mainly classic authors from the horror, science fiction and occult genres such as Walpole,

Ann Radcliffe, Bram Stoker, Monk Lewis, Sheridan La Fanu and Edgar Allan Poe. About 40 titles in 2005. Proposals accepted by e-mail only. See website for details.

QueenSpark Books
49 Grand Parade, Brighton BN2 9QA
☎01273 571710   Fax 01273 571710
✉ info@queensparkbooks.org.uk
www.queensparkbooks.org.uk
A community writing and publishing group. Since the early 1970s QueenSpark Books has published 80 titles, mainly featuring the lives of local people. Writing workshops and groups held on a regular basis. No unsolicited mss, please.

Radikal Phase Publishing House Ltd
Willow Court, Cordy Lane, Underwood NG16 5FD
☎01773 764288   Fax 01773 764282
✉ sales@radikalbooks.com
www.radikalbooks.com
Joint Managing Directors *Philip Gardiner, Kevin Marks*
Founded 2001. Publishes radical revelation and technical electrical books. IMPRINTS **William Ernest** *Kevin Marks*; **Radikal Phase** *Philip Gardiner*. Welcomes unsolicited material; approach in writing in the first instance.
ROYALTIES twice-yearly.

The Riverside Press
PO Box 388A, Surbiton KT7 0ZT
☎020 8339 0945   Fax 020 8339 0945
✉ mruswords@aol.com
www.good-writing-matters.co.uk
Managing Editor *Michael Russell*
Founded 1998 to publish short-run titles from new writers. Mainly fiction but also special interest non-fiction. No poetry or film. Editorial support service provided. No unsolicited mss. Send synopsis and three chapters only with covering letter.

The Robinswood Press
30 South Avenue, Stourbridge DY8 3XY
☎01384 397475   Fax 01384 440443
✉ info@robinswoodpress.com
www.robinswoodpress.com
Managing Editor *Christopher J. Marshall*
Founded 1985. Publishes education, particularly teacher resources, SEN, including the

Spotlight and Lifeboat Read and Spell ranges. Also collaborative publishing, e.g. with Camphill Foundation. About 12–15 titles a year. Unsolicited mss, synopses and ideas welcome.
ROYALTIES paid.

Romer Publications
PO Box 10120, NL–1001 EC Amsterdam, The Netherlands
☎00 31 20 676 9442
Fax 00 31 20 676 9442
✉ harrymelkman@hotmail.com
Managing Editor *Hubert de Brouwer*
Founded 1986. Publishes critical reflection on origins and legitimacy of established institutions; law and history. Assessment of unsolicited material is suspended until further notice.
ROYALTIES paid.

St James Publishing
Suite 213 Parkway House, Sheen Lane, East Sheen, London SW14 8LS
☎0870 870 8797   Fax 0870 870 8798
www.stjamespublishing.co.uk
Managing Editors *Linda Smith, David Smith*
Founded 1995 to provide teaching materials with spiritual substance for St James Independent Schools: 'Good Books for Fine Minds'. Also many workbooks and texbooks for the study of English and mathematics. No unsolicited mss, synopses or ideas.

Serendipity
Suite 530, 14 Tottenham Court Road, London W1T 1JY
☎0845 130 2434   Fax 0845 130 2434
✉ serendipity530@tiscali.co.uk
Managing Director *Kimberley Wheatley*
Founded 2001. Publishes fiction, academic, memoirs, poetry, children's and religion.About 40 titles a year. Unsolicited mss and synopses welcome.
ROYALTIES twice-yearly.

Serif
47 Strahan Road, London E3 5DA
☎020 8981 3990   Fax 020 8981 3990
✉ stephen@serif.demon.co.uk
Managing Editor *Stephen Hayward*
Founded 1993. Publishes cookery, Irish and African studies, travel writing and modern history; no fiction. Ideas and synopses welcome; no unsolicited mss.
ROYALTIES paid.

Sherlock Publications
6 Bramham Moor, Hill Head, Fareham PO14 3RU
☎01329 667325
✉ sales@sherlockpublications.biz
Managing Editor *Philip Weller*
Founded to supply publishing support to a number of Sherlock Holmes societies. Publishes Sherlock Holmes and other Conan Doyle studies only. About 10 titles a year. No unsolicited mss; synopses and ideas welcome.
ROYALTIES not paid.

Shield Publications
PO Box 5, Low Fell, Gateshead NE9 7YS
☎0191 4823222
Managing Director *Norman L. Middlemiss*
Founded 1977. Publishes nautical books only – the *Merchant Fleet* series (44 vols.). Unsolicited mss and fleet lists welcome.
ROYALTIES paid.

Spacelink Books
115 Hollybush Lane, Hampton TW12 2QY
☎020 8979 3148
www.spacelink.fsworld.co.uk
Managing Director *Lionel Beer*
Founded 1967. Named after a UFO magazine published in the 1960/70s. Publishes nonfiction titles connected with UFOs, Fortean phenomena and paranormal events. Publishers of *TEMS News* for the Travel and Earth Mysteries Society and *MWB Railway Society News Brief* newsletters. Distributors of a wide range of related titles and magazines. No unsolicited mss; send synopses and ideas.
ROYALTIES AND FEES according to contract.

Stenlake Publishing Limited
54–58 Mill Square, Catrine KA5 6RD
☎01290 552233
www.stenlake.co.uk
Publishes illustrated local history, railways, shipping, aviation and industrial. 40 titles in 2004. Unsolicited mss, synopses and ideas welcome if accompanied by s.a.e. Freelance writers with experience in above fields also sought for specific commissions.
ROYALTIES OR FIXED FEE paid.

Stone Flower Limited
PO Box 1513, Ilford IG1 3QU
✉ stoneflower10622@aol.com
Managing Editor *L. G. Norman*
Founded 1989. Publishes biography, humour

and general fiction. Will consider mss, synopses and ideas only if sent with s.a.e. or IRC. Approach in writing in the first instance. 'No anthropomorphism, please.'

Stride
11 Sylvan Road, Exeter EX4 6EW
✉ editor@stridebooks.co.uk
www.stridebooks.co.uk
Managing Editor *Rupert Loydell*

Founded in 1982 as a magazine and booklet series. Since the mid-1980s, the press has published paperback editions of imaginative new writing. Publishes poetry, prose-poems, criticism, reviews, interviews, arts (particularly experimental music and literary criticism). No unsolicited submissions required at this time.

ROYALTIES sometimes paid; free copies usually.

Superscript
404 Robin Square, Newtown SY16 1HP
☎01588 650452
✉ drjbford@yahoo.co.uk
Editor *Julie Ford*
Chair *Bernard Burgoyne*

Founded 2002. Publishes literary, philosophical and political fiction, autobiography and wartime memoirs, humanities and social sciences. 7 titles in 2004. All suitable ideas, synopses or mss are submitted to the editorial board who are looking for 'well-crafted material that exposes injustice, challenges stereotypes and promotes human dignity'. Will also consider new editions of out-of-print titles at author's request. Initial enquiries by letter, telephone or e-mail to the editor.

ROYALTIES vary with each contract.

Tamarind Ltd
PO Box 52, Northwood HA6 1UN
☎020 8866 8808   Fax 020 8866 5627
✉ info@tamarindbooks.co.uk
www.tamarindbooks.co.uk
Managing Editor *Verna Wilkins*

Founded 1987 to publish picture books which give a high, positive profile to black children. They feature on the SATs List for National Curriculum, on BBC Words and Pictures, CBBC and 'Balamory'. Regularly chosen among the Best Books of the Year. All titles sold into both trade and educational markets. Age range: 2–12.

Tarquin Publications
99 Hatfield Road, St Albans Al1 4EG
☎0870 143 2568   Fax 0845 456 6385
✉ enquiries@tarquin-books.demon.co.uk

www.tarquin-books.demon.co.uk
Managing Editor *Andrew Griffin*

Founded 1970 as a hobby which gradually grew and now publishes mathematical, cut-out models, teaching and pop-up books. Other topics covered if they involve some kind of paper cutting or pop-up scenes. 5 titles in 2004. No unsolicited mss; letter with 1–2 page synopses welcome.

ROYALTIES paid.

Tartarus Press
Coverley House, Carlton-in-Coverdale,
Leyburn DL8 4AY
☎01969 640399   Fax 01969 640399
✉ tartarus@pavilion.co.uk
www.tartaruspress.com
Proprietor *Raymond Russell*
Editor *Rosalie Parker*

Founded 1987. Publishes fiction, short stories, reprinted classic supernatural fiction and reference books. About 12 titles a year. 'Please do not send submissions. We cater to a small, collectable market and commission the fiction we publish.'

Tindal Street Press Ltd
217 The Custard Factory, Gibb Street,
Birmingham B9 4AA
☎0121 773 8157   Fax 0121 693 5525
✉ emma@tindalstreet.co.uk
www.tindalstreet.co.uk
Managing Editor *Emma Hargrave*

Founded in 1998 to publish contemporary original fiction from the English regions. Publishes original fiction only – novels and short story anthologies. No local history, memoirs or poetry. Published *Astonishing Splashes of Colour* by Clare Morrall, shortlisted for the 2003 **Man Booker Prize for Fiction**.6 titles in 2004. Approach with a letter, synopsis and three chapters and include s.a.e. for return of ms.

ROYALTIES paid.

Tournesol Books
BP14, Lauzerte 82110, France
✉ editor@tournesolbooks.com
www.tournesolbooks.com
Managing Editors *Paul M. Muller, PhD, Sara Gill Costelloe, BA Hons*

Founded 2004, initially to publish the works of Paul Muller, Tournesol Books provides pre-publication services, including editing, to self-publishing authors accepted by **Sunflower Literary Agency**, as an imprint of **Pen Press**

Publishers Ltd. All contact must be via Sunflower Literary Agency only (see entry under *UK Literary Agents*).

Wakefield Historical Publications
19 Pinder's Grove, Wakefield WF1 4AH
☎01924 372748
✉ kate@airtime.co.uk
Managing Editor *Kate Taylor*
Founded 1977 by the Wakefield Historical Society to publish well-researched, scholarly works of regional (namely West Riding) historical significance. 1–2 titles a year. Unsolicited mss, synopses and ideas for books welcome.
ROYALTIES not paid.

Watling Street Publishing Ltd
The Glen, Southrop, Nr Lechlade GL7 3NY
☎01367 850558
✉ watlingst@btinternet.com
Managing Director *Chris McLaren*
Editorial Head *Christine Kidney*
Founded 2001. Publishes non-fiction titles on London and its history; children's and adult. 14 titles in 2004. No unsolicited mss. Ideas and synopses welcome. Approach in writing or by e-mail with a one-page proposal. 'Not interested in anything not related to London.'

Waywiser Press
9 Woodstock Road, London N4 3ET
☎020 8374 5526   Fax 020 8374 5736
✉ waywiserpress@aol.com
www.waywiser-press.com
Editor *Philip Hoy*
Founded 2002. A literary press, publishing poetry and prose of distinction. The backlist includes books by well-known figures such as Al Alvarez, Peter Dale, Anthony Hecht, Richard Wilbur and Richard Wollheim, as well as works by newcomers such as Neil Berry, Joseph Harrison, Dan Rifenburgh, Deborah Warren and Clive Watkins. Submissions and proposals welcome; follow guidelines on website.
ROYALTIES paid.

Whitchurch Books Ltd
67 Merthyr Road, Whitchurch, Cardiff CF14 1DD
☎029 2052 1956   Fax 029 2062 3599
✉ whitchurchbooks@btconnect.com
Managing Director *Gale Canvin*
Founded 1994. Publishes local interest, particularly local history. Welcomes unsolicited mss,

synopses and ideas on relevant subjects. Approach first by phone or in writing.
ROYALTIES twice-yearly.

White Ladder Press
Great Ambrook, Near Ipplepen TQ12 5UL
☎01803 813343   Fax 01803 813928
✉ enquiries@whiteladderpress.com
www.whiteladderpress.com
Publishers *Roni Jay, Richard Craze*
Founded 2002. Publishes non-fiction books which present a new angle on everyday living. Welcomes synopses and ideas by mail or e-mail. No fiction, poetry or children's titles.
ROYALTIES quarterly.

Whittles Publishing
Dunbeath Mains Cottages, Dunbeath KW6 6EY
☎01593 731333   Fax 01593 731400
✉ info@whittlespublishing.com
www.whittlespublishing.com
Publisher *Dr Keith Whittles*
Publisher in civil and structural engineering and geomatics disciplines plus maritime, military history, nature writing and selected fiction. Unsolicited mss, synopses and ideas welcome on appropriate themes.
ROYALTIES annually.

William Ernest
See **Radikal Phase Publishing House Ltd**

Witan Books
Cherry Tree House, 8 Nelson Crescent, Cotes Heath, via Stafford ST21 6ST
☎01782 791673
✉ witan@mail.com
Managing Editor *Jeff Kent*
Founded in 1980 for self-publishing and commenced publishing other writers in 1991. Publishes general books, including biography, education, environment, geography, history, politics, popular music and sport. 1 or 2 titles a year. Unsolicited mss, synopses and ideas welcome (include s.a.e.)
ROYALTIES paid.

Worple Press
PO Box 328, Tonbridge TN9 1WR
☎01732 368958
✉ theworpleco@aol.com
Managing Editors *Peter Carpenter, Amanda Knight*
Founded 1997. Independent publisher special-

ising in poetry, art and alternative titles. Write or phone for catalogue and flyers. 4 titles a year. ROYALTIES paid.

Writers' Bookshop

Remus House, Coltsfoot Drive, Woodston, Peterborough PE2 9JX
☎01733 898105   Fax 01733 313524
✉ info@forwardpress.co.uk
www.forwardpress.co.uk

Writers' Bookshop is an imprint of **Forward Press** (see entry under *Poetry Presses*). Publishes writers' aids in the form of directories and how-to guides.

Zymurgy Publishing

Hoults Estate, Walker Road, Newcastle upon Tyne NE6 2HL
☎0191 276 2425   Fax 0191 276 2425
✉ martin.ellis@ablibris.com
zymurgypublishing.com

Chairman *Martin Ellis*

Founded 2000. Publishes adult non-fiction, ranging from full colour illustrated hardbacks to mass market paperbacks. Synopses and ideas for books welcome but no unsolicited mss. Contact by telephone or e-mail.

ROYALTIES twice-yearly.

Electronic Publishing and Other Services

ABCtales
5 Stucley Place, London NW1 8NS
☎020 7209 2607   Fax 020 7209 2594
✉ markbrown@abctales.com
www.abctales.com
Owner *Burgeon Creative Ideas Ltd*
Editor *Mark Brown*

Founded by A. John Bird, MBE, co-founder of the *Big Issue* magazine, Tony Cook and Gordon Roddick. ABCtales is a free website dedicated to publishing and developing new writing. Content is predominantly short stories and poetry but includes interviews and lifestyle features, photo essays, reviews (games, websites, film, music) and competitions. Anyone can upload creative writing to the website.

Authors OnLine
See entry under *UK Publishers*

BeWrite Books
32 Bryn Road South, Wigan WN4 8QR
☎00 334 9335 9531 (editorial base in France)
Fax 00 334 9341 3509
✉ info@bewrite.net
www.bewrite.net
Managing Director *Cait Myers*
Editorial Director *Neil Marr*

A multi-genre publishing house founded in 1999 and especially geared toward the encouragement and publication in electronic and print formats of first-time authors. Unsolicited mss and synopses welcome (using the online form on the website). 'All offers promptly acknowledged and draft manuscript-to-publication time shorter than most other publishing houses.'
ROYALTIES quarterly (no advance).

Books 4 Publishing
Lasyard House, Underhill Street, Bridgnorth WV16 4BB
☎0870 777 3339   Fax 01746 761298
✉ editor@books4publishing.com
www.books4publishing.com
Owner *Dreamstar Books*
Managing Director *Mark Horton-Oliver*

Founded 2000. Specialises in helping new and unpublished authors gain recognition for their work by displaying synopses and up to 5000 words on the Books 4 Publishing website and promoting them to publishers and agents. Mss, synopses and ideas welcome; initial enquiries by e-mail or post.

Chameleon HH Publishing
The Quarry House, East End, Witney OX29 6QA
☎01993 880223   Fax 01993 880236
✉ marion@chameleonhh.co.uk *and* david@chameleonhh.co.uk
www.chameleonhh.co.uk
Directors *David Hall, Marion Hebblethwaite*

Founded 1997. CD-ROM publishers on behalf of commercial publishers, institutes, associations and government bodies. Produces web-updateable CDs – CD and DVD duplication, plus all artwork undertaken. Files prepared for print-on-demand. Consulting and advice on CD-ROM and Web publishing. Welcomes unsolicited mss for electronic publishing from self-publishers and print-on-demand. 'Small runs particularly catered for, whether book or CD.'

Claritybooks.com
Colt Farm, Bromley Green Road, Ashford TN26 2EQ
✉ ed@claritybooks.com
www.claritybooks.com

Internet e-book publisher and distributor. Has proprietary e-book technology which simplifies the process of downloading and reading of purchased works for the reader while still providing authors with copyright protection/encryption. Mss or synopses welcomed from new or published authors. No charges to authors. Will consider all works of a good standard. E-mail communication preferred. If paper submission, please include s.a.e.

Context Limited
Grand Union House, 20 Kentish Town Road, London NW1 9NR
☎020 7267 8989   Fax 020 7267 1133
✉ tenders@context.co.uk

www.context.co.uk
Founded 1986. Electronic publisher of UK and European legal and offical information on CD-ROM, online and the Internet.

Deunant Books

PO Box 25, Denbigh LL16 5ZQ
☎01745 870259   Fax 01745 870259
✉ mail@deunantbooks.com
www.deunantbooks.com

Managing Director *Les Broad*

Founded 2001. Internet e-book publisher of biography, fiction, history, horror, humour, philosophy, poetry, politics, science fiction, short story compendia, theology, travel. 90 titles in 2004. 'Our interactive book format allows us to publish single short stories or poems as well as full-length books. Technical manuals and any unusual publishing ideas welcome.'

50 Connect – www.50connect.co.uk

5 Church Street, Windsor SL4 1PE
☎01753 850606   Fax 01753 840112
✉ admin@50connect.com
www.50connect.co.uk

Owner *Phil Cooper*
Editor *Rachael Hannan*

Launched in 2000, www.50connect.co.uk is an over-45's web portal with a large community section. Daily updates. Check the website for topics covered. Approach with ideas by e-mail in the first instance.

Fledgling Press Limited

7 Lennox Street, Edinburgh EH4 1QB
☎0131 332 6867
✉ info@fledglingpress.co.uk
www.fledglingpress.co.uk

Director *Zander Wedderburn*

Founded 2000. Internet publisher, aiming to be 'a launching pad for new authors. Special interest in authentic writing about the human condition, including autobiography, diaries, poetry and fictionalised variations on these.' Monthly online competition (www.canyouwrite. com) with small prizes for short pieces. Also free books and reports in the areas of shiftwork and working time. Send mss and other details by e-mail from the website or by post. Links into short-run book production.

The Good Web Guide Ltd

See entry under *UK Publishers*

New Authors Showcase

See **Barrie James Literary Agency** under *UK Literary Agents*

NoSpine.com

26 Sunningdale Way, Bletchley MK3 7SB
✉ info@nospine.com
www.nospine.com

Managing Director *Andrew Gardner*

Founded 2000. An electronic self-publishing venture 'designed by authors for authors'. NoSpine accepts electronic mss and arranges sales and distribution in return for a commission on each sale. Authors retain complete control over their work, full copyright, and set their own sale prices of which they retain 80%. 'We are not a vanity publisher, nor a subsidy publisher. No author ever pays us a penny: in effect we are a writers' cooperative.' All new submissions are refereed by the founding authors to screen out unacceptable or illegal material. Over 500 titles currently available.

Online Originals

Priory Cottage, Wordsworth Place, London NW5 4HG
☎020 7267 4244
✉ editor@onlineoriginals.com
www.onlineoriginals.com

Managing Director *David Gettman*
Technical Director *Neill Sanders*

Publishes book-length works on the Internet and as print-on-demand. Acquires global electronic rights (including print-on-demand) in literary fiction, intellectual non-fiction, drama and youth fiction (ages 8–16). No poetry, fantasy, how-to, self-help, picture books, cookery, hobbies, crafts or local interest. TITLES *Being and Becoming* Christopher Macann (7 vols.); *Starkey* Paul R. Hyde; *Quintet* Frederick Forsyth. 6 titles in 2004. Unsolicited mss, synopses and ideas for books welcome. *All* authors must have Internet access. Unique peer-review, automated submissions system, accessed via the website address above. Please no submissions on paper or disk.

ROYALTIES paid annually (50% royalties on e-book price of £6).

WritersServices

See entry under *Useful Websites*

Goblins in My Living Room

*Andrew S. Walsh explains what it takes
to write for computer games*

Your breathing is shallow. Smoke obscures your sight, but you can hear something moving, the scrape of steel on leather as a sword is drawn. Your pulse quickens. Suddenly, through the smoke, you see goblins charging towards you! Valiantly, you raise your weapon, a small, grey, plastic gizmo with the power to liberate kingdoms, win the FA Cup and save the universe.

The story so far ...

Computer games have come a long way from their early beginnings as bat and ball bonanzas, or completely text-based adventures. Now goblins as real as those in the cinema hurl themselves against your television screen in a bid to break into the real world. But surely that's all games are – graphics and pretty pictures. Why would they need a writer? It's simple to write a game, isn't it?

In the early days of home-video gaming, graphics just about qualified as awful. If you got a goblin at all, it was static and had the look of a badly constructed 2D Lego model – all boxes and primary colours. So, from *Adventure* to Douglas Adams's game version of *The Hitchhiker's Guide to the Galaxy*, text-based games ruled. Then the silicon revolution began and to conquer the world it sent forth a pixelated horde. Graphics had arrived. Games became purely visual, the console and computer were relegated to poster-lined bedrooms and kids were seen as the main audience. But the kids have grown up and haven't stopped playing. In fact, Playstation 2 was marketed for 20–35 year olds, and this more mature audience brings with it a demand for more sophisticated games.

To meet this demand, the games industry is realising they need to employ professional directors, actors and writers. *Enter the Matrix,* for example, was written and directed by the Wachowski Brothers, while Tom Clancy is behind a range of games, most notably the hugely successful *Splinter Cell* series. From manuals to captions, level briefings, character design, character biogs, ingame dialogue, storylining and level design, the skills of the writer are being called upon to create worlds which are more immersive, believable and entertaining.

Current highscores

Current estimates put the computer games industry as worth $19 billion a year and growing. On top of that there's interactive TV (niche, low pay, but evolving very quickly); mobile technology (currently primitive and recycling a lot of material but evolving into a market for new content) and interactive DVDs (also niche, primarily supportive content for existing films, most new content appears to be in the music and … er … porn industry). This article deals solely with the video-games industry (PC, console, mobile) and contains no porn at all.

Training level

Back in the seventies, games were restricted to the smoky pub corner and the rich kid on your street. Nowadays arcade games are way behind in-home gaming and most kids have access to one game machine or another. The living-room invader is the gaming console. Cause of many late nights and the occasional divorce, these are dedicated gaming machines such as the X-Box or Playstation 2. Stray further into the house and you find computer games. Contrary to popular opinion, these are often far in advance of the consoles in terms of technology. It's also easier to access online games through them, although consoles are catching up. Online games split between simple (normally free) flash type games; online multiplayer versions of games you can play at home; and huge roleplaying games hosting several thousand players in the same world, all of whom you can interact with.

Leave the house and you're surrounded by handheld games – from mobile phones to Gameboy, and Playstation PSP. These are far behind their living-room counterparts in terms of technology. Most of the dialogue will be text only and the content is often recycled from elsewhere.

So, games are everywhere, but what is everyone playing? Do all games involve space aliens and goblins? Actually, there's a huge range of games available to tap a wide variety of pockets. The major categories are:

Roleplaying games (RPGs) Take on a personality in order to go on a quest, which can be fantasy, sci-fi or more down to earth. These are the most dialogue heavy type of game – *Fable* (200,000+ lines of dialogue).

Action games These can have a tiny amount of text, e.g. *Doom 3*, *Mortal Combat*, or they can have their own movie-style storyline like *Metalgear Solid*.

Sims Take over someone's life or business and be God for the day, probably for months actually – *Sims*, *Populous*.

Strategy games Before lifestyle sims, we had (and still have) strategy games. Be Napoleon Bonaparte and conquer swathes of land without the worry of UN sanctions – *Command and Conquer*, *Cossacks*.

Platform The traditional jump-around game from old-style side scrollers such as *Sonic the Hedgehog* to newer 3D games such as *Crash Bandicoot*.

Sports Play your favourite sport without the need for deodorant. These often have commentaries even if there isn't interaction between the characters.

Racing games These aren't just sports games, many take an approach that is more *Fast and Furious* than Formula One. They sometimes have a background story and a small amount of dialogue in them.

Flight sims Pilot a Sopwith, a 747 or a starcruiser. Often little or no dialogue.

Children's games Often niche versions of the above, generally with lower budgets and text rather than the spoken word.

Educational High text, specialised games.

Start new game

Okay, so who creates the goblins and launches invasion forces against Earth? Primarily, games are produced by developers. Many of these are small, single-title operations prone to financial collapse and takeover. These developers provide content to publishers who then release it to the world. There are a number of big players such as Electronic Arts (EA) and Sony that both develop and publish games.

Unlike other media, it's not worth sending computer games companies original ideas. It is extremely rare for a company to accept ideas from the outside. It's also worth saying that with ideas and scripts, companies buy your creations outright rather than allowing residual deals, though with some of the big-name writers beginning to demand residual rights for their creations this is something which may well change as computer firms start to ape the movie industry.

In terms of pay, every company has their own scale and every project differs wildly. Some games are as short as 100 words, while others, such as *X-Files,* need a 250-page shooting script. Check what size the game is then compare this with rates for equivalent TV or radio projects (if you don't know what these are try the Writers' Guild website).

Jobs are sometimes advertised through companies' websites, on gaming websites, through recruitment agencies and very occasionally in newspapers. There are also some all-in-one agencies that offer developers a one-stop shop for script writing through to recording. When approaching a company, select something that shows your writing ability. A television, film, or even theatre script can do. You don't have to write a games script. What's more important is matching the script you send to the genre of game you're applying to write (action to action for instance).

Is there specific equipment you'll need? Not necessarily. Where you're only required to supply text you can bash this out on anything. However, as writing jobs often require more than just scribbling, it is best to have a high specification computer and to make this a PC. Most computer games come out on PCs and are only translated to Macs. When buying a PC, check what the current minimum requirements are for new games and then add some. Remember, games you will be working on are games that will be released in the future and so are likely to demand better specifications than those for games out now. The major limiting factors are: processor speed, amount of memory and type of video/graphics card. The graphics card is the part of the computer that handles, well ... er ... the graphics. The vast percentage of writers working in gaming also have at least one console in addition to their PC. Companies do not expect you to have every games console that exists and will often lend you one if it is needed to develop the game.

Do you need to be a programmer? While you're not expected to be a computer expert (you're a writer remember) it is best to take heed of the true story of the writer who tried to get a job in the games industry but didn't have e-mail and get yourself a good basic knowledge of how a home PC works. You won't be programming the game, but at the very least you will be called upon to download all manner of programs from things to uncompress files to specific audio packages to listen to clips. Knowing how the scripting (a confusing term for a type of programming, the scripting of the scripting ...) works can help you to make the dialogue better, but you can learn this on the job.

Load game

So, how to approach games writing? First off, take your games seriously. Learn the medium and the language. That doesn't mean you have to become a code monkey (a junior programmer), but you should have a good understanding of what games are out there, of games genre and of what different platforms can do. Beginners think you can do anything in a game, but remember every animation and line of dialogue has to be programmed and so costs time and money. In addition, the game's engine (the coding framework that defines the game's world and its physics) will have limits that stop you doing certain things.

Select mission

What does a games script look like? Surprise, surprise, there's no standard layout. Some scripts appear in Excel spreadsheets, others as film scripts, while I've worked on ones with play-script format with a dialogue code before each line so that the line and speaker can be identified and programmed. If you have to put these codes in then the games company will tell you how these work. They'll also tell you if they want a particular script format, otherwise, it's up to you. What you do need to know are the types of dialogue found in games scripts.

Cutscene dialogue

A cutscene is any part of the game which is an animation/video insert and is not playable. They are there to tell the game's story and to entertain. The most obvious ones are story inserts between levels and these often contain higher quality graphics than the rest of the game.

Pool dialogue

This is a dialogue that can appear anywhere in a particular level or indeed anywhere in the game. It is a set of words, sounds (argghh!) or sentences triggered by an event such as the character scoring a goal, or coming under attack (though these probably won't both happen in the same game!). This dialogue provides environment as well as making the world the player is in more believable, engaging and entertaining.

Standard dialogue

A type of pool dialogue, standard dialogue is a definition sometimes used to explain a set of standard responses for a non-player character (NPC). A non-player character is literally any character that the player is not controlling.

Interactive dialogue

In some games the player is able to interact directly with the NPCs to ask them questions, or even just chat to them. This is the truly 'interactive' dialogue, prompted by the player.

Select character

Many writers are asked to do several jobs on the same game, not just write the script. These jobs can range from story development to in-game dialogue, character design, manuals, level design or even writing advertising copy.

The most specialised of these jobs is level design which demands a greater knowledge of gameplay. Designing levels will sometimes be split between the writer, a dedicated level designer, the programmer and the graphic artist. A writer's involvement can be as basic as setting the starting point of the level and the objective of it: get a key from the goblins; rescue a captured squad member; open the magic box of poddling insanity, etc. Once you go beyond this it gets a lot more complicated. You have to know what the game's engine is capable of so as to not design levels that can't happen, or at least that will look bad. You should know what levels are clichés in order to avoid them (there are still many games which ask you to get a key, but these have become a really formulaic objective so people often seek to avoid this). Game balancing (making sure a level isn't too easy or difficult) is also an important part of designing a level.

Writing doesn't always start as early as level design, some games exist prior to the employment of a writer and you can be asked either to create a story and dialogue to match the existing game or to regionalise a game that was developed in another country. This regionalisation could be as simple as smoothing out the translation into better-sounding dialogue, or it could be a complete redesign to better suit the English-speaking market.

Select difficulty

Boiled down, computer games are just another medium. Skills learned elsewhere will transfer to interactive storytelling, but just as film or radio need to be learned as media, so do games. The main difference comes when you encounter non-linear sections in the game. This is where the player can choose what to do next. The amount of choice to give a player is a constant balancing act in games. Do you let Frodo hand the ring over to some goblins he meets? Can Luke destroy the Death Star before he's rescued Princess Leia? What happens if they do? So, if a screenwriter decides to snub you because you write for 'games' remember, while they're struggling with one linear story, you're the one keeping four non-linear plots spinning at the same time – now which medium is child's play?

Save game to memory card?

The hero strides through the smoke, the bodies of the slain goblins around him. Where does he go now? That's up to the player, and you. A story with ten hours of interactive dialogue ... games are not just about pretty pictures. With an audience as wide as that for big-budget movies waiting for you, with the chance to create a truly interactive immersive world for your story and the excuse to play games as research ... pick up your plastic gizmo, turn on the goblins in your living room and see where they take you.

Useful Websites

Many of these and other useful websites for writers can be found in *The Internet for Writers* by Nick Daws (ISBN 1-84025-308-8), one of a series of books published by Internet Handbooks; *The Incredibly Indispensable Web Directory* by Clive and Bettina Zietman, published by Kogan Page (ISBN 0-7494-3617-4); *thegoodwebguide for writers* by Paul Chronnell, published by The Good Web Guide Limited (ISBN 1-903282-38-1).

A2A Access to Archives
www.a2a.org.uk
Database of UK archive catalogues dating from the 900s to the present day.

AbeBooks
www.abebooks.co.uk
Includes new and second-hand books search engine and 'The Rare Book Room' for antiquarian, rare and collectible titles online. 'Textbook Central' offers a search engine for textbooks and reference publications, both new and second-hand.

Academi (Welsh Academy/ Yr Academi Gymreig)
www.academi.org
News of events, publications and funding for Welsh-based literary events. (See entry under *Professional Associations*.)

Alibris
www.alibris.com
Over 40 million used, new and hard-to-find books online. Bargain books, text and reference listings and auction pages for rare books. ISBN search engine.

Alliance of Literary Societies
www.sndc.demon.co.uk/als.htm
Details of societies and events. (See entry under *Professional Associations*.)

Amazon Bookshop
www.amazon.co.uk
The online shop for books, music, videos and DVDs, electronics, toys and games, travel, and home and kitchen-ware.

Ancestry
www.ancestry.com
Family history information – databases, articles and other sources of genealogical data.

Arvon Foundation
www.arvonfoundation.org
Information on the four Arvon centres in the UK. (See entry under *UK Writers' Courses*.)

Association for Scottish Literary Studies
www.asls.org.uk
The educational charity promoting the languages and literature of Scotland. (See entry under *Professional Associations*.)

Association of Authors' Agents (AAA)
www.agentsassoc.co.uk
UK agents' organisation including list of current members. (See entry under *Professional Associations*.)

Association of Authors' Representatives (AAR)
www.aar-online.org
US agents' organisation including list of current members. (See entry under *Professional Associations*.)

Authorbank
www.authorbank.com
Registration for a fee enables authors to present book ideas to publishers online. Also offers assistance with publishers' contracts and a free advice service.

Author.co.uk
www.author.co.uk
Advice and information for writers, articles, contacts, writers' circles, online bookshop, authors' websites and reviews.

AuthorHouse UK
www.authorhouse.co.uk
Self-publishing company founded in 1997 by an

aspiring author who 'saw a need for a simple and effective self-publishing process'. Services for authors include Standard Paperback Publishing (£525). (See entry under *UK Publishers*.)

Authors' Licensing and Collecting Society Limited (ALCS)
www.alcs.co.uk
Details of membership, news, publications, legal issues and rights, plus links to related sites. (See entry under *Professional Associations*.)

Author-Network
www.author-network.com
Writers' resource site run by Karen Scott and Diana Hayden.

Bartleby.com
www.bartleby.com
An ever-expanding list of books published online for reference, free of charge.

BBC
www.bbc.co.uk
Access to all BBC departments and services.

bibliofind
www.bibliofind.com
Over 20 million second-hand and rare books, periodicals and ephemera for sale online via Amazon.com.

Bibliomania
www.bibliomania.com
Over 2000 texts, study guides and reference resources available online for free. Also selected books for sale in the Bibliomania shop.

BOL
www.bol.com
Internet shopping; a database of over 1.5 million titles.

Book2Book
www.book2book.co.uk
Established by a group of publishers, booksellers, website developers and trade journalists to provide up-to-date news, features and useful information for the book trade.

Booktrust
www.booktrust.org.uk
Book information service, guide to prizes and awards, links to other book organisations, factsheets for writers. (See entry under *Professional Associations*.)

British Association of Picture Libraries and Agencies (BAPLA)
www.bapla.org.uk
Website includes the BAPLA Online Database with a search facility by category or name. (See entry under *Professional Associations*.)

British Centre for Literary Translation
www.literarytranslation.com
A joint website (currently under construction) with the British Council containing workshops by leading translators, contacts and networks, and listings of translation conferences, seminars and events. (See entry under *Professional Associations*.)

The British Council
www.britishcouncil.org
Information on the Council's English Language services, education programmes, science and health links, and information exchange. (See entry under *Professional Associations*.)

British Film Institute (bfi)
www.bfi.org.uk
Information on the services offered by the Institute. (See entry under *Professional Associations*.)

British Library
www.bl.uk
Reader service enquiries, access to main catalogues, information on collections, links to the various reading rooms and exhibitions. (See related entries under *Library Services*.)

Children's Writing Resource Center
www.write4kids.com
US website for children's writers', whether published or beginners. Includes special reports, advice, chat links, news on the latest bestsellers and links to related sites.

CILIP
www.cilip.org.uk
The professional body for librarians and information professionals. (See entry under *Professional Associations*.)

Complete Works of William Shakespeare
www-tech.mit.edu/Shakespeare/works.html
Access to the text of the complete works with search facility, quotations and discussion pages.

Copyright Licensing Agency Ltd (CLA)
www.cla.co.uk
Copyright information, customer support and information on CLA services. (See entry under *Professional Associations*.)

Crime Writers' Association (CWA)
www.thecwa.co.uk
Website of the professional crime writers' association. (See entry under *Professional Associations*.)

Daily Mirror
www.mirror.co.uk
The *Daily Mirror* newspaper online.

Dictionary of Slang
dictionaryofslang.co.uk
A guide to slang 'from a British perspective' Research information and search facility.

The Dramatic Exchange
www.dramex.org
Script exchange site; over 400 unpublished plays online for producers and readers to search through.

The Eclectic Writer
www.eclectics.com/writing/writing.html
US website offering a selection of articles on advice for writers on topics such as 'Proper Manuscript Format', 'What is a Regency Romance Novel?', 'How to Write a Synopsis' and 'Setting'. Also an online discussion board.

Electronic Telegraph
www.telegraph.co.uk
The *Daily Telegraph* online – one of the first UK national newspapers to establish itself on the web.

Encyclopædia Britannica
www.britannica.com
Subscription access to the entire *Encyclopædia Britannic*. EB online also gives links to more than 130,000 sites selected, rated and reviewed by Britannica editors.

Arts Council England
www.artscouncil.org.uk
Includes information on funding applications, publications and the National Lottery. (See entry under *Arts Councils and Regional Offices*.)

The English Association
www.le.ac.uk/engassoc

News, publications, conference and membership information. (See entry under *Professional Associations*.)

Federation of Worker Writers and Community Publishers (FWWCP)
myweb.tiscali.co.uk/thefwwcp/Info.htm
Links to members of the FWWCP, the Federation magazine, information on membership. (See entry under *Professional Associations*.)

Film Angel
www.filmangel.co.uk
Established in conjunction with Hammerwood Films to create a shop window for writers and would-be film angels alike. Writers submit a short synopsis which can be displayed for a predetermined period, for a fee, while would-be angels are invited to finance a production of their choice.

Filmmaker Store
www.filmmakerstore.com
Scriptwriting resources, listings and advice.

Financial Times
www.ft.com
Financial Times online.

Frankfurt Book Fair
www.frankfurt-book-fair.com/en/portal.html
Provides latest news and market analysis of the book business plus information on the annual Book Fair.

The Guardian
www.guardian.co.uk
Website of the *Guardian* and the *Observer* newspapers online.

Guide to Grammar and Style
www.andromeda.rutgers.edu/~jlynch/Writing
A guide to grammar and style which is organised alphabetically, plus articles and links to other grammatical reference sites.

Hansard
www.parliament.the-stationery-office.co.uk/pa/cm/cmhansrd.htm
The official record of debates and written answers in the House of Commons. The transcript of each day's business appears at noon on the following weekday.

House of Commons Research Library
www.parliament.uk/parliamentary_publications_and_archives/research_paperscfm

Gives access to the text of research reports prepared for MPs on a wide range of current issues.

The HTML Writers Guild
www.hwg.org
US organisation offering resources, support, representation and education for web authors. (See entry under *Professional Associations*.)

The Independent
www.independent.co.uk
The Independent newspaper online.

IngentaConnect
www.ingentaconnect.com
A comprehensive online UK academic research service The site offers access to almost 18 million articles, chapters and reports online.

Institute of Linguists
www.iol.org.uk
Discussion forum, news on regional societies, job opportunities, `Find a Linguist' service and *The Linguist* magazine. (See entry under *Professional Associations*.)

Institute of Translation and Interpreting (ITI)
www.iti.org.uk
Website of the professional association of translators and interpreters, with the ITI Directory, publications, training and membership information. (See entry under *Professional Associations*.)

Internet Movie Database (IMDb)
www.imdb.com
Essential resource for film buffs and researchers with search engine for cast lists, screenwriters, directors and producers; film and television news, awards, film preview information, video releases.

Internet Classics Archive
classics.mit.edu
Includes 441 works of classical literature by 59 different authors. Mostly Greek and Roman works with some Chinese and Persian. All are in English translation

The Irish Arts Council/ An Chomhairle Ealaíon
www.artscouncil.ie
Monthly e-mail newsletter available giving latest information on grants and awards, news and

events, etc. (See entry under *Arts Councils and Regional Offices*.)

Journalism UK
www.journalismuk.co.uk
A website for UK-based journalists who write for text-based publications. Includes links to newspapers, magazines, e-zines, news sources plus information on jobs, training and organisations.

The Library Association
See **CILIP**

Location Register of 20th-Century English Literary Manuscripts and Letters
www.library.rdg.ac.uk/colls/projects/locreg.html
Reference source for the study of English literature. Information about the manuscript holdings of repositories of all sizes, from the British Library to small-town museums, of literary authors – from major poets to minor science fiction writers.

Mr William Shakespeare and the Internet
shakespeare.palomar.edu
Guide to scholarly Shakespeare resources on the Internet.

National Union of Journalists (NUJ)
www.nuj.org.uk
Represents those journalists who work in all sectors of publishing, print and broadcasting. (See entry under *Professional Associations*.)

Newnovelist
www.newnovelist.com
Software that helps you write a novel. Embraces tuition used in university creative writing courses helping experienced and novice writers alike. Aids research, characterisation, structure and plot, and breaks down the process of writing a novel into manageable chunks. Planning to launch 'Story Wizard' software that helps children write creative stories (www.storywizard.co.uk).

New Writers Consultancy
www.new-writers-consultancy.com
Advice for writers and critiques, offered by Diana Hayden and Karen Scott.

New Writing North
www.newwritingnorth.com
Essentially for writers based in the north of

England but also a useful source of advice and guidelines.

Arts Council of Northern Ireland
www.artscouncil-ni.org
Includes the 'Infodesk – International Arts & Culture', an enquiry service based in Belfast and Dublin with access to a database of international arts contacts, information on funding, etc. (See entry under *Arts Councils and Regional Offices*.)

Novel Advice Newsletter
www.noveladvice.com
A free US journal aimed at the fiction writer; full text of current and past issues online.

PEN
www.englishpen.org
Website of the English Centre of International PEN. News of events, membership details. (See entry under *Professional Associations*.)

PlaysOnTheNet
www.playsonthenet.com
Information and help for new playwrights. Launched in association with Oneword Radio in 2002, the site offers the chance to get involved, whether as a writer or someone who enjoys reading and listening to new plays. The site features new works that can be downloaded.

Poets and Writers
www.pw.org
A US site containing publishing advice, a directory of writers, online bookstore, literary links, news, articles on aspects of writing, grants and awards.

Producers Alliance for Cinema and Television (PACT)
www.pact.co.uk
Publications, jobs in the industry, production companies, membership details. (See entry under *Professional Associations*.)

Publish-This.Com
www.publish-this.com
Provides a venue on which authors, for a fee, may post submissions for the attention of publishers and literary agents registered with the site. Submissions are arranged by genre for easy identification.

Publishers Association
www.publishers.org.uk
Information about the Association and careers

in publishing; also 'Getting Published' pages. (See entry under *Professional Associations*.)

RefDesk.com
refdesk.com
Facts and statistics on every country in the world plus charts and maps, illustrations and related sources.

Royal Society of Literature
www.rslit.org
Information on lectures, discussions and readings; membership details and prizes. (See entry under *Professional Associations*.)

Save Our Short Story Campaign
www.saveourshortstory.org.uk
An Arts Council England and Scottish Arts Council campaign to increase the number and visibility of high quality outlets for short fiction; give the short story form more prestige and a higher profile; enable writers to specialise in the short story form; and encourage and promote exciting short fiction.

Science Fiction Foundation Collection
www.liv.ac.uk/~asawyer/sffchome.html
The research library of the Science Fiction Foundation, based at the University of Liverpool. Includes links to the Foundation, the John Wyndham archive, the Foundation's journal and other SF collections and associations. (See entry under *Library Services*.)

Scottish Arts Council
www.sac.org.uk
Information on funding and events. (See entry under *Arts Councils and Regional Offices*.)

Scottish Book Trust
www.scottishbooktrust.com
Information on the Trust's activities and a link to their Book Information Service. (See entry under *Professional Associations*.)

Scottish Library Association (SLAINTE: Information & Libraries Scotland)
www.slainte.org.uk
Links to various services and major Scottish websites and information on people, organisations, libraries, events and resources of Scottish interest. (See entry under *Professional Associations*.)

Scottish Publishers Association
www.scottishbooks.org

Links to websites of members of the Association, information on activities and publications. (See entry under *Professional Associations*.)

Screenwriters Online
screenwriter.com/insider/news.html
Described as the 'only professional screenwriter's site run by major screenwriters who get their scripts and screenplays made into movies'. Contains screenplay analysis, expert articles and The Insider Report.

Shots Magazine
www.shotsmag.co.uk
Electronic magazine of crime and mystery fiction.

Society for Editors and Proofreaders (SfEP)
www.sfep.org.uk
Information about the Society including online directory of members. (See entry under *Professional Associations*.)

The Society of Authors
www.societyofauthors.org
Includes FAQs for new writers, diary of events, membership details, links to publishers' and other societies' websites. (See entry under *Professional Associations*.)

Society of Indexers
www.socind.demon.co.uk
Indexing information for publishers and authors, `Indexers Available' pages. Membership information. (See entry under *Professional Associations*.)

South Bank Centre, London
www.sbc.org.uk
Links to the Royal Festival Hall, the Hayward Gallery and Poetry Library; news of literature events.

Story Wizard
See **Newnovelist**

The Sun
www.thesun.co.uk
Website of the *Sun* newspaper.

The Times
www.thetimes.co.uk
Website of *The Times* newspaper.

trAce Online Writing Centre
www.trace.ntu.ac.uk
Based at Nottingham Trent University, trAce is an online centre for writers and readers worldwide to share and critique their work, discuss favourite books and talk. Also holds occasional (live) conferences and workshops. Links to a wide range of sites for writers.

UK Children's Books Directory
www.ukchildrensbooks.co.uk
Website created by Steve and Diana Kimpton to 'increase the profile of UK children's books on the Internet'.

The UK Public Libraries Page
dspace.dial.pipex.com/town/square/ac940/weblibs.html
Website links to public libraries throughout the UK, compiled by Sheila and Robert Harden.

Arts Council of Wales
www.ccc-acw.org.uk
Information on publications, council meetings, the arts in Wales. Links to other arts websites. (See entry under *Arts Councils and Regional Offices*.)

Webster Dictionary/Thesaurus
www.m-w.com/home.htm
Merriam-Webster Online. Includes a search facility for words in the Webster Dictionary or Webster Thesaurus; word games and 'Word of the Day'.

Welsh Academy
See **Academi**

Welsh Books Council (Cyngor Llyfrau Cymru)
www.cllc.org.uk and www.gwales.com
Information about books from Wales, editorial and design services, 'Wales Book Day'. (See entry under *Professional Associations*.)

The Word Pool
www.wordpool.co.uk
Children's book site with information on writing for children and a thriving discussion group for children's writers.

Word Pool Design
www.wordpooldesign.co.uk
Web design for writers, illustrators and publishers.

WordCounter
www.wordcounter.com
Highlights the most frequently used words in a given text. Use as a guide to see what words are overused.

Writers' Guild of Great Britain
www.writersguild.org.uk
A wide range of information including rates of pay, articles on topics such as copyright, news, writers' resources and industry regulations. (See entry under *Professional Associations*.)

Writers, Artists and their Copyright Holders (W.A.T.C.H.)
tyler.hrc.utexas.edu
Database of copyright holders in the UK and North America. (See entry under *Professional Associations*.)

Writers' Circles
www.writers-circles.com
Offers free pages to writers' circles. Listings and information.

Writernet
www.writernet.org.uk

Information, advice and guidance for writers on all aspects of live and recorded performance.

WritersNet
www.writers.net
A directory of writers, editors, publishers and literary agents.

WritersServices
www.WritersServices.com
Established in March 2000 by Chris Holifield, former deputy managing director and publisher at Cassell. Offers factsheets, book reviews, advice, links and other resources for writers including editorial services, contract vetting and self-publishing. (Enquiries to: info@writersservices.com)

Writing-World.com
writing-world.com
'A world of writing tips ... for writers around the world.'

UK Packagers

Aladdin Books Ltd
2/3 Fitroy Mews, London W1T 6DF
☎020 7383 2084   Fax 020 7388 6391
Managing Director *Charles Nicholas*

Founded in 1979 as a packaging company but with joint publishing ventures in the UK and USA. Commissions children's fully illustrated, non-fiction reference books. IMPRINTS **Aladdin Books** *Bibby Whittaker* Children's reference; **Nicholas Enterprises** *Charles Nicholas* Adult non-fiction; **The Learning Factory** *Charles Nicholas* Early learning concepts 0–4 years. TITLES *World Issues; Science Readers; The Atlas of Animals.* About 40 titles a year. Will consider synopses and ideas for children's non-fiction with international sales potential only. No fiction.

FEES usually paid instead of royalties.

The Albion Press Ltd
Spring Hill, Idbury OX7 6RU
☎01993 831094   Fax 01993 831982
Chairman/Managing Director *Emma Bradford*

Founded 1984. Commissions illustrated trade titles, particularly children's. TITLES *From a Distance* Jane Ray and Julie Gold; *The Little Mermaid and Other Fairy Stories* Isabelle Brent. About 4 titles a year. Unsolicited synopses and ideas for books not welcome.

ROYALTIES paid; fees paid for introductions and partial contributions.

Alphabet & Image Ltd
See **Marston House** under *UK Publishers*

Amber Books Ltd
Bradleys Close, 74–77 White Lion Street, London N1 9PF
☎020 7520 7600   Fax 020 7520 7606/7
✉ enquiries@amberbooks.co.uk
www.amberbooks.co.uk
Managing Director *Stasz Gnych*
Rights Director *Sara Ballard*
Publishing Manager *Charles Catton*

Founded 1989. Commissions history, encyclopedias, military, aviation, transport, sport, combat, survival and fitness, cookery, lifestyle, naval history, crime and general reference. No fiction.

IMPRINT **Brown Books**. 120 titles in 2004. No unsolicited material.
FEES paid.

Archival Facsimiles
See **Erskine Press**

AS Publishing
73 Montpelier Rise, London NW11 9DU
☎020 8458 3552   Fax 020 8458 0618
Managing Director *Angela Sheehan*

Founded 1987. Commissions children's illustrated non-fiction. No unsolicited synopses or ideas for books, but approaches welcome from experienced authors, editors and illustrators in this field.

FEES paid.

BCS Publishing Ltd
2nd Floor, Temple Court, 109 Oxford Road, Cowley OX4 2ER
☎01865 770099   Fax 01865 770050
✉ bcs-publishing@dsl.pipex.com
Managing Director *Steve McCurdy*
Approx. Annual Turnover £150,000

Commissions general interest non-fiction for the international co-edition market.

Bender Richardson White
PO Box 266, Uxbridge UB9 5BD
☎01895 832444   Fax 01895 835213
✉ brw@brw.co.uk
Partners *Lionel Bender, Kim Richardson, Ben White*

Founded 1990 to produce illustrated non-fiction for children, adults and family reference for publishers in the UK and abroad. 80 titles in 2004. Unsolicited material not welcome.
FEES paid.

Book House
See **Salariya Book Company Ltd**

Book Packaging and Marketing
1 Church Street, Blakesley, Towcester NN12 8RA
☎01327 861300   Fax 01327 861300
✉ martin@marixevans.freeserve.co.uk

Contact *Martin F. Marix Evans*

Founded 1989. Essentially a project management service, handling books demanding close designer/editor teamwork or complicated multi-contributor administration, for publishers, business 'or anyone who needs one'. Illustrated adult non-fiction: mostly military history and other historical and reference books. No fiction or poetry. Proposals considered but rarely come to fruition; most books are bespoke by publishers. Additional writers are sometimes required for projects in development. TITLES *A Terrible Beauty: An Illustrated History of Irish Battlefields; The Fall of France 1940; Forgotten Battlefronts of the First World War; The Vital Guide to Major Battles of World War II; Encyclopedia of the Boer War; The Military Heritage of Britain and Ireland; Guide to South Georgia; American Voices of World War I.* 3–6 titles a year.

PAYMENT Authors contract direct with client publishers; fees paid on first print usually and royalties on reprint but this depends on publisher.

Breslich & Foss Ltd

Unit 2A, Union Court, 20–22 Union Road, Clapham, London SW4 6JP

☎020 7819 3990   Fax 020 7819 3998

✉ sales@breslichfoss.com

Directors *Paula Breslich, K.B. Dunning*

Approx. Annual Turnover £650,000

Packagers of adult non-fiction titles, including interior design, crafts, gardening, health and children's non-fiction and picturebooks. Unsolicited mss welcome but synopses preferred. Include s.a.e. with all submissions.

ROYALTIES paid twice-yearly.

Brown Books

See **Amber Books Ltd**

Brown Wells and Jacobs Ltd

Forresters Hall, 25–27 Westow Street, London SE19 3RY

☎020 8771 5115   Fax 020 8771 9994

✉ graham@bwj-ltd.com

www.bwj.org

Managing Director *Graham Brown*

Founded 1979. Commissions non-fiction, novelty, pre-school and first readers, natural history and science. About 40 titles a year. Unsolicited synopses and ideas for books welcome.

FEES paid.

Cameron & Hollis

PO Box 1, Moffat DG10 9SU

☎01683 220808   Fax 01683 220012

✉ info@cameronbooks.co.uk

www.cameronbooks.co.uk

Directors *Ian A. Cameron, Jill Hollis*

Approx. Annual Turnover £400,000

Commissions contemporary art, film (serious critical works only), design, collectors' reference, decorative arts, architecture and children's non-fiction About 6 titles a year.

PAYMENT varies with each contract.

Compendium Publishing Ltd

See entry under *UK Publishers*

Roger Coote Publishing

Gissing's Farm, Fressingfield, Eye IP21 5SH

☎01379 588044   Fax 01379 588055

✉ rgc@ndirect.co.uk

Director *Roger Goddard-Coote*

Founded 1993. Packager of children's and adult non-fiction for trade, school and library markets. No fiction. About 40 titles a year. Include s.a.e. for return.

FEES paid; no royalties.

Diagram Visual Information Ltd

195 Kentish Town Road, London NW5 2JU

☎020 7482 3633   Fax 020 7482 4932

✉ brucerobertson@diagramgroup.com

Managing Director *Bruce Robertson*

Founded 1967. Producer of library, school, academic and trade reference books. About 10 titles a year.

FEES paid; no payment for sample material/submissions for consideration.

Duncan Petersen Publishing Limited

See entry under *UK Publishers*

Eddison Sadd Editions

St Chad's House, 148 King's Cross Road, London WC1X 9DH

☎020 7837 1968   Fax 020 7837 2025

✉ reception@eddisonsadd.co.uk

Managing Director *Nick Eddison*

Editorial Director *Ian Jackson*

Approx. Annual Turnover £2.5 million

Founded 1982. Produces a wide range of popular illustrated non-fiction – mind, body, spirit and complementary therapies are particular strengths – with books published in 30 countries. Ideas and synopses are welcome but titles must have international appeal.

ROYALTIES paid twice yearly; flat fees paid when appropriate.

Erskine Press
The Old Bakery, Banham, Norwich NR16 2HW
☎01953 887277   Fax 01953 888361
✉ erskpres@aol.com
www.erskine-press.com
Chief Executive *Crispin de Boos*

Founded 1986. Specialist publisher of books on Antarctic exploration – facsimiles, diaries, previously unpublished works and first English translations of European expeditions of the late 19th and early 20th centuries. Publisher of general interest autobiographies with special reference to Norfolk and medical–related 'Patient's Guides' (*Hip & Knee Replacement*; *Chronic Fatigue Syndrome*). Recent publications include three Second World War related subjects (*Living With Heroes*; *The Story of the Dam Busters*). **Archival Facsimiles**, the parent company, produces scholarly reprints and limited edition publications for academic/business organisations ranging from period print reproductions to facsimiles of rare and important books no longer available. No unsolicited mss. Ideas welcome.

ROYALTIES paid twice-yearly.

Expert Publications Ltd
Sloe House, Halstead CO9 1PA
☎01787 474744   Fax 01787 474700
✉ expert@lineone.net
Chairman *Dr. D.G. Hessayon*

Founded 1993. Produces the *Expert* series of books by Dr. D.G. Hessayon. Currently 24 titles in the series, including *The Flower Expert*; *The Evergreen Expert*; *The Vegetable & Herb Expert*; *The Flowering Shrub Expert*; *The Container Expert*. No unsolicited material.

Haldane Mason Ltd
PO Box 34196, London NW10 3YB
☎020 8459 2131   Fax 020 8728 1216
✉ info@haldanemason.com

Founded 1994. Commissions mainly children's illustrated non-fiction and some young children's fiction. Children's books are published under the **Red Kite Books** imprint. Adult list consists mainly of mind, body and spirit plus alternative

health books under the Neals' Yard Remedies banner; children's age range 0–5. Unsolicited synopses and ideas welcome; approach in writing or by e-mail in the first instance. No adult fiction.

FEES paid.

The Ilex Press Limited
3 St Andrews Place, Lewes BN7 1UP
☎01273 487440   Fax 01273 487441
✉ surname@ilex-press.com
Managing Director *Stephen Paul*

Founded 1999. Sister company of **The Ivy Press Limited**. Commissions titles on digital art, design and photography as well as on all aspects of website design and graphics software. No fiction. Unsolicited synopses and ideas welcome; send a *brief* idea outline (3 or 4 pages) and a letter.

FEES paid.

The Ivy Press Limited
The Old Candlemakers, West Street, Lewes BN7 2NZ
☎01273 487440   Fax 01273 487441
✉ surname@ivypress.co.uk
Managing Director *Stephen Paul*

Founded 1996. Sister company of **The Ilex Press Limited**. Commissions illustrated non-fiction books covering subjects such as art, health, self-help, mind, body and spirit, and general reference. No fiction. Unsolicited synopses and ideas welcome; send a *brief* idea outline (3 or 4 pages) and a letter.

FEES paid.

The Learning Factory
See **Aladdin Books Ltd**

Lexus Ltd
60 Brook Street, Glasgow G40 2AB
☎0141 556 0440   Fax 0141 556 2202
✉ peterterrell@lexusforlanguages.co.uk
www.lexusforlanguages.co.uk
Managing/Editorial Director *P.M. Terrell*

Founded 1980. Compiles bilingual reference, language and phrase books. TITLES *Harrap Study Aids*; Langenscheidt dictionaries; *HarperCollins English-Chinese*; *Oxford Italian Pocket Dictionary*. Own series of *Travelmates* published in 2004. About 5 titles a year. No unsolicited material. Books are mostly commissioned. Freelance contributors employed for a wide range of languages.

PAYMENT Generally flat fee.

Lionheart Books

10 Chelmsford Square, London NW10 3AR
☎020 8459 0453   Fax 020 8451 3681
✉ Lionheart.Brw@btinternet.com

Senior Partner *Lionel Bender*
Partner *Madeleine Samuel*

A design/editorial packaging team. Titles are primarily commissioned from publishers. Highly illustrated non-fiction for children aged 8–14, mostly natural history, history and general science. See also **Bender Richardson White**. About 20 titles a year.
PAYMENT Generally flat fee.

M&M Publishing Services

33 Warner Road, Ware SG12 9JL
☎01920 466003
✉ MikeMoran@moran19.fsnet.co.uk
www.mikemoranphotography.co.uk

Proprietors *Mike Moran, Maggie Copeland*

Project managers, production and editorial, packagers and publishers. TITLES *MM Publisher Database; MM Printer Database* (available in UK, European and international editions).

Market House Books Ltd

2 Market House, Market Square, Aylesbury HP20 1TN
☎01296 484911   Fax 01296 437073
✉ books@mhbref.com
www.mhbref.com

Directors *Dr John Daintith, Peter Sapsed*

Founded 1970. Formerly Laurence Urdang Associates. Compiles dictionaries, encyclopedias and reference. TITLES *Collins English Dictionary*; Facts on File dictionaries; *Grolier Bibliographical Encyclopedia of Scientists* (10 vols); *Larousse Thematica* (6 vols); *The Macmillan Encyclopedia*; Macmillan Dictionaries; Oxford Dictionaries of: *Business, Science, Medicine*, etc.; *Penguin Dictionary of Electronics*; *Penguin Rhyming Dictionary*. About 15 titles a year. Unsolicited material not welcome as most books are compiled in-house.
FEES paid.

Marshall Editions Ltd

See **Quarto Publishing**

Monkey Puzzle Media Ltd

Gissing's Farm, Fressingfield IP21 5SH
☎01379 588044   Fax 01379 588055
✉ info@monkeypuzzlemedia.com

Chairman/Managing Director *Roger Goddard-Coote*
Commissioning and List Development *Paul Mason*

Founded 1998. Packager of adult and children's non-fiction for trade, school, library and mass markets. No fiction or textbooks. About 80 titles a year. Synopses and ideas welcome. Include s.a.e. for return.
FEES paid; no royalties.

Nicholas Enterprises

See **Aladdin Books Ltd**

Orpheus Books Limited

2 Church Green, Witney OX28 4AW
☎01993 774949   Fax 01993 700330
✉ info@orpheusbooks.com
www.orpheusbooks.com

Chairman *Nicholas Harris*

Founded 1993. Commissions children's non-fiction. 12 titles in 2004. No unsolicited material.
FEES paid.

Playne Books Limited

Park Court Barn, Trefin, Haverfordwest SA62 5AU
☎01348 837073   Fax 01348 837063
✉ playne.books@virgin.net

Editorial Director *Gill Davies*
Design & Production *David Playne*

Founded 1987. Commissions early learning titles for young children – fun ideas with an educational slant and novelty books. Also highly illustrated and practical books on any subject. Synopses and ideas by prior arrangement only. Vanity publications considered.
ROYALTIES paid 'on payment from publishers'. Fees sometimes paid instead of royalties.

PRC Publishing Ltd

The Chrysalis Building, Bramley Road, London W10 6SP
☎020 7314 1400   Fax 020 7314 1596
✉ jmessham@chrysalisbooks.co.uk *or* fhopkinson@chrysalisbooks.co.uk
www.chrysalisbooks.co.uk

Head of Contract Division *Joanne Messham*
Senior Commissioning Editor *Frank Hopkinson*

PRC Publishing is an imprint within the packaging division of **Chrysalis Books** (see entry under **UK Publishers**). Publishes a wide array of subjects including architecture, history and natural history, lifestyle, art, hobbies, military and transport. Up to 50 new titles worldwide.

Mathew Price Ltd
The Old Glove Factory, Bristol Road, Sherborne DT9 4HP
☎01935 816010   Fax 01935 816310
✉ mathewp@mathewprice.com
Chairman/Managing Director *Mathew Price*
Approx. Annual Turnover £650,000

Commissions full-colour novelty and picture books and fiction for young children plus children's non-fiction for all ages. TITLES *Magnificent Mazes*; *Creepies*; *Tractor Factory*; *Join-In Stories for the Very Young*; *Treasure Hunt*. Mss should be double-spaced, typed on one side of paper. Enclose s.a.e. with submission and keep a copy of everything that is sent.

FEES sometimes paid instead of royalties.

Quarto Publishing plc
The Old Brewery, 6 Blundell Street, London N7 9BH
☎020 7700 6700   Fax 020 7700 4191
www.quarto.com
Chairman & CEO *Laurence Orbach*
Director of Co-edition Publishing *Piers Spence*

Founded 1976. Britain's largest book packager. Acquired Marshall Editions in 2002. Commissions illustrated non-fiction, including painting, graphic design, how-to, lifestyle, visual arts, history, cookery, gardening, crafts. Publishes under the Apple imprint. Unsolicited synopses/ideas for books welcome.

PAYMENT Flat fees paid.

Red Kite Books
See **Haldane Mason Ltd**

Regency House Publishing Limited
See entry under *UK Publishers*

Salariya Book Company Ltd
25 Marlborough Place, Brighton BN1 1UB
☎01273 603306   Fax 01273 693857
✉ salariya@salariya.com
www.salariya.com
www.book-house.co.uk
Managing Director *David Salariya*

Founded 1989. Children's information books – fiction, history, art, music, science, architecture, education and picture books. Publishes under its IMPRINT **Book House** Publisher *David Salariya*

Highly illustrated non-fiction in all subjects for children, from pre-school to teenage.
PAYMENT by arrangement.

Savitri Books Ltd
25 Lisle Lane, Ely CB7 4AS
☎01353 654327   Fax 01353 654327
✉ munni@savitribooks.demon.co.uk
Managing Director *Mrinalini S. Srivastava*
Approx. Annual Turnover £200,000

Founded 1983 and since 1998, Savitri Books has also become a publisher in its own right (textile crafts). Keen to work 'very closely with authors/illustrators and try to establish long-term relationships with them, doing more books with the same team of people'. Commissions illustrated non-fiction: biography, history, travel. About 7 titles a year. Unsolicited synopses and ideas for books 'very welcome'.

Small Packages
20 Carisbrooke Road, London E17 7EF
☎020 8520 6073   Fax 020 8926 4585
✉ mail@smallpackage.co.uk
www.smallpackage.co.uk
Partners *Adam Hibbert, Clare Hibbert*

Founded 2002. Packages children's illustrated non-fiction for trade, school and library markets, UK and co-editions. A mix of project management commissions and packaging. No unsolicited mss.

FLAT FEES paid.

Stonecastle Graphics Ltd/ Touchstone
Battle Cross Studio, Comp Lane, Offham, West Malling ME19 5PP
☎01732 220064   Fax 01732 220112
✉ paul@stonecastle-graphics.co.uk *or* sue@stonecastle-graphics.co.uk
www.stonecastle-graphics.co.uk
www.touchstone-books.com
Partner *Paul Turner*
Editorial Head *Sue Pressley*
Approx. Annual Turnover £300,000

Founded 1976. Formed additional design/packaging partnership, Touchstone, in 1983. Commissions illustrated non-fiction general books – motoring, health, sport, leisure, lifestyle and children's non-fiction. TITLES *The Cocktail Bible*; *Guide to Knots*; *Royal Britain*; *The Ultimate History of Mercedes-Benz*; *The Ultimate History of Corvette*; *Learn to Play the Guitar*; 20 titles in 2004. Unsolicited synopses and ideas for books welcome

FEES paid.

Templar Publishing

Pippbrook Mill, London Road, Dorking
RH4 1JE
☎01306 876361   Fax 01306 889097
✉ editorial@templarco.co.uk
www.templarco.co.uk
Managing Director/Editorial Head *Amanda Wood*
Approx. Annual Turnover £10 million

Founded 1981. A division of The Templar Company plc. Commissions quality novelty and gift books, picture books and children's illustrated non-fiction. 100 titles a year. Synopses and ideas for books welcome. 'We are particularly interested in picture book mss and ideas for new novelty concepts.'
ROYALTIES by arrangement.

Toucan Books Ltd

Third Floor, 89 Charterhouse Street, London
EC1M 6HR
☎020 7250 3388   Fax 020 7250 3123
Managing Director *Ellen Dupont*
Approx. Annual Turnover £1.2 million

Founded 1985. Specialises in international co-editions and fee-based editorial, design and production services. Commissions illustrated non-fiction for children and adults. No fiction or non-illustrated titles. About 5–10 titles a year.
ROYALTIES paid twice-yearly; fees paid in addition to or instead of royalties.

Touchstone

See **Stonecastle Graphics Ltd**

David West Children's Books

7 Princeton Court, 55 Felsham Road, London
SW15 1AZ
☎020 8780 3836   Fax 020 8780 9313
✉ dww@btinternet.com

www.davidwestchildrensbooks.com
Founded 1992. Commissions children's illustrated reference books. No fiction or adult books. 70 titles in 2004. Unsolicited ideas and synopses welcome; approach in writing in the first instance
FEES AND ROYALTIES paid annually.

Working Partners Ltd

1 Albion Place, London W6 0QT
☎020 8748 7477   Fax 020 8748 7450
✉ enquiries@workingpartnersltd.co.uk
www.workingpartnersltd.co.uk
Chairman *Ben Baglio*
Managing Director *Chris Snowdon*
Contact *James Noble*

Specialises in quality mass-market fiction for leading children's publishers including Hodder, Bloomsbury, HarperCollins, Orchard, OUP, Macmillan, Random House and Scholastic. First chapter books to young adult. No picture books. Welcomes approaches from interested writers.
PAYMENT Both fees and royalties by arrangement.

Zoë Books Ltd

15 Worthy Lane, Winchester SO23 7AB
☎01962 851318
✉ enquiries@zoebooks.co.uk
www.zoebooks.co.uk
Managing Director *Imogen Dawson*

Founded 1990. Specialises in full-colour information and reference books for schools and libraries worldwide. Does *not* publish picture books or fiction. No freelance work available. Unsolicited material not considered.
FEES paid.

Book Clubs

David Arscott's Sussex Book Club
Dolphin House, 51 St Nicholas Lane, Lewes
BN7 2JZ
☎01273 470100   Fax 01273 470100
✉ sussexbooks@aol.com
Founded January 1998. Specialises in books
about the county of Sussex. Represents all the
major publishers of Sussex books and offers a
wide range of titles. Free membership without
obligation to buy.

Artists' Choice
PO Box 3, Huntingdon PE28 0QX
☎01832 710201   Fax 01832 710488
www.artists-choice.co.uk
Specialises in books for the amateur artist at all
levels of ability.

Baker Books
Manfield Park, Cranleigh GU6 8NU
☎01483 267888   Fax 01483 267409
✉ bakerbooks@dial.pipex.com
www.bakerbooks.co.uk
Book clubs for schools: Funfare for ages 3–8
and Bookzone, ages 8–13. Four issues per year
operated in the UK and overseas.

BCA (Book Club Associates)
Greater London House, Hampstead Road,
London NW1 7TZ
☎020 7760 6500   Fax 020 7760 6505
With two million members, BCA is Britain's
largest book club organisation, consisting of over
20 book and software clubs as well as bol.com.
These include: Ancient & Medieval History
Book Club, The Arts Guild, The Book Club of
Ireland, Books For Children, Escape (female fic-
tion), Fantasy Science Fiction, History Guild,
Home Software World, Just Good Books,
Mango, Military and Aviation Book Society,
Mind, Body & Spirit, Mystery and Thriller Club,
Quality Paperbacks Direct, Railway Book Club,
Taste, TSP, World Books.

Bibliophile Books
5 Thomas Road, London E14 7BN
☎020 7515 9222   Fax 020 7538 4115
✉ orders@bibliophilebooks.com
www.bibliophilebooks.com

New books covering a wide range of subjects at
discount prices. Write, phone or fax for free
catalogue issued 10 times a year.

Cygnus Books
PO Box 15, Llandeilo SA19 6YX
☎01550 777701   Fax 01550 777569
✉ enquiries@cygnus-books.co.uk
www.cygnus-books.co.uk
'Bookseller offering books for your next step in
spirituality and complementary health care. See
website for over 1000 hand-picked titles.'
Publishes *The Cygnus Review* magazine which
features 50–60 reviews on new mind, body and
spirit titles each month.

The Folio Society
44 Eagle Street, London WC1R 4FS
☎020 7400 4222   Fax 020 7400 4242
✉ enquiries@foliosoc.co.uk
www.foliosociety.com
Fine editions of classic fiction, history and
memoirs; also some children's classics.

Letterbox Library
71–73 Allen Road, London N16 8RY
☎020 7503 4801   Fax 020 7503 4800
✉ info@letterboxlibrary.com
www.letterboxlibrary.com
Children's book cooperative. Hard and soft-
cover, non-sexist and multi-cultural books for
children from one to teenage.

Poetry Book Society
See entry under *Organisations of Interest to
Poets*

Readers' Union Ltd
Brunel House, Forde Close, Newton Abbot
TQ12 4PU
☎01626 323200   Fax 01626 323318
Ten book clubs, all dealing with specific in-
terests: Anglers' Book Club, The Craft Club,
Craftsman's Book Club, Country Sports Book
Club, Equestrian Society, The Gardeners
Society, Needlecrafts with Cross Stitch, Painting
for Pleasure, Photographers' Book Club, Puzzles
Plus.

Scholastic Book Clubs
See **Scholastic Ltd** under *UK Publishers*

Writers' News Bookshelf
First Floor, Victoria House, 143–145 The
Headrow, Leeds LS1 5RL
☎0113 200 2929   Fax 0113 200 2928
✉ janet.davison@writersnews.co.uk
www.writersnews.co.uk

Specialises in books for writers.

UK Literary Agents

★ = Members of the **Association of Authors' Agents**

Aaron, Goldberg & Rothschild Literary Agency
28 Cochrane House, Cowley Road, Uxbridge UB8 2DA
☎0870 199 7573   Fax 0870 199 7573
Contact *Don A. Williams*

Founded 2002. Handles literary fiction and non-fiction; science fiction, crime, horror, fantasy, biography, lifestyle, self-help. Philosophy and esoteric material also considered as well as drama, comedy and documentary scripts for film, TV and radio. No children's, cookery, crafts, hobbies, gardening or poetry. COMMISSION Home 15%; US & Translation 20%. ASSOCIATES Cheeks Media (USA); Docurama (UK).Prefers authors to have some form of previous publication but will consider those who do not. Synopsis and first three chapters welcome; send letter with personal background, publication history and proposal for material submitted. S.a.e. essential. No reading fee.

Sheila Ableman Literary Agency★
122 Arlington Road, London NW1 7HP
☎020 7485 3409   Fax 020 7485 3409
✉ sheila@ableman.freeserve.co.uk
Contact *Sheila Ableman*

Founded 1999. Handles non-fiction including history, science, biography and autobiography. Specialises in TV tie-ins and celebrity ghost writing. No poetry, children's, cookery, gardening or sport. COMMISSION Home 15%; US & Translation 20%. Unsolicited mss welcome. Approach in writing with publishing history, c.v., synopsis, three chapters and s.a.e. for return. No reading fee.

The Agency (London) Ltd★
24 Pottery Lane, London W11 4LZ
☎020 7727 1346   Fax 020 7727 9037
✉ info@theagency.co.uk
Contacts *Stephen Durbridge, Leah Schmidt, Norman North, Julia Kreitman, Bethan Evans, Hilary Delamere, Katie Haines, Ligeia Marsh, Faye Webber, Nick Quinn*

Founded 1995. Handles writers and rights for TV, film, theatre, radio scripts and children's fic-

tion. Only existing clients for adult fiction or non-fiction. COMMISSION Home 10%; US by arrangement. Send letter with s.a.e. No unsolicited mss. No reading fee.

Gillon Aitken Associates Ltd★
18–21 Cavaye Place, London SW10 9PT
☎020 7373 8672   Fax 020 7373 6002
✉ recep@gillonaitken.co.uk
www.gillonaitkenassociates.co.uk
Contacts *Gillon Aitken, Clare Alexander, Lesley Thorne* (also film/TV)
Associated Agents *Anthony Sheil, Mary Pachnos*

Founded 1977. Handles fiction and non-fiction. No plays, scripts or children's fiction unless by existing clients. CLIENTS include Caroline Alexander, John Banville, Pat Barker, Nicholas Blincoe, Gordon Burn, Jung Chang, John Cornwell, Josephine Cox, Sarah Dunant, Susan Elderkin, Sebastian Faulks, Helen Fielding, John Fowles, Russell Grant, Jane Goldman, Germaine Greer, Mark Haddon, Susan Howatch, Liz Jensen, John Keegan, V.S. Naipaul, Jonathan Raban, Piers Paul Read, Michèle Roberts, Nicholas Shakespeare, Gillian Slovo, Matt Thorne, Colin Thubron, Sally Vickers, A.N. Wilson, Robert Wilson. COMMISSION Home 10%; US & Translation 20%; Film/TV 10%. Send preliminary letter, with half-page synopsis and first 30pp of sample material, and adequate return postage, in the first instance. No reading fee.

Michael Alcock Management★
See **Johnson & Alcock Ltd**

The Ampersand Agency
Ryman's Cottages, Little Tew OX7 4JJ
☎01608 683677   Fax 01608 683449
✉ peter@theampersandagency.co.uk
www.theampersandagency.co.uk
Contact *Peter Buckman*

Founded 2003. Handles literary and commercial fiction and non-fiction; contemporary and historical novels, crime, thrillers, biography, women's fiction, history, cookery, memoirs. No scripts unless by existing clients. No poetry, science fiction or illustrated children's books. CLIENTS

Georgette Heyer estate, Barbara Else, Beryl Kingston, Naomi Shepherd, Rita Piper, Philip Purser, Justin Elliott, Vikas Swarup, Kirby Wright. COMMISSION Home 10–15%; US 15–20%; Translation 20%. Translation rights handled by The Buckman Agency. Unsolicited mss, synopses and ideas welcome; send sample chapters and synopsis by e-mail or post (s.a.e. required if material is to be returned). No reading fee.

Darley Anderson Literary, TV & Film Agency*

Estelle House, 11 Eustace Road, London SW6 1JB
☎020 7385 6652   Fax 020 7386 5571
✉ enquiries@darleyanderson.com
www.darleyanderson.com

Contacts *Darley Anderson* (crime, mystery & thrillers), *Lucie Whitehouse* (women's fiction & foreign rights), *Elizabeth Wright* (agent), *Julia Churchill* (children's fiction), *Emma White* (non-fiction, US, foreign & TV rights), *Rosi Bridge* (finance)

Run by an ex-publisher with a knack for spotting talent and making great deals – many for six and seven figure advances. Handles commercial fiction and non-fiction, children's fiction; also selected scripts for film and TV. No academic books or poetry. Special fiction interests: all types of thrillers and crime (American/hard boiled/cosy/historical); women's fiction (sagas, chick-lit, contemporary, love stories, 'tear jerkers', women in jeopardy) and all types of American and Irish novels. Also comic fiction. Non-fiction interests: celebrity autobiographies, biographies, sports books, 'true life' women in jeopardy, revelatory history and science, popular psychology, self improvement, diet, beauty, health, finance, fashion, animals, humour/cartoon, gardening, cookery, inspirational and religious. CLIENTS Liz Allen, Anne Baker, Alex Barclay, Constance Briscoe, Paul Carson, Caroline Carver, Cathy Cassidy, Lee Child, Kira Cochrane, Martina Cole, John Connolly, Margaret Dickinson, Joan Jonker, Danny King, Astrid Longhurst, Rani Manicka, Carole Matthews, Lesley Pearse, Lynda Page, Adrian Plass, Sheila Quigley, Carmen Reid, Rebecca Shaw, Peter Sheridan, Kwong Kuen Shan, Linda Taylor, Elizabeth Waite, Patrick Woodrow. COMMISSION Home 15%; US & Translation 20%; Film/TV/Radio 20%. OVERSEAS ASSOCIATES APA Talent and Literary Agency (LA/Hollywood); Liza Dawson Literary Agency (New York); and leading foreign agents throughout the world. Send letter, synopsis and first three chapters; return postage/s.a.e. essential

for reply. Disk and e-mailed submissions cannot be considered.

Anubis Literary Agency

6 Birdhaven Close, Lighthorne, Warwick CV35 0BE
☎01926 642588   Fax 01926 642588
✉ writerstuff2@btinternet.com

Contacts *Steve Calcutt*

Founded 1994. Handles genre fiction in the following categories: science fiction, fantasy, horror thrillers and crime. No other material considered. CLIENTS include Lesley Asquith, Christopher Golden, J.F. Gonzalez, Anthea Ingham, Tim Lebbon, Sarah Pinborough, Adam Roberts, Steve Savile, Brett A. Savory, Zoe Sharp. COMMISSION Home 15%; US & Translation 20%. Works with the Marsh Agency on translation rights. In the first instance send 50 pages with a one-page synopsis (s.a.e. essential). No telephone calls. No reading fee. The agency runs regular writers' workshops/seminars aimed at helping writers better understand the industry and also improve their writing. For further information, e-mail *Steve Calcutt*.

Artellus Limited

30 Dorset House, Gloucester Place, London NW1 5AD
☎020 7935 6972   Fax 020 7487 5957
✉ artellus@artellusltd.co.uk

Chairman *Gabriele Pantucci*
Director *Leslie Gardner*
Associates *Darryl Samaraweera, Michael Kindellan*

Founded 1986. Full-length and short mss. Handles crime, science fiction, historical, contemporary and literary fiction; non-fiction: art history, current affairs, biography, general history, science. Charges reading fee 'selectively'. Works directly in the USA and with agencies internationally. COMMISSION Home 10%; Overseas 20%. Will suggest revision. Return postage essential.

Author Literary Agents

53 Talbot Road, London N6 4QX
☎020 8341 0442/07989 318245 (mobile)
Fax 020 8341 0442
✉ agile@authors.co.uk

Contact *John Havergal*

Founded 1997. New animation, character, graphics and family entertainment concepts for digital media. COMMISSION Writing: Home 15%; Overseas & Translation 25%; Non-Writing

Media: Publishing or production 25%; Sales promotion one-third.VAT extra.Send a half-to-one-page outline plus first chapter, scene or section only for saleability appraisal. S.a.e. essential for reply. No reading fee.

The Bell Lomax Agency

James House, 1 Babmaes Street, London SW1Y 6HF
☎020 7930 4447   Fax 020 7925 0118
✉ agency@bell-lomax.co.uk
Executives *Eddie Bell, Pat Lomax, Paul Moreton, June Bell*

Established 2002. Handles quality fiction and non-fiction, biography, children's, business and sport. No unsolicited mss without preliminary letter. No scripts. No reading fee.

Lorella Belli Literary Agency (LBLA)★

54 Hartford House, 35 Tavistock Crescent, Notting Hill, London W11 1AY
☎020 7727 8547   Fax 0870 787 4194
✉ info@lorellabelliagency.com
www.lorellabelliagency.com
Contact *Lorella Belli*

Founded 2002. Handles full length fiction (from literary to genre) and general non-fiction. Particularly interested in first novelists, journalists, multi-cultural and international writing, books on or about Italy. No children's, fantasy, science fiction, poetry, plays, scripts or academic books. CLIENTS include Sean Bidder, Zöe Brân, Scott Capurro, Annalisa Coppolaro-Nowell, Sean Coughlan, Nino Filastò, Dario Fo (winner of the 1997 Nobel Prize for Literature), Jacopo Fo, Emily Giffin, Paul Martin, Nisha Minhas, Robet Ray, Rupert Steiner, Marcello Vannucci, Diana Winston. COMMISSION Home 15%; US & Translation 20%. Works in conjunction with leading associate agencies in most countries. REPRESENTS Italy: Boroli Editore Group; Studio Nabu Literary Agency; USA: The Imprint Agency, Marmur Associates Ltd, Norris Literary Agency, LLC; Canada: The Harding Agency; Seventh Avenue Literary Agency. Welcomes approaches from new authors. Send outline plus two chapters for non-fiction, and short synopsis plus first three chapters for fiction. S.a.e. essential. No reading fee. Revision suggested where appropriate.

Blake Friedmann Literary Agency Ltd★

122 Arlington Road, London NW1 7HP
☎020 7284 0408   Fax 020 7284 0442

✉ firstname@blakefriedmann.co.uk
www.blakefriedmann.co.uk
Contacts *Carole Blake* (books), *Julian Friedmann* (film/TV), *Conrad Williams* (original scripts/radio), *Isobel Dixon* (books)

Founded 1977. Handles all kinds of fiction from genre to literary; a varied range of specialised and general non-fiction, plus scripts for TV, radio and film. No poetry, science fiction or short stories (unless from existing clients). Special interests: commercial women's fiction, literary fiction, upmarket non-fiction. CLIENTS include Jane Asher, Edward Carey, Elizabeth Chadwick, Barbara Erskine, Maeve Haran, Ken Hom, Billy Hopkins, Glenn Meade, Lawrence Norfolk, Gregory Norminton, Joseph O'Connor, Siân Rees, Michael Ridpath, Craig Russell. COMMISSION Books: Home 15%; US & Translation 20%. Radio/TV/Film: 15%. OVERSEAS ASSOCIATES worldwide. Unsolicited mss welcome but initial letter with synopsis and first two chapters preferred. Letters should contain as much information as possible on previous writing experience, aims for the future, etc. No reading fee.

Luigi Bonomi Associates Limited (LBA)★

91 Great Russell Street, London WC1B 3PS
☎020 7637 1234   Fax 020 7637 2111
✉ info@bonomiassociates.co.uk
Contacts *Luigi Bonomi, Amanda Preston*

Handles commercial and literary fiction, thrillers, crime and women's fiction; non-fiction: history, science, parenting, mind, body & spirit, gardening, cookery, lifestyle, diet, health, sport, TV tie-ins. All types of journalism. Also TV, film, radio and theatre scripts. No poetry, science fiction/fantasy, children's storybooks. CLIENTS include James Barrington, Chris Beardshaw, John Humphrys, Dr Gillian McKeith, Richard Madeley & Judy Finnigan, Melanie Phillips, Esther Rantzen, Colin Shindler, Prof. Bryan Sykes, Mitch Symons, Alan Titchmarsh, Kim Woodburn & Aggie MacKenzie, Sally Worboyes. COMMISSION Home 15%; US & Translation 20%.'We are very keen to find new authors and help them develop their careers.' Send preliminary letter, synopsis and first three chapters. Return postage/s.a.e. essential for reply. No reading fee.

BookBlast Ltd

PO Box 20184, London W10 5AU
☎020 8968 3089   Fax 020 8932 4087
www.bookblast.com

Contact *Address material to the Company*

Handles fiction and non-fiction. No scripts, horror, crime, children's, science fiction, fantasy, poetry, health, cookery, gardening, short stories, academic or articles. COMMISSION Home 12%; US & Translation 20%; TV & Radio 15%; Film 20%. No unsolicited approaches at present. No new authors taken on except by recommendation. Film, TV and radio rights mainly sold in works by existing clients. No reading fee.

Alan Brodie Representation Ltd
6th Floor, Fairgate House, 78 New Oxford Street, London WC1A 1HB
☎020 7079 7990   Fax 020 7079 7999
✉ info@alanbrodie.com
www.alanbrodie.com

Contacts *Alan Brodie, Sarah McNair, Lisa Foster*

Founded 1989. Handles theatre, film and TV scripts. No books. COMMISSION Home 10%; Overseas 15%. Preliminary letter plus professional recommendation and c.v. essential. No reading fee but s.a.e. required.

Rosemary Bromley
Literary Agency
Avington, Near Winchester SO21 1DB
☎01962 779656   Fax 01962 779656
✉ juvenilia@clara.co.uk

Contact *Rosemary Bromley*

Founded 1981. Handles non-fiction. Scripts for TV and radio by existing clients only. No poetry or short stories. Special interests: natural history, leisure, biography and cookery. CLIENTS include Elisabeth Beresford, Linda Birch, Teresa Collard, estate of Fanny Cradock, Glenn Hamilton, Cathy Hopkins, Keith West, John Wingate. COMMISSION Home 10%; US 15%; Translation 20%. No unsolicited mss. No fax, telephone or e-mail enquiries. Enquiries unaccompanied by return postage will not be answered. Client list is currently full.

Jenny Brown Associates
42 The Causeway, Edinburgh EH15 3PZ
☎0131 620 1556   Fax 0131 620 1556
✉ jenny-brown@blueyonder.co.uk
www.jennybrownassociates.com

Contacts *Jenny Brown, Mark Stanton*

Founded 2002. Emphasis on Scottish-based writers. Handles literary fiction; non-fiction: biography, history, sport, music, popular culture. No children's books, poetry, science fiction, fantasy or academic. CLIENTS include Des Dillon,

Jennie Erdal, Diana Hendry, Anne MacLeod, Laura Marney, Janet Morgan, Tom Pow, Suhayl Saadi, Christopher Whyte. COMMISSION Home 10%; US & Translation 20%. Works with The Marsh Agency. No unsolicited mss. Approach in writing with letter, synopsis and first two chapters. Include c.v. and s.a.e.

Felicity Bryan★
2A North Parade, Banbury Road, Oxford OX2 6LX
☎01865 513816   Fax 01865 310055
Agents *Felicity Bryan, Catherine Clarke*
Contact *Michele Topham*

Founded 1988. Handles fiction of various types and non-fiction with emphasis on history, biography, science and current affairs. No scripts for TV, radio or theatre. No crafts, how-to, science fiction or light romance. CLIENTS include Karen Armstrong, Simon Blackburn, Michael Buerk, Artemis Cooper, Isla Dewar, John Dickie, A.C. Grayling, Julie Hearn, Angela Huth, Colin Jones, Liz Kessler, Diarmaid MacCulloch, James Naughtie, John Julius Norwich, Gemma O'Connor, Iain Pears, Robin Pilcher, Rosamunde Pilcher, Matt Ridley, Meg Rosoff, Miriam Stoppard, Roy Strong, John Sulston, Eleanor Updale and the estates of Robertson Davies and Humphrey Carpenter. COMMISSION Home 10%; US & Translation 20%. OVERSEAS ASSOCIATES Andrew Nurnberg, Europe; several agencies in US. No unsolicited mss. Best approach by letter. No reading fee.

The Buckman Agency
Ryman's Cottages, Little Tew OX7 4JJ
☎01608 683677   Fax 01608 683449
✉ r.buckman@talk21.com *or*
j.buckman@talk21.com
Partners *Rosie Buckman, Jessica Buckman*

Founded in the early 1970s, the agency specialises in foreign rights and represents leading authors and agents from the UK and US. COMMISSON 20% (including sub-agent's commission). No unsolicited mss.

Brie Burkeman★
14 Neville Court, Abbey Road, London NW8 9DD
☎0709 223 9113/0870 199 5002
Fax 0709 223 9111/0870 199 1029
✉ brie.burkeman@mail.com
Contact *Brie Burkeman*

Founded 2000. Handles commercial and literary full-length fiction and non-fiction. Film and theatre scripts. No academic, text, poetry, short stories, musicals or short films. Also associated with Serafina Clarke Ltd and independent film/TV consultant to literary agents. CLIENTS include Richard Askwith, Alexandra Carew, Kitty Ferguson, Joanne Harris, Shaun Hutson, David Savage, Gerald Wilson. COMMISSION Home 15%; Overseas 20%. Unsolicited e-mail attachments will be deleted without opening. No reading fee but return postage essential.

Juliet Burton Literary Agency
2 Clifton Avenue, London W12 9DR
☎020 8762 0148   Fax 020 8743 8765
✉ juliet.burton@virgin.net
Contact *Juliet Burton*

Founded 1999. Handles fiction and non-fiction. Special interests crime and women's fiction. No plays, film scripts, articles, poetry or academic material. COMMISSION Home 10%; US & Translation 20%. Approach in writing in the first instance; send synopsis and two sample chapters with s.a.e. No e-mail submissions. No unsolicited mss. No reading fee.

Campbell Thomson & McLaughlin Ltd★
1 King's Mews, London WC1N 2JA
☎020 7242 0958   Fax 020 7242 2408
Contacts *John McLaughlin, Charlotte Bruton*

Founded 1931. Handles fiction and general non-fiction, excluding children's. No plays, film/TV scripts, articles, short stories or poetry. OVERSEAS ASSOCIATES Fox Chase Agency, Pennsylvania; Raines & Raines, New York. No unsolicited mss or synopses. Preliminary letter with s.a.e. essential. No reading fee.

Capel & Land Ltd★
29 Wardour Street, London W1D 6PS
☎020 7734 2414   Fax 020 7734 8101
✉ robert@capelland.co.uk
www.capelland.com
Contact *Georgina Capel*

Handles fiction and non-fiction. Also film, TV, theatre and radio scripts. CLIENTS Kunal Basu, Julie Burchill, John Gimlette, Andrew Greig, Dr Tristram Hunt, Andrew Roberts, Simon Sebag Montefiore, Diana Souhami, Louis Theroux, Lucy Wadham. COMMISSION Home, US & Translation 15%. Send sample chapters and syn-

opsis with covering letter and s.a.e. (if return required) in the first instance. No reading fee.

Casarotto Ramsay and Associates Ltd
National House, 60–66 Wardour Street, London W1V 4ND
☎020 7287 4450   Fax 020 7287 9128
✉ agents@casarotto.uk.com
www.casarotto.uk.com
Film/TV/Radio *Jenne Casarotto, Charlotte Kelly, Jodi Shields, Elinor Burns, Miriam James, Holly Nicholson*
Stage *Tom Erhardt, Mel Kenyon*

Handles scripts for TV, theatre, film and radio. CLIENTS include: **Theatre** Alan Ayckbourn, Caryl Churchill, Christopher Hampton, David Hare, Sarah Kane estate, Mark Ravenhill. **Film** Laura Jones, Neil Jordan, Nick Hornby, Shane Meadows, Purvis & Wade, Lynne Ramsay. **TV** Howard Brenton, Amy Jenkins, Susan Nickson, Jessica Stevenson. COMMISSION Home 10%. OVERSEAS ASSOCIATES worldwide. No unsolicited material without preliminary letter.

Celia Catchpole
56 Gilpin Avenue, London SW14 8QY
☎020 8255 4835
Contact *Celia Catchpole*

Founded 1996. Handles children's books – artists and writers. No TV, film, radio or theatre scripts. No poetry. COMMISSION Home 10% (writers) 15% (artists); US & Translation 20%. Works with associate agents abroad. No unsolicited mss.

Chapman & Vincent★
The Mount, Sun Hill, Royston SG8 9AT
☎01763 245005   Fax 01763 243033
✉ info@chapmanvincent.co.uk
Contacts *Jennifer Chapman, Gilly Vincent*

A small agency whose clients come mainly from personal recommendation. The agency looks after only a limited number of predominantly non-fiction writers and is not actively seeking clients but happy to consider really original work. Does not handle poetry, thrillers, adventure, children's books or genre fiction. CLIENTS include George Carter, Leslie Geddes-Brown, Sara George, Rowley Leigh, Eve Pollard. COMMISSION Home 15%; US & Europe 20%. Please do not telephone or submit by fax or e-mail. Write with two sample chapters and enclose s.a.e.

Mic Cheetham Literary Agency

11–12 Dover Street, London W1S 4LJ
☎020 7495 2002   Fax 020 7495 5777
www.miccheetham.com

Contacts *Mic Cheetham, Simon Kavanagh*

Established 1994. Handles general and literary fiction, crime and science fiction, and some specific non-fiction. No film/TV scripts apart from existing clients. No children's, illustrated books or poetry. CLIENTS include Iain Banks, Carol Birch, Anita Burgh, Laurie Graham, M. John Harrison, Toby Litt, Ken MacLeod, China Miéville, Antony Sher, Janette Turner Hospital. COMMISSION Home 15%; US & Translation 20%. Works with The Marsh Agency for all translation rights. No unsolicited mss. Approach in writing with publishing history, first two chapters and return postage. No reading fee.

Judith Chilcote Agency★

8 Wentworth Mansions, Keats Grove, London NW3 2RL
☎020 7794 3717
✉ judybks@aol.com

Contact *Judith Chilcote*

Founded 1990. Handles commercial fiction, TV tie-ins, health and nutrition, popular psychology, biography and celebrity autobiography and current affairs. COMMISSION Home 15%; Overseas 20–25%. *No* academic, science fiction, children's, short stories, film scripts or poetry. *No approaches by e-mail.* Send letter with c.v., synopsis, three chapters and s.a.e. for return. No reading fee.

Teresa Chris Literary Agency Ltd★

43 Musard Road, London W6 8NR
☎020 7386 0633

Contacts *Teresa Chris, Charles Brudenell-Bruce*

Founded 1989. Handles crime, general, women's, commercial and literary fiction, and non-fiction: history, biography, health, cookery, lifestyle, sport and fitness, gardening, etc. Specialises in crime fiction and commercial women's fiction. No scripts. Film and TV rights handled by co-agent. No poetry, short stories, fantasy, science fiction or horror. CLIENTS include Stephen Booth, Tamara McKinley, Marguerite Patten, Eileen Ramsay, Danuta Reah, Kate Tremayne. COMMISSION Home 10%; US 15%; Translation 20%. OVERSEAS ASSOCIATES Thompson & Chris Literary Agency, USA; representatives in most other countries. Unsolicited mss welcome. Send query letter with first two chapters plus two-page synopsis (s.a.e. *essential*) in first instance. No reading fee.

Mary Clemmey Literary Agency★

6 Dunollie Road, London NW5 2XP
☎020 7267 1290   Fax 020 7482 7360

Contact *Mary Clemmey*

Founded 1992. Handles fiction and non-fiction – high-quality work with an international market. No science fiction, fantasy or children's books. TV, film, radio and theatre scripts from existing clients only. US clients: Frederick Hill Bonnie Nadell Inc., Lynn C. Franklin Associates Ltd, The Miller Agency, Roslyn Targ, Weingel-Fidel Agency Inc. COMMISSION Home 10%; US & Translation 20%. OVERSEAS ASSOCIATE Elaine Markson Literary Agency, New York. No unsolicited mss. Approach by letter only in the first instance giving a description of the work (include s.a.e.). No reading fee.

Sappho Clissitt Literary Agency

Seamere Cottage, Seamere Green, Diss IP21 4XA
☎01379 741861
✉ sappho@sapholiterary.co.uk

Contact *Sappho Clissitt*

Handles general fiction and non-fiction, excluding science fiction, technical, children's books or poetry. COMMISSION Home 15%; US & Translation 20% Unsolicited mss welcome. Send covering letter, synopsis, approx first 50 pages and s.a.e. No electronic submissions.

Jonathan Clowes Ltd★

10 Iron Bridge House, Bridge Approach, London NW1 8BD
☎020 7722 7674   Fax 020 7722 7677

Contacts *Ann Evans, Lisa Whadcock*

Founded 1960. Pronounced 'clewes'. Now one of the biggest fish in the pond, and not really for the untried unless they are true high-flyers. Fiction and non-fiction, plus scripts. No text-books or children's. Special interests: situation comedy, film and television rights. CLIENTS include David Bellamy, Bill Dare, Len Deighton, Elizabeth Jane Howard, David Lawrence, Doris Lessing, David Nobbs, Gillian White and the estate of Kingsley Amis. COMMISSION Home & US 15%; Translation 19%. OVERSEAS ASSOCIATES Andrew Nurnberg Associates; Sane Töregard Agency. No unsolicited mss; authors come by recommendation or by successful follow-ups to preliminary letters.

Elspeth Cochrane
Personal Management
16 Old Town, Clapham, London SW4 0JY
☎020 7819 6256   Fax 020 7819 4297
✉ info@elspethcochrane.co.uk
Contact *Elspeth Cochrane*

Founded 1960. Handles fiction, non-fiction, biographies, screenplays and plays. No children's fiction. CLIENTS include Alex Jones, Dominic Leyton, Royce Ryton, F.E. Smith, Robert Tanitch, Gerald Vaughn-Hughes. COMMISSION 12½%. No unsolicited mss. Phone before submitting work.

Rosica Colin Ltd
1 Clareville Grove Mews, London SW7 5AH
☎020 7370 1080   Fax 020 7244 6441
Contact *Joanna Marston*

Founded 1949. Handles all full-length mss, plus theatre, film, television and sound broadcasting but few new writers being accepted. COMMISSION Home 10%; US 15%; Translation 20%. Preliminary letter with return postage essential; writers should outline their writing credits and whether their mss have previously been submitted elsewhere. May take 3–4 months to consider full mss; synopsis preferred in the first instance. No reading fee.

Conville & Walsh Limited★
2 Ganton Street, London W1F 7QL
☎020 7287 3030   Fax 020 7287 4545
✉ firstname@convilleandwalsh.com
Directors *Clare Conville, Patrick Walsh* (book rights), *Peter Tallack* (popular science)

Established in 2000 by Clare Conville (ex-A.P. Watt) and Patrick Walsh (ex-Christopher Little Literary Agency). Handles literary and commercial fiction plus serious and narrative non-fiction. Clare Conville also represents many successful children's authors. Particularly interested in first-time novelists, scientists, historians and journalists. CLIENTS John Burningham, Kate Cann, Helen Castor, Tom Conran, Michael Cordy, Mike Dash, Belle de Jour, Professor John Emsley, Steve Erikson, Kitty Fitzgerald, Katy Gardner, Sarah Hall, Christopher Hart, Dermot Healy, James Holland, Tom Holland, Sebastian Horsley, David Huggins, Dee Jarrett-Macauley, Richard T. Kelly, Guy Kennaway, Daren King, Manjit Kumar, P.J. Lynch, Hector Macdonald, Andrew Marshall, Mark Mason, Harland Miller, Joshua Mowll, Jacqui Murhall, Ruth Padel, D.B.C. Pierre, Rebecca Ray, Patrick Redmond, Candace Robb,

Philip Robinson, Mark Sanderson, Saira Shah, Tahir Shah, Nicky Singer, Simon Singh, Michael Smith, Doron Swade, Steve Voake, Nick Wright, Dr Richard Wiseman, Adam Wishart, Isabel Wolff and the estate of Francis Bacon. COMMISSION Home 15%; US & Translation 20%. Send first three chapters, one-page synopsis, covering letter and s.a.e.

Jane Conway-Gordon Ltd★
1 Old Compton Street, London W1D 5JA
☎020 7494 0148   Fax 020 7287 9264
Contact *Jane Conway-Gordon*

Founded 1982. Works in association with Andrew Mann Ltd. Handles fiction and general non-fiction. No poetry or science fiction. COMMISSION Home 15%; US & Translation 20%. OVERSEAS ASSOCIATES McIntosh & Otis, Inc., New York; plus agencies throughout Europe and Japan. Unsolicited mss welcome; preliminary letter and return postage essential. No reading fee.

Rupert Crew Ltd★
1A King's Mews, London WC1N 2JA
☎020 7242 8586   Fax 020 7831 7914
✉ info@rupertcrew.co.uk *(correspondence only)*
www.rupertcrew.co.uk
Contacts *Doreen Montgomery, Caroline Montgomery*

Founded 1927. International representation, handling volume and subsidiary rights in fiction and non-fiction properties. No plays or poetry, journalism or short stories, science fiction or fantasy. COMMISSION Home 15%; Elsewhere 20%. Preliminary letter and return postage essential. No reading fee.

Curtis Brown Group Ltd★
Haymarket House, 28/29 Haymarket, London SW1Y 4SP
☎020 7393 4400   Fax 020 7393 4401
✉ cb@curtisbrown.co.uk
www.curtisbrown.co.uk
CEO *Jonathan Lloyd*
Director of Operations *Ben Hall*
Directors *Jacquie Drewe, Jonny Geller, Nick Marston, Peter Robinson*
Books *Jonny Geller* (MD, Book Division), *Ali Gunn, Camilla Hornby, Jonathan Lloyd, Anthea Morton-Saner, Jonathan Pegg, Peter Robinson, John Saddler, Vivienne Schuster, Janice Swanson, Euan Thorneycroft*
Foreign Rights (books) *Kate Cooper, Carol Jackson*

Film/TV/Theatre *Nick Marston* (MD, Media Division), *Tally Garner, Ben Hall, Joe Phillips, Sally Whitehill* Actors *Grace Clissold, Maxine Hoffman, Sarah MacCormick, Sarah Spear, Kate Staddon, Claire Stannard, Frances Williams* Presenters *Jacquie Drewe*

Founded 1899. Agents for the negotiation in all markets of novels, general non-fiction, children's books and associated rights (including multimedia) as well as film, theatre, TV and radio scripts. COMMISSION Home 15%; Overseas 20%. OVERSEAS ASSOCIATES in Australia and the US. Send outline for non-fiction and short synopsis for fiction with two/three sample chapters and autobiographical note. No reading fee. Return postage essential. No submissions by e-mail. See submission guidelines on website. Also represents playwrights, film and TV writers and directors, theatre directors and designers, TV and radio presenters and actors.

Judy Daish Associates Ltd

2 St Charles Place, London W10 6EG
☎020 8964 8811   Fax 020 8964 8966

Contacts *Judy Daish, Sara Stroud, Tracey Elliston*

Founded 1978. Theatrical literary agent. Handles scripts for film, TV, theatre and radio. No books. Preliminary letter essential. No unsolicited mss.

Caroline Davidson Literary Agency

5 Queen Anne's Gardens, London W4 1TU
☎020 8995 5768   Fax 020 8994 2770

Contact *Caroline Davidson*

Founded 1988. Handles fiction and non-fiction, including archaeology, architecture, art, astronomy, biography, design, gardening, health, history, medicine, natural history, reference, science. CLIENTS Peter Barham, Nigel Barlow, Andrew Dalby, Emma Donoghue, Cindy Engel, Chris Greenhalgh, Tom Jaine, Paul Luff, Huon Mallalieu, Brij Sharma, Linda Sonntag. COMMISSION Home & Commonwealth, US, Translation 12½%; 20% if sub-agents are involved in foreign sales. Finished, polished first novels positively welcomed. No thrillers, crime, occult, short stories, children's, plays or poetry. Writers should send an initial letter giving details of their project and/or book proposal, including the first 50 pages of their novel if a fiction writer, together with c.v. and s.a.e. Submissions without the latter (or those sent by fax or e-mail) are not considered or returned.

Merric Davidson Literary Agency

12 Priors Heath, Goudhurst, Cranbrook TN17 2RE
☎01580 212041   Fax 01580 212041
✉ authors@mdla.co.uk

Contacts *Merric Davidson, Wendy Suffield*

Founded 1990. Handles fiction. No scripts. No academic, short stories or articles. CLIENTS include Alys Clare, Francesca Clementis, Murray Davies, Alison Habens, Frankie Park, Simon Scarrow. COMMISSION Home 10%; US 15%; Translation 20%. No unsolicited mss. Send preliminary letter with synopsis and biographical details. S.a.e. essential for response. No reading fee.

Felix de Wolfe

Kingsway House, 103 Kingsway, London WC2B 6QX
☎020 7242 5066   Fax 020 7242 8119
✉ info@felixdewolfe.com

Contact *Felix de Wolfe*

Founded 1938. Handles quality fiction only, and scripts. No non-fiction or children's. CLIENTS include Jan Butlin, Robert Cogo-Fawcett, Jeff Dowson, Carolina Giametta, Brian Glover, Sheila Goff, Aileen Gonsalves, John Kershaw, Bill MacIlwraith, Angus Mackay, Gerard McLarnon, Braham Murray, Julian Slade, Malcolm Taylor, David Thompson, Paul Todd, Dolores Walshe. COMMISSION Home 12½%; US 20%. No unsolicited mss. No reading fee.

The Dench Arnold Agency

10 Newburgh Street, London W1F 7RN
☎020 7437 4551   Fax 020 7439 1355
www.dencharnold.co.uk

Contacts *Elizabeth Dench, Michelle Arnold*

Founded 1972. Handles scripts for TV and film. CLIENTS include Peter Chelsom. COMMISSION Home 10–15%. OVERSEAS ASSOCIATES include: William Morris/Sanford Gross and C.A.A., Los Angeles. Unsolicited mss will be read, but a letter with sample of work and c.v. (plus s.a.e.) is required.

Dorian Literary Agency (DLA)★

Upper Thornehill, 27 Church Road, St Marychurch, Torquay TQ1 4QY
☎01803 312095   Fax 01803 312095

Contact *Dorothy Lumley*

Founded 1986. Handles popular genre fiction: romance, historicals, sagas; crime and thrillers; science fiction, fantasy, horror; some general fiction. No short stories, poetry, autobiography, film/TV scripts or plays. CLIENTS include Gillian Bradshaw, Gary Gibson, Stephen Jones, Brian Lumley, Amy Myers, Rosemary Rowe, Lyndon Stacey. COMMISSION Home 12½% for new clients; US 15%;Translation 20–25%.Works with agents in most countries for translation. 'Reading only *very selectively*.' Introductory letter with outline and 1–3 chapters (with return postage/s.a.e.) only, please. No enquiries or submissions by fax or e-mail. No reading fee.

Toby Eady Associates Ltd
9 Orme Court, London W2 4RL
☎020 7792 0092   Fax 020 7792 0879
✉ toby@tobyeady.demon.co.uk *or* jessica@tobyeady.demon.co.uk
www.tobyeadyassociates.co.uk

Contacts *Toby Eady, Jessica Woollard*

Handles fiction, and non-fiction. Special interests: China, Middle East, Africa, India. CLIENTS include Nada Awar Jarrar, Julia Blackburn, Mark Burnell, Robert Carter, Chris Cleave, Bernard Cornwell, Rana Dasgupta, Fadia Faqir, Xiaolu Guo, Liu Hong, Hitomi Kanehara, Francesca Marciano, Rachel Seiffert, John Carey, Kuki Gallmann, Julia Lovell, Robert Macfarlane, Kanan Makiya, Linda Polman, Fiammetta Rocco, Deborah Scroggins, Samia Serageldin, Xinran Xue, Amy Yamada. COMMISSION Home 15%; Elsewhere 20%. OVERSEAS ASSOCIATES France: La Nouvelle Agence; Holland: Jan Michael; Italy, Spain, Portugal and Scandinavia: The Buckman Agency; China: Joanne Wang; Eastern Europe/Russia: Prava I Prevodi; Czech Republic: Kristin Olson; Hungary: Katai & Bolza; Greece: JLM. Approach by personal recommendation. No film/TV scripts or poetry.

Eddison Pearson Ltd
West Hill House, 6 Swains Lane, London N6 6QS
☎020 7700 7763   Fax 020 7700 7866
✉ enquiries@eddisonpearson.com

Contact *Clare Pearson*

Founded 1995. Small, personally-run agency. Handles children's books and scripts, literary fiction and non-fiction, poetry. CLIENTS include Valerie Bloom, Sue Heap, Robert Muchamore. COMMISSION Home 10%; US & Translation 15–20%.Please e-mail for up-to-date submission guidelines by return. Or post writing sample enclosing s.a.e. No reading fee.

Edwards Fuglewicz★
49 Great Ormond Street, London WC1N 3HZ
☎020 7405 6725   Fax 020 7405 6726
Contacts *Ros Edwards, Helenka Fuglewicz, Julia Forrest*

Founded 1996. Handles literary and commercial fiction (not children's, science fiction, horror or fantasy); non-fiction: biography, history, popular culture. COMMISSION Home 15%; US & Translation 20%. No unsolicited mss or e-mail submissions.

Faith Evans Associates★
27 Park Avenue North, London N8 7RU
☎020 8340 9920   Fax 020 8340 9410

Founded 1987. Small agency. Handles fiction and non-fiction. No scripts. CLIENTS include Melissa Benn, Shyam Bhatia, Cherie Booth, Eleanor Bron, Carolyn Cassady, Caroline Conran, Helen Falconer, Alicia Foster, Midge Gillies, Ed Glinert, Vesna Goldsworthy, Cate Haste, Jim Kelly, Helena Kennedy, Seumas Milne, Tom Paulin, Sheila Rowbotham, the estate of Lorna Sage, Rebecca Stott, Harriet Walter, Francesca Weisman, Elizabeth Wilson. COMMISSION Home 15%; US & Translation 20%. OVERSEAS ASSOCIATES worldwide. New clients by personal recommendation only; no unsolicited mss or phone calls, please.

Lisa Eveleigh Literary Agency★
3rd Floor, 11/12 Dover Street, London W1S 4LJ
☎020 7399 2803   Fax 020 7399 2801
✉ lisaeveleigh@dial.pipex.com

Contact *Lisa Eveleigh*

Founded 1996. Handles literary and commercial fiction and non-fiction. No children's picture books, plays, scripts or poetry or horror. CLIENTS include Christina Balit, Robin Brooks, Samit Basu, Philip Casey, Jonathan Gornall, Jonathan Meres, Relate, Lori Reid, Grace Wynne-Jones. COMMISSION Home 15%; US & Translation 20%. Send synopsis with covering letter and c.v. rather than full mss. No reading fee but return postage essential. Please restrict e-mail contact to preliminary letter only.

Laurence Fitch Ltd
Mezzanine, Quadrant House, 80–82 Regent Street, London W1B 5AU
☎020 7734 9911
✉ information@laurencefitch.com
www.laurencefitch.com

Contact *Brendan Davis*

Founded 1952, incorporating the London Play Company (1922) and in association with Film

Rights Ltd (1932). Handles children's and horror books, scripts for theatre, film, TV and radio only. CLIENTS include Carlo Ardito, Hindi Brooks, John Chapman & Ray Cooney, Jeremy Lloyd, Dave Freeman, John Graham, Robin Hawdon, Glyn Robbins, Lawrence Roman, John Rooney, Gene Stone, the estate of Dodie Smith, Edward Taylor. COMMISSION UK 10%; Overseas 15%. OVERSEAS ASSOCIATES worldwide. No unsolicited mss. Send synopsis with sample scene(s)/ first chapters in the first instance. No reading fee.

Jill Foster Ltd

9 Barb Mews, Brook Green, London W6 7PA
☎020 7602 1263   Fax 020 7602 9336
✉ agents@jflagency.com

Contacts *Jill Foster, Alison Finch, Simon Williamson, Dominic Lord, Gary Wild*

Founded 1976. Handles scripts for TV, drama and comedy. No fiction, short stories or poetry. CLIENTS include Ian Brown, Jan Etherington and Gavin Petrie, Phil Ford, Nev Fountain and Tom Jaimeson, Rob Gittins, Jenny Lecoat, Jim Pullin and Fraser Steele, Pete Sinclair, Peter Tilbury, Susan Wilkins. COMMISSION Home 12½%; Books, US & Translation 15%. No unsolicited mss; approach by letter in the first instance. No approaches by e-mail. No reading fee.

Fox & Howard Literary Agency

4 Bramerton Street, London SW3 5JX
☎020 7352 8691   Fax 020 7352 8691

Contacts *Chelsey Fox, Charlotte Howard*

Founded 1992. A small agency, specialising in non-fiction, that prides itself on 'working closely with its authors'. Handles biography, history and popular culture, reference, business, mind, body and spirit, health and fitness. COMMISSION Home 15%; US & Translation 20%. No unsolicited mss; send letter and synopsis with s.a.e. for response. No reading fee.

Fraser Ross Associates

6 Wellington Place, Edinburgh EH6 7EQ
☎0131 657 4412/0131 553 2759
✉ kjross@tiscali.co.uk *and* lindsey.fraser@tiscali.co.uk

Contact *Lindsey Fraser, Kathryn Ross*

Founded 2002. Handles children's books, adult literary and mainstream fiction. No poetry, short stories, adult fantasy and science fiction, academic, scripts. CLIENTS include Thomas Bloor, Chris Fisher, Vivian French, Michaela Morgan. COMMISSION Home 10%; USA & Translation 20%. Send preliminary letter, synopsis, first three

chapters or equivalent, c.v. and s.a.e. No reading fee.

Futerman, Rose & Associates★

17 Deanhill Road, London SW14 7DQ
☎020 8255 7755   Fax 020 8286 4860
✉ guy@futermanrose.co.uk
www.futermanrose.co.uk

Contact *Guy Rose*

Founded 1984. Handles fiction; scripts for film and TV; biography; show business; current affairs and teenage fiction. No science fiction, fantasy or young children's. CLIENTS include Joanne & Jerry Dryansky, Royston Ellis, Adam Hamdy, Paul Hendy, Eric MacInnes, Paul Marx, Francis Matthews, Paul Rattigan, Liz Rettig, Yvonne Ridley, Pat Silver-Lasky, Iain Duncan Smith, Toyah Willcox, Simon Woodham. COMMISSION 15–20%. No unsolicited mss. Send preliminary letter with brief resumé, detailed synopsis, first 20 pages (approx.) and s.a.e.

Jüri Gabriel

35 Camberwell Grove, London SE5 8JA
☎020 7703 6186   Fax 020 7703 6186

Contact *Jüri Gabriel*

Handles quality fiction and non-fiction and (almost exclusively for existing clients) film, TV and radio rights. Jüri Gabriel worked in television, wrote books for 20 years and is chairman of Dedalus publishers. No short stories, articles, verse or books for children. CLIENTS include Maurice Caldera, Diana Constance, Miriam Dunne, Pat Gray, Mikka Haugaard, Robert Irwin, John Lucas, David Madsen, Richard Mankiewicz, David Miller, Andy Oakes, John Outram, Philip Roberts, Dr Stefan Szymanski, Frances Treanor, Dr Terence White, Chris Wilkins, Dr Robert Youngson. COMMISSION Home 10%; US & Translation 20%. Unsolicited mss ('two-page synopsis and three sample chapters in first instance, please') welcome if accompanied by return postage and letter giving sufficient information about author's writing experience, aims, etc.

Eric Glass Ltd

25 Ladbroke Crescent, London W11 1PS
☎020 7229 9500   Fax 020 7229 6220
✉ eglassltd@aol.com

Contacts *Janet Glass, Sissi Lichtenstein*

Founded 1934. Handles fiction, non-fiction and scripts for publication or production in all media. No poetry, short stories or children's works. CLIENTS include Pierre Chesnot, Charles

Dyer, Henry Fleet, Tudor Gates, Ronald Millar, and the estates of Rodney Ackland, Marc Camoletti, Jean Cocteau, Wawick Deeping, William Douglas Home, Philip King, Robin Maugham, Beverley Nichols, Jack Popplewell, Jean-Paul Sartre. COMMISSION Home 15%; US & Translation 20%. OVERSEAS ASSOCIATES in the US, Australia, France, Germany, Greece, Holland, Italy, Japan, Poland, Scandinavia, South Africa, Spain. No unsolicited mss. Return postage required. No reading fee.

David Godwin Associates

55 Monmouth Street, London WC2H 9DG
☎020 7240 9992   Fax 020 7395 6110
✉ assistant@davidgodwinassociates.co.uk
www.davidgodwinassociates.co.uk
Contact *David Godwin*

Founded 1996. Handles literary and general fiction, non-fiction, biography. No scripts, science fiction or children's. No reading fee. COMMISSION Home 10%; Overseas 20%. 'Please contact the office before making a submission.'

Annette Green Authors' Agency★

1 East Cliff Road, Tunbridge Wells TN4 9AD
☎01892 514275   Fax 01892 518124
✉ annettekgreen@aol.com
www.annettegreenagency.co.uk
Contact *Address material to the Agency*

Founded 1998. Handles literary and general fiction and non-fiction, popular culture and current affairs, science, music, film, history, biography, children's and teenage fiction. No dramatic scripts or poetry. CLIENTS include Andrew Baker, Nick Barlay, Bill Broady, Simon Conway, Terry Darlington, Fiona Gibson, Justin Hill, Anvar Khan, Maria McCann, Adam Macqueen, Ian Marchant, Professor Charles Pasternak, Kirsty Scott, Bernadette Strachan, Elizabeth Woodcraft. COMMISSION Home 15%; US & Translation 20%. Letter, synopsis, sample chapters and s.a.e. essential. No reading fee.

Christine Green Authors' Agent★

6 Whitehorse Mews, Westminster Bridge Road, London SE1 7QD
☎020 7401 8844   Fax 020 7401 8860
✉ info@christinegreen.co.uk
www.christinegreen.co.uk
Contact *Christine Green*

Founded 1984. Handles fiction (general and literary) and general non-fiction. No scripts, poetry or children's. COMMISSION Home 10%;

US & Translation 20%. No unsolicited mss; initial letter and synopsis preferred. No reading fee but return postage essential.

Louise Greenberg Books Ltd★

The End House, Church Crescent, London N3 1BG
☎020 8349 1179   Fax 020 8343 4559
✉ louisegreenberg@msn.com
Contact *Louise Greenberg*

Founded 1997. Handles full-length literary fiction and serious non-fiction only. COMMISSION Home 15%; US & Translation 20%. DRAMATIC ASSOCIATE Micheline Steinberg Associates; CHILDREN'S ASSOCIATE Sarah Mason Literary Agent. *No telephone approaches.* No reading fee. S.a.e. essential.

Greene & Heaton Ltd★

37 Goldhawk Road, London W12 8QQ
☎020 8749 0315   Fax 020 8749 0318
www.greeneheaton.co.uk
Contacts *Carol Heaton, Judith Murray, Antony Topping, Linda Davis* (children's), *Will Francis*

A medium-sized agency with a broad range of clients. Handles all types of fiction and non-fiction. No original scripts for theatre, film or TV. CLIENTS include Mark Barrowcliffe, Bill Bryson, Jan Dalley, Marcus du Sautoy, Hugh Fearnley-Whittingstall, Michael Frayn, P.D. James, William Leith, Mary Morrissy, C.J. Sansom, William Shawcross, Sarah Waters. COMMISSION Home 15%; US & Translation 20%. OVERSEAS ASSOCIATES worldwide. No reply to unsolicited submissions without s.a.e. and/or return postage.

Gregory & Company, Authors' Agents★ (formerly Gregory & Radice)

3 Barb Mews, London W6 7PA
☎020 7610 4676   Fax 020 7610 4686
✉ info@gregoryandcompany.co.uk
www.gregoryandcompany.co.uk
Contact *Jane Gregory*
Editorial Manager *Anna Valdinger*
Rights Manager *Claire Morris*
Administration *Jemma McDonagh*

Founded 1987. Handles all kinds of fiction and general non-fiction. Special interest fiction – literary, commercial, women's fiction, crime, suspense and thrillers. 'We are particularly interested in books which will also sell to publishers abroad.' No original plays, film or TV scripts (only published books are sold to film and TV). No science fiction, fantasy, poetry, academic or children's books. No reading fee. Editorial advice given to own authors. COMMISSION Home 15%; US, Translation, Radio/TV/Film 20%. Is well represented throughout Europe, Asia and US. No unsolicited mss; send a preliminary letter with c.v., synopsis, first three chapters and future writing plans (plus return postage). Short submissions by fax or e-mail in the first instance (max. five pages).

David Grossman Literary Agency Ltd

118b Holland Park Avenue, London W11 4UA
☎020 7221 2770   Fax 020 7221 1445

Contact *Submissions Dept.*

Founded 1976. Handles full-length fiction and general non-fiction – good writing of all kinds and anything healthily controversial. No verse or technical books for students. No original screenplays or teleplays (only works existing in volume form are sold for performance rights). Generally works with published writers of fiction only but 'truly original, well-written novels from beginners' will be considered. COMMISSION Rates vary for different markets. OVERSEAS ASSOCIATES throughout Europe, Asia, Brazil and the US. Best approach by preliminary letter giving full description of the work and, in the case of fiction, with the first 50 pages. 'Please ensure material is printed in at least 1½ spacing on one side of paper only; that all pages are numbered consecutively throughout and in minimum 11pt typeface.' All material must be accompanied by return postage. No approaches or submissions by fax or e-mail. No unsolicited mss. No reading fee.

The Rod Hall Agency Limited

3 Charlotte Mews, London W1T 4DZ
☎020 7637 0706   Fax 020 7637 0807
✉ office@rodhallagency.com
www.rodhallagency.com

Contact *Charlotte Mann*

Founded 1997. Handles drama for film, TV and theatre and writers-directors. Does not represent writers of episodes for TV series where the format is provided but represents originators of series. CLIENTS include Simon Beaufoy (*The Full Monty*), Jeremy Brock (*Mrs Brown*), Liz Lochhead (*Perfect Days*), Martin McDonagh (*The Pillowman*), Simon Nye (*Men Behaving Badly*). COMMISSION Home 10%; US 15%; Translation 20%. No reading fee.

Margaret Hanbury Literary Agency★

27 Walcot Square, London SE11 4UB
☎020 7735 7680   Fax 020 7793 0316
✉ maggie@hanburyagency.demon.co.uk

Contact *Margaret Hanbury*

Personally run agency representing quality fiction and non-fiction. No plays, scripts, poetry, children's books, fantasy, horror. CLIENTS include J.G. Ballard, Simon Callow, George Alagiah, Judith Lennox, Jane Glover, Jordan. COMMISSION Home 15%; Overseas 20%. No unsolicited approaches.

Roger Hancock Ltd

4 Water Lane, London NW1 8NZ
☎020 7267 4418   Fax 020 7267 0705
✉ info@rogerhancock.com

Contact *Material should be addressed to the Company*

Founded 1960. Special interests: comedy drama and light entertainment. Scripts only. No books. COMMISSION Home 10%; Overseas 15%. Unsolicited mss not welcome. Initial phone call required. No reading fee.

Antony Harwood Limited

103 Walton Street, Oxford OX2 6EB
☎01865 559615   Fax 01865 310660
✉ mail@antonyharwood.com
www.antonyharwood.com

Contacts *Antony Harwood, James Macdonald Lockhart*

Founded 2000. Handles fiction and non-fiction. CLIENTS Amanda Craig, Peter F. Hamilton, Alan Hollinghurst, A.L. Kennedy, Douglas Kennedy, Chris Manby, George Monbiot, Tim Parks. COMMISSION Home 15%; US & Translation 20%. Send letter and synopsis with return postage in the first instance. No reading fee.

A.M. Heath & Co. Ltd★

6 Warwick Court, London WC1R 5DJ
☎020 7242 2811   Fax 020 7242 2711
www.amheath.com

Contacts *Bill Hamilton, Sara Fisher, Sarah Molloy, Victoria Hobbs*

Founded 1919. Handles fiction, general non-fiction and children's. No dramatic scripts, poetry or short stories. CLIENTS include Christopher Andrew, Bella Bathurst, Anita Brookner, Helen Cresswell, Patricia Duncker, Geoff Dyer, Katie Fforde, Lesley Glaister, Graham Hancock, Conn Iggulden, Hilary Mantel, Hilary Norman, Susan Price, John Sutherland, Adam Thorpe, Barbara

Trapido. COMMISSION Home 10–15%; US & Translation 20%; Film & TV 15%. OVERSEAS ASSOCIATES in the US, Europe, South America, Japan and the Far East. Preliminary letter and synopsis essential. No reading fee.

Rupert Heath Literary Agency

The Beeches, Furzedown Lane, Amport SP11 8BW
☎020 7788 7807   Fax 020 7691 9331
✉ emailtheagency@rupertheath.com

Contact *Rupert Heath*

Founded 2000. Handles literary and general fiction and non-fiction, including history, biography and autobiography, current affairs, popular science, the arts and popular culture. No scripts or poetry. COMMISSION Home 15%; US & Translation 20%. OVERSEAS ASSOCIATES worldwide. Approach with e-mail or letter (sample chapter and s.a.e.). E-mail submission preferred. No reading fee.

Henser Literary Agency

174 Pennant Road, Llanelli SA14 8HN
☎01554 753520
✉ henserliteraryagency@btopenworld.com

Contact *Steve Henser*

Founded 2002. Handles mystery, mainstream, literary fiction, fantasy, science fiction. Also film, TV, radio and theatre scripts. No horror. Specialises in translations from Japanese into English – especially literary fiction. CLIENTS include John Campbell, Mary Matsumoto. COMMISSION Home 15%; Foreign & Translation 20%. No unsolicited mss, synopses or ideas as not looking for additional clients at this time.

hhb agency ltd

6 Warwick Court, London WC1R 5DJ
☎020 7405 5525   Fax 020 7405 5525
✉ heather@hhbagency.com
www.hhbagency.com

Contact *Heather Holden-Brown*

Founded in 2005 by Heather Holden-Brown, a publishing editor for 20 years with Waterstone's, Harrap, BBC Books and Headline. Handles non-fiction: journalism, history and politics, contemporary autobiography/biography, entertainment and TV, mainstream business, family memoir, cookery and diet; fiction: commercial women's and some historical. No scripts. COMMISSION Home 15%. No unsolicited mss; please contact by e-mail or telephone before sending any material. No reading fee.

David Higham Associates Ltd★

5–8 Lower John Street, Golden Square, London W1F 9HA
☎020 7434 5900   Fax 020 7437 1072
✉ dha@davidhigham.co.uk
www.davidhigham.co.uk

Books *Anthony Goff, Bruce Hunter, Jacqueline Korn, Veronique Baxter, Lizzy Kremer, Caroline Walsh* (children's)
Scripts *Nicky Lund, Georgina Ruffhead, Gemma Hirst*

Founded 1935. Handles fiction, general non-fiction (biography, history, current affairs, etc.) and children's books. Also scripts. CLIENTS include John le Carré, J.M. Coetzee, Stephen Fry, Jane Green, James Herbert, Alexander McCall Smith, Jacqueline Wilson. COMMISSION Home 15%; US & Translation 20%; Scripts 10%. Preliminary letter with synopsis essential in first instance. No reading fee.

Vanessa Holt Ltd★

59 Crescent Road, Leigh-on-Sea SS9 2PF
☎01702 473787   Fax 01702 471890
✉ vanessa@holtlimited.freeserve.co.uk

Contact *Vanessa Holt*

Founded 1989. Handles general fiction, non-fiction and non-illustrated children's books. No scripts, poetry, academic or technical. Specialises in crime fiction, commercial and literary fiction, and particularly interested in books with potential for sales abroad and/or to TV. COMMISSION Home 15%; US & Translation 20%; Radio/TV/Film 15%. Represented in all foreign markets. No unsolicited mss. Representation by arrangement only.

Kate Hordern Literary Agency

18 Mortimer Road, Clifton, Bristol BS8 4EY
☎0117 923 9368   Fax 0117 973 1941
✉ katehordern@blueyonder.co.uk

Contact *Kate Hordern*

Founded 1999. Handles quality literary and commercial fiction including women's, suspense and genre fiction; also general non-fiction. CLIENTS Richard Bassett, Jeff Dawson, Leigh Eduardo, Kylie Fitzpatrick, Duncan Hewitt, J.T. Lees, Will Randall. COMMISSION Home 15%; US & Translation 20%. OVERSEAS ASSOCIATES Carmen Balcells Agency, Spain; Synopsis Agency, Russia and various agencies in Asia. Approach in writing in the first instance with details of project. New clients taken on very selectively. Synopsis required for fiction; proposal/chapter breakdown for non-fiction.

Sample chapters on request only. S.a.e. essential. No reading fee.

Valerie Hoskins Associates Limited
20 Charlotte Street, London W1T 2NA
☎020 7637 4490   Fax 020 7637 4493
✉ vha@vhassociates.co.uk

Contacts *Valerie Hoskins, Rebecca Watson*

Founded 1983. Handles scripts for film, TV and radio. Special interests feature films, animation and TV. COMMISSION Home 12½%; US 20% (maximum). No unsolicited scripts; preliminary letter of introduction essential. No reading fee.

ICM
Oxford House, 76 Oxford Street, London W1D 1BS
☎020 7636 6565   Fax 020 7323 0101
✉ admin@icmlondon.co.uk

Contacts *Sue Rodgers, Jessica Sykes, Cathy King, Greg Hunt, Hugo Young, Michael McCoy, Duncan Heath, Paul Lyon-Maris*

Founded 1973. Specialises in scripts for film, theatre, TV and radio. No reading fee. COMMISSION 10%. OVERSEAS ASSOCIATES ICM, New York/Los Angeles.

ICM Books
International Creative Management Ltd, 4–6 Soho Square, London W1D 3PZ
☎020 7432 0800   Fax 020 7432 0808
www.icmtalent.com

Contact *Kate Jones*

Handles fiction and non-fiction; no plays or scripts. OVERSEAS ASSOCIATE International Creative Management Inc., 40 West 57th Street, New York, NY 10019, USA. Submissions must include sample chapters and letter. No reading fee.

The Inspira Group
5 Bradley Road, Enfield EN3 6ES
☎020 8292 5163   Fax 0870 139 3057
✉ darin@theinspiragroup.com
www.theinspiragroup.com

Managing Director *Darin Jewell*

Founded 2001. Handles children's books, fiction, humour, lifestyle/relationships, science fiction/fantasy. No scripts. CLIENTS Paul Rogan, Jasmine Birtles, Mike Anderiesz. COMMISSION Home & US 15%. Unsolicited mss and synopses welcome; approach by e-mail or telephone. No reading fee but do ask authors to pay for editing, if required.

Intercontinental Literary Agency★
33 Bedford Street, London WC2E 9ED
☎020 7379 6611   Fax 020 7379 6790
✉ ila@ila-agency.co.uk

Contacts *Nicki Kennedy, Sam Edenborough*

Founded 1965. Handles translation rights only for, among others, the authors of PFD, London; PFD, New York; LAW Ltd, London; Harold Matson Co. Inc., New York.

International Scripts
1A Kidbrooke Park Road, London SE3 0LR
☎020 8319 8666   Fax 020 8319 0801

Contacts *Bob Tanner, Pat Hornsey, Jill Lawson*

Founded 1979 by Bob Tanner. Handles most types of books (non-fiction and fiction) and scripts for most media. No poetry, articles or short stories. CLIENTS include Jane Adams, Zita Adamson, Ashleigh Bingham, Simon Clark, Dr James Fleming, June Gadsby, Ed Gorman, Julie Harris, Robert A. Heinlein, Anna Jacobs, Anne Jones, Richard Laymon, Trevor Lummis, Nick Oldham, Chris Pascoe, Christine Poulson, John and Anne Spencer, Janet Woods. COMMISSION Home 15%; US & Translation 20%. OVERSEAS ASSOCIATES include Ralph Vicinanza, USA; Thomas Schlück, Germany; Eliane Benisti, France. Preliminary letter plus s.a.e. required. An editorial contribution plus return postage may be requested for reading mss.

Barrie James Literary Agency
(including **New Authors Showcase**)
Rivendell, Kingsgate Close, Torquay TQ2 8QA
☎01803 326617
✉ mail@newauthors.org.uk
www.newauthors.org.uk

Contact *Barrie James*

Founded 1997. No unsolicited mss. First approach should be made by sending s.a.e. or e-mail. No reading fee but small charge is made for display on the Internet.

Janklow & Nesbit (UK) Ltd
33 Drayson Mews, London W8 4LY
☎020 7376 2733   Fax 020 7376 2915
✉ queries@janklow.co.uk

Contacts *Tif Loehnis, Claire Paterson*

Founded 2000. Handles fiction and non-fiction; commercial and literary. (See also Janklow & Nesbit Associates, New York, under *US Literary Agents*.) No unsolicited mss. Send full outline (non-fiction), synopsis and three sample chapters (fiction) plus informative covering letter and return postage.

Johnson & Alcock★

Clerkenwell House, 45–47 Clerkenwell Green, London EC1R 0HT
☎020 7251 0125   Fax 020 7251 2172
✉ info@johnsonandalcock.co.uk

Contacts *Michael Alcock, Andrew Hewson, Anna Power, Merel Reinink*

Founded 1956. Handles literary and commercial fiction, children's fiction; general non-fiction including current affairs, biography and memoirs, history, lifestyle, health and personal development. No poetry, screenplays, science fiction, technical or academic material. COMMISSION Home 15%; US & Translation 20%. No unsolicited mss; approach by letter in the first instance giving details of writing and other media experience, plus synopsis. For fiction send one-page synopsis and first three chapters. S.a.e. essential for response. No reading fee.

Jane Judd Literary Agency★

18 Belitha Villas, London N1 1PD
☎020 7607 0273   Fax 020 7607 0623

Contact *Jane Judd*

Founded 1986. Handles general fiction and non-fiction: women's fiction, crime, thrillers, literary fiction, humour, biography, investigative journalism, health, women's interests and travel. 'Looking for good contemporary women's fiction but not Mills & Boon-type; also historical fiction and non-fiction.' No scripts, academic, gardening, short stories or DIY. CLIENTS include Andy Dougan, Cliff Goodwin, Jill Mansell, Jonathon Porritt, Rosie Rushton, Manda Scott, David Winner. COMMISSION Home 10%; US & Translation 20%. Approach with letter, including synopsis, first chapter and s.a.e. Initial telephone call helpful in the case of non-fiction.

Juvenilia

Avington, Near Winchester SO21 1DB
☎01962 779656   Fax 01962 779656
✉ juvenilia@clara.co.uk

Contact *Rosemary Bromley*

Founded 1973. Handles young/teen fiction and picture books; non-fiction. Scripts for TV and radio by existing clients only. No poetry or short stories unless part of a collection or picture book material. CLIENTS include Paul Aston, Elisabeth Beresford, Linda Birch, Denis Bond, Katie Cumm, Terry Deary, Ann Evans, Gaye Hicyilmaz, Cathy Hopkins, Tony Maddox, Phil McMylor, Anna Perara, Elizabeth Pewsey, Fran

and John Pickering, Saviour Pirotta, Kelvin Reynolds, James Riordan, Peter Riley, Susan Rollings, Malcolm Rose, Cathy Simpson, Keith West. COMMISSION Home 10%; US 15%; Translation 20%. No unsolicited mss. 'Client list is currently full.' Enquiries by phone, fax or e-mail will not be answered.

Tamar Karet Literary Agency

56 Priory Road, London N8 7EX
☎020 8340 6460   Fax 020 8348 8638
✉ tamar.karet.agent@btinternet.com

Contact *Tamar Karet*

Specialises in fiction, travel, leisure, biography, history, social affairs and politics. No academic, children's, poetry, science fiction, horror, militaria or scripts. COMMISSION Home 15%; US & Translation 20%. No unsolicited mss; no submissions by e-mail. Send synopsis and brief sample with s.a.e.

Michelle Kass Associates★

36–38 Glasshouse Street, London W1B 5DL
☎020 7439 1624   Fax 020 7734 3394
✉ office@michellekass.co.uk

Contacts *Michelle Kass, Julia Johnson*

Founded 1991. Handles literary fiction, film and television primarily. COMMISSION Home 10%; US & Translation 15–20%. No mss accepted without preliminary phone call/e-mail. No reading fee.

Frances Kelly★

111 Clifton Road, Kingston upon Thames KT2 6PL
☎020 8549 7830   Fax 020 8547 0051

Contact *Frances Kelly*

Founded 1978. Handles non-fiction, including illustrated: biography, history, art, self-help, food & wine, complementary medicine and therapies, finance and business books; and academic non-fiction in all disciplines. No scripts except for existing clients. COMMISSION Home 10%; US & Translation 20%. No unsolicited mss. Approach by letter with brief description of work or synopsis, together with c.v. and return postage.

Knight Features

20 Crescent Grove, London SW4 7AH
☎020 7622 1467   Fax 020 7622 1522
✉ peter@knightfeatures.co.uk

Contacts *Peter Knight, Samantha Ferris, Gaby Martin, Andrew Knight*

Founded 1985. Handles motor sports, cartoon

books, puzzles, business, history, factual and bio-graphical material. No poetry, science fiction or cookery. CLIENTS include Frank Dickens, Gray Jolliffe, Angus McGill, Chris Maslanka, Barbara Minto. COMMISSION dependent upon authors and territories. OVERSEAS ASSOCIATES United Media, US; Auspac Media, Australia; Puzzle Co., New Zealand. No unsolicited mss and no e-mail submissions. Send letter accompanied by c.v. and s.a.e. with synopsis of proposed work.

LAW★

14 Vernon Street, London W14 0RJ
☎020 7471 7900   Fax 020 7471 7910

Contacts *Mark Lucas, Julian Alexander, Araminta Whitley, Alice Saunders, Celia Hayley, Lucinda Cook, Peta Nightingale, Lizzie Jones, Katie Mankin, Philippa Milnes-Smith* (children's), *Helen Norris* (children's)

Founded 1996. Handles full-length commercial and literary fiction, non-fiction and children's books. No fantasy (except children's), plays, poetry or textbooks. Film and TV scripts handled for established clients only. COMMISSION Home 15%; US & Translation 20%. OVERSEAS ASSOCIATES worldwide. Unsolicited mss considered; send brief covering letter, short synopsis and two sample chapters. S.a.e. essential. No e-mailed or disk submissions.

LBA

See **Luigi Bonomi Associates Limited**

Barbara Levy Literary Agency★

64 Greenhill, Hampstead High Street, London NW3 5TZ
☎020 7435 9046   Fax 020 7431 2063

Contacts *Barbara Levy, John Selby*

Founded 1986. Handles general fiction, non-fiction, and film and TV rights. COMMISSION Home 10%; US 20%; Translation by arrange-ment, in conjunction with The Marsh Agency. US ASSOCIATE Writers House, New York. No unsolicited mss. Send detailed preliminary letter in the first instance. No reading fee.

Limelight Management★

33 Newman Street, London W1T 1PY
☎020 7637 2529   Fax 020 7637 2538
✉ limelight.management@virgin.net
www.limelightmanagement.com

Contacts *Fiona Lindsay, Linda Shanks*

Founded 1991. Handles general non-fiction: cookery, gardening, antiques, interior design, wine, art and crafts and health. No fiction, TV, film, radio or theatre. Specialises in illustrated books. COMMISSION Home 15%; US & Translation 20%. Unsolicited mss welcome; send preliminary letter (s.a.e. essential). No reading fee.

The Christopher Little Literary Agency★

10 Eel Brook Studios, 125 Moore Park Road, London SW6 4PS
☎020 7736 4455   Fax 020 7736 4490
✉ info@christopherlittle.net *or* firstname@christopherlittle.net
www.christopherlittle.net

Contacts *Christopher Little, Kellee Nunley, Emma Schlesinger, Neil Blair* (legal)

Founded 1979. Handles commercial and literary full-length fiction and non-fiction. No poetry, plays, science fiction, fantasy, textbooks, illus-trated children's or short stories. Film scripts for established clients only. AUTHORS include Steve Barlow and Steve Skidmore, Paul Bajoria, Andrew Butcher, Will Daws, Janet Gleeson, Carol Hughes, Alastair MacNeill, Robert Mawson, Haydn Middleton, A.J. Quinnell, Robert Radcliffe, J.K. Rowling, Darren Shan, Wladyslaw Szpilman, John Watson. COMMISSION Home 15%; US, Canada, Translation, Audio & Motion Picture 20%. Send detailed preliminary letter in the first instance with synopsis, first 2–3 chapters and s.a.e. No reading fee.

London Independent Books

26 Chalcot Crescent, London NW1 8YD
☎020 7706 0486   Fax 020 7724 3122

Proprietor *Carolyn Whitaker*

Founded 1971. A self-styled 'small and idiosyn-cratic' agency. Handles fiction and non-fiction reflecting the tastes of the proprietor. All subjects considered (except computer books and young children's), providing the treatment is strong and saleable. Scripts handled only if by existing clients. Special interests: boats, travelogues, com-mercial fiction, science fiction and fantasy, teenage fiction. COMMISSION Home 15%; US & Translation 20%. No unsolicited mss; letter, syn-opsis and first two chapters with return postage the best approach. No reading fee.

The Andrew Lownie Literary Agency★

17 Sutherland Street, London SW1V 4JU
☎020 7828 1274   Fax 020 7828 7608
✉ lownie@globalnet.co.uk
www.andrewlownie.co.uk

Contact *Andrew Lownie*

Founded 1988. Specialises in non-fiction, especially history, biography, current affairs, military history, UFOs, reference and packaging celebrities and journalists for the book market. No poetry, short stories or science fiction. Formerly a journalist, publisher and himself the author of 12 non-fiction books, Andrew Lownie's CLIENTS include Richard Aldrich, Juliet Barker, the Joyce Cary estate, Tom Divine, Jonathan Fryer, Laurence Gardner, Timothy Good, Robert Holden, Lawrence James, Robert Jobson, Julian Maclaren-Ross estate, Patrick MacNee, Norma Major, Sir John Mills, Tom Pocock, Nick Pope, John Rae, Richard Rudgley, Desmond Seward, David Stafford, Alan Whicker, Lawrence James, editors of the *Oxford Classical Dictionary* and *Cambridge Guide to Literature in English*. Translation rights handled by The Marsh Agency. COMMISSION Worldwide 15%. Approach with letter, synopsis, sample chapter and s.a.e.

Lucas Alexander Whitley
See **LAW**

Lutyens and Rubinstein★
231 Westbourne Park Road, London
W11 1EB
☎020 7792 4855   Fax 020 7792 4833

Partners *Sarah Lutyens, Felicity Rubinstein*
Submissions *Susannah Godman*

Founded 1993. Handles adult fiction and non-fiction books. No TV, film, radio, theatre scripts. COMMISSION Home 15%; US & Translation 20%. Unsolicited mss accepted; send introductory letter with c.v., two chapters and return postage for all material submitted. No reading fee.

Duncan McAra
28 Beresford Gardens, Edinburgh EH5 3ES
☎0131 552 1558   Fax 0131 552 1558
✉ duncanmcara@hotmail.com

Contact *Duncan McAra*

Founded 1988. Handles fiction (literary fiction) and non-fiction, including art, architecture, archaeology, biography, military, travel and books of Scottish interest. COMMISSION Home 10%; Overseas 20%. Preliminary letter, synopsis and sample chapter (including return postage) essential. No reading fee.

Bill McLean Personal Management Ltd
23B Deodar Road, London SW15 2NP
☎020 8789 8191

Contact *Bill McLean*

Founded 1972. Handles scripts for all media. No books. CLIENTS include Dwynwen Berry, Graham Carlisle, Pat Cumper, Jane Galletly, Patrick Jones, Tony Jordan, Bill Lyons, John Maynard, Michael McStay, Les Miller, Ian Rowlands, Jeffrey Segal, Richard Shannon, Ronnie Smith, Barry Thomas, Garry Tyler, Frank Vickery, Laura Watson, Mark Wheatley. COMMISSION Home 10%. No unsolicited mss. Phone call or introductory letter essential. No reading fee.

Eunice McMullen Children's Literary Agent Ltd
Low Ibbotsholme Cottage, Off Bridge Lane, Troutbeck Bridge, Windermere LA23 1HU
☎01539 448551   Fax 01539 442289
✉ eunicemcmullen@totalise.co.uk
www.eunicemcmullen.co.uk

Contact *Eunice McMullen*

Founded 1992. Handles all types of children's material. Has 'an excellent' list of picture book authors and illustrators. CLIENTS include Wayne Anderson, Sam Childs, Caroline Jayne Church, Jason Cockcroft, Ross Collins, Charles Fuge, Susie Jenkin-Pearce, Angela McAllister, David Melling, Sue Porter, Angie Sage, Susan Winter, David Wood. COMMISSION Home 10%; US 15%; Translation 20%. *No unsolicited scripts.* Telephone enquiries only.

Andrew Mann Ltd★
1 Old Compton Street, London W1D 5JA
☎020 7734 4751   Fax 020 7287 9264
✉ manscript@onetel.com

Contacts *Anne Dewe, Tina Betts, Sacha Elliot*

Founded 1975. Handles fiction, general non-fiction, children's and film, TV, theatre, radio scripts. COMMISSION Home 15%; US & Translation 20%. OVERSEAS ASSOCIATES various. No unsolicited mss. Preliminary letter, synopsis and s.a.e. essential. E-mail submissions for synopses only. No reading fee.

Sarah Manson Literary Agent
6 Totnes Walk, London N2 0AD
☎020 88442 0396
✉ info@sarahmanson.com
www.sarahmanson.com

Contact *Sarah Manson*

Founded 2002. Handles quality fiction for children and young adults. COMMISSION Home 10%; Overseas & Translation 20%. Please consult website or submission guidelines. No reading fee.

Marjacq Scripts Ltd
34 Devonshire Place, London W1G 6JW
☎020 7935 9499   Fax 020 7935 9115
✉ subs@marjacq.com
www.marjacq.com
Contact *Philip Patterson* (books), *Luke Speed* (film/TV)
Handles fiction and non-fiction, literary and commercial as well as film, TV, radio scripts. No poetry. COMMISSION Home 10%; Overseas 20%. New work welcome; send brief letter, synopsis and approx. first 50 pages plus s.a.e. No reading fee.

The Marsh Agency Ltd★
11/12 Dover Street, London W1S 4LJ
☎020 7399 2800   Fax 020 7399 2801
✉ enquiries@marsh-agency.co.uk
www.marsh-agency.co.uk
Contacts *Paul Marsh, Chris Van Raaijen, Camilla Ferrier, Caroline Hardman*
Founded 1994. International rights specialists selling English and foreign language writing. No TV, film, radio or theatre. CLIENTS include several British and American agencies and publishers, and some individual authors. See also Paterson Marsh Ltd. Unsolicited mss considered; send brief covering letter, short synopsis and three sample chapters. S.a.e. essential.

MBA Literary Agents Ltd★
62 Grafton Way, London W1T 5DW
☎020 7387 2076   Fax 020 7387 2042
✉ firstname@mbalit.co.uk
www.mbalit.co.uk
Contacts *Diana Tyler, John Richard Parker, Meg Davis, Laura Longrigg, David Riding, Sophie Gorell, Susan Smith, Jean Kitson*
Founded 1971. Handles fiction and non-fiction, TV, film, radio and theatre scripts. Works in conjunction with agents in most countries. Also UK representative for Donald Maass Agency, Frances Collin Literary Agency, Martha Millard Literary Agency and the JABberwocky Agency. COMMISSION Home 15%; Overseas 20%; Theatre/TV/Radio 10%; Film 10–20%. No unsolicited mss.

Christy Moore Ltd
See **Sheil Land Associates Ltd**

William Morris Agency (UK) Ltd★
52/53 Poland Street, London W1F 7LX
☎020 7534 6800   Fax 020 7534 6900
www.wma.com

Managing Director *Stephanie Cabot*
London office founded in 1965. Worldwide theatrical and literary agency with offices in New York, Beverly Hills, Nashville, Miami and Shanghai. Handles fiction, general non-fiction, TV and film scripts. COMMISSION TV 10%; UK Books 15%; US Books & Translation 20%. Mss for books including covering letter to Book Department; single page synopsis, s.a.e. Limit submission to one title; sample to 50 pages or less. No reading fee.

Michael Motley Ltd
The Old Vicarage, Tredington, Tewkesbury GL20 7BP
☎01684 276390   Fax 01684 297355
Contact *Michael Motley*
Founded 1973. Handles only full-length mss (i.e. 60,000+). No short stories or journalism. No science fiction, horror, poetry or original dramatic material. COMMISSION Home 10%; US 15%; Translation 20%. OVERSEAS ASSOCIATES in all publishing centres. New clients by referral only: no unsolicited material considered. No reading fee.

Judith Murdoch Literary Agency★
19 Chalcot Square, London NW1 8YA
☎020 7722 4197
Contact *Judith Murdoch*
Founded 1993. Handles full-length fiction only, especially accessible literary and commercial women's fiction. No science fiction/fantasy, children's, poetry or short stories. CLIENTS include Alison Bond, Meg Hutchinson, Lisa Jewell, Pamela Jooste, Eve Makis. Translation rights handled by The Marsh Agency. COMMISSION Home 15%; US & Translation 20%. No unsolicited mss; approach in writing only enclosing first two chapters and brief synopsis. Submissions by e-mail cannot be considered. Return postage/s.a.e. essential. Editorial advice given. No reading fee.

The Narrow Road Company
182 Brighton Road, Coulsdon CR5 2NF
☎020 8763 9895   Fax 020 8763 2558
✉ richardireson@narrowroad.co.uk
Contacts *Richard Ireson, James Ireson*
Founded 1986. Part of the Narrow Road Group. Theatrical literary agency. Handles scripts for TV, theatre, film and radio. No novels or poetry. CLIENTS include Geoff Aymer, Steve Gooch, David Halliwell, Ian Kershaw, Simon McAllum, Marty Ross, Tim Sanders, Andy

Smith. No unsolicited mss; approach by letter with c.v. only. Interested in writers with some experience and original ideas.

The Maggie Noach Literary Agency★

22 Dorville Crescent, London W6 0HJ
☎020 8748 2926   Fax 020 8748 8057
✉ m-noach@dircon.co.uk

Contact *Maggie Noach*

Founded 1982. Pronounced 'no-ack'. Recommended for promising young writers but very few new clients taken on as it is considered vital to give individual attention to each author's work. Will consider high quality full-length fiction; general non-fiction (especially travel and history); children's books (text only) for reading age 8 and upwards. No short stories, poetry, plays, screenplays, cookery, gardening, mind, body & spirit, scientific/academic or specialist non-fiction. 'Absolutely *no* illustrated books.' COMMISSION Home 15%; US & Translation 20%. 'No submissions from authors resident outside the UK as we work very closely with our clients.' Initial approach should consist of a brief description of the book plus two/three sample chapters. Return postage essential. 'We do *not* open e-mail attachments or consider faxed submissions.' No reading fee.

Andrew Nurnberg Associates Ltd★

Clerkenwell House, 45–47 Clerkenwell Green, London EC1R 0QX
☎020 7417 8800   Fax 020 7417 8812
✉ all@nurnberg.co.uk

Directors *Andrew Nurnberg, Sarah Nundy, D. Roger Seaton, Vicky Mark*

Founded in the mid-1970s. Specialises in foreign rights, representing leading authors and agents. Branches in Moscow, Budapest, Prague, Sofia, Warsaw, Riga, Beijing and Taipei. COMMISSION Home 15%; US & Translation 20%.

Alexandra Nye

'Craigower', 6 Kinnoull Avenue, Dunblane FK15 9JG
☎01786 825114

Contact *Alexandra Nye*

Founded 1991. Handles fiction and topical non-fiction. Special interests: literary fiction and history. CLIENTS include Dr Tom Gallagher, Harry Mehta, Robin Jenkins. COMMISSION Home 10%; US 20%; Translation 15%. Un-

solicited mss welcome (s.a.e. essential for return). No phone calls. Preliminary approach by letter, with synopsis, preferred. Reading fee for supply of detailed report.

David O'Leary Literary Agents

10 Lansdowne Court, Lansdowne Rise, London W11 2NR
☎020 7229 1623   Fax 020 7229 1623
✉ d.o'leary@virgin.net

Contact *David O'Leary*

Founded 1988. Handles fiction, both popular and literary, and non-fiction. Areas of interest include thrillers, history, popular science, Russia and Ireland (history and fiction). No poetry or science fiction. CLIENTS include David Crackanthorpe, James Kennedy, Nick Kochan, Jim Lusby, Derek Malcolm, Ken Russell. COMMISSION Home & US 10%. OVERSEAS ASSOCIATES Lennart Sane, Scandinavia/Spain/ South America; Tuttle Mori, Japan. No unsolicited mss but happy to discuss a proposal. Ring or write in the first instance. No reading fee.

Deborah Owen Ltd★

78 Narrow Street, Limehouse, London E14 8BP
☎020 7987 5119/5441   Fax 020 7538 4004

Contacts *Deborah Owen*

Founded 1971. Small agency specialising in representing authors direct around the world. Handles international fiction and non-fiction (books which can be translated into a number of languages). *No new authors.* CLIENTS Amos Oz and Delia Smith. COMMISSION Home 10%; US & Translation 15%.

Paterson Marsh Ltd★

11/12 Dover Street, London W1S 4LJ
☎020 7399 2800   Fax 020 7399 2801
✉ steph@patersonmarsh.co.uk
www.patersonmarsh.co.uk

Contacts *Mark Paterson* (☎01206 825433; ✉ mark@patersonmarsh.co.uk), *Paul Marsh, Stephanie Ebdon*

Formerly Mark Paterson & Associates, founded 1961. World rights representatives of authors and publishers handling many subjects, with specialisation in psychoanalysis and psychotherapy. CLIENTS range from Balint, Bion, Casement and Ferenczi, through to Freud and Winnicott; plus Hugh Brogan, Peter Moss and the estates of Sir Arthur Evans, Hugh Schonfield and Dorothy Richardson. No fiction, scripts, poetry, children's, articles, short stories or 'unsaleable mediocrity'. COMMISSION 20% (including sub-agent's commission). No unsolicited mss, but preliminary letter and synopsis with s.a.e. welcome.

John Pawsey

60 High Street, Tarring, Worthing BN14 7NR
☎01903 205167   Fax 01903 205167

Contact *John Pawsey*

Founded 1981. Experience in the publishing business has helped to attract some top names here, but the door remains open for bright, new ideas. Handles non-fiction: biography, politics, current affairs, popular culture, travel, sport, business; also fiction: crime, thrillers, suspense but not science fiction, fantasy or horror. Special interests: sport and biography. No children's, drama scripts, poetry, short stories, journalism or academic. CLIENTS include David Rayvern Allen, David Ashforth, Jennie Bond, Elwyn Hartley Edwards, William Fotheringham, Don Hale, Patricia Hall, Dr David Lewis, Anne Mustoe. COMMISSION Home 12½%; US & Translation 19–25%. OVERSEAS ASSOCIATES in the US, Japan, South America and throughout Europe. Preliminary letter with s.a.e. essential (no e-mail submissions). No reading fee.

Maggie Pearlstine Associates Ltd★

31 Ashley Gardens, Ambrosden Avenue, London SW1P 1QE
☎020 7828 4212   Fax 020 7834 5546
✉ post@pearlstine.co.uk

Contact *Maggie Pearlstine*

Founded 1989. Small, selective agency. Handles general non-fiction and fiction. Special interests: history, current affairs, biography and health. No children's, poetry, horror, science fiction, short stories or scripts. Seldom takes on new authors. CLIENTS Matthew Baylis, Kate Bingham, Menzies Campbell, Robin Cook, Frank Dobson, Kim Fletcher, Roy Hattersley, Rachel Holmes, Charles Kennedy, Mark Leonard, Quentin Letts, Claire Macdonald, Prof. Raj Persaud, Prof. Lesley Regan, Hugo Rifkind, Winifred Robinson, Jackie Rowley, Henrietta Spencer-Churchill, Prof. Alan Stewart, Prof. Kathy Sykes, Prof. Robert Winston. Translation rights handled by Gillon Aitken Associates Ltd. COMMISSION Home 12½% (fiction), 10% (non-fiction); US & Translation 20%; TV, Film & Journalism 20%. Prospective clients should write an explanatory letter and enclose s.a.e. and the first three chap-

ters only. No submissions accepted by fax, e-mail or from abroad. No reading fee.

Peters Fraser & Dunlop Group Ltd

See **PFD**

PFD★

Drury House, 34–43 Russell Street, London WC2B 5HA
☎020 7344 1000
Fax 020 7836 9539/7836 9541
✉ postmaster@pfd.co.uk
www.pfd.co.uk

Joint Chairmen *Anthony Jones, Tim Corrie*
Managing Director *Anthony Baring*
Books *Caroline Dawnay, Michael Sissons, Pat Kavanagh, Charles Walker, Rosemary Canter, Robert Kirby, Simon Trewin, James Gill*
Serial *Pat Kavanagh, Carol MacArthur*
Film/TV *Anthony Jones, Tim Corrie, Charles Walker, St. John Donald, Rosemary Scoular, Natasha Galloway, Jago Irwin, Louisa Thompson, Lynda Mamy*
Actors *Maureen Vincent, Dallas Smith, Lindy King, Ruth Young, Lucy Brazier, Kathryn Fleming*
Theatre *Kenneth Ewing, St John Donald, Nicki Stoddart, Rosie Cobbe*
Children's *Rosemary Canter*
Multimedia *Rosemary Scoular*

Founded 1988 as a result of the merger of A.D. Peters & Co. Ltd and Fraser & Dunlop, and was later joined by the June Hall Literary Agency. Handles all sorts of books including fiction and children's, plus scripts for film, theatre, radio and TV material. CLIENTS include Julian Barnes, Alan Bennett, Alain de Botton, estate of C.S. Forester, Nicci Gerrard, Robert Harris, Nick Hornby, Clive James, Russell Miller, estate of Nancy Mitford, John Mortimer, Andrew Motion, Douglas Reeman, Ruth Rendell, estate of Anthony Sampson, Gerald Seymour, Tom Stoppard, Emma Thompson, Joanna Trollope, estate of Evelyn Waugh. COMMISSION Home 10%; US & Translation 20%. Prospective clients should write 'a full letter, with an account of what he/she has done and wants to do and enclose, when possible, a detailed outline and sample chapters'. Screenplays and TV scripts should be addressed to the Film & Script Dept. Enclose return postage. No reading fee. The Children's Dept. accepts unsolicited written material in the form of a covering letter, three initial chapters (works over 1000 words) or entire text; submissions from illustrators also welcome.

Pollinger Limited★
9 Staple Inn, London WC1V 7QH
☎020 7404 0342   Fax 020 7242 5737
✉ info@pollingerltd.com
www.pollingerltd.com
Chairman *Paul Woolf*
Managing Director *Lesley Pollinger*
Agents *Lesley Pollinger, Joanna Devereux*
Permissions *permissions@pollingerltd.com*
Rights Manager *rightsmanager@pollingerltd.com*
Consultants *Leigh Pollinger, Joan Deitch*

Founded 2002. A successor of Laurence Pollinger Limited (founded 1958) and Pearn, Pollinger & Higham. Handles all types of general trade adult and children's fiction and non-fiction books; intellectual property development, illustrators and photographers. CLIENTS include Derry Brabbs, Michael Coleman, Teresa Driscoll, Catherine Fisher, Philip Gross, Catherine Johnson, Kelly McKain, Gary Latham, Sue Mongredien, Gary Paulsen, Nicholas Rhea and Sue Welford. Also the estates of H.E. Bates, Vera Chapman, Louis Bromfield, Erskine Caldwell, D.H. Lawrence, John Masters, W.H. Robinson, Eric Frank Russell, Clifford D. Simak and other notables. COMMISSION Home 15%; Translation 20%. Overseas theatrical, and media associates. No unsolicited material.

Shelley Power
Literary Agency Ltd★
13 rue du Pré Saint Gervais, 75019 Paris, France
☎00 33 1 42 38 36 49
Fax 00 33 1 40 40 70 08
✉ shelley.power@wanadoo.fr
Contact *Shelley Power*

Founded 1976. Shelley Power works between London and Paris. This is an English agency with London-based administration/accounts office and the editorial office in Paris. Handles general commercial fiction, quality fiction, business books, self-help, true crime, investigative exposés, film and entertainment. No scripts, short stories, children's or poetry. COMMISSION Home 10%; US & Translation 19%. Preliminary letter with brief outline of project (plus return postage as from UK or France) essential. 'We do not consider submissions by e-mail.' No reading fee.

Puttick Agency★
46 Brookfield Mansions, Highgate Hill West, London N6 6AT
☎020 8340 6383   Fax 0870 751 8098
✉ agency@puttick.com
www.puttick.com

Contact *Liz Puttick*
Founded 1995. Handles general non-fiction (including illustrated books) with special interest in self-help, mind-body-spirit, health and fitness. Also interested in current affairs, popular culture, biography, history, philosophy, science. No fiction, poetry, scripts, drama or children's books. CLIENTS include William Bloom, Cornel Chin, Mike Fisher, Ann-Marie Gallagher, Nirmala Heriza, Diane Ladd, Martin Lewis, Steve Nobel, Emma Restall Orr, Lorraine Thomas. COMMISSION Home 15%; US & Translation 20%. Works with associates in the US and with The Marsh Agency for translation rights. Preliminary enquiries and c.v. by e-mail. No reading fee, but s.a.e. essential.

PVA Management Limited
Hallow Park, Worcester WR2 6PG
☎01905 640663   Fax 01905 641842
✉ pvamanltd@aol.com
Managing Director *Paul Vaughan*

Founded 1978. Handles non-fiction only. COMMISSION 15%. Send synopsis and sample chapters together with return postage.

Real Creatives Worldwide
14 Dean Street, London W1D 3RS
☎020 7437 4188
✉ malcolm.rasala@realcreatives.com
Contacts *Mark Maco, Malcolm Rasala*

Founded 1984. Specialises in drama, science, technology, factual and entertainment. Represents Hollywood TV/film writers and directors, as well as designers, editors, producers and composers. Has a production arm making motion pictures, television, etc. 'Send letter or e-mail requesting a writer's submission agreement covering libel, defamation, plagiarism, etc.' Reading fee: £125.

Redhammer
186 Bickenhall Mansions, Bickenhall Street, London W1U 6BX
☎020 7224 1748   Fax 020 7224 1802
✉ info@redhammer.biz
www.redhammer.biz
Vice President *Peter Cox*
Vice President *Barbara Gorna*

'Provides in-depth management for a small number of highly talented authors.' Willing to take on unpublished authors who are professional in their approach and who have major international potential, ideally for, book, film and/or tv. CLIENTS Martin Bell OBE, Mihir Bose, Brian Clegg, Caris Davis, Audrey Eyton, Senator Orrin Hatch, Gill Hudson, Amanda Lees, Josh McHugh, David McIntee, Michelle Paver, Saxon Roach, Fiona Ross, Carolyn Soutar, David Soul, Donald Trelford, Justin Wintle. Submissions considered only if the guidelines given on the website have been followed. Do not send unsolicited mss by post. No radio or theatre scripts. No reading fee.

Rogers, Coleridge & White Ltd★

20 Powis Mews, London W11 1JN
☎020 7221 3717   Fax 020 7229 9084

Contacts *Deborah Rogers, Gill Coleridge, Patricia White, Peter Straus, David Miller, Zoe Waldie*
Foreign Rights *Laurence Laluyaux, Stephen Edwards*

Founded 1967. Handles fiction, non-fiction and children's books. No TV or film scripts, plays or technical books. Rights representative in UK and translation for several New York agents. COMMISSION Home 10%; US & Translation 20%. OVERSEAS ASSOCIATE Melanie Jackson Agency, New York. No unsolicited mss, please and no submissions by fax or e-mail.

Uli Rushby-Smith Literary Agency

72 Plimsoll Road, London N4 2EE
☎020 7354 2718   Fax 020 7354 2718

Contact *Uli Rushby-Smith*

Founded 1993. Handles fiction and non-fiction, commercial and literary, both adult and children's. Film and TV rights handled in conjunction with a sub-agent. No plays or poetry. COMMISSION Home 15%; US & Translation 20%. Represents UK rights for Curtis Brown, New York (children's), 2.13.61 USA and Columbia University Press. Approach with an outline, two or three sample chapters and explanatory letter in the first instance (s.a.e. essential). No disks. No reading fee.

Rosemary Sandberg Ltd

6 Bayley Street, London WC1B 3HB
☎020 7304 4110   Fax 020 7304 4109
✉ rosemary@sandberg.demon.co.uk

Contact *Rosemary Sandberg*

Founded 1991. In association with Ed Victor Ltd. Specialises in children's writers and illustrators. COMMISSION 10%. No unsolicited mss as client list is currently full.

The Sayle Literary Agency★

8b King's Parade, Cambridge CB2 1SJ
☎01223 303035   Fax 01223 301638
Proprietor *Rachel Calder*

Handles fiction, crime and general. Non-fiction: current affairs, social issues, travel, biographies, historical. No plays, poetry, children's, textbooks, technical, legal or medical books. CLIENTS Stephen Amidon, Billy Bragg, Pete Davies, Margaret Forster, Georgina Hammick, Andy Kershaw, Phillip Knightley, Denise Mina, Malcolm Pryce, Kate Pullinger, Ronald Searle, Gitta Sereny, Stanley Stewart, William Styron. COMMISSION Home 15%; US & Translation 20%. OVERSEAS ASSOCIATES Dunow & Carlson Literary Agency; Darhansoff, Verrill and Feldman; Anne Edelstein Literary Agency; Sally Wofford-Girand Agency; New England Publishing Associates, USA; translation rights handled by The Marsh Agency; film rights by Sayle Screen Ltd. No unsolicited mss. Preliminary letter essential, including a brief biographical note and a synopsis plus two or three sample chapters. Return postage essential. No reading fee.

Sayle Screen Ltd

11 Jubilee Place, London SW3 3TD
☎020 7823 3883   Fax 020 7823 3363
✉ info@saylescreen.com
www.saylescreen.com

Agents *Jane Villiers, Matthew Bates, Toby Moorcroft*

Specialises in writers and directors for film and television. Also deals with theatre and radio. Works in association with The Sayle Literary Agency and Greene & Heaton Ltd representing film and TV rights in novels and non-fiction. CLIENTS include Shelagh Delaney, Marc Evans, Margaret Forster, Rob Green, Mark Haddon, Christopher Monger, Paul Morrison, Gitta Sereny, Sue Townsend. No unsolicited material without preliminary letter. No e-mail submissions.

The Sharland Organisation Ltd

The Manor House, Manor Street, Raunds NN9 6JW
☎01933 626600   Fax 01933 624860
✉ tsoshar@aol.com
www.sharlandorganisation.co.uk

Contacts *Mike Sharland, Alice Sharland*

Founded 1988. Specialises in national and international film and TV negotiations. Also negotiates multimedia, interactive TV deals and computer game contracts. Handles scripts for film, TV, radio and theatre; also non-fiction. Markets books for film and handles stage, radio, film and TV rights for authors. No scientific, technical or poetry. COMMISSION Home 15%; US & Translation 20%. OVERSEAS ASSOCIATES various. No unsolicited mss. Preliminary enquiry by letter or phone essential.

Sheil Land Associates Ltd★

(incorporating **Richard Scott Simon Ltd 1971** and **Christy Moore Ltd 1912**)
52 Doughty Street, London WC1N 2LS
☎020 7405 9351   Fax 020 7831 2127
✉ info@sheilland.co.uk
Agents, UK & US *Sonia Land, Vivien Green*
Film/Theatrical/TV *Emily Hayward, Sophie Janson*
Foreign *Jenny Bateman, Gaia Banks*

Founded 1962. Handles full-length general, commercial and literary fiction and non-fiction, including: social politics, business, history, science, military history, gardening, thrillers, crime, romance, drama, biography, travel, cookery and humour, UK and foreign estates. Also theatre, film, radio and TV scripts. CLIENTS include Peter Ackroyd, Hugh Bicheno, Melvyn Bragg, Stephanie Calman, David Cohen, Catherine Cookson estate, Anna del Conte, Seamus Deane, Greg Dyke, Erik Durschmied, Alan Garner, Bonnie Greer, Susan Hill, Richard Holmes, HRH The Prince of Wales, Mark Irving, Simon Kernick, Richard Mabey, Patrick O'Brian estate, Jean Rhys estate, Martin Riley, Catherine Sampson, Tom Sharpe, Martin Stephen, Brian Sykes, Jeffrey Tayler, Andrew Taylor, Alan Titchmarsh, Rose Tremain, Phil Vickery, John Wilsher, Toby Young. COMMISSION Home 15%; US & Translation 20%. OVERSEAS ASSOCIATES Georges Borchardt, Inc. (Richard Scott Simon). US film and TV representation: CAA, APA, and others. Welcomes approaches from new clients either to start or to develop their careers. Preliminary letter with s.a.e. essential. No reading fee.

Caroline Sheldon Literary Agency★

Thorley Manor Farm, Thorley, Yarmouth, Isle of Wight PO41 0SJ
☎01983 760205
Also at: 70–75 Cowcross Street, London EC1M 6EJ
Contacts *Caroline Sheldon, Penny Holroyde*

Founded 1985. Handles adult fiction, in particular women's (both commercial and literary) and human-interest non-fiction. Also full-length children's fiction, younger children's fiction, picture books and picture book artists. No TV/film scripts unless by book-writing clients. COMMISSION Home 10–15%; US & Translation 20%. Submissions should be sent to Isle of Wight address and include a letter 'describing your ambitions', a well-written synopsis, the first three chapters of proposed book and an s.a.e. with sufficient postage for return. No reading fee.

Dorie Simmonds Agency★

67 Upper Berkeley Street, London W1H 7QX
☎020 7569 8686   Fax 020 7569 8696
✉ dhsimmonds@aol.com
Contact *Dorie Simmonds*

Handles a wide range of subjects including general non-fiction and commercial fiction, children's books and associated rights. Specialities include contemporary personalities and historical biographies. COMMISSION Home & US 15%; Translation 20%. Outline required for non-fiction; a short synopsis for fiction with 2–3 sample chapters, and a c.v. with writing experience/publishing history. No reading fee. Return postage essential.

Jeffrey Simmons

15 Penn House, Mallory Street, London NW8 8SX
☎020 7224 8917   Fax 020 7224 8918
✉ jas@london-inc.com
Contact *Jeffrey Simmons*

Founded 1978. Handles biography and autobiography, cinema and theatre, fiction (both quality and commercial), history, law and crime, politics and world affairs, parapsychology and sport (but not exclusively). No science fiction/fantasy, children's books, cookery, crafts, hobbies or gardening. Film scripts handled only if by book-writing clients. Special interest in personality books of all sorts and fiction from young writers (i.e. under 40) with a future. COMMISSION Home 10–15%; US & Foreign 15%. Writers become clients by personal introduction or by letter, enclosing a synopsis if possible, a brief biography, a note of any previously published books, plus a list of any publishers and agents who have already seen the mss.

Richard Scott Simon Ltd

See **Sheil Land Associates Ltd**

Sinclair-Stevenson
3 South Terrace, London SW7 2TB
☎020 7581 2550   Fax 020 7581 2550
Contact *Christopher Sinclair-Stevenson*
Founded 1995. Handles biography, current affairs, travel, history, fiction, the arts. No scripts, children's, academic, science fiction/fantasy. CLIENTS include Jennifer Johnston, J.D.F. Jones, Ross King, Christopher Lee, Andrew Sinclair and the estates of Alec Guinness, John Cowper Powys and John Galsworthy. COMMISSION Home 10%; US 15%; Translation 20%. OVERSEAS ASSOCIATE T.C. Wallace Ltd, New York. Translation rights handled by David Higham Associates. Send synopsis with s.a.e. in the first instance. No reading fee.

Robert Smith
Literary Agency Ltd*
12 Bridge Wharf, 156 Caledonian Road, London N1 9UU
☎020 7278 2444   Fax 020 7833 5680
✉ robertsmith.literaryagency@virgin.net
Contact *Robert Smith*
Founded 1997. Handles non-fiction; biography, memoirs, current affairs, entertainment, true crme, cookery and lifestyle. No scripts, fiction, poetry, academic or children's books. CLIENTS Martin Allen, Kevin Booth, Carol Clerk, Stewart Evans, Neil and Christine Hamilton, James Haspiel, Roberta Kray, Mike Reid, Professor Bill Rubinstein, Keith Skinner, Douglas Thompson. COMMISSION Home 15%; US & Translation 20%. OVERSEAS ASSOCIATE Thomas Schlück Literary Agency (Germany). No unsolicited mss. Send a letter and synopsis in the first instance. No reading fee.

The Standen Literary Agency
41b Endymion Road, London N4 1EQ
☎020 8245 3053   Fax 020 8245 3053
✉ info@standenliteraryagency.com
www.standenliteraryagency.com
Contact *Mrs Yasmin Standen*
Founded 2004. Handles fiction, both adult and children's. No non-fiction, academic or science except for law. No TV/radio scripts. Interested in first time writers. COMMISSION Home 15%; Overseas 20%. See website for submissions procedure. No reading fee.

Elaine Steel
110 Gloucester Avenue, London NW1 8HX
☎020 8348 0918   Fax 020 8341 9807
✉ ecmsteel@aol.com

Contact *Elaine Steel*
Founded 1986. Handles scripts, screenplays and books. No technical or academic. CLIENTS include Les Blair, Anna Campion, Michael Eaton, Pearse Elliott, Gwyneth Hughes, Brian Keenan, Troy Kennedy Martin, Rob Ritchie, Albie Sachs, Ben Steiner. COMMISSION Home 10%; US & Translation 20%. Initial phone call preferred.

Abner Stein*
10 Roland Gardens, London SW7 3PH
☎020 7373 0456   Fax 020 7370 6316
Contact *Arabella Stein*
Founded 1971. Mainly represents US agents and authors but handles some full-length fiction and general non-fiction. No scientific, technical, etc. No scripts. COMMISSION Home 10%; US & Translation 20%.

Micheline Steinberg Associates
104 Great Portland Street, London W1W 6PE
☎020 7631 1310   Fax 020 7631 1146
✉ info@steinplays.com
www.steinplays.com
Contacts *Micheline Steinberg, Ginny Sennett, Matt Connell*
Founded 1988. Specialises in plays for stage, TV, film, animation and radio. Dramatic associate for other book agents. COMMISSION Home 10%; Elsewhere 15%. Best approach by preliminary letter (with s.a.e.).

Shirley Stewart Literary Agency
3rd Floor, 21 Denmark Street, London WC2H 8NA
☎020 7836 4440   Fax 020 7836 3482
Director *Shirley Stewart*
Founded 1993. Handles fiction and non-fiction. No scripts, children's, science fiction, fantasy or poetry. COMMISSION Home 10–15%; US & Translation 20%. OVERSEAS ASSOCIATE Curtis Brown Ltd, New York; Carolyn Swayze Agency, Canada. Will consider unsolicited material; send letter with two or three sample chapters in the first instance. S.a.e. essential. Submissions by fax or on disk not accepted. No reading fee.

Sunflower Literary Agency
106 Mansfield Drive, Redhill RH1 3JN
✉ contact@sunflowerliteraryagency.com
www.sunflowerliteraryagency.com
Senior Editor *Philip Adams*
Correspondence Secretary *David Sherriff*

Founded 2003. Handles full-length fiction, especially thrillers (techno a plus); literary fiction, especially political and/or social satire (controversy a plus); erotica, in any of the above genres. No poetry, screenplays, non-fiction, short fiction, 'who-dunnits' or autobiography. COMMISSION Home 15% (first book), 10% (later books); USA & Translation additional 5% to base rate. 'We *only* consider work from *unpublished* authors (or major changes of genre).' Electronic submissions preferred: contact via the website only. All requirements listed on the web page must be fulfilled before e-mail contact is made. No fees charged. Provides editing and pre-publication services via **Tournesol Books** (see entry under *Small Presses*) and facilitates self-publication and promotion through **Pen Press Limited** (see entry under *Small Presses*).

The Susijn Agency Ltd

3rd Floor, 64 Great Titchfield Street, London W1W 7QH
☎020 7580 6341   Fax 020 7580 8626
✉ info@thesusijnagency.com
www.thesusijnagency.com

Contacts *Laura Susijn, Charles Buchan, Elaine Wishart*

Founded April 1998. Specialises in selling rights worldwide in literary fiction and non-fiction. Also represents non-English language authors and publishers for UK, US and translation rights worldwide. COMMISSION Home 15%; US & Translation 15–20%. Send preliminary letter, synopsis and first two chapters by post. No reading fee.

The Tennyson Agency

10 Cleveland Avenue, Wimbledon Chase, London SW20 9EW
☎020 8543 5939
✉ letterbox@tenagy.co.uk
www.tenagy.co.uk

Contact *Christopher Oxford*

Founded 2001. Specialises in theatre, radio, television and film scripts. Related material considered on an ad hoc basis. No short stories, children's, poetry, travel, military/historical, academic or sport. CLIENTS Vivienne Allen, Tony Bagley, Alastair Cording, Iain Grant, Jonathan Holloway, Julian Howell, Philip Hurd-Wood, Joanna Leigh, John Ryan, Walter Saunders, Diana Ward. COMMISSION Home 12½–15%; Overseas 17½–20%. No unsolicited material; send introductory letter with résumé and proposal/outline of work. No reading fee.

Lavinia Trevor Literary Agency★

The Glasshouse, 49A Goldhawk Road, London W12 8QP
☎020 8749 8481   Fax 020 8749 7377

Contact *Lavinia Trevor*

Founded 1993. Handles general fiction (literary and commercial) and non-fiction, including popular science. No fantasy, science-fiction, poetry, academic, technical or children's books. No TV, film, radio, theatre scripts. COMMISSION rate by agreement with author. Approach with a preliminary letter, a brief autobiography and first 50–60 typewritten pages. S.a.e. essential. No reading fee.

Jane Turnbull★

Mailing address: Barn Cottage, Veryan, Truro TR2 5QA
☎01872 5013170
✉ jane.turnbull@btinternet.com

London office: 58 Elgin Crescent, London W11 2JJ ☎020 7727 9409

Contact *Jane Turnbull*

Founded 1986. Handles fiction and non-fiction but specialises in biography, history, current affairs, self-help and humour. Translation rights handled by Gillon Aitken Associates Ltd. COMMISSION Home 10%; US & Foreign 20%. No unsolicited mss. Approach with letter in the first instance. No reading fee.

Ed Victor Ltd★

6 Bayley Street, Bedford Square, London WC1B 3HE
☎020 7304 4100   Fax 020 7304 4111

Contacts *Ed Victor, Maggie Phillips, Sophie Hicks, Grainne Fox*

Founded 1976. Handles a broad range of material but leans towards the more commercial ends of the fiction and non-fiction spectrums. Excellent children's book list. No poetry, scripts or academic. Takes on very few new writers and does not accept unsolicited submissions. After trying his hand at book publishing and literary magazines, Ed Victor, an ebullient American, found his true vocation. Strong opinions, very pushy and works hard for those whose intelligence he respects. Loves nothing more than a good title auction. CLIENTS include Herbie Brennan, Eoin Colfer, Frederick Forsyth, A.A. Gill, Josephine Hart, Jack Higgins, Nigella Lawson, Kathy Lette, Allan Mallinson, Andrew Marr, Janet Street-Porter and the estates of Douglas Adams, Raymond Chandler, Dame Iris Murdoch, Sir Stephen Spender and Irving

Wallace. COMMISSION Home & US 15%; Translation 20%. No unsolicited mss.

Wade & Doherty Literary Agency Ltd
33 Cormorant Lodge, Thomas More Street, London E1W 1AU
☎020 7488 4171   Fax 020 7488 4172
✉ rw@rwla.com *or* bd@rwla.com
www.rwla.com
Contacts *Robin Wade, Broo Doherty*

Founded 2001. Handles general fiction and non-fiction including children's books. Specialises in military history and crime books. No scripts, poetry, plays or short stories. CLIENTS include Louise Cooper, Adam Guillain, Helen Oyeyemi, Ewen Southby-Tailyour. COMMISSION Home 10%; Overseas & Translation 20%. 'Fees negotiable if a contract has already been offered.' Send detailed synopsis and two specimen chapters by e-mail with a brief biography. No reading fee.

Cecily Ware Literary Agents
19C John Spencer Square, London N1 2LZ
☎020 7359 3787   Fax 020 7226 9828
✉ info@cecilyware.com
Contacts *Cecily Ware, Gilly Schuster, Warren Sherman*

Founded 1972. Primarily a film and TV script agency representing work in all areas: drama, children's, series/serials, adaptations, comedies, etc. COMMISSION Home 10%; US 10–20% by arrangement. No unsolicited mss or phone calls. Approach in writing only. No reading fee.

Watson, Little Ltd★
Capo Di Monte, Windmill Hill, London NW3 6RJ
☎020 7431 0770   Fax 020 7431 7225
✉ enquiries@watsonlittle.com
Contacts *Mandy Little, Sugra Zaman*

Handles fiction, commercial women's fiction, crime and literary fiction. Non-fiction special interests include history, science, popular psychology, self-help and general leisure books. Also children's fiction and non-fiction. No short stories, poetry, TV, play or film scripts. Not interested in purely academic writers. COMMISSION Home 15%; US 24%; Translation 19%. OVERSEAS ASSOCIATES worldwide. FILM & TV ASSOCIATES The Sharland Organisation Ltd; MBA Literary Agents. No e-mails or unsolicited mss. Informative preliminary letter and synopsis with return postage essential.

A.P. Watt Ltd★
20 John Street, London WC1N 2DR
☎020 7405 6774   Fax 020 7831 2154
✉ apw@apwatt.co.uk
www.apwatt.co.uk
Directors *Caradoc King, Linda Shaughnessy, Derek Johns, Georgia Garrett, Nick Harris, Natasha Fairweather, Sheila Crowley*

Founded 1875. The oldest-established literary agency in the world. Handles full-length typescripts, including children's books, screenplays for film and TV. No poetry, academic or specialist works. CLIENTS include Trezza Azzopardi, David Baddiel, Quentin Blake, Marika Cobbold, Helen Dunmore, Nicholas Evans, Giles Foden, Esther Freud, Janice Galloway, Martin Gilbert, Nadine Gordimer, Linda Grant, Reginald Hill, Michael Holroyd, Michael Ignatieff, Mick Jackson, Philip Kerr, Dick King-Smith, India Knight, John Lanchester, Alison Lurie, Jan Morris, Jill Murphy, Andrew O'Hagan, Susie Orbach, Tony Parsons, Caryl Phillips, Philip Pullman, Jancis Robinson, Jon Ronson, Elaine Showalter, Zadie Smith, Graham Swift Fiona Walker and the estates of Wodehouse, Graves and Maugham. COMMISSION Home 10%; US & Translation 20%. No unsolicited mss accepted.

Josef Weinberger Plays
12–14 Mortimer Street, London W1T 3JJ
☎020 7580 2827   Fax 020 7436 9616
✉ general.info@jwmail.co.uk
www.josef-weinberger.com
Contact *Michael Callahan*

Josef Weinberger is both agent and publisher of scripts for the theatre. CLIENTS include Ray Cooney, John Godber, Peter Gordon, Debbie Isitt, Arthur Miller, Sam Shepard, John Steinbeck. OVERSEAS REPRESENTATIVES in the US, Canada, Australia, New Zealand, India, South Africa and Zimbabwe. No unsolicited mss; introductory letter essential. No reading fee.

John Welch, Literary Consultant & Agent
Mill Cottage, Calf Lane, Chipping Camden GL55 6JQ
☎01386 840237   Fax 01386 840568
✉ johnwelch@waitrose.com
Contact *John Welch*

Founded 1992. Handles military aviation and naval history, and history in general. No fiction, poetry, children's books or scripts for radio, TV, film or theatre. Already has a full hand of authors so no new authors being considered. CLIENTS include Alexander Baron, Michael Calvert, Patrick Delaforce, Timothy Jenkins, Sybil Marshall, Ewart Oakeshott, Norman Scarfe, Anthony Trew, Peter Trew, David Wragg. COMMISSION Home 10%.

Eve White Literary Agent

Irish Hill House, Hamstead Marshall,
Newbury RG20 0JB
☎01488 657656
✉ evewhite@btinternet.com

Contact *Eve White*

Founded 2003. Handles full-length adult and children's fiction and non-fiction. No poetry, short stories or textbooks. CLIENTS Jimmy Docherty, Peter J. Murray, Gillian Rogerson, Carol Sinclair, Andy Stanton. COMMISSION Home 15%; US & Translation 20%.No unsolicited mss. Send introductory letter (enclose résumé, brief synopsis, one-page writing sample) with e-mail address and phone number. No initial approach by e-mail. No reading fee.

Dinah Wiener Ltd*

12 Cornwall Grove, Chiswick, London
W4 2LB
☎020 8994 6011   Fax 020 8994 6044

Contact *Dinah Wiener*

Founded 1985. Handles fiction and general non-fiction: auto/biography, popular science, cookery. No scripts, children's or poetry. CLIENTS include Valerie-Anne Baglietto, Malcolm Billings, Hugh Brune, Guy Burt, Victoria Corby, David Deutsch, Jenny Hobbs, Mark Jeffery, Tania

Kindersley, Michael Lockwood, Sarah Mason, Daniel Snowman, Peta Tayler, Mitchell Tonks, Rachel Trethewey, Marcia Willett. COMMISSION Home 15%; US & Translation 20%. Approach with preliminary letter in first instance, giving full but brief c.v. of past work and future plans. Mss submitted must include s.a.e. and be typed in double-spacing.

Rebecca Winfield Literary Agency

5B Walpole Court, Ealing Studios, London
W5 5ED
☎020 8567 6738   Fax 020 8567 6738
✉ rebecca.winfield@btopenworld.com

Contact *Rebecca Winfield*

Founded 2003. Handles quality fiction and non-fiction; biography, social politics and narrative non-fiction. No science fiction, fantasy, horror or poetry. COMMISSION Home 15%; US & Translation 20%. Send letter, synopsis and no more than three sample chapters in the first instance together with s.a.e. for return of material. Submissions on disk or by e-mail not accepted. No reading fee.

The Wylie Agency (UK) Ltd

17 Bedford Square, London WC1B 3JA
☎020 7908 5900   Fax 020 7908 5901
✉ mail@wylieagency.co.uk

Handles fiction and non-fiction. No scripts or children's books. COMMISSION Home 10%; US 15%;Translation 20%.The Wylie Agency does not accept unsolicited submissions. Enquire by letter or e-mail before submitting. Any submission must be accompanied by return postage/s.a.e.

UK Literary Scouts

Literary scouts gather information from UK agents, publishers and editors on behalf of foreign clients. They are not literary agents and work only with material that is already commissioned or being handled by an agent. They do **not** accept unsolicited material and do **not** deal directly with writers.

Louise Allen-Jones
40 Lillieshall Road, London SW4 0LP
☎020 7720 2453   Fax 020 7498 1818
✉ louise@louiseallenjones.com
Contact *Louise Allen-Jones*
Scouts for Ullstein, List/Claassen/Marion von Schröder, Econ, Propyläen, Germany; The English Agency, Japan; AW Bruna, Signature, vip and DeBoekerij, M Publishers, Forum, The Netherlands; Distribuidora Record, Brazil; The Film Council, UK.

Badcock & Rozycki
Literary Scouts
1 Old Compton Street, London W1D 5JA
☎020 7734 7997   Fax 020 7734 6886
Contacts *June Badcock* (june@badcock-rozycki.co.uk), *Barbara Rozycki* (barbara@badcock-rozycki.co.uk), *Claire Holt* (claire@badcock-rozycki.co.uk)

Scouts for Wilhelm Heyne Verlag and Diana Verlag, Germany; Unieboek BV and Prometheus/Bert Bakker, The Netherlands; RCS Libri Group, Italy; Editions Jean-Claude Lattès, France; Ediciones Salamandra, Spain; Ellinika Grammata, Greece; Werner Söderström Osakeyhtiö, Finland; Forum, Sweden; NW Damm & Son A/S, Norway; Aschehoug Dansk Forlag, Denmark; Edda Media, Iceland.

Natasha Farrant
77 Starfield Road, London W12 9SN
☎020 8746 1857
✉ natasha.farrant@btinternet.com
Contact *Natasha Farrant*
Scouts for children's fiction on behalf of Hachette Jeunesse, France; Edizione Piemme, Italy; Presenca, Portugal; Lerner Publishing Group, USA.

Anne Louise Fisher
and Suzy Lucas
29 D'Arblay Street, London W1F 8EP
☎020 7494 4609   Fax 020 7494 4611
✉ annelouise@alfisher.co.uk
Contacts *Anne Louise Fisher, Suzy Lucas*
Scouts for Doubleday/Broadway Books/Nan Talese, US; Doubleday/Bond Street Books, Canada; Librarie Plon/Perrin, Pocket, Pocket Jeunesse, France; Karl Blessing Verlag, Germany; Arnoldo Mondadori Editore and Mondadori Ragazzi, Italy; Albert Bonniers Forlag, Sweden; Otava, Finland; Gyldendal Norsk Forlag, Norway; Mouria, Holland; Random House Mondadori, Spain; Patakis Publications, Greece, Heday Films, UK.

Koukla MacLehose
Arundel House, 3 Westbourne Road, London N7 8AR
☎020 7607 1336   Fax 020 7609 7775
✉ koukla@btopenworld.com
Contact *Koukla MacLehose*
Scouts for Tammi, Finland; Wählström & Widstrand, Sweden; Pax, Norway; Rosinante, Samlerens and Forum/Fremad, Denmark; De Bezige Bij, The Netherlands; Hanser, Zsolnay, Sans Souci and Nagel & Kimche, Germany; Gallimard and Denoël, France; Einaudi, Italy; Anagrama, Spain; Asa, Portugal; Psichogios, Greece; Keter, Israel.

Folly Marland
6 Elmcroft Street, London E5 0SQ
☎020 8986 0111   Fax 020 8986 0111
✉ fmarland@pobox.com
Contact *Folly Marland*
Scouts for Scherz Verlag, Krüger Verlag, Germany; Uitgeverij Het Spectrum, The Netherlands; Sony Magazines, Japan; Livani, Greece.

Rosalind Ramsay Limited

First Floor, 2 Ingate Place, London SW8 3NS
☎020 7622 3336
✉ ros@rosalindramsay.com
www.rosalindramsay.com

Contacts *Rosalind Ramsay*

Scouts for Kiepenheuer & Witsch, Germany; Sperling & Kupfer, Italy; Ambo Anthos, The Netherlands; Norstedts, Sweden; Kadokawa, Japan; Dioptra, Greece; Kinneret-Zmora, Israel.

Heather Schiller

✉ heather.schiller@virgin.net

Contact *Heather Schiller*

Scouts for BZZTÔH, The Netherlands; Cappelen, Norway; Piper, Germany; Lindhardt & Ringhof, Denmark; Prisma, Sweden.

Petra Sluka

21 Denmark Street, London WC2H 8NA
☎020 7836 9028   Fax 020 7836 3982
✉ petrasluka@aol.com

Also at: 3 Dry Bank Road, Tonbridge TN10 3BS
☎01732 353694 Fax 01732 359225

Contact *Petra Sluka*

Scouts for Verlagsgruppe Lübbe, Gemany; De Fontein/De Kern, Holland; J'ailu, France; Bra Böcker, Sweden; Japan Uni Agency, Inc., Japan.

Jane Southern

11 Russell Avenue, Bedford MK40 3TE
☎01234 400147   Fax 01234 400146
✉ jane.southern@ntlworld.com

Contact *Jane Southern*

UK Scout for Hoffmann und Campe Verlag, Germany; Bertelsmann Club, Germany; The House of Books, The Netherlands; Belfond, Presses de la Cité and France Loisirs, France.

Van Lear Limited

PO Box 21816, London SW6 5ZU
☎020 7385 1199   Fax 020 7385 6262
✉ evl@vanlear.co.uk

Contact *Liz Van Lear*

Scouts for Droemer Knaur, Germany; Planeta Group, Spain and Latin America; Richters, Sweden; Artist House, Japan; Oceanida, Greece; Dom Quixote, Portugal; il Saggiatore, Italy; Veen Bosch & Keuning, The Netherlands.

Sylvie Zannier-Betts

114 Springfield Road, Brighton BN1 6DE
☎01273 557370   Fax 01273 557370
✉ szannier@lineone.net

Contact *Sylvie Zannier-Betts*

Scouts for Uitgeverij De Geus, The Netherlands; S. Fischer Verlag, Germany; Gummerus Publishers, Finland. Agent in the UK for S. Fischer Verlag, Germany.

Words on Pictures

Craig McGill reveals a booming market for
writers who are team workers

Let's get the obvious bits out the road first: Zap! Bam! Biff! Kapow! You may
smile, but that's the general perception of comics at the moment. Yes, there have
been a number of recent hit movies – *X-Men* and *Spider-Man* – and *Batman
Begins* and *Superman Returns* recently completed shooting, but for most people
the old cheesy 1960s *Batman* show is what they remember. The good news for
writers is that comics are nothing like that. No matter what you want to write
about, there's a comic company for you. Of course, like every other area of publishing competition is harsh, but the rewards can be worthwhile.

Comics have been around for over a century – since the Stone Age if you consider a sequence of artwork to be a comic – and most people in the UK remember picking up a copy of *Roy of the Rovers, Beano, Dandy, 2000AD* or an American
comic with the likes of Superman, Batman, Spiderman or the Hulk in it.

Many UK publications have since gone to the wall, victims of rising costs and
trying to compete with films, DVDs and computer games, but the American,
European and Far East publications are still going incredibly strong. Of course,
in America and the UK the general perception is that comics are for children but,
just as people used to think that about computer games, the attitude is changing.
In other parts of the world, like mainland Europe and Japan, comics are as celebrated as any other art form. Indeed, in Europe, new graphic novels (as they are
called there) can be the top-selling publication for months, selling in their millions.
But even that pales in comparison with the Far East where Manga publications
can sell over seventeen million copies a month.

Breaking into those two markets can be done, but it's not for the newcomer
and the best way to become established is to get into the American market and
boost your exposure before tackling the other areas, which is what we'll be looking at here.

But why would anyone want to write comics in the first place? First off, it's a
medium that presents incredible storytelling possibilities, far wider than that just
of text alone. Secondly, it's a market that is still relatively free from corporate
censorship. Thirdly, the rewards can be fantastic. Not only is Hollywood and the
computer-gaming industry adapting more and more comics each year, but there's
also the ability to get a dedicated audience for your work, allowing you to build
up a fanbase relatively easily on a monthly basis. That fanbase can be important
when you go into other areas, say novels, as it means you have a built-in readership. Lastly, European and especially British writers are very much in demand. It
is only in the last twenty-five years that British writers (and artists to be fair, but

this article is for the writers) have broken into the lucrative American industry, but they have turned it upside down, bringing a dark, European sensibility to a medium that beforehand was normally very manichean and where the bad guy was always caught at the end of the story. Writers like Alan Moore, Grant Morrison, Neil Gaiman, Mark Millar, Warren Ellis, Garth Ennis and Eddie Campbell have shown what comics are capable of, taking them from children's reads to works that can be appreciated and enjoyed by adults.

As for financial rewards, as a newcomer to the industry you might not get rich – $1,000 being the average payment to a newcomer for a single comic – but that sum can quickly rise if you are seen as a hot talent. Nowadays it is not uncommon to see many writers earning over $4,000 a comic per month, plus royalties. There are also many exclusive deals where companies like Marvel or DC will pay up to $100,000 – as well as a monthly wage – to ensure that a writer will work for them exclusively for a two- or three-year period. In the early 1990s, there was so much money going around that one writer was able to buy his own private plane, so you'll agree that there are possibilities.

But of course, the main reason for wanting to write comics should be because you have a tale that just has to be told, a story so good that you have to get it out there for everyone to read.

So that's *why* you should write comics, the next question is *how* do you write comics? It's not as simple as filling in the word balloons to what the artist has drawn (that's actually a letterer's job). Just like a writer anywhere else you come up with the story, the themes, the dialogue and so on. The difference here is that the only part the public sees as words is the dialogue. Here's the average creative team on a comic:

Writer: comes up with the concept, words and so on.
Penciller: takes the writers words and turns them into pictures
Inker: improves upon the pencils for reproduction, adds mood
Colourist: turns the black and white art into colour
Letterer: takes the writers dialogue and turns it into speech balloons, sound effects and caption boxes
Editor: oversees the whole process

The writer's role in creating a comic has been said to be more like making a movie than writing a book because the comic-book writer can – if they wish – choose to be the writer, director and set designer. Look at this example for one image on a page:

Page One
Our hero, in the middle of the massive alien invasion force, fights his way through with his sword. Alien blood and guts everywhere.
(no dialogue)

At the same time that could be written as:

Page One

Our hero's in the thick of it, looking grim and determined as he takes on the alien hordes. He's trying to hack them, kick them and head-butt them as he makes his way through them, but there's obviously some blood on him from his wounds – though there's far more alien blood being spilled. At the top of the page we have flying aliens dive-bombing him while on the left-hand side – where there is also an exit sign (that's what he's fighting to get to) – there are some aliens looking very determined. One of them is tying the alien equivalent of shoelaces (for some comic relief).

In the background, the walls lined with alien technology are all flashing wildly and there's a smattering of light from the broken skylight, making some areas darker than others. *(no dialogue.)*

Both of those describe the same thing. There is no set amount of detail needed for an artist – some prefer lots, some don't. As you work with artists you'll get to see how much detail they like. The golden rule to remember is that while you may spend twenty minutes typing a scene description, an artist may have to spend days on it.

The average comic is twenty-two pages long – and each page is broken down into scenes called panels. To give you an idea of this, here's the opening page from my upcoming graphic novel (a graphic novel is a comic over fifty pages in length) called *Know the Provo*, which is about a loyalist hit-list I uncovered when I was a journalist at the *Sunday Mirror*. It is in the standard format for a comic script. First you describe the scene, then any dialogue, then any captions and special effect, SFX, noises. The best way to think of it is like breaking the story down into beats: in that you want certain things to happen on each page. Each page should also contain your contact details so that editors and art teams can speak to you about any problems or queries they may have.

Know the Provo

by Craig McGill

Page One

This page will have six panels on it, all the same size, There won't be any dialogue, but caption boxes in each panel. Letterer, I'll leave it to you to choose the best positioning for the captions.

P1:

Lets have a shot of looking over someone's shoulder. They're sitting at a keyboard and computer. Their back is obviously to us, but we can tell that it's a tall-ish male with dark hair. Make the computer a Mac – running the old OS9

– as we're going for realism. We can see on the screen that they've typed the following:

JOURNALISM CAN BE A GREAT CAREER

P2:
A shot of a bunch of people at a top event – make it something that will be easily recognisable for people on both sides of the Atlantic, a pop show with celebs, a presidential swearing in, something like that. Have the person from panel one there. *(no dialogue)*

CAPTION: YOU CAN BE AT THE FRONT OF ALL THE TOP EVENTS

P3:
Same dark-haired journo with some famous people, notepad or dictaphone out as if he is interviewing them. Again, go for someone with global appeal. *(no dialogue)*

CAPTION: MEET ALL THE TOP PEOPLE

P4:
Similar shot to panel 1, but different words on the screen.

BUT IT'S NOT ALL FUN AND GAMES

P5:
We're in a lane here. At the front of the panel there are two mean-looking guys. We can only tell they are mean by their general build, because their backs are to us and their hands at their sides are balled up into fists.
Between them – practically in the middle of the panel – is the journo, he's got a bloody nose, has been punched down to the ground and looks absolutely terrified for his life.

CAPTION: IT CAN GET YOU KILLED

P6:
Flip the view. We now have the close up of one of the mean-looking guys throwing a punch towards the panel – as if punching the reader. Every indication is that this is one sore punch being thrown (not that there are many other kinds). Then at the end of the page, have a block of black as if the reporter has been knocked out – or worse.

Craig McGill: cmcgill@gmail.com
AIM: scribblercraig

By specifying the exact panel sizes and so on, I'm being quite restrictive with the artist. Here's another example which was more loose for the artist, taken from Variance Press's *Last Orders*, written by me:

P1:
Establishing shot of a lot of people in a busy pub. In the background there's the usual stuff going on – guys trying to chat up girls (what we'll be doing is following one couple in the background from chat-up to ... (well, we'll see, but feel free to sneak them in whenever you can), folk sitting on their own, people being knocked back for being under age. And in some part of the panel, we have a guy with blond hair sitting, sipping a pint. There's also a telly on the wall (bracket-mounted) and it looks as if there's something wrong with the picture.

CAP: NO ONE BELIEVED IT WHEN THE ALIENS CAME ON OUR TELLIES AND TOLD US WE WERE GOING TO DIE.

P2:
Do this like we are looking directly at a telly. The static is clearing away and we have a plain shot of an alien – no open pores on this thing (it has a closed biological system) – but how it looks is up to you. I like that bottom sketch you did – but without the neck-type markings. This race don't go in for aesthetics, so no clothing, no decoration or marks on them.

ALIEN (don't have a tail coming out the speech balloon, just the circular balloon): PEOPLE OF EARTH LISTEN TO US.

P3:
More alien. In any shot with the aliens, make the panel look spotless, pristine, as opposed to the busypanels with humans in them.

ALIEN: WE ARE YOUR CREATORS AND HAVE DECIDED YOUR TIME AS A BIOLOGICAL EXPERIMENT IS UP. YOU HAVE ONE YEAR.

P4:
Back to a shot of the pub, everyone in stunned silence, watching

ALIEN: WE ARE TRANSMITTING THIS ON EVERY FREQUENCY AND LANGUAGE YOU USE.

P5:
Pub people burst into laughter – after it all, it's fecking ridiculous innit?

SOUND EFFECTS (SFX): HAHAHAHAHAHA.
ALIEN: WE DO NOT EXPECT YOU TO BELIEVE US. BUT YOU WILL TOMORROW WHEN WE STERILISE AUSTRALIA.

Craig McGill: cmcgill@gmail.com
AIM: scribblercraig

But knowing what you have to do and how you have to do it is only half the battle. Newcomers to comics do it the hard way just like in everything else. Granted there are exceptions. If you are established in another field, you may be invited to write comics. This has happened to the likes of sci-fi author Richard Morgan, TV producer J.M. Straczynski and also John Cleese. But the odds are you aren't as high-profile as them, so you will have do this by the romantic route, i.e. from the bottom. And it's here that being a writer in comics, to borrow an Americanism, sucks. The reason is that comics are primarily a visual medium, so people see the artwork first and the words second.

As with any medium you need to have samples to show an editor. Now script samples are OK, but getting an artist to draw your stuff for you makes a far better impression. How do you find an artist? Fortunately the internet takes a lot of work out of that. Websites like www.digitalwebbing.com, http://forums.delphiforums.com/comicwriter/start, www.millarworld.net and http://forums.delphiforums.com/variance/start are all good places to start looking. Search engines like Google will also provide other sites to look at, like www.comicbookresources.com and www.silverbulletcomicbooks.com which are also good to go to see what is happening in the industry. It can also give you pointers for the sort of people you should talk to for help in letting the world know about your comic when completed, like Rich Johnston, who is arguably the premier comics journalist today.

Anyway, once you have the script – and remember if you are sending it to an American firm to spellcheck with a US dictionary – and perhaps artwork ready, what do you do? The best thing is to attach not only a short letter about yourself but also a one-page summary of the comic and a pitch-line for it. Think of it like a Hollywood sales pitch where you have to sum up your idea in one or two sentences. For example, *Alien* would be described as 'A haunted house story set on a space ship' or the tag for the horror *30 Days of Night*, 'Vampires descend upon a town up north where the sun won't shine for thirty days', or *Know the Provo* would be, 'It's *The Crying Game* and *The Long Good Friday* meets *All the President's Men* as a journalist uncovers an Irish loyalist hit-list containing the details of top politicians and American stars.'

One thing you have to be warned about though is copyright. In every project, once it has been submitted and accepted, check out the copyright situation. The traditional rule of 'you created it, you keep the copyright' doesn't always apply here. Some companies work under the concept of work for hire, meaning you are paid for what you write – as well as potential royalties – but not for spin-offs and so on. Also, not every company guarantees royalties so check that in a contract as well. Never assume that comic publishing is the same as other publishing areas; it isn't.

This may not seem like a big deal at first, but what if other writers want to use your characters or a movie studio wants them? If you haven't clarified the copyright and the company operates work-for-hire policies then you could get nothing – or perhaps a small payment depending on the generosity of the company.

The next trick is to find out which company is most likely to publish your ideas. There's a list of the best comic companies in the US and UK at the end of this article and using Google will allow you to see what is currently in vogue for each of them to publish. In the UK, the main place to send submissions to is *2000AD* magazine which concentrates on sci-fi stories. However, *2000AD* is swamped with submissions so many creators skip it and go straight to the European or American companies.

But you don't just have to post work off and hope for the best. As the world of comics is fairly small compared to other areas of publishing, it's also fairly easy to start arranging face-to-face meetings with people in the industry. Every year there are three main events. The first of these, every January/February, is called Le Festival International de la bande dessinee at Anglouême in France. This is the largest gathering for comic fans, writers and artists outside Japan, attracting more than 200,000 visitors in 2003 alone. The next event is expected to take place in May in Bristol and is a lot more low-key, but tends to attract more editors and publishers from the US, giving you the chance to talk to them. The last is in San Diego in July or August and can attract up to 100,000 people. This is by far the most commercial of the three, but also traditionally attracts the most publishers and editors from the American market.

The best advice I can give you is never walk up to editors and just hand them a bundle of pages or pitches. If possible, speak to them in advance by phone or e-mail and ask if you can give them something. Failing that, approach them at the event, give them a business card or something to remember you by and ask if you can send them something when they return to the office.

It sounds like a lot of work, but as with all writing endeavours when you see your name in print or get the royalty cheque it will have been worth it, especially as the growing trend in comics is to serialise stories and then collect them into what is known as a trade paperback, which normally consists of at least six issues of a comic. This lets you get royalties twice – once for the original comic and once for the trade paperback. Some trade paperbacks are also collected into hardback, giving you three bites from the same story.

So, good luck, and remember, whatever you do, there's no need for Zap! Bam! Biff! Kapow! This is a format designed to let your imagination run wild, so go for it.

Companies

AiT/Planet Lar
2034 47th Avenue, San Francisco,
CA 94116, USA
www.ait-planetlar.com

Avatar Press
9 Triumph Drive, Urbana, IL 61802, USA
Fax 001-217-384-2216
www.avatarpress.com

DC Comics and Vertigo Comics
1700 Broadway, New York,
NY 10019, USA
www.dccomics.com

Humanoids Publishing
P.O. Box 931658, Hollywood,
CA 90093, USA
www.humanoids-publishing.com

IDW Publishing Editorial Offices
4411 Morena Blvd., Suite 106, San Diego,
CA 92117, USA
www.idwpublishing.com/

Marvel Comics
Marvel Enterprises, Inc., 10 East 40th Street,
New York, NY 10016, USA
www.marvel.com

Oni Press
6336 SE Milwaukie Ave, PMB 30, Portland,
OR 97202, USA
www.onipress.com

Platinum Studios
9744 Wilshire Boulevard, Suite 210, Beverly
Hills, California 90212, USA
platinumstudios.com/index.php

(The Platinum website also has an excellent
mini-site about how to present comic ideas
and scripts to publishers)

Tokyopop
Editorial Submissions Dept., Tokyopop, Inc.,
5900 Wilshire Blvd. # 2000, Los Angeles,
CA 90036, USA
www.tokyopop.com

2000 AD Submissions Editor
The Studio, Brewer Street, Oxford OX1 1QN

National Newspapers

Departmental e-mail addresses are too numerous to include in this listing. They can be obtained from the newspaper's main switchboard or the department in question

The Business
292 Vauxhall Bridge Road, London
SW1V 1SS
☎020 7961 0000
Owner *Barclay Brothers*
Editor-in-Chief *Andrew Neil*
Circulation 189,441
Launched in 1998. Sunday national newspaper dedicated to business, finance and politics. No unsolicited material. All ideas must be discussed with the department's editor in advance.
   Political Editor *Fraser Nelson*

Daily Express
The Northern & Shell Building, No. 10
Lower Thames Street, London EC3R 6EN
☎0871 434 1010
www.express.co.uk
Owner *Northern & Shell Media/Richard Desmond*
Editor *Peter Hill*
Circulation 926,438
Under owner Richard Desmond, publisher of *OK!* magazine, the paper features a large amount of celebrity coverage. The general rule of thumb is to approach in writing with an idea; all departments are prepared to look at an outline without commitment. Ideas welcome but already receives many which are 'too numerous to count'.
   News Editor *Greg Swift*
   Diary (Hickey Column) *Kathryn Spencer*
   Features Editor *Heather Preen*
   City Editor *Stephen Kahn*
   Political Editor *Patrick O'Flynn*
   Sports Editor *Bill Bradshaw*
   Planning Editor (News Desk) should be circulated with copies of official reports, press releases, etc., to ensure news desk cover at all times.
Saturday magazine. Editor *Graham Bailey*
PAYMENT negotiable.

Daily Mail
Northcliffe House, 2 Derry Street, London
W8 5TT
☎020 7938 6000

Owner *Associated Newspapers/Lord Rothermere*
Editor *Paul Dacre*
Circulation 2.4 million
In-house feature writers and regular columnists provide much of the material. Photo-stories and crusading features often appear; it's essential to hit the right note to be a successful Mail writer. Close scrutiny of the paper is strongly advised. Not a good bet for the unseasoned. Accepts news on savings, building societies, insurance, unit trusts, legal rights and tax.
   News Editor *Tony Gallagher*
   City Editor *Alex Brummer*
   'Money Mail' Editor *Tony Hazell*
   Political Editor *David Hughes*
   Education Correspondent *Sarah Harris*
   Diary Editor *Richard Kay*
   Features Editor *Leaf Kalfayan*
   Literary Editor *Jane Mays*
   Head of Sport *Tim Jotischky*
   Femail *Lisa Collins*
Weekend Saturday supplement. Editor *Heather McGlone*

Daily Mirror
1 Canada Square, Canary Wharf, London
E14 5AP
☎020 7293 3000 Fax 020 7293 3409
www.mirror.co.uk
Owner *Trinity Mirror plc*
Editor *Richard Wallace*
Circulation 1.72 million
No freelance opportunities for the inexperienced, but strong writers who understand what the tabloid market demands are always needed.
   Deputy Editor *Conor Hanna*
   News Editor *Anthony Harwood*
   Features Editor *Matt Kelly*
   Political Editor *Kevin Maguire*
   Business Editor *Clinton Manning*
   Showbusiness Diary Editor *Jessica Callan*
   Sports Editor *Dean Morse*

Daily Record
One Central Quay, Glasgow G3 8DA
☎0141 309 3000 Fax 0141 309 3340

www.record-mail.co.uk
Owner *Trinity Mirror plc*
Editor *Bruce Waddell*
Circulation 503,077

Mass-market Scottish tabloid. Freelance material is generally welcome.
News Editor *Tom Hamilton*
Features Editor *Melanie Harvey*
Business Editor *John Penman*
Political Editor *Paul Sinclair*
Assistant Editor (Sport) *James Traynor*
Magazine Editor *Angela Dewar*

Scotland Means Business Quarterly business magazine, launched 2002. Editor *Magnus Gardham*

Daily Sport
19 Great Ancoats Street, Manchester
M60 4BT
☎0161 236 4466   Fax 0161 236 4535
www.dailysport.co.uk
Owner *Sport Newspapers Ltd*
Editor *David Beevers*
Circulation 200,000

Tabloid catering for young male readership. Unsolicited material welcome; send to News Editor, *Jane Field*
Sports Editor *Marc Smith*

Lads Mag Monthly glossy magazine. Editor *Mark Harris.*

Daily Star
The Northern & Shell Building, No. 10
Lower Thames Street, London EC3R 6EN
☎0871 434 1010
Owner *Northern & Shell Media/Richard Desmond*
Editor *Dawn Neesom*
Circulation 850,936

In competition with *The Sun* for off-the-wall news and features. Freelance opportunities available.
Deputy Editor *Jim Mansell*
Assistant Editor, Features *Samm Taylor*
Sports Editor *Howard Wheatcroft*

Daily Star Sunday
The Northern & Shell Building, No. 10
Lower Thames Street, London EC3R 6EN
☎0871 434 1010
Owner *Northern & Shell Media/Richard Desmond*
Editor *Gareth Morgan*
Circulation 556,751

New Sunday, launched in September 2002 in direct competition with *News of the World* and *The People.*
Supplement: *Take5* Lifestyle/showbiz magazine.

The Daily Telegraph
1 Canada Square, Canary Wharf, London
E14 5DT
☎020 7538 5000   Fax 020 7513 2506
www.telegraph.co.uk
Owner *Telegraph Group Ltd*
Editor *Martin Newland*
Circulation 912,497

Unsolicited mss not generally welcome – 'all are carefully read and considered, but very few published'. Contenders should approach the paper in writing, making clear their authority for writing on that subject. No fiction.
Home Editor *Richard Preston* Tip-offs or news reports from *bona fide* journalists. Must phone the news desk in first instance. Maximum 200 words. Payment minimum £40 (tip).
Arts Editor *Sarah Crompton*
City Editor *Neil Collins*
Political Editor *George Jones*
Diary Editor *Celia Walden* Always interested in diary pieces.
Education *John Clare*
Environment *Charles Clover*
Features Editor *Richard Preston* Most material supplied by commission from established contributors. New writers are tried out by arrangement with the features editor. Approach in writing. Maximum 1500 words.
Literary Editor *Sam Leith*
Sports Editor *Keith Perry* Occasional opportunities for specialised items.
Style Editor *Rachel Forder*
PAYMENT by arrangement.

Daily Telegraph Weekend Saturday supplement.
Editor *Michele Lavery*

Financial Times
1 Southwark Bridge, London SE1 9HL
☎020 7873 3000   Fax 020 7873 3076
✉ firstname.lastname@ft.com
www.ft.com
Owner *Pearson*
Editor *Andrew Gowers*
Circulation 426,803

Founded 1888. UK and international coverage of business, finance, politics, technology, management, marketing and the arts. All feature ideas must be discussed with the department's editor in advance. Not snowed under with unsolicited contributions – they get less than any other national newspaper. Approach by e-mail with ideas in the first instance.

News Editors *Tracy Corrigan, Deborah Hargreaves*
Features Editor *Andrew Hill*
Arts Editor *Peter Aspden*
Financial Editor *Deborah Hargreaves*
Literary Editor *Jan Dalley*
Notebook Editor *Robert Shrimsley*
Education *Miranda Green*
Environment *Fiona Harvey*
Political Editor *James Blitz*
Sports Correspondent *David Owen*

Weekend FT Editor *Richard Addis*

How to Spend It Monthly magazine. Editor *Gillian de Bono*

The Guardian
119 Farringdon Road, London EC1R 3ER
☎020 7278 2332   Fax 020 7837 2114
✉ firstname.secondname@guardian.co.uk
www.guardian.co.uk
Owner *The Scott Trust*
Editor *Alan Rusbridger*
Circulation 367,478

Of all the nationals *The Guardian* probably offers the greatest opportunities for freelance writers, if only because it has the greatest number of specialised pages which use freelance work. But mss must be directed at a specific slot.

Deputy Editor *Georgina Henry*
Deputy Editor (News) *Paul Johnson* No opportunities except in those regions where there is presently no local contact for news stories.
Home News *Ed Pilkington*
Arts Editor *Charlie English*
Literary Editor *Claire Armitstead*
Financial Editor *Paul Murphy*
City Editor *Julia Finch*
Life Editor *Simon Rogers* Thursday supplement, published in association with *Nature*. Science, technology, medicine, environment and other issues. Incorporates *Online* science and computing. Computing/communications (Internet) articles should be addressed to *Jack Schofield*; science articles to *Tim Radford*. Mss on disk or by e-mail (neil.mcintosh@guardian.co.uk).
Diary Editor *Marina Hyde*
Education Editor *Will Woodward* Expert pieces on modern education welcome.
Environment *John Vidal*
Features Editor *Ian Katz* Receives up to 50 unsolicited mss a day; these are passed on to relevant page editors.
Guardian Society Patrick Butler Focuses on

social change – the forces affecting us, from environment to government policies. Top journalists and outside commentators.

Media Editor *Matt Wells* Nine pages a week, plus 'New Media'. Outside contributions are considered. All aspects of modern media, advertising and PR. Background insight important. Best approach is by e-mail (janine.gibson@guardian.co.uk).
Political Editor *Mike White*
Sports Editor *Ben Clissitt*
Women's Page *Clare Margetson* Runs three days a week. Unsolicited ideas used if they show an appreciation of the page in question. Maximum 800–1000 words. Write, e-mail (clare.margetson@guardian.co.uk) or fax on 020 7239 9935.

The Guardian Weekend Glossy Saturday issue. Editor *Katharine Viner*
The Guide Editor *Tim Lusher*

The Herald (Glasgow)
200 Renfield Street, Glasgow G2 3PR
☎0141 302 7000   Fax 0141 302 7070
www.theherald.co.uk
Owner *Gannett UK Ltd*
Editor *Mark Douglas-Home*
Circulation 83,083

One of the oldest national newspapers in the English-speaking world, *The Herald*, which dropped its 'Glasgow' prefix in February 1992, was bought by Scottish Television in 1996 and by Newsquest in 2003. Lively, quality, national Scottish daily broadsheet. Approach with ideas in writing or by phone in first instance.

News Editor *Magnus Llewellin*
Arts Editor *Keith Bruce*
Business Editor *Ian McConnell*
Diary *Ken Smith*
Education *Andrew Denholm*
Sports Editor *Donald Cowey*
Herald Magazine Editor *Kathleen Morgan*

The Independent
Independent House, 191 Marsh Wall, London E14 9RS
☎020 7005 2000   Fax 020 7005 2999
www.independent.co.uk
Owner *Independent Newspapers*
Editor *Simon Kelner*
Circulation 262,004

Founded 1986. Particularly strong on its arts/media coverage, with a high proportion of feature material. Theoretically, opportunities for freelancers are good. However, unsolicited mss are not welcome; most pieces originate in-house or from known and trusted outsiders. Ideas should be submitted in writing.

News Editor *John Mullin*
Features *Adam Leigh*
Arts Editor *Ian Irvine*
Business Editor *Jeremy Warner*
Education *Richard Garner*
Environment *Michael McCarthy*
Literary Editor *Boyd Tonkin*
Political Editor *Andrew Grice*
Sports Editor *Matt Tench*
Travel Editor *Simon Calder*

The Independent Magazine Saturday supplement. Editor *Laurence Earle*

The Independent Traveller 32-page Saturday magazine

The Information Editor *Jo Ellison*

Independent on Sunday

Independent House, 191 Marsh Wall, London E14 9RS
☎020 7005 2000   Fax 020 7005 2999
www.independent.co.uk
Owner *Independent Newspapers*
Editor *Tristan Davies*
Circulation 210,198

Founded 1986. Regular columnists contribute most material but feature opportunites exist. Approach with ideas in first instance.

News Editor *Andy Malone*
Focus Editor *Cole Moreton*
Arts Editor *Marcus Field*
Comment Editor *James Hanning*
Business Editor *Jason Nissé*
Literary Editor *Suzi Feay*
Environment *Geoffrey Lean*
Political Editor *Andy McSmith*
Sports Editor *Neil Morton*
Travel Editor *Kate Simon*

The Sunday Review supplement. Editor *Andrew Tuck*

ABC Arts, books and culture supplement.

International Herald Tribune

6 bis, rue des Graviers, 92521 Neuilly, Paris
☎0033 1 4143 9300
Fax 0033 1 4143 9338 (editorial)
✉ iht@iht.com
www.iht.com
Executive Editor *Walter Wells*
Managing Editor *Alison Smale*
Features Editor *Katherine Knorr*
Circulation 245,223

Published in France, Monday to Saturday, and circulated in Europe, the Middle East, North Africa, the Far East and the USA. General news, business and financial, arts and leisure. Uses regular freelance contributors. Contributor policy can be found on the website at: www.iht.com/contributor.htm

The Mail on Sunday

Northcliffe House, 2 Derry Street, London W8 5TS
☎020 7938 6000   Fax 020 7937 3829
Owner *Associated Newspapers/Lord Rothermere*
Editor *Peter Wright*
Circulation 2.4 million

Sunday paper with a high proportion of newsy features and articles. Experience and judgement required to break into its band of regular feature writers.

News Editor *Sebastian Hamilton*
Financial Editor *Lisa Buckingham*
Diary Editor *Katie Nicholl*
Features Editor/Women's Page *Sian James*
Books *Marilyn Warnick*
Political Editor *Simon Walters*
Sports Editor *Malcolm Vallerius*
Night & Day Editor *Christena Appleyard*
Review Editor *Jim Gillespie*

You – The Mail on Sunday Magazine Colour supplement. Many feature articles, supplied entirely by freelance writers. Editor *Sue Peart*. Features Editor *Rosalind Lowe*

Morning Star

William Rust House, 52 Beachy Road, London E3 2NS
☎020 8510 0815   Fax 020 8986 5694
✉ morsta@geo2.poptel.org.uk
Owner *Peoples Press Printing Society*
Editor *John Haylett*
Circulation 9000

Not to be confused with the *Daily Star*, the *Morning Star* is the farthest left national daily. Those with a penchant for a Marxist reading of events and ideas can try their luck, though feature space is as competitive here as in the other nationals.

News Editor *Dan Coysh*
Features & Arts Editor/Political Editor *Richard Bagley*
Foreign Editor *Dave Williams*
Sports Editor *Mark Barber*

News of the World

1 Virginia Street, London E98 1NW
☎020 7782 1000   Fax 020 7583 9504
www.newsoftheworld.co.uk

Owner *News International plc/Rupert Murdoch*
Editor *Andy Coulson*
Circulation 3.64 million

Highest circulation Sunday paper. Freelance contributions welcome. News and features editors welcome tips and ideas.

Deputy Editor *Neil Wallis*
News Editor *Gary Thompson*
Features Editor *Jules Stenson*
Business/City Editor *Peter Prendergast*
Political Editor *Ian Kirby*
Sports Editor *Mike Dunn*

Sunday Magazine Colour supplement. Editor *Judy McGuire*. Showbiz interviews and strong human-interest features make up most of the content, but there are no strict rules about what is 'interesting'. Unsolicited mss and ideas welcome.

The Observer

3–7 Herbal Hill, London EC1R 5EJ
☎020 7278 2332   Fax 020 7837 7817
✉ editor@observer.co.uk
www.observer.co.uk

Owner *Guardian Newspapers Ltd*
Editor *Roger Alton*
Circulation 453,197

Founded 1791. Acquired by Guardian Newspapers from Lonrho in May 1993. Occupies the middle ground of Sunday newspaper politics.

Unsolicited material is not generally welcome, 'except from distinguished, established writers'. Receives far too many unsolicited offerings already. No news, fiction or special page opportunities. The newspaper runs annual competitions which change from year to year. Details are advertised in the newspaper.

Executive Editor, News *Kamal Ahmed*
Arts Editor *Sarah Donaldson*
Review Editor *Jane Ferguson*
Comment Editor *Barbara Gunnell*
Deputy Business Editor/City Editor *Richard Wachman*
Business Editor *Frank Kane*
Personal Finance Editor *Maria Scott*
Science Editor *Robin McKie*
Education Editor *Martin Bright*
Environment Correspondent *Juliette Jowit*
Literary Editor *Robert McCrum*
Travel Editor *Joanne O'Connor*
Sports Editor *Brian Oliver*

The Observer Magazine Glossy arts and lifestyle supplement. Editor *Allan Jenkins*

The Observer Sport Monthly Magazine supplement launched in 2000. Editor *Jason Cowley*

The Observer Food Monthly Launched in 2001. Editor *Nicola Jeal*

The Observer Music Monthly Launched in 2003. Editor *Caspar Llewellyn Smith*

The People

1 Canada Square, Canary Wharf, London E14 5AP
☎020 7293 3614   Fax 020 7293 3887
www.people.co.uk

Owner *Trinity Mirror plc*
Editor *Mark Thomas*
Circulation 941,026

Slightly up-market version of *The News of the World*. Keen on exposés and big-name gossip. Interested in ideas for investigative articles. Phone in first instance.

News Editor *David Jeff*
Features Editor *Katy Weitz*
Political Editor *Nigel Nelson*
Sports Editor *Lee Horton*
Travel Associate Editor *Trisha Harbord*

Take It Easy Magazine supplement. Editor *Maria Coole* Approach by phone with ideas in first instance.

Scotland on Sunday

Barclay House, 108 Holyrood Road, Edinburgh EH8 8AS
☎0131 620 8620   Fax 0131 620 8491
www.scotlandonsunday.com

Owner *Scotsman Publications Ltd*
Editor *Iain Martin*
Circulation 82,265

Scotland's top-selling quality broadsheet. Welcomes ideas rather than finished articles.

News Editor *Peter Laing*
Arts Editor *Fiona Leith*

Spectrum Colour supplement. Features on personalities, etc. Editor *Eilidh MacAskill*

The Scotsman

Barclay House, 108 Holyrood Road, Edinburgh EH8 8AS
☎0131 620 8620   Fax 0131 620 8616
(Editorial)
www.scotsman.com

Owner *Scotsman Publications Ltd*
Editor *John McGurk*
Circulation 67,327

Scotland's national newspaper. Many unsolicited mss come in, and stand a good chance of being read, although a small army of regulars supply much of the feature material not written in-house. See website for contact details.

News Editor *James Hall*
Business Editor *Nick Bevens*
Education *Kevin Schofield*
Features Editor *Emma Cowing*
Book Reviews *David Robinson*
Sports Editor *Donald Walker*

The Sun

1 Virginia Street, London E98 1SN
☎020 7782 4000   Fax 020 7782 4108
✉ firstname.lastname@the-sun.co.uk
www.the-sun.co.uk
Owner *News International Ltd/Rupert Murdoch*
Editor *Rebekah Wade*
Circulation 3.26 million

Highest circulation daily. Populist outlook; very keen on gossip, pop stars, TV soap, scandals and exposés of all kinds. No room for non-professional feature writers; 'investigative journalism' of a certain hue is always in demand, however.
Head of News *Chris Pharo*
Head of Features *Dominic Mohan*
Head of Sport *Steve Waring*
Woman's Editor *Sharon Hendry*
Health Editor *Jane Symons*
Fashion Editor *Erica Davies*

Sunday Express

The Northern & Shell Building, No. 10
Lower Thames Street, London EC3R 6EN
☎0871 434 1010   Fax 0871 434 7300
Owner *Northern & Shell Media/Richard Desmond*
Editor *Martin Townsend*
Circulation 912,089

The general rule of thumb is to approach in writing with an idea; all departments are prepared to look at an outline without commitment.
News Editor *Stuart Winter*
Features Editor *Giulia Rhodes*
Business Editor *David Parsley*
Political Editor *Julia Hartley-Brewer*
Sports Editor *Scott Wilson*

S Fashion and lifestyle magazine for women. Editor *Louise Robinson*. No unsolicited mss. All contributions are commissioned. Ideas in writing only.
PAYMENT negotiable.

Sunday Herald

200 Renfield Street, Glasgow G2 3QB
☎0141 302 7800   Fax 0141 302 7815
✉ editor@sundayherald.com
www.sundayherald.com
Owner *Newsquest*

Editor *Richard Walker*
Circulation 58,303
Also at: 9/10 St Andrew Square, Edinburgh EH2 2AF
☎0131 718 6040 Fax 0131 718 6105
Launched February 1999. Scottish seven-section broadsheet.
Joint Deputy Editors *David Milne, David Dick*
News Editor *Charlene Sweeney*
Political Editor *Paul Hutcheon*
Sports Editor *Stephen Penman*
Entertainment Editor *Andrew Burnet*
Magazine Editor *Jane Wright*

Sunday Mail

One Central Quay, Glasgow G3 8DA
☎0141 309 3000   Fax 0141 309 3587
www.sundaymail.co.uk
Owner *Trinity Mirror plc*
Editor *Allan Rennie*
Circulation 605,743

Popular Scottish Sunday tabloid.
News Editor *Brendan McGinty*
Features Editor *Susie Cormack*
Sports Editor *George Cheyne*

7Days Weekly supplement. Editor *Liz Steele*

Sunday Mirror

1 Canada Square, Canary Wharf, London E14 5AP
☎020 7293 3000
Fax 020 7293 3939 (news desk)
www.sundaymirror.co.uk
Owner *Trinity Mirror*
Editor *Tina Weaver*
Circulation 1.53 million

In general terms contributions are welcome, though the paper patiently points out it has more time for those who have taken the trouble to study the market. Initial contact in writing preferred, except for live news situations. No fiction.
News Editor *James Saville* The news desk is very much in the market for tip-offs and inside information. Contributors would be expected to work with staff writers on news stories. Approach by telephone or fax in the first instance.
Finance *Melanie Wright*
Features Editor *Nicky Dawson* 'Anyone who has obviously studied the market will be dealt with constructively and courteously.' Cherishes its record as a breeding ground for new talent.
Sports Editor *Craig Tregurtha*

Celebs on Sunday Colour supplement. Editor *Mel Brodie*

Sunday Post

2 Albert Square, Dundee DD1 9QJ
☎01382 223131   Fax 01382 201064
✉ mail@sundaypost.com
www.sundaypost.com

Owner *D.C. Thomson & Co. Ltd*
Editor *David Pollington*
Circulation 497,800

Contributions should be addressed to the editor.

post plus Monthly colour supplement. Editor *Jan Gooderham*

Sunday Sport

19 Great Ancoats Street, Manchester M60 4BT
☎0161 236 4466   Fax 0161 236 4535
www.sundaysport.com

Owner *David Sullivan*
Editor *Paul Carter*
Circulation 178,740

Founded 1986. Sunday tabloid catering for a particular sector of the male 15–35 readership. As concerned with 'glamour' (for which, read: 'page 3') as with human interest, news, features and sport. Unsolicited mss are welcome; receives about 90 a week. Approach should be made by phone in the case of news and sports items, by letter for features. All material should be addressed to the news editor.

News Editor *Nick Appleyard* Off-beat news, human interest, preferably with photographs.

Showbiz Editor *Alice Walker* Regular items: showbiz, television, films, pop music and gossip.

Sports Editor *Marc Smith* Hard-hitting sports stories on major soccer clubs and their personalities, plus leading clubs/people in other sports. Strong quotations to back up the news angle essential.

PAYMENT negotiable and on publication.

The Sunday Telegraph

1 Canada Square, Canary Wharf, London E14 5DT
☎020 7538 5000   Fax 020 7538 6242
www.telegraph.co.uk

Owner *Press Holdings Limited*
Editor *Dominic Lawson*
Circulation 686,270

Right-of-centre quality Sunday paper which, although traditionally formal, has pepped up its image to attract a younger readership. Unsolicited material from untried writers is rarely ever used. Contact with idea and details of track record.

News Editor *Richard Ellis*
Features Editor *Susannah Herbert*

City Editor *Robert Peston*
Political Editor *Patrick Hennessy*
Education Editor *Julie Henry*
Arts Editor *Lucy Tuck*
Environment Editor *David Harrison*
Literary Editor *Michael Prodger*
Diary Editor *Tim Walker*
Sports Editor *Jon Ryan*

Sunday Telegraph Magazine Colour supplement. Editor *Anna Murphy*

The Sunday Times

1 Pennington Street, London E98 1ST
☎020 7782 5000   Fax 020 7782 5658
www.sunday-times.co.uk

Owner *News International plc/Rupert Murdoch*
Editor *John Witherow*
Circulation 1.36 million

Founded 1820. Tendency to be anti-establishment, with a strong crusading investigative tradition. Approach the relevant editor with an idea in writing. Close scrutiny of the style of each section of the paper is strongly advised before sending mss. No fiction. All fees by negotiation.

News Editor *Charles Hymas* Opportunities are very rare.

News Review Editor *Eleanor Mills* Submissions are always welcome, but the paper commissions its own, uses staff writers or works with literary agents, by and large. The features sections where most opportunities exist are *Style* and *The Culture*.

Culture Editor *Helen Hawkins*
Business Editor *William Lewis*
City Editor *Richard Fletcher*
Education Editor *Geraldine Hackett*
Science/Environment *Jonathan Leake*
Literary Editor *Caroline Gascoigne*
Sports Editor *Alex Butler*
Style Editor *Tiffanie Darke*

Sunday Times Magazine Colour supplement. Editor *Robin Morgan* No unsolicited material. Write with ideas in first instance.

The Times

1 Pennington Street, London E98 1TT
☎020 7782 5000   Fax 020 7488 3242
www.thetimes.co.uk

Owner *News International plc/Rupert Murdoch*
Editor *Robert Thomson*
Circulation 685,448

Generally right (though features can range in tone from diehard to libertarian). *The Times* receives a great many unsolicited offerings.

Writers with feature ideas should approach by letter in the first instance. No fiction.

Deputy Editor *Ben Preston*
News Editor *John Wellman*
Features Editor *Michael Harvey*
Associate Editor *Brian MacArthur*
City/Financial Editor *Patience Wheatcroft*
Diary Editor *Andrew Pierce*

Arts Editor *Richard Halledge*
Literary Editor *Erica Wagner*
Political Editor *Phil Webster*
Sports Editor *Tim Hallissey*
Weekend Review Editor *Ben MacIntyre*
The Times Magazine Saturday supplement. Editor *Gill Morgan*
Times 2 Editor *Sandra Parsons*

Regional Newspapers

ENGLAND

Berkshire

Reading Evening Post
8 Tessa Road, Reading RG1 8NS
☎0118 918 3000 Fax 0118 959 9363
✉ editorial@reading-epost.co.uk
Owner *Guardian Media Group*
Editor *Andy Murrill*
Circulation 18,681

Unsolicited mss welcome; one or two received every day. Fiction rarely used. Interested in local news features, human interest, well-researched investigations. Special sections include holidays & travel (Mon); food page; children's page (Tues); style page (Wed); business (Wed & Fri); motoring and motorcycling; gardening; rock music (Fri).

Cambridgeshire

Cambridge Evening News
Winship Road, Milton, Cambridge CB4 6PP
☎01223 434434 Fax 01223 434415
Owner *Cambridge Newspapers Ltd*
Editor *Murray Morse*
Circulation 32,830

> Deputy Editor *James Foster*
> News Editor *John Deex*
> Business Editor *Jenny Chapman*
> Sports Editor *Chris Gill*

Cheshire

Trinity Mirror Cheshire
Chronicle House, Commonhall Street, Chester CH1 2AA
☎01244 340151 Fax 01244 606498
✉ eric.langton@cheshirenews.co.uk
www.iccheshireonline.co.uk
Owner *Trinity Mirror Plc*
Editor-in-Chief *Eric Langton*

All unsolicited feature material will be considered.

Cleveland

Hartlepool Mail
New Clarence House, Wesley Square, Hartlepool TS24 8BX
☎01429 239333 Fax 01429 869024
✉ mail.news@northeast-press.co.uk
www.hartlepooltoday.co.uk
Owner *Johnston Press Plc*
Editor *Paul Napier*
Circulation 20,719

> News Editor *Pete McCusker*
> Sports Editor *Roy Kelly*

Cumbria

News & Star
Newspaper House, Dalston Road, Carlisle CA2 5UA
☎01228 612600 Fax 01228 612601
Owner *Cumbrian Newspaper Group Ltd*
Editor *Keith Sutton*
Circulation 25,029

> Deputy Editor *Nick Turner*
> Sports Editor *Vic Gibson*
> Women's Page *Jane Loughran*

North West Evening Mail
Abbey Road, Barrow in Furness LA14 5QS
☎01229 821835 Fax 01229 840164
✉ news@nwemail.co.uk
www.nwemail.co.uk
Owner *Robin Burgess*
Editor *Stephen Brauner*
Circulation 19,752

All editorial material should be addressed to the editor.

> Sports Editor *Leo Clarke*

Derbyshire

Derby Evening Telegraph
Northcliffe House, Meadow Road, Derby DE1 2DW
☎01332 291111 Fax 01332 253027
Owner *Northcliffe Newspapers Group Ltd*
Editor *Mike Norton*
Circulation 50,133

News Editor *Cheryl Hague* (newsdesk@derbytelegraph.co.uk)
News Features Editor *Sarah Newton* (sarahnewton@derbytelegraph.co.uk)
Sports Editor *Peter Green* (sports@derbytelegraph.co.uk)
Motoring Editor *Bob Maddox*

Devon

Evening Herald

17 Brest Road, Derriford Business Park, Derriford, Plymouth PL6 5AA
☎01752 765500 Fax 01752 765527
✉ news@eveningherald.co.uk
www.thisisplymouth.co.uk
Owner *Northcliffe Newspapers Group Ltd*
Editor *Alan Qualtrough*
Circulation 41,865

All editorial material to be addressed to the editor or the News Editor *James Garnett*.

Express & Echo

Heron Road, Sowton, Exeter EX2 7NF
☎01392 442211 Fax 01392 442287 (editorial)
✉ echonews@expressandecho.co.uk
www.thisisexeter.co.uk
Owner *Westcountry Publications Limited*
Editor *Steve Hall*
Circulation 25,270

Weekly supplements: *Business Week*; *Property Echo*; *Wheels*; *Weekend Echo*.
  Head of Content *Sue Kemp*
  Features Editor *Lynne Turner*
  Sports Editor *Richard Davies* (Fax 01392 442416)

Herald Express

Harmsworth House, Barton Hill Road, Torquay TQ2 8JN
☎01803 676000 Fax 01803 676228 (editorial)
✉ newsdesk@heraldexpress.co.uk
www.thisissouthdevon.co.uk
Owner *Northcliffe Newspapers Group Ltd*
Editor *B. Hanrahan*
Circulation 26,095

Drive scene, property guide, *On The Town* – leisure and entertainment guide, Monday sports, special pages, rail trail, Saturday surgery, nature and conservation column, dance scene, shop scene, The Business. Supplements: *Gardening* (weekly); *Visitors Guide* and *Antiques & Collectables* (fortnightly). Unsolicited mss

generally not welcome. All editorial material should be addressed to the editor in writing.

Sunday Independent

Burrington Way, Plymouth PL5 3LN
☎01752 206600 Fax 01752 206164
Owner *Tindle Newspapers*
Editor *John Noble*
Circulation 28,434

Tabloid Sunday covering the whole of the West Country from Bristol to Weymouth and Land's End. News stories/tips, news features. All editorial should be addressed to the editor. PAYMENT by arrangement.

Western Morning News

17 Brest Road, Derriford Business Park, Derriford, Plymouth PL6 5AA
☎01752 765500 Fax 01752 765535
✉ wmnnewsdesk@westernmorningnews.co.uk
www.thisisplymouth.co.uk
Owner *Northcliffe Newspapers Group Ltd*
Editor *Barrie Williams*
Circulation 46,189

Unsolicited mss welcome, but must be of topical and local interest and addressed to the Assistant Editor (News) *Mark Hughes*.
  Features Editor *Su Carroll*
  Sports Editor *Mark Stephens*

Dorset

Daily Echo

Richmond Hill, Bournemouth BH2 6HH
☎01202 554601 Fax 01202 299543
Owner *Newsquest Media Group Ltd (a Gannett company)*
Editor *Neal Butterworth*
Circulation 34,359

Founded 1900. Has a strong news and features content and invites specialist articles, particularly on unusual subjects, either contemporary or historical, but only with a local angle or flavour. Special review sections each day, including sport, property, entertainment and culture, heritage, motoring, gardening, the environment and the coastline. Also *Saturday Magazine* and monthly *Society* glossy magazine. All editorial material should be addressed to the Editor *Neal Butterworth*. PAYMENT on publication.

Dorset Echo

Fleet House, Hampshire Road, Granby Industrial Estate, Weymouth DT4 9XD
☎01305 830930 Fax 01305 830956

Owner *Newsquest Media Group Ltd (a Gannett company)*
Editor *David Murdock*
Circulation 21,507

By-gone days, films, arts, showbiz, brides, motoring, property, weekend leisure and entertainment including computers and gardening and weekend magazine.

News Editor *Paul Thomas*
Sports Editor *Paul Baker*

Durham

The Northern Echo
Priestgate, Darlington DL1 1NF
☎01325 381313 Fax 01325 380539
✉ echo@nne.co.uk
www.thisisthenortheast.co.uk
Owner *Newsquest (North East) Ltd (a Gannett company)*
Editor *Peter Barron*
Circulation 55,675

Founded 1870. Freelance pieces welcome but telephone first to discuss submission.

News Editor *Nigel Burton* Interested in reports involving the North East or North Yorkshire. Preferably phoned in.

Features Editor *Nick Morrison* Background pieces to topical news stories relevant to the area. Must be arranged with the features editor before submission of any material.

Business Editor *Julia Breen*
Sports Editor *Nick Loughlin*
PAYMENT and length by arrangement.

Essex

Evening Echo
Newspaper House, Chester Hall Lane, Basildon SS14 3BL
☎01268 522792 Fax 01268 469281
Owner *Newsquest Media Group (a Gannett company)*
Editor *Martin McNeill*
Circulation 38,081

Relies almost entirely on staff and regular outside contributors, but will very occasionally consider material sent on spec. Approach the editor in writing with ideas. Although the paper is Basildon-based, its largest circulation is in the Southend area.

Evening Gazette (Colchester)
Oriel House, 43–44 North Hill, Colchester CO1 1TZ
☎01206 506000 Fax 01206 508274

✉ gazette_newsdesk@nqe.com
www.thisisessex.co.uk
Owner *Newsquest (Essex) Ltd*
Editor *Irene Kettle*
Circulation 26,179

Monday to Friday daily newspaper servicing north and mid-Essex including Colchester, Harwich, Clacton, Braintree, Witham, Maldon and Chelmsford. Unsolicited mss not generally used. Relies heavily on regular contributors.

Features Editor *Iris Clapp*

Gloucestershire

The Citizen
St John's Lane, Gloucester GL1 2AY
☎01452 424442
Fax 01452 420664 (Editorial)
Owner *Northcliffe Newspapers Group Ltd*
Editor *Ian Mean*
Circulation 28,587

News or features material should be addressed to News Editor, *Bev Hawes* or Features Editor, *Victoria Temple*.

Gloucestershire Echo
1 Clarence Parade, Cheltenham GL50 3NY
☎01242 271900 Fax 01242 271848
Owner *Northcliffe Newspapers Group Ltd*
Editor *Anita Syvret*
Circulation 23,419

All material, other than news, should be addressed to the editor.

News Editor *Tanya Gledhill*

Hampshire

The News
The News Centre, Hilsea, Portsmouth PO2 9SX
☎023 9266 4488 Fax 023 9267 3363
✉ newsdesk@thenews.co.uk
www.portsmouth.co.uk
Owner *Portsmouth Printing & Publishing Ltd*
Editor *Mike Gilson*
Circulation 60,663

Unsolicited mss not generally accepted. Approach by letter.

Assistant Editor *Colin McNeill*
Features Editor *John Millard* General subjects of S.E. Hants interest. Maximum 600 words. No fiction.

Sports Editor *Colin Channon* Sports background features. Maximum 600 words.

The Southern Daily Echo

Newspaper House, Test Lane, Redbridge,
Southampton SO16 9JX
☎023 8042 4777   Fax 023 8042 4545
www.thisishampshire.net
Owner *Newsquest Plc*
Editor *Ian Murray*
Circulation 42,137

Unsolicited mss 'tolerated'. Approach the editor
in writing with strong ideas; staff supply almost
all the material.

Kent

Kent Messenger

6 & 7 Middle Row, Maidstone ME14 1TG
☎01622 695666   Fax 01622 757227
✉ rdimond@thekmgroup.co.uk
www.kentonline.co.uk
Owner *Kent Messenger Group*
Editor *Bob Dimond*
Circulation 57,450

Very little freelance work is commissioned.

Medway Messenger

Medway House, Ginsbury Close, Sir Thomas
Longley Road, Medway City Estate, Strood,
Rochester ME2 4DU
☎01634 227800   Fax 01634 715256
✉ medwaymessenger@thekmgroup.co.uk
www.kentonline.co.uk
Owner *Kent Messenger Group*
Editor *Bob Dimond*
Circulation 13,560

Published Mondays and Fridays with the free
Medway Extra on Wednesday.
  Business Editor *Trevor Sturgess*
  Community Editor *David Jones*
  Sports Editor *Mike Rees*

Lancashire

Bolton Evening News

Newspaper House, Churchgate, Bolton
BL1 1DE
☎01204 522345   Fax 01204 365068
✉ bennewsdesk@boltoneveningnews.co.uk
www.thisisbolton.co.uk
Owner *Newsquest Media Group Ltd (a Gannett
  company)*
Editor *Steve Hughes*
Circulation 35,350

Business, children's page, travel, local services,
motoring, fashion and cookery.

News Editor *John Horne*
Features Editor/Women's Page *Andrew
  Mosley*

The Gazette (Blackpool)

PO Box 20, Avroe House, Avroe Crescent,
Blackpool FY4 2DP
☎01253 400888   Fax 01253 361870
✉ editorial@blackpoolgazette.co.uk
www.blackpooltoday.co.uk
Owner *Johnston Press plc*
Managing Director *Philip Welsh*
Editor *David Helliwell*
Circulation 34,890

Unsolicited mss welcome in theory. Approach
in writing with an idea. Supplements: *Eve*
(women, Tues); *All Stars* (football, Wed); *Homes*
(Thurs); *The Weekend* (entertainment, Fri);
Wheels (motoring, Fri); *Life!* magazine (entertainment & leisure, Sat); *Jobs Plus* (jobs and
careers, Sat).

Lancashire Evening Post

Olivers Place, Eastway, Fulwood, Preston
PR2 9ZA
☎01772 254841   Fax 01772 880173
www.prestontoday.net
Owner *Johnston Press plc*
Editor *Simon Reynolds*
Circulation 40,010

Unsolicited mss are not generally welcome;
many are received and not used. All ideas in
writing to the editor.

Lancashire Evening Telegraph

Newspaper House, High Street, Blackburn
BB1 1HT
☎01254 678678   Fax 01254 680429
www.thisislancashire.co.uk
Owner *Newsquest Media Group Ltd (a Gannett
  company)*
Editor *Kevin Young*
Circulation 36,026

News stories and feature material with an East
Lancashire flavour (a local angle, or written by
local people) welcome. Approach in writing
with an idea in the first instance. No fiction.
  News Editor *Andrew Turner*
  Features Editor *John Anson*

Oldham Evening Chronicle

PO Box 47, Union Street, Oldham OL1 1EQ
☎0161 633 2121   Fax 0161 652 2111
✉ editorial@oldham-chronicle.co.uk
Owner *Hirst Kidd & Rennie Ltd*

Editor *Jim Williams*
Circulation 25,957

Motoring, food and wine, lifestyle supplement, business page.
News Editor *Mike Attenborough*

Leicestershire

Leicester Mercury

St George Street, Leicester LE1 9FQ
☎0116 251 2512 Fax 0116 253 0645
www.thisisleicestershire.co.uk
Owner *Northcliffe Newspapers Group Ltd*
Editor *Nick Carter*
Circulation 84,419

News Editor *Mark Charlton*
Features Editor *Alex Dawson*

Lincolnshire

Grimsby Telegraph

80 Cleethorpe Road, Grimsby DN31 3EH
☎01472 360360 Fax 01472 372257
✉ newsdesk@grimsbytelegraph.co.uk
Owner *Northcliffe Newspapers Group Ltd*
Editor *Michelle Lalor*
Circulation 39,681

Sister paper of the *Scunthorpe Evening Telegraph*. Unsolicited mss generally welcome. Approach in writing. No fiction. Weekly supplements: *Business Telegraph*; *Homes and Gardens*; *Drive* (motoring); *Sports Telegraph* (Sat). All material to be addressed to the News Editor *D. Laister*. Particularly welcomes hard news stories – approach in haste by telephone.
Special Publications Editor *B. Farnsworth*

Lincolnshire Echo

Brayford Wharf East, Lincoln LN5 7AT
☎01522 820000 Fax 01522 804493
✉ editor@lincolnshireecho.co.uk
Owner *Northcliffe Newspapers Group Ltd*
Editor *Michael Sassi*
Circulation 25,169

Best buys, holidays, motoring, dial-a-service, restaurants, sport, leisure, home improvement, record reviews, gardening corner, stars. All editorial material to be addressed to the editor.

Scunthorpe Telegraph

4–5 Park Square, Scunthorpe DN15 6JH
☎01724 273273 Fax 01724 273101
Owner *Northcliffe Newspapers Group Ltd*

Editor *Jon Grubb*
Circulation 22,432

All correspondence should go to the Deputy Editor *Jane Manning*.

London

Evening Standard

Northcliffe House, 2 Derry Street, London W8 5EE
☎020 7938 6000 Fax 020 7937 2648
www.standard.co.uk/e-editions
Owner *Associated Newspapers/Lord Rothermere*
Editor *Veronica Wadley*
Circulation 343,314

Long-established evening paper, serving Londoners with both news and feature material. Genuine opportunities for London-based features. Produces a weekly colour supplement, *ES The Evening Standard Magazine*, a weekly listings magazine, *MetroLife* and regular weekly supplements: *Just the Job* (Mon) and *Homes & Property* (Wed).
Joint Deputy Editors *Andrew Bordiss, Ian MacGregor*
Executive Editor *Anne McElvoy*
Managing Editor *Doug Wills*
Assistant Editor (Features) *Guy Eaton*
News Editor *Ian Walker*
Assistant Editor (Arts) *Norman Lebrecht*
Assistant Editor (Sport) *Martin Chilton*
Editor, *ES Catherine Ostler*
Editor, *MetroLife Mark Booker*

Manchester

Manchester Evening News

164 Deansgate, Manchester M60 2RD
☎0161 832 7200 Fax 0161 834 3814
www.manchesteronline.co.uk
Owner *Manchester Evening News Ltd*
Editor *Paul Horrocks*
Circulation 141,737

One of the country's major regional dailies. Initial approach in writing preferred. No fiction. *Personal Finance* (Mon); *Health* (Tues); *Homes & Property* (Wed); *Small Business* (Thurs); *Lifestyle* (Fri/Sat); *Holidays* (Sat).
News Editor *Ian Wood*
Features Editor *Deanna Delamotta* Regional news features, personality pieces and showbiz profiles considered. Maximum 1200 words.
Sports Editor *Peter Spencer*
Women's Page *Helen Tither*
PAYMENT based on house agreement rates.

Merseyside

Liverpool Daily Post

PO Box 48, Old Hall Street, Liverpool
L69 3EB
☎0151 227 2000 Fax 0151 236 4682
www.icliverpool.co.uk
Owner *Trinity Mirror Plc*
Editor *Jane Wolstenholme*
Circulation 20,199

Unsolicited mss welcome. Receives about six a day. Approach in writing with an idea. No fiction. Local, national/international news, current affairs, profiles – with pictures. Maximum 800–1000 words.

Features Editor *Louise Douglas*
News Editor *Greg Fray*
Business Editor *Bill Gleeson*
Sports Editor *Richard Williamson*
Women's Page *Penny Fray*

Liverpool Echo

PO Box 48, Old Hall Street, Liverpool
L69 3EB
☎0151 227 2000 Fax 0151 236 4682
✉ letters@liverpoolecho.co.uk
Owner *Trinity Mirror Merseyside*
Editor *Alastair Machray*
Circulation 129,681

One of the country's major regional dailies. Unsolicited mss welcome; initial approach with ideas in writing preferred.

News Editor *Alison Gow*
Features Editor *Jane Haase*
Sports Editor *John Thompson*
Women's Editor *Susan Lee*

Norfolk

Eastern Daily Press

Prospect House, Rouen Road, Norwich
NR1 1RE
☎01603 628311 Fax 01603 623872
www.EDP24.co.uk
Owner *Archant Regional*
Editor *Peter Franzen, OBE*
Circulation 71,095

Most pieces by commission only. Supplements: Centro (daily); education, motoring, business, property pages, agriculture, employment (all weekly); *Event* full-colour magazine (Fri); *Saturday* full colour magazine.

Deputy Editor *James Ruddy*
Assistant Editor (News) *Paul Durrant*
Head of Features Content *Sarah Hardy*

Sports Editor *David Thorpe*
Assistant Editor (*Saturday*) *Steve Snelling*

Evening News

Prospect House, Rouen Road, Norwich
NR1 1RE
☎01603 628311 Fax 01603 219060
✉ david.bourn@archant.co.uk
www.eveningnews24.co.uk
Owner *Archant Ltd*
Editor *David Bourn*
Circulation 28,420

Includes special pages on local property, motoring, pop, fashion, arts, entertainments and TV, gardening, local music scene, home and family.

Deputy Editor *Tim Williams*
(tim.williams@archant.co.uk)
Assistant Editor *Amanda Patterson*
(amanda.patterson@archant.co.uk)
Features Editor *Derek James*
(derek.james@archant.co.uk)

Northamptonshire

Chronicle and Echo

Upper Mounts, Northampton NN1 3HR
☎01604 467000 Fax 01604 467190
Owner *Northamptonshire Newspapers*
Editor *Mark Edwards*
Circulation 24,434

Unsolicited mss are 'not necessarily unwelcome but opportunities to use them are rare'. Approach in writing with an idea. No fiction. Supplements: *Sport on Monday*; *Business Week* (Tues); *Property Week* (Wed); *Job Search* (Thurs); *Weekend Motors* and *The Guide* (Friday); *TV Week* (Sat).

News Editor *Richard Edmondson*
Features Editor/Women's Page *Angela Pownall*
Sports Editor *Steve Pitts*

Evening Telegraph

Newspaper House, Ise Park, Rothwell Road, Kettering NN16 8GA
☎01536 506100
Fax 01536 506195 (editorial)
✉ etnewsdesk@northantsnews.co.uk
www.northantsnews.com
Owner *Johnston Press Plc*
Managing Editor *David Penman*
Circulation 27,536

Northamptonshire Business Guide (weekly); *Entertainment Guide* and *Jobs* supplements (Thurs); films and eating out (Fri); and *Home & Garden*

– monthly lifestyle supplement including gardening, etc.

Assistant Editor *Nick Tite*
  Deputy News Editor *Kristy Ward*
  Sports Editor *Mark Lea*

Nottinghamshire

Evening Post Nottingham
Castle Wharf House, Nottingham NG1 7EU
☎0115 948 2000   Fax 0115 964 4032
Owner *Northcliffe Newspapers Group Ltd*
Editor *Graham Glen*
Circulation 72,269

Unsolicited mss occasionally used. Good local interest only. Maximum 800 words. No fiction. Send ideas in writing.
  News Editor *Claire Catlow*
  Deputy Editor *Marc Astley*
  Sports Editor *Dave Parkinson*

Oxfordshire

Oxford Mail
Osney Mead, Oxford OX2 0EJ
☎01865 425262   Fax 01865 425554
✉ nqonews@nqo.com
www.thisisoxfordshire.co.uk
Owner *Newsquest (Oxfordshire) Ltd*
Editor *Simon O'Neill*
Circulation 26,428

Unsolicited mss are considered but a great many unsuitable offerings are received. Approach in writing with an idea, rather than by phone. No fiction.
PAYMENT All fees negotiable.

Shropshire

Shropshire Star
Ketley, Telford TF1 5HU
☎01952 242424   Fax 01952 254605
Owner *Shropshire Newspapers Ltd*
Editor *Sarah-Jane Smith*
Circulation 79,460

No unsolicited mss; approach the editor with ideas in writing in the first instance. No news or fiction.
  Head of Features *Sharon Walters, Carl Jones*
Limited opportunities; uses mostly in-house or syndicated material. Maximum 1200 words.
  Sports Editor *Dave Ballinger*

Somerset

The Bath Chronicle
Windsor House, Windsor Bridge Road, Bath
BA2 3AU
☎01225 322322   Fax 01225 322291
www.thisisbath.com
Owner *Northcliffe Newspapers Group Ltd*
Editor *David Gledhill* (editor@bathchron.co.uk)
Circulation 13,871

Local news and features especially welcomed (news@bathchron.co.uk).
  Deputy Editor *John McCready*
  News Editor *Paul Wiltshire*
  Features Editor *Georgette McCready*
  Sports Editor *Julie Riegal*

Evening Post
Temple Way, Bristol BS99 7HD
☎0117 934 3000   Fax 0117 934 3575
✉ epnews@bepp.co.uk
www.thisisbristol.com
Owner *Northcliffe Newspapers Group Ltd*
Editor *Mike Lowe*
Circulation 63,870
  News Editor *Kevan Blackadder*
  Features Editor *Bill Davis*
  Sports Editor *Chris Bartlett*

Western Daily Press
Temple Way, Bristol BS99 7HD
☎0117 934 3000   Fax 0117 934 3574
✉ WDEditor *or* WDNews *or*
WDFeats@bepp.co.uk
www.westpress.co.uk
Owner *Bristol Evening Post & Press Ltd*
Editor *Terry Manners*
Circulation 48,097
  Sports Editor *Chris Spittles*
  Women's Page *Susie Weldon* (Features
  Production)

Staffordshire

Burton Mail
65–68 High Street, Burton upon Trent
DE14 1LE
☎01283 512345   Fax 01283 515351
✉ editorial@burtonmail.co.uk
Owner *Staffordshire Newspapers Ltd*
Editor *Paul Hazeldine*
Circulation 15.960

Fashion, health, wildlife, environment, nostalgia, financial/money (Mon); consumer (Tues);

women's world, rock (Wed); property (Thurs); motoring, farming, what's on (Fri); what's on, leisure (Sat).

News *Steve Doohan*
Features *Louise Worrell*
Sports Editor *Rex Page*

The Sentinel/Sentinel Sunday

Sentinel House, Etruria, Stoke on Trent
ST1 5SS
☎01782 602525 Fax 01782 280781
(Sentinel)/201167 (Sentinel Sunday)
www.thisisstaffordshire.co.uk
Owner *Staffordshire Sentinel Newspapers Ltd*
Editor-in-Chief *Sean Dooley*
Circulation 73,210 (Sentinel)/13,140
(Sentinel Sunday)

Weekly sports final supplement. All material should be sent to the Head of Content *Martin Tideswell*.

Suffolk

East Anglian Daily Times

Press House, 30 Lower Brook Street, Ipswich
IP4 1AN
☎01473 230023 Fax 01473 324776
✉ eadt@eadt.co.uk
www.eadt.co.uk
Owner *Archant Ltd*
Editor *Terry Hunt*
Circulation 39,297

Founded 1874. Unsolicited mss generally not welcome; three or four received a week and almost none are used. Approach in writing in the first instance. No fiction. Supplements: sport (Mon); business (Tues); jobs (Wed); property (Thurs); motoring (Fri); magazine (Sat).

News Editor *Aynsley Davidson* Hard news stories involving East Anglia (Suffolk, Essex particularly) or individuals resident in the area are always of interest.

Features *Julian Ford* Mostly in-house, but will occasionally buy in when the subject is of strong Suffolk/East Anglian interest. Photo features preferred (extra payment). Special advertisement features are regularly run. Some opportunities here. Maximum 1000 words.

Sports Editor *Nick Garnham*
Women's Page *Victoria Hawkins*

Evening Star

30 Lower Brook Street, Ipswich IP4 1AN
☎01473 230023 Fax 01473 324850
Owner *Archant Ltd*

Editor *Nigel Pickover*
Circulation 24,896

News Editor *Martin Davey*

East Sussex

The Argus

Argus House, Crowhurst Road, Hollingbury, Brighton BN1 8AR
☎01273 544544 Fax 01273 505703
✉ michael.beard@theargus.co.uk
www.theargus.co.uk
Owner *Newsquest (Sussex) Ltd*
Editor-in-Chief *Michael Beard*
Circulation 38,361

News Editor *Melanie Dowding*
Sports Editor *Chris Giles*

Teesside

Evening Gazette

Borough Road, Middlesbrough TS1 3AZ
☎01642 234242 Fax 01642 232014
www.icTeesside.co.uk
Owner *Trinity Mirror plc*
Editor *Steve Dyson*
Circulation 58,446

Special pages: health, education, family, business, property, entertainment, leisure, motoring, recruitment.

News Editor *Jim Horsley*
Features Editor/Women's Page *Kathryn Armstrong*
Business *Helen Logan*
Sports Editor *Allan Boughey*
Councils *Sandy McKenzie*
Consumer *Babara Argument*
Health *Helen Sturdy*
Crime *Mike Underwood*

Tyne & Wear

Evening Chronicle

Groat Market, Newcastle upon Tyne
NE1 1ED
☎0191 232 7500 Fax 0191 232 2256
✉ ec.news@ncjmedia.co.uk
www.icnewcastle.co.uk
Owner *Trinity Mirror Plc*
Editor *Paul Robertson*
Circulation 89,074

Receives a lot of unsolicited material, much of which is not used. Family issues, gardening, pop, fashion, cooking, consumer, films and entertainment guide, home improvements, motoring, property, angling, sport and holidays. Approach in writing with ideas. Limited opportunities for features due to full-time feature staff.

News Editor *John Howe*
Sports Editor *Paul New*
Women's Interests *Jennifer Bradbury*

Gazette

Chapter Row, South Shields NE33 1BL
☎0191 427 4800 Fax 0191 456 8270
www.southtynesidetoday.co.uk

Owner *Northeast Press Ltd*
Editor *John Szymanski*
Circulation 20,967

News Editor *Gary Welford*
Sports Editor *Mick Worrall*
Feature's Editor *Janie Blower*

The Journal

Groat Market, Newcastle upon Tyne NE1 1ED
☎0191 232 7500/201 6344 (Newsdesk)
Fax 0191 232 2256/201 6044
✉ jnl.newsdesk@ncjmedia.co.uk
www.icnewcastle.co.uk

Owner *Trinity Mirror Plc*
Editor *Brian Aitken*
Circulation 41,665

Daily platforms include farming and business.
Deputy Editor *Graham Pratt*
Sports Editor *Kevin Dinsdale*
Arts & Entertainment Editor *David Whetstone*
Environment Editor *Tony Henderson*
Business Editor *Iain Laing*

Sunday Sun

Newcastle Chronicle & Journal Ltd, Thomson House, Groat Market, Newcastle upon Tyne NE1 1ED
☎0191 201 6158 Fax 0191 201 6180
✉ peter.montellier@ncjmedia.co.uk

Owner *Trinity Mirror Plc*
Editor *Peter Montellier*
Circulation 80,066

All material should be addressed to the appropriate editor (phone to check), or to the editor.
Sports Editor *Darren Kelso*

Sunderland Echo

Echo House, Pennywell, Sunderland SR4 9ER
☎0191 501 5800 Fax 0191 534 4861
✉ rob.lawson@northeast-press.co.uk

Owner *Johnston Press Plc*
Editor *Rob Lawson*
Circulation 47,184

Address any editorial material to the News Editor *Patrick Lavelle* (echo.news@northeast-press.co.uk).

Warwickshire

Coventry Evening Telegraph

Corporation Street, Coventry CV1 1FP
☎024 7663 3633 Fax 024 7655 0869
✉ news@coventry-telegraph.co.uk
www.IcCoventry.co.uk

Owner *Trinity Mirror Plc*
Editor *Alan Kirby*
Circulation 58,217

Unsolicited mss are read, but few are published. Approach in writing with an idea. No fiction. All unsolicited material should be addressed to the editor. Maximum 600 words for features.
News Managers *Steve Chilton, Steve Williams*
Features Manager/Women's Page *Paula Irish*
Sports Editor *Rob Madill*
PAYMENT negotiable.

Leamington Spa Courier

32 Hamilton Terrace, Leamington Spa CV32 4LY
☎01926 457755 Fax 01926 339960
✉ editorial@leamingtoncourier.co.uk
www.leamingtontoday.co.uk

Owner *Heart of England Newspapers (Johnston Press)*
Editor *Martin Lawson*
Circulation 16,270

One of the Leamington Spa Courier series which also includes the Warwick Courier and Kenilworth Weekly News. Unsolicited feature articles considered, particularly matter with a local angle. Telephone with idea first.
News Editor *Peter Gawthorpe*

West Midlands

Birmingham Evening Mail

PO Box 78, Weaman Street, Birmingham B4 6AT
☎0121 236 3366
Fax 0121 234 5878 (editorial)

Owner *Trinity Mirror Plc*
Editor *Roger Borrell*
Circulation 96,143

Freelance contributions are welcome, particularly topics of interest to the West Midlands and Women's Page pieces offering original and lively comment.

Deputy Editor *Colin Clark*
Features Editor *Alison Handley*
Women's Page *Diane Parkes*

Birmingham Post

Weaman Street, Birmingham B4 6AT
☎0121 236 3366 Fax 0121 234 5667

Owner *Trinity Mirror Plc*
Editor *Fiona Alexander*
Circulation 12,936

One of the country's leading regional newspapers. Freelance contributions are welcome. Topics of interest to the West Midlands and pieces offering lively, original comment are particularly welcome.

News Editor *Mo Ilyas*
Features Editor *Sid Langley*

Express & Star

Queen Street, Wolverhampton WV1 1ES
☎01902 313131 Fax 01902 319721

Owner *Midlands News Association*
Editor *Adrian Faber*
Circulation 157,783

Deputy Editor *Keith Harrison*
Assistant Editor *Roy Williams*
Head of News *Mark Drew*
Features Editor *Dylan Evans*
Business Editor *Jim Walsh*
Sports Editor *Tim Walters*
Women's Editor *Elured Bowen*

Sunday Mercury (Birmingham)

Weaman Street, Birmingham B4 6AY
☎0121 234 5567 Fax 0121 234 5877
✉ sundaymercury@mrn.co.uk

Owner *Trinity Mirror Plc*
Editor *David Brookes*
Circulation 75,049

Deputy Editor (Features) *Paul Cole*
Head of Content *Tony Larner*
Assistant Editor (Sport) *Lee Gibson*

Wiltshire

Evening Advertiser

100 Victoria Road, Swindon SN1 3BE
☎01793 528144 Fax 01793 501888
✉ editor@newswilts.co.uk
www.thisiswiltshire.co.uk

Owner *Newsquest (Wiltshire & Oxfordshire) Ltd*
Editor *Mark Waldron*
Circulation 23,204

Copy and ideas invited. 'All material must be

strongly related or relevant to the town of Swindon or the county of Wiltshire.' Little scope for freelance work. Fees vary depending on material.

Deputy Editor *Pauline Leighton*
News Editor *Catherine Turnbull*
Sports Editor *Neville Smith*

Worcestershire

Evening News

Berrow's House, Hylton Road, Worcester WR2 5JX
☎01905 748200 Fax 01905 748009

Owner *Newsquest (Midlands South) Ltd*
Editor *Stewart Gilbert*
Circulation 19,427

Local events (Tues); jobs/careers (Wed); property (Thurs); showbiz/what's on, motoring and Pulse pop page (Fri); holidays/what's on (Sat).

News Editor *Sala Lloyd*
Features Editor *Mike Pryce*
Sports Editor *Paul Ricketts*

Yorkshire

The Doncaster Star

Sunny Bar, Doncaster DN1 1NB
☎01302 348500 Fax 01302 348528
✉ rob.hollingworth@sheffieldnewspapers.co.uk

Owner *Sheffield Newspapers Ltd*
Editor/News Editor *Rob Hollingworth*
Circulation 5,638

Editorial material to be addressed to the editor.

Sports Writer *Steve Hossack*

Evening Press

PO Box 29, 76–86 Walmgate, York YO1 9YN
☎01904 653051 Fax 01904 612853
✉ newsdesk@ycp.co.uk
www.thisisyork.co.uk

Owner *Newsquest Media Group (a Gannett company)*
Editor *Kevin Booth*
Circulation 36,555

Unsolicited mss not generally welcome, unless submitted by journalists of proven ability. *Business Press Pages* (Tues); *Property Press* (Thurs); *Friday Night Fever* – what's on (Fri); *8 Days* TV supplement (Sat).

Assistant Editor *Fran Clee*
News Editor *Scott Armstrong*
Picture Editor *Martin Oates*
Sports Editor *Martin Jarred*
PAYMENT negotiable.

Huddersfield Daily Examiner

Queen Street South, Huddersfield
HD1 2TD
☎01484 430000 Fax 01484 437789
Owner *Trinity Mirror Plc*
Editor *Roy Wright*
Circulation 29,953

Home improvement, home heating, weddings, dining out, motoring, fashion, services to trade and industry.

Assistant Editor *Michael O'Connell*
Head of Content *Jenny Parkin*
News Editor *Neil Atkinson*
Features Editor *Andrew Flynn*
Sports Editor *John Gledhill*
Women's Page *Hilarie Stelfox*

Hull Daily Mail

Blundell's Corner, Beverley Road, Hull
HU3 1XS
☎01482 327111 Fax 01482 315353
✉ news@hdmp.co.uk
www.thisishullandeastriding.co.uk
Owner *Northcliffe Newspapers Group Ltd*
Editor *John Meehan*
Circulation 66,608

News Editor *Jeremy Deacon*
Features Editor *Paul Johnson*

Scarborough Evening News

17–23 Aberdeen Walk, Scarborough
YO11 1BB
☎01723 363636 Fax 01723 383825
✉ editorial@scarboroughEveningnews.co.uk
www.scarboroughtoday.co.uk
Owner *Yorkshire Regional Newspapers Ltd*
Editor *Ed Asquith*
Circulation 14,889

Special pages include property (Mon); jobs (Thurs); motors (Fri).

Deputy Editor *Sue Wilkinson*
News Editor *Neil Pickford*
Sports Editor *Charles Place*
All other material should be addressed to the editor.

The Star

York Street, Sheffield S1 1PU
☎0114 276 7676 Fax 0114 272 5978
Owner *Sheffield Newspapers Ltd*
Editor *Alan Powell*
Circulation 68,261

Unsolicited mss not welcome, unless topical and local.

News Editor *Bob Westerdale* Contributions only accepted from freelance news reporters if they relate to the area.

Features Editor *John Highfield* Very rarely requires outside features, unless on specialised local subjects.

Sports Editor *Martin Smith*
Women's Page *Jo Davison*
PAYMENT negotiable.

Telegraph & Argus (Bradford)

Hall Ings, Bradford BD1 1JR
☎01274 729511 Fax 01274 723634
www.thisisbradford.co.uk
Owner *Newsquest Media Group Ltd (a Gannett company)*
Editor *Perry Austin-Clarke*
Circulation 45,069

No unsolicited mss – approach in writing with samples of work. No fiction.

Head of News *Martin Heminway*
Features Editor *David Barnett* Local features and general interest. Showbiz pieces. 600–1000 words (maximum 1500).

Yorkshire Evening Post

Wellington Street, Leeds LS1 1RF
☎0113 243 2701 Fax 0113 238 8536
✉ eped@ypn.co.uk
Owner *Johnson Press*
Editor *Neil Hodgkinson*
Circulation 68,635

Evening sister of the Yorkshire Post.

News Editor *Gilian Haworth*
Features Editor *Anne Pickles*
Sports Editor *Phil Rostron*
Women's Page *Jayne Dawson*

Yorkshire Post

Wellington Street, Leeds LS1 1RF
☎0113 243 2701 Fax 0113 238 8537
✉ yp.editor@ypn.co.uk
Owner *Johnston Press*
Editor *Peter Charlton*
Circulation 57,976

A serious-minded, quality regional daily with a generally conservative outlook. Three or four unsolicited mss arrive each day; all will be considered but initial approach in writing preferred. All submissions should be addressed to the editor. No fiction, poetry or family histories.

Deputy Editor *Duncan Hamilton*
Features Editor *Catherine Scott* Open to suggestions in all fields (though ordinarily commissioned from specialist writers).
Sports Editor *Matt Reeder*

NORTHERN IRELAND

Northern Ireland

Belfast News Letter
46–56 Boucher Crescent, Belfast BT12 6QY
☎028 9068 0000   Fax 028 9066 4412

Owner *Century Newspapers Ltd*
Editor *Austin Hunter*

Weekly supplements: *Farming Life; Business News Letter, Female Times; The Guide; Sports Ulster.*
News Editors *Ric Clark, Steven Moore*
Features Editor *Geoff Hill*
Sports Editor *Brian Millar*
Fashion & Lifestyle/Property Editor *Sandra Chapman*
Business Editor *Adrienne McGill*
Agricultural Editor *David McCoy*
Political Editor *Stephen Dempster*

Belfast Telegraph
Royal Avenue, Belfast BT1 1EB
☎028 9026 4000   Fax 028 9055 4506/4540

Owner *Independent News & Media (UK)*
Editor *Edmund Curran*
Circulation 94,540

Weekly business, property and recruitment supplements.
Deputy Editor *Jim Flanagan*
News Editor *Paul Connolly*
Features Editor *Gail Walker*
Sports Editor *John Laverty*
Business Editor *Nigel Tilson*

The Irish News
113/117 Donegall Street, Belfast BT1 2GE
☎028 9032 2226   Fax 028 9033 7505
✉ newsdesk@irishnews.com

Owner *Irish News Ltd*
Editor *Noel Doran*
Circulation 50,007

All material to appropriate editor (phone to check), or to the news desk.
Assistant Editor *Fiona McGarry*
Sports Editor *Thomas Hawkins*
Arts Editor/Women's Page *Joanna Braniff*
Scotland

Sunday Life
124–144 Royal Avenue, Belfast BT1 1EB
☎028 9026 4300   Fax 028 9055 4739
✉ betty.arnold@belfasttelegraph.co.uk
www.sundaylife.co.uk

Owner *Independent News & Media (UK)*
Editor/General Manager *Martin Lindsay*

Circulation 82,850
Deputy Editor *Martin Hill*
Sports Editor *Jim Gracey*
More2Life Colour supplement. Editor *Stephanie Bell*

SCOTLAND

The Courier and Advertiser
80 Kingsway East, Dundee DD4 8SL
☎01382 223131   Fax 01382 454590
✉ courier@dcthomson.co.uk
www.thecourier.co.uk

Owner *D.C. Thomson & Co. Ltd*
Editor *Bill Hutcheon*
Circulation 81,002

Circulates in East Central Scotland. Features occasionally accepted on a wide range of subjects, particularly local/Scottish interest – including finance, insurance, agriculture, motoring, modern homes, lifestyle and fitness. Maximum length, 500 words.
News Editor *Arliss Rhind*
Features Editor/Women's Page *Catriona McInnes*
Sports Editor *Graeme Dey*

Daily Record (Glasgow)
See *National Newspapers*

Evening Express (Aberdeen)
PO Box 43, Lang Stracht, Mastrick, Aberdeen AB15 6DF
☎01224 690222   Fax 01224 699575
✉ ee.news@ajl.co.uk

Owner *Northcliffe Newspapers Group Ltd*
Editor *Donald Martin*
Circulation 57,893

Circulates in Aberdeen and the Grampian region. Local, national and international news and pictures, sport. Family platforms include *What's On, Counter* (consumer news), *Eating Out Guide, Family Days Out.* Unsolicited mss welcome 'if on a controlled basis'.
Assistant Editor *Richard Prest* Freelance news contributors welcome.
PAYMENT negotiable.

Evening News
Barclay House, 108 Holyrood Road, Edinburgh EH8 8AS
☎0131 620 8620   Fax 0131 620 8696

www.edinburghnews.com
Owner *Scotsman Publications Ltd*
Editor *Ian Stewart*
Circulation 63,771

Founded 1873. Circulates in Edinburgh, Fife, Central and Lothian. Coverage includes: entertainment, gardening, motoring, shopping, fashion, health and lifestyle, showbusiness. Occasional platform pieces, features of topical and/or local interest. Unsolicited feature material welcome. Approach the appropriate editor in writing.
  News Editor *Euan McGrory*
  Sports Editor *Graham Lindsay*
  PAYMENT NUJ/house rates.

Evening Telegraph
80 Kingsway East, Dundee DD4 8SL
☎01382 223131 Fax 01382 454590
✉ general@eveningtelegraph.co.uk
www.eveningtelegraph.co.uk

Owner *D.C. Thomson & Co. Ltd*
Editor *Alan Proctor*
Circulation 25,545

Circulates in Tayside, Dundee and Fife. All material should be addressed to the editor.

Evening Times
200 Renfield Street, Glasgow G2 3QB
☎0141 302 7000 Fax 0141 302 6677
✉ times@eveningtimes.co.uk

Owner *Newsquest*
Editor *Charles McGhee*
Circulation 91,613

Circulates in Glasgow and the west of Scotland. Supplements: *Job Search*; *City Living*; *Drive times*; *Extra times*; *Times Out*; *et* magazine.
  News Editor *Hugh Boag*
  Features Editor *Garry Scott*
  Sports Editor *David Stirling*

Greenock Telegraph
2 Crawfurd Street, Greenock PA15 1LH
☎01475 726511 Fax 01475 783734

Owner *Clyde & Forth Press Ltd*
Editor *Martin Biddle*
Circulation 18,806

Circulates in Greenock, Port Glasgow, Gourock, Kilmacolm, Langbank, Bridge of Weir, Inverkip, Wemyss Bay, Skelmorlie, Largs. Unsolicited mss considered 'if they relate to the newspaper's general interests'. No fiction. All material to be addressed to the editor.

The Herald/Sunday Herald (Glasgow)
See *National Newspapers*

Paisley Daily Express
14 New Street, Paisley PA1 1YA
☎0141 887 7911 Fax 0141 887 6254
✉ pde@s-un.co.uk
Owner *Scottish & Universal Newspapers Ltd*
Editor *Jonathan Russell*
Circulation 11,091

Circulates in Paisley, Linwood, Renfrew, Johnstone, Elderslie, Neilston and Barrhead. Unsolicited mss welcome only if of genuine local (Paisley) interest. The paper does not commission work and will consider submitted material. Maximum 1000–1500 words. All submissions to the editor.
  News Editor *Anne Dalrymple*
  Sports Reporters *Michelle Evans, Paul Behan*

The Press and Journal
PO Box 43, Lang Stracht, Mastrick, Aberdeen AB15 6DF
☎01224 690222 Fax 01224 663575
Owner *Northcliffe Newspapers Group Ltd*
Editor *Derek Tucker*
Circulation 87,858

A well-established daily that circulates in Aberdeen, Grampians, Highlands, Tayside, Orkney, Shetland and the Western Isles. Most material is commissioned but will consider ideas.
  News Editor *Fiona McWhirr* Wide variety of hard or off-beat news and features relating especially, but not exclusively, to the north of Scotland.
  Sports Editor *Alex Martin*
  Women's Page *Victoria Banks*
  Your Life *Sonja Cox* Saturday lifestyle tabloid pullout. Features food, fashion, travel, books, arts and lifestyle.
  PAYMENT by arrangement.

Scotland on Sunday (Edinburgh)
See *National Newspapers*

Sunday Mail (Glasgow)
See *National Newspapers*

The Scotsman (Edinburgh)
See *National Newspapers*

Sunday Post (Dundee)
See *National Newspapers*

WALES

Daily Post
PO Box 202, Vale Road, Llandudno Junction,
Conwy LL31 9ZD
☎01492 574455   Fax 01492 574433
✉ welshnews@dailypost.co.uk
Owner *Trinity Mirror Plc*
Editor in Chief *To be appointed*
Circulation 40,835

> Features Editor *Jill Tunstall*
> News Editor *Maria Breslyn*
> Sports Editor *Steve Macmillan*

Evening Leader
Mold Business Park, Wrexham Road, Mold
CH7 1XY
☎01352 707707   Fax 01352 752180
✉ news@eveningleader.co.uk
Owner *North Wales Newspapers*
Editor-in-Chief *Richard Williams*
Circulation 26,331

Circulates in Wrexham, Flintshire, Deeside and
Chester. Special pages/features: motoring,
travel, arts, women's, children's, photography,
local housing, information and news for the
disabled, music and entertainment.

> Assistant Editor *Barrie Jones*
> Head of Content *Joanne Shone*
> Sports Editor *Nick Harrison*

South Wales Argus
Cardiff Road, Maesglas, Newport
NP20 3QN
☎01633 810000   Fax 01633 777202
www.thisisgwent.co.uk
Owner *Newsquest*
Editor *Gerry Keighley*
Circulation 30,788

Circulates in Newport, Gwent and surrounding
areas.

> News Editor *Mark Templeton*
> Sports Editor *Phil Webb*

South Wales Echo
Thomson House, Havelock Street, Cardiff
CF10 1XR
☎029 2058 3622   Fax 029 2058 3624
www.icwales.co.uk
Owner *Trinity Mirror Plc*
Editor *Richard Williams*
Circulation 57,852

Circulates in South and Mid Glamorgan and
Gwent.

Head of News *Cathy Owen*
Head of Features *Jonah Webb, Alison Stokes*
Head of Sport *Delme Parfitt*

South Wales Evening Post
Adelaide Street, Swansea SA1 1QT
☎01792 510000   Fax 01792 514697
✉ postbox@swwp.co.uk
www.thisissouthwales.co.uk
Owner *Northcliffe Newspapers Group Ltd*
Editor *Spencer Feeney*
Circulation 56,487

Circulates throughout south west Wales.

> News Editor *Peter Slee*
> Features Editor *Catherine Ings*
> Sports Editor *David Evans*

Wales on Sunday
Thomson House, Havelock Street, Cardiff
CF10 1XR
☎029 2022 3333   Fax 029 2058 3725
Owner *Trinity Mirror plc*
Editor *Tim Gordon*
Circulation 48,060

Launched 1989. Tabloid with sports supplement. Does not welcome unsolicited mss.

> News Editor *Laura Kemp*
> Show Biz/Features Editor *Rachel Mainwaring*
> Sports Editor *Nick Rippington*

Western Mail
Thomson House, Havelock Street, Cardiff
CF10 1XR
☎029 2058 3583   Fax 029 2058 3652
www.icwales.com
Owner *Trinity Mirror Plc*
Editor *Alan Edmunds*
Circulation 43,247

Circulates in Cardiff, Merthyr Tydfil, Newport,
Swansea and towns and villages throughout
Wales. Mss welcome if of a topical nature, of
Welsh interest. No short stories or travel.
Approach in writing to the editor. 'Usual sub-
jects already well covered, e.g. motoring, travel,
books, gardening. We look for the unusual.'
Maximum 1000 words. Opportunities also on
women's page. Supplements: *Saturday Magazine*;
Education; *WM*; *Box Office*; *Welsh Homes*;
Business; *Sport*; *Motoring*; *Country & Farming*.

> Deputy Editor *Ceri Gould*
> News Editor *Pal Carey*
> Sports Editor *Philip Blanche*
> Features Editor *Duncan Higgitt*

CHANNEL ISLANDS

Guernsey Press & Star

Braye Road, Vale, Guernsey GY1 3BW
☎01481 240240   Fax 01481 240235
✉ newsroom@guernsey-press.com
www.guernsey-press.com

Owner *Guiton Group*
Editor *Richard Digard*
Circulation 16,291

Special pages include children's and women's interest, gardening and fashion.

News Editor *James Falla*
Sports Editor *Rob Batiste*
Features Editor *Suzanne Heneghan*

Jersey Evening Post

PO Box 582, Jersey JE4 8XQ
☎01534 611611   Fax 01534 611622
✉ editorial@jerseyeveningpost.com
www.thisisjersey.com

Owner *Claverley Company*
Editor *Chris Bright*
Circulation 22,037

Special pages: gardening, motoring, property, boating, technology, young person's (16–25), women, food and drink, personal finance, rock reviews, health, business.

News Editor *Sue Le Ruez*
Features Editor *Elaine Hanning*
Sports Editor *Ron Felton*

Magazines

Abraxas

57 Eastbourne Road, St Austell PL25 4SU
☎01726 64975   Fax 01726 64975
✉ LordCrashingbore@aol.com *or*
palnew7@hotmail.com
www.stormloader.com/users/abrax7

Owner *Paul Newman*
Editors *Paul Newman, Pamela Smith-Rawnsley*

Founded 1991. Regularly features a lead article by *Colin Wilson* combined with short stories, poems, translations and articles on philosophy, existentialism and ideas. Favours challenging essays on the new and radical slants on the old. Contributors include Gary Lachman, D.M. Thomas, Ramond Tallis, Adam Daly and Colin Stanley.

FICTION One story per issue; approx. 1000 words. 'Think of a writer like Wolfgang Borchert who wrote briefly, vividly and fiercely.'

POETRY Open to all styles, rhymed and irregular but prefers a creative, original use of language rather than prosy verse.

Acclaim

See **The New Writer**

Accountancy

145 London Road, Kingston Upon Thames
KT2 6SR
☎020 8247 1387   Fax 020 8247 1424
www.accountancymagazine.com

Owner *Wolters Kluwer UK*
Editor *Chris Quick*
Circulation 51,482

Founded 1889. MONTHLY. Written ideas welcome.

FEATURES *Lesley Bolton* Accounting, tax, business-related articles of high technical content aimed at professional/managerial readers. Maximum 2000 words. PAYMENT by arrangement.

Accountancy Age

32–34 Broadwick Street, London W1A 2HG
☎020 7316 9190   Fax 020 7316 9250
✉ accountancy_age@vnu.co.uk
www.accountancyage.com

Owner *VNU Business Publications*

Editor *Damian Wild*
Deputy Editor *Gavin Hinks* (☎020 7316 9242)
Circulation 70,092

Founded 1969. WEEKLY. Unsolicited mss welcome. Ideas may be suggested in writing provided they are clearly thought out.

FEATURES *Rachel Fielding* Topics right across the accountancy, business and financial world. Max. 2000 words. PAYMENT negotiable.

ACE Tennis Magazine

IG House, Palliser Road, London W14 9EB
☎020 7381 7100   Fax 020 7610 2794
✉ Nigel.Billen@acemag.co.uk

Owner *Tennis GB*
Editor *Nigel Billen*
Circulation 46,140

Founded 1996. MONTHLY specialist tennis magazine. News (250 words max.) and features (2000 words max.). No unsolicited mss; send feature synopses by e-mail in the first instance. No tournament reports. PAYMENT £200 per 1000 words.

Acumen

See under *Poetry Magazines*

Aeroplane

IPC Media Ltd., King's Reach Tower, Stamford Street, London SE1 9LS
☎020 7261 5849   Fax 020 7261 5269
✉ aeroplane_monthly@ipcmedia.com
www.aeroplanemonthly.com

Owner *IPC Country & Leisure Media Ltd*
Editor *Michael Oakey*
Circulation 36,656

Founded 1973. MONTHLY. Historic aviation and aircraft preservation from its beginnings to the 1960s. No post-1960 aircraft types; no poetry. Will consider news items and features written with authoritative knowledge of the subject, illustrated with good quality photographs.

NEWS *Tony Harsmworth* Max. 500 words.
FEATURES *Michael Oakey* Max. 3000 words.
Approach by letter in the first instance.

PAYMENT £60 per 1000 words; £10–40 per picture used.

Air International

PO Box 100, Stamford PE9 1XQ
☎01780 755131 Fax 01780 757261
✉ malcolm.english@keypublishing.com
www.airinternational.com
Owner *Key Publishing Ltd*
Editor *Malcolm English*
Circulation 13,249

Founded 1971. MONTHLY. Civil and military aircraft magazine. Unsolicited mss welcome but initial approach by phone or in writing preferred.

AirForces Monthly

PO Box 100, Stamford PE9 1XQ
☎01780 755131 Fax 01780 757261
✉ edafm@keypublishing.com
Owner *Key Publishing Ltd*
Editor *Alan Warnes*
Circulation 20,571

Founded 1988. MONTHLY. Modern military aviation magazine. Unsolicited mss welcome but initial approach by phone or in writing preferred.

Amateur Gardening

Westover House, West Quay Road, Poole BH15 1JG
☎01202 440840 Fax 01202 440860
Owner *IPC Media (A Time Warner Company)*
Editor *Tim Rumball*
Circulation 49,763

Founded 1884. WEEKLY. New contributions are welcome especially if they are topical and informative. All articles/news items should be supported by colour pictures (which may or may not be supplied by the author).

FEATURES Topical and practical gardening articles; will only consider those accompanied by photos. Max. 1000 words.

NEWS Compiled and edited in-house generally but all stories welcomed.

PAYMENT negotiable.

Amateur Photographer

IPC Media Ltd., King's Reach Tower, Stamford Street, London SE1 9LS
☎020 7261 5100/0870 444 5000 (switchboard) Fax 020 7261 5404
✉ amateurphotographer@ipcmedia.com
Owner *IPC Media (A Time Warner Company)*
Editor *Garry Coward-Williams*
Circulation 26,698

Founded 1884. WEEKLY. For the competent amateur with a technical interest. Freelancers

are used but writers should be aware that there is ordinarily no use for words without pictures.

Amateur Stage

Hampden House, 2 Weymouth Street, London W1W 5BT
☎020 7636 4343 Fax 020 7636 2323
✉ cvtheatre@aol.com
Owner *Platform Publications Ltd*
Editor *Charles Vance*

Some opportunity here for outside contributions. Topics of interest include amateur premières, technical developments within the amateur forum and items relating to landmarks or anniversaries in the history of amateur societies. Approach in writing only (include s.a.e. for return of mss). No PAYMENT.

Ancestors

See **The National Archives** under *UK Publishers*

Angler's Mail

IPC Media Ltd., King's Reach Tower, Stamford Street, London SE1 9LS
☎020 7261 5778 Fax 020 7261 6016
✉ anglersmail@ipcmedia.com
Owner *IPC Media (A Time Warner Company)*
Editor *Tim Knight*
Circulation 45,237

Founded 1965. WEEKLY. Angling news and matches. Interested in pictures, stories, tip-offs and features. Approach the news desk by telephone. PAYMENT £10–40 per 200 words; pictures, £20–40.

Animal Action

Wilberforce Way, Southwater, Horsham RH13 9RS
☎0870 010 1181 Fax 0870 753 0048
✉ publications@rspca.org.uk
www.rspca.org.uk
Owner *RSPCA*
Editor *Sarah Evans*
Circulation 80,000

BI-MONTHLY RSPCA youth membership magazine. Articles (pet care, etc.) are written in-house. Good-quality animal photographs welcome.

Animalprints

Worthing Animal Aid, 56 Cissbury Gardens, Worthing BN14 0DZ
☎01903 877144
✉ WorthingAnimalAid@btinternet.com
Owner *Worthing Animal Aid*

Editor *Lilian Taylor*
Circulation 500
Founded 1999. QUARTERLY magazine that aims to advance the animal movement. Welcomes contributions that are well researched, subtly thought provoking and have the potential for stimulating discussion. Approach in writing. PAYMENT Complimentary copies of relevant issue.

The Antique Dealer and Collectors' Guide
PO Box 805, Greenwich, London SE10 8TD
☎020 8691 4820   Fax 020 8691 2489
✉ antiquedealercollectorsguide@ukbusiness. com
www.antiquecollectorsguideco.uk
Owner *Statuscourt Ltd*
Publisher *Philip Bartlam*
Circulation 12,500

Founded 1946. SIX ISSUES YEARLY. Covers all aspects of the antiques and fine art worlds. Unsolicited mss welcome.
FEATURES Practical but readable articles on the history, design, authenticity, restoration and market aspects of antiques and fine art. Max. 2000 words.
NEWS Items on events, sales, museums, exhibitions, antique fairs and markets. Max. 300 words.
PAYMENT rates for features by arrangement.

Antiquesnews incorporating
Antiques & Art Independent
PO Box 1945, Comely Bank, Edinburgh EH4 1AB
☎07000 268478
✉ antiquesnews@hotmail.com
www.antiquesnews.co.uk
Owner *Antiquesnews Ltd*
Publisher/Editor *Tony Keniston*
Founded 1997. WEEKLY. Up-to-date information online for the British antiques and art trade. News, photographs, gossip and controversial views on all aspects of the fine art and antiques world welcome. Articles on antiques and fine arts themselves are not featured. Approach in writing with ideas.

Apex Advertiser
PO Box 7086, Clacton-on-Sea CO15 5WN
☎01255 428500   Fax 0870 046 6536
✉ enquiry@apexadvertiser.co.uk
www.apexadvertiser.co.uk
Owner *Apex Publishing Ltd*
Editor *Susan Kidby*

Circulation 12,000
Founded 2002. MONTHLY advertising magazine including guides and information, features, listings and reviews. Approach by post, only.

Apollo Magazine
20 Theobald's Road, London WC1X 8PF
☎020 7430 1900   Fax 020 7404 7386
✉ editorial@apollomag.com
www.apollo-magazine.com
Owner *The Spectator (1828) Ltd*
Editor *Michael Hall*
Publisher *Kimberly Quinn*
FOUNDED 1925. MONTHLY. Specialist articles on art and antiques, exhibition and book reviews, exhibition diary, information on dealers and auction houses. Unsolicited mss welcome. Interested in specialist, usually new research in fine arts, architecture and antiques.

The Architects' Journal
151 Rosebery Avenue, London EC1R 4GB
☎020 7505 6700   Fax 020 7505 6701
www.ajplus.co.uk
Owner *Emap Construct*
Editor *Isabel Allen*
Circulation 13,587
WEEKLY trade magazine dealing with all aspects of the industry. No unsolicited mss. Approach in writing with ideas.

Architectural Design
John Wiley & Sons, 4th Floor, International House, Ealing Broadway Centre, London W5 5DB
☎020 8326 3800   Fax 020 8326 3801
Owner *John Wiley & Sons Ltd*
Editor *Helen Castle*
Senior Production Editor *Mariangela Palazzi-Williams*
Circulation 5,000
Founded 1930. BI-MONTHLY. Sold as a book as well as a journal, *AD* charts theoretical and topical developments in architecture. Format consists of 128pp, the first part dedicated to a theme compiled by a specially commissioned guest-editor; the back section (AD+) carries series and more current one-off articles. Unsolicited mss not welcome generally, though journalistic contributions will be considered for the back section.

The Architectural Review
151 Rosebery Avenue, London EC1R 4GB
☎020 7505 6725   Fax 020 7505 6701

www.arplus.com
Owner *Emap Construct*
Editor *Paul Finch*
Circulation 22,049

MONTHLY professional magazine dealing with architecture and all aspects of design. No unsolicited mss. Approach in writing with ideas.

Arena

Endeavour House, 189 Shaftesbury Avenue, London WC2H 8JG
☎020 7437 9011
Owner *Emap East*
Editor *Anthony Noguera*
Circulation 44,347

MONTHLY style and general interest magazine for men. Intelligent articles and profiles.

FEATURES Fashion, lifestyle, film, television, politics, business, music, media, design, art, architecture and sport.

Art Monthly

4th Floor, 28 Charing Cross Road, London WC2H 0DB
☎020 7240 0389 Fax 020 7497 0726
✉ info@artmonthly.co.uk
www.artmonthly.co.uk
Owner *Britannia Art Publications Ltd*
Editor *Patricia Bickers*
Circulation 6000

Founded 1976. TEN ISSUES YEARLY. News and features of relevance to those interested in modern and contemporary visual art. Unsolicited mss welcome. Contributions should be addressed to the deputy editor, accompanied by s.a.e.

FEATURES Always commissioned. Interviews and articles of up to 2000 words on art theory, individual artists, contemporary art history and issues affecting the arts (e.g. funding and arts education). Exhibition reviews of 750–1000 words; book reviews of 750–1000 words.

NEWS Brief reports (250–300 words) on art issues.

PAYMENT negotiable.

The Art Newspaper

70 South Lambeth Road, London SW8 1RL
☎020 7735 3331 Fax 020 7735 3332
✉ contact@theartnewspaper.com
www.theartnewspaper.com
Owner *Umberto Allemandi & Co. Publishing*
Editor *Cristina Ruiz*
Circulation 22,000

Founded 1990. MONTHLY. Tabloid format with hard news on the international art market, news, museums, exhibitions, archaeology, conservation, books and current debate topics. Length 250–2000 words. No unsolicited mss. Approach with ideas in writing. Commissions only. PAYMENT £120 per 1000 words.

Art Review

Hereford House, 23–24 Smithfield Street, London EC1A 9LF
☎020 7246 3350 Fax 020 7246 3351
✉ info@art-review.co.uk
www.art-review.co.uk
Owner *Dennis Hotz*
Editor *Rebecca Wilson*
Deputy Editor *Charlotte Edwards*
Circulation 35,000

Founded 1949. MONTHLY magazine of international contemporary art. Features, profiles, previews and reviews of artists and exhibitions worldwide. 'We have a very international focus so it's important that the artist is exhibiting internationally and has good gallery representation.'

FEATURES *Rebecca Wilson, Charlotte Edwards* Max. 1500 words. E-mail pitch and c.v. to editor@art-review.co.uk at least three months in advance of related show/publication. PAYMENT £400–500.

NEWS All items written in-house.

The Artist

Caxton House, 63–65 High Street, Tenterden TN30 6BD
☎0158076 3673 Fax 0158076 5411
www.theartistmagazine.co.uk
Owner/Editor *Sally Bulgin*
Circulation 21,500

Founded 1931. MONTHLY. Art journalists, artists, art tutors and writers with a good knowledge of art materials are invited to write to the editor with ideas for practical and informative features about art, materials, techniques and artists.

Asian Times

Unit 2, 65 Whitechapel Road, London E1 1DU
☎020 7650 2000 Fax 020 7650 2001
✉ asiantimes@ethnicmedia.co.uk
www.asiantimesonline.co.uk
Owner *Ethnic Media Group*
Editor *Burhan Ahmad*
Circulation 28,525

Founded 1981. WEEKLY community paper for the Asian community in Britain. Interested in

relevant general, local and international issues.
Approach in writing with ideas for submission.

Athletics Weekly
83 Park Road, Peterborough PE1 2TN
☎01733 898440   Fax 01733 898441
✉ results@athletics-weekly.co.uk
www.athleticsweekly.com
Owner *Descartes Publishing*
Editor *Jason Henderson*
Circulation 14,000
Founded 1945. WEEKLY. Covers track and field, road, fell, cross-country, race walking, athletic features and sports politics.
NEWS *Steve Landells* Max. 400 words.
FEATURES *Tony Ward* Max. 2000 words.
Approach in writing.
PAYMENT negotiable.

Attitude
Northern & Shell Tower, City Harbour,
4 Selsdon Way, London E14 9GL
☎020 7308 5090   Fax 020 7308 5384
✉ attitude@attitudemag.co.uk
Owner *Remnant Media*
Editor *Adam Mattera*
Deputy Editor *Jamie Hakim*
Circulation 60,000
Founded 1994. MONTHLY. Style magazine aimed primarily, but not exclusively, at gay men. Celebrity, fashion and cultural coverage. Brief summaries of proposed features, together with details of previously published work, should be sent by post or e-mail only. 'It sounds obvious, but anyone wanting to contribute to the magazine should read it first.'

The Author
84 Drayton Gardens, London SW10 9SB
☎020 7373 6642
Owner *The Society of Authors*
Editor *Andrew Taylor*
Manager *Kate Pool*
Circulation 8500
Founded 1890. QUARTERLY journal of the **Society of Authors**. Most articles are commissioned.

Auto Express
30 Cleveland Street, London W1T 4JD
☎020 7907 6200   Fax 020 7907 6234
✉ editorial@autoexpress.co.uk
www.autoexpress.co.uk
Owner *Dennis Publishing*
Editor *David Johns*

Associate Editor *Richard Yarrow*
Circulation 101,013
Founded 1989. WEEKLY consumer motoring title with news, drives, tests, investigations, etc.
NEWS News stories and tip-offs welcome. Fillers 150 words max.; leads 300 words. Approach by e-mail.
FEATURES Ideas welcome. No fully-written articles – features will be commissioned if appropriate and good enough. Max. 2000 words.
PAYMENT £350 per 1000 words.

Autocar
Somerset House, Somerset Road, Teddington TW11 8IU
☎020 8943 5630   Fax 020 8267 5759
✉ autocar@haynet.com
www.autocar.co.uk
Owner *Haymarket Publishing Ltd*
Editor *Rob Aherne*
News Editor *Hilton Holloway*
Circulation 66,661
Founded 1895. WEEKLY. All news stories, features, interviews, scoops, ideas, tip-offs and photographs welcome. PAYMENT negotiable.

Aviation News
HPC, Drury Lane, St Leonards on Sea TN38 9BJ
☎01424 720477   Fax 01424 443693
✉ editor@aviation-news.co.uk
www.aviation-news.co.uk
Owner *Hastings Printing Company*
Editor *Barry C. Wheeler*
Circulation 21,000
Founded 1939. MONTHLY review of aviation for those interested in military, commercial and business aircraft and equipment – old and new. Will consider articles on military and civil aircraft, airports, air forces, current and historical subjects. No fiction.
FEATURES 'New writers always welcome and if the copy is not good enough it is returned with guidance attached.' Max. 5000 words.
NEWS Items are always considered from new sources. Max. 300 words.
PAYMENT negotiable.

B Magazine
64 North Row, London W1K 7LL
☎020 7150 7020   Fax 020 7150 7677
✉ letters@bmagazine.co.uk
www.bmagazine.co.uk
Owner *Hachette Filipacchi (UK) Ltd*

Editor *Nina Ahmad*
Circulation 166,145

MONTHLY glossy magazine aimed at women in their mid–twenties. Will consider real–life stories, emotional issues and celebrity features. Ideas for features should be sent to *Laura Millar*. No short stories. Approach in writing or by e-mail.

Balance

Diabetes UK, 10 Parkway, London NW1 7AA
☎020 7424 1000   Fax 020 7424 1001
✉ balance@diabetes.org.uk

Owner *Diabetes UK*
Editor *Martin Cullen*
Circulation 250,000

Founded 1935. BI-MONTHLY. Unsolicited mss are not accepted. Writers may submit a brief proposal in writing. Only topics relevant to diabetes will be considered.

NEWS Short pieces about activities relating to diabetes and the lifestyle of people with diabetes. Max. 150 words.

FEATURES Medical, diet and lifestyle features written by people with diabetes or with an interest and expert knowledge in the field. General features are mostly based on experience or personal observation. Max. 1500 words.

PAYMENT NUJ rates.

The Banker

Tabernacle Court, 16–28 Tabernacle Street, London EC2A 4DD
☎020 7382 8507   Fax 020 7382 8586
✉ stephen.timewell@ft.com
www.thebanker.com

Owner *FT Business*
Editor-in-Chief *Stephen Timewell*
Circulation 24,701

Founded 1926. MONTHLY. News and features on banking, finance and capital markets worldwide and technology.

BBC Gardeners' World Magazine

Woodlands, 80 Wood Lane, London W12 0TT
☎020 8433 3959   Fax 020 8433 3986
✉ adam.pasco@bbc.co.uk
www.gardenersworld.com

Owner *BBC Worldwide Publishing Ltd*
Editor *Adam Pasco*
Deputy Editor *Lucy Hall*
Features Editor *Harriet Smith*
Circulation 257,628

Founded 1991. MONTHLY. Gardening advice, ideas and inspiration. No unsolicited mss. Approach by phone or in writing with ideas –

interested in features about exceptional small gardens. Also interested in any exciting new gardens showing good design and planting ideas as well as new plants and the stories behind them. 'The magazine aims to be the first to bring news of new trends and developments, and always welcomes ideas from contributors.'

BBC Good Food

Woodlands, 80 Wood Lane, London W12 0TT
☎020 8433 2000   Fax 020 8433 3931
✉ goodfood.magazine@bbc.co.uk

Owner *BBC Worldwide Publishing Ltd*
Editor *Gillian Carter*
Circulation 342,677

Founded 1989. MONTHLY food and drink magazine with television and radio links. No unsolicited mss.

BBC Good Homes Magazine

Woodlands, 80 Wood Lane, London W12 0TT
☎020 8433 2391   Fax 020 8433 2691
www.bbcgoodhomes.com

Owner *BBC Worldwide Publishing Ltd*
Editor *Lisa Allen*
Circulation 129,778

Founded 1998. MONTHLY. Decorating, interiors, readers' homes, shopping, makeovers, property and consumer information. No non-homes related features, food, fiction or puzzles.

Features *Chris Haslam*
PROPERTY & READERS' HOMES *Rachel Watson* Property features from specialists. Approach by letter with cuttings.

BBC History Magazine
(incorporating **Living History**)

14th Floor, Tower House, Fairfax Street, Bristol BS1 3BN
☎0117 927 9009
www.originpublishing.co.uk

Owner *BBC Worldwide Publishing Ltd*
Editor *Dave Musgrove*
Circulation 54,067

Founded 2000. MONTHLY. General news and features on British and international history, with books and CD reviews, listings of history events, TV and radio history programmes and regular features for those interested in history and current affairs. Winner, British Society of Magazine Editors 'Editor of the Year Award', 2002, for general interest and current affairs titles. Will consider submissions from academic or otherwise expert historians/archaeologists as well as, occasionally, from historically literate journalists who include expert analysis and historiography with a well-told narrative. Ideas for regular features are welcome. Also publishes cartoons, quizzes and crosswords. 'We cannot guarantee to acknowledge all unsolicited mss immediately.'

FEATURES should be pegged to anniversaries or forthcoming books/TV programmes, current affairs topics, etc. 750–3000 words.

NEWS 400–500 words. Send short letter or e-mail with synopsis, giving appropriate sources, pegs for publication dates, etc.

PAYMENT negotiable.

BBC Homes & Antiques

Woodlands, 80 Wood Lane, London W12 0TT
☎020 8433 3490　Fax 020 8433 3867
www.bbcworldwide.com/antiques

Owner *BBC Worldwide Publishing Ltd*
Editor *Mary Carroll*
Circulation 120,141

Founded 1993. MONTHLY traditional home interest magazine with a strong bias towards antiques and collectibles. Opportunities for freelancers are limited; most features are commissioned from regular stable of contributors. No fiction, health and beauty, fashion or general showbusiness. Approach with ideas by phone or in writing.

FEATURES *Caroline Wheater* At-home features: inspirational houses – people-led items. Pieces commissioned on recce shots and cuttings. Guidelines available on request. Send cuttings of relevant work published. Max. 1500 words. PAYMENT negotiable.

BBC Music Magazine

14th Floor, Tower House, Fairfax Street, Bristol BS1 3BN
☎0117 927 9009
www.originpublishing.co.uk

Owner *BBC Worldwide Publishing Ltd*
Editor *Oliver Condy*
Circulation 56,096

Founded 1992. MONTHLY. All areas of classical music. Not interested in unsolicited material. Approach with ideas by e-mail or fax.

BBC Top Gear Magazine

Room A1004, Woodlands, 80 Wood Lane, London W12 0TT
☎020 8433 3716　Fax 020 8433 3754
www.topgear.com

Owner *BBC Worldwide Publishing Ltd*
Editor *Michael Harvey*
Circulation 146,073

Founded 1993. MONTHLY companion maga-

zine to the popular TV series. No unsolicited material as most features are commissioned.

BBC Wildlife Magazine

14th Floor, Tower House, Fairfax Street, Bristol BS1 3BN
☎0117 927 9009
www.originpublishing.co.uk

Owner *BBC Worldwide Publishing Ltd*
Editor *Sophie Stafford*
Circulation 46,094

Founded 1963 (formerly *Wildlife*, née *Animals*). MONTHLY. Unsolicited mss generally not welcome.

FEATURES Most features commissioned from writers with expert knowledge of wildlife or conservation subjects. Max. 2500 words.

NEWS Most news stories commissioned from known freelancers. Max. 400 words. PAYMENT features, £200–450; news, £80–120

Bee World

IBRA, 18 North Road, Cardiff CF10 3DT
☎029 2037 2409　Fax 029 2066 5522
✉ mail@ibra.org.uk
www.ibra.org.uk

Owner *International Bee Research Association*
Editor *Dr P.A. Munn*
Circulation 1700

Founded 1919. QUARTERLY. High-quality factual journal, including peer-reviewed articles, with international readership. Features on apicultural science and technology. Unsolicited mss welcome but authors should write to the editor for guidelines before submitting material.

Bella

H. Bauer Publishing, Academic House, 24–28 Oval Road, London NW1 7DT
☎020 7241 8000　Fax 020 7241 8056

Owner *H. Bauer Publishing*
Editor-in-Chief *Jayne Marsden*
Circulation 428,028

Founded 1987. WEEKLY. Women's magazine specialising in real-life, human interest stories.

FEATURES *Clare Swatman* Contributions welcome for some sections of the magazine: readers' letters, 'Blush with Bella'.

FICTION *Linda O'Byrne* Max. 1000–1500 words. Send s.a.e. for guidelines.

Best

72 Broadwick Street, London W1F 9EP
☎020 7439 5000　Fax 020 7312 4175
✉ best@acp-natmag.co.uk

Owner *National Magazine Company/ACP*
Editor *Louise Court*
Circulation 411,060

Founded 1987. WEEKLY women's magazine. Multiple features, news, short stories on all topics of interest to women. Important for would-be contributors to study the magazine's style which differs from many other women's weeklies. Approach in writing with s.a.e.

FEATURES *Helen Garston, Charlotte Seligman* Max. 1500 words. No unsolicited mss.

FICTION *Pat Richardson* Short story slot – 900–1200 words. Send s.a.e. for guidelines. PAYMENT negotiable.

Best of British

Church Lane Publishing Ltd, Bank Chambers, 27a Market Place, Market Deeping PE6 8EA
☎01778 342814
✉ mail@british.fsbusiness.co.uk
www.bestofbritishmag.co.uk

Owner *Church Lane Publishing Ltd*
Editor-in-Chief *Ian Beacham*

Founded 1994. MONTHLY magazine celebrating all things British, both past and present. Emphasis on nostalgia – memories from the 1940s, 1950s and 1960s. Study of the magazine is advised in the first instance. All preliminary approaches should be made in writing.

The Big Issue

1–5 Wandsworth Road, London SW8 2LN
☎020 7526 3200 Fax 020 7526 3201
✉ editorialinfo@bigissue.com
www.bigissue.com

Editor-in-Chief *A. John Bird*
Editor *Matt Ford*
Circulation 155,575

Founded 1991. WEEKLY. An award-winning campaigning and street-wise general interest magazine sold in London, the Midlands, the North East and South of England. Separate regional editions sold in Manchester, Scotland, Wales and the South West.

NEWS *Judy Kerr* Hard-hitting exclusive stories with emphasis on social injustice aimed at national leaders.

ARTS *Charles Howgego* Interested in interviews and analysis ideas. Reviews written in-house. Send synopses to arts editor.

FEATURES Interviews, campaigns, comment, opinion and social issues reflecting a varied and informed audience. Balance includes social issues but mixed with arts and cultural features. Freelance writers used each week – commissioned from a variety of contributors. Best approach is to e-mail or post synopses to assistant deputy editor *Charles Howgego* with examples of work in the first instance. Max. 1500 words. PAYMENT £165 for 1000 words.

The Big Issue Cymru

55 Charles Street, Cardiff CF10 2GD
☎029 2025 5670 Fax 029 2025 5672
✉ edit@bigissuecymru.fsnet.co.uk
www.bigissuecymru.co.uk

Editor *Cathryn Scott*
Circulation 10,000

Founded 1993. WEEKLY. Hard-hitting social and news features plus arts and entertainment.

FEATURES/NEWS *Cathryn Scott* Welcomes contributions but must be relevant to a Welsh readership. Approach by e-mail. Lead in of four to six weeks. Max. 1000 words (features); 550 (news). No poetry or fiction.

The Big Issue in Scotland

Mir Village, 71 Oxford Street, Glasgow G5 9EP
☎0141 418 7000 Fax 0141 418 7061
✉ editorial@bigissuescotland.com
www.bigissuescotland.com

Editor *Claire Black*
Circulation 35,000

WEEKLY. Coverage of social issues, arts and culture, sport, interviews; news and hard-hitting journalism.

The Big Issue in the North

135–141 Oldham Street, Manchester M4 1LN
☎0161 834 6300 Fax 0161 832 3237
✉ editorial@bigissueinthenorth.com
www.thebiglifecompany.com

Owner *The Big Life Company*
Editor *Ato Erzan-Essien*
Circulation 32,000

Launched 1992. WEEKLY. Entertainment, celebrity interviews, environmental issues and issues from the social sector as well as homelessness. Welcomes news stories not covered by the national press; approach by e-mail.

The Big Issue South West

5 Brunswick Court, Brunswick Square, Bristol BS2 8PT
☎0117 916 6593 Fax 0017 916 6599
✉ editorial@bigissuesouthwest.co.uk

Editor *Cathryn Scott*
Circulation 18,000

Founded 1994. WEEKLY. Hard-hitting, socially aware news and features, local arts and entertainment. Welcomes news features with a regional relevance. No poetry or fiction.

FEATURES/NEWS *Cathryn Scott* Items must be regionally specific, date pegged, new information and people-based. Approach by e-mail. Max. 1000 words (features); 550 (news).

Bike
Emap Automotive Ltd, Media House, Lynch Wood, Peterborough PE2 6EA
☎01733 468181   Fax 01733 468196
✉ bike@emap.com
Owner *Emap Plc*
Editor *Tim Thompson*
Circulation 89,325

Founded 1971. MONTHLY. Broad-based motorcycle magazine. Approach by e-mail.

Bird Life Magazine
The RSPB, UK Headquarters, The Lodge, Sandy SG19 2DL
☎01767 680551   Fax 01767 683262
✉ derek.niemann@rspb.org.uk
Owner *Royal Society for the Protection of Birds*
Editor *Derek Niemann*
Circulation 90,000

Founded 1965. BI-MONTHLY. Bird, wildlife and nature conservation for 8–12-year-olds (RSPB Wildlife Explorers members). No unsolicited mss. No 'captive/animal welfare' articles.

FEATURES Unsolicited material rarely used.

NEWS News releases welcome. Approach in writing in the first instance.

Bird Watching
Emap Active, Bretton Court, Peterborough PE3 8DZ
☎0870 062 0200   Fax 01733 465376
✉ david.cromack@emap.com
www.birdwatching.co.uk
Owner *Emap Active*
Editor *David Cromack*
Circulation 20,380

Founded 1986. MONTHLY magazine for birdwatchers at all levels of experience. Offers practical advice of where and when to see birds, how to identify them, product reviews (particularly binoculars and telescopes), extensive bird sightings, 'Go Birding' walks (10 each issue), news and general articles.

FEATURES Interested in authoratative articles on bird behaviour and bird watching/sites in the UK. Please send synopsis, not the whole piece. Max. 1000 words.

NEWS UK news pre-eminent, preferably with pictures. Max. 350 words.

FEES negotiable.

Birds
The RSPB, UK Headquarters, The Lodge, Sandy SG19 2DL
☎01767 680551   Fax 01767 683262
✉ rob.hume@rspb.org.uk
Owner *Royal Society for the Protection of Birds*
Editor *R.A. Hume*
Circulation 620,780

QUARTERLY magazine which covers not only wild birds but also other wildlife and related conservation topics. No interest in features on pet birds or 'rescued' sick/injured/orphaned ones. Content refers mostly to RSPB work so opportunities for freelance work on other subjects are limited but some freelance submissions are used in most issues. Phone or e-mail to discuss.

Birdwatch
B403A The Chocolate Factory, 5 Clarendon Road, London N22 6XJ
☎020 8881 0550   Fax 020 8881 0990
✉ editorial@birdwatch.co.uk
www.birdwatch.co.uk
Owner *Solo Publishing*
Editor *Dominic Mitchell*
Circulation 13,000

Founded 1992. MONTHLY magazine featuring illustrated articles on all aspects of birds and birdwatching, especially in Britain. No unsolicited mss. Approach in writing with synopsis of 100 words max. Annual **Birdwatch Bird Book of the Year** award (see entry under *Prizes*).

FEATURES *Dominic Mitchell* Unusual angles/personal accounts, if well-written. Articles of an educative or practical nature suited to the readership. Max. 2000 words.

FICTION *Dominic Mitchell* Very little opportunity although occasional short story published. Max. 1500 words.

NEWS *Steve Hay* Very rarely use external material.

PAYMENT £50 per 1000 words.

Bizarre
30 Cleveland Street, London W1T 4JD
☎020 7907 6000   Fax 020 7907 6020
✉ bizarre@dennis.co.uk
www.bizarremag.com
Owner *Dennis Publishing*
Editor *Alex Godfrey*

Circulation 85,852

Founded 1997. MONTHLY magazine featuring amazing stories and images from around the world. No fiction, poetry, illustrations, short snippets.
FEATURES *Kate Hodges* No unsolicited mss. Send synopsis by post or e-mail.
PAYMENT negotiable.

Black Beauty & Hair

2nd Floor, Culvert House, Culvert Road, Battersea, London SW11 5HD
☎020 7720 2108 Fax 020 7498 3023
✉ info@blackbeautyandhair.com
www.blackbeautyandhair.com
Owner *Hawker Consumer Publications Ltd*
Editor *Irene Shelley*
Circulation 18,279

BI-MONTHLY with one annual special: *The Hairstyle Book* in October; and a *Bridal Supplement* in the April/May issue. Black hair and beauty magazine with emphasis on authoritative articles relating to hair, beauty, fashion, health and lifestyle. Unsolicited contributions welcome.
FEATURES Beauty and fashion pieces welcome from writers with a sound knowledge of the Afro-Caribbean beauty scene plus bridal features. Minimum 1000 words.
PAYMENT £100 per 1000 words.

Bliss Magazine

Endeavour House, 189 Shaftesbury Avenue, London WC2H 8JG
☎020 7208 3478 Fax 020 7208 3591
✉ diana.best@emap.com
Owner *Emap élan*
Editor *Lisa Smosarski*
Deputy Editor *Chantelle Horton*
Circulation 285,061

Founded 1995. MONTHLY teenage lifestyle magazine for girls. No unsolicited mss; 'call the Features Editor (*Emma Deeks*) with an idea and then send it in.'
NEWS Worldwide teenage news. Max. 200 words.
FEATURES Real life teenage stories with subjects willing to be photographed. Reports on teenage issues. Max. 2000 words.
PAYMENT news, £50–100; feaures, £350.

The Book Collector

PO Box 12426, London W11 3GW
☎020 7792 3492 Fax 020 7792 3492
✉ info@thebookcollector.co.uk
www.thebookcollector.co.uk

Owner *The Collector Ltd*
Editor *Nicolas J. Barker*

Founded 1950. QUARTERLY magazine on bibliography and the history of books, book-collecting, libraries and the book trade.

Book World Magazine

2 Caversham Street, London SW3 4AH
☎020 7351 4995 Fax 020 7351 4995
Owner *Christchurch Publishers Ltd*
Editor *James Hughes*
Circulation 5500

Founded 1980. MONTHLY news and reviews for serious book collectors, librarians, antiquarian and other booksellers. No unsolicited mss. Interested in material relevant to literature, art and book collecting. Send letter in the first instance.

Bookdealer

11 Gainsborough Court, College Road, Dulwich, London SE21 7LT
☎020 8693 5685 Fax 020 8693 5685
✉ wernershawltd@btinternet.com
Editor *Barry Shaw*

WEEKLY trade paper which acts almost exclusively as a platform for people wishing to buy or sell rare/out-of-print books. Twelve-page editorial only; occasional articles and book reviews by regular freelance writers.

The Bookseller

Endeavour House, 5th Floor, 189 Shaftesbury Avenue, London WC2H 8TJ
☎020 7420 6006 Fax 020 7420 6103
www.theBookseller.com
Owner *VNU Entertainment Media*
Editor-in-Chief *Neill Denny*

Trade journal of the publishing book trade and libraries – the essential guide to what is being done to whom. Trade news and features, including special features, company news, publishing trends, bestseller data, etc. Unsolicited mss rarely used as most writing is either done in-house or commissioned from experts within the trade. Approach in writing first.
Features *Liz Bury*
Deputy Editor/News *Joel Rickett*

Boxing Monthly

40 Morpeth Road, London E9 7LD
☎020 8986 4141 Fax 020 8986 4145
✉ mail@boxing-monthly.demon.co.uk
www.boxing-monthly.co.uk
Owner *Topwave Ltd*

Editor *Glyn Leach*
Circulation 25,000

Founded 1989. MONTHLY. International coverage of professional boxing; previews, reports and interviews. Unsolicited material welcome. Interested in small hall shows and grass-roots knowledge. No big fight reports. Approach in writing in the first instance.

Boyz

18 Brewer Street, London W1F 0SH
☎020 7025 6120   Fax 020 7025 6109
✉ hudson@boyz.co.uk

Editor *David Hudson*
Circulation 55,000

Founded 1991. WEEKLY entertainment and features magazine aimed at a gay readership covering clubs, fashion, TV, films, music, theatre, celebrities and the UK gay scene in general. Unsolicited mss are looked at but not often used.

Brides

Vogue House, Hanover Square, London
W1S 1JU
☎020 7499 9080   Fax 020 7152 3369
www.bridesuk.net

Owner *Condé Nast Publications Ltd*
Editor *Liz Savage*
Circulation 67,385

Founed 1955. BI-MONTHLY. Much of the magazine is produced in-house, but a good, relevant feature on cakes, jewellery, music, flowers, etc. is always welcome. Max. 1000 words. Prospective contributors should telephone with an idea in the first instance.

British Birds

The Banks, Mountfield, Robertsbridge
TN32 5JY
☎01580 882039   Fax 01580 882038
✉ editor@britishbirds.co.uk

Editor *Dr R. Riddington*
Circulation 6,000

Founded 1907. MONTHLY ornithological journal. Features main papers on topics such as behaviour, distribution, ecology, identification and taxonomy; annual *Report on Rare Birds in Great Britain* and *Rare Breeding Birds in the UK*; sponsored competition for Bird Photograph of the Year. Unsolicited mss welcome from ornithologists.

FEATURES Well-researched, original material relating to Western Palearctic birds welcome.

NEWS *Adrian Pitches* (adrian.pitches@blueyonder.co.uk) Items ranging from conser-

vation to humour. Max. 200 words.

PAYMENT for photographs, drawings, paintings and main papers.

British Chess Magazine

The Chess Shop, 44 Baker Street, London
W1U 7RT
☎020 7486 8222   Fax 020 7486 3355
✉ bcmchess@compuserve.com
www.bcmchess.co.uk

Director/Editor *John Saunders*

Founded 1881. MONTHLY. Emphasis on tournaments, the history of chess and chess-related literature. Approach in writing with ideas. Unsolicited mss not welcome unless from qualified chess experts and players.

British Medical Journal

BMA House, Tavistock Square, London
WC1H 9JR
☎020 7387 4499   Fax 020 7383 6418
✉ editor@bmj.com
www.bmj.com

Owner *British Medical Association*
Editor *Dr Fiona Goodlee*

One of the world's leading general medical journals.

British Philatelic Bulletin

Royal Mail, 148 Old Street, London
EC1V 9HQ
☎020 7250 2038   Fax 020 7250 2389

Owner *Royal Mail*
Editor *John Holman*
Circulation 22,000

Founded 1963. MONTHLY bulletin giving details of forthcoming British stamps, features on older stamps and postal history, and book reviews. Welcomes photographs of interesting, unusual or historic letter boxes.

FEATURES Articles on all aspects of British philately. Max. 1500 words.

NEWS Reports on exhibitions and philatelic events. Max. 500 words. Approach in writing in the first instance.

PAYMENT £65 per 1000 words.

British Railway Modelling

The Maltings, West Street, Bourne PE10 9PH
☎01778 391027   Fax 01778 425437
✉ johne@warnersgroup.co.uk
www.brmodelling.com

Owner *Warners Group Publications Plc*
Managing Editor *David Brown*
Editor *John Emerson*

Assistant Editor *Tony Wright*
Circulation 22,500

Founded 1993. MONTHLY. A general magazine for the practising modeller. No unsolicited mss but ideas are welcome. Interested in features on quality models, from individual items to complete layouts. Approach in writing.

FEATURES Articles on practical elements of the hobby, e.g. locomotive construction, kit conversions, etc. Layout features and articles on individual items which represent high standards of the railway modelling art. Max. length 6000 words (single feature).

NEWS News and reviews containing the model railway trade, new products, etc. Max. length 1000 words.

PAYMENT up to £60 per published page.

Broadcast

33-39 Bowling Green Lane, London EC1R 0DA
☎020 7505 8045 Fax 020 7505 8050
Owner *Emap Communications*
Editor *Conor Dignam*
Circulation 11,462

Founded 1960. WEEKLY. Opportunities for freelance contributions. Write to the relevant editor in the first instance.

FEATURES *Lisa Campbell* Any broadcasting issue. Max. 1500 words.

NEWS *Colin Robertson* Broadcasting news. Max. 350 words.

PAYMENT £250 per 1000 words.

Build It

1 Canada Square, Canary Wharf, London E14 5AP
☎020 7772 8440 Fax 020 7772 8584
✉ buildit@mrn.co.uk
www.self-build.co.uk
Owner *Inside Communications*
Editor *Catherine Monk*
Circulation 23,663

Founded 1990. MONTHLY magazine covering self-build, conversion and renovation. Unsolicited material welcome on self-build case studies as well as articles on technical construction, architecture and design and dealing with builders. Max. length 2500 words. Approach by phone, post or e-mail.

The Burlington Magazine

14–16 Duke's Road, London WC1H 9SZ
☎020 7388 1228 Fax 020 7388 1230
✉ editorial@burlington.org.uk
www.burlington.org.uk

Owner *The Burlington Magazine Publications Ltd*
Managing Director *Kate Trevelyan*
Editor *Richard Shone*
Associate Editors *Bart Cornelis, Jane Martineau*

Founded 1903. MONTHLY. Contributions welcome on the subject of art history provided they are previously unpublished. All preliminary approaches should be made in writing.

EXHIBITION REVIEWS Usually commissioned, but occasionally unsolicited reviews are published if appropriate. Max. 1000 words.

ARTICLES Max. 4500 words.

SHORTER NOTICES Max. 2000 words.

PAYMENT articles, £140 (max.); shorter notices, £80 (max.).

Business Brief

PO Box 582, Five Oaks, St Saviour JE4 8XQ
☎01534 611600 Fax 01534 611610
✉ mspeditorial@msppublishing.com
Owner *MSP Publishing*
Editor *Peter Body*
Circulation 6500 (Jersey & Guernsey)

Founded 1989. MONTHLY magazine covering business developments in the Channel Islands and how they affect the local market. Styles itself as the magazine for business people rather than just a magazine about business. Interested in business-orientated articles only – 800 words max. Approach the editor by e-mail in the first instance with telephone follow-up.

PAYMENT negotiable.

Business Traveller

Nestor House, Playhouse Yard, London EC4V 5EX
☎020 7778 0000 Fax 020 7778 0022
✉ editorial@businesstraveller.com
www.businesstraveller.com
Owner *Euromoney Institutional Investor Plc*
Editor-in-Chief *Tom Otley*
Circulation 500,000 (worldwide)

MONTHLY. Consumer publication. Opportunities exist for freelance writers but unsolicited contributions tend to be about leisure travel rather than business travel. Would-be contributors are strongly advised to study the magazine or the website first. Approach in writing with ideas.

PAYMENT varies.

Camcorder User

Highbury Entertainment London,
53–79 Highgate Road, London NW5 1TW
☎020 7331 1000 Fax 020 7331 1273
✉ rob.hull@highburygroup.com

www.camuser.co.uk
Owner *Highbury Entertainment*
Editor *Robert Hull*
Circulation 15,000
Founded 1988. MONTHLY magazine dedicated to camcorders, with features on creative technique, shooting advice, new equipment, accessory round-ups and interesting applications on location. Unsolicited mss, illustrations and pictures welcome. PAYMENT negotiable.

Campaign
22 Bute Gardens, London W6 7HN
☎020 8267 4683   Fax 020 8267 4914
✉ campaign@haynet.com
www.brandrepublic.com
Owner *Haymarket Publishing Ltd*
Editor *Claire Beale*
Circulation 11,062
Founded 1968. WEEKLY. Lively magazine serving the advertising and related industries. Freelance contributors are best advised to write in the first instance.
FEATURES Ideas welcome.
NEWS Relevant news stories of up to 320 words.
PAYMENT negotiable.

Camping and Caravanning
Greenfields House, Westwood Way, Coventry CV4 8JH
☎024 7647 5448   Fax 024 7647 5413
Owner *The Camping and Caravanning Club*
Editor *Nick Harding*
Circulation 194,437
Founded 1901. MONTHLY. Interested in journalists with camping and caravanning knowledge. Write with ideas for features in the first instance.
FEATURES Outdoor pieces in general, plus items on specific regions of Britain. Max. 1200 words. Illustrations to support text essential.

Canal and Riverboat
PO Box 618, Norwich NR7 0QT
☎01603 708930
✉ bluefoxfilms@themag.fsnet.co.uk
www.canalandriverboat.com
Owner *A.E. Morgan Publications Ltd*
Editor *Chris Cattrall*
Circulation 14,000
Covers all aspects of waterways, narrow boats and cruisers. Contributions welcome. Make initial approach by post or e-mail.
FEATURES Waterways, narrow boats and

motor cruisers, cruising reports, practical advice, etc. Unusual ideas and personal comments are particularly welcome. Max. 2000 words. Articles should be supplied in PC Windows format disk or e-mailed with JPEG images.
NEWS Items of up to 200 words welcome on the Inland Waterways System, plus photographs if possible.
PAYMENT features, around £60 per page; news, £20.

Car Mechanics
Kelsey Publishing Group, Cudham Tithe Barn, Berry's Hill, Cudham TN16 3AG
☎01959 541444   Fax 01959 541400
✉ cm.mag@kelsey.co.uk
Owner *Kelsey Publishing Group*
Editor *Peter Simpson*
Circulation 35,000
MONTHLY. Practical guide to maintenance and repair of post-1978 cars for DIY and the motor trade. Unsolicited mss, with good-quality colour prints or transparencies, sent 'at sender's risk'. Initial approach by letter or phone strongly recommended, 'but please read a recent copy for style first'. No cartoons or fiction.
FEATURES Good, entertaining and well-researched technical material welcome, especially anything presenting complex matters clearly and simply. PAYMENT negotiable.

Caravan Life
Warners Group Publications plc, The Maltings, West Street, Bourne PH10 9PH
☎01778 391165   Fax 01778 425437
✉ mikelec@warnersgroup.co.uk
Editor *Michael Le Caplain*
Circulation 12,926
Founded 1987. Magazine for experienced caravanners and enthusiasts providing practical and useful information and product evaluation. Opportunities for caravanning, relevant touring and travel material, also monthly reviews of the best tow cars, all with good-quality colour photographs.

Caravan Magazine
IPC Media Ltd, Leon House, 233 High Street, Croydon CR9 1HZ
☎020 8726 8000   Fax 020 8726 8299
✉ caravan@ipcmedia.com
www.caravanmagazine.co.uk
Owner *IPC Media (A Time Warner Company)*
Editor *Steve Rowe*
Circulation 15,926

Founded 1933. MONTHLY. Unsolicited mss welcome. Approach in writing with ideas. All correspondence should go direct to the editor.

FEATURES Touring with strong caravan bias, technical/DIY features and how-to section. Max. 1500 words.

PAYMENT by arrangement.

Caribbean Times

Unit 2, 65 Whitechapel Road, London E1 1DU
☎020 7650 2000 Fax 020 7650 2001
✉ caribbeantimes@ethnicmedia.co.uk
www.ethnicmedia.co.uk

Owner *Ethnic Media Group*
Editor *Ron Shillingford*
Circulation 25,190

Founded 1981. WEEKLY community paper for the African and Caribbean communities in Britain. Interested in general, local and international issues relevant to these communities.

Cat World

Ancient Lights, 19 River Road, Arundel BN18 9EY
☎01903 884988 Fax 01903 885514
✉ editor@catworld.co.uk
www.catworld.co.uk

Owner *Ashdown Publishing Ltd*
Editor *Jo Rothery*
Circulation 20,000

Founded 1981. MONTHLY. Unsolicited mss welcome but initial approach in writing preferred. No poems or fiction.

FEATURES Lively, first-hand experience features on every aspect of the cat. Breeding features and veterinary articles by acknowledged experts only. Preferred length 750 or 1700 words. Accompanying pictures should be good quality and sharp. Submissions on disk (MS Word) if possible, with accompanying hard copy and s.a.e. for return or by e-mail.

The Catholic Herald

Lamb's Passage, Bunhill Row, London EC1Y 8TQ
☎020 7448 3603 Fax 020 7256 9728
✉ editorial@catholicherald.co.uk
www.catholicherald.co.uk

Editor *Luke Coppen*
Features Editor *Christina Farrell*
Literary Editor *Damian Thompson*
Circulation 22,000

WEEKLY. Interested mainly in straight Catholic issues but also in general humanitarian matters, social policies, the Third World, the arts and books. PAYMENT by arrangement.

Chapman

4 Broughton Place, Edinburgh EH1 3RX
☎0131 557 2207 Fax 0131 556 9565
✉ chapman-pub@blueyonder.co.uk
www.chapman-pub.co.uk

Owner/Editor *Joy Hendry*
Circulation 2000

Founded 1970. Scotland's quality literary magazine. Features poetry, short works of fiction, criticism, reviews and articles on theatre, politics, language and the arts. Gives priority to Scottish writers but also has work from UK and international authors. Unsolicited material welcome if accompanied by s.a.e. Approach in writing unless discussion is needed. Priority is given to full-time writers.

FEATURES Topics of literary interest, especially Scottish literature, theatre, culture or politics. Max. 5000 words.

FICTION Short stories, occasionally novel extracts if self-contained. Max. 6000 words.

SPECIAL PAGES Poetry, both UK and non-UK in translation (mainly, but not necessarily, European).

PAYMENT by negotiation.

Chat

IPC Media Ltd., King's Reach Tower, Stamford Street, London SE1 9LS
☎020 7261 6565 Fax 020 7261 6534
www.ipcmedia.com/pubs/chat.htm

Owner *IPC Connect*
Editor *June Smith-Sheppard*
Circulation 636,310

Founded 1985. WEEKLY general interest women's magazine. Unsolicited mss considered; approach in writing with ideas. Not interested in contributors 'who have never bothered to read *Chat* and therefore don't know what type of magazine it is. *Chat* does not publish fiction.'

FEATURES *Ingrid Millar* Human interest and humour. Max. 1000 words.

PAYMENT up to £1500 maximum.

Chemist & Druggist

Sovereign House, Sovereign Way, Tonbridge TN9 1RW
☎01732 377487 Fax 01732 367065
✉ chemdrug@cmpinformation.com
www.dotpharmacy.com

Owner *CMP Information*
Editor *Charles Gladwin*
Circulation 13,920

Founded 1859. WEEKLY news magazine for community pharmacy.

FEATURES practice, politics, professional matters, clinical articles and business advice. Contact by phone or e-mail to discuss features ideas.

NEWS Contact News Editor with news articles relating to local pharmacy matters, local pharmaceutical industry events and pharmacists in the news. Max. 200 words.

PAYMENT standard rates.

Child Education

Scholastic Ltd, Villiers House, Clarendon Avenue, Leamington Spa CV32 5PR
☎01926 887799   Fax 01926 883331
www.scholastic.co.uk

Owner *Scholastic Ltd*
Editor *Helen Freeman*
Circulation 21,121

Founded 1923. MONTHLY magazine aimed at teachers of children aged 4–7 years. Practical articles from teachers about education for this age group are welcome. Max. 900 words. Approach in writing with synopsis.

Choice

First Floor, 2 King Street, Peterborough PE1 1LT
☎01733 555123   Fax 01733 427500
✉ editorial@choicemag.co.uk

Owner *Choice Publishing Ltd*
Editor *Norman Wright*
Circulation 90,000

Monthly full-colour, lively and informative magazine for people aged 50 plus which helps them get the most out of their lives, time and money after full-time work.

FEATURES Real-life stories, hobbies, interesting (older) people, British heritage and countryside, involving activities for active bodies and minds, health, relationships, book/entertainment reviews. Unsolicited mss read (s.a.e. for return of material); write with ideas and copies of cuttings if new contributor. No phone calls, please.

RIGHTS/MONEY All items affecting the magazine's readership are written by experts. Areas of interest include pensions, state benefits, health, finance, property, legal. PAYMENT by arrangement.

Christian Herald

Christian Media Centre, Garcia Estate, Canterbury Road, Worthing BN13 1EH
☎01903 821082   Fax 01903 821081
✉ news@christianherald.org.uk

www.christianherald.org.uk

Owner *Christian Media Centre Ltd*
Editor *Russ Bravo*
Circulation 14,000

WEEKLY. Evangelical, inter-denominational newspaper for committed Christians. News, bible-based comment and incisive features. No poetry. Contributors' guidelines available. PAYMENT Christian Media rates.

Church Music Quarterly

Cleveland Lodge, Westhumble, Dorking RH5 6BW
☎01306 872800   Fax 01306 887260
✉ cmq@rscm.com
www.rscm.com

Owner *Royal School of Church Music*
Editor *Esther Jones*
Circulation 16,000

QUARTERLY. Contributions welcome. Phone in the first instance.

FEATURES Articles on church music or related subjects considered. Max. 2000 words.

PAYMENT £60 per page.

Church of England Newspaper

20–26 Brunswick Place, London N1 6DZ
☎020 7417 5800   Fax 020 7216 6410
✉ cen@parlicom.com
www.churchnewspaper.com

Owner *Parliamentary Communications Ltd*
Editor *Colin Blakely*
Circulation 9,500

Founded 1828. WEEKLY. Almost all material is commissioned but unsolicited mss considered.

FEATURES *Emma Garrow* Preliminary enquiry essential. Max. 1200 words.

NEWS *Jonathan Wynne-Jones* Items must be sent promptly and should have a church/ Christian relevance. Max. 200–400 words.

PAYMENT negotiable.

Church Times

33 Upper Street, London N1 0PN
☎020 7359 4570   Fax 020 7226 3073
✉ news@churchtimes.co.uk *or* features@churchtimes.co.uk
www.churchtimes.co.uk

Owner *Hymns Ancient & Modern*
Editor *Paul Handley*
Circulation 31,570

Founded 1863. WEEKLY. Unsolicited mss considered.

FEATURES *Nick Ericsson* Articles and pictures

(any format) on religious topics. Max. 2000 words.

NEWS *Helen Saxbee* Occasional reports (commissions only) and up-to-date photographs.

PAYMENT features, £120 per 1000 words; news, by arrangement.

Classic & Sports Car

Somerset House, Somerset Road, Teddington TW11 8RT

☎020 8267 5399 Fax 020 8267 5318

✉ letters.c&sc@haynet.com

www.classicandsportscar.com

Owner *Haymarket Publishing Ltd*

Editor *James Elliott*

Circulation 81,125

Founded 1982. MONTHLY. Best-selling classic car magazine covering all aspects of buying, selling, owning and maintaining historic vehicles. Will consider news stories and features involving classic cars but 'be patient as hundreds of unsolicited material received monthly'. Initial contact by e-mail (james.elliott@haynet.com).

Classic Bike

EMAP Automotive, Media House, Lynchwood, Peterborough Business Park, Peterborough PE2 6EA

☎01733 468465 Fax 01733 468466

✉ classic.bike@emap.com

Owner *Emap Automotive Ltd*

Editor *Hugo Wilson*

Circulation 42,315

Founded 1978. MONTHLY. Mainly pre-1980 classic motorcycles with a heavy bias to British marques. Freelancers must contact the editor before making submissions. Approach in writing.

NEWS Genuine news with good illustrations, if possible, suitable for a global audience. Max. 400 words.

FEATURES British motorcycle industry inside stories, technical features 'that can be understood by all', German, Spanish and French machine features, people. Max. 2000 words.

SPECIAL PAGES How-to features, oddball machines, stunning pictures, features with a fresh slant.

PAYMENT £100–125 per 1000 words, plus pictures.

Classic Boat

IPC Media Ltd, Leon House, 233 High Street, Croydon CR9 1HZ

☎020 8726 8000

✉ cb@ipcmedia.com

www.classicboat.co.uk

Owner *IPC Media (A Time Warner Company)*

Editor *Dan Houston*

Circulation 13,211

Founded 1987. MONTHLY. Traditional boats and classic yachts, old and new; maritime history. Unsolicited mss, particularly if supported by good photos, are welcome. Sail and power boat pieces considered. Approach in writing with ideas. Interested in well-researched stories on all nautical matters. News reports welcome. Contributor's notes available (send s.a.e.).

FEATURES Boatbuilding, boat history and design, events, yachts and working boats. Material must be well-informed and supported where possible by good-quality or historic photos. Max. 3000 words. Classic is defined by excellence of design and construction – the boat need not be old and wooden!

NEWS New boats, restorations, events, boatbuilders, etc. Max. 500 words.

PAYMENT features, £75–100 per published page; news, according to merit.

Classic Cars

Media House, Peterborough Business Park, Lynchwood, Peterborough PE2 6EA

☎01733 468219 Fax 01733 468888

✉ classic.cars@emap.com

www.classiccarsmagazine.co.uk

Owner *Emap Automotive Ltd*

Editor *Martyn Moore*

Circulation 48,133

Founded 1973. TWELVE ISSUES YEARLY. International classic car magazine containing entertaining and informative articles about classic cars, events and associated personalities. Contributions welcome. PAYMENT negotiable.

Classical Guitar

1 & 2 Vance Court, Trans Britannia Enterprise Park, Blaydon on Tyne NE21 5NH

☎0191 414 9000 Fax 0191 414 9001

✉ classicalguitar@ashleymark.co.uk

www.classicalguitarmagazine.com

Owner *Ashley Mark Publishing Co.*

Editor *Macer Hall*

Founded 1982. MONTHLY.

FEATURES *Macer Hall* Usually written by staff writers. Max. 1500 words.

NEWS *Thérèse Wassily Saba* Small paragraphs and festival concert reports welcome.

REVIEWS *Tim Panting* Concert reviews of up to 250 words usually written by staff reviewers.

PAYMENT features, by arrangement; no payment for news.

Classical Music
241 Shaftesbury Avenue, London WC2H 8TF
☎020 7333 1742   Fax 020 7333 1769
✉ classical.music@rhinegold.co.uk
www.rhinegold.co.uk
Owner *Rhinegold Publishing Ltd*
Editor *Keith Clarke*

Founded 1976. FORTNIGHTLY. A specialist magazine using precisely targeted news and feature articles aimed at the music business. Most material is commissioned but professionally written unsolicited mss are occasionally published. Freelance contributors may approach in writing with an idea but should familiarise themselves beforehand with the style and market of the magazine. PAYMENT negotiable.

Classics
Berwick House, 8–10 Knoll Rise, Orpington BR6 0PS
☎01689 887268   Fax 01689 876438
✉ classics@highburyleisure.co.uk
Owner *Highbury Leisure*
Editor *Gary Stretton*

Founded 1997. MONTHLY how-to magazine for classic car owners, featuring everything from repairing and restoring to buying, selling and enjoying all types of cars from the 1950s to 1980s. Includes vehicle comparison tests, price guide, practical advice and technical know-how from experts and owners, plus hundreds of readers' free ads.
FEATURES Illustrated features on classic car maintenance, repair and restoration with strong technical content and emphasis on DIY.
NEWS All classic car related news stories and topical photos.

Climber
Warners Group Publications plc, West Street, Bourne PE10 9PH
☎01778 391117
✉ bernard@warnersgroup.co.uk
www.climber.co.uk
Owner *Warners Group Publications plc*
Editor *Bernard Newman*

Founded 1962. MONTHLY. Features articles and news on climbing and mountaineering in the UK and abroad. No unsolicited mss.

Closer
Endeavour House, 189 Shaftesbury Avenue, London WC2H 8JG
☎020 7437 9011   Fax 020 7859 8600
✉ closer@emap.com

Owner *Emap élan Ltd*
Editor *Jane Johnson*
Circulation 504,350

Launched 2002. WEEKLY celebrity magazine with a 'tongue-in-cheek' approach. No unsolicited material; approach by e-mail with idea in the first instance.

Club International
2 Archer Street, London W1D 7AW
☎020 7292 8000   Fax 020 7734 5030
✉ mattb@pr-org.co.uk
Owner *Paul Raymond*
Editor *Matt Berry*
Circulation 180,000

Founded 1972. MONTHLY. Features and short humorous items aimed at young male readership aged 18–30.
FEATURES Max. 1000 words.
SHORTS 200–750 words.
PAYMENT negotiable.

Co-op Traveller
Wrap Communications Ltd, The Bake House, J108 TBBC, 100 Clements Road, London SE16 4DG
☎020 7231 0707   Fax 020 7231 1232
✉ info@wrapcom.com
www.wrapcom.com
Owner *United Co-op Travel Division/Wrap Communications*
Editor *Jo Swinnerton*
Circulation 150,000

Founded 2001. BIANNUAL. Magazine for Co-op Travel customers. Travel articles and travel-related news for the independent traveller. No unsolicted material; approach by telephone, fax, letter or e-mail in the first instance.
FEATURES Ideas for exciting travel features, including destinations, accommodation, activities etc. Max. 1000 words.
News Stories that reveal fascinating facts for holidaymakers, including interesting products, new destinations and developments in the travel market. Max. 300 words.
PAYMENT negotiable.

Coach and Bus Week
Emap Active Ltd, Bretton Court, Bretton, Peterborough PE3 8DZ
☎01733 467778   Fax 01733 467770
✉ jacqui.grobler@emap.com
www.cbwnet.co.uk
Owner *Emap Active Ltd*
Editor *Mark Williams*

Circulation 4575

WEEKLY magazine, aimed at coach and bus operators. Interested in coach and bus industry-related items only; contact by letter, e-mail, telephone or via website.

Coin News
Token Publishing Ltd, Orchard House, Duchy Road, Heathpark, Honiton EX14 1YD
☎01404 46972 Fax 01404 44788
✉ info@tokenpublishing.com
www.tokenpublishing.com
Owners *J. W. Mussell, Carol Hartman*
Editor *J. W. Mussell*
Circulation 10,000
Founded 1964. MONTHLY. Contributions welcome. Approach by phone in the first instance.
FEATURES Opportunity exists for well-informed authors 'who know the subject and do their homework'. Max. 2000 words.
PAYMENT by arrangement.

Company
National Magazine House, 72 Broadwick Street, London W1F 9EP
☎020 7439 5000 Fax 020 7312 3797
✉ company.mail@natmags.co.uk
www.company.co.uk
Owner *National Magazine Co. Ltd*
Editor *Victoria White*
Circulation 332,603
MONTHLY. Glossy women's magazine appealing to the independent and intelligent young woman. A good market for freelancers: 'We look for great newsy features relevant to young British women'. Keen to encourage bright, new, young talent, but uncommissioned material is rarely accepted. Feature outlines are the only sensible approach in the first instance. Max. 1500–2000 words. Send to *Claire Askew*, Features Editor. PAYMENT £250 per 1000 words.

Compass Sport
Ballencrieff Cottage, Ballencrieff Toll, Bathgate EH48 4LD
☎01506 632728 Fax 01506 632728
✉ editor@compasssport.com
www.compasssport.com
Owner *Pages Editorial & Publishing Services*
Editor *Suse Coon*
BI-MONTHLY orienteering magazine covering all disciplines of the sport including mountain marathons, mountain bike, ski and trail orienteering. Includes profiles and articles on relevant top-ics, with subsections on fixtures, junior news, adventure racing and mountain marathons which are compiled by sub-editors. Letters, puzzles and competition. Phone or e-mail to discuss content and timing. PAYMENT by arrangement.

Computer Arts
30 Monmouth Street, Bath BA1 2BW
☎01225 442244 Fax 01225 732295
✉ ca.mail@futurenet.co.uk
www.computerarts.co.uk
Owner *The Future Network*
Editor *Gillian Carson*
Founded 1995. MONTHLY. The world of computer arts – 3D, web design, photoshop, digital video. No unsolicited mss. Interested in tutorials, profiles, tips, software and hardware reviews. Approach by post or e-mail.

Computer Weekly
Quadrant House, The Quadrant, Sutton SM2 5AS
☎020 8652 3122 Fax 020 8652 8979
✉ computer.weekly@rbi.co.uk
www.computerweekly.com
Owner *Reed Business Information*
Editor *Hooman Bassirian*
Circulation 143,000
Founded 1966. Freelance contributions welcome.
FEATURES Always looking for good new writers with specialised industry knowledge. Max. 1800 words.
NEWS *Mike Simons* Some openings for regional or foreign news items. Max. 300 words. PAYMENT negotiable.

Computeractive
VNU Business Publications, VNU House, 32–34 Broadwick Street, London W1A 2HG
☎020 7316 9000 Fax 020 7316 9520
✉ news@computeractive.co.uk
www.computeractive.co.uk
Owner *VNU Business Publications Ltd*
Editor *Dylan Armbrust*
Circulation 236,026
Launched 1998. FORTNIGHTLY. Consumer and computer technology magazine. No unsolicited material.

Computing, The IT Newspaper
VNU Business Publications, VNU House, 32–34 Broadwick Street, London W1A 2HG
☎020 7316 9000 Fax 020 7316 9160
✉ computing@vnu.co.uk

www.computing.co.uk
Owner *VNU Business Publications Ltd*
Editor-in-Chief *Toby Wolpe*
Managing Editor *Bryan Glick*
Circulation 115,000

Founded 1973. WEEKLY newspaper for IT professionals. Unsolicited articles welcome. Please enclose s.a.e. for return.
NEWS *Emma Nash*
PAYMENT up to £350 per 1000 words.

Condé Nast Traveller
Vogue House, Hanover Square, London
W1S 1JU
☎020 7499 9080   Fax 020 7493 3758
✉ editorcntraveller@condenast.co.uk
www.cntraveller.co.uk
Owner *Condé Nast Publications*
Editor *Sarah Miller*
Circulation 83,092

Founded 1997. MONTHLY travel magazine. Proposals rather than completed mss preferred. Approach in writing in the first instance. No unsolicited photographs. 'The magazine has a no freebie policy and no writing can be accepted on the basis of a press or paid-for trip.'

Conservative Heartland
The Spectator (1828) Ltd, 56 Doughty Street, London WC1N 2LL
☎020 7440 9240   Fax 020 7831 6468
✉ editor@hearlandmag.co.uk
Owner *The Conservative Party*
Editor *Martin Vander Weyer*
Circulation 250,000

Founded 1999. ANNUAL. Conservative Party magazine. Lifestyle articles, political comment and information. No unsolicited material; approach by telephone or e-mail with idea in the first instance.

Contemporary Review
PO Box 1242, Oxford OX1 4FJ
☎01865 201529   Fax 01865 201529
✉ editorial@contemporaryreview.co.uk
www.contemporaryreview.co.uk
Owner *Contemporary Review Co. Ltd*
Editor *Dr Richard Mullen*

Founded 1866. MONTHLY. Covers international affairs and politics, literature and the arts, history and religion. No fiction. Max. 3000 words.
Literary Editor *Dr James Munson* Monthly book section with reviews which are always commissioned. PAYMENT £5 per page.

CosmoGIRL!
National Magazine House, 72 Broadwick Street, London W1F 9EP
☎020 7439 5000   Fax 020 7439 5400
✉ cosmogirl.mail@natmags.co.uk
www.cosmogirl.co.uk
Owner *National Magazine Co. Ltd*
Editor *Celia Duncan*
Circulation 213,311

Founded 2001. THREE-WEEKLY glossy magazine for 'fun, fearless teens'. Fashion, beauty advice and boys.
FEATURES *Miranda Eason* Interested in ideas – send synopsis by mail – no finished articles.

Cosmopolitan
National Magazine House, 72 Broadwick Street, London W1F 9EP
☎020 7439 5000   Fax 020 7439 5016
✉ cosmo.mail@natmags.co.uk
www.cosmopolitan.co.uk
Owner *National Magazine Co. Ltd*
Editor *Sam Baker*
Deputy Editor *Lou Ford*
Circulation 478,394

MONTHLY. Designed to appeal to the mid-twenties, modern-minded female. Popular mix of articles, with emphasis on relationships and careers, and hard news. No fiction. Will rarely use unsolicited mss but always on the look-out for 'new writers with original and relevant ideas and a strong voice'. Send short synopsis of idea to features' writer *Catherine Gray*. All would-be writers should be familiar with the magazine.

Counselling at Work
Association for Counselling at Work, BACP, BACP House, 35–37 Albert Street, Rugby CV21 2SG
☎0870 443 5252
✉ acw@bacp.co.uk
Owner *British Association for Counselling and Psychotherapy*
Editor *Rick Hughes*
Circulation 1600

Founded 1993. QUARTERLY official journal of the Association for Counselling at Work, a Division of BACP. Looking for well-researched articles (500–2400 words) about *any* aspect of workplace counselling. Mss from those employed as counsellors or in welfare posts are particularly welcome. Photographs accepted. No fiction or poetry. Send A4 s.a.e. for writer's guidelines and sample copy of the journal. No PAYMENT.

Country Homes and Interiors

IPC Media Ltd., King's Reach Tower,
Stamford Street, London SE1 9LS
☎020 7261 6451 Fax 020 7261 6895
✉ countryhomes@ipcmedia.com
Owner *IPC Media*
Editor *Rhoda Parry*
Circulation 94,204

Founded 1986. MONTHLY. The best approach
for prospective contributors is with an idea in
writing as unsolicited mss are not welcome.

FEATURES *Jean Carr* Monthly personality
interviews of interest to an intelligent, affluent
readership (women and men), aged 25–44. Max.
1200 words.

HOUSES *Rhoda Parry* Country-style homes
with excellent design ideas. Length 1000 words.

PAYMENT negotiable.

Country Life

IPC Media Ltd., King's Reach Tower,
Stamford Street, London SE1 9LS
☎020 7261 6400 Fax 020 7261 5139
www.countrylife.co.uk
Owner *IPC Media (A Time Warner Company)*
Editor *Clive Aslet*
Circulation 42,693

Established 1897. WEEKLY. *Country Life* features
articles which relate to architecture, countryside,
wildlife, rural events, sports, arts, exhibitions, current events, property and news articles of interest
to town and country dwellers. Strong informed
material rather than amateur enthusiasm.
'Uncommissioned material is rarely accepted. We
regret we cannot be liable for the safe custody or
return of any solicited or unsolicited materials.'

Country Living

National Magazine House, 72 Broadwick
Street, London W1F 9EP
☎020 7439 5000 Fax 020 7439 5093
www.countryliving.co.uk
Owner *National Magazine Co. Ltd*
Editor *Susy Smith*
Circulation 185,136

Magazine aimed at both country dwellers and
town dwellers who love the countryside.
Covers people, conservation, wildlife, houses
(gardens and interiors) and rural businesses. No
unsolicited mss

Country Smallholding

Archant Publishing, Fair Oak Close, Exeter
Airport Business Park, Clysts Honiton, Nr
Exeter EX5 2UL
☎01392 888475 Fax 01392 888550
✉ editorial.csh@archant.co.uk
www.countrysmallholding.com
Owner *Archant Publishing*
Editor *Diane Cowgill*
Circulation 18,966

Founded 1975. MONTHLY magazine for small
farmers, smallholders, practical landowners and
for anyone interested in self sufficiency at all
levels both in town and in the country. Articles
welcome on organic growing, keeping poultry,
livestock and other animals, crafts, cookery, herbs,
building and energy. Articles should be detailed
and practical, based on first-hand knowledge and
experience. Approach in writing or by e-mail.

Country Walking

Bretton Court, Bretton, Peterborough
PE3 8DZ
☎01733 282614 Fax 01733 282654
✉ country.walking@emap.com
Owner *Emap Plc*
Editor *Jonathan Manning*
Circulation 47,774

Founded 1987. MONTHLY magazine focused on
walking in the finest landscapes of the UK and
Europe. News, gear tests and profiles of celebrity
walkers also feature. Special monthly pull-out
section of 28 detailed walking routes. Original
high quality photography and ideas for features
considered, although very few unsolicited mss
accepted. Approach by letter or e-mail.

FEATURES *Danny Hopkins*

SPECIAL PAGES 'Down your way' section of
walk routes, including outline map and step-by-
step directions. Accurately and recently researched walk and fact file including photographs
and points of interest en route. Please contact
Trevor Rickwood for guidelines (unsolicited submissions generally not accepted for this section).

PAYMENT not negotiable.

The Countryman

PO Box 5956, Sherborne DT9 9AA
☎01935 812434
✉ editorial@thecountryman.co.uk
www.thecountryman.co.uk
Owner *Country Publications Ltd*
Editor *Bill Taylor*
Circulation 22,870

Founded 1927. MONTHLY. Feature ideas welcome by e-mail. Contributors are strongly advised to study the magazine's content in the
first instance. Articles supplied with top quality
illustrations (colour transparencies, archive b&w

prints and line drawings) are far more likely to be used. Max. article length 1200 words.

The Countryman's Weekly
(incorporating **Gamekeeper and Sporting Dog**)
Yelverton PL20 7PE
☎01822 855281 Fax 01822 855372
✉ cmansweekly@aol.com
Managing Director *Vic Gardner*
Editor *David Venner*
Founded 1895. WEEKLY. Unsolicited material welcome.
FEATURES on any country sports topic. Max. 1000 words.
PAYMENT rates available on request.

Countryside Alliance Campaign Update
The Old Town Hall 367 Kennington Road, London SE1 4PT
☎020 7582 5432 Fax 020 7793 8484
www.countryside-alliance.org
Owner *Countryside Alliance*
Editor *Georgina Kester*
Circulation 70,000
Founded 1996. QUARTERLY membership magazine on country sports and conservation issues. No unsolicited mss.

County
26C High Street, Watlington OX49 5PY
☎01491 614040 Fax 01491 614041
✉ sales@icpmagazines.com
www.icpmagazines.com
Owners *Mr and Mrs R. Watts*
Editor *Mrs Ashlyn Watts*
Circulation 50,000
Founded 1986. QUARTERLY lifestyle magazine featuring homes, interiors, gardening, fashion and beauty, motoring, leisure and dining. Welcomes unsolicited mss. All initial approaches should be made in writing.

The Cricketer International
See **The Wisden Cricketer**

Crimewave
5 Martins Lane, Witcham, Ely CB6 2LB
✉ ttapress@aol.com
www.ttapress.com
Owner *TTA Press*
Editor *Andy Cox*
Founded 1998. QUARTERLY B5 colour maga-

zine of crime fiction. 'The UK's only magazine specialising in crime short stories, publishing the very best from across the spectrum.' Every issue contains stories by authors who are household names in the crime fiction world but room is found for lesser known and unknown writers. *Taking Care of Frank* by Antony Mann (Crimewave 2) and *Prussian Snowdrops* by Marion Arnott (Crimewave 4) won the **CWA/ Macallan Short Story Dagger** award in 1999 and 2001 respectively. Submissions welcome (not via e-mail) with appropriate return postage. Potential contributors are advised to study the magazine. Contracts exchanged upon acceptance. PAYMENT on publication.

Cumbria
The Water Mill, Broughton Hall, Skipton BD23 3AG
☎01756 701381 Fax 01756 701326
✉ editorial@dalesman.co.uk
www.dalesman.co.uk
Owner *Country Publications Ltd*
Editor *Terry Fletcher*
Circulation 13,713
Founded 1951. MONTHLY. County magazine of strong regional and countryside interest, focusing on the Lake District. Unsolicited mss welcome. Max. 1500 words. Approach in writing, by phone or e-mail with feature ideas. PAYMENT negotiable.

Cycle Sport
IPC Media Ltd, Leon House, 233 High Street, Croydon CR9 1HZ
☎020 8726 8463
✉ cyclesport@ipcmedia.com
www.cyclesport.co.uk
Owner *IPC Media (A Time Warner Company)*
Managing Editor *Robert Garbutt*
Deputy Editor *Nigel Wynn*
Circulation 21,447
Founded 1993. MONTHLY magazine dedicated to professional cycle racing. Unsolicited ideas for features welcome.

Cycling Weekly
IPC Media Ltd, Leon House, 233 High Street, Croydon CR9 1HZ
☎020 8774 0600
✉ cycling@ipcmedia.com
www.cyclingweekly.co.uk
Owner *IPC Media (A Time Warner Company)*
Publishing Director *Keith Foster*
Editor *Robert Garbutt*

Circulation 26,429

Founded 1891. WEEKLY. All aspects of cycle sport covered. Unsolicited mss and ideas for features welcome. Approach in writing with ideas. Fiction rarely used.

FEATURES Cycle racing, coaching, technical material and related areas. Max. 2000 words. Most work commissioned but interested in seeing new work.

NEWS Short news pieces, local news, etc. Max. 300 words.

PAYMENT features, around £60–120 per 1000 words (quality permitting); news, £15 per story.

Dalesman

The Water Mill, Broughton Hall, Skipton BD23 3AG

☎01756 701381 Fax 01756 701326

✉ editorial@dalesman.co.uk

www.dalesman.co.uk

Owner *Country Publications Ltd*

Editor *Terry Fletcher*

Circulation 43,935

Founded 1939. Now the biggest-selling regional publication of its kind in the country. MONTHLY magazine with articles of specific Yorkshire interest. Unsolicited mss welcome; receives approximately ten per day. Initial approach in writing, by phone or e-mail. Max. 1500 words. PAYMENT negotiable.

Dance Theatre Journal

Laban, Creekside, London SE8 3DZ

☎020 8691 8600 Fax 020 8691 8400

✉ dtj@laban.org

www.laban.org

Owner *Laban*

Editor *Martin Hargreaves*

Circulation 2000

Founded 1982. QUARTERLY. Interested in features on every aspect of the contemporary dance scene, particularly issues such as the funding policy for dance, critical assessments of choreographers' work and the latest developments in the various schools of contemporary dance. Unsolicited mss welcome. Length 1000–3000 words

Dance Today!

The Dancing Times Ltd, Clerkenwell House, 45–47 Clerkenwell Green, London EC1R 0EB

☎020 7250 3006 Fax 020 7253 6679

✉ dancetoday!@dancing-times.co.uk

www.dancing-times.co.uk

Owner *The Dancing Times Ltd*

Editor *Sylvia Boerner*

Circulation 2500

Founded 1956 as *Ballroom Dancing Times.* Relaunched as *Dance Today!* in 2001. MONTHLY magazine for anyone interested in ballroom and social dancing. Unsolicited contributions welcome; send c.v. with sample work by post or e-mail.

The Dancing Times

The Dancing Times Ltd, Clerkenwell House, 45–47 Clerkenwell Green, London EC1R 0EB

☎020 7250 3006 Fax 020 7253 6679

✉ editorial@dancing-times.co.uk

www.dancing-times.co.uk

Owner *The Dancing Times Ltd*

Editor *Mary Clarke*

Founded 1910. MONTHLY. Freelance suggestions welcome from specialist dance writers and photographers only. Approach in writing.

Darts World

81 Selwood Road, Croydon CR0 7JW

☎020 8650 6580 Fax 020 8654 4343

✉ dartsworld@blueyonder.co.uk

www.dartsworld.com

Owner *World Magazines Ltd*

Editor *A.J. Wood*

Circulation 12,263

FEATURES Single articles or series on technique and instruction. Max. 1200 words.

FICTION Short stories with darts theme. Max. 1000 words.

NEWS Tournament reports and general or personality news required. Max. 800 words.

PAYMENT negotiable.

Day by Day

Woolacombe House, 141 Woolacombe Road, London SE3 8QP

☎020 8856 6249

Owner *Loverseed Press*

Editor *Patrick Richards*

Circulation 25,000

Founded 1963. MONTHLY. News commentary and digest of national and international affairs, with reviews of the arts (books, plays, art exhibitions, films, opera, musicals) and county cricket and Test reports among regular slots. Unsolicited mss welcome (s.a.e. essential). Approach in writing with ideas. Contributors are advised to study the magazine in the first instance. (Specimen copy £1.20) UK subscription £14.65; Europe £18.65; RoW £22.65.

NEWS *Ronald Mallone* Interested in themes connected with non-violence and social justice only. Max. 600 words.

FEATURES No scope for freelance contributions here.

POEMS *Michael Gibson* Short poems in line with editorial principles considered. Max. 20 lines.

PAYMENT negotiable.

Dazed & Confused
112 Old Street, London EC1V 1BG
☎020 7336 0766 Fax 020 7336 0966
✉ dazed@confused.co.uk
www.confused.co.uk
Owner *Waddell Ltd*
Editor *Callum McGeoch*
Circulation 80,000

Founded 1992. MONTHLY. Cutting edge fashion, music, art interviews and features. No unsolicited material. Approach in writing with ideas in the first instance.

Debrett's
See **Debrett's Ltd** under *UK Publishers*

Decanter
First Floor, Broadway House, 2–6 Fulham Broadway, London SW6 1AA
☎020 7610 3929 Fax 020 7381 5282
✉ decanter_editorial@decanter.com
www.decanter.com
Editor *Amy Wislocki*
Circulation 35,000

FOUNDED 1975. Glossy wines magazine. Feature ideas welcome; send to editor by post or fax (not e-mail). No fiction.

NEWS/FEATURES All items and articles should concern wines, food and related subjects. PAYMENT £230 per 1000 words.

Delicious
Seven Publishing, 20 Upper Ground, London SE1 9PD
☎020 7775 7757 Fax 020 7775 7705
✉ info@deliciousmagazine.co.uk
www.deliciousmagazine.co.uk
Owner *Seven Publishing*
Editor *Mitzie Wilson*
Circulation 102,095

Launched 2003. MONTHLY publication for those who love food and cooking. Recipes – from the simple to the sophisticated – plus features on food and where it comes from. Welcomes freelance contributions; approach by e-mail.

Derbyshire Life and Countryside
Heritage House, Lodge Lane, Derby DE1 3HE
☎01332 347087 Fax 01332 290688
✉ editorials@hhgroup.co.uk
Owner *B.C. Wood*
Editor *Vivienne Irish*
Circulation 12,140

Founded 1931. MONTHLY county magazine for Derbyshire. Unsolicited mss and photographs of Derbyshire welcome, but written approach with ideas preferred.

Descent
Wild Places Publishing, PO Box 100, Abergavenny NP7 9WY
☎01873 737707 Fax 01873 737707
✉ descent@wildplaces.co.uk
www.caving.uk.com
Owner *Wild Places Publishing*
Editor *Chris Howes*
Assistant Editor *Judith Calford*

Founded 1969. BI-MONTHLY magazine for cavers and mine enthusiasts. Submissions welcome from freelance contributors who can write accurately and knowledgeably on any aspect of caves, mines or underground structures.

FEATURES General interest articles of under 1000 words welcome, as well as short foreign news reports, especially if supported by photographs/illustrations. Suitable topics include exploration (particularly British, both historical and modern), expeditions, equipment, techniques and regional British news. Max. 2000 words.

PAYMENT on publication according to page area filled.

Desire
9 Harmsworth Street, London SE17 3TJ
☎020 7820 8844 Fax 020 7820 9944
www.desire.co.uk
Owner *Moondance Media Ltd*
Editor *Ian Jackson*

Founded 1994. FIVE ISSUES YEARLY. Britain's only erotic magazine for both women and men, celebrating sex and sensuality with a mix of features, reviews, interviews, photography, reports and erotic fantasy. For a sample copy of the magazine plus contributors' guidelines and rates, please enclose four first class stamps.

Director
116 Pall Mall, London SW1Y 5ED
☎020 7766 8950 Fax 020 7766 8840
✉ director-ed@iod.com

Editor *Joanna Higgins*
Circulation 58,271

1991 Business Magazine of the Year. Published by Director Publications Ltd. for members of the Institute of Directors. Wide range of features from political and business profiles and management thinking to employment and financial issues. Also book reviews. Regular contributors used. Send letter with synopsis/published samples rather than unsolicited mss.
PAYMENT negotiable.

Disability Now

6 Market Road, London N7 9PW
☎020 7619 7323   Fax 020 7619 7331
✉ editor@disabilitynow.org.uk
www.disabilitynow.org.uk

Owner *SCOPE*
Acting Editor *Sarah Hobson*
Circulation 20,034

Founded 1984. Leading MONTHLY newspaper with fortnightly supplement for disabled people in the UK – people with a wide range of physical disabilities, as well as their families, carers and relevant professionals. Freelance contributions welcome. No fiction. Approach in writing.

FEATURES Covering new initiatives and services, personal experiences and general issues of interest to a wide national readership. Max. 900 words. Disabled contributors welcome.

NEWS Max. 300 words.

SPECIAL PAGES Possible openings for cartoonists.

PAYMENT by arrangement.

Disabled Motorist

DDMC, Cottingham Way, Thrapston NN14 4PL
☎01832 734724   Fax 01832 733816
✉ info@ddmc.org.uk
www.ddmc.org.uk

Owner *Disabled Drivers' Motor Club*
Editor *Ed Passant*
Circulation 18,000

MONTHLY publication of the Disabled Drivers' Motor Club, an organisation which aims to promote and protect the interests and welfare of disabled people and help and encourage them in gaining increased mobility. Various discounts available for members; membership costs £12 p.a. (single), £18 (joint). The magazine includes information for members plus members' letters. Approach in writing with ideas. Unsolicited mss welcome.

Diva, lesbian life and style

Spectrum House, 32–34 Gordon House Road, London NW5 1LP
☎020 7424 7400   Fax 020 7424 7401
✉ edit@divamag.co.uk
www.divamag.co.uk

Owner *Millivres-Prowler Ltd*
Editor *Jane Czyzselska*

Founded 1994. MONTHLY glossy magazine featuring lesbian news and culture including fashion, lifestyle and satire. Welcomes news, features and photographs. No poetry. Contact the news editor at the e-mail address above with news items and feature ideas and photo/fashion photographs.

Dog World

Somerfield House, Wotton Road, Ashford TN23 6LW
☎01233 621877   Fax 01233 645669
www.dogworld.co.uk

Owner *Dog World Ltd*
Editor *Stuart Baillie*
Circulation 21,157

Founded 1902. WEEKLY newspaper for people who are seriously interested in pedigree dogs. Unsolicited mss occasionally considered but initial approach in writing preferred.

FEATURES Well-researched historical items or items of unusual interest concerning dogs. Max. 1000 words. Photographs of unusual 'doggy' situations occasionally of interest.

NEWS Freelance reports welcome on court cases and local government issues involving dogs.

PAYMENT features, up to £50; photos £15.

Dogs Monthly

Ascot House, High Street, Ascot SL5 7HG
☎0870 730 8433   Fax 0870 730 8431
✉ dm@rtc-mail.org.uk
www.dogsmonthly.co.uk

Owner *Mr D. Cavill*
Editor *Meriel France*
Circulation 17,000

Founded 1983. MONTHLY magazine suitable for serious dog owners whose dog is more than just a pet.

FEATURES Articles on breeds and topical news. Approach the editor first by e-mail. Max. length for features, news, fiction or other articles 2000 words.

PAYMENT £35 per published page for illustrated articles.

Eastern Eye
Unit 2, 65 Whitechapel Road, London E1 1DU
☎020 7650 2000   Fax 020 7650 2001
www.ethnicmedia.co.uk
Owner *Ethnic Media Group*
Editor *Amar Singh*
Circulation 21,197

Founded 1989. WEEKLY community paper for
the Asian community in Britain. Interested in
relevant general, local and international issues.
Approach in writing with ideas for submission.

Easy Gardening
BBC Worldwide, AG 192, 80 Wood Lane,
London W12 0TT
☎020 8433 2000
✉ easygardening@bbc.co.uk
www.bbcworldwide.co.uk
Owner *BBC Worldwide Publishing Ltd*
Editor *Ceri Thomas*
Circulation 62,000

TEN ISSUES YEARLY. Down-to-earth and easy to
follow gardening advice 'that gets results'. Will
consider 'reader gardens' contributions; approach
by e-mail. No transparencies; digital images only.

Easy Living
68 Old Bond Street, London W1S 4PH
☎020 7499 9080   Fax 020 7399 2625
www.easylivingmagazine.com
Owner *Condé Nast*
Editor *Susie Forbes*

Launched 2005. MONTHLY magazine aimed at
women aged 30–50-plus. Focuses on aspects of
home life, beauty and health, food, relationships; stylish and glossy with real-life, practical
and useful items.

The Ecologist
Unit 18, Chelsea Wharf, 15 Lots Road,
London SW10 0QJ
☎020 7351 3578   Fax 020 7351 3617
✉ editorial@theecologist.org
www.theecologist.org
Owner *Ecosystems Ltd*
Managing Editor *Harry Ram*
Editor *Zac Goldsmith*
Circulation 20,000

Founded 1970. MONTHLY. Unsolicited mss
welcome but best approach is a brief proposal
to the editor by e-mail (address above), outlining experience and background and summarising suggested article.
    FEATURES Radical approach to political,

economic, social and environmental issues, with
an emphasis on rethinking the basic assumptions that underpin modern society. Articles of
between 500 and 3000 words.
    PAYMENT negotiable.

The Economist
25 St James's Street, London SW1A 1HG
☎020 7830 7000   Fax 020 7839 2968
www.economist.com
Owner *Pearson/individual shareholders*
Editor *Bill Emmott*
Circulation 204,869 (Continental Europe)

Founded 1843. WEEKLY. Worldwide circulation.
Approaches should be made in writing to the
editor. No unsolicited mss.

The Edge
65 Guinness Buildings, Hammersmith,
London W6 8BD
☎020 8563 1310
✉ davec@theedge.abelgratis.co.uk
www.theedgeabelgratis.co.uk
Editor *Dave Clark*

QUARTERLY. Reviews and features: film (indie,
arts), books, popular culture. Fiction: modern
crime/horror/SF/erotica/slipstream.   Sample
issue £4 post-free (cheques payable to 'The
Edge'). Writers' guidelines available on website,
for s.a.e. or by e-mail.
    PAYMENT up to £60 per 1000 words.

Electrical Times
Nexus House, Swanley BR8 8HU
☎01322 611282   Fax 01322 616376
✉ b.evett@highburybiz.com
Owner *Highbury Business*
Managing Editor *Bill Evett*
Circulation 10,623

Founded 1891. MONTHLY. Aimed at electrical
contractors, designers and installers. Unsolicited
mss welcome but initial approach preferred.

Elle
64 North Row, London W1K 7LL
☎020 7150 7000   Fax 020 7150 7670
Owner *Hachette Filipacchi*
Editor *Lorraine Candy*
Features Editor *Anna Pursglove*
Circulation 202,074

Founded 1985. MONTHLY fashion glossy. Prospective contributors should approach the relevant editor in writing in the first instance,
including cuttings.
    FEATURES Max. 2000 words.

HOT LIST Short articles on hot trends, events, fashion and beauty. Max. 500 words. PAYMENT negotiable.

Embroidery

PO Box 42B, East Molesley KT8 9BB
☎01260 295735
✉ jhall@embroiderersguild.com
www.embroiderersguild.com

Owner *Embroiderers' Guild*
Editor *Joanne Hall*
Circulation 12,000

Founded 1933. BI-MONTHLY. Features articles on historical and foreign embroidery, and contemporary artists' work with illustrations. Covers all forms of textile art, historical and contemporary. Also reviews. Unsolicited material welcome. Max. 1000 words.
PAYMENT negotiable.

Empire

4th Floor, Mappin House, 4 Winsley Street, London W1W 8HF
☎020 7436 1515   Fax 020 7343 8703
✉ empire@emap.com
www.empireonline.co.uk

Owner *Emap East*
Editor *Colin Kennedy*
Circulation 205,587

Founded 1989. Launched at the Cannes Film Festival. MONTHLY guide to the movies which aims to cover the world of films in a 'comprehensive, adult, intelligent and witty package'. Although most of *Empire* is devoted to films and the people behind them, it also looks at the developments and technology behind television and DVDs plus music, multimedia and books. Wide selection of in-depth features and stories on all the main releases of the month, and reviews of over 100 films and videos. Contributions welcome but approach in writing first.
FEATURES Behind-the-scenes features on films, humorous and factual features.
PAYMENT by agreement.

The Engineer

50 Poland Street, London W1F 7AX
☎020 7970 4000   Fax 020 7970 4189
✉ andrew.lee@centaur.co.uk
www.e4engineering.com

Owner *Centaur Communications*
Editor *Andrew Lee*
Circulation 41,000

FOUNDED 1856. FORTNIGHTLY news magazine for technology and innovation.

FEATURES Most outside contributions are commissioned but good ideas are always welcome. Max. 2000 words.
NEWS Scope for specialist regional freelancers, and for tip-offs. Max. 500 words.
TECHNOLOGY Technology news from specialists, and tip-offs. Max. 500 words.
PAYMENT by arrangement.

The English Garden

Archant Specialist, Jubilee House, 2 Jubilee Place, London SW3 3QT
☎020 7751 4800   Fax 020 7751 4848
✉ englishgarden@archant.co.uk
www.theenglishgarden.co.uk

Owner *Archant Specialist*
Acting Editor *Janine Wookey*
Circulation 35,651

Founded 1996. MONTHLY. Features on beautiful gardens with practical ideas on design and planting. No unsolicited mss.
FEATURES *Jackie Bennett* Max. 1000–1200 words. Approach in writing in the first instance; send synopsis of 150 words with strong design and planting ideas, feature proposals, or sets of photographs of interesting gardens.

English Nature Magazine

English Nature, Northminster House, Peterborough PE1 1UA
☎01733 455100   Fax 01733 455436
✉ amanda.giles@english-nature.org.uk
www.english-nature.org.uk

Owner *English Nature*
Editor *Amanda Giles*
Circulation 16,000

Founded 1992. BI-MONTHLY magazine which explains the work of English Nature, the government adviser on wildlife and conservation policies. No unsolicited material.

Erotic Review

30 Cleveland Street, London W1T 4JD
☎020 8956 2799
✉ info@theeroticreview.co.uk
www.theeroticreview.co.uk

Owner *Alton Russell International*
Circulation 20,000

Founded 1997. MONTHLY erotic literary magazine containing articles, humour, fiction, poetry and art work. Unsolicited material welcome, but please read magazine first. No clichéd pornography. Approach in writing in the first instance enclosing a brief sample of work and s.a.e.

FEATURES Esoteric, humorous or real-life experiences. Max. 2000 words.
FICTION Erotic short stories. Max. 2000 words.
PAYMENT features, £40–100; fiction, £50–100.

ES (Evening Standard magazine)
See **Evening Standard** under *Regional Newspapers*

Esquire
National Magazine House, 72 Broadwick Street, London W1F 9EP
☎020 7439 5000 Fax 020 7439 5675
Owner *National Magazine Co. Ltd*
Editor *Simon Tiffin*
Circulation 71,401

Founded 1991. MONTHLY. Quality men's general interest magazine. No unsolicited mss or short stories.

Essentials
IPC Media Ltd., King's Reach Tower, Stamford Street, London SE1 9LS
☎020 7261 6970 Fax 020 7261 5262
Owner *IPC Media (A Time Warner Company)*
Editor *Julie Barton-Breck*
Circulation 128,844

Founded 1988. MONTHLY women's interest magazine. Unsolicited mss (not originals) welcome if accompanied by s.a.e. Initial approach in writing preferred. Prospective contributors should study the magazine thoroughly before submitting anything. No fiction.
FEATURES Max. 2000 words (double-spaced on A4).
PAYMENT negotiable.

The Essex Magazine
See **The Journal Magazines**

Eve
Griffin House, 161 Hammersmith Road, London W6 8BS
☎020 8267 5000 Fax 020 8267 8222
✉ evemagazine@haynet.com
www.evemagazine.co.uk
Owner *Haymarket Publishing*
Editor *Sara Cremer*
Deputy Editor *Lucy Dunn*
Features Director *Victoria Woodhall*
Circulation 160,210

Founded 2000. MONTHLY. Wide-ranging general interest – aimed at the intelligent 30+

woman. No unsolicited material. Send introductory letter, *recent* writings and outlines for ideas aimed at a specific section. It is essential that would-be contributors familiarise themselves with the magazine.

Eventing
See **Horse and Hound**

Evergreen
PO Box 52, Cheltenham GL50 1YQ
☎01242 537900 Fax 01242 537901
Editor *R. Faiers*
Circulation 75,000

Founded 1985. QUARTERLY magazine featuring articles and poems about Britain. Unsolicited contributions welcome.
FEATURES Britain's natural beauty, towns and villages, nostalgia, wildlife, traditions, odd customs, legends, folklore, crafts, etc. Length 250–2000 words.
PAYMENT £15 per 1000 words; poems £4.

Everything France
Westgate, 120-128 Station Road, Redhill RH1 1ET
☎01737 786800 Fax 01737 786801
✉ martin.hedges@brooklandsgroup.com
www.brooklandsgroup.com
Owner *Brooklands Group Limited*
Editor *Martin Hedges*

Founded 2001. MONTHLY. 'The premier magazine for French property, travel, touring, food and drink.' Welcomes French-based features on property – buying, lifestyle and gardens; tourism, cities and regions, personalities and French culture. Words and picture packages welcome. Approach by e-mail. Max. 3000 words.
PAYMENT negotiable.

Executive Woman
2 Chantry Place, Harrow HA3 6NY
☎020 8420 1210 Fax 020 8420 1691
✉ info@execwoman.com
www.execwoman.com
Owner *Saleworld*
Managing Editor *Angela Giveon*
Circulation 85,000

Founded 1987. BI-MONTHLY magazine for female executives in the corporate field and female entrepreneurs.
FEATURES New and interesting business issues and 'Women to Watch'. Health and con-

ferencing, profiles, technology, beauty, fashion, training and arts items. 700 words per page. LEGAL/FINANCIAL Opportunities for lawyers/accountants to write on issues in their field. Max. 600 words.

Fairgame Magazine
The Baltic Business Centre, Gateshead NE8 3DA
☎0191 442 4001 Fax 0191 442 4002
www.fairgamemagazine.com

Editor *Jennifer O'Neill*
Circulation 15,000

Founded 2003. BI-MONTHLY magazine for women football players. Contributions welcome.

FEATURES *Claire Foy* International reports, player and team profiles, interviews, diet, health and fitness, tactics, training advice, play improvement, fund-raising. Max. 1500 words.

NEWS *Wilf Frith* Match reports, team news, transfers, injuries, results and fixtures. Max. 600 words.

Family Circle
IPC Media Ltd., King's Reach Tower, Stamford Street, London SE1 9LS
☎0870 444 5000 Fax 020 7261 5929

Owner *IPC Media (A Time Warner Company)*
Editor *Karen Livermore*
Circulation 140,305

Founded 1964. MONTHLY. Women's general interest. Little scope for freelancers as most material is produced in-house or by published journalists.

Features *Emma Burstall*
Health & Consumer *Sarah Touquet*
Food & Drink *Catherine Hill*

Family Tree Magazine
61 Great Whyte, Ramsey, Huntingdon PE26 1HJ
☎01487 814050 Fax 01487 711361
✉ sue.f@family-tree.co.uk
www.family-tree.co.uk

Owner *ABM Publishing Ltd*
Editor *Peter Watson*
Circulation 50,000

Founded 1984. MONTHLY. News and features on matters of genealogy. Not interested in own family histories. Approach in writing with ideas. All material should be addressed to *Sue Fearn*.

FEATURES Any genealogically related subject. Max. 2000 words. No puzzles or fictional articles.

PAYMENT news and features, £45 per 1000 words.

Fancy Fowl
The Publishing House, Station Road, Framlingham IP13 9EE
☎01728 622030 Fax 01728 622031
✉ ff@prestige.typo.co.uk

Owner *TP Publications*
Editor *Liz Fairbrother*
Circulation 3000

Founded 1979. MONTHLY. Devoted entirely to poultry, waterfowl, turkeys, geese, pea fowl, etc. – management, breeding, rearing and exhibition. Outside contributions of knowledgeable, technical poultry-related articles and news welcome. Max. 1000 words. Approach by letter.

PAYMENT negotiable.

Farmers Weekly
Quadrant House, Sutton SM2 5AS
☎020 8652 4911 Fax 020 8652 4005
✉ farmers.weekly@rbi.co.uk
www.fwi.co.uk

Owner *Reed Business Information*
Editor *Jane King*
Circulation 75,158

WEEKLY. 1996 Business Magazine of the Year. For practising farmers and those in the ancillary industries. Unsolicited mss considered.

FEATURES A wide range of material relating to farmers' problems and interests: specific sections on arable and livestock farming, farm life, practical and general interest, machinery and business.

NEWS General farming news.

PAYMENT negotiable.

Fast Car
Berwick House, 8–10 Knoll Rise, Orpington BR6 0PS
☎01689 887200 Fax 01689 838844
✉ fastcar@highburyleisure.co.uk
www.fastcar.co.uk

Owner *Highbury Leisure*
Editor *Gez Jones*
Circulation 117,359

Founded 1987. THIRTEEN ISSUES YEARLY. Lad's magazine about performance tuning and modifying cars. Covers all aspects of this youth culture including the latest street styles and music. Features cars and their owners, product tests and in-car entertainment. Also includes a free reader ads section.

NEWS Any item in line with the above.

FEATURES Innovative ideas in line with the above and in the *Fast Car* writing style. Generally four pages in length. No Kit-car features, race reports or road test reports of standard cars. Copy should be as concise as possible. PAYMENT negotiable.

FHM
Mappin House, 4 Winsley Street, London W1W 8HF
☎020 7182 8028   Fax 020 7182 8021
✉ general@fhm.com
www.fhm.com
Owner *Emap Plc*
Editor *Ross Brown*
Circulation 580,027

Founded in 1986 as a free fashion magazine, FHM evolved to become more male oriented but without much public acclaim until Emap bought the title in the 1994. Since then it has become the best-selling men's magazine in the world covering all areas of men's lifestyle. Published MONTHLY with 18 international editions worldwide. No unsolicited mss. Synopses and ideas welcome by e-mail. PAYMENT negotiable.

The Field
IPC Media Ltd., King's Reach Tower, Stamford Street, London SE1 9LS
☎020 7261 5198   Fax 020 7261 5358
✉ beatrice_gray@ipcmedia.com
www.thefield.co.uk
Owner *IPC Media (A Time Warner Company)*
Editor-in-Chief *Jonathan Young*
Circulation 30,867

Founded 1853. MONTHLY magazine for those who are serious about the British countryside and its pleasures. Unsolicited mss (and transparencies) welcome but initial approach should be made in writing or by phone on 020 7261 6225.

FEATURES Exceptional work on any subject concerning the countryside. Most work tends to be commissioned.
PAYMENT varies.

50 Connect –
www.50connect.co.uk
See entry under *Electronic Publishing and Other Services*

Film Review
Visual Imagination Ltd, 9 Blades Court, Deodar Road, London SW15 2NU
☎020 8875 1520   Fax 020 8875 1588
✉ filmreview@visimag.com
www.visimag.com
Owner *Visual Imagination Ltd*
Editor *Grant Kempster*

Circulation 50,000
FOUR-WEEKLY. Reviews, profiles, interviews and special reports on films. Unsolicited material considered. PAYMENT negotiable.

Fishing News
4th Floor, Albert House 1–4 Singer Street, London EC2A 4LQ
☎020 7017 4531   Fax 020 7017 4536
✉ tim.oliver@informa.com
www.fishingnews.co.uk
Owner *Informa Group Plc*
Editor *Tim Oliver*
Circulation 9,578

Founded 1913. WEEKLY. All aspects of the commercial fishing industry in the UK and Ireland. No unsolicited mss; telephone inquiry in the first instance. Max. 600 words for news and 1500 words for features. PAYMENT £100 per 1000 words.

The Fix
5 Martins Lane, Witcham, Ely CB6 2LB
✉ ttapress@aol.com
www.ttapress.com
Owner *TTA Press*

Founded 1994. BI-MONTHLY. Features detailed contributors' guidelines and reviews of international short story publications, plus varied articles, news, views and interviews.

FEATURES Unsolicited articles welcome on any aspect of short story publishing: market information, writing, editing, illustrating, interviews and reviews. All genres. Submissions should include adequate return postage. 'Please study the magazine: this will greatly enhance your chances of acceptance.' No fiction or poetry.

Flight International
Quadrant House, The Quadrant, Sutton SM2 5AS
☎020 8652 3842   Fax 020 8652 3840
✉ flight.international@rbi.co.uk
www.flightinternational.com
Owner *Reed Business Information*
Editor *Murdo Morrison*
Circulation 52,222

Founded 1909. WEEKLY. International trade magazine for the aerospace industry, including civil, military and space. Unsolicited mss considered. Commissions preferred – phone with ideas and follow up with letter. E-mail submissions encouraged.

FEATURES *Murdo Morrison* Technically informed articles and pieces on specific geographical areas with international appeal. Analytical, in-depth coverage required, preferably supported by interviews. Max. 1800 words.

NEWS *Andrew Doyle* Opportunities exist for news pieces from particular geographical areas on specific technical developments. Max. 350 words.

PAYMENT NUJ rates.

Flora International

The Fishing Lodge Studio, 77 Bulbridge Road, Wilton, Salisbury SP2 0LE
☎01722 743207 Fax 01722 743207
✉ floramag@aol.com
Publisher/Editor *Maureen Foster*
Circulation 16,000

Founded 1974. BI-MONTHLY magazine for flower arrangers and florists. Unsolicited mss welcome. Approach in writing with ideas. Not interested in general gardening articles.

FEATURES Fully illustrated: colour photographs, transparencies or CD. Flower arranging, flower arrangers' gardens and flower crafts. Floristry items written with practical knowledge and well illustrated are particularly welcome. Max. 1000 words.

PROFILES/REVIEWS Personality profiles and book reviews.

PAYMENT £50 per 1000 words plus additional payment for suitable photographs.

FlyPast

PO Box 100, Stamford PE9 1XQ
☎01780 755131 Fax 01780 757261
✉ flypast@keypublishing.com
Owner *Key Publishing Ltd*
Editor *Ken Ellis*
Circulation 39,863

Founded 1981. MONTHLY. Historic aviation and aviation heritage, mainly military, Second World War period up to c.1970. Unsolicited mss welcome.

Focus

See **British Science Fiction Association** under *Professional Associations*

Focus

Origin Publishing, 14th Floor, Tower House, Fairfax Street, Bristol BS1 3BN
☎0117 927 9009 Fax 0117 934 9008
www.originpublishing.co.uk
Owner *Origin Publishing*
Editor *Paul Parsons*
News Editor *Graham Southorn*
Circulation 55,000

Founded 1992. MONTHLY. Popular science and discovery. Welcomes *relevant* summaries of original feature ideas by e-mail.

For Women

Fantasy Publications, 4 Selsdon Way, London E14 9EL
☎020 7308 5090
Editor *Liz Beresford*
Circulation 60,000

Founded 1992. SIX-WEEKLY magazine of erotic and sex interest for women – health and sex, erotic fiction and photography. No homes and gardens articles. Approach in writing in the first instance. Send s.a.e. for submission guidelines.

FICTION *Elizabeth Coldwell* Erotic short stories. Max. 3000 words.

PAYMENT £150 total.

Fortean Times: The Journal of Strange Phenomena

PO Box 2409, London NW5 4NP
☎020 7907 6235 Fax 020 7907 6406
✉ david_sutton@dennis.co.uk
www.forteantimes.com
Editor *David Sutton*
Circulation 27,115

Founded 1973. THIRTEEN ISSUES YEARLY. Accounts of strange phenomena and experiences, curiosities, mysteries, prodigies and portents. Unsolicited mss welcome. Approach in writing with ideas. No fiction, poetry, rehashes or politics.

FEATURES Well-researched and referenced material on current or historical mysteries, or first-hand accounts of oddities. Max. 3000 words, preferably with good relevant photos/illustrations.

NEWS Concise copy with full source references essential.

PAYMENT negotiable.

FQ Magazine

Seymour House, South Street, Bromley BR1 1RH
☎020 8460 6060 Fax 020 8460 6050
✉ matt@touchline.com
www.fqmagazine.co.uk
Owner *3D Media Ltd*
Editor *Matt Weiner*

Launched 2003. BI-MONTHLY. Lifestyle magazine for young fathers. Interviews, reviews, finance, kids' toys, child issues, parenting tips and general fatherhood advice. Ideas welcome; contact the editor by e-mail.

France Magazine

Archant House, Oriel Road, Cheltenham
GL50 1BB
☎01242 216050   Fax 01242 216074
✉ editorial@francemag.com
www.francemag.com
Owner *Archant (Life South) Ltd*
Editor *Nick Wall*
Circulation 47,488

FOUNDED 1989. MONTHLY magazine containing all things of interest to Francophiles – in English. Approach by e-mail in the first instance.

Freelance Market News

Sevendale House, 7 Dale Street, Manchester
M1 1JB
☎0161 228 2362, ext 210
Fax 0161 228 3533
✉ fmn@writersbureau.com
www.writersbureau.com/fmn
Editor *Angela Cox*

MONTHLY. News and information on the free-lance writers' market, both inland and overseas. Includes market information, competitions, seminars, courses, overseas openings, etc. Short articles (700 words max.). Unsolicited contributions welcome.
   PAYMENT by negotiation.

The Freelance

See **National Union of Journalists** under *Professional Associations*

Garden Answers

Bretton Court, Bretton, Peterborough
PE3 8DZ
☎01733 264666   Fax 01733 282695
Owner *Emap Active Publications Ltd*
Deputy Editor *Daniella Delaney*
Circulation 49,419

Founded 1982. MONTHLY. 'It is unlikely that unsolicited manuscripts will be used, as articles are usually commissioned and must be in the magazine style.' Prospective contributors should approach the editor in writing. Interested in hearing from gardening writers on any subject, whether flowers, fruit, vegetables, houseplants or greenhouse gardening.

Garden Life

Seven Publishing, Sea Containers House,
20 Upper Ground, London SE1 9PD
☎020 7775 7775
✉ message@gardenlifemagazine.co.uk
www.gardenlifemagazine.co.uk

Owner *Seven Publishing*
Editor *Tiffany Daneff*
Circulation 80,000

Launched 2004. MONTHLY gardening magazine for the novice as well as the more experienced gardener. 'Easy to use and free of jargon.'

Garden News

Bretton Court, Bretton, Peterborough
PE3 8DZ
☎01733 264666   Fax 01733 282695
Owner *Emap Active Publications Ltd*
Editor *Sarah Page*
Circulation 50,361

Founded 1958. Britain's biggest-selling, full-colour gardening WEEKLY. News and advice on growing flowers, fruit and vegetables, plus colourful features on all aspects of gardening especially for the committed gardener. News and features welcome, especially if accompanied by top-quality photos or illustrations. Contact the editor before submitting any material.

The Garden, Journal of the Royal Horticultural Society

RHS Publications, 4th Floor, Churchgate
New Road, Peterborough PE1 1TT
✉ thegarden@rhs.org.uk
www.rhs.org.uk
Owner *The Royal Horticultural Society*
Editor *Ian Hodgson*
Circulation 345,728

Founded 1866. MONTHLY journal of the Royal Horticultural Society. Covers all aspects of the art, science and practice of horticulture and garden making. 'Articles must have depth and substance.' Approach by letter with a synopsis in the first instance. Max. 2500 words.

Gardens Illustrated

BBC Worldwide, Woodlands, 80 Wood Lane,
London W12 0TT
☎020 8433 1352   Fax 020 8433 2680
www.gardensillustrated.com
Owner *BBC Worldwide Publishing Ltd*
Acting Editor *Juliet Roberts*
Circulation 30,106

Founded 1993. TEN ISSUES YEARLY. 'Britain's most distinguished garden magazine' with a world-wide readership. The focus is on garden design, with a strong international flavour. Unsolicited mss are rarely used and it is best that prospective contributors approach the editor with ideas in writing, supported by photographs.

Gardens Monthly

Berwick House, 8–10 Knoll Rise, Orpington BR6 0PS
☎01689 887200 Fax 01689 896847
✉ hgriffin@highburyleisure.co.uk
Owner *Highbury Leisure Publishing*
Editor *Helen Griffin*
Circulation 32,978

Launched 2002. MONTHLY consumer magazine for amateur gardeners with some experience. New plants and equipment, garden design and problem-solving advice. Welcomes big garden features with pictures; e-mail in the first instance.

Gay Times

Unit M, Spectrum House, 32–34 Gordon House Road, London NW5 1LP
☎020 7424 7400 Fax 020 7424 7401
✉ edit@gaytimes.co.uk
www.gaytimes.co.uk
Owner *Millivres-Prowler Group*
Editor *Vicky Powell*
Circulation 65,000

Covers all aspects of gay life, plus general interest likely to appeal to the gay community, art reviews and news. Regular freelance writers used. PAYMENT negotiable.

Gibbons Stamp Monthly

Stanley Gibbons, 7 Parkside, Christchurch Road, Ringwood BH24 3SH
☎01425 472363 Fax 01425 470247
✉ hjefferies@stanleygibbons.co.uk
www.gibbonsstampmonthly.com
Owner *Stanley Gibbons Ltd*
Editor *Hugh Jefferies*
Circulation 22,000

Founded 1890. MONTHLY. News and features. Unsolicited mss welcome. Make initial approach in writing by telephone or e-mail to avoid disappointment.

FEATURES *Hugh Jefferies* Unsolicited material of specialised nature and general stamp features welcome. Max. 3000 words but longer pieces can be serialised.

NEWS *John Moody* Any philatelic news item. Max. 500 words.

PAYMENT features, £40–50 per 1000 words; news, no payment.

Girl About Town

Independent House, 191 Marsh Wall, London E14 9RS
☎020 7005 5550 Fax 020 7005 5777

www.londoncareers.net
Owner *Independent Magazines*
Editor-in-Chief *Bill Williamson*
Circulation 85,000

Founded 1972. Free WEEKLY magazine for women aged 18 to 45. Unsolicited mss may be considered. No fiction.

FEATURES Standards are 'exacting'. Commissions only. Some chance of unknown writers being commissioned. Max. 1500 words.

PAYMENT negotiable.

Glamour

6–8 Old Bond Street, London W1S 4PH
☎020 7499 9080 Fax 020 7491 2551
www.condenast.co.uk
Owner *Condé Nast*
Editor *Jo Elvin*
Circulation 620,391

Founded 2001. Handbag-size glossy women's magazine – fashion, beauty and celebrities. No unsolicited mss; send ideas for features in synopsis form to the Features Editor *Rachel Pask*.

The Golf+

IPC Media Ltd, Leon House, 233 High Street, Croydon CR9 1HZ
☎020 8726 8000
✉ thegolfmag@ipcmedia.com
www.thegolf.co.uk
Owner *IPC Media (A Time Warner Company)*
Editor *Steve Kirk*
Circulation 25,000

Founded 1995. MONTHLY features Volkswagen Golfs and other VAG cars. Articles on tuning, styling, performance, technical and potential feature cars. 'Not interested in anything to do with the game of golf.' Submissions should be made directly to the editor. Articles must show excellent specialist knowledge of the subject matter. PAYMENT by negotiation.

Golf Monthly

IPC Media Ltd., King's Reach Tower, Stamford Street, London SE1 9LS
☎020 7261 7237 Fax 020 7261 7240
✉ golfmonthly@ipcmedia.com
golf-monthly.co.uk
Owner *IPC Media (A Time Warner Company)*
Editor *Jane Carter*
Circulation 77,766

Founded 1911. MONTHLY. Player profiles, golf instruction, general golf features and columns. Not interested in instruction material from outside contributors. Unsolicited mss welcome. Approach in writing with ideas. FEATURES Max. 1500–2000 words. PAYMENT by arrangement.

Golf Weekly

Bushfield House, Orton Centre, Peterborough PE2 5UW
☎01733 288011   Fax 01733 288025
✉ golf.weekly@emap.com
Owner *Emap Active Ltd*
Editor *Peter Masters*
Circulation 10,000

Founded 1890. WEEKLY. Unsolicited material welcome from full-time journalists only. 'Always looking for photographic and written news contributions.' For features, approach in writing in first instance; for news, e-mail, fax or phone.
FEATURES Max. 1500 words.
NEWS Max. 300 words.
PAYMENT negotiable.

Golf World

Bushfield House, Orton, Peterborough PE2 5UW
☎01733 237111   Fax 01733 288025
✉ peter.masters@emap.com
www.email.golfworldmagazine.co.uk
Owner *Emap Active Ltd*
Editor *Adam Duckworth*
Deputy Editor *Peter Masters*
Circulation 47,079

Founded 1962. MONTHLY. No unsolicited mss. Approach in writing with ideas.

Good Holiday Magazine

27A High Street, Esher KT10 9RL
☎01372 468140   Fax 01372 470765
✉ info@goodholidayideas.com
Editor *John Hill*
Circulation 100,000

Founded 1985. QUARTERLY aimed at better-off holiday-makers rather than travellers. Worldwide destinations including Europe and domestic. No unsolicited material but approach in writing or by e-mail with ideas and/or synopsis. PAYMENT negotiable.

Good Housekeeping

National Magazine House, 72 Broadwick Street, London W1F 9EP
☎020 7439 5000   Fax 020 7439 5616
✉ firstname.lastname@natmags.co.uk
www.natmags.co.uk
Owner *National Magazine Co. Ltd*

Editor-in-Chief *Lindsay Nicholson*
Circulation 435,076
Founded 1922. MONTHLY glossy. No unsolicited mss. Write with ideas in the first instance to the appropriate editor.
FEATURES *Lucy Moore* Most work is commissioned but original ideas are always welcome. No ideas are discussed on the telephone. Send short synopsis, plus relevant cuttings, showing previous examples of work published. No unsolicited mss.
HEALTH *Julie Powell*. Submission guidelines as for features; no unsolicited mss.

Good Motoring

Station Road, Forest Row RH18 5EN
☎01342 825676   Fax 01342 824847
✉ dh@motoringassist.com
www.roadsafety.org.uk
Owner *Gem Motoring Assist*
Editor *Derek Hainge*
Circulation 52,000

Founded 1932. QUARTERLY motoring, road safety, travel and general features magazine. 1500 words max. Prospective contributors should approach in writing only.

Good News

50 Loxwood Avenue, Worthing BN14 7RA
☎01903 824174   Fax 01903 824174
www.goodnews-paper.org.uk
Owner *Good News Fellowship*
Editor *Donald Banks*
Circulation 50,000

Founded 2001. MONTHLY evangelistic newspaper which welcomes contributions. No fiction. Send for sample copy of writers' guidelines in the first instance. No poetry or children's stories.
NEWS Items of up to 500 words (preferably with pictures) 'showing God at work, and human interest photo stories. "Churchy" items not wanted. Testimonies of how people have come to personal faith in Jesus Christ and the difference it has made are always welcome. They do not need to be dramatic!'
WOMEN'S PAGE Relevant items of interest welcome.
PAYMENT negotiable.

Good Ski Guide

PPL, 5th Floor, Mermaid House, 2 Puddle Dock, London EC4V 3DR
☎020 7332 2000
✉ info@goodskiguide.com
www.goodskiguide.com

Owner *Profile Media Group plc*
Editor *Cate Langmuir*
Circulation 50,000

Founded 1976. FOUR ISSUES YEARLY. Unsolicited mss welcome from writers with a knowledge of skiing and ski resorts. Prospective contributors are best advised to make initial contact in writing as ideas and work need to be seen before any discussion can take place.
PAYMENT negotiable.

GQ

Vogue House, Hanover Square, London
W1S 1JU
☎020 7499 9080   Fax 020 7495 1679
www.gq-magazine.co.uk
Owner *Condé Nast Publications Ltd*
Editor *Dylan Jones*
Circulation 125,016

Founded 1988. MONTHLY. Men's style magazine. No unsolicited material. Write or fax with an idea in the first instance.

Granta

2–3 Hanover Yard, Noel Road, London
N1 8BE
☎020 7704 9776   Fax 020 7704 0474
✉ editorial@granta.com
www.granta.com

Editor *Ian Jack*
Deputy Editor *Matt Weiland*

QUARTERLY magazine of new writing, including fiction, memoirs, reportage and photography published in paperback book form. Highbrow, diverse and contemporary, with a thematic approach. Unsolicited mss (including fiction) considered. A lot of material is commissioned. Vital to read the magazine first to appreciate its very particular fusion of cultural and political interests. No reviews or news articles. No poetry. Access the website for submission guidelines.
PAYMENT negotiable.

Grazia

Emap Consumer Media, Endeavour House,
189 Shaftesbury Avenue, London WC2H 8JG
☎020 7437 9011
www.graziamagazine.co.uk
Owner *Emap Consumer Media*
Editor *Jane Bruton*

Launched February 2005. Britain's first WEEKLY glossy aimed at women aged 25 to 45. Features articles on fashion, celebrity, news, beauty and lifestyle. Approach by e-mail.

The Great Outdoors
See **TGO**

The Great War

PO Box 202, Scarborough YO11 3GE
☎01723 581329   Fax 01723 581329
✉ books@greatnorthernpublising.co.uk
www.greatnorthernpublishing.co.uk
Owner *Great Northern Publishing*
Editor *Mark Marsay*

Founded 2001. BI-MONTHLY subscription only, non-academic magazine published in A5 format. 'The little magazine dedicated to the Great War (1914–19) and to those who perished and those who returned.' Articles, personal stories and accounts of those who served (men and women of all nationalities) and their families: diaries, anecdotes, letters, postcards, poetry, unit histories, events and memorials, etc. Absolutely no fiction or long academic works expounding historian's personal views. New material welcome but contact editor prior to sending. See website for submission guidelines and editorial content. 'Open door policy: all welcome regardless of ability to write to high standard as all work is carefully edited. No subject or topic excluded.' Sample copy £5.

Guardian Weekend
See **The Guardian** under *National Newspapers*

Guiding magazine

17–19 Buckingham Palace Road, London
SW1W 0PT
☎020 7834 6242   Fax 020 7828 5791
✉ guiding@girlguiding.org.uk
www.girlguiding.org.uk
Owner *The Guide Association*
Editor *Wendy Kewley*
Circulation 72,500

Founded 1914. MONTHLY. Unsolicited mss welcome provided topics relate to the Movement and/or women's role in society. Ideas in writing appreciated in first instance. No nostalgic, 'when I was a Guide', pieces, please.

ACTIVITY IDEAS Interesting, contemporary ideas and instructions for activities for girls aged 5 to 18+ to do during unit meetings – crafts, games (indoor/outdoor), etc.

FEATURES Topics relevant to today's girls and young women. 650 words.

NEWS Items likely to be of interest to members. Max. 100–150 words.

PAYMENT £70 per 1000 words.

H&E Naturist

Burlington Court, Carlisle Street, Goole
DN14 5EG
☎01405 760298/766769   Fax 01405 763815
✉ editor@henaturist.co.uk
www.healthandefficiency.co.uk
Owner *New Freedom Publications Ltd*
Editor *Sara Backhouse*
Circulation 20,000

Founded 1898. MONTHLY naturist magazine.
FEATURES Will consider short features on social
nudism, longer features on nudist holidays and
nudist philosophy. 90% of every issue is by freelance contributors. 8000–10,500 words.

NEWS 'We are always on the lookout for
national and international nudist news stories.'
250–500 words. No soft porn, 'sexy' stories or
sleazy photographs. Approach by post, e-mail or
telephone.

Hair

IPC Media Ltd., King's Reach Tower,
Stamford Street, London SE1 9LS
☎020 7261 6975   Fax 020 7261 7382
Owner *IPC Media (A Time Warner Company)*
Editor *Zoe Richards*
Circulation 131,735

Founded 1977. BI-MONTHLY hair and beauty
magazine. No unsolicited mss, but always interested in good photographs. Approach with
ideas in writing.
FEATURES Fashion pieces on hair trends and
styling advice. Max. 1000 words.
PAYMENT negotiable.

Hairflair

Hairflair Magazines Ltd, Freebournes House,
Freebournes Road, Witham CM8 3US
☎01376 534540   Fax 01376 534546
Owner *Hairflair Magazines Ltd*
Editor *Ruth Page*
Circulation 60,000

Founded 1982. BI-MONTHLY. Original and
interesting hair and beauty-related features written in a young, lively style to appeal to a readership aged 16–35 years. Unsolicited mss not
welcome, although freelancers are used.
FEATURES Hair and beauty. Max. 2500
words. PAYMENT negotiable.

Harpers & Queen

National Magazine House, 72 Broadwick
Street, London W1F 9EP
☎020 7439 5000   Fax 020 7439 5506

Owner *National Magazine Co. Ltd*
Editor *Lucy Yeomans*
Circulation 98,100

MONTHLY. Up-market glossy combining the
stylish and the streetwise. Approach in writing
(not phone) with ideas.
FEATURES *Harriet Green* Ideas only in the first
instance.
NEWS Snippets welcome if very original.
PAYMENT negotiable.

Health & Fitness Magazine

53–79 Highgate Road, London NW5 1TW
☎020 7331 1000   Fax 020 7331 1181
✉ editorial@htonline.co.uk
www.hfonline.co.uk
Owner *Highbury-WV*
Editor *Mary Comber*
Circulation 65,000

Founded 1983. MONTHLY. Target reader: active,
health-conscious women aged 25–40.
FEATURES news and articles on nutrition,
exercise, healthy eating, holistic health and well-
being. Will consider ideas; approach in writing
in the first instance.

Healthy

River Publishing, 14 Leicester Place, London
WC2H 7BZ
☎020 7413 9359
✉ ameggeson@riverltd.co.uk
Owner *River Publishing*
Editor *Annabel Meggeson*
Circulation 280,075

BI-MONTHLY health magazine with authoritative and accessible information and advice. Will
consider holistic health and lifestyle features;
approach by e-mail.

Heat

Endeavour House, 189 Shaftesbury Avenue,
London WC2H 8JG
☎020 7437 9011   Fax 020 7859 8670
✉ heat@emap.com
Owner *Emap Entertainment*
Editor *Mark Frith*
Circulation 552,215

Founded January 1999. WEEKLY entertainment
magazine dealing with TV, film and radio information, fashion and features, with an emphasis
on celebrity interviews and news. Targets 18 to
40-year-old readership, male and female.
Articles written both in-house and by trusted
freelancers. No unsolicited mss.

Hello!
Wellington House, 69–71 Upper Ground, London SE1 9PQ
☎020 7667 8700 Fax 020 7667 8716
www.hellomagazine.com

Owner *Hola! (Spain)*
Editor *Ronnie Whelan*
Commissioning Editor *Linda Newman*
Circulation 382,391

WEEKLY. Owned by a Madrid-based publishing family, *Hello!* has grown faster than any other British magazine since its launch here in 1988. The magazine has editorial offices both in Madrid and London. Major colour features plus regular news pages. Although much of the material is provided by regulars, good proposals do stand a chance. Approach the commissioning editor with ideas in the first instance. No unsolicited mss.

FEATURES Interested in celebrity-based features with a newsy angle, and exclusive interviews from usually unapproachable personalities. PAYMENT by arrangement.

Hi-Fi News
IPC Media Ltd, Leon House, 233 High Street, Croydon CR9 1HZ
☎020 8726 8000
✉ hi-finews@ipcmedia.com

Owner *IPC Media (A Time Warner Company)*
Editor *Steve Harris*
Circulation 17,211

Founded 1956. MONTHLY. Write in the first instance with suggestions based on knowledge of the magazine's style and subject. All articles must be written from an informed technical or enthusiast viewpoint. PAYMENT negotiable, according to technical content.

High Life
37–43 Sackville Street, London W1S 3EH
☎020 7534 2400 Fax 020 7534 2555
✉ high.life@cedarcom.co.uk
www.cedarcom.co.uk

Owner *Cedar Communications*
Editor *Scott Manson*
Circulation 206,834

Founded 1973. MONTHLY glossy. British Airways in-flight magazine. Almost all the content is commissioned. No unsolicited mss. Few opportunities for freelancers.

History Today
20 Old Compton Street, London W1D 4TW
☎020 7534 8000
✉ p.furtado@historytoday.com

www.historytoday.com

Owner *History Today Trust for the Advancement of Education*
Editor *Peter Furtado*
Circulation 27,919

Founded 1951. MONTHLY. General history and archaeology worldwide, history behind the headlines. Serious submissions only; no 'jokey' material. Approach by post only with s.a.e.

Home
Jordan House, 47 Brunswick Place, London N1 6EB
☎020 7608 6576 Fax 020 7608 6560
✉ joanne.wooderson@highburygroup.com

Owner *Highbury Lifestyle Ltd*
Editor *Joanne Wooderson*
Circulation 47,341

MONTHLY magazine with ideas, information and inspiration for the home. Features include style, design, home products, shopping, lifestyle and entertaining. Synopses and ideas welcome; approach in writing. No health and lifestyle articles.

Home & Country
104 New Kings Road, London SW6 4LY
☎020 7731 5777 Fax 020 7736 4061

Owner *National Federation of Women's Institutes*
Editor *Joanna Remmer*
Circulation 50,000

Founded 1919. MONTHLY. Official full-colour journal of the Federation of Women's Institutes, containing articles on a wide range of subjects of interest to women. Strong environmental country slant with crafts and cookery plus gardening appearing every month. Unsolicited mss, photos and illustrations welcome. PAYMENT by arrangement.

Home & Family
Mary Sumner House, 24 Tufton Street, London SW1P 3RB
☎020 7222 5533 Fax 020 7222 1591

Owner *MU Enterprises Ltd*
Editor *Jill Worth*
Circulation 54,450

Founded 1976. QUARTERLY. Unsolicited mss considered. No fiction or poetry. Features on family life, social problems, marriage, Christian faith, etc. Max. 1000 words. PAYMENT 'modest'.

Homes & Gardens
IPC Media Ltd., King's Reach Tower, Stamford Street, London SE1 9LS

☎020 7261 5000   Fax 020 7261 6247
www.homesand gardens.com
Owner *IPC Media (A Time Warner Company)*
Editor *Deborah Barker*
Circulation 149,683

Founded 1919. MONTHLY. Almost all published articles are specially commissioned. No fiction or poetry. Best to approach in writing with an idea, enclosing snapshots if appropriate.

Horse

Room 2303, IPC Country & Leisure Media Ltd, King's Reach Tower, Stamford Street, London SE1 9LS
☎020 7261 7969   Fax 020 7261 7979
✉ amanda_williams@ipcmedia.com
www.ipcmedia.com
Owner *IPC Media (A Time Warner Company)*
Editor *Amanda Williams*
Circulation 26,679

Founded 1997. MONTHLY magazine which aims at people who ride regularly and are committed to learning more about current issues in the equestrian world such as riding concepts, vetinary developments and horse care as well as offering practical advice. Regular contributors provide a lot of reader interaction. Articles on leading equestrian celebrities. Send examples of published work with c.v. to the editor.

Horse and Hound

IPC Media Ltd., King's Reach Tower, Stamford Street, London SE1 9LS
☎020 7261 6315   Fax 020 7261 5429
✉ jenny_sims@ipcmedia.com
Owner *IPC Media (A Time Warner Company)*
Editor *Lucy Higginson*
Circulation 71,128

Founded 1884. WEEKLY. The oldest equestrian magazine on the market. Contains regular veterinary advice and instructional articles, as well as authoritative news and comment on fox hunting, international and national showjumping, horse trials, dressage, driving and endurance riding. Also weekly racing and point-to-points, breeding reports and articles. Regular books and art reviews, and humorous articles and cartoons are frequently published. Plenty of opportunities for freelancers. Unsolicited contributions welcome.

Also publishes a sister monthly publication, *Eventing*, which covers the sport of horse trials comprehensively; Acting Editor *Julie Harding*.
PAYMENT NUJ rates.

Horse and Rider

Headley House, Headley Road, Grayshott GU26 6TU
☎01428 601020   Fax 01428 601030
✉ djm@djmurphy.co.uk
www.horseandridermagazine.co.uk
Owner *D.J. Murphy (Publishers) Ltd*
Editor *Alison Bridge*
Assistant Editor *Danielle Pascoe*
Circulation 46,000

Founded 1949. MONTHLY. Adult readership, largely horse-owning. News and instructional features, which make up the bulk of the magazine, are almost all written in-house or commissioned. New contributors and unsolicited articles are occasionally used. Approach the editor in writing with ideas.

Hotline

The River Group, Victory House, Leicester Square, London WC2H 7BZ
☎020 7306 0304
✉ rstanley@riverltd.co.uk
Editor *Rod Stanley*

Founded 1997. QUARTERLY on-board magazine for Virgin trains. UK celebrity and travel-based features. Ideas and outlines welcome by post or e-mail.

House & Garden

Vogue House, Hanover Square, London W1S 1JU
☎020 7499 9080   Fax 020 7629 2907
www.houseandgarden.co.uk
Owner *Condé Nast Publications Ltd*
Editor *Susan Crewe*
Circulation 144,547

Founded 1947. MONTHLY. Most feature material is produced in-house but occasional specialist features are commissioned from qualified freelancers, mainly for the interiors, wine and food sections and travel.

FEATURES *Liz Elliot* Suggestions for features, preferably in the form of brief outlines of proposed subjects, will be considered.

House Beautiful

National Magazine House, 72 Broadwick Street, London W1F 9EP
☎020 7439 5000   Fax 020 7439 5141
Owner *National Magazine Co. Ltd*
Editor *Kerryn Harper*
Circulation 215,360

Founded 1989 and recently relaunched in November 2003. MONTHLY. Lively magazine offering sound, practical information and plenty of inspiration for those who want to make the most of where they live. Over 100 pages of easy-reading editorial. Regular features about decoration, DIY, food, gardening and occasionally property, plus topical features with a newsy slant to fit the 'Hot Topics' slot. Approach in writing with synopses in the first instance including a brief outline of areas of specialism and examples of previously published articles in a similar vein.

i-D Magazine

124 Tabernacle Street, London EC2A 4SA
☎020 7490 9710   Fax 020 7251 2225
✉ editor@i-dmagazine.co.uk
www.i-dmagazine.com

Owner *Levelprint*
Editor *Glenn Waldron*
Circulation 68,304

Founded 1980. MONTHLY lifestyle magazine for both sexes with a fashion bias. International. Very hip. Does not accept unsolicited contributions but welcomes new ideas in the fields of fashion, music, clubs, art, film, technology, books, sport, etc. No fiction or poetry. Always 'looking for free-lance non-fiction writers with new or unusual ideas.' A different theme each issue – past themes have included Green politics, taste, films, sex, love and loud dance music – means it is advisable to discuss feature ideas in the first instance.

Ideal Home

IPC Media Ltd., King's Reach Tower, Stamford Street, London SE1 9LS
☎020 7261 6505   Fax 020 7261 6494

Owner *IPC Media (A Time Warner Company)*
Editor *Susan Rose*
Circulation 260,439

Founded 1920. MONTHLY glossy. Unsolicited feature ideas are welcome only if appropriate to the magazine. Prospective contributors wishing to submit ideas should do so in writing to the editor. No fiction.

FEATURES Furnishing and decoration of houses, kitchens or bathrooms; interior design, soft furnishings, furniture and home improvements, lifestyle, consumer, gardening, property, food and readers' homes. Length to be discussed with editor.

PAYMENT negotiable.

The Illustrated London News

20 Upper Ground, London SE1 9PF
☎020 7805 5562   Fax 020 7805 5911
✉ iln@ilng.co.uk
www.ilng.co.uk

Owner *James Sherwood*
Editor *Alison Booth*
Circulation 47,547

Founded 1842. BIANNUAL: Christmas and Summer issues, plus the occasional special issue to coincide with particular events. Although the *ILN* covers issues concerning the whole of the UK, its emphasis remains on the capital and its life. Travel, wine, restaurants, events, cultural and current affairs are all covered. There are few opportunities for freelancers but all unsolicited mss are read (receives about five a week). The best approach is with an idea in writing to the editor. Particularly interested in articles relating to events and developments in contemporary London, and about people working in the capital. All features are illustrated, so ideas with picture opportunities are particularly welcome.

Image Magazine

Upper Mounts, Northampton NN1 3HR
☎01604 467000   Fax 01604 467190
✉ image@northantsnews.co.uk
www.northantsnews.com

Owner *Northamptonshire Newspapers Ltd*
Editor *Ruth Supple*
Circulation 12,000

Founded 1905. MONTHLY general interest regional magazine. No unsolicited mss.

FEATURES Local issues, personalities, businesses, etc., of Northamptonshire, Bedfordshire, Buckinghamshire interest. Max. 500 words.

NEWS No hard news as such, just monthly diary column.

OTHER Regulars on motoring, fashion, beauty, lifestyle, travel and horoscopes. Max. 500 words.

PAYMENT for features negotiable.

In Britain

Jubilee House, 2 Jubilee Place, London SW3 3TQ
☎020 7751 4800   Fax 020 7751 4848
✉ inbritain@archant.co.uk

Editor *Andrea Spain*
Circulation 47,000

Founded in the 1930s. BI-MONTHLY. Travel magazine of 'VisitBritain'. Not much opportunity for unsolicited work – approach (by e-mail) with ideas and samples. Words and picture packages preferred (good quality transparencies only).

Independent Magazine

See **The Independent** under *National Newspapers*

Inspirations

Jordan House, 47 Brunswick Place, London
N1 6EB
☎020 7608 6553   Fax 020 7608 6704
Owner *Highbury Leisure Ltd*
Acting Editor *Rowena Medlow*
Circulation 50,000

Homes and interiors covering decorating, design, house features, makeovers, cookery, property, DIY advice and gardens. Will consider unsolicited synopses on these subjects.

InStyle

IPC Media Ltd., 12th Floor, Kings Reach Tower, Stamford Street, London SE1 9LS
☎020 7261 5000   Fax 020 7261 6664
✉ firstname_lastname@instyleuk.com
Owner *IPC Media (A Time Warner Company)*
Editor *Louise Chunn*
Senior Features Editor *Kate O'Donnell*
Fashion Director *Tamasin Doe*
Circulation 191,001

Launched March 2001. MONTHLY. UK edition of US fashion, beauty, celebrity and lifestyle magazine. Unsolicited material welcome; send by e-mail to individual editors.

The International Journal of Erotica

Diverse Publications, Unit 56, 3 Courthill House, 60 Water Lane, Wilmslow SK9 5AJ
✉ diversepublications@yahoo.co.uk
www.diversepublications.co.uk
Owner *Diverse Publications Ltd*
Editors *Robin Barratt, Inna Zabrodskaya*
Circulation 25,000

Founded 2003. QUARTERLY publication focusing on erotic art, poetry, photography and fiction. 'From India to Russia, from the UK to South Africa and Asia, we will be discussing and exploring the full range of erotic art and writing from a variety of countries and cultures.' Unsolicited contributions welcome, particularly from outside the UK – prose, fiction or poetry, up to 5000 words. Also monochrome or colour photographic portfolios. Absolutely *no* pornography.

Interzone: Science Fiction & Fantasy

TTA Press, 5 Martins Lane, Witcham, Ely CB6 2LB
www.ttapress.com
Editor *Andy Cox*

Circulation 10,000

Founded 1982. BI-MONTHLY magazine of science fiction and fantasy. Unsolicited mss are welcome 'from writers who have a knowledge of the magazine and its contents'. S.a.e. essential for return.

FICTION 2000–6000 words.

FEATURES Book/film reviews, interviews with writers and occasional short articles. Length by arrangement.

PAYMENT fiction, £30 per 1000 words; features, negotiable.

Investors Chronicle

Tabernacle Court, 16–28 Tabernacle Street, London EC2A 4DD
☎020 7382 8607   Fax 020 7382 8105
www.investorschronicle.co.uk
Owner *Pearson*
Editor *Matthew Vincent*
Deputy Editor *Rosie Carr*
Circulation 40,096

Founded 1860. WEEKLY. Opportunities for freelance contributors in the survey section only. All approaches should be made in writing. Over forty surveys are published each year on a wide variety of subjects, generally with a financial, business or investment emphasis. Copies of survey list and synopses of individual surveys are obtainable from the surveys editor. PAYMENT negotiable.

Irish Pages

The Linen Hall Library, 17 Donegall Square North, Belfast BT1 5GB
☎028 90 321 707
✉ irishpages@yahoo.co.uk
www.irishpages.org
Editor *Chris Agee*
Circulation 1400

Founded 2002. BIANNUAL non-partisan, non-sectarian journal publishing writing from Ireland and abroad. 'The most important cultural journal in Ireland at the present moment' (Jonathan Allison, Director of the Yeats Summer School).

FEATURES Poetry, short fiction, essays, non-fiction, memoirs, nature-writing, translated work, literary journalism and other autobiographical, historical and scientific writing of literary distinction. Irish language and Ulster Scots writing are published in the original, with English translations. Equal editorial attention is given to established, emergent and new writers. Send submissions to the editor by post.

IRRV Valuer

The IRRV, 41 Doughty Street, London
WC1N 2LF
☎01992 505529 Fax 01992 505547
✉ katemiller@globalnet.co.uk
www.irrv.org.uk

Owner *Institue of Revenues, Rating and Valuation*
Managing Editor *Kate Miller*
Circulation 1322

Founded 2001. FOUR issues yearly for property valuation professionals. Well-qualified commentary, analysis and news covering issues affecting valuers, including reforms, legislation and technology. Small amount of appropriate lifestyle coverage. No unsolicited material; approach first by telephone, fax, letter or e-mail.
FEATURES Ideas for stories must be well sourced and informed. Max. 1000 words.
NEWS Stories relevant to property professionals. Max. 300 words.
PAYMENT negotiable.

It's Hot! Magazine

Rm A1136, BBC Worldwide, Woodlands, 180 Wood Lane, London W12 0TT
☎020 8433 3910 Fax 020 8433 2763
✉ itshot@bbc.co.uk

Owner *BBC Worldwide Publishing Ltd*
Editor *Rosalie Snaith*
Deputy Editor *Shelley Moulden*
Circulation 101,547

Founded 2002. MONTHLY magazine aimed at celebrity-mad 9–13 year old girls featuring music, film & TV gossip. Interested in exclusive celebrity interviews relevant to their market, and quizzes. Approach the deputy editor with ideas by e-mail (shelley.moulden@bbc.co.uk) but 'please read the magazine first for style'. PAYMENT negotiable.

Jade

PO Box 202, Scarborough YO11 3GE
☎01723 581329 Fax 01723 581329
✉ books@greatnorthernpublishing.co.uk
www.greatnorthernpublishing.co.uk

Owner *Great Northern Publishing*
Editor *Mark Marsay*

Founded 2002. MONTHLY uncensored, adult subscription only magazine in A5 format. 'Erotica for the modern age.' Features new and established international photographers, artists, sculptors and writers in all erotic genres from around the world. No editorial articles, features or advice columns. Prides itself on minimal advertising stance. Contributors (photographers, artists, sculptors, writers) should consult the website for submission guidelines and current requirements; contact the editor prior to sending material. Sample copy £5 (contains strong adult content).

Jane's Defence Weekly

Sentinel House, 163 Brighton Road, Coulsdon CR5 2YH
☎020 8700 3700 Fax 020 8763 1007
✉ jdw@janes.com
www.janes.com

Owner *Jane's*
Editor *Peter Felstead*
Circulation 25,500

Founded 1984. WEEKLY. No unsolicited mss. Approach in writing with ideas in the first instance.
FEATURES Current defence topics of worldwide interest. No history pieces. Most features are commissioned. Max. 4000 words.

Jazz Journal International

3 & 3A Forest Road, Loughton IG10 1DR
☎020 8532 0456/0678 Fax 020 8532 0440

Owner *Jazz Journal Ltd*
Editor *Janet Cook*
Circulation 8000+

Founded 1948. MONTHLY. A specialised jazz magazine, for record collectors, principally using expert contributors whose work is known to the editor. Unsolicited mss not welcome, with the exception of news material (for which no payment is made). It is not a gig guide, nor a free reference source for students.

Jersey Now

PO Box 582, Five Oaks, St Saviour JE4 8XQ
☎01534 611743 Fax 01534 611610
✉ mspeditorial@msppublishing.com

Owner *MSP Publishing*
Managing Editor *Peter Body*
Circulation 24,000

Founded 1987. QUARTERLY lifestyle magazine for Jersey covering homes, gardens, the arts, heritage, motoring, boating, fashion and technology. Upmarket glossy aimed at an informed and discerning readership. Interested only in Jersey-orientated articles; 1200 words max. Approach the editor initially. PAYMENT negotiable.

Jewish Chronicle

25 Furnival Street, London EC4A 1JT
☎020 7415 1500 Fax 020 7405 9040
✉ editorial@thejc.com
www.thejc.com

Owner *Kessler Foundation*
Editor *Jeff Barack*
Circulation 35,427

WEEKLY. Unsolicited mss welcome if 'the specific interests of our readership are borne in mind by writers'. Approach in writing, except for urgent current news items. No fiction. Max. 1500 words for all material.

Features *Gerald Jacobs*
Leisure/Lifestyle *Alan Montague*
Home News *Barry Toberman*
Foreign News *Joe Millis*
Supplements *Angela Kiverstein*
PAYMENT negotiable.

Jewish Quarterly

PO Box 37645, London NW7 1WB
☎020 8343 4675 Fax 020 8343 4675
✉ editor@jewquart.freeserve.co.uk
www.jewishquarterly.org

Publisher *Jewish Literary Trust Ltd*
Editor *Matthew Reisz*

Founded 1953. QUARTERLY illustrated magazine featuring Jewish literature and fiction, politics, art, music, film, poetry, history, dance, community, autobiography, Hebrew, Yiddish, Israel and the Middle East, Judaism, interviews, Zionism, philosophy and holocaust studies. Features a major books and arts section. Unsolicited mss welcome but letter or phone call preferred in first instance.

Jewish Telegraph

Jewish Telegraph Group of Newspapers, 11 Park Hill, Bury Old Road, Prestwich, Manchester M25 0HH
☎0161 740 9321 Fax 0161 740 9325
✉ editor@jewishtelegraph.com
www.jewishtelegraph.com

Editor *Paul Harris*
Circulation 16,000

Founded 1950. WEEKLY publication with local, national and international news and features. (Separate editions published for Manchester, Leeds, Liverpool and Glasgow.) Unsolicited features on Jewish humour and history welcome.

The Journal Magazines (Norfolk, Suffolk, Cambridgeshire)/ The Essex Magazine

Cambridge Newspapers Ltd, Winship Road, Milton CB4 6PP
☎01223 434434 Fax 01223 434415

Owner *Cambridge Newspapers Ltd*
Editor *Pippa Bastin*

Circulation 12,000 each

Founded 1990. MONTHLY magazines covering items of local interest – history, people, conservation, business, places, food and wine, fashion, homes and sport.

FEATURES 750–1500 words max., plus pictures. Approach the editor with ideas in the first instance.

Kerrang!

Mappin House, 4 Winsley Street, London W1W 8HR
☎020 7436 1515 Fax 020 7182 8910
www.kerrang.com

Owner *Emap Performance*
Editor *Paul Brannigan*
Circulation 61,844

Founded 1980. WEEKLY rock, punk and metal magazine. 'Written by fans for fans.' Will consider ideas for features but not actively seeking new contributors unless expert in specialist fields such as Black metal and nu-metal.

The Lady

39–40 Bedford Street, London WC2E 9ER
☎020 7379 4717 Fax 020 7836 4620

Editor *Arline Usden*
Circulation 35,013

Founded 1885. WEEKLY. Unsolicited mss are accepted provided they are not on the subject of politics or religion, or on topics covered by staff writers or special correspondents, i.e. fashion and beauty, health, cookery, household, gardening, finance and shopping.

FEATURES Well-researched pieces on British and foreign travel, historical subjects or events; interviews and profiles and other general interest topics. Max. 1200 words for illustrated two-page articles; 900 words for one-page features; 430 words for first-person 'Viewpoint' pieces. All material should be addressed to the editor with s.a.e. enclosed. Photographs supporting features may be supplied as colour transparencies, b&w prints or on disk. Telephone enquiries about features are not encouraged.

Land Rover World

IPC Media Ltd, Leon House, 233 High Street, Croydon CR9 1HZ
☎020 8774 0600

Owner *IPC Media (A Time Warner Company)*
Editor *John Carroll*
Circulation 30,000

Founded 1994. MONTHLY. Incorporates *Practical Land Rover World* and *Classic Land Rover*

World. Unsolicited material welcome, especially if supported by high-quality illustrations.
FEATURES All articles with a Land Rover theme of interest. Potential contributors are strongly advised to examine previous issues before starting work. PAYMENT negotiable.

Let's Talk
Archant Norfolk, Prospect House, Rouen Road, Norwich NR1 1RE
☎01603 772455
✉ letstalk@archant.co.uk
Owner *Archant Regional*
Editor *Cathy Brown*
Circulation 30,000
Launched 2002. MONTHLY. Norfolk's biggest selling consumer magazine, aimed at the over-50s. Topical features, nostalgia, fiction and puzzles.
FEATURES 'Suggestions always welcome', particularly profiles of older people doing extraordinary things – adventurous hobbies, new businesses, community involvement, etc. No poetry or articles emphasising the problems of growing older. Max. 1500 words.
FICTION Short stories for the monthly magazine and seasonal fiction specials. All styles considered; regional themes preferred. Approach by letter or e-mail. Max. 1500 words.
PAYMENT From £50 upwards.

LG
Upper Mounts, Northampton NN1 3HR
☎01604 467043 Fax 01604 467190
Owner *Northamptonshire Newspapers Ltd*
Editor *Ruth Supple*
Circulation 10,000
Formerly *Looking Good*, founded 1984. Relaunched in 2002 as *LG*, a MONTHLY magazine aimed at women aged 18–30. Fashion and beauty, lifestyle, true life stories. Contributions occasionally considered but majority of work is done in-house.

Lincolnshire Life
County Life Ltd, PO Box 81, Lincoln LN1 1HD
☎01522 527127 Fax 01522 560035
✉ editorial@lincolnshirelife.co.uk
www.lincolnshirelife.co.uk
Publisher *A.L. Robinson*
Executive Editor *Judy Theobald*
Circulation 10,000
Founded 1961. MONTHLY county magazine featuring geographically relevant articles on local culture, history, personalities, etc. Max. 1500 words. Contributions supported by three

or four good-quality photographs welcome. Approach in writing. PAYMENT varies.

The Lincolnshire Poacher
County Life Ltd, PO Box 81, Lincoln LN1 1HD
☎01522 527127 Fax 01522 560035
✉ editorial@lincolnshirelife.co.uk
www.lincolnshirelife.co.uk
Publisher *A.L. Robinson*
Executive Editor *Judy Theobald*
Circulation 5000
QUARTERLY county magazine featuring geographically relevant but nostalgic articles on history, culture and personalities of Lincolnshire. Max. 2000 words. Contributions supported by three or four good-quality photography/illustrations appreciated. Approach in writing. PAYMENT varies.

The List
14 High Street, Edinburgh EH1 1TE
☎0131 558 1191 Fax 0131 557 8500
✉ editor@list.co.uk
www.list.co.uk
Owner *The List Ltd*
Publisher *Robin Hodge*
Editor *Nick Barley*
Circulation 17,500
Founded 1985. FORTNIGHTLY. Events guide covering Glasgow and Edinburgh. Interviews and profiles of people working in film, theatre, music and the arts. Max. 1200 words. No unsolicited mss. Phone with ideas. News material tends to be handled in-house. PAYMENT £100.

Literary Review
44 Lexington Street, London W1F 0LW
☎020 7437 9392 Fax 020 7734 1844
✉ litrev@dircon.co.uk
Editor *Nancy Sladek*
Circulation 15,000
Founded 1979. MONTHLY. Publishes book reviews (commissioned), features and articles on literary subjects. Prospective contributors are best advised to contact the editor in writing. Unsolicited mss not welcome. Runs a monthly competition for 'poems which rhyme, scan and make sense'. PAYMENT 'miniscule'.

Living France Magazine
Archant House, Oriel Road, Cheltenham GL50 1BB
☎01242 216050 Fax 01242 216074
✉ editorial@livingfrance.com

www.livingfrance.com
Owner *Archant Life*
Editor *Lucy-Jane Cypher*

Founded 1989. MONTHLY. A magazine for people who are considering or actively purchasing a home in France. Editorial consists of practical, friendly information and advice on becoming an owner of French property. Will consider articles describing different regions of France, interviews with owners of property and aspects of living in France. Interested in hearing from professional writers who could do interviews. No unsolicited mss; approach in writing or by e-mail with an idea.

Living History
See **BBC History Magazine**

Loaded
IPC Media Ltd., King's Reach Tower, Stamford Street, London SE1 9LS
☎020 7261 5562   Fax 020 7261 5557
✉ andrew_woods@ipcmedia.com
Owner *IPC Media (A Time Warner Company)*
Editor *Martin Daubney*
Features Editor *Andrew Woods*
Circulation 220,057

Founded 1994. MONTHLY men's lifestyle magazine featuring music, sport, sex, humour, travel, fashion, hard news and popular culture. Will consider material which comes into these categories; approach the features editor in writing or by e-mail in the first instance. No fiction or poetry.

Logos
5 Beechwood Drive, Marlow SL7 2DH
☎01628 433871   Fax 01628 477577
✉ logos-marlow@dial.pipex.com
Owner *Whurr Publishers Ltd*
Editor *Gordon Graham*
Associate Editor *Betty Graham*

Founded 1990. QUARTERLY. Aims to 'deal in depth with issues which unite, divide, excite and concern the world of books', with an international perspective. Each issue contains 6 to 8 articles of between 3500 and 7000 words. 'Logos is a non-profit making professional forum, not a scholarly journal.' Suggestions and ideas for contributions are welcome, and should be addressed to the editor. 'Guidelines for Contributors' available. Contributors write from their experience as authors, publishers, booksellers, librarians, etc.
PAYMENT Contributors receive 25 off-prints,

a copy of the issue in which their article appears and a 50% concession on the subscription rate.

The London Magazine
32 Addison Grove, London W4 1ER
☎020 8400 5882   Fax 020 8994 1713
✉ admin@thelondonmagazine.net
www.londonmagazine.net
Owner *Christopher Arkell*
Editor *Sebastian Barker*
Circulation 1200

Founded originally in 1732 and relaunched in 2002. BI-MONTHLY review of literature and the arts. Publishes poems, short stories, features, memoirs, and book and performance reviews. Not interested in overtly political material. Do *not* send anything by e-mail or fax. No phonecalls. All submissions should be made by post with an s.a.e. to the editor.
FEATURES Max. 6000 words.
FICTION Max. 6000 words.
POEMS 'Any length within reason.'
PAYMENT negotiable.

London Review of Books
28 Little Russell Street, London WC1A 2HN
☎020 7209 1101   Fax 020 7209 1102
✉ edit@lrb.co.uk
www.lrb.co.uk
Owner *LRB Ltd*
Editor *Mary-Kay Wilmers*
Circulation 42,907

Founded 1979. FORTNIGHTLY. Reviews, essays and articles on political, literary, cultural and scientific subjects. Also poetry. Unsolicited contributions welcome (approximately 50 received each week). No pieces under 2000 words. Contact the editor in writing. Please include s.a.e.
PAYMENT £150 per 1000 words; poems, £75.

Looking Good
See **LG**

Lothian Life
Ballencrieff Cottage, Ballencrieff Toll, Bathgate EH48 4LD
☎01506 632728   Fax 01506 632728
✉ editor@lothianlife.co.uk
www.lothianlife.co.uk
Owner *Pages Editorial & Publishing Services*
Editor *Susan Coon*

QUARTERLY county magazine for people who live, work or have an interest in the Lothians. Includes three or four major features (1500 words) on successful people, businesses or initiatives. A local walk takes up the centre spread. Regular articles by experts on collectibles, property, interior design, cookery, health and local gardening, plus news items, letters and a competition. Freelance writers used only for main features. Phone first to discuss content and timing.

PAYMENT by arrangement.

Machine Knitting Monthly
PO Box 1479, Maidenhead SL6 8YX
☎01628 783080 Fax 01628 633250
✉ rpa@surf3.net
www.machineknittingmonthly.co.uk

Owner *RPA Publishing Ltd*
Editor *Anne Smith*

Founded 1986. MONTHLY. Unsolicited mss considered 'as long as they are applicable to this specialist publication. We have our own regular contributors each month but we're always willing to look at new ideas from other writers.' Approach in writing in the first instance.

MacUser
30 Cleveland Street, London W1T 4JD
☎020 7907 6000
✉ mailbox@macuser.co.uk
www.macuser.co.uk

Owner *Dennis Publishing*
Editor *Nik Rawlinson*
Circulation 20,401

Launched 1985. FORTNIGHTLY computer magazine.

Management Today
174 Hammersmith Road, London W6 7JP
☎020 8267 5000
✉ management.today@haynet.com

Owner *Haymarket Business Publications Ltd*
Managing Director *Rufus Olins*
Editor *Matthew Gwyther*
Circulation 100,464

General business topics and features. Ideas welcome. Send brief synopsis to the editor.

marie claire
13th Floor, King's Reach Tower, Stamford Street, London SE1 9LS
☎020 7261 5240 Fax 020 7261 5277
✉ marieclaire@ipcmedia.com
www.ipcmedia.com

Owner *European Magazines Ltd*
Editor *Marie O'Riordan*
Circulation 384,502

Founded 1988. MONTHLY. An intelligent glossy magazine for women, with strong international features and fashion. No unsolicited mss. Approach with ideas in writing or by e-mail (marieclaireideas@ipcmedia.com). No fiction.

FEATURES *Charlotte Moore* Detailed proposals for feature ideas should be accompanied by samples of previous work.

Marketing Week
St Giles House, 50 Poland Street, London W1F 7AX
☎020 7970 4000 Fax 020 7970 6721
✉ mw.editorial@centaur.co.uk
www.mad.co.uk/publication/mw/

Owner *Centaur Communications*
Editor *Stuart Smith*
Circulation 37.029

WEEKLY trade magazine of the marketing industry. Features on all aspects of the business, written in a newsy and up-to-the-minute style. Approach with ideas in the first instance.

FEATURES *Daney Parker*
PAYMENT negotiable.

Match
Bushfield House, Orton Centre, Peterborough PE2 5UW
☎01733 237111 Fax 01733 288150
✉ match.magazine@emap.com
www.matchmag.co.uk

Owner *Emap Active Ltd*
Acting Editor *Ian Foster*
Circulation 95,806

Founded 1979. WEEKLY. The UK's biggest-selling football magazine aimed at 10–15-year-olds. All material is generated in-house by a strong news and features team. Work experience placements often given to trainee journalists and students; the majority of staff are recruited through this route. Approach in writing or by phone.

Match Angling Plus
Emap Active, Bushfield House, Orton Centre, Peterborough PE2 5UW
☎01733 465705 Fax 01733 465658
✉ steve.cole@emap.com

Owner *Emap Active*
Editor *Steve Cole*
Circulation 16,601

Founded 1992. MONTHLY magazine aimed at match anglers and advanced pleasure anglers. Coarse fishing only.

FEATURES only. Please send relevant articles, with or without pictures, by e-mail to the editor. Max. 2500 words.

Matrix
See **British Science Fiction Association** under *Professional Associations*

Maxim
30 Cleveland Street, London W1T 4JD
☎020 7907 6410   Fax 020 7907 6439
✉ editorial@maxim-magazine.co.uk
Owner *Dennis Publishing*
Editor *Greg Gutfeld*
Circulation 234,183

Established 1995. MONTHLY glossy men's lifestyle magazine featuring sex, travel, health, motoring and fashion. No fiction or poetry. Approach in writing in the first instance, sending outlines of ideas only together with examples of published work.

Mayfair
2 Archer Street, Piccadilly Circus, London W1D 7AW
☎020 7292 8000   Fax 020 7734 5030
✉ mayfair@pr-org.co.uk
www.sexclub.co.uk
Owner *Paul Raymond Publications*
Editor *David Ryder*
Circulation 331,760

Founded 1966. THIRTEEN ISSUES YEARLY. Unsolicited material accepted if pertinent to the magazine and if accompanied by suitable illustrative material. 'We will *only* publish work if we can illustrate it.' Interested in features and humour aimed at men aged 18–80; 800–1000 words. Punchy, bite-sized humour, top ten features, etc. 'Must make the editor laugh.' Also considers erotica.

Mayfair Times
1 Blandel Bridge House, 56 Sloane Square, London SW1W 8AX
☎020 7259 1050   Fax 020 7901 9042
✉ erik.brown@pubbiz.com
www.pubbiz.com
Owner *Publishing Business Ltd*
Editor *Erik Brown*
Circulation 17,000

Founded 1985. MONTHLY. Features on Mayfair of interest to residents, local workers, visitors and shoppers.

Medal News
Orchard House, Duchy Road, Heathpark, Honiton EX14 1YD
☎01404 46972   Fax 01404 44788
✉ info@tokenpublishing.com

www.tokenpublishing.com
Owners *J.W. Mussell, Carol Hartman*
Editor *J.W. Mussell*
Circulation 5,500

Founded 1989. TEN ISSUES YEARLY. Unsolicited material welcome but initial approach by phone or in writing preferred.
FEATURES 'Opportunities exist for well-informed authors who know the subject and do their homework.' Max. 2500 words.
PAYMENT £25 per 1000 words.

Media Week
Griffin House, 161 Hammersmith Road, London W6 8BS
☎020 8267 5000
www.mediaweek.co.uk
Owner *Haymarket Publishing Ltd*
Editor *Philip Smith*
Circulation 16,297

Founded 1986. WEEKLY trade magazine. UK and international coverage on all aspects of commercial media. Approach in writing with ideas. See website for e-mail addresses.

Melody Maker
See **New Musical Express**

Men's Health
National Magazine House, 72 Broadwick Street, London W1F 9EP
☎020 7339 4400   Fax 020 7339 4444
www.menshealth.co.uk
Owner *Natmag-Rodale Publishing*
Editor *Morgan Rees*
Circulation 229,116

Founded 1994. MONTHLY men's healthy lifestyle magazine covering health, fitness, nutrition, stress and sex issues. No unsolicited mss; will consider ideas and synopses tailored to men's health. No fiction or extreme sports. Approach in writing in the first instance.

MiniWorld Magazine
IPC Media Ltd, Leon House, 233 High Street, Croydon CR9 1HZ
☎020 8726 8000   Fax 020 8726 8399
✉ miniworld@ipcmedia.com
www.miniworld.co.uk
Owner *IPC Media (A Time Warner Company)*
Editor *Monty Watkins*
Circulation 37,000

Founded 1991. MONTHLY car magazine devoted to the Mini. Unsolicited material welcome but prospective contributors are advised to contact the editor.

FEATURES Maintenance, tuning, restoration, technical advice, classified, sport, readers' cars and social history of this cult car.

PAYMENT negotiable.

Mizz

IPC Media Ltd, 27th Floor, King's Reach Tower, Stamford Street, London SE1 9LS
☎020 7261 6319 Fax 020 7261 6032

Owner *IPC Media (A Time Warner Company)*
Editor *Lucie Tobin*
Deputy Editor *Cassie Whittell*
Circulation 70,320

Founded 1985. FORTNIGHTLY magazine for the 10–14-year-old girl.

FEATURES 'We have a full features team and thus do not accept freelance features.'

Model Collector

IPC Focus Network, Leon House, 233 High Street, Croydon CR9 1HZ
☎020 8726 8000
✉ modelcollector@ipcmedia.com
www.modelcollector.com

Owner *AOL Time Warner/IPC Media*
Editor *Lindsey Amrani*
Circulation 14,622

Founded 1987. THIRTEEN ISSUES YEARLY Britain's best selling die cast magazine. From the latest models to classic 1930's Dinkys. Interested in historical articles about particular models or ranges and reviews of the latest products. Photographs welcome. Not interested in radio controlled models or model railways.

FEATURES Freelancers should contact the editor. Unsolicited material may be considered.

NEWS Trade news welcome. Call *Lindsey Amrani* (Tel 020 8726 8238) to discuss details.

Mojo

Mappin House, 4 Winsley Street, London W1W 8HF
☎020 7436 1515 Fax 020 7182 8596
✉ mojo@emap.com
www.mojo4music.com

Owner *Emap Performance*
Editor-in-Chief *Phil Alexander*
Circulation 111,815

Founded 1993. MONTHLY magazine containing features, reviews and news stories about rock music and its influences. Receives about five mss per day. No poetry, think-pieces on dead rock stars or similar fan worship.

FEATURES Amateur writers discouraged except as providers of source material, contacts, etc.

NEWS All verifiable, relevant stories considered.

REVIEWS Write to Reviews Editor *Jenny Bulley* with relevant specimen material.

PAYMENT negotiable.

Moneywise

1st Floor, Dashwood House, 69 Old Broad Street, London EC2M 1QS
☎020 7382 4300 Fax 020 7374 4520
www.moneywise.co.uk

Owner *Capital Accumulation Services Ltd*
Editor *Emma-Lou Montgomery*
Circulation 47,183

Founded 1990. MONTHLY. No unsolicited mss; ideas welcome. Make initial approach in writing to Editorial Department (c.v. preferred).

More!

Endeavour House, 189 Shaftesbury Avenue, London WC2H 8JG
☎020 7208 3165 Fax 020 7208 3595
✉ emma.patterson@emap.com
www.moremagazine.co.uk

Owner *Emap élan Publications*
Editor *Emma Patterson*
Features Director *Hannah Verdier*
Editorial Enquiries *Abby Woolf*
Circulation 274,635

Founded 1988. FORTNIGHTLY women's magazine aimed at the working woman aged 18–25. Features on sex and relationships plus celebrity news, style and fashion. Most items are commissioned; approach features director with idea. Prospective contributors are strongly advised to study the magazine's style before submitting anything.

Mother and Baby

Greater London House, Hampstead Road, London NW1 7EJ
☎020 7347 1869 Fax 020 7347 1888
✉ mother&baby@emap.com

Owner *Emap Esprit*
Editor *Elena Dalrymple*
Circulation 81,083

Founded 1956. MONTHLY. Welcomes suggestions for feature ideas about pregnancy, newborn basics, practical babycare, baby development and childcare subjects. Approaches may be made by telephone, e-mail or in writing to the Features Editor *Lucy Dimbylow*.

Motor Boat & Yachting

IPC Media Limited, King's Reach Tower, Stamford Street, London SE1 9LS
☎020 7261 5333   Fax 020 7261 5030
✉ mby@ipcmedia.com
www.mby.com
Owner *Time Warner*
Editor *Tom Isitt*
Circulation 16,911

Founded 1904. MONTHLY for those interested in motor boats and motor cruising.

FEATURES *Tom Isitt* Cruising features and practical features especially welcome. Illustrations/ photographs (mostly colour) are just as important as text. Max. 3000 words.

NEWS *Kate Brunel-Cohen* Factual pieces. Max. 200 words.

PAYMENT features: from £100 per 1000 words or by arrangement; news: up to £50 per item.

Motor Caravan Magazine

IPC Media Ltd, Leon House, 233 High Street, Croydon CR9 1HZ
☎020 8726 8000
✉ simon_collis@ipcmedia.com
www.motorcaravanmagazine.co.uk
Owner *IPC Media (A Time Warner Company)*
Editor *Simon Collis*
Circulation 15,000

Founded 1986. MONTHLY consumer magazine delivering test reports, touring ideas and practical advice to motor caravanners. Unsolicited material welcome. Interested in holiday reports, interesting or unusual caravans, practical step-by-step motor caravanning features. Phone the editor or e-mail outlining basic ideas. Max. 2500 words. PAYMENT £60 a page.

Motor Cycle News

Media House, Lynchwood, Peterborough Business Park, Peterborough PE2 6EA
☎01733 468000   Fax 01733 468028
✉ MCN@emap.com
www.motorcylenews.com
Owner *Emap plc*
Editor *Marc Potter*
Circulation 139,105

Founded 1955. WEEKLY. Interested in short news stories and features on motorcyles and motorcycle racing. No race reports. Contact relevant desks direct.

Motorcaravan Motorhome Monthly (MMM)

PO Box 88, Tiverton EX16 7ZN
✉ mmmeditor@warnersgroup.co.uk
www.mmmonline.co.uk
Owner *Warners Group Publications Plc*
Editor *Mike Jago*
Circulation 34,803

Founded 1966. MONTHLY. 'There's no money in motorcaravan journalism but for those wishing to cut their first teeth ...' Unsolicited mss welcome if relevant, but ideas in writing preferred in first instance.

FEATURES Caravan site reports. Max. 500 words.

TRAVEL Motorcaravanning trips (home and overseas). Max. 2000 words.

NEWS Short news items for miscellaneous pages. Max. 200 words.

FICTION Must be motorcaravan-related and include artwork/photos if possible. Max. 2000 words.

SPECIAL PAGES DIY – modifications to motorcaravans. Max. 1500 words.

OWNER REPORTS Contributions welcome from motorcaravan owners. Contact the editor for requirements. Max. 2000 words.

PAYMENT varies.

Mslexia (For Women Who Write)

PO Box 656, Newcastle upon Tyne NE99 2XD
☎0191 261 6656   Fax 0191 261 6636
✉ postbag@mslexia.demon.co.uk
www.mslexia.co.uk
Owner *Mslexia Publications Limited*
Editor *Debbie Taylor*
Circulation 10,000

Founded 1997. QUARTERLY. Articles, advice, reviews, interviews, events for women writers plus new poetry and prose. Will consider fiction, poetry, features and letters but contributors *must* send for guidelines first.

Music Week

Ludgate House, 245 Blackfriars Road, London SE1 9UR
☎020 7921 5000   Fax 020 7921 8326
www.musicweek.com
Owner *CMP Information*
Editor *Martin Talbot*
Circulation 9,622

Britain's only WEEKLY music business magazine. No unsolicited mss. Approach in writing with ideas.

FEATURES Analysis of specific music business events and trends.
NEWS Music industry news only.

Musical Opinion

2 Princes Road, St Leonards on Sea
TN37 6EL
☎01424 715167   Fax 01424 712214
✉ musicalopinion2@aol.com
www.musicalopinion.com
Owner *Musical Opinion Ltd*
Editor *Denby Richards*
Circulation 6000

Founded 1877. Glossy, full-colour BI-MONTHLY magazine. Classical music content, with topical features on music, musicians, festivals, etc., and reviews (concerts, festivals, opera, ballet, jazz, CDs, DVDs, videos, books and printed music). International readership. No unsolicited mss; commissions only. Ideas always welcome though; approach by phone, fax or e-mail, giving telephone number. Visit the website for full information.
PAYMENT negotiable.

My Weekly

80 Kingsway East, Dundee DD4 8SL
☎01382 223131   Fax 01382 452491
✉ myweekly@dcthomson.co.uk
Owner *D.C. Thomson & Co. Ltd*
Editor *Harrison Watson*
Circulation 244,218

A traditional women's WEEKLY. D.C. Thomson has long had a policy of encouragement and help to new writers of promise. Ideas welcome. Approach in writing.
FEATURES Particularly interested in human interest pieces (1000–1500 words) which by their very nature appeal to the 50-plus age-group.
FICTION Three stories a week, ranging in content from the emotional to the off-beat and unexpected. 1000–4000 words.
PAYMENT negotiable.

The National Trust Magazine

36 Queen Anne's Gate, London SW1H 9AS
☎020 7222 9251   Fax 020 7222 5097
✉ enquiries@thenationaltrust.org.uk
Owner *The National Trust*
Editor *Gaynor Aaltonen*
Circulation 1.66 million

Founded 1968. THREE ISSUES YEARLY. Conservation of historic houses, coast and countryside in England, Northern Ireland and

Wales. No unsolicited mss. Approach in writing with ideas.

The Naturalist

c/o University of Bradford, Bradford BD7 1DP
☎01274 234212   Fax 01274 234231
✉ m.r.d.seaward@bradford.ac.uk
Owner *Yorkshire Naturalists' Union*
Editor *Prof. M.R.D. Seaward*
Circulation 5000

Founded 1875. QUARTERLY. Natural history, biological and environmental sciences for a professional and amateur readership. Unsolicited mss and b&w illustrations welcome. Particularly interested in material – scientific papers – relating to the north of England. No PAYMENT.

Nature

The Macmillan Building, 4–6 Crinan Street, London N1 9XW
☎020 7833 4000   Fax 020 7843 4596
✉ nature@nature.com
www.nature.com/nature
Owner *Nature Publishing Group*
Editor *Philip Campbell*
Circulation 65,000

Covers all fields of science, with articles and news on science and science policy only. Scope only for freelance writers with specialist knowledge in these areas.

New Beacon

105 Judd Street, London WC1H 9NE
☎020 7388 1266   Fax 020 8438 9092
www.rnib.org.uk
Owner *Royal National Institute of the Blind*
Editor *Ann Lee*
Circulation 6000

Founded 1917. MONTHLY (except August). Published in print, braille and on tape, disk and e-mail. Unsolicited mss welcome. Approach with ideas in writing. Personal experiences by writers who have sight problems (partial sight or blindness), and authoritative items by professionals or volunteers working in the field of sight loss welcome. Max. 1500 words.
PAYMENT negotiable.

New Humanist

1 Gower Street, London WC1E 6HD
☎020 7436 1151
✉ editor@newhumanist.org.uk
Owner *Rationalist Press Association*
Editor *Frank Jordans*
Circulation 5000

Founded 1885. BI-MONTHLY. Unsolicited mss welcome. No fiction.

FEATURES Articles with a humanist perspective welcome in the following fields: religion (critical), humanism, human rights, philosophy, current events, literature, history and science. 2000 words.

BOOK REVIEWS 750–1000 words, by arrangement with the editor.

PAYMENT for features is nominal, but negotiable.

New Impact

Diversity Leaders UK, Courtyard Offices, 140 Oxford Road, Marlow SL7 2NT
☎01628 481581 Fax 01628 475570
✉ info@diversityleaders.org.uk
www.diversityleaders.org.uk
Owner *D.E. Sihera*
Owner/Editor *Elaine Sihera*
Features Editor *Alex Wing*
Circulation 10,000

Founded 1993. QUARTERLY. Celebrates diversity, enterprise and achievement from a minority ethnic perspective. Unsolicited mss welcome. Interested in training, arts, features, personal achievement, small business features, profiles of personalities especially for a multicultural audience. Promotes the British Diversity Awards each June and the Windrush Awards each October, the Register of Diversity Managers among employers and managing the diversity maze for practitioners.

NEWS Local training/business features – some opportunities. Max. length 550 words.

FEATURES Original, interesting pieces with a deliberate multicultural/diversity focus. Personal/professional successes and achievements welcome. Max. length 1000 words.

FICTION Short stories, poems, especially from minority writers. Not interested in romantic/sexual narratives. Max. length 1500 words.

SPECIAL PAGES Interviews with personalities, especially Asian, African Caribbean and Chinese. Max. length 1200 words.

PAYMENT negotiable.

New Internationalist

55 Rectory Road, Oxford OX4 1BW
☎01865 728181 Fax 01865 793152
✉ ni@newint.org
www.newint.org/
Owner *New Internationalist Trust*
Co-Editors *Vanessa Baird, David Ransom, Katharine Ainger, Adam Ma'anit*
Circulation 80,000

Radical and broadly leftist in approach, but unaligned. Concerned with world poverty and global issues of peace and politics, feminism and environmentalism, with emphasis on the Third World. Difficult to use unsolicited material as they work to a theme each month and features are commissioned by the editor on that basis. The way in is to send examples of published or unpublished work; writers of interest are taken up.

New Musical Express

IPC Media Ltd., King's Reach Tower, Stamford Street, London SE1 9LS
☎020 7261 6472 Fax 020 7261 5185
www.nme.com
Owner *IPC Media (A Time Warner Company)*
Editor *Conor McNicholas*
Circulation 70,017

Britain's best-selling musical WEEKLY. Now incorporates *Melody Maker*. Freelancers used, but always for reviews in the first instance. Specialisation in areas of music (or film, which is also covered) is a help.

REVIEWS: LPs *Anthony Thornton* LIVE *Pat Long* Send in examples of work, either published or specially written samples.

New Nation

Unit 2, 65 Whitechapel Road, London E1 1DU
☎020 7650 2000 Fax 020 7650 2001
www.ethnicmedia.co.uk
Owner *Ethnic Media Group*
Editor *Michael Eboda*
Circulation 21,630

Founded 1996. WEEKLY community paper for the Black community in Britain. Interested in relevant general, local and international issues. Approach in writing with ideas for submission.

New Scientist

8th Floor, Lacon House, 84 Theobalds Road, London WC1X 8NS
☎020 8652 3500 Fax 020 7611 1200 (News)
www.newscientist.com
Owner *Reed Business Information Ltd*
Editor-in-Chief *Dr Alun Anderson*
Editor *Jeremy Webb*
Circulation 151,661

Founded 1956. WEEKLY. No unsolicited mss. Approach with ideas – one A4-page synopsis – by fax or e-mail.

FEATURES Commissions only, but good ideas welcome. Max. 3500 words.

NEWS *Matt Walker* Mostly commissions, but

ideas for specialist news welcome. Max. 1000 words.
REVIEWS *Maggie McDonald* Reviews are commissioned.
OPINION *Michael Bond* Unsolicited material welcome if of general/humorous interest and related to science. Max. 1000 words.
PAYMENT negotiable.

The New Shetlander
11 Mounthooly Street, Lerwick ZE1 0BJ
☎01595 693816 Fax 01595 696787
✉ shetlandcss@zetnet.co.uk
www.shetlandcss.co.uk
Owner *Shetland Council of Social Service*
Editors *Brian Smith, Laureen Johnson*
Circulation 1900

Founded 1947. QUARTERLY literary magazine containing short stories, essays, poetry, historical articles, literary criticism, political comment, arts and books. The magazine has two editors and an editorial committee who all look at submitted material. Interested in considering short stories, poetry, historical articles with a northern Scottish or Scandinavian flavour, literary pieces and articles on Shetland. As a rough guide, items should be between 1000 and 2000 words although longer mss are considered. Initial approach in writing, please.
PAYMENT Complimentary copy.

New Statesman
3rd Floor, 52 Grosvenor Gardens, London SW1W 0AU
☎020 7730 3444 Fax 020 7259 0181
www.newstatesman.co.uk
Publisher *Spencer Neal*
Editor *John Kampfner*
Deputy Editor *Sue Matthias*
Circulation 24,860

WEEKLY magazine, the result of a merger (1988) of *New Statesman* and *New Society*. Coverage of news, book reviews, arts, current affairs, politics and social reportage. Unsolicited contributions with s.a.e. will be considered. No short stories.
Arts Editor *Rosie Millard*
Books Editor *William Skidelsky*

New Theatre Quarterly
Oldstairs, Kingsdown, Deal CT14 8ES
☎01304 373448
✉ simontrussler@btinternet.com
www.uk.cambridge.org
Publisher *Cambridge University Press*
Editors *Clive Barker, Simon Trussler, Maria Shevtsova*

Founded 1985 (originally launched in 1971 as *Theatre Quarterly*). Articles, interviews, documentation and reference material covering all aspects of live theatre. Recommend preliminary e-mail enquiry before sending contributions. No theatre reviews or anecdotal material.

New Welsh Review
PO Box 170, Aberystwyth SY23 1WZ
☎01970 626230 Fax 01970 626230
✉ editor@newwelshreview.co.uk
www.newwelshreview.co.uk
Owner *New Welsh Review Ltd*
Editor *Francesca Rhydderch*
Circulation 900

Founded 1988. QUARTERLY Welsh literary magazine in the English language. Welcomes material of literary and cultural relevance to Welsh readers and those with an interest in Wales. Approach in writing in the first instance.
FEATURES Max. 3000 words.
FICTION Max. 5000 words.
REVIEWS Max. 800 words.
PAYMENT average of £150 (features); £75 (fiction); £40 (reviews); £25 per poem.

New Woman
Endeavour House, 189 Shaftesbury Avenue, London WC2H 8JG
☎020 7437 9011 Fax 020 7208 3585
✉ sarah.williams@emap.com
www.newwoman.co.uk
Owner *Emap élan Ltd*
Editor *Margi Conklin*
Circulation 280,448

MONTHLY women's interest magazine. Winner of the Emap 'Magazine of the Year' award in 2002 and the BSME 'Editor of the Year' in 2001. Aimed at women aged 25–35. An 'entertaining, informative and intelligent' read. Main topics of interest include men, sex, love, health, careers, beauty and fashion. Uses mainly established freelancers but unsolicited ideas submitted in synopsis form will be considered. Welcomes ideas from male writers for humorous 'men's opinion' pieces.
FEATURES/NEWS *Katie Masters* Articles must be original and look at subjects or issues from a new or unusual perspective.

The New Writer
PO Box 60, Cranbrook TN17 2ZR
☎01580 212626 Fax 01580 212041
✉ editor@thenewwriter.com
www.thenewwriter.com
Publisher *Merric Davidson*

Editor *Suzanne Ruthven*

Founded 1996. Published BI-MONTHLY following the merger between *Acclaim* and *Quartos* magazines. TNW continues to offer practical 'nuts and bolts' advice on poetry and prose but with the emphasis on *forward-looking* articles and features on all aspects of the written word that demonstrate the writer's grasp of contemporary writing and current editorial/publishing policies. Plenty of news, views, competitions, reviews; writers' guidelines available with s.a.e. Regular e-mail Newsletter included in subscription package.

FEATURES Unsolicited mss welcome. Interested in lively, original articles on writing in its broadest sense. Approach with ideas in writing in the first instance. No material is returned unless accompanied by s.a.e.

FICTION Publishes short-listed entries from competitions and subscriber-only submissions.

POETRY Unsolicited poetry welcome. Both short and long unpublished poems, providing they are original and interesting.

PAYMENT features, £20 per 1000 words; fiction, £10 per story; poetry, £3 per poem.

New Writing Scotland

Association for Scottish Literary Studies, c/o Department of Scottish History, 9 University Gardens, University of Glasgow G12 8QH
☎0141 330 5309   Fax 0141 330 5309
✉ nws@asls.org.uk
www.asls.org.uk

Contact *Duncan Jones*

ANNUAL anthology of contemporary poetry and prose in English, Gaelic and Scots, produced by the **Association for Scottish Literary Studies** (see entry under *Professional Associations*). Will consider poetry, drama, short fiction or other creative prose but not full-length plays or novels, though self-contained extracts are acceptable. Contributors should be Scottish by birth or upbringing, or resident in Scotland. Max. length of 3500 words is suggested. Send no more than two short stories and six poems. Submissions should be accompanied by two s.a.e.s (one for receipt, the other for return of mss). Mss, which must be sent by 30 September, should be typed, double-spaced, on one side of the paper only with the sheets secured at top left-hand corner. Provide covering letter with full contact details but do not put name or address on individual work(s). Prose pieces should carry an approximate word count.

NewBooks

15 Scots Drive, Wokingham RG41 3XF
✉ guy@newbooksmag.com
www.newbooksmag.com

Owner/Editor *Guy Pringle*
Circulation 20,000

Founded 2000. BI-MONTHLY magazine for readers and reading groups with extracts from the best new fiction and free copies to be claimed. No unsolicited contributions. Also publishes *myBOOKSmag* for 5–7-year-olds and *tBkmag* for 8–12-year-olds.

The North

See under *Poetry Magazines*

Now

IPC Media Ltd., King's Reach Tower, Stamford Street, London SE1 9LS
☎020 7261 6274

Owner *IPC Media (A Time Warner Company)*
Editor *Jane Ennis*
Circulation 619,186

Founded 1996. WEEKLY magazine of celebrity gossip, news and topical features aimed at the working woman. Unlikely to use freelance contributions due to specialist content – e.g. exclusive showbiz interviews – but ideas will be considered. Approach in writing; no faxes.

Nursery Education

Scholastic Ltd, Villiers House, Clarendon Avenue, Leamington Spa CV32 5PR
☎01926 887799   Fax 01926 883331
✉ earlyyears@scholastic.co.uk
www.scholastic.co.uk

Owner *Scholastic Ltd*
Editor *Sarah Sodhi*
Circulation 20,000

Founded 1997. MONTHLY magazine for early years professionals. Welcomes contributions from freelance journalists specialising in education.

FEATURES Early years issues explored. Max. 1500 words.

NEWS Relevant and timely news for the early years sector. Max. 400 words.

PRACTICAL IDEAS Themed activities that support the Foundation Stage curriculum. Max. 800 words. Approach by letter or e-mail.

Nursing Times

Greater London House, Hampstead Road, London NW1 7EJ
☎020 7874 0500   Fax 020 7874 0505
www.nursingtimes.net

Owner *Emap Healthcare*
Editor *Rachel Downey*
Circulation 71,274

Some of *Nursing Times'* feature content is from unsolicited contributions sent on spec. Articles on all aspects of nursing and health care, including clinical information, written in a contemporary style, are welcome.

Nuts

IPC Media Ltd., King's Reach Tower, Stamford Street, London SE1 9LS
☎020 7261 5660   Fax 020 7261 5480
✉ nutsmagazine@ipcmedia.com
www.nuts.co.uk
Owner *IPC Media (A Time Warner Company)*
Editor *Phil Hilton*
Circulation 275,459

Launched 2004. WEEKLY magazine for men aged 16–45 'who like chat, women, gossip, cars and football'. Welcomes true life stories and items on gadgets but *no* fashion, grooming or health matters. Approach by e-mail in the first instance.

OK! Magazine

The Northern & Shell Building, 10 Lower Thames Street, London EC3R 6EN
☎0871 434 1010   Fax 0871 434 7305
✉ firstname.lastname@express.co.uk
Owner *Northern & Shell Media/Richard Desmond*
Editor *Lisa Palta*
Circulation 529,492

Founded 1996. WEEKLY celebrity-based magazine. Welcomes interviews and pictures on well known personalities, and ideas for general features. Approach the editor by phone or fax in the first instance.

Old Glory

Mortons Heritage Media, Newspaper House, Morton Way, Horncastle LN9 6JR
☎01507 529300   Fax 01507 529495
✉ ctyson@mortons.co.uk
www.oldglory.co.uk
Owner *Mortons Media Ltd*
Editor *Colin Tyson*

Founded 1988. MONTHLY magazine covering all aspects of transport and industrial heritage both in the UK and overseas. Specialises in vintage vehicles and steam preservation. Unsolicited articles are welcome. Approach by letter addressed to the editor.

FEATURES Restoration projects from steam rollers to windmills. Max. 1000 words.

NEWS Steam and transport rally reports. News concerning industrial and heritage sites and buildings.

The Oldie

65 Newman Street, London W1T 3EG
☎020 7436 8801   Fax 020 7436 8804
✉ theoldie@theoldie.co.uk
www.theoldie.co.uk
Owner *Oldie Publications Ltd*
Editor *Richard Ingrams*
Circulation 25,606

Founded 1992. MONTHLY general interest magazine with a strong humorous slant for the older person. Submissions welcome; enclose s.a.e. No poetry.

Olive

BBC Worldwide, 80 Wood Lane, London W12 0TT
☎020 8433 1389
✉ firstname.surname@bbc.co.uk
www.olivemag.co.uk
Owner *BBC Worldwide Publishing Ltd*
Editorial Coordinator *Paula Stain*
Features Editor *Jenny McIvor*
Food Editor *Lulu Grimes*
Circulation 63,550

Launched 2003. MONTHLY food magazine. Recipes, restaurants and food lovers' travel. Unsolicited contributions not welcome; 'generally only commission features from regular freelancers. It's impossible to respond to all the pitches we receive.'

Opera

36 Black Lion Lane, London W6 9BE
☎020 8563 8893   Fax 020 8563 8635
✉ editor@operamag.clara.co.uk
www.opera.co.uk
Owner *Opera Magazine Ltd*
Editor *John Allison*
Circulation 11,500

Founded 1950. MONTHLY review of the current opera scene. Almost all articles are commissioned and unsolicited mss are not welcome. All approaches should be made in writing.

Opera Now

241 Shaftesbury Avenue, London WC2H 8TF
☎020 7333 1740   Fax 020 7333 1769
✉ opera.now@rhinegold.co.uk
www.rhinegold.co.uk
Publisher *Rhinegold Publishing Ltd*

Editor-in-Chief *Ashutosh Khandekar*
Deputy Editor *Antonia Couling*
Founded 1989. BI-MONTHLY. News, features and reviews aimed at those involved as well as those interested in opera. No unsolicited mss. All work is commissioned. Approach with ideas in writing.

Orbis
See under *Poetry Magazines*

Organic Gardening
Sandvoe, North Roe, Shetland ZE2 9RY
☎01806 533319   Fax 01806 533319
✉ organic.gardening@virgin.net
Editor *Gaby Bartai Bevan*
Circulation 20,000

Founded 1988. MONTHLY. Articles and features on all aspects of gardening based on organic methods. Unsolicited material welcome; 800–2000 words for features and 100–300 for news items. Poetry not published. Prefers 'hands-on' accounts of projects, problems, challenges and how they are dealt with. Approach in writing.
PAYMENT by arrangement.

OS (Office Secretary) Magazine
First Floor, 63 High Street, Witney OX28 6HS
☎01993 775545   Fax 01993 778884
Owner *Peebles Media Group Ltd*
Editor *Cath Janes*
Circulation 35,000

Founded 1986. BI-MONTHLY. Features articles of interest to secretaries and personal assistants aged 25–60. No unsolicited mss.
FEATURES Informative pieces on technology and practices, office and employment-related topics. Length 1000 words. Approach with ideas by telephone or in writing.
PAYMENT by negotiation.

Palmtop User Magazine
Palmtop Publications, PO Box 188, Bicester OX26 6GP
☎01869 249287   Fax 01869 246043
✉ editor@palmtop.co.uk
www.palmtop.co.uk
Owners *Mr S. Clack, Miss R.A. Rolfe*
Editor *Mr S. Clack*
Circulation 10,000

Founded 1994. BI-MONTHLY users' magazine for hand-held computers. No unsolicited mss; approach by telephone or e-mail in the first instance.

Park Home & Holiday Caravan
IPC Media Ltd, Leon House, 233 High Street, Croydon CR9 1HZ
☎020 8774 0600
✉ anne_webb@ipcmedia.com
www.phhc.co.uk
Owner *IPC Country & Leisure Media*
Editor *Anne Webb*
Circulation 15,000

Founded 1960. THIRTEEN ISSUES YEARLY. News of parks, models, legislation, accessories, lifestyle for those living in residential park homes or owning holiday caravans. Welcomes material specifically related to park home and holiday caravan sites; no general touring features. Approach by letter or telephone.

PC Format
Future Publishing, 30 Monmouth Street, Bath BA1 2BW
☎01225 442244   Fax 01225 732295
✉ pcfmail@futurenet.co.uk
www.futurenet.co.uk
Owner *Future Publishing*
Publisher *James Binns*
Editor *Adam Oxford*
Circulation 39,269

Founded 1991. FOUR-WEEKLY magazine covering everything for the consumer PC – games, hardware. Welcomes feature and interview ideas in the first instance; approach by telephone, e-mail or in writing.

Pensions World
2 Addiscombe Road, Croydon CR9 5AF
☎020 8212 1946   Fax 020 8212 1970
Owner *Reed Elsevier*
Editor *Stephanie Hawthorne*
Circulation 6817

Launched 1972. MONTHLY magazine for pensions professionals. Pensions, law, investment and retirement issues. Specialist contributors only. No consumer pension stories. Approach by e-mail.
FEATURES Max. 1500 words.
NEWS Max. 400 words.
PAYMENT negotiable.

People Management
Personnel Publications Limited, 1 Benjamin Street, London EC1M 5EA
☎020 7880 6200   Fax 020 7296 4215
✉ editorial@peoplemanagement.co.uk
www.peoplemanagement.co.uk
Editor *Steve Crabb*
Deputy Editor *Rima Manocha*

Circulation 120,110

FORTNIGHTLY magazine on human resources, industrial relations, employment issues, etc. Welcomes submissions but apply for 'Guidelines for Contributors' in the first instance.

Features *Jane Pickard/Claire Warren*
News *Zoe Roberts*
Law at Work *Jill Evans*

The People's Friend
80 Kingsway East, Dundee DD4 8SL
☎01382 462276/223131 Fax 01382 452491
✉ peoplesfriend@dcthomson.co.uk
Owner *D.C. Thomson & Co. Ltd*
Editor *Margaret McCoy*
Circulation 372,743

A fiction magazine, with two serials and several short stories each week. Founded in 1869, it has always prided itself on providing 'a good read for all the family'. Stories should be about ordinary, identifiable characters with the kind of problems the average reader can understand and sympathise with. 'We look for the romantic and emotional developments of characters, rather than an overcomplicated or contrived plot. We regularly use period serials and, occasionally, mystery/adventure.' Guidelines on request with s.a.e.

SHORT STORIES Can vary in length from 1000 words or less to 4000.
SERIALS Serials of 8–12 instalments.
ARTICLES Short fillers welcome.
PAYMENT on acceptance.

Period Living & Traditional Homes
Mappin House, 4 Winsley Street, London W1W 8HF
☎020 7343 8775 Fax 020 7343 8710
✉ period.living@emap.com
Owner *Emap East*
Editor *Sharon Parsons*
Deputy Editor *Andrew Lilwall-Smith*
Circulation 63,584

Founded 1992. Formed from the merger of *Period Living* and *Traditional Homes*. Covers interior decoration in a period style, period house profiles, traditional crafts, renovation of period properties.

PAYMENT varies according to length/type of article.

Personal Finance
Arnold House, 36–41 Holywell Lane, London EC2A 3SF
☎020 7827 5454 Fax 020 7827 0567

Owner *Charterhouse Communications plc*
Editor *Martin Fagan*
Circulation 40,000

Founded 1994. MONTHLY finance magazine.
NEWS All items written in-house.
FEATURES All issues relating to personal finance, particularly investment, insurance, banking, mortgages, savings, borrowing, health care and pensions. No corporate articles or personnel issues. Write to the editor with ideas in the first instance. No unsolicited mss. PAYMENT £200 per 1000 words.

The Philosopher
Centre for Lifelong Learning, Newcastle University, Newcastle upon Tyne NE1 7RU
✉ docmartincohen@yahoo.co.uk
www.the-philosopher.co.uk
Owner *The Philosophical Society*
Editor *Martin Cohen*

Founded 1913. BIANNUAL journal of the Philosophical Society of Great Britain with an international readership made up of members, libraries and specialist booksellers. Wide range of interests, but leaning towards articles that present philosophical investigation which is relevant to the individual and to society in our modern era. Accessible to the non-specialist. Will consider articles and book reviews. Notes for Contributors available; send s.a.e., e-mail or see website. As well as short philosophical papers, will accept:

NEWS about lectures, conventions, philosophy groups. Ethical issues in the news. Max. 1000 words.
REVIEWS of philosophy books (max. 600 words); discussion articles of individual philosophers and their published works (max. 2000 words).
MISCELLANEOUS items, including graphics, of philosophical interest and/or merit.
PAYMENT Free copies.

Piano
241 Shaftesbury Avenue, London WC2H 8TF
☎020 7333 1724 Fax 020 7333 1736
✉ piano@rhinegold.co.uk
www.rhinegold.co.uk
Owner *Rhinegold Publishing*
Editor *Jeremy Siepmann*
Deputy Editor *Sarah Smith*
Circulation 11,000

Founded 1993. BI-MONTHLY magazine containing features, profiles, technical information, news, reviews of interest to those with a serious amateur or professional concern with pianos or their playing. No unsolicited material. Approach with ideas in writing only.

Picture Postcard Monthly
15 Debdale Lane, Keyworth, Nottingham NG12 5HT
☎0115 937 4079 Fax 0115 937 6197
✉ reflections@argonet.co.uk
www.postcardcollecting.co.uk
Owners *Brian & Mary Lund*
Editor *Brian Lund*
Circulation 4000

Founded 1978. MONTHLY. News, views, clubs, diary of fairs, sales, auctions, and well-researched postcard-related articles. Might be interested in general articles supported by postcards. Unsolicited mss welcome. Approach by phone or in writing with ideas.

Pilot
Archant Specialist, The Mill, Bearwalden Business Park, Wendens Ambo, Saffron Walden CB11 4GB
☎01799 544200 Fax 01799 544201
✉ dave.calderwood@pilotweb.co.uk
www.pilotweb.co.uk
Publisher *Archant Specialist*
Editor-in-Chief *Dave Calderwood*
Deputy Editor *Nick Bloom*
Circulation 22,308

Founded 1968. MONTHLY magazine for private plane pilots. Much of the magazine is written by outside contributors – mostly regulars. Unsolicited mss welcome but ideas in writing preferred. Perusal of any issue of the magazine will reveal the type of material bought. 700 words of 'Advice to would-be contributors' sent on receipt of s.a.e. (mark envelope 'Advice'), or see the website for details.

NEWS Contributions need to be as short as possible. See *Pilot Notes* and *Old-Timers* in the magazine.

FEATURES Many articles are unsolicited personal experiences/travel accounts from pilots of private planes; good photo coverage is very important. Max. 5000 words.

Pink Paper
Unit M, Spectrum House, 32–34 Gordon House Road, London NW5 1LPG
☎020 7424 7400 Fax 020 7424 7401
✉ tris@pinkpaper.com
Owner *Millivres Prowler Group*
Editor *Tris Reid-Smith*
Circulation 55,000

Founded 1987. FORTNIGHTLY. Only national newspaper for lesbians and gay men covering politics, social issues, health, the arts and all areas of concern to lesbian/gay people. Unsolicited mss welcome. Initial approach by post with an idea preferred. Interested in profiles, reviews, in-depth features and short news pieces.
PAYMENT by arrangement.

Planet: The Welsh Internationalist
See **Planet** under *Small Presses*

PN Review
See under *Poetry Magazines*

Poetry Ireland Review
See under *Poetry Magazines*

Poetry Review
See under *Poetry Magazines*

Poetry Scotland
See under *Poetry Magazines*

Poetry Wales
See under *Poetry Magazines*

Pony
D.J. Murphy (Publishers) Ltd, Headley House, Headley Road, Grayshott GU26 6TU
☎01428 601020 Fax 01428 601030
✉ djm@djmurphy.co.uk (text only)
www.ponymag.com
Owner *D.J. Murphy (Publishers) Ltd*
Editor *Janet Rising*
Assistant Editor *Zoe Cannon*
Circulation 35,857

Founded 1948. Lively MONTHLY aimed at 10–16-year-olds. News, instruction on riding, stable management, veterinary care, interviews. Approach in writing with an idea.
FEATURES welcome. Max. 900 words.
NEWS Written in-house. Photographs and illustrations (serious/cartoon) welcome.
PAYMENT £65 per 1000 words.

Popular Crafts
Highbury Leisure, Berwick House, 8–10 Knoll Rise, Orpington BR6 0PS
☎01689 886674 Fax 01689 886666
✉ mbegumhossain@highburyleisure.co.uk
Editor *To be appointed*

Founded 1980. MONTHLY. Covers crafts of all kinds. Freelance contributions welcome – copy needs to be lively and interesting. Approach in writing or by e-mail with an outline of idea and photographs.

FEATURES Project-based under the following headings: Homecraft; Needlecraft; Popular Craft; Kidscraft; News and Columns. Any craft-related material including projects to make, with full instructions/patterns supplied in all cases; profiles of crafts people and news of craft group activities or successes by individual persons; articles on collecting crafts; personal experiences and anecdotes.
PAYMENT on publication.

post plus
See **Sunday Post** under *National Newspapers*

PR Week
174 Hammersmith Road, London W6 7JP
☎020 8267 4429 Fax 020 8267 4509
www.prweek.com
Owner *Haymarket Business Publications Ltd*
Editor *Daniel Rodgers*
Circulation 16,448
Founded 1984. WEEKLY. Contributions accepted from experienced journalists. Approach in writing with an idea.
PAYMENT negotiable.

Practical Boat Owner
Westover House, West Quay Road, Poole BH15 1JG
☎01202 440820 Fax 01202 440860
www.pbo.co.uk
Owner *IPC Media (A Time Warner Company)*
Editor *Sarah Norbury*
Circulation 50,977
Founded 1967. MONTHLY magazine of practical information for cruising boat owners. Receives about 1500 mss per year. Interested in hard facts about gear, equipment, pilotage and renovation, etc. from experienced yachtsmen.
FEATURES Technical articles about maintenance, restoration, modifications to cruising boats, power and sail up to 45ft, or reader reports on gear and equipment. European pilotage articles and cruising guides. Approach in writing with synopsis in the first instance.
PAYMENT negotiable.

Practical Caravan
60 Waldegrave Road, Teddington TW11 8LG
☎020 8267 5629 Fax 020 8267 5725
✉ practical.caravan@haynet.com
www.practicalcaravan.com
Owner *Haymarket Magazines Ltd*
Editor *Alex Newby*
Circulation 43,189
Founded 1967. MONTHLY. Contains caravan reviews, travel features, investigations, products, park reviews. Unsolicited mss welcome on travel relevant only to caravanning/touring vans. No motorcaravan or static van stories. Approach with ideas by phone, letter or e-mail.
FEATURES Must refer to caravanning. Written in friendly, chatty manner. Pictures essential. Max. length 2000 words.
PAYMENT negotiable.

Practical Fishkeeping
Bretton Court, Bretton, Peterborough PE3 8DZ
☎01733 264666 Fax 01733 465246
✉ karen.youngs@emap.com
www.practicalfishkeeping.co.uk
Owner *Emap Active Publications Ltd*
Editor *Karen Youngs*
Circulation 15,493
MONTHLY. Practical articles on all aspects of fishkeeping. Unsolicited mss welcome; approach in writing with ideas. Quality photographs of fish always welcome. No fiction or verse.

Practical Parenting
IPC Media Ltd., King's Reach Tower, Stamford Street, London SE1 9LS
☎020 7261 5058 Fax 020 7261 6542
Owner *IPC Media (A Time Warner Company)*
Editor *Mara Lee*
Circulation 50,456
Founded 1987. MONTHLY. Practical advice on pregnancy, birth, babycare and childcare, 0–4 years. Submit ideas in writing with synopsis or send mss on spec. Interested in feature articles of up to 3000 words in length, and in readers' experiences/personal viewpoint pieces of between 750–1000 words. All material must be written for the magazine's specifically targeted audience and in-house style.
PAYMENT negotiable.

Practical Photography
Bretton Court, Bretton, Peterborough PE3 8DZ
☎01733 264666 Fax 01733 465246
✉ practical.photography@emap.com
Owner *Emap Active Publications Ltd*
Editor *Andrew James*
Circulation 56,202
MONTHLY All types of photography, particularly technique-orientated pictures. No unsolicited mss. Preliminary approach may be made by e-mail. Always interested in new, especially unusual, ideas.
FEATURES Anything relevant to the world of

photography, but not 'the sort of feature produced by staff writers. Features on technology, digital imaging techniques and humour are three areas worth exploring. Bear in mind that there is a three-month lead-in time.' Max. 2000 words. PAYMENT varies.

Practical Wireless

Arrowsmith Court, Station Approach, Broadstone BH18 8PW
☎0870 224 7810   Fax 0870 224 7850
✉ name@pwpublishing.ltd.uk
www.pwpublishing.ltd.uk
Owner *PW Publishing Ltd*
Editor *Rob Mannion*
Circulation 20,000

Founded 1932. MONTHLY. News and features relating to amateur radio, radio construction and radio communications. Unsolicited mss welcome. Author's guidelines available (send s.a.e.). Approach by phone or e-mail with ideas in the first instance. Only interested in hearing from people with a thorough knowledge of radio. Copy (typed only) should be supported where possible by artwork, either illustrations, diagrams or photographs.
PAYMENT £54–70 per page.

Practical Woodworking

Highbury Leisure, Berwick House, 8–10 Knoll Rise, Orpington BR6 0PS
☎01923 286421   Fax 01923 286421
✉ practicalwoodworking@getwoodworking.com
www.getwoodworking.com
Owner *Highbury House Communications*
Editor *Mark Chisholm*
Circulation 9,500

Founded 1965. MONTHLY. Contains articles relating to woodworking: projects, techniques, new products, tips, letters, etc. Unsolicited mss welcome. No fiction. Approach with ideas in writing, by phone or e-mail.
FEATURES Projects, techniques, etc.
PAYMENT by arrangement.

Prediction

IPC Media Ltd, Leon House, 233 High Street, Croydon CR9 1HZ
☎020 8726 8000
✉ prediction@ipcmedia.com
www.predictionmagazine.co.uk
Owner *IPC Media (A Time Warner Company)*
Editor *Tania Ahsan*
Circulation 14,543

Founded 1936. MONTHLY. Covering astrology and mind, body, spirit topics. Unsolicited material in these areas welcome (about 200–300 mss received every year). Writers' guidelines available on request.
ASTROLOGY Pieces should be practical and of general interest. Charts and astro data should accompany them, especially if profiles.
FEATURES Articles on divination, shamanism, alternative healing, psychics and other supernatural phenonema considered. Please read a recent copy of the magazine before sending unsolicited material.

Pregnancy & Birth

Greater London House, Hampstead Road, London NW1 7EJ
☎020 7347 1885   Fax 020 7347 1888
✉ elin.tough@emap.com
Owner *Emap Esprit*
Editor *Kaye McIntosh*
Features Editor *Susanna Wood*
Circulation 53,341

MONTHLY magazine covering all aspects of pregnancy from health to fashion. Regularly commissions features from health journalists. Freelancers should approach by post in the first instance. PAYMENT varies.

Pregnancy, Baby & You

Jordan House, 47 Brunswick Place, London N1 6EB
☎020 7608 6412
✉ claire.roberts@highburygroup.com
Owner *Highbury Lifestyle*
Editor *Claire Roberts*
Deputy Editor *Tessa Taylor*

MONTHLY publication that focuses on issues affecting the family as a whole.

Press Gazette

Quantum House, 19 Scarbrook Road, Croydon CR9 1LX
☎020 8565 4473   Fax 020 8565 4395
✉ pged@pressgazette.co.uk
www.pressgazette.co.uk
Owner *Press Gazette Limited*
Editor *Ian Reeves*
Deputy Editor *Jon Slattery*
Circulation 9500

WEEKLY magazine for all journalists – in regional and national newspapers, magazines, broadcasting, and online – containing news, features and analysis of all areas of journalism, print and broadcasting. Unsolicited mss welcome; interested in profiles of magazines, broadcasting companies and news agencies, personality profiles, technical and current affairs relating to the world of journalism. Approach with ideas by phone, e-mail, fax or in writing.

Pride
Hamilton House, 55 Battersea Bridge Road, London SW11 3AX
☎020 7228 3110 Fax 020 7228 3129
✉ info@pridemagazine.com
Owner *Carl Cushnie Junior*
Editor *Sherry Dixon*
Circulation 40,000

Founded 1991. MONTHLY lifestyle magazine for Black women with features, beauty, arts and fashion. Approach in writing or by e-mail with ideas.
FEATURES Issues pertaining to the Black community. 'Ideas and solicited mss are welcomed from new freelancers.' Max. 2000 words.
FICTION Publishes the occasional short story. Max. 3000 words.
HEALTH, BEAUTY, LIFESTYLE *Sherry Dixon* Freelancers used for short features. Max. 1000 words.

Prima
National Magazine House, 72 Broadwick Street, London W1F 9EP
☎020 7439 5000
✉ prima@natmags.co.uk
www.natmags.co.uk
Owner *National Magazine Company*
Editor *Maire Fahey*
Circulation 317,308

Founded 1986. MONTHLY women's magazine.
HEALTH & FEATURES Coordinator *Ruth Tierney* Mostly practical and written by specialists, or commissioned from known freelancers. Unsolicited mss not welcome.

Private Eye
6 Carlisle Street, London W1D 3BN
☎020 7437 4017 Fax 020 7437 0705
✉ strobes@private-eye.co.uk
www.private-eye.co.uk
Owner *Pressdram*
Editor *Ian Hislop*
Circulation 200,872

Founded 1961. FORTNIGHTLY satirical and investigative magazine. Prospective contributors are best advised to approach the editor in writing. News stories and feature ideas are always welcome, as are cartoons. All jokes written in-house.

PAYMENT in all cases is 'not great', and length of piece varies as appropriate.

Prospect
2 Bloomsbury Place, London WC1A 2QA
☎020 7255 1344 (editorial)/1281 (publishing)
Fax 020 7255 1279
✉ editorial@prospect-magazine.co.uk *or*
publishing@prospect-magazine.co.uk
www.prospect-magazine.co.uk
Owner *Prospect Publishing Limited*
Editor *David Goodhart*
Circulation 24,400

Founded 1995. MONTHLY. Essays, reviews, short fiction and research on current/international affairs and cultural issues. No news features. Unsolicited contributions welcome, although more useful to approach in writing with ideas in the first instance.

Psychic News
The Coach House, Stansted Hall, Stansted CM24 8UD
☎01279 817050 Fax 01279 817051
✉ pnadv@snu.org.uk
www.psychicnewsbookshop.co.uk
Owner *Psychic Press 1995 Ltd*
Editor *Tony Ortzen*
Circulation 40,000

Founded 1932. *Psychic News* is the world's only WEEKLY spiritualist newspaper. It covers subjects such as psychic research, hauntings, ghosts, poltergeists, spiritual healing, survival after death and paranormal gifts. Unsolicited material considered.

Publishing News
7 John Street, London WC1N 2ES
☎0870 870 2345 Fax 0870 870 0385
✉ mailbox@publishingnews.co.uk
www.publishingnews.co.uk
Editor *Liz Thomson*

WEEKLY newspaper of the book trade. Hardback and paperback reviews and extensive listings of new paperbacks and hardbacks. Interviews with leading personalities in the trade, authors, agents and features on specialist book areas.

Q
Mappin House, 4 Winsley Street, London W1W 8HF
☎020 7436 1515 Fax 020 7182 8547
www.q4music.com
Owner *Emap Performance*

Editor *Paul Rees*
Circulation 162,574

Founded 1986. MONTHLY. Glossy aimed at educated popular music enthusiasts of all ages. Few opportunities for freelance writers. Unsolicited mss are strongly discouraged. Prospective contributors should approach in writing only.

Q-News, The Muslim Magazine

PO Box 4295, London W1A 7YH
☎07985 143263
✉ info@q-news.com
www.q-news.com

Owner *Fuad Nahdi*
Editor *Fareena Alam*
Circulation 40,000

Founded 1992. MONTHLY British Muslim community magazine concerned with shaping the debate about Muslims in Britain. Covers recruitment, news, opinion and reviews.

FEATURES *Abdul-Rehman Maik* 'Writers wishing to focus on areas of interest to our readership will gain access and credibility among the relevant people.' Max. 3000 words.

OTHER *Fareena Alam* Analysis on news and current affairs – alternative rather than mainstream viewpoint preferred. Max. 2000 words.

PAYMENT None.

Quartos Magazine

See **The New Writer**

QWF Magazine

PO Box 1768, Rugby CV21 4ZA
☎01788 334302
✉ jo@qwfmagazine.co.uk
www.qwfmagazine.co.uk

Editor *Jo Good*

BI-MONTHLY small press magazine. Founded in 1994, as a showcase for the best in women's short story writing – original and thought-provoking. Only considers stories that are previously unpublished and of less than 4000 words; articles must be less than 1000 words and of interest to the writer. Include covering letter, s.a.e. and brief biography with mss. Before submission of material send s.a.e. (50p stamp) with request for free back copy. Also runs script appraisal service and regular short story competitions. For further information and detailed guidelines for contributors please access the website or contact the editor at the address above. Submissions should be sent to Assistant Editor, *Sally Zigmond* (18 Warwick Crescent, Harrogate HG2 8JA) with s.a.e.

RA Magazine (Royal Academy of Arts Magazine)

Royal Academy of Arts, Burlington House, Piccadilly, London W1J 0BD
☎020 7300 5820   Fax 020 7300 5882
✉ ramagazine@royalacademy.org.uk
www.ramagazine.org.uk

Owner *Royal Academy of Arts*
Editor *Sarah Greenberg*
Circulation 100,000

Founded 1983. QUARTERLY visual arts, architecture and culture magazine distributed to Friends of the RA, promoting exhibitions and publishing articles on art shows, books and news worldwide. 'There are opportunities for freelancers who can write about art in an accessible way. Most articles need to be tied in to forthcoming exhibitions, books and projects.' No unsolicited contributions. Approach by telephone or e-mail.

Racecar Engineering

IPC Media Ltd, Leon House, 233 High Street, Croydon CR9 1HZ
☎020 8726 8000
✉ racecar@ipcmedia.com
www.racecar-engineering.co.uk

Owner *IPC Media (A Time Warner Company)*
Editor *Charles Armstrong-Wilson*
Circulation 15,000

Founded 1990. MONTHLY. In-depth features on motorsport technology plus news and products. Interested in receiving news and features from freelancers.

FEATURES Informed insight into current motorsport technology. 3000 words max.

NEWS New cars, products or business news relevant to motorsport. No items on road cars or racing drivers. 500 words max. Call or e-mail to discuss proposal.

Racing Post (incorporating The Sporting Life)

1 Canada Square, Canary Wharf, London E14 5AP
☎020 7293 3000   Fax 020 7293 3758
✉ editor@racingpost.co.uk
www.racingpost.co.uk

Owner *Trinity Mirror Plc*
Editor *Chris Smith*

Founded 1986. DAILY horse racing paper with some general sport. In 1998, following an agreement between the owners of *The Sporting Life* and the *Racing Post*, the two papers merged.

Radio Times
80 Wood Lane, London W12 0TT
☎020 8433 3400 Fax 020 8433 3160
✉ radio.times@bbc.co.uk
www.radiotimes.com
Owner *BBC Worldwide Limited*
Editor *Gill Hudson*
Circulation 1.11 million

WEEKLY. UK's leading broadcast listings magazine. The majority of material is provided by freelance and retained writers, but the topicality of the pieces means close consultation with editors is essential. Very unlikely to use unsolicited material. Detailed BBC, ITV, Channel 4, Channel 5 and satellite television and radio listings are accompanied by feature material relevant to the week's output.
PAYMENT by arrangement.

Rail
Bretton Court, Bretton, Peterborough PE3 8DZ
☎01733 264666 Fax 01733 282720
✉ rail@emap.com
Owner *Emap Active Publications Ltd*
Managing Editor *Nigel Harris*
Circulation 27,087

Founded 1981. FORTNIGHTLY magazine dedicated to modern railway. News and features, and topical newsworthy events. Unsolicited mss welcome. Approach by phone with ideas. Not interested in personal journey reminiscences. No fiction.
FEATURES By arrangement with the editor. All modern railway British subjects considered. Max. 2000 words.
NEWS Any news item welcome. Max. 500 words.
PAYMENT features, varies/negotiable; news, up to £100 per 1000 words.

Railway Gazette International
Quadrant House, Sutton SM2 5AS
☎020 8652 8608 Fax 020 8652 3738
www.railwaygazette.com
Owner *Reed Business Information*
Editor *Murray Hughes*
Circulation 9760

Founded 1835. MONTHLY magazine written for senior railway managers and engineers worldwide. 'No material for railway enthusiast publications.' Telephone to discuss ideas in the first instance.

The Railway Magazine
IPC Media Ltd., King's Reach Tower, Stamford Street, London SE1 9LS
☎020 7261 5533/5821 Fax 020 7261 5269
✉ railway@ipcmedia.com
www.ipcmedia.com
Owner *IPC Media (A Time Warner Company)*
Editor *Nick Pigott*
Circulation 30,501

Founded 1897. MONTHLY. Articles, photos and short news stories of a topical nature, covering modern railways, steam preservation and railway history, welcome. Max. 2000 words, with sketch maps of routes, etc., where appropriate. Unsolicited mss welcome. No poetry.
PAYMENT negotiable.

Reader's Digest
11 Westferry Circus, Canary Wharf, London E14 4HE
☎020 7715 8000 Fax 020 7715 8716
www.readersdigest.co.uk
Owner *Reader's Digest Association Ltd*
Editor-in-Chief *Katherine Walker*
Circulation 773,731

Although in theory, a good market for general interest features of around 2500 words very few are ever accepted. However, 'a tiny proportion' comes from freelance writers, all of which are specially commissioned. Opportunities exist for short humorous contributions to regular features – 'Life's Like That', 'Laughter, the Best Medicine', 'All in a Day's Work'. Issues a helpful booklet called 'Writing for Reader's Digest', available by post at £4.50.
PAYMENT up to £100.

The Reader
Reader Office, 19 Abercromby Square, Liverpool L69 7ZG
✉ readers@liv.co.uk
www.thereader.co.uk
Editor *Jane Davis*
Circulation 1200

Founded 1997. QUARTERLY. Poetry, short fiction, literary articles and essays, thought, reviews, recommendations. Contributions from internationally lauded and new voices. Welcomes articles/essays about reading, max. 2000 words. Recommendations for good reading, max. 1000 words. Short stories, max. 2500 words. No theoretical style literary discourses. Approach in writing.
PAYMENT negotiable.

Real

Essential Publishing, Phoenix Square, Colchester CO4 9HU
☎01206 851117
www.essentialpublishing.co.uk
Owner *Essential Publishing Ltd*
Editor *Sally Narraway*
Circulation 197,031

FORTNIGHTLY women's magazine. Real life stories

Record Collector

Unit 101, 140 Wales Farm Road, Acton, London W3 6UG
☎0870 732 8080   Fax 0870 732 6060
✉ alan.lewis@metropolis.co.uk
www.recordcollectormag.com
Owner *Metropolis*
Editor *Alan Lewis*

Founded 1979. MONTHLY. Detailed, well-researched articles welcome on any aspect of record collecting or any collectable artist in the field of popular music (1950s to present day), with complete discographies where appropriate. Unsolicited mss welcome. Approach with ideas by phone or e-mail.

PAYMENT negotiable.

Red

64 North Row, London W1K 7LL
☎020 7150 7000   Fax 020 7150 7684
✉ sally.mann@hf-uk.com
www.redmagazine.co.uk
Owner *Hachette Filipacchi UK Ltd*
Editor *Trish Halpin*
Circulation 210,027

Founded 1998. MONTHLY magazine aimed at the 30-something woman. Will consider ideas sent in 'on spec' but tends to rely on regular contributors.

Report

ATL, 7 Northumberland Street, London WC2N 5RD
☎020 7930 6441   Fax 020 7782 1618
Owner *Association of Teachers and Lecturers*
Joint Editors *Guy Goodwin, Miranda Green*
Circulation 160,000

Founded 1978. TEN ISSUES YEARLY during academic terms. Contributions welcome. All submissions should go directly to the editor. Articles should be no more than 800 words and must be of practical interest to the classroom teacher and F.E. lecturers.

Reveal

National Magazine Co., National Magazine House, 72 Broadwick Street, London W1F 9EP
☎020 7339 4500   Fax 020 7339 4529
✉ sarah@acp-natmag.co.uk
www.natmags.co.uk
Owner *National Magazines & Australian Consolidated Press*
Editor *Sarah Edwards*
Circulation 239,907

Launched 2004. WEEKLY glossy lifestyle magazine with celebrities, real-life stories, cookery, beauty and seven-day TV guide. No unsolicited contributions.

Right Now!

Box 361, 78 Marylebone High Street, London W1U 5AP
☎0845 601 3243   Fax 0845 601 3243
✉ editor@right-now.org
www.right-now.org
Owner *Right Now! Press Ltd*
Editor *Derek Turner*
Circulation 3000

Founded 1993. BI-MONTHLY right-wing conservative commentary. Welcomes well-documented disputations, news stories and features about British heritage ('the more politically incorrect, the better!'). No fiction or poems. Initial approach in writing. No PAYMENT.

Rugby World

IPC Media Ltd., 23rd Floor, King's Reach Tower, Stamford Street, London SE1 9LS
☎020 7261 6830   Fax 020 7261 5419
www.rugbyworld.com
Owner *IPC Media (A Time Warner Company)*
Editor *Paul Morgan*
Circulation 44,496

Founded 1960. MONTHLY. Features of special rugby interest only. Unsolicited contributions welcome but s.a.e. essential for return of material. Prior approach by phone or in writing preferred.

Runner's World

72 Broadwick Street, London W1F 9EP
☎020 7339 4400   Fax 020 7339 4220
✉ rwedit@natmag-rodale.co.uk
www.runnersworld.co.uk
Owner *Rodale Press*
Editor *Steven Seaton*
Circulation 77,671

Founded 1979. MONTHLY magazine giving practical advice on all areas of distance running including products and training, travel features, news and cross-training advice. Personal running-related articles, famous people who run or off-beat travel articles are welcome. No elite athlete or training articles. Approach with ideas in writing in the first instance.

Running Fitness
1st Floor, South Wing, Broadway Court, Broadway, Peterborough PE1 1RP
☎01733 347559 Fax 01733 352749
✉ rf.ed@kelsey.co.uk
www.running-fitness.com
Owner *Kelsey Publishing*
Editor *Paul Larkins*
Circulation 26,000

Founded 1985. MONTHLY. Instructional articles on running, fitness, and lifestyle, plus running-related activities and health.
FEATURES Specialist knowledge an advantage. Opportunities are wide, but approach with ideas in first instance.
NEWS Opportunities for people stories, especially if backed up by photographs.

Saga Magazine
Saga Publishing Ltd, Middelburg Square, Folkstone CT21 1AZ
☎01303 771523 Fax 01303 776699
www.saga.co.uk
Owner *Saga Publishing Ltd*
Editor *Emma Soames*
Circulation 1.25 million

Founded 1984. MONTHLY magazine that sets out to celebrate the role of older people in society, reflecting their achievements, promoting their skills, protecting their interests, and campaigning on their behalf. A warm personal approach, addressing the readership in an upbeat and positive manner. It has a hard core of celebrated commentators/writers (e.g. Keith Waterhouse, Alexander Chancellor, Angela Rippon) as regular contributors. Articles mostly commissioned or written in-house but exclusive celebrity interviews welcome if appropriate/relevant. Length 1000–1200 words (max. 1600). No short stories or poems, please.

Sailing Today
4 Chapel Row, Bath BA1 1HN
☎01225 470074 Fax 01225 313325
✉ feedback@sailingtoday.co.uk
Owner *Edisey Ltd*
Editor *John Goode*
Founded 1997. MONTHLY practical magazine for cruising sailors. *Sailing Today* covers owning and buying a boat, equipment and products for sailing and is about improving readers' skills, boat maintenance and product tests. Most articles are commissioned but will consider practical features and cruise stories with photos. Approach by telephone or in writing in the first instance.

Sainsbury's Magazine
20 Upper Ground, London SE1 9PD
☎020 7633 0266 Fax 020 7401 9423
✉ edit@newcrane.co.uk
Owner *New Crane Ltd*
Editor *Sue Robinson*
Consultant Director *Delia Smith*
Circulation 340,126

Founded 1993. MONTHLY featuring a main core of food and cookery with features, health, beauty, home and gardening. No unsolicited mss. Approach in writing with ideas only in the first instance.

The Salisbury Review
33 Canonbury Park South, London N1 2JW
☎020 7226 7791 Fax 020 7354 0383
✉ salisburyreview@tiscali.co.uk
www.salisbury-review.co.uk
Editor *Dennis O'Keeffe*
Managing Editor *Merrie Cave*
Consulting Editors *Roger Scruton, Sir Richard Body, Myles Harris*
Circulation 1700

Founded 1982. QUARTERLY magazine of conservative thought. Editorials and features from a right-wing viewpoint. Unsolicited material welcome. No fiction or poetry.
FEATURES Max. 2000 words.
REVIEWS Max. 1000 words.
SMALL PAYMENT.

Scotland in Trust
5 Windsor Place, Edinburgh EH15 2AJ
☎0131 657 4612 Fax 0131 657 4612
✉ trust@cmyk-design.co.uk
Owner *National Trust for Scotland*
Editor *Iain Gale*
Circulation 153,773

Founded 1983. THREE ISSUES YEARLY. Magazine containing heritage/conservation features. No unsolicited mss.

Scotland on Sunday Magazine
See **Scotland on Sunday** under *National Newspapers*

The Scots Magazine

D.C. Thomson & Co., 2 Albert Square,
Dundee DD1 9QJ
☎01382 223131   Fax 01382 322214
✉ mail@scotsmagazine.com
www.scotsmagazine.com
Owner *D.C. Thomson & Co. Ltd*
Editor *John Methven*
Circulation 45,664

Founded 1739. MONTHLY. Covers a wide field of Scottish interests ranging from personalities to wildlife, climbing, reminiscence, history and folklore. Outside contributions welcome; 'staff delighted to discuss in advance by letter or e-mail'.

The Scottish Farmer

SMG Magazines, 200 Renfield Street,
Glasgow G2 3PR
☎0141 302 7700   Fax 0141 302 7799
✉ firstname.surname@thescottishfarmer.co.uk
Owner *SMG Magazines*
Editor *Alasdair Fletcher*
Circulation 21,220

Founded 1893. WEEKLY. Farmer's magazine covering most aspects of Scottish agriculture. Unsolicited mss welcome. Approach with ideas in writing, by fax or e-mail.

FEATURES *Ken Fletcher* Technical articles on agriculture or farming units. 1000–2000 words.

NEWS *Ken Fletcher* Factual news about farming developments, political, personal and technological. Max. 800 words.

WEEKEND FAMILY PAGES Rural and craft topics.

Scottish Field

Special Publications, Craigcrook Castle,
Craigcrook Road, Edinburgh EH4 3PE
☎0131 312 4550   Fax 0131 312 4551
✉ editor@scottishfield.co.uk
Owner *Oban Times*
Editor *Claire Grant*
Circulation 14,082

Founded 1903. MONTHLY. Scotland's quality lifestyle magazine. Unsolicited mss welcome but writers should study the magazine first.

FEATURES Articles of general interest on Scotland and Scots abroad with good photographs or, preferably, e-mailed images at 300 DPI. Approx. 1000 words.

PAYMENT negotiable.

Scottish Home & Country

42 Heriot Row, Edinburgh EH3 6ES
☎0131 225 1724   Fax 0131 225 8129

✉ magazine@swri.demon.co.uk
Owner *Scottish Women's Rural Institutes*
Editor *Liz Ferguson*
Circulation 11,000

Founded 1924. MONTHLY. Scottish or rural-related issues, health, travel, women's issues and general interest. Unsolicited mss welcome. Commissions are rare and tend to go to established contributors only.

Scouting Magazine

Gilwell House, Gilwell Park, Chingford
E4 7QW
☎020 8433 7100   Fax 020 8433 7103
✉ scouting.magazine@scout.org.uk
www.scouts.org.uk
Owner *The Scout Association*
Editors *Chris James, Hilary Galloway,
   Matthew Oakes*
Circulation 72,000+

BI-MONTHLY magazine for adults connected to or interested in the Scout Movement. Interested in Scouting-related submissions only. PAYMENT by negotiation.

Screen

Gilmorehill Centre for Theatre, Film and Television, University of Glasgow, Glasgow
G12 8QQ
☎0141 330 5035   Fax 0141 330 3515
✉ screen@arts.gla.ac.uk
www.screen.arts.gla.ac.uk
Publisher *Oxford University Press*
Editors *Annette Kuhn, John Caughie, Simon
   Frith, Karen Lury, Jackie Stacey, Sarah Street*
Editorial Assistant *Caroline Beven*
Circulation 1200

QUARTERLY refereed academic journal of film and television studies for a readership ranging from undergraduates to screen studies academics and media professionals. There are no specific qualifications for acceptance of articles. Straightforward film reviews are not normally published. Check the magazine's style and market in the first instance.

Screen International

33–39 Bowling Green Lane, London
EC1R 0DA
☎020 7505 8000
✉ michael.gubbins@emap.com
www.screendaily.com
Owner *Emap Communications*
Editor *Michael Gubbins*

The voice of the international film industry.

Expert freelance writers used in all areas. No unsolicited mss. Approach by e-mail.
Features *Louise Tutt*
International *Patrick Frater*
PAYMENT negotiable on NUJ basis.

Screentrade Magazine

Screentrade Media Ltd, PO Box 144, Orpington BR6 6LZ
☎01689 833117 Fax 01689 833117
✉ philip@screentrademagazine.co.uk
www.screentrademagazine.co.uk
Owner *Screentrade Media Ltd*
Editor *Philip Turner*
Circulation 3000+

Founded 2002. QUARTERLY journal for British, European and American exhibitors and film distributors.

FEATURES Items on cinema management, technical, cinema building history, nostalgia, showmanship, book reviews, concession supply, ticketing issues, trade articles including seating, screening, projection/career tips and other managerial matters. Also film and producer/director opinions. Some film reviews but no 'film star' interviews. Most contributions are from within the industry. Items on the state of cinema exhibition, film distribution, cinema architecture, interviews with key industry personnel frequently undertaken. 1500–3000 words.

NEWS Topical items (if substantiated) welcome. Events coverage (e.g. festivals, premières) from an exhibitor's viewpoint preferred.

ScriptWriter Magazine

2 Elliott Square, London NW3 3SU
☎020 7586 4853 Fax 020 7586 4853
✉ julian@scriptwritermagazine.com
www.scriptwritermagazine.com
Owner *Scriptease Ltd*
Editor *Julian Friedmann*
Circulation 1500

Launched November 2001. SIX ISSUES PER YEAR. Magazine for professional scriptwriters covering all aspects of the business and craft of writing for the small and large screen. Interested in serious, in–depth analysis; max. 1500–3500 words. E-mail with synopsis sample material and c.v.
PAYMENT £20 per 1000 words.

Sea Breezes

Mannin Media Group Ltd, Media House, Cronkbourne IM4 4SB
☎01624 696566 Fax 01624 661655
✉ seabreezes@manninmedia.co.im
www.seabreezes.co.im

Owner *Print Centres*
Editor *Captain A.C. Douglas*
Circulation 17,000

Founded 1919. MONTHLY. Covers virtually everything relating to ships and seamen. Unsolicited mss welcome; they should be thoroughly researched and accompanied by relevant photographs. No fiction, poetry, or anything which 'smacks of the romance of the sea'.

FEATURES Factual tales of ships, seamen and the sea, Royal or Merchant Navy, sail or power, nautical history, shipping company histories, epic voyages, etc. Length 1000–4000 words. 'The most readily acceptable work will be that which shows it is clearly the result of first-hand experience or the product of extensive and accurate research.'
PAYMENT £14 per page (about 800 words).

The Second World War – WWII (1939–1945)

PO Box 202, Scarborough YO11 3GE
☎01723 581329 Fax 01723 581329
✉ books@greatnorthernpublishing.co.uk
www.greatnorthernpublishing.co.uk
Owner *Great Northern Publishing*
Editor *Mark Marsay*

Launched October 2005. BI-MONTHLY subscription only non-academic magazine published in A5 format. 'The magazine dedicated to the struggle for freedom – the voice and record of those who died between 1939 and 1945.' Articles, personal stories and accounts of those who served (men and women of all nationalities) and their families; diaries, anecdotes, letters postcards, poetry, unit histories, events and memorials, etc. Absolutely no fiction or academic works expounding historian's personal views. New material welcome; contact the editor prior to sending. Submission guidelines and editorial content on the website. 'Open door policy: all welcome regardless of ability to write to a high standard as all work is carefully edited. No subject or topic excluded.' Sample copy £5.

She Magazine

National Magazine House, 72 Broadwick Street, London W1F 9EP
☎020 7439 5000 Fax 020 7312 3981
www.natmags.co.uk
Owner *National Magazine Co. Ltd*
Editor *Terry Tavner*
Circulation 180,160

Glossy MONTHLY for the thirty-something woman, addressing her needs as an individual, a partner and a parent. Talks to its readers in an intelligent, humorous and sympathetic way. FEATURES should be about 1200 words long. Approach with ideas in writing or e-mail *Natasha Cook*, Features Editor (natasha.cook@natmags.co.uk). No unsolicited material. PAYMENT negotiable.

Ships Monthly
IPC Country & Leisure Media Ltd, 222 Branston Road, Burton-upon-Trent DE14 3BT
☎01283 542721 Fax 01283 546436
✉ shipsmonthly@ipcmedia.com
Owner *IPC Country & Leisure Media Ltd*
Editor *Iain Wakefield*
Circulation 22,000

Founded 1966. MONTHLY A4 format magazine for ship enthusiasts and maritime professionals. News, photographs and illustrated articles on all kinds of ships – mercantile and naval, past and present. No yachting. Most articles are commissioned; prospective contributors should telephone or e-mail in the first instance.

Shoot Monthly Magazine
IPC Media Ltd., King's Reach Tower, Stamford Street, London SE1 9LS
☎020 7261 6287 Fax 020 7261 6019
✉ shoot@ipcmedia.com
Owner *IPC Media (A Time Warner Company)*
Editor *Colin Mitchell*
Circulation 30,316

Founded 1969. MONTHLY football magazine. No unsolicited mss. Present ideas for news, features or colour photo-features to the editor by letter or e-mail.
FEATURES Hard-hitting, topical and off-beat.
NEWS Items welcome, especially exclusive gossip and transfer speculation.
PAYMENT negotiable.

Shooting and Conservation
BASC, Marford Mill, Rossett, Wrexham LL12 0HL
☎01244 573000 Fax 01244 573001
Owner *The British Association for Shooting and Conservation (BASC)*
Editor *Jeffrey Olstead*
Circulation 120,000

SIX ISSUES PER YEAR. Good articles and stories on shooting, conservation and related areas may be considered although most material is produced in-house. Max. 1500 words. PAYMENT negotiable.

Shooting Times & Country Magazine
IPC Media Ltd., King's Reach Tower, Stamford Street, London SE1 9LS
☎020 7261 6180 Fax 020 7261 7179
✉ steditorial@ipcmedia.com
Owner *IPC Media (A Time Warner Company)*
Editor *Camilla Collinson*
Circulation 27,720

Founded 1882. WEEKLY. Covers shooting, fishing and related countryside topics. Unsolicited contributions considered.
PAYMENT negotiable.

Shortwave Magazine
Arrowsmith Court, Station Approach, Broadstone BH18 8PW
☎0870 224 7810 Fax 0870 224 7850
✉ name@pwpublishing.ltd.uk
www.pwpublishing.ltd.uk
Owner *PW Publishing Ltd*
Editor *Kevin Nice*
Circulation 20,000

Founded 1937. MONTHLY. Specialist electronics and radio enthusiasts' magazine. Features, news, regular columns and projects. Will consider contributions but recommends that contact be made prior to submission to check publishing plans.

Shout Magazine
D.C. Thomson & Co., Albert Square, Dundee DD1 9QJ
☎01382 223131 Fax 01382 200880
✉ shout@dcthomson.co.uk
Owner *D.C. Thomson Publishers*
Editor *Maria T. Welch*
Circulation 67,466

Founded 1993. FORTNIGHTLY. Pop music, quizzes, emotional, beauty, fashion, soap features.
FICTION *Maria Welch* Supernatural/spooky stories welcome. Approach by telephone in the first instance. Max. 1500 words. PAYMENT £100.

Shout!
PO Box YR46, Leeds LS9 6XG
☎0113 248 5700 Fax 0113 295 6097
✉ shout.magazine@ntlworld.com
www.shout.connectfree.co.uk
Owner/Editor *Mark Michalowski*
Circulation 7000

Founded 1995. MONTHLY lesbian/gay and bisexual news, views, arts and scene for Yorkshire; lgb health and politics. Interested in reviews of Yorkshire lgb events, happenings, news, analysis – 300 to 1000 words max. No fiction, fashion or items with no reasonable relevance to Yorkshire and the north. PAYMENT £40 per 1000 words.

Showing World

The Publishing House, Station Road, Framlingham IP13 9EE
☎01728 622030   Fax 01728 622031
✉ todaymagazine@btopeworld.com
Owner *T.P. Publications*
Editor *Charlotte Knight*
Circulation 3000
Founded 1991. Features every aspect of showing horses and ponies plus natives, miniatures and donkeys. Knowledgeable and how-to-do-it articles welcome. Photos essential.
PAYMENT negotiable.

Shropshire Magazine

Waterloo Road, Telford TS1 5HU
☎01952 288822   Fax 01952 288820
Owner *Shropshire Newspapers Ltd*
Editor *Henry Carpenter*
Founded 1950. MONTHLY. Unsolicited mss welcome but ideas in writing preferred.
FEATURES Personalities, topical items, historical (e.g. family) of Shropshire; also general interest: homes, weddings, antiques, etc. Max. 1000 words. PAYMENT negotiable 'but modest'.

Sight & Sound

British Film Institute, 21 Stephen Street, London W1T 1LN
☎020 7255 1444   Fax 020 7436 2327
www.bfi.org.uk/sightandsound
Owner *British Film Institute*
Editor *Nick James*
Founded 1932. MONTHLY. Topical and critical articles on international cinema, with regular columns from the USA and Europe. Length 1000–5000 words. Relevant photographs appreciated. Also book, film and video release reviews. Approach in writing with ideas.
PAYMENT by arrangement.

The Sign

See **Hymns Ancient & Modern Ltd** under *UK Publishers*

Ski and Board

The White House, 57–63 Church Road, Wimbledon, London SW19 5SB
☎020 8410 2000   Fax 020 8410 2001
✉ info@skiandboard.co.uk

www.skiclub.co.uk
Owner *Ski Club of Great Britain*
Editor *Arnie Wilson*
Founded 1903. FOUR ISSUES YEARLY. Features from established ski/snowboard writers only.

The Skier and Snowboarder Magazine

Mountain Marketing Ltd., PO Box 386, Sevenoaks TN13 1AQ
☎0845 310 8303   Fax 01732 779266
✉ skierandsnowboarder@hotmail.com
Publisher *Mountain Marketing Ltd*
Editor *Frank Baldwin*
Circulation 30,000
SEASONAL (from July to May). FIVE ISSUES YEARLY. Outside contributions welcome.
FEATURES Various topics covered, including race reports, resort reports, fashion, equipment update, dry slope, club news, new products, health and safety. Crisp, tight, informative copy of 800 words or less preferred.
NEWS All aspects of skiing news covered.
PAYMENT negotiable.

Slightly Foxed: The Real Reader's Quarterly

67 Dickinson Court, 15 Brewhouse Yard, London EC1V 4JX
☎020 7549 2121/2111   Fax 0870 199 1245
✉ all@foxedquarterly.com
www.foxedquarterly.com
Owner *Slightly Foxed Ltd*
Editors *Gail Pirkis, Hazel Wood*
Circulation 3300
Founded 2004. 'Reviews of books (fiction and non-fiction) that have stood the test of time or books that have been published recently and are of real quality but which have been overlooked by reviewers and bookshops.' Unsolicited contributions of 'lively, personal, idiosyncratic writing of real quality' are welcome but it is recommended that would-be contributors read the magazine first to gauge its approach. Send e-mail with sample work in the first instance. Not interested in anything that is not actually a review of a book or author.

Slimming

Greater London House, Hampstead Road, London NW1 7EJ
☎020 7347 1700   Fax 020 7347 1863
✉ katy.salter@emap.com
Owner *Emap Esprit*
Editor *Marie Farquharson*

Circulation 64,587

Founded 1969. TWELVE ISSUES YEARLY. Leading magazine about slimming, diet and health. Opportunities for freelance contributions on general health, relationships and well being (diet-related); general lifestyle and fitness. It is best to approach with an idea by e-mail. PAYMENT negotiable.

Smallholder

Hook House, Wimblington March PE15 0QL
☎01354 741182   Fax 01354 741182
✉ edit@smallholder.co.uk
www.smallholder.co.uk
Owner *Newsquest Plc*
Editor *Liz Wright*
Circulation 20,000

Founded 1982. MONTHLY. Outside contributions welcome. Send for sample magazine and editorial schedule before submitting anything. Follow up with samples of work to the editor so that style can be assessed for suitability. No poetry or humorous, unfocused personal tales; no puzzles.

FEATURES New writers always welcome, but must have high level of technical expertise – 'not textbook stuff'. 'How to do it' articles with photos welcome. Illustrations and photos paid for. Length 750–1500 words.

NEWS All agricultural and rural news welcome. Length 200–500 words.

PAYMENT negotiable.

Smash Hits

Mappin House, 4 Winsley Street, London W1W 8HF
☎020 7182 8000   Fax 020 7636 5792
✉ letters@smashhits.net
www.smashhits.net
Owner *Emap Performance*
Editor *Lisa Smosarski*
Editorial Director *Jennifer Cawthron*
Circulation 126,100

Founded 1978. FORTNIGHTLY. Top of the mid-teen market. Unsolicited mss are not accepted, but prospective contributors may approach in writing with ideas.

Sneak Magazine

Mappin House, 4 Winsley Street, London W1W 8HF
☎020 7436 1515   Fax 020 7312 8229
✉ michelle.garnett@emap.com
www.sneakmagazine.com
Owner *EMAP*

Editor *Michelle Garnett*
Editorial Director *Jennifer Cawthron*
Circulation 90,946

Founded 2002. WEEKLY magazine for teenagers providing gossip and entertainment. Unsolicited material welcome.

FEATURES *Leo Roberts*
NEWS *Jenna Good*

Snooker Scene

Hayley Green Court, 130 Hagley Road, Halesowen, Birmingham B63 1DY
☎0121 585 9188   Fax 0121 585 7117
✉ clive.everton@talk21.com
www.snookersceneonline.com
Owner *Everton's News Agency*
Editor *Clive Everton*
Circulation 10,000

Founded 1971. MONTHLY. No unsolicited mss. Approach in writing with an idea.

Songs of Praise Magazine

Origin Publishing, Tower House, Fairfax Street, Bristol BS1 3BN
☎0117 927 9009
✉ songsofpraisemagazine@originpublishing.co.uk
www.songsofpraisemagazinecom
Owner *BBC Magazines*
Editor *Liz Vercoe*
Circulation 20,000

Launched 2003. QUARTERLY magazine complementing the weekly BBC *Songs of Praise* programme and its guests. Welcomes contributions: moving true stories, short 'words of inspiration', A-list interviews linked to faith. Approach by letter or e-mail.

The Spectator

56 Doughty Street, London WC1N 2LL
☎020 7405 1706   Fax 020 7242 0603
✉ editor@spectator.co.uk
www.spectator.co.uk
Owner *The Spectator (1828) Ltd*
Editor *Boris Johnson*
Deputy Editor *Stuart Reid*
Circulation 66,105

Founded 1828. WEEKLY political and literary magazine. Prospective contributors should write in the first instance to the relevant editor. Unsolicited mss welcome, but no 'follow up' phone calls, please.

Books *Mark Amory*
PAYMENT nominal.

The Sporting Life
See **Racing Post**

Staffordshire Life
The Publishing Centre, Derby Street, Stafford ST16 2DT
☎01785 257700 Fax 01785 253287
✉ editor@staffordshirelife.co.uk
Owner *Staffordshire Newspapers Ltd*
Editor *Philip Thurlow-Craig*
Circulation 20,000
Founded 1982. ELEVEN ISSUES YEARLY. Full-colour county magazine devoted to Staffordshire, its surroundings and people. Contributions welcome. Approach in writing with ideas.
FEATURES Max. 1200 words.
PAYMENT NUJ rates.

The Stage (incorporating Television Today)
Stage House, 47 Bermondsey Street, London SE1 3XT
☎020 7403 1818 Fax 020 7357 9287
✉ editor@thestage.co.uk
www.thestage.co.uk
Owner *The Stage Newspaper Ltd*
Editor *Brian Attwood*
Circulation 29,841
Founded 1880. WEEKLY. No unsolicited mss. Prospective contributors should write with ideas in the first instance.
FEATURES Preference for middle-market, tabloid-style articles. 'Puff pieces', PR plugs and extended production notes will not be considered. Max. 800 words. Profiles: 1200 words.
NEWS News stories from outside London are always welcome. Max. 300 words.
PAYMENT £100 per 1000 words.

Stamp Lover
National Philatelic Society, 107 Charterhouse Street, London EC1M 6PT
☎020 7490 9610
✉ nps@ukphilately.org.uk
Owner *National Philatelic Society*
Editor *Michael Furnell*
Circulation 1000
Founded 1908. SIX ISSUES YEARLY. Magazine of the National Philatelic Society. Welcomes articles about the hobby; stamps, old and new. Approach by letter.
FEATURES Max. 1500 words. PAYMENT £10
NEWS Information about worldwide philately. Max. 1000 words.

Stamp Magazine
IPC Media Ltd, Leon House, 233 High Street, Croydon CR9 1HZ
☎020 8726 8000
✉ steve_fairclough@ipcmedia.com
Owner *IPC Media (A Time Warner Company)*
Editor *Steve Fairclough*
Circulation 12,000
Founded 1934. MONTHLY news and features on the world of stamp collecting from the past to the present day. Interested in articles by experts on particular countries or themes such as subject matter illustrated on stamps – dogs, politics, etc. Approach in writing.
NEWS *Deborah Lees* News of latest stamp issues or industry news. Max. 500 words.
FEATURES *Steve Fairclough* Any features welcome on famous stamps, rarities, postmarks, postal history, exhibitions, postcards, personal collections, auctions. Must be illustrated with colour images ('we can arrange for photography of original stamps'). Max. 2500 words, or 5000 for 2-part expert piece.
PAYMENT negotiable.

Stand Magazine
See under *Poetry Magazines*

Staple
See under *Poetry Magazines*

Steam Railway Magazine
Bretton Court, Bretton, Peterborough PE3 8DZ
☎01733 264666 Fax 01733 282720
✉ steam.railway@emap.com
Owner *Emap Active Limited*
Editor *Tony Streeter*
Circulation 32,831
Founded 1979. FOUR-WEEKLY magazine targeted at all steam enthusiasts interested in the modern preservation movement. Unsolicited material welcome. News reports, photographs, steam-age reminiscences. Approach in writing or by e-mail.

The Strad
Orpheus Publications, Newsquest Specialist Media Ltd, 2nd Floor, 30 Cannon Street, London EC4M 6YJ
☎020 7618 3095 Fax 020 7618 3483
✉ thestrad@orpheuspublications.com
www.thestrad.com
Owner *Newsquest Specialist Media Group*
Editor *Naomi Sadler*
Circulation 17,500

Founded 1890. MONTHLY for classical string musicians, makers and enthusiasts. Unsolicited mss accepted occasionally 'though acknowledgement/return not guaranteed'.

FEATURES Profiles of string players, teachers, luthiers and musical instruments, also relevant research. Max. 2000 words.

REVIEWS *Ariane Todes, Catherine Nelson*
PAYMENT £150 per 1000 words.

Stuff

38–42 Hampton Road, Teddington TW11 0JE
☎020 8267 5036
✉ stuff.magazine@haynet.com
www.stuffmagazine.co.uk

Owner *Haymarket Publishing Ltd*
Editor *Oliver Irish*
Circulation 74,750

Launched 1998. MONTHLY guide to new technology with information on all the latest gadgets and gear. Includes a 'Buyers' Guide' with information about the top tried and tested items. No unsolicited contributions.

Suffolk and Norfolk Life

The Publishing House, Framlingham IP13 9EE
☎01728 622030   Fax 01728 622031

Owner *Today Magazines Ltd*
Editor *Kevin Davis*
Circulation 17,000

Founded 1989. MONTHLY. General interest, local stories, historical, personalities, wine, travel, food. Unsolicited mss welcome. Approach by phone or in writing with ideas. Not interested in anything which does not relate specifically to East Anglia.

FEATURES *Kevin Davis* Max. 1500 words, with photos.

NEWS *Kevin Davis* Max. 1000 words, with photos.

SPECIAL PAGES *William Locks* Study the magazine for guidelines. Max. 1500 words.

PAYMENT £35–50.

Sugar Magazine

64 North Row, London W1K 7LL
☎020 7150 7050   Fax 020 7150 7678

Owner *Hachette Filipacchi (UK)*
Editor *Annabel Brog*
Editorial Director *Lysanne Currie*
Circulation 295,364

Founded 1994. MONTHLY. Everything that might interest the teenage girl. No unsolicited mss. Will consider ideas or contacts for real-life features. No fiction. Approach in writing in the first instance.

Sunday Times Magazine

See **The Sunday Times** under *National Newspapers*

SuperBike Magazine

IPC Media Ltd, Leon House, 233 High Street, Croydon CR9 1HZ
☎020 8774 0600
www.ipcmedia.com

Owner *IPC Media (A Time Warner Company)*
Publishing Director *Keith Foster*
Editor *Kenny Pryde*
Circulation 63,890

Founded 1977. MONTHLY. Dedicated to all that is best and most exciting in the world of high-performance motorcycling. Unsolicited mss, synopses and ideas welcome.

Sussex Life

Baskerville Place, 28 Teville Road, Worthing BN11 1UG
☎01903 218719   Fax 01903 820193
✉ jonathan.keeble@sussexlife.co.uk
www.sussexlife.com

Owner *Archant Life*
Editor *Jonathan Keeble*
Circulation 42,000

Founded 1965. MONTHLY. Sussex and general interest magazine. Regular supplements on education, fashion, homes and gardens. Interested in investigative, journalistic pieces relevant to the area and celebrity profiles. Unsolicited mss, synopses and ideas welcome but approach by telephone in the first instance.

Swimming Magazine

41 Granby Street, Loughborough LE11 3DU
☎01509 632230   Fax 01509 632233

Owner *Amateur Swimming Association*
Editor *P. Hassall*
Circulation 20,000

Founded 1923. MONTHLY about competitive swimming and associated subjects. Unsolicited mss welcome.

FEATURES Technical articles on swimming, water polo, diving or synchronised swimming. Length and payment negotiable.

The Tablet

1 King Street Cloisters, Clifton Walk, London W6 0QZ
☎020 8748 8484   Fax 020 8748 1550
✉ thetablet@tablet.co.uk
www.thetablet.co.uk

Owner *The Tablet Publishing Co Ltd*

Editor *Catherine Pepinster*
Circulation 22,274

Founded 1840. WEEKLY. Quality international Roman Catholic magazine featuring articles (political, social, cultural, theological or spiritual) of interest to concerned Christian laity and clergy.'We welcome ideas for articles; please send a brief outline in advance, setting out what you propose to write about and explaining your credentials.' Unsolicited material is not accepted.
PAYMENT from about £75.

Take a Break
Academic House, 24–28 Oval Road, London NW1 7DT
☎020 7241 8000
✉ tab.features@bauer.co.uk
Owner *H. Bauer Publishing Ltd*
Editor *John Dale*
Circulation 1.22 million

Founded 1990. WEEKLY. True-life feature magazine. Approach with ideas in writing.
NEWS/FEATURES Always on the look-out for good, true-life stories. Max. 1200 words.
FICTION Sharp, succinct stories which are well told and often with a twist at the end. All categories, provided it is relevant to the magazine's style and market. Max. 1000 words.
PAYMENT negotiable.

Tate Etc
Millbank, London SW1P 4RG
☎020 7887 8030 Fax 020 7887 8729
✉ tateetc@tate.org.uk
www.tate.org.uk
Owner *Tate*
Editorial Director *Bice Curiger*
Editor *Simon Grant*
Circulation 90,000

Relaunched May 2004. THREE ISSUES YEARLY. Visual arts magazine aimed at a broad readership with articles blending the historic and the contemporary. Please send material by post.

Tatler
Vogue House, Hanover Square, London W1S 1JU
☎020 7499 9080 Fax 020 7493 1641
www.tatler.co.uk
Owner *Condé Nast Publications Ltd*
Editor *Geordie Greig*
Circulation 86,051

Up-market glossy from the Condé Nast stable. New writers should send in copies of either

published work or unpublished material; writers of promise will be taken up. The magazine works largely on a commission basis: they are unlikely to publish unsolicited features, but will ask writers to work to specific projects.
Features Director *Vassi Chamberlain*

The Teacher
Hamilton House, Mabledon Place, London WC1H 9BD
☎020 7380 4708 Fax 020 7383 7230
✉ teacher@nut.org.uk
www.teachers.org.uk
Owner *National Union of Teachers*
Editor *Mitch Howard*
Circulation 300,000

Journal of the National Union of Teachers, published EIGHT TIMES YEARLY. News, advice, information and special features on educational matters relating to classroom teaching. Will consider 'anything on spec'. Approach by letter or e-mail.

TGO (The Great Outdoors)
Newsquest Magazines, 200 Renfield Street, Glasgow G2 3QB
☎0141 302 7700 Fax 0141 302 7799
✉ catherine.pepinster@tgomagazine.co.uk
Owner *Newsquest*
Editor *Catherine Pepinster*
Circulation 22,000

Founded 1978. MONTHLY. Deals with walking, backpacking and wild country topics. Unsolicited mss are welcome.
FEATURES Well-written and illustrated items on relevant topics. Max. 2500 words. Colour photographs only, please.
NEWS Short topical items (or photographs). Max. 300 words.
PAYMENT negotiable.

That's Life!
Academic House, 24–28 Oval Road, London NW1 7DT
☎020 7241 8000 Fax 020 7241 8008
✉ firstname.lastname@bauer.co.uk
Owner *H. Bauer Publishing Ltd*
Editor *Jo Checkley*
Circulation 601,806

Founded 1995. WEEKLY. True-life stories, puzzles, health, homes, parenting, cookery and fun.
FEATURES *Karen Bryans* Max. 1600 words.
FICTION *Emma Fabian* 1200 words.
PAYMENT features, varies; fiction, £300.

Therapy Weekly

Emap Healthcare, Greater London House, Hampstead Road, London NW1 7EJ
☎020 7874 0362   Fax 020 7874 0368
www.therapyweekly.co.uk
Owner *Emap Healthcare*
Editor *Nina Lovelace*
Circulation 15,000

Founded 1974. WEEKLY professional magazine for physiotherapists, occupational therapists and speech and language therapists. Will consider topical articles of professional interest to the reader. No fiction. Approach by telephone.

The Third Alternative

5 Martins Lane, Witcham, Ely CB6 2LB
☎01353 777931
✉ ttapress@aol.com
www.ttapress.com
Owner *TTA Press*
Editor *Andy Cox*

Founded 1993. QUARTERLY A4 colour magazine of horror, fantasy, science fiction and cross-genre fiction, plus interviews, profiles, comment, cinema and artwork. Publishes talented newcomers alongside famous authors. Unsolicited mss welcome if accompanied by s.a.e. or e-mail address for overseas submissions (no length restriction but no novels or serialisations). Queries and letters welcome via e-mail but submissions as hard copy only. Potential contributors are advised to study the magazine. Contracts are exchanged upon acceptance; payment is upon acceptance. Winner of several British Fantasy Awards.

This England

PO Box 52, Cheltenham GL50 1YQ
☎01242 537900   Fax 01242 537901
Owner *This England Ltd*
Editor *Roy Faiers*
Circulation 200,000

Founded 1968. QUARTERLY, with a strong overseas readership. Celebration of England and all things English: famous people, natural beauty, towns and villages, history, traditions, customs and legends, crafts, etc. Generally a rural basis, with the 'Forgetmenots' section publishing readers' recollections and nostalgia. Up to a hundred unsolicited pieces received each week. Unsolicited mss/ideas welcome. Length 250–2000 words.

PAYMENT £25 per 1000 words.

Time

Brettenham House, Lancaster Place, London WC2E 7TL
☎020 7499 4080
✉ edit_office@timemagazine.com
www.timeeurope.com
Owner *Time Warner*
Editor (Europe, Middle East, Africa) *Eric Pooley*
Circulation 555,205 (Europe)

Founded 1923. WEEKLY current affairs and news magazine. There are few opportunities for freelancers on *Time* as almost all the magazine's content is written by staff members from various bureaux around the world. No unsolicited mss.

Time Out

Universal House, 251 Tottenham Court Road, London W1T 7AB
☎020 7813 3000   Fax 020 7813 6001
www.timeout.com
Publisher *Lesley Gill*
Editor *Gordon Thomson*
Circulation 88,279

Founded 1968. WEEKLY magazine of news, arts, entertainment and lifestyle in London plus listings.

FEATURES *Jessica Cargill Thompson* 'Usually written by staff writers or commissioned, but it's always worth submitting an idea by post if particularly apt to the magazine.' Word length varies; up to 2000 max.

CONSUMER SECTION Fashion, shopping, travel, design, property.

PAYMENT negotiable.

The Times Educational Supplement

Admiral House, 66–68 East Smithfield, London E1W 1BX
☎020 7782 3000   Fax 020 7782 3200
✉ newsdesk@tes.co.uk *or* editor@tes.co.uk
www.tes.co.uk
Owner *News International*
Editor *Bob Doe*
Circulation 76,696

Founded 1910. WEEKLY. New contributors are welcome and should fax or e-mail ideas on one sheet of A4 for news, features or reviews, or e-mail the editor or newsdesk. The main newspaper accepts contributions in the following sections:

OPINION 'Platform': a weekly slot for a well-informed and cogently argued viewpoint. Max. 1200 words. 'Another Voice': a shorter comment on an issue of the day by non-education professionals. Max. 700 words.

LEADERSHIP Weekly pages on practical issues for school governors and managers. Max. 800 words.

FE FOCUS Weekly pull-out section covering post-16 education and training in colleges, work and the wider community. Aimed at everyone from teachers/lecturers to leaders and opinion formers in lifelong learning. News, features, comment and opinion on all aspects of college life welcome. Length from 350 words (news) to 1000 max. (features). Contact ian.nash@tes.co.uk

Friday A weekly magazine with *The TES* which focuses on whole school issues, good practice, teaching as a career and the work/life balance (friday@tes.co.uk):

FEATURES Unsolicited features are rarely accepted but ideas are welcome accompanied by cuttings and/or c.v. Length from 1000–2000 words. Strong storylines are expected.

TALKBACK Short, first person pieces, max. 650 words, are welcome for consideration. Humour from teachers is encouraged, especially for the 'Thank God it's Friday' column.

TES Teacher Weekly magazine for classroom teachers focusing on what individual teachers do in the classroom to teach pupils and subjects. Specific subject section each week. Max. 800 words. (teacher@tes.co.uk)

Online (Computers in Education) A magazine devoted to information and communications technology appearing with *The TES* six times a year. (merlin.john@tes.co.uk)

SPECIAL ISSUES Occasional pull-out magazines on topics including newly qualified teachers (fiona.flynn@tes.co.uk), business links (ian.nash@tes.co.uk), school visits – *Going Places* (thomas.watson@tes.co.uk).

The Times Educational Supplement Scotland

Scott House, 10 South St Andrew Street, Edinburgh EH2 2AZ
☎0131 557 1133 Fax 0131 558 1155
✉ scoted@tes.co.uk
www.tes.co.uk/scotland

Owner *TSL Education Ltd*
Editor *Neil Munro*
Circulation 6,600

Founded 1965. WEEKLY. Unsolicited mss welcome.

FEATURES Articles on education in Scotland. Max. 1000 words.

NEWS Items on education in Scotland. Max. 600 words.

The Times Higher Education Supplement

Admiral House, 66–68 East Smithfield, London E1W 1BX
☎020 7782 3000 Fax 020 7782 3300
✉ editor@thes.co.uk
www.thes.co.uk

Owner *News International*
Editor *John O'Leary*
Circulation 23,902

Founded 1971. WEEKLY. Unsolicited items are welcome but most articles and almost all book reviews are commissioned. 'In most cases it is better to write or e-mail, but in the case of news stories it is all right to phone.'

FEATURES *Mandy Garner* Most articles commissioned from academics in higher education.

NEWS *Lee Eliot-Major* Freelance opportunities very occasionally.

Books *Andrew Robinson*
Science *Steve Farrar*
Science Books *Andrew Robinson*
Foreign *David Jobbins*
PAYMENT by negotiation.

The Times Literary Supplement

Admiral House, 66–68 East Smithfield, London E1W 1BX
☎020 7782 3000 Fax 020 7782 3100
www.the-tls.co.uk

Owner *TSL Education Ltd*
Editor *Peter Stothard*
Circulation 34,229

Founded 1902. WEEKLY review of literature, history, philosophy, science and art. Contributors should approach in writing and be familiar with the general level of writing in the *TLS*.

Literary Discoveries *Alan Jenkins*
Poems *Mick Imlah*
NEWS Reviews and general articles concerned with literature, publishing and new intellectual developments anywhere in the world. Length by arrangement.
PAYMENT by arrangement.

Titbits

2 Caversham Street, London SW3 4AH
☎020 7351 4995 Fax 020 7351 4995

Owner *Sport Newspapers Ltd*
Editor *James Hughes*
Circulation 150,000

Founded 1895. MONTHLY. Consumer magazine for men covering show business and general interests. Ideas in writing welcome. Max. 3000 words. News, features, particularly photofeatures (colour) and fiction. Always send letter or telephone first. PAYMENT negotiable.

Today's Golfer

Bushfield House, Orton Centre, Peterborough PE2 5UW
☎01733 237111   Fax 01733 288014
Owner *Emap Active Ltd*
Editor *Andy Calton*
Associate Editor *John McKenzie*
Circulation 100,078

Founded 1988. MONTHLY. Golf instruction, features, player profiles and news. Most features written in-house but unsolicited mss will be considered. Approach in writing with ideas. Not interested in instruction material from outside contributors.

FEATURES/NEWS *Kevin Brown* Opinion, player profiles and general golf-related features.

Top of the Pops Magazine

Room A1136, Woodlands, 80 Wood Lane, London W12 0TT
☎020 8433 3910   Fax 020 8433 2694
www.beeb.com/totp
Owner *BBC Worldwide Publishing Ltd*
Editor *Peter Hart*
Circulation 200,907

Founded 1995. FORTNIGHTLY teenage pop music magazine with a lighthearted and humorous approach. No unsolicited material apart from pop star interviews.

Total Film

99 Baker Street, London W1U 6FP
☎020 7317 2600   Fax 020 7317 2642
✉ totalfilm@futurenet.co.uk
Owner *Future Publishing*
Editor *Matt Mueller*
Circulation 82,810

Founded 1997. MONTHLY reviews-based movie magazine. Interested in ideas for features, not necessarily tied in to specific releases, and humour items. No reviews or interviews with celebrities/directors. Approach by post or e-mail.

Total TV Guide

H. Bauer Publishing, Academic House, 24–28 Oval Road, London NW1 8DT
☎020 7241 8000   Fax 020 7241 8042
✉ barbara.miller@bauer.co.uk
www.bauer.co.uk
Owner *H. Bauer Publishing*
Editor *Jon Peake*
Circulation 103,560

Founded 2003. WEEKLY TV listings for those with access to multichannel television, covering everything from movies to sport, drama to children's programmes.

FEATURES *Ben Lawrence* Commissions features relating to current TV programmes; chiefly celebrity interviews and set visits. No unsolicited contributions.

Total Vauxhall

Future Publishing, 30 Monmouth Street, Bath BA1 2BW
☎01225 442244   Fax 01225 446019
✉ info@totalvauxhall.co.uk
www.totalvauxhall.co.uk
Owner *Future Publishing*
Editor *Barton Brisland*
Circulation 20,000

Founded 2001. MONTHLY independent newsstand magazine aimed at the Vauxhall enthusiast. Covers new, modified, historical/classic, race and rally Vauxhalls of all kinds. Substantial amount of technical content. Also covers the more interesting parts of the GM family, particularly Opel and Holden. Uses a lot of freelance contributors; 'those who hit deadlines and fulfill the brief get regular work and lots of it.' Feature ideas, news items, historical pieces and potential feature cars welcome but must have a Vauxhall/GM tilt. Call the editor directly for an informal discussion on style, approach and angle.

PAYMENT 'surprisingly generous'.

Traditional Woodworking

151 Station Street, Burton on Trent DE14 1BG
☎01283 742950   Fax 01283 742957
✉ enquiries@twonline.co.uk
Owner *Waterways World*
Editor *Alison Bell*
Circulation 8,034

Founded 1988. MONTHLY. Features workshop projects, techniques, reviews of the latest woodworking tools and equipment, general articles on woodworking and furniture making. Supplement: *Power Tool Guide*.

FEATURES Technical features and furniture projects welcome. The latter must include drawings and cutting lists. A photograph of the piece is required before commissioning. Approach in writing in the first instance.

PAYMENT negotiable.

Trail

Bretton Court, Bretton, Peterborough PE3 8DZ
☎01733 264666   Fax 01733 282653
www.trailroutes.com

Owner *Emap Active Publishing Ltd*
Editor *Guy Proctor*
Circulation 40,307

Founded 1990. MONTHLY. Gear reports, where to walk and practical advice for the hillwalker and long distance walker. Inspirational reads on people and outdoor/walking issues. Health, fitness and injury prevention for high level walkers and outdoor lovers. Approach by phone or in writing in the first instance.

FEATURES *Will Cockrell* Very limited requirement for overseas articles, 'written to our style'. Ask for guidelines. Max. 2000 words. Limited requirement for guided walks articles. Specialist writers only. Ask for guidelines. 750–2000 words (depending on subject).

PAYMENT £100 per 1000 words.

Traveller
45–49 Brompton Road, London SW3 1DE
☎020 7589 0500 Fax 020 7581 1357
www.traveller.org.uk

Owner *Wexas International Ltd*
Editor *Jonathan Lorie*
Deputy Editor *Amy Sohanpaul*
Circulation 37,000

Founded 1970. QUARTERLY travel magazine.

FEATURES High quality, personal narratives of remarkable journeys. Articles should be off-beat, adventurous, authentic. No mainstream destinations. For guidelines, see website. Articles may be accompanied by professional quality, original slides. Freelance articles considered. Max. 1000 words. Initial contact by e-mail.

PAYMENT £200 per 1000 words.

Trout Fisherman
EMAP Active Ltd, Bushfield House, Orton Centre, Peterborough PE2 5UW
☎01733 237111 Fax 01733 465820
✉ russell.hill@emap.com

Owner *Emap Active Ltd*
Editor *Russell Hill*
Circulation 34,553

Founded 1977. MONTHLY instructive magazine on trout fishing. Most of the articles are commissioned, but unsolicited mss and quality colour transparencies welcome.

FEATURES Max. 2500 words.
PAYMENT varies.

TVTimes
IPC Media Ltd., King's Reach Tower, Stamford Street, London SE1 9LS
☎020 7261 7000 Fax 020 7261 7888

Owner *IPC Media (A Time Warner Company)*
Editor *Mike Hollingsworth*
Circulation 473,956

Founded 1955. WEEKLY magazine of listings and features serving the viewers of independent television, BBC, satellite and radio. Freelance contributions by commission only. No unsolicited contributions.

Ulster Tatler
39 Boucher Road, Belfast BT12 6UT
☎028 9068 1371 Fax 028 9038 1915
✉ info@ulstertatler.com
www.ulstertatler.com

Owner/Editor *Richard Sherry*
Circulation 11,995

Founded 1965. MONTHLY. Articles of local interest and social functions appealing to Northern Ireland's ABC1 population. Welcomes unsolicited material; approach by phone or in writing in the first instance.

FEATURES *Noreen Dorman* Max. 1500 words.
FICTION *Richard Sherry* Max. 3000 words

Uncut
King's Reach Tower, Stamford Street, London SE1 9LS
☎020 7261 6992 Fax 020 7261 5573
✉ farah_ishaq@ipcmedia.com
www.uncut.co.uk

Owner *IPC Media (A Time Warner Company)*
Editor *Allan Jones*
Circulation 114,034

Launched 1997. MONTHLY music and film magazine with free CD each issue. Welcomes music and film reviews; approach by e-mail.

The Universe
St James's Buildings, Oxford Street, Manchester M1 6FP
☎0161 236 8856 Fax 0161 236 8892
✉ joseph.kelly@the-universe.com
www.totalcatholic.com

Owner *Gabriel Communications Ltd*
Editor *Joe Kelly*
Circulation 60,000

Occasionally uses new writers, but a substantial network of regular contributors already exists. Interested in a wide range of material: all subjects which might bear on Christian life. Fiction not normally accepted. PAYMENT negotiable.

Vector
See **British Science Fiction Association** under *Professional Associations*

The Vegan

Donald Watson House, 7 Battle Road,
St Leonards on Sea TN37 7AA
☎01424 427393   Fax 01424 717064
✉ editor@vegansociety.com
www.vegansociety.com
Owner *Vegan Society*
Editor *Catriona Toms*
Circulation 5000

Founded 1944. QUARTERLY. Deals with the ecological, ethical and health aspects of veganism. Unsolicited mss welcome. Max. 2000 words. PAYMENT negotiable.

Verbatim The Language Quarterly

PO Box 156, Chearsley, Aylesbury HP18 0DQ
☎01844 208474
✉ verbatim.uk@tesco.net
www.verbatimmag.com
Owner *Word, Inc.*
Editor *Erin McKean*

Founded in 1974 by Laurence Urdang. QUARTERLY journal devoted to what is amusing, interesting and engaging about the English language and languages in general. Will consider unsolicited material but send for writer's guidelines in the first instance. For a sample copy of the magazine, send 50p (stamp or IRC).

PAYMENT ranges from £20–300, 'depending on length, wit and other merit'.

Vogue

Vogue House, Hanover Square, London
W1S 1JU
☎020 7499 9080   Fax 020 7408 0559
www.vogue.co.uk
Owner *Condé Nast Publications Ltd*
Editor *Alexandra Shulman*
Circulation 206,834

Launched 1916. Condé Nast Magazines tend to use known writers and commission what's needed, rather than using unsolicited mss. Contacts are useful.

FEATURES *Jo Craven* Upmarket general interest rather than 'women's'. Good proportion of highbrow art and literary articles, as well as travel, gardens, food, home interest and reviews.

The Voice Newspaper

Blue Star House, 234–244 Stockwell Road, London SW9 9UG
☎020 7737 7377   Fax 020 7274 8994
✉ newsdesk@the-voice.co.uk
www.voice-online.co.uk
Deputy Managing Director *George Ruddock*

Group Editor *Deidre Forbes*
Circulation 40,000

Founded 1982. Leading WEEKLY newspaper for black Britons. Includes news, features, arts, sport and a comprehensive jobs section. Also includes a weekly glossy entertainment section. Illustrations: colour and b&w photos. Open to ideas for news and features on sport, business, community events and the arts.

Voyager

Redwood Publishing, 7 St Martin's Place, London WC2N 4HA5AD
☎020 7747 0700   Fax 020 7747 7299
✉ danlinstead@redwoodgroup.net
www.redwoodgroup.net
Owner *Redwood Group*
Editor *Dan Linstead*
Circulation 60,000

TEN ISSUES PER YEAR. In-flight magazine of bmi british midland. Lifestyle features and profiles, plus British Midland information. Approach in writing with ideas in the first instance.

walk

2nd Floor, Camelford House, 87–90 Albert Embankment, London SE1 7TW
☎020 7339 8500   Fax 020 7339 8501
✉ ramblers@london.ramblers.org.uk
Owner *Ramblers' Association*
Editor *Christopher Sparrow*
Circulation 103,689

QUARTERLY. Official magazine of the Ramblers' Association, available to members only. Unsolicited mss welcome. S.a.e. required for return.

FEATURES Freelance features are invited on any aspect of walking in Britain. Length 450–650 words, preferably with good photographs. No general travel articles.

The War Cry

101 Newington Causeway, London SE1 6BN
☎020 7367 4900   Fax 020 7367 4710
✉ warcry@salvationarmy.org.uk
www.salvationarmy.org.uk/warcry
Owner *The Salvation Army*
Editor *Major Nigel Bovey*
Circulation 58,000

Founded 1879. WEEKLY full-colour magazine containing Christian comment on current issues. Unsolicited mss welcome if appropriate to contents. No fiction or poetry. Approach by phone with ideas.

NEWS relating to Christian Church or social issues. Max. length 500 words.

FEATURES Human interest articles aimed at the 'person-in-the-street'. Max. 500 words. PAYMENT negotiable.

Wasafiri

School of English & Drama, Queen Mary, University of London, Mile End Road, London E1 4NS
☎020 7882 3120   Fax 020 7882 3120
✉ wasafiri@qmul.ac.uk
www.wasafiri.org
Editor *Susheila Nasta*
Managing Editor *Richard Dyer*
Reviews Editor *Mark Stein*

TRI-ANNUAL literary journal of African, Asian, Black British and Caribbean culture. Short stories, poetry, reviews, interviews, criticism and cross cultural debate, film and literature. Illustrations in b&w. Send double-spaced mss, in duplicate, with s.a.e. No e-mail submissions. PAYMENT negotiable.

Waterways World

151 Station Street, Burton on Trent DE14 1BG
☎01283 742950   Fax 01283 742957
✉ admin@wwonline.co.uk
Owner *Waterways World Ltd*
Editor *Hugh Potter*
Circulation 17,648

Founded 1972. MONTHLY magazine for inland waterway enthusiasts. Unsolicited mss welcome, provided the writer has a good knowledge of the subject. No fiction.

FEATURES *Hugh Potter* Articles (preferably illustrated) are published on all aspects of inland waterways in Britain and abroad, including recreational and commercial boating on rivers and canals.

NEWS *Chris Daniels* Max. 500 words.
PAYMENT £42 per 1000 words.

Web User

IPC Media, Room 0305, King's Reach Tower, Stamford Street, London SE1 9LS
☎020 7261 7294   Fax 020 7261 7878
✉ letters@web-user.co.uk
www.web-user.co.uk
Owner *IPC Media (A Time Warner Company)*
Editor *Richard Clark*
Circulation 44,211

Founded 2001. FORTNIGHTLY bestseller Internet magazine for all users of the Internet. No unsolicited material; send e-mail or letter of enquiry in the first instance.

Wedding

IPC Media Ltd., King's Reach Tower, Stamford Street, London SE1 9LS
☎020 7261 7471   Fax 020 7261 7459
✉ wedding@ipcmedia.com
Owner *IPC Media (A Time Warner Company)*
Editor *Kate Barlow*
Circulation 50,000

Founded 1985. BI-MONTHLY offering ideas and inspiration for women planning their wedding. Most features are written in-house or commissioned from known freelancers. Unsolicited mss not welcome; approach in writing.

Weekly News

D.C. Thomson & Co. Ltd., Albert Square, Dundee DD1 9QJ
☎01382 223131   Fax 01382 201390
✉ dburness@dcthomson.co.uk
Owner *D.C. Thomson & Co. Ltd*
Editor *David Burness*
Circulation 102,504

Founded 1855. WEEKLY. Newsy, family-orientated magazine designed to appeal to the busy housewife. 'We receive a lot of unsolicited articles and there is great loss of life among them.' Usually commissions, but writers of promise will be taken up. Series include showbiz, royals and television. Limited general interest fiction. PAYMENT negotiable.

Welsh Country Magazine

Aberbanc, Llandysul SA44 5NP
☎01559 372010   Fax 01559 371995
✉ editor@welshcountry.co.uk
www.welshcountry.co.uk
Owner *Equine Marketing Limited*
Editor *Kath Rhodes*
Circulation 11,500

Founded 2004. BI-MONTHLY. Outside contributions welcome. Contact the editor with samples of work before submitting full article. The magazine does have some Welsh language in it but is predominantly written in English.

FEATURES Pesonal experiences or viewpoints, historical or modern, but there needs to be a strong Welsh connection in some form.

NEWS All Welsh news welcome; anything at all commercial is not paid for.
PAYMENT negotiable.

What Car?

60 Waldegrave Road, Teddington TW11 8LG
☎020 8267 5683   Fax 020 8267 5750
✉ whatcar@haynet.com

www.whatcar.com
Owner *Haymarket Motoring Publications Ltd*
Editor *David Motton*
Circulation 137,411

MONTHLY. The car buyer's bible, *What Car?* concentrates on road test comparisons of new cars, news and buying advice on used cars, as well as a strong consumer section. Some scope for freelancers. No unsolicited mss.
PAYMENT negotiable.

What Hi-Fi? Sound & Vision
38–42 Hampton Road, Teddington TW11 0JE
☎020 8943 5000 Fax 020 8267 5019
www.whathifi.com
Owner *Haymarket Magazines Ltd*
Managing Director *Kevin Costello*
Editor *Clare Newsome*
Circulation 67,531

Founded 1976. THIRTEEN ISSUES YEARLY. Features on hi-fi and home cinema. No unsolicited contributions. Prior consultation with the editor essential.

FEATURES General or more specific items on hi-fi and home cinema pertinent to the consumer electronics market.

REVIEWS Specific product reviews. All material is now generated by in-house staff. Freelance writing no longer accepted.

What Investment
4th Floor, Arnold House, 36–41 Holywell Lane, London EC2A 3SF
☎020 7827 5454 Fax 020 7827 0567
Owner *Charterhouse Communications*
Editor-in-Chief *Keiron Root*
Circulation 37,000

Founded 1982. MONTHLY. Features articles on a variety of savings and investment matters. All approaches should be made in writing.
FEATURES Max. 2500 words.
PAYMENT NUJ rates minimum.

What Mortgage
Arnold House, 36–41 Holywell Lane, London EC2A 3SF
☎020 7827 5454 Fax 020 7827 0567
✉ vhartley@charterhouse-communications.co.uk
www.whatmortgage.co.uk
Owner *Charterhouse Communications*
Editor *Victoria Hartley*

Founded 1982. MONTHLY magazine on property purchase and finance. No unsolicited material;

prospective contributors may make initial contact with ideas either by telephone or in writing.
FEATURES Particularly welcomes new angles, ideas or specialities relevant to mortgages.
PAYMENT £200 per 1000 words.

What Satellite and Digital TV
Highbury Entertainment London, 53–79 Highgate Road, London NW5 1TW
☎020 7331 1000 Fax 020 7331 1286
✉ wotsat@wvip.co.uk
www.wotsat.com
Owner *Highbury Entertainment London*
Editor *Alex Lane*
Circulation 40,000

Founded 1986. MONTHLY including news, technical information, equipment tests, programme background, listings. Contributions welcome – phone first.

FEATURES *Alex Lane* Unusual installations and users. In-depth guides to popular/cult shows. Technical tutorials.

NEWS *Alex Lane* Industry and programming. Max. 250 words.

What's New in Building
Ludgate House, 245 Blackfriars Road, London SE1 9UY
☎020 7921 8228 Fax 020 7921 8247
✉ mpennington@cmpinformation.com
Owner *CMP Information*
Editor *Mark Pennington*
Circulation 29,000

MONTHLY. Specialist magazine covering new products for building. Unsolicited mss not generally welcome. The only freelance work available is rewriting press release material. This is offered on a monthly basis of 25–50 items of about 150 words each. PAYMENT £5.25 per item.

What's On in London
180 Pentonville Road, London N1 9JP
☎020 7278 4393 Fax 020 7837 5838
✉ editorial@whatsoninlondon.co.uk
www.whatsoninlondon.co.uk
Owner *Where to Go Ltd*
Managing Editor *Roger Foss*
Circulation 40,000

WEEKLY entertainment-based guide and information magazine. Features, celebrity interviews, listings and reviews. Always interested in well-thought-out and well-presented mss. Articles should have London/Home Counties connection, except during the summer when they can be of much wider tourist/historic interest, relating to unusual traditions and events. Approach the managing editor by telephone in the first instance.

Features *Graham Hassell*
Cinema *Jim Healy*
Pop Music *John Coleman*
Classical Music *Michael Darvell*
Theatre *Contact the Theatre Desk*
Events *Adam Lay*
Eating Out *Michael Darvell*
PAYMENT by arrangement.

Wild Times
The RSPB, UK Headquarters, The Lodge, Sandy SG19 2DL
☎01767 680551 Fax 01767 683262
✉ derek.niemann@rspb.org.uk
Owner *Royal Society for the Protection of Birds*
Editor *Derek Niemann*

Founded 1965. BI-MONTHLY. Bird, wildlife and nature conservation for under 8-year-olds (RSPB Wildlife Explorers members). No unsolicited mss. No 'captive/animal welfare' articles.
FEATURES Unsolicited material rarely used.
NEWS News releases welcome. Approach in writing in the first instance.

Wine Magazine
Quest Magazines Ltd., 6–14 Underwood Street, London N1 7JQ
☎020 7549 2572 Fax 020 7549 2550
✉ wine@wineint.com
www.wineint.com
Owner *Wilmington Publishing*
Editor *Catharine Lowe*
Circulation 35,000

Founded 1983. MONTHLY. No unsolicited mss.
NEWS/FEATURES Wine, spirits, cigars, food and food/wine-related travel stories. Prospective contributors should approach in writing.

Wingbeat
The RSPB, UK Headquarters, The Lodge, Sandy SG19 2DL
☎01767 680551 Fax 01767 683262
✉ derek.niemann@rspb.org.uk
Owner *Royal Society for the Protection of Birds*
Editor *Derek Niemann*

Founded 1965. BI-MONTHLY. Bird, wildlife and nature conservation for 14–18-year-olds (RSPB Wildlife Explorers members). No unsolicited mss. No 'captive/animal welfare' articles.
FEATURES Unsolicited material rarely used.

NEWS News releases welcome. Approach in writing in the first instance.

The Wisden Cricketer
14 Shepherds Building, Charecroft Way, London W14 0EE
☎020 7471 6900 Fax 020 7471 6901
✉ twc@wisdengroup.com
Owner *Wisden Cricketer Publishing Ltd*
Editor *John Stern*
Circulation 35,000

Founded 2003. MONTHLY. Result of a merger between *The Cricketer International* (1921) and *Wisden Cricket Monthly* (1979). Very few uncommissioned articles are used, but would-be contributors are not discouraged. Approach in writing. PAYMENT varies.

Woman
IPC Media Ltd, King's Reach Tower, Stamford Street, London SE1 9LS
☎020 7261 7023 Fax 020 7261 5997
Owner *IPC Media (A Time Warner Company)*
Editor *To be appointed*
Acting Editor *Lisa Burrow*
Circulation 527,764

Founded 1937. WEEKLY. Long-running, popular women's magazine which boasts a readership of over 2.5 million. No unsolicited mss. Most work commissioned. Approach with ideas in writing.
FEATURES *Judy Yorke* Max. 1250 words.
Books *Sue Thomas*

Woman and Home
IPC Media Ltd., King's Reach Tower, Stamford Street, London SE1 9LS
☎020 7261 5176 Fax 020 7261 7346
Owner *IPC Media (A Time Warner Company)*
Editor *Sue James*
Circulation 332,646

Founded 1926. MONTHLY. No unsolicited mss. Prospective contributors are advised to write with ideas, including photocopies of other published work or details of magazines to which they have contributed. S.a.e. essential for return of material. Most freelance work is specially commissioned.

Woman's Own
IPC Media Ltd., King's Reach Tower, Stamford Street, London SE1 9LS
☎020 7261 5500 Fax 020 7261 5346
Owner *IPC Media (A Time Warner Company)*

Editor *Elsa McAlonan*
Features Editor *Jackie Hatton*
Circulation 449,688

Founded 1932. WEEKLY. Prospective contributors should contact the features editor *in writing* in the first instance before making a submission. No unsolicited fiction.

Woman's Realm

Merged with *Woman's Weekly* in 2001.

Woman's Weekly

IPC Media Ltd., King's Reach Tower,
Stamford Street, London SE1 9LS
☎0870 444 5000   Fax 020 7261 6322

Owner *IPC Media (A Time Warner Company)*
Editor *Gilly Sinclair*
Deputy Editor *Geoffrey Palmer*
Circulation 447,696

Founded 1911. Mass-market women's WEEKLY.

FEATURES Inspiring, positive human interest stories, especially first-hand experiences, of up to 1200 words. Freelancers used regularly but only experienced magazine journalists. Synopses and ideas should be submitted in writing.

FICTION *Gaynor Davies* Short stories 1000–2500 words; serials 12,000–30,000 words. Guidelines for serials: 'a strong emotional theme with a conflict not resolved until the end'; short stories should have warmth and originality.

Woman's Weekly Fiction Special

IPC Media Ltd., King's Reach Tower,
Stamford Street, London SE1 9LS
☎020 7261 6701

Owner *IPC Media (A Time Warner Company)*
Editor *Olwen Rice*
Fiction Editor *Gaynor Davis*

Launched 1998. BI-MONTHLY. Welcomes short stories but would-be contributors should contact the Fiction Department with an s.a.e. for guidelines in the first instance.

Women & Golf

24th Floor, IPC Media Ltd., King's Reach Tower, Stamford Street, London SE1 9LS
☎020 7261 7237   Fax 020 7261 7240
✉ women&golf@ipcmedia.com

Owner *IPC Media (A Time Warner Company)*
Editor *Jane Carter*
Circulation 24,000

Founded 1991. MONTHLY consumer magazine aimed at amateur lady golfers of all ability

levels. Features and photography and news welcome; approach by e-mail or post.

Woodworker

Highbury Leisure, Berwick House, 8–10 Knoll Rise, Orpington BR6 0PS
☎01689 886656
www.getwoodworking.com

Owner *Highbury Leisure*
Editor *Mark Ramuz*
Circulation 45,000

Founded 1901. MONTHLY. Contributions welcome; approach with ideas in writing.

FEATURES Articles on woodworking with good photo support appreciated. Max. 2000 words.

PAYMENT £150+ per 1000 words.

World Fishing

Media House, Azalea Drive, Swanley BR8 8HU
☎01322 660070   Fax 01322 616324
✉ pilar.santamaria@nexusmedia.com

Owner *Highbury Business*
Editor *Pilar Santamaria*
Circulation 4185

Founded 1952. MONTHLY. Unsolicited mss welcome; approach by phone or in writing with an idea.

NEWS/FEATURES of a technical or commercial nature relating to the commercial fishing and fish processing industries worldwide (the magazine is read in 126 different countries). Max. 1500 words.

PAYMENT by arrangement.

The World of Interiors

Vogue House, Hanover Square, London W1S 1JU
☎020 7499 9080   Fax 020 7493 4013
✉ interiors@condenast.co.uk
www.worldofinteriors.co.uk

Owner *Condé Nast Publications Ltd*
Editor *Rupert Thomas*
Circulation 65,748

Founded 1981. MONTHLY. Best approach by fax or letter with an idea, preferably with reference snaps or guidebooks.

FEATURES *Rupert Thomas* Most feature material is commissioned. 'Subjects tend to be found by us, but we are delighted to receive suggestions of interiors, archives, little-known museums, collections, etc. unpublished elsewhere, and are keen to find new writers.'

World Ski and Wintersports Guide

27a High Street, Esher KT10 9RL
☎01372 468140   Fax 01372 470765
✉ info@goodholidayideas.com
Editor *John Hill*
Circulation 65,000
Founded 2002. BI-ANNUAL destination guide for skiers and winter sports enthusiasts covering the top 100 ski and winter sports resorts. No unsolicited mss. Approach with ideas and/or synopsis in writing or by e-mail. PAYMENT negotiable.

World Soccer

IPC Media Ltd., King's Reach Tower, Stamford Street, London SE1 9LS
☎020 7261 5737   Fax 020 7261 7474
✉ world_soccer@ipcmedia.com
www.worldsoccer.com
Owner *IPC Media (A Time Warner Company)*
Editor *Gavin Hamilton*
Circulation 47,922
Founded 1960. MONTHLY. Unsolicited material welcome but initial approach by e-mail or in writing. News and features on world soccer.

Writers' Forum incorporating World Wide Writers

PO Box 3229, Bournemouth BH1 1ZS
☎01202 589828   Fax 01202 587757
✉ editorial@writers-forum-com
www.worldwidewriters.com
Owner *Writers International Ltd*
Editor *John Jenkins*
Deputy Editor *Mary Hogarth*
Founded 1993. MONTHLY. Magazine covers all aspects of the craft of writing. Well written articles welcome. Write to the editor in the first instance.

Writers Forum Short Story Competition Prizes: £300 (1st), £150 (2nd), £100 (3rd) with an annual trophy and a cheque for £1,000 for the best story of the year. Entrance fee: non-subscribers: £10; subscribers: £6. Winners published in every issue.

Writers' Forum Poetry Competition First prize £100; runners up receive a dictionary. Entrance fee: £5 for one poem or £7 for two. Winners published in every issue. Annual subscription: £33 UK; £44 Worldwide. Send s.a.e. with 66p in stamps for free back issue.

Writers' News/Writing Magazine

First Floor, Victoria House, 143–144 The Headrow, Leeds LS1 5RL
☎0113 200 2929   Fax 0113 200 2928
www.writersnews.co.uk
Owner *Warners Group Publications plc*
Publishing Editor *Derek Hudson*
Founded 1989. MONTHLY magazines containing news and advice for writers. *Writers' News* is exclusive to mail-order members who also receive *Writing Magazine*, a full-colour glossy publication, which is available on newsstands. No poetry or general items on 'how to become a writer'. Receive 1000 mss each year. Approach in writing or by e-mail.

NEWS Exclusive news stories of interest to writers. Max. 350 words.

FEATURES How-to articles of interest to professional writers. Max. 1000 words.

Yachting Monthly

IPC Media Ltd., King's Reach Tower, Stamford Street, London SE1 9LS
☎020 7261 6040   Fax 020 7261 7555
✉ paul_gelder@ipcmedia.com
www.yachtingmonthly.com
Owner *IPC Media (A Time Warner Company)*
Editor *Paul Gelder*
Circulation 36,174
Founded 1906. MONTHLY magazine for yachting and cruising enthusiasts – not racing. Unsolicited mss welcome, but many are received and not used. Prospective contributors should make initial contact in writing.

FEATURES A wide range of features concerned with maritime subjects and cruising under sail; well-researched and innovative material always welcome, especially if accompanied by colour transparencies. Max. 1800 words.

PAYMENT £80–110 per 1000 words.

Yachting World

IPC Media Ltd., King's Reach Tower, Stamford Street, London SE1 9LS
☎020 7261 6800   Fax 020 7261 6818
✉ yachtingworld@ipcmedia.com
www.yachtingworld.com
Owner *IPC Media (A Time Warner Company)*
Editor *Andrew Bray*
Circulation 28,699
Founded 1894. MONTHLY with international coverage of yacht racing, cruising and yachting events. Will consider well researched and written sailing stories. Preliminary approaches should be by phone for news stories and in writing for features.

PAYMENT by arrangement.

Yorkshire Women's Life Magazine
PO Box 113, Leeds LS8 2WX
✉ ywlmagenquiries@btinternet.com
Editor/Owner *Dawn Maria France*
Fashion *Sky Taylor*
Magazine PA *Anna Jenkins*
Diary *Giles Smith*

Founded 2001. THREE ISSUES YEARLY. Features of interest to women along with regional, national, international news and lifestyle articles. Past issues have covered anorexia nervosa, mental health, stress management, children in US chain gangs, women living in pain, Windrush awards. 'It is important to study the style of the magazine before submitting material. Send A4 s.a.e. with 46p stamp for copy of submission guidelines. Unsolicited mss and new writers actively encouraged; approach in writing in the first instance with s.a.e.' Magazine available on subscription.

You & Your Wedding
National Magazine Company, 72 Broadwick Street, London W1F 9EP
☎020 7439 5000 (editorial)
Fax 020 7439 2985

Owner *The National Magazine Company Ltd*
Editor *Carole Hamilton*
Circulation 62,145

Founded 1985. BI-MONTHLY. Anything relating to weddings, setting up home, and honeymoons. No unsolicited mss. Submit ideas by e-mail only, especially travel features. No phone calls.

You – The Mail on Sunday Magazine
See **The Mail on Sunday** under *National Newspapers*

Young Voices
Voice Group Limited, Blue Star House, 234–244 Stockwell Road, London SW9 9UG
☎020 7737 7377 Fax 020 7274 8894
www.young-voices.co.uk
Editor-in-Chief *Deidre Forbes*
Editor *Emelia Kenlock*

Founded 2003. MONTHLY glossy magazine aimed at 11–19-year-olds. 'Provides a new outlet for today's youth.' Latest news features, showbiz insight and reviews. Also covers current affairs topics that affect readers' lives.

Young Writer
Glebe House, Weobley, Hereford HR4 8SD
☎01544 318901 Fax 01544 318901
✉ editor@youngwriter.org

www.youngwriter.org
Editor *Kate Jones*

Describing itself as 'The Magazine for Children with Something to Say', *Young Writer* is issued three times a year, at the back-to-school times of September, January and April. A forum for young people's writing – fiction and non-fiction, prose and poetry – the magazine is an introduction to independent writing for young writers aged 5–18. PAYMENT from £20 to £100 for freelance commissioned articles (these can be from adult writers).

Your Cat Magazine
Roebuck House, 33 Broad Street, Stamford PE9 1RB
☎01780 766199 Fax 01780 766416
✉ yourcat@bournepublishinggroup.co.uk
www.yourcat.co.uk
Owner *BPG (Stamford) Ltd*
Editor *Sue Parslow*

Founded 1994. MONTHLY magazine giving practical information on the care of cats and kittens, pedigree and non-pedigree, plus a wide range of general interest items on cats. Will consider 'true life' cat stories (max. 900 words) and quality fiction. Send synopsis in the first instance. 'No articles written as though by a cat.'

Your Dog Magazine
Roebuck House, 33 Broad Street, Stamford PE9 1RB
☎01780 766199 Fax 01780 766416
Owner *BPG (Stamford) Ltd*
Editor *Sarah Wright*
Circulation 26,000

Founded 1995. MONTHLY. Practical advice for pet dog owners. Will consider practical features and some personal experiences (no highly emotive pieces or fiction). Telephone in the first instance.
NEWS Max. 300–400 words.
FEATURES Max. 2500 words; limited opportunities.
PAYMENT negotiable.

Your Horse
Bretton Court, Bretton, Peterborough PE3 8DZ
☎01733 264666 Fax 01733 465200
www.yourhorse.co.uk
Owner *Emap Active Ltd*
Editor *Natasha Simmonds*
Circulation 56,030

'The magazine that aims to make owning and

riding horses more rewarding.' Most writing produced in-house but well-targeted articles will always be considered.

Yours Magazine

Emap Esprit, Bretton Court, Bretton, Peterborough PE3 8DZ
☎01733 264666   Fax 01733 465266

Owner *Emap Esprit*
Editor *Valery McConnell*
Circulation 438,872

Founded 1973. MONTHLY plus various special issues. Aimed at a readership aged 50 and over.
FEATURES Unsolicited mss welcome but must enclose s.a.e. Max. 1500 words.
FICTION One or two short stories used in each issue. Max. 1500 words.
PAYMENT negotiable.

Zembla Magazine

319 Portobello Road, London W10 5SY
☎020 8969 4333
✉ mail@zemblamagazine.com
www.zemblamagazine.com

Owners *Simon Finch, Dan Crowe*
Editor *Dan Crowe*
Circulation 30,000

Founded 2003. BI-MONTHLY literary magazine featuring fiction, non-fiction, reviews, interviews and 'all sorts of fun with words'. Welcomes fiction and non-fiction ideas and review material. Approach by e-mail in the first instance.

Zest

National Magazine House, 72 Broadwick Street, London W1F 9EP
☎020 7439 5000   Fax 020 7312 3750
✉ zest.mail@natmags.co.uk
www.zest.co.uk

Owner *National Magazine Company*
Editor *Alison Pylkkanen*
Deputy Editors *Rebecca Frank, Susie Whalley*
Circulation 110,764

Founded 1994. MONTHLY. Health, beauty, fitness, nutrition and general well-being. No unsolicited mss. Prefers ideas in synopsis form; approach in writing.

Zoo

Emap Consumer Media, Endeavour House, 189 Shaftesbury Avenue, London WC2H 8JG
☎020 7437 9011
www.zooweekly.co.uk

Owner *Emap Consumer Media*
Editor *Paul Merrill*
Circulation 240,215

Launched 2004. WEEKLY men's lifestyle magazine featuring showbiz, sport, humour, sex, fashion and news. Will consider ideas; see 'Work for Us' page on the website for freelance guidelines.

News Agencies

Associated Press Limited
12 Norwich Street, London EC4A 1BP
☎020 7353 1515
Fax 020 7353 8118 (Newsdesk)

Material is either generated in-house or by regulars. Hires the occasional stringer. No unsolicited mss.

Dow Jones Newswires
10 Fleet Place, London EC4M 7QN
☎020 7842 9900   Fax 020 7842 9361

A real-time financial and business newswire operated by Dow Jones & Co., publishers of *The Wall Street Journal*. No unsolicited material.

Hayters Teamwork Sports Agency
6 Sharman Walk, Apperknowle, Sheffield S18 4BJ
☎01246 414767/07970 284848 (mobile)
Fax 01246 414767
✉ Nicksport1@aol.com

Contact *Nick Johnson*

Provides written/broadcast coverage of sport in the South Yorkshire area.

National News Press and Photo Agency
4–5 Academy Buildings, Fanshaw Street, London N1 5LQ
☎020 7684 3000   Fax 020 7684 3030
✉ news@nationalnews.co.uk

All press releases are welcome. Most work is ordered or commissioned. Coverage includes courts, tribunals, conferences, general news, etc. – words and pictures – as well as PR.

Press Association Ltd
292 Vauxhall Bridge Road, London SW1V 1AE
☎020 7963 7000   Fax 020 7963 7090
✉ copy@pa.press.net

www.pa.press.net

No unsolicited material. Most items are produced in-house though occasional outsiders may be used. A phone call to discuss specific material may lead somewhere 'but this is rare'.

Reuters
30 South Colonnade, Canary Wharf, London E14 5EU
☎020 7250 1122

No unsolicited material.

Solo Syndication Ltd
17–18 Hayward's Place, London EC1R 0EQ
☎020 7566 0360   Fax 020 7566 0388
✉ tyork@solosyndication.com
www.solosyndication.com

Founded 1978. Specialises in worldwide newspaper syndication of photos, features and cartoons. Professional contributors only.

Space Press News and Pictures
Bridge House, Blackden Lane, Goostrey CW4 8PZ
☎01477 533403   Fax 01477 535756
✉ Scoop2001@aol.com

Editor *John Williams*
Pictures *Emma Williams*

Founded 1972. Press and picture agency covering Cheshire and the North West, North Midlands, including Knutsford, Macclesfield, Congleton, Crewe and Nantwich, Wilmslow, Alderley Edge, serving national, regional and local press, TV, radio, and digital picture transmission. Copy and pictures produced for in-house publications and PR. Property, countryside and travel writing. A member of the National Association of Press Agencies (NAPA).

Television and Radio

For the latest information on broadcast rates for freelancers access the following websites: the National Union of Journalists' 'The Rate for the Job' database link (www.gn.apc.org/media); the Producers Alliance for Cinema and Television (www.pact.co.uk); the Society of Authors (www.societyofauthors.org); and the Writers' Guild (www.writersguild.org.uk).

BBC TV and Radio

www.bbc.co.uk
Director-General *Mark Thompson*
Deputy Director-General *Mark Byford*

The BBC structure consists of the following: Television Division - responsible for the network television channels and for commissioning in most genres; Drama, Entertainment and Children's; Factual and Learning; Radio and Music; News; Sport; Nations and Regions; and the New Media division which develops the BBC's interactive television and online activities.

TELEVISION
BBC Television Centre, Wood Lane, London W12 7RJ
☎020 8743 8000

TV commissioning:
www.bbc.co.uk/commissioning/structure

Director, Television *Jana Bennett*
Controller, BBC1 *Peter Fincham*
Controller, BBC2 *Roly Keating*
Controller, Daytime *Alison Sharman*
DIGITAL TELEVISION
Controller, BBC Three *Stuart Murphy*
Controller, BBC Four *Janice Hadlow*

BBC Three, launched in 2003, broadcasts a wide range of entertainment aimed at a 25–34-year-old audience. BBC Four, launched in 2002, is devoted solely to the arts. Programmes include *Readers and Writers*, a weekly book programme.

RADIO
Broadcasting House, Portland Place, London W1A 1AA
☎020 7580 4468

Radio commissioning:
www.bbc.co.uk/commissioning/structure/ process_radio.shtml

Radio 4 proposals must be submitted through an in-house department or a registered inde-

pendent production company (list available on website above).

Director of Radio & Music *Jenny Abramsky*
Controller, Radio 1 *Andy Parfitt*
Executive Producer, Speech & Campaigns Radio 1 *Sam Steele*
Controller, Radio 2 & 6 Music *Lesley Douglas*
Commissions & Schedules Manager, Radio 2 *Julian Grundy*
Controller, Radio 3 *Roger Wright*
Commissions & Schedules Manager, Radio 3 *David Ireland*
Controller, Radio 4 & BBC 7 *Mark Damazer*
Controller, Radio 5 Live *Bob Shennan*
Commissioning Editor, Radio 5 Live *Moz Dee*

DIGITAL RADIO
BBC 1Xtra
BBC Five Live Sports Extra
BBC 6 Music
BBC 7 (comedy, drama and books)
BBC Asian Network

Drama, Entertainment and Children's Division

Creative Director *Alan Yentob*

BBC *writersroom* champions new writers across all BBC platforms for Drama, Comedy and CBBC, running targeted schemes and workshops linked directly to production. It accepts and assesses unsolicited scripts for film, TV drama, narrative comedy and radio drama. The *writersroom* website (www.bbc.co.uk/writersroom) offers a diary of events, opportunities, competitions, interviews with established writers, submission guidelines and free formatting software. BBC *writersroom* also runs *northern exposure* which focuses on new writing in the north of England. Writers should address hard copies of original, completed scripts to: Development Manager, BBC *writersroom*, 1 Mortimer Street, London W1T 3JA. Before sending in scripts, please log on to the website, or send a large s.a.e. to *writersroom* at the Mortimer

Street address above for the latest guidelines on submitting unsolicited work. See also www.bbc.co.uk/commissioning/structure/public.shtml

DRAMA

Controller, Drama Commissioning *Jane Tranter*
Controller, Continuing Drama Series/Head of Independent Drama *John Yorke*
Head of Drama Series and Serials *Laura Mackie*
Acting Head of Development, Drama Series and Serials *Lisa Osborne*
Head of Films and Single Drama *David Thompson*
Creative Director, New Writing *Kate Rowland*
Head of Radio Drama *Alison Hindell*
Executive Producer (Birmingham) & Editor, The Archers *Vanessa Whitburn*
Executive Producer (World Service Drama) *Marion Nancarrow*
Executive Producer (Manchester) *Sue Roberts*

ENTERTAINMENT

Controller, Entertainment Commissioning *Jane Lush*
Acting Head of Comedy Commissioning *Lucy Lumsden*
Commissioning Executive *Lucy Lumsden*
Head of Comedy Entertainment, Television *Jon Plowman*
Head of Comedy *Sophie Clarke-Jervoise*
Editor, Comedy Development *Micheal Jacob*
Head of Radio Entertainment *John Pidgeon*

CBBC (CHILDREN'S)

Controller, CBBC *Alison Sharman*
Head of CBBC Drama *Elaine Sperber*
Head of Entertainment *Anne Gilchrist*
Head of CBBC Pre-school *Clare Elstow*
Head of CBBC Education *Sue Nott*
Head of CBBC Creates *Amanda Gabbitas*

Factual and Learning Division

Director, Factual TV & Learning *John Willis*
Controller, Learning & Interactive *Liz Cleaver*
Controller, Documentaries and Contemporary Factual *Anne Morrison*
Commissioner, Specialist Factual *Keith Scholey*

News Division

www.bbc.co.uk/news
news.bbc.co.uk

BBC News is the world's largest news-gathering organisation with over 2500 journalists, 45 bureaux worldwide and 15 networks and services across TV, radio and new media.

Director, News *Helen Boaden*

Controller of Production/Deputy Director, News *Adrian Van Klaveren*
Head of Current Affairs *Peter Horrocks*
Head of Newsgathering *Fran Unsworth*
Head of News Interactive *Richard Deverell*
Head of Political Programmes, Analysis and Research *Sue Inglish*
Head of Radio News *Stephen Mitchell*
Head of Television News *Roger Mosey*
Deputy Head of Television News *Rachel Attwell*

TELEVISION

Editor, 1 o'clock News *Chris Rybczynski*
Editor, 6 o'clock News *Amanda Farnsworth*
Editor, 10 o'clock News *Kevin Bakhurst*
Editor, Newsnight *Peter Barron*
Editor, Breakfast *David Kermode*
Editor, Breakfast With Frost *Barney Jones*
Editor, This World *Karen O'Connor*
Managing Editor, World Service News Programmes *Alan Le Breton*

RADIO

Editor, Today *Kevin Marsh*
Editor, The World at One/World This Weekend *Colin Hancock*
Editor, PM/Broadcasting House *Peter Rippon*
Head of News, Five Live *Matt Morris*
Editor, The World Tonight *Alistair Burnett*

CEEFAX

Room 7540, BBC Television Centre, Wood Lane, London W12 7RJ
☎020 8576 1801

Editor, Ceefax *Paul Brannan*

SUBTITLING

Room BC3A5, Broadcast Centre, Wood Lane, London W12 7TP
☎020 8008 0596/0141 339 8844 ext. 2128

A rapidly expanding service available via Ceefax page 888. Units based in both London and Glasgow.

Sport Division

Acting Director, Sport *Dave Gordon*

Sports news and commentaries across television and Radios 1, 4 and 5 Live, with the majority of output on Radio 5 Live.

BBC Religion

New Broadcasting House, Oxford Road, Manchester M60 1SJ
☎0161 200 2020   Fax 0161 244 3183

Head of Religion and Ethics *Alan Bookbinder*

Regular programmes for television include *Heaven & Earth*; *Songs of Praise*; *A Seaside Parish*.

Radio output includes *Good Morning Sunday*; *Sunday Half Hour, Thought for the Day*; *The Daily Service.*

BBC New Talent
www.bbc.co.uk/newtalent

The BBC's search for new talent covers a constantly changing range of outlets that has included radio producers, presenters, young storytellers, filmmakers and comedy writers. Access the website for latest information.

BBC World Service
PO Box 76, Bush House, Strand, London WC2B 4PH
☎020 7240 3456 Fax 020 7557 1900
www.bbc.co.uk/worldservice

Director, World Service *Nigel Chapman*
Director, English Networks & News, BBCWS *Phil Harding*

The World Service broadcasts in English and 42 other languages. The English service is round-the-clock, with news and current affairs as the main component. With over 145 million listeners, excluding countries where research is not possible, it reaches a bigger audience than its five closest competitors combined. The World Service is increasingly available throughout the world on local FM stations, via satellite and online as well as through short-wave frequencies. Coverage includes world business, politics, people/events/opinions, development issues, the international scene, developments in science and technology, sport, religion, music, the arts. BBC World Service broadcasting is financed by a grant-in-aid voted by Parliament amounting to £225 million for 2004/2005.

BBC writersroom
See **Drama, Entertainment and Children's Division**

BBC Nations

BBC Northern Ireland
Broadcasting House, Ormeau Avenue, Belfast BT2 8HQ
☎028 9033 8000
www.bbc.co.uk/northernireland

Controller *Anna Carragher*
Head of Broadcasting *Peter Johnston*
Managing Editor, Television *Peter McCann*
Head of Programme Operations *Stephen Beckett*

Head of News & Current Affairs *Andrew Colman*
Editor, News Gathering *Michael Cairns*
Editor, Television News *Angelina Fusco*
Editor, Radio News *Kathleen Carragher*
Head of Drama *Patrick Spence*
Head of Programme Production *Mike Edgar*
Editor, Entertainment *Alex Johnston*
Editor, Sport *Edward Smith*
Head of Creative Development *Bruce Batten*
Head of Interactive Services & Learning *Kieran Hegarty*
Managing Editor, Radio *Susan Lovell*
Producer, Religion *Bert Tosh*
Editor, Political Programmes *Lena Ferguson*
Managing Editor, Foyle *Ana Leddy*

Regular television programmes include *BBC Newsline 6.30* and a wide range of documentary, popular factual and entertainment programmes. Radio stations: BBC Radio Foyle and BBC Radio Ulster (see entries). For further details on television and film scripts contact: *Susan Carson*, Development Co-ordinator Television, BBC Northern Ireland Drama, Room 3.07, Blackstaff House, Great Victoria Street, Belfast, BT2 7BB. (☎028 9033 8498 ✉ tvdrama.ni@bbc.co.uk) Radio scripts contact: *Anne Simpson*, Manager, Radio Drama at the same address.

BBC Scotland
Broadcasting House, Queen Margaret Drive, Glasgow G12 8DG
☎0141 338 2000
www.bbc.co.uk/scotland

Controller *Ken MacQuarrie*
Head of Programme and Services *Donalda MacKinnon and Maggie Cunningham*
Head of Drama, Television *Barbara McKissack*
Head of Drama, Radio *Patrick Rayner*
Head of Factual Programmes *Andrea Miller*
Head of Gaelic *Margaret Mary Murray*
Head of Radio *Jeff Zycinski*
Head of News and Current Affairs *Blair Jenkins*
Commissioning Editor, Television *Ewan Angus*

Headquarters of BBC Scotland with centres in Aberdeen, Dundee, Edinburgh, Dumfries, Inverness, Orkney, Shetland and Stornaway. Regular and recent programmes include *Reporting Scotland, Sportscene* and *Monarch of the Glen* on television and *Good Morning Scotland* and *Fred Macaulay* on radio.

Aberdeen
Broadcasting House, Beechgrove Terrace, Aberdeen AB9 2ZT
☎01224 625233

Dundee
Nethergate Centre, 66 Nethergate, Dundee
DD1 4ER
☎01382 202481

Edinburgh
The Tun, Holyrood Road, Edinburgh EH8 8JF
☎0131 557 5677

Dumfries
Elmbank, Lover's Walk, Dumfries DG1 1NZ

Inverness
7 Culduthel Road, Inverness 1V2 4ADT
☎01463 720720
Editor *Ishbel MacLennan*

Orkney
Castle Street, Kirkwall, Orkney KW15 1DF

Shetland
Pitt Lane, Lerwick, Shetland ZE1 0DW

Stornaway
Rosebank, Church Street, Stornoway, Isle of
Lewis PA87 2LS
☎01851 705000

Radio Nan Gaidheal
Rosebank, Church Street, Stornoway, Isle of
Lewis PA87 2LS
☎01851 705000

BBC Wales
Broadcasting House, Llandaff CF5 2YQ
☎029 2032 2000   Fax 029 2055 2973
www.bbc.co.uk/wales

Controller *Menna Richards*
Head of Programmes (Welsh Language) *Keith Jones*
Head of Programmes (English Language) *Clare Hudson*
Head of News & Current Affairs *Mark O'Callaghan*
Head of Drama *Julie Gardner*
Commissioning Editor, Independents and BBC2W *Martyn Ingram*
Producer, Pobol y Cwm *Bethan Jones*
Editor, New Media *Iain Tweedale*

Headquarters of BBC Wales, with regional centres in Bangor, Aberystwyth, Carmarthen, Wrexham and Swansea. BBC Wales television produces up to 12 hours of English language programmes a week, 12 hours in Welsh for transmission on **S4C** and an increasing number of hours on network services. BBC2W, the digital channel, was launched in 2001. Regular programmes include *Wales Today*; *Newyddion* (Welsh-language daily news); *Week In Week Out*, *The Exchange* and *Pobol y Cwm* (Welsh-language soap)

on television and *Good Morning Wales*; *Good Evening Wales*; *Post Cyntaf* and *Post Prynhawn* on Radio Wales and Radio Cymru. Ideas for programmes should be submitted either by post to *Martyn Ingram*, Commissioning Editor, Room 3021 at the address above or by e-mail to commissioning@bbc.co.uk

Bangor
Broadcasting House, Meirion Road, Bangor
LL57 2BY
☎01248 370880 Fax 01248 351443
Head of Centre *Marian Wyn Jones*

BBC Regions

BBC Asian Network
The Mailbox, Birmingham B1 1RF
☎0121 567 6767
✉ asian.network@bbc.co.uk
www.bbc.co.uk/asiannetwork
Managing Editor *Vijay Sharma*

Commenced broadcasting in November 1996. Broadcasts to a Midlands audience during the day and nationwide coverage in the evening. Programmes in English, Bengali, Gujerati, Hindi, Punjabi and Urdu.

BBC Birmingham
The Mailbox, Birmingham B1 1RF
☎0121 567 6767   Fax 0121 567 6875
www.bbc.co.uk/birmingham
Head of Regional and Local Programmes
   David Holdsworth
Output Editor *Charles Watkin*

Output for the network includes: TELEVISION *Coast*; *Doctors*; *Countryfile*; *Top Gear*; *Dalziel and Pascoe*; *Gardener's World*; *Big Strong Boys*; *Trading Up*. RADIO *The Archers*; *Shake, Rattle and Roll*; *Farming Today*; *Late Night Currie*; *Ramblings With Clare Balding*.

BBC East Midlands (Nottingham)
East Midlands Broadcasting Centre, London Road, Nottingham NG2 4UU
☎0115 955 0500 Fax 0115 902 1983
www.bbc.co.uk/nottingham
Head of Regional Programming *Alison Ford*
Output Editor *Lisa Lambden*

BBC East (Norwich)
The Forum, Millennium Plain, Norwich
NR2 1AW
☎01603 284700 Fax 01603 284399

Website www.bbc.co.uk/norfolk
Head of Regional Programming *Tim Bishop*
Output Editor *Dave Betts*

BBC Bristol

Broadcasting House, Whiteladies Road, Bristol
BS8 2LR
☎0117 973 2211

Managing Editor *Jenny Lacey*
Head of General Factual & Learning *Tom Archer*
Head of Natural History Unit *Neil Nightingale*

BBC Bristol is the home of the BBC's Natural History Unit, producing programmes such as *Blue Planet*; *Life of Mammals*; *British Isles, A Natural History*; *Abyss* and *The Really Wild Show* for BBC1 and BBC2. It also produces natural history programmes for Radio 4 and Radio 5 Live. The Factual department produces a wide range of television programmes, including *DIY SOS*; *Antiques Roadshow*; *Bargain Hunt* and *Life of Grime* in addition to radio programmes specialising in history, travel, literature and human interest features for Radio 4.

BBC London

35 Marylebone High Street, London
W1U 4QA
☎020 7224 2424
www.bbc.co.uk/london

Executive Editor *Mike MacFarlane*
   (Responsible for BBC tri-media: BBC London News, BBC London 94.9FM and the BBC London website)
Planning Editor *Duncan Williamson*

BBC South East (Tunbridge Wells)

The Great Hall, Mount Pleasant, Tunbridge Wells TN1 1QQ
☎01892 670000

Head of Regional and Local Programmes
   Mike Hapgood (Responsible for BBC South East [TV], BBC Radio Kent and BBC Southern Counties Radio)
Editor, South East Today *Quentin Smith*
Managing Editor, Southern Counties Radio *Neil Pringle*
Managing Editor, Radio Kent *Paul Leaper*
Editor, Newsgathering *Talya Robertson*
Producer, Inside Out *Linda Bell*

BBC West/BBC South/ BBC South West

The three regional television stations, BBC West, BBC South and BBC South West pro-duce the lunchtime and nightly news magazine programmes, as well as regular 30-minute local current affairs programmes and parliamentary programmes. Each of the regions operates a comprehensive local radio service as well as a range of correspondents specialising in subjects such as health, education, business, local government, home affairs and the environment.

BBC West (Bristol)

Broadcasting House, Whiteladies Road, Bristol
BS8 2LR
☎0117 973 2211

Head of Regional and Local Programmes
   Andrew Wilson (Responsible for the BBC West region. TV: BBC Points West (regional news programme), Inside Out West (regional current affairs series) and The Politics Show West. Local Radio: BBC Radio Bristol, BBC Somerset Sound, BBC Radio Gloucestershire, BBC Radio Wiltshire, BBC Radio Swindon and the regional BBC Where I Live websites)
Daily TV Output Editors *Jane Kinghorn, Stephanie Marshall*
TV Features Editor *Roger Farrant*
Political Editor *Dave Harvey*

BBC South (Southampton)

Broadcasting House, Havelock Road,
Southampton SO14 7PU
☎023 8022 6201

Head of Regional and Local Programmes *Eve Turner* (Responsible for BBC South TV, BBC Radio Berkshire, BBC Radio Oxford, BBC Radio Solent and BBCi Southampton)
Output Editor, BBC South Today *Lee Desty*
Newsgathering Editor *Cathy Burnett*
Series Producer, Inside Out *Jane French*

BBC South West (Plymouth)

Broadcasting House, Seymour Road,
Mannamead, Plymouth PL3 5BD
☎01752 229201

Head of Regional and Local Programmes *John Lilley* (Responsible for the BBC South West region. TV: BBC Spotlight (regional news programme), Inside Out (regional current affairs series) and The Politics Show South West. Local Radio: BBC Radio Devon, BBC Radio Cornwall, BBC Radio Guernsey, BBC Radio Jersey and the regional BBC Where I Live websites)
Output Editor *Simon Read*
Series Producer *Simon Willis*

BBC Yorkshire/BBC North West/ BBC North East & Cumbria

The regional centres at Leeds, Manchester and Newcastle make their own programmes on a bi-media approach, each centre having its own head of regional and local programmes.

BBC Yorkshire

Broadcasting Centre, 2 St Peter's Square, Leeds LS9 8AH
☎0113 244 1188

Head of Regional and Local Programmes
Tamsin O'Brien
Editor, Newsgathering *Kate Watkins*
Output Editor, Look North Yorkshire *Jake Fowler*/Acting Editor *Gary Keown*
Output Editor, Look North East Yorkshire and Lincolnshire *Steve Punter*
Assistant News Editors, Look North *Denise Wallace*/Acting Editor *Graham Moorby*
Political Editor, North of Westminster *Len Tingle*
Senior Broadcast Journalist, North of Westminster *Rod Jones*
Weeklies Editor, Close Up North *Ian Cundall*
Producers, Close Up North *Richard Taylor, Paul Greenan*

BBC North West (Manchester)

New Broadcasting House, Oxford Road, Manchester M60 1SJ
☎0161 200 2020

Head of Regional and Local Programmes
Martin Brooks
Editor, Newsgathering *Michelle Mayman*
Output Editor *Cerys Griffiths*
Producer, Northwest Tonight *Jim Clarke*
Producer, Inside Out *Deborah van Bishop*
Producer, The Politics Show *Liam Fogarty*

BBC North East & Cumbria (Newcastle upon Tyne)

Broadcasting Centre, Barrack Road, Newcastle Upon Tyne NE99 2NE
☎0191 232 1313

Head of Regional and Local Programmes
Wendy Pilmer
Editor, Newsgathering *Andrew Lambert*
Output Editor, Look North *Andy Cooper*

BBC Local Radio

There are 40 local BBC radio stations in England transmitting on FM and medium wave. These present local news, information and entertainment to local audiences and reflect the life of the communities they serve. Each has its own newsroom which supplies local bulletins and national news service. Many have specialist producers. A comprehensive list of programmes for each is unavailable and would soon be out of date. For general information on programming, contact the relevant station direct.

BBC Radio Berkshire

PO Box 104.4, Reading RG4 8FH
☎0118 9464200   Fax 0118 9464555
www.bbc.co.uk/berkshire
Editor *Marianne Bell*

BBC Radio Bristol

PO Box 194, Bristol BS99 7QT
☎0117 974 1111   Fax 0117 923 8323
✉ radio.bristol@bbc.co.uk
www.bbc.co.uk/england/radiobristol
Managing Editor *Jenny Lacey*
Wide range of feature material used.

BBC Radio Cambridgeshire

104 Hills Road, Cambridge CB2 1LD
☎01223 259696   Fax 01223 460832
✉ cambs@bbc.co.uk
www.bbc.co.uk/radiocambridgeshire
Editor *David Martin*
Commenced broadcasting in May 1982.

BBC Radio Cleveland

PO Box 95FM, Broadcasting House, Newport Road, Middlesbrough TS1 5DG
☎01642 225211   Fax 01642 211356
✉ bbcradiocleveland@bbc.co.uk
www.bbc.co.uk/england/radiocleveland
Managing Editor *Andrew Glover*
Material used is mainly local to Teesside, Co. Durham and North Yorkshire, and is almost exclusively news and current affairs.

BBC Radio Cornwall

Phoenix Wharf, Truro TR1 1UA
☎01872 275421   Fax 01872 240679
✉ radio.cornwall@bbc.co.uk
www.bbc.co.uk/radiocornwall
Editor *Pauline Causey*
On air from 1983 serving Cornwall and the Isles of Scilly. Broadcasts 117 hours of local programmes weekly including news, phone-ins and specialist music.

BBC Coventry and Warwickshire

Priory Place, Coventry CV1
✉ coventry.warwickshire@bbc.co.uk

www.bbc.co.uk/coventrywarwickshire

Managing Editor *David Clargo*

Commenced broadcasting in January 1990 as CWR. News, current affairs, public service information and community involvement, relevant to its broadcast area. (Moving to new premises in September 2005; phone number unavailable at time of going to press.)

BBC Radio Cumbria

Annetwell Street, Carlisle CA3 8BB
☎01228 592444   Fax 01228 511195
✉ cumbria@bbc.co.uk
www.bbc.co.uk/cumbria

Editor *Nigel Dyson*

Occasional opportunities for plays and short stories are advertised on-air.

BBC Radio Cymru

Broadcasting House, Llandaff, Cardiff CF5 2YQ
☎029 20 322018   Fax 029 20 322473
✉ radio.cymru@bbc.co.uk
www.bbc.co.uk/radiocymru

Editor *Aled Glynne Davies*

Welsh language station serving Welsh speaking communities. Rich mix of news, music, sport, features, current affairs, drama, comedy, religion and education. Writing Opportunities: DRAMA Daily 10 minute soap *Rhydeglwys* and over nine further hours of new radio drama each year. COMEDY Occasional series during the year (for details of independent commissions see www.bbc.co.uk/wales/commissioning/).

BBC Radio Derby

PO Box 104.5, Derby DE1 3HL
☎01332 361111   Fax 01332 290794
✉ radio.derby@bbc.co.uk
www.bbc.co.uk/derby

Editor *Simon Cornes*

News, sport, information and entertainment.

BBC Radio Devon

PO Box 1034, Broadcasting House, Seymour Road, Mannamead, Plymouth PL3 5YQ
☎01752 260323   Fax 01752 234599
✉ radio.devon@bbc.co.uk
www.bbc.co.uk/devon

Also at: Walnut Gardens, St David's Hill, Exeter EX4 4DB
☎01392 215651 Fax 01392 425570

Managing Editor *Robert Wallace*

Head of Programmes *Ian Timms*

Head of News *Sarah Solftley*

On air since 1983.

BBC Essex

PO Box 765, Chelmsford CM2 9XB
☎01245 616000   Fax 01245 492983
✉ essex@bbc.co.uk
www.bbc.co.uk/essex

Managing Editor *Margaret Hyde*

Broadcasts local and regional programmes for 20 hours every day aimed at a mature audience. Programmes are a mix of news, interviews, expert contributors, phone-ins, sport and special interest such as gardening.

BBC Radio Foyle

8 Northland Road, Londonderry BT48 7GD
☎028 7137 8600   Fax 028 7137 8666
www.bbc.co.uk/northernireland

Managing Editor *Ana Leddy*
News Producer *Paul McFadden*
Arts/Book Reviews *Colum Arbuckle*
Features *Michael Bradley*

Radio Foyle broadcasts about seven hours of original material a day, seven days a week to the north west of Northern Ireland. Other programmes are transmitted simultaneously with Radio Ulster. The output ranges from news, sport, and current affairs to live music recordings and arts reviews.

BBC Radio Gloucestershire

London Road, Gloucester GL1 1SW
☎01452 308585   Fax 01452 309491
✉ radio.gloucestershire@bbc.co.uk
www.bbc.co.uk/radiogloucestershire

Managing Editor *Mark Hurrell*

News and information covering the large variety of interests and concerns in Gloucestershire. Leisure, sport and music, plus African Caribbean and Asian interests. Regular book reviews and interviews with local authors in the *Trish Campbell Show*.

BBC GLR

See **BBC London 94.9FM**

BBC GMR

PO Box 951, Oxford Road, Manchester M60 1SD
☎0161 200 2000   Fax 0161 228 6110
✉ gmr@bbc.co.uk
www.bbc.co.uk/gmr

Managing Editor *Mike Briscoe*
News Editor *Mark Elliot*

On air from 1970 as Radio Manchester, becoming BBC GMR in 1988. One of the largest of the BBC local radio stations, broadcasting news, current affairs, phone-ins, help, advice and sport.

BBC Radio Guernsey
Broadcasting House, Bulwer Avenue,
St Sampson's, Guernsey GY2 4LA
☎01481 200600   Fax 01481 200361
✉ radio.guernsey@bbc.co.uk
www.bbc.co.uk/radioguernsey
Managing Editor *David Martin*

Opened with its sister station, BBC Radio Jersey, in March 1982. Broadcasts 80 hours of local programming a week.

BBC Hereford & Worcester
Hylton Road, Worcester WR2 5WW
☎01905 748485   Fax 01905 748006
✉ bbchw@bbc.co.uk
www.bbc.co.uk/herefordworcester
Also at: 43 Broad Street, Hereford HR4 9HH
☎01432 355252 Fax 01432 356446
Managing Editor *James Coghill*

Has an interest in writers/writing with local connections

BBC Radio Humberside
Queen's Court, Queen's Gardens, Hull
HU1 3RH
☎01482 323232   Fax 01482 621403
✉ radio.humberside@bbc.co.uk
www.bbc.co.uk/radiohumberside
Managing Editor *Simon Pattern*

On air since 1971. Occasionally broadcasts short stories by local writers and, from time to time, looks for short stories for Radio Drama.

BBC Radio Jersey
18 Parade Road, St Helier, Jersey JE2 3PL
☎01534 870000   Fax 01534 732569
✉ jersey@bbc.co.uk
www.bbc.co.uk/jersey
Managing Editor *Denzil Dudley*
Assistant Editor *Matthew Price*

Local news, current affairs and community items.

BBC Radio Kent
The Great Hall, Mount Pleasant Road,
Tunbridge Wells TN1 1QQ
☎01892 670000   Fax 01892 549118
✉ radio.kent@bbc.co.uk
www.bbc.co.uk/radiokent

Managing Editor *Paul Leaper*
Occasional commissions are made for local interest documentaries and other one-off programmes.

BBC Radio Lancashire
20–26 Darwen Street, Blackburn BB2 2EA
☎01254 262411   Fax 01254 680821
✉ radio.lancashire@bbc.co.uk
www.bbc.co.uk/radiolancashire
Editor *John Clayton*

Journalism-based radio station, interested in interviews with local writers. Contact *Alison Brown*, Daily Programmes Producer, Monday to Friday (alison.brown@bbc.co.uk).

BBC Radio Leeds
2 St Peters Square, Leeds LS9 8AH
☎0113 244 2131   Fax 0113 224 7316
✉ radioleeds@bbc.co.uk
www.bbc.co.uk/radioleeds
Managing Editor *John Ryan*

BBC Radio Leeds is the station for West Yorkshire, serving 1.3 million potential listeners since 1968. Broadcasts a mix of news, sport, talk, music and entertainment, 24 hours a day.

BBC Radio Leicester
9th Floor, Epic House, Charles Street,
Leicester LE1 3SH
☎0116 251 6688   Fax 0116 251 1463
✉ radioleicester@bbc.co.uk
www.bbc.co.uk/radioleicester
Managing Editor *Kate Squire*

The first local station in Britain. Occasional interviews with local authors.

BBC Radio Lincolnshire
PO Box 219, Newport, Lincoln LN1 3XY
☎01522 511411   Fax 01522 511058
✉ radio.lincolnshire@bbc.co.uk
www.bbc.co.uk/radiolincolnshire
Managing Editor *Charlie Partridge*

Unsolicited material considered only if locally relevant. Maximum 1000 words: straight narrative preferred, ideally with a topical content.

BBC London 94.9FM
PO Box 94.9, 35 Marylebone High Street,
London W1Y 4QA
☎020 7224 2424   Fax 020 7486 2442
✉ yourlondon@bbc.co.uk
www.bbc.co.uk/london
Managing Editor *David Robey*

Formerly Greater London Radio (GLR), launched in 1988, BBC London 94.9 broadcasts news, information, travel bulletins, sport and music to Greater London and the Home Counties.

BBC Radio Manchester
See **BBC GMR**

BBC Radio Merseyside
55 Paradise Street, Liverpool L1 3BP
☎0151 708 5500   Fax 0151 794 0988
✉ radio.merseyside@bbc.co.uk
www.bbc.co.uk/radiomerseyside
www.bbc.couk/liverpool

Acting Editor *Liam Fogarty*

First Friday – a monthly poetry slot between 1.30 pm and 2.00 pm on the first Friday of every month in the Roger Phillips lunchtime programme. Merseyside writers can offer poetry by e-mailing roger.phillips@bbc.co.uk or send copies with name/address attached, to 'First Friday Poetry', c/o BBC Radio Merseyside at the address above. Only the poets used will be acknowledged and contacted.

BBC Radio Newcastle
Broadcasting Centre, Barrack Road, Newcastle upon Tyne NE99 1RN
☎0191 232 4141
✉ radio.newcastle@bbc.co.uk
www.bbc.co.uk/tyne
www.bbc.co.uk/wear

Editor *Graham Moss*
Senior Producer (Programmes) *Sarah Miller*

LAUNCHED January 1971. One of the BBC's big city radio stations in England, Radio Newcastle reaches an audience of 233,000.

BBC Radio Norfolk
The Forum, Millennium Plain, Norwich NR2 1BH
☎01603 617411   Fax 01603 633692
✉ radionorfolk@bbc.co.uk
www.bbc.co.uk/radionorfolk

Editor *David Clayton*

Good local ideas and material welcome for features and documentaries *if* directly related to Norfolk.

BBC Radio Northampton
Broadcasting House, Abington Street, Northampton NN1 2BH
☎01604 239100   Fax 01604 230709
✉ radionorthampton@bbc.co.uk

www.bbc.co.uk/radionorthampton
Managing Editor *Laura Moss*

Books of local interest are regularly featured. Authors and poets are interviewed on merit. Poems and short stories are reviewed occasionally, but not broadcast. Runs occasional competitions for local writers.

BBC Radio Nottingham
London Road, Nottingham NG2 4UU
☎0115 955 0500   Fax 0115 902 1983
✉ radio.nottingham@bbc.co.uk
www.bbc.co.uk/radionottingham

Editor *Mike Bettison*

Rarely broadcasts scripted pieces of any kind but interviews with authors form a regular part of the station's output.

BBC Radio Orkney
Castle Street, Kirkwall KW15 1DF
☎01856 873939   Fax 01856 872908
✉ radio.orkney@bbc.co.uk

Senior Producer *John Fergusson*

Regular programmes include *Around Orkney* (news magazine programme), *Bruck* (swapshop and general features), *Tatties & Point* (food) and *Orky-Ology* (archaeology magazine). As a BBC Community station, all Radio Orkney's programme material is generated from within the Orkney Islands.

BBC Radio Oxford
PO Box 95.2, Oxford OX2 7YL
☎08459 311444   Fax 08459 311555
✉ radio.oxford@bbc.co.uk
www.bbc.co.uk/radiooxford

Executive Editor *Steve Taschini*

Restored to its original name in 2000 having been merged with BBC Radio Berkshire in 1995 to create BBC Radio Thames Valley. The station frequently carries interviews with local authors and offers books as prizes.

BBC Radio Scotland (Dumfries)
Elmbank, Lover's Walk, Dumfries DG1 1NZ
☎01387 268008   Fax 01387 252568
✉ dumfries@bbc.co.uk

Senior Producer *Willie Johnston*

Previously Radio Solway. The station mainly outputs news bulletins (four daily) although it has become more of a production centre with programmes being made for Radio Scotland as well as BBC Radio 2 and 5 Live. Freelancers of a high standard, familiar with Radio Scotland, should contact the producer.

BBC Radio Scotland (Selkirk)

Municipal Buildings, High Street, Selkirk
TD7 4JX
☎01750 21884   Fax 01750 22400
Senior Broadcaster *Ninian Reid*

Formerly BBC Radio Tweed. Local news bulletins.

BBC Radio Sheffield

54 Shoreham Street, Sheffield S1 4RS
☎0114 273 1177   Fax 0114 267 5454
✉ radio.sheffield@bbc.co.uk
www.bbc.co.uk/radiosheffield
Managing Editor *Gary Keown*
Programmes Editor *Angus Morat*
News Editor *Michael Woodcock*

Writer interviews, writing-related topics and readings on Rony Robinson's show at 11.00 am.

BBC Radio Shetland

Pitt Lane, Lerwick ZE1 0DW
☎01595 694747   Fax 01595 694307
✉ radio.shetland@bbc.co.uk
Senior Producer *Caroline Moyes*

Regular programmes include *Good Evening Shetland.* An occasional books programme highlights the activities of local writers and writers' groups.

BBC Radio Shropshire

2–4 Boscobel Drive, Shrewsbury SY1 3TT
☎01743 248484   Fax 01743 237018
✉ radio.shropshire@bbc.co.uk
bbc.co.uk/shropshire
Managing Editor *Tim Pemberton*

On air since 1985. Unsolicited literary material rarely used, and then only if locally relevant.

BBC Radio Solent

Broadcasting House, Havelock Road,
Southampton SO14 7PW
☎023 8063 2811   Fax 023 8033 9648
✉ radio.solent@bbc.co.uk
www.bbc.co.uk/radiosolent
Managing Editor *Mia Costello*
Broadcasting since 1970.

BBC Somerset Sound

Broadcasting House, Park Street, Taunton
TA1 4DA
☎01823 348920   Fax 01823 332539

✉ somerset.sound@bbc.co.uk
www.bbc.co.uk/somerset
Managing Editor *Jenny Lacey*
Assistant Editor *Simon Clifford*

Informal, speech-based programming with strong news and current affairs output and regular local interest features, including local writing. Poetry and short stories on the *Adam Thomas Programme.*

BBC Southern Counties Radio

Broadcasting Centre, Guildford GU2 7AP
☎01483 306306   Fax 01483 304952
✉ southern.counties.radio@bbc.co.uk
www.bbc.co.uk/southerncounties
Also at: Broadcasting House, 40–42 Queens
Road, Brighton BN1 3XB
Managing Editor *Neil Pringle*

Regular programmes include three individual breakfast shows: *Breakfast Live in Brighton with Sarah Gorrell/in Surrey with Ed Douglas/in Sussex with John Radford.*

BBC Radio Stoke

Cheapside, Hanley, Stoke on Trent ST1 1JJ
☎01782 208080   Fax 01782 289115
✉ radio.stoke@bbc.co.uk
www.bbc.co.uk/radiostoke
Editor *Sue Owen*

On air since 1968, one of the first eight 'experimental' BBC stations. Emphasis on news, current affairs and local topics. Music represents one fifth of total output. Unsolicited material of local interest is welcome – send to *Tim Wedgwood.*

BBC Radio Suffolk

Broadcasting House, St Matthew's Street,
Ipswich IP1 3EP
☎01473 250000   Fax 01473 210887
✉ radiosuffolk@bbc.co.uk
www.bbc.co.uk/suffolk
Managing Editor *Gerald Main*

Strongly locally speech-based, dealing with news, current affairs, community issues, the arts, agriculture, commerce, travel, sport and leisure. Programmes sometimes carry interviews with writers.

BBC Radio Swindon

BBC Broadcasting House, Prospect Place,
Swindon SN1 3RW
☎01793 513626   Fax 01793 513650
✉ radio.swindon@bbc.co.uk
www.bbc.co.uk/england/radiowiltshire

Editor *Tony Worgan*

Local news and current affairs. Local authors are interviewed on Mark Seaman's *Afternoon Show*.

BBC Three Counties Radio

1 Hastings Street, Luton LU1 5XL
☎01582 637400   Fax 01582 401467
✉ threecounties@bbc.co.uk
www.bbc.co.uk/threecounties

Managing Editor *Mark Norman*

Encourages freelance contributions from the community across a wide range of radio output, including interview and feature material. Interested in local history topics (five minutes maximum).

BBC Radio Ulster

Broadcasting House, Ormeau Avenue, Belfast BT2 8HQ
☎028 9033 8000   Fax 028 9033 8116

Managing Editor *Susan Lovell*

Programmes broadcast from 6.30 am to midnight weekdays and from 6.55 am to midnight at weekends. Radio Ulster has won seven Sony awards in recent years. Programmes include: *Good Morning Ulster*; *Gerry Anderson*; *Talk Back*; *Just Jones*; *Evening Extra*; *On Your Behalf*; *Your Place and Mine* and *Across the Line*.

BBC Radio Wales

Broadcasting House, Llandaff, Cardiff CF5 2YQ
☎029 2032 2000   Fax 029 2032 2674
✉ radio.wales@bbc.co.uk
www.bbc.co.uk/radiowales

Editor *Julie Barton*
Editor, Radio Wales News *Geoff Williams*

Broadcasts news on the hour and half hour throughout weekday daytime programmes; hourly bulletins in the evenings and at weekends. Programmes include *Good Morning Wales*; *Roy Noble & Nicola Heywood-Thomas*. Access line number: 08700 100110.

BBC Radio Wiltshire

BBC Broadcasting House, Prospect Place, Swindon SN1 3RW
☎01793 513626   Fax 01793 513650
✉ radio.wiltshire@bbc.co.uk
www.bbc.co.uk/england/radiowiltshire

Editor *Tony Worgon*

Sister company of BBC Radio Swindon. Regular programmes include Mark Seaman's *Afternoon Show* (reviews and author interviews).

BBC WM

The Mailbox, Birmingham B1 1RF
☎08453 009956   Fax 0121 567 6025
✉ bbcwm@bbc.co.uk
www.bbc.co.uk/radiowm

Managing Editor *Keith Beech*

Commenced broadcasting in November 1970 as BBC Birmingham and has won four gold Sony awards in recent years. Speech-based station broadcasting to the West Midlands, South Staffordshire and North Worcestershire.

BBC Radio York

20 Bootham Row, York YO30 7BR
☎01904 641351   Fax 01904 610937
✉ radio.york@bbc.co.uk
www.bbc.co.uk/northyorkshire

Editor *Matt Youdale*

Books of local interest are sometimes previewed.

Independent Television

Carlton
See **ITV London**

Channel 4

124 Horseferry Road, London SW1P 2TX
☎020 7396 4444   Fax 020 7306 8356
www.channel4.com

Chief Executive *Andy Duncan*
Director of Television *Kevin Lygo*
Head of E4 and Factual Entertainment *Julian Bellamy*
Head of Features *Sue Murphy*
Head of History, Science, Religion and Arts *Hamish Mykura*
Head of News, Current Affairs *Dorothy Byrne*
Head of Commissioning Management (Managing Editor, Commissioning) *Janey Walker*
Director of Acquisitions *Jeff Ford*
Head of Education *Heather Rabbatts*
Head of More4 and Documentary Events *Peter Dale*

COMMISSIONING EDITORS
Head of Drama and Film Four *Tessa Ross*
Head of Comedy and Films *Caroline Leddy*
Head of Entertainment *Andrew Newman*
Head of Sport *David Kerr*
Controller of Broadcasting *Rosemary Newell*
Head of Schedules, Music, Youth and T4 *Julie Oldroyd*

Commissioning Editor, Daytime *Adam McDonald*

Head of Documentaries *Danny Cohen*

Channel 4 started broadcasting as a national channel in November 1982. It enjoys unique status as the world's only major public service broadcaster funded entirely by its own commercial activities. All programmes are commissioned from independent production companies and are broadcast across the whole of the UK except those parts of Wales covered by S4C. Its FilmFour channel, launched in 1998, is a premium pay-TV channel featuring modern independent cinema. A second digital channel, E4, was launched in January 2001, broadcasting a range of programmes similar to Channel 4.

Channel Television

Television Centre, La Pouquelaye, St Helier, Jersey JE1 3ZD

☎01534 816816   Fax 01534 816817

www.channeltv.co.uk

Also at: Television House, Bulwer Avenue, St Sampsons, Guernsey GY2 4LA

☎01481 241888 Fax 01481 241878

Managing Director *Michael Lucas*
Director of Programmes *Karen Rankine*
Director of Sales *Don Miller*
Director of Resources & Transmission *Kevin Banner*

Channel Television is the independent television broadcaster to the Channel Islands, serving 143,000 residents, most of whom live on the main islands, Jersey, Guernsey, Alderney and Sark. The station has a weekly reach of more than 94% with local programmes (in the region of five and a half hours each week) at the heart of the ITV service to the islands.

Five

22 Long Acre WC2E 9LY

☎020 7550 5555   Fax 020 7550 5554

www.five.tv

CEO *Jane Lighting*
Director of Programmes *Dan Chambers*
Controller of Children's and Religious Programmes *Nick Wilson*
Senior Programme Controller *Chris Shaw*
Controller of Drama Programmes *Jeff Ford*

Channel 5 Broadcasting Ltd won the franchise for Britain's third commercial terrestrial television station in 1995 and came on air at the end of March 1997. Regular programmes include *Family Affairs* (Monday to Friday soap opera) and

The Wright Stuff (weekday morning chat show), plus documentaries, drama, films, children's programmes, sport and entertainment.

GMTV

The London Television Centre, Upper Ground, London SE1 9TT

☎020 7827 7000   Fax 020 7827 7249

✉ talk2us@gm.tv

www.gmtv.co.uk

Managing Director *Paul Corley*
Director of Programmes *Peter McHugh*
Managing Editor *John Scammell*
Editor *Martin Frizell*

Winner of the national breakfast television franchise. Jointly owned by ITV plc and Disney. GMTV took over from TV-AM on 1 January 1993, with live programming from 6.00 am to 9.25 am. Regular news bulletins, current affairs, topical features, showbiz and lifestyle. Plus competitions, travel and weather reports. Launched its digital service, GMTV2, in January 1999, with daily broadcasts from 6.00 am to 9.25 am. News reports, travel, health and lifestyle features, some simulcast with GMTV1. Children's programming on Saturdays. The week's news and political issues reviewed on Sundays, followed by children's programming.

Grampian TV

Craigshaw Business Park, West Tullos, Aberdeen AB12 3QH

☎01224 848848   Fax 01224 848800

www.grampiantv.co.uk

Managing Director *Derrick Thomson*
Head of News and Current Affairs *Craig Wilson*

Extensive regional news and reports including farming, fishing and sports, interviews and leisure features, various light entertainment, Gaelic and religious programmes, and live coverage of the Scottish political, economic and industrial scene. Serves the area stretching from Fife to Shetland. Regular programmes include *North Tonight* and other varied genre shows strongly reflecting the regionality of the north of Scotland.

HTV

See **ITV West**

ITN (Independent Television News Ltd)

200 Gray's Inn Road, London WC1X 8XZ

☎020 7833 3000   Fax 020 7430 4868

✉ contact@itn.co.uk

www.itn.co.uk

Chief Executive *Mark Wood*
Editor-in-Chief, ITV News *David Mannion*
Editor, Channel 4 News *Jim Gray*
Provider of the main national and international news for ITV and Channel 4 and radio news for IRN. Programmes on ITV: *Lunchtime News*; *London Today*; *Evening News*; *London Tonight*; *News at 10.30*, plus regular news summaries and three programmes a day at weekends. Programmes on Channel 4 include the in-depth news analysis programmes *Channel 4 News at Noon* and *Channel 4 News*. ITN also has operating control of *Euronews*, Europe's only pan-European broadcaster. Since August 2000, ITN broadcasts in its own right on ITV News Channel, a 24-hour news service available for television, video, audio and text format.

ITV plc

The London Television Centre, Upper Ground, London SE1 9LT
☎020 7620 1620
www.itvplc.com
Chief Executive *Charles Allen*

ITV Broadcasting
200 Gray's Inn Road, London WC1X 8HF
☎020 7843 8000
www.itv.com
Chief Executive *Mick Desmond*
Programme Director *Nigel Pickard*
See below for listings for ITV Anglia, ITV Border, ITV Central, ITV Granada, ITV London, ITV Meridian, ITV Tyne Tees, ITV Wales, ITV West, ITV Westcountry and ITV Yorkshire.

ITV Network

ITV plc holds the eleven English and Welsh regional ITV licences (Anglia, Border, Central, Granada, London, Meridian, Tyne Tees, Wales, West, Westcountry and Yorkshire) as well as the digital channels, ITV2 and ITV3. The remaining three ITV licences belong to: SMG plc (Grampian and Scottish), Ulster Television plc (UTV) and Channel Television. Granada is the production arm of ITV plc.

ITV Anglia Television

Anglia House, Norwich NR1 3JG
☎01603 615151   Fax 01603 761245
www.angliatv.com
Managing Director *Graham Creelman*
Controller of Programmes *Neil Thompson*
Broadcasting to the east of England, Anglia

Television is a major producer of programmes for the ITV network. Its network factual department currently boasts the largest portfolio of North American documentary commissions for a UK-based production company.

ITV Border Television

Television Centre, Durranhill, Carlisle CA1 3NT
☎01228 525101   Fax 01228 541384
www.border-tv.com
Managing Director *Douglas Merrall*
Border's region covers three different cultures – English, Scottish and Manx. Programming concentrates on documentaries rather than drama. Most scripts are supplied in-house but occasionally there are commissions. Apart from notes, writers should not submit written work until their ideas have been fully discussed.

ITV Central

Gas Street, Birmingham B1 2JT
☎0121 643 9898
Managing Director *Ian Squires*
Formed in 2004 by the merger of Carlton and Granada, ITV Central is the largest of the UK commercial television networks.

ITV Granada

Quay Street, Manchester M60 9EA
☎0161 832 7211   Fax 0161 827 2180
www.granadatv.com
Director of Programmes *John Whiston*
Director of Production *Claire Poyser*
Controller of Regional Programmes *Kieron Collins*
Controller of Drama *Carolyn Reynolds*
Controller of Current Affairs and Features *Jeff Anderson*
Controller of Documentaries, History and Science *Bill Jones*
The longest continuous ITC licence holder, broadcasting for over 40 years. Programmes include *Coronation Street* and *Disappearing World*. See also **Granada Drama** under ***Film, TV and Radio Producers***.

ITV London

The London Television Centre, Upper Ground, London SE1 9LT
☎020 7621 8163
Managing Director *Christy Swords*
ITV London was formed in 2004 by the merger of Carlton and LWT, broadcasting to the London region.

ITV Meridian

Solent Business Park, Whiteley PO15 7PA
☎01489 442000   Fax 01489 442200
www.meridiantv.com

Managing Director *Lindsay Charlton*
Controller of Regional Programmes *Mark Southgate*

Serves five and a half million listeners spread across the South Coast, Thames Valley, Sussex and Kent. Long-running programmes include *Country Ways* and *Monkey Business.*

ITV Tyne Tees

Television Centre, Newcastle upon Tyne NE1 2AL
☎0191 261 0181   Fax 0191 261 2302
www.tynetees.tv

Managing Director/Controller of Programmes *Graeme Thompson*
Editor, Current Affairs and Features *Jane Bolesworth*
Managing Editor, News *Graham Marples*
Executive Producer & Head of Development, Yorkshire Tyne Tees Features *Mark Robinson*
Head of Regional Affairs *Norma Hope*
Head of Sport *Roger Tames*

Programming covers religion, politics, news and current affairs, regional documentaries, business, entertainment, sport and arts. Regular programmes include *North East Tonight with Mike Neville* and *Around the House* (politics).

ITV Wales

The Television Centre, Culverhouse Cross, Cardiff CF5 6XJ
☎029 2059 0590   Fax 029 2059 7183
✉ info@itvwales.com

Managing Director *Roger Lewis*

Fomerly HTV Wales. Programmes include the consumer affairs magazine, *The Ferret* and current affairs series, *Wales this Week.* The company also makes Welsh language programming for S4C, including the series voted the most popular with viewers on the Welsh channel – *Cefn Gwlad* and the current affairs series, *Y Byd ar Bedwar.*

ITV West

Television Centre, Bath Road, Bristol BS4 3HG
☎0117 972 2722   Fax 0117 971 7685
✉ itvwestnews@itv.com (newsdesk)

Managing Director *Mark Haskell*
Director of Programmes *Jane McCloskey*

Formerly HTV. Broadcasts to over two million listeners in the West of England.

ITV West Country

Langage Science Park, Western Wood Way, Plymouth PL7 5BQ
☎01752 333333   Fax 01752 333444

Managing Director *Mark Haskell*
Director of Programmes *Jane McCloskey*

Broadcasts to Cornwall, Devon, Somerset and west Dorset. Produces eight and a half hours of regional news, current affairs and features programmes each week.

ITV Yorkshire

The Television Centre, Leeds LS3 1JS
☎0113 243 8283   Fax 0113 244 5107
www.itv.com

Managing Director *David Croft*
Director of Drama, Kids & Arts *John Whiston*
Controller of Drama, Leeds *Keith Richardson*
Controller of Comedy Drama and Drama Features *David Reynolds*

Drama series, situation comedies, film productions and long-running series like *Emmerdale* and *Heartbeat.* Always looking for strong writing in these areas, but prefers to find it through an agent. Documentary/current affairs material tends to be supplied by producers; opportunities in these areas are rare but adaptations of published work as a documentary subject are considered. In theory, opportunity exists within series, episode material. Best approach is through a good agent.

LWT

See **ITV London**

S4C

Parc Ty Glas, Llanishen CF14 5DU
☎029 2074 7444   Fax 029 2075 4444
✉ s4c@s4c.co.uk
www.s4c.co.uk

Chief Executive *Huw Jones*
Director of Programmes *Iona Jones*

The Welsh 4th Channel, established by the Broadcasting Act 1980, is responsible for a schedule of Welsh and English programmes on the Fourth Channel in Wales. Known as S4C, the analogue service is made up of about 34 hours per week of Welsh language programmes and more than 85 hours of English language output from Channel 4. S4C digidol broadcasts in Welsh exclusively for 80 hours per week. Ten hours a week of the Welsh programmes are provided by the BBC; the remainder are purchased from ITV1 Wales and independent producers.

Drama, comedy and documentary are all part of S4C's programming. Commissioning guidelines can be viewed on the website given above.

Scottish Television Ltd
200 Renfield Street, Glasgow G2 3PR
☎0141 300 3000   Fax 0141 300 3030
www.scottishtv.co.uk

Managing Director, Scottish TV *Bobby Hain*
Head of Features & Entertainment *Agnes Wilkie*
Head of News & Current Affairs *Gordon Macmillan*
Head of Sport *Henry Eagles*

Scottish TV produces 12 hours of television a week for the central Scotland region. This is made up of news, current affairs and sport, and a wide-ranging portfolio of other programmes ranging from entertainment, documentary and drama. Scottish Television together with Grampian TV and Scottish Screen make a number of short films under the banner of New Found Land as well as feature films under the New Found Land production scheme. The same partners also produce documentaries through their annual This Scotland initiative.

Teletext Ltd
Building 10, Chiswick Park, 566 Chiswick High Road, London W4 5TS
☎0870 731 3000   Fax 0870 731 3001
www.teletext.co.uk

Managing Director *Mike Stewart*
Editor-in-Chief *John Sage*

Broadcasts TV text services on analogue TV on ITV, Channel 4 and Five. It also broadcasts digital text services on Freeview and satellite on Channel 4 and, from summer 2005, on ITV. In addition, Teletext runs a holidays website and mobile services.

UTV (Ulster Television)
Havelock House, Ormeau Road, Belfast BT7 1EB
☎028 9032 8122   Fax 028 9024 6695
✉ info@u.tv
www.u.tv

Director of Television *Alan Bremner*
Head of News, Current Affairs and Sport *Rob Morrison*

Regular programmes on news and current affairs, politics, sport, education, music, light entertainment, arts, health and local culture.

Cable and Satellite Television

Artsworld
Great West House, Great West Road, Brentford TW8 9DF
☎020 7805 2424
✉ tv@artsworld.com
www.artsworld.com

Chairman *John Hambley*
Programme Controller *Kate Potter*

Satellite arts channel, launched in November 2000. Broadcasts from 7.00 pm to midnight (repeated from 2.00 pm to 7.00 pm the following day) via BSkyB. Programmes include the series, *Great Books*.

British Sky Broadcasting Ltd (BSkyB)
6 Centaurs Business Park, Grant Way, Isleworth TW7 5QD
☎020 7705 3000   Fax 020 7705 3030
www.sky.com

Chief Executive *James Murdoch*
Managing Director, Sky Networks *Dawn Airey*
Chief Operating Officer *Richard Freudenstein*
Head of Sky News *Nick Pollard*
Managing Director, Sky Sports *Vic Wakeling*

Launched in 1989, British Sky Broadcasting gives over 15 million viewers (in more than 7 million households) access to movies, news, entertainment and sports channels, and interactive services on Sky digital. Launched in October 1998, Sky digital has more than 400 channels and offers a range of innovative interactive services. 2001 saw the introduction of the next-generation integrated digital satellite set-top box/personal video recorder, Sky+.

WHOLLY-OWNED SKY CHANNELS
Sky Movies 1–9/Sky Cinema 1&2
Largest TV movie service outside the US. Sky Movies 1–9 show over 90% of the top 100 grossing box-office films of the previous year. Sky Cinema 1&2 shows classic films, from Westerns to Film Noir, Chaplin to Chevy Chase, as well as a World Cinema strand that includes UK premières of new and old movies.

Sky News
Award winning 24-hours news service with hourly bulletins and expert comment.

Sky One/Sky One Mix
The most frequently watched non-terrestrial channel with the accent on entertainment for 16–34-year-olds.

Sky Sports 1/Sky Sports 2/Sky Sports 3/ Sky Sports News/Sky Sports Extra

Over 30,000 hours of sport are broadcast every year across the five Sky Sports channels. Sky Sports 1, 2 and 3 are devoted to live events, support programmes and in-depth sports coverage seven days a week. Sky Sports News provides sports news and the latest results and information 24 hours a day. Sky Sports Extra carries additional sports programming including the award-winning live interactive coverage.

Sky Travel/Sky Travel Extra

Magazine shows, documentaries and teleshopping.

JOINT VENTURES:
National Geographic; Nickelodeon; Nick Jr; The History Channel; Paramount Comedy Channel; QVC; MUTV; Music Choice Europe; Granada Men & Motors; Granada Plus; Artsworld; Adventure One; The Biography Channel; Attheraces; Chelsea Digital Media.

CNBC Europe

10 Fleet Place, London EC4M 7QS
☎020 7653 9300   Fax 020 7653 5956
www.cnbceurope.com
Managing Director *Tim Popplewell*
A service of NBC and Dow Jones. 24-hour business and financial news service. Programmes include *Today's Business*; *Morning Exchange*; *Capital Ideas*; *Europe Squawk Box*.

CNN International

Turner House, 16 Great Marlborough Street, London W1F 7HS
☎020 7693 1000   Fax 020 7693 1001
edition.cnn.com
Managing Editor, CNN International Europe, Middle East & Africa *Nick Wrenn*

CNN, the leading global 24-hour news network, is available to one billion people worldwide via the 26 CNN branded TV, Internet, radio and mobile services produced by CNN News Group, a Time Warner company. CNN has major production centres in Atlanta, New York, Los Angeles, London, Hong Kong and Mexico City. The London bureau, the largest outside the USA, is CNN's European headquarters and produces over 50 hours of programming per week. Live business and news programmes, including *CNN Today*; *Business International*; *World News* and *World Business Today*.

MTV Networks Europe

180 Oxford Street, London W1D 1DS
☎020 7284 7777   Fax 020 7284 7788
www.mtv.co.uk
President & Chief Executive *Brent Hansen*
Established 1987. Europe's 24-hour music and youth entertainment channel, available on cable, via satellite and digitally.Transmitted from London in English across Europe.

Travel Channel

66 Newman Street, London W1T 3EQ
☎020 7636 5401
✉ enquiries@travelchannel.co.uk ·
www.travelchannel.co.uk

Launched in February 1994. Broadcasts programmes and information on the world of travel. Destinations reports, lifestyle programmes plus food and drink, sport and leisure pursuits. Transmits from 7.00 am to 1.00 am throughout Europe and Africa.

National Commercial Radio

Classic FM

7 Swallow Place, London W1B 2AG
☎020 7343 9000   Fax 020 7344 2700
www.classicfm.com
Station Manager *Darren Henley*

Classic FM, Britain's largest national commercial radio station, started broadcasting in September 1992. Plays accessible classical music 24 hours a day and broadcasts news, weather, travel, business information, political/celebrity/general interest talks, features and interviews. Classic has gone well beyond its expectations, attracting 6.2 million listeners a week. Winner of the 'Station of the Year' Sony Award in 2000.

Digital One

7 Swallow Place, London W1B 2AG
☎020 7288 4600   Fax 020 7288 4601
✉ info@digitalone.co.uk
www.ukdigitalradio.com

The UK's only national commercial digital radio multiplex operator. Backed by radio group GCap Media and cable supplier ntl, Digital One began broadcasting on 15 November 1999. Stations include **Classic FM**, **Virgin Radio**, **TalkSport** and digital-only stations, **Oneword**, Planet Rock, Core, PrimeTime Radio and Life.

Oneword

Landseer House, 19 Charing Cross Road,
London WC2H 0ES
☎020 7976 3030   Fax 020 7930 9460
✉ info@oneword.co.uk
www.oneword.co.uk

Station Manager *Simon Blackmore*
Head of Programmes *Paul Kent*

The first commercial radio station dedicated solely to the transmission of plays, books, comedy and reviews. Broadcasts on Sky Digital (channel 877), Freeview (channel 87), ntl (channel 893) in Europe, DAB Digital Radio (Digital One – 18 hours a day) in the UK and worldwide on the Internet. Programmes include *Between the Lines*, a twice-daily conversation by Paul Blezard with different authors. Winner of the 'Station of the Year' Sony Radio Awards in 2001 and 2002.

TalkSport

PO Box 1089, London SE1 8WQ
☎020 7959 7800
✉ pressreleases@talksport.co.uk
www.talksport.net

Programme Director *Bill Ridley*

Commenced broadcasting in February 1995 as Talk Radio UK. Re-launched January 2000 as TalkSport, the UK's first sports radio station. Acquired by Ulster Television in 2005. Broadcasts 24 hours a day. News items can be e-mailed via the website.

Virgin Radio

1 Golden Square, London W1F 9DJ
☎020 7434 1215   Fax 020 7434 1197
www.virginradio.co.uk

Programme Director *Paul Jackson*

Music-based station launched in 1973, bought by Chris Evans' Ginger Media Group in December 1997 and acquired by the Scottish Media Group in March 2000.

Independent Local Radio

95.8 Capital FM

30 Leicester Square, London WC2H 7LA
☎020 7766 6000   Fax 020 7766 6100
www.capitalfm.com

Managing Director *Keith Pringle*

Commenced broadcasting in October 1973 as the country's second commercial radio station (the first being LBC, launched a week earlier). Europe's largest commercial radio station.

Central FM Ltd

201–203 High Street, Falkirk FK1 1DU
☎01324 611164   Fax 01324 611168
✉ email@centralfm.co.uk
www.centralfm.co.uk

Brand Manager and Programme Controller
   Tom Bell

Broadcasts music, sport and local news to central Scotland, 24 hours a day.

Century FM

Century House, PO Box 100, Church Street,
Gateshead NE8 2YY
☎0191 477 6666   Fax 0191 477 5660

Programme Controller *Paul Drogan*

Music, talk, news and interviews, 24 hours a day.

Clyde 1/Clyde 2

Clydebank Business Park, Clydebank
G81 2RX
☎0141 565 2200   Fax 0141 565 2265
www.clyde1.com
www.clyde2.com

Owner *Radio Clyde*
Managing Director *Paul Cooney*

Programmes usually originate in-house or by commission. All documentary material is made in-house. Good local news items always considered. There are three book programmes presented by Alex Dickson each week on Clyde 2 at 10.00 pm – 10.30 pm: *Authors* (Monday) features author interviews while *Hardback Bookcase* (Tuesday) and *Paperback Bookcase* (Wednesday) review latest titles.

Cool FM

See **Downtown Radio**

Downtown Radio/Cool FM

Newtownards, Co. Down BT23 4ES
☎028 9181 5555   Fax 028 9181 5252
✉ programmes@downtown.co.uk
www.downtown.co.uk

Managing Director *David Sloan*

Downtown Radio first ran a highly successful short story competition in 1988, attracting over 400 stories. The competition is now an annual event and writers living within the station's transmission area are asked to submit material during the winter and early spring. The competition is promoted in association with Eason Shops. For further information, write to *Anita Downey* at the station.

Essex FM/Classic Gold
Radio House, 31 Glebe Road, Chelmsford
CM1 1QG
☎01245 524500   Fax 01245 524 559
www.musicradio.com
Programme Controller *Chris Cotton*

Music-based stations. No real opportunities for
writers' work as such, but will occasionally interview local authors of published books. Contact
Lee Murphy, News Editor.

Forth One/Forth 2
Forth House, Forth Street, Edinburgh
EH1 3LF
☎0131 556 9255   Fax 0131 475 1221
✉ scott@forth2.com
www.forthonline.co.uk
Controller, Forth One & Forth 2 *Luke
McCullough*
Programme Producer, Forth 2 *Moira Millar*
News Editor *Paul Robertson*
Book Reviewer *Lesley Fraser-Taylor*

News stories welcome from freelancers. Music-
based programming.

Galaxy 102.2
See **100.7 Heart FM**

GWR FM
PO Box 2000, 1 Passage Street, Bristol
BS99 7SN
☎0117 984 3200   Fax 0117 984 3202
www.musicradio.com
Programme Controller *Paul Andrew*

Very few opportunities for writers. Almost all
material originates in-house.

Hallam FM/Magic AM
Radio House, 900 Herries Road, Sheffield
S6 1RH
☎0114 209 1000
www.hallamfm.co.uk
Programme Director *Gary Stein*

Launched in 1974. Music, news and features, 24
hours a day.

100.7 Heart FM/Galaxy 102.2
1 The Square, 111 Broad Street, Birmingham
B15 1AS
☎0121 695 0000   Fax 0121 695 0055
✉ mail@heartfm.co.uk *or*
mail@galaxy1022.co.uk
www.heartfm.co.uk
www.galaxy1022.co.uk
Managing Director *Paul Fairburn*

Programme Director, Heart FM *Alan Carruthers*
Programme Director, Galaxy *Neil Greenslade*

Heart FM commenced broadcasting music,
regional news and information in September
1994. Galaxy broadcasts today's dance and
R&B, news and information.

Isle of Wight Radio
Dodnor Park, Newport PO30 5XE
☎01983 822557   Fax 01983 821690
✉ tom.stroud@iwradio.co.uk
www.iwradio.co.uk
Managing Director *Andy Shier*
Programme Manager *Tom Stroud*

Part of The Local Radio Company, Isle of
Wight Radio is the island's only radio station
broadcasting local news, music and general
entertainment including phone-ins and interview based shows. Music, television, film, popular culture are the main areas of interest.

KM-fm
Medway House, Ginsbury Close, St Thomas
Longley Road, Medway City Estate, Strood,
Rochester ME2 4DU
☎01634 227800   Fax 01634 297272
www.kentonline.co.uk/kmfm
Group Programme Director *Mike Osborne*

A wide range of music programming plus
news, views and local interest. Part of the Kent
Messenger Group.

LBC News 1152 AM
See **LBC Radio Ltd**

LBC Radio Ltd
The Chrysalis Building, Bramley Road,
London W10 6SP
☎020 7314 7300
www.lbc.co.uk
Deputy Programme Director *Scott Solder*
Editorial Director *Jonathan Richards*

LBC 97.3 FM is a talk-based station broadcasting 24 hours a day, providing entertainment,
interviews, celebrity guests, music, chat shows,
local interest, news and sport. LBC News 1152
AM, the sister station of LBC 87.3 FM, provides 24-hour rolling news.

105.4 FM Leicester Sound
6 Dominus Way, Meridian Business Park,
Leicester LE19 1RP
☎0116 256 1300
Fax 0116 256 1303/1309 (news)
Programme Controller *Craig Boddy*

Predominantly a music station. Very occasionally, unsolicited material of local interest – 'targeted at our particular audience' – may be broadcast.

Magic 1152AM
(Newcastle upon Tyne)
See **Metro Radio**

Magic 1548
See **Radio City Ltd**

Magic AM
See **Hallam FM**

Marcher Radio Group
The Studios, Mold Road, Wrexham
LL11 4AF
☎01978 752200   Fax 01978 722209
www.musicradio.com
Programme Controller *Lisa Marrey*

Occasional features and advisory programmes. Hour-long Welsh language broadcasts are aired weekdays at 6.00 pm on Classic Gold Marcher 1260.

Metro Radio/Magic 1152AM
Swalwell, Newcastle upon Tyne NE99 1BB
☎0191 420 0971   Fax 0191 488 8611
www.metroradio.co.uk
Deputy Programme Director *Alex Rowland*

Very few opportunities for writers, but phone-in programmes may interview authors.

NorthSound Radio
Abbotswell Road, Aberdeen AB12 4AJ
☎01224 337000   Fax 01224 400003
www.northsound1.com
andwww.northsound2.com
Managing Director *Iain McKenna*
Programme Controller *Chris Thomson*

Features and music programmes 24 hours a day including, mid-morning (9.00 am – midday), *Northsound 2* feature programme.

Premier Radio
22 Chapter Street, London SW1P 4NP
☎020 7316 1300   Fax 020 7233 6706
✉ premier@premier.org.uk
www.premier.org.uk
Managing Director *Peter Kerridge*

Broadcasts programmes that reflect the beliefs and values of the Christian faith, 24 hours a day on 1305, 1413, 1332 MW, Sky digital 873, ntl 886, Freeview channel 96 and on the Web.

Radio City Ltd/Magic 1548
St John's Beacon, 1 Houghton Street,
Liverpool L1 1RL
☎0151 472 6800   Fax 0151 472 6821
www.radiocity.co.uk
Managing Director *Tom Hunter*
Programme Director *Richard Maddock*

Opportunities for writers are very few and far between as this is predominantly a music station.

Radio XL 1296 AM
KMS House, Bradford Street, Birmingham
B12 0JD
☎0121 753 5353   Fax 0121 753 3111
Managing Director *Arun Bajaj*

Asian broadcasting for the West Midlands, 24 hours a day. Broadcasts *Love Express* featuring love stories and poems. Writers should send material for the attention of *Hardev Nara*.

Sabras Radio
Radio House, 63 Melton Road, Leicester
LE4 6PN
☎0116 261 0666   Fax 0116 266 7776
www.sabrasradio.com
Programme Controller *Don Kotak*

Programmes for the Asian community, broadcasting 24 hours a day.

Spectrum Radio
4 Ingate Place, London SW8 3NS
☎020 7627 4433   Fax 020 7627 3409
✉ enquiries@spectrumradio.net
www.spectrumradio.net
Managing Director *Toby Aldrych*

Programmes for a broad spectrum of ethnic groups in London.

Spire FM
City Hall Studios, Malthouse Lane, Salisbury
SP2 7QQ
☎01722 416644   Fax 01722 416688
www.spirefm.co.uk
Station Director *Ceri Herford-Jones*

Music, news current affairs, quizzes and sport. Won the Sony Award for the best local radio station in 1994 and 1996.

Sunrise Radio (Yorkshire)
Sunrise House, 30 Chapel Street, Bradford
BD1 5DN
☎01274 735043   Fax 01274 728534
www.sunriseradio.fm

Programme Controller, Chief Executive & Chairman *Usha Parmar*

Programmes for the Asian community in West Yorkshire.

Sunshine 855

South Shropshire Communications Ltd., Unit 11, Burway Trading Estate, Bromfield Road, Ludlow SY8 1EN

☎01584 873795   Fax 01584 875900

www.sunshine855.com

Operations Director *Mrs G. Murfin*

Music, news and information, broadcast 24 hours a day.

Swansea Sound 1170 MW/ 96.4 FM The Wave

Victoria Road, Gowerton, Swansea SA4 3AB

☎01792 511170 (MW)/ 511964 (FM)

Fax 01792 511171 (MW)/511965 (FM)

www.swanseasound.co.uk

Station Director *Carrie Mosley*

Programme Controller *Steve Barnes*

News Editor *Emma Thomas*

Music-based programming on FM while Swansea Sound is interested in a wide variety of material, though news items must be of local relevance. An explanatory letter, in the first instance, is advisable.

2CR-FM/Classic Gold 828

5–7 Southcote Road, Bournemouth BH1 3LR

☎01202 234900   Fax 01202 234909

✉ newsbournemouth@creation.com

www.musicradio.com

Programme Controller *Graham Mack*

Serves Dorset and Hampshire. All reviews/ topicality/press releases to the Programme Controller, 2CR-FM at the address above.

96.4 FM The Wave

See **Swansea Sound 1170 MW**

Putting the Soap into Opera

Bob G. Ritchie reveals the secrets of writing popular TV

Writers, like the rest of the population, can be divided into two groups: those who have a favourite TV soap and those who don't. If you are one of the latter, stop reading now. If you don't enjoy watching a soap, you won't enjoy writing for it. And if you don't enjoy writing for it, no producer is going to enjoy reading what you write, no matter how desperate he may be for new writers.

It hardly needs to be said that soaps – or continuing drama series, as people in the business prefer to call them – are hugely popular. More people watch them than almost any other programme on television, apart from special events like the Olympics, royal weddings and England losing World Cup football matches. The other obvious thing is that there are an awful lot of them. Aside from the big three – *EastEnders, Coronation Street* and *Emmerdale* – there are *Hollyoaks, Family Affairs, Casualty, Holby City, The Bill, Doctors*, children's series like *Grange Hill* and those that hover on the brink of being soaps, like *Down to Earth, The Royal, Bad Girls* and *Footballers' Wives*. And these are only the ones on the five main terrestrial channels.

For the aspiring TV drama writer soaps therefore represent an enormous opportunity. At any given time, each probably employs a minimum of ten writers. Some, like *EastEnders*, use maybe four times that number. Some of these writers will be writing their first episodes, still not quite sure what they can get away with and what they can't. Others will be on their tenth, confident that they have finally got to know their characters' distinctive voices and how much dialogue can be squeezed in on a walk from the Queen Vic to the bookies. The remaining few will have written so many episodes they'll be thinking desperately either of retirement or the next series they can move on to, deaf to the pleas of the executive producer to hang around a little longer because, despite the fact that over the five years they've been writing for the series they've been sucked dry of original ideas, at least their scripts come in on time and more or less to length and don't require buildings to be expensively blown up or fifty extras to appear dressed in rabbit costumes.

In other words, there is a high turnover. Though it may not seem so, commissioning editors are always looking for new writers. First, they ask the existing writers if they know of any – a vain hope, given that writers generally lead lonely, isolated, friendless lives. Failing that, they rely on agents, who keep a steady stream of sample scripts flowing into production offices. Finally, they simply steal writers from other soaps. What few of them do, unfortunately for those aspiring writers who have yet to gain a credit, is look for completely new blood (one exception is *Doctors*, which actually has a policy of encouraging untried talent).

That said, a new writer stands a much better chance of getting onto a soap than having a one-off drama commissioned, no matter how brilliant it may be.

So what are the characteristics of soaps that make them different from other kinds of TV drama? The most obvious difference is that the characters and the world they inhabit are already firmly established. In addition, the main storylines have usually been decided well in advance. Contrary to what many new writers may believe, soap producers don't in general expect you to come up with Pauline Fowler's long-lost cousins from Australia, the overdue gentrification of Albert Square or the miraculous third coming of Den Watts. That's all in the pipeline, thanks very much.

A new writer may therefore wonder what is left for him or her to do. A few people in the business, it has to be said, share that wonder. A script editor once told me, only half-joking, that my task was to 'make it look pretty on the page.' In fact, there is quite enough for the writer to do, especially when you discover how little time you are given in which to do it. The characters may be familiar to millions, but it's the writer who puts words in their mouths and tells them in which part of the set to say them. While the story outline may indicate that an episode must start at event A and end at event B, it's the writer's job to get from one to the other in the most dramatically convincing and entertaining way.

Nevertheless, it's important for the new writer to realise that producing an episode of a soap is first and last a team process. When I walked into my first planning meeting there were more than thirty people sitting round the table: story developers, producers, directors, schedulers, script editors, as well as the writers. We had already been provided with a fifty-page planning document outlining the stories in each of sixteen episodes, but I, like many of my fellow-writers, had had only a couple of days in which to digest how the characters were going to get from the episode I had watched the previous night to where they would be when my episode went out in six months time. It was my first taste of the pressure under which all continuing drama series are produced.

The main purpose of a planning meeting is to make sure that each writer understands the overall arc of the stories, and where their episode fits into that arc. In theory it's possible to suggest changes to a story at this stage, but it's a brave writer who attempts to do so. It would be like the flap of a butterfly's wings. Even a small change would produce huge ramifications in subsequent episodes, perhaps even in preceding ones. So unless you want to look like the person who asks for the ketchup in a Michelin restaurant, don't even think about it.

After the planning meeting comes what many writers regard as the most interesting part of the writing process: working out how to turn five or six separate stories into a coherent episode. This is when you have to say to yourself, 'OK, I know this, this and this happens, but what is the episode actually about?' Fortunately, it will usually be obvious which is the strongest story and, from that, who is the central character in that story. The journey that character travels therefore becomes the 'spine' of your episode, the central thread which holds the whole thing together.

You then pitch your approach to the commissioning meeting, a smaller affair than the planning meeting because it covers only one week's episodes. This is when you get your first lesson in what it means to have a thick skin. If you can't take criticism, believe me, choose another career. At my first commissioning meeting, confident that I had found a novel and exciting way of telling my stories, I instead suffered the ignominy of having my chosen spine story rejected in favour of another and the humiliation of needing two other stories explained to me again because I had completely got the wrong end of the stick. In theory, a writer can be sacked at this meeting, but obviously you have to do something really bad before that happens.

Producing a soap is an industrial process, a non-stop production line driven by the demands of the transmission schedule. At least two months before your episode is beamed out to a few million homes, filming needs to be completed. At least a month before that, your script will need to be finished and approved. If you're lucky you'll get maybe ten weeks in which to write it. This may sound generous, but it isn't. In that time you may be required to produce six, eight, even ten drafts.

If, like many writers, you believe your first draft to be such a work of genius it requires mere tweaking to be ready for handover to the cast, prepare to have your spirit crushed. The reams of notes that will inevitably arrive a few days later come via your script editor, the person many writers believe exists only to make their otherwise happy, carefree lives a misery. The truth is that script editors are put-upon middlemen, struggling to turn your draft into something halfway decent without hurting your feelings, juggling contradictory comments from all and sundry, trying to second-guess the sudden changes of mind of the executive producer, while at the same time firefighting script problems on a previous set of episodes now being filmed and trying to read all the other scripts on which your episode may have an impact.

A rule of first drafts is that your favourite bits will be the least liked. That scene you turned into a witty take on *The Taming of the Shrew* or *Reservoir Dogs*? By draft three it will have been reduced to a glance. More frustratingly, you won't even be able to moan about it to anyone. The big soaps – in particular *EastEnders* – are produced under conditions of secrecy the planners of D-Day might have envied. You don't want to be the one who spills the beans to *Heat* magazine, so you can't even try out a tricky bit of dialogue on your spouse or your mates down the pub. This is where your script editor comes in handy. Indeed, some writers use them as emotional crutches for every aspect of their lives. One script editor was woken up at two o'clock in the morning to hear a writer sobbing over the phone, 'My husband's left me!'

The third or fourth draft may sometimes be referred to as the final draft, though usually it is final only in the sense that your script editor has come to the conclusion that from now on you are likely to make things worse rather than better, so your script might as well be put in front of the executive producer. Depending on what sort of mood he or she is in, i.e. how many of the cast were arrested for being drunk and disorderly the previous weekend, your script may have to go through up to six more drafts.

Finally, when you have almost despaired of ever getting it right, the call will come: your script has been approved. A perfect excuse for a celebratory drink – unless you are already working on your next episode, in which case you'll probably resent the interruption. A few days later and the pukka version of your script arrives in the post, a lot thicker than you remember it because it's been formatted with more white space and lots of additional pages to do with the cast and filming, etc. – pages which you ignore because the only thing you are interested in is the front page, the page which has your name on, preceded by that magical word 'by'.

A week or so later filming starts. Writers are usually welcome to attend, but their status is uncertain. Yes, you wrote the dialogue the cast are desperately trying to speak convincingly, but don't expect anyone to take any notice of you. It's probably best to keep a low profile anyway, because actors tend to let it be known when they have a line they don't like. This can be very disheartening, particularly when they decide to ad lib a speech every word of which you have spent the last ten weeks honing.

But never mind, because if, when two months later you are proudly watching your first episode in the company of your family, your friends and half the street, they like it, then you can claim every word as your own, and if they don't, then you can always say it was ruined by the cast. The important thing, the reason you struggled through this long process, is that you are now – if only among your immediate circle – famous.

This happy conclusion assumes, of course, that nothing goes wrong. In practice, the world of continuing drama series is a continuing drama series in itself. I was in the middle of a fourth draft when I was told that the actor playing the leading character in my episode was no longer available, indeed was no longer in the country. Three months' worth of stories had to be rewritten. Filming of another of my episodes was actually underway when a leading actress had to be hospitalised. Even if no disaster strikes, writing for a soap is hedged with constraints. Most soaps are transmitted pre-watershed and are watched by huge numbers of children, so the writer must be careful to stay within bounds of taste, decency and language. How to make a working-class East Ender lose his temper without mouthing obscenities? Yes, it may be unrealistic and yes, it is difficult, but it has to be done.

Writing for a soap is a continual challenge and not, as some aspiring writers may believe, something that can be knocked off with one hand tied behind their backs. Some of our best TV writers spent many years writing for soaps: Alan Plater on *Z Cars*, Jimmy McGovern on *Brookside*, Paul Abbott on *Coronation Street*, to name only three. It is in many ways the best training a new writer could have. Where else would you find yourself writing about domestic violence in one episode, the consequences of rape in another, the breakdown of a marriage in the next, poverty, racism, illegitimacy and football in a fourth?

For some writers the main problem with soaps is, perversely, their very popularity. In our elitist view of culture it has always been a given that the worthiest art should be appreciated by only a few. Apparently it therefore follows that art which is enjoyed by many has little merit. This is simply snobbery under another name. Soaps may sometimes appear to be peopled by mouthy, outrageous characters in bizarre situations, but at their heart they are actually about ordinary, usually working-class people struggling with the problems of daily life, the kind of people whose opinions are rarely heard, who are often inarticulate and who are typically spoken about only in generalisations as being either the salt of the earth or shiftless.

Soaps give these people individual voices, as Dickens did 150 years ago, or as Timothy Spall once said in praise of Mike Leigh's films, 'They let the smallest characters have epic lives.' To be a writer for a soap, to be part of a team that tells the most watched stories on TV, is therefore neither a prostitution of one's talents nor a period of marking time until one's real genius is recognised. It is, despite the lost weekends, the impossible deadlines and the cast ruining your finest speeches, one of the best TV writing jobs going.

Film, TV and Radio Producers

Aardman

Gas Ferry Road, Bristol BS1 6UN
☎0117 984 8485   Fax 0117 984 8486
www.aardman.com

Head of Development (Features) *Richelle Wilder*
Script Editor (Television) *Dick Hansom*

Founded 1972. Award-winning animation studio producing films, television series, videos, commercials and new media properties. OUTPUT includes: *Rex the Runt*; *Morph Files*; *Creature Comforts*; *Wallace and Gromit*; *Angry Kid*; *Chicken Run*; *The Presentators*. No unsolicited submissions.

Above The Title

Level 2, 10/11 St Georges Mews, London NW1 8XE
☎020 7916 1984   Fax 020 7722 5706
✉ mail@abovethetitle.com
www.abovethetitle.com

Contacts *Bruce Hyman, Helen Chattwell*

Producer of radio drama and documentary programmes. OUTPUT includes *The Hitchhiker's Guide to the Galaxy* (Radio 4); *Clive Anderson's Chat Room* (Radio 2); *The Joy of Sax* (Radio 3) Unsolicited mss and ideas welcome. Approach in the first instance by e-mail. 'We encourage and support new writing in every way we can.'

Abstract Images

117 Willoughby House, Barbican, London EC2Y 8BL
☎020 7638 5123
✉ productions@abstract-images.co.uk

Contact *Howard Ross*

Television documentary and drama programming. Also theatre productions. OUTPUT includes *Balm in Gilead* (drama); *Road* (drama); *Bent* (drama); *God: For & Against* (documentary); *This Is a Man* (drama/doc). New writers should send synopsis in the first instance.

Acacia Productions Ltd

80 Weston Park, London N8 9Tb
☎020 8341 9392   Fax 020 8341 4879
✉ acacia@dial.pipex.com
www.acaciaproductions.co.uk

Contact *J. Edward Milner*

Producer of award-winning television and video documentaries; also news reports, corporates and programmes for educational charities. Undertakes basic video training and has a video manual in preparation. OUTPUT includes documentary series entitled *Last Plant Standing*; *A Farm in Uganda*; *Montserrat: Under the Volcano*; *Spirit of Trees* (8 progs.); *Vietnam: After the Fire*; *Macroeconomics – the Decision-makers*; *Greening of Thailand*; *A Future for Forests*. No unsolicited mss.

Acrobat Television

107 Wellington Road North, Stockport SK4 2LP
☎0161 477 9090   Fax 0161 477 9191
✉ info@acrobat-tv.co.uk

Contacts *David Hill, Annie Broom*

Specialises in training and promotional scripts, comedy and drama-based material. OUTPUT includes *Make a Stand* (Jack Dee, Gina Bellman and John Thompson); *The Customer View* (Roy Barraclough); *Serious About Waves* series (Peter Hart). No unsolicited mss.

Actaeon Films Ltd

24 Park Avenue, London NW2 5AP
☎020 8459 0955   Fax 0870 134 7980
✉ info@actaeonfilms.com
www.actaeonfilms.com

Producer *Daniel Cormack*
Head of Development *Rebecca Connell*

Founded 2004. Specialises in films for viewing and distribution via new media such as third generation mobile phones, p2p networks, e-mail and the Internet. OUTPUT includes *Darwinism, Death's Door* and *Response Time* (short comedies); *Fruit* (short drama). In development: *Golden Apples* (feature-length drama). Actaeon Films is a member of the **New Producers Alliance** and **The Script Factory**. 'We actively encourage new writers and new writing. However, we can only give feedback on scripts with strong potential for developments (all mss are read by a professional reader within two weeks of submission). Scripts returned only if accompanied by s.a.e.'

All Out Productions

50 Copperas Street, Manchester M4 1HS
☎0161 834 9955   Fax 0161 834 6978
✉ mail@allout.co.uk
www.allout.co.uk

Contact *David Cook*

Producer of documentaries, features and current affairs programmes for radio. OUTPUT includes *Five Live Report* (BBC Five Live – weekly news documentary); *Lamacq Live* (BBC Radio One – music and social affairs). Ideas welcome but not mss. Approach by e-mail.

Anglo/Fortunato Films Ltd

170 Popes Lane, London W5 4NJ
☎020 8932 7676   Fax 020 8932 7491

Contact *Luciano Celentino*

Film, television and video producer/director of action comedy and psych-thriller drama. No unsolicited mss.

Ariel Productions Ltd

46 Melcombe Regis Court, 59 Weymouth Street, London W1G 8NT
☎020 7935 6636   Fax 020 7935 6636

Producer *Otto Plaschkes*

Feature film and television producer. OUTPUT includes *Georgy Girl*; *Hopscotch*; *In Celebration*; *Butley*; *Doggin' Around*. Encourages new writers through involvement with the **National Film and Television School** and Screen Laboratory. No unsolicited mss.

Arlington Productions Limited

Cippenham Court, Cippenham Lane, Cippenham, Nr Slough SL1 5AU
☎01753 516767   Fax 01753 691785

Television producer. Specialises in popular international drama, with *occasional* forays into other areas. 'We have an enviable reputation for encouraging new writers but only accept unsolicited submissions via agents.'

The Ashford Entertainment Corporation Ltd

20 The Chase, Coulsdon CR5 2EG
✉ info@ashford-entertainment.co.uk
www.ashford-entertainment.co.uk

Managing Director *Frazer Ashford*

Founded in 1996 by award-winning film and TV producer Frazer Ashford whose credits include *Great Little Trains* (Mainline Television for Westcountry/Ch4, starring the late Willie Rushton); *Street Life* and *Make Yourself at Home* (both for

WTV). Produces theatrical films and television: drama, lifestyle and documentaries. Happy to receive ideas for documentaries but submit a one-page synopsis only in the first instance, enclosing s.a.e. 'Be patient, allow up to four weeks for a reply. Be precise with the idea; specific details rather than vague thoughts. Attach a back-up sheet with credentials and supporting evidence, i.e., can you ensure that your idea is feasible?'

Assembly Film and Television Ltd

Riverside Studios, Crisp Road, London W6 9RL
☎020 8237 1075   Fax 020 8237 1071
✉ judithmurrell@riversidestudios.co.uk

Contacts *William Burdett-Coutts, Judith Murrell*

Television documentary producer. OUTPUT includes the Prudential Awards for the Arts; the London Comedy Festival; Ch4's Black Season, *In Exile: Sitcom*; BAFTA award-winning *Black Books, Series 1, 2 & 3: Sitcom* and Jo Brand's *Hot Potatoes* for BBC1.

Beckmann International Ltd

1 The Courtyard, Court Row, Ramsey IM8 1AS
☎01624 816585   Fax 01624 816589
✉ sales@beckmanngroup.co.uk
www.beckmanngroup.co.uk

Contacts *Jo White, Stuart Semark*

Isle of Man-based company. Video and television documentary distributor. OUTPUT *Practical Guide to Europe* (travel series); *Maestro* (12-part series on classical composers); *Ivory Orphans*.

Big Heart Media

✉ info@bigheartmedia.com
www.bigheartmedia.com

Contacts *Colin Izod, Beth Newell*

Producers of drama and documetaries for television, radio and video. Ideas/outlines welcome by e-mail, but not unsolicited mss. 'We will respond as soon as we can. We're very keen to enourage new writing – particularly for radio drama.'

Blackwatch Productions Limited

3 Royal Exchange Court, 17 Royal Exchange Square, Glasgow G1 3DB
☎0141 222 2640/2641   Fax 0141 222 2646
✉ info@blackwatchtv.com
www.blackwatchtv.com

Company Director *Nicola Black*
Head of Production *Paul Gallagher*
Production Manager *Amanda Keown*

Film, television, video producer of drama and documentary programmes. OUTPUT includes *The Paranormal Peter Sellers*; *Snorting Coke with the BBC*; *When Freddie Mercury Met Kenny Everett*; *Designer Vaginas*; *Bonebreakers*; *Luv Bytes*; and *Can We Carry On, Girls?* for Ch4. Also coordinates *Mesh*, animation scheme. Does not welcome unsolicited mss.

Bona Broadcasting Ltd
3rd Floor, 21 Albert Square, Dundee DD1 1DJ
☎01382 225403   Fax 01382 225408
✉ ideas@bonabroadcasting.com
www.bonabroadcasting.com

Contact *Turan Ali*

Producer of award winning-drama and documentary programmes for BBC Radio, TV and film projects. No unsolicited mss but send a one-paragraph summary by e-mail in the first instance. 'Writers new to BBC radio should expect to write a whole script on spec to win a commission.' Runs radio and TV drama training courses in the UK and internationally.

Buccaneer Films
5 Rainbow Court, Oxhey WD19 4RP
☎01923 254000
✉ michael@gosling.com

Contact *Michael Gosling*

Corporate video production and still photography specialists in education and sport. No unsolicited mss.

Carnival (Films & Theatre) Ltd
12 Raddington Road, Ladbroke Grove, London W10 5TG
☎020 8968 0968   Fax 020 8968 0155
✉ info@carnival-films.co.uk
www.carnival-films.co.uk

Contact *Brian Eastman, Gareth Neame*

Film, TV and theatre producer. OUTPUT FILM: *The Mill on the Floss* (BBC); *Firelight* (Hollywood Pictures/Wind Dancer Productions); *Up on the Roof* (Rank/Granada); *Shadowlands* (Savoy/Spelling); *The Infiltrator* (Home Box Office); *Under Suspicion* (Columbia/Rank/LWT). TELEVISION: *The Grid* (BBC/TNT); *Rosemary & Thyme* (ITV/Granada); *As If* (Ch4/Columbia); *Lucy Sullivan is Getting Married* (ITV); *The Tenth Kingdom* (Sky/NBC); *Agatha Christie's Poirot* (ITV/LWT/A&E); *Every Woman Knows a Secret* and *Oktober* (both for ITV Network Centre); *The Fragile Heart* (Ch4); *Crime Traveller* (BBC); *Bugs 1–4* (BBC); *Anna Lee* (LWT); *All Or Nothing At All* (LWT); *Head Over Heels* (Carlton); *Jeeves &*

Wooster I–IV (Granada); *Traffik* (Ch4); *Porterhouse Blue* (Ch4); *Blott on the Landscape* (BBC). Theatre: *What a Performance*; *Juno & the Paycock*; *Murder is Easy*; *Misery*; *Ghost Train*; *Map of the Heart*; *Shadowlands*; *Up on the Roof*.

Cartwn Cymru
32 Wordsworth Avenue, Roath, Cardiff CF24 3FR
☎029 2046 3556/07771 640400
✉ production@cartwn-cymru.com

Contact *Naomi Jones*

Animation production company. OUTPUT *Toucan 'Tecs* (YTV/S4C); *Funnybones* and *Turandot: Operavox* (both for S4C/BBC); *Testament: The Bible in Animation* (BBC2/S4C); *The Miracle Maker* (S4C/BBC/British Screen/Icon Entertainment International); *Faeries* (HIT Entertainment plc for CITV); *Otherworld* (animated feature film for S4C Films, British Screen, Arts Council of Wales).

Celador
39 Long Acre, London WC2E 9LG
☎020 7240 8101   Fax 020 7845 6977
✉ tvhits@celador.co.uk
www.celador.co.uk

Head of Entertainment *Colman Hutchinson*
Development Executives, Comedy *Humphrey Barclay, Vanessa Haynes*
Head of Radio *Liz Anstee*

Producer of TV and radio comedy and light entertainment. OUTPUT *You Are What You Eat*; *Who Wants to be a Millionaire*; *Winning Lines*; *Commercial Breakdown*; *Britain's Brainiest ...*; *All About Me*; *It's Been a Bad Week*. 'We are interested in original comedy and radio scripts but do not accept unsolicited entertainment formats. As a relatively small company our script-reading capacity is limited.'

Celador Films
39 Long Acre, London WC2E 9LG
☎020 7845 6988   Fax 020 7497 9541
✉ sbaker@celador.co.uk
www.celador.co.uk

Head of Production and Development *Christian Colson*
Development Executive *Ivana MacKinnon*
Development Assistant *Sarah Baker*

Producer of feature films. OUTPUT includes *Dirty Pretty Things* and Julian Fellowes-helmed romantic drama, *Separate Lives*. Currently in post-production on Neil Marshall's horror feature, *The Descent*. No unsolicited mss.

Celtic Films Ent. Ltd

22 Grafton Street, London W1S 4EX
☎020 7409 2080   Fax 020 7409 2383
✉ info@celticfilms.co.uk

Contact *Stuart Sutherland*

Film and television drama producer. OUTPUT includes 14 feature-length *Sharpe* TV films for Carlton and *A Life for a Life – The True Story of Stefan Kiszko* TV film for ITV. Devised *Hornblower* series for ITV. Supports new writing and welcomes unsolicited mss.

Chameleon Television Ltd

Great Minster House, Lister Hill, Horsforth, Leeds LS18 5DL
☎0113 205 0040   Fax 0113 281 9454
✉ allen@chameleontv.com

Contacts *Allen Jewhurst, Qyuen Muu, Simon Wells*

Film and television drama and documentary producer. OUTPUT includes *Edge of the City*; 'Dispatches' – *Killing for Honour, College Girls*; *Ken Dodd in the Dock* (all for Ch4); *Divorces From Hell*; *Shipman*; *Love to Shop*; *The Marchioness* (all for ITV); *Ted & Sylvia – Love, Loss* (BBC); *Liverpool Poets* (Ch5). Scripts not welcome unless via agents but new writing is encouraged.

Chatsworth Television Limited

4 Great Chapel Street, London W1F 8FD
☎020 7734 4302   Fax 020 7437 3301
✉ television@chatsworth-tv.co.uk
www.chatsworth-tv.co.uk

Managing Director *Malcolm Heyworth*

Entertainment and factual entertainment television producer. No drama or comedy scripts.

The Children's Film & Television Foundation Ltd

The John Maxwell Building, Elstree Film & TV Studios, Shenley Road, Borehamwood WD6 1JG
☎020 8953 0844   Fax 020 8207 0860
✉ annahome@cftf.onyxnet.co.uk

Chief Executive *Anna Home*

Involved in the development and co-production of films for children and the family, both for the theatric market and for TV.

Cinécosse

North Meadows, Oldmeldrum AB51 OGQ
☎01651 873311   Fax 01651 873300
✉ admin@cinecosse.co.uk
www.cinecosse.co.uk

Contact *Graeme Mowat*

Television and video documentary and corporate productions. OUTPUT includes *Scotland's Larder* and *Rising to the Challenge* (Scottish/Grampian TV); safety and training videos for industry; tourism promotional and sales information, interactive multimedia and DVD authoring. All scripts are commissioned; no unsolicited material.

Cinema Verity Productions Ltd

11 Addison Avenue, London W11 4QS
☎020 7460 2777   Fax 020 7371 3329

Contact *Verity Lambert*

Leading television drama producer whose credits include *She's Out* by Lynda la Plante; *Class Act* by Michael Aitkens; *May to December* (BBC series); *Running Late* by Simon Gray (Screen 1); *The Cazalets* adapt. of *The Cazalet Chronicle* by Elizabeth Jane Howard (BBC).

Cleveland Productions

5 Rainbow Court, Oxhey, Near Watford WD19 4RP
☎01923 254000
✉ michael@gosling.com

Contact *Michael Gosling*

Communications in sound and vision A/V production and still photography specialists in education and sport. No unsolicited mss.

COI

Hercules Road, London SE1 7DU
☎020 7928 2345

Government advertising and marketing communications, and public information films.

Collingwood O'Hare Entertainment Ltd & Convergence Productions Ltd

10–14 Crown Street, London W3 8SB
☎020 8993 3666   Fax 020 8993 9595
✉ info@crownstreet.co.uk

Producers *Christopher O'Hare, Terence Clegg, Tony Collingwood*

Head of Development *Helen Stroud*

Film and TV. Convergence Productions produces live action, drama documentaries; Collingwood O'Hare Entertainment specialises in children's animation. OUTPUT **Convergence**: *Theo* (film drama series); *Plastic Fantastic* (UK cosmetic surgery techniques, Ch5); *David Starkey's Henry VIII* (Ch4 historical documentary) and *On the Road Again* (BBC2 documentary travel series).

Collingwood: *RARG* (award-winning animated film); *Yoko! Jakamoko! Toto!* (CITV); *Daisy-Head Mayzie* (Dr Seuss animated series for Turner Network and Hanna-Barbera); *Gordon the Garden Gnome* (CBBC); *Eddy and the Bear* (CITV) and *The King's Beard* (CITV). Unsolicited mss not welcome 'as a general rule as we do not have the capacity to process the sheer weight of submissions this creates. We therefore tend to review material from individuals recommended to us through personal contact with agents or other industry professionals. We like to encourage new writing and have worked with new writers but our ability to do so is limited by our capacity for development. We can usually only consider taking on one project each year, as development/finance takes several years to put in place.'

The Comedy Unit

Glasgow TV & Film Studios, Glasgow Media Park, Craigmont Street, Glasgow G20 9BT
☎0141 305 6666   Fax 0141 305 6600
✉ comedyunit@comedyunit.co.uk
www.comedyunit.co.uk

Contacts *April Chamberlain, Colin Gilbert*

Producers of comedy entertainment for children's TV, radio, video and film. OUTPUT *Still Game*; *Karen Dunbar Show*; *Offside*; *Chewin' the Fat*; *Only An Excuse*; *Yo! Diary* and *Watson's Wind Up*. Unsolicited mss welcome by post or e-mail.

Convergence Productions Ltd

See **Collingwood O'Hare Entertainment Ltd & Convergence Productions Ltd**

Cosgrove Hall Films

8 Albany Road, Chorlton–cum–Hardy M21 0AW
☎0161 882 2500   Fax 0161 882 2555
✉ animation@chf.co.uk

Contact *Lee Marriott*

Children's animation producer; film video and television. OUTPUT includes *Noddy* and *Rotten Ralph* (both for BBC); *Lavender Castle* by Gerry Anderson; *The Fox Busters; Animal Shelf; Rocky & the Dodos*; Alison Uttley's *Little Grey Rabbit* (all for children's ITV); Terry Pratchett's *Discworld* (Ch4). 'We try to select writers on a project-by-project basis.'

Creative Channel Ltd

Channel TV, Television Centre, St Helier, Jersey JE1 3ZD
☎01534 816873   Fax 01534 816889
✉ david@channeltv.co.uk

www.channeltv.co.uk
Senior Producer *David Evans*

Producer of TV commercials and corporate material: information, promotional, sales, training and events coverage. CD and DVD production; promotional videos for all types of businesses throughout Europe. No unsolicited mss; new writing/scripts commissioned as required. Interested in hearing from local writers resident in the Channel Islands.

The Creative Partnership

13 Bateman Street, London W1D 3AF
☎020 7439 7762
✉ sallyc@thecreativepartnership.co.uk
www.thecreativepartnership.co.uk

Contacts *Christopher Fowler, Sally Chapman*

'Europe's largest "one-stop shop" for advertising and marketing campaigns for the film and television industries.' Clients include most major and independent film companies. No scripts. 'We train new writers in-house, and find them from submitted c.v.s. All applicants must have previous commercial writing experience.'

Cricket Ltd

Medius House, 63–69 New Oxford Street, London WC1A 1EA
☎020 7845 0300   Fax 020 7845 0303
✉ team@cricket-ltd.com
www.cricket-ltd.com

Head of Production (Film & Video) *Jonathan Freer*

Film and video, live events and conferences, print and design. 'Communications solutions for business clients wishing to influence targeted external and internal audiences.'

CSA Word

6A Archway Mews, 241A Putney Bridge Road, London SW15 2PE
☎020 8871 0220   Fax 020 8877 0712
✉ victoria@csaword.co.uk
www.csaword.co.uk

Contacts *Victoria Williams, Clive Stanhope*

Producer of drama, documentaries and readings for radio. OUTPUT *Alfie Elkins & His Little Life* (drama for BBC World Service); *Lucky Man* (reading for BBC R4); *A Stable Relationship* (feature for BBC R4); *Decline and Fall* (reading for BBC R2); *It's a Girl; Chat Snaps; Videotape – Two* (documentaries for BBC World Service Learning); *The Glenn Miller Story* (documentary for BBC Radio 2). Unsolicited mss and ideas welcome by post or e-mail. 'We encourage new drama, short story writing and documentary/ feature ideas.'

Cutting Edge Productions Ltd
27 Erpingham Road, London SW15 1BE
☎020 8780 1476   Fax 020 8780 0102
✉ juliannorridge@btconnect.com

Contact *Julian Norridge*

Corporate and documentary video and television. OUTPUT includes US series on evangelicalism, 'Dispatches' on US tobacco and government videos. No unsolicited mss; 'we commission all our writing to order, but are open to ideas.'

Dakota Films Ltd
4 Junction Mews, London W2 1PN
☎020 7706 9407   Fax 020 7402 6111
✉ info@o-spi.com

Managing Director *Jonathan Olsberg*

Film and television drama. Feature films include: *Head in the Clouds; Me Without You; Janice Beard 45wpm; Let Him Have It; Othello*. Currently developing a slate of films including John Sayles' *Fade to Black* and a number of projects by new writers. Interested in working with new talent but does not consider unsolicited material.

Diverse Production Limited
6 Gorleston Street, London W14 8XS
☎020 7603 4567   Fax 020 7603 2148
www.diverse.tv

Independent production company specialising in popular prime-time formats, strong documentaries, specialist factual, historical, cultural, religious, arts, music and factual entertainment. Recent OUTPUT includes *Musicality; Operatunity; Who Wrote the Bible; Make Me a Perfect Wife; Who You Callin' Nigger?; In Search of Tony Blair; Britain AD; Shock Treatment; Status Anxiety*.

DMS Films Ltd
89 Sevington Road, London NW4 3RU
☎020 8203 5540   Fax 0870 762 5871
✉ danny@dmsfilms.co.uk

Producer *Daniel San*

Film drama producer. OUTPUT includes *Understanding Jane; Hard Edge; Strangers*. Unsolicited screenplays not welcome: phone, fax or e-mail synopsis or outline in first instance.

Double Exposure
See **Flashback Television Limited**

DoubleBand Films
Crescent Arts Centre, 2–4 University Road, Belfast BT7 1NH
☎028 9024 3331   Fax 028 9023 6980
✉ info@doublebandfilms.com
www.doublebandfilms.com

Contacts *Michael Hewitt, Dermot Lavery*

Specialises in documentaries and drama. Recent productions include *Seven Days that Shook the World* and *War in Mind* (both for Ch4); *Christine's Children* (BBC Northern Ireland; nominated for both the RTS and Celtic Film Festival). Currently working on documentary about Rwanda for Ch4's 'The Slot' and a Landmark D-Day documentary, *D-Day: Triumph and Tragedy* (for BBC NI).

Drake A-V Video Ltd
89 St Fagans Road, Fairwater, Cardiff CF5 3AE
☎029 2056 0333   Fax 029 2055 4909
www.drakeav.com

Contact *Ian Lewis*

Corporate A-V film and video, mostly promotional, training or educational. Scripts in these fields welcome. Design and installation of AV systems.

Charles Dunstan Communications Ltd
42 Wolseley Gardens, London W4 3LS
☎020 8994 2328   Fax 020 8994 2328

Contact *Charles Dunstan*

Producer of film, video and TV for documentary and corporate material. OUTPUT *Renewable Energy* for broadcast worldwide in *Inside Britain* series; *The Far Reaches* travel series; *The Electric Environment*. No unsolicited scripts.

Electric Airwaves Ltd (Ladbroke Radio)
Essel House, 29 Foley Street, London W1W 7JW
☎020 7323 2770   Fax 020 7079 2080
✉ neil@electricairwaves.com
www.electricairwaves.com

Contacts *Neil Gardner, Richard Bannerman*

Producer of radio drama, documentary, corporate, music, music documentaries and readings. OUTPUT includes *The Woman in White; The Darling Buds of May; The True History of British Pop; The World on a String; The Colour of Music* (all for BBC Radio 2); *Don Carlos; In the Company of Men* (BBC Radio 3 drama); *Sitting in Limbo*

(BBC World Service drama); *Your Vote Counts* (Electoral Commision audio CDs). Unsolicited mss and ideas welcome; send letter in the first instance. 'We are willing to help develop for possible submission to the BBC.'

Ruth Evans Productions
4 Offlands Cottages, Moulsford OX10 9HP
☎01491 651331
✉ ruth@ruthgevans.com

Contact *Ruth Evans*

Producer of features and documentaries for the World Service and BBC Radio 4. Unsolicited ideas welcome by e-mail.

Fairline Productions Ltd
15 Royal Terrace, Glasgow G3 7NY
☎0141 331 0077   Fax 0141 331 0066
✉ fairprods@aol.com

Contact *Mr R. Walker*

Television and video producer of documentary and corporate programmes and commercials. OUTPUT includes *Hooked*, a 15-part angling series (Discovery Channel) plus training and instructional videos for Forbo-Nairn Ltd, Royal Bank of Scotland, and Health & Safety Executive. No unsolicited scripts.

Farnham Film Company Ltd
34 Burnt Hill Road, Lower Bourne, Farnham GU10 3LZ
☎01252 710313   Fax 01252 725855
www.farnfilm.com

Contact *Ian Lewis*

Television and film: children's drama and documentaries. Unsolicited mss usually welcome but prefers a letter to be sent in the first instance. Check website for current requirements.

Fast Films
Christmas House, 213 Chester Road, Castle Bromwich, Solihull B36 0ET
☎0121 749 7147/4144
✉ ukfastfilms@yahoo.co.uk

Contact *Gavin Prime*

Film and television: comedy, entertainment and animation. No unsolicited mss.

Festival Film and Television Ltd
Festival House, Tranquil Passage, Blackheath, London SE3 0BJ
☎020 8297 9999   Fax 020 8297 1155
✉ info@festivalfilm.com
www.festivalfilm.com

Managing Director *Ray Marshall*
Producer *Matt Marshall*
Development *Johanna Devereaux*

Best known for the Catherine Cookson dramas, produced for ITV. First feature film, *Man Dancin'*, was distributed in 2004. The company is looking for television drama (primarily two-parters or single films) and feature films for international theatrical distribution. Prefers submissions through an agent. Unsolicited work must be professionally presented.

Festival Productions Limited
PO Box 70, Brighton BN1 1YJ
☎01273 669595   Fax 01273 669596
✉ steve@festivalradio.com
www.festivalradio.com

Managing Director *Steve Stark*

Producer of globally syndicated music shows, Sony Award winning radio campaigns, contemporary spoken word productions and a dedicated net radio service at www.totallyradio.com

Fiction Factory
14 Greenwich Church Street, London SE10 9BJ
☎020 8853 5100   Fax 020 8293 3001
✉ radio@fictionfactory.co.uk
www.fictionfactory.co.uk

Creative Director *John Taylor*

Producer of drama and documentaries for radio. OUTPUT includes Proust's *A La Recherche du Temps Perdu* (BBC R4 Classic Serial); Jonathan Myerson's *Kidnap*; Rob John's *Little Queen of England* and R.L. Stevenson's *Markheim* (new plays for R4); *Changing the Guards* (R4 feature) and Nela Larsen's *Passing* (R4 Classic Serial). Ideas considered if sent by e-mail. Mss only from agents or writers with a professional track record in the broadcast media.

Film and General Productions Ltd
4 Bradbrook House, Studio Place, London SW1X 8EL
☎020 7235 4495   Fax 020 7245 9853
✉ cparsons@filmgen.co.uk

Contacts *Clive Parsons, Davina Belling*

Film and television drama. Feature films include *True Blue, Tea with Mussolini* and *I Am David*. Also *Seesaw* (ITV drama), *The Greatest Store in the World* (family drama, BBC) and *The Queen's Nose* (children's series, BBC). Interested in considering new writing but subject to prior telephone conversation.

Firehouse Productions
42 Glasshouse Street, London W1B 5DW
☎020 7439 2220   Fax 020 7439 2210
✉ postie@firehouse.biz
www.firehouse.biz

Contacts *Julie-anne Edwards, Gavin Knight*

Corporate films and websites, commercials and DRTV. OUTPUT includes work for De Beers; Prudential; government and various agencies.

The First Film Company Ltd
3 Bourlet Close, London W1W 7BQ
☎020 7436 9490   Fax 020 7637 1290
✉ info@firstfilmcompany.com

Producers *Roger Randall-Cutler, Robert Cheek*

Founded 1984. Cinema screenplays. All submissions should be made through an agent.

First Writes Theatre Company
Lime Kiln Cottage, High Starlings, Banham, Norwich NR16 2BS
☎01953 888525   Fax 01953 888974
✉ ellen@firstwrites.fsnet.co.uk
www.first-writes.co.uk

Contact *Ellen Dryden*

Producer of numerous afternoon, Friday and Saturday plays, classic serials and comedy narrative series for BBC Radio 3, 4 and World Service. Welcomes unsolicited mss or ideas by post. 'As an independent company it is difficult to obtain commissions for new writers and in-house should be your first port of call. However, we are committed to producing new work by established writers.'

Flannel
21 Berwick Street, London W1F 0PZ
☎020 7287 9277   Fax 020 7287 7785
✉ mail@flannel.net

Contact *Kate Haldane*

Producer of drama, documentaries and comedy for television and radio. OUTPUT includes *Women's Hour* (BBC R4); *The Hendersons' Christmas Party* (five-part Christmas drama, BBC R4). No unsolicited mss. 'Keen to encourage new writing, but must come via an agent. Particularly interested in 45–50 minute dramas for radio. Not in a position to produce plays for stage, but very happy to consider adaptations. Welcomes comedy with some track record.'

Flashback Television Limited
11 Bowling Green Lane, London EC1R 0BG
☎020 7490 8996   Fax 020 7490 5610
✉ mailbox@flashbacktv.co.uk
www.flashbacktv.com

Contact *Tim Ball*

Producer of documentaries and factual entertainment since 1982. Based in London and Bristol. Acquired education producer Double Exposure in 2004. Recent credits include *Battlestations/Heavy Metal* (AETN, Ch4); *Superhomes* (BBC); *The Badness of King George IV* (Ch4); and *Top Tens* (Discovery).

Flicks Films Ltd
101 Wardour Street, London W1F 0UG
☎020 7734 4892   Fax 020 7734 4892
www.flicksfilms.com

Managing Director/Producer *Terry Ward*

Film and video: children's animated series and specials. OUTPUT *The Mr Men; Little Miss; Bananaman; The Pondles; Nellie the Elephant; See How They Work With Dig and Dug; Timbuctoo; Busy Buses*. Scripts specific to their needs will be considered. 'Always willing to read relevant material.'

Flying Scotsman Films Ltd
The Producers' Centre, 61 Holland Street, Glasgow G2 4NJ
☎0141 287 6817   Fax 0141 287 6817
✉ broncofilm@btinternet.com
www.broncofilms.co.uk

Contact *Peter Broughan*

Film and television drama. OUTPUT includes *Rob Roy* (feature film) and *Young Person's Guide to Becoming a Rock Star* (TV series). No unsolicited mss.

Focus Films Ltd
The Rotunda Studios,
Rear of 116–118 Finchley Road,
London NW3 5HT
☎020 7435 9004   Fax 020 7431 3562
✉ focus@focusfilms.co.uk
www.focusfilms.co.uk

Contacts *David Pupkewitz, Malcolm Kohll* (Head of Development)

Film producer. OUTPUT *The Book of Eve* (Canadian drama); *The Bone Snatcher* (Horror, UK/Can/SA); *Julia's Ghost* (German co-production); *The 51st State* (feature film); *Secret Society* (comedy drama feature film); *Crimetime* (feature thriller); *Diary of a Sane Man; Othello*. Projects in development include *Barry; Dogwatch; Indibindie; Tainted Desert; Big Time; The Complete History of the Beast; Triomf*. No unsolicited scripts.

Mark Forstater Productions Ltd
27 Lonsdale Road, London NW6 6RA
☎020 7624 1123   Fax 020 7624 1124

Contact *Mark Forstater*

Active in the selection, development and production of material for film and TV. OUTPUT *Monty Python and the Holy Grail; The Odd Job; The Grass is Singing; Xtro; Forbidden; Separation; The Fantasist; Shalom Joan Collins; The Silent Touch; Grushko; The Wolves of Willoughby Chase; Between the Devil and the Deep Blue Sea; Doing Rude Things.* No unsolicited scripts.

FremantleMedia Ltd
1 Stephen Street, London W1T 1AL
☎020 7691 6000   Fax 020 7691 6100
www.fremantlemedia.com

Chief Executive *Tony Cohen*
Chief Executive, UK Production *Lorraine Heggessey*

FremantleMedia, formerly known as Pearson Television, is the production arm of the RTL Group, Europe's largest TV and radio company. Acquired Thames Television in 1993 (producer of *The Bill*) and Grundy Worldwide (*Neighbours*) in 1995. Further acquisitions were Witzend Productions (*Lovejoy*) and Alomo Productions in 1996 and TalkBack Productions in 2000. FremantleMedia produces more than 260 programmes in over 40 countries and territories a year.

Gaia Communications
Sanctuary House, 35 Harding Avenue, Eastbourne BN22 8PL
☎01323 734809/727183   Fax 01323 734809
✉ production@gaiacommunications.co.uk
www.gaiacommunications.co.uk

Producer *Robert Armstrong*
Script Editor *Loni Webb*

Established 1987. Video and TV corporate and documentary. OUTPUT *Discovering* (south east regional tourist and local knowledge series); *Holistic* (therapies and general information); local interest audiobooks.

Noel Gay Television
Shepperton Studios, Studios Road, Shepperton TW17 0QD
☎01932 592569   Fax 01932 592172
✉ charles.armitage@virgin.net

CEO *Charles Armitage*

OUTPUT *The Fear* (BBC Choice); *Second Chance* (Ch4); *Hububb* Series 1–5 (BBC); *I-Camcorder* (Ch4); *Frank Stubbs Promotes* (Carlton/ITV);

10%ers Series 2 (Carlton/ITV); *Call Up the Stars* (BBC1); *Smeg Outs* (BBC video); *Red Dwarf* 8xseries; *Dave Allen* (ITV); *Windrush* (BBC2). Joint ventures and companies include a partnership with Odyssey, a leading Indian commercials, film and TV producer, and the Noel Gay Motion Picture Company, whose credits include *Virtual Sexuality; Trainspotting* (with Ch4 and Figment Films); *Killer Tongue; Dog Soldiers; Fast Sofa;* and *Pasty Faces.* Associate NGTV companies are Grant Naylor Productions and Pepper Productions. NGTV is willing to accept unsolicited material from writers but 1–2-page treatments only. No scripts, please.

Ginger Television
See **SMG & Ginger TV Productions Ltd**

Goldcrest Films International Ltd
65–66 Dean Street, London W1D 4PL
☎020 7437 8696   Fax 020 7437 4448
✉ mailbox@goldcrestfilms.com

Chairman *John Quested*
Contact *Stephen Johnston*

Founded in the late 1970s. Formerly part of the Brent Walker Leisure Group but independent since 1990 following management buy-out led by John Quested. The company's core activities are film production, post-production facilities and worldwide distribution. Scripts via agents only.

The Good Film Company Ltd
The Studio, 5–6 Eton Garages, Lambolle Place, London NW3 4PE
☎020 7794 6222   Fax 020 7794 4651
✉ yanina@goodfilms.co.uk
www.goodfilms.co.uk

Contact *Yanina Barry*

Commercials and pop videos. Clients include Hugo Boss, Cadbury's, Wella, National Express Coaches, Camel Cigarettes, Tunisian Tourist Board. *No* unsolicited mss.

Granada Drama
The London Television Centre, Upper Ground, South Bank, London SE1 9LT
☎020 7620 1620   Fax 020 7261 3041

Controller of Granada Drama, London *Michele Buck*

Granada Productions, **ITV plc**'s production arm, is the largest commercial TV production company in the UK. Produces original programmes, co-productions and TV movies for ITV channels and other broadcasters, both in the UK and abroad. OUTPUT includes *Hornblower; Poirot; Miss*

Marple; Touching Evil; Where the Heart Is; The Last Detective; William and Mary; Jericho; and Sex Traffic.

Granite Film & Television Productions Ltd
Vigilant House, 120 Wilton Road, London SW1V 1JZ
☎020 7808 7230   Fax 020 7808 7231
Contact *Simon Welfare*

Producer of television documentary programmes such as *Nicholas & Alexandra; Victoria & Albert* and *Arthur C. Clarke's Mysterious Universe.*

Green Umbrella Ltd
The Old Post Office, 67 Stoke Hill, Stoke Bishop, Bristol BS9 1EP
☎0117 962 7910   Fax 0117 968 8788
✉ postmaster@umbrella.co.uk
www.umbrella.co.uk

Film producers specialising in science and natural history documentaries. OUTPUT includes episodes for *The Natural World, Wildlife on One* and original series such as *Living Europe* and *Triumph of Life.* Unsolicited treatments relating to natural history and science subjects are welcome.

Greenwich Village Productions
14 Greenwich Church Street, London SE10 9BJ
☎020 8853 5100   Fax 020 8293 3001
✉ info@greenwichvillage.tv
www.greenwichvillage.tv
Contact *John Taylor*

Producer of drama documentaries, arts features and educational programmes. OUTPUT *An Arundel Tomb* (video treatment of Philip Larkin's poem); *Adlestrop* (video treatment of Edward Thomas' poem); and *The Secret Places of the Four Quartets.* Welcomes ideas by e-mail. Mss only from agents or writers with a professional track record in the chosen medium.

H2 Business Communications
Shepperton Studios, Shepperton TW17 0QD
☎01932 593717   Fax 01932 593718
✉ bob@hthc.co.uk
www.h2bc.co.uk
Contact *Bob Carson*

Conferences, videos, awards presentations and speaker training.

Hammer Film Productions Ltd
☎020 7637 2322   Fax 020 7323 2307
Contact *Terry Ilott*

Television and feature films. Please do not send unsolicited scripts or treatments.

Hammerwood Film Productions
110 Trafalgar Road, Portslade BN41 1GS
☎01273 277333   Fax 01273 705451
✉ filmangels@freenetname.co.uk
www.filmangel.co.uk
Contacts *Ralph Harvey, Petra Ginman*

Film, video and TV drama. OUTPUT *Iceni – Queen of Death* (film; co-production with Pan-European Film Productions and Boudicca Film Productions Ltd); *Boudicca – A Celtic Tragedy* (TV series). In pre-production: *Road to Nirvana* (Ealing-style comedy); *The Black Egg* (witchcraft in 17th century England); *The Ghosthunter; Iceni* (documentary of the rebellion of AD61); *No Case to Answer* (legal series). 'Authors are recommended to access www.filmangel.co.uk' (see *Useful Websites*).

Hartswood Films Ltd
Twickenham Studios, The Barons, St Margarets TW1 2AW
☎020 8607 8736   Fax 020 8607 8744
✉ films.tv@hartswoodfilms.co.uk
Contact *Elaine Cameron*

Film and TV production for drama, comedy and documentary. OUTPUT (all for BBC) *Border Cafe; Coupling; Carrie & Barry; Men Behaving Badly.*

Hat Trick Productions Ltd
10 Livonia Street, London W1F 8AF
☎020 7437 2907   Fax 020 7287 9791
www.hattrick.com
Contact *Denise O'Donoghue*
Television programmes.

Healthcare Productions Limited
The Great Barn, Godmersham, Canterbury CT4 7DT
☎01227 738279   Fax 01227 732145
✉ penny@healthcareproductions.co.uk
www.healthcareproductions.co.uk
Contact *Penny Webb*

Television and video: documentary and drama. Produces training and educational material, in text, video and CD-ROM, mostly health-related, social care issues, law and marriage.

The Jim Henson Company
30 Oval Road, Camden NW1 7DE
☎020 7428 4000   Fax 020 7428 4001
www.henson.com
Contact *Martin Baker, Executive Producer*

Feature films and TV: family entertainment and children's, fantasy and sci-fi. OUTPUT *Good Boy!*; *Buddy*; *Rat*; *The Dark Crystal*; *Labyrinth*; *The Witches* (films); *Dinosaurs* (ABC); *Muppet Tonight* (BBC/Sky); *The Muppet Show* (ITV); *The Storyteller* (Ch4/BBC); *Dr Seuss*; *The Secret Life of Toys* (BBC); *The Animal Show* (BBC); *Mopatop's Shop* (ITV); *Brats of the Lost Nebula* (WB); *Farscape* (Sci-Fi/USA/BBC); *Bear in the Big Blue House* (Disney Channel/Ch5); *Jim Henson's Construction Site* (ITV); *The Hoobs* (Ch4); *Jack and the Beanstalk: The Real Story* (CBS); *Telling Stories with Tomie de Paola* and *Donna's Day* (both for Odyssey); *The Fearing Mind* (Fox); *It's a Very, Merry Muppet Christmas* (NBC); *Kermit's Swamp Years* (CTHV); *Animal Jam* (Discovery); *Bambaloo* (Seven Network); *The Wubbulous World of Dr Seuss* (BBC); *Gulliver's Travels* (CBS). Scripts via agents only.

Heritage Theatre Ltd
8 Clanricarde Gardens, London W2 4NA
☎020 7243 2750   Fax 020 7792 8584
✉ rm@heritagetheatre.com
www.heritagetheatre.com

Contact *Robert Marshall*

Video recordings of successful stage plays for distribution on DVD and broadcast.

John Holloway
53 Daybrook Road, London SW19 3DJ
☎020 8542 7721
✉ holliesx2@aol.com

Contact *John Holloway*

Corporate video and promotional articles. Clients include the Post Office, IBM, British Gas, Freemans, Eastern Electricity, Customs & Excise.

Holmes Associates
The Studio, 37 Redington Road, London NW3 7QY
☎020 7813 4333
✉ holmesassociates@blueyonder.co.uk

Contact *Andrew Holmes*

Prolific originator, producer and packager of documentary, drama and music television and films. See also **Open Road Films**. OUTPUT has included *Prometheus* (Ch4 'Film on 4'); *The Shadow of Hiroshima* (Ch4 'Witness'); *The House of Bernarda Alba* (Ch4/WNET/Amaya); *Piece of Cake* (LWT); *The Cormorant* (BBC/Screen 2); *John Gielgud Looks Back*; *Rock Steady*; *Well Being*; *Signals*; *Ideal Home?* (all Ch4); *Timeline* (with

MPT, TVE Spain & TRT Turkey); *Seven Canticles of St Francis* (BBC2).

Hourglass Productions
27 Prince's Road, London SW19 8RA
☎020 8540 8786
✉ productions@hourglass.co.uk
www.hourglass.co.uk

Directors *Martin Chilcott, Jacqueline Chilcott*

Film and video; documentary and drama. OUTPUT BAFTA nominated scientific television documentaries and educational programming. Also current affairs, health and social issues.

Icon Films
10 Redland Terrace, Bristol BS6 6TD
☎0117 924 8535   Fax 0117 974 4971
✉ info@iconfilms.co.uk
www.iconfilms.co.uk

Contact *Harry Marshall*

Film and TV documentaries. OUTPUT *Holy Cow!* (WNET); *The King Cobra & I* (BBC 'Natural World'); *The Riddle of Einstein's Brain* (Ch4/National Geographic Channels International). Specialises in factual documentaries. Open-minded to new filmmakers. Proposals welcome.

Imari Entertainment Ltd
PO Box 158, Beaconsfield HP9 1AY
☎01494 677147   Fax 01494 677147
✉ info@imarientertainment.com

Contact *Jonathan Fowke*

TV and video producer, covering all areas of drama, documentary and corporate productions.

Isis Productions
106 Hammersmith Grove, London W6 7HB
☎020 8748 3042   Fax 020 8748 3046
✉ isis@isis-productions.com
www.isisproductions.co.uk

Directors *Nick de Grunwald, Jamie Rugge-Price*
Production Coordinator *Catriona Lawless*

Formed in 1991, Isis Productions focuses on the production of music and documentary programmes. OUTPUT *Ray Davies – The World from My Window*; *James Brown – Soul Survivor* (Ch4); *Pink Floyd* (ITV 'Classic Albums 4'); *Bernie Taupin* (ITV 'South Bank Show'); *Iron Maiden, Judas Priest* (Five 'Rock Classics'); Films on *Deep Purple, Metallica, Def Leppard, Lou Reed, Elton John, Elvis Presley, Sex Pistols* (ITV 'Classic Albums 3'); *Nosey Series 3* (Five – Children's); *The Genesis Songbook* (Five); *England's Other Elizabeth – Elizabeth Taylor* (BBC 'Omnibus').

Isolde Films
28 Twyford Avenue, London W3 9QB
☎020 8896 2860
✉ isolde@btinternet.com
www.tonypalmer.org
Contact *Michela Antonello*

Film and TV documentaries. OUTPUT *Wagner*; *Menuhin*; *Maria Callas*; *Testimony*; *In From the Cold*; *Pushkin*; *England, My England* (by John Osborne). Unsolicited material is read, but please send a written outline first.

JAM Pictures and Jane Walmsley Productions
8 Hanover Street, London W1S 1YE
☎020 7290 2676   Fax 020 7290 2677
✉ producers@jampix.com
Contacts *Jane Walmsley, Michael Braham*

JAM Pictures was founded in 1996 to produce drama for film, TV and stage. Projects include: *Hillary's Choice* (TV film, A&E Network); *Son of Pocahontas* (TV film, ABC); *Rudy: the Rudy Giuliani Story* (TV film, USA Network); *One More Kiss* (feature, directed by Vadim Jean); *Bad Blood* (UK theatre tour). Jane Walmsley Productions, formed in 1985 by TV producer, writer and broadcaster, Jane Walmsley, has completed award-winning documentaries and features such as *Hot House People* (Ch4). No unsolicited mss. 'Letters can be sent to us, asking if we wish to see mss; we are very interested in quality material, from published or produced writers only, please'

Justice Entertainment Ltd
PO Box 4377, London W1A 7SX
☎020 7467 5450   Fax 020 7467 5451
✉ info@timwestwood.com
www.timwestwood.com

Producer of shows for Radio 1. No unsolicited material.

Keo Films.com Ltd
Studio 2B, 151–157 City Road, London EC1V 1JH
☎020 7490 3580   Fax 020 7490 8419
✉ keo@keofilms.com
www.keofilms.com
Contact *Katherine Perry*

Television documentaries and factual entertainment. OUTPUT includes *Atlantic Britain* and *Surviving Extremes* (both for Ch4/NatGeo Europe); *Beyond River Cottage*; *Where's Your F***ing Manners?*; *Road Trip*; *Tales From River Cottage*; *How To Be a Man*; *Running for God*;

Heavy; *My Body My Business*; *A Dangerous Obsession*; *Sperm Bandits* (all for Ch4); *10 Years Younger* (Discovery Health). No unsolicited mss.

Kingfisher Television Productions Ltd
Martindale House, The Green, Ruddington, Nottingham NG11 6HH
☎0115 945 6581   Fax 0115 921 7750
Contact *Tony Francis*

Broadcast television production.

Kismet Film Company
PO Box 42847, Tufnell Park, London N19 4WQ
☎020 7281 7121   Fax 020 7281 2251
✉ kismetfilms@dial.pipex.com
Producer *Michele Camarda*

Feature films. OUTPUT includes *Photographing Fairies*; *This Year's Love*; *Wonderland*; *Born Romantic*; *Doctor Sleep*; *River King*. Involved in workshops such as PAL Writer's Workshop, Equinoxe Screenwriting Workshops and North by Northwest. Kismet can no longer accept unsolicited material.

Kudos Film and Televison Ltd
12/14 Amwell Street, London EC1R 1UQ
☎020 7812 3270   Fax 020 7812 3271
✉ info@kudosfilmandtv.com
www.kudosfilmandtv.com
Joint Managing Directors *Jane Featherstone, Stephen Garrett*
General Manager *Daniel Isaacs*

Television dramas include *Spooks*; *Hustle*; and *The Magician's House* (BBC1 series); *Psychos* (Ch4 series); *Comfortably Numb* and *Pleasureland* (Ch4). Feature films such as *Among Giants* and *Pure*. No unsolicited mss.

Lagan Pictures Ltd
21 Tullaghbrow, Tullaghgarley, Ballymena BT42 2LY
☎028 2563 9479/077 9852 8797
Fax 028 2563 9479
✉ laganpictures@tullaghbrow.freeserve.co.uk
Producer/Director *Stephen Butcher*

Film, video and TV: drama, documentary and corporate. OUTPUT *A Force Under Fire* (Ulster TV). In development: *Into the Bright Light of Day* (drama-doc); *The £10 Float* (feature film); *The Centre* (drama series). 'We are always interested in hearing from writers originating from or based in Northern Ireland or anyone with, preferably unstereotypical, projects relevant to Northern

Ireland. We do not have the resources to deal with unsolicited mss, so please write with a brief treatment/synopsis in the first instance.'

Landseer Film Productions Ltd

140 Royal College Street, London NW1 0TA
☎020 7485 7333
✉ mail@landseerfilms.com
www.landseerfilms.com

Directors *Derek Bailey, Ken Howard*

Film and video production: documentary, drama, music and arts. OUTPUT *Should Accidentally Fall* (BBC/Arts Council); *Nobody's Fool* ('South Bank Show' on Danny Kaye for LWT); *Swinger* (BBC2/Arts Council); *Auld Lang Syne* and *Retying the Knot – The Incredible String Band* (both for BBC Scotland); *Benjamin Zander* ('The Works', BBC2); *Zeffirelli, Johnnie Ray, Petula Clark* and *Bing Crosby* (all for 'South Bank Show', LWT); *Death of a Legend – Frank Sinatra* ('South Bank Show' special); *Routes of Rock* (Carlton); *See You in Court* (BBC); *Nureyev Unzipped, Gounod's Faust, The Judas Tree, Ballet Boyz, 4Dance* and *Bourne to Dance* (all for Ch4), *Proms in the Park* (Belfast).

Lilyville Screen Entertainment Ltd

7 Lilyville Road, London SW6 5DP
☎020 7371 5940   Fax 020 7736 9431
✉ tony.cash@btclick.com

Contact *Tony Cash*

Drama and documentaries for TV. OUTPUT *Poetry in Motion* (series for Ch4); 'South Bank Show': *Ben Elton* and *Vanessa Redgrave*; *Musique Enquête* (drama-based French language series, Ch4); *Landscape and Memory* (arts documentary series for the BBC); Jonathan Miller's production of the *St Matthew Passion* for the BBC; major documentary on the BeeGees for the 'South Bank Show'. Scripts with an obvious application to TV may be considered. Interested in new writing for documentary programmes.

Loftus Productions Ltd

2A Aldine Street, London W12 8AN
☎020 8740 4666
✉ ask@loftusproductions.co.uk
www.loftusproductions.co.uk

Contact *Nigel Acheson*

Producer of radio documentaries, audio guides and non-fiction readings. OUTPUT includes *Josiah Wedgwood* and *Kandahar Cookery* for Radio 4's 'Book of the Week'.'We are interested in new, commissioned non-fiction titles suitable

for abridgement for R4's Book of the Week.' Send e-mail with brief synopsis for feature or documentary ideas; also advance information on commissioned non-fiction titles.

London Scientific Films Ltd

Mill Studio, Crane Mead, Ware SG12 9PY
☎01920 444399
✉ lsf@londonscientificfilms.co.uk

Contact *Mike Cockburn*

Film and video documentary and corporate programming. No unsolicited mss.

Lucida Productions

49 Sunderland Road, London SE23 2PS
☎020 8699 9470
✉ paul.lucida@ntlworld.com

Contact *Paul Joyce*

Television and cinema: arts, adventure, current affairs, documentary, drama and music. OUTPUT has included *Motion and Emotion: The Films of Wim Wenders; Dirk Bogarde – By Myself; Sam Peckinpah – Man of Iron; Kris Kristofferson – Pilgrim; Wild One: Marlon Brando; Stanley Kubrick: 'The Invisible Man'; 2001: the Making of a Myth* (Ch4); *Mantrap – Straw Dogs, the final cut* (with Dustin Hoffman). Currently in development for documentary and drama projects.

Malone Gill Productions Ltd

27 Campden Hill Road, London W8 7DX
☎020 7937 0557   Fax 020 7376 1727
✉ malonegill@aol.com

Contact *Georgina Denison*

Mainly documentary but also some drama. OUTPUT includes *The Face of Russia* (PBS); *Vermeer* ('South Bank Show'); *Highlanders* (ITV); *Storm Chasers*; *Nature Perfected* and *The Feast of Christmas* (all for Ch4); *The Buried Mirror: Reflections on Spain and the New World* by Carlos Fuentes (BBC2/Discovery Channel). Approach by letter with proposal in the first instance.

Marchmont Films

24 Three Cups Yard, Sandland Street, London WC1R 4PZ
☎020 7681 0324
✉ web@marchmontfilms.com
www.marchmonfilms.com

Contact *Andrew Cussens*

Producer of short films and feature projects. OUTPUT includes *Out In the Cold; Platinum; Murdering Howard.* .Welcomes new writers. See website for current submission criteria.

Jane Marshall Productions
The Coach-House, Westhill Road,
Blackdown, Leamington Spa CV32 6RA
☎01926 831680
✉ jane@jmproduction.freeserve.co.uk

Contact *Jane Marshall*

Producer of readings of published work both
fiction and non-fiction for BBC Radio.
Published work only.

Maverick Television
Units 1 & 4, Progress Works, The Custard
Factory, Heath Mill Lane, Birmingham
B9 4AL
☎0121 771 1812   Fax 0121 771 1550
✉ mail@mavericktv.co.uk
www.mavericktv.co.uk

Contact *Clare Welch*

Founded 1994. High quality and innovative
DVC programming in both documentary and
drama. Expanding into light entertainment and
more popular drama. OUTPUT includes *Extreme
Engineering* (Ch5); *Trade Secrets*; *Picture This:
Accidental Hero* (both for BBC2); *Born Too Soon*;
Up Your Street; *The Property Chain*; *Motherless
Daughters*; *Highland Bollywood: Black Bag*; *Health
Alert: My Teenage Menopause*; *Embarrassing
Illnesses*; *Vee-TV* and *Home From Home* (all for
Ch4); *Long Haul* (Scottish Screen/STV); *Learning
to Love the Grey* (BBC/OU).

Maya Vision International Ltd
43 New Oxford Street, London WC1A 1BH
☎020 7836 1113   Fax 020 7836 5169
www.mayavisionint.com

Contact *John Cranmer*

Film and TV: drama and documentary. OUTPUT
Saddam's Killing Fields (for 'Viewpoint', Central
TV); *3 Steps to Heaven* and *A Bit of Scarlet* (fea-
ture films for BFI/Ch4); *A Place in the Sun* and
North of Vortex (dramas for Ch4/Arts Council);
The Real History Show (Ch4); *In Search of Myths
and Heroes*; *In Search of Shakespeare*; *In the
Footsteps of Alexander the Great*; *Conquistadors*
(BBC documentaries); *Hitler's Search for the Holy
Grail* (Ch4 documentary). Absolutely no un-
solicited material; commissions only.

MBP TV
Saucelands Barn, Coolham, Horsham
RH13 8QG
☎01403 741620   Fax 01403 741647
✉ info@mbptv.com
www.mbptv.com

Contact *Phil Jennings*

Maker of film and video specialising in programmes covering equestrianism and the countryside. No unsolicited scripts, but always looking
for new writers who are fully acquainted with
the subject.

Melendez Films
Julia House, 44 Newman Street, London
W1T 1QD
☎020 7323 5273   Fax 020 7323 5373

Contact *Steven Melendez*

Independent production company specialising
in 2D animation. Also involved in production
and film design for clients in England, Spain,
Sweden, India and the US, plus website design
and 3D animation on the web. Clients include
book publishers, TV companies and advertisers.
Winner of international awards for films, particularly of classic books, stories and comic
characters. 'We will look at unsolicited projects
in outline or synopsis form only. Enclose s.a.e.'

Mendoza Film Productions
3–5 Barrett Street, London W1U 1AY
☎020 7935 4674   Fax 020 7935 4417
✉ office@mendozafilms.com
www.mendozafilms.com

Contacts *Wynn Wheldon, Debby Mendoza*

Commercials, title sequences (e.g. Alan
Bleasdale's *G.B.H.*); party political broadcasts.
Currently in pre-production on a feature-length
comedy film. Involved with the **Screenwriters'
Workshop**. Unsolicited mss welcome but
'comedies only, please'. Material will not be
returned without s.a.e.

Mersey Television Company Ltd
Campus Manor, Childwall Abbey Road,
Liverpool L16 0JP
☎0151 722 9122   Fax 0151 722 1969
www.merseytv.com

Chairman *Prof. Phil Redmond*

The best known of the independents in the
north of England. Makers of television drama.
OUTPUT *Hollyoaks* and *The Courtroom* (Ch4);
Grange Hill (BBC).

Moonstone Films Ltd
5 Linkenholt Mansions, Stamford Brook
Avenue, London W6 0YA
☎020 8846 8511   Fax 0870 005 6839
✉ info@moonstonefilms.co.uk

Contact *Tony Stark*

Television: current affairs, science and history

documentaries. OUTPUT *Arafat's Authority* and *Arafat Investigated*, both for BBC 'Correspondent'. Plus various Ch4 News commissions. Unsolicited mss welcome.

Neon
Studio One, 19 Marine Crescent, Glasgow
G51 1HD
☎0141 429 6366   Fax 0141 429 6377
✉ stephy@go2neon.com
www.go2neon.com

Contact *Stephanie Pordage*

Television and radio: drama and documentary producers. OUTPUT includes *The Brand New Opry*; *Man in a Briefcase*; *Peeking Past the Gates of Skibo*. Supports and encourages new writing 'at every opportunity'. Welcomes unsolicited material but telephone in the first instance.

Number 9 Films
Linton House, 24 Wells Street, London
W1T 3PH
☎020 7323 4060   Fax 020 7323 0456
✉ info@number9films.co.uk

Contacts *Stephen Woolley, Elizabeth Karlsen*

Leading feature film producer. OUTPUT includes *Return to Sender*; *Purely Belter*; *Little Voice*. Forthcoming productions: *Mrs Harris*; *The Wild and Wicked World of Brian Jones*. No unsolicited material.

Octopus TV
See **Octopus Publishing Group** under *UK Publishers*

Odyssey Productions Ltd
72 Tay Street, Newport-on-Tay DD6 8AP
☎01382 542070   Fax 01382 542070
✉ billykay@sol.co.uk

Contact *Billy Kay*

Producer of radio documentaries. OUTPUT includes *Scotland's Black History*; *Gentle Shepherds* (oral history); *Street Kids* (Scottish missionaries working with street kids in Brazil).Ideas for radio documentaries welcome; send letter with one page outlining the idea and programme content.

Omnivision
Pinewood Studios, Iver Heath SL0 0NH
☎01753 656329   Fax 01753 631146
✉ info@omnivision.co.uk
www.omnivision.co.uk

Contact *Christopher Morris*

TV and video producers of documentary, corporate, news and sport programming. Also equipment and facilities hire. Interested in ideas; approach by letter or e-mail.

ON Communication
5 East St Helen Street, Abingdon, Oxford
OX14 5EG
☎01235 537400   Fax 01235 530581
✉ ON@oncommication.com
www.oncommunication.com

Contact *Martine Benoit*

An independent production company founded in 1985 to produce high-quality factual programming, including science, current affairs, authored documentaries for television, as well as for corporate and heritage markets.

Open Media
The Mews Studio, 8 Addison Bridge Place, London W14 8XP
✉ contact@openmedia.co.uk
www.openmedia.co.uk

Contact *Laura Cook*

Broadcast television. OUTPUT *After Dark*; *The Secret Cabaret*; *James Randi Psychic Investigator*; *Opinions*; *Is This Your Life?*; *Don't Quote Me*; *Brave New World*; *The Talking Show*; *Natural Causes*; *Equinox*; *Dispatches*.

Open Road Films
The Studio, 37 Redington Road, London
NW3 7QY
☎020 7813 4333
✉ openroadfilms@blueyonder.co.uk

Development Executive *Elizabeth King*
Producer *Andrew Holmes*

Company, formed by **Holmes Associates**, to produce low to medium budget British feature films. OUTPUT *Chunky Monkey*; *Ashes & Sand*. Four projects in development. Unsolicited treatments/synopses by e-mail will be considered but may take some time for response.

Orlando TV Productions
Up-the-Steps, Little Tew, Chipping Norton
OX7 4JB
☎01608 683218   Fax 01608 683364
✉ info@orlandodigital.co.uk
www.orlandodigital.co.uk

Contact *Mike Tomlinson*

Producer of TV documentaries and digital multimedia content, with science and information technology subjects as a specialisation.

Approaches by established writers/ journalists to discuss proposals for collaboration are welcome.

Orpheus Productions
6 Amyand Park Gardens, Twickenham TW1 3HS
☎020 8892 3172   Fax 020 8892 4821
✉ richard-taylor@blueyonder.co.uk
Contact *Richard Taylor*

Television documentaries and corporate work. OUTPUT has included programmes for the BBC, ITV and Ch4 as well as documentaries for the United Nations, the Shell Film Unit and Video Arts. Unsolicited scripts are welcomed with caution. 'Our preference is for the more classically structured documentary that, while being hard-hitting, explores the subtleties and the paradox of an issue – and is not presented by unqualified celebrities.'

Outcast Production
92 Buckhold Road, London SW18 4AP
✉ andythewise@aol.com
Contact *Andreas Wisniewski*

Low-budget feature films. No unsolicited mss; send synopsis or treatment only. 'We are actively searching for and encouraging new writing.'

Ovation
One Prince of Wales Passage, 117 Hampstead Road, London NW1 3EF
☎020 7387 2342   Fax 020 7380 0404
Contact *John Plews*

Corporate video and conference scripts. Unsolicited mss not welcome. 'We talk to new writers from time to time.' Ovation also runs the fringe theatre, 'Upstairs at the Gatehouse' in Highgate, north London.

Oxford Scientific (OSF)
Station Yard, Thame OX9 3UH
☎01844 262370   Fax 01844 262380
✉ enquiries@osf.com
www.osf.com
CEO *Glenn Parker*
Sales Director *James Cape*

Established media company with specialist knowledge and expertise in award-winning natural history films and science-based programmes. Film, video and TV documentaries. Scripts welcome. Operates an extensive stills and film footage library specialising in wildlife and special effects (see entry under *Picture Libraries*).

Paper Moon Productions
Wychwood House, Burchetts Green Lane, Littlewick Green, Nr. Maidenhead SL6 3QW
☎01628 829819   Fax 01628 825949
✉ david@paper-moon.co.uk
Contact *David Haggas*

Broadcast documentaries and corporate communications. Recent OUTPUT includes *Bilbo & Beyond*, an affectionate glimpse into the life and work of the dedicated philologist and fantasy writer J.R.R. Tolkien.

Parallax Independent Ltd
7 Denmark Street, London WC2H 8LZ
☎020 7836 1478   Fax 020 7497 8062
www.parallaxindependent.co.uk
Contact *Sally Hibbin*

Feature films/television drama. OUTPUT *A Very British Coup*; *Riff-Raff*; *Bad Behaviour*, *Raining Stones*; *Ladybird, Ladybird*; *i.d.*; *Land and Freedom*; *The Englishman Who Went up a Hill But Came Down a Mountain*; *Bliss*; *Jump the Gun*; *Carla's Song*; *The Governess*; *My Name Is Joe*; *Stand and Deliver*; *Dockers*; *Hold Back the Night*; *Bread and Roses*; *Princesa*; *The Navigators*; *Sweet Sixteen*; *Innocence*; *The Intended*; *Blind Flight*; *Yasmin*.

Passion Pictures
3rd Floor, 33–34 Rathbone Place, London W1T 1JN
☎020 7323 9933   Fax 020 7323 9030
✉ info@passion-pictures.com
Managing Director *Andrew Ruhemann*

Documentary and drama includes: *One Day in September* (Academy Award-winner for Best Feature Documentary, 2000); also commercials and music videos: Carphone Warehouse, Mini, Aero, Gorillaz, Coldplay and Robbie Williams. Unsolicited mss welcome.

Pathé Pictures
14–17 Kenthouse, Market Place, London W1W 8AR
☎020 7323 5151   Fax 020 7631 3568
Head of Creative Affairs *Celine Haddad*
Development & Acquisitions Executive *Erol Arguden*
Story Editor *Charlie Mitchell*

Produces 4–6 theatrical feature films each year. 'We are pleased to consider all material that has representation from an agent or production company.'

Pearson Television
See **FremantleMedia Ltd**

Pelicula Films
59 Holland Street, Glasgow G2 4NJ
☎0141 287 9522   Fax 0141 287 9504

Contact *Mike Alexander*

Television producer. Maker of drama documentaries and music programmes for the BBC and Ch4. OUTPUT *As an Eilean (From the Island)*; *The Trans-Atlantic Sessions 1 & 2*; *Nanci Griffith, Other Voices 2*; *Follow the Moonstone*.

Pennine Productions LLP
2 Grimeford Lane, Anderton, Nr Chorley
PR6 9HL
☎01257 482559
✉ mike@pennine.biz
www.pennine.biz

Contact *Mike Hally*

Producer of radio documentaries, features and short story readings. OUTPUT includes *Red Games*; *Still Angry After All these Years*; *After the Silver* (all or Radio 4). No unsolicited material.

Photoplay Productions Ltd
21 Princess Road, London NW1 8JR
☎020 7722 2500   Fax 020 7722 6662
✉ photoplay@compuserve.com

Contact *Patrick Stanbury*

Documentaries for film, television and video plus restoration of silent films and their theatrical presentation. OUTPUT includes *The Cat and the Canary*; *Orphans of the Storm*; *Cecil B. DeMille: American Epic* and the 'Channel 4 Silents' series of silent film restoration, including *The Wedding March* and *The Iron Mask*. Recently completed *The Tramp and the Dictator*; *So Funny It Hurt: Buster Keaton & MGM*. No unsolicited mss;'we tend to create and write all our own programmes.'

Picardy Media & Communication
1 Park Circus, Glasgow G3 6AX
☎0141 333 5554   Fax 0141 332 6002
✉ jr@picardy.co.uk
www.picardy.co.uk

Head of Production *John Rocchiccioli*

Television and video: arts documentaries, training and promotional videos, education projects, multi-media productions, and TV and cinema commercials. Unsolicited mss welcome; 'keen to encourage new writing.'

Picture Palace Films Ltd
13 Egbert Street, London NW1 8LJ
☎020 7586 8763   Fax 020 7586 9048
✉ info@picturepalace.com
www.picturepalace.com

Contacts *Malcolm Craddock, Katherine Hedderly*

Leading independent producer of film and TV drama. OUTPUT *Rebel Heart* (BBC1); *Extremely Dangerous*; *A Life for A Life* and *Frances Tuesday* (all for ITV); *Sharpe's Rifles* (14 films for Carlton TV); *Little Napoleons* (comedy drama, Ch4); *The Orchid House* (drama serial, Ch4); *Tandoori Nights; 4 Minutes; When Love Dies* (all for Ch4); *Ping Pong* (feature film); *Acid House* (Picture Palace North). Material will only be considered if submitted through an agent.

Plantagenet Films Limited
Ard–Daraich Studio B, Ardgour, Nr Fort William PH33 7AB
☎01855 841384   Fax 01855 841384
✉ plantagenetfilms@aol.com

Contact *Norrie Maclaren*

Film and television: documentary and drama programming such as *Dig* (gardening series for Ch4); various 'Dispatches' for Ch4 and 'Omnibus' for BBC. Keen to encourage and promote new writing; unsolicited mss welcome.

Portobello Pictures
Eardley House, 4 Uxbridge Street, London W8 7SY

Contact *Eric Abraham*

Film drama, including Jan Sverak's *Dark Blue World* and *Kolya*; Jez Butterworth's *Mojo* and Tim Roth's *The War Zone*, plus BBC1's *Dalziel & Pascoe* (series 1–3).

Pozzitive Television
Paramount House, 162–170 Wardour Street, London W1F 8AB
☎020 7734 3258   Fax 020 7437 3130
✉ pozzitive@pozzitive.co.uk

Contact *David Tyler*

Producer of comedy and entertainment for television and radio. OUTPUT *Dinner Ladies*; *Coogan's Run*; *The 99p Challenge*. Unsolicited mss of TV and radio comedy only welcome. 'No screenplays or stage plays, please. Send hard copy of full sample script. We read everything submitted this way.'

Promenade Enterprises Limited
6 Russell Grove, London SW9 6HS
☎020 7582 9354   Fax 020 7587 1564
✉ info@promenadeproductions.com

www.promenade productions.com

Contact *Nicholas Newton*

Producer of drama for radio and theatre predominantly. Supports new writing but only accepts unsolicited mss via agents or producers.

Redweather

Easton Business Centre, Felix Road, Easton BS5 0HE

☎0117 941 5854   Fax 0117 941 5851

✉ production@redweather.co.uk

Broadcast documentaries on arts and disability, corporate video and CD-ROM, Water Aid, British Oxygen, etc.

Renaissance Vision

256 Fakenham Road, Taverham, Norwich NR8 6QW

☎01603 260280   Fax 01603 864853

✉ bfg@renvision.co.uk

Contact *B. Gardner*

Video: full range of corporate work (training, sales, promotional, etc.). Producers of educational and special-interest video publications. Willing to consider good ideas and proposals.

Richmond Films & Television Ltd

PO Box 33154, London NW3 4AZ

☎020 7722 6464   Fax 020 7722 6232

✉ mail@richmondfilms.com

Contact *Development Executive*

Film and TV: drama and comedy. OUTPUT *Press Gang; The Lodge; The Office; Wavelength; Privates; in2minds*. No unsolicited scripts.

Brenda Rowe Productions

42 Wellington Park, Clifton BS8 2UW

☎0117 973 0390

✉ br007b3169@blueyonder.co.uk

Contact *Brenda Rowe*

Produces observational, investigative, current affairs TV documentaries, and training and promotional videos for business organisations. Open to new work; unsolicited mss welcome.

RS Productions

191 Trewhitt Road, Newcastle upon Tyne NE6 5DY

☎0191 224 4301/00 49 89 5111 5895/ 07710 064632 (Mobile)   Fax 0191 224 4301

✉ enquiries@rsproductions.co.uk

www.rsproductions.co.uk

Contact *Mark Lavender*

Feature films and television: drama series/serials and singles. TV documentaries and series. Working with established and new talent.

Sands Films

119 Rotherhithe Street, London SE16 4NF

☎020 7231 2209   Fax 020 7231 2119

www.sandsfilms.co.uk

Contacts *Christine Edzard, Olivier Stockman*

Film and TV drama. OUTPUT *Little Dorrit; The Fool; As You Like It; A Dangerous Man; The Long Day Closes; A Passage to India; Topsy Turvy; Nicholas Nickleby; The Gangs of New York; The Children's Midsummer Night's Dream*. No unsolicited scripts.

Scala Productions Ltd

4th Floor, Portland House, 4 Great Portland Street, London W1W 8QJ

☎020 7612 0060   Fax 020 7612 0031

✉ scalaprods@aol.com

Contacts *Ian Prior*

Production company set up by ex-Palace Productions Nik Powell and Stephen Woolley, who have an impressive list of credits including *Company of Wolves; Absolute Beginners; Mona Lisa; Scandal; The Crying Game; Backbeat; Neon Bible; 24:7; Little Voice; Divorcing Jack; The Last September; Wild About Harry; Last Orders; A Christmas Carol – The Movie; Black and White; Leo; One Love; The Night We Called It A Day; Ladies in Lavender*. In development: *The Wild and Wicked World of Brian Jones; The Queen & I; Meek; The Coat; Train to Glory; Du Cane's Boys; Shang-a-Lang; Johnny Bollywood; English Passengers; He Kills Coppers; Eden's Team*.

Scope Productions Ltd

123 Blythswood Street, Glasgow G2 4EN

☎0141 332 7720   Fax 0141 332 1049

✉ laurakingwell@scopeproductions.co.uk

www.scopeproductions.co.uk

Corporate *Laura Kingwell*

Corporate film and video; broadcast documentaries and sport; TV commercials.

Screen First Ltd

The Studios, Funnells Farm, Down Street, Nutley TN22 3LG

☎01825 712034   Fax 01825 713511

✉ paul.madden@virgin.net

Contacts *M. Thomas, P. Madden*

Television dramas, documentaries, arts and animation programmes. Developing major drama series, feature films, animated specials and series. No unsolicited scripts.

Screen Ventures Ltd
49 Goodge Street, London W1T 1TE
☎020 7580 7448
✉ sales@screenventures.com

Contacts *Christopher Mould, Michael Evans*

Film and TV sales and production: documentary, music videos and drama. OUTPUT *Life and Limb* (documentary, Discovery Health Channel); *Pavement Aristocrats* (SABC); *Woodstock Diary*; *Vanessa Redgrave* and *Genet* (both for LWT 'South Bank Show'); *Mojo Working*; *Burma: Dying for Democracy* (Ch4); *Dani Dares* (Ch4 series on strong women); *Pagad* (Ch4 news report).

Screenhouse Productions Ltd
Chapel Allerton House, 114 Harrogate Road, Leeds LS7 4NY
☎0113 266 8881   Fax 0113 266 8882
✉ paul.bader@screenhouse.co.uk
www.screenhouse.co.uk

Contacts *Paul Bader, Barbara Govan*

Specialises in science TV, documentary, stunts and events, including outside broadcasts. Science prop. and demo workshop supplying working models to, e.g., BBC History *What the Past Did For Us*; ITV, Discovery and museums. Output includes *Stardate* (BBC2 astronomy series); *Zapped* (Discovery/US/Canada 2hr-special); *The Man Who Invented the Aeroplane* (UKTV/BBC North); *Science Shack, Local Heroes*, BBC2, presented by Adam Hart-Davis.'More likely to consider written up proposals.'

Screenprojex.com – a division of Screen Production Associates Ltd
✉ enquiries@screenprojex.com
screenprojex.com

Contacts *Doug Abbott, John Jaquiss*

Feature films: *The Fourth Man*; *The Case*; *Black Badge*; *The Truth Game*; *Club Le Monde*; *Midnight Warriors*; *Strong Language*; *Holding On*; *Chunky Monkey*; *Sixty-three Closure*. No unsolicited mss. Send preliminary letter outlining project and c.v.

September Films Ltd
Glen House, 22 Glenthorne Road, London W6 0NG
☎020 8563 9393   Fax 020 8741 7214
✉ september@septemberfilms.com
www.septemberfilms.com

Director of Production *Elaine Day*

Factual entertainment and documentary specialists. Feature film output includes *Breathtaking*; *House of America*; *Solomon & Gaenor*.

Serendipity Picture Company
Media Centre, Emma-Chris Way, Abbeywood Park, Bristol BS34 7JU
☎0117 906 6541   Fax 0117 906 6542
✉ tony@serendipitypictures.com

Contacts *Tony Yeadon, Nick Dance*

Television and video; corporate and documentary programming. Encourages new writing and will consider proposals for documentaries.

Shell Like
81 Whitfield Street, London W1T 4HG
☎020 7255 5204   Fax 020 7255 5255
✉ enquiries@shellike.com
www.shelllike.com

Contact *Nicola Warman-Johnston*

Produces radio commercials. Unsolicited mss and ideas welcome; send by e-mail.

Sianco Cyf
36 Y Maes, Caernarfon LL55 2NN
☎01286 676100/07831 726111 (mobile)
Fax 01286 677616
✉ post@sianco.tv

Contact *Siân Teifi*

Children's, youth and education programmes, children's drama, people-based documentaries for adults. 'Please note that we do not accept unsolicited scripts.'

SilentSound Films Ltd
Cambridge Court, Cambridge Road, Frinton on Sea CO13 9HN
☎01255 676381   Fax 01255 676381
✉ thj@silentsoundfilms.co.uk
www.silentsoundfilms.co.uk
www.londonfoodfilmfiesta.co.uk

Contact *Timothy Foster*

Active in European film co-production with mainstream connections in the USA. Special interest in developing stage and film musicals, art house and documentaries on the arts. Synopses considered via e-mail or post.

Siriol Productions
3 Mount Stuart Square, Butetown, Cardiff CF10 5EE
☎029 2048 8400   Fax 029 2048 5962
✉ enquiries@siriol.co.uk
www.siriolproductions.com

Contact *Andrew Offiler*

Animated series, mainly for children. OUTPUT includes *Meeow*; *Hilltop Hospital*; *The Hurricanes*;

Tales of the Toothfairies; *Billy the Cat*; *The Blobs*, as well as the feature films, *Under Milk Wood* and *The Princess and the Goblin*. Write with ideas and sample script in the first instance.

Skyline Productions
10 Scotland Street, Edinburgh EH3 6PS
☎0131 557 4580   Fax 0131 556 4377
✉ leslie@skyline.uk.com
www.skyline.uk.com
Producer/Writer *Leslie Hills*

Produces film and television drama and documentary.

SMG & Ginger TV Productions Ltd
SMG: 200 Renfield Street, Glasgow G2 3PR
☎0141 300 3000
www.ginger.com

Also: Ginger TV Productions,
3 Waterhouse Square, 138–142 Holborn
London EC1N 2NY
☎020 7882 1020

Managing Director (SMG) *Elizabeth Partyka*
Head of Drama *Eric Coulter*
Head of Factual Programming *Helen Alexander*

SMG (Scottish Media Group) TV Productions Ltd, which incorporates Ginger Television, makes programmes for the national television networks, including ITV, Ch4 and Sky. Specialises in drama, factual entertainment and children's programming. OUTPUT includes *Taggart*; *Rebus*; *Our Daughter Holly*; *Club Reps*.

So Television Ltd
18 Hatfields, London SE1 8GN
☎020 7960 2000   Fax 020 7960 2095
Contact *Nina Gosling*

Producer of a entertainment comedy show for television. Developing comedy entertainment and comedy narrative. No unsolicited mss.

Somethin Else
Units 1–4, 1A Old Nichol Street, London
E2 7HR
☎020 7613 3211   Fax 020 7739 9799
✉ info@somethin-else.com
www.somethin-else.com
Contact *Jez Nelson*

Producer of television, video and radio documentaries, DVD and interactive content. Ideas for TV shows welcome; send letter in the first instance.

Soundplay Limited
17 Gleneagles Drive, Henbury, Bristol
BS10 7PS
☎07818 271659
✉ enquiries@soundplay.co.uk
www.soundplay.co.uk
Contact *Tom Bennett*

Producer of radio drama and documentaries. OUTPUT *In Search of the Picturesque* (dramatised feature by Tom Bennett); *The Hearts and Lives of Men* (radio drama by Fay Weldon); *Remember the Day* (radio thriller by Tom Bennett).

Specific Films
25 Rathbone Street, London W1T 1NQ
☎020 7580 7476   Fax 020 7494 2676
✉ info@specificfilms.com
Contacts *Michael Hamlyn*

Founded 1991. OUTPUT includes *Mr Reliable* (feature film co-produced by PolyGram and the AFFC); *The Adventures of Priscilla, Queen of the Desert*, co-produced with Latent Image (Australia) and financed by PolyGram and AFFC; *U2 Rattle and Hum*, full-length feature – part concert film/part cinema verité documentary; *Paws* (executive producer); *The Last Seduction 2* (Polygram); and numerous pop promos for major international artists.

Spellbound Productions Ltd
90 Cowdenbeath Path, Islington, London
N1 0LG
☎020 7713 8066   Fax 020 7713 8066
✉ phspellbound@hotmail.com
Contact *Paul Harris*

Specialises in feature films for cinema and drama for television. Keen to support and encourage new writing. Material will only be considered if in correct screenplay format and accompanied by s.a.e.

Spice Factory (UK) Ltd
81 The Promenade, Brighton BN10 8LS
☎01273 585275   Fax 01273 585304
✉ shirine@spicefactory.co.uk
Contacts *Lucy Shuttleworth, Shirine Best*

Founded 1995. Film producers. OUTPUT *Plots With a View* (Christopher Walken, Brenda Blethyn, Alfred Molina, Lee Evans); *Bollywood Queen* (Preeya Kallidas, James McAvoy, Ian McShane); *The Bridge of San Luis Rey* (Robert De Niro, Kathy Bates, Harvey Keitel); *A Different Loyalty* (Sharon Stone, Rupert Everett); *Head in the Clouds* (Charlize Theron, Penelope Cruz); *The*

Merchant of Venice (Al Pacino, Jeremy Irons, Joseph Fiennes, Lynn Collins). No unsolicited material accepted.

'Spoken' Image Ltd
8 Hewitt Street M15 4GB
☎0161 236 7522   Fax 0161 236 0020
✉ multimedia@spoken-image.com
www.spoken-image.com

Contacts *Geoff Allman, Steve Foster*

Film, video and TV production for documentary and corporate material. Specialises in high-quality brochures and reports, CD-ROMs, exhibitions, conferences, film and video production for broadcast, industry and commerce.

Starz! – Film and Theatre Performing Arts
See entry under *UK Writers' Courses*

Tony Staveacre Productions
Channel View, Blagdon BS40 7TP
☎01761 462161   Fax 01761 462161
✉ staving@dircon.co.uk

Contact *Tony Staveacre*

Producer of dramas and documentaries as well as music, arts and comedy progammes. OUTPUT *The Wodehouse Notebooks; The Liberation of Daphne, Speaking from the Belly* (Radio Four); *The Very Thought of You* (theatre); *Tango Maestro* (BBC4). Welcomes unsolicited mss by mail or e-mail, 'especially from those who understand that it is hard to find a path through the commissioning maze and that a well-researched and targeted proposal will be more successful than a multiple submission.'

Stirling Film & TV Productions Limited
137 University Street, Belfast BT7 1HP
☎028 9033 3848   Fax 028 9043 8644
✉ anne@stirlingtelevision.co.uk

Contact *Anne Stirling*

Producer of broadcast and corporate programming – documentary, sport, entertainment and lifestyle programmes.

Storm Film Productions Ltd
2nd Floor, 20 Kingly Street, London W1B 5PZ
☎020 7439 1616   Fax 020 7439 4477
✉ sophie.storm@btclick.com
www.stormfilms.tv

Contact *Nic Auerbach*

Producer of commercials for clients such as British Airways and Shell. Unsolicited mss welcome.

Straight Forward Film & Television Productions Ltd
Building 2, Lesley Office Park, 393 Hollywood Road, Belfast BT4 2LS
☎028 9065 1010   Fax 028 9065 1012
✉ enquiries@straightforward.co.uk

Contacts *John Nicholson, Ian Kennedy*

Northern Ireland-based production company specialising in documentary, feature and lifestyle series for both regional and network transmission. OUTPUT includes *We Shall Overcome* (winner of Best Documentary at 1999 Celtic Television Festival for BBC); *Conquering the Normans* (Ch4 Learning – history of Normans in Ireland); *Gift of the Gab* (Ch4 Learning – contemporary Irish writing); *Fire School* (BBC NI – training of a team of fire-fighters); *On Eagle's Wing* (full stage musical/TV material; story of the Scots/Irish in America); *Just Jones* (BBC Radio Ulster daily show); *Sportsweek* (BBC Radio Ulster); *School Challenge* (3rd series, BBC NI); *World Indoor Bowls* (BBC NI); *Awash With Colour* (series, BBC Daytime).

Strawberry Productions Ltd
36 Priory Avenue, London W4 1TY
☎020 8994 4494   Fax 020 8742 7675

Contact *John Black*

Film, video and TV: drama and documentary; corporate and video publishing.

Sunset + Vine Productions Ltd
30 Sackville Street, London W1S 3DY
☎020 7478 7300   Fax 020 7478 7403
www.sunsetvine.co.uk

Sports, children's and music programmes for television. No unsolicited mss. 'We hire freelancers only upon receipt of a commission.'

Table Top Productions
1 The Orchard, Chiswick, London W4 1JZ
☎020 8742 0507   Fax 020 8742 0507
✉ alvin@tabletopproductions.com

Contact *Alvin Rakoff*

TV and film. OUTPUT *Paradise Postponed; The Adventures of Don Quixote; A Voyage Round My Father; The First Olympics 1896; Dirty Tricks; A Dance to the Music of Time; Too Marvellous for Words*. Also Dancetime Ltd. No unsolicited mss.

talkbackTHAMES Productions

20–21 Newman Street, London W1T 1PG
☎020 7861 8000   Fax 020 7861 8001
✉ reception@talkbackthames.tv

Chief Executive Officer *Lorraine Heggessey*
Chief Operating Officer *Sally Debonnaire*
Commercial Director *Alex Mahon*

talkackTHAMES Productions is a **Fremantle-Media** company. Specialises in comedy, comedy drama and drama; also feature lifestyle programmes. OUTPUT *Smith and Jones; Murder Most Horrid; The Day Today; Knowing Me Knowing You with Alan Partridge; I'm Alan Partridge; They Think It's All Over; Never Mind the Buzzcocks; Brass Eye; House Doctor; She's Gotta Have It; Grand Designs; Sword of Honour; In a Land of Plenty; Shooting the Past; 11 o'clock Show; Smack the Pony; Big Train; Los Dos Bros; Your Money or Your Life; Property Ladder; Would Like to Meet.*

Talkingheads Production Ltd

2–4 Noel Street, London W1F 8GB
☎020 7292 7575   Fax 020 7292 7576
✉ johnsachs@talkingheadsproductions.com
www.talkingheadsproductions.com

Contact *John Sachs*

Feature films. OUTPUT includes *The Merchant of Venice* starring Al Pacino. Will consider scripts; contact by e-mail. 'Somewhere out there is the new Tom Stoppard.'

Tandem TV & Film Ltd

Suite 206, Charleston House, Hemel Hempstead HP1 3AA
☎01442 261576   Fax 01442 219250
✉ info@tandemtv.com
www.tandemtv.com

Contact *Barbara Page*

Produces training videos, especially health and safety; construction and civil engineering documentaries; drama-doc life stories for satellite television; Christian church and charity documentary, training and promotional programmes. Welcomes unsolicited mss.

Taylor Made Broadcasts Ltd

PO Box 100, Woodstock OX20 1XE
☎01608 677777
✉ post@tmtv.co.uk

Contact *Trevor Taylor*

Producer of corporate videos and documentaries for television and radio. OUTPUT includes *Gardeners' Question Time* (BBC Radio 4). No unsolicited mss.

Telemagination Ltd

Royalty House, 72–74 Dean Street, London W1D 3SG
☎020 7434 1551   Fax 020 7434 3344
✉ mail@tmation.co.uk
www.telemagination.co.uk

Contact *Beth Parker*

Producer of television animation. OUTPUT includes *The Animals of Farthing Wood; Noah's Island; The Last Polar Bears; Little Ghosts; Pongwiffy.* In production: *Heidi.* No unsolicited material.

Tern Television Productions Ltd

73 Crown Street, Aberdeen AB11 6EX
☎01224 211123   Fax 01224 211199
✉ office@terntv.com
www.terntv.com

Also at: RWF House, 5 Renfield Street, Glasgow G2 5EZ
☎0141 243 5678

Contacts *David Strachan, Gwyneth Hardy* (Aberdeen), *Harry Bell* (Glasgow)

Broadcast, television and corporate video productions. Specialises in factual entertainment. Currently developing drama.

Testbed Productions

Fifth Floor, 14–16 Great Portland Street, London W1W 8QW
☎020 7436 0555   Fax 020 7436 2800
✉ mail@testbed.co.uk
www.testbed.co.uk

Contacts *Viv Black, Nick Baker*

Producer of documentaries, light entertainment, factual and spoken word programmes for radio.

Testimony Films

12 Great George Street, Bristol BS1 5RS
☎0117 925 8589   Fax 0117 925 7608
✉ stevehumphries@testimonyfilms.force9.co.uk

Contact *Steve Humphries*

TV documentary producer. Specialises in social history exploring Britain's past using living memory. OUTPUT includes *Hooked: History of Addictions; Married Love* (both Ch4 series); *A Secret World of Sex* (BBC series); *The 50s & 60s in Living Colour; Some Liked It Hot* (both ITV series). Welcomes ideas from those working on life stories and oral history.

Theatre of Comedy Company

See *Theatre Producers*

Tiger Aspect Productions

7 Soho Square, London W1D 3DQ
☎020 7434 6700   Fax 020 7434 1798
✉ jonathanhall@tigeraspect.co.uk
www.tigeraspect.co.uk

Contact *Charles Brand*

Television producer for comedy, drama, documentary and entertainment. OUTPUT *Births, Marriages & Deaths; Kid in the Corner, Country House; Gimme Gimme Gimme; Harry Enfield & Chums; Howard Goodalls' Big Bangs; Playing the Field I, II & III; Streetmate I & II; Let Them Eat Cake; The Vicar of Dibley*. Only considers material submitted via an agent or from writers with a known track record.

Tonfedd Eryri

Hen Ysgol Aberpwll, Y Felinheli, Bangor
LL56 4JS
☎01248 671167   Fax 01248 671172
✉ swyddfa@tonfedd-eryri.com

Contacts *Hefin Elis, Norman Williams*

Light entertainment, comedy, music and drama.

Touch Productions Ltd

The Malt House Studios, Donhead St Mary,
Shaftesbury SP7 9DN
☎01747 828030   Fax 01747 828004
✉ erica@touchproductions.co.uk

Contacts *Erica Wolfe-Murray, Malcolm Brinkworth*

Over the past 18 years has produced 'investigative documentary films, history-based films with a strong contemporary relevance, powerful observational series and innovative films that stretch the form.'Television documentaries such as *Life of a £10 Note; Afghan Warrior – the Life & Death of Abdul Haq; Falklands 20th Anniversary; OJ – The Untold Story; Simon Weston V; Siege Doctors* (all for BBC); *The Good Life; The Surgery; Coast of Dreams; A French Affair, Watching the Detectives; Brown Babies* (all for Ch4); *Fame School* and *Fame School – the Graduates* (both for Meridian). Also has a drama section based on real-life stories and unsolicited mss are welcome.

Transatlantic Films Production and Distribution Company

Studio One, 3 Brackenbury Road, London
W6 0BE
☎020 8735 0505   Fax 020 8735 0605
✉ mail@transatlanticfilms.com
www.transatlanticfilms.com

Executive Producer *Revel Guest*

Producer of TV documentaries. OUTPUT *Belzoni* (Ch4 Schools); *Science of Sleep and Dreams; Science of Love* and *Extreme Body Parts* (all for Discovery Health); *Legends of the Living Dead* (Discovery Travel/S4C International); *2025* (Discovery Digital); *How Animals Tell the Time* (Discovery); *Trailblazers* (Travel Channel). Interested in new writers to write 'the book of the series', e.g. for *Greek Fire* and *The Horse in Sport*, but not usually drama script writers. No unsolicited scripts.

TV Choice Ltd

PO Box 597, Bromley BR2 OYB
☎020 8464 7402   Fax 020 8464 7845
✉ tvchoiceuk@aol.com
www.tvchoice.uk.com

Contact *Norman Thomas*

Produces a range of educational videos for schools and colleges on subjects such as history, geography, business studies and economics. No unsolicited mss; send proposals only.

Twentieth Century Fox Film Co

Twentieth Century House, 31–32 Soho Square, London W1D 3AP
☎020 7437 7766   Fax 020 7734 3187
www.fox.co.uk

London office of the American giant.

Twofour Productions Limited

Twofoour Studios, Estover, Plymouth
PL6 7RG
☎01752 727400   Fax 01752 727450
✉ enq@twofour.co.uk
www.twofour.co.uk

Managing Director *Charles Wace*
Director of Broadcast *Jill Lourie*

Specialises in factual and leisure programming for Britain's network and digital TV channels; business communications for national/international business and public sector; special interest videos for retail/mail order; and, through its subsidiary twofourtv, webcasting and Intrantet or Intranet-based TV.

Tyburn Film Productions Limited

Cippenham Court, Cippenham Lane,
Cippenham, Nr Slough SL1 5AU
☎01753 516767   Fax 01753 691785

Feature films. Subsidiary of **Arlington Productions Limited**. No unsolicited submissions.

UBA Ltd

21 Alderville Road, London SW6 2EE
☎01984 623619   Fax 01984 623733

Contacts *Peter Shaw, Joanna Shaw*

Feature films and TV for an international market. OUTPUT includes *Windprints; The Lonely Passion of Judith Hearne* (co-production with HandMade Films Ltd); *Taffin*; *Castaway*; *Turtle Diary*; *Sweeney Todd*; *Keep the Aspidistra Flying*. In development: *Kinder Garden*; *Rebel Magic*; *No Man's Land*. Prepared to commission new writing whether adapted from another medium or based on a short outline/treatment. Concerned with the quality of the script (*Turtle Diary* was written by Harold Pinter) and breadth of appeal. 'Exploitation material' not welcome.

UK Film and TV Production Company Plc

3 Colville Place, London W1T 2BH
☎020 7255 1650

Contact *Henrietta Fudakowski*

Film producers. Currently looking for feature films, with a preference for stories with humour. No TV formats, please. Return postage and list of credits essential. Please phone before submitting material.

Vera Productions

66–68 Margaret Street, London W1W 8SR
☎020 7436 6116   Fax 020 7436 6117

Contact *Cree Jones*

Produces television comedy such as *Rory Bremner*.

Video Enterprises

12 Barbers Wood Road, High Wycombe HP12 4EP
☎01494 534144/07831 875216 (Mobile)
Fax 01494 534145
✉ videoenterprises@ntlworld.com
www.videoenterprises-uk.co.uk

Contact *Maurice R. Fleisher*

Video and TV, mainly corporate: business and industrial training, promotional material and conferences. No unsolicited material 'but always ready to try out good new writers'.

VIP Broadcasting

8 Bunbury Way, Epsom KT17 4JP
☎01372 721196   Fax 01372 726697
✉ mail@vipbroadcasting.co.uk

Contact *Chris Vezey*

Produces a wide range of radio programmes, particularly interviews, documentaries, music programmes and live concerts. Won award for

'Best Sound' at New York Festival 2000. Approach with idea by e-mail in the first instance; no unsolicited mss.

Wall to Wall

8–9 Spring Place, London NW5 3ER
☎020 7485 7424   Fax 020 7267 5292
www.walltowall.co.uk

Chief Executive *Alex Graham*

Factual and drama programming. OUTPUT includes *Who Do You Think You Are?*; *New Tricks*; *A Rather English Marriage*; *Glasgow Kiss*; *Sex, Chips & Rock 'n' Roll*; *The 1940s House*; *Body Story* and *Neanderthal*.

Jane Walmsley Productions
See **JAM Pictures**

Walsh Bros. Limited

4 The Heights, London SE7 8JH
☎020 8858 6870/8854 5557/07879 816426
Fax 020 8858 6870/8854 5557
✉ john@walshbros.co.uk
www.walshbros.co.uk

Producer/Director *John Walsh*
Producer/Head of Finance *David Walsh, ACA*
Producer/Head of Development *Maura Walsh*

Producer of television, film drama and documentaries. OUTPUT *Monarch* (feature film); *Headhunting the Homeless* (BBC programme on the perception of homeless people in the work place); *Trex* (factual series on teenagers at work in China, Mexico, Vancouver and Alaska); *Trex2* (follow-up series covering Romania, India, Iceland and Louisiana); *Boyz & Girlz*, (Derbyshire dairy farm documentary series); *Cowboyz & Cowgirlz* (US sequel to hit series of Brit teens working on a ranch in Montana). Also arts documentaries: *The Comedy Store* and *Ray Harryhausen* (the work of Hollywood special effects legend). Drama: *The Sleeper, The Sceptic and the Psychic; A State of Mind*.

Paul Weiland Film Company

14 Newburgh Street, London W1F 7RT
☎020 7287 6900   Fax 020 7434 0146
✉ action@paulweiland.com

Television commercials and pop promos.

Whistledown Productions Ltd

66 Southwark Bridge Road, London SE1 0AS
☎020 7922 1120   Fax 020 7261 0939
✉ david.prest@whistledown.net
www.whistledown.net

Contact *David Prest*

Producer of Sony Award Winning Landmark Series for BBC Radio 4: *Evacuation, The Child Migrants*. Features and documentaries on wide range of social and historical subjects, contemporary issues and popular culture. OUTPUT includes *Questions Questions* and *The Reunion* (Radio 4); music-based documentaries for Radio 2. 'We welcome contributions and ideas, but phone or e-mail first.'

Windrush Productions Ltd

Moving to new premises, details not available at time of going to press
✉ writers@oomgallery.net

Contacts *Emma Jeffares, Pogus Caesar*

Television documentaries, including a multicultural series for Carlton TV *Xpress*. Also for Carlton produced and directed *Respect; An Eye on X; The A-Force* (BBC); *I'm Black in Britain* (Central TV) and the music film *Xpress Urself Thru Muzik*. Produces films, documentaries, pop promos, corporate videos for a range of clients. 'We encourage new writing, especially from the regions and seek scripts from writers interested in developing new Black fiction/ comedy.'

Working Title Films Ltd

Oxford House, 76 Oxford Street, London W1D 1BS
☎020 7307 3000   Fax 020 7307 3001/2/3

Co-Chairmen (Films) *Tim Bevan, Eric Fellner*
Head of Development (Films) *Debra Hayward*
Development Coordinator *Luke Parker Bowles*
Television *Simon Wright*

Feature films, TV drama; also family/children's entertainment and TV comedy. OUTPUT: FILMS *Wimbledon; Bridget Jones 2; Edge of Reason; Shaun of the Dead; Love Actually; Thunderbirds; Ned Kelly; Johnny English; Bridget Jones's Diary; Captain Corelli's Mandolin; Ali G in dahouse; Notting Hill; Elizabeth; Fargo; Dead Man Walking; French Kiss; Four Weddings and a Funeral; The Hudsucker Proxy; The Tall Guy; Wish You Were Here; My Beautiful Laundrette.* TELEVISION *More Tales of the City; The Borrowers I & II; Armisted Maupin's Tales of the City;*

News Hounds; Randall & Hopkirk Deceased; Doomwatch. No unsolicited mss at present.

Wortman Productions UK

48 Chiswick Staithe, London W4 3TP
☎020 8994 8886/07976 805976 (Mobile)
✉ nevillewortman@beeb.net

Producer *Neville Wortman*

Co-producers with Polestar Pictures Ltd. Feature film and TV production for drama, documentary, entertainment and corporate. OUTPUT *House in the Country* John Julius Norwich (ITV series); *Tribute to Ellington* (jazz special); *Lost Ships* (maritime historical drama series; Discovery Channel); *The Assassination of Julius Caesar* (Discovery/History Channel/Five); *Events That Shook the World* (BBCTV). Open to new writing, preferably through agents; single page outline, some pages of dialogue; s.a.e. for reply.

WT2

Oxford House, 76 Oxford Street, London W1D 1BS
☎020 7307 3000   Fax 020 7307 3004

Head of WT2 *Natascha Wharton*
Head of Development *Rachael Prior*
Development Coordinator *Hannah Farrell*

Lower budget film division of **Working Title Films**. Feature films only. OUTPUT includes *Billy Elliot; Long Time Dead; Ali G Indahouse; My Little Eye; Shaun of the Dead; Inside I'm Dancing.* No unsolicited screenplays at present.

Zenith Entertainment Ltd

43–45 Dorset Street, London W1U 7NA
☎020 7224 2440   Fax 020 7224 3194
✉ general@zenith-entertainment.co.uk

Head of Drama *Adrian Bate*

Feature films and TV drama. OUTPUT: FILMS Todd Haynes' *Velvet Goldmine; Wisdom of Crocodiles;* Nicole Holofcener's *Walking and Talking.* TELEVISION *Hamish Macbeth; Rhodes; Bodyguards; Bomber; Two Thousand Acres of Sky; Hear the Silence; Roman Road; 55 Degrees North.* No unsolicited scripts.

Theatre Producers

For latest minimum rates for writers of plays for subsidised repertory theatres (not Scotland) access the following websites: Theatrical Management Association at www.tmauk.org; and the Writers' Guild at www.writersguild.org.uk

Almeida Theatre Company

The Almeida Theatre, Almeida Street, London
N1 1TA
☎020 7288 4900   Fax 020 7288 4901
www.almeida.co.uk

Artistic Director *Michael Attenborough*

Founded 1980. Now in its fifteenth year as a full-time producing theatre, presenting a year-round theatre and music programme in which international writers, composers, performers, directors and designers are invited to work with British artists on challenging new and classical works. Previous productions: *Ivanov; Naked; The Iceman Cometh; The Jew of Malta; Celebration; Richard II; Coriolanus; The Shape of Things; King Lear, The Lady from the Sea The Goat, or Who is Sylvia?; The Mercy Seat; Festen*. No unsolicited mss: 'our producing programme is very limited and linked to individual directors and actors'.

Alternative Theatre Company Ltd

Bush Theatre, Shepherds Bush Green, London
W12 8QD
☎020 7602 3703   Fax 020 7602 7614
✉ info@bushtheatre.co.uk
www.bushtheatre.co.uk

Literary Manager *Abigail Gonda*

Founded 1972. Trading as The Bush Theatre. Produces nine new plays a year (principally British) including up to three visiting companies also producing new work: 'we are a writer's theatre'. Previous productions: *Kiss of the Spiderwoman* Manuel Puig; *Raping the Gold* Lucy Gannon; *The Wexford Trilogy* Billy Roche; *Love and Understanding* Joe Penhall; *This Limetree Bower* Conor McPherson; *Discopigs* Enda Walsh; *The Pitchfork Disney* Philip Ridley; *Caravan* Helen Blakeman; *Beautiful Thing* Jonathan Harvey; *Killer Joe* Tracy Letts; *Shang-a-Lang* Catherine Johnson; *Howie the Rookie* Mark O'Rowe; *The Glee Club* Richard Cameron; *Adrenalin ... Heart* Georgia Fitch. Scripts are read by a team of associates, then discussed with the management, a process which takes about four months. The theatre offers a small number of commissions, recommissions to

ensure further drafts on promising plays, and a guarantee against royalties so writers are not financially penalised even though the plays are produced in a small house. Writers should send scripts (full-length plays only) with small s.a.e. for acknowledgement and large s.a.e. for return of script.

ATC (Actors Touring Company)

15–16 Nassau Street, London W1W 7AB
☎020 7580 7723   Fax 020 7580 7724
✉ info@atc-online.com
www.atc-online.com

Artistic Director *Gordon Anderson*

Collaborates with writers on adaptation and/or translation work and unsolicited mss will be considered in this category as well as new writing. 'We endeavour to read mss but do not have the resources to do so quickly.' As a small-scale company, all plays must have a cast of six or less.

Birmingham Repertory Theatre

Centenary Square, Broad Street, Birmingham
B1 2EP
☎0121 245 2000   Fax 0121 245 2100
www.birmingham-rep.co.uk

Literary Officer *Caroline Jester*

The Birmingham Repertory Theatre aims to provide a platform for the best work from new writers from both within and beyond the West Midlands region. The Rep is committed to the production of new work which reflects the diversity of contemporary experience and approaches to writing for the stage. The commissioning of new plays takes place across the full range of the theatre's activities: in the Main House, The Door (which is a dedicated new writing space) and on tour to community venues in the region. The theatre runs a programme of writers' attachments every year in addition to its commissioning policy and maintains close links with *Script* (the regional writers' training agency) and the MA in Playwriting Studies at the University of Birmingham. For more information contact the Literary Officer.

Black Theatre Co-op
See **NITRO**

Bootleg Theatre Company
23 Burgess Green, Bishopdown, Salisbury
SP1 3El
☎01722 421476
✉ colin@thebootlegtheatrecompany.fsnet.co.uk
Contact *Colin Burden*
Founded 1984. Tries to encompass as wide an audience as possible and has a tendency towards plays with socially relevant themes. Unsolicited mss are very welcome. 'Our policy is to produce new and/or rarely seen plays and anything received is given the most serious consideration.' Actively seeks to obtain grants to commission new writers for the company. Productions include: *Clubland* by Giles, Harris, Suthers and Mordell; *Hanging Hanratty* Michael Burnham; *The Truth About Blokes* Trevor Suthers; *Cool Blokes: Decent Suits* Russell Mardell; *Rainy Night in Soho* Stephen Giles; *Grass* Russell Mardell.

Borderline Theatre
Darlington New Church, North Harbour Street, Ayr KA8 8AA
☎01292 281010   Fax 01292 263825
✉ enquiries@borderlinetheatre.co.uk
www.borderlinetheatre.co.uk
Producer *Eddie Jackson*
Founded 1974. Borderline is one of Scotland's leading touring companies. Committed to new writing, it tours an innovative programme of new plays and radical adaptations/translations of classic texts in an accessible and entertaining style. Tours to main-house theatres and small venues throughout Scotland. Productions include the world premières of *The Angels' Share* by Chris Dolan; *The Prince and the Pilot* Anita Sullivan. Previous writers have included Dario Fo, Liz Lochhead and John Byrne. Borderline is also committed to commissioning and touring new plays for young people. Please contact the company before submitting synopsis or script.

Bristol Old Vic Theatre Company
(Old Vic, Studio & Basement)
King Street, Bristol BS1 4ED
☎0117 949 3993   Fax 0117 949 3996
✉ admin@bristol-old-vic.co.uk
www.bristol-old-vic.co.uk

Bristol Old Vic actively seeks new writers for development and commission. 'We do not offer a formal reading service but are keen to build relationships with local writers in particular.'

Bush Theatre
See **Alternative Theatre Company Ltd**

Carnival (Films & Theatre) Ltd
See entry under *Film, TV and Radio Producers*

Guy Chapman Productions Ltd
33 Southampton Street, London WC2E 7HE
☎020 7379 7474   Fax 020 7379 8484
✉ admin@g-c-a.co.uk
Contacts *Guy Chapman*
Performs to young audiences with innovative, experimental theatre. Productions include: *Shopping and Fucking*; *Love Upon the Throne*; *Crave*; *Disco Pigs*; *Resident Alien*; *Corpus Christi*; *New Boy*.

Citizens Theatre
Gorbals, Glasgow G5 9DS
☎0141 429 5561   Fax 0141 429 7374
✉ info@citz.co.uk
www.citz.co.uk
Artistic Director *Jeremy Raisen*
General Manager *Anna Stapleton*
No formal new play policy. The theatre has a play reader but opportunities to do new work are limited.

Clwyd Theatr Cymru
Mold, Flintshire CH7 1YA
☎01352 756331   Fax 01352 701558
✉ drama@celtic.co.uk
www.clwyd-theatr-cymru.co.uk
Literary Manager *William James*
(william.james@clwyd-theatr-cymru.co.uk)
Clwyd Theatr Cymru produces plays performed by a core ensemble in Mold and tours them throughout Wales (in English and Welsh). Productions are a mix of classics, revivals and contemporary drama. Recent new writing includes: *The Rabbit* Meredydd Barker; *The Journey of Mary Kelly* Siân Evans; *And Now What?* by Tim Baker and Sarah Argent; *Pocketful of Memories*, *The Ballad of Megan Morgan*, *Flora's War/Rhyfel Flora*, *Word for Word/Gair am Air* and *The Secret/Y Gyfrinach* all by Tim Baker. Plays by Welsh writers or on Welsh themes will be considered.

Michael Codron Plays Ltd
Aldwych Theatre Offices, Aldwych, London WC2B 4DF
☎020 7240 8291   Fax 020 7240 8467
General Manager *Paul O'Leary* (Productions)

Michael Codron Plays Ltd manages the Aldwych Theatre in London's West End. The plays it produces don't necessarily go into the Aldwych but always tend to be big-time West End fare. Previous productions: *Bedroom Farce*; *Blue Orange*; *Copenhagen*; *The Invention of Love*; *Hapgood*; *Uncle Vanya*; *Rise and Fall of Little Voice*; *Arcadia*; *Dead Funny*; *My Brilliant Divorce*; *Dinner*. No particular rule of thumb on subject matter or treatment. The acid test is whether 'something appeals to Michael'. Straight plays rather than musicals.

Colchester Mercury Theatre Limited

Balkerne Gate, Colchester CO1 1PT
☎01206 577006   Fax 01206 769607
✉ info@mercurytheatre.co.uk
www.mercurytheatre.co.uk
Chief Executive *Dee Evans*
Associate Director *Adrian Stokes*

Producing theatre with a wide-ranging audience. Unsolicited scripts welcome. The theatre has a free playwright's group for adults with a serious commitment to writing plays.

The Coliseum, Oldham

Fairbottom Street, Oldham OL1 3SW
☎0161 624 1731   Fax 0161 624 5318
Chief Executive/Artistic Director *Kevin Shaw*

The artistic policy of the theatre is to present a high quality and diverse theatre programme with the ambition to commission a new play each year. Unsolicited scripts will be read but only returned if s.a.e. included.

Concordance

c/o Finborough Theatre, 118 Finborough Road, London SW10 9ED
☎020 7244 7439   Fax 020 7835 1853
✉ admin@concordance.org.uk
www.concordance.org.uk
Artistic Director *Neil McPherson*

Founded in 1981, Concordance is one of two resident companies based at the **Finborough Theatre** (see entry). Presents world premières of new writing and revivals of neglected work with a special commitment to music theatre as well as integrating music into its work and productions featuring the writing of non-theatrical artists – poets, artists, novelists, etc. – presenting their work in a theatrical setting. Unsolicited scripts not welcome, 'although we offer dramaturgical services through our website'.

Contact Theatre Company

Oxford Road, Manchester M15 6JA
☎0161 274 3434   Fax 0161 274 0640
✉ info@contact-theatre.org.uk
www.contact-theatre.org
Artistic Director *John E. McGrath*

'In partnership with the BBC, we are investing in innovative approaches to the discovery of new writers – and new kinds of writing – for stage, screen, radio and new media.' In general, Contact works primarily with the 13–30 age group and is particularly interested in materials that relate to the lives and culture of young people. 'We welcome work from writers of all ages. Hearing from a variety of voices, from different cultures and backgrounds, is also important to us. We encourage concise pitches from writers (no more than ten pages) including a summary and some sample pages.'

Crucible Theatre

55 Norfolk Street, Sheffield S1 1DA
☎0114 249 5999   Fax 0114 249 6003
Artistic Director *Sam West*
Literary Associate *Matthew Byam Shaw*

'Most of the new work we present will be the result of commissions or a prolonged exchange of ideas and script development with writers in whom we have expressed an interest. However, we are interested in all new work and offer a free script reading service for unsolicited scripts. NB We do not offer readers' reports. Please ring or send s.a.e. for full details of script reading service.'

Derby Playhouse

Eagle Centre, Derby DE1 2NF
☎01332 363271   Fax 01332 547200
www.derbyplayhouse.co.uk
Chief Executive *Karen Hebden*
Creative Producer *Stephen Edwards*

Derby Playhouse is interested in new work and has produced several world premières over the last year. 'We have a discrete commissioning budget but already have several projects under way. Due to the amount of scripts we receive, we now ask writers to send a letter accompanied by a synopsis of the play, a résumé of writing experience and any ten pages of the script they wish to submit. We will then determine whether we think it is suitable for the Playhouse, in which case we will ask for a full script.' Writers are welcome to send details of rehearsed readings and productions as an alternative means of introducing the theatre to their work.

Druid Theatre Company

Flood Street, Galway, Republic of Ireland
☎00 353 91 568660   Fax 00 353 91 563109
✉ info@druidtheatre.com
www.druidtheatre.com

Contact *Literary Manager*

Founded 1975. Based in Galway and playing nationally and internationally, the company operates a major programme for the development of new writing. While focusing on Irish work, the company also accepts unsolicited material from outside Ireland.

The Dukes

Moor Lane, Lancaster LA1 1QE
☎01524 598505   Fax 01524 598519
www.dukes-lancaster.org

Chief Executive *Amanda Belcham*
Artistic Director *Ian Hastings*

Founded 1971. The only producing house in Lancashire. Wide target market for cinema and theatre. Plays in a 313-seater end-on auditorium and in a 198-seater in-the-round studio. Host for **Litfest** – Lancaster's annual festival of literature. In the summer months open-air promenade performances are held in Williamson Park. Also, community based Youth Arts Centre.

Dundee Repertory Theatre

Tay Square, Dundee DD1 1PB
☎01382 227684   Fax 01382 228609
✉ hwatson@dundeereptheatre.co.uk
www.dundeereptheatre.co.uk

Artistic Directors *Dominic Hill, James Brining*

Founded 1939. Plays to a varied audience. Translations and adaptations of classics, and new local plays. Most new work is commissioned. Interested in contemporary plays in translation and in new Scottish writing. No scripts except by prior arrangement.

Eastern Angles Theatre Company

Sir John Mills Theatre, Gatacre Road, Ipswich IP1 2LQ
☎01473 218202   Fax 01473 384999
✉ admin@easternangles.co.uk
www.easternangles.co.uk

Artistic Director *Ivan Cutting*
General Manager *Jill Streatfeild*

Founded 1982. Plays to a rural audience for the most part. New work only: some commissioned, some devised by the company, some researched documentaries. Unsolicited mss welcome but scripts or writers need to have some connection with East Anglia. 'We are always keen to develop and produce new writing, especially that which is germane to a rural area.'

Edinburgh Royal Lyceum Theatre

See **Royal Lyceum Theatre Company**

English Touring Theatre

25 Short Street, London SE1 8LJ
☎020 7450 1990   Fax 020 7450 1991
✉ admin@englishtouringtheatre.co.uk
www.englishtouringtheatre.co.uk

Artistic Director *Stephen Unwin*

Founded 1993. National touring company visiting middle-scale receiving houses and arts centres throughout the UK. Mostly mainstream. Largely classical programme, but with increasing interest to tour one modern English play per year. Strong commitment to education work. No unsolicited mss.

Finborough Theatre

118 Finborough Road, London SW10 9ED
☎020 7244 7439   Fax 020 7835 1853
✉ admin@finboroughtheatre.co.uk
www.finboroughtheatre.co.uk

Artistic Director *Neil McPherson*

Founded 1980. 'One of London's leading new writing venues' (*Time Out*). Presents revivals of neglected work from 1850 onwards, music theatre and UK premières of foreign work, particularly from Ireland, the United States and Canada. The theatre is available for hire and the fee is sometimes negotiable to encourage interesting work, though unsolicted mss are no longer accepted. Premièred work by Chris Lee, Anthony Neilson, Naomi Wallace, Tony Marchant, Diane Samuels and Mark Ravenhill.

Robert Fox Ltd

6 Beauchamp Place, London SW3 1NG
☎020 7584 6855   Fax 020 7225 1638
✉ info@robertfoxltd.com

Contact *Robert Fox*

Producer and co-producer of work suitable for West End production. Previous productions: *Another Country; Chess; Lettice and Lovage; Burn This; When She Danced; The Ride Down Mount Morgan; The Importance of Being Earnest; The Seagull; Goosepimples; Vita & Virginia; The Weekend; Three Tall Women; Skylight; Who's Afraid of Virginia Woolf; Masterclass; A Delicate Balance; Amy's View; Closer; The Lady in the Van; The Caretaker; The Breath of Life.* Also Broadway productions, recently: *Gypsy; The Boy From Oz; Salome: The Reading*, and films including *Iris* and *The Hours*.

Scripts, while usually by established playwrights, are always read.

Gate Theatre Company Ltd

11 Pembridge Road, London W11 3HQ
☎020 7229 5387   Fax 020 7221 6055
✉ gate@gatetheatre.co.uk
www.gatetheatre.co.uk

Artistic Director *Thea Sharrock*

Founded 1979. Plays to a mixed, London-wide audience, depending on production. Aims to produce British premières of plays which originate from abroad and translations of neglected classics. Most work is with translators. Runs a biennial Translation Award. Recent productions: *Tshepang* by Lara Foot Newton; *Woyzeck* by George Büchner, adapted by Daniel Kramer; *Tejas Verdes* by Fermín Cabal, transl. by Robert Shaw. Positively encourages writers from abroad to send in scripts or translations. Most unsolicited scripts are read but it is extremely unlikely that new British plays will have any future at the theatre due to emphasis on plays translated from foreign languages. Please address submissions to the Literary Manager. Always enclose s.a.e. if play needs returning.

Graeae Theatre Company

LVS Resource Centre, 356 Holloway Road, London N7 6PA
☎020 7700 2455   Fax 020 7609 7324
✉ info@graeae.org
www.graeae.org

Minicom 020 7700 8184

Artistic Director *Jenny Sealey*
Executive Producer *Roger Nelson*

Europe's premier theatre company of disabled people, the company tours nationally and internationally with innovative theatre productions highlighting both historical and contemporary disabled experience. Graeae also runs educational programmes available to schools, youth clubs, students and disabled adults nationally and provides vocational training in theatre arts (including playwriting). Unsolicited scripts, from disabled writers, welcome. New work is commissioned.

Hampstead Theatre

Eton Avenue, Swiss Cottage, London NW3 3EU
☎020 7449 4200   Fax 020 7449 4201
✉ literary@hampsteadtheatre.com
www.hampsteadtheatre.com

Contact *Pippa Ellis*

A brand new Hampstead Theatre opened in 2003. The building is an intimate space with a flexible stage and an auditorium capable of expanding to seat 325. The artistic policy continues to be the production of British and international new plays and the development of important young writers. 'We are looking for writers who recognise the power of theatre and who have a story to tell. All plays are read and discussed. We give feedback to all writers with potential.' Writers produced at Hampstead include Michael Frayn, Roy Williams, Shelagh Stephenson, Simon Block, Philip Ridley, Frank McGuinness, Rona Munro, Brad Fraser, Tim Firth and Abi Morgan.

Harrogate Theatre Company

Oxford Street, Harrogate HG1 1QF
☎01423 502710   Fax 01423 563205
✉ firstname.surname@harrogatetheatre.co.uk

Artistic Director *Hannah Chissick*

Produces four to five productions a year on the main stage, one of which may be a new play but is most likely to be commissioned. Annual mainstage Youth Theatre production may also be commissioned. Over the next two years it is planned to workshop and read new plays by local writers and possibly stage them in the studio. Unsolicited scripts from outside Yorkshire are unlikely to receive a production or workshop. Please write with a brief synopsis initially.

Heritage Theatre Ltd

See entry under *Film, TV and Radio Producers*

The Hiss & Boo Company Ltd

1 Nyes Hill, Wineham Lane, Bolney RH17 5SD
Fax 01444 882057
✉ hissboo@msn.com
www.hissboo.co.uk

Contact *Ian Liston*

Particularly interested in new thrillers, comedy thrillers, comedy and melodrama – must be commercial full-length plays. Also interested in plays/plays with music for children. No one-acts. Previous productions: *The Shakespeare Revue*; *Come Rain Come Shine*; *Sleighrider*; *Beauty and the Beast*; *An Ideal Husband*; *Mr Men's Magical Island*; *Mr Men and the Space Pirates*; *Nunsense*; *Corpse!*; *Groucho: A Life in Revue*; *See How They Run*; *Christmas Cat and the Pudding Pirates*; *Pinocchio* and traditional pantos written by Roy Hudd for the company. 'We are keen on revue-type shows and compilation shows but *not* tribute-type performances.' No unsolicited scripts; no telephone calls.

Send synopsis and introductory letter in the first instance.

Hull Truck Theatre Company

Spring Street, Hull HU2 8RW
☎01482 224800   Fax 01482 581182
Executive Director *Joanne Gower*

John Godber, of *Teechers, Bouncers, Up 'n' Under* fame, the artistic director of this high-profile Northern company since 1984, has very much dominated the scene in the past with his own successful plays. The emphasis is still on new writing but Godber's work continues to be toured extensively. Most new plays are commissioned. Previous productions: *Confessions of a City Supporter* Alan Plater; *Like a Virgin* and *Kissing Married Women* Gordon Steel; *Be My Baby* Amanda Whittington; *Life's a Beach* Alison Watt; and various family shows by Nick Lane. The company receives a large number of unsolicited scripts but cannot guarantee a quick response. Bear in mind the artistic policy of Hull Truck, which is 'accessibility and popularity'. In general they are not interested in musicals, or in plays with casts of more than eight.

Stephen Joseph Theatre

Westborough, Scarborough YO11 1JW
☎01723 370540   Fax 01723 360506
www.sjt.uk.com
Artistic Director *Alan Ayckbourn*
Literary Manager *Laura Harvey*

A two-auditoria complex housing a 165-seat end stage theatre/cinema (the McCarthy) and a 400-seat theatre-in-the-round (the Round). Positive policy on new work. For obvious reasons, Alan Ayckbourn's work features quite strongly but a new writing programme ensures plays from other sources are actively encouraged. Also runs a lunchtime season of one-act plays each summer. Writers are advised however that the SJT is very unlikely to produce an unsolicited script – synopses are preferred. Recent commissions and past productions include: *Soap* Sarah Woods; *Fields of Gold* Alex Jones; *For Starters* Nick Warburton; *Bedtime Stories* Lesley Bruce; *Making Waves* Stephen Clark; *Larkin with Women* Ben Brown; *Amaretti Angels* Sarah Phelps; *Something Blue* Gill Adams; *Clockwatching* and *A Listening Heaven* Torben Betts; *The Star Throwers* Paul Lucas; *Safari Party* Tim Firth; *Drowning on Dry Land*; *Private Fears in Public Places* and *My Sister Sadie* Alan Ayckbourn. 'Writers are welcome to send details of rehearsed readings and productions as an alternative means of introducing the theatre to their work.' Submit to *Laura Harvey* enclosing an s.a.e. for return of mss.

Bill Kenwright Ltd

BKL House, 106 Harrow Road, London W2 1RR
☎020 7446 6200   Fax 020 7446 6222
Contact *Bill Kenwright*

Presents both revivals and new shows for West End and touring theatres. Although new work tends to be by established playwrights, this does not preclude or prejudice new plays from new writers. Scripts should be addressed to Bill Kenwright with a covering letter and s.a.e. 'We have enormous amounts of scripts sent to us although we very rarely produce unsolicited work. Scripts are read systematically. Please do not phone; the return of your script or contact with you will take place in time.'

Komedia

Gardner Street, North Lane, Brighton BN1 1UN
☎01273 647101   Fax 01273 647102
✉ info@komedia.co.uk
www.komedia.co.uk
Contact *David Lavender*

Founded in 1994, Komedia promotes, produces and presents new work. Mss of new plays welcome.

Leeds Playhouse

See **West Yorkshire Playhouse**

Leicester Haymarket Theatre

Belgrave Gate, Leicester LE1 3YQ
☎0116 253 0021   Fax 0116 251 3310
✉ enquiry@leicesterhaymarkettheatre.org
www.leicesterhaymarkettheatre.org
Artistic Directors *Kully Thiarai, Paul Kerryson*

Leicester Haymarket Theatre aims for a balanced programme of original and established works. It is a multi-cultural integrated company with educational projects that support all productions and areas of work. Productions include *West Side Story*; *Singin' In the Rain*; *To Kill a Mockingbird*; *Master Harold and the Boys* and new commissions such as *Palace of Fear* and *The Fortune Club*. Works with other arts organisations in the city and county to provide external productions.

Library Theatre Company

St Peter's Square, Manchester M2 5PD
☎0161 234 1913   Fax 0161 228 6481
✉ ltc@libraries.manchester.gov.uk

www.librarytheatre.com

Artistic Director *Chris Honer*

Produces new and contemporary work, as well as occasional classics. No unsolicited mss. Send outline of the nature of the script first. Encourages new writing through the commissioning of new plays and through a programme of rehearsed readings to help writers' development.

Live Theatre Company

7/8 Trinity Chare, Newcastle upon Tyne NE1 3DF

☎0191 261 2694   Fax 0191 232 2224

✉ info@live.org.uk

www.live.org.uk

Artistic Director *Max Roberts*

Executive Director *Jim Beirne*

Founded 1973. Produces shows at its refurbished 200-seat venue, and also tours regionally and nationally. Company policy is to produce work that is rooted in the culture of the region, particularly for those who do not normally get involved in the arts. The company is particularly interested in promoting new writing. As well as full-scale productions the company organises workshops, rehearsed readings and other new writing activities. The company also enjoys a close relationship with **New Writing North** and is funded to support new writing through the BBC's *Northern Exposure* project. Productions include: *Falling Together* Tom Hadaway; *Cooking With Elvis* Lee Hall; *Bones* Peter Straughan; *ne1*; *Tales From the Backyard* Alan Plater; *Double Lives* Julia Darling and Sean O'Brien; *Smack Family Robinson* Richard Bean; *Keepers of the Flame* and *Laughter When We're Dead* Sean O'Brien.

Llwyfan Gogledd Cymru (North Wales Stage)

c/o Theatr Gwynedd, Ffordd Deiniol, Bangor LL57 2TL

☎01248 370088/07855 758264 (mobile)

Fax 01248 370121

www.llwyfan-gogledd-cymru.com

Contact *Artistic Director*

Founded 2003, Llwyfan Gogledd Cymru is an Arts Council Wales revenue funded company dedicated to producing work about and for North Wales with a brief to tour both nationally and internationally. Though primarily a Welsh language mid-scale theatre company, it recognises the importance of placing both the Welsh language and its culture in a broader context. As a consequence, the work the company has lined up over the next three years is largely multilingual,

reflecting the changing demographic of the region and the growing confidence of Welsh Wales to express itself on an international stage.

London Bubble Theatre Company

5 Elephant Lane, London SE16 4JD

☎020 7237 4434   Fax 020 7231 2366

✉ admin@londonbubble.org.uk

www.londonbubble.org.uk

Artistic Director *Jonathan Petherbridge*

Produces workshops, plays and events for a mixed audience of theatregoers and non-theatregoers, wide-ranging in terms of age, culture and class. Previous productions: *Punchkin, Enchanter, You Can't Say You Can't Play*. Unsolicited mss are received but 'our reading service is extremely limited and there can be a considerable wait before we can give a response'. Commissions approximately one new project a year, often inspired by a promenade site, specific community of interest or workshop group.

Lyric Theatre Hammersmith

Lyric Square, King Street, London W6 0QL

☎08700 500 5111   Fax 020 8741 5965

✉ enquiries@lyric.co.uk

www.lyric.co.uk

Artistic Director *Neil Bartlett*

Executive Director *Simon Mellor*

The main theatre stages an eclectic programme of new and revived classics. Interested in developing projects with writers, translators and adaptors. The Lyric does not accept unsolicited scripts. Its 110-seat studio focuses on work for children, young people and families.

mac

Cannon Hill Park, Birmingham B12 9QH

☎0121 440 4221   Fax 0121 446 4372

✉ info@mac-birmingham.org.uk

www.macarts.co.uk

Minicom: 0121 440 4923

Director *Dorothy Wilson*

Innovative creative arts activities, including theatre, music, comedy, plays for children, literature and poetry events, family show at Christmas, films and free exhibitions.

Manchester Library Theatre

See **Library Theatre Company**

New Vic Theatre

Etruria Road, Newcastle under Lyme ST5 0JG

☎01782 717954   Fax 01782 712885

✉ admin@newvictheatre.org.uk

Artistic Director *Gwenda Hughes*

The New Vic is a purpose-built theatre-in-the-round. Produces ten in-house plays each year and is active within the education sector and community. New plays produced are the result of specific commissions. Send synopses *not* unsolicited scripts. 'We cannot guarantee that unsolicited scripts will be read; they will be returned on receipt of an s.a.e.'

Newpalm Productions

26 Cavendish Avenue, London N3 3QN
☎020 8349 0802   Fax 020 8346 8257

Contact *Lionel Chilcott*

Very rarely produces new plays (*As Is* by William M. Hoffman, which came from Broadway to the Half Moon Theatre, was an exception to this). National tours and West End productions such as *Peter Pan (The Musical); Noises Off, Seven Brides for Seven Brothers* and *Rebecca*, at regional repertory theatres, are more typical examples of Newpalm's work. Both plays and musicals are, however, welcome; synopses are preferable to scripts.

NITRO

6 Brewery Road, London N7 9NH
☎020 7609 1331   Fax 020 7609 1221
✉ info@nitro.co.uk
www.nitro.co.uk

Artistic Director *Felix Cross*

Founded 1978. Formerly Black Theatre Co-op. Plays to a mixed audience, approximately 65% female. Usually tours nationally twice a year. 'A music theatre company, we are committed in the first instance to new writing by Black British writers and work which relates to the Black culture and experience throughout the Diaspora.' Unsolicited mss welcome.

Northcott Theatre

Stocker Road, Exeter EX4 4QB
☎01392 223999   Fax 01392 223996
www.northcott-theatre.co.uk

Artistic Director *Ben Crocker*

Founded 1967. The Northcott is the South-west's principal subsidised producing theatre, situated on the University of Exeter campus. Describes its audience as 'geographically diverse, with a core audience of AB1s (40–60 age range)'. Continually looking to broaden the base of its audience profile, targeting younger and/or non-mainstream theatregoers. Aims to develop, promote and produce quality new writing which reflects the life of the region and addresses the audience it serves. Generally

works on a commission basis but occasionally options existing new work. Unsolicited mss welcome – current turnaround on script-reading service is approximately three months and no mss can be returned unless a correct value s.a.e. is included with the original submission.

Norwich Puppet Theatre

St James, Whitefriars, Norwich NR3 1TN
☎01603 615564   Fax 01603 617578
✉ info@puppettheatre.co.uk
www.puppettheatre.co.uk

Artistic Director *Luis Boy*
General Manager *Ian Woods*

Plays to a young audience (aged 3–12) but developing shows for adult audiences interested in puppetry. All year round programme plus tours to schools and arts venues. Most productions are based on traditional stories but unsolicited mss welcome if relevant.

Nottingham Playhouse

Nottingham Theatre Trust, Wellington Circus, Nottingham NG1 5AF
☎0115 947 4361   Fax 0115 947 5759
www.nottinghamplayhouse.co.uk

Artistic Director *Giles Croft*

Aims to make innovation popular, and present the best of world theatre, working closely with the communities of Nottingham and Nottinghamshire. Unsolicited mss will be read. It normally takes about six months, however, and 'we have never yet produced an unsolicited script. All our plays have to achieve a minimum of 60 per cent audiences in a 732-seat theatre. We have no studio.'

Nottingham Playhouse Roundabout Theatre in Education

Wellington Circus, Nottingham NG1 5AF
☎0115 947 4361
✉ andrewb@nottinghamplayhouse.co.uk
www.nottinghamplayhouse.co.uk

Contact *Andrew Breakwell*

Founded 1973. Theatre-in-Education company of the **Nottingham Playhouse**. Plays to a young audience aged 5–18 years of age. 'We are committed to the encouragement of new writing and commission at least two new plays for young people each year. With other major producers in the East Midlands we share the resources of the *Theatre Writing Partnership* which is based at the Playhouse. See website for philosophy and play details. Please make contact before submitting scripts.'

N.T.C. Touring Theatre Company

The Playhouse, Bondgate Without, Alnwick
NE66 1PQ
☎01665 602586   Fax 01665 605837
✉ admin@ntc-touringtheatre.co.uk
www.ntc-touringtheatre.co.uk
Contact *Gillian Hambleton*
General Manager *Anna Flood*

Founded 1978. Formerly Northumberland
Theatre Company. An Arts Council England
revenue funded organisation. Predominantly
rural, small-scale touring company, playing to
village halls and community centres throughout
the Northern region, the Scottish Borders and
countrywide. Productions range from established classics to new work and popular comedies, but must be appropriate to their audience.
Unsolicited scripts welcome but are unlikely to
be produced. All scripts are read and returned
with constructive criticism within six months.
Writers whose style is of interest may then be
commissioned. The company encourages new
writing and commissions when possible.
Financial constraints restrict casting to a *maximum* of five.

Nuffield Theatre

University Road, Southampton SO17 1TR
☎023 8031 5500   Fax 023 8031 5511
✉ info@nuffieldtheatre.co.uk
www.nuffieldtheatre.co.uk
Artistic Director *Patrick Sandford*
Script Executive *John Burgess*

Well known as a good bet for new playwrights,
the Nuffield gets an awful lot of scripts. They
do a couple of new main stage plays every season. Previous productions: *Exchange* by Yuri
Trifonov (transl. Michael Frayn) which transferred to the Vaudeville Theatre; *The Floating
Light Bulb* Woody Allen (British première); new
plays by Claire Luckham: *Dogspot; The Dramatic
Attitudes of Miss Fanny Kemble;* and by Claire
Tomalin: *The Winter Wife.* Open-minded about
subject and style, producing musicals as well as
straight plays. Also opportunities for some
small-scale fringe work. Scripts preferred to
synopses in the case of writers new to theatre.
All will, eventually, be read 'but please be
patient. We do not have a large team of paid
readers. We read everything ourselves.'

Octagon Theatre Trust Ltd

Howell Croft South, Bolton BL1 1SB
☎01204 529407   Fax 01204 556502
✉ info@octagonbolton.co.uk
www.octagonbolton.co.uk

Executive Director *John Blackmore*

Founded in 1967, the award-winning Octagon
Theatre stages at least eight main auditorium
home-produced shows a year, and hosts UK
touring companies such as the National Theatre,
John Godber's Hull Truck Theatre Company,
Peshkar Productions and Alan Ayckbourn's
Stephen Joseph Theatre. Also hosts the work of
partner companies as part of its commitment to
creative partnerships. The theatre boasts a thriving
and constantly developing participatory department, activ8, which operates a highly successful
Youth Theatre as well as initiating and facilitating
exciting education and outreach programmes.
The theatre is keen to encourage new writing
but, due to the lack of a dedicated literary department, is unable to accept and process new and
unsolicited scripts; the theatre uses **North West
Playwrights** as a reading service instead.

Orange Tree Theatre

1 Clarence Street, Richmond TW9 2SA
☎020 8940 0141   Fax 020 8332 0369
✉ admin@orange-tree.demon.co.uk
www.orangetreetheatre.co.uk
Artistic Director *Sam Walters*

The Orange Tree, a theatre-in-the-round
venue, presents a broad cross section of work.
Past productions have included plays by
Rodney Ackland, John Galsworthy and a new
translation of Lorca as well as a new play by
Oliver Ford Davies. The theatre no longer considers unsolicited mss; writers who may wish to
approach the theatre are asked to write first.

Out of Joint

7 Thane Works, Thane Villas, London N7 7NU
☎020 7609 0207   Fax 020 7609 0203
✉ ojo@outofjoint.co.uk
www.outofjoint.co.uk
Director *Max Stafford-Clark*
Producer *Graham Cowley*
Literary Associate *Alex Roberts*

Founded 1993. Award-winning theatre com-
pany with new writing central to its policy.
Produces new plays which reflect society and its
concerns, placing an emphasis on education
activity to attract young audiences. Welcomes
unsolicited mss. Productions include: *Blue Heart*
Caryl Churchill; *Our Lady of Sligo, The Steward
of Christendom* and *Hinterland* Sebastian Barry;
Shopping and Fucking and *Some Explicit Polaroids*
Mark Ravenhill; *Rita, Sue and Bob Too* Andrea
Dunbar; *A State Affair* and *Talking to Terrorists*
Robin Soans; *Sliding with Suzanne* Judy Upton;
The Positive Hour and *A Laughing Matter* April

de Angelis; *Duck* Stella Feehily; *The Permanent Way* David Hare.

Oxford Stage Company
Chertsey Chambers, 12 Mercer Street, London WC2H 9QD
☎020 7438 9940   Fax 020 7438 9941
www.oxfordstage.co.uk
Artistic Director *Dominic Dromgoole*

A middle-scale touring company producing established and new plays. On average, one new play or new adaptation a year. Due to forthcoming projects the company is not considering unsolicited scripts at present.

Paines Plough
4th Floor, 43 Aldwych, London WC2B 4DN
☎020 7240 4533   Fax 020 7240 4534
✉ office@painesplough.com
www.painesplough.com
Artistic Director *Roxana Silbert*
Associate Director *John Tiffany*
Literary Manager *Lucy Morrison*

Tours new plays nationally. Works with writers to develop their skills and voices through workshops, rehearsed readings and playwriting projects. Provides a supportive environment for commissioned writers to push themselves and challenge their craft. Will consider unsolicited material from UK writers (please send s.a.e. for return of script).

Perth Repertory Theatre Ltd
185 High Street, Perth PH1 5UW
☎01738 472700   Fax 01738 624576
✉ info@horsecross.co.uk
www.horsecross.co.uk
Creative Directors *Ian Grieve, Graham McLaren*
General Manager *Paul Hackett*

Founded 1935. Combination of one- to four-weekly repertoire of plays and musicals, incoming tours and studio productions. Unsolicited mss are read when time permits, but the timetable for return of scripts is lengthy. New plays staged by the company are usually commissioned under the SAC scheme.

Plymouth Theatre Royal
See **Theatre Royal**

Polka Theatre for Children
240 The Broadway, Wimbledon SW19 1SB
☎020 8545 8320   Fax 020 8545 8365
✉ info@polkatheatre.com
www.polkatheatre.com

Artistic Director *Annie Wood*
Executive Director *Stephen Midlane*
Associate Director, New Writing *Richard Shannon*

Founded in 1967 and moved into its Wimbledon base in 1979. Leading children's theatre committed to commissioning and producing new plays. Programmes are planned two years ahead and at least three new plays are commissioned each year. 'Many of our scripts are commissioned from established writers. We are, however, keen to develop work from writers new to children's and young people's theatre. We run a new writing programme which includes master classes and workshops. Potential new writers' work is read and discussed on a regular basis; thus we constantly add to our pool of interesting and interested writers. This department is headed by *Richard Shannon*, Associate Director for New Writing.'

Queen's Theatre, Hornchurch
Billet Lane, Hornchurch RM11 1QT
☎01708 462362   Fax 01708 462363
✉ info@queens-theatre.co.uk
www.queens-theatre.co.uk
Artistic Director *Bob Carlton*

The Queen's Theatre is a 503-seat theatre producing up to nine in-house productions per year, including pantomime. Aims for distinctive and accessible performances in an identifiable house style focused upon actor/musician shows but, in addition, embraces straight plays, classics and comedies. 'New play/musical submissions are welcome but should be submitted in treatment and not script form.' Also runs a writers' group which meets on the first Thursday of each month, and playwright David Eldridge runs the 'Beginning Writers' Group' for adults (contact the Education Manager for information). These groups have close links with the Queen's community company which workshops and showcases the groups' work. Summer 2005 saw the staging of a large-scale community play by a local writer.

The Really Useful Group Ltd
22 Tower Street, London WC2H 9TW
☎020 7240 0880   Fax 020 7240 1204
www.reallyuseful.com

Commercial/West End, national and international theatre producer/co-producer whose output has included *Joseph and the Amazing Technicolor Dreamcoat*; *Jesus Christ Superstar*; *Cats*; *Song & Dance*; *Daisy Pulls It Off*; *Lend Me a Tenor*; *Starlight Express*; *The Phantom of the Opera*; *Aspects of Love; Sunset Boulevard; By Jeeves; Whistle Down the Wind; The Beautiful Game; Tell Me On a Sunday; Bombay Dreams; The Woman in White.*

Red Ladder Theatre Company

3 St Peter's Buildings, York Street, Leeds LS9 8AJ
☎0113 245 5311   Fax 0113 245 5351
✉ wendy@redladder.co.uk
www.redladder.co.uk

Artistic Director/Literary Manager *Wendy Harris*
Administrator *Janis Smyth*

Founded 1968. Commissioning company touring 2–3 shows a year with a strong commitment to new work and new writers. Aimed at an audience of young people aged between 14–25 years who have little or no access to theatre. Performances held in youth clubs and theatre venues. Recent productions: *Soulskin* Esther Wilson; *Tagged* Louise Wallwein; *Silent Cry* Madani Younis; *Free Falling* Madani Younis. The company is particularly keen to enter into a dialogue with writers with regard to creating new work for young people. E-mail the artistic director for more information at the address above.

Red Shift Theatre Company

TRG2 Trowbray House, 108 Weston Street, London SE1 3QB
☎020 7378 9787   Fax 020 7378 9789
✉ mail@redshifttheatreco.co.uk
www.redshifttheatreco.co.uk

Contact *Jonathan Holloway* (Artistic Director)
General Manager *Emma Rees*

Founded 1982. Small-scale touring company which plays to a theatre-literate audience. Welcomes contact with writers – 'we try to see their work' – and receipt of c.v.s and treatments. Occasionally runs workshops bringing new scripts, writers and actors together. These can develop links with a reservoir of writers who may feed the company. Interested in new plays with subject matter which is accessible to a broad audience and concerns issues of importance; also new translations and adaptations. Recent productions: *The Third Man* and *Bartleby: A Story of Wall Street.*

Ridiculusmus

c/o Your Imagination, BAC, Lavender Hill, London SW11 5TN
✉ ridiculusmus@yourimagination.org
www.ridiculusmus.com

Artistic Directors *Jon Haynes, David Woods*
Founded 1992. Touring company which plays

to a wide range of audiences. Productions have included adaptations of *The Importance of Being Earnest; Three Men In a Boat; The Third Policeman; At Swim Two Birds* and original work: *The Exhibitionists; Yes, Yes, Yes; Say Nothing* and *Ideas Men.* Unsolicited scripts not welcome.

Royal Court Theatre

Sloane Square, London SW1W 8AS
☎020 7565 5050
Fax 020 7565 5002 (Literary office)
www.royalcourttheatre.com

Literary Manager *Graham Whybrow*

The Royal Court is a leading international theatre producing up to 17 new plays each year in its 400-seat proscenium theatre and 80-seat studio. In 1956 its first director George Devine set out to find 'hard-hitting, uncompromising writers whose plays are stimulating, provocative and exciting'. This artistic policy helped transform post-war British theatre, with new plays by writers such as John Osborne, Arnold Wesker, John Arden, Samuel Beckett, Edward Bond and David Storey, through to Caryl Churchill, Jim Cartwright, Kevin Elyot and Timberlake Wertenbaker. Since 1994 it has produced a new generation of playwrights such as Joe Penhall, Rebecca Prichard, Sarah Kane, Jez Butterworth, Martin McDonagh, Mark Ravenhill, Ayub Khan-Din, Conor McPherson, Roy Williams and many other first-time writers. The Royal Court has programmes for young writers and international writers, and it is always searching for new plays and new playwrights.

Royal Exchange Theatre Company

St Ann's Square, Manchester M2 7DH
☎0161 615 6709   Fax 0161 832 0881
✉ jo.combes@royalexchange.co.uk
www.royalexchange.co.uk

Associate Artistic Director *Sarah Frankcom*
Associate Director (Literary) *Jo Combes*

Founded 1976. The Royal Exchange has developed a new writing policy which it finds is attracting a younger audience to the theatre. The company has produced new plays by Simon Stephens, Shelagh Stephenson, Brad Fraser, Simon Burke, Jim Cartwright, Peter Barnes and Owen McCafferty. Currently has Gurpreet Bhatti, Nick Leather, Owen McCafferty, Abi Morgan, Chloe Moss, Lavinia Murray and Roy Williams on commission. Runs WRITE, a new playwriting competition, details of which are available on the website. 'If you would like to submit your script to us, please enclose the appropriate postage if you would like it returned.'

Royal Lyceum Theatre Company
Grindlay Street, Edinburgh EH3 9AX
☎0131 248 4800　Fax 0131 228 3955
www.lyceum.org.uk
Artistic Director *Mark Thomson*
Administration Manager *Ruth Butterworth*

Founded 1965. Repertory theatre which plays to a mixed urban Scottish audience. Produces classic, contemporary and new plays. Would like to stage more new plays, especially Scottish. No full-time literary staff to provide reports on submitted scripts.

Royal National Theatre
South Bank, London SE1 9PX
☎020 7452 3333　Fax 020 7452 3350
www.nationaltheatre.org.uk
Literary Manager *Jack Bradley*

The majority of the National's new plays come about as a result of direct commission or from existing contacts with playwrights. There is no quota for new work, though many of the plays presented have been the work of living playwrights especially in the Cottesloe Theatre which is dedicated to new plays. Writers new to the theatre would need to be of exceptional talent to be successful with a script here, however the Royal National Theatre Studio helps a limited number of playwrights, through readings, workshops and discussions. Scripts considered (send s.a.e).

Royal Shakespeare Company
1 Earlham Street, London WC2H 9LL
☎020 7845 0515
www.rsc.org.uk
Literary Manager *Jeanie O'Hare*

The RSC is a classical theatre company based in Stratford upon Avon. As well as Shakespeare, the RSC produces English classics, foreign classics in translation and new plays. The literary department is proactive rather than reactive and seeks out the plays and playwrights it wishes to commission. 'We can only read contemporary works where the writer is known. Sadly we are unable to read unsolicited work from less established writers but we do monitor the work of emerging playwrights in production nationally and internationally.' In 2006 the company is presenting an ambitious year-round Complete Works of Shakespeare Festival. All these RSC

productions, classics and new plays, transfer to a variety of West End venues in London.

7:84 Theatre Company Scotland
333 Woodlands Road, Glasgow G3 6NG
☎0141 334 6686　Fax 0141 334 3369
✉ admin@784theatre.com
www.784theatre.com
Artistic Director *Lorenzo Mele*

Founded 1973. One of Scotland's foremost touring theatre companies committed to producing work that addresses current social, cultural and political issues. Recent productions include commissions by Scottish playwrights such as Stephen Greenhorn, Rona Munro and Martin McArdie (*Reasons to be Cheerful*); Christopher Dean (*Boiling a Frog*); Peter Arnott (*A Little Rain*); Stephen Greenhorn (*Dissent*); David Greig (*Caledonia Dreaming*) and the Scottish premières of Tony Kushner's *Angels in America* and Athol Fugard's *Valley Song*. 'The company is committed to a new writing policy that encourages and develops writers at every level of experience, to get new voices and strong messages on to the stage.' New writing development has always been central to 7:84's core activity and has included Summer Schools and rehearsed readings. The company continues to be committed to this work and its development. 'Happy to read unsolicited scripts.'

Shared Experience
The Soho Laundry, 9 Dufour's Place, London W1F 7SJ
☎020 7434 9248　Fax 020 7287 8763
✉ admin@sharedexperience.org.uk
www.sharedexperience.org.uk
Joint Artistic Directors *Nancy Meckler, Polly Teale*

Founded 1975. Varied audience depending on venue, since this is a touring company. Recent productions have included: *Anna Karenina, Mill on the Floss*, and *War and Peace* (all adapt. by Helen Edmundson); *The Danube* Maria Irene Fornes; *Desire Under the Elms* Eugene O'Neill; *The Tempest* William Shakespeare; *Jane Eyre* (adapt. Polly Teale); *I Am Yours* Judith Thompson; *The House of Bernarda Alba* (transl. Rona Munro); *Mother Courage* (transl. Lee Hall); *A Doll's House* (transl. Michael Meyer); *The Magic Toyshop* (adapt. Bryony Lavery); *The Clearing* Helen Edmundson; *A Passage to India* (adapt. Martin Sherman). No unsolicited mss. Primarily not a new writing company but 'we are interested in innovative new scripts'.

Sherman Theatre Company

Senghennydd Road, Cardiff CF24 4YE
☎029 2064 6901   Fax 029 2064 6902
www.shermantheatre.co.uk

Artistic Director *Phil Clark*

Founded 1973. Theatre for Young People, with main house and studio. Encourages new writing; has produced 86 new plays in the last ten years. Previous productions include a David Wood adaptation of Roald Dahl's *Danny the Champion of the World*, plays by Frank Vickery (*Pullin the Wool*); Helen Griffin (*Flesh and Blood*); Patrick Jones (*Everything Must Go*); Terry Deary (*Horrible Histories Crackers Christmas*); Mike Kenny (*Puff the Magic Dragon*); Brendan Murray (*Something Beginning With ...*); Roald Dahl (*The Enormous Crocodile*); Roger Williams (*Pop*); Arnold Wesker (*Break, My Heart*). Runs a new scheme called WriteHere for which scripts can be submitted. Interesting ideas go through to ScriptSlam during which an audience votes for their favourite excerpt to be developed further.

Show of Strength

74 Chessel Street, Bedminster, Bristol BS3 3DN
☎0117 902 0235   Fax 0117 902 0196
✉ sheila@showofstrength.freeserve.co.uk
www.showofstrength.org.uk

Artistic Director *Sheila Hannon*

Founded 1986. Plays to an informal, younger than average audience. Aims to stage at least one new play each season with a preference for work from Bristol and the South West. Will read unsolicited scripts but a lack of funding means they are unable to provide written reports. Output: *The Wills Girls* by Amanda Whittington; *Lags* by Ron Hutchinson; *So Long Life* and *Nicholodeon* by Peter Nichols. Also, rehearsed readings of new work.

Snap People's Theatre Trust

29 Raynham Road, Bishop's Stortford CM23 5PE
☎01279 461607   Fax 01279 506694
✉ info@snaptheatre.co.uk
www.snaptheatre.co.uk

Contacts *Andy Graham, Gill Bloomfield*

Founded 1979. Plays to young people (5–11; 12–19), and for the under 25s. New writing, young people and new media are the priorities. Writers should make contact in advance of sending material. New writing is encouraged and should involve, be written for or by young people. 'Projects should reflect the writer's own beliefs, be thought-provoking, challenging and accessible. The writer should be able to work with designers, directors and musicians in the early stages to develop the text and work alongside other disciplines.'

Soho Theatre Company

21 Dean Street, London W1D 3NE
☎020 7287 5060   Fax 020 7287 5061
✉ writers@sohotheatre.com
www.sohotheatre.com

Artistic Director *Abigail Morris*

Dedicated to new writing, the company has an extensive research and development programme consisting of a free script-reading service, workshops and readings. Also runs many courses for new writers. Soho Young Writers hold free 'Taster Workshops' and longer courses for promising playwrights aged 15–25. The company produces around four plays a year. Recent productions include: *A Night At the Dogs* Matt Charman (winner of the 2000 Verity Bargate Award); *Colder Than Here* Laura Wade; *Thom Pain* Will Eno (Pulitzer Prize for Drama nominee). Runs the **Verity Bargate Award**, a biennial competition (see entry under *Prizes*).

Sphinx Theatre Company

25 Short Street, London SE1 8LJ
☎020 7401 9993   Fax 020 7401 9995
✉ admin@sphinxtheatre.co.uk
www.sphinxtheatre.co.uk

Artistic Director *Sue Parrish*
General Manager *Susannah Kraft Levene*
Administrator *Bonnie Mitchell*

Founded 1973. Tours new plays by women nationally to small and mid-scale venues. Synopses and ideas are welcome by e-mail or post with s.a.e.

The Steam Industry

c/o/ Finborough Theatre, 118 Finborough Road, London SW10 9ED
☎020 7244 7439   Fax 020 7835 1853
✉ admin@finboroughtheatre.co.uk
www.steamindustry.co.uk

Artistic Director *Phil Willmott*

Since June 1994, the multi-awards-winning production company The Steam Industry has become known for its diverse and prolific productions of both new writing, radical adaptations of classic texts and musicals at many venues including the Finborough Theatre, BAC, The Bridewell, The Drill Hall and Riverside Studios. Unsolicited scripts are no longer welcome.

Black, Asian and Irish). Looks for a strong narrative drive with popular appeal, not 'studio' plays. Fee: £12 per script. Supplies written reader's report. Can only return scripts if postage coupons or s.a.e. are enclosed with original submission.

Tron Theatre Company

63 Trongate, Glasgow G1 5HB
☎0141 552 3748   Fax 0141 552 6657
✉ neil@tron.co.uk
www.tron.co.uk

Director *Neil Murray*

Founded 1981. Plays to a broad cross-section of Glasgow and beyond, including international tours. Recent productions: *Standing Wave: Delia Derbyshire in the 60s* Nicola McCartney (co-production with Reeling & Writhing); *The Wonderful World of Dissocia* Anthony Neilson (co-production with Edinburgh International Festival and Theatre Royal, Plymouth); *San Diego* David Greig (co-production with Edinburgh International Festival). Interested in ambitious plays by UK and international writers. No unsolicited scripts.

Unicorn Theatre for Children

From Oct. 2005: Tooley Street, Southwark, London SE1
☎020 7700 0702   Fax 020 7700 3870
✉ admin@unicorntheatre.com
www.unicorntheatre.com

Artistic Director *Tony Graham*
Literary Manager *Carl Miller*

Founded 1947, resident at the Arts Theatre from 1967 to 1999 and now based (from October 2005) at the new Unicorn Children's Centre with two theatres. Produces full-length professionally performed plays for children, aged 4–12, their teachers and families. Recent work includes *Old King Cole* by Ken Campbell; *Rama and Sita: Path of Flames* and *Clockwork* by Philip Pullman, adapt. David Wood and Stephen McNeff. Does not produce unsolicited scripts but works with commissioned writers. Writers interested in working with the company should send details of relevant previous work and why they would like to write for Unicorn.

Upstairs at the Gatehouse

See **Ovation Productions** under *Film, TV and Radio Producers*

Charles Vance Productions

Hampden House, 2 Weymouth Street, London W1W 5BT
☎020 7636 4343   Fax 020 7636 2323

✉ cvtheatre@aol.com
Contact *Charles Vance*

In the market for medium-scale touring productions and summer-season plays. Hardly any new work and no commissions but writing of promise stands a good chance of being passed on to someone who might be interested in it. Occasional try-outs for new work in the Sidmouth repertory theatre. Send s.a.e. for return of mss.

Warehouse Theatre

Dingwall Road (adjacent to East Croydon Station), Croydon CR0 2NF
☎020 8681 1257
✉ info@warehousetheatre.co.uk
www.warehousetheatre.co.uk

Artistic Director *Ted Craig*

South London's new writing theatre seats 90–100 and produces up to six new plays a year. Also co-produces with, and hosts, selected touring companies who share the theatre's commitment to new work. The theatre continues to build upon a tradition of discovering and nurturing new writers through the **International Playwriting Festival** (see entry under *Festivals*). Also runs a vigorous writers' workshop at the end of each month and hosts youth theatre workshops and Saturday morning children's theatre. Scripts will get a faster response if submitted through the International Playwriting Festival.

Watford Palace Theatre

Clarendon Road, Watford WD17 1JZ
☎01923 235455   Fax 01923 819664
✉ enquiries@watfordtheatre.co.uk
www.watfordtheatre.co.uk

Artistic Director *Lawrence Till*
Literary Director *Joyce Branagh*

Recently reopened following an £8.7 million refurbishment. An important part of artistic and cultural policy is the commissioning of new plays and to discover major new playwrights and new plays of enduring stature to be produced in the region. Recent new plays: *Flying Under Bridges* Sarah Daniels; *Get Ken Barlow* Ian Kershaw; *Elton John's Glasses* David Farr (1997 Writers' Guild Best Regional Play award); *The Talented Mr Ripley* Phyllis Nagy; *The Dark* Jonathan Holloway; *The Late Middle Classes* Simon Gray (1999 Barclays/TMA Best New Play Award); *Morning Glory* Sarah Daniels; *The True-Life Fiction of Mata Hari* Diane Samuels;

Full House and *The Hairless Diva* (after Ionesco) John Mortimer; *Big Night Out at the Little Palace Theatre* Sandi Toksvig and Dillie Keane.

West Yorkshire Playhouse

Playhouse Square, Leeds LS2 7UP
☎0113 213 7800   Fax 0113 213 7250
✉ alex.chisholm@wyp.org.uk
www.wyp.org.uk

Literary Manager *Alex Chisholm*

Committed to working with new writing originating from or set in the Yorkshire and Humberside region. New writing from outside the region is programmed usually where writer or company is already known to the theatre. The Playhouse runs workshops, courses and writers' events including Thursday Night Live, an open platform held at the theatre for local writers and performers. For more information contact the Literary Manager, ☎0113 213 7286 or e-mail to address above. Scripts should be submitted with s.a.e. for return. 'Not all submitted scripts will be read. You are strongly advised to check guidelines on the website *before* submitting.'

Whirligig Theatre

14 Belvedere Drive, Wimbledon, London SW19 7BY
☎020 8947 1732   Fax 020 8879 7648
✉ whirligig-theatre@virgin.net

Contact *David Wood*

Occasional productions and tours to major theatre venues, usually a musical for primary school audiences and weekend family groups. Interested in scripts which exploit the theatrical nature of children's tastes. Previous productions: *The See-Saw Tree*; *The Selfish Shellfish*; *The Gingerbread Man*; *The Old Man of Lochnagar*, *The Ideal Gnome Expedition*; *Save the Human*; *Dreams of Anne Frank*; *Babe, the Sheep-Pig*.

White Bear Theatre Club

138 Kennington Park Road, London SE11 4DJ
Administration: 3 Dante Road, Kennington, London SE11 4RB
☎020 7793 9193   Fax 020 7793 9193

Contact *Michael Kingsbury*
Administrator *Julia Parr*

Founded 1988. Output primarily new work for an audience aged 20–35. Unsolicited scripts welcome, particularly new work with a keen eye on contemporary issues, though not agitprop. *Absolution* by Robert Sherwood was nominated by the Writers' Guild for 'Best Fringe Play' and *Spin* by the same author was the *Time Out* Critics' Choice in 2000. The theatre received the *Time Out* award for Best Fringe Venue in 2001 and a Peter Brook award for best up-and-coming venue. In 2004 *Round the Horne ... Revisited* transferred to The Venue, Leicester Square.

Windsor Theatre Royal
See **Theatre Royal Windsor**

The Young Vic

Kennington Park, 2nd Floor, Chester House, 1–3 Brixton Road, London SW9 6DE
☎020 7820 3350   Fax 020 7820 3355
✉ info@youngvic.org
www.youngvic.org

Artistic Director *David Lan*
Executive Director *Kevin Fitzmaurice*

Founded 1970. The Young Vic is a theatre for everyone but, above all, for younger artists and audiences. Produces revivals of classics – old and new – as well as new plays and annual events that embrace both young people and adults. From July 2004 the theatre will be closed for two years for rebuilding but will maintain a programme of productions in other venues in the borough (check website for details).

Festivals

Aberdeen Arts Carnival

Aberdeen Arts Centre, 33 King Street,
Aberdeen AB24 5AA
☎01224 635208
www.aberdeenartscentre.org.uk
Venue Manager *Arthur Deans*

Performances – mainly by local amateurs and arts workshops in drama, music, art, dance and creative writing – take place each summer during the school holidays.

The Aldeburgh Literary Weekend

44 High Street, Aldebugh IP15 5AB
☎01728 452389   Fax 01728 452389
www.aldeburghbookshop.co.uk
Festival Organisers *John and Mary James*

Founded 2002. Held on the first weekend in March. The programme includes creative writing workshops, a literary dinner and lunch, and talks. Previous speakers have included Beryl Bainbridge, Alan Bennett, Craig Brown, Richard Dawkins, Lady Antonia Fraser, Anthony Horowitz, P.D. James, Doris Lessing, Christopher Matthew, Harold Pinter, Matt Ridley, Alexander McCall Smith, Libby Purves, Salley Vickers, V.S. Naipaul, A.N. Wilson and David Lodge.

Aldeburgh Poetry Festival

The Cut, 9 New Cut, Halesworth IP19 8BY
☎01986 835940   Fax 01986 835949
✉ info@thepoetrytrust.org
www.thepoetrytrust.org
Director *Naomi Jaffa*

Founded 1989. An annual celebration of international contemporary poetry, held annually on the first weekend in November. Features poetry readings, performances, talks, public masterclass, workshops, discussions, Writer-in-Residence and a children's event. Also includes a reading by the winner of the annual **Jerwood Aldeburgh First Collection Prize** (see entry under *Prizes*).

Annual Writers' Conference, Bookfair & Workshops, Winchester

See entry under *UK Writers' Courses*

Aspects Literature Festival

North Down Borough Council, Town Hall,
The Castle, Bangor BT20 4BT
☎028 9127 8032   Fax 028 9127 1370
✉ gail.prentice@northdown.gov.uk
Festival Coordinator/Arts Officer *Gail Prentice*

Founded 1992. 'Ireland's Premier Literary Festival' is held at the end of September and celebrates the richness and diversity of living Irish writers with occasional special features on past generations. It draws upon all disciplines – fiction (of all types), poetry, theatre, non-fiction, cinema, song-writing, etc. It also includes a day of writing for young readers and sends writers to visit local schools during the festival. Highlights of recent festivals include appearances by Bernard MacLaverty, Marion Keyes, Alice Taylor, Frank Delaney, Seamus Heaney, Brian Keenan and Fergal Keane.

Bath Literature Festival

Administration Office: Bath Festivals Trust,
5 Broad Street, Bath BA1 5LJ
☎01225 462231   Fax 01225 445551
✉ info@bathfestivals.org.uk
www.bathlitfest.org.uk
Box Office: Bath Festivals Box Office,
2 Church Street, Abbey Green, Bath BA1 1NL
☎01225 463362
✉ boxoffice@bathfestivals.org.uk
Artistic Director *Sarah LeFanu*

Founded 1995. This annual festival (4–12 March in 2006) programmes over 100 different literary events from debates and lectures to readers' groups and workshops in venues throughout the city. In addition there are a number of events for children and young people. Previous featured writers include Tony Benn, Kazuo Ishiguro, Andrea Levy, Peter Porter, Oliver Sacks and Sue Townsend.

Bay Lit

Academi, Mount Stuart House, Mount Stuart Square, Cardiff CF10 5FQ
☎029 2047 2266   Fax 029 2049 2930
✉ post@academi.org
www.academi.org
Chief Executive *Peter Finch*

Annual literature festival held in Cardiff Bay, featuring writers from Wales and beyond. Lectures, readings, performances, workshops and book launches in English and Welsh. Dates and further details available on the Academi website. Writers who appeared at the 2005 Festival included: Ian McMillan, Fay Weldon, Simon Singh, Helen Oyeyemi and Will Self.

Belfast Festival at Queen's
8 Fitzwilliam Street, Belfast BT9 6AW
☎028 9097 2600   Fax 028 9097 2630
✉ festival@qub.ac.uk
www.belfastfestival.com
Director *Stella Hall*

Founded 1964. Annual three-week festival held in October/November. Organised by Queen's University in association with the **Arts Council of Northern Ireland**, the festival covers a wide variety of events, including literature. Programme available in September.

Between the Lines – Belfast Literary Festival
Crescent Arts Centre, 2–4 University Road, Belfast BT7 1NH
☎028 9024 2338   Fax 028 9024 6748
✉ btl.cac@btconnect.com
www.crescentarts.org
Artistic Director *John Brown*

Founded 1998. Annual 7–10-day international event held in March/April. Features readings, workshops, open platforms, quizzes and performance. All genres covered: playwriting, prose, poetry, screenwriting, etc. and special events for children. Previous guests include David Lodge, Lemn Sissay, Sheila O'Flanagan, Matthew Sweeney, Medbh McGuckian, Conor O'Callaghan, Merlin Holland, Ciaran Carson. Telephone to join free mailing list.

Birmingham Book Festival
c/o Book Communications, Unit 116, The Custard Factory, Gibb Street, Birmingham B9 4AA
☎0121 246 2777/2770   Fax 0121 246 2771
✉ jonathan@bookcommunications.co.uk
Contacts *Helen Thomas, Jonathan Davidson*

Founded 1999. Annual nine-day festival held during October at venues around Birmingham. Also promotes events throughout the year. Includes performances, lectures, discussion events and workshops.

Book Now!
The Arts Team, Orleans House Gallery, Riverside, Twickenham TW1 3DJ
✉ artsinfo@richmond.gov.uk

www.richmond.gov.uk/arts

Founded 1992. Annual festival which runs throughout the month of November, administered by the Arts Section of Richmond Council. Events cover serious fiction, poetry, biography, writing for theatre, children's writing. Programme includes readings, discussions, workshops, debates, exhibitions, schools events. Writers who appeared at past festivals include Kate Adie, Sir Roy Strong, Humphrey Carpenter, David Starkey, Salley Vickers, Virginia Ironside, Tobias Hill, Redmond O'Hanlon, Sheila Hancock, Simon Hoggart, Christian Wolmar, Mavis Cheek and John Humphrys.

Bradford Book Festival
Central Library, Princes Way, Bradford BD1 1NN
☎01274 433915
✉ paula.truman@bradford.gov.uk
Contact *Paula Truman*

Founded 1999. Month-long festival organised by Bradford Libraries, held during May/June.

Brighton Festival
Festival Office, 12a Pavilion Buildings, Castle Square, Brighton BN1 1EE
☎01273 700747   Fax 01273 707505
✉ info@brighton-festival.org.uk
www.brighton-festival.org.uk
Contact *General Manager*

Founded 1966. For 24 days every May, Brighton hosts England's largest mixed arts festival. Music, dance, theatre, film, opera, literature, comedy and exhibitions. Literary enquiries will be passed to the literature officer. Deadline October for following May.

Bristol Poetry Festival
The Poetry Can, Unit 11, 20–23 Hepburn Road, Bristol BS2 8UD
☎0117 942 6976   Fax 0117 944 1478
✉ festival@poetrycan.demon.co.uk
www.poetrycan.co.uk
Festival Director *Colin Brown*

Founded 1995. Annual festival taking place across the city every September (8–18th in 2005). A celebration of the best in local, national and international contemporary poetry, from readings and performances to cabaret and slam and open mic. 'Where words mean more than a spin in th dark.'

Broadstairs Dickens Festival
10 Lanthorne Road, Broadstairs CT10 3NH
☎01843 861827   Fax 01843 861827

www.broadstairs.gov.uk/DickensFestival.html

Organiser *Sylvia Hawkes*

Founded 1937 to commemorate the 100th anniversary of Charles Dickens' first visit to Broadstairs in 1837, which he continued to visit until 1859. The Festival lasts for nine days in June and events include an opening gala concert, a parade, a performance of a Dickens play (*Great Expectations* in 2005), duels, melodramas, Dickens readings, a Victorian cricket match, Victorian bathing parties, talks, music hall, three-day Victorian country fair. Costumed Dickensian ladies in crinolines with top-hatted escorts promenade during the week.

Cambridge History Festival

Indicombe, West Buckland, Barnstaple EX32 0SE

☎01598 760367

✉ wh@histfest.com

www.histfest.com

Contacts *Derek Wilson, Ruth Wilson*

Annual three-day festival held in September in the heart of the university (not held in 2005). The major networking event for all popular history enthusiasts – academics, historical novelists, popular historians, TV producers and presenters, museum and gallery staff. Varied programme includes talks, presentations, displays, discussions, concerts of period music, publishers' receptions, etc. Programmes available from April. Among the speakers who have appeared are David Starkey, Beryl Bainbridge, Louis de Bernières, Timothy West, Tracy Chevalier, Diarmaid MacCulloch, John Guy, Richard Holmes, Felipe Fernández-Armesto, Conn Iggulden, Lisa Jardine, Prunella Scales and Terry Jones.

Cambridge Wordfest

☎01954 212255

✉ cam.wordfest@btinternet.com

www.cambridgewordfest.co.uk

Festival Director *Cathy Moore*

An annual spring festival for writers as well as readers which takes place at various venues across Cambridge and the surrounding area. A weekend event packed with the best of contemporary writing, political debate, events for children and writing workshops.

Camelford Poetry Festival

The Indian King, Garmoe Cottage, Trefrew Road, Camelford PL32 9TP

☎01840 212161

✉ indianking@btconnect.com

Director *Helen Wood*

Founded 1997 as the Jon Silkin Memorial Poetry Festival. Jon Silkin taught annual poetry workshops and readings to raise funds for the Centre, and the festival was held to honour his life and work. Held annually close to Easter in Camelford, the central town in North Cornwall, the festival includes workshops, poetry readings and performances, writing and literary walks, and a dinner in memory of Jon Silkin on the Friday evening. Previous guests have included Fred d'Aguilar, Sara Jane Arbury, John Branfield, Ann Gray, John Greening, Philip Gross, Derrek Hines, Christopher Logue, William Oxley, Ian Parks, Fiona Sampson, Myra Schneider and Dilys Wood. Book for individual events or buy a weekend ticket.

Canterbury Festival

Christ Church Gate, The Precincts, Canterbury CT1 2EE

☎01227 452853 Fax 01227 781830

✉ info@canterburyfestival.co.uk

Festival Director *Rosie Turner*

Founded 1984. Annual two-week festival held in October (8–22 Oct. 2005). A mixed programme of events including concerts in the cathedral by international artistes, opera, dance, drama, jazz and folk, visual arts open-house trail, community events and street theatre, talks and walks.

Centre for Creative & Performing Arts Spring Literary Festival at UEA

University of East Anglia, School of Literature and Creative Writing, Norwich NR4 8TJ

☎01603 592810

✉ v.striker@uea.ac.uk

www.uea.ac.uk/eas/events/intro.shtml

Contact *Val Striker*

Founded 1993. Annual event held in the spring.

Charleston Festival

The Charleston Trust, Charleston, Nr Firle, Lewes BN8 6LL

☎01323 811626

✉ info@charleston.org.uk

www.charleston.org.uk

Festival Programmer *Diana Reich*

Annual literary festival held in May over nine days. Novelists, biographers, travel writers, broadcasters, poets, food writers, actors and artists gather at Charleston, the country home of the Bloomsbury Group. Past speakers: Margaret Atwood, Alan Bennett, Jeanette Winterson, Patti

Smith, Paula Rego, Clive James, Roger McGough, Germaine Greer, Harold Pinter.

The Cheltenham Festival of Literature

Town Hall, Imperial Square, Cheltenham GL50 1QA
☎01242 263494   Fax 01242 256457
✉ adam.pushkin@cheltenham.gov.uk
www.cheltenhamfestivals.co.uk

Festival Organiser *Adam Pushkin*

Founded 1949. Annual festival held in October. The first purely literary festival of its kind, this festival has over the past decade developed from an essentially local event into the largest and most popular in Europe. A wide range of events including talks and lectures, poetry readings, novelists in conversation, exhibitions, discussions and a large bookshop.

Chester Literature Festival

8 Abbey Square, Chester CH1 2HU
☎01244 319985   Fax 01244 341200
✉ freda@chesterfestivals.co.uk

Chairman *John Scrivener*

Founded 1989. Annual festival commencing the first weekend in October (1st–29th in 2005). Events include international and nationally known writers, as well as events by local literary groups. There is a Literary Lunch and a Festival Dinner, events for children, workshops and competitions. Free mailing list.

Children's Books Ireland – Annual Festival

See **Children's Books Ireland** under *Professional Associations*

Dartington Literary Festival

See **Ways With Words**

Derbyshire Literature Festival

c/o Arts Office, Derbyshire County Council, Cultural & Community Services Department, Alfreton Library, Severn Square, Alfreton DE55 7BQ
☎01773 832497   Fax 01773 831359
✉ ann.wright@derbyshire.gov.uk
www.derbyshire.gov.uk

Festival Organiser *Ann Wright*

Founded 2000. The festival takes place in June every two years and covers the whole county. The festival programming includes all types of live literature events; performance poetry, theatre, talks, readers' groups, workshops, dramatised readings,

signings, song, readings, storytelling and literary trails, as well as a number of cross-art form events. The festival takes place in libraries and many other community venues including heritage centres, industrial buildings, stately homes, parks and moors, churches and schools and is specifically designed to reach as many different communities and geographical areas in the county as possible.

Dorchester Festival

Dorchester Arts Centre, School Lane, The Grove, Dorchester DT1 1XR
☎01305 266926   Fax 01305 266143
www.dorchesterarts.org.uk

Artistic Director *Sharon Hayden*

Founded 1996. A biennial five-day international festival over early May Bank Holiday (next to be held in 2006) which includes performance, live music and visual arts with associated educational and community projects. Also three days of free events in the Borough Gardens with a wide range of activities, and events at over 40 venues around the town, including literature and poetry.

The Daphne du Maurier Festival of Arts & Literature

Restormel Borough Council, Penwinnick Road, St Austell PL25 5DR
☎01726 223535
www.dumaurier.org/festival.html

Founded 1997. Annual festival, held in Fowey over ten days in May. Guests at the 2005 Festival included Bryan Appleyard, Joan Bakewell, Ray Galton and Alan Simpson, Anthony Holden, D.M. Thomas, Jacqueline Tong.

Dumfries and Galloway Arts Festival

Gracefield Arts Centre, 28 Edinburgh Road, Dumfries DG1 1JQ
☎01387 260447   Fax 01387 260447
✉ info@dgartsfestival.org.uk
www.dgartsfestival.org.uk

Festival Organiser *Mrs Barbara Kelly*

Founded 1980. Annual week-long festival held at the end of May with a variety of events including classical and folk music, theatre, dance, literary events, exhibitions and children's events.

Durham Literature Festival

Durham City Arts, Byland Lodge, Hawthorn Terrace, Durham City DH1 4TD
☎0191 301 8245   Fax 0191 301 8821
✉ info@durhamcityarts.org

Festival Coordinator *Alison Lister*
Founded 1989. Annual 2–3-week festival now held in September/October at various locations in the city. Performances and readings plus workshops, cabaret, exhibitions and other events.

Edinburgh International Book Festival
Scottish Book Centre, 137 Dundee Street, Edinburgh EH11 1BG
☎0131 228 5444   Fax 0131 228 4333
✉ admin@edbookfest.co.uk
www.edbookfest.co.uk
Director *Catherine Lockerbie*
Founded 1983. The world's largest and most dynamic annual book event takes place over 17 days in Edinburgh each August. An extensive programme showcases the work of the world's top authors and thinkers to an audience of over 200,000 adults and children. Featuring workshops, readings, lectures and a high profile debate and discussion series.

Everybody's Reading
Leicester City Council, Libraries, A12 New Walk Centre, Leicester LE1 6ZG
☎0116 252 7347
✉ waltd001@leicester.gov.uk
Literature Development Officer *Damien Walter*
Annual celebration of words and reading held in October. Aims to engage the city's diverse communities with reading.

Fife Festival of Authors
Fife Council Libraries – Central Area, Libraries HQ, East Fergus Place, Kirkcaldy KY1 1XT
☎01592 412930
✉ david.spalding@fife.gov.uk
Contact *David Spalding*
Founded 1996. Annual festival running in March/April for adults and children (not held in 2005). Aims to bring the best of modern writing to the public as well as stimulate and foster creative writing within the local communities. Author readings, poetry events, writing workshops, literary competitions and dramatic presentations feature in the programme.

Folkestone Literary Festival
Church Street Studios, 11 Church Street, Folkestone CT20 1SE
☎01303 211300
✉ info@folkestonelitfest.com

www.folkestonelitfest.com
Festival Director *Camilla Swift*
The Folkestone Literary Festival brings outstanding writers to this beautiful seaside town for a week packed with tours, discussions, talks and readings. Annual festival held in the last full week of September.

Frome Festival
25 Market Place, Frome BA11 1AH
☎01373 453889   Fax 01373 471574
✉ fromefestival@ukonline.co.uk
www.fromefestival.co.uk
Festival Director *Martin Bax*
An annual festival held from the first Friday in July for ten days celebrating all aspects of visual and performing arts and entertainment and with a strong literary element. Features music, film, dance, drama and visual arts plus readings, talks and workshops. Previous literary guests have included nationally renowned writers as well as local authors.

Graham Greene Festival
See **Graham Greene Birthplace Trust** under *Literary Societies*

Greenwich + Docklands Festivals
6 College Approach, London SE10 9HY
☎020 8305 1818   Fax 020 8305 1188
✉ info@festival.org
www.festival.org
Executive Director *Mathew Russell*
Artistic Director *Bradley Hemmings*
Greenwich + Docklands Festivals (GDF) is a festival and event-producing organisation working across east London in the boroughs of Greenwich, Tower Hamlets, Newham and more recently further afield. GDF's portfolio includes the International Festival, London's largest multi-artform festival and First Night, a celebration of the new year through the arts.

The Guardian Hay Festival
25 Lion Street, Hay-on-Wye HR3 5AD
☎0870 787 2848   Fax 01497 821066
www.hayfestival.com
Festival Director *Peter Florence*
Founded 1988. Annual May festival sponsored by *The Guardian*. Also has a children's programme which began in 2003. The event coincides with half term and caters for young children through to teenage. Guests have included Paul McCartney, Bill Clinton, Salman Rushdie, Toni

Morrison, Stephen Fry, Joseph Heller, Carlos Fuentes, Maya Angelou, Amos Oz, Arthur Miller.

Guildford Book Festival

c/o Tourist Information Centre, 15 Tunsgate, Guildford GU1 3QT
☎01483 444334
✉ director@guildfordbookfestival.co.uk
www.guildfordbookfestival.co.uk
Book Festival Director *Glenis Pycraft*
Founded 1990. Patrons: Elizabeth Buchan, Michael Buerk, Sandi Toksvig, Fay Weldon, Timothy West and Jacqueline Wilson. Held annually, during October in venues throughout the ancient town of Guildford. The festival includes events with established and new writers, workshops, poetry performances, children's events, adult short story competition and the **Pendleton May First Novel Award** (see entry under *Prizes*). This diverse festival aims to involve, instruct and entertain all who care about literature. Guest authors in 2004 included Rory Bremner, Margaret Drabble, Robert Goddard, Sally Vickers, Barbara Trapido, Julian Fellowes, Ken Follett, Max Hastings, Terry Jones, Tom Conti and Joan Collins.

Haringey Literature Festival

Collage Arts, The Chocolate Factory, Clarendon Road, London N22 6XJ
☎020 8829 1317   Fax 020 8365 8686
✉ dana@collage-arts.org
www.collage-arts.org
Festival Organiser *Dana Captainino*
Founded 1995. Annual literature programme is a mixture of poetry and literature in the form of readings, discussions, workshops and residencies. A regular feature is *Poetry and Poppadums* featuring top and up-and-coming poets in the setting of La Kera, an Indian restaurant in the Chocolate Factory. Writers who have appeared at past festivals include Patience Agbabi, John Hegley, Matthew Sweeney, Fay Weldon.

Harrogate Crime Writing Festival

See **Theakston's Old Peculier Harrogate Crime Writing Festival**

Harrogate International Festival

1 Victoria Avenue, Harrogate HG1 1EQ
☎01423 562303   Fax 01423 521264
✉ info@harrogate-festival.org.uk
www.harrogate-festival.org.uk
Festival Director *William Culver-Dodds*
Festival Manager *Sharon Canavar*

Founded 1966. Annual two-week festival at the end of July and beginning of August. Events include international symphony orchestras, chamber concerts, ballet, celebrity recitals, contemporary dance, opera, drama, jazz and comedy.

Harwich Festival of the Arts

2A Kings Head Street, Harwich CO12 3EG
☎01255 503571
✉ anna@rendell-knights.freeserve.co.uk
Contact *Anna Rendell-Knights*
Founded 1980. Annual ten-day summer festival held in June/July. Events include concerts, drama, film, dance, art, exhibitions, historic town walks and children's competitions. The 2005 Festival celebrated the 200th anniversary of the Battle of Trafalgar.

Hastings International Poetry First of All

'The Snoring Cat', 16 Marianne Park, Dudley Road, Hastings TN35 5PU
Contact *Josephine Austin*
Founded 1968. Annual weekend poetry festival held in November in the White Rock Hotel (formerly the Yelton Hotel), White Rock, Hastings. Runs the Hastings National Poetry Competition; entry forms available from the address above. Issues *First Time*, a biannual poetry magazine for first-time poets and others.

The Hay Festival

See **The Guardian Hay Festival**

Hebden Bridge Arts Festival

New Oxford House, Albert Street, Hebden Bridge HX7 4AH
☎01422 842684
✉ hbartsfestival@hotmail.com *or* enid.stephenson@3-c.coop
www.hebdenbridge.co.uk/festival
Contact *Enid Stephenson*
Founded 1994. Annual arts festival with increasingly strong adult and children's literature events. Previous guest writers include Roger McGough, Benjamin Zephaniah, Anne Fine, Juliet Barker, Jacqueline Wilson, Pete McCarthy, Ian McMillan, Adele Geras.

Humber Mouth – Hull Literature Festival

City Arts Unit, Central Library, Albion Street, Kingston upon Hull HU1 3TF
☎01482 616961   Fax 01482 616961
✉ humber.mouth@hullcc.gov.uk

www.humbermouth.org.uk

Contact *Maggie Hannan*, City Arts Unit

Founded 1992. Hull's largest festival, held in the summer, and one of the region's liveliest events. Features readings, talks, performances and workshops by writers and artists from around the world and from the city.

Ilkley Literature Festival

The Manor House, 2 Castle Hill, Ilkley LS29 9DT

☎01943 601210   Fax 01943 817079

✉ admin@ilkelyliteraturefestival.org.uk

www.ilkleyliteraturefestival.orguk

Director *Rachel Feldberg*

Founded 1973. Major literature festival in the north held over 17 days every October. Includes children's literature weekend and Festival fringe. Recent guests include Alan Bennett, Benjamin Zephaniah, Liz Lochhead, Donna Tartt, Kate Adie, Ian Rankin. Telephone or e-mail to join free mailing list.

Imagine: Writers and Writing for Children

See **Royal Festival Hall Literature & Talks**

The International Festival of Mountaineering Literature

56 Conduit Road, Sheffield S10 1EW

☎0114 266 8813 (Festival venue)

Fax 0133 343 9148

✉ terry@gifford9.wanadoo.co.uk

www.festivalofmountaineeringliterature.couk

Director *Terry Gifford*

Founded 1987. Annual one-day festival held at the University of Leeds, Bretton Hall Campus in Wakefield. Taking place in March, the Festival celebrates recent books, commissions new writing, gives overviews of national literatures, holds debates of issues, book signings and discussion with the Chair of Judges of the adjudication of the annual **Boardman Tasker Award** for the best mountaineering book of the year. Announces the winner of the festival writing competition run in conjunction with *Climb* magazine. Write to join free mailing list.

International Playwriting Festival

Warehouse Theatre, Dingwall Road, Croydon CR0 2NF

☎020 8681 1257   Fax 020 8688 6699

✉ info@warehousetheatre.co.uk

www.warehousetheatre.co.uk

Festival Administrator *Rose Marie Vernon*

Founded 1985. Annual competition for full-length unperformed plays, judged by a panel of theatre professionals. Finalists given rehearsed readings during the festival week in November. Entries welcome from all parts of the world. Scripts plus two s.a.e.s (one script-sized) should reach the theatre by the end of June, accompanied by an entry form (available online or from the theatre). Previous winners produced at the theatre include: Kevin Hood *Beached*; Ellen Fox *Conversations with George Sandburgh After a Solo Flight Across the Atlantic*; Guy Jenkin *Fighting for the Dunghill*; James Martin Charlton *Fat Souls*; Peter Moffat *Iona Rain*; Dino Mahoney *YoYo*; Simon Smith *Fat Janet is Dead*; Dominic McHale *The Resurrectionists*; Philip Edwards *51 Peg*; Roumen Shomov *The Dove*; Maggie Nevill *The Shagaround*; Andrew Shakeshaft *Just Sitting*. Shares plays with its partner festival in Italy, the Premio Candoni Arta Terme.

Isle of Man Literature Festival

Isle of Man Arts Council, 10 Villa Marina Arcade, Douglas IM1 2HN

☎01624 611316   Fax 01624 615423

✉ dawn.maddrell@iomartscouncil.dtl.gov.im

Contact *Arts Development Manager*

Founded 1997. Regular programme of literature events throughout the year.

King's Lynn, The Fiction Festival

19 Tuesday Market Place, King's Lynn PE30 1JW

☎01553 691661 (office hours) or 761919

Fax 01553 691779

Contact *Anthony Ellis*

Founded 1989. Annual weekend festival held in March. Over the weekend there are readings and discussions, attended by guest writers of which there are usually eight. Guests in 2005 included Beryl Bainbridge, Louis de Bernière, John Buchan, Jane Gardam, Maggie Gee, Adele Geras, Julian Rathbone, William Riviere, Toby Litt and David Mitchell.

King's Lynn, The Poetry Festival

19 Tuesday Market Place, King's Lynn PE30 1JW

☎01553 691661 (office hours) or 761919

Fax 01553 691779

Contact *Anthony Ellis*

Founded 1985. Annual weekend festival held at the end of September, with guest poets (usually eight). Guests in 2004 included U.A. Fanthorpe,

Jo Shapcott, Matthew Sweeney, Julia Copus, Anthony Thwaite, John Whitworth, John Hartley Williams. Helen Ivory, Michael Laskey, Pascale Petit, Bejan Matur and John Welch.

Knutsford Literature Festival

☎01565 652445

✉ sarah@ganc.u-net.com

www.knutsfordlitfest.co.uk

Contact *Sarah Leigh*

An annual two-week festival, held at the beginning of October to celebrate writing and performance by distinguished national, international and local authors. Events include readings and discussions, a literary lunch and theatrical performances.

Lancaster LitFest

26 Castle Park, Lancaster LA1 1YQ

☎01524 62166

✉ andy.darby@litfest.org

www.litfest.org

Founded 1978. Regional Literature Development Agency, organising workshops, readings, residencies, publications. Year-round programme of literature-based events and annual festival in November featuring a wide range of writers from the UK and overseas.

Leamington Festival

Warwick Arts Society, Pageant House, 2 Jury Street, Warwick CV34 4EW

☎01926 410747   Fax 01926 409050

✉ admin@warwickarts.org.uk

www.warwickarts.org.uk

Festival Director *Richard Phillips*

Launched 2003, the Festival has grown from an annual themed chamber music weekend to include jazz and world music events. Held in early May, it features literary events, many of which reflect the theme of the overall Festival. Extensive educational programme including workshops.

Ledbury Poetry Festival

Town Council Offices, Church Lane, Ledbury HR8 1DH

☎0845 458 1743

✉ info@poetry-festival.com

www.poetry-festival.com

Contact *Charles Bennett*

Founded 1997. Annual ten-day festival held in July. Includes readings, discussions, workshops, exhibitions, music and walks. There is also an extensive year-round community programme

and a national poetry competition. Past guests have included Andrew Motion, Benjamin Zephaniah, Simon Armitage, Roger McGough, John Hegley and Germaine Greer. Full programme available in May.

Lewes Live Literature Festival

PO Box 2766, Lewes BN7 2WF

☎01273 401100   Fax 01273 401100

✉ info@leweslivelit.co.uk

www.leweslivelit.co.uk

Artistic Director *Mark Hewitt*

Founded 1995. Lewes Live Literature Festival is a three-day intensive event, held in late October/early November. Areas of programming include poetry, fiction, non-fiction, art, art history, music, theatre, film, TV. Events include readings, performances, lectures, workshops, screenings of film and video, exhibitions. LLL also runs year-round creative writing workshops and courses led by established professionals.

Lichfield Festival

7 The Close, Lichfield WS13 7LD

☎01543 306270   Fax 01543 306274

✉ lichfield.fest@lichfield-arts.org.uk

www.lichfieldfestival.org

Festival Director *Richard Hawley*

Founded 1982. Annual July festival with events taking place in the 13th century Cathedral, the new Lichfield Garrick Theatre, and various country churches and outdoor venues. Mainly music but a growing programme of literary events such as poetry, plays and talks.

City of London Festival

230 Bishopsgate, London EC2M 4HW

☎020 7377 0540   Fax 020 7377 1972

✉ admin@colf.org

www.colf.org

Director *Ian Ritchie*

Founded 1962. Annual three-week festival held in June and July. Features over fifty classical and popular music events alongside poetry and prose readings, street theatre and open-air extravaganzas, in some of the most outstanding performance spaces in the world.

Lowdham Book Festival

4th Floor Arts, County Hall, West Bridgford NG2 7QP

☎0115 977 4435

✉ ross.bradshaw@nottsscc.gov.uk

www.lowdhambookfestival.co.uk

Contact *Ross Bradshaw*

Founded 1999. Annual week-long festival combining a village fête atmosphere with that of a major literature festival. Guests have included Carol Ann Duffy, Pete McCarthy, Ian McMillan, Alan Sillitoe, Jackie Kay, Sarah Harrison and Carole Blake. Talks on everything from St Kilda to the Jewish roots of rock 'n' roll. Free mailing list includes *County Lit* magazine.

Ludlow Festival
Castle Square, Ludlow SY8 1AY
☎01584 875070 (Admin)/872150 (Box Office)
Fax 01584 877673
✉ admin@ludlowfestival.co.uk
www.ludlowfestival.co.uk
Contact *Festival Manager*

Now in its 46th year, the 2005 Festival ran for two weeks with two open-air Shakespeare productions held at Ludlow Castle, street events and a varied programme including recitals, opera, dance, popular and classical concerts, literary and historical lectures.

Manchester Poetry Festival
3rd Floor, 24 Lever Street, Stevenson Square, Manchester M1 1D2
☎0161 236 5725   Fax 0161 236 5719
✉ info@manchesterpoetryfestival.co.uk
www.manchesterpoetryfestival.co.uk
Contact *The Coordinator*

Held in the autumn, Manchester Poetry Festival is the largest urban poetry festival outside of London with nationally recognised poets and local poets and groups.

Mere Literary Festival
Lawrence's, Old Hollow, Mere BA12 6EG
☎01747 860475/861211 (Tourist Information)
www.merewilts.org.uk
Contact *Adrienne Howell*

Founded 1997. Annual festival held in the second week of October in aid of registered charity, The Mere & District Linkscheme. Events include readings, quiz, workshop, writer's lunch and talks. Finale is adjudication of the festival's writing competition (see entry under *Prizes*) and presentation of awards.

Arthur Miller Centre Literary Festival at UEA
University of East Anglia, School of American Studies, Norwich NR4 8TJ
☎01603 592810
✉ v.striker@uea.ac.uk

www.uea.ac.uk/eas/events/intro.shtml
Contact *Val Striker*
Founded 1991. Annual festival, held in the autumn

National Association of Writers' Groups (NAWG) Open Festival of Writing
The Arts Centre, Washington NE38 2AB
☎01262 609228
✉ nawg@tesco.net
www.nawg.co.uk
Festival Administrator *Mike Wilson*

Founded 1995. Annual festival held at St Aidan's College, University of Durham in September or October. Three days of creative writing tuition covering poetry, short and long fiction, playwriting, journalism, TV sitcom and many other subjects all led by professional writer-tutors. 36 workshops, 32 one-to-one tutorials and fringe events. Saturday gala dinner and awards ceremony. Full or part-residential weekend, or single workshops only. Open to all, no qualifications or NAWG membership required.

National Eisteddfod of Wales
40 Parc Ty Glas, Llanishen, Cardiff CF14 5WU
☎029 2076 3777   Fax 029 2076 3737
www.eisteddfod.org.uk

The National Eisteddfod, held in August, is the largest arts festival in Wales, attracting over 170,000 visitors during the week-long celebration of more than 800 years of tradition. Competitions, bardic ceremonies and concerts.

National Student Drama Festival
See **University of Hull** under *UK Writers' Courses*

New Hall School Festival of Literature
New Hall School, Chelmsford CM3 3HS
✉ library@newhallschool.co.uk
www.newhallschool.co.uk
Contact *Jenny Bignold*

Founded 1992, the festival is open to parents, staff and friends. The aim is to widen students' horizons and students from other schools in the town are invited to join in an array of events.

Northern Children's Book Festival
Schools Library Service, Sandhill Centre, Grindon Lane, Sunderland SR3 4EN
☎0191553 8866/7/8   Fax 0191 553 8869

schools.library@sunderland.gov.uk
www.ncbf.org.uk

Secretary *Eleanor Dowley*

Founded 1984. Annual two-week festival during November. Events in schools and libraries for children in the North East region. One Saturday during the festival sees the staging of a large book event hosted by one of the local authorities involved.

Off the Page Literature Festival

County Library Support Services, Glaisdale Parkway, Nottingham NG8 4GP
☎0115 928 6029   Fax 0115 928 6400
✉ alison.hirst@nottscc.gov.uk

Contact *Alison Hirst*

Author visits aimed at making authors accessible to readers. Programme is available from late summer/early autumn.

Off the Shelf Literature Festival

Central Library, Surrey Street, Sheffield
S1 1XZ
☎0114 273 4716/4400   Fax 0114 273 5009
✉ offtheshelf@sheffield.gov.uk
www.offtheshelf.org.uk

Festival Organisers *Maria de Souza, Susan Walker, Lesley Webster*

Founded 1992. Annual two-week festival held during the last fortnight in October. Lively and diverse mix of readings, workshops, children's events, storytelling and competitions. Previous guests have included Nick Hornby, Doris Lessing, Benjamin Zephaniah, Terry Pratchett, Michael Palin, Carol Ann Duffy and Louis de Bernières.

Oundle Festival of Literature

34 South Road, Oundle PE8 4BU
☎01832 275146
✉ enquiries@oundlelitfest.org.uk
www.oundlelitfest.org.uk

Festival Chairman *Nick Turnbull*

Founded 2002. Annual festival running in the second week of March for adults and children. Features talks by high profile authors, writing workshops, poetry and prose showcases for local writers, children's writing competitions, school events, drama productions and community readings for young and old.

Oxford Literary Festival

See *The Sunday Times* **Oxford Literary Festival**

Poetry Otherwise

Emerson College, Forest Row RH18 5JX
☎01342 822238   Fax 01342 826055
✉ mail@emerson.org.uk
www.emerson.org.uk
www.poetryotherwise.org

Director *Paul Matthews*

Held in August. A summer gathering of poets, writers and all lovers of language. Workshops, readings, talks, conversation, practice in the art of speaking poetry. Contributors have included Andrea Hollander Budy, John Freeman, Ashley Ramsden, Andie Lewenstein, Paul Matthews, Peter Abbs, Katherine Pierpoint, Fiona Owen, Lee Harwood, Jay Ramsay, Mimi Khalvati and Roselle Angwin. 'Wholesome food, wonderful Sussex countryside.'

ProudWords Writing Festival

PO Box 181, Newcastle upon Tyne NE6 5XG
☎07973 8949 12
✉ pwcwf@hotmail.com
www.proudwords.org.uk

Contact *Mary Lowe*

Founded 1998. The only writing festival in the UK to celebrate the diversity of literary talent that exists within the gay community. Held annually, the festival includes workshops, bus trips, walking tours, readings, discussions and performances of both writing and music. ProudWords encourages participation, lively debate, an interest in literature-related activity and offers opportunities for gay people to express themselves in writing in a supportive, friendly atmosphere. Writers at past festivals include Jackie Kay, Julia Darling, Sarah Waters, Jake Arnott, P-P Hartness, Emma Donaghue, Paul Magrs, Stella Duffy, Julia Bell, Val McDermid, Chrissie Glazebrook and Cathal O Searcaigh. 'Lesbians, gay men and bisexuals are invited to Newcastle to discover for themselves the thriving writing culture that exists here.'

Purple Patch Poetry Convention

25 Griffiths Road, West Bromwich B71 2EH
✉ ppatch66@hotmail.com
www.poetrywednesbury.co.uk

Contact *Geoff Stevens*

Held at the Barlow Theatre near Birmingham this event celebrates the strength of small press poets. The next Purple Patch Poetry Convention, due to take place in 2006, is a three-day event of poetry readings, talks, workshops and discussions and admission charges are kept very low, payments to participants being low to non-existent. The Convention's aims are quality and an opportunity to participate. Poets at past festivals have included Ray Avery, R.G. Bishop, Tilla Brading, Gerald England, J.F Haines, Brendan Hawthorne, Martin Holroyd, Mike Hoy, Eamer O'Keeffe, Carolyn King, Paul McDonald, Bob Mee, Les Merton, Michael Newman, Simon Pitt, Andy Robson, Sam Smith and Steve Sneyd. Monthly poetry readings are held at the Barlow Theatre with open mic, guest poet, music and residents Unleaded Petrels.

Redbridge Literature Festival

Arts & Events, Leisure Services, 8th Floor, Lynton House, 255–259 High Road, Ilford IG1 1NY
☎020 8708 3041   Fax 020 8708 3178
www.redbridge.gov.uk

Founded in 2003, the festival celebrates literature in all its forms, and takes place annually over two weeks in March/April. Features a programme of author readings, book signings, creative writing classes, school-based workshops, community events, performance poetry evenings, competitions, exhibitions and a 'Children's Day'.

Royal Court Young Writers Programme

The Site, Royal Court Theatre, Sloane Square, London SW1W 8AS
☎020 7565 5050   Fax 020 7565 5001
✉ ywp@royalcourttheatre.com
www.royalcourttheatre.com

Associate Director *Ola Animashawun*

Open to young people up to the age of 25. The YWP focuses on the process of playwriting by running a series of writers' groups throughout the year at its base in Sloane Square. Additionally the YWP welcomes unsolicited scripts from all young writers from across the country. 'We are always looking for scripts for development and possible production (not film scripts).'

Royal Festival Hall Literature & Talks

Performing Arts Department, Royal Festival Hall, London SE1 8XX
☎020 7921 0906   Fax 020 7928 2049
✉ awhitehead@rfh.org.uk
www.sbc.org.uk

Head of Literature & Talks *Ruth Borthwick*

The Royal Festival Hall presents a year-round literature programme covering all aspects of writing. Regular series range from A Life Indeed! to Fiction International and there are two biennial festivals: Poetry International and

Imagine: Writers and Writing for Children. Literature events are now programmed in the Voice Box, Purcell Room and Queen Elizabeth Hall. To join the free mailing list, call 020 7921 0971 or ✉ Literature&Talks@rfh.org.uk

Rye Festival

PO Box 33, Rye TN31 7YB
☎01797 224442
✉ info@ryefestival.co.uk
www.ryefestival.co.uk

Director *Tony Clamp*

Founded 1972. Annual two-week September arts event, plus short winter series. Covers music, visual arts, theatre and literature. Write or phone for more information.

Salisbury International Arts Festival

Festival Office, 87 Crane Street, Salisbury SP1 2PU
☎01722 332241   Fax 01722 410552
✉ info@salisburyfestival.co.uk
www.salisburyfestival.co.uk

Director *Jo Metcalf-Shore*

Founded 1972. Annual festival held at the end of May/beginning of June, including classical music, theatre, jazz and exhibitions.

The Scottish Book Town Festival

Wigtown Book Town Company, County Buildings, Wigtown DG8 9JH
☎01988 402036   Fax 01988 402506
✉ info@wigtown-booktown.co.uk
www.wigtown-booktown.co.uk

Contact *Jennifer Bradley*

Founded 1999. A rural literary festival which takes place annually at the end of September in Wigtown town centre, many of the town's bookshops and the nearby Bladnoch Distillery. Authors' readings, including children's authors, debates, poetry, music and film.

Southwell Poetry Festival

4th Floor Arts, County Hall, West Bridgford NG2 7QP
☎0115 977 4435
✉ ross.bradshaw@nottscc.gov.uk
www.southwellpoetryfestival.co.uk

Contact *Ross Bradshaw*

This festival returned in 2003 after a trial run in 2000 and is now established as an annual event.

Southwold Festival

See **Ways with Words**

StAnza: Scotland's Poetry Festival

Registered Office: 57 Lade Braes, St Andrews
KY16 9DA
☎01333 360491
✉ info@stanzapoetry.org
www.stanzapoetry.org

Festival Director *Brian Johnstone*

The only regular festival dedicated to poetry in Scotland, StAnza is international in outlook. Held annually in the ancient university town of St Andrews, the festival is an opportunity to hear world class poets reading in exciting and atmospheric venues. The 2006 festival themes are 'Poetry & the Land' and 'Celtic Voices'. The festival, to be held 16th–19th March, features, readings, discussions, conversations, performance poetry, poetry in exhibition, workshops and children's poetry. It will feature a strong showing of Irish and Welsh poets and leading Scottish poets as well as the festival's signature foreign language readings. Tickets can be purchased from the Byre Theatre box office on 01334 475000 early in 2006. Free programmes can be ordered from Fife Council Arts on 01592 414714 or by ✉ to arts.development@fife.gov.uk

Stratford-upon-Avon Poetry Festival

The Shakespeare Centre, Henley Street, Stratford-upon-Avon CV37 6QW
☎01789 204016/292176 (box office)
Fax 01789 296083
✉ director@shakespeare.org.uk

Festival Director *Roger Pringle*

Founded 1953. Annual festival held on nine Sunday evenings during July and August. Readings by poets and professional actors by invitation.

Strokestown International Poetry Festival

See **Strokestown International Poetry Prize** under *Prizes*

The Sunday Times Oxford Literary Festival

301 Woodstock Road, Oxford OX2 7NY
☎01865 514149   Fax 01865 514804
✉ oxford.literary.festival@ntlworld.com
www.sundaytimes-oxfordliteraryfestival.co.uk

Directors *Sally Dunsmore, Angela Prysor-Jones*

Founded 1997. Annual six-day festival held two weekends prior to Easter. Authors speaking about their books, covering a wide variety of writing: fiction, poetry, biography, travel, food, gardening, children's art. Previous guests have included William Boyd, Andrew Motion, Beryl Bainbridge, Sophie Grigson, Philip Pullman, Doris Lessing, Seamus Heaney, Richard Dawkins, Zandra Rhodes, Kazuro Ishiguro.

Swansea Festivals

Dylan Thomas Centre, Somerset Place, Swansea SA1 1RR
☎01792 463980   Fax 01792 463993
✉ dylan.thomas.lit@swansea.gov.uk
www.dylanthomas.org
www.dylanthomasfestival.com

Contacts *David Woolley, Jo Furber*

Wordplay (3rd–8th October): eleventh annual festival of literature and arts for young people. The Dylan Thomas Celebration (27th October–9th November) is two weeks of performances, talks, lectures, films, music, poetry, exhibitions and celebrity guests. The Dylan Thomas Centre also runs a year-round programme of literary events; please e-mail for details.

Swindon Festival of Literature

Lower Shaw Farm, Shaw, Swindon SN5 5PJ
☎01793 771080   Fax 01793 771080
✉ swindonlitfest@lowershawfarm.co.uk
www.swindonfestivalofliterature.co.uk

Festival Director *Matt Holland*

Founded 1994. Annual festival held in May, starting with 'Dawn Chorus' at sunrise on May Day. Includes a wide range of authors, speakers, discussions, performances and workshops, plus the Clive Brain Memorial Lecture and the Swindon Performance Poetry Slam competition. Guests at th 2005 Festival included Julian Clary, Fergal Keene, Jon Snow, Anne Michaels, John Berger, Lisa Jardine, Nick Hornby, John Pilger, Simon Hoggart and Michael Eavis.

Tears in the Fence Festival

38 Hod View, Stourpaine, Blandford Forum DT11 8TN
☎01258 456803
✉ esp@euphony.net
www.wanderingdog.co.uk

Festival Director *David Caddy*
Festival Manager *Jonathan Ward*

Founded 1995. Annual international poetry festival based in London with readings, talks, discussions and workshops continuing the work begun by the Wessex Poetry Festivals, 1995–2001.

Previous guests have included Lee Harwood, Elizabeth Cook, Jeremy Reed, Alice Notley, Fred Voss, Joan Jobe Smith, Irina Ratushinskaya, Michele Roberts, Edwin Morgan and Kim Taplin.

Theakston's Old Peculier Harrogate Crime Writing Festival

1 Victoria Avenue, Harrogate HG1 1EQ
☎01423 562303   Fax 10423 521264
✉ crime@harrogate-festival.org.uk
www.harrogate-festival.org.uk

Festival Director *William Culver Dodds*
Festival Manager *Sharon Canavar*

Launched 2003. Weekend of events at the end of July each year featuring the best of British and American crime writers. The inaugural winner of the **Theakston's Old Peculier Prize for the Crime Novel of the Year** was announced at the 2005 Festival (see entry under *Prizes*). Events also include industry 'How to ...' sessions, social events and late night shows. Part of the **Harrogate International Festival**.

The Dylan Thomas Celebration

See **Swansea Festivals**

Ty Newydd Festival

Ty Newydd, Llanystumdwy, Criccieth LL52 0LW
☎01766 522811   Fax 01766 523095
✉ post@tynewydd.org
www.tynewydd.org

Director *Sally Baker*

Biennial, bilingual literature festival held on alternate years with the Academi's **Bay Lit Festival**. Held in April and run by the National Writers' Centre for Wales, it is located at Ty Newydd Writers' Centre and other venues near Criccieth. Features writers and poets from Wales (working in both English and Welsh) and worldwide. Ty Newydd also holds an annual weekend festival in November devoted solely to Cynghanedd – Welsh strict meter poetry.

Warwick Festival

Warwick Arts Society, Pageant House, 2 Jury Street, Warwick CV34 4EW
☎01926 410747   Fax 01926 409050
✉ admin@warwickarts.org.uk
www.warwickarts.org.uk

Festival Director *Richard Phillips*

Founded 1980, this annual festival has had four names but since 2003 events have only taken place in Warwick town, using Warwick Castle and other historic buildings, plus new theatres The Dream Factory and Bridge House Theatre on the outskirts. Primarily a music festival but embraces drama, opera, dance, puppets, art exhibitions, poetry readings and other literary events. Extensive educational programme including workshops.

Warwick Words

Warwick Events Group, Northgate, Warwick CV34 4JL
☎01926 497000   Fax 01926 407606
✉ admin@warwickarts.org.uk
www.WarwickLive.com

Founded 2002. Annual venture featuring both living writers and those who have had connections with Warwick – Tolkien, Larkin and Landor in particular. Also workshops and an education programme. A weekend festival of literature and spoken word for all the family. Events at The Dream Factory, Bridge House Theatre, St Mary's Church, the Lord Leycester Hospital and other historic buildings around Warwick over the first weekend in October. 2005 Festival: 6th–9th October.

Ways with Words

Droridge Farm, Dartington, Totnes TQ9 6JQ
☎01803 867373   Fax 01803 863688
✉ admin@wayswithwords.co.uk
www.wayswithwords.co.uk

Festival Director *Kay Dunbar*

Ways with Words runs a major literature festival at Dartington Hall in south Devon for ten days in July each year. Features over 200 writers giving lectures, readings, interviews, discussions, performances, masterclasses and workshops. Also, Words by the Water, a Cumbrian literature festival held in Keswick. There is a regular festival in held in Southwold, Suffolk (2005: 10–14th November). Also organises writing, reading and painting courses in Italy.

Wellington Literary Festival

Civic Offices, Larkin Way, Tan Bank, Wellington, Telford TF1 1LX
☎01952 222935   Fax 01952 222936
✉ WellTownCl@aol.com
www.wellington-shropshire.gov.uk

Contact *Derrick Drew*

Founded 1997. Annual festival held throughout October. Events include storytelling, writers' forum, 'Pints and Poetry', children's poetry competition, story competition, theatre review and guest speakers.

Wells Festival of Literature

25 Chamberlain Street, Wells BA5 2PQ
☎01749 670929
www.somersite.co.uk/wellsfest.htm

Founded 1992. Annual weekend-plus festival held at the end of October. Main venue is the historic, moated Bishop's Palace. A wide range of speakers caters for different tastes in reading. Recent guests include: Shirley Vickers, Kate Adie, Libby Purves, Melvyn Bragg, Margaret Drabble, William Dalrymple, Timothy West. Short story and poetry competitions and writing workshops are run in conjunction with the Festival.

Wessex Poetry Festival

See **Tears in the Fence Festival**

westwords festival

c/o London Borough of Hammersmith & Fulham, Arts Team, Munster Centre, Filmer Road, London SW6 6AS
☎020 7736 0864

Currently under development; telephone for further information.

Wonderful Words Book Festival

c/o Bude Library, The Wharf, Bude EX23 8LQ
☎01288 359242
www.cornwall.gov.uk

Festival Organiser *Rebecca Rowland*

Founded 1994. Biennial two-month festival hosted throughout Cornwall. The next and seventh Festival will be in 2006. The festival, organised by the library service, has grown into a prestigious two-month event for children and adults. Offers author talks, writers' workshops, poetry performances, theatre and storytelling. Guest authors have included Doris Lessing,

Ruth Rendell, Margaret Drabble and Dick King-Smith.

Wordfest: A Festival of Words in Basingstoke and Deane

Basingstoke & Deane Borough Council, Civic Offices, London Road, Basingstoke RG21 4AH
☎01256 845686
✉ c.gibson@basingstoke.gov.uk
www.basingstoke.gov.uk/wordfest

Contact *Ceri Gibson*

Founded 1999. Annual celebration of words held over ten days in October. A range of events and activities including author appearances, participatory workshops, theatre and community projects, which take place throughout the borough at a variety of venues.

Wordplay

See **Swansea Festivals**

Words by the Water

See **Ways with Words**

Wordsworth Trust

The Wordsworth Trust, Dove Cottage, Grassmere LA22 9SH
☎015394 35544   Fax 015394 35748
✉ enquiries@wordsworth.org.uk
www.wordsworth.org.uk

Contemporary poetry programme held over 30 weeks. Past readers have included Paul Muldoon, Philip Pullman, Simon Armitage and Don Paterson. The Trust also operates a writers-in-residence programme throughout the year, giving time and space for important new writers to develop their work. Past poets in residence include Henry Shukman, Owen Sheers, Jacob Polley and Jack Mapanje

European Publishers

Austria

Springer-Verlag GmbH
Postfach 89, A–1201 Vienna
☎00 43 1 3302415   Fax 00 43 1 3302426
✉ springer@springer.at
www.springer.at
Founded 1924. Publishes academic and text-books, journals and translations: anthropology, architecture, art, business, chemistry, computer science, communications, electronics, economics, education, environmental studies, engineering, law, mathematics, dentistry, medicine, nursing, philosophy, physics, psychology, technology and general science.

Verlag Carl Ueberreuter GmbH
Postfach 306, A–1091 Vienna
☎00 43 1 404440   Fax 00 43 1 404445
www.ueberreuter.de
Founded 1548. Publishes fiction and general non-fiction; art, astrology, biography, government, history, economics, political science, general science, health and nutrition, science fiction, fantasy, music and dance.

Paul Zsolnay Verlag GmbH
Postfach 142, A–1040 Vienna
☎00 43 1 50576610
Fax 00 43 1 505766110
✉ info@zsolnay.at
www.zsolnay.at
Founded 1923. Publishes biography, fiction, general non-fiction, history, poetry.

Belgium

Brepols Publishers NV
Begijnhof 67, B–2300 Turnhout
☎00 32 14 448020   Fax 00 32 14 428919
✉ info@brepols.net
www.brepols.net
Founded 1796. Publishes academic – architecture, archaeology, art, interior design, Asian studies, history, language arts, linguistics, literature, literary criticism, essays, philosophy, religion and biblical studies.

Facet NV
Willem Linnigstr 13, B–2060 Antwerp
☎00 32 3 2274028   Fax 00 32 3 2273792
Founded 1986. Publishes children's books.

Uitgeverij Lannoo NV
Kasteelstr 97, B–8700 Tielt
☎00 32 51 424211   Fax 00 32 51 401152
✉ lannoo@lannoo.be
www.lannoo.be
Founded 1909. Publishes general non-fiction, art, architecture and interior design, cookery, biography, economics, gardening, health and nutrition, history, management, photography, self-help, poetry, government, political science, religion, travel.

Standaard Uitgeverij
Belgiëlei 147a, B–2018 Antwerp
☎00 32 3 2857200   Fax 00 32 3 2857299
www.standarduitgeverij.be
Founded 1919. Publishes education, fiction, poetry, humour, children's and young adult.

Denmark

Forlaget Apostrof ApS
Postboks 2580, DK–2100 Copenhagen O
☎00 45 39 208420   Fax 00 45 39 208453
www.apostrof.dk
Founded 1980. Publishes psychology and psychiatry.

Aschehoug Dansk Forlag A/S
Postbox 2179, DK–1017 Copenhagen K
☎00 45 33 305522   Fax 00 45 33 305822
www.aschehoug.dk
Founded 1977. Merged with Egmont Lademann A/S in 2003. Publishes reference, directories, dictionaries, encyclopedias, young adult, textbooks, fiction, biography, cookery, children's, how-to, health and nutrition, maritime.

Blackwell Munksgaard
1 Rosenørns Alle, DK–1970 Frederiksberg C
☎00 45 77 333333   Fax 00 45 77 333377
www.blackwellmunksgaard.com

Founded 1917. Part of **Blackwell Publishing**. Publishes academic books and journals for higher education, research and professional markets.

Borgens Forlag A/S
Valbygardsvej 33, DK–2500 Valby
☎00 45 36 153615   Fax 00 45 36 153616
www.borgens.dk
Founded 1948. Publishes fiction and general non-fiction: bibliography, children's and young adult, illustrated, journals, textbooks, literature, literary criticism, art, astrology, child care, crafts, education, environmental studies, essays, games, hobbies, health and nutrition, how-to, humour, music, dance, occult, philosophy, poetry, psychology, psychiatry, self-help, religion.

Forlaget Forum
PO Box 2252, DK–1019 Copenhagen K
☎00 45 33 411830   Fax 00 45 33 411831
✉ kontakt@forlagetforum.dk
www.forlagetforum.dk
Founded 1940. Part of **Gyldendalske Boghandel-Nordisk Forlag A/S**. Publishes fiction, bibliography, history, humour, mysteries, children's and young adults.

Gyldendal
PO Box 11, DK–1001 Copenhagen K
☎00 45 33 755555   Fax 00 45 33 755556
✉ gyldendal@gyldendal.dk
www.gyldendal.dk
Founded 1770. Publishes fiction, children's and young adult, directories, art, biography, dance, dentistry, education, history, how-to, medicine, music, poetry, nursing, philosophy, psychology, psychiatry, reference, general and social sciences, sociology, textbooks.

Hekla Forlag
Valbygaardsvej 33, DK–2500 Valby
☎00 45 36 153615   Fax 00 45 36 153616
✉ post@borgen.dk
www.borgen.dk
Founded 1979. Part of **Borgens Verlag A/S**. Publishes general fiction and non-fiction.

Høst & Søn Publishers Ltd
PO Box 2212, DK–1018 Copenhagen K
☎00 45 33 382888   Fax 00 45 33 382898
Founded 1836. Publishes fiction, children's, crafts, environmental studies, games, hobbies, history.

Lindhardt og Ringhof
Frederiksborggade 1, DK–1360 Copenhagen K
☎00 45 33 695000   Fax 00 45 33 695001

www.lrforlag.dk
Founded 1971. Publishes fiction and general non-fiction.

Nyt Nordisk Forlag Arnold Busck A/S
Købmagergade 49, DK–1150 Copenhagen K
☎00 45 33 733575   Fax 00 45 33 733576
www.nytnordiskforlag.dk
Founded 1896. Publishes fiction, art, biography, dance, dentistry, directories, history, how-to, music, philosophy, religion, medicine, nursing, psychology, psychiatry, general and social sciences, sociology, textbooks.

Samlerens Forlag A/S
Postboks 2252, DK–1019 Copenhagen K
☎00 45 33 411800   Fax 00 45 33 411801
✉ samleren@samleren.dk
www.samleren.dk
Founded 1943. Publishes essays, translations, fiction, government, history, literature, literary criticism, political science.

Det Schønbergske Forlag
Landemaerket 5, DK–1119 Copenhagen K
☎00 45 33 733585   Fax 00 45 33 733586
www.nytnordiskforlag.dk
Founded 1857. Part of **Nyt Nordisk Forlag Arnold Busck A/S**. Publishes art, biography, careers, directories, fiction, history, humour, philosophy, poetry, psychology, psychiatry, reference, textbooks, travel

Spektrum Forlagsaktieselskab
PO Box 2252, DK–1019 Copenhagen K
☎00 45 33 147714   Fax 00 45 33 147791
Founded 1990. Publishes general non-fiction.

Tiderne Skifter Forlag A/S
Laederstraede 5, 1, DK–1201 Copenhagen K
☎00 45 33 186390   Fax 00 45 33 186391
✉ tiderneskifter@tiderneskifter.dk
www.tiderneskifter.dk
Founded 1973. Publishes fiction, literature and literary criticism, essays, ethnicity, photography.

Finland

Gummerus Publishers
PO Box 749, SF–00101 Helsinki
☎00 358 9 584301   Fax 00 358 9 58430200
www.gummerus.fi
Founded 1872. Publishes fiction and general non-fiction.

Karisto Oy
PO Box 102, SF–13101 Hämeenlinna
☎00 358 3 6163151   Fax 00 358 3 6161565
www.karisto.fi
Founded 1900. Publishes fiction and general non-fiction, juvenile and young adult.

Kirjayhtymä Oy
Urho Kekkosen Katu 4–6E, SF–00100 Helsinki
☎00 358 9 6937641   Fax 00 358 9 69376366
Founded 1958. Publishes fiction and general non-fiction, textbooks.

Kustannusosakeyhtiö Tammi
PO Box 410, SF–00101 Helsinki
☎00 358 9 6937621   Fax 00 358 9 69376266
✉ tammi@tammi.net
www.tammi.net
Founded 1943. Publishes fiction, general non-fiction, children's and young adult, illustrated. Part of the Bonnier Group.

Otava Publishing Co. Ltd
Uudenmaankatu 8–12, SF–00120 Helsinki
☎00 358 9 19961   Fax 00 358 9 643136
www.otava.fi
Founded 1890. Publishes fiction, translations, general non-fiction, children's and young adult, CD-ROMs, dictionaries, directories, encyclopedias, textbooks, art, architecture and interior design, history, how-to.

Werner Söderström Osakeyhtiö (WSOY)
PO Box 222, SF–00121 Helsinki
☎00 358 9 61681   Fax 00 358 9 6163566
Founded 1878. Publishes fiction, general non-fiction, education, dictionaries, encyclopedias, textbooks, young adult.

France

Editions Arthaud SA
26 rue Racine, F–75006 Paris
☎00 33 1 4051 3008   Fax 00 33 1 4325 0118
Founded 1890. Imprint of Flammarion SA.

Editions Belfond
12 avenue d'Italie, F–75627 Paris Cedex 13
☎00 33 1 4416 0500
www.belfond.fr
Founded 1963. Publishes fiction and general non-fiction.

Editions Bordas
21 blvd du Montparnasse, F–75006 Paris
☎00 33 1 4656 5266   Fax 00 33 1 4656 0476
www.editions-bordas.com
Founded 1945. Publishes education and general non-fiction: dictionaries, directories, encyclopedias, reference.

Editions Calmann-Lévy-Stock SA
3 rue Auber, F–75009 Paris
☎00 33 1 4742 3833   Fax 00 33 1 4742 7781
Founded 1836. Publishes fiction, science fiction, fantasy, biography, history, humour, economics, philosophy, psychology, psychiatry, social sciences, sociology, sport.

Editions Denoël
9 rue du Cherche-Midi, F–75006 Paris
☎00 33 1 4439 7373   Fax 00 33 1 4439 7390
Founded 1932. Part of Editions Gallimard. Publishes fiction, science fiction, fantasy, art, directories, economics, government, history, illustrated, philosophy, political science, psychology, psychiatry, reference.

Editions Larousse
21 rue de Montparnasse, F–75283 Paris Cedex 06
☎00 33 1 4439 4400   Fax 00 33 1 4439 4343
www.larousse.fr
Founded 1852. Publishes animals, bilingual, children's and young adult, childcare, cookery, dictionaries, directories, encyclopedias, gardening, history, medicine, nursing, dentistry, music, dance, self-help, psychology, psychiatry, reference, general science, social sciences, sociology, language arts, linguistics, sport, technology, textbooks.

Librairie Arthème Fayard
75 rue des Saints-Pères, F–75279 Paris Cedex 6
☎00 33 1 4549 8200   Fax 00 33 1 4222 4017
www.editions-fayard.fr
Founded 1854. Publishes fiction, biography, directories, maps, atlases, history, dance, music, philosophy, religion, reference, social sciences, sociology, general science, technology.

Flammarion SA
26 rue Racine, F–75006 Paris
☎00 33 1 4051 3008   Fax 00 33 1 4325 0118
www.flammarion.com
Founded 1875. Publishes general fiction and non-fiction, art, architecture, children's, garden-

ing, plants, CD-ROMs, bilingual, literature, literary criticism, essays, medicine, nursing, dentistry, wine and spirits.

Editions Gallimard
5 rue Sébastien-Bottin, F–75328 Paris Cedex 07
☎00 33 1 4954 4200   Fax 00 33 1 4544 9403
www.gallimard.fr
Founded 1911. Publishes fiction, poetry, art, biography, dance, history, music, philosophy, young adult.

Editions Grasset et Fasquelle
61 rue des Saints-Pères, F–75006 Paris
☎00 33 1 4439 2200   Fax 00 33 1 4222 6418
✉ editorial@edition-grasset.fr
www.edition-grasset.fr
Founded 1907. Publishes fiction and general non-fiction, essays, literature, literary criticism, philosophy.

Hachette-Livre
43 quai de Grenelle, F–75905 Paris Cedex 15
☎00 33 1 4392 3000   Fax 00 33 1 4392 3030
Founded 1826. Publishes fiction and general non-fiction, architecture and interior design, art, bibliographies, bilingual, directories, economics, education, general engineering, government, history, language and linguistics, political science, philosophy, reference, general science, self-help, social sciences, sociology, sport, textbooks, travel.

Robert Laffont
24 ave Marceau, F–75381 Paris Cedex 08
☎00 33 1 5367 1400   Fax 00 33 1 5367 1414
www.laffont.fr
Founded 1987. Publishes fiction.

Editions Jean-Claude Lattès
17 rue Jacob, F–75006 Paris
☎00 33 1 4441 7400   Fax 00 33 1 4325 3047
Founded 1968. Part of **Hachette-Livre**. Publishes fiction and general non-fiction.

Magnard SA
20 rue Berbier-du-Mets, F–75647 Paris Cedex 13
☎00 33 1 4408 8585   Fax 00 33 1 4408 4979
www.magnard.fr
Founded 1933. Publishes education, foreign language and bilingual books, juvenile and young adults, textbooks.

Michelin Editions des Voyages
46 ave de Breteuil, F–75324 Paris

☎00 33 1 4566 1234   Fax 00 33 1 4566 1163
Founded 1900. Publishes travel: maps and atlases.

Les Editions de Minuit SA
7 rue Bernard-Palissy, F–75006 Paris
☎00 33 1 4439 3920   Fax 00 33 1 4544 8236
✉ contact@leseditionsdeminuit.fr
www.leseditionsdeminuit.fr
Founded 1942. Publishes fiction, essays, literature, literary criticism, philosophy, social sciences, sociology.

Editions Fernand Nathan
9 rue Méchain, F–75014 Paris
☎00 33 1 4587 5000   Fax 00 33 1 4537 5300
www.nathan.fr
Founded 1881. Publishes dictionaries, directories, education, encyclopedias, history, philosophy, psychology, psychiatry, reference, general and social sciences, sociology, textbooks.

Presses de la Cité
12 ave d'Italie, F–75627 Paris Cedex 13
☎00 33 1 4416 0500   Fax 00 33 1 4416 0505
www.pressesdelacite.com
Founded 1947. Imprint of **Editions Belfond**. Publishes fiction and general non-fiction, science fiction, fantasy, history, mysteries, romance, biography.

Presses Universitaires de France (PUF)
6 ave Reille, F–75685 Paris Cedex 14
☎00 33 1 5810 3100   Fax 00 33 1 5810 3182
www.puf.com
Founded 1921. Publishes art, biography, dance, dentistry, dictionaries, directories, encyclopedias, government, general engineering, geography, geology, history, journals, law, medicine, music, nursing, philosophy, psychology, psychiatry, religion, political science, reference, social science, sociology, textbooks.

Editions Seghers
24 ave Marceau, F–75381 Paris Cedex 08
☎00 33 1 5367 1400   Fax 00 33 1 5367 1414
Paperback imprint of **Robert Laffont**.

Editions du Seuil
27 rue Jacob, F–75006 Paris
☎00 33 1 4046 5050   Fax 00 33 1 4046 4300
✉ contact@seuil.com
www.seuil.com
Founded 1935. Publishes fiction, literature, literary criticism, essays, poetry, art, biography,

dance, government, illustrated, political science, history, how-to, music, photography, philosophy, psychology, psychiatry, religion, general and social sciences, sociology, textbooks.

Les Editions de la Table Ronde
7 rue Corneille, F–75006 Paris
☎00 33 1 4046 7070
Fax 00 33 1 4046 7101
Founded 1944. Publishes fiction and general non-fiction, biography, history, psychology, psychiatry, religion.

Librairie Vuibert
20 rue Berbier-du-Mets, F–75647 Paris Cedex 13
☎00 33 1 4408 4900
Fax 00 33 1 4408 4939
www.vuibert.com
Founded 1877. Publishes biological and earth sciences, chemistry, chemical engineering, children's, economics, law, mathematics, physics, textbooks.

Germany

Verlag C.H. Beck (OHG)
Postfach 400340, 80703 Munich
☎00 49 89 381890   Fax 00 49 89 38189402
www.beck.de
Founded 1763. Publishes general non-fiction, anthropology, archaeology, art, CD-ROMs, dance, dictionaries, directories, economics, essays, encyclopedias, history, illustrated, journals, language arts, law, linguistics, literature, literary criticism, music, philosophy, professional, reference, social sciences, sociology, textbooks, theology.

Bertelsmann
Verlagsgruppe Random House, Neumarkter Strasse 28, 81673 Munich
☎00 49 89 41360
www.randomhouse.de
Founded 1835. Part of the **Random House Group**. Publishes fiction and general non-fiction, art, biography, government and political science.

Carlsen Verlag GmbH
Postfach 500380, 22703 Hamburg
☎00 49 40 398040   Fax 00 49 40 39804390
www.carlsen.de
Founded 1953. Publishes children's and comic books.

Deutscher Taschenbuch Verlag GmbH & Co. KG (dtv)
Postfach 400422, 80704 Munich
☎00 49 89 38167-0   Fax 00 49 89 346428
www.dtv.de
Founded 1961. Publishes fiction and general non-fiction; art, astronomy, biography, child care and development, children's, dance, dictionaries, directories, education, encyclopedias, government, history, large print, music, poetry, psychiatry, psychology, philosophy, political science, reference, religion, social sciences, literature, literary criticism, essays, humour, translations, young adult.

Econ-Verlag GmbH
Paul-Heyse-Strasse 28, 80336 Munich
☎00 49 89 5148-0
Fax 00 49 89 5148-2229
www.econ-verlag.de
Founded 1950. Publishes general non-fiction and fiction, CD-ROMs, directories, economics, professional, reference and general science.

S Fischer Verlag GmbH
Postfach 700355, 60553 Frankfurt am Main
☎00 49 69 6062-0   Fax 00 49 69 606214
www.fischerverlage.de
Founded 1886. Part of the **Holtzbrinck Group**. Publishes fiction, general non-fiction, directories, essays, literature, literary criticism, reference.

Carl Hanser Verlag
Kolbergerstrasse 22, 81679 Munich
☎00 49 89 998300
Fax 00 49 89 984809
✉ info@hanser.de
www.hanser.de/verlag
Founded in 1928 in Munich. Publishes international and German contemporary literature; children's and juveniles; specialist books on engineering, natural science, plastics, computers and computer science, economics and management, dentistry; CD-ROMs, journals, academic, textbooks, translations.

Wilhelm Heyne Verlag
Postfach 200143, 80001 Munich
☎00 49 89 4136-0
Fax 00 49 89 5148-2229
www.heyne.de
Founded 1934. Publishes fiction, mystery, romance, humour, science fiction, fantasy, astrology, biography, cookery, film, history, how-to, occult, psychology, psychiatry, video, illustrated.

Hoffmann und Campe Verlag GmbH

Harvestehuder Weg 42, 20149 Hamburg
☎00 49 40 441880   Fax 00 49 40 44188-290
www.hoca.de

Founded 1781. Publishes fiction and general non-fiction; art, biography, dance, history, illustrated, music, poetry, philosophy, psychology, psychiatry, general science, social sciences, sociology.

Verlagsgruppe Georg von Holtzbrinck GmbH

Gänsheidestrasse 26, 70184 Stuttgart
☎00 49 711 21500   Fax 00 49 711 215269
✉ info@holtzbrinck.com
www.holtzbrinck.com

Founded 1948. One of the world's largest publishing groups with 12 book publishing houses and 40 imprints. Also publishes the newspapers, *Handelsblatt* and *Die Zeit*.

Hüthig GmbH & Co. KG

Postfach 102869, 69018 Heidelberg
☎00 49 6221 489-0   Fax 00 49 6221 489-279
✉ info@huethig.de
www.huethig.de

Founded 1925. Germany's fourth largest professional publisher: CD-ROMs, journals, academic, textbooks, translations.

Ernst Klett Verlag GmbH

Postfach 106016, 70049 Stuttgart
☎00 49 711 6672-0
Fax 00 49 711 6672-2000
www.klett.de

Founded 1897. Publishes dictionaries, encyclopedias, maps and atlases, education, geography, geology; textbooks.

Langenscheidt KG

Postfach 401120, 80711 Munich
☎00 49 89 36096-0   Fax 00 49 89 36096-222
www.langenscheidt.de

Founded 1856. Publishes dictionaries, encyclopedias, reference, bilingual, language, textbooks.

Gustav Lübbe Verlag GmbH

Postfach 200180, 51431 Bergisch Gladbach
☎00 49 2202 121330
Fax 00 49 2202 121920
www.lubbe.de

Founded 1963. Publishes fiction and general non-fiction, audio, archaeology, biography, history, how-to.

Propylän Verlag, Zweigniederlassung Berlin der Ullstein Buchverlage GmbH

Charlottenstrasse 13, 10969 Berlin
☎00 49 30 25913570
Fax 00 49 30 25913533

Founded 1903. Publishes fiction and general non-fiction, romance, mysteries, architecture and interior design, art, biography, dance, dictionaries, encyclopedias, film, video, education, essays, ethnology, geography, geology, government, health, history, how-to, humour, literature, literary criticism, maritime, military science, music, nutrition, poetry, political science, general science, social sciences, sociology, translations, travel.

Rowohlt Verlag GmbH

Hamburgerstr 17, 21465 Reinbeck
☎00 49 30 72720   Fax 00 49 40 7272319
✉ info@rowohlt.de
www.rowohlt.de

Founded 1908. Publishes general non-fiction.

Springer GmbH

Tiergartenstrasse 17, 69121 Heidelberg
☎00 49 6221 4870   Fax 00 49 6221 487-8366
www.springer.de

Also at: Heidelberger Platz 3, 14197 Berlin
☎00 49 30 827870 Fax 00 49 30 8214091

Founded 1842. Part of Springer Science+Business Media. Leading scientific publisher. Subjects range from natural sciences, mathematics, engineering and computer science, medicine, psychology, economics, law, arts and social sciences – with eighty per cent of publications in English.

Suhrkamp Verlag

Postfach 101945, 60019 Frankfurt am Main
☎00 49 69 756010   Fax 00 49 69 75601314
www.suhrkamp.de

Founded 1950. Publishes fiction, poetry, biography, philosophy, psychology, psychiatry, general science.

Taschen GmbH

Hohenzollernring 53, 50672 Cologne
☎00 49 221 201800   Fax 00 49 221 254919
✉ contact@taschen.com
www.taschen.com

Founded 1980. Publishes photography, art, erotica, architecture and interior design.

WEKA Firmengruppe GmbH & Co KG

Römerstr. 4, 86438 Kissing
☎00 49 8233 230   Fax 00 49 8233 237500

Founded 1973. Germany's largest professional publisher.

Italy

Adelphi Edizioni SpA
Via S. Giovanni sul Muro 14, 20121 Milan
☎00 39 2 725731   Fax 00 39 2 89010337
✉ info@adelphi.it
www.adelphi.it
Founded 1962. Publishes fiction, literature, literary criticism, essays, mysteries, poetry, anthropology, biography, history, mathematics, philosophy, physics, psychology, religion, general science.

Bompiani–RCS Libri
Via Mecenate 91, 20138 Milan
☎00 39 2 50951   Fax 00 39 2 5065361
www.rcslibri.it
Founded 1929. Publishes fiction and general non-fiction, dictionaries, encyclopedias, juvenile and young adult.

Bulzoni Editore SRL (Le Edizioni Universitarie d'Italia)
Via Dei Liburni 14, 00185 Rome
☎00 39 6 4455207   Fax 00 39 6 4450355
✉ bulzoni@bulzoni.it
www.bulzoni.it
Founded 1969. Publishes fiction, literature, literary criticism, essays, art, drama, general engineering, film, law, language, linguistics, philosophy, general science, social sciences, sociology, textbooks, theatre, video.

Cappelli Editore
Via Farini 14, 40124 Bologna
☎00 39 51 239060   Fax 00 39 51 239286
✉ info@cappellieditore.com
www.cappellieditore.com
Founded 1851. Publishes fiction, art, biography, drama, film, government, history, music, dance, directories, poetry, medicine, nursing, dentistry, juvenile and young adult, philosophy, political science, psychology, psychiatry, reference, religion, general science, social sciences, sociology, textbooks, theatre, video.

Garzanti Libri
Via Gasparotto 1, 20124 Milan
☎00 39 2 674171   Fax 00 39 2 67417323
Founded 1861. Publishes fiction, literature, literary criticism, essays, art, biography, dictionaries, directories, encyclopedias, history, poetry,

government, political science, reference, textbooks.

Giunti Gruppo Editoriale
Via Bolognese 165, 50139 Florence
☎00 39 55 5062376   Fax 00 39 55 5062397
www.giunti.it
Founded 1840. Publishes fiction, literature, literary criticism, essays, art, chemistry, chemical engineering, dictionaries, directories, education, encyclopedias, history, how-to, language arts, linguistics, mathematics, psychology, psychiatry, reference, general science. Italian publishers of National Geographical Society books.

Ernesto Gremese Editore SRL
Via Virginia Agnelli 88, Via le de Collei Portuensi 537, 00151 Rome
☎00 39 6 657 40507   Fax 00 39 6 657 40509
www.liberiagremese.com
Founded 1954. Publishes fiction, art, erotica, astrology, cookery, crafts, dance, drama, film, video, fashion, games, hobbies, illustrated, essays, literature, literary criticism, bilingual, dictionaries, directories, encyclopedias, health and nutrition, house and home, how-to, music, occult, reference, sport, travel, theatre, television, radio, wine and spirits.

Longanesi & C
Corso Italia 13, 20122 Milan
☎00 39 2 80206310   Fax 00 39 2 72000306
✉ info@longanesi.it
www.longanesi.it
Founded 1946. Mass market paperback publisher of fiction, art, biography, dance, history, how-to, medicine, nursing, dentistry, music, philosophy, psychology, psychiatry, religion, general and social sciences, sociology.

Arnoldo Mondadori Editore SpA
Via Mondadori 1, 20090 Segrate (Milan)
☎00 39 2 75421   Fax 00 39 2 75422302
www.mondadori.it
Founded 1907. Publishes fiction, mystery, romance, art, biography, dance, dentistry, directories, history, how-to, medicine, music, poetry, philosophy, psychology, psychiatry, reference, religion, nursing, general science, education, textbooks.

Società Editrice Il Mulino
Str Maggiore 37, 40125 Bologna
☎00 39 51 256011   Fax 00 39 51 256034
✉ info@mulino.it
www.mulino.it

Founded 1954. Publishes economics, government, history, law, language arts, linguistics, philosophy, political science, psychology, psychiatry, social sciences, sociology, textbooks, journals.

Gruppo Ugo Mursia Editore SpA
Via Melchiorre Gioia 45, 20124 Milan
☎00 39 2 6737 8500   Fax 00 39 2 6737 8605
✉ info@mursia.com
www.mursia.com
Founded 1922. Publishes fiction, poetry, art, biography, directories, education, history, maritime, philosophy, reference, religion, sport, general science, social sciences, sociology, textbooks, juvenile and young adult.

RCS Rizzoli Libri SpA
Via Mecenate 91, 20138 Milan
☎00 39 2 50951   Fax 00 39 2 5065361
Founded 1945. Publishes art, crafts, dance, business, dictionaries, directories, encyclopedias, games, hobbies, history, music, medicine, nursing, dentistry, general science, textbooks, juvenile and young adult.

Società Editrice Internazionale – SEI
Corso Regina Margherita 176, 10152 Turin
☎00 39 11 52271   Fax 00 39 11 5211320
Founded 1908. Publishes literature, literary criticism, essays, children's, dictionaries, encyclopedias, education, geography, geology, history, mathematics, philosophy, physics, religion, psychology, psychiatry, textbooks.

Sonzogno
Via Mecenate 91, 20138 Milan
☎00 39 2 50951   Fax 00 39 2 5065361
Founded 1818. Publishes fiction, mysteries, and general non-fiction.

Sperling e Kupfer Editori SpA
Via Durazzo 4, 20134 Milan
☎00 39 2 217211   Fax 00 39 2 21721277
www.sperling.it
Founded 1899. Publishes fiction and general non-fiction, biography, economics, health, how-to, management, nutrition, general science, sport, travel.

Sugarco Edizioni SRL
Via Gnocchi 4, 21048 Milan
☎00 39 2 407 8370   Fax 00 39 2 407 8493
Founded 1956. Publishes fiction, biography, history, how-to, philosophy.

Todariana Editrice
Via Gardone 29, 20139 Milan
☎00 39 2 56812953   Fax 00 39 2 55213405
Founded 1967. Publishes fiction, poetry, science fiction, fantasy, literature, literary criticism, essays, language arts, linguistics, psychology, psychiatry, social sciences, sociology, travel.

The Netherlands

A.W. Bruna Uitgevers BV
Postbus 40203, 3504 AA Utrecht
☎00 31 30 247 0411   Fax 00 31 30 241 0018
www.awbruna.nl
Founded 1868. Publishes fiction and general non-fiction; mysteries, computer science, CD-ROMs, history, philosophy, psychology, psychiatry, general science, social sciences, sociology.

BZZTÔH Publishers
Laan van Meerdervoort 10, 2517 AJ The Hague
☎00 31 70 363 2934   Fax 00 31 70 363 1932
✉ info@bzztoh.nl
www.bzztoh.nl
Founded 1970. Publishes fiction, mysteries, literature, romance, literary criticism, essays, foreign language, bilingual, general non-fiction, animals, astrology, biography, cookery, dance, humour, journals, music, philosophy, self-help, health and nutrition, occult, pets, religion, sport, translations, travel, women's studies.

Elsevier Science BV
Sara Burgehartst. 25, 1055 KV Amsterdam
☎00 31 20 586 2560   Fax 00 31 20 485 2457
www.elsevier.nl
Founded 1946. Parent company Reed Elsevier. Publishes sciences (all fields), medicine, nursing, dentistry, economics, engineering (chemical and general), mathematics, physics, technology.

Uitgeversmaatschappij J. H. Kok BV
PO Box 5019, 8260 GA Kampen
☎00 31 38 339 2555   Fax 00 31 38 331 1776
www.kok.nl
Founded 1894. Publishes fiction, poetry, history, religion, directories, reference, general science, social sciences, sociology, textbooks, journals, juvenile and young adult.

J.M. Meulenhoff BV
Postbus 100, 1000 AC Amsterdam
☎00 31 20 553 3500   Fax 00 31 20 625 8511
✉ info@meulenhoff.nl

www.meulenhoff.nl

Founded 1895. Publishes international co-productions, fiction and general non-fiction. Specialises in Dutch and translated literature.

Pearson Education Benelux

Concertgebouwplein 25, 1071 LM Amsterdam
☎00 31 20 575 5800   Fax 00 31 20 664 5334
www.pearsoneducation.nl

Founded 1942. Publishes education, business, computer science, directories, economics, management, reference, textbooks, technology.

Uitgeverij Het Spectrum BV

Postbus 2073, 3500 GB Utrecht
☎00 31 30 265 0650   Fax 00 31 30 262 0850
www.spectrum.nl

Founded 1935. Publishes science fiction, fantasy, literature, literary criticism, essays, mysteries, criminology, general non-fiction, computer science, dictionaries, encyclopedias, history, illustrated, astrology, occult, management, environmental studies, travel.

Springer Science+Business Media BV

Postbus 322, 3300 AH Dordrecht
☎00 31 78 657 6736

Formerly Kluwer Academic Publishers. Founded 1889. Publishes ebooks, CD-ROMs, databases and journals, medicine, nursing, dentistry, social sciences, sociology, technology.

Unieboek BV

Postbus 97, 3990 DB Houten
☎00 31 30 637 7660   Fax 00 31 30 637 7600
✉ info@unieboek.nl
www.unieboek.nl

Founded 1891. Publishes fiction, mysteries, romance, general non-fiction, children's, directories, reference, animals, architecture and interior design, childcare, crafts, hobbies, games, how-to, literature, literary criticism, essays, cookery, history, self-help, photography, travel, women's studies.

Uniepers BV

Postbus 69, 1390 AB Abcoude
☎00 31 29 428 5111   Fax 00 31 29 428 3013
✉ info@uniepers.nl
www.uniepers.nl

Founded 1961. Publishes (mostly in co-editions) antiques, anthropology, archaeology, architecture and interior design, art, dance, history, music, natural history, photography.

Norway

H. Aschehoug & Co (W. Nygaard) A/S

Postboks 363, Sentrum, N–0102 Oslo
☎00 47 22 400400
Fax 00 47 22 206395
✉ epost@aschehoug.no
www.aschehoug.no

Founded 1872. Publishes fiction and general non-fiction; juvenile and young adult; antiques, architecture and interior design, art, business, directories, economics, education, gardening, health and nutrition, how-to, language arts, linguistics, law, mathematics, philosophy, poetry, reference, general science, science fiction and fantasy, self-help, social sciences, sociology, textbooks, travel.

J.W. Cappelens Forlag A/S

Postboks 350, Sentrum, N–0101 Oslo
☎00 47 22 365000
Fax 00 47 22 365040
www.cappelen.no

Founded 1829. Publishes fiction, general non-fiction, maps and atlases, juvenile and young adult, dictionaries, directories, encyclopedias, reference, religion, textbooks.

N.W. Damm og Søn A/S

Fridtjof Nansenvei 14, N–0055 Oslo
☎00 47 24 051000   Fax 00 47 24 051290
www.damm.no

Founded 1845. Owned by the Egmont Group. Publishes general non-fiction, reference, dictionaries, encyclopedias and translated fiction.

Ex Libris Forlag A/S

Tordenskioldsgt 6B, N–0055 Oslo
☎00 47 22 471100   Fax 00 47 22 471149

Founded 1982. Publishes cookery, health, nutrition, humour, human relations, publishing and book trade reference.

Gyldendal Norsk Forlag A/S

Postboks 6860, St Olavs Plass, N–0130 Oslo
☎00 47 22 034100   Fax 00 47 22 034105
www.gyldendal.no

Founded 1925. Publishes fiction, science fiction, fantasy, art, dance, biography, children's, dictionaries, directories, encyclopedias, government, journals, political science, history, how-to, music, social sciences, sociology, poetry, philosophy, psychology, psychiatry, reference, religion, textbooks.

Tiden Norsk Forlag
Postboks 6704, St Olavs Plass, N–0130 Oslo
☎00 47 22 2332 7660
Fax 00 46 22 2332 7697
✉ tiden@tiden.no
www.tiden.no
Founded 1933. Publishes fiction, general nonfiction; essays, literature, literary criticism, science fiction, fantasy, directories, management, reference.

Portugal

Bertrand Editora Lda
Rua Anchieta 29–1, 1200 Lisbon
☎00 351 21 320084   Fax 00 351 21 3468286
Founded 1727. Publishes art, essays, literature, literary criticism, bilingual, dictionaries, encyclopedias, juvenile and young adult, social sciences, sociology.

Editorial Caminho SARL
Al Santo Antonio dos Capuchos 6B, 1100 Lisbon
☎00 351 1 3152683   Fax 00 351 1 534346
Founded 1977. Publishes fiction, government, political science, juvenile and young adult.

Livraria Civilização (Américo Fraga Lamares & Ca Lda)
Rua Dr Alberto Aires de Gouveia 27, 4000 Porto
☎00 351 22 0002286
Fax 00 351 22 312382
Founded 1921. Publishes fiction, art, economics, history, political science, government, sociology, social sciences, juvenile and young adult.

Publicações Dom Quixote Lda
Rua Luciano Cordeiro 116–2, 1098 Lisbon
☎00 351 21 538079   Fax 00 351 21 574595
Founded 1965. Publishes fiction, poetry, children's, directories, education, history, philosophy, reference, general science, social sciences, sociology.

Publicações Europa-América Lda
Estrada Lisboa-Sintra, Km 14, 2725 Mem Martins
☎00 351 21 921 1461
Fax 00 351 21 921 7846
Founded 1945. Publishes fiction, poetry, art, biography, children's, dance, directories, education, general engineering, history, how-to, music, philosophy, medicine, nursing, dentistry, psychology, psychiatry, reference, general science, social sciences, sociology, technology, textbooks.

Gradiva–Publicações Lda
Rua Almeida e Sousa 21–r/c Esq, 1399–041 Lisbon
☎00 351 1 3974067   Fax 00 351 1 3953471
www.gravida.pt
Founded 1981. Publishes fiction, literature, literary criticism, essays, science fiction, fantasy, romance, anthropology, Asian studies, astronomy, behavioural sciences, biological science, children's, communications, computer science, crafts, directories, earth sciences, education, games, hobbies, economics, general engineering, geography, geology, government, political studies, journalism, natural history, history, humour, environmental studies, human relations, illustrated, management, mathematics, philosophy, general science, physics, psychology, psychiatry, reference, self-help, social sciences, sociology, translations.

Livros Horizonte Lda
Rua Chagas 17 - 1 Dto, 1200 Lisbon
☎00 351 1 3466917   Fax 00 351 1 3326921
Founded 1953. Publishes art, children's, education, history, psychology, psychiatry, social sciences, sociology, textbooks.

Editorial Verbo SA
Av Antonio Augusto de Aguiar 148–6, 1069–019 Lisbon
☎00 351 21 380 2131
Fax 00 351 21 386 1122
www.editorialverbo.pt
Founded 1959. Publishes dictionaries, education, encyclopedias, history, general science, juvenile and young adult.

Spain

Alianza Editorial SA
Juan Ignacio Luca de Tena 15, 28027 Madrid
☎00 349 1 393 8888   Fax 00 349 1 320 7480
www.alianzaeditorial.es
Founded 1966. Publishes fiction, poetry, art, history, mathematics, dance, music, philosophy, government, political science, social sciences, sociology, general science.

Ediciones Anaya SA
Juan Ignacio Luca de Tena 15, 28027 Madrid
☎00 349 1 393 8600   Fax 00 349 1 742 6631
www.anaya.es
Founded 1959. Publishes education.

EDHASA (Editora y Distribuidora Hispano – Americana SA)
Av Diagonal 519–521, 2 piso, 08029 Barcelona
☎00 349 3 494 9720   Fax 00 349 3 419 4584
✉ info@edhasa.es
www.edhasa.es
Founded 1946. Publishes fiction, literature, literary criticism, essays, history.

Editorial Espasa–Calpe SA
Apdo de correos 547, Carreterade Irún Km 12, 200, 28049 Madrid
☎00 349 1 358 9689   Fax 00 349 1 358 9364
www.espasa.com
Founded 1925. Publishes fiction, science fiction, fantasy, English as a second language, general non-fiction, academic, art, children's, child care and development, cookery, biography, essays, history, literature, literary criticism, self-help, social sciences, sociology, CD-ROMs, dictionaries, encyclopedias, reference, maps and atlases.

Grijalbo Mondadori SA
Arago 385, 08013 Barcelona
☎00 349 3 476 7110   Fax 00 349 3 476 7121
www.grijalbo.com
Founded 1962. Publishes fiction, general non-fiction, architecture and interior design, children's, dictionaries, directories, encyclopedias, gardening, plants, humour, literature, literary criticism, essays, poetry, human relations, reference.

Grupo Editorial CEAC SA
Paseig Manel Girona, 71 Baixos, 08034 Barcelona
☎00 349 3 247 2424   Fax 00 349 3 231 5115
www.editorialceac.com
Founded 1957. Publishes children's, education, technology, young adult, science fiction, fantasy.

Ediciónes Hiperión SL
Calle Salustiano Olózaga 14, 28001 Madrid
☎00 349 1 557 6015   Fax 00 349 1 435 8690
✉ info@hiperion.com
www.hiperion.com
Founded 1976. Publishes literature, literary criticism, essays, poetry, bilingual, language arts and linguistics, children's, religion (Islamic and Jewish), translations.

Editorial Luis Vives (Edelvives)
63a Feria del Libro, 28034 Madrid
☎00 349 1 334 4883   Fax 00 349 1 334 4893
Founded 1890. Publishes education.

Editorial Molino
Calabria 166, 08015 Barcelona
☎00 349 3 226 0625   Fax 00 349 3 226 6998
www.editorialmolino.com
Founded 1933. Publishes children's, education, mysteries, sport, fiction.

Pearson Educacion SA
Nunez de Balboa 120, 28006 Madrid
☎00 349 1 590 3432   Fax 00 349 1 590 3448
Founded 1942. Publishes art, children's, education, history, language arts, linguistics, medicine, nursing, dentistry, general science, psychology, psychiatry, philosophy, textbooks.

Editorial Planeta SA
Edifici Planeta Diagonal 662–664, 08034 Barcelona
☎00 349 3 228 5800   Fax 00 349 3 217 7140
www.planeta.es
Founded 1952. Publishes fiction and general non-fiction.

Editorial Seix Barral SA
Avda Diagonal 662–664, 7a, 08034 Barcelona
☎00 349 3 496 7003   Fax 00 349 3 496 7004
✉ editorial@seix-barral.es
www.seix-barral.es
Founded 1911. Part of Grupo Planeta. Foreign language publisher of literature.

Tusquets Editores
Cesare Cantù 8, 08017 Barcelona
☎00 349 3 253 0400   Fax 00 349 3 417 6703
✉ general@tusquets-editores.com
www.tusquets-editores.com
Founded 1969. Publishes fiction, biography, history, essays, literature, literary criticism, general science.

Sweden

Albert Bonniers Förlag
PO Box 3159, S-103 63 Stockholm
☎00 46 8 696 8620   Fax 00 46 8 696 8369
www.albertbonniersforlag.com
Founded 1837. Publishes fiction and general non-fiction.

Bokförlaget Bra Böcker AB
PO Box 890, S-20180 Malmo
☎00 46 40 665 4600   Fax 00 46 40 665 4622
www.bbb.se
Founded 1965. Publishes fiction, dictionaries, encyclopedias, geography, geology, history, illustrated.

Brombergs Bokförlag AB
PO Box 12886, S-112 98 Stockholm
☎00 46 8 5626 2080
Fax 00 46 8 5626 2085
✉ info@brombergs.se
www.brombergs.se
Founded 1973. Publishes fiction and general non-fiction.

Bokförlaget Forum AB
PO Box 70321, S-107 23 Stockholm
☎00 46 8 696 8440   Fax 00 46 8 696 8367
Founded 1944. Publishes fiction and general non-fiction.

Bokförlaget Natur och Kultur
PO Box 27323, S-102 54 Stockholm
☎00 46 8 453 8600   Fax 00 46 8 453 8790
✉ info@nok.se
www.nok.se
Founded 1922. Publishes fiction and general non-fiction; biography, children's, dictionaries, encyclopedias, history, psychology, psychiatry and general science, social sciences and sociology, textbooks.

Norstedts Förlag
Box 2052, S-103 12 Stockholm
☎00 46 8 769 8850   Fax 00 46 8 769 8864
www.norstedt.se
Founded 1823. Publishes fiction and general non-fiction.

Rabén och Sjögren Bokförlag
PO Box 2052, S-103 12 Stockholm
☎00 46 8 769 8800   Fax 00 46 8 769 8813
www.raben.se
Founded 1942. Publishes general non-fiction and children's books.

Richters Egmont
Sallerupsvaegen 9, 205 75 Malmö
☎00 46 40 380600   Fax 00 46 40 933708
✉ egmont@egmont.com
www.egmont.com
Founded 1942. Publishes fiction and non-fiction; children's, dictionaries, directories, reference.

B. Wählströms
PO Box 30022, S-104 25 Stockholm
☎00 46 8 6198600   Fax 00 46 8 6189761
✉ info@wahlstroms.se
www.wahlstroms.se
Founded 1911. Publishes fiction and general non-fiction, juvenile and young adult.

Switzerland

Arche Verlag AG
Niederdorfstr 90, CH-8001 Zurich
☎00 41 1 2522410   Fax 00 41 1 2611115
✉ info@arche-verlag.com
www.arche-verlag.com
Founded 1944. Publishes literature and literary criticism, essays, biography, fiction, poetry, music, dance, travel.

Diogenes Verlag AG
Sprecherstr 8, CH-8032 Zurich
☎00 41 1 2548511   Fax 00 41 1 2528407
✉ info@diogenes.ch
www.diogenes.ch
Founded 1952. Publishes fiction, essays, literature, literary criticism, illustrated, mysteries, art, children's, drama, theatre, philosophy.

Langenscheidt AG Zürich-Zug
Postfach 326, CH-8021 Zurich
☎00 41 1 2115000   Fax 00 41 1 2122149
Part of **Langenscheidt Group**, Germany. Publishes language arts and linguistics.

Larousse (Suisse) SA
c/o Acces-Direct, 3 Route du Grand-Mont, CH-1052 Le Mont-sur-Lausanne
☎00 41 21 335336
Publishes dictionaries, directories, encyclopedias, reference and textbooks. Part of **Librairie Larousse**, France.

Neptun-Verlag
Postfach 1220, CH-8280 Kreuzlingen
☎00 41 71 6779655   Fax 00 41 72 6779650
www.neptunart.ch
Founded 1946. Publishes children's, history and travel.

Orell Füssli Verlag
Dietzingerstr 3, CH-8036 Zurich
☎00 41 1 466 7711   Fax 00 41 1 466 7412
✉ info@ofv.ch
www.ofv.ch

Founded 1519. Publishes accountancy, art, biography, business, children's, economics, education, geography, geology, history, how-to, illustrated, law.

Editions Payot Lausanne

CP 529, CH-1001 Lausanne
☎00 41 21 329 0264
Fax 00 41 21 329 0266

Founded 1875. Publishes general non-fiction, anthropology, archaeology, architecture and interior design, dance, history, law, medicine, nursing, dentistry, music, philosophy, literature, literary criticism, essays, scholarly, general science, social sciences and sociology, textbooks.

Sauerländer AG

Ausserfeldstr. 9, CH-5036 Oberentfelden
☎00 41 64 2836 8686
Fax 00 41 64 2836 8620
✉ verlag@sauerlaender.ch
www.sauerlaender.ch

Founded 1807. Publishes education and general non-fiction.

Scherz Verlag AG

Postfach 850, CH-3000 Berne 7
☎00 41 31 3277117   Fax 00 41 31 3277171
✉ scherz@scherzverlag.ch

Founded 1938. Publishes biography, history, psychology, psychiatry, philosophy, parapsychology.

European Television Companies

Austria

ORF (Österreichisher Rundfunk)
Würzburggasse 30, A–1136 Vienna
☎00 43 1 87 8780   Fax 00 43 1 87 8782550
www.orf.at

Belgium

Radio-Télévision Belge de la Communauté Française (RTBF)
Boulevard Auguste Reyers 52, B–1044 Brussels
☎00 32 2 737 2111   Fax 00 32 2 737 2936
www.rtbf.be

Vlaamse Radio en Televisieomroep (VRT)
Omroepcentrum, Reyerslaan 52, B–1043 Brussels
☎00 32 2 741 3111   Fax 00 32 2 739 9351
www.vrt.be

Vlaamse Televisie Maatschappij (VTM) (cable)
Medialaan 1, B–1800 Vilvoorde
☎00 32 2 255 3211   Fax 00 32 2 252 5141
✉ info@vtm.be   www.vtm.be

Denmark

Danmarks Radio–TV
TV-Byen, DK–2860 Søborg
☎00 45 35 20 3040   Fax 00 45 35 20 2644
✉ dr@dr.dk   www.dr.dk

TV Danmark
Mileparken 20A, DK–2740 Skovlunde
☎00 45 70 10 1010   Fax 00 45 70 10 1002
✉ info@tvdanmark.dk   www.tvdanmark.dk

TV–2 Danmark
Rugaardsvej 25, DK–5100 Odense C
☎00 45 65 91 9191   Fax 00 45 65 91 3322
✉ tv2@tv2.dk   www.tv2.dk

Finland

MTV3 Finland
Ilmalantori 2, FIN–00240 Helsinki

☎00 358 9 15001   Fax 00 358 9 1500707
www.mtv3.fi

Yleisradio Oy (YLE)
PO Box 90, FIN–00024 Yleisradio
☎00 358 9 14801   Fax 00 358 9 14803215
www.yle.fi

France

Arte France (cable & satellite)
8 rue Marceau, 92785 Issy les Moulineaux Cedex 9
☎00 33 1 55 00 77 77
Fax 00 33 1 55 00 77 00
www.artefrance.fr

Canal + (pay TV)
85–89 quai André Citroën, 75711 Paris Cedex 15
☎00 33 1 44 25 10 00   www.cplus.fr

France 5
10–12 rue Horace-Vernet, 92785 Issy-les-Moulineaux Cedex 9
☎00 33 1 56 22 91 91
Fax 00 33 1 56 22 95 95   www.france5.fr

France Télévision (France 2/France 3)
7 Esplanade Henri de France, 75907 Paris Cedex 15
☎00 33 1 56 22 42 42(France 2)/30 30 (France 3)
www.france2.fr and www.france3.fr

M6 (Métropole Télévision)
89 ave Charles de Gaulle, 92575 Neuilly-sur-Seine Cedex
☎00 33 1 41 92 66 66
Fax 00 33 1 41 92 66 10   www.m6.fr

RFO (Radio Télévision Française d'Outre-mer)
5 ave du Recteur Poincaré, 75016 Paris
☎00 33 1 42 15 71 00   www.rfo.fr

TF1 (Télévision Française 1)
1 quai du Pont du Jour, 92656 Boulogne

☎00 33 1 41 41 12 34
Fax 00 33 1 41 41 28 40   www.tf1.fr

Germany

ARD – Das Erste
ARD Büro, Bertramstr 8, 60320 Frankfurt
am Main
☎00 49 69 59 0607   Fax 00 49 69 15 52075
www.daserste.de

Arte Germany (cable & satellite)
Postfach 10 02 13, 76530 Baden-Baden
☎00 49 7221 93690
Fax 00 49 7221 936970   www.arte.de

ZDF (Zweites Deutsches Fernsehen)
Postfach 40 40, 55100 Mainz
☎00 49 61 31/701   Fax 00 49 61 31 702157
www.zdf.de

Republic of Ireland

Radio Telefís Éireann (RTE – RTE 1)
Donnybrook, Dublin 4
☎00 353 1 208 3111   Fax 00 353 1 208 3080
www.rte.ie

Teilefís na Gaelige
Baile na hAbhann, Co. na Gaillimhe
☎00 353 91 505050   Fax 00 353 91 505021
www.tg4.ie

Italy

RAI (RadioTelevisione Italiana)
Viale Mazzini 14, 00195 Rome
☎00 39 06 3878-1   Fax 00 39 06 372 5680
www.rai.it

The Netherlands

AVRO (Algemene Omroep Vereniging)
Postbus 2, 1200 JA Hilversum
☎00 31 35 671 79 11
Fax 00 31 35 671 74 39
www.central.avro.nl/index.asp

IKON
Postbus 10009, 1201 DA Hilversum
☎00 31 35 672 72 72
Fax 00 31 35 621 51 00   ✉ ikon@ikon.nl
www.omroep.nl/ikon

NCRV (Nederlandse Christelijke Radio Vereniging)
Postbus 25000, 1202 HB Hilversum
☎00 31 35 671 99 11
Fax 00 31 35 671 92 85   info.omroep.nl/ncrv

NOS (Nederlandse Omroep Stichting)
Sumatralaan 45, 1217 GP Hilversum
☎00 31 35 677 92 22
Fax 00 31 35 677 4863   www.nos.nl

NPS (Nederlandse Programma Stichting)
Postbus 29000, 1202 MA Hilversum
☎00 31 35 677 9333
Fax 00 31 35 677 4959   www.omroep.nl/nps

VARA
Postbus 175, 1200 AD Hilversum
☎00 31 35 671 19 11
Fax 00 31 35 671 13 40   www.omroep.nl/vara

VPRO
Postbus 11, 1200 JC Hilversum
☎00 31 35 671 29 11
Fax 00 31 35 671 21 00   ✉ info@vpro.nl
www.vpro.nl

Norway

NRK (Norsk Rikskringkasting),
N–0340 Oslo
☎00 47 23 04 7000   Fax 00 47 23 04 7575
✉ info@nrk.no   www.nrk.no

TVNorge
Postboks 11, Sentrum, N–0101 Oslo
☎00 47 21 02 2000   Fax 00 47 22 05 1000
✉ tvnorge@tvnorge.no   www.tvnorge.no

TV2
Postboks 7222, N–5020 Bergen
☎00 47 55 90 8070   ✉ info@tv2.no
www.tv2.no

Portugal

Radiotelevisão Portuguesa (RTP)
Avenida Marechal, Gomes da Costa 37,
1849–030 Lisbon
☎00 351 21 794 7000   www.rtp.pt

TVI (Televisão Independente)
Rua Mário Castelhano 40, Queluz de Baixo,
2734–502 Barcarena

☎00 351 21 434 7500
Fax 00 351 21 434 7654   www.tvi.pt

Spain

RTVE (RadioTelevision Española)
Edificio Prado del Rey, E–28223 Madrid
☎00 349 1 581 7000   www.rtve.es

Sweden

Sveriges Television AB–SVT
Oxenstierngatan 26–34, S–105 10 Stockholm
☎00 46 8 784 0000   Fax 00 46 8 784 1500
www.svt.se

TV4
Tegeluddsvägen 3, S–115 79 Stockholm
☎00 46 8 459 4000   Fax 00 46 8 459 4444
www.tv4.se

Switzerland

RTR (Radio e Televisiun Rumantscha) (Romansch language TV)
Via dal Teater 1, CH–7002 Cuira

☎00 41 81 255 7575   Fax 00 41 81 255 7500
✉ contact@rtr.ch   www.rtr.ch

RTSI (Radiotelevisione svizzera di lingua Italiana) (Italian language TV)
Casella postale, CH–6903 Lugano
☎00 41 91 803 51 11
Fax 00 41 91 803 53 55   ✉ info@rtsi.ch
www.rtsi.ch

SF DRS (Schweizer Fernsehen)
(German language TV)
Postfach, CH–8052 Zurich
☎00 41 1 305 66 11   Fax 00 41 1 305 56 60
✉ sfdrs@sfdrs   www.sfdrs.ch

SRG SSR idée suisse (Swiss Broadcasting Corp.)
Postfach 26, CH–3000 Berne15
☎00 41 31 350 91 11
Fax 00 41 31 350 92 56   www.srg-ssr.ch

TSR (Télévision Suisse Romande)
Quai Ernest Ansermet 20, CH–1211 Geneva 8
☎00 41 22 708 20 20
Fax 00 41 22 708 98 00   www.tsr.ch

US Publishers

Anyone corresponding with the big American publishers should know that following the terrorist attacks of 2001 they are wary of any package or letter that looks in any way suspicious. This, of course, begs the question what is or what is not suspicious which is as difficult to answer as what makes or does not make a good novel. The best policy is to make an initial enquiry by email.

International Reply Coupons (IRCs)
For return postage, send IRCs, available from post offices. Letters, 60 pence; mss according to weight. For current postal rates to the UK, go to the United States Postal Service website at www.usps.com and click on 'Calculate Postage'.

ABC–CLIO
PO Box 1911, Santa Barbara, CA 93116–1911
☎001 805 968 1911   Fax 001 805 685 9685
✉ sales@abc-clio.com
www.abc-clio.com
CEO *Ronald J. Boehm*

Founded 1953. Publishes academic and reference, focusing on history and social studies; books and multimedia. UK SUBSIDIARY **ABC-Clio Ltd**, Oxford. No unsolicited mss; synopses and ideas welcome.
ROYALTIES annually.

Abingdon Press
PO Box 801, Nashville, TN 37202–0801
☎001 615 749 6290   Fax 001 615 749 6056
www.abingdonpress.com
Snr. VP/Editorial Director *Harriett Jane Olson*

Founded 1789. Publishes non-fiction: religious (Protestant), reference, professional and academic texts. Over 100 titles a year.

Harry N. Abrams, Inc.
100 Fifth Avenue, New York, NY 10011
☎001 212 206 7715   Fax 001 212 645 8437
www.abramsbooks.com
VP/Editor-in-Chief *Eric Himmel*

Founded 1950. Publishes illustrated books: art, natural history, photography. No fiction. About 200 titles a year.

Academy Chicago Publishers
363 W. Erie Street, Chicago, IL 60610
☎001 312 751 7300   Fax 001 312 751 7306
✉ info@academychicago.com
www.academychicago.com
President & Senior Editor *Anita Miller*

Founded 1975. Publishes mainstream fiction; non-fiction: art, history, mysteries. No romance, children's, young adult, religious, sexist or avant-garde.
ROYALTIES twice-yearly.

Access
See **HarperCollins Publishers, Inc.**

Ace
See **Penguin Group (USA) Inc.**

Addison Wesley
75 Arlington Street, Suite 300, Boston, MA 02116
☎001 617 848 7500   Fax 001 617 848 6016
✉ firstname.lastname@pearsoned.com
www.aw-bc.com

A division of Pearson Education. Publishes academic textbooks, multimedia and learning programs in computer science, economics, finance, mathematics and statistics. See the website for submission guidelines.

University of Alabama Press
Box 870380, Tuscaloosa, AL 35487–0380
☎001 205 348 5180   Fax 001 205 348 9201
Director *Daniel J.J. Ross*

Founded 1945. Publishes American history, Latin American history, American religious history; African-American and Native American studies, Judaic studies, archaeology, anthropology, enthnohistory and American letters.

About 60 titles a year. Submissions are not invited in poetry, fiction or drama.

Aladdin Books
See **Simon & Schuster Children's Publishing**

University of Alaska Press
PO Box 756240, University of Alaska, Fairbanks, AK 99775–6240
☎001 907 474 5831   Fax 001 907 474 5502
✉ fypress@uaf.edu
www.uaf.edu/uapress
Executive Editor *Jennifer Collier*
Acquisitions *Erica Hill*

Publishes scholarly works about Alaska and the North Pacific rim, with a special emphasis on circumpolar regions, history, anthropology, natural history. No fiction or poetry.
DIVISIONS **Rasmuson Library Historical Translation Series; Oral Biography Series; Classic Reprint Series** Informal non-fiction covering Northern interest. 10 titles a year. Queries and proposals welcome.

Alyson Books
PO Box 4371, Los Angeles, CA 90078
☎001 323 860 6065   Fax 001 323 467 0152
✉ mail@alyson.com
www.alyson.com
Publisher *Greg Constante*
Editor-in-Chief *Angela Brown*

Founded 1980. Publishes fiction and non-fiction books of general interest to the gay and lesbian community. No unsolicited mss. Synopses and ideas for books welcome; initial contact by mail or e-mail.
ROYALTIES twice-yearly.

AMACOM Books
1601 Broadway, New York, NY 10019–7406
☎001 212 586 8100   Fax 001 212 903 8168
www.amanet.org
President & Publisher *Harold V. Kennedy*

Founded 1972. Owned by American Management Association. Publishes business books only, including general management, business communications, sales and marketing, finance, computers and information systems, human resource management and training, career/personal growth skills. About 80 titles a year.

Amistad
See **HarperCollins Publishers, Inc.**

Anchor Books
See **Doubleday Broadway Publishing Group**

Anvil
See **Krieger Publishing Co.**

Shaye Areheart Books
See **Crown Publishing Group**

University of Arizona Press
355 S. Euclid Avenue, Suite. 103, Tucson, AZ 85719–6654
☎001 520 621 1441   Fax 001 520 621 8899
✉ uapress@uapress.arizona.edu
www.uapress.arizona.edu
Director & Editor-in-Chief *Christine Szuter*

Founded 1959. Publishes academic non-fiction, particularly with a regional/cultural link, plus Native-American and Hispanic literature. About 50 titles a year.

University of Arkansas Press
McIlroy House, 201 Ozark Avenue, Fayetteville, AR 72701
☎001 479 575 3246
Fax 001 479 575 6044
www.uapress.com
Director *Lawrence J. Malley*

Founded 1980. Publishes scholarly monographs, poetry and general trade books. Particularly interested in scholarly works in history, politics and literary criticism. About 30 titles a year.
ROYALTIES annually.

ASM Press
1752 N. Street NW, Washington, DC 20036–2904
☎001 202 737 3600
Fax 001 202 942 9342
✉ books@asmusa.org
www.asmpress.org
Director *Jeffrey Holtmeier*

Founded 1899. The book publishing division of the American Society for Microbiology. Publishes monographs, texts, reference books and manuals in microbiological sciences.

Aspect
See **Warner Books Inc.**

Atheneum Books for Young Readers
See **Simon & Schuster Children's Publishing**

Atlantic Monthly Press
See **Grove/Atlantic Inc.**

Atria Books
See **Simon & Schuster Adult Publishing Group**

Avalon Publishing Group
1400 65th Street, Suite 250, Emeryville, CA 94608
www.avalonpub.com
Also at: 245 West 17th Street, 11th floor, New York, NY 10011–5300
Chairman *Charlie Winton*

Founded 1994. Leading independent publisher of fiction and non-fiction; current affairs, history, politics, psychology, self-help, health, science, women's studies, gay and lesbian, travel, music, mystery and popular culture.

DIVISIONS
Avalon Publishing Group California IMPRINTS **Avalon Travel Publishing** (guide books); **Seal Press** (books by and about women); **Shoemaker & Hoard Publishers** (literature, fiction, history, biography); **Avalon Publishing Group New York** IMPRINTS **Carroll & Graf Publishers** (history, current affairs, literature, fiction, mystery); **Thunder's Mouth Press** (current affairs, popular culture, film, music, fiction, science); **Nation Books** (current world affairs, politics, cultural studies); **Marlowe & Company** (psychology, self-help, health). 438 titles in 2004. No unsolicited material.

Avery
375 Hudson Street, New York, NY 10014
☎001 212 366 2000   Fax 001 212 366 2738
www.penguinputnam.com
Publisher *Megan Newman*

Founded 1976. Imprint of **Penguin Group (USA) Inc.** Publishes alternative and complementary health care, nutrition, disease prevention, diet, supplements, functional foods, mind/body therapies, holistic healing. About 30 titles a year. No unsolicited mss; synopses and ideas welcome if accompanied by s.a.e./IRCs.
ROYALTIES twice-yearly.

Avon
See **HarperCollins Publishers, Inc.**

Baker Publishing Group
PO Box 6287, Grand Rapids, MI 49516–6287
☎001 616 676 9185   Fax 001 616 676 9573
www.bakerpublishinggroup.com

President *Dwight Baker*

Founded 1939. Began life as a used-book store and began publishing in earnest in the 1950s, primarily serving the evangelical Christian market. Additional information for authors on website.

DIVISIONS/IMPRINTS
Baker Books Publishes religious non-fiction and fiction, Bible reference, professional (pastors and church leaders) books, children's books. About 80 titles a year. No unsolicited proposals.
Baker Academic *Jim Kinney* Publishes college/seminary textbooks, religious reference books, biblical studies monographs. About 45 titles a year. No unsolicited proposals.
Revell *Lonnie Hull Du Pont* Founded 1870. Publishes adult fiction and non-fiction for evangelical Christians. About 75 titles a year. No unsolicited proposals.
Brazos Press *Rodney Clapp* Publishes academic and trade books in theology, biblical studies, ethics, cultural criticism and spirituality (trade editions only). About 20 titles a year. No unsolicited mss.
Chosen *Jane Campbell* Founded 1971; joined Baker Book House in 1992. Publishes charismatic adult non-fiction for evangelical Christians. About 30 titles a year. No unsolicited proposals.

Ballantine Books
See **Random House Publishing Group**

Banner Books
See **University Press of Mississippi**

Bantam Dell Publishing Group
1745 Broadway, New York, NY 10019
☎001 212 782 9000   Fax 001 212 302 7985
www.randomhouse.com/bantamdell
President & Publisher *Irwyn Applebaum*

Founded 1945. The largest mass market paperback publisher in the USA. A division of the **Random House Publishing Group.** Publishes general commercial fiction and non-fiction, young readers and children's: mysteries, science fiction and fantasy, romance, health and nutrition, self-help. DIVISIONS/IMPRINTS **Dell**; **Bantam Classics; Delacorte Press; Delta Books; Dial Press**.

Barron's Educational Series, Inc.
250 Wireless Boulevard, Hauppauge, NY 11788–3917
☎001 631 434 3311   Fax 001 631 434 3723
✉ waynebarr@barronseduc.com

www.barronseduc.com
Chairman/CEO *Manuel H. Barron*
President *Ellen Sibley*
Acquisitions Editor *Wayne Barr*
Founded 1942. *Publishes* adult non-fiction, children's fiction and non-fiction, test preparation materials and language materials, cookbooks, pets, hobbies, sport, photography, health, business, law, computers, travel, business, art and painting. No adult fiction. 400 titles a year. Unsolicited mss, synopses and ideas for books welcome.
ROYALTIES twice-yearly.

Basic Books
See **Perseus Books Group**

Beacon Press
25 Beacon Street, Boston, MA 02108
☎001 617 742 2110   Fax 001 617 723 3097
www.beacon.org
Director *Helene Atwan*
Founded 1854. Publishes general non-fiction. About 60 titles a year. Does not accept unsolicited mss. For further information, refer to website page.

Belknap Press
See **Harvard University Press**

Berkley
See **Penguin Group (USA) Inc.**

Bison Books
See **University of Nebraska Press**

Blackbird Press
See **Thomson Gale**

Blackwell Publishing
2121 State Avenue, Ames, IA 50014
☎001 515 292 0140   Fax 001 515 292 3348
✉ acquisitions@blackwellprofessional.com
www.blackwellprofessional.com
Publishing Director *Antonia Seymour*
Formerly Iowa State Press. Founded 1934 as an offshoot of the Iowa State University's journalism department. Publishes reference books and textbooks on food science, human dentistry, aquaculture, agriculture, animal science and veterinary medicine. No fiction, trade books or poetry.
ROYALTIES annually.

H.&R. Block
See **Simon & Schuster Adult Publishing Group**

Boyds Mills Press
815 Church Street, Honesdale, PA 18431
☎001 570 253 1164   Fax 001 570 253 0179
www.boydsmillspress.com
Publisher *Kent Brown*
A subsidiary of Highlights for Children, Inc. Founded 1990 as a publisher of children's trade books. Publishes children's and young adult's fiction, non-fiction and poetry. About 60 titles a year.

Brassey's, Inc.
See **Potomac Books, Inc.**

Brazos Press
See **Baker Publishing Group**

Broadway Books
See **Doubleday Broadway Publishing Group**

Caedmon
See **HarperCollins Publishers, Inc.**

University of California Press
2120 Berkeley Way, Berkeley, CA 94720
☎001 510 642 4247   Fax 001 510 643 7127
✉ askucp@ucpress.edu
www.ucpress.edu
Director *Lynne Withey*
Founded 1893. Publishes scholarly and scientific non-fiction; some fiction in translation. Preliminary letter with outline preferred.

Canongate US
See **Grove/Atlantic Inc.**

Carolrhoda Books, Inc.
241 First Avenue N, Minneapolis, MN 55401
☎001 612 332 3344   Fax 001 612 332 7615
www.lernerbooks.com
VP & Editor-in-Chief *Mary M. Rodgers*
Founded 1969. A division of the **Lerner Publishing Group**. Publishes: animals, biography, earth sciences, ethnology, history, geography, geology, general science, historical fiction and picture books. Please send s.a.e. for author guidelines, making sure guideline requests are clearly marked on the envelope or they will be returned. 'We are *only* accepting submissions once a year – November 1st–30th only. Submissions postmarked with other dates will be returned unopened. Also, only submissions with s.a.e./IRCs will receive a response.'

Carroll & Graf Publishers
See **Avalon Publishing Group**

Charlesbridge Publishing
85 Main Street, Watertown, MA 02472
☎001 617 926 0329   Fax 001 617 926 5720
✉ books@charlesbridge.com
www.charlesbridge.com
President/Publisher *Brent Farmer*
Vice President, School Division *Elena Dworkin Wright*
Founded 1980 as an educational publisher focused on a strategic approach to reading, writing, maths and science. Publishes children's educational programmes, non-fiction picture books and fiction for 3 to 12-year-olds. School division publishes mathematical fiction, *Maths Adventures*, in picture-book format and astronomy-related picture books.

University of Chicago Press
1427 East 60th Street, Chicago, IL 60637
☎001 773 702 7700   Fax 001 773 702 9756
www.press.uchicago.edu
Founded 1891. Publishes academic non-fiction only.

Children's Press
See **Scholastic Library Publishing**

Chosen
See **Baker Publishing Group**

Chronicle Books LLC
85 Second Street, Sixth Floor, San Francisco, CA 94105
☎001 415 537 4200   Fax 001 415 437 4460
✉ frontdesk@chroniclebooks.com
www.chroniclebooks.com
President/Publisher *Jack Jensen*
Founded 1966. Publishes illustrated and non-illustrated adult trade and children's books as well as stationery and gift items. About 400 titles a year. Query or submit outline/synopsis and sample chapters and artwork. Guidelines for ms submissions on the website.
ROYALTIES twice-yearly.

Clarkson Potter
See **Crown Publishing Group**

Columbia University Press
61 West 62nd Street, New York, NY 10023
☎001 212 459 0600   Fax 001 212 459 3679
www.columbia.edu/cu/cup
Managing Director *James D. Jordan*

Editorial Director *Jennifer Crewe*
Founded 1893. Publishes scholarly and general interest non-fiction, reference, translations of Asian literature. No fiction or poetry. Welcomes unsolicited material if the subject fits their programme (see website). Approach by regular mail only.

Joanna Cotler Books
See **HarperCollins Publishers, Inc.**

Counterpoint Press
See **Perseus Books Group**

Crocodile Books, USA
See **Interlink Publishing Group, Inc.**

Crown Publishing Group
1745 Broadway, New York, NY 10019
☎001 212 782 9000   Fax 001 212 940 7408
www.randomhouse.com/crown
Founded 1933. Division of the **Random House Publishing Group**. Publishes popular trade fiction and non-fiction. IMPRINTS **Clarkson Potter** Illustrated books: cookery, gardening, style, decorating and design; **Crown Business** *Steve Ross* Business books; **Crown** *Steve Ross* General fiction and non-fiction; **Harmony Books** *Shaye Areheart* New Age, spirituality, religion, some fiction; **Shaye Areheart Books** *Shaye Areheart* Fiction; **Three Rivers Press** *Steve Ross* Non-fiction paperbacks.

Cumberland House Publishing
431 Harding Industrial Drive, Nashville, TN 37211
☎001 615 832 1171   Fax 001 615 832 0633
✉ information@cumberlandhouse.com
www.cumberlandhouse.com
Founded 1996. Publishes general non-fiction, humour, travel cookery and sports.

Currency
See **Doubleday Broadway Publishing Group**

Da Capo Press
See **Perseus Books Group**

Dark Alley
See **HarperCollins Publishers, Inc.**

DAW Books, Inc.
375 Hudson Street, 3rd Floor, New York, NY 10014–3658
☎001 212 366 2096/Submissions: 366 2095

Fax 001 212 366 2090
daw@penguingroup.com
www.dawbooks.com

Publishers *Elizabeth R. Wollheim, Sheila E. Gilbert*
Submissions Editor *Peter Stampfel*

Founded 1971 by Donald and Elsie Wollheim as the first mass-market publisher devoted to science fiction and fantasy. An imprint of **Penguin Group (USA) Inc.** Publishes science fiction/fantasy, and some horror. No short stories, anthology ideas or non-fiction. Unsolicited mss, synopses and ideas for books welcome. About 36 titles a year. ROYALTIES twice-yearly.

DD Equestrian Library
See **Doubleday Broadway Publishing Group**

Dearborn Trade Publishing
30 S. Wacker Drive, Chicago, IL 60606–1719
☎001 312 836 4400   Fax 001 312 836 1021
contactus@dearborn.com
www.dearborn.com

President *Roy Lipner*

Founded 1967. Publishes professional, textbooks, finance, law, business, marketing and investment reference for the consumer (personal finance, real estate) and small business owner. About 200 titles a year.

Del Rey
See **Random House Publishing Group**

Delacorte Press
See **Bantam Dell Publishing Group**

Dell
See **Bantam Dell Publishing Group**

Delta Books
See **Bantam Dell Publishing Group**

Dial Books for Young Readers
345 Hudson Street, New York, NY 10014–3657
☎001 212 366 2800

Queries *Submissions Coordinator*

Founded 1961. A division of Penguin Books for Young Readers. Publishes children's books, including picture books, beginning readers, fiction and non-fiction for middle grade and young adults. IMPRINTS Hardcover only: **Dial Books for Young Readers; Dial Easy-to-Read.** 50 titles a year. Accepts unsolicited picture book mss and up to ten pages for longer works with query letter. ROYALTIES twice-yearly.

Dial Press
See **Bantam Dell Publishing Group**

Doubleday Broadway Publishing Group
1745 Broadway, New York, NY 10019
☎001 212 782 9000   Fax 001 212 302 7985
www.randomhouse.com

President & Publisher *Stephen Rubin*

The Doubleday Broadway Publishing Group, a division of the **Random House Publishing Group**, was formed by a merger of Doubleday and Broadway Books in 1999. Publishes fiction and non-fiction. DIVISION/IMPRINTS **The Anchor Bible; Anchor Books; Currency; DD Equestrian Library; Galilee Books; Image Books; Made Simple Books; Main Street/Back List; New Jerusalem Bible; Nan A. Talese Books; Outdoor Bible Series.** No unsolicited material.

Downtown Press
See **Simon & Schuster Adult Publishing Group**

Lisa Drew Books
See **Simon & Schuster Adult Publishing Group**

Thomas Dunne Books
See **St Martin's Press LLC**

Sanford J. Durst Publications
106 Woodcleft Avenue, Freeport, NY 11520
☎001 516 867 3333   Fax 001 516 867 3397

Owner *Sanford J. Durst*

Founded 1975. Publishes non-fiction: numismatic and related, philatelic, legal, classical history and art. Also children's books. About 12 titles a year. ROYALTIES twice-yearly.

Dutton/Dutton's Children's Books
See **Penguin Group (USA) Inc.**

Ecco
See **HarperCollins Publishers, Inc.**

William B. Eerdmans Publishing Co.
255 Jefferson Avenue SE, Grand Rapids, MI 49503
☎001 616 459 4591   Fax 001 616 459 6540
www.eerdmans.com
www.eerdmans.com/youngreaders

President *William B. Eerdmans Jr*

Vice President/Editor-in-Chief *Jon Pott*

Founded 1911 as a theological and reference publisher. Gradually began publishing in other genres with authors like C.S. Lewis, Dorothy Sayers and Malcolm Muggeridge on its lists. Publishes religious: theology, biblical studies, ethical and social concern, social criticism and children's, religious history, religion and literature.

DIVISIONS **Children's** *Judy Zylstra* Picture books, novels and biographies for the general trade market; **Other** *Jon Pott.* About 120 titles a year. Unsolicited mss, synopses and ideas welcome. ROYALTIES twice-yearly.

Eos
See **HarperCollins Publishers, Inc.**

M. Evans & Co., Inc.
216 East 49th Street, New York, NY 10017
☎001 212 688 2810   Fax 001 212 486 4544
✉ editorial@mevans.com
www.mevans.com

Associate Publisher *Harry McCullough*

Founded 1954 as a packager. Began publishing in 1962. Best known for its popular psychology and health books, with titles like *Dr Atkins' New Diet Revolution*, *This is How Love Works*, *Bragging Rights* and *Robert Crayhon's Nutrition Made Simple.* Publishes general non-fiction and fiction. About 30 titles a year. No unsolicited mss; query first. See website for ms submission guidelines.

Faber & Faber, Inc.
19 Union Square West, New York, NY 10003
☎001 212 741 6900   Fax 001 212 633 9385
www.fsgbooks.com/faberandfaber.htm

Senior Editor *Denise Oswald*

Founded 1976. An affiliate of **Farrar, Straus & Giroux, Inc.** Publishes primarily non-fiction books for adults with a focus on film, theatre, music, popular culture and literary and cultural criticism. Unsolicited mss accepted; please query first and include IRCs with letter.

Facts On File, Inc.
132 West 31st Street, New York, NY 10001
☎001 212 967 8800   Fax 001 212 967 9196

President *Mark McDonnell*
Publisher *Laurie E. Likoff*

Started life in the early 1940s with News Digest subscription series to libraries. Began publishing on specific subjects with the Facts On File imprint and developed its current reference and trade book programme in the 1970s. Publishes

general trade, young adult trade and academic reference for the school and library markets. Specialises in single subject encyclopedias, atlases and biographical dictionaries. No fiction, cookery or popular non-fiction.

DIVISIONS **General Reference** *Laurie Likoff;* **Academic Reference** *Owen Lancer;* **Adult Trade** *James Chambers;* **Young Adult & US History** *Nicole Bowen;* **Electronic Publishing** *James Housley;* **Literary Studies** *Jeff Soloway.* About 250 titles a year. Unsolicited synopses and ideas welcome; no mss. Send query letter in the first instance.

ROYALTIES twice-yearly.

Farrar, Straus & Giroux, Inc.
19 Union Square West, New York, NY 10003
☎001 212 741 6900   Fax 001 212 741 6973
www.fsgbooks.com

Founded 1946. Publishes general fiction, non-fiction, poetry, juveniles. No unsolicited material.

Fireside
See **Simon & Schuster Adult Publishing Group**

First Avenue Editions
See **Lerner Publishing Group**

The Free Press
See **Simon & Schuster Adult Publishing Group**

Samuel French, Inc.
45 West 25th Street, New York,
NY 10010–2751
☎001 212 206 8990   Fax 001 212 206 1429
✉ samuelfrench@earthlink.net
www.samuelfrench.com

Editor *Roxanne Hintz*

Founded 1830. Publishes plays in paperback: London, Broadway and off-Broadway hits, light comedies, mysteries, one-act plays and plays for young audiences. Unsolicited mss welcome. No synopses. OVERSEAS ASSOCIATES in London, Toronto, Sydney and Johannesburg.

ROYALTIES annually (books); twice-yearly (amateur productions); monthly (professional productions).

Gale
See **Thomson Gale**

Galilee Books
See **Doubleday Broadway Publishing Group**

Laura Geringer Books
See **HarperCollins Publishers, Inc.**

The Globe Pequot Press
PO Box 480, Guilford, CT 06437–0480
☎001 203 458 4500   Fax 001 203 458 4601
✉ info@gobepequot.com
www.globepequot.com
President & Publisher *Linda Kennedy*
Founded 1947. Publishes regional and international travel, how-to, regional and outdoor recreation. Also publishes the *Insiders'* guides. About 500 titles a year. Unsolicited mss, synopses and ideas welcome, particularly for travel and outdoor recreation books.

Gotham
See **Penguin Group (USA) Inc.**

Great Source Education Group
See **Houghton Mifflin Co.**

Greenhaven Press
See **Thomson Gale**

Greenlight Readers
See **Harcourt Trade Publishers**

Greenwillow Books
See **HarperCollins Publishers, Inc.**

Griffin
See **St Martin's Press LLC**

Grolier Educational
See **Scholastic Library Publishing**

Grosset & Dunlap
See **Penguin Group (USA) Inc.**

Grove/Atlantic Inc.
841 Broadway, 4th Floor, New York,
NY 10003–4793
☎001 212 614 7850   Fax 001 212 614 7886
www.groveatlantic.com
President/Publisher *Morgan Entrekin*
Managing Editor *Michael Hornburg*
Founded 1952. Publishes general fiction and non-fiction. IMPRINTS **Atlantic Monthly Press**; **Canongate US**; **Grove Press**.

Harcourt School Publishers
6277 Sea Harbor Drive, Orlando, FL 32887
☎001 407 345 2000   Fax 001 407 352 3445
www.harcourtschool.com

President/CEO *Jan Spalding*
A division of Harcourt Inc., founded 1919. Publishes education materials – books, CD-ROMs, Internet and audio.

Harcourt Trade Publishers
525 'B' Street, Suite 1900, San Diego,
CA 92101
☎001 619 231 6616
www.harcourtbooks.com
Also at: 15 East 26th Street, 15th Floor, New York, NY 10010
☎001 212 592 1000
President/CEO *Dan Farley*
A division of Harcourt Inc. Publishes fiction, poetry and non-fiction covering a wide range of subjects: biography, history, humour, music, dance, philosophy, psychology, religion, science, social sciences and sociology, sport, wine and spirits, women's studies.
IMPRINTS **Greenlight Readers**; **Harvest Books**; **Libros Viajeros**; **Magic Carpet Books**; **Odyssey Classics**; **Red Wagon Books**; **Silver Whistle Books**; **Voyager Books**. About 300 titles a year. No unsolicited mss.

Harlequin Historicals
See **Silhouette Books**

Harmony Books
See **Crown Publishing Group**

HarperCollins Publishers, Inc.
10 East 53rd Street, New York, NY 10022
☎001 212 207 7000   Fax 001 212 207 7145
www.harpercollins.com
President/Chief Executive Officer *Jane Friedman*
Founded 1817. Subsidiary of News Corporation. Publishes general and literary fiction, general non-fiction, business, children's, reference and religious books.
DIVISIONS/IMPRINTS **Adult Trade**; **Harper-Collins/ HarperCollins Children's Books**; **HarperAudio**; **HarperBusiness**; **Harper Design**; **HarperEntertainment**; **Harper-Festival**; **HarperTempest**; **HarperTorch**; **HarperTrophy**; **Access**; **Amistad**; **Avon**; **Caedmon**; **Joanna Cotler Books**; **Dark Alley**; **Laura Geringer Books**; **Greenwillow Books**; **Perennial**; **Rayo**; **ReganBooks**; **Ecco**; **Eos**; **Katherine Tegen Books**; **Tempest**; **William Morrow**.
SUBSIDIARY **Zondervan** (see entry). About 1700 titles a year. No unsolicited material.

Harvard University Press

79 Garden Street, Cambridge, MA 02138–1499
☎001 617 495 2600   Fax 001 617 495 5898
✉ firstname_lastname@harvard.edu
www.hup.harvard.edu

Director *William P. Sisler*

Founded 1913. Publishes scholarly non-fiction only; humanities, social sciences, sciences. IMPRINT **Belknap Press**.

Harvest Books

See **Harcourt Trade Publishers**

University of Hawai'i Press

2840 Kolowalu Street, Honolulu, HI 96822
☎001 808 956 8255   Fax 001 808 988 6052
✉ uhpbooks@hawaii.edu
www.uhpress.hawaii.edu

Director *William Hamilton*
Executive Editor *Patricia Crosby*

Founded 1947. Publishes scholarly books pertaining to East Asia, Southeast Asia, Hawaii and the Pacific. IMPRINT **Latitude 20**. Unsolicited synopses and ideas welcome; approach by mail. No poetry, children's books or any topics other than Asia and the Pacific.

ROYALTIES twice-yearly.

HiddenSpring

See **Paulist Press**

Hill Street Press

191 E. Broad Street, Suite 209, Athens, GA 30601–2848
☎001 706 613 7200   Fax 001 706 613 7204
www.hillstreetpress.com

Senior Editor *Patrick Allen*

Founded 1998. Publishes books on the American South – fiction and non-fiction. No poetry, erotica, romance, children's or young adults. Unsolicited material welcome; approach in writing in the first instance.

Hippocrene Books, Inc.

171 Madison Avenue, New York, NY 10016
☎001 212 685 4371   Fax 001 212 779 9338
✉ hippocrene.books@verizon.net
www.hippocrenebooks.com

President/Editorial Director *George Blagowidow*
Foreign Language Editor *Robert Martin*
Cookbook Editor *Rebecca Cole*
History Editor *Sophie Fels*

Founded 1971. Publishes general non-fiction and reference books. Particularly strong on foreign language dictionaries, language studies and international cookbooks. No fiction. Send brief summary, table of contents and one chapter for appraisal. S.a.e. essential for response. For manuscript return include sufficient postage cover (IRCs).

Holiday House, Inc.

425 Madison Avenue, New York, NY 10017
☎001 212 688 0085   Fax 001 212 421 6134

Vice President/Editor-in-Chief *Regina Griffin*

Publishes children's general fiction and non-fiction (pre-school to secondary). About 50 titles a year. Send query letters only. IRCs for reply must be included.

Henry Holt & Company

115 West 18th Street, New York, NY 10011
☎001 212 886 9200   Fax 001 212 633 0748
www.henryholt.com

President/Publisher *John Sterling*
Editor-in-Chief *Jennifer Barth*

Founded in 1866, Henry Holt is one of the oldest publishers in the United States. Part of Holtzbrinck Publishing Holdings. Publishes fiction, by both American and international authors, biographies, children's and books on history and politics, ecology and psychology.

DIVISIONS/IMPRINTS **Adult Trade**; **Books for Young Readers**; **Metropolitan Books** *Sara Bershtel*; **Owl Books**; **Times Books**. About 250 titles a year.

Houghton Mifflin Co.

222 Berkeley Street, Boston, MA 02116–3764
☎001 617 351 5000   Fax 001 617 351 1125
www.hmco.com

Contact *Submissions Editor*

Founded 1832. Acquired by Vivendi in June 2001. Publishes literary fiction and general non-fiction, including autobiography, biography and history. Also school and college textbooks; children's fiction and non-fiction. DIVISIONS/SUBSIDIARY COMPANIES **Houghton Mifflin College Division**; **Houghton Mifflin School Division**; **Houghton Mifflin Trade & Reference Division**; **Great Source Education Group**; **McDougal Littell Inc.**; **The Riverside Publishing Co.**; **Promissor Inc**. About 100 titles a year. Unsolicited adult mss no longer accepted. Send synopses, outline and sample chapters for children's non-fiction; complete mss for children's fiction. IRCs required with all submissions/queries.

HPBooks
See **Penguin Group (USA) Inc.**

Hudson Street Press
See **Penguin Group (USA) Inc.**

Humanity Books
See **Prometheus Books**

Hydra
See **Northwestern University Press**

University of Illinois Press
1325 South Oak Street, Champaign,
IL 61820–6903
☎001 217 333 0950   Fax 001 217 244 8082
✉ uipress@uillinois.edu
www.press.uillinois.edu
Director *Willis Regier*

Publishes non-fiction, scholarly and general, with special interest in Americana, women's studies, African-American studies, film, religion, American music and regional books. About 140–150 titles a year.

Image Books
See **Doubleday Broadway Publishing Group**

Indiana University Press
601 North Morton Street, Bloomington,
IN 47404–3797
☎001 812 855 8817   Fax 001 812 855 8507
✉ iupress@indiana.edu
www.indiana.edu/~iupress
Director *Janet Rabinowitch*

Publishes scholarly non-fiction in the following subject areas: African studies, anthropology, Asian studies, African-American studies, bioethics, environment and ecology, film, folklore, history, Jewish studies, music, Middle East studies, military history, music, paleontology, philanthropy, philosophy, politics, religion, Russian and East European studies, women's studies. Query in writing in first instance.

Interlink Publishing Group, Inc.
46 Crosby Street, Northampton, MA 01060
☎001 413 582 7054   Fax 001 413 582 7057
✉ info@interlinkbooks.com
www.interlinkbooks.com
Publisher *Michel Moushabeck*

Founded 1987. Publishes fiction, travel, politics, cookbooks. Specialises in Middle East titles and ethnicity. IMPRINTS **Crocodile Books, USA** Editorial Head *Ruth Lane Moushabeck* Children's books; **Olive Branch Press** Editorial Head *Phyllis Bennis* Political books. About 50–60 titles a year.See submission guidelines on the website before making an approach. ROYALTIES annually.

University of Iowa Press
100 Kuhl House, 119 West Park Road, Iowa City, IA 52242–1000
☎001 319 335 2000   Fax 001 319 335 2055
✉ uipress@uiowa.edu
www.uiowapress.org
Director *Holly Carver*

Founded 1969 as a small scholarly press publishing about five books a year. Now publishing about 35 annually in a variety of scholarly fields, plus local interest, short stories, creative nonfiction and poetry anthologies. No unsolicited mss; query first. Unsolicited ideas and synopses welcome. ROYALTIES annually.

Iowa State University Press
See **Blackwell Publishing**

Jove
See **Penguin Group (USA) Inc.**

University Press of Kansas
2502 Westbrooke Circle, Lawrence,
KS 66049–3905
☎001 785 864 4154   Fax 001 785 864 4586
✉ upress@ku.edu
www.kansaspress.ku.edu
Director *Fred M. Woodward*

Founded 1946. Became the publishing arm for all six state universities in Kansas in 1976. Publishes scholarly books in American history, legal studies, presidential studies, American studies, political philosophy, political science, military history and environmental history. About 55 titles a year. Proposals welcome. ROYALTIES annually.

Kar-Ben Publishing
See **Lerner Publishing Group**

Kent State University Press
307 Lowry Hall, Terrace Drive, Kent,
OH 44242
☎001 330 672 7913   Fax 001 330 672 3104
www.kentstateuniversitypress.com
Director *Will Underwood*
Editor-in-Chief *Joanna Hildebrand Craig*

Founded 1965. Publishes scholarly works in history, literary studies and general non-fiction with an emphasis on American history and literature. 25–30 titles a year. Queries welcome; no mss. ROYALTIES annually.

KidHaven Press
See **Thomson Gale**

Krieger Publishing Co.
PO Box 9542, Melbourne, FL 32902–9542
☎001 321 724 9542   Fax 001 321 951 3671
✉ info@krieger-publishing.com
www.krieger-publishing.com
Chairman *Robert E. Krieger*
President *Donald E. Krieger*
Vice-President *Maxine D. Krieger*

Founded 1970. Publishes science, education, ecology, humanities, history, mathematics, space science, chemistry, technology and engineering. IMPRINTS/SERIES **Anvil**; **Orbit**; **Exploring Community History**; **Public History**; **Open Forum**; **Professional Practices**. Unsolicited mss welcome. Not interested in synopses/ideas or trade type titles.
ROYALTIES annually.

Latino Voices
See **Northwestern University Press**

Latitude 20
See **University of Hawai'i Press**

Lerner Publishing Group
241 First Avenue N., Minneapolis, MN 55401
☎001 612 332 3344   Fax 001 612 332 7615
✉ info@lernerbooks.com
www.lernerbooks.com
Chairman *Harry J. Lerner*
President & Publisher *Adam M. Lerner*

Founded 1959. Publishes children's non-fiction, fiction and curriculum material for all grade levels. DIVISIONS/IMPRINTS **Lerner Publications**; **Carolrhoda Books** (see entry); **LernerClassroom**; **First Avenue Editions**; **Millbrook Press**; **Twenty-First Century Books**; **Kar-Ben Publishing**. No puzzle, song or alphabet books, text books, workbooks, religious subject matter or plays. Submissions accepted only during the month of November; all others returned unopened. S.a.e./IRCs required for return of authorised submission material. Allow eight months for a response. No phone calls.
ROYALTIES annually.

Libros Viajeros
See **Harcourt Trade Publishers**

Little Simon
See **Simon & Schuster Children's Publishing**

Little, Brown and Company
1271 Avenue of the Americas, New York, NY 10020
☎001 212 522 8700   Fax 001 212 522 2067
www.twbookmark.com

Subsidiary of Time Warner Book Group. Founded 1837. Publishes fiction, non-fiction and children's. DIVISIONS **Adult Trade** VP/Publisher *Michael Pietsch*; **Children's Books** VP/Editor-in-Chief *Maria Modugno*. No unsolicited mss.

Llewellyn Publications
PO Box 64383, St Paul, MN 55164–0383
☎001 612 291 1970   Fax 001 612 291 1908
✉ lwlpc@llewellyn.com
www.llewellyn.com
President/Publisher *Carl L. Weschcke*

Division of Llewellyn Worldwide Ltd. Founded 1901. Publishes self-help and how-to: astrology, alternative health, tantra, Fortean studies, tarot, yoga, Santeria, dream studies, metaphysics, magic, witchcraft, herbalism, shamanism, organic gardening, women's spirituality, graphology, palmistry, parapsychology. Also fiction with an authentic magical or metaphysical theme. About 100 titles a year. Unsolicited mss welcome; proposals preferred. IRCs essential in all cases.

Louisiana State University Press
PO Box 25053, Baton Rouge, LA 70894–5053
☎001 225 578 6295   Fax 001 225 578 6461
✉ lsupress@lsu.edu
www.lsu.edu/lsupress
Director *MaryKatherine Calloway*

Publishes non-fiction: Southern history, American history, Southern literary criticism, American literary criticism, biography, political science, music (jazz) and Latin American studies. About 80 titles a year. Send IRCs for mss guidelines.

Love Inspired
See **Silhouette Books**

Lucent Books
See **Thomson Gale**

Luna Books
See **Silhouette Books**

The Lyons Press Inc.
246 Goose Lane, Guilford, CT 06347
☎001 203 458 4500
www.lyonspress.com
Editorial Director *Jay Cassell*

Managing Editor *Alicia Solis*
Founded 1978. Imprint of The Globe Pequot Press. Publishes non-fiction; outdoor (hunting, fishing, survival), natural history, sports, pets, equestrian, history and self-reliant living. About 200 titles a year. Unsolicited mss, synopses and ideas welcome. ROYALTIES twice-yearly.

McDougal Littell Inc.
See **Houghton Mifflin Co.**

Margaret K. McElderry Books
See **Simon & Schuster Children's Publishing**

McFarland & Company, Inc., Publishers
PO Box 611, Jefferson, NC 28640
☎001 336 246 4460   Fax 001 336 246 5018
✉ info@mcfarlandpub.com
www.mcfarlandpub.com
President/Editor-in-Chief *Robert Franklin*
Executive Vice President *Rhonda Herman*
Executive Editor *Steve Wilson*
Editorial Development Chief *Virginia Tobiassen*
Founded 1979. A library reference and upper-end speciality market press publishing scholarly books in many fields: international studies, performing arts, popular culture, sports, automotive history, women's studies, music and fine arts, chess, history and librarianship. Specialises in general reference. Especially strong in cinema studies. No fiction, poetry, children's, New Age or inspirational/devotional works. About 275 titles a year. No unsolicited mss; send query letter first. Synopses and ideas welcome; submissions by mail preferred. ROYALTIES annually.

The McGraw-Hill Companies, Inc.
1221 Avenue of the Americas, 50th Floor, New York, NY 10020
☎001 212 512 2000
www.mcgraw-hill.com
Chairman/President/CEO *Harold W. McGraw*
Founded 1888. Parent of **McGraw-Hill Education** which has offices in the UK (see entry under **UK Publishers**). Publishes a wide range of educational, professional, business, science, engineering and computing books.

Macmillan Reference USA
See **Thomson Gale**

Made Simple Books
See **Doubleday Broadway Publishing Group**

Magic Carpet Books
See **Harcourt Trade Publishers**

Main Street
See **Doubleday Broadway Publishing Group**

Marlowe & Company
See **Avalon Publishing Group**

University of Massachusetts Press
PO Box 429, Amherst, MA 01004–0429
☎001 413 545 2217   Fax 001 413 545 1226
✉ info@umpress.umass.edu
www.umass.edu/umpress
Director *Bruce Wilcox*
Senior Editor *Clark Dougan*
Founded 1964. Publishes scholarly, general interest, African-American, ethnic, women's and gender studies, cultural criticism, economics, fiction, literary criticism, poetry, philosophy, biography, history. About 40 titles a year. Unsolicited mss considered but query letter preferred in the first instance. Synopses and ideas welcome.

Metropolitan Books
See **Henry Holt & Company**

The University of Michigan Press
839 Greene Street, Ann Arbor, MI 48104–3209
☎001 734 764 4388   Fax 001 734 615 1540
✉ um.press@umich.edu
www.press.umich.edu
Founded 1930. Publishes scholarly non-fiction, fiction, textbooks, translation, literary criticism, theatre, music, current affairs, economics, political science, history, classics, anthropology, law studies, gender studies, English as a second language.

Millbrook Press
See **Lerner Publishing Group**

University of Minnesota Press
111 Third Avenue South, Suite 290, Minneapolis, MN 55401–2520
☎001 612 627 1970
www.upress.umn.edu
Director *Douglas Armato*
Associate Editor, Cinema & Media Studies
   Jason Weidemann
Associate Editor, Architecture & Public Art
   Pieter Martin
Acquisitions Editor, American Studies, Cultural Theory, Gay & Lesbian Studies, Art & Visual Cultures, Humanities *Richard Morrison*
Senior Editor, Regional Trade Books, Regional

Natural History, Scandinavian Studies *Todd Orjala*

Executive Editor, Anthropology, Geography, Political & Social Theory, Race & Ethnic Studies, Sociology, Urban Studies, Native American Studies *Carrie Mullen*

Founded 1927. Publishes academic books for scholars and selected general interest titles: art and aesthetics, American studies, anthropology, cultural theory, film and media studies, gay and lesbian studies, geography, literary theory, political and social theory, race and ethnic studies, sociology and urban studies. No fiction or poetry. About 110 titles a year. No unsolicited mss. Welcomes synopses and proposals sent by mail (*no e-mails*). See website for submission details.

Minotaur
See **St Martin's Press LLC**

University Press of Mississippi
3825 Ridgewood Road, Jackson,
MS 39211–6492
☎001 601 432 6205   Fax 001 601 432 6217
✉ press@ihl.state.ms.us
www.upress.state.ms.us

Director *Seetha Srinivasan*
Editor-in-Chief *Craig Gill*

Founded 1970. Non-profit book publisher partially supported by the eight State universities. Publishes scholarly and trade titles in literature, history, American culture, Southern culture, African-American, women's studies, popular culture, folklife, ethnic, performance, art, architecture and photography and other liberal arts.
IMPRINTS **Muscadine Books** *Craig Gill* Regional trade titles. **Banner Books** Paperback reprints of significant fiction and non-fiction. REPRESENTED worldwide. UK representatives: **Roundhouse Publishing Group**. About 60 titles a year. Send letter of enquiry, prospectus, table of contents and sample chapter prior to submission of full mss. ROYALTIES annually.

University of Missouri Press
2910 LeMone Boulevard, Columbia,
MO 65201
☎001 573 882 7641   Fax 001 573 884 4498
www.system.missouri.edu/upress

Director *Beverly Jarrett*

Founded 1958. Publishes academic: history, literary criticism, intellectual history and related humanities disciplines and occasional volumes of short stories. About 60 titles a year. Best approach is by letter. Send synopses for academic work together with author c.v.

Modern Library
See **Random House Publishing Group**

William Morrow
See **HarperCollins Publishers, Inc.**

Muscadine Books
See **University Press of Mississippi**

Mysterious Press
See **Warner Books Inc.**

NAL
See **Penguin Group (USA) Inc.**

Nation Books
See **Avalon Publishing Group**

University of Nebraska Press
233 North 8th Street, Lincoln, NE 68588–0255
☎001 402 472 3581   Fax 001 402 472 6214
✉ pressmail@unl.edu
www.nebraskapress.unl.edu

Interim Director *Gary H. Dunham*

Founded 1941. Publishes scholarly, Native American studies, history of the American West, literary and cultural studies, music, Jewish studies, military history, sports history, environmental history. IMPRINT **Bison Books**. 152 titles in 2004. No unsolicited mss; welcomes synopses and ideas for books. Send enquiry letter in the first instance with description of project and sample material. No original fiction, children's books or poetry.
ROYALTIES annually.

University of Nevada Press
MS 166, Reno, NV 89557–0076
☎001 775 784 6573   Fax 001 775 784 6200
www.nvbooks.nevada.edu

Director *Joanne O'Hare*

Founded 1961. Publishes scholarly and popular books; serious fiction, Native American studies, natural history, Western Americana, Basque studies and regional studies. About 25 titles a year. Unsolicited material welcome if it fits in with areas published, or offers a 'new and exciting' direction.

New American Library
See **Penguin Group (USA) Inc.**

University Press of New England
One Court Street, Suite 250, Lebanon,
NH 03766
☎001 603 448 1533   Fax 001 603 448 7006

www.upne.com

Director *Richard Abel*

Editor-in-Chief *Phyllis Deutsch*

Founded 1970. A scholarly books publisher sponsored by six institutions of higher education in the region: Brandeis, Dartmouth, University of Vermont, Tufts, the University of New Hampshire and Northeastern. Publishes general and scholarly non-fiction and Hardscrabble Books fiction of New England. OVERSEAS ASSOCIATES Canada: University of British Columbia; UK, Europe, Middle East: Eurospan University Press Group; Australia, New Zealand, Asia & the Pacific: East-West Export Books. About 80 titles a year. Unsolicited material welcome.

ROYALTIES annually.

University of New Mexico Press

1601 Randolph Road SE, Albuquerque, NM 87106

☎001 505 277 2346   Fax 001 505 277 9270

www.unmpress.com

Director *Luther Wilson*

Editor-in-Chief *David V. Holtby*

Founded 1929. Publishes scholarly, regional books and fiction. No how-to, humour, self-help or technical.

University of North Texas Press

PO Box 311336, Denton, TX 76203–1336

☎001 940 565 2142   Fax 001 940 565 4590

✉ rchrisman@unt.edu

www.unt.edu/untpress

Director *Ronald Chrisman*

Founded 1987. Publishes folklore, regional interest, contemporary, social issues, Texas history, military history, women's issues, multicultural. Publishes annually the winners of the Vassar Miller Poetry Prize and the Katherine Anne Porter Prize in Short Fiction. About 15 titles a year. No unsolicited mss; synopses and ideas welcome.

ROYALTIES annually.

Northwestern University Press

629 Noyes Street, Evanston, IL 60208

☎001 847 491 2046   Fax 001 847 491 8150

✉ nupress@northwestern.edu

www.nupress.northwestern.edu

Chairman *Peter Hayes*

Managing Director *Donna Shear*

Publishes general and academic books: philosophy, theatre and performance studies, Slavic studies, Latino fiction and biography, contemporary fiction, poetry. No children's, art books.

IMPRINTS **Hydra**; **Latino Voices** Editorial Head *Susan Betz*. 60 titles in 2004. Unsolicited mss, synopses and ideas welcome; approach by mail.

ROYALTIES annually.

W.W. Norton & Company, Inc.

500 Fifth Avenue, New York, NY 10110–0017

☎001 212 354 5500   Fax 001 212 869 0856

www.wwnorton.com

Vice-President/Managing Editor *Nancy K. Palmquist*

Founded 1923. Publishes fiction and non-fiction, college textbooks and professional books. About 400 titles a year.

Odyssey Classics

See **Harcourt Trade Division**

Ohio University Press

Scott Quadrangle, Athens, OH 45701

☎001 740 593 1155   Fax 001 740 593 4536

www.ohiou.edu/oupress

Managing Director *David Sanders*

Founded 1964. Publishes academic, regional and general trade books. IMPRINT **Swallow Press**. 50 titles in 2004. Synopses and ideas for books welcome. Send detailed synopsis, sample chapters and c.v. with covering letter. See website for author guidelines. No children's, how-to or genre fiction.

ROYALTIES twice-yearly.

University of Oklahoma Press

2800 Venture Drive, Norman, OK 73069–8216

☎001 405 325 2000   Fax 001 405 325 4000

www.oupress.com

Director *John N. Drayton*

Founded 1928. Publishes general scholarly non-fiction only: American Indian studies, American West, classical studies, anthropology, natural history and political science. About 100 titles a year.

Olive Branch Press

See **Interlink Publishing Group, Inc.**

One World

See **Random House Publishing Group**

Onyx

See **Penguin Group (USA) Inc.**

Open Forum

See **Krieger Publishing Co.**

Orbit
See **Krieger Publishing Co.**

Outdoor Bible Series
See **Doubleday Broadway Publishing Group**

Owl Books
See **Henry Holt & Company**

Palgrave
See **St Martin's Press LLC**

Paragon House
1925 Oakcrest Avenue, Suite 7, St Paul, MN 55113–2619
☎001 651 644 3087   Fax 001 651 644 0997
✉ paragon@paragonhouse.com
www.paragonhouse.com
Executive Director *Dr Gordon L. Anderson*

Founded 1982. Publishes non-fiction: reference and academic. Subjects include history, religion, philosophy, spirituality, Jewish interest, political science, international relations, psychology.
ROYALTIES twice-yearly.

Paulist Press
997 Macarthur Boulevard, Mahwah, NJ 07430
☎001 201 825 7300   Fax 001 201 825 8345
✉ sales@paulistpress.com
www.paulistpress.com
Owner *Missionary Society of St Paul the Apostle, New York*
Publisher *Fr. Lawrence Boadt*
Managing Editor *Paul McMahon*

Founded in 1866 by the Paulist Fathers as the Catholic Publication Society, it is now one of the largest Catholic publishing houses in the world. Publishes religious, spiritual, theology and children's religious books. IMPRINTS **Paulist Press** *Paul McMahon* Spirituality, ministry resources, ethics and social issues, ecumenical and inter-religious; *Nancy de Flon* Theology and philosophy; *Susan O'Keefe* Children's religious. **HiddenSpring** *Paul McMahon* General religious trade books. 90 titles a year. Unsolicited mss, synopses and ideas welcome; approach through direct mail with IRCs for return postage of material and/or letter. No New Age, Evangelical Christian books.

Pearson Scott Foresman
1900 E Lake Avenue, Glenview, IL 60025
☎001 847 729 3000
✉ firstname.lastname@scottforesman.com
www.scottforesman.com

President *Paul McFall*

Founded 1896. Part of Pearson Education. Publishes elementary education materials. No unsolicited material.

Pelican Publishing Company
100 Burmaster Street, Gretna, LA 70053
☎001 504 368 1175
www.pelicanpub.com
Editor-in-Chief *Nina Kooij*

Publishes general non-fiction: popular history, cookbooks, travel, art, business, biography, children's, editorial cartoon, architecture, golf, Scottish interest, collectibles guides and motivational. About 75 titles a year. Initial enquiries required for all submissions.

Pelion Press
See **The Rosen Publishing Group, Inc.**

Penguin Group (USA) Inc.
375 Hudson Street, New York, NY 10014
☎001 212 366 2000   Fax 001 212 366 2666
✉ online@penguingroup.com
www.penguin.com
CEO *David Shanks*
President *Susan Petersen Kennedy*

The second-largest trade book publisher in the world. Publishes fiction and non-fiction in hardback and paperback; adult and children's.

ADULT DIVISION
IMPRINTS Hardcover: **Avery** (see entry); **Dutton**; **G.P. Putnam's Sons**; **Gotham**; **Hudson Street Press**; **Jeremy P. Tarcher/Putnam**; **The Penguin Press**; **Portfolio**; **Riverhead Books**; **Viking**; Trade Paperback: **Ace**; **Berkley**; **HPBooks**; **New American Library (NAL)**; **Perigee**; **Penguin Books**; **Plume**; **Riverhead**; **Roc**. Mass Market Paperback: **Ace**; **Berkley**; **DAW Books** (see entry); **Jove**; **Onyx**; **Roc**; **Signet**.

CHILDREN'S DIVISION
Hardcover: **Dial Books for Young Readers** (see entry); **Dutton Children's Books**; **Frederick Warne**; **G.P. Putnam's Sons** (see entry); **Philomel Books**; **Viking Children's Books**. Paperback: **Puffin Books**; **Razorbill**. Mass Merchandise: **Grosset & Dunlap**; **Price Stern Sloan**. No unsolicited mss.
ROYALTIES twice-yearly.

University of Pennsylvania Press
4200 Pine Street, Philadelphia, PA 19104–4011
☎001 215 898 6261   Fax 001 215 898 0404

www.upenn.edu/pennpress

Director *Eric Halpern*

Founded 1890. Publishes serious non-fiction: scholarly, reference, professional, textbooks and semi-popular trade. No original fiction or poetry. About 75 titles a year. No unsolicited mss but synopses and ideas for books welcome.

Perennial
See **HarperCollins Publisers, Inc.**

Perigee
See **Penguin Group (USA) Inc.**

Perseus Books Group
387 Park Avenue S, 12th Floor, New York, NY 10016
☎001 212 340 8100   Fax 001 212 340 8115
www.perseusbooksgroup.com
President/CEO *David Steinberger*

Founded 1997. Subsidiary of Perseus Capital LLC. Publishes general, academic and professional. IMPRINTS **Basic Books**; **Counterpoint Press**; **Da Capo Press**; **PublicAffairs**; **Running Press**. No unsolicited mss.

Philomel Books
See **Penguin Group (USA) Inc.**

Picador USA
See **St Martin's Press LLC**

Players Press
PO Box 1132, Studio City, CA 91614-0132
☎001 818 789 4980
CEO *William-Alan Landes*

Founded 1965 as a publisher of plays; now publishes across the entire range of performing arts: plays, musicals, theatre, film, cinema, television, costume, puppetry, plus technical theatre and cinema material. OVERSEAS SUBSIDIARIES in Canada, Australia, Germany and the UK. No unsolicited mss; synopses/ideas welcome. Send query letter s.a.e. for response.
ROYALTIES twice-yearly.

Plume
See **Penguin Group (USA) Inc.**

Pocket Books
See **Simon & Schuster Adult Publishing Group**

Portfolio
See **Penguin Group (USA) Inc.**

Potomac Books, Inc.
22841 Quicksilver Drive, Dulles, VA 20166
☎001 703 661 1548   Fax 001 703 661 1547
✉ djacobs@booksintl.com
www.potomacbooksinc.com
Publisher *Don McKeon*

Formerly Brassey's, Inc., founded 1984 (acquired in 1999 by Books International of Dulles, Virginia). Publishes non-fiction titles on topics of history (especially military history), world and US affairs, US foreign policy, defence, intelligence, biography and sports. About 60 titles a year. No unsolicited mss; synopses and ideas welcome. ROYALTIES annually.

Presidio Press
See **Random House Publishing Group**

Price Stern Sloan
See **Penguin Group (USA) Inc.**

Primary Source Microfilm
See **Thomson Gale**

Princeton University Press
41 William Street, Princeton, NJ 08540–5237–6305
☎001 609 258 4800
www.pup.princeton.edu
Managing Director *Walter Lippincott*
Editor-in-Chief *Sam Elworthy*
Approx. Annual Turnover $20 million

Founded 1905. Publishes academic and trade books. About 200 titles a year. No unsolicited mss. Synopses and ideas considered. Send letter to editor-in-chief in the first instance. No fiction. OVERSEAS ASSOCIATE Princeton University Press, 3 Market Place, Woodstock OX20 1SY, UK.
ROYALTIES annually.

Professional Practices
See **Krieger Publishing Co.**

Prometheus Books
59 John Glenn Drive, Amherst, NY 14228–2197
☎001 800 421 0351   Fax 001 716 691 0137
✉ marketing@prometheusbooks.com
www.prometheusbooks.com
www.pyrsf.com
Chairman *Paul Kurtz*
Editor-in-Chief *Steven L. Mitchell*
Acquisitions Editor *Ann O'Hear*

Founded 1969. Publishes books and journals: educational, scientific professional, library, popular science, science fiction and fantasy, philosophy and young readers. IMPRINTS **Humanity Books**; **Pyr™**.About 100 titles a year. Unsolicited mss, synopses and ideas for books welcome. ROYALTIES twice-yearly.

Promissor Inc
See **Houghton Mifflin Co.**

Public History
See **Krieger Publishing Co.**

PublicAffairs
See **Perseus Books Group**

Puffin Books
See **Penguin Group (USA) Inc.**

G.P. Putnam's Sons (Children's)
345 Hudson Street, New York, NY 10014
☎001 212 366 2000
www.penguingroup.com
President/Publisher *Nancy Paulsen*
Executive Editor *Kathryn Dawson*

A children's book imprint of Penguin Young Readers Group, a member of **Penguin Group (USA) Inc.** Publishes picture books, middlegrade fiction and young adult fiction.

Pyr™
See **Prometheus Books**

Rand McNally
PO Box 7600, Chicago, IL 60680
☎001 847 329 8100   Fax 001 847 673 0539
www.randmcnally.com
President/CEO *Rob Apatoff*

Founded 1856. Publishes world atlases and maps, road atlases of North America and Europe, city and state maps of the United States and Canada, educational wall maps, atlases and globes, plus children's products. Includes electronic multimedia products. IMPRINT **Rand McNally for Kids**.

Random House Publishing Group
1745 Broadway, New York, NY 10019
☎001 212 782 9000
www.randomhouse.com
President/Publisher *Gina Centrello*

Publishes fiction, non-fiction, science fiction in hardcover, trade paperback and mass market. IMPRINTS **Ballantine Books**; **Del Rey**; **Modern Library**; **One World**; **Presidio Press**; **Random House**; **Random House Trade Paperbacks**; **Villard**.No unsolicited mss.

Rawson Associates
See **Simon & Schuster Adult Publishing Group**

Rayo
See **HarperCollins Publishers, Inc.**

Razorbill
See **Penguin Group (USA) Inc.**

Reader's Digest Association Inc
Reader's Digest Road, Pleasantville, NY 10570–7000
☎001 914 238 1000   Fax 001 914 238 4559
www.rd.com
Chairman/CEO *Thomas Ryder*

Publishes home maintenance reference, cookery, DIY, health, gardening, children's books; videos and magazines.

Red Wagon Books
See **Harcourt Trade Division**

ReganBooks
See **HarperCollins Publishers, Inc.**

Revell
See **Baker Publishing Group**

Riverhead Books
See **Penguin Group (USA) Inc.**

The Riverside Publishing Co.
See **Houghton Mifflin Co.**

Roc
See **Penguin Group (USA) Inc.**

The Rosen Publishing Group, Inc.
29 East 21st Street, New York, NY 10010
☎001 212 777 3017   Fax 001 212 777 0277
✉ info@rosenpublishing.com
www.rosenpublishing.com
President *Roger Rosen*
Vice-President *Gina Strazzabosco-Hayn*

Founded 1950. Publishes non-fiction books (supplementary to the curriculum, reference and self-help) for a young adult audience. Reading levels are years 7–12, 4–6 (books for teens with literacy problems), and 5–9. Subjects include conflict resolution, character building, health, safety, drug abuse prevention, self-help and multicultural titles. IMPRINT **Pelion Press**.For all imprints, write with outline and sample chapters.

Running Press
See **Perseus Books Group**

Rutgers University Press

100 Joyce Kilmer Avenue, Piscataway,
NJ 08854–8099
☎001 732 445 7762   Fax 001 732 445 7039
rutgerspress.rutgers.edu

Director *Marlie Wasserman*
Associate Director/Editor-in-Chief *Leslie Mitchner*

Founded 1936. Publishes scholarly books, regional, social sciences and humanities. About 80 titles a year. Unsolicited mss, synopses and ideas for books welcome. No original fiction or poetry.

St Martin's Press LLC

175 Fifth Avenue, New York, NY 10010
☎001 212 674 5151   Fax 001 212 420 9314
✉ inquiries@stmartins.com
www.stmartins.com

CEO (Holtzbrinck) *John Sargent*
President/Publisher (Trade Division) *Sally Richardson*

Founded 1952. A subsidiary of **Macmillan Publishers** (UK), St Martin's Press made its name and fortune by importing raw talent from the UK to the States and has continued to buy heavily in the UK. Publishes general fiction, especially mysteries and crime; and adult non-fiction: history, self-help, political science, travel, biography, scholarly, popular reference, college textbooks.

IMPRINTS **Picador USA**; **Griffin** (Trade paperbacks); **St Martin's Paperbacks** (Mass market); **Thomas Dunne Books**; **Minotaur**; **Palgrave**; **Truman Talley Books**. All submissions via legitimate literary agents only.

Scarecrow Press Inc.

4501 Forbes Boulevard, Suite 200, Lanham,
MD 20706
☎001 301 459 3366   Fax 001 301 429 5747
www.scarecrowpress.com

President *Jed Lyons*
Vice President/Publisher *Edward Kurdyla*

Founded 1950 as a short-run publisher of library reference books. Acquired by **University Press of America, Inc.** in 1995 which is now part of Rowman and Littlefield Publishing Group. Publishes reference, scholarly and monographs (all levels) for libraries. Reference books in all areas except sciences, specialising in the performing arts, music, cinema and library science. About 160 titles a year. Unsolicited mss welcome but material will not be returned unless requested and accompanied by return postage. Unsolicited synopses and ideas for books welcome.

Scholastic Library Publishing

90 Old Sherman Turnpike, Danbury,
CT 06816
☎001 203 797 3500   Fax 001 203 797 3657
www.scholasticlibrary.com

President *Greg Worrell*

Publishes juvenile non-fiction, encyclopedias, speciality reference sets and picture books.

DIVISIONS/IMPRINTS **Children's Press**; **Grolier Educational**; **Franklin Watts**. About 500 titles a year.

Scribner

See **Simon & Schuster Adult Publishing Group**

Charles Scribner's Sons

See **Thomson Gale**

Seal Press

See **Avalon Publishing Group**

Seven Stories Press

140 Watts Street, New York, NY 10013
☎001 212 226 8760   Fax 001 212 226 1411
✉ info@sevenstories.com
www.sevenstories.com

CEO *Daniel Simon*

Founded 1995. Named by *Publishers Weekly* in 2001 as the fastest growing independent publisher in America. Publishes fiction, literature, literary translations, memoirs, political non-fiction, health, history, current affairs. No unsolicited mss; synopses and ideas from agents welcome or send query letter. No children's or business books. OVERSEAS SUBSIDIARIES Turnaround Publishing Services, UK; Tower Books, Australia; Hushion House, Canada.

Shoemaker & Hoard Publishers

See **Avalon Publishing Group**

Signet

See **Penguin Group (USA) Inc.**

Silhouette Books

233 Broadway, Suite 1001, New York,
NY 10279
☎001 212 553 4200   Fax 001 212 227 8969

Executive Editor *Mary Theresa Hussey*

Founded 1979 as an imprint of Simon & Schuster and was acquired by a wholly owned subsidiary of Toronto-based Harlequin Enterprises Ltd in 1984. Publishes category, contemporary romance fiction and historical romance fiction only.

IMPRINTS **Silhouette Romance** *Ann Leslie Tuttle*; **Silhouette Bombshell** *Natasha Wilson*; **Silhouette Desire** *Melissa Jeglinski*; **Silhouette Special Edition** *Gail Chasan*; **Silhouette Intimate Moments** *Patience Smith*; **Harlequin Historicals** *Ann Leslie Tuttle*; **Luna Books** *Theresa Hussey*; **Steeple Hill** *Joan Marlow Golan*; **Love Inspired** publishes a line of inspirational contemporary romances with stories designed to 'lift readers' spirits and gladden their hearts'. See also **Harlequin Mills & Boon Ltd** under **UK Publishers**. OVERSEAS ASSOCIATES worldwide. Over 360 titles a year across a number of lines. No unsolicited mss. Submit query letter in the first instance or write for detailed submission guidelines/tip sheets. ROYALTIES twice-yearly.

Silver Whistle Books
See **Harcourt Trade Division**

Simon & Schuster Adult Publishing Group (Division of Simon & Schuster, Inc)
1230 Avenue of the Americas, New York, NY 10020
☎001 212 698 7000   Fax 001 212 698 7007
www.simonsays.com
President *Carolyn K. Reidy*
Publishes fiction and non-fiction.
DIVISIONS
Atria Books VP & Executive Editorial Director *Emily Bestler*; **The Free Press** VP & Editorial Director *Dominick Anfuso*; **Fireside/Touchstone** VP & Editor-in-Chief Trish Todd; **Pocket Books** VP & Editorial Director *Maggie Crawford*; **Scribner** VP & Editor-in-Chief *Nan Graham*; **Simon and Schuster** Senior VP & Editor-in-Chief *Michael V. Korda*.
IMPRINTS
Atria Books; **H.&R. Block**; **Downtown Press**; **Lisa Drew Books**; **Fireside**; **The Free Press**; **Pocket Books**; **Rawson Associates**; **Scribner**; **Scribner Classics**; **Scribner Paperback Fiction**; **S&S Libros eñ Espanol**; **Simon & Schuster**; **Touchstone**; **Washington Square Press**. No unsolicited mss.
ROYALTIES twice-yearly.

Simon & Schuster Children's Publishing
1230 Avenue of the Americas, New York, NY 10020
☎001 212 698 7200
www.simonsayskids.com

President/Publisher *Rick Richter*
VP/Publisher, Hardcover Imprints *Suzanne Harper*
A division of the Simon & Schuster Consumer Group. Publishes pre-school to young adult, picture books, hardcover and paperback fiction, non-fiction, trade, library and mass-market titles.
IMPRINTS
Aladdin Books *Ellen Krieger* Picture books, paperback fiction and non-fiction reprints and originals, and limited series for ages pre-school to young adult; **Atheneum Books for Young Readers** *Ginee Seo* Picture books, hardcover fiction and non-fiction books across all genres for ages three to young adult; **Little Simon** *Robin Corey* Mass-market novelty books (pop-ups, board books, colouring & activity) and merchandise (book and audio cassette) for ages birth through eight; **Margaret K. McElderry Books** *Margaret K. McElderry, Emma Dryden* Picture books, hardcover fiction and non-fiction trade books for children ages three to young adult; **Simon & Schuster Books for Young Readers** *Elizabeth Law* Picture books, hardcover fiction and non-fiction for children ages three to young adult. **Simon Spotlight** *Jennifer Bergstrom* New imprint devoted exclusively to children's media tie-ins and licensed properties. About 480 titles a year. For submissions to all imprints: send envelope (US size 10) for guidelines, attention: 'Manuscript Submissions Guidelines'.

Simon Spotlight
See **Simon & Schuster Children's Publishing**

Southern Illinois University Press
PO Box 3697, Carbondale, IL 62902–3697
☎001 618 453 2281   Fax 001 618 453 1221
www.siu.edu/~siupress
Director *John F. Stetter*
Founded 1956. Publishes scholarly and general interest non-fiction books and educational materials. 50 titles a year.

Stackpole Books
5067 Ritter Road, Mechanicsburg, PA 17055
☎001 717 796 0411   Fax 001 717 796 0412
www.stackpolebooks.com
President *David Ritter*
Vice President/Editorial Director *Judith Schnell*
Founded 1933. Publishes outdoor sports, fishing, hunting, nature, crafts, Pennsylvania and

regional, military reference, history. About 100 titles a year.
ROYALTIES twice-yearly.

Stanford University Press
1450 Page Mill Road, Palo Alto,
CA 94304–1124
☎001 650 723 9434   Fax 001 650 725 3457
www.sup.org
Managing Director *Geoffrey R.H. Burn*

Founded 1925. Publishes non-fiction: scholarly works in all areas of the humanities, social sciences, history and literature, also professional lists in business, economics and law. About 120 titles a year. No unsolicited mss; query in writing first.

Steeple Hill
See **Silhouette Books**

Sterling Publishing Co. Inc.
387 Park Avenue South, 5th Floor, New York,
NY 10016–8810
☎001 212 532 7160   Fax 001 212 213 2495
www.sterlingpub.com
VP/Publisher *Andrew Martin*
President/CEO *Charles Nurnberg*
VP, Editorial *Steve Magnuson*

Founded 1949. Publishes illustrated non-fiction: reference and information books, science, business, nature, arts and crafts, home improvement, history, photography, children's humour, complementary health, wine and food, sports, music, psychology, New Age, woodworking, pets, hobbies, gardening, puzzles. Submission guidelines available.

Swallow Press
See **Ohio University Press**

Syracuse University Press
621 Skytop Road, Suite 110, Syracuse,
NY 13244–5290
☎001 315 443 5534   Fax 001 315 443 5545
www.SyracuseUniversityPress.syr.edu
Director *Peter B. Webber*

Founded 1943. Publishes scholarly books in the following areas: Middle East studies, Middle East literature in translation,Irish studies, Jewish studies, sports, gender and globalisation, Iroquois studies, women and religion, medieval studies, religion and politics, television, geography and regional books. Distributes for the Moshe Dayan Center, Jusoor. About 50 titles a year. No unsolicited mss. Send query letter with IRCs.
ROYALTIES annually.

The Taft Group
See **Thomson Gale**

Nan A. Talese
See **Doubleday Broadway Publishing Group**

Jeremy P. Tarcher
See **Penguin Group (USA) Inc.**

Katherine Tegan Books
See **HarperCollins Publishers, Inc.**

Tempest
See **HarperCollins Publishers, Inc.**

Temple University Press
1601 N. Broad Street, 083–42, Philadelphia,
PA 19122–6099
☎001 215 204 8787   Fax 001 215 204 4719
www.temple.edu/tempress
Editor-in-Chief *Janet M. Francendese*

Founded 1969. Publishes scholarly books. Authors generally academics. Letter of inquiry with brief outline. Include fax/e-mail address. About 60 titles a year.

University of Tennessee Press
110 Conference Center Bldg., Knoxville,
TN 37996–4108
☎001 865 974 3321   Fax 001 865 974 3724
www.utpress.org
Managing Editor *Stan Ivester*
Acquisitions Editor *Scott Danforth*

Founded in 1940. Publishes scholarly and regional non-fiction. Submission guidelines are posted on the website.

University of Texas Press
PO Box 7819, Austin, TX 78713-7819
☎001 512 471 7233/471 4278 (editorial)
Fax 001 512 232 7178
www.utexas.edu/utpress/
www.utexaspress.com
Director *Joanna Hitchcock*
Assistant Director/Editor-in-Chief *Theresa J. May*

Publishes scholarly and regional non-fiction: anthropology, architecture, classics, environmental studies, humanities, social sciences, geography, language studies, literary modernism; Latin American/Latino/Mexican American/Middle Eastern/Native American studies, natural history and ornithology, regional books (Texas and the southwest). Unsolicited material welcome in

above subject areas only. About 90 titles a year and 11 journals.
ROYALTIES annually.

Thomson Gale
27500 Drake Road, Farmington Hills, MI 48331
☎001 248 699 4253   Fax 001 248 699 8070
www.gale.com
CEO *Charles Siegel*
Founded 1954. A subsidiary of The Thomson Corporation, Gale is a world leader in e-information publishing. Publishes electronic, print and microfiche reference material for libraries, schools and businesses. BRANDS/IMPRINTS **Blackbird Press; Charles Scribner's Sons; Greenhaven Press; KidHaven Press; Lucent Books; Macmillan Reference USA; Primary Source Microfilm; The Taft Group; Thorndike Press; UXL; Wheeler Publishing**.

Thorndike Press
See **Thomson Gale**

Three Rivers Press
See **Crown Publishing Group**

Thunder's Mouth Press
See **Avalon Publishing Group**

Times Books
See **Henry Holt & Company**

Touchstone
See **Simon & Schuster Adult Publishing Group**

Transaction Publishers Ltd
c/o Rutgers – The State University of New Jersey, 35 Berrue Circle, Piscataway, NJ 08854–8042
☎001 732 445 2280   Fax 001 732 445 3138
✉ ihorowitz@transactionpub.com
www.transactionpub.com
Chairman *I.L. Horowitz*
President *Mary E. Curtis*
Founded 1962. Independent publisher of academic social scientific books, periodicals and serials. 160 titles in 2004. All unsolicited material should be submitted in hard copy and full draft. E-mail submissions are not accepted. 'Decision-making is rapid.'

Truman Talley Books
See **St Martin's Press LLC**

Twenty-First Century Books
See **Lerner Publishing Group**

Tyndale House Publishers, Inc.
PO Box 80, Wheaton, IL 60189–0080
☎001 630 668 8303
www.tyndale.com
President *Mark D. Taylor*
Founded 1962. Books cover a wide range of categories from non-fiction to gift books, theology, doctrine, Bibles, fiction, children's and youth. Also produces video material, calendars and audio books for the same market. No poetry. Non-denominational religious publisher of around 300 titles a year for the evangelical Christian market. No unsolicited mss. Synopses and ideas considered. Send query letter summarising contents of book and length. Include a brief biography, detailed outline and three sample chapters. IRCs essential for response or return of material. No audio cassettes, disks or video tapes in lieu of mss. Response time around 12–16 weeks. No phone calls or e-mail submissions. Send s.a.e. for submission guidelines.

University Press of America, Inc.
4501 Forbes Boulevard, Suite 200, Lanham, MD 20706
☎001 301 459 3366   Fax 001 301 429 5748
www.univpress.com
President/Publisher *James E. Lyons*
VP/Editorial Director *Judith L. Rothman*
Founded 1974. Publishes scholarly monographs, college and graduate level textbooks. No children's, elementary or high school. About 400 titles a year. Submit outline or request proposal questionnaire.

UXL
See **Thomson Gale**

Viking/Viking Children's Books
See **Penguin Group (USA) Inc.**

Villard
See **Random House Publishing Group**

University of Virginia Press
PO Box 400318, Charlottesville, VA 22904–4318
☎001 434 924 3468   Fax 001 434 982 2655
✉ upressvirginia@virginia.edu
www.upress.virginia.edu
Director *Penelope J. Kaiserlian*
Founded 1963. Publishes academic books in

humanities and social science with concentrations in American history, African-American studies, architecture, Victorian literature, Caribbean literature and ecocriticism. No unsolicited mss; will consider synopses and ideas for books if in their specific areas of concentration. Approach by mail for full proposal; e-mail for short inquiry. No fiction, children's, poetry or academic books outside interests specified above. ROYALTIES annually.

Voyager Books
See **Harcourt Trade Division**

J. Weston Walch, Publisher
PO Box 658, Portland, ME 04104
☎001 207 772 2846   Fax 001 207 772 3105
www.walch.com
President *John Thoreson*
Editor-in-Chief *Susan Blair*
Founded 1927. Publishes supplementary educational materials for middle and secondary schools across a wide range of subjects, including English/language arts, literacy, special needs, mathematics, social studies, science and school-to-career. Always interested in ideas from secondary school teachers who develop materials in the classroom. Proposal letters, synopses and ideas welcome.

Walk Worthy Press
See **Warner Books Inc.**

Walker & Co.
104 Fifth Avenue, 7th Floor, New York, NY 10011
☎001 212 727 8300   Fax 001 212 727 0984
www.walkerbooks.com (trade non-fiction)
www.walkeryoungreaders.com (BFYR)
Contact *Submissions Editor*
Founded 1959. Publishes children's fiction and non-fiction and adult non-fiction. Please contact the following editors in advance before sending any material to be sure of their interest, then follow up as instructed: **Trade Non-fiction** *George Gibson* Permission and documentation must be available with mss. Submit prospectus first, with sample chapters and marketing analysis. **Books for Young Readers** *Emily Easton* Fiction and non-fiction for all ages. Query before sending non-fiction proposals. Especially interested in picture books – fiction and non-fiction, historical and contemporary fiction for middle grades and young adults. BFYR will consider unsolicited submissions.

Frederick Warne
See **Penguin Group (USA) Inc.**

Warner Books Inc.
1271 Avenue of the Americas, New York, NY 10020
☎001 212 522 7200   Fax 001 212 522 7991
www.twbookmark.com
Senior Vice-President/Publisher *Jamie Raab*
Associate Publishers *Les Pockell, Ivan Held*
Founded 1961. A subsidiary of Time Warner Book Group. Publishes fiction and non-fiction, audio books.
IMPRINTS **Aspect; Mysterious Press; Walk Worthy Press; Warner Vision; Warner Faith; Warner Forever.** About 250 titles a year. No unsolicited mss.

Washington Square Press
See **Simon & Schuster Adult Publishing Group**

Washington State University Press
PO Box 645910, Pullman, WA 99164-5910
☎001 509 335 3518   Fax 001 509 335 8568
✉ wsupress@wsu.edu
www.wsu.edu/wsupress
Editor-in-Chief *Glen Lindeman*
Founded 1928. Publishes hardcover originals, trade paperbacks and reprints. Publishes mainly on the history, prehistory, culture, politics and natural history of the Northwest United States (Washington, Idaho, Oregon, Montana, Alaska) and British Columbia, but works that focus on national topics or other regions may also be considered if they have a Northwest connection. Subjects include history, biography, cooking/food history, nature/environment, politics. 8–10 titles a year. Queries welcome.

Franklin Watts
See **Scholastic Library Publishing**

Wheeler Publishing
See **Thomson Gale**

John Wiley & Sons, Inc.
111 River Street, Hoboken, NJ 07030–5774
☎001 201 748 6000   Fax 001 201 748 6088
✉ info@wiley.com
www.wiley.com
President/CEO *William J. Pesce*
Founded 1807. Wiley's core publishing programme includes scientific, technical and medical journals, encyclopedias, books and online

products and services; professional and consumer books and subscription services; and educational materials for undergraduate, graduate students and life-long learners. About 1500 titles a year.Unsolicited mss not accepted.

The University of Wisconsin Press

1930 Monroe Street, 3rd Floor, Madison, WI 53711

☎001 608 263 1110   Fax 001 608 263 1120

✉ uwiscpress@uwpress.wisc.edu

www.wisc.edu/wisconsinpress

Director *Robert A. Mandel*

Founded 1936. Publishes scholarly, general interest non-fiction and regional books about Wisconsin and the mid-west. About 50 titles a year. No unsolicited mss; proposals (sent by mail) welcome. 'No unrevised dissertations, no Festschrifts, no genre, no how-to.'

Zondervan

5300 Patterson Avenue SE, Grand Rapids, MI 49530

☎001 616 698 6900   Fax 001 616 698 3454

www.zondervan.com

President/Chief Executive *Bruce E. Ryskamp*

Founded 1931. Subsidiary of **HarperCollins Publishers, Inc.** Publishes Protestant religion, Bibles, books, audio & video, computer software, calendars and speciality items.

US Literary Agents

International Reply Coupons (IRCs)
For return postage, send IRCs, available from post offices. Letters, 60 pence; mss according to weight. For current postal rates to the UK, go to the United States Postal Service website at www.usps.com and click on 'Calculate Postage'.

★ = Members of the **Association of Authors' Representatives, Inc.**

Dominick Abel
Literary Agency, Inc★
146 West 82nd Street, Suite 1B, New York, NY 10024
☎001 212 877 0710   Fax 001 212 595 3133
✉ agency@dalainc.com
Contact *Dominick Abel*
Established 1975. No scripts, children's books or poetry. COMMISSION Home 15%; Translation 20%. No unsolicited material. Send query letter with s.a.e. in the first instance. No reading fee.

Miriam Altshuler
Literary Agency★
53 Old Post Road North, Red Hook, NY 12571
☎001 845 758 9408
Contact *Sara McGhee*
Founded 1994. Handles literary and commercial fiction; general non-fiction, narrative non-fiction, memoirs, psychology, biography. No romance, science fiction, mysteries, poetry, westerns, fantasy, how-to, techno thrillers or self-help. COMMISSION Home 15%; Foreign/Translation 20%. Send query letter and synopsis in the first instance with return postage or s.a.e. (no e-mail or fax queries). No reading fee.

Bart Andrews & Associates Inc
7510 Sunset Boulevard, Suite 100, Los Angeles, CA 90046–3418
☎001 310 271 9916
Contact *Bart Andrews*
Founded 1982. General non-fiction: show business, biography and autobiography, film books, trivia, TV, nostalgia. No scripts. No fiction, poetry, children's or science. No books of less than major commercial potential. Specialises in working with celebrities on autobiographies. COMMISSION Home & Translation 15%. OVERSEAS ASSOCIATE Abner Stein, UK. No unsolicited mss. 'Send a brilliant letter (with IRCs for response) extolling your manuscript's virtues. Sell me!' No reading fee.

Malaga Baldi Literary Agency
233 West 99th Street, Suite 19C, New York, NY 10025
☎001 212 222 3213
✉ MBALDI@aol.com
Contact *Malaga Baldi*
Founded 1986. Handles quality fiction and non-fiction. No scripts. No westerns, men's adventure, science fiction/fantasy, romance, how-to, young adult or children's. COMMISSION 15%. OVERSEAS ASSOCIATES **Abner Stein**, UK; Owl Agency; Eliane Benisti, France; **Marsh Agency**. Writers of fiction should send query letter describing the novel plus IRCs. For non-fiction, approach in writing with a proposal, table of contents and two sample chapters. No reading fee.

The Balkin Agency, Inc.★
PO Box 222, Amherst, MA 01004
☎001 413 548 9835   Fax 001 413 548 9836
✉ rick62838@crocker.com
Contact *Richard Balkin*
Founded 1973. Handles adult non-fiction only. COMMISSION Home 15%; Foreign 20%. No reading fee for outlines and synopses.

Loretta Barrett Books, Inc.★
101 Fifth Avenue, New York, NY 10003
☎001 212 242 3420   Fax 001 212 807 9579
Contacts *Loretta Barrett, Nick Mullendore*
Founded 1990. Handles all non-fiction and fiction genres except children's, poetry, science fiction/fantasy. Specialises in women's fiction, history, spirituality. No scripts. COMMISSION Home 15%; Foreign 20%. No e-mail submissions. Send query letter with biography and return postage only in the first instance.

Meredith Bernstein Literary Agency, Inc.★

2112 Broadway, Suite 503A, New York, NY 10023

☎001 212 799 1007   Fax 001 212 799 1145

Contacts *Meredith Bernstein*

Founded 1981. Handles commercial and literary fiction, mysteries and non-fiction (women's issues, business, memoirs, health, current affairs, crafts). COMMISSION Home & Dramatic 15%; Translation 20%. OVERSEAS ASSOCIATES **Abner Stein**, UK; Lennart Sane, Holland, Scandinavia and Spanish language; Thomas Schluck, Germany; Bardon Chinese Media Agency; William Miller, Japan; Frederique Porretta, France; Agenzia Letteraria, Italy.

Bleecker Street Associates, Inc.★

532 LaGuardia Place, #617, New York, NY 10012

☎001 212 677 4492   Fax 001 212 388 0001

Founded 1984. Handles fiction – women's, mystery, suspense, literary; non-fiction – history, women's interests, parenting, health, relationships, psychology, sports, sociology, current events, biography, spirituality, New Age, business. No poetry, children's, westerns, science fiction, professional, academic. COMMISSION Home 15%; Foreign 25%. Send query letter in the first instance. Will only respond if envelope and return postage enclosed. No phone calls, faxes or e-mails. No reading fee.

The Blumer Literary Agency★

350 Seventh Avenue, Suite 1003, New York, NY 10001

☎001 212 749 8853   Fax 001 212 749 0460

Contact *Olivia Blumer*

Founded 2002. Handles a broad range of commercial and literary fiction and non-fiction. Strong background in memoir, inspiration, commercial, literary fiction, illustrated and non-fiction. Specialist subject: cookery. No TV, film, radio or theatre scripts. No children's, science fiction and fantasy or romances. COMMISSION Home 15%; Foreign & Translation 20%. Send initial introductory letter. No reading fee.

Georges Borchardt, Inc.★

136 East 57th Street, New York, NY 10022

☎001 212 753 5785   Fax 001 212 838 6518

Founded 1967. Works mostly with established/published authors. Specialises in fiction, biography, and general non-fiction of unusual interest. COMMISSION Home, UK & Dramatic 15%; Translation 20%. UK ASSOCIATE **Sheil Land Associates Ltd** (Richard Scott Simon), London. Unsolicited mss not read.

Brandt & Hochman Literary Agents, Inc.★

1501 Broadway, Suite 2310, New York, NY 10036

☎001 212 840 5760

Contacts *Carl D. Brandt, Gail Hochman, Marianne Merola, Charles Schlessiger*

Founded 1914. Handles non-fiction and fiction. No poetry. COMMISSION Home & Dramatic 15%; Foreign 20%. UK ASSOCIATE A.M. Heath & Co. Ltd. No unsolicited mss. Approach by letter describing background and ambitions; include return postage. No reading fee.

Barbara Braun Associates, Inc★

104 Fifth Avenue, 7th Floor, New York, NY 10011

☎001 212 604 9023   Fax 001 212 604 9041

✉ bba.230@earthlink.net

www.barbarabraunagency.com

Contacts *Barbara Braun, John Baker*

Founded 1995. Handles literary and mainstream, women's and historical fiction, also serious non-fiction, including psychology and biography. Also young adult and mystery books. Specialises in art history, archaeology, architecture and cultural history. No scripts, self-help, science fiction. COMMISSION Home 15%; Foreign 20%. OVERSEAS ASSOCIATE Chandler Crawford Literary Agency. No unsolicited mss; send query letter in the first instance. No reading fee.

Browne & Miller Literary Associates

410 S. Michigan Avenue, Suite 460, Chicago, IL 60605

☎001 312 922 3063   Fax 001 312 922 1905

✉ mail@browneandmiller.com

www.browneandmiller.com

President *Danielle Egan-Miller*

Founded 1971. Formerly known as Multimedia Product Development. Handles commercial and literary fiction, and practical non-fiction with wide appeal. No scripts, juvenile, science fiction or poetry. COMMISSION Home 15%; Foreign & Translation 20%. OVERSEAS ASSOCIATES in Europe, Latin America, Japan and Asia. In the first instance, send query letter with return postage. No unsolicited material. No reading fee.

Pema Browne Ltd, Illustration and Literary Agents

11 Tena Place, Valley Cottage, NY 10989
☎001 845 268 0029
✉ ppbltd@optonline.net
www.pemabrowneltd.com

Contacts *Pema Browne, Perry Browne*

Founded 1966. ('Pema rhymes with Emma.') Handles mass–market mainstream and hardcover fiction: romance, business, children's picture books and young adult; non-fiction: how-to and reference. COMMISSION Home 15%; Translation 20%; Overseas authors 20%. No unsolicited mss; send query letter with IRCs. No fax or e-mail queries. Also handles illustrators' work. No longer accepting screenplays. 'We are accepting very few new clients at this time.'

Sheree Bykofsky Associates, Inc.★

16 West 36th Street, 13th Floor, New York, NY 10018
☎001 212 244 4144
✉ shereebee@aol.com

Contact *Sheree Bykofsky*

Founded 1991. Handles adult fiction and non-fiction. No scripts. No children's, young adult, horror, science fiction, romance, westerns, occult or supernatural. COMMISSION Home 15%; UK (including sub-agent's fee) 20%. No unsolicited mss. Send query letter first with brief synopsis or outline and writing sample (1–3 pp) for fiction. IRCs essential for reply or return of material. 'Please do not send material via methods that require signature, such as FedEx, etc.' No phone calls. No reading fee.

Maria Carvainis Agency, Inc.★

1350 Avenue of the Americas, Suite 2905, New York, NY 10019
☎001 212 245 6365   Fax 001 212 245 7196
✉ mca@mariacarvainisagency.com

President *Maria Carvainis*

Founded 1977. Handles fiction: literary and mainstream, contemporary women's, mystery, suspense, historical, young adult novels; non-fiction: business, finance, women's issues, politics, film, memoirs, reportage, biography, medicine, psychology and popular science. No film scripts unless from writers with established credits. No science fiction. COMMISSION Domestic & Dramatic 15%; Translation 20%. No faxed or e-mailed queries. No unsolicited mss; they will be returned unread. Queries only, with IRCs for response. No reading fee.

Castiglia Literary Agency★

1155 Camino del mar, #510, Del Mar, CA 92014
☎001 858 755 8761   Fax 001 858 755 7063
✉ jaclagency@aol.com

Contacts *Julie Castiglia, Winifred Golden, Sally van Haitsma*

Founded 1993. Handles fiction: literary, mainstream, ethnic; non-fiction: narrative, biography, science, health, parenting, memoirs, psychology, women's and contemporary issues. Specialises in science, biography and literary fiction. No scripts, horror or true crime. COMMISSION Home 15%; Foreign & Translation 25%. No unsolicited material; send query letter only in the first instance. No reading fee.

The Catalog Literary Agency

PO Box 2964, Vancouver, WA 98668
☎001 360 694 8531

Contact *Douglas Storey*

Founded 1986. Handles popular, professional and textbook material in all subjects, especially business, health, money, science, technology, computers, electronics and women's interests; also how-to, self-help. No fiction. No scripts, articles, screenplays, plays, poetry or short stories. COMMISSION 15%. No unsolicited mss. Query with an outline and sample chapters, and include IRCs. No reading fee.

Jane Chelius Literary Agency, Inc.★

548 Second Street, Brooklyn, New York, NY 11215
☎001 718 499 0236   Fax 001 718 832 7335
✉ queries@janechelius.com
www.janechelius.com

Contacts *Jane Chelius, Mark Chelius*

Founded 1995. No children's, young adult, screenplays, scripts and poetry. COMMISSION Home 15% Foreign 20%. Send first three chapters/synopsis via post or e-mail. No reading fee.

Linda Chester & Associates★

Rockefeller Center, 630 Fifth Avenue, New York, NY 10111
☎001 212 218 3350   Fax 001 212 218 3343
✉ lcassoc@mindspring.com
www.lindachester.com

Contact *Linda Chester*

Founded 1978. Handles literary and commercial fiction and non-fiction in all subjects. No scripts, children's or textbooks. COMMISSION Home & Dramatic 15%; Translation 25%. No unsolicited mss or queries. No reading fee for solicited material.

Frances Collin Literary Agent★
PO Box 33, Wayne, PA 19087–0033
☎001 610 254 0555   Fax 001 610 254 5029

Contact *Frances Collin*

Founded 1948. Successor to Marie Rodell. Handles general fiction and non-fiction. No scripts. OVERSEAS ASSOCIATES worldwide. No unsolicited mss. Send query letter only, with IRCs for reply, for the attention of *Marsha Kear*. No fax or telephone queries, please. No reading fee. Rarely accepts non-professional writers or writers not represented in the UK.

Don Congdon Associates, Inc.★
156 Fifth Avenue, Suite 625, New York,
NY 10010–7002
☎001 212 645 1229   Fax 001 212 727 2688

Contacts *Don Congdon, Michael Congdon, Susan Ramer, Cristina Concepcion*

Founded 1983. Handles fiction and non-fiction. No academic, technical, romantic fiction or scripts. COMMISSION Home 15%; UK & Translation 19%. OVERSEAS ASSOCIATES worldwide. No unsolicited mss. Query letter with return postage in the first instance. No reading fee.

Cornerstone Literary Agency★
4500 Wilshire Boulevard, Los Angeles,
CA 90010
☎001 323 930 6039   Fax 001 323 930 0407
✉ info@cornerstoneliterary.com
www.cornerstoneliterary.com

Contact *Helen Breitwieser*

Founded 1998. Handles literary and commercial fiction. Specialises in thrillers and commercial women's fiction. No scripts, children's, self-help, science fiction or fantasy. COMMISSION Home 15%; Foreign & Translation 20%. No unsolicited mss via mail, e-mail or fax; send query letter and one-page synopsis via mail only (enclosing return postage). No reading fee.

Curtis Brown Ltd★
10 Astor Place, New York, NY 10003
☎001 212 473 5400

Book Rights *Laura Blake Peterson, Ellen Geiger, Peter L. Ginsberg, Emilie Jacobson, Ginger Knowlton, Maureen Walters, Mitchell Waters, Elizabeth Harding*
Film & TV Rights *Timothy Knowlton, Edwin Wintle*
Translation *Dave Barbor*

Founded 1914. Handles general fiction and non-fiction. Also some scripts for film, TV and theatre. OVERSEAS ASSOCIATES Representatives in all major foreign countries. No unsolicited mss; queries only, with IRCs for reply. No reading fee.

Joan Daves Agency
21 West 26th Street, New York,
NY 10010-1003
☎001 212 685 2400   Fax 001 212 685 1781

Director *Jennifer Lyons*

Founded 1952. See also **Writers House LLC**. Literary fiction and non-fiction. No romance or textbooks. No scripts. Send query letter in the first instance. COMMISSION Home 15%; Dramatic/Film 15%; Foreign 20%. 'A detailed synopsis seems valuable only for non-fiction work. Material submitted should specify the author's background, publishing credits and similar pertinent information.' No reading fee.

Sandra Dijkstra Literary Agency★
PMB 515, 1155 Camino Del Mar, Del Mar,
CA 92014
☎001 858 755 3115   Fax 001 858 794 2822

Contact *Taryn Fagerness*

Founded 1981. Handles quality and commercial non-fiction and fiction, including some genre fiction. No scripts. No westerns, contemporary romance or poetry. Willing to look at children's projects. Specialises in quality fiction, mystery/thrillers, narrative non-fiction, psychology, self-help, science, health, business, memoirs, biography, current affairs. 'Dedicated to promoting new and original voices and ideas.' COMMISSION Home 15%; Translation 20%. OVERSEAS ASSOCIATES **Abner Stein**, UK; Ursula Bender, Agence Hoffman, Germany; Licht & Burr, Scandinavia; Luigi Bernabo, Italy; Sandra Bruna, Spain; Caroline Van Gelderen, Netherlands; M. Kling (La Nouvelle Agence), France; The English Agency, Japan; Bardon-Chinese Media Agency, China/Taiwan; Prava I Prevodi, Eastern Europe. For fiction: send brief synopsis (one page) and first 50 pages; for non-fiction: send proposal with overview, chapter outline, author biog, two sample chapters and profile of competition. All submissions should be accompanied by IRCs. No reading fee.

Dunham Literary Inc★
156 Fifth Avenue, Suite 625, New York,
NY 10010
☎001 212 929 0994   Fax 001 212 929 0904
www.dunhamlit.com

Contacts *Jennie Dunham, Ashley Johnston*

Founded 2000. Handles literary fiction and non-fiction, New Age spirituality, mysteries and children's (from picture books through young adult). No scripts, romance, westerns, horror, science-fiction/fantasy or poetry. COMMISSION Home 15%; Foreign & Translation 20%. OVERSEAS ASSOCIATE UK & Europe: **A.M. Heath & Co. Ltd.** The Rhoda Weyr Agency is now a division of Dunham Literary Inc. No unsolicited material. Send query letter (with return postage) giving information on the author and ms. No e-mail or faxed queries; see the website for further contact information. No reading fee.

Dystel & Goderich Literary Management★

One Union Square West, Suite 904, New York, NY 10003
☎001 212 627 9100   Fax 001 212 627 9313
www.dystel.com

Contacts *Jane Dystel, Miriam Goderich, Stacey Glick, Michael Bourret, Jim McCarthy*

Founded 1991. Handles non-fiction and fiction. Specialises in politics, history, biography, cookbooks, current affairs, celebrities, commercial and literary fiction. No reading fee.

Anne Edelstein Literary Agency LLC★

20 West 22nd Street, #1603, New York, NY 10010
☎001 212 414 4923   Fax 001 212 414 2930
www.aeliterary.com

Contact *Emilie Stewart*

Founded 1990. No film, TV, theatre or radio scripts. COMMISSION Home 15%; Translation 20%. OVERSEAS ASSOCIATES Ulf Toregard; Eliane Benisti; Caroline van Gelderen; Luigi Bernabo; Rachel Calder, **The Sayle Literary Agency**; Mercedes Casanovas; Petra Eggers; Lucia Riff, BMSR. Unsolicited material welcome; send query letter in the first instance.

Educational Design Services, Inc.

7238 Treviso Lane, Boynton Beach, FL 33437
☎001 561 739 9402
✉ linder.eds@adelphia.net

President *Bertram Linder*

Founded 1979. Specialises in educational material and textbooks for sale to school markets. COMMISSION Home 15%; Foreign 25%. IRCs must accompany submissions.

Ethan Ellenberg Literary Agency★

548 Broadway, #5E, New York, NY 10012
☎001 212 431 4554   Fax 001 212 941 4652
✉ agent@ethanellenberg.com
www.ethanellenberg.com

Contact *Ethan Ellenberg*

Founded 1984. Handles fiction: commercial, genre, literary and children's; non-fiction: history, biography, business, science, health, cooking, current affairs. Specialises in commercial fiction, thrillers, suspense and romance. No scripts, poetry or short stories. COMMISSION Home 15%; Translation 20%. Prefers submissions by mail with return postage. For fiction send synopsis and three chapters; for non-fiction send proposal and sample chapters, if available. No reading fee. For e-mail submissions send query letter only; no attachments.

Ann Elmo Agency, Inc.★

60 East 42nd Street, New York, NY 10165
☎001 212 661 2880/1
Fax 001 212 661 2883

Contacts *Lettie Lee, Mari Cronin, Andree Abecassis*

Founded in the 1940s. Handles literary and romantic fiction, mysteries and mainstream; also non-fiction in all subjects, including biography and self-help. Some children's (8–12-year-olds). COMMISSION Home 15–20%. Query letter with outline of project in the first instance. No reading fee.

The Fogelman Literary Agency★

7515 Greenville Avenue, Suite 712, Dallas, TX 75231
☎001 214 361 9956   Fax 001 214 361 9553
✉ info@aol.com
www.fogelman.com

Also at: 445 Park Avenue, 9th Floor, New York, NY 10022

Contacts *Evan Fogelman, Linda Kruger*

Founded 1989. Handles non-fiction and fiction: romance (including historical and contemporary) and some mystery/suspense. No scripts, poetry, westerns, science fiction/fantasy or children's books. COMMISSION Home 15%; Foreign & Translation 10%. OVERSEAS ASSOCIATES Thomas Schluck Agency; Shin Won Literary Agency; Bastei Lubbe Taschenbucher; Big Apple Tuttle-Mori Agency. No unsolicited material. Published authors are welcome to call but unpublished authors should send query by e-mail or letter with return postage. No reading fee.

ForthWrite Literary Agency & Speakers Bureau

A subsidiary of Keller Media, Inc,
23852 W Pacific Coast Highway, Suite 701,
Malibu, CA 90265
☎001 310 394 9840   Fax 001 310 394 9857
✉ agent@kellermedia.com
www.kellermedia.com
Contact *Wendy L. Keller*

Founded 1988. Specialises in promoting the careers of speakers and authors in the categories of biography, business (marketing, finance, management and sales), alternative health, cookery, gardening, nature, popular psychology, history, self-help, home and health, crafts, computer, how-to. Handles electronic, foreign (translation and distribution) and resale rights for previously published books. COMMISSION Foreign 20%. Send query letter with IRCs. No reading fee.

Jeanne Fredericks Literary Agency, Inc.★

221 Benedict Hill Road, New Canaan,
CT 06840
☎001 203 972 3011   Fax 001 203 972 3011
✉ jfredrks@optonline.net
Contact *Jeanne Fredericks*

Founded 1997. Handles quality adult non-fiction, usually of a practical and popular nature by authorities in their fields. Specialises in health, gardening, business, self-help, reference. No fiction, juvenile, poetry, essays, politics, academic or textbooks. COMMISSION Home 15%; Foreign 25% (with co-agent) or 20% (direct). No unsolicited material; send query by e-mail (no attachments) or letter with return postage in the first instance. No reading fee.

Robert A. Freedman Dramatic Agency, Inc.★

Suite 2310, 1501 Broadway, New York,
NY 10036
☎001 212 840 5760
President *Robert A. Freedman*
Senior Vice-President *Selma Luttinger*
Vice-President *Robin Kaver*
Associate *Marta Praeger*

Founded 1928 as Brandt & Brandt Dramatic Department, Inc. Took its present name in 1984. Works mostly with established authors. Specialises in plays, film and TV scripts. COMMISSION Dramatic 10%. Unsolicited mss not read.

Gelfman Schneider Literary Agents, Inc.★

250 West 57th Street, Suite 2515, New York,
NY 10107
☎001 212 245 1993   Fax 001 212 245 8678
Contacts *Deborah Schneider, Jane Gelfman*

Founded 1919 (London), 1980 (New York). Formerly John Farquharson Ltd. Works mostly with established/published authors. Specialises in general trade fiction and non-fiction. No poetry, short stories or screenplays. COMMISSION Home 15%; Dramatic 15%; Foreign 20%. OVERSEAS ASSOCIATE **Curtis Brown Group Ltd**, UK. No reading fee for outlines. Submissions must be accompanied by IRCs. No e-mail queries please.

Sanford J. Greenburger Associates, Inc.★

55 Fifth Avenue, 15th Floor, New York,
NY 10003
☎001 212 206 5600   Fax 001 212 463 8718
www.greenburger.com
Contacts *Heide Lange, Faith Hamlin, Daniel Mandel, Matt Bialer, Peter McGuigan*

Handles fiction and non-fiction. No unsolicited mss. First approach with query letter, sample chapter and synopsis. No reading fee.

The Charlotte Gusay Literary Agency

10532 Blythe Avenue, Los Angeles, CA 90064
☎001 310 559 0831   Fax 001 310 559 2639
✉ gusay1@aol.com (queries only)
www.mediastudio.com/gusay
Contact *Charlotte Gusay*

Founded 1988. Handles fiction, both literary and commercial, books to film and screenplays, plus non-fiction: children's and adult humour, parenting, gardening, women's and men's issues, feminism, psychology, memoirs, biography, travel. No science fiction, horror, short pieces or collections of stories. COMMISSION Home 15%; Dramatic 15%; Translation & Foreign 25%. No unsolicited mss; send query letter by snailmail first, then if material is requested, send succinct outline and first three sample chapters for fiction, or proposal for non-fiction. No response without IRCs or self-addressed stamped envelope. No reading fee but may require a minimal processing fee to cover handling of material.

Joy Harris Literary Agency, Inc.★

156 Fifth Avenue, Suite 617, New York,
NY 10010
☎001 212 924 6269   Fax 001 212 924 6609

✉ gen.office@jhlitagent.com

Contacts *Joy Harris, Stephanie Abou, Leslie Daniels, Sara Lustig*

Handles adult non-fiction and fiction. COMMISSION Home 15%; Foreign 20%. No unsolicited mss. Query letter in the first instance. No reading fee.

John Hawkins & Associates, Inc.*
71 West 23rd Street, Suite 1600, New York, NY 10010
☎001 212 807 7040   Fax 001 212 807 9555
✉ jha@jhaliterary.com

Contacts *John Hawkins, William Reiss*

Founded 1893. Handles film and TV rights. COMMISSION Apply for rates. No unsolicited mss; send queries with 1–3-page outline and one-page c.v. IRCs necessary for response. No reading fee.

The Jeff Herman Agency, LLC
PO Box 1522, Stockbridge, MA 01262
☎001 413 298 0077   Fax 001 413 298 8188
✉ jeff@jeffherman.com
www.jeffherman.com

Contact *Jeffrey H. Herman*

Handles all areas of non-fiction, textbooks and reference, business, spiritual and psychology. No scripts. COMMISSION Home 15%; Translation 10%. No unsolicited mss. Query letter with IRCs in the first instance. No reading fee. Jeff Herman publishes a useful reference guide to the book trade called *Herman's Guide to Book Editors, Publishers & Literary Agents* (Kalmbach).

Frederick Hill Bonnie Nadell Inc.
1842 Union Street, San Francisco, CA 94123
☎001 415 921 2910   Fax 001 415 921 2802

Contacts *Fred Hill, Bonnie Nadell*

Founded 1979. General fiction and non-fiction. No scripts. COMMISSION Home & Dramatic 15%; Foreign 20%. OVERSEAS ASSOCIATE **Mary Clemmey Literary Agency**, UK. No longer accepting unsolicited queries.

Janklow & Nesbit Associates
445 Park Avenue, New York, NY 10022
☎001 212 421 1700   Fax 001 212 980 3671

Partners *Morton L. Janklow, Lynn Nesbit*
Senior Vice-President *Anne Sibbald*
Agents *Tina Bennett, Luke Janklow, Richard Morris, Eric Simonoff*

Founded 1989. Handles fiction and non-fiction;

commercial and literary. See also **Janklow & Nesbit (UK) Ltd** under *UK Literary Agents*. No unsolicited mss.

JCA Literary Agency, Inc*
174 Sullivan Street, New York, NY 10012
☎001 212 807 0888

Contacts *Jeff Gerecke, Tony Outhwaite, Peter Steinberg*

Founded 1978. Handles general fiction and non-fiction. No scripts, poetry, science fiction/fantasy or children's books. COMMISSION Home 15%; Foreign 20%. OVERSEAS ASSOCIATE **Vanessa Holt Ltd**, UK. No unsolicited mss; send query letter with return postage. No reading fee.

The Karpfinger Agency
357 West 20th Street, New York, NY 10011
☎001 212 691 2690   Fax 001 212 691 7129

Agent *Barney M. Karpfinger*

Founded 1985. Handles quality fiction and non-fiction. No scripts, poetry, romance, horror, science fiction/fantasy, children's picture books. COMMISSION Home 15%; Foreign & Translation 20%.No unsolicited mss. Send query letter with synopsis and writing samples (not exceeding 30 pages). No reading fee.

Kirchoff/Wohlberg, Inc.*
866 United Nations Plaza, Suite 525, New York, NY 10017
☎001 212 644 2020   Fax 001 212 223 4387
www.kirchoffwohlberg.com

Authors' Representative *Elizabeth Pulitzer-Voges*

Founded 1930. Handles books for children and young adults, specialising in children's picture books. No adult material. No scripts for TV, radio, film or theatre. Send letter of enquiry with synopsis or outline and writing sample plus IRCs for reply or return. No reading fee.

Harvey Klinger, Inc.*
301 West 53rd Street, New York, NY 10019
☎001 212 581 7068   Fax 001 212 315 3823
✉ queries@harveyklinger.com
www.harveyklinger.com

Contact *Harvey Klinger*

Founded 1977. Handles mainstream fiction and non-fiction. Specialises in commercial and literary fiction, psychology, health and science. No scripts, poetry, computer or children's books. COMMISSION Home 15%; Foreign 25%. OVERSEAS ASSOCIATES in all principal countries. Welcomes unsolicited material; send by e-mail or post (no faxes). No reading fee.

Linda Konner Literary Agency★
10 West 15 Street, Suite 1918, New York,
NY 10011
☎001 212 691 3419
✉ ldkonner@cs.com
Contact *Linda Konner*

Founded 1996. Handles non-fiction only, specialising in health, self-help, diet/fitness, pop psychology, relationships, parenting, personal finance. Also some pop culture/celebrities. COMMISSION Home 15%; Foreign 25%. Books must be written by or with established experts in their field. No scripts, fiction, poetry or children's books. No unsolicited material; send one-page query with return postage. No reading fee.

Peter Lampack Agency, Inc.
551 Fifth Avenue, Suite 1613, New York,
NY 10176
☎001 212 687 9106
✉ ALampack@verizon.net
Contact *Andrew Lampack*

Founded in 1977. Handles commercial fiction: male action and adventure, contemporary relationships, historical, mysteries and suspense, literary fiction; also non-fiction from recognised experts in a given field, plus biographies, autobiographies. Also handles theatrical, motion picture, and TV rights from book properties. No original scripts or screenplays, series or episodic material. COMMISSION Home & Dramatic 15%; Translation & UK 20%. Best approach by letter in first instance. No reply without s.a.e. 'We will respond within three weeks and invite the submission of manuscripts which we would like to examine.' No reading fee. No unsolicited mss.

Michael Larsen/Elizabeth Pomada Literary Agency★
1029 Jones Street, San Francisco, CA 94109
☎001 415 673 0939
✉ larsenpoma@aol.com
www.larsenpomada.com
Contact (non-fiction) *Michael Larsen*
Contact (fiction) *Elizabeth Pomada*

Founded 1972. Handles adult fiction and non-fiction – literary and commercial. No scripts, poetry, children's, science fiction. COMMISSION Home 15%; Foreign 20–30%. OVERSEAS ASSOCIATES **David Grossman Literary Agency Ltd**, British rights; Chandler Crawford (foreign rights). Fiction: send first ten pages with 2-page synopsis and s.a.e.; non-fiction: e-mail title and promotion plan. Consult website for guidelines.

Sarah Lazin Books★
126 Fifth Avenue, Suite 300, New York,
NY 10011
☎001 212 989 5757   Fax 001 212 989 1393
Contact *Sarah Lazin*

Handles adult narrative non-fiction in pop culture, biography, social issues, music reference, photography, fiction. Specialises in music and biography. COMMISSION Home 15%; Foreign 10%. Send query letter with references and writing sample.

The Ned Leavitt Agency★
70 Wooster Street, Suite 4F, New York,
NY 10012
www.nedleavittagency.com
President *Ned Leavitt*
Agent *Britta Steiner Alexander*

Ned Leavitt specialises in creativity, spirituality, health and literary fiction; Britta Alexander specialises in smart non-fiction for 20 and 30-somethings (dating, relationships, business) and commercial ficton. No screenplays or genre fiction. COMMISSION Home 15%. Send 2–3 sample chapters with synopsis, by post, with s.a.e. No reading fee.

Lescher & Lescher Ltd★
47 East 19th Street, New York, NY 10003
☎001 212 529 1790   Fax 001 212 529 2716
Contact *Robert Lescher*

Founded 1964. Handles a broad range of serious non-fiction including current affairs, history, biography, memoir, government, politics, law, contemporary issues, sociology, psychology, popular culture, food and wine, literary and commercial fiction including mysteries and thrillers; some children's books. Specialises in wine books and cookbooks. No poetry, science fiction, New Age, spiritual, romance. COMMISSION Home 10%; Foreign 20%. No unsolicited manuscripts – please query first. No reading fee.

Sterling Lord Literistic, Inc.
65 Bleecker Street, New York, NY 10012
☎001 212 780 6050   Fax 001 212 780 6095
www.sll.com
Contacts *Philippa Brophy, Chris Calhoun*

Founded 1979. Handles all genres, fiction and non-fiction, plus scripts for TV and film. COMMISSION Home 15%; UK & Translation 20%. No unsolicited mss. Prefers letter outlining all non-fiction. No reading fee.

Lowenstein–Yost Associates Inc★

121 West 27th Street, Suite 601, New York,
NY 10001
☎001 212 206 1630   Fax 001 212 727 0280
www.lowensteinyost.com
Agents *Barbara Lowenstein, Nancy Yost, Eileen
Cope, Dorian Karchmar*

Founded 1976. Handles fiction: literary and
commercial, women's, mainstream, romance,
mystery, thrillers. Non-fiction: narrative, health,
business, women's issues, adventure travel, science, spirituality, psychology, social issues, ethnic and cultural issues, history, biography and
the arts. No textbooks, westerns, science fiction, cookery or children's books. COMMISSION
Home 15%; Foreign & Translation 20%.
OVERSEAS ASSOCIATES in all major countries.
Fiction: send query letter, synopsis and first
chapter; non-fiction: send query with proposal,
if available, or overview. Include return postage.
No reading fee.

Carol Mann Agency★

55 Fifth Avenue, New York, NY 10003
☎001 212 206 5635   Fax 001 212 675 4809
✉ carol.mann@carolmannagency.com *or*
kristy@carolmannagency.com *or*
emily@carolmannagen
Contacts *Carol Mann, Emily Nurkin, Kristy Mayer*

Founded 1977. Handles literary fiction and narrative non-fiction, including psychology, biography, memoirs, history, pop culture, spirituality.
No scripts or genre fiction. COMMISSION
Home 15%; Foreign 20%. No unsolicited material; send query letter with return postage. No
reading fee.

Manus & Associates Literary Agency, Inc.★

425 Sherman Avenue, Suite 200, Palo Alto,
CA 94306
✉ ManusLit@ManusLit.com
www.ManusLit.com
Also at: 445 Park Avenue, New York, NY 10022
Contacts (California) *Jillian Manus, Jandy Nelson,
Stephanie Lee, Donna Levin, Penny Nelson*
Contact (New York) *Janet Manus*

Handles commercial and literary fiction; non-
fiction, including true crime, self-help, memoirs, history, pop culture and popular science.
No scripts, science fiction/fantasy, westerns,
romance, horror, poetry or children's books.
COMMISSION Home 15%; Foreign 25%. No
unsolicited mss. Fiction: send query letter and

first 30 pages; non-fiction: query letter and proposal. Include return postage. No reading fee.

The Evan Marshall Agency★

Six Tristam Place, Pine Brook, NJ 07058–9445
☎001 973 882 1122   Fax 001 973 882 3099
✉ evanmarshall@thenovelist.com
www.TheNovelist.com
Contact *Evan Marshall*

Founded 1987. Handles general adult fiction.
COMMISSION Home 15%; UK & Translation
20%. No unsolicited mss; send query letter first.
No reading fee.

Mews Books Ltd

c/o Sidney B. Kramer, 20 Bluewater Hill,
Westport, CT 06880
☎001 203 227 1836   Fax 001 203 227 1144
✉ mewsbooks@aol.com (initial contact only;
submission by regular mail)
Contacts *Sidney B. Kramer, Fran Pollak*

Founded 1970. Handles adult fiction and non-
fiction, children's, pre-school and young adult.
No scripts, short stories or novellas (unless by
established authors). Specialises in cookery, medical, health and nutrition, scientific non-fiction,
children's and young adult. COMMISSION Home
15%; Film & Translation 20%. OVERSEAS ASSOCI-
ATE **Abner Stein**, UK. Unsolicited material
welcome. Presentation must be professional and
should include summary of plot/characters, one
or two sample chapters, personal credentials and
brief on target market, all suitable for forwarding
to a publisher. No reading fee. Charges for photocopying, postage expenses, telephone calls and
other direct costs. Principal agent is an attorney
and former publisher (a founder of Bantam
Books, Corgi Books). Offers consultation service
through which writers can get advice on a contract or on publishing problems.

Doris S. Michaels Literary Agency Inc.★

1841 Broadway, Suite 903, New York,
NY 10023
☎001 212 265 9474   Fax 001 212 265 9480
✉ info@dsmagency.com
www.dsmagency.com
Contact *Doris Michaels*

Handles literary fiction that has a commercial
appeal and strong screen potential and women's
fiction; non-fiction: current affairs, biography and
memoirs, self-help, business, history, health, classical music, sports, women's issues, computers and
pop culture. No action/adventure, suspense, sci-

ence fiction, romance, New Age, religion/spirituality, gift books, art books, fantasy, thrillers, mysteries, westerns, occult and supernatural, horror, historical fiction, poetry, children's literature, humour or travel books. COMMISSION Home 15% Send query letter via e-mail with a one-page synopsis and include a short paragraph detailing credentials. No reading fee. .

Howard Morhaim Literary Agency★

11 John Street, Suite 407, New York, NY 10038
☎001 212 529 4433   Fax 001 212 995 1112
Contact *Howard Morhaim*

Founded 1979. Handles general adult fiction and non-fiction. No scripts. No children's or young adult material, poetry or religious. COMMISSION Home 15%; UK & Translation 20%. OVERSEAS ASSOCIATES worldwide. No unsolicited mss. Send query letter with synopsis and sample chapters for fiction; query letter with outline or proposal for non-fiction. Include return postage. No reading fee.

Henry Morrison, Inc.

PO Box 235, Bedford Hills, NY 10507–0235
☎001 914 666 3500   Fax 001 914 241 7846
Contact *Henry Morrison*

Founded 1965. Handles general fiction, crime and science fiction, and non-fiction. No scripts unless by established writers. COMMISSION Home 15%; UK & Translation 25%. Unsolicited material welcome but send query letter with outline (1–5 pp) in the first instance. No reading fee.

The Jean V. Naggar Literary Agency★

216 East 75th Street, Suite 1-E, New York City, NY 10021
Contacts *Jean Naggar, Alice Tasman, Mollie Glick, Jennifer Weltz*

Founded 1978. Handles strong mainstream fiction, literary fiction, memoir, biography, sophisticated self-help, popular science and psychology. No scripts. COMMISSION Home 15%; Foreign 20%. No unsolicited material; send query letter *only* with return postage initially. No reading fee.

B.K. Nelson Literary Agency

84 Woodland Road, Pleasantville, NY 10570
☎001 914 741 1322   Fax 001 914 741 1324
✉ bknelson4@cs.com
www.bknelson.com

Also at: 1565 Paseo Vida, Palm Springs, CA 92264
☎001 760 880 7800 Fax 001 760 778 0034
President *Bonita K. Nelson*
Vice President *Leonard 'Chip' Ashbach*
Editorial Director *John W. Benson*

Founded 1979. Specialises in novels, business, self-help, how-to, political, autobiography, celebrity biography. Major motion picture and TV documentary success. COMMISSION 20%. Lecture Bureau for Authors founded 1994; Foreign Rights Catalogue established 1995; BK Nelson Infomercial Marketing Co. 1996, primarily for authors and endorsements, and BKNelson, Inc. for motion picture production in 1998. Signatory to Writers Guild of America, West (WGAW). No unsolicited mss. Letter of inquiry. Reading fee charged.

New England Publishing Associates, Inc.★

Box 5, Chester, CT 06412
☎001 860 345 7323   Fax 001 860 345 3660
✉ nepa@nepa.com
www.nepa.com
Contacts *Elizabeth Frost-Knappman, Edward W. Knappman, Kris Schiavi, Ron Formica, Victoria S. Harlow* (photo/research editor)

Founded 1983. Handles non-fiction. Specialises in current affairs, business, history, science, women's studies, reference, psychology, politics, biography, true crime and literature. No textbooks or anthologies. No scripts, poetry or fiction. COMMISSION Home 15%. OVERSEAS ASSOCIATES throughout Europe and Japan; Rachel Calder, UK. Dramatic rights: Joel Gotler, Intellectual Property Group, Los Angeles. Unsolicited mss considered but query letter or phone call preferred first. No reading fee.

Richard Parks Agency★

PO Box 693, Salem, NY 12865
☎001 518 854 9466   Fax 001 518 854 9466
✉ rp@richardparksagency.com
Contact *Richard Parks*

Founded 1989. Handles general trade fiction and non-fiction: literary novels, mysteries and thrillers, commercial fiction, science fiction, biography, pop culture, psychology, self-help, parenting, medical, cooking, gardening, history, etc. No scripts. No technical or academic. COMMISSION Home 15%; UK & Translation 20%. OVERSEAS ASSOCIATES **The Marsh Agency; Barbara Levy Literary Agency**. No unsolicited mss. Fiction read by referral only.

Non-fiction query with s.a.e. Faxed or e-mail queries will *not* be considered. No reading fee.

James Peter Associates, Inc.*
PO Box 358, New Canaan, CT 06840
☎001 203 972 1070   Fax 001 203 972 1759
✉ gene_brissie@msn.com
President *Eugene Brissie*
Founded 1971. Non-fiction only. 'Many of our authors are historians, psychologists, physicians – all are writing trade books for general readers.' No scripts. No fiction or children's books. Specialises in history, popular culture, business, health, biography and politics. COMMISSION 15%. No unsolicited mss. Send query letter first with brief project outline, samples and biographical information. No reading fee.

Alison J. Picard Literary Agent
PO Box 2000, Cotuit, MA 02635
☎001 508 477 7192
Fax 001 508 477 7192 (notify before faxing)
✉ ajpicard@aol.com
Contact *Alison Picard*
Founded 1985. Handles mainstream and literary fiction, contemporary and historical romance, children's and young adult, mysteries and thrillers; plus non-fiction. No short stories or poetry. Rarely any science fiction and fantasy. Particularly interested in expanding non-fiction titles. COMMISSION 15%. OVERSEAS ASSOCIATE **John Pawsey**, UK. Approach with written query. No reading fee.

Pinder Lane & Garon-Brooke Associates Ltd*
159 West 53rd Street, Suite 14–E, New York, NY 10019
☎001 212 489 0880   Fax 001 212 489 7104
✉ pinderl@interport.net
Owner Agents *Dick Duane, Robert Thixton*
Founded 1951. Fiction and non-fiction. No category romance, westerns or mysteries. COMMISSION Home 15%; Dramatic 10–15%; Foreign 30%. OVERSEAS ASSOCIATES **Abner Stein**, UK; Translation: Rights Unlimited. No unsolicited mss. First approach by query letter. No reading fee.

PMA Literary & Film Management, Inc.
PO Box 1817, Old Chelsea Sta., New York, NY 10011
☎001 212 929 1222   Fax 001 212 206 0238
✉ pmalitfilm@aol.com

www.pmalitfilm.com
President *Peter Miller*
Associates *Scott Hoffman, Lisa Silverman*
Founded 1976. Commercial fiction and non-fiction. Specialises in books with motion picture and television potential, and in true crime. No poetry, pornography, non-commercial or academic. COMMISSION Home 15%; Dramatic 10–15%; Foreign 20–25%. No unsolicited mss. Approach by letter with one-page synopsis.

The Aaron M. Priest Literary Agency*
708 Third Avenue, 23rd Floor, New York, NY 10017
☎001 212 818 0344   Fax 001 212 373 9417

Founded 1974. Handles literary and commercial fiction. No scripts, children's fantasy or sci-fi. Submissions by mail only. No reading fee.

Susan Ann Protter Literary Agent*
110 West 40th Street, Suite 1408, New York, NY 10018
☎001 212 840 0480
Contact *Susan Ann Protter*
Founded 1971. Handles general fiction, mysteries, thrillers, science fiction and fantasy; non-fiction: history, general reference, biography, science, health and parenting. No romance, poetry, westerns, religious, children's or sport manuals. No scripts. COMMISSION Home & Dramatic 15%. OVERSEAS ASSOCIATES **Abner Stein**, UK; agents in all major markets. First approach with letter, including IRCs. No reading fee.

Quicksilver Books, Literary Agents
508 Central Park Avenue, #5101, Scarsdale, NY 10583
☎001 914 722 4664   Fax 001 914 722 4664
President *Bob Silverstein*
Founded 1973. Handles literary fiction and mainstream commercial fiction: blockbuster, suspense, thriller, contemporary, mystery and historical; and general non-fiction, including self-help, psychology, holistic healing, ecology, environmental, biography, fact crime, New Age, health, nutrition, cookery, enlightened wisdom and spirituality. No scripts, science fiction and fantasy, pornographic, children's or romance. COMMISSION Home & Dramatic 15%; Translation 20%. UK material being submitted must have universal appeal for the US market.

Unsolicited material welcome but must be accompanied by IRCs for response, together with biographical details, covering letter, etc. No reading fee.

Raines & Raines*
103 Kenyon Road, Medusa, NY 12120
☎001 518 239 8311   Fax 001 518 239 6029

Contacts *Theron Raines, Joan Raines, Keith Korman*

Founded 1961. Handles general non-fiction. No scripts. COMMISSION Home 15%; Foreign & Translation 20%. No unsolicited material; send one-page letter in the first instance. No reading fee.

Reece Halsey North*
98 Main Street, #704, Tiburon, CA 94920
☎001 415 789 9191   Fax 001 415 789 9177
✉ info@reecehalseynorth.com
www.kimberleycameron.com

Also: Reece Halsey Agency, 8733 Sunset Blvd. #101, Los Angeles, CA 90069
☎001 310 652 2409 Fax 001 310 652 7595

Contact (Tiburon) *Kimberley Cameron*
Contact (Los Angeles) *Dorris Halsey*

Founded 1957. Represents literary and mainstream fiction, non-fiction. No scripts, poetry or children's books. COMMISSION Home 15%; Foreign 20%. Send query letter with first ten pages together with return postage. No e-mail submissions. No reading fee.

Helen Rees Literary Agency*
376 North Street, Boston, MA 02113–2103
☎001 617 227 9014   Fax 001 617 227 8762
✉ agent10702@aol.com

Contact *Helen Rees*
Associates *Ann Collette, Lorin Rees*

Founded 1982. Specialises in books on health and business; also handles biography, autobiography and history; quality fiction. No scholarly or technical books. No scripts, science fiction, children's, poetry, photography, short stories, cooking. COMMISSION Home 15%; Foreign 20%. No unsolicited mss; no e-mail queries or attachments. Send query letter with IRCs. No reading fee.

Rights Unlimited, Inc.*
101 West 55th Street, Suite 2D, New York, NY 10019
☎001 212 246 0900   Fax 001 212 246 2114
✉ alongden@rightsunlimited.com

Contacts *Raymond Kurman, John Sansevere*

Founded 1985. Handles adult fiction, non-fiction. No scripts, poetry, short stories, educa-

tional or literary works. COMMISSION Home & Translation 20%. Query letter with synopsis preferred in the first instance. No reading fee.

The Angela Rinaldi Literary Agency*
PO Box 7877, Beverly Hills, CA 90212–7877
☎001 310 842 7665   Fax 001 310 837 8143
✉ amr@rinaldiliterary.com

Contact *Angela Rinaldi*

Founded 1995. Handles commercial and literary fiction; narrative non-fiction, practical and pro-active self-help. No scripts, cookery, science fiction, westerns, romance, poetry, children's/young adult. COMMISSION Home 15%; Foreign 20%. Send brief e-mail or query letter with return postage in the first instance. No reading fee.

B.J. Robbins Literary Agency*
5130 Bellaire Avenue, North Hollywood, CA 91607
☎001 818 760 6602   Fax 001 818 760 6616
✉ robbinsliterary@aol.com

Contact *B.J. Robbins*

Founded 1992. Handles literary fiction, narrative and general non-fiction. No scripts, genre fiction, romance, horror, science fiction or children's books. COMMISSION Home 15%; Foreign & Translation 20%. OVERSEAS ASSOCIATES **Abner Stein** and **The Marsh Agency**, UK. Send covering letter with first three chapters or e-mail query in the first instance. No reading fee.

Linda Roghaar Literary Agency, Inc.*
133 High Point Drive, Amherst, MA 01002
☎001 413 256 1921   Fax 001 413 256 2636
✉ contact@lindaroghaar.com
www.lindaroghaar.com

Contact *Linda L. Roghaar*

Founded 1997. Handles fiction and non-fiction, specialising in religious titles. No science fiction or horror. COMMISSION Home 15%; Foreign & Translation rate varies. Send query by e-mail or letter with return postage (for fiction, include the first five pages). No reading fee.

The Rosenberg Group*
23 Lincoln Avenue, Marblehead, MA 01945
www.rosenberggroup.com

Contact *Barbara Collins Rosenberg*

Founded 1998. Handles non-fiction (please see website for areas of interest), fiction, specialising in romance (single title and category) and women's; non-fiction, specialising in college textbooks. No scripts, science fiction, true crime, inspirational fiction, children's and young adult. COMMISSION Home 15%; Foreign 25%. No unsolicited material; send query letter by post only. No reading fee.

Rosenstone/Wender★
38 East 29th Street, 10th Floor, New York, NY 10016
☎001 212 725 9445   Fax 001 212 725 9447
Contacts *Phyllis Wender, Susan Perlman Cohen, Sonia E. Pabley*
Founded 1981. Handles fiction, non-fiction, children's, and scripts for film, TV and theatre. No material for radio. COMMISSION Home 15%; Dramatic 10%; Foreign 20%. OVERSEAS ASSOCIATES La Nouvelle Agence, France; Andrew Nurnberg, Netherlands; The English Agency, Japan; Mohrbooks, Germany; Ole Licht, Scandinavia. No unsolicited mss. Send letter outlining the project, credits, etc. No reading fee.

The Sagalyn Literary Agency★
7201 Wisconsin Avenue, Suite 675, Bethesda, MD 20814
☎001 301 718 6440   Fax 001 301 718 6444
✉ info@sagalyn.com
www.sagalyn.com
Founded 1980. Handles mostly upmarket non-fiction with some fiction. No screenplays, romance, science fiction/fantasy, children's literature. No unsolicited material. See website for submissions procedure. No reading fee.

Victoria Sanders & Associates LLC★
241 Avenue of the Americas, Suite 11H, New York, NY 10014
☎001 212 633 8811   Fax 001 212 633 0525
✉ queriesvsa@hotmail.com
www.victoriasanders.com
Contacts *Victoria Sanders, Diane Dickensheid*
Founded 1993. Handles general trade fiction and non-fiction, plus ancillary film and television rights. COMMISSION Home & Dramatic 15%; Translation 20%. Please send all queries via e-mail.

Jack Scagnetti Talent & Literary Agency
5118 Vineland Avenue, Suite 102, North Hollywood, CA 91601
☎001 818 762 3871
Contact *Jack Scagnetti*

Founded 1974. Works mostly with established/published authors. Handles non-fiction, fiction, film and TV scripts. No reading fees. COMMISSION Home & Dramatic 10% (scripts), 15% (books); Foreign 15%.

Schiavone Literary Agency, Inc.
236 Trails End, West Palm Beach, FL 33413–2135
☎001 561 966 9294   Fax 001 561 966 9294
✉ profschia@aol.com
www.publishersmarketplace.com/members/profschia
Branch office (June/July/Aug. only): 3671 Hudson Manor Terrace, Suite 11H, Bronx, NY 10463
☎/Fax 001 718 548 5332
President *James Schiavone*
Vice-President *Jennifer Duvall*
Founded 1996. Handles fiction and non-fiction (all genres). Specialises in biography, autobiography, celebrity memoirs. No poetry. COMMISSION Home 15%; Foreign & Translation 20%. OVERSEAS ASSOCIATES in Europe and Asia. No unsolicited mss; send query letter only with s.a.e. and IRCs. No response without s.a.e. For fastest response, e-mail queries of one page (no attachments) are encouraged. No reading fee.

Susan Schulman, A Literary Agency★
454 West 44th Street, New York, NY 10036
☎001 212 713 1633/4/5
Fax 001 212 581 8830
✉ schulman@aol.com
www.susanschulmanagency.com
Submissions Editor (books) *Emily Uhry*
Submissions Editor (plays) *Linda Migalti*
Foreign Rights Director *Eleanora Tevis*
Founded 1979. Specialises in non-fiction of all types but particularly in health and psychology-based self-help for men, women and families. Other interests include business, memoirs, the social sciences, biography, language and international law. Fiction interests include contemporary fiction, including women's, mysteries, historical and thrillers 'with a cutting edge'. Always looking for 'something original and fresh'. Represents properties for film and theatre, and works with agents in appropriate territories for translation rights. COMMISSION Home & Dramatic 15%; Translation 20%. OVERSEAS ASSOCIATES Plays: **Rosica Colin Ltd** and **The Agency Ltd**, UK; Commercial fiction: Laura Morris, UK. No unsolicited mss. Query first, including outline and three sample chapters with IRCs. No reading fee.

Scovil Chichak Galen Literary Agency, Inc.*

381 Park Avenue South, Suite 1020, New York, NY 10016
☎001 212 679 8686   Fax 001 212 679 6710
✉ mailroom@scglit.com
www.scglit.com

Contacts *Russell Galen, Anna M. Ghosh, Jack Scovil*

Founded 1993. Handles all categories of books. No scripts. COMMISSION Home 15%; Foreign 20%. No unsolicited material; send query by e-mail or letter. No reading fee.

Scribblers House LLC Literary Agency

PO Box 1007 Cooper Station, New York, NY 10276–1007
☎001 212 714 7747
✉ query@scribblershouse.net
www.scribblershouse.net

Agents *Stedman Mays, Garrett Gambino*

Founded 2003 by Stedman Mays, founding member of Clausen, Mays & Tahan Literary Agency. Handles health, medical, diet, nutrition, the brain, psychology, self-help, how-to, business, personal finance, memoirs, biography, history, politics, writing books, language, relationships, sex, pop culture, spirituality, gender issues, parenting. No fiction, young adult or screenplays. COMMISSION 15%.Send e-mail query letter with brief description of the book, what's fresh and new about it, and a brief author biog including credentials for writing it. Consult the website for more submission information.

Shapiro-Lichtman – Talent Agency

8827 Beverly Boulevard, Los Angeles, CA 90048
☎001 310 859 8877   Fax 001 310 859 7153
Founded 1969. Works mostly with established/published authors. Handles film and TV scripts. COMMISSION Home & Dramatic 10%; Foreign 20%. Unsolicited mss will not be read.

Rosalie Siegel, International Literary Agency, Inc.*

1 Abey Drive, Pennington, NJ 08534
☎001 609 737 1007   Fax 001 609 737 3708

Contact *Rosalie Siegel*

Founded 1978. A one-woman, highly selective agency that takes on only a limited number of new projects. Handles fiction and non-fiction (especially narrative). Specialises in French history and literature; Europe in general; American history, social history. No science fiction, photography, illustrated art books or children's. COMMISSION Home 15%; Foreign 20%. OVERSEAS ASSOCIATE **Louise Greenberg**, UK; plus associates worldwide. No unsolicited material; send query letter citing background, previously published books and brief description of current book. Include return postage. No reading fee.

Michael Snell Literary Agency

PO Box 1206, Truro, MA 02666–1206
☎001 508 349 3718

President *Michael Snell*
Vice President *Patricia Smith*

Founded 1980. Adult non-fiction, especially psychology, science, business and women's issues. Specialises in business and pet and animal books (professional and reference to popular trade how-to); general how-to and self-help on all topics, from diet and exercise to parenting, relationships, health, sex, psychology, personal finance and dogs, cats and horses, plus literary and suspense fiction. COMMISSION Home 15%. No unsolicited mss. Send outline and sample chapter with return postage for reply. No reading fee for outlines. Brochure available on how to write a book proposal. Author of *From Book Idea to Bestseller*, published by Prima. Rewriting, developmental editing, collaborating and ghostwriting services available on a fee basis. Send IRCs.

Spectrum Literary Agency*

320 Central Park West, Ste. 1-D, New York, NY 10025
☎001 212 362 4323   Fax 001 212 362 4562
www.spectrumliteraryagency.com

President and Agent *Eleanor Wood*
Agent *Lucienne Diver*

Founded 1976. Handles science fiction, fantasy, mystery, suspense and romance. No scripts. Not interested in self-help, New Age, religious fiction/non-fiction, children's books, poetry, short stories, gift books or memoirs. COMMISSION Home 15%; Translation 20%. Send query letter in first instance with s.a.e. Faxed or electronic submissions are not accepted. No reading fees.

The Spieler Agency

154 West 57th Street, Room 135, New York, NY 10019
☎001 212 757 4439
✉ spieleragency@spieleragency.com

The Spieler Agency/West, 4096 Piedmont Avenue, Oakland, CA 94611
☎001 510 985 1422 Fax 001 510 985 1323

Contacts *Joseph Spieler, John Thornton, Lisa M.*

Ross, Dierdre Mullane, Katya Balter (NY); *Victoria Shoemaker* (Oakland)

Founded 1980. Handles literary fiction and non-fiction. No how-to, genre romance, humour or science fiction. Specialises in history, science, ecology, social and political issues and business. No scripts. COMMISSION Home 15%; Translation 20%. OVERSEAS ASSOCIATES **Abner Stein**; **The Marsh Agency**, UK. Approach in writing with IRCs. No reading fee.

Philip G. Spitzer Literary Agency, Inc.*

50 Talmage Farm Lane, East Hampton, NY 11937

☎001 631 329 3650   Fax 001 631 329 3651

✉ spitzer516@aol.com

Contact *Philip Spitzer*

Founded 1969. Works mostly with established/published authors. Specialises in general non-fiction and fiction – thrillers. COMMISSION Home & Dramatic 15%; Foreign 20%. No reading fee for outlines.

Steele-Perkins Literary Agency*

26 Island Lane, Canandaigua, NY 14424

☎001 585 396 9290   Fax 001 585 396 3579

✉ pattiesp@aol.com

Contact *Pattie Steele-Perkins*

Handles mainstream women's fiction, genre romance, inspirational romances. No scripts. COMMISSION Home 15%. Send query letter, synopsis, three chapters and return postage. No reading fee.

Gloria Stern Agency (Hollywood)

12535 Chandler Boulevard, Suite 3, North Hollywood, CA 91607

☎001 818 508 6296   Fax 001 818 508 6296

✉ wryter21@excite.com

Contact *Gloria Stern*

Founded 1984. Handles film scripts, genre (romance, detective, thriller and sci-fi) and mainstream fiction; electronic media. Accepts interactive material, games and electronic data. COMMISSION Home 15%; Offshore 20%. Currently not accepting unsolicited material. Fee required for critique.

Stimola Literary Studio*

308 Chase Court, Edgewater, NJ 07020

☎001 201 945 9353   Fax 001 201 945 9353

✉ LtryStudio@aol.com

Contact *Rosemary B. Stimola*

Founded 1997. Handles children's books – pre-school through young adult – fiction and non-fiction. Specialises in picture books, middle/young adult novels. No adult fiction. COMMISSION Home 15%; Foreign 20%. No unsolicited material; send query e-mail. No reading fee.

Barbara W. Stuhlmann Author's Representative

PO Box 276, Becket, MA 01223–0276

☎001 413 623 5170

Contact *Barbara Ward Stuhlmann*

Founded 1954. Handles literary fiction, biography and serious non-fiction. 'At the present time we are not taking on any new clients.' No short stories, detective, romance, adventure, poetry, technical or computers. COMMISSION Home 10%; Foreign 15%; Translation 20%. Query first with IRCs, including sample chapters and synopsis of project. No reading fee.

Mary M. Tahan Literary Agency LLC*

PO Box 1060 Gracie Station, New York, NY 10028–1060

☎001 646 375 2483

✉ querymarytahan@earthlink.net

Contact *Mary M. Tahan*

Founded 2004 by Mary M. Tahan who is also co-owner of Clausen, Mays & Tahan Literary Agency since 1997. Specialises in mainstream commercial fiction: thrillers, suspense, romance, mysteries, science fiction; narrative non-fiction: history, biography, autobiography, heroic true stories, entrepreneurial business books, health and nutrition (prospective authors must have expertise in their field). No scripts, children's, fundamental religious, humour. COMMISSION Home 15%; Foreign 25%. For non-fiction submissions send proposal and sample chapters; for fiction, synopsis and first three chapters. Include s.a.e for return of material. Initial approach should be by e-mail or post; no phone calls.

Roslyn Targ*

105 West 13th Street, Suite 15-E, New York, NY 10011

☎001 212 206 9390   Fax 001 212 989 6233

✉ roslyntarg@aol.com

Contact *Roslyn Targ*

Founded 1970. Handles non-fiction, particularly biography, self-help and literary fiction. No screenplays or cookbooks. COMMISSION Home 15%; Foreign 20%. No unsolicited material; send query e-mail or letter describing the work. No reading fee.

Patricia Teal Literary Agency★
2036 Vista del Rosa, Fullerton, CA 92831
☎001 714 738 8333   Fax 001 714 738 8333
Contact *Patricia Teal*

Founded 1978. Handles women's fiction: series and single-title works; commercial and popular non-fiction. Specialises in romantic fiction. No scripts, science fiction, fantasy, horror, academic texts. COMMISSION Home 15%; Foreign 20%. No unsolicited material. Send query letter in the first instance. No reading fee.

S©ott Treimel NY★
434 Lafayette Street, New York, NY 10003
☎001 212 505 8353   Fax 001 212 505 0664
✉ st.ny@verizon.net

Founded 1995. Handles children's books only, from concept/board books to teen fiction. No filmscripts. COMMISSION Home 15%; Foreign 20%. No unsolicited material. 'Not accepting anyone unless recommended by professional authors or editors.' No reading fee.

2M Communications Ltd
121 West 27th Street, Suite 601, New York, NY 10001
☎001 212 741 1509   Fax 001 212 691 4460
✉ morel@bookhaven.com
www.2mcommunications.com
Contact *Madeleine Morel*

Founded 1982. Handles non-fiction only: everything from pop psychology and health to cookery books, biographies and pop culture. No scripts. No fiction, children's, computers or science. COMMISSION Home & Dramatic 15%; Translation 20%. OVERSEAS ASSOCIATES Thomas Schluck Agency, Germany; Asano Agency, Japan; EAIS, France; Living Literary Agency, Italy; Nueva Agencia Literaria Internacional, Spain. No unsolicited mss; send letter with sample pages and IRCs. No reading fee.

The Vines Agency, Inc.★
648 Broadway, Suite 901, New York, NY 10012
☎001 212 777 5522   Fax 001 212 777 5978
✉ jv@vinesagency.com
www.vinesagency.com
Contact *James C. Vines*

Founded 1995. Handles fiction – literary, women's, thrillers, love stories; narrative non-fiction, historical, biography, advice, how-to. Specialises in women's fiction and thrillers. No children's picture books or poetry. COMMISSION Home 15%; Foreign & Translation 25%.

OVERSEAS ASSOCIATE Baror International (foreign rights). Unsolicited mss, synopses and sample chapters welcome. Send query with one-page letter and return postage. No reading fee.

Wales Literary Agency, Inc.★
PO Box 9428, Seattle, WA 98109–0428
☎001 206 284 7114
✉ waleslit@waleslit.com
www.waleslit.com
Contacts *Elizabeth Wales, Adrienne Reed, Josie Di Bernardo*

Founded 1988. Handles quality fiction and non-fiction. No genre fiction, westerns, romance, science fiction or horror. Special interest in 'Pacific Rim', West Coast and Pacific Northwest stories. COMMISSION Home 15%; Dramatic & Translation 20%. No unsolicited mss; send query letter with publication list and writing sample. No e-mail queries longer than one page and no attachments. No reading fee.

John A. Ware Literary Agency
392 Central Park West, New York, NY 10025
☎001 212 866 4733   Fax 001 212 866 4734
Contact *John Ware*

Founded 1978. Specialises in non-fiction: biography, history, current affairs, investigative journalism, science, nature, inside looks at phenomena, medicine and psychology (academic credentials required). No personal memoirs. Also handles literary fiction, mysteries/ thrillers, sport, oral history, Americana and folklore. COMMISSION Home & Dramatic 15%; Foreign 20%. Unsolicited mss not read. Send query letter first with IRCs to cover return postage. No reading fee.

Watkins Loomis Agency, Inc.
133 East 35th Street, Suite 1, New York, NY 10016
☎001 212 532 0080   Fax 001 212 889 0506
Contact *Katherine Fausset*

Founded 1904. Handles fiction and non-fiction. No scripts for film, radio, TV or theatre. No science fiction, fantasy or horror. COMMISSION Home 15%; UK & Translation 20%. OVERSEAS ASSOCIATES **Abner Stein**; **The Marsh Agency**, UK. No unsolicited mss. Approach in writing with enquiry or proposal and s.a.e. No reading fee.

Wecksler-Incomco
170 West End Avenue, New York, NY 10023
☎001 212 787 2239   Fax 001 212 496 7035
✉ jacinny@aol.com

Contacts *Sally Wecksler, Joann Amparan-Close*
Founded 1971. Handles literary fiction and
non-fiction: business, reference, biography, performing arts, history and heavily illustrated
books; also children's books (picture to young
adult). Foreign rights. COMMISSION Home
15%; UK & Translation 20%. Send queries only.
No unsolicited mss. No submissions by fax or
e-mail; hard copy only. No reading fee.

Cherry Weiner Literary Agency
28 Kipling Way, Manalapan, NJ 07726
☎001 732 446 2096 Fax 001 732 792 0506
✉ cherry8486@aol.com
Contact *Cherry Weiner*
Founded 1977. Handles all types of fiction: science fiction and fantasy, mainstream, romance,
mystery, westerns. COMMISSION 15%. No submissions except through referral. No reading
fee.

Wieser & Elwell, Inc.
80 Fifth Avenue, Suite 1101, New York,
NY 10011
☎001 212 260 0860
President *Jake Elwell*
Founded 1976. Works mostly with
established/published authors. Specialises in literary and mainstream fiction, serious and popular
historical fiction, and general non-fiction: business, finance, aviation, sports, travel and popular
medicine. No poetry, children's, science fiction or
religious. COMMISSION Home & Dramatic 15%;
Foreign 20%. No unsolicited mss. First approach
by letter with IRCs. No reading fee for outlines.

Ann Wright Representatives
165 West 46th Street, Suite 1105, New York,
NY 10036–2501
☎001 212 764 6770   Fax 001 212 764 5125
Contact *Dan Wright*
Founded 1961. Specialises in material with
strong film potentical. Handles screenplays
and novels, drama and fiction. No academic,
scientific or scholarly. COMMISSION Literary
10–20%; Screenplays 10% of gross. Approach by
letter; no reply without IRCs. Include outline
and credits only. 'Has reputation for encouraging new writers.' No reading fee. Signatory to
the Writers Guild of America Agreement.

Writers House, LLC.*
21 West 26th Street, New York, NY 10010
☎001 212 685 2400   Fax 001 212 685 1781
www.writershouse.com

Contacts *Albert Zuckerman, Amy Berkower,
Merrilee Heifetz, Susan Cohen, Susan
Ginsburg, Robin Rue, Simon Lipskar, Steven
Malk, Jennifer Lyons, Jodi Reamer*
Founded 1974. See also **Joan Daves Agency**.
Handles all types of fiction, including children's
and young adult, plus narrative non-fiction: history, biography, popular science, pop and rock
culture as well as how-to, business and finance,
and New Age. Specialises in popular and literary fiction, women's novels, thrillers and children's. No scripts. No professional or scholarly.
COMMISSION Home & Dramatic 15%; Foreign
20%. Albert Zuckerman is author of *Writing the
Blockbuster Novel*, published by Little, Brown &
Co. and Warner Paperbacks. For consideration
of unsolicited mss, send one-page letter of
enquiry, 'explaining why your book is wonderful, briefly what it's about and outlining your
writing background'. No reading fee.

The Zack Company, Inc.*
243 West 70th Street, Suite 8D, New York,
NY 10023–4366
www.zackcompany.com
www.literaryagent.info
Contact *Andrew Zack*
Founded 1996. Handles serious narrative non-
fiction by qualified experts: history, particularly
military, politics, current affairs, science and technology, biography, autobiography, memoirs, personal finance, parenting, health and medicine,
business, relationships. Commercial fiction –
thrillers, mysteries, crime, science fiction/fantasy.
No women's fiction, westerns, gay or lesbian,
scripts. COMMISSION Home 15% (published
authors)/20% (new, unpublished); Foreign &
Translation 25%. See website for full listing of
areas of representation and submission guidelines.
No unsolicited material. No reading fee.

Susan Zeckendorf Associates, Inc*
171 West 57th Street, Suite 11B, New York,
NY 10019
☎001 212 245 2928
Contact *Susan Zeckendorf*
Founded 1979. Handles non-fiction of all kinds:
self help, social history, biography; fiction. No
scripts, romance, science fiction or children's
books. COMMISSION Home 15%; Foreign &
Translation 20%. ASSOCIATES Rosemarie
Buckman (translation); **Abner Stein**, UK. No
unsolicited material; send query letter with s.a.e.
in the first instance. No reading fee.

US Media Contacts in the UK

ABC News Intercontinental Inc.
3 Queen Caroline Street, Mail Code 2303,
London W6 9PE
☎020 8222 5000   Fax 020 8222 5020
Bureau Chief & Director of News Coverage,
   Europe, Middle East & Africa *Marcus Wilford*

The Associated Press
12 Norwich Street, London EC4A 1BP
☎020 7353 1515   Fax 020 7353 8118 (news)
Vice President – Global Business for Europe,
   Africa & Middle East *Barry Renfrew*

The Baltimore Sun
11 Kensington Court Place, London W8 5BJ
☎020 7460 2200
Bureau Chief *Todd Richissin*

Bloomberg Business News
City Gate House, 39–45 Finsbury Square,
London EC2A 1PQ
☎020 7330 7500   Fax 020 7392 6666
Print – London Bureau Chief *Chris Collins*

Boston Globe
6 Holly Mount, London NW3 6SG
☎020 7431 5797   Fax 020 7431 5807
✉ sennott@globe.com
Bureau Chief *Charles Sennott*

Business Week
20 Canada Square, Canary Wharf, London
E14 5LH
☎020 7176 6060   Fax 020 7176 6070
Bureau Chief *Stanley Reed*

Cable News Network Inc. (CNN)
Turner House, 16 Great Marlborough Street,
London W1P 1DF
☎020 7693 1000   Fax 020 7693 1552
Office Manager *Rosalind Jackman*

CBC Television and Radio
43/51 Great Titchfield Street, London
W1P 8DD
☎020 7412 9200   Fax 020 7412 9226
London Bureau Manager *Ann Macmillan*

CBS News
68 Knightsbridge, London SW1X 7LL
☎020 7581 4801   Fax 020 7581 4431
Vice President/Bureau Chief *John Paxson*

Chicago Tribune Press Service
116 Brompton Road, London SW3 1JJ
☎020 7225 0345
Chief European Correspondent *Tom Hundley*

CNBC
10 Fleet Place, Limeburner Lane, London
EC4M 7QS
☎020 7653 9451   Fax 020 7653 9393
Assignments Manager *Harry Fuller*

Dallas Morning News
5 Rylett Crescent, London W12 9RP
☎020 8248 4924
✉ trobberson@dallasnews.com
European Bureau Chief *Tod Robberson*

Dow Jones Newswires
10 Fleet Place, Limeburner Lane, London
EC4M 7QN
☎020 7842 9900
Editor (Europe, Middle East, Africa) *Jan Boucek*

Fairchild Publications
of New York
20 Shorts Gardens, London WC2H 9AU
☎020 7240 0420   Fax 020 7240 0290
Bureau Chief *Samantha Conti*

Forbes Magazine
Malta House, 36/38 Picadilly, London
W1J 0DP
☎020 7534 3900
Managing Director & Publisher (Europe,
   Middle East & Africa) *Bob Crozier*

Fortune
Brettenham House, Lancaster Place, London
WC2E 7TL
☎020 7322 1068   Fax 020 7322 1097
Europe Editor *Nelson Schwartz*

Fox News Channel
6 Centaurs Business Park, Grant Way,
Isleworth TW7 5QD
☎020 7805 7143   Fax 020 7805 1111
Bureau Chief *Scott Norvell*

International Herald Tribune
40 Marsh Wall, London E14 9TP
☎020 7510 5718   Fax 020 7987 3470
London Correspondent *Eric Pfanner*
See entry under **National Newspapers**

Los Angeles Times
Moreau House, 116–118 Brompton Road,
London SW3 1JJ
☎020 7823 7315   Fax 020 7823 7308
Bureau Chief *John Daniszewski*

Market News International
Ocean House, 10–12 Little Trinity Lane,
London EC4A 2AR
☎020 7634 1655   Fax 020 7236 7122
✉ ukeditorial@marketnews.com
Senior UK Political Correspondent *David Robinson*

National Public Radio
Room G-10 East Wing, Bush House, Strand,
London WC2B 4PH
☎020 7557 1087   Fax 020 7379 6486
Bureau Chief *Anthony Kuhn*

NBC News Worldwide Inc.
4th Floor, 3 Shortlands, Hammersmith,
London W6 8HX
☎020 8600 6600   Fax 020 8600 6601
Bureau Chief *Chris Hampson*

The New York Times
66 Buckingham Gate, London SW1E 6AU
☎020 7799 5050   Fax 020 7799 2962
Acting Bureau Chief *Alan Cowell*

Newsweek
Academy House, 36 Poland Street, London
W1F 7LU
☎020 7851 9750   Fax 020 7851 9762
Bureau Chief *Stryker McGuire*

People Magazine
Brettenham House, Lancaster Place, London
WC2E 7TL
☎020 7499 4080   Fax 020 7322 1125
Bureau Chief *Bryan Alexander*

Reader's Digest Association Ltd
11 Westferry Circus, Canary Wharf, London
E14 4HE
See entries under **UK Publishers** and
Magazines

Time Magazine
Brettenham House, Lancaster Place, London
WC2E 7TL
☎020 7499 4080   Fax 020 7322 1230
Bureau Chief *Jef McAllister*
See entry under **Magazines**

Voice of America
☎020 7410 0960   Fax 020 7410 0966
Bureau Chief *Michael Drudge*

Wall Street Journal
10 Fleet Place, Limeburner Lane, London
EC4M 7QN
☎020 7842 9200   Fax 020 7842 9201
London Bureau Chief *Paul Beckett*

Washington Post
17 Dartmouth Street, London SW1H 9BL
☎020 7222 8512   Fax 020 7233 4597
✉ frankelg@washpost.com
Bureau Chief *Glenn Frankel*

US Writers' Courses

In general, courses are open to students from overseas though the financial aid situation varies for international students.

Arkansas

University of Arkansas
Programs in Creative Writing, 333 Kimpel Hall, Fayetteville, AR 72701
☎001 479 575 4401
www.uark.edu/depts/english/PCWT.html
Contact *Course Director*

MFA in *Creative Writing*, offering small, intensive workshops and innovative classes in fiction and poetry.

California

American Film Institute
2021 N. Western Avenue, Los Angeles, CA 90027
☎001 323 856 7628
✉ jjackman@afi.com
Admissions Manager *J.J. Jackman*

Screenwriting at AFI focuses on narrative storytelling in an environment designed to stimulate the world of the professional screenwriter. Screenwriting Fellows in the First Year are immersed in the production process in order to learn how screenplays are visualised. Initially writing short screenplays – one of which will be the basis for a first year production – writers collaborate with Producing and Directing Fellows to see their work move from page to screen. The remainder of the first year is devoted to the completion of a feature-length screenplay. Second Year Fellows may write a second feature-length screenplay, or develop materials for television, including biopics, television movies and spec scripts for sitcoms and one-hour dramas. They also have the opportunity to work closely with other disciplines by writing a Second Year thesis script.

California Institute for the Arts
MFA Writing Program, School of Critical Studies, 24700 McBean Parkway, Valencia, CA 91355-2397
☎001 661 253 7701
✉ writing@calarts.edu

Contact *Program Coordinator*

The two-year MFA Writing Programme is rooted in principles of critical thought, experimentation and innovation. It is intended as an alternative to traditional programmes, with a founding premise that distinctions between creative and critical writing should be suspended. Students are encouraged to work across genres and often work in various multi-media forms in addition to their literary production.

Chapman University
Master of Fine Arts Degree, Dept. of English and Comparative Literature, Office of Admissions, One University Drive, Orange, CA 92866
☎001 714 997 6750
www.chapman.edu
Contact *Admissions*

Three-year Master of Fine Arts (MFA) degree in *Creative Writing* is intended for graduate students who wish to pursue writing as a career and is aimed toward publishing as well as development of writing techniques.

Saint Mary's College of California
MFA Program in Creative Writing, PO Box 4686, Moraga, CA 94575–4686
☎001 925 631 4762
✉ writers@stmarys-ca.edu
www.stmarys-ca.edu
Programme Coordinator *Thomas Cooney*

Two-year MFA course in *Fiction, Non-fiction* or *Poetry*. The core of the programme is the Writing Workshop which provides the opportunity for students to work with established writers.

San Francisco State University
Creative Writing Department, College of Humanities, 1600 Holloway Avenue, San Francisco, CA 94132–4162
☎001 415 338 1891
✉ cwriting@sfsu.edu
www.sfsu.edu/~cwriting/rl

Offers BA and MA in *English:* with a concentration on *Creative Writing;* and MFA in *Creative*

Writing. Undergraduate classes include feature writing, short story writing, the craft of poetry and the craft of playwriting while graduate classes include advanced story writing, advanced poetry writing, advanced playwriting, experimental fiction, playwright's theatre workshop and workshops in fiction, poetry and playwriting.

University of Southern California (USC)

School of Cinema-Television, University Park, LUC 301, Los Angeles, CA 90089–2211
☎001 213 740 3303   Fax 001 213 740 8035
✉ writing@cinema.usc.edu
www-cntv.usc.edu

Offers a Bachelor of Fine Arts or Master of Fine Arts degree in *Writing for Screen and Television.* Each spring, the most advanced graduating students have the opportunity to pitch their best scripts to industry professionals at a special Writing Division event called 'First Pitch'. The Division has a strong international presence, having accepted students from over 44 countries.

Strawberry Mansion Films

13586 Mahogany Place, Tustin, CA 92780
☎001 714 997 6586
✉ axelrod@chapman.edu
Contact *Mark Axelrod*

One-day, three-day and five-day seminar/workshops in *Screenwriting.* A practising screenwriter, Mark Axelrod has conducted such programmes at the Escuela Internacional de Cine y TV in San Antonio de los Baños, Cuba (founded by García Márquez); the Goethe Institute, Santiago, Chile (with Antonio Skármeta – *Il Postino*); the National Film School of Denmark, as well as the University of East Anglia in Norwich, Columbia College, Chicago, and the Film Stadium der Universität, Hamburg, Germany. Latest film books include: *Aspects of the Screenplay* and *Character and Conflict.*

Colorado

Colorado State University

Department of English, Creative Writing Program, Fort Collins, CO 80523
☎001 970 491 6428   Fax 001 970 491 5601
✉ english@lamar.colostate.edu
www.colostate.edu/Depts/English/programs/mfa.htm
Contact *Assistant to the Director of Creative Writing or Director of Creative Writing*

Three-year Master of Fine Arts (MFA) programme in creative writing with concentrations in fiction or poetry. The programme offers a balance of intimate and intensive writing and translation. Course work culminates in a thesis – a collection of poetry or short stories or a novel. Students have the opportunity to teach introductory creative-writing courses, intern with literary journals including the *Colorado Review* and be a part of a thriving community.

Florida

University of West Florida

Department of English and Foreign Languages, College of Arts and Sciences, 11000 University Parkway, Pensacola, FL 32514
☎001 850 474 2923   Fax 001 850 474 2935
✉ English@uwf.edu
www.uwf.edu/english

BA in *English (Writing Specialization)*: students who choose to develop their creative writing skills or editing can take courses in poetry, fiction, creative non-fiction, magazine writing and editing, and feature writing. *MA in English (Creative Writing Specialization)*: workshop courses in the specialisation include fiction, creative non-fiction, poetry, editing, teaching creative writing and special topics in creative writing. Students also have the opportunity to work on the literary magazine *Bayou.*

Georgia

Georgia State University

Department of English, MSC 8R0322, 33 Gilmer Street SE, Unit 8, Atlanta, GA 30303–3088
☎001 404 651 2900   Fax 001 404 651 1710
✉ engjwh@langate.gsu.edu
www.gsu.edu/~wweng/
Contact *Director of Creative Writing*

BA, MA, MFA and PhD programmes in *Creative Writing* – fiction or poetry. The writing faculty includes poet and novelist David Bottoms; poet Beth Gylys, fiction writers Sheri Joseph, John Holman and Josh Russell; poet Leon Stokesbury.

Illinois

Southern Illinois University

Department of English, Carbondale, IL 62901–4503
☎001 618 453 6849   Fax 001 618 453 3253
✉ gradengl@siu.edu

Contact *Professor Allison Joseph*

Three-year MFA in *Creative Writing*. The programme accepts a maximum of eight students each year, so workshops are small and faculty members work closely with students.

Indiana

University of Notre Dame

Creative Writing Program, Department of English, 356 O'Shaughnessy Hall, Notre Dame, IN 46556
☎001 574 631 7526   Fax 001 574 631 4795
✉ creativewriting@nd.edu
www.nd.edu/~alcwp/
Director *William O'Rourke*

Offers a MFA *Creative Writing* programme which includes workshops with nationally acclaimed writers and literature classes with a distinguished Dept of English faculty. Admits ten writers annually. All students write a thesis – a collection of stories or creative non-fiction, a novel or a collection of poetry – and work closely with a thesis adviser. Publishes *The Notre Dame Review*, a nationally distributed literary journal, providing editorial training in print and online publishing. All accepted students receive full tuition waivers. Applicants are also considered for additional support including teaching and administrative assistantships and the Nicholas Sparks Fellowship.

Taylor University

Department of English, 1025 West Rudisill Blvd, Fort Wayne, IN 46807–2170
☎001 260 744 8647
✉ DNHensley@TaylorU.edu
Contact *Dr Dennis E. Hensley*

Summer Honours Programme one-week seminars in *Professional Writing*; evening courses in *Freelance Writing* and *Fiction Writing*; one year college certificate in *Professional Writing*. Dr Hensley is a professor of English and director of the professional writing major.

Louisiana

Louisiana State University

English Department, 260 Allen Hall, Baton Rouge, LA 70803
www.english.lsu.edu
Contacts *James Wilcox, Judy Kahn*

Master of Fine Arts (MFA) course with a focus in *Poetry*, *Fiction*, *Playwriting*, *Screenwriting* or *Creative Non-fiction*. Includes opportunity to edit literary journals.

Maryland

Goucher College

Welch Center for Graduate Studies, 1021 Dulaney Valley Road, Baltimore, MD 21204–2794
☎001 800 697 4646   Fax 001 410 337 6085
✉ center@goucher.edu
Programme Director *Patsy Sims* (☎001 800 697 4646)

The two-year MFA Program in *Creative Non-fiction* is a limited-residency programme that allows students to complete most of the requirements off campus while developing their skill as non-fiction writers under the close supervision of a faculty mentor. Provides instruction in the following areas: the personal essay, memoir, literary journalism, travel/nature/science writing, biography/profiles and narrative non-fiction.

Johns Hopkins University

The Writing Seminars, 3400 N. Charles Street, Baltimore, MD 21218
☎001 410 516 7563
✉ regina@jhu.edu

Two-year Master of Fine Arts in *Creative Writing*: concentrates on fiction or poetry. One-year Master of Arts in *Creative Writing*: concentrates on science writing.

Massachusetts

Boston University

Creative Writing Programme, 236 Bay State Road, Boston, MA 02215
☎001 617 353 2510   Fax 001 617 353 3653
✉ crwr@bu.edu
www.bu.edu/writing
Director *Leslie Epstein*
Contact *Matthew Yost*

One-year MA programme in *Creative Writing*: fiction, poetry or drama. The Creative Writing Programme is one of the oldest in the country. Students participate in workshops or seminars concentrating on their chosen specialisation and are expected to balance that work with an equal number of graduate literature courses. Internships at the literary journal *AGNI*, assistantships at the Boston Arts Academy, as well as teaching fellowships are available on a limited basis.

Emerson College

120 Boylston Street, Boston, MA 01226
☎001 617 824 8610
✉ gradapp@emerson.edu

www.emerson.edu/graduate_admission
Programme Director *Douglas Whynott*
Offers MFA in *Creative Writing* with a focus on writing fiction, non-fiction and poetry. Includes writing workshops, internship opportunities, a student reading series and student teaching opportunities. Publishes literary magazines, *Ploughshares* and *Redivider*. Contact the Graduate Admission Office for more information.

Michigan

Western Michigan University
Department of English, 1903 W. Michigan Avenue, Kalamazoo, MI 49008-5331
☎001 269 387 2572
✉ larson@wmich.edu
www.wmich.edu/english
Director of Graduate Studies *Jil Larson*

BA English Major/Minor with *Creative Writing Emphasis* (poetry, fiction, playwriting). The English Major aims at giving students intensive practice in writing and criticism in various genres in a workshop format; for general writing careers or for prospective candidates for the MFA in Creative Writing.

MFA in *Creative Writing* (poetry, fiction, playwriting, non-fiction) For students who wish to become professional writers of poetry, fiction, drama or non-fiction. Qualifies them to teach the craft at college or university level.

Minnesota

Minnesota State University Moorhead
Graduate Studies Office, MSUM, 1104 7th Avenue South, Moorhead, MN 56563
☎001 218 477 2344
✉ graduate@mnstate.edu
www.mnstate.edu/finearts
Programme Coordinator *John Early*

MFA in *Creative Writing (Fiction, Non-fiction, Playwriting, Poetry, Screenwriting)*. The programme offers the opportunity to take workshops, seminars and tutorials in chosen areas and to work with New Rivers Press (www.newriverspress.com) or with *Red Weather*, the campus literary magazine.

Minnesota State University, Mankato
Department of English, 230 Armstrong Hall, Mankato, MN 56001
☎001 507 389 2117

✉ mfa@mnsu.edu
www.english.mnsu.edu/web/gradCreativeWriting.htm
Programme Director *Richard Robbins*
The MFA programme in *Creative Writing* meets the needs of students who want to strike a balance between the development of individual creative talent and the close study of literature and language. The programme gives appropriate training for careers in freelancing, college-level teaching, editing and publishing and arts administration.

Missouri

University of Missouri–Columbia
Creative Writing Program, Department of English, 107 Tate Hall, Columbia, MO 65211-1500
☎011 573 884 7773
✉ creativewriting@missouri.edu/~cwp
www.missouri.edu/~cwp
Contact *Sharon Fisher*

Creative Writing MA and PhD in English programmes in fiction, poetry and non-fiction. Access the website for further information.

New York

New York University
19 University Place, Room 219, New York, NY 10003
✉ creative.writing@nyu.edu
www.nyu.edu/gsas/program/cwp
Contact *Russell Carmony*
Director *Melissa Hammerle*

Offers MFA in *Creative Writing* and MA in *English* with focus in *Creative Writing* in poetry and fiction. Includes writing workshops and craft courses, literary outreach programmes, a public reading series, student readings, special literary seminars and student teaching opportunities. Publishes a literary journal, *Washington Square*. Contact the department via e-mail.

North Carolina

University of North Carolina at Greensboro
MFA Writing Program, English Department, 134 McIver Building, UNCG, PO Box 26170, Greensboro, NC 27402-6170
☎001 336 334 5459
✉ jlclark@uncg.edu
www.uncg.edu/eng/mfa

Contact *Jim Clark, Director*

MFA in Creative Writing (poetry, fiction) One of the oldest of its kind in the country, the MFA Writing Program at Greensboro is a two-year residency with an emphasis on providing students with studio time in which to study the writing of poetry or fiction with a flexibility that permits students to develop their particular talents through small classes in writing, literature and the arts.

University of North Carolina at Wilmington

Department of Creative Writing, 601 S. College Road, Wilmington, NC 28403–5938
☎001 910 962 7711
✉ mfa@uncw.edu
www.uncw.edu/mfa

Contact *MFA Coordinator*

An intensive studio-academic programme in the writing of fiction, poetry and creative non-fiction leading to either the Master of Fine Arts or Bachelor of Fine Arts degree in *Creative Writing*. Courses include workshops in the three genres, special topics and forms courses as well as a range of courses in literature. Course work in publishing and editing is also offered in the Publishing Laboratory, a university press imprint which supports local, regional and national publishing projects.

Ohio

Bowling Green State University,

Bowling Green, OH 43403
☎001 419 372 8370   Fax 001 419 372 6805
www.bgsu.edu/departments/creative-writing/

Director of Creative Writing *Dr Lawrence Coates*

Undergraduate BFA programme: a four-year programme which offers comprehensive and rigorous training in the art of writing and develops students' skills in preparation for numerous post-graduate careers.

Graduate MFA programme: a two-year studio/academic composite, mostly work in writing itself in either poetry or fiction. Also offers ten new teaching assistantships each autumn. See the website for details on both programms.

Philadelphia

Seton Hill University

1 Seton Hill Drive, Greensburg, PA 15601
☎001 724 838 4221
✉ gadmit@setonhill.edu

www.setonhill.edu

Contact *Dane Dornin*

The MA in *Writing Popular Fiction* programme at Seton Hill University allows students to earn a graduate degree by writing fiction that people *actually* read. Students attend week-long residencies in January and June and complete writing projects off-campus, working with a faculty mentor who is a published author in the chosen genre. Students can choose to specialise in science fiction, fantasy, horror, children's literature, romance or mystery. Programmes can be completed in 24 months.

Rhode Island

Brown University

Literary Arts, Box 1923, Providence, RI 02912
☎001 401 863 3260
✉ Writing@brown.edu

Contact *Director of Literary Arts*

Two-year MFA in *Fiction, Poetry, Playwriting and Electronic Writing*. Students take three workshops, four electives and one independent study (through which they complete a thesis project).

Virginia

Virginia Commonwealth University

Department of English, PO Box 842005, Richmond, VA 23284–2005
☎001 804 828 1329
✉ eng-grad@vcu.edu
www.has.vcu.edu/eng

Graduate Programmes Coordinator *Jeff Lodge*

Three-year MFA in *Creative Writing* with tracks in fiction and poetry and workshops in short fiction, the novel, poetry, drama, screenwriting and creative non-fiction. Opportunities to work with *Blackbird*: an online journal of literature and the arts (www.blackbird.vcu.edu), *Stand Magazine*, the Levis Reading Prize and the First Novelist Award.

Washington

Eastern Washington University

Inland Northwest Center for Writers, Creative Writing, 705 W. 1st Avenue, Spokane, WA 99201
☎001 509 623 4221
✉ writing@mail.ewu.edu
www.creativewriting.ewu.edu

Director *Jonathan Johnson*

The MFA Program is an intensive two-year, pre-professional course of study with an emphasis on the practise of literature as a fine art. Includes course work in the study of literature from the vantage point of its composition and history, but the student's principal work is done in advanced workshops and in the writing of a book-length thesis of publishable quality in fiction, literary non-fiction or poetry. Students have the opportunity to work as interns on several projects: the literary magazine, *Willow Springs*; the community outreach programme, Writers in the Community; and Eastern Washington University Press. The MFA is a terminal degree programme.

Commonwealth Publishers

Australia

ACER Press
Private Bag 55, Camberwell, Victoria 3124
☎00 61 3 9277 5555   Fax 00 61 3 9277 5500
www.acer.edu.au
Founded 1930. Publishes education, human relations, psychology, psychiatry.

Allen & Unwin Pty Ltd
PO Box 8500, St Leonards, Sydney, NSW 1590
☎00 61 2 8425 0100   Fax 00 61 2 9906 2218
www.allenandunwin.com
Founded 1976. Publishes fiction, literature, literary criticism, essays; general non-fiction, art, Asian studies, behavioural sciences, business, children's, cookery, earth sciences, economics, education, gay and lesbian, government, labour, political science, health and nutrition, history, industrial relations, general science.

Edward Arnold (Australia) Pty Ltd
PO Box 885, Kew, Victoria 3101
☎00 61 3 985 9011   Fax 00 61 3 985 9141
Founded 1966. Part of Hodder & Stoughton (Australia) Pty Ltd. Publishes general non-fiction: accountancy, Asian studies, behavioural sciences, career development, computer science, cookery, geography, geology, government, political science, health and nutrition, law, mathematics, psychology and psychiatry, technology, textbooks.

Blackwell Science Publishing (Asia)
PO Box 378, South Carlton, Victoria 3053
☎00 61 3 8359 1011   Fax 00 61 3 8359 1120
www.blacksci.co.uk
Founded 1971. Part of Blackwell Science Ltd, UK. Publishes academic books, journals and CD-ROMs; general science, medicine, nursing, dentistry, earth sciences, general engineering, computer science, mathematics, physical sciences, physics, professional, psychology, psychiatry, textbooks.

Currency Press Pty Ltd
PO Box 2287, Strawberry Hills, NSW 2012
☎00 61 2 9319 5877   Fax 00 61 2 9319 3649
✉ enquiries@currency.com.au
www.currency.com.au
Founded 1971. Performing arts publisher – directories and reference – drama, theatre, music, dance, film and video.

Dangaroo Press
GPO Box 1209, New Lambton, NSW 2001
☎00 61 2 4954 5938   Fax 00 61 2 4954 6531
Founded 1978. Publishes general non-fiction, art, literature, literary criticism, essays, poetry, social sciences, sociology, women's studies.

HarperCollins Publishers (Australia) Pty Ltd
PO Box 321, Pymble, NSW 2073
☎00 61 2 9952 5000
Fax 00 61 2 9952 5555
www.harpercollins.com.au
Founded 1872. Part of the HarperCollins Publishers Group. Publishes fiction and general non-fiction, biography, children's, gardening, humour, government, political science, regional interests, literature, literary criticism, essays, women's studies.

Hodder Headline Australia
Level 22, 207 Kent Street, Sydney, NSW 2000
☎00 61 2 8248 0800   Fax 00 61 2 8248 0810
www.hha.com.au
Founded 1958. Owned by **Hodder Headline**, UK. Publishes general non-fiction and fiction (adult and children's), education.

Hyland House Publishing Pty Ltd
PO Box 122, Flemington, Victoria 3031
☎00 61 3 9376 4461   Fax 00 61 3 9376 4461
Founded 1976. Publishes general non-fiction, Asian studies, juvenile and young adult, animals, pets, fiction, gardening, how-to.

LexisNexis Butterworths Australia
Tower 2, 475–495 Victoria Avenue,
Chatswood, NSW 2067
☎00 61 2 9422 2222   Fax 00 61 2 9422 2444
www.lexisnexis.com.au
Founded 1910. A division of Reed Elsevier. Publishes accountancy, business and law.

Thomas C. Lothian Pty Ltd
Level 5, 132–136 Albert Road, South
Melbourne, Victoria 3205
☎00 61 3 9694 4900   Fax 00 61 3 9645 0705
✉ books@lothian.com.au
www.lothian.com.au
Founded 1888. Publishes general non-fiction:
biography, business, health and nutrition, children's, self-help, sport.

Macmillan Education Australia Pty Ltd
Level 4, 627 Chapel Street, South Yarra,
Victoria 3141
☎00 61 3 9825 1025   Fax 00 61 3 9825 1010
www.macmillan.com.au
Founded 1896. Part of **Macmillan Publishers**,
UK. Publishes accountancy, behavioural sciences,
children's, economics, education, geography,
geology, government, political science, history,
management, mathematics, physics, professional,
general science, social sciences, sociology, textbooks.

McGraw-Hill Australia Pty Ltd
Locked Bag 2233, Business Centre, North
Ryde, NSW 1670
☎00 61 2 9900 1800   Fax 00 61 2 9878 8280
www.mcgraw-hill.com.au
Founded 1964. Owned by **McGraw-Hill Inc.**,
USA. Publishes accountancy, education, health
and nutrition, advertising, aeronautics, aviation,
anthropology, architecture and interior design,
art, behavioural sciences, chemistry, chemical
engineering, child care and development, computer science, criminology, disability, earth
sciences, economics, electronics, electrical engineering, general engineering, English as a second
language, environmental studies, film and video,
geography, geology, journalism, industrial relations, labour, language arts, linguistics, management, marketing, maritime, mathematics,
mechanical engineering, medicine, nursing,
dentistry, philosophy, photography, physics, professional, psychology, psychiatry, sport, social
sciences and sociology, textbooks.

Melbourne University Press
PO Box 1167, Carlton South, Victoria 3053
☎00 61 3 9342 0300   Fax 00 61 3 9342 0399
✉ mup-info@mup.unimelb.edu.au
www.mup.unimelb.edu.au
Founded 1922. Academic publishers; general
non-fiction, biography, essays, history, literature,
literary criticism, natural history, psychology,
psychiatry, travel.

Oxford University Press (Australia, New Zealand, Singapore & the Pacific)
GPO Box 2784Y, Melbourne, Victoria 3001
☎00 61 3 9934 9123   Fax 00 61 3 9934 9100
www.oup.com.au
Founded 1908. Owned by **Oxford University
Press**, UK. Publishes for the college, school and
trade markets.

Pan Macmillan Australia Pty Ltd
Level 18, St Martin's Tower, 31 Market Street,
Sydney, NSW 2000
☎00 61 2 9285 9100   Fax 00 61 2 9285 9190
www.panmacmillan.com.au
Founded 1983. Part of **Macmillan Publishers**,
UK. Publishes fiction, essays, literature, literary
criticism; general non-fiction, biography, children's, health and nutrition, humour, self-help,
travel.

Pearson Education Australia
Locked Bag 507, Frenchs Forest, NSW 1640
☎00 61 3 9454 2200   Fax 00 61 3 9453 0089
www.awl.com.au
Australia's largest educational publisher, formed
in 1998 from a merger of Addison Wesley
Longman Australia and Prentice Hall Australia.

Penguin Books Australia Ltd
PO Box 701, Hawthorn, Victoria 3122
☎00 61 3 9811 2400   Fax 00 61 3 9811 2620
www.penguin.com.au
Founded 1946. Publishes general non-fiction
and fiction; biography, children's, cookery,
humour, literature, literary criticism, essays, science fiction, fantasy, self-help, travel.

University of Queensland Press
PO Box 6042, St Lucia, Queensland 4067
☎00 61 7 3365 2127   Fax 00 61 7 3365 7579
✉ uqp@uqp.uq.edu.au
www.uqp.uq.edu.au
Founded 1948. Publishes academic, textbooks,
children's, general non-fiction and fiction, literature, literary criticism, essays, poetry, biography, history, sport, travel.

Random House Australia
20 Alfred Street, Milsons Point, NSW 2061
☎00 61 2 9954 9966   Fax 00 61 2 9954 4562
✉ random@randomhouse.com.au
www.randomhouse.com.au
Subsidiary of **Bertelsmann AG**. Publishes fiction and non-fiction.

Reader's Digest (Australia) Pty Ltd

GPO Box 4353, Sydney, NSW 2001
☎00 61 2 9690 6935   Fax 00 61 2 9690 6390
Founded 1946. Associate company of **Reader's Digest Association, Inc.** (USA). Educational publisher.

Reed Educational Publishing Australia

PO Box 460, Port Melbourne, Victoria 3207
☎00 61 3 9245 7188   Fax 00 61 3 9245 7265
✉ admin@reededucation.com.au
www.reededucation.com.au
Founded 1982. Publishes art, CD-ROMs, chemistry, chemical engineering, children's, dictionaries, encyclopedias, environmental studies, geography, geology, health and nutrition, history, maps and atlases, mathematics, physics, textbooks.

Scholastic Australia Pty Limited

PO Box 579, Gosford, NSW 2250
☎00 61 2 4328 3555   Fax 00 61 2 4323 3827
www.scholastic.com.au
Founded 1968. Educational publisher.

Science Press

Unit 16, 102 Edinburgh Road, Marrickville, NSW 2204
☎00 61 2 9516 1122   Fax 00 61 2 9550 1915
Founded 1945. Educational publisher.

Simon & Schuster Australia Pty Ltd

PO Box 507, East Roseville, NSW 2069
☎00 61 2 9415 9900   Fax 00 61 2 9417 3188
www.simonandschuster.com.au'
Founded 1987. Part of **Simon & Schuster Inc.**, USA. Publishes general non-fiction; animals and pets, anthropology, childcare, children's, cookery, crafts, games and hobbies, health and nutrition, history, how-to, management, natural history, self-help.

University of Western Australia Press

35 Stirling Highway, Crawley, WA 6009
☎00 61 8 9380 3670   Fax 00 61 8 9380 1027
www.uwapress.uwa.edu.au
Founded 1954. Publishes general non-fiction, essays, literature, literary criticism, science fiction, fantasy, history, social sciences, sociology, natural history, children's, directories, biography, reference, textbooks, women's studies.

John Wiley & Sons Australia Ltd

PO Box 1226, Milton, Queensland 4064
☎00 61 7 3859 9755   Fax 00 61 7 3859 9715
✉ brisbane@johnwiley.com.au
www.johnwiley.com.au
Founded 1954. Owned by **John Wiley & Sons Inc.**, USA. Publishes general non-fiction and education books, dictionaries, encyclopedias, maps and atlases, textbooks.

Canada

Canadian Scholars' Press, Inc

180 Bloor Street W, Suite 801, Toronto, Ontario M5S 2V6
☎001 416 929 2774   Fax 001 416 929 1926
✉ info@cspi.org
www.cspi.org
Founded 1987. Publishes academic books in English and French.

Fenn Publishing Co Ltd

34 Nixon Road, Bolton, Ontario L7E 1W2
☎001 905 951 6600   Fax 001 905 951 6601
www.hbfenn.com
Founded 1977. Publishes fiction and non-fiction, children's.

Firefly Books Ltd

66 Leek Crescent, Richmond Hill, Ontario L4B 1H1
☎001 416 499 8412   Fax 001 416 499 1142
www.fireflybooks.com
Founded 1976. Publishes dictionaries, juvenile and young adult, encyclopedias, general non-fiction, aviation, art, astronomy, cookery, crafts, games and hobbies, home interest, how-to, science, sport, transport.

Fitzhenry & Whiteside Limited

195 Allstate Parkway, Markham, Ontario L3R 4T8,
☎001 905 477 9700   Fax 001 905 477 9179
✉ godwit@fitzhenry.ca
www.fitzhenry.ca
Founded 1966. Publishes trade, reference and children's books; educational material.

Gage Learning Corporation

1120 Birchmount Road, Scarborough, Ontario M1K 5G4
☎001 416 752 9448   Fax 001 416 752 8101
✉ inquire@nelson.com
www.nelson.com
Founded 1844. Owned by Thomson Nelson,

part of The Thomson Corporation. Publishes dictionaries and encyclopedias.

Harcourt Canada Ltd
55 Horner Avenue, Toronto, Ontario M8Z 4X6
☎001 416 255 4491   Fax 001 416 255 6708
www.harcourtcanada.com
Founded 1922. Acquired by Thomson Nelson in April 2005. Publishes educational material.

Harlequin Enterprises Ltd
225 Duncan Mill Road, Don Mills, Ontario M3B 3K9
☎001 416 445 5860   Fax 001 416 445 8655
www.eharlequin.com
Founded 1949. Canada's second largest publishing house. Publishes romantic fiction.

HarperCollins Publishers Limited
2 Bloor Street E, 20th Floor, Toronto, Ontario M4W 1A8
☎001 416 975 9334   Fax 001 416 975 9884
www.harpercanada.com
Founded 1989. Publishes fiction and non-fiction, children's and religious.

LexisNexis Canada Ltd
123 Commerce Valley Drive E, Suite 700, Markham, Ontario L3T 7W8
☎001 905 479 2665   Fax 001 905 479 2826
www.lexisnexis.ca
Founded 1912. Publishes law books, CD-ROMs, journals, newsletters, law reports.

McClelland & Stewart Ltd
481 University Avenue, Suite 900, Toronto, Ontario M5G 2E9
☎001 416 598 1114   Fax 001 416 598 7764
✉ mail@mcclelland.com
www.mcclelland.com
Founded 1906. Publishes fiction and general non-fiction, poetry.

McGraw-Hill Ryerson Ltd
300 Water Street, Whitby, Ontario L1N 9B6
☎001 905 430 5000   Fax 001 905 430 5020
www.mcgrawhill.ca
Founded 1944. Subsidiary of **McGraw-Hill Education**. Publishes education and professional.

Nelson
1120 Birchmount Road, Scarborough, Ontario M1K 5G4
☎001 416 752 9448   Fax 001 416 752 8101
✉ inquire@nelsom.com

www.nelson.com
Founded 1914. Division of Thomson Canada Ltd. Leading educational publisher. Also publishes professional and reference.

New Star Books Ltd
107–3477 Commercial Street, Vancouver, BC V5N 4E8
☎001 604 738 9429   Fax 001 604 738 9332
✉ info@newstarbooks.com
www.newstarbooks.com
Founded 1974. Publishes literature, literary criticism, essays, environmental studies, geography, geology, government and political science, history, industrial relations, journalism, labour, women's studies, gay and lesbian studies, sociology, social sciences.

Oxford University Press, Canada
70 Wynford Drive, Don Mills, Onatario M3C 1J9
☎001 416 441 2941   Fax 001 416 444 0427
www.oup.com/ca
Founded 1904. Owned by **Oxford University Press**, UK. Publishes for college, school and trade markets.

Pearson Education Canada Inc.
26 Prince Andrew Place, Don Mills, Ontario M3C 2T8
☎001 416 447 5101   Fax 001 416 443 0948
www.pearsoned.com
Founded 1966. Fourth-largest educational publisher in Canada. Publishes in English and French.

Penguin Group Canada
10 Alcorn Avenue, Suite 300, Toronto, Ontario M4V 3B2
☎001 416 925 2249   Fax 001 416 925 0068
www.penguin.ca
Founded 1974. Publishes fiction and non-fiction books and audio cassettes.

Random House of Canada Ltd
One Toronto Street, Unit 300, Toronto, Ontario M5C 2V6
☎001 416 364 4449   Fax 001 416 364 6863
www.randomhouse.ca
Founded 1944. Publishes fiction and non-fiction and children's.

Reader's Digest Association (Canada)
1100 Rene Levesque Blvd. W, Montreal, Quebec H3B 5H5

☎001 514 940 0751   Fax 001 514 940 3637
www.readersdigest.ca
Founded 1943. Publishes reference; altases and maps, dictionaries, directories, encyclopedias.

Scholastic Canada Ltd
175 Hillmount Road, Markham, Ontario
L6C 1Z7
☎001 905 887 7323   Fax 001 905 887 1131
www.scholastic.ca
Founded 1957. Publishes (in English and French) children's books and educational material.

Thomson Nelson
1120 Birchmount Road, Scarborough,
Ontario M1K 5G4
☎001 416 752 9448   Fax 001 416 752 8101
✉ inquire@nelson.com
www.nelson.com
Part of the Thomson Corporation. Publishes directories, education, professional, reference, textbooks.

University of Toronto Press
10 St Mary's Street, Suite 700, Toronto,
Ontario M4Y 2W8
☎001 416 978 2239   Fax 001 416 978 4738
www.utpress.utoronto.ca
Founded 1901. Publishes scholarly books and journals.

Tundra Books
481 University Avenue, Suite 900, Toronto,
Ontario M5G 2E9
☎001 416 598 4786   Fax 001 416 598 0247
www.tundrabooks.com
Founded 1967. Division of **McClelland & Stewart Ltd**. Publishes (in English and French) children's and young adult books.

John Wiley & Sons Canada Ltd
6045 Fremont Blvd, Mississauga, Ontario
L5R 4J3
☎001 416 236 4433   Fax 001 416 236 4447
✉ canada@wiley.com
www.wiley.ca
Founded 1968. Subsidiary of **John Wiley & Sons Inc.**, USA. Publishes professional, reference and textbooks.

India

Affiliated East West Press Pvt Ltd
105 Nirmal Tower, 26 Barakhamba Road,
New Delhi 110 001

☎00 91 11 331 5398   Fax 00 91 11 326 0538
Founded 1962. Publishes aeronautics, aviation, agriculture, anthropology, biological sciences, chemistry, engineering (chemical, civil, electrical, mechanical), computer science, economics, electronics, geography, geology, mathematics, management, microcomputers, physical sciences, physics, psychology, psychiatry, general science, textbooks, veterinary science, women's studies.

Arnold Heinman Publishers (India) Pvt Ltd
AB-9, 1st Floor, Safdaoung Enclave, New
Delhi 110 029
☎00 91 11 638 3422   Fax 00 91 11 687 7571
Founded 1969. Associate company of Edward Arnold (Publishers) Ltd, UK. Publishes fiction, poetry, essays, literature, literary criticism, directories, reference, textbooks, art, dentistry, general engineering, government, political science, philosophy, religion, medicine, nursing, social sciences and sociology.

S. Chand & Co Ltd
PO Box 5733 Ram Nagar, New Delhi 110 055
☎00 91 11 367 2080   Fax 00 91 11 367 7446
Founded 1917. Publishes art, business, economics, government, political science, medicine, nursing, dentistry, philosophy, social sciences, sociology, general science, technology.

Current Books
DC Bookshop, Pooma Complex, Thrissur
680 001
☎00 91 487 244 4322
Founded 1952. Publishes fiction and general non-fiction.

General Book Depot
PO Box 1220, Delhi 110 006
☎00 91 11 2326 3695
Fax 00 91 11 2394 0861
Founded 1936. Publishes general non-fiction, reference, textbooks; business, career development, dictionaries, directories, encyclopedias, how-to, English as a second language, language arts, linguistics, self-help, travel.

Hind Pocket Books Private Ltd
18–19 Dilshad Garden G T Road, Shadar,
Delhi 110 095
Fax 00 91 11 228 2332
Founded 1957. Publishes fiction and general non-fiction; biography, how-to and self-help.

Jaico Publishing House
127 Mahatma Gandhi Road, Mumbai 400 023
☎00 91 22 267 6702   Fax 00 91 22 265 6412
www.jaicobooks.com
Founded 1946. Publishes biography, behavioural sciences, language arts, linguistics, health and nutrition, cookery, law, criminology, astrology, directories, reference, self-help, occult, philosophy, religion, general engineering, economics, humour, history, government, political science, psychology, psychiatry.

LexisNexis India
14th Floor, Vijaya Building, 17 Barakhamba Road, New Delhi 110 001
☎00 91 11 373 9614   Fax 00 91 11 332 6456
✉ info@lexisnexis.co.in
www.lexisnexis.co.in
Publishes law, taxation and business books.

Macmillan India Ltd
315/316 Raheja Chambers, 12 Museum Road, Bangalore 560 052
☎00 91 80 558 7878   Fax 00 91 80 558 8713
www.macmillan-india.com
Founded 1903. Part of **Macmillan Publishers**, UK. Educational publisher.

Munshiram Manoharlal Publishers Pvt Ltd
PO Box 5715, New Delhi 110 055
☎00 91 11 367 1668   Fax 00 91 11 361 2745
www.mrmlbooks.com
Founded 1952. Publishes academic, dictionaries, encyclopedias, professional, art, architecture and interior design, anthropology, archaeology, astrology, occult, religion (Buddhist, Hindu, Islamic), philosophy, history, language arts and linguistics, music, dance, drama, theatre, Asian studies.

National Book Trust India
A5 Green Park, New Delhi 110 016
☎00 91 11 651 8378   Fax 00 91 11 685 1795
www.nbtindia.com
Founded 1957. Publishes human relations.

National Publishing House
23 Daryaganj, New Delhi 110 002
☎00 91 11 327 4161
Founded 1950. Publishes human relations, ethnicity, social sciences, sociology.

Orient Paperbacks
1590 Madarsa Road, Kashmere Gate, Delhi 110 006
☎00 91 11 2386 2267
Fax 00 91 11 2386 2935
www.orientpaperbacks.com
Founded 1977. Publishes fiction and general non-fiction; business, career development, cookery, crafts, games, hobbies, humour, drama, theatre, health and nutrition, how-to, poetry, astrology, occult, self-help, sport.

Oxford University Press India
YMCA Library Building, 1st Floor, 1 Jai Singh Road, New Delhi 110 001
☎00 91 11 202 1029
Fax 00 91 11 373 2312
Founded 1912. Owned by **Oxford University Press**, UK. Academic publishers.

Rajpal & Sons
1590 Madarasa Road, Kashmere Gate, Delhi 110 006
☎00 91 11 296 3904
Fax 00 91 11 296 7791
Founded 1947. Publishes fiction, literature, literary criticism, essays, human relations, general science, children's, dictionaries, encyclopedias, textbooks.

Tata McGraw-Hill Publishing Company
7 West Patel Nagar, New Delhi 110 008
☎00 91 11 2588 2743
www.tatamcgrawhill.com
Founded 1970. Publishes general engineering and science, business, social sciences, sociology, management and textbooks.

Vidyarthi Mithram Press
Market Road, Kochi 11
☎00 91 481 354 003
Fax 00 91 481 562 616
Founded 1928. Publishes children's, CD-ROMs, dictionaries, directories, encyclopedias, cookery, drama and theatre, economics, biography, biological sciences, chemistry and chemical engineering, computer science, reference.

A.H. Wheeler & Co Ltd
23 Lal Bahadur Shasti Marg, Allahabad 211 001
☎00 91 11 331 2629
Fax 00 91 11 335 7798
Founded 1879. Publishes CD-ROMs, professional, textbooks; computer science, behavioural sciences, accountancy, advertising, business, career development, civil engineering, communications.

New Zealand

Auckland University Press
University of Auckland, Private Bag 92019, Auckland
☎00 64 9 373 7528   Fax 00 64 9 373 7465
✉ aup@auckland.ac.nz
www.auckland.ac.nz/aup
Founded 1966. Publishes academic, art, archaeology, biography, dictionaries, encyclopedias, government, political science, history, social sciences, sociology, women's studies, essays, poetry, literature, literary criticism.

Butterworths New Zealand Ltd
PO Box 472, Wellington 1
☎00 64 4 385 1479   Fax 00 64 4 385 1598
www.butterworths.co.nz
Founded 1914. Publishes law, professional and textbooks.

Canterbury University Press
University of Canterbury, Private Bag 4800, Christchurch
☎00 64 3 364 2914   Fax 00 64 3 364 2044
✉ mail@cup.canterbury.ac.nz
www.cup.canterbury.ac.nz
Founded 1964. Academic publishers; general non-fiction; biography, biological sciences, history, natural history.

The Caxton Press
113 Victoria Street, Christchurch
☎00 64 3 366 8516   Fax 00 64 3 365 7840
www.caxton.co.nz
Founded 1935. Publishes general non-fiction; biography, gardening and plants, illustrated, textbooks.

HarperCollins Publishers (New Zealand) Ltd
31 View Road, Auckland
☎00 64 9 443 9400   Fax 00 64 9 443 9403
✉ editors@harpercollins.co.nz
www.harpercollins.co.nz
Founded 1888. Publishes fiction, children's, art, dictionaries, directories, encyclopedias, history, humour, natural history, biography, cookery, plants, gardening, reference, sport, travel, self-help.

Hodder Moa Beckett Publishers Ltd
PO Box 100–749, North Shore Mail Centre, Auckland 1330
☎00 64 9 478 1000   Fax 00 64 9 478 1010
Founded 1971. Owned by **Hodder Headline**,

UK. Publishes fiction and general non-fiction; biography, business, cookery, humour, sport.

Huia Publishers
PO Box 17335, Aotearoa, Wellington
☎00 64 4 473 9262   Fax 00 64 4 473 9265
www.huia.co.nz
Founded 1991. Publishes Maori cultural history and language, children's books in Maori and English, histories of colonisation in New Zealand, textbooks, drama and theatre, fiction.

LexisNexis New Zealand
PO Box 472, Wellington
☎00 64 4 385 1479   Fax 00 64 4 385 1598
www.lexisnexis.com.au/nz
Publishes accountancy, business and law.

Macmillan Publishers New Zealand Ltd
6 Ride Way, Albany, Auckland
☎00 64 9 414 0350   Fax 00 64 9 414 0351
Education publishers – general, school and academic books; fiction and non-fiction for all ages.

University of Otago Press
PO Box 56, Dunedin
☎00 64 3 479 8807   Fax 00 64 3 479 8385
✉ university.press@otago.ac.nz
www.otago.ac.nz
Founded 1958. Publishes fiction, academic, textbooks, essays, literature, literary criticism, poetry, art, history, education, biography, anthropology, natural history, environmental studies, photography, psychology, psychiatry, government and political science.

Pearson Education New Zealand Ltd
Private Bag 102908, North Shore Mail Centre, Auckland 10
☎00 64 9 444 4968   Fax 00 64 9 444 4957
www.pearson.co.nz
Founded 1968. Educational publishers.

Penguin Books (NZ) Ltd
Private Bag 102–902, North Shore Mail Centre, Auckland 1310
☎00 64 9 415 4700   Fax 00 64 9 415 4703
www.penguin.co.nz
Founded 1976. Owned by **Penguin UK**.

Random House New Zealand
18 Poland Road, Glenfield, Auckland
☎00 64 9 444 7197   Fax 00 64 9 444 7524

www.randomhouse.co.nz
Publishes fiction and non-fiction and children's.

Reed Publishing (NZ) Ltd
Private Bag 34901, Birkenhead, Auckland 10
☎00 64 9 441 2960   Fax 00 64 9 480 4999
✉ info@reed.co.nz
www.reed.co.nz
Founded 1988. Publishes fiction and general non-fiction, biography, children's, cookery, directories, history, natural history, regional interests, reference, textbooks, travel.

Southern Press Ltd
PO Box 50–134, Porirua 6221
☎00 64 4 233 1899
Founded 1971. Publishes aviation, aeronautics, maritime, transport, technology, mechanical and civil engineering, archaeology.

Tandem Press
PO Box 34–272, Birkenhead, Auckland
☎00 64 9 480 1452
Fax 00 64 9 480 1455
www.tandempress.co.nz
Founded 1990. Publishes fiction and general non-fiction; cookery, business, health and nutrition, photography, psychology, psychiatry, self-help, travel, women's studies.

Victoria University Press
PO Box 600, Wellington
☎00 64 4 463 6580   Fax 00 64 4 463 6581
✉ victoria-press@vuw.ac.nz
www.vup.vuw.ac.nz
Founded 1979. Publishes government, political science, essays, poetry, literature, literary criticism, drama, theatre, history, social sciences and sociology, anthropology, language and linguistics, law, architecture and interior design.

Viking Sevenseas NZ Ltd
PO Box 152, Paraparaumu 6150, Wellington
☎00 64 4 902 8240
Fax 00 64 4 902 8240
Founded 1957. Publishes natural history and ethnicity.

Bridget Williams Books Ltd
PO Box 5482, Wellington
☎00 64 4 473 8317
Fax 00 64 4 473 8417
Founded 1990. Publishes academic, general non-fiction, biography, government, political science, history, women's studies.

South Africa

W.J. Flesch & Partners
PO Box 3473, Cape Town 8001
☎00 27 21 461 7472   Fax 00 27 21 461 3758
Founded 1966. Publishes reference, aviation, aeronautics, directories, maritime, animals, pets, business.

Heinemann Educational Publishers Southern Africa
PO Box 781940, Sandton, Johannesburg 2146
☎00 27 11 322 8600   Fax 00 27 11 322 8716
www.heinemann.co.za
Founded 1986. Parent company: Reed Educational & Professional Publishing, UK. Publishes economics, education, English as a second language, mathematics, mechanical engineering, textbooks.

University of Kwa-Zulu–Natal Press
PB X01, Scottsville, Pietermaritzburg 3209
☎00 27 331 260 5226
Fax 00 27 331 260 5801
✉ info@ukzn.ac.za
www.ukznpress.co.za
Founded 1947. Academic publishers; biography, biological sciences, education, essays, genealogy, government, political science, literature and literary criticism, poetry, health and nutrition, psychology, psychiatry, women's studies, sociology, social sciences.

LexisNexis Butterworths South Africa
PO Box 792, Durban 4000
☎00 27 31 268 3111   Fax 00 27 31 268 3108
www.lexisnexis.co.za
Owned by Butterworth & Co. UK. Publishes professional and text books; general science, medicine, nursing and dentistry, economics, education, law.

Maskew Miller Longman
PO Box 396, Cape Town 8000
☎00 27 21 531 7750   Fax 00 27 21 531 4877
www.mml.co.za
Founded 1893. Publishes academic, education, children's, language arts and linguistics, essays, literature, literary criticism, textbooks.

Oxford University Press Southern Africa
PO Box 12119, N1 City 7463
☎00 27 21 595 4400   Fax 00 27 21 595 4430
✉ oxford.za@oup.com

www.oup.com/za

Founded 1915. Parent company: **Oxford University Press**, UK. Publishes academic, educational and general books.

Ravan Press (Pty) Ltd

PO Box 32484, Braamfontein,
Johannesburg 2017
☎00 27 11 484 0916
Fax 00 27 11 484 42631

Founded 1972. Part of Hodder & Stoughton Educational Southern Africa. Publishes fiction and general non-fiction; children's, anthropology, biography, business, economics, education, environmental studies, government, political science, history, labour, industrial relations, management, music, dance, sociology, social sciences, women's studies.

Shuter & Shooter (Pty) Ltd

PO Box 109, Pietermaritzburg 3200
☎00 27 33 394 8881   Fax 00 27 33 342 7419

Founded 1925. Publishes general non-fiction; biography, history, ethnicity, foreign language, bilingual, general science, technology, social sciences, sociology, textbooks.

Struik Publishers (Pty) Ltd

Cornelis Struik House, 80 McKenzie Street, Cape Town 8001
☎00 27 21 462 4360
Fax 00 27 21 462 4379
✉ admin@struik.co.za

Founded 1962. Publishes child care and development, general non-fiction, children's, cookery, directories, gardening, plants, environmental studies, illustrated, maps and atlases, humour, natural history, reference, travel.

Witwatersrand University Press

PO Wits, Johannesburg 2050
☎00 27 11 717 1000
Fax 00 27 11 717 1065
www.wirs.ac.za/wup.html

Founded 1922. Publishes academic, dictionaries, textbooks, encyclopedias, education, economics, essays, finance, literature and literary criticism, drama, theatre, history, business, anthropology, archaeology, crafts, games and hobbies, government, political science, language arts, linguistics, law, general science, natural history, religion (Jewish), medicine, nursing and dentistry.

Professional Associations and Societies

ABSW

Wellcome Wolfson Building, 165 Queen's Gate, London SW7 5HE
☎0870 770 3361
✉ absw@absw.org.uk
www.absw.org.uk
Chairman *Toby Murcott*
Administrator & EUSJA Board Member
Barbara Drillsma
MEMBERSHIP £40 (full) p.a.; £36 (associate); £5 (student)

ABSW has played a central role in improving the standards of science journalism in the UK over the last 40 years. The Association seeks to improve standards by means of networking, lectures and organised visits to institutional laboratories and industrial research centres. Puts members in touch with major projects in the field and with experts worldwide. A member of the European Union of Science Journalists' Associations, ABSW is able to offer heavily subsidised places on visits to research centres in most other European countries, and hosts reciprocal visits to Britain by European journalists. Membership open to those who are considered to be *bona fide* science writers/editors, or film/TV/radio equivalents, who earn a substantial part of their income by promoting public interest in and understanding of science. Runs the administration and judging of the **Glaxo Science Writers' Awards**, for outstanding science journalism in newspapers, journals and broadcasting and, with The Wellcome Trust, awards bursaries for science undergraduates taking a science communication course.

Academi (Yr Academi Gymreig)

3rd Floor, Mount Stuart House, Mount Stuart Square, Cardiff CF10 5FQ
☎029 2047 2266   Fax 029 2049 2930
✉ post@academi.org
www.academi.org

North West Wales office: Ty Newydd, Llanystumdwy, Criccieth, Gwynedd LL52 0LW
☎01766 522817 Fax 01766 523095
✉ olwen@academi.org

West Wales office: Dylan Thomas Centre, Somerset Place, Swansea SA1 1RR
☎01792 463980 Fax 01792 463993

✉ academi.dylan.thomas@business.ntl.com
Chief Executive *Peter Finch*

Academi is the trading name of Yr Academi Gymreig, the Welsh National Literature Promotion Agency and Society for Writers. Yr Academi Gymreig was founded in 1959 as an association of Welsh language writers. An English language section was established in 1968. Membership, for those who have made a significant contribution to the literature of Wales, is by invitation. Membership currently stands at 500. The Academi runs courses, competitions (including the **Cardiff International Poetry Competition**), conferences, tours by authors, festivals and represents the interests of Welsh writers and Welsh writing both inside Wales and beyond. Its publications include *Taliesin*, a quarterly literary journal in the Welsh language, *The Oxford Companion to the Literature of Wales*, *The Welsh Academy English-Welsh Dictionary* and a variety of translated works.

The Academi won the franchise from the Arts Council of Wales to run the Welsh National Literature Promotion Agency. The new, much enlarged organisation now administers a variety of schemes including bursaries, the annual **Book of the Year Award**, critical services, writers' mentoring, Writers on Tour, Writers Residencies and a number of literature development projects. It promotes an annual literary festival alternating between North and South Wales, runs its own programme of literary activity and publishes *A470*, a bi-monthly literature information magazine. The Academi is also in receipt of a lottery grant to publish the first Welsh National Encyclopedia. This is expected to be ready in 2006.

Those with an interest in literature in Wales can become an associate of the Academi (which carries a range of benefits). Rates are £15 p.a. (waged); £7.50 (unwaged).

ALCS

See **Authors' Licensing & Collecting Society Limited**

Alliance of Literary Societies

22 Belmont Grove, Havant PO9 3PU
☎023 9247 5855
✉ rosemary@sndc.demon.co.uk

www.allianceofliterarysocieties.org
Honorary Secretary *Mrs Rosemary Culley*
Founded 1974. Aims to help and support its 100+ member societies and, when necessary, to act as a pressure group. Produces a handbook which holds useful information that is deemed important for the successful running of a literary society. It also contains details of the member societies to publicise them to the ALS members and the wider public. In addition, the Alliance produces two newsletters and *The Open Book*, an annual publication.

Arts & Business (A&B)

Nutmeg House, 60 Gainsford Street, Butlers Wharf, London SE1 2NY
☎020 7378 8143   Fax 020 7407 7527
✉ head.office@AandB.org.uk
www.AandB.org.uk
P.R. Manager *Jonathan Tuchner*

The purpose of Arts & Business (formerly the Association for Business Sponsorship of the Arts) is to help strengthen communities by developing creative and effective partnership between Business and the Arts. It provides a wide range of services to over 350 business members as well as to 700 arts organisations and museums through the Development Forum. The Arts & Business Skills Bank, Board Bank and mentoring schemes enable individual business people to share their skills with arts managers. On behalf of the Department for Culture, Media and Sport, it manages the Arts & Business New Partners Programme, an incentive programme for new and established sponsors of the arts. Arts & Business is working with forward-looking businesses to determine the future of business/arts partnerships. With the support of its President, HRH The Prince of Wales, it is exploring and developing new ways for business, the arts and society to interact. Arts & Business has 15 offices offering a range of services throughout the UK.

Arvon Foundation

See entry under *UK Writers' Courses*

ASLS

See **Association for Scottish Literary Studies**

Association for Scottish Literary Studies

c/o Department of Scottish History,
9 University Gardens, University of Glasgow,
Glasgow G12 8QH
☎0141 330 5309   Fax 0141 330 5309

✉ office@asls.org.uk
www.asls.org.uk
Contact *Duncan Jones*
SUBSCRIPTION £38 (individual);
£67 (institutional)
Founded 1970. ASLS is an educational charity promoting the languages and literature of Scotland. Publishes works of Scottish literature; essays, monographs and journals; and *Scotnotes*, a series of comprehensive study guides to major Scottish writers. Also produces *New Writing Scotland*, an annual anthology of contemporary poetry and prose in English, Gaelic and Scots (see entry under *Magazines*).

Association of American Correspondents in London

c/o Time Magazine, Brettenham House,
Lancaster Place, London WC2E 7TL
☎020 7322 1084   Fax 020 7322 1230
Secretary/Treasurer *Monique Jessen*
SUBSCRIPTION £100 (organisations)
Founded 1919 to serve the professional interests of its member organisations, promote social cooperation among them, and maintain the ethical standards of the profession. (An extra £40 is charged for each department of an organisation which requires separate listing in the Association's handbook and a charge of £10 for each full-time editorial staff listed, up to a maximum of £120 regardless of the number listed.)

Association of American Publishers, Inc

71 Fifth Avenue, 2nd Floor, New York,
NY 10003–3004, USA
☎001 212 255 0200   Fax 001 212 255 7007
www.publishers.org
Also at: 50 f Street, NW, Washington,
DC 20001–1564
☎001 202 347 3375 Fax 001 202 347 3690
Contact *Judith Platt*
Founded 1970. For information, visit the Association's website.

Association of Authors' Agents (AAA)

A.P. Watt Ltd, 20 John Street, London
WC1N 2DR
☎020 7405 6774   Fax 020 7831 2154
✉ aaa@apwatt.co.uk
www.agentsassoc.co.uk
President *Derek Johns*
Membership £50 p.a.

Founded 1974. Membership voluntary. The AAA maintains a code of practice, provides a forum for discussion and represents its members in issues affecting the profession. For a full list of members and a list of frequently asked questions visit the AAA website. The AAA is a voluntary body and unable to operate as an information service to the public.

Association of Authors' Representatives (AAR)

PO Box 237201, Ansonia Station, New York, NY 10003, USA
☎001 212 252 3695
✉ info@aar-online.org
www.aar-online.org

Administrative Secretary *Leslie Carroll*

Founded in 1991 through the merger of the Society of Authors' Representatives and the Independent Literary Agents Association. Membership of this US organisation is restricted to agents of at least two years' operation. Provides information, education and support for its members and works to protect their best interests.

Association of British Editors
See **Society of Editors**

Association of British Science Writers
See **ABSW**

Association of Canadian Publishers

161 Eglinton Avenue East, Suite 702, Toronto, Ontario M4P 1J5, Canada
☎001 416 487 6116   Fax 001 416 487 8815
✉ admin@canbook.org
www.publishers.ca

Executive Director *Margaret Eaton*

Founded 1971. ACP represents more than 140 Canadian-owned book publishers country-wide from the literary, general trade, scholarly and education sectors. Aims to encourage the writing, publishing, distribution and promotion of Canadian books and to support the development of a 'strong, independent and vibrant Canadian-owned publishing industry'. The website has information on getting published and links to many of their member publishers' websites.

Association of Christian Writers

All Saints Vicarage, 43 All Saints Close, London N9 9AT
☎020 8884 4348   Fax 020 8884 4348
✉ admin@christianwriters.org.uk
www.christianwriters.org.uk

Administrator *Mrs Jenny Kyriacou*
SUBSCRIPTION single: £20 (£17 Direct Debit); joint husband/wife: £23 (£20 DD); overseas: £27 (£24 DD on UK a/c)

Founded in 1971 'to inspire and equip men and women to use their talents and skills with integrity to devise, write and market excellent material which comes from a Christian worldview. In this way we seek to be an influence for good and for God in this generation.' Publishes a quarterly magazine. Runs three training events each year, biennial conference, competitions, postal workshops, area groups, prayer support and manuscript criticism. Charity No. 1069839.

Association of Freelance Editors, Proofreaders & Indexers (Ireland)

3 The Lawn, Oldtown Mill, Celbridge, Co. Kildare, Republic of Ireland
☎00 353 1 601 2846
www.afepi.ie

Contacts *Priscilla O'Connor, Brenda O'Hanlon*
SUBSCRIPTION €40 p.a. (full); €20 (associate)

The organisation was established in Ireland to protect the interests of its members and to provide information to publishers on freelancers working in the relevant fields. Full membership is restricted to freelancers with experience and/or references (but the association does not test or evaluate the skills of members). A new category of membership, Associate Member, is available for trainees in proofreading/editing who are taking the Publishing Training Centre correspondence courses in Proofreading and Copy-editing.

Association of Freelance Journalists

107 Marlborough Road, Hadley, Telford TF1 5LJ
Fax 0870 133 7210
✉ afj_info@yahoo.com
www.afj.home-page.org

Official Patron *Dr Carl Chinn, PhD, MBE*
Founding President *Martin Scholes*
SUBBSCRIPTION £30 p.a.

Offers membership to all who work in the field of journalism but especially local correspondents, stringers, freelance journalists, news photographers, those at the beginning of their careers or long established. Also welcomes those who make a modest income writing for the specialist press or who self-publish; who have written for a hobby but now wish to make a career of their writing. Members receive a regular e-mail newsletter, a laminated press card, a free postal/e-mail advice service, the opportunity to network with other members (through the newsletter and a special Internet service) and editors who contact the AFJ. There are discounts on products and services, including the AFJ writing course.

Association of Freelance Writers

Sevendale House, 7 Dale Street, Manchester
M1 1JB
☎0161 228 2362, ext 210
Fax 0161 228 3533
✉ fmn@writersbureau.com
www.writersbureau.com/fmn

Contact *Angela Cox*
SUBSCRIPTION £29 p.a.

Founded in 1995 to help and advise new and established freelance writers. Members receive a copy of *Freelance Market News* each month which gives news, views and the latest advice and guidelines about publications at home and abroad. Other benefits include one free appraisal of prose or poetry each year, reduced entry to **The Writers Bureau** writing competition, reduced fees for writing seminars and discounts on books for writers.

Association of Golf Writers

1 Pilgrims Bungalow, Mulberry Hill, Chilham
CT4 8AH
☎01227 732496   Fax 01227 732496
✉ andyfarrell@compuserve.com

Honorary Secretary *Andy Farrell*

Founded 1938. Aims to cooperate with golfing bodies to ensure best possible working conditions.

Association of Illustrators

81 Leonard Street, London EC2A 4QS
☎020 7613 4328   Fax 020 7613 4417
✉ info@theaoi.com
www.theaoi.com

Contact *Membership & Publications Secretary*

Founded 1973 to promote illustration, protect illustrators' rights, and encourage professional standards. The AOI is a non-profit-making trade association dedicated to its members, to protecting their interests and promoting their work. Talks, seminars, bi-monthly journal, regional groups, legal and portfolio advice as well as a number of related publications such as *Rights, Contact Directories, The Illustrator's Guide to Professional Practice, Survive, The Illustrator's Guide to a Professional Career* and *Images*, the only jury-selected annual of British illustration.

Association of Independent Libraries

Leeds Library, 18 Commercial Street, Leeds
LS1 6AL
☎0113 245 3071
www.independentlibraries.co.uk

Chairman *Geoffrey Forster*
Secretary *Krystyna Smithers*

Established to 'further the advancement, conservation and restoration of a little-known but important living portion of our cultural heritage'. Members include the **London Library, Devon & Exeter Institution, Linen Hall Library** and **Plymouth Proprietary Library**.

Association of Learned and Professional Society Publishers

South House, The Street, Clapham, Worthing
BN13 3UU
☎01903 871686   Fax 01903 871457
✉ chief-exec@alpsp.org
www.alpsp.org

Chief Executive *Sally Morris*
Member Services Manager *Nick Evans*
Editors, Learned Publishing *Robert Welham* (UK), *Alma Wills* (USA)

The Association of Learned and Professional Society Publishers (ALPSP) is the international trade association for not-for-profit publishers and those who work with them. It currently has over 300 members in more than 30 countries. ALPSP provides representation of its sector, cooperative services such as the award-winning ALPSP Learned Journals Collection, professional development activities and a wealth of information and advice.

Association of Scottish Motoring Writers

c/o Scottish and Universal Newspapers,
5/15 Bank Street, Airdrie ML6 6AF
☎01236 748048   Fax 01236 748098
✉ jmurdoch@s-un.co.uk

Secretary *John Murdoch*
SUBSCRIPTION £45 (full); £25 (associate)

Founded 1961. Aims to co-ordinate the activities of, and provide shared facilities for, motoring writers resident in Scotland. Membership is by invitation only.

Audiobook Publishing Association

c/o 18 Green Lanes, Hatfield AL10 9JT
www.theapa.net

Chairman *Barry Clark*
Administrator *Charlotte McCandlish*

Founded 1994. The Audiobook Publishing Association (formerly the Spoken Word Publishing Association) is the UK trade association for the audiobook industry with membership open to all those involved in the publishing of spoken word audio. Publishes *APA Resources Directory*, available from the address above.

Australian Copyright Council

PO Box 1986, Strawberry Hills, NSW 2016, Australia
☎00 61 29318 1788   Fax 00 61 29698 3536
✉ info@copyright.org.au
www.copyright.org.au
Contact *Customer Service*

Founded 1968. The Council's activities and services include a range of publications, organising and speaking about copyright at seminars, research, consultancies and free legal advice. Aims include assistance for copyright owners to exercise their rights effectively, raising awareness about the importance of copyright and seeking changes to the law of copyright.

Australian Publishers Association

60/89 Jones Street, Ultimo, NSW 2007, Australia
☎00 61 2 9281 9788
✉ apa@publishers.asn.au
www.publishers.asn.au
Chief Executive *Susan Bridge*
SUBSCRIPTION Annual membership subscription open to Australian publishers

Founded 1948. The APA initiates programmes that contribute to the development of publishing in Australia, vigorously protects and furthers the interests of copyright owners, agents and licensees and actively represents members' interests to government and other organisations as appropriate. The Association encourages excellence in writing, editing, design, production, marketing and distribution of published works in Australia, protects freedom of expression and manages members' funds to further the interests of the industry.

Australian Society of Authors

PO Box 1566, Strawberry Hills, NSW 2012, Australia
☎00 61 2 9318 0877   Fax 00 61 2 9318 0530
✉ asa@asauthors.org
www.asauthors.org
Executive Director *Dr Jeremy Fisher*

Founded 1963. The ASA aims to promote and protect the professional interests of Australian authors. Provides contract advice and assists authors on industry standards and practices. Publishes *Australian Author* magazine.

Authors' Club

40 Dover Street, London W1S 4NP
☎020 7499 8581   Fax 020 7409 0913
✉ secretary@authorsclub.co.uk
www.authorsclub.co.uk
Secretary *Lucy Jane Tetlow*

Founded in 1891 by Sir Walter Besant, the Authors' Club welcomes as members writers, agents, publishers, critics, journalists, academics and anyone involved with literature and the written word. Administers the **Authors' Club Best First Novel Award** and **Sir Banister Fletcher Award**, and organises regular talks and dinners with well-known guest speakers. Membership fee: apply to secretary.

Authors' Licensing & Collecting Society Limited (ALCS)

Marlborough Court, 14–18 Holborn, London EC1N 2LE
☎020 7395 0600   Fax 020 7395 0660
✉ alcs@alcs.co.uk
www.alcs.co.uk
Chief Executive *Jane Carr*
SUBSCRIPTION £10.00 incl. VAT (UK; free to members of Society of Authors, Writers' Guild, NUJ, BAJ and CIOJ)

Founded 1977. The UK collective rights management society for writers and their successors, ALCS is a non-profit organisation whose principal purpose is to ensure that hard-to-collect revenues due to writers are efficiently collected and speedily distributed. Established to give assistance to writers through the protection and exploitation of collective rights, ALCS has distributed over £105 million in secondary royalties to writers since its creation.

ALCS represents all types of writer, fiction and non-fiction, including educational, research and academic authors, scriptwriters, playwrights, poets, editors and freelance journalists across the print and broadcast media. On joining, members give ALCS a mandate to administer on their behalf those rights which the law determines must be received or which are best handled collectively. Chief among these are: photocopying, cable retransmission (including the fees for BBC Prime and BBC World Service programming), rental and lending rights (but not British Public Lending Right), off-air recording, electronic rights, the performing right and public reception of broadcasts. The society is a prime resource and a leading authority on copyright matters and writers' collective interests. It maintains a watching brief on all matters affecting copyright both in Britain and abroad, making representations to UK government authorities and the EU. Visit the ALCS website or contact the office for registration forms and further information.

BAPLA (British Association of Picture Libraries and Agencies)
18 Vine Hill, London EC1R 5DZ
☎020 7713 1780   Fax 020 7713 1211
✉ enquiries@bapla.org.uk
www.bapla.org

Everything you need to know about finding, buying and selling pictures. Represents over 450 members.

The Bibliographical Society
c/o Institute of English Studies, University of London, Room 304, Senate House, Malet Street, London WC1E 7HU
☎020 7862 8679   Fax 020 7862 8720
✉ secretary@bibsoc.org.uk
President *J.L. Flood*
Honorary Secretary *M.L. Ford*
SUBSCRIPTION £33 p.a.

Aims to promote and encourage the study and research of historical, analytical, descriptive and textual bibliography, and the history of printing, publishing, bookselling, bookbinding and collecting; to hold meetings at which papers are read and discussed; to print and publish works concerned with bibliography; to form a bibliographical library. Awards grants and bursaries for bibliographical research. Publishes a quarterly magazine called *The Library*.

Booksellers Association of the UK & Ireland Ltd
Minster House, 272 Vauxhall Bridge Road, London SW1V 1BA
☎020 7802 0802   Fax 020 7802 0803
✉ mail@booksellers.org.uk
www.booksellers.org.uk
Chief Executive *Tim Godfray*

Founded 1895. The BA helps 3200 independent, chain and multiple members to sell more books, reduce costs and improve efficiency. It represents members' interests to the UK Government, European Commission, publishers, authors and others in the trade as well as offering marketing assistance, conferences, seminars and exhibitions. Together with **The Publishers Association**, coordinates World Book Day. Publishes directories, catalogues, surveys and various other publications connected with the book trade and administers the **Whitbread Book Awards**.

Booktrust
Book House, 45 East Hill, London SW18 2QZ
☎020 8516 2977   Fax 020 8516 2978
✉ info@booktrust.org.uk
www.booktrust.org.uk
www.booktrusted.com
Director *Chris Meade*
Head of Promotions *Helen Hayes*

Founded 1925. Booktrust, the independent educational charity promoting books and reading, runs the Book Information Line giving accurate facts about topical books and the book world (☎0906 516 1193, weekdays 10.00 am to 1.00 pm; calls charged at £1.50 per minute). Runs Booktrusted.com, their website for all those who care what young people read which includes details of Children's Book Week. Administers many literary prizes such as the **Orange** and **Booktrust Teenage Prize** for fiction only, creative reading projects like Bookscapes, and runs Bookstart, the acclaimed national scheme which aims to supply a free introductory bag of baby books to all babies at their eight-month health check.

British Academy of Composers and Songwriters
2nd Floor, British Music House, 25–27 Berners Street, London W1T 3LR
☎020 7636 2929   Fax 020 7636 2212
✉ info@britishacademy.com
www.britishacademy.com
Head of Membership *Kizzy Donaldson*

The Academy represents the interests of music writers of all genres, providing advice on professional and artistic matters. Publishes bi-monthly magazines and administers the annual Ivor Novello Awards and British Composer Awards.

British Association of Communicators in Business (CiB)
Suite A, First Floor, The Auriga Building, Davy Avenue, Knowhill, Milton Keynes MK5 8HG
☎0870 121 7606   Fax 0870 121 7601
✉ enquiries@cib.uk.com
www.cib.uk
Secretary General *Kathie Jones*

Founded 1949. The Association aims to be the

'market leader for those involved in corporate media management and practice by providing professional, authoritative, dynamic, supportive and innovative services'.

British Association of Journalists
89 Fleet Street, London EC4Y 1DH
☎020 7353 3003   Fax 020 7353 2310
✉ office@bajunion.org.uk
General Secretary *Steve Turner*
SUBSCRIPTION National newspaper staff, national broadcasting staff, national news agency staff: £17.50 per month. Other seniors, including magazine journalists, PRs and freelances who earn the majority of their income from journalism: £10 p.m. Journalists under 24: £7.50 p.m.

Founded 1992. Aims to protect and promote the industrial and professional interests of journalists.

British Association of Picture Libraries and Agencies
See **BAPLA**

British Centre for Literary Translation
University of East Anglia, Norwich NR4 7TJ
☎01603 592785   Fax 01603 592737
✉ bclt@uea.ac.uk
www.uea.ac.uk
Contact *Catherine Fuller*

Founded 1989, BCLT is funded jointly by Arts Council England and the University of East Anglia. It aims to raise the profile of literary translation in the UK through events, publications, activities and research aimed at professional translators, students and the general reader. Member of the international RECIT literary translation network. Activities include the annual NESTA Sebald Lecture in London, Summer School, translator in residence scheme funded by the EC Culture 2000 programme and a joint website with the British Council (www.literarytranslation.com). BCLT has a PhD programme in literary translation as well as an MA in Literary Translation and other units at undergraduate and postgraduate level. Joint sponsor with BCLA of the **John Dryden Translation Prize**. Publishes a journal *In Other Words* and *New Books in German*. Free mailing list.

British Copyright Council
Copyright House, 29–33 Berners Street, London W1T 3AB
☎01986 788122   Fax 01986 788847
✉ secretary@britishcopyright.org

Contact *Janet Ibbotson*
Works for the national and international acceptance of copyright and acts as a lobby/watchdog organisation on behalf of creators, publishers and performers on copyright and associated matters. Publications include *Guide to the Law of Copyright and Rights in Performances in the UK.*

The British Council
10 Spring Gardens, London SW1A 2BN
☎020 7389 3166 (Literature Dept)
Fax 020 7839 6347
www.britishcouncil.org

The British Council promotes Britain abroad. It provides access to British ideas, expertise and experience in education, the English language, literature and the arts, science and technology and governance. Works in 110 countries running a mix of offices, libraries, resource centres and English teaching operations.

British Equestrian Writers' Association
Priory House, Station Road, Swavesey, Cambridge CB4 5QJ
☎01954 232084   Fax 01954 231362
✉ gnewsumn@aol.com
Contact *Gillian Newsum*
SUBSCRIPTION £15

Founded 1973. Aims to further the interests of equestrian sport and improve, wherever possible, the working conditions of the equestrian press. Membership is by invitation of the committee. Candidates for membership must be nominated and seconded by full members and receive a majority vote of the committee.

British Film Institute
21 Stephen Street, London W1T 1LN
☎020 7255 1444   Fax 020 7436 0439
www.bfi.org.uk
Chair *Anthony Minghella CBE*
Director *Amanda Nevill*
24-hour *bfi* events line: 0870 240 4050

Established in 1933 to champion moving image culture in all its richness and diversity across the UK, for the benefit of as wide an audience as possible and to create and encourage debate. Visit the website for more information on *bfi* services.

British Guild of Beer Writers
68b Elmwood Road, London SE24 9NR
✉ peterhaydon@onetel.com
www.beerwriters.co.uk
Secretary *Peter Haydon*

SUBSCRIPTION £40 p.a.

Founded 1988. Aims to improve standards in beer writing and at the same time extend public knowledge of beers and brewing. Publishes a directory of members with details of their publications and their particular areas of interest; this is then circulated to newspapers, magazines, trade press and broadcasting organisations. Also publishes a monthly newsletter, the *BGBW Newsletter*. As part of the plan to improve writing standards and to achieve a higher profile for beer, the Guild offers annual awards, The Gold and Silver Tankard Awards, to writers and broadcasters judged to have made the most valuable contribution towards this end in their work. Meetings are held regularly.

British Guild of Travel Writers

51b Askew Crescent, London W12 9DN
☎020 8749 1128   Fax 020 8181 6663
✉ charlotte.c@virtualnecessities.com
www.bgtw.org
Chairman *Melissa Shales*
Secretariat *Charlotte Copeman*
SUBSCRIPTION £100 p.a.

The professional association of travel writers, broadcasters, photographers and editors which aims to serve its members' professional interests by acting as a forum for debate, discussion and 'networking'. The Guild publishes an annual Year Book and has a website giving full details of all its members and useful trade contacts, holds monthly meetings and has a monthly newsletter. Members are required to spend a significant proportion of their working time on travel.

British Science Fiction Association

1 Long Row Close, Everdon, Daventry
NN11 3BE
☎01327 361661
✉ bsfa@enterprise.net
Chair *Paul and Elizabeth Billinger*
SUBSCRIPTION £21 p.a. (reduction for unwaged)

Founded originally in 1958 by a group of authors, readers, publishers and booksellers interested in science fiction. With a worldwide membership, the Association aims to promote the reading, writing and publishing of science fiction and to encourage SF fans to maintain contact with each other. *Publishes Matrix* bimonthly newsletter with comment and opinions, news of conventions, etc. Contributions from members welcomed; *Vector* bi-monthly

critical journal – reviews of books and magazines; *Focus* biannual magazine with articles, original fiction and letters column. Also offers postal writer's workshop. For further information, contact the Membership Secretary Estelle Roberts at 97 Sharp Street, Newland Avenue, Hull HU5 2AE or via e-mail.

British Society of Comedy Writers

61 Parry Road, Ashmore Park,
Wolverhampton WV11 2PS
☎01902 722729   Fax 01902 722729
✉ comedy@bscw.co.uk
www.bscw.co.uk
Contact *Ken Rock*

Founded 1999. The Society aims to develop good practice and professionalism among comedy writers while bringing together the best creative professionals, and working to standards of excellence agreed with the light entertainment industry. Offers a network of industry contacts and a range of products, services and training initiatives including specialised workshops, an annual international conference, script assessment service and opportunities to visit international festivals.

British Society of Magazine Editors (BSME)

137 Hale Lane, Edgware HA8 9QP
☎020 8906 4664   Fax 020 8959 2137
✉ admin@bsme.com
www.bsme.com
Contact *Gill Branston*

Holds regular industry forums and events as well as an annual awards dinner.

British Universities Film & Video Council

See **Learning on Screen**

Broadcasting Press Guild

Tiverton, The Ridge, Woking GU22 7EQ
☎01483 764895   Fax 01483 765882
✉ torin.douglas@bbc.co.uk
Membership Secretary *Richard Last*
Lunch Secretary *Torin Douglas*
SUBSCRIPTION £15 p.a.

Founded 1974 to promote the professional interests of journalists specialising in writing or broadcasting about the media. Organises monthly lunches addressed by leading industry figures, and annual TV and radio awards. Membership by invitation.

BSME

See **British Society of Magazine Editors**

Bureau of Freelance Photographers

Focus House, 497 Green Lanes, London
N13 4BP
☎020 8882 3315   Fax 020 8886 5174
✉ info@thebfp.com
Membership Secretary *Emma Farrell*
SUBSCRIPTION £49 p.a. (UK);
£65 p.a. (overseas)
Founded 1965. Assists members in selling their pictures through monthly *Market Newsletter*, and offers advisory, legal assistance and other services.

Campaign for Press and Broadcasting Freedom

Second Floor, 23 Orford Road, London
E17 9NL
☎020 8521 5932
✉ freepress@cpbf.org.uk
www.cpbf.org.uk
SUBSCRIPTION £15 p.a. (concessions available);
£25 p.a. (institutions/organisations)
Broadly based pressure group working for more accountable and accessible media in Britain. Advises on right of reply and takes up the issue of the portrayal of minorities. Members receive *Free Press* (bi-monthly), discounts on publications and news of campaign progress.

Canada Cuba Literary Alliance

109 Bayshore Road, RR#4, Brighton,
Ontario K0K 1H0, Canada
☎001 613 475 2368   Fax 001 801 751 1837
✉ richardgrove@canadacubaliteraryalliance.org
www.CanadaCubaLiteraryAlliance.org
President *Richard M. Grove*
A not-for-profit organisation established to advance literary solidarity between Canada and Cuba through the creative expression of poetry, prose and photography. Publishes a members anthology (in English and Spanish) and runs poetry contests. 'We are always looking for poetry, prose, art, photography, articles and reviews; international submissions welcome (e-mail only); see website for details.

Canadian Authors Association

National Office: Box 419, 320 South Shores
Road, Campbellford, Ontario K0L 1L0,
Canada
☎001 705 653 0323   Fax 001 705 653 0593
✉ admin@canauthors.org
www.canauthors.org

Contact *The Administrator*
Founded 1921. The CAA was founded to promote recognition of Canadian writers and their works, and to foster and develop a climate favourable to the creative arts. It is Canada's national association for writers of every kind; for those actively seeking to become writers and for those who want to support writers. The Association has branches across the country providing support to local members in the form of advice, local contests, publications and writers' circles. Publishes *National Newsline* (quarterly) and *The Canadian Writer's Guide*.

Canadian Publishers' Council

250 Merton Street, Suite 203, Toronto
M4S 1B1, Canada
☎001 416 322 7011   Fax 001 416 322 6999
✉ pubadmin@pubcouncil.ca
www.pubcouncil.ca
Executive Director, External Relations
Jacqueline Hushion
Founded 1910. Trade association of English-language publishers which represents the domestic and international interests of member companies.

Careers Writers' Association

www.careerswriters.co.uk
Founded 1979. 'An association of professional careers writers whose work in careers writing reaches high standards of accuracy and impartiality. Membership is open only to writers with an established reputation for providing objective and up-to-date careers information.' See website for details.

Chartered Institute of Journalists

2 Dock Offices, Surrey Quays Road, London
SE16 2XU
☎020 7252 1187   Fax 020 7232 2302
✉ memberservices@cioj.co.uk
www.ioj.co.uk
General Secretary *Dominic Cooper*
SUBSCRIPTION £195 p.a.; £16 (monthly)
Founded 1884. The Institute is concerned with professional journalistic standards and with safeguarding the freedom of the media. It is open to writers, broadcasters and journalists (including self-employed) in all media. Affiliate membership (£133) is available to part-time or occasional practitioners and to overseas journalists who can join the Institute's International Division. Members also belong to the IOJ (TU), an inde-

pendent trade union which protects, advises and represents them in their employment or freelance work; negotiates on their behalf and provides legal assistance and support. The IOJ (TU) is a certificated independent trade union which represents members' interests in the workplace, and the CIOJ is also a constituent member of the National Council for the Training of Journalists, the **British Copyright Council** and the Journalists Copyright Fund. Editor of the Institute's quarterly magazine is *Andrew Smith*.

Children's Book Circle

✉ childrensbookcircle@hotmail.co.uk
www.childrensbookcircle.org.uk

Membership Secretary *Alison Kain*

The Children's Book Circle provides a discussion forum for anybody involved with children's books. Regular meetings are addressed by a panel of invited speakers and topics focus on current and controversial issues. Administers the **Eleanor Farjeon Award**.

Children's Books Ireland

17 Lower Camden Street, Dublin 2, Republic of Ireland
☎00 353 1 475 0445   Fax 00 353 1 475 3716
✉ info@childrensbooksireland.com
www.childrensbooksireland.com

Contact *Mags Walsh*
SUBSCRIPTION €25 p.a. (individual);
€35 (institution); €15 (student);
€45/US$40 (overseas)

Aims to promote quality children's books and reading. Holds annual summer school as well as other occasional seminars and events. Quarterly magazine, *Inis* and bi-monthly newsletter, *Children's Book News*. Annual children's book festival in October; **Bisto/CBI Book of the Year Award** (see entry under *Prizes*). Publishes *Book Choice for Primary Schools*; *Book Choice for Post Primary Schools*; *The Big Guide 2: Irish Children's Books, What's The Story? The Reading Choices of Young People in Ireland*.

CiB

See **British Association of Communicators in Business**

CILIP in Scotland

1st Floor, Building C, Brandon Gate, Leechlee Road, Hamilton M13 6AU
☎01698 458888   Fax 01698 283170
✉ cilips@slainte.org.uk
www.slainte.org.uk

Director *Elaine Fulton*

CILIP in Scotland (Chartered Institute of Library and Information Professionals in Scotland) – formerly the Scottish Library Association – aims to bring together everyone engaged in or interested in library work in Scotland. The Association has over 2300 members, covering all aspects of library and information work. Its main aims are the promotion of library services and the qualifications and status of librarians.

CILIP: The Chartered Institute of Library and Information Professionals

7 Ridgmount Street, London WC1E 7AE
☎020 7255 0500   Fax 020 7255 0501
✉ info@cilip.org.uk
www.cilip.org.uk

Chief Executive *Bob McKee*

The leading membership body for library and information professionals, formed in 2002 following the unification of The Library Association and the Institute of Information Scientists. **Facet Publishing** (successor to LA Publishing) produces 25–30 new titles each year and has over 150 titles in print from the LA's back catalogue. Further information from Marketing & External Relations, CILIP.

Circle of Wine Writers

166 Meadvale Road, London W5 1LS
☎020 8930 0181
✉ administration@winewriters.org
www.winewriters.org

Administrator *Andrea Warren*
MEMBERSHIP £35 p.a.

Founded 1960. Membership is open to all those professionally engaged in communicating about wines and spirits, with the exception of people primarily doing so for promotional purposes. Aims to improve the standard of writing, broadcasting and lecturing about wines, spirits and beers; to contribute to the growing knowledge and interest in wine; to promote wines and spirits of quality and to comment adversely on faulty products or dubious practices; to establish and maintain good relations with the news media and the wine trade; to provide members with a strong voice with which to promote their views; to provide a programme of workshops, meetings, talks and tastings.

Cleveland Arts

See **Tees Valley Arts**

Clé – Irish Book Publishers' Association

25 Denzille Lane, Dublin 2, Republic of Ireland
☎00 353 56 775 6333
✉ info@publishingireland.com
www.publishingireland.com

President *Fergal Tobin*
Administrator *Jolly Ronan*

Founded 1970 to promote Irish publishing, protect members' interests and train the industry.

Comedy Writers' Association UK

118 Forest Edge, Buckhurst Hill IG9 5AB
☎020 8505 2476
www.cwauk.co.uk

Honorary President *Ken Dodd*
Membership Secretary *Doreen Friend*

Founded 1981 to assist and promote the work of comedy writers, the Association has grown to become the largest group of independent comedy writers in the UK. Holds annual and one-day seminars. Members receive a monthly newsletter and regular market opportunities.

Comhairle nan Leabhraichean/ The Gaelic Books Council

22 Mansfield Street, Glasgow G11 5QP
☎0141 337 6211   Fax 0141 341 0515
✉ brath@gaelicbooks.net
www.gaelicbooks.net

Chairman *Dr Martin MacGregor*
Director *Ian MacDonald*

Founded 1968 and now a charitable company with its own bookshop. Encourages and promotes Gaelic publishing by giving grants to publishers and writers; providing editorial and word-processing services; retailing Gaelic books; producing a catalogue of all Gaelic books in print and answering enquiries about them; mounting occasional literary evenings and training courses.

Commercial Radio Companies Association

77 Shaftesbury Avenue, London W1D 5DU
☎020 7306 2603   Fax 020 7470 0062
✉ info@crca.co.uk
www.crca.co.uk

Chairman *David Elstein*
Chief Executive *Paul Brown, CBE*
Research and Communications Manager *Alison Winter*
External Affairs Manager *Lisa Kerr*

The CRCA is the trade body for UK commercial radio companies. It represents members' interests to government, Ofcom, the European Commission, the European Parliament, copyright organisations and other bodies concerned with radio and broadcasting.

The Copyright Licensing Agency Ltd

90 Tottenham Court Road, London W1T 4LP
☎020 7631 5555   Fax 020 7631 5500
✉ cla@cla.co.uk
www.cla.co.uk

Chief Executive *Peter Shepherd*

CLA is the UK's reproduction rights organisation which looks after the interests of authors, publishers and artists in the photocopying and scanning of extracts from books, journals and periodicals. Founded in 1982 by the **Authors' Licensing and Collecting Society Limited (ALCS)** and the **Publishers Licensing Society Ltd (PLS)** to promote and enforce intellectual property rights of UK rightsholders both at home and abroad. CLA works closely with Reproductive Rights Organizations (RROs) from other countries and has close ties with the Design and Artists Copyright Society (DACS) which represents artists and illustrators. A not-for-profit organisation, CLA licenses the use of copyright text by business, education and government and distributes fees collected via authors, publishers and artists collective societies. CLA has also developed licences which enable digitisation of existing print material The licence enables users to scan and electronically send extracts from copyright works. Scanning and e-mail distribution is only available for UK works at present. Since its inception in 1982, CLA has distributed over £100 million.

Council for British Archaeology

St Mary's House, 66 Bootham, York YO30 7BZ
☎01904 671417   Fax 01904 671384
✉ info@britarch.ac.uk
www.britarch.ac.uk

Information Officer *Jonathan Bateman*

Founded 1944 to represent and promote archaeology at all levels. Its aims are to improve the public's awareness in and understanding of Britain's past; to carry out research; to survey, guide and promote the teaching of archaeology at all levels of education; to publish a wide range of academic, educational, general and bibliographical works (see **CBA Publishing** under *UK Publishers*).

Council of Academic and Professional Publishers
See **The Publishers Association**

Crime Writers' Association (CWA)
PO Box 273, Boreham Wood WD6 2XA
✉ secretary@thecwa.co.uk
www.thecwa.co.uk

Hon. Secretary *Liz Evans*
Membership Secretary *Rebecca Tope* (at
   Crossways Cottage, Walterstone HR2 0DX)
MEMBERSHIP £45, £60 (associate)

Full membership is limited to professional crime writers, but publishers, literary agents, booksellers, etc. who specialise in crime, are eligible for Associate membership. The Association has regional chapters throughout the country, including Scotland. Meetings are held regularly with informative talks frequently given by police, scenes of crime officers, lawyers, etc., and a weekend conference is held annually in different parts of the country. Produces a monthly newsletter for members called *Red Herrings* and presents various annual awards (see entries under *Prizes*).

The Critics' Circle
c/o Catherine Cooper, 69 Marylebone Lane, London W1U 2PH
☎020 7224 1410
www.criticscircle.org.uk

President *Mike Dixon*
Honorary General Secretary *Charles Hedges*
SUBSCRIPTION £25 p.a.

Membership by invitation only. Aims to uphold and promote the art of criticism (and the commercial rates of pay thereof) and preserve the interests of its members: professionals involved in criticism of film, drama, music and dance.

Cyngor Llyfrau Cymru
See **Welsh Books Council**

Department for Culture, Media and Sport
2–4 Cockspur Street, London SW1Y 5DH
☎020 7211 6000   Fax 020 7211 6270
✉ lauren.mcgovern@culture.gsi.gov.uk
Head of News *Paddy Feeny*

The Department for Culture, Media and Sport has responsibilities for Government policies relating to the arts, museums and galleries, public libraries, sport, gambling, broadcasting, Press standards, the built heritage, the film and music industries, tourism and the National Lottery. It funds the **Arts Council**, national museums and galleries, the **British Library**, the **Public Lending Right** and the Royal Commission on Historical Manuscripts. It is responsible within Government for the public library service in England, and for library and information matters generally, where they are not the responsibility of other departments.

Directory & Database Publishers Association
Queen's House, 28 Kingsway, London WC2B 6JR
☎020 7405 0836
✉ christine.scott@dpassoc.org
www.directory-publisher.co.uk

Contact *Christine Scott*
SUBSCRIPTION £120 – £1200 p.a.

Founded 1970 to promote the interests of *bona fide* directory and database publishers and protect the public from disreputable and fraudulent practices. The objectives of the Association are to maintain a code of professional practice to safeguard public interest; to raise the standard and status of directory publishing throughout the UK; to promote business directories as a medium for advertising; to protect the legal and statutory interests of directory publishers; to foster bonds of common interest among responsible directory publishers and to provide for the exchange of technical, commercial and management information between members. Meetings, seminars, conference, newsletter, awards, statistics, business support helpline.

DOI Registration Agency
3rd Floor, Midas House, 62 Goldsworth Road, Woking GU21 6LQ
☎0870 777 8712   Fax 0870 777 8714
✉ doi@nielsenbookdata.co.uk
www.doi.nielsenbookdata.co.uk

A service to publishers seeking to ensure effective discovery of their publications via the Internet. DOI (Digital Object Identifier) captures and records metadata for books (and other publications which qualify for an ISBN), serial publications and individual chapters of books, and issues of serials where they are available separately.

Drama Association of Wales
The Old Library Building, Singleton Road, Splott, Cardiff CF24 2ET
☎029 2045 2200   Fax 029 2045 2277
✉ aled.daw@virgin.net
Contact *Teresa Hennessy*

Runs a large playscript lending library; holds an

annual playwriting competition (see entry under *Prizes*); offers a script-reading service (£15 per script) which usually takes three months from receipt of play to issue of reports. From plays submitted to the reading service, selected scripts are considered for publication of a short run (70–200 copies). Writers receive a percentage of the cover price on sales and a percentage of the performance fee.

Edinburgh Bibliographical Society

National Library of Scotland, George IV Bridge, Edinburgh EH1 1EW
✉ warrenmcdougall@aol.com
www.edbibsoc.lib.ed.ac.uk

Honorary Secretary *Warren McDougall*
SUBSCRIPTION £10; £15 (institution); £7 (student)

Founded 1890. Organises lectures on bibliographical topics and visits to libraries. Publishes an occasional journal called *Transactions*, which is free to members, and other occasional publications.

Educational Publishers Council

See **The Publishers Association**

Electronic Publishers' Forum

See **The Publishers Association**

The English Association

University of Leicester, University Road LE1 7RH
☎ 0116 252 3982   Fax 0116 252 2301
✉ engassoc@le.ac.uk
www.le.ac.uk/engassoc/

Chief Executive *Helen Lucas*

Founded 1906 to promote understanding and appreciation of the English language and its literatures. Activities include sponsoring a number of publications and organising lectures and conferences for teachers, plus annual sixth-form conferences. Publications include *Year's Work in Critical and Cultural Theory, English, Use of English, English 4–11, Essays and Studies* and *Year's Work in English Studies*.

English PEN

6–8 Amwell Street, London EC1R 1UQ
☎ 020 7713 0023   Fax 020 7837 7838
✉ enquiries@englishpen.org
www.englishpen.org

Director *Susanna Nicklin*
MEMBERSHIP Cheque/standing order: £45/ £40 (London/overseas); £40/£35 (country); £15 (students)

English PEN is part of International PEN, a worldwide association of writers and other literary professionals which promotes literature, fights for freedom of expression and speaks out for writers who are imprisoned or harassed for having criticised their governments, or for publishing other unpopular views.

Founded in London in 1921, International PEN now consists of over 130 centres in almost 100 countries. PEN originally stood for poets, essayists and novelists, but membership is now open to all literary professionals. It is also possible to become a 'Friend of English PEN'. A programme of talks and discussions, and other activities such as social gatherings, is supplemented by mailings, website and annual congress at one of the centre countries.

Federation of Entertainment Unions

1 Highfield, Twyford, Nr Winchester SO21 1QR
☎ 01962 713134   Fax 01962 713134
✉ harris.s@btconnect.com

Secretary *Steve Harris*

Plenary meetings six times annually. Additionally, there are Training & European Committees. Represents the following unions: British Actors' Equity Association; Broadcasting Entertainment Cinematograph and Theatre Union; Musicians' Union; AMICUS; Professional Footballers' Association; **National Union of Journalists**; **The Writers' Guild of Great Britain**.

The Federation of Worker Writers and Community Publishers (FWWCP)

Burslem School of Art, Queen Street, Stoke on Trent ST6 3EJ
☎ 01782 822327
✉ thefwwcp@tiscali.co.uk
www.thefwwcp.org.uk

Administrator/Coordinator *Tim Diggles*

The FWWCP is a federation of writing groups committed to writing and publishing based on working-class experience and creativity. The FWWCP is the membership's collective national voice and has for some time been given funding by the **Arts Council**. Founded in 1976, it comprises around 80 member groups, each one with its own identity, reflecting its community and membership. These groups represent over 5000 people who regularly (often weekly) meet to offer constructive criticism, produce books and tapes, perform and share skills, offering creative and critical support. There are writers' workshops of long standing; adult literacy organisations; groups working mainly in oral and local history; groups and local networks of writers who come together to publish, train or perform; groups with a specific remit to further the aims of a section of the community such as the homeless or disabled.

Although diverse in nature, member organisations share the aim of making writing and publishing accessible to people and encourage them to take an active, cooperative and democratic role in writing, performing and publishing. The main activities include training days and weekends to learn and share skills, a quarterly magazine, a quarterly broadsheet of members' writing, a major annual festival of writing and networking between member organisations.

The FWWCP has published a number of anthologies and is willing to work with other organisations on publishing projects. Membership is open only to groups but individuals will be put in touch with groups which can help them, and become friends of the Federation. Contact the address above for an information leaflet.

Fellowship of Authors and Artists

PO Box 158, Hertford SG13 8FA
☎0870 747 2514   Fax 0870 199 1469
✉ fellowship@compassion-in-business.co.uk
www.author-fellowship.co.uk

Contact *Graham Irwin*

Founded in 2000 to promote and encourage the use of writing and all art forms as a means of therapy and self healing; to provide a valuable resource and meeting point for all interested parties including, but not limited to, writers, artists, counsellors and healers; to publish as web pages or e-books any suitable works that may help to support or promote the aims of the fellowship.

Foreign Press Association in London

11 Carlton House Terrace, London SW1Y 5AJ
☎020 7930 0445   Fax 020 7925 0469
✉ secretariat@foreign-press.org.uk
www.foreign-press.org.uk

General Manager *Andrew Jarrett*
MEMBERSHIP (incl. VAT) Full Members: £155 (entrance fee); £158 (annual subscription); Associate Journalists: £130 (entrance fee); £146 (annual sub.) Associate Non-journalists: £220 (entrance fee); £220 (annual sub.)

Founded 1888. Non-profit-making service association for foreign correspondents based in London, providing a variety of press-related services.

The Gaelic Books Council

See **Comhairle nan Leabhraichean**

The Garden Writers' Guild

c/o Institute of Horticulture, 14/15 Belgrave Square SW1X 8PS
☎020 7245 6943
✉ gwg@horticulture.org.uk
www.gardenwriters.co.uk

Contact *Angela Clarke*
SUBSCRIPTION £45; (£40 to Institute of Horticulture members); £55 (associate members)

Founded 1990. Aims to raise the quality of gardening communication, to help members operate efficiently and profitably, to improve liaison between garden communicators and the horticultural industry. Administers an annual awards scheme. Operates a mailing service and organises press briefing days.

Guild of Agricultural Journalists

Isfield Cottage, Church Road, Crowborough TN6 1BN
☎01892 611618   Fax 01892 613394
✉ don.gomery@farmingline.com
www.gaj.org.uk

Honorary General Secretary *Don Gomery*
SUBSCRIPTION £40 p.a.

Founded 1944 to promote a high professional standard among journalists who specialise in agriculture, horticulture and allied subjects. Represents members' interests with representative bodies in the industry; provides a forum through meetings and social activities for members to meet eminent people in the industry; maintains contact with associations of agricultural journalists overseas; promotes schemes for the education of members and for the provision of suitable entrants into agricultural journalism.

Guild of Editors

See **Society of Editors**

The Guild of Food Writers

48 Crabtree Lane, London SW6 6LW
☎020 7610 1180   Fax 020 7610 0299
✉ gfw@gfw.co.uk
www.gfw.co.uk

Administrator *Christina Thomas*
SUBSCRIPTION £70

Founded 1985. The objects of the Guild are to

bring together professional food writers including journalists, broadcasters and authors, to extend the range of members' knowledge and experience by arranging discussions, tastings and visits, and to encourage new writers through competitions and awards. The Guild aims to contribute to the growth of public interest in, and knowledge of, the subject of food and to campaign for improvements in the quality of food.

Guild of Motoring Writers
39 Beswick Avenue, Ensbury Park,
Bournemouth BH10 4EY
☎01202 518808   Fax 01202 518808
✉ gensec@gomw.co.uk
www.guildofmotoringwriters.co.uk
General Secretary *Patricia Lodge*

Founded 1944. Represents members' interests and provides a forum for members to exchange information.

Horror Writers Association
UK Contact: 24 Pearl Road, London
E17 4QZ
✉ hwa@horror.org
www.horror.org

US Contact: HWA Membership,
PO Box 50577, Palo Alto, CA 94303, USA
☎001 650 561 9511

Contact (UK) *Jo Fletcher*

Founded 1987. World-wide organisation of writers and publishers dedicated to promoting the interests of writers of horror and dark fantasy. Publishes a bi-monthly newsletter, issues e-mail bulletins, gives access to lists of horror agents, reviewers and bookstores; and keys to the 'Members Only' area of the HWA website. Presents the annual **Bram Stoker Awards** (see entry under *Prizes*).

HWA
See **Horror Writers Association**

Independent Publishers Guild
PO Box 93, Royston SG8 5GH
☎01763 247014   Fax 01763 246293
✉ info@ipg.uk.com
www.ipg.uk.com
Executive Director *Bridget Shine*
Subscription £150 + VAT p.a.

Founded 1962. Membership open to independent publishers, packagers and suppliers, i.e. professionals in allied fields. Regular meetings,

annual conference, seminars, mailings and e-mail bulletin.

Independent Theatre Council
12 The Leathermarket, Weston Street, London
SE1 3ER
☎020 7403 1727   Fax 020 7403 1745
✉ admin@itc-arts.org
www.itc-arts.org
Chief Executive *Charlotte Jones*

The management association and representative body for small/middle-scale performing arts organisations and individuals. Publications available from ITC include *A Guide for Writers and Companies*. Negotiates contracts and has established standard agreements for theatre professionals with Equity. The rights and fee structure agreement, reached with **The Writers' Guild** in 1991, was updated in December 2002. Contact The Writers' Guild for details.

Institute of Copywriting
Honeycombe House, Bagley, Wedmore
BS28 4TD
☎01934 713563   Fax 01934 713492
✉ copy@inst.org
www.inst.org/copy
Secretary *Lynn Hall*

Founded 1991 to promote copywriters and copywriting (writing publicity material). Maintains a code of practice. Membership is open to students as well as experienced practitioners. Runs training courses (see entry under **UK Writers' Courses**). Has a list of approved copywriters. Answers queries relating to copywriting. Contact the Institute for a free booklet.

Institute of Linguists
Saxon House, 48 Southwark Street, London
SE1 1UN
☎020 7940 3100   Fax 020 7940 3101
✉ info@iol.org.uk
www.iol.org.uk
Chief Executive Officer *Henry Pavlovich*
Membership Services Manager *Stephen Eden*

Founded 1910. Professional association for translators, interpreters and trainers; examining body for languages at degree level and above for vocational purposes; the National Register of Public Service Interpreters is managed by NRPSI Limited, an IoL subsidiary. Subscription rates on application. The Institute's limited company, Language Services Ltd, provides customised assessments of language-oriented requirements, skills, etc.

Institute of Translation and Interpreting (ITI)

Fortuna House, South Fifth Street, Milton Keynes MK9 2EU
☎01908 325250   Fax 01908 325259
✉ info@iti.org.uk
www.iti.org.uk

Founded 1986. The ITI is an association of translators and interpreters to promote the highest standards in their field. It has strong corporate membership and runs professional development courses and conferences. Membership is open to those with a genuine and proven involvement in translation and interpreting (including students). ITI's bi-monthly *Bulletin* and other publications are available from the Secretariat, which also offers a free referral service for those in need of a professional translator/interpreter. ITI's *Directory of Members* is available online. ITI is a full and active member of FIT (International Federation of Translators).

Irish Book Publishers' Association

See **Clé**

Irish Copyright Licensing Agency Ltd

25 Denzille Lane, Dublin 2, Republic of Ireland
☎00 353 1 662 4211   Fax 00 353 1 662 4213
✉ info@icla.ie
www.icla.ie

Executive Director *Samantha Holman*

Founded 1992 by writers and publishers in Ireland to provide a scheme through which rights holders can give permission, and users of copyright material can obtain permission, to copy.

Irish Playwrights and Screenwriters Guild

Art House, The Curved Street, Temple Bar, Dublin 2, Republic of Ireland
☎00 353 1 492 3808   Fax 00 353 1 492 3808
✉ david.cavanagh@script.ie
www.script.ie

Contact *David Cavanagh*
SUBSCRIPTION details available on request

Founded in 1969 to safeguard the rights of scriptwriters for radio, stage and screen.

Irish Translators' & Interpreters' Association (ITIA)

Irish Writers' Centre, 19 Parnell Square, Dublin 1, Republic of Ireland
☎00 353 1 872 1302   Fax 00 353 1 872 6282

✉ itiasecretary@eircom.net
www.translatorsassociation.ie

Chairperson *Annette Schiller*
Honorary Secretary *Mary Phelan*
Treasurer *Mirian Watchorn*
Annual Membership €120 (corporate); €75 (professional); €40 (ordinary); €20 (student)

Founded 1986. The Association is open to all translators: technical, commercial, literary and cultural, and to all classes of interpreters. It is also for those with an interest in translation such as teachers and third-level students. Information on the profession of interpreting and translation and a Register of members are available on the website. Publishes a newsletter, *Translation Ireland* and an eZine, the *ITIA Bulletin*.

Irish Writers' Union

Irish Writers' Centre, 19 Parnell Square, Dublin 1, Republic of Ireland
☎00 353 1 872 1302   Fax 00 353 1 872 6282
✉ info@writerscentre.ie
www.ireland-writers.com

Chairman *Peter McKim*
Secretary *Anthony P. Quinn*
SUBSCRIPTION €45 p.a.; €25 (associate)

Founded 1986 to promote the interests and protect the rights of writers in Ireland.

ISBN Agency

3rd Floor, Midas House, 62 Goldsworth Road, Woking GU21 6LQ
☎0870 777 8712   Fax 0870 777 8714
✉ isbn@nielsenbookdata.co.uk
www.isbn.nielsenbookdata.co.uk

ISBNs are product numbers used by all sections of the book trade for ordering and listing purposes. While ISBNs have no links to copyright and carry no form of legal protection for the book, they enable books to be listed on bibliographic databases and may therefore help sales. The UK ISBN Agency is responsible for assigning ISBN prefixes to publishers based in the UK or Republic of Ireland. Applications for ISBNs for new publishers, help with calculating ISBNs and additional prefixes are all available from the Agency.

Isle of Man Authors

11 Christian Close, Ballastowell Gardens, Ramsey IM8 2AU
☎01624 815634

Secretary *Mrs Beryl Sandwell*
SUBSCRIPTION £5 p.a.

An association of writers living on the Isle of Man, which has links with the **Society of Authors**.

ITC
See **Independent Theatre Council**

ITI
See **Institute of Translation and Interpreting**

IVCA (International Visual Communication Association)
19 Pepper Street, Glengall Bridge, London E14 9RP
☎020 7512 0571   Fax 020 7512 0591
✉ info@ivca.org
www.ivca.org
Chief Executive *Wayne Drew*
Publications and Information Officer *Louise Miller*
The IVCA is a professional association representing the interests of the users and suppliers of visual communications. In particular it pursues the interests of producers, commissioners and manufacturers involved in the non-broadcast and independent facilities industries and also business event companies. It represents all sizes of company and freelance individuals, offering information and advice services, publications, a professional network, special interest groups, a magazine and a variety of events including the UK's Film and Video Communications Festival.

Learning on Screen (British Universities Film & Video Council)
77 Wells Street, London W1T 3QJ
☎020 7393 1500   Fax 020 7393 1555
www.bufvc.ac.uk/learningonscreen.ac.uk
Learning on Screen is the title used by the Society for Screen-Based Learning (SSBL) for its courses and conferences. In January 2004 the SSBL merged with the British Universities Film & Video Council (BUFVC). The title Learning on Screen, now adopted by the BUFVC, will continue for a range of practical, 'hands-on' one-day courses and events around the country as well as the annual Learning on Screen conference and Awards. The BUFCV promotes the production, study and use of moving images and related media for learning, teaching and research. It offers a specialist information service, publications, online services and the unique Off-Air Recording Back-Up Service, recording 44,000 hours per year of UK television.

Lewes Live Literature
See **Lewes Live Literature Festival** under *Festivals*

The Library Association
See **CILIP: The Chartered Institute of Library and Information Professionals**

literaturetraining
PO Box 23595, Leith, Edinburgh EH6 7YX
☎0131 553 2210
✉ info@literaturetraining.com
www.literaturetraining.com
Director *Philippa Johnston*
A group of eight literature organisations working in partnership to provide information, advice and guidance on professional development for writers and others involved with new writing and literature. Their easy to use, fully searchable website provides a central source of information on literature training and professional development opportunities in the UK and is supported by a range of advisory services. The literaturetraining partners are **The National Association of Writers in Education, The National Association for Literature Development, Writernet, The Federation of Worker Writers and Community Publishers**, Lapidus, **Survivors' Poetry, Apples & Snakes** and **Scottish Book Trust**. literaturetraining is a partner in the CreativePeople Network.

Medical Journalists' Association
Fairfield, Cross in Hand, Heathfield TN21 0SH
☎01435 868786   Fax 01435 865714
✉ pigache@globalnet.co.uk
www.mja-uk.org
Chairman *Pete Moore*
Honorary Secretary *Philippa Pigache*
SUBSCRIPTION £40 p.a. (full); £30 (associate); £10 (junior)
Founded 1967. Aims to improve the quality and practice of medical and health journalism and to improve relationships and understanding between medical and health journalists and the health and medical professions. Regular meetings with senior figures in medicine and medico politics; educational workshops on important subject areas or issues of the day; debates; awards for medical journalists from commercial sponsors, plus the MJA's own annual awards for journalism and books. Publishes a newsletter five times a year.

Medical Writers' Group
The Society of Authors, 84 Drayton Gardens, London SW10 9SB

☎020 7373 6642   Fax 020 7373 5768
✉ info@societyofauthors.org
www.societyofauthors.org/medical
Contact *Dorothy Sym*

Founded 1980. A specialist group within the **Society of Authors** offering advice and help to authors of medical books.

Mystery Writers of America, Inc.
17 East 47th Street, 6th Floor, New York, NY 10017, USA
☎001 212 888 8171   Fax 001 212 888 8107
✉ mwa@mysterywriters.org
www.mysterywriters.org
Office Manager *Margery Flax*
SUBSCRIPTION $95(US)

Founded 1945. Aims to promote and protect the interests of writers of the mystery genre in all media; to educate and inform its membership on matters relating to their profession; to uphold a standard of excellence and raise the profile of this literary form to the world at large. Holds an annual banquet at which the 'Edgars' are awarded (named after Edgar Allan Poe).

National Association for Literature Development
PO Box 140, Ilkley LS29 7ET
☎01943 862107
✉ steve@nald.org
www.nald.org
Coordinator *Steve Dearden*

NALD exists to enable literature professionals to talk to each other, develop their professional skills and make the case for increased investment in their work. Offers individual, organisational or corporate membership.

National Association of Writers Groups
The Arts Centre, Biddick Lane, Washington NE38 2AB
☎01262 609228
✉ nawg@tesco.net
www.nawg.co.uk
Secretary *Diane Wilson*
SUBSCRIPTION £25 p.a. + £5 registration (group); £12 p.a. (individual)

Founded 1995 with the object of furthering the interests of writers' groups throughout the UK. A registered charity, No: 1059047, NAWG is strictly non-sectarian and non-political. *Publishes* a bi-monthly newsletter, distributed to member groups; gives free entry to competitions for group anthologies, poetry, short stories, articles, novels and sketches; holds an annual open festival of writing with 36 workshops, seminars, individual surgeries led by professional, high-profile writers. Membership is open to all writers' groups and individual writers – there are no restrictions or qualifications required for joining; 160 groups are affiliated to-date.

National Association of Writers in Education
PO Box 1, Sheriff Hutton, York YO60 7YU
☎01653 618429
✉ info@nawe.co.uk
www.nawe.co.uk
Contact *Paul Munden*
SUBSCRIPTION £20 p.a. (individual); £10 (student); £60 (institution); £30 (overseas)

Founded 1991. Aims to promote the contribution of living writers to education and to encourage both the practice and the critical appreciation of creative writing. Has over 700 members. Organises national conferences and training courses. A directory of writers who work in schools, colleges and the community is available online. Publishes a magazine, *Writing in Education*, issued free to members three times per year.

National Campaign for the Arts
Pegasus House, 37–43 Sackville Street, London W1S 3EH
☎020 7333 0375   Fax 020 7333 0660
✉ nca@artscampaign.org.uk
www.artscampaign.org.uk
Director *Victoria Todd*

The UK's only independent lobbying organisation representing the arts. Founded in 1984 it seeks to safeguard, promote and develop the arts and win public and political recognition for the importance of the arts as a key element in the national culture. As a membership organisation it relies on subscription to sustain its work, receiving no public subsidy. Members have access to the NCA's information, advice, networks, seminars, conferences and publications. Membership is open to organisations and individuals working in or with an interest in the arts. Literature subscriptions available.

National Literacy Trust
Swire House, 59 Buckingham Gate, London SW1E 6AJ
☎020 7828 2435   Fax 020 7931 9986
✉ contact@literacytrust.org.uk
www.literacytrust.org.uk
www.rif.org.uk

Director *Neil McClelland*

Founded 1993. Independent registered charity (No: 1015539) 'dedicated to building a literate nation in which everyone enjoys the skills, confidence and pleasures that literacy can bring.' The only organisation concerned with raising literacy standards for all age groups throughout the UK. Maintains an extensive website with literacy news, summaries of key issues, research and examples of practice nationwide; organises an annual conference, courses and training events and runs a range of initiatives to turn promising ideas into effective action. These include the National Reading Campaign, funded by the government; Reading Is Fundamental, UK, which provides free books to children; Reading The Game, involving the professional football community; the Talk To Your Baby campaign; the Literacy and Social Inclusion Project, a partnership wth the Basic Skills Agency.

National Union of Journalists

Headland House, 308 Gray's Inn Road, London WC1X 8DP
☎020 7278 7916   Fax 020 7837 8143
✉ acorn.house@nuj.org.uk
www.nuj.org.uk

General Secretary *Jeremy Dear*
SUBSCRIPTION £177 p.a. (freelance) or 1% of annual income if lower; or 0.5% if income less than £13,600 p.a.

Represents journalists in all sectors of publishing, print and broadcast. Responsible for wages and conditions agreements which apply across the industry. Provides advice and representation for its members, as well as administering unemployment and other benefits. Publishes various guides and magazines: *On-Line Freelance Directory, Fees Guide, The Journalist* and *The Freelance*.

New Playwrights Trust

See **Writernet**

New Producers Alliance (NPA)

9 Bourlet Close, London W1W 7BP
☎020 7580 2480   Fax 020 7580 2484
✉ queries@npa.org.uk
www.npa.org.uk

Founded 1993. National membership and training organisation for independent new filmmakers, the NPA provides a forum and focus for over 800 members, ranging from students and first timers to highly experienced feature filmmakers and industry affiliates. Services include: producer training from 'entrance' to 'advanced' levels; seminars, masterclasses, business breakfasts, themed networking evenings and preview screenings; in addition the NPA supports its members at film festivals including Cannes and Edinburgh with events and industry receptions. Provides free advice services including Legal and Tax & Accounting; the NPA also publishes a monthly newsletter and online members directory included in the website.

The New SF Alliance (NSFA)

c/o BBR, PO Box 625, Sheffield S1 3GY
www.bbr-online.com/catalogue

Contact *Chris Reed*

Founded 1989. Committed to supporting the work of new writers and artists by promoting independent and small press publications worldwide. 'Helps with finding the right market for your material by providing a mail-order service which allows you to sample magazines, quickly and conveniently from a single address, to help you to find the ones best suited to your needs. What's more, you'll find useful information about many more outlets in the review pages of these magazines, whilst *Light's List* provides contact addresses for a whole host of small press publications.'

New Writing North

2 School Lane, Whickham, Newcastle upon Tyne NE16 4SL
☎0191 488 8580   Fax 0191 488 8576
✉ mail@newwritingnorth.com
www.newwritingnorth.com

Director *Claire Malcolm*
Administrator *Holly Hooper*

New Writing North is the literature development agency for the Arts Council North East region and offers many useful services to writers, organising events, readings and courses. NWN produces writing guides and has a website with literary news, events and opportunities. Administers the **Northern Rock Foundation Writer's Award** (see entry under *Bursaries, Fellowships and Grants*) and the Northern Writers' Awards, which include tailored development packages (mentoring and financial help). NWN works to develop theatre writing and creative radio writing projects within the region as well as a strong education programme, working with schools and LEAS.

The Newspaper Society

Bloomsbury House, 74–77 Great Russell Street, London WC1B 3DA
☎020 7636 7014   Fax 020 7631 5119
✉ ns@newspapersoc.org.uk

www.newspapersoc.org.uk

Director *David Newell*

Founded in 1836, the Newspaper Society is the voice of Britain's regional press, a £3 billion advertising medium read by over 40 adults a week. The Society works to protect and improve the regulatory and commercial environment for its members while providing a range of services.

NPA
See **New Producers Alliance**

NSFA
See **The New SF Alliance**

Outdoor Writers' Guild
PO Box 118, Twickenham TW1 2XB
☎020 8538 9468   Fax 020 8538 9468
✉ sec@owg.org.uk
www.owg.org.uk
Secretary *Hazelle Jackson*
SUBSCRIPTION £66 p.a.

Founded 1980 to promote, encourage and assist the development and maintenance of professional standards among those involved in all aspects of outdoor journalism. Members include writers, photographers, broadcasters, filmmakers, editors, publishers and illustrators. Publishes a quarterly journal, *Bootprint*, and an annual *Directory* (£30; free to members). Presents five Awards for Excellence plus other awards in recognition of achievement. Maintains a website of members' details; informal members' e-mail 'chatline' to exchange news and information; sends out regular media press releases; organises press trips.

PACT (Producers Alliance for Cinema and Television)
The Eye, 2nd Floor, 1 Procter Street, London WC1V 6DW
☎020 7067 4367   Fax 020 7067 4377
✉ enquiries@pact.co.uk
www.pact.co.uk
Chief Executive *John McVay*
Information Manager *David Alan Mills*

Founded 1991. PACT is the trade association of the UK independent feature film, television, animation and interactive media production sector and is a key contact point for foreign producers seeking British co-production, co-finance partners and distributors. Works for producers in the industry at every level and operates a members' regional network throughout the UK with a divisional office in Scotland. Membership services include: a dedicated industrial relations unit; discounted legal advice; a varied calendar of events; business advice; representation at international film and television markets; a comprehensive research programme; various publications: a monthly magazine, an annual members' directory; affiliation with European and international producers' organisations; extensive information and production advice. Lobbies actively with broadcasters, financiers and governments to ensure that the producer's voice is heard and understood in Britain and Europe on all matters affecting the feature film, television, animation and interactive production industry.

PEN
See **English PEN**

Performing Right Society
29–33 Berners Street, London W1T 3AB
☎020 7580 5544   Fax 020 7306 4455
✉ info@prs.co.uk
www.prs.co.uk

PRS collects licence fees for the public performance and broadcast of musical works and distributes this money to its members –writers and publishers of music.

Periodical Publishers Association (PPA)
Queens House, 28 Kingsway, London WC2B 6JR
☎020 7404 4166   Fax 020 7404 4167
✉ info1@ppa.co.uk
www.ppa.co.uk

Founded 1913 to promote and protect the interests of its members in particular and the magazine industry as a whole.

The Personal Managers' Association Ltd
1 Summer Road, East Molesey KT8 9LX
☎020 8398 9796   Fax 020 8398 9796
✉ info@thepma.com
Co-chairs *Michelle Kass, Alan Brodie, Nicholas Young*
Secretary *Angela Adler*
SUBSCRIPTION £250 p.a.

An association of artists' and dramatists' agents (membership not open to individuals). Monthly meetings for exchange of information and discussion. Maintains a code of conduct and acts as a lobby when necessary. Applicants screened. A high proportion of play agents are members of the PMA.

The Picture Research Association
c/o 1 Willow Court, off Willow Street, London EC2A 4QB
☎020 7739 8544   Fax 020 7782 0011
✉ chair@picture-research.org.uk
www.picture-research.org.uk

Chair *Veneta Bullen*
Membership Secretary *Wendy Wilders*
SUBSCRIPTION Members: £45 (introductory); £55 (full); £50 (associate). Magazine only: £25

Founded 1977 as the Society of Picture Researchers & Editors. The Picture Research Association is a professional body for picture researchers, managers, picture editors and all those involved in the research, management and supply of visual material to all forms of the media. The Association's main aims are to promote the interests and specific skills of its members internationally; to promote and maintain professional standards; to bring together those involved in the research and publication of visual material; to provide a forum for the exchange of information and to provide guidance to its members. Free advisory service for members, regular meetings, quarterly magazine, monthly newsletter and Freelance Register.

Player–Playwrights
9 Hillfield Park, London N10 3QT
☎020 8883 0371
✉ P-P@dial.pipex.com
www.playerplaywrights.co.uk

Presidents *Laurence Marks, Maurice Gran*
Contact *Peter Thompson* (at the address above)
SUBSCRIPTION £10 (joining fee); £6 p.a. thereafter, plus £2 per attendance

Founded 1948. A society giving opportunity for writers new to stage, radio, television and film, as well as others finding difficulty in achieving results, to work with writers established in those media. At weekly meetings (7.30 pm–10.00 pm, Mondays, upstairs at the Horse and Groom, 128 Great Portland Street, London W1), members' scripts are read or performed by actor members and afterwards assessed and dissected in general discussion. New writers and new acting members are always welcome.

PLR
See **Public Lending Right**

PLS
See **Publishers Licensing Society Ltd**

PMA
See **The Personal Managers' Association Ltd**

Poetry Book Society
See under *Organisations of Interest to Poets*

Poetry Ireland
See under *Organisations of Interest to Poets*

The Poetry Society
See under *Organisations of Interest to Poets*

Press Complaints Commission
1 Salisbury Square, London EC4Y 8JB
☎020 7353 1248   Fax 020 7353 8355
✉ pcc@pcc.org.uk
www.pcc.org.uk

Director *Tim Toulmin*
Information Officer *Tonia Milton*

Founded in 1991 to deal with complaints from members of the public about the editorial content of newspapers and magazines. Administers the editors' Code of Practice covering such areas as accuracy, privacy, harrassment and intrusion into grief. Publications available: *Code of Practice, How to Complain* and *Annual Review*.

Private Libraries Association
55 Hamilton Park West, London N5 1AE
☎020 7503 9827   Fax 020 7503 9876
✉ pla@illuminata.co.uk

Honorary Secretary *James Brown*
MEMBERSHIP £25 p.a.

Founded 1956. An international society of book collectors. The Association's objectives are to promote and encourage the awareness of the benefits of book ownership, and the study of books, their production and ownership; to publish works concerned with this, particularly those which are not commercially profitable, to hold meetings at which papers on cognate subjects can be read and discussed. Lectures and exhibitions are open to non-members.

Producers Alliance for Cinema and Television
See **PACT**

Public Lending Right
Richard House, Sorbonne Close, Stockton-on-Tees TS17 6DA
☎01642 604699   Fax 01642 615641
✉ authorservices@plr.com
www.plr.uk.com

Registrar *Jim Parker*

Founded 1979. Public Lending Right is funded by the Department for Culture, Media and Sport to recompense authors for books borrowed from public libraries. Authors and books can be registered for PLR only when application is made during the author's lifetime. To qualify, an author must be resident in a European Union member state, or in Iceland, Liechtenstein or Norway, and the book must be printed, bound and put on sale with an ISBN. In 2005, £6.55 million was distributed to over 18,600 authors (£6.4 million in the previous year) with 291 authors reaching the maximum payment threshold of £6000. The Rate Per Loan was raised in 2005 to 5.26 pence, its highest level to date. Consult the website for further information.

The Publishers Association

29B Montague Street, London WC1B 5BW
☎020 7691 9191   Fax 020 7691 9199
✉ mail@publishers.org.uk
www.publishers.org.uk
Chief Executive *Ronnie Williams, OBE*

The national UK trade association for books, learned journals, and electronic publications, with around 200 member companies in the industry. Very much a trade body representing the industry to Government and the European Commission, and providing services to publishers. Publishes the *Directory of Publishing* in association with **Continuum**. Also home of the Educational Publishers Council (school books), PA's International Division (BDCI), the Council of Academic and Professional Publishers, the Trade Publishers Council and the Electronic Publishers' Forum.

Publishers' Association of South Africa

PO Box 15277, Vlaberg 8018, Cape Town, South Africa
☎00 27 21 426 1726   Fax 00 27 21 426 1733
✉ pasa@publishsa.co.za
www.publishsa.co.za

Founded in 1992 to represent publishing in South Africa, a key industry sector. With a membership of 162 companies, the Association includes commercial organisations, university presses, one-person privately-owned publishers as well as importers and distributors.

Publishers Licensing Society Ltd

37–41 Gower Street, London WC1E 6HH
☎020 7299 7730   Fax 020 7299 7780
✉ pls@pls.org.uk
www.pls.org.uk

Chief Executive *Alicia Wise*
Manager *Caroline Elmslie*

Founded in 1981, the PLS obtains mandates from publishers which grant PLS the authority to license photocopying of pages from published works. Some licences for digitisation of printed works are available. PLS aims to maximise revenue from licences for mandating publishers and to expand the range and repertoire of mandated publishers available to licence holders. It supports the **Copyright Licensing Agency Ltd (CLA)** in its efforts to increase the number of legitimate users through the issuing of licences and vigorously pursues any infringements of copyright works belonging to rights' holders.

Publishers Publicity Circle

65 Airedale Avenue, London W4 2NN
☎020 8994 1881
✉ ppc-@lineone.net
www.publisherspublicitycircle.co.uk
Contact *Heather White*

Enables book publicists from both publishing houses and freelance PR agencies to meet and share information regularly. Meetings, held monthly in central London, provide a forum for press journalists, television and radio researchers and producers to meet publicists collectively. A directory of the PPC membership is published each year and distributed to over 2500 media contacts.

The Radio Academy

5 Market Place, London W1W 8AE
☎020 7255 2010   Fax 020 7255 2029
✉ info@radioacademy.org
www.radioacademy.org
Director *John Bradford*
SUBSCRIPTIONS £18 p.a., payable by direct debit at £1.50 per month, or a one-off payment of £55 by cheque or credit card

Founded 1983. The professional body for people working in the radio industry, the Academy is dedicated to the encouragement, recognition and promotion of excellence throughout the UK radio industry. Membership ranges from students to Governors of the BBC. Hosts the annual Radio Festival which features speakers from all aspects of the industry; holds events in London and the regions; runs masterclasses for those who aspire to enter the radio industry, and seminars for the further development of professionals within the industry at various levels. Services include a directory covering all aspects of the industry, a quarterly newsletter and the Academy website.

Romance Writers of America

1600 Stuebner Airline Road, Suite 140, Spring, TX 77379, USA
☎001 832 717 5200   Fax 001 832 717 5201
✉ info@rwanational.org
www.rwanational.org
PR Coordinator *Nicole Kennedy*
MEMBERSHIP $75 p.a. plus $25 joining fee

Founded 1980. RWA, a non-profit association with more than 9000 members worldwide, provides a service to authors at all stages of their careers as well as to the romance publishing industry and its readers. Anyone pursuing a career in romantic fiction may join RWA. Holds an annual conference, and provides contests for both published and unpublished writers through the RITA Awards and Golden Hearts Awards.

The Romantic Novelists' Association

Tyddyn Chwarel, 5/6 Cymro Street, Carneddi, Bethesda LL57 3SA
✉ julietsirona@myisp.co.uk
www.rna-uk.org
Contact *Juliet Greenwood*
SUBSCRIPTION £40 p.a. (full members);
   £45 (full, non-EU); £50 (associate); full and
   associate members who pay by standing
   order receive a £3 discount

Membership is open to published writers of romantic fiction (modern or historical), or those who have had one or more full-length serials published. Associate membership is open to publishers, editors, literary agents, booksellers, librarians and others having a close connection with novel writing and publishing. Membership in the New Writers' Scheme is available to writers who have not yet had a full-length novel published. New Writers must submit a manuscript each year. The mss receive a report from experienced published members and the reading fee is paid with the annual subscription of £90 (£95 for non-EU members). Meetings are held in London and the regions with guest speakers. The *RNA News* is published bi-monthly and issued free to members. The Association makes three annual awards: **The FosterGrant Romantic Novel of the Year**; The New Writers Award for the best published novel by a new writer who has gone through the New Writers' Scheme, and the Romance Prize for category romances.

Royal Festival Hall Literature & Talks

See entry under *Festivals*

Royal Society of Literature

Somerset House, Strand, London WC2R 1LA
☎020 7845 4676   Fax 020 7845 4679
✉ info@rslit.org
www.rslit.org
Chairman *Maggie Gee, FRSL*
SUBSCRIPTION £30 p.a.

Founded 1820. Membership by application to the Secretary. Fellowships are conferred by the Society on the proposal of two Fellows. Membership benefits include lectures, discussion meetings and poetry readings. Lecturers have included Jung Chang, Michael Holroyd, Don Paterson, Zadie Smith and Tom Stoppard. Presents the **Royal Society of Literature Ondaatje Prize**, the **Royal Society of Literature/Jerwood Awards** and the **V.S. Pritchett Memorial Prize**.

Royal Television Society

Holborn Hall, 100 Gray's Inn Road, London WC1X 8AL
☎020 7430 1000   Fax 020 7430 0924
✉ info@rts.org.uk
www.rts.org.uk
MEMBERSHIP from £65 p.a.

Founded 1927. Covers all disciplines involved in the television industry. Provides a forum for debate and conferences on technical, social and cultural aspects of the medium. Presents various awards including journalism, programmes, technology and design. Publishes *Television Magazine* nine times a year for members and subscribers.

SAN Agency

3rd Floor, Midas House, 62 Goldsworth Road, Woking GU21 6LQ
☎0870 777 8712   Fax 0870 777 8714
✉ san@nielsenbookdata.co.uk
www.san.nielsenbookdata.co.uk

The SAN Agency issues Standard Address Numbers and Global Location Numbers (GLNs) to organisations such as booksellers, libraries or publishers, enabling commercial transactions to be made more efficient and accurate. The numbers identify specific geographic locations and are recognised throughout the bookselling and publishing industries.

Science Fiction Foundation

37 Coventry Road, Ilford IG1 5QR
www.sf-foundation.org

Founded 1970. The SFF is an international academic body for the furtherance of science fiction studies. Publishes a thrice-yearly magazine, *Foundation* (see entry under *Magazines*), which features academic articles and reviews of new fiction. It also has a reference library (see entry under *Library Services*), housed at Liverpool University.

Scottish Book Trust

Sandeman House, Trunk's Close, 55 High Street, Edinburgh EH1 1SR
☎0131 524 0160   Fax 0131 524 0161
✉ info@scottishbooktrust.com
www.scottishbooktrust.com

Contact *Marc Lambert*

Founded 1956. Scottish Book Trust exists to serve readers and writers in Scotland. 'We work to ensure that everyone has access to good books and to related resources and opportunities. We do this by operating 'Live Literature Scotland' which funds over 1400 visits a year by Scottish writers to a variety of institutions and groups; by supporting Scottish writing through a programme of professional training opportunities for writers; by publishing a wide variety of resources and leaflets to support readership; by promoting initiatives such as World Book Day and other readership development opportunities; through our Book Information Service providing free advice and support to readers and writers and the general public.'

Scottish Daily Newspaper Society

48 Palmerston Place, Edinburgh EH12 5DE
☎0131 220 4353   Fax 0131 220 4344
✉ info@sdns.org.uk

Director *Mr J.B. Raeburn*

Founded 1915. Trade association representing publishers of Scottish daily and Sunday newspapers including the major Scottish editions of UK national newspapers.

Scottish Library Association

See **CILIP in Scotland**

Scottish Newspaper Publishers Association

48 Palmerston Place, Edinburgh EH12 5DE
☎0131 220 4353   Fax 0131 220 4344
✉ info@snpa.org.uk
www.snpa.org.uk

Director *Mr J.B. Raeburn*

The representative body for the publishers of paid-for weekly and associated free newspapers in Scotland. Represents the interests of the industry to government, public and other bodies and provides a range of services including marketing of *The Scottish Weekly Press*, industrial relations, and education and training. It is an active supporter of the Press Complaints Commission.

Scottish Print Employers Federation

48 Palmerston Place, Edinburgh EH12 5DE
☎0131 220 4353   Fax 0131 220 4344
✉ info@spef.org.uk
www.spef.org.uk

Director *Mr J.B. Raeburn*

Founded 1910. Employers' organisation and trade association for the Scottish printing industry. Represents the interests of the industry to government, public and other bodies and provides a range of services including industrial relations, education, training and commercial activities. Negotiates a national wages and conditions agreement with Amicus EPM Sector. The Federation is a member of Intergraf, the international confederation for employers' associations in the printing industry. In this capacity its views are channelled on the increasing number of matters affecting print businesses emanating from the European Union.

Scottish Publishers Association

Scottish Book Centre, 137 Dundee Street, Edinburgh EH11 1BG
☎0131 228 6866   Fax 0131 228 3220
✉ carol.lothian@scottishbooks.org
www.scottishbooks.org

Director *Lorraine Fannin*
Member Services Manager *Liz Small*
Financial and Office Administrator *Carol Lothian*
Information and Professional Development Administrator *Katherine A. Naish*

The Association represents over 80 Scottish publishers, from multinationals to small presses, in a number of capacities, but primarily in the cooperative promotion and marketing of their books. The SPA also acts as an information and advice centre for both the trade and general public. Publishes membership lists and the annual *Directory of Publishing in Scotland*. Represents members at international book fairs; runs an extensive training programme in publishing skills; carries out market research; and encourages export initiatives.

Scottish Screen

2nd Floor, 249 West George Street, Glasgow
G2 4QE
☎0141 302 1700   Fax 0141 302 1711
✉ info@scottishscreen.com
www.scottishscreen.com

Infomation Manager *Isabella Edgar*

Founded 1997. Scottish Screen develops, encourages and promotes every aspect of film, television and new media in Scotland through script development, short film production, distribution of national lottery film production finance, training, education, exhibition funding, film commission locations support and the Scottish Screen Archive.

Society for Editors and Proofreaders (SfEP)

1 Riverbank House, 1 Putney Bridge
Approach, London SW6 3JD
☎020 7736 3278/7736 0901 (training dept.)
Fax 020 7736 3318
✉ administration@sfep.org.uk
www.sfep.org.uk

Chair *Penny Williams*
Vice-Chair *Shena Deuchars*
Secretary *Val Rice*
SUBSCRIPTION £67.50 p.a. (individuals) plus £25 joining fee; corporate membership available.

Founded 1988 in response to the growing number of freelance editors and their increasing importance to the publishing industry. Aims to promote high editorial standards by disseminating information through advice and training, and to achieve recognition of the professional status of its members. The Society also supports moves towards recognised standards of training and accreditation for editors and proofreaders. It launched its own Accreditation in Proofreading test in 2002.

Society for Technical Communications (STC)

901 N. Stuart Street, Suite 904, Arlington,
Virginia 22203, USA
☎001 703 522 4114   Fax 001 703 522 2075
www.stc.org
www.stc-europe.org/uk
UK Chapter Contact *Liz Hale*
(liz35.hale@virgin.net)

Dedicated to advancing the arts and sciences of technical communication, the STC has 25,000 members worldwide, including technical writers, editors, graphic designers, videographers, multimedia artists, Web and intranet page information designers, translators and others whose work involves making technical information available to those who need it. Publishes a quarterly scholarly journal, *Technical Communications* and the magazine, *Intercom*, ten times a year (both available to members only). The UK Chapter, which has about 140 members, hosts meetings and seminars, runs an annual technical publications competition, and publishes its own newsletter six times a year.

The Society of Authors

84 Drayton Gardens, London SW10 9SB
☎020 7373 6642   Fax 020 7373 5768
✉ info@societyofauthors.org
www.societyofauthors.org

General Secretary *Mark Le Fanu*
SUBSCRIPTION £80/75 p.a.

The Society of Authors is an independent trade union, chaired by Antony Beevor in 2005, with some 7700 members. As well as campaigning for the profession, it advises members on negotiations with publishers, agents, broadcasting organisations, theatre managers and film companies and on queries or concerns members may have about the business aspects of their writing. The Society assists with complaints and takes action for breach of contract, copyright infringement, etc. Among the Society's publications are *The Author* (quarterly) and the *Quick Guides* series to various aspects of writing (all free of charge to members). Other services include vetting of contracts, emergency funds for writers, and various special discounts. There are groups within the Society for broadcasters, children's writers and illustrators, educational writers, academic writers, medical writers and translators, as well as some regional groups. Authors under 35 or over 65, not earning a significant income from their writing, may apply for lower subscription rates (after their first year, in the case of over-65s). Contact the Society for a free booklet and a copy of *The Author* or visit the website.

The Society of Authors in Scotland

8 Briar Road, Kirkintilloch, Glasgow G66 3SA
☎0141 776 4280   Fax 0141 776 4280
✉ brian@bdosborne.fsnet.co.uk
www.writersorg.co.uk

Secretary *Brian D. Osborne*

The Scottish branch of the **Society of Authors**, which organises business meetings, social and bookshop events throughout Scotland.

Society of Children's Book Writers & Illustrators

36 Mackenzie Road, Beckenham BR3 4RU
✉ scbwi_bi@hotmail.com
www.wordpool.co.uk/scbwi

British Isles Regional Advisor *Natascha Biebow*
Scotland Regional Advisor *Lowri Potts*
(flying.pizza@virgin.net)

Founded in 1968 by a group of Los Angeles-based writers, the SCBWI is the only international professional organisation for the exchange of information between writers, illustrators, editors, publishers, agents and others involved with literature for young people. With a membership of 18,000 worldwide, it holds three annual international conferences plus a number of regional events, publishes a bi-monthly newsletter and awards grants for works in progress. The British Isles region meets quarterly for speaker events and holds an Illustrator's Day in the spring and a Writer's Day in the autumn. It facilitates critique groups and publishes a quarterly regional newsletter. For membership enquiries, contact the address above.

Society of Civil and Public Service Writers

17 The Green, Corby Glen, Grantham
NG33 4NP
✉ joan@lewis5634.fsnet.co.uk
www.scpsw.co.uk

Membership Secretary *Mrs Joan Lewis*
SUBSCRIPTION £15 p.a.

Founded 1935. Welcomes serving and retired members of the Civil Service, armed forces, Post Office, BT, nursing profession and other public servants who are aspiring or published writers. Offers competitions for short story, article and poetry; postal folios for short story and article; AGM, occasional meetings and luncheon held in London; quarterly magazine, *Civil Service Author*, to which members may submit material; Poetry Workshop (extra £3) offers annual weekend outside London, anthology, newsletter, postal folio, competitions. S.a.e. to Secretary for details.

Society of Editors

University Centre, Granta Place, Mill Lane,
Cambridge CB2 1RU
☎01223 304080   Fax 01223 304090
✉ info@societyofeditors.org
www.societyofeditors.org

Executive Director *Bob Satchwell*

Formed by a merger of the Association of British Editors and the Guild of Editors, the Society of Editors has nearly 500 members in national, regional and local newspapers, magazines, broadcasting, new media, journalism education and media law. Campaigns for media freedom and self-regulation. For further information contact *Bob Satchwell* at the address above.

Society of Indexers

Blades Enterprise Centre, John Street,
Sheffield S2 4SU
☎0114 292 2350   Fax 0114 292 2351
✉ admin@indexers.org.uk
www.indexers.org.uk

Secretary *Ann Kingdom*
Administrator *Wendy Burrow*
SUBSCRIPTION £60 p.a.; Institutions: from £120

Founded 1957. Publishes *The Indexer* (biannual, April and October) and a quarterly newsletter. Issues an annual list of members and *Indexers Available (IA)*, which lists members and their subject expertise. In addition, the Society runs an open-learning course entitled *Training in Indexing* and recommends rates of pay (currently £16–30 per hour or £1.20–£5 per page).

Society of Medical Writers

31 Meriden Road, Hampton-in-Arden,
Solihull B92 0BS
✉ rcharlton@doctors.org.uk
www.somw.org.uk

Contact *Dr Rodger Charlton*
SUBSCRIPTION £40 p.a.

Founded in 1986 and expanding rapidly in membership and influence. Exists to promote and improve professional and lay writing activities for all health care professionals; also to professional journalists writing on anything pertaining to clinical practice. Keen to develop input from interested parties who work mainly outside the profession. Regular workshops held around Britain. Publishes a twice-yearly journal (*The GP Writer*), anthologies and books from members, and a register of members and their writing interests.

Society of Picture Researchers & Editors

See **The Picture Research Association**

Society of Women Writers & Journalists

Broadlea House, Heron Way, Hickling
NR12 0YQ
☎01692 598287
✉ zoe@zoeking.com

www.swwj.co.uk

Acting Secretary *Zoe King*

SUBSCRIPTION £35 (town); £30 (country); £25 (overseas). £10 joining fee

Founded 1894. The first of its kind to be run as an association of women engaged in journalism. Aims to encourage literary achievement, uphold professional standards, and establish social contacts with other writers. Offers advice to members and has regular seminars, etc. Publishes a society journal, *The Woman Writer.*

Society of Young Publishers

c/o The Bookseller, Endeavour House, 189 Shaftesbury Avenue, London WC2H 8JT

✉ info@thesyp.org.uk

www.thesyp.org.uk

SUBSCRIPTION £30 p.a.; £20 (student/unwaged); £35 (associate)

Provides facilities whereby members can increase their knowledge and widen their experience of all aspects of publishing, and holds regular social events. Run entirely by volunteers, it is open to those in related occupations, students, and associate membership is available for over-35s. Publishes a monthly newsletter called *Inprint* and holds meetings on the last Wednesday of each month featuring trade professionals. For other events see the website. Please enclose an s.a.e. when writing to the Society.

The South and Mid-Wales Association of Writers (SAMWAW)

c/o I.M.C. Consulting Group, Denham House, Lambourne Crescent, Cardiff CF14 5ZW

☎029 2076 1170   Fax 029 2076 1304

✉ info@imcconsultinggroup.co.uk

SUBSCRIPTION £15 (single); £20 (joint)

Founded 1971 to foster the art and craft of writing in all its forms. Provides a common meeting ground for writers, critics, editors, adjudicators from all over the UK and abroad. Organises residential weekend conferences and day seminars throughout the year. Holds competitions, two for members only and two which are open to the public, in addition to **The Mathew Prichard Award for Short Story Writing** (see entry under *Prizes*).

Spoken Word Publishing Association

See **Audiobook Publishing Association**

Sports Journalists' Association of Great Britain

c/o Sport England Events, 3rd Floor, Victoria House, Bloomsbury Square, London WC1B 4SE

☎020 7273 1789   Fax 020 7383 0273

✉ trevjanbond1@aol.com (Secretary)

www.sportsjournalists.org.uk

Secretary *Trevor Bond* (244 Perry Street, Billericay CM12 0QP ☎01277 651708 Fax 01277 622890)

SUBSCRIPTION £23.50 p.a. incl. VAT (London); £11.75 (regional)

Founded in 1948 as the Sports Writers' Association of Great Britain to promote and maintain a high professional standard among journalists who specialise in sport in all its branches and to serve members' interests. Publishes a biannual bulletin, a quarterly *Newsletter* and an annual *Handbook* for members, and promotes jointly with Sport England the annual British Sports Personalities of the Year Awards, the British Sports Journalism Awards and the Sports Photographer of the Year award.

Tees Valley Arts

Third Floor, Melrose House, Melrose Street, Middlesbrough TS1 2HZ

☎01642 264651   Fax 01642 264955

✉ info@teesvalleyarts.org.uk

www.teesvalleyarts.org.uk

Contact *Director*

Tees Valley Arts is a cultural education agency working throughout the Tees Valley. The company works in partnership with local authorities, public agencies, the business sector, schools, colleges, individuals and organisations to co-ordinate, promote and develop the arts – crafts, film, video, photography, music, drama, dance, literature, public arts, disability, diverse arts, community arts.

Theatre Writers' Union
See **The Writers' Guild of Great Britain**

Trade Publishers Council
See **The Publishers Association**

The Translators Association

84 Drayton Gardens, London SW10 9SB

☎020 7373 6642   Fax 020 7373 5768

✉ info@societyofauthors.org

www.societyofauthors.org/translators

Secretary *Dorothy Sym*

Founded 1958 as a subsidiary group within the

Society of Authors to deal exclusively with the special problems of literary translators into the English language. Benefits to members include free legal and general advice and assistance on all business matters relating to translators' work, including the vetting of contracts and advice on rates of remuneration. Membership is normally confined to translators who have had their work published in volume or serial form or produced in this country for stage, television or radio. The Association administers several prizes for translators of published work (see *Prizes*) and maintains a database to enable members' details to be supplied to publishers who are seeking a translator for a particular work.

UK Film Council

10 Little Portland Street, London W1W 7JG
☎020 7861 7861 Fax 020 7861 7862
✉ info@ukfilmcouncil.org.uk
www.ukfilmcouncil.org.uk

The UK's leading film body. Uses lottery money and Government Grant-in-Aid to encourage the development of new talent, skills and creative and technological innovation in UK film; help new and established filmmakers make distinctive British films; support the creation and growth of stable businesses in the film sector; provide access to finance and help the UK film industry to compete in the global marketplace. Also promotes enjoyment and understanding of the cinema and ensures that film's economic and creative and cultural interests are properly represented in public policy making.

Voice of the Listener & Viewer Ltd (VLV)

101 Kings Drive, Gravesend DA12 5BQ
☎01474 352835 Fax 01474 351112
✉ info@vlv.org.uk
www.vlv.org.uk
Chairman *Jocelyn Hay*
Administrative Secretary *Sue Washbrook*

VLV represents the citizen and consumer interests in broadcasting. It is an independent, non-profit-making society working to ensure independence, quality and diversity in broadcasting. VLV is the only consumer body speaking for listeners and viewers on the full range of broadcasting issues. It is funded by its members and is free from sectarian, commercial and political affiliations. Holds public lectures, seminars and conferences, and has frequent contact with MPs, civil servants, the BBC and independent broadcasters, regulators, academics and other consumer groups. Provides an independent forum where all with an interest in broadcasting can speak on equal terms. Produces a quarterly news bulletin and regular briefings on broadcasting issues. Holds its own archive and those of the former Broadcasting Research Unit (1980–90) and BACTV (British Action for Children's Television). Maintains a panel of speakers, the VLV Forum for Children's Broadcasting, the VLV Forum for Educational Broadcasting, and acts as secretariat for the European Alliance of Listeners' and Viewers' Associations (EURALVA). VLV has responded to all major public enquiries on broadcasting since 1984. The VLV does not handle complaints.

W.A.T.C.H.

See **Writers, Artists and their Copyright Holders**

Welsh Academy

See **Academi**

Welsh Books Council (Cyngor Llyfrau Cymru)

Castell Brychan, Aberystwyth SY23 2JB
☎01970 624151 Fax 01970 625385
✉ castellbrychan@cllc.org.uk
www.cllc.org.uk
www.gwales.com
Director *Gwerfyl Pierce Jones*
Head of Editorial Department *Dewi Morris Jones*

Founded 1961 to stimulate interest in books from Wales and to support publishing in Wales. The Council distributes publishing grants and promotes and fosters all aspects of book production in Wales in both Welsh and English. Its Editorial, Design, Marketing and Children's Books departments and wholesale distribution centre offer central services to publishers in Wales. Writers in Welsh and English are welcome to approach the Editorial Department for advice on how to get their manuscripts published.

Welsh National Literature Promotion Agency

See **Academi**

West Country Writers' Association

Barton House, Newton St Cyres, Exmouth EX5 5DA
☎01392 851301 Fax 01392 851556
✉ ebrat@globalnet.co.uk
www.westcountrywriters.co.uk

President *Christopher Fry*
Honorary Secretary *Sarah Hughes*
Founded 1951 in the interest of published authors with an interest in the West Country. Meets to discuss news and views and to listen to talks. Conference and newsletters.

Women in Publishing
Membership Secretary: PO Box 46816, London SW11 3XL
✉ membership@wipub.org.uk *and* info@wipub.org.uk
www.wipub.org.uk
Membership Secretary *Bridget Clark*

Aims to promote the status of women working in publishing and related trades by helping them to develop their careers. Through WiP there are opportunities for members to learn more about their area of work, share information and expertise, give and receive support and partake in a practical forum for the exchange of information about different industry sectors. Monthly meetings provide a forum for discussion on various topics of interest within the industry. Meetings are held on the second Wednesday of each month. See website for further information. Publishes monthly newsletter, *WiPlash* and *Women in Publishing Directory*.

Women Writers Network (WWN)
23 Prospect Road, London NW2 2JU
☎020 7794 5861
www.womenwriters.org.uk
Membership Secretary *Cathy Smith*
SUBSCRIPTION £45 p.a. (incl. meeting admissions & 6 newsletters p.a., WWN website and online directory access); £35 p.a. (overseas); £30 p.a. ('newsletter only' UK membership')

Founded 1985. Provides a forum for the exchange of information, support, career and networking opportunities for working women writers. Meetings, seminars, excursions, newsletter and directory. Full membership includes free admission to monthly meetings and a monthly newsletter. Details from the Membership Secretary at the address above.

Writernet
Cabin V, Clarendon Buildings, 25 Horsell Road, London N5 1XL
☎020 7609 7474 Fax 020 7609 7557
✉ info@writernet.org.uk
www.writernet.org.uk
Executive Director *Jonathan Meth*

SUBSCRIPTION (information on rates available by post or on website)

Writernet (formerly the New Playwrights Trust) is the national research and development organisation for writing for all forms of live and recorded performance. Publishes a range of information pertinent to writers on all aspects of development and production in the form of pamphlets, and a six-weekly journal which also includes articles and interviews on aesthetic and practical issues. Writernet also runs a script-reading service and a link service between writers and producers, organises seminars and conducts research projects.

The Writers' Guild of Great Britain
15 Britannia Street, London WC1X 9JN
☎020 7833 0777 Fax 020 7833 4777
✉ admin@writersguild.org.uk
www.writersguild.org.uk
President *David Nobbs*
Chair *Graham Lester George*
General Secretary *Bernie Corbett*
Assistant General Secretaries *Anne Hogben, Christine Paris*
SUBSCRIPTION Full member: 1% of earnings from professional writing (min. £150, max. £1500); Candidate member: £90; Student member: £20; Affiliate member (agent or writers' group): £275; Life member: voluntary contribution

Founded in 1959 as the Screenwriters' Guild, the Writers' Guild is a trade union, affiliated to the TUC, representing professional writers in television, radio, theatre, film, books and new media. It negotiates Minimum Terms Agreements governing writers' contracts and covering minimum fees; advances; repeat fees; royalties and residuals; rights; credits; number of drafts; script alterations and the resolution of disputes. The most important MTAs cover BBC TV Drama; BBC Radio Drama; ITV Companies; **PACT** (independent TV and film producers); TAC (Welsh language independent TV producers); Theatrical Management Association; **Independent Theatre Council**; the **Royal National Theatre**, **Royal Shakespeare Company**, and **Royal Court Theatre**. These agreements are regularly re-negotiated and in most cases the minimum fees are reviewed annually.

The Guild advises members on all aspects of their working lives, including contract vetting, legal advice, help with copyright problems and representation in disputes with producers, publishers or other writers.

Events organised by the Guild include a seminar on writing sitcoms, a networking evening for TV soap writers, a panel discussion on marketing theatre plays and lectures on forensic science aimed at TV series writers. Runs a series of 'Variety Nights' at which members perform/read their work to an audience of writers. *UK Writer*, the Guild's quarterly magazine, is free to members and contains features about professional writing, Guild news and details of work opportunities, training courses, literary competitions, etc. A detailed e-mail of news, opportunities and other information is sent to members every Friday.

Full Membership is open to anyone who has received payment for a piece of written work under a contract with terms not less than those negotiated by the Guild. Writers who do not qualify can join as Candidate Members and those on accredited writing courses or theatre attachments can become Student Members. Aged writers and those with long service in the Guild are entitled to free Life Membership.

Writers, Artists and their Copyright Holders (W.A.T.C.H.)

The Library, The University of Reading, PO Box 223, Whiteknights, Reading RG6 6AE
☎0118 378 8783   Fax 0118 378 6636
www.watch-file.com

Contact *Dr David Sutton*

Founded 1994. Provides an online database of information about the copyright holders of literary authors and artists. The database is available free of charge on the Internet and the Web. W.A.T.C.H. is the successor project to the Location Register of English Literary Manuscripts and Letters, and continues to deal with location register enquiries.

Yachting Journalists' Association

Sutton's, Church Lane, Eastergate PO20 3UZ
☎01243 542196   Fax 01243 555562
✉ maggie@yja.co.uk
Honorary Secretary *Maggie Milne*
SUBSCRIPTION £40 p.a.

To further the interest of yachting, sail and power, and to provide support and assistance to journalists in the field; current membership is just over 260 with 31 from overseas. A handbook, listing details of members and subscribing PR organisations, press facility recommendations, forthcoming events and other useful information, is published annually at a cost to non-members and non-advertisers of £10. Information for inclusion should be submitted by the end of August. The YJA organises the Yachtsman of the Year and Young Sailor of the Year Awards, presented annually at the beginning of January.

Yr Academi Gymreig

See **Academi**

Copyright in Chaos

If anything is likely to cause legal merriment it is the prospect of a fight over copyright. Like all affairs that send a tremor of financial excitement through the courts, the ground rules for copyright are quite simple, thus tempting the aggrieved to seek protection and compensation. But the reality is a legislative quagmire into which the richest plaintiff can sink without trace.

Start with what is in the formal agreements. Britain along with other EU members offers protection on all original material during the author's lifetime and for seventy years after the author's death. Why seventy? No good reason except that when the EU got round to coordinating its creative affairs a few years ago, the longest period of national copyright was adopted as the common standard. For literary works, Germany held the record so British copyright was extended by twenty years. By the same reasoning, Italy had to change its copyright on musical recordings from thirty to fifty years to match the British law.

This makes the system all very neat and tidy but, of course, the point about copyright law is not so much what it says as whether it can be enforced. Serious worries on that score started with the advent of the mass-produced photocopier. The first victim was the education market. Librarians who were used to buying six or sixty copies of a publication found they could make do with one. Similarly, students were spared the expense of book purchase when, cheaply and quickly, they were able to copy relevant pages. A rescue for struggling authors came in the shape of the Authors' Licensing and Collecting Society (ALCS, see page 505), a non-profit organisation set up to collect and distribute secondary royalties which might otherwise remain in limbo. Last year the licensing scheme for reprographic rights brought in £14,739,792.

There are similar programmes in other countries but not all work so smoothly. In Germany, for example, there is a copying tariff built into the charging system of each machine, but details of the distribution of monies are hard to come by and, of a certainty, no compensation is currently paid to foreign authors. A complicating factor is the changing perception of just how much it is permissible to copy from a particular volume. It used to be thought that one or two pages were the limit. Now it is not uncommon for whole books to be reproduced. Is this wrong? An author who receives a substantial cheque from the ALCS may not give a damn, but his publisher will feel aggrieved at the loss of income. For academic books the reaction has been to cut joint sums and raise prices, but clearly there is a point at which the whole business becomes uneconomic.

A not entirely unrelated problem is the consensus or, rather, the lack of it, on the interpretation of fair usage. In this country it is perfectly legitimate for a writer to quote from someone else's work for 'purposes of criticism or review' as long as 'sufficient acknowledgement' is given. What he must not do is to lift 'a substantial part' to incorporate into his own work without seeking permission and paying an agreed fee. But what is substantial? In one case, four lines from a thirty-two line poem were held to amount to 'a substantial part'. On the other hand, even a substantial quotation from a copyright work may be acceptable if a student or critic is engaged in 'fair dealing with a literary work for the purposes of research or music study'.

Commonsense suggests basing the assessment on the length and importance of the quotation; the amount quoted in relation to the text as a whole; the extent to which the work competes with the work quoted; and the extent to which the words quoted are saving a writer time and trouble. The Society of Authors and the Publishers' Association regard as fair usage a single extract of up to 400 words, or a series of extracts (of which none exceeds 300 words) to a total of 800 words from a prose work, or of extracts to a total of forty lines from a poem, provided that this does not exceed a quarter of the poem.

Authors or their descendants who are rewarded for permission to quote are all in favour of tightening the law. Those who have to pay are less sure. Since copyright was extended to the author's life plus seventy years, there have been cases where work taken back into copyright has suddenly been put under embargo, to be released only at a substantial price. An even greater sense of outrage is created by those who reassert copyright by editing or otherwise amending work that has long since been in the public domain. Some translations fall into this category. Nobody denies that the expertise and creative skill of a translator need to be protected, but there is reasonable cause for complaint when a proprietorial right is extended over the work of a classic writer in a foreign language, thus frustrating the efforts of other translators to break into the market. So far in Britain, these issues have not caused great controversy but elsewhere in Europe, particularly in Germany and Sweden, consumer pressure groups are arguing for a more generous interpretation of 'fair usage' and for shortening of the period of copyright. Judged by the anti lobby, it is not altogether clear why often distant relatives of great writers should continue to profit from their work long after the creative minds have ceased to be.

But the challenges or, if you like, the threats to copyright law discussed so far are minor irritants compared to the mighty force for change released by the World Wide Web. At one extreme, the media guru Nicholas Negroponte predicts that the new technology will eradicate the traditional constraints on the copying of material at the click of a mouse:

> Most people worry about copyright in terms of the ease of making copies. In the digital world, not only the ease is at issue, but also the fact that the digital copy is as perfect as the original and, with some fancy computing, even better.... We see a new kind of fraud, which may not be fraud at all. When I read something on the Internet and, like a clipping from a newspaper, wish to send a copy of it to somebody else or to a mailing list of people, this seems harmless. But, with less than a dozen

keystrokes, I could redeliver that material to literally thousands of people all over the world.

Duplication is not only efficient, it is incredibly cheap, which is why publishers find it hard to make money from the Internet. Even if in the future some rational economic model is laid on top of the Internet, it may cost a penny or two to distribute a million bits to a million people. It certainly will not cost anything like postage. Negroponte concludes: 'Copyright law is totally out of date. It is a Gutenberg artefact. Since it is a reactive process, it will probably have to break down completely before it is corrected.'

The more advanced publishers are already thinking along these lines. As one chief executive put it to me, 'We may have to abandon any thought of making money from a backlist. As soon as a book or a journal is out in the market, it is liable to be targeted by the Internet. Our income will come from new work presented in a way that makes it more attractive than getting it off the screen. The whole nature of publishing will change.'

And not just for publishers. By association, authors too will have to rethink their money-making potential. Income may be derived less from copies of books sold in shops or, indeed, over the Internet and more from what are currently known as secondary rights – press serialisation, film and television adaptations, merchandising. The book will not disappear but it will change its market appeal with more emphasis on expensive presentation volumes, the ideal gift, and, at the other end of the line, cheap and easy to read paperbacks to wile away long-distance travel.

There is another scenario. Computer boffins are hard at work on new metering systems which will allow publishers to monitor and record the use of copyright material on the Internet. But this could be like an arms race. As soon as an effective policing system is in place, along will come a powerful antidote. The World Intellectual Property Organisation, the UN agency responsible for administering copyright conventions, requires member states to outlaw devices aimed at avoiding detection of unauthorised copying. But is anyone taking any notice? Certainly not in the Far East, China or Russia where the precedent for Internet piracy is already set by the unauthorised reproduction of hard print, said to be costing British publishers and their authors up to £200 million a year.

And back we come to the question, does it really matter? There are those who argue that a more liberal copyright regime would best serve education, economic growth and international cooperation. Foremost of these radicals are the scientists who used to be restricted to expensive journals to promote their ground-breaking ideas. Now they have the Internet as a cheaper, more efficient means of communication. They are not likely to give that up.

Meanwhile, urged on by authors, the publishers, either individually or through their federations, are spending millions in legal fees on trying to hold back the tide. It is a fair guess that before long they will conclude that they are wasting their money.

Literary Societies

Margery Allingham Society

2B Higham Green, Winchelsea TN36 4HB
☎01797 222363   Fax 01797 222363
www.margeryallingham.org.uk
Contact *Mrs Pamela Bruxner*
SUBSCRIPTION £14 p.a.

Founded 1988 to promote interest in and study of the works of Margery Allingham. The Society publishes two issues of the journal, *The Bottle Street Gazette*, per year. Contributions welcome. Two social events a year. Open membership.

Jane Austen Society

22 Belmont Grove, Bedhampton, Havant PO9 3PU
☎023 9247 5855
✉ rosemary@sndc.demon.co.uk
www.janeaustensociety.org.uk
Membership Secretary *Mrs Rosemary Culley*
SUBSCRIPTION UK: £7.50 (student);
£15 (annual); £20 (joint); £45 (corporate);
£250 (life); Overseas: £18 (annual by credit card or UK banker's order only);
£50 (corporate); overseas membership
£50/€75 (for 3 years); £300/€450 (life)

Founded 1940 to promote interest in and enjoyment of Jane Austen's novels and letters. The society has branches in Bath and Bristol, the Midlands, London, Oxford, Norfolk, Kent, Hampshire, Isle of Wight and northern Scotland. There are independent Societies in North America and Australia.

The Baskerville Hounds

6 Bramham Moor, Hill Head, Fareham PO14 3RU
☎01329 667325
Chairman *Philip Weller*
SUBSCRIPTION £6 p.a.

Founded 1989. An international Sherlock Holmes society specialising solely in studies of *The Hound of the Baskervilles* and its Dartmoor associations. Publishes an annual journal and specialist monographs. It also organises many social functions, usually on Dartmoor. Open membership.

The BB Society

8 Park Road, Solihull B91 3SU
☎01564 741847
✉ bryan@barbryn.co.uk
Chairman *Bill Humphreys*
Secretary *Bryan Holden*
SUBSCRIPTION £10 (individual);
£17.50 (family); £50 (corporate);
£5 (student); £17.50 (overseas)

Founded in 2000 to bring together devotees of the writer/illustrator BB (Denys Watkins-Pitchford). BB's oeuvre included books on wildfowling, angling, children's fantasy and the countryside. The Society holds two meetings a year and publishes newsletters and an annual journal, *Sky Gypsy*. BB's centenary year will be celebrated in 2005 with a series of special events and Society publications.

The Beckford Society

The Timber Cottage, Crockerton, Warminster BA12 8AX
☎01985 213195
✉ Sidney.Blackmore@btinternet.com
Secretary *Sidney Blackmore*
SUBSCRIPTION £10 (minimum) p.a.

Founded 1995 to promote an interest in the life and works of William Beckford (1760–1844) and his circle. Encourages Beckford studies and scholarship through exhibitions, lectures and publications, including an annual journal, *The Beckford Journal* and occasional newsletters.

Thomas Lovell Beddoes Society

9 Amber Court, Belper DE56 1HG
☎01773 828066   Fax 01773 828066
✉ john@beddoes.demon.co.uk
www.beddoes.org
Chairman *John Lovell Beddoes*
Secretary *Christine Hunkinson*

Formed to research the life, times and work of poet Thomas Lovell Beddoes (1803–1849), encourage relevant publications, further the reading and appreciation of his works by a wider public and liaise with other groups and organisations. Publishes an annual journal.

The Adrian Bell Society

3 The Maltings, Church Close, Coltishall NR12 7DZ
☎01603 737168
Secretary *Moya Leighton*

SUBSCRIPTION £5 p.a.

Founded 1995, the Society aims to promote the study and enjoyment of the writing of Adrian Bell (1901–80); to publish journals twice a year and hold meetings to help members obtain copies of out of print titles; to assemble a collection of photocopies of his 1500 *Countryman's Notebooks* that appeared in the *Eastern Daily Press* and to index them; to commemorate his career as *The Times* first crossword compiler; to share knowledge of the places and factual background mentioned in his books. The society has 250 members worldwide who keep in touch through the journal *A Centenary Countryman's Notebook*, published 2001 (£7.00 + p&p).

Hilaire Belloc Society

1 Hillview, Elsted, Midhurst GU29 0JX
☎01730 825575
✉ HilaireBelloc1@aol.com

Contact *Dr Grahame Clough*

Founded in 1996 to promote the life and work of Hilaire Belloc through the publication of newsletters containing rare and previously unpublished material. Organises walks, social events, a Belloc weekend and a three-day conference. Currently 70 members, of which 30% are from overseas.

Arnold Bennett Society

4 Field End Close, Trentham, Stoke on Trent ST4 8DA
✉ arnoldbennettsociety@btinternet.com
www.arnoldbennettsociety.org.uk

Secretary *Mrs Carol Gorton*
SUBSCRIPTION £9 p.a. (single); £11 (family) plus £2 for membership outside the UK; £5 (student)

Aims to promote interest in the life and works of 'Five Towns' author Arnold Bennett and other North Staffordshire writers. Annual dinner. Regular functions and talks in and around Burslem, plus annual seminar at Wedgwood College, Barlaston and annual conference at Staffordshire University.

E.F. Benson Society

The Old Coach House, High Street, Rye TN31 7JF
☎01797 223114
www.efbensonsociety.org

Secretary *Allan Downend*
SUBSCRIPTION £7.50 (UK/Europe); £12.50 (overseas)

Founded 1985 to promote the life and work of

E.F. Benson and the Benson family. Organises social and literary events, exhibitions, talks and Benson interest walks in Rye. Publishes a quarterly newsletter and annual journal, *The Dodo*, postcards and reprints of E.F. Benson articles and short stories in a series called 'Bensoniana' plus other books of Benson interest. Holds an archive which includes the Seckersen Collection (transcriptions of the Benson collection at the Bodleian Library in Oxford).

E.F. Benson/The Tilling Society

5 Friars Bank, Guestling, Hastings TN35 4EJ
Fax 01424 813237
www.tilling.org.uk/society

Contact *Cynthia Reavell*
SUBSCRIPTION Full starting membership (members receive all back newsletters) £36 (UK); £40 (overseas); or Annual Membership (members receive only current year's newsletters) £8 (UK); £10 (overseas)

Founded 1982 for the exchange of news, information and speculation about E.F. Benson, his works and, in particular, his *Mapp & Lucia* novels. Readings, talks and journal-length biannual newsletter. Acts as a clearing house for every sort of news and activity concerning E.F. Benson, also studies his family and friends.

The Betjeman Society

35 Eaton Court, Boxgrove Avenue, Guildford GU1 1XH
☎01483 560882

Chairman *John Heald*
SUBSCRIPTION £10 (individual); £12 (family); £3 (student); £3 additional for overseas members

Aims to promote the study and appreciation of the work and life of Sir John Betjeman. Annual programme includes poetry readings, lectures, discussions, visits to places associated with Betjeman, and various social events. Meetings are held in London and other centres. Regular newsletter and annual journal, *The Betjemanian*.

The Bewick Society

c/o The Hancock Museum, Newcastle upon Tyne NE2 4PT
☎01207 562196
✉ juneholmes@lineone.net
www.bewicksociety.org

Membership Secretary *June Holmes*
SUBSCRIPTION £7 p.a. (individual); £10 (family)

Founded 1988 to promote an interest in the life and work of Thomas Bewick, wood-engraver and naturalist (1753–1828). Organises related events and meetings, and is associated with the Bewick birthplace museum at Cherryburn, Northumberland.

Birmingham Central Literary Association

23 Arden Grove, Ladywood, Birmingham
B16 8HG
☎0121 454 9352
✉ bakerbrum@aol.com

Contact *The Secretary*

Holds fortnightly meetings in central Birmingham to discuss the lives and work of authors and poets. Holds an annual dinner to celebrate Shakespeare's birthday.

The George Borrow Society

60 Upper Marsh Road, Warminster BA12 9PN
www.clough5.fsnet.co.uk/gb.html

Chairman/Bulletin Editor *Dr Ann M. Ridler*
Membership Secretary *Michael Skillman*
Honorary Treasurer *David Pattinson*
Bulletin Editor: St Mary's Cottage, 61 Thame Road, Warborough, Wallingford, Oxford OX10 7EA ☎01865 858379 Fax 01865 858575
SUBSCRIPTION £15 p.a.

Founded 1991 to promote knowledge of the life and works of George Borrow (1803–81), traveller, linguist and writer. The Society holds biennial conferences (with published proceedings) and informal intermediate gatherings, all at places associated with Borrow. Publishes the *George Borrow Bulletin* twice yearly, containing scholarly articles, reviews of publications relating to Borrow, reports of past events and news of forthcoming events. Member of the **Alliance of Literary Societies** and corporate associate member of the Centre of East Anglian Studies (CEAS) at the University of East Anglia, Norwich (Borrow's home city for many years).

Elinor Brent-Dyer

See **Friends of the Chalet School** and **The New Chalet Club**

British Fantasy Society

201 Reddish Road, South Reddish, Stockport
SK5 7HR
☎0161 476 5368 (after 6pm)
✉ faliol@yahoo.com
www.britishfantasysociety.org.uk

President *Ramsey Campbell*
Chairman *Marie O'Regan*
Secretary *Robert Parkinson*

SUBSCRIPTION from £25 p.a.

Founded 1971 for devotees of fantasy, horror and related fields in literature, art and the cinema. Publishes a regular newsletter with information and reviews of new books and films, plus related fiction and non-fiction magazines. Annual conference at which the **British Fantasy Awards** are presented. These awards are voted on by the membership and are not an open competition.

The Brontë Society

Brontë Parsonage Museum, Haworth,
Keighley BD22 8DR
☎01535 642323   Fax 01535 647131
✉ bronte@bronte.org.uk
www.bronte.info

Contact *Membership Officer*
SUBSCRIPTION £18.50 p.a. (UK/Europe);
£10.50 (student); £5 (junior – up to age 14); £27.50 (overseas); joint subscriptions available

Founded 1893. Aims and activities include the preservation of manuscripts and other objects related to or connected with the Brontë family, and the maintenance and development of the museum and library at Haworth. The society holds regular meetings, lectures and exhibitions; and publishes information relating to the family and a triannual *Gazette*. Freelance contributions for either publication should be sent to the Publications Secretary at the address above. Members can receive the journal, *Brontë Studies*, at a reduced subscription of £13.50 p.a.

The Rupert Brooke Society

The Orchard, 45/47 Mill Way, Grantchester
CB3 9ND
☎01223 551118   Fax 01223 551119
✉ rbs@callan.co.uk
www.rupertbrooke.com

Contacts *Claire Pidoux, Karen Smith*
SUBSCRIPTION £7.50 (UK); £10.50 (overseas)

Founded in 1999 to foster an interest in the work of Rupert Brooke, help preserve places associated with him and to increase the knowledge and appreciation of the village of Grantchester. Members receive a newsletter with information about events, new books and activities.

The Browning Society

9 Duncan Terrace, London N1 8BZ
☎020 7833 4228   Fax 020 7833 5834
✉ anneke.berrill@btconnect.com

Honorary Secretary *Anneke Berrill*

SUBSCRIPTION £15 p.a.

Founded 1969 to promote an interest in the lives and poetry of Robert and Elizabeth Barrett Browning. Meetings are arranged in the London area, one of which occurs in December at Westminster Abbey to commemorate Robert Browning's death.

The John Buchan Society

Greenmantle, Main Street, Kings Newton, Melbourne DE73 8BX
☎01332 865315
✉ kenhbsoc@moonfleet69.freeserve.co.uk
Secretary *Kenneth Hillier*
SUBSCRIPTION £12 (full/overseas); £5 (associate); £6 (junior); £20 (corporate); £100 (10 years)

To perpetuate the memory of John Buchan and to promote a wider understanding of his life and works. Holds regular meetings and social gatherings, publishes a journal, and liaises with the John Buchan Centre at Broughton in the Scottish borders.

The Robert Burns World Federation Ltd

Dean Castle Country Park Dower House, Kilmarnock KA3 1XB
☎01563 572469   Fax 01563 572469
✉ robertburnsfederation@kilmarnock26. freeserve.co.uk
www.robertburnsfederation.co.uk
Chief Executive *Shirley Bell*
SUBSCRIPTION £23 p.a.(individual); £25 (family); £46 (club subscription)

Founded 1885 to encourage interest in the life and work of Robert Burns and keep alive the old Scottish Tongue. The Society's interests go beyond Burns himself in its commitment to the development of Scottish literature, music and arts in general. Publishes the triannual *Burns Chronicle*.

Randolph Caldecott Society

Clatterwick House, Little Leigh, Northwich CW8 4RJ
☎01606 891303 (day)/781731 (evening)
Honorary Secretary *Kenneth N. Oultram*
SUBSCRIPTION £10–£15 p.a.

Founded 1983 to promote the life and work of artist/book illustrator Randolph Caldecott. Meetings held in the spring and autumn in Caldecott's birthplace, Chester. Guest speakers, outings, newsletter, exchanges with the Society's American counterpart. (Caldecott died and was buried in St Augustine, Florida.) A medal in his memory is awarded annually in the US for children's book illustration.

Lewis Carroll Society

69 Cromwell Road, Hertford SG13 7DP
☎01992 584530
✉ alanwhite@tesco.net
www.lewiscarrollsociety.org.uk
Secretary *Alan White*
SUBSCRIPTION from £15 p.a. (individual); apply to Secretary

Founded 1969 to bring together people with an interest in Charles Dodgson and promote research into his life and works. Publishes bi-annual journal *The Carrollian*, featuring scholarly articles and reviews; a newsletter (*Bandersnatch*) which reports on Carrollian events and the Society's activities; and *The Lewis Carroll Review*, a book-reviewing journal. Regular meetings held in London with lectures, talks, outings, etc.

Lewis Carroll Society (Daresbury)

Clatterwick House, Little Leigh, Northwich CW8 4RJ
☎01606 891303 (day)/781731 (evening)
Honorary Secretary *Kenneth N. Oultram*
SUBSCRIPTION £5 p.a.

Founded 1970. To promote the life and work of Charles Dodgson, author of the world-famous *Alice's Adventures*. Holds meetings in the spring and autumn in Carroll's birthplace, Daresbury, Cheshire. Guest speakers and theatre visits.

The New Chalet Club

18 Nuns Moor Crescent, Newcastle upon Tyne NE4 9BE
www.newchaletclub.co.uk
Membership Secretary *Mrs Rona S.S. Falconer*
SUBSCRIPTION £6 p.a. (UK under 18); £10 (UK adult & Europe); £12 (RoW)

Founded 1995 for all those with an interest in the books of Elinor Brent-Dyer. Publishes a quarterly journal and occasional supplements, including *Children's Series Fiction*, and regularly holds local and national meetings.

Friends of the Chalet School

4 Rock Terrace, Coleford, Bath BA3 5NF
☎01373 812705
✉ focs@rockterrace.demon.co.uk
www.rockterrace.demon.co.uk/FOCS
Contacts *Ann Mackie-Hunter, Clarissa Cridland*
SUBSCRIPTION £7.50 p.a.; £6 (under-18); outside UK: details on application

Founded 1989 to promote the works of Elinor Brent-Dyer. The society has members worldwide; publishes four magazines a year and runs a lending library.

The Chesterton Society UK
11 Lawrence Leys, Bloxham, Near Banbury
OX15 4NU
☎01295 720869/07766 711984 (mobile)
Fax 01295 720869
Honorary Secretary *Robert Hughes, KHS*
SUBSCRIPTION £12.50 p.a.

Founded 1964 to promote the ideas and writings of G.K. Chesterton.

The Children's Books History Society
26 St Bernards Close, Buckfast, Buckfastleigh
TQ11 0EP
☎01364 643568
✉ cbhs@abcgarrett.demon.co.uk
Chair/Membership Secretary *Mrs Pat Garrett*
SUBSCRIPTION £10 p.a. (UK/Europe); write for overseas subscription details

Established 1969. Aims to promote an appreciation of children's books and to study their history, bibliography and literary content. The Society holds approximately six meetings per year in London and a summer meeting to a collection, or to a location with a children's book connection. Three substantial newsletters issued annually, with an occasional paper. Review copies should be sent to Newsletter co-editor *Mrs Pat Garrett* (address above). The Society constitutes the British branch of the Friends of the Osborne and Lillian H. Smith Collections in Toronto, Canada, and also liaises with **CILIP** (formerly The Library Association). In 1990, the Society established its biennial Harvey Darton Award for a book, published in English, which extends our knowledge of some aspect of British children's literature of the past. 2004 winner: Jane Cooper for her book on Mrs Molesworth.

The John Clare Society
9 The Chase, Ely CB6 3DR
☎01353 668438
vzone.virgin.net/linda.curry/jclaresociety.htm
human.ntu.ac.uk/clare/clare.html
Honorary Secretary *Miss Sue Holgate*
SUBSCRIPTION £10 (individual); £13 (joint);
£8 (fully retired); £10 (joint retired);
£13 (group); £15 (library); £5 (student, full-time); £15 sterling draft/$30/€25 (eurocheque) (overseas)

Founded 1981 to promote a wider appreciation of the life and works of the poet John Clare (1793–1864). Organises an annual festival in Helpston in July; arranges exhibitions, poetry readings and conferences; and publishes an annual society journal and quarterly newsletter.

William Cobbett Society
10 Grenehurst Way, Petersfield GU31 4AZ
☎01730 262060
✉ williamcobbett@fsmail.web
Chairman *Molly Townsend*
Also: Boynell House, Outlands Lane,
Curdridge, Southampton SO30 2HR
☎01489 782453
Contact *David Chun*
SUBSCRIPTION £8 p.a.

Founded in 1976 to bring together those with an interest in the life and works of William Cobbett (1763–1835) and to extend the interest to a wider public. Society activities include an annual Memorial Lecture; publication of an annual journal (*Cobbett's New Register*) containing articles on various aspects of his life and times; an annual expedition retracing routes taken by Cobbett on his Rural Rides in the 1820s; visits to his birthplace and his tomb in Farnham, Surrey. In association with the Society, the Museum of Farnham holds bound volumes of *Cobbett's Political Register*, a large collection of Cobbett's works, books about Cobbett, and has various Cobbett artefacts on display.

The Friends of Coleridge
87 Richmond Road, Montpelier, Bristol
BS6 5EP
☎0117 942 6366
✉ gcddavidson@compuserve.com
www.friendsofcoleridge.com
Membership Secretary *Paul Cheshire* (74 Wells Road, Bath BA2 3AR,
✉ paul.cheshire@btclick.com)
Editor (Coleridge Bulletin) *Graham Davidson*
SUBSCRIPTION £10 (UK); £15 or £20 (overseas)

Founded in 1987 to advance knowledge about the life, work and times of Samuel Taylor Coleridge and his circle, and to support his Nether Stowey Cottage, with the National Trust, as a centre of Coleridge interest. Holds literary evenings, study weekends and a biennial international academic conference. Publishes *The Coleridge Bulletin* biannually. Short articles on Coleridge-related topics may be sent to the editor at the (Bristol) address above.

Wilkie Collins Society
4 Ernest Gardens, London W4 3QU
✉ paul@wilkiecollins.org
www.wilkiecollins.org
Chairman *Andrew Gasson*
Membership Secretary *Paul Lewis* (at address above)
SUBSCRIPTION £10 (UK/Europe); £18 (RoW – remittance must be made in UK sterling)

Founded 1980 to provide information on and promote interest in the life and works of Wilkie Collins, one of the first English novelists to deal with the detection of crime. *The Woman in White* appeared in 1860 and *The Moonstone* in 1868. Publishes newsletters, reprints of Collins' work and an annual academic journal.

The Arthur Conan Doyle Society
PO Box 1360, Ashcroft, British Columbia, Canada V0K 1A0
☎ 001 250 453 2045   Fax 001 250 453 2075
✉ ashtree@ash-tree.bc.ca
www.ash-tree.bc.ca/acdsocy.html
Joint Organisers *Christopher Roden, Barbara Roden*

Founded 1989 to promote the study and discussion of the life and works of Sir Arthur Conan Doyle. Occasional meetings, functions and visits. Publishes an occasional journal together with reprints of Conan Doyle's writings.

Joseph Conrad Society (UK)
c/o P.O.S.K., 238–246 King Street, Hammersmith, London W6 0RF
Fax 020 8240 4365
✉ theconradian@aol.com
www.josephconradsociety.org
Secretary *Hugh Epstein*
Treasurer/Editor (*The Conradian*) *Allan Simmons*
SUBSCRIPTION £20 p.a. (individual); £20 (institution)

Founded in 1973 to promote the study of the works and life of Joseph Conrad (1857–1924). A scholarly society, supported by the Polish Library at the Polish Cultural Association where a substantial library of Conrad texts and criticism is held in the Study Centre. Publishes a journal of Conrad studies (*The Conradian*) biannually and holds an annual International Conference in the first week of July. Awards an essay prize and travel and study grants to scholars on application.

The Rhys Davies Trust
10 Heol Don, Whitchurch, Cardiff CF14 2AU
☎ 029 2062 3359
Contact *Professor Meic Stephens*

SUBSCRIPTION
Founded 1990 to perpetuate the literary reputation of the Welsh prose writer, Rhys Davies (1901–78), and to foster Welsh writing in English. Organises competitions in association with other bodies such as the **Welsh Academy**, puts up plaques on buildings associated with Welsh writers, offers grant-aid for book production, etc.

The Walter de la Mare Society
Flat 15, Trinity Court, Vicarage Road, Twickenham TW2 5TY
www.bluetree.co.uk/wdlmsociety
Honorary President *Professor John Bayley, CBE*
Honorary Secretary & Treasurer *Julie de la Mare*
SUBSCRIPTION £15 p.a.

Founded in 1997 to honour the memory of Walter de la Mare; to promote the study and deepen the appreciation of his works; to widen the readership of his works; to facilitate research by making available the widest range of contacts and information about de la Mare; and to encourage and facilitate new Walter de la Mare publications. Produces a regular newsletter and organises events. Membership information from the address above.

Warwick Deeping Appreciation Society
23 Merton Road, Enfield EN2 0LS
☎ 020 8367 0263
✉ geoffrey@gillam.fsworld.co.uk
Secretary *Geoffrey Gillam*
SUBSCRIPTION £3.50 p.a.

Open to all with an interest in the life and work of Warwick Deeping who produced 70 novels and many short stories. A quarterly newsletter includes reviews of his books and results of research into his life.

The Dickens Fellowship
48 Doughty Street, London WC1N 2LX
☎ 020 7405 2127   Fax 020 7831 5175
✉ arwilliams33@compuserve.com
www.dickens.fellowship.btinternet.co.uk
Joint Honorary General Secretaries *Mrs Thelma Grove, Dr Tony Williams*
SUBSCRIPTION £6 (first year); £12 (renewal)

Founded 1902. The Society's particular aims and objectives are: to bring together lovers of Charles Dickens; to spread the message of Dickens, his love of humanity ('the keynote of all his work'); to remedy social injustice for the poor and oppressed; to assist in the preservation of material and buildings associated with Dickens. Annual conference. Publishes journal called *The Dickensian* (founded 1905 and available at special rate to members) and organises a full programme of lectures, discussions, visits and conducted walks throughout the year. Branches worldwide.

Dymock Poets
See **The Friends of the Dymock Poets**

Early English Text Society
Lady Margaret Hall, Oxford OX2 6QA
Fax 01865 286581
www.eets.org.uk

Executive Secretary *Professor Vincent Gillespie* (at address above)
Editorial Secretary *Dr H.L. Spencer* (at Exeter College, Oxford OX1 3DP)
Membership Secretary *Mrs J.M. Watkinson* (at 12 North End, Durham DH1 4NJ)
SUBSCRIPTION £20 p.a. (UK); $30 (US); $35 (Canada)

Founded 1864. Concerned with the publication of early English texts. Members receive annual publications (one or two a year) or may select titles from the backlist in lieu.

The George Eliot Fellowship
71 Stepping Stones Road, Coventry CV5 8JT
☎024 7659 2231
www.george-eliot-fellowship.com
Contact *Mrs Kathleen Adams*
SUBSCRIPTION £10 p.a.; £100 (life); concession for pensioners

Founded 1930. Exists to honour George Eliot and promote interest in her life and works. Readings, memorial lecture, birthday luncheon and functions. Issues a quarterly newsletter and an annual journal. Awards an annual prize for a George Eliot essay.

Rev. G. Bramwell Evens
See **The Romany Society**

The John Meade Falkner Society
Greenmantle, Main Street, Kings Newton, Melbourne DE73 8BX
☎01332 865315
✉ kenjmfsoc@moonfleet69.freeserve.co.uk
Secretary *Kenneth Hillier*
SUBSCRIPTION £5 (UK); $10 (overseas)

Founded in 1999 to promote the appreciation and study of John Meade Falkner's life, times and works. Produces three newsletters a year and an annual journal.

Folly (Fans of Light Literature for the Young)
21 Warwick Road, Pokesdown, Bournemouth BH7 6JW
☎01202 432562
✉ folly@sims.abel.co.uk
Contact *Mrs Sue Sims*
SUBSCRIPTION £9 p.a. (UK); £11 (Europe); £14 (worldwide)

Founded 1990 to promote interest in a wide variety of children's authors – with a bias towards writers of girls' books and school stories. Publishes three magazines a year.

The Ford Madox Ford Society
c/o Dr Sara Haslam, Dept of Literature, The Open University, Milton Keynes MK7 6AA
☎01908 653453   Fax 01908 653750
✉ s.haslam@open.ac.uk
www.rialto.com/fordmadoxford_society
Chairman *Professor Max Saunders*
Treasurer *Dr Sara Haslam*
SUBSCRIPTION £12 or £6 concession

Founded 1996 to promote the works of Ford Madox Ford and to increase knowledge of his writing and impact on writing in the 20th century. Meets for academic conferences and more popular events annually. Distributes *International Ford Madox Ford Studies* free to members. Welcomes all with an interest in Ford and his works. Has members in the UK, USA, Italy, France and Germany and holds events in as many different places as possible.

C.S. Forester Society
11 Park Town, Oxford OX2 6SN
☎01865 512111   Fax 01865 515292
✉ csforester@hotmail.com
www.csforester.com
Contact *Colin Blogg*
SUBSCRIPTION £10 or $15 p.a.

Founded in 1999 to provide an informal forum to promote knowledge and enjoyment of the works and life of C.S. Forester; to write a definitive bibliography and, ultimately, a biography. Publishes a newsletter 3 or 4 times a year containing contributions from members, and holds meetings for film shows, readings and lectures and a literary supplement, *Reflections* (editor: David Stead ☎0114 233 1255).

The Franco-Midland Hardware Company
6 Bramham Moor, Hill Head, Fareham PO14 3RU

☎01329 667325
✉ fmhc@acd-221b.info
www.btinternet.com/~sherlock.fmhc
Chairman *Philip Weller*
SUBSCRIPTION £5 p.a. (UK); £10 (Europe);
£15 (RoW)

Founded 1989. 'The world's leading Sherlock Holmes correspondence study group and the most active Holmesian society in Britain.' Publishes annual journal, a biannual news magazine and an individual case study as a subscription package. Also publishes at least two specialist monographs a year. It provides certificated self-study courses and organises monthly functions at Holmes-associated locations. Open membership.

The Friends of Shandy Hall (The Laurence Sterne Trust)

Shandy Hall, Coxwold, York YO61 4AD
☎01347 868465   Fax 01347 868465
www.asterisk.org.uk
Curator *Patrick Wildgust*
SUBSCRIPTION £7 (annual); £70 (life)

Promotes interest in the works of Laurence Sterne and aims to preserve the house in which they were created (open to the public). Publishes annual journal, *The Shandean*. An Annual Memorial Lecture is delivered each summer.

The Friends of the Dymock Poets

19 The Southend, Ledbury HR8 2EY
☎01531 634796
✉ cateluck2003@yahoo.com
www.dymockpoets.co.uk
Chairman *Roy Palmer*
Hon. Secretary *Catharine Luck*
Membership Secretary *Jeff Cooper*
SUBSCRIPTION £7 (individual); £12 (couple);
£3 (student); £12 (society/family)

Founded 1993. Established to foster an interest in the work of the Dymock Poets – Edward Thomas, Robert Frost, Wilfrid Gibson, Rupert Brooke, John Drinkwater, Lascelles Abercrombie; help preserve places and things associated with them; keep members informed of literary and other matters relating to the poets; increase knowledge and appreciation of the landscape between May Hill (Gloucestershire) and the Malvern Hills. Members are offered lectures, poetry readings, social meetings, newsletters and annual journal, guided walks in the countryside around Dymock; links with other literary societies; and annual event to commemorate the first meeting between Edward Thomas and Robert Frost on 6 October 1913.

The Gaskell Society

Far Yew Tree House, Chester Road, Tabley, Knutsford WA16 0HN
☎01565 634668
✉ joanleach@aol.com
gaskellsociety.users.btopenworld.com
lang.nagoya-u.ac.jp/~matsuoka/EG-Society.html
Honorary Secretary *Joan Leach*
SUBSCRIPTION £15 p.a.; £20 (corporate & overseas)

Founded 1985 to promote and encourage the study and appreciation of the life and works of Elizabeth Cleghorn Gaskell. Meetings held in Knutsford, Manchester, Bath and London; annual journal and biannual newsletter. On alternate years holds either a residential weekend conference or overseas visit.

The Ghost Story Society

PO Box 1360, Ashcroft, British Columbia, Canada V0K 1A0
☎001 250 453 2045   Fax 001 250 453 2075
✉ nebuly@telus.net
www.ash-tree.bc.ca/GSS.html
Joint Organisers *Barbara Roden, Christopher Roden*
SUBSCRIPTION UK: £24 (airmail); $38 (US$);
$42 (Canadian$)

Founded 1988. Devoted mainly to supernatural fiction in the literary tradition of M.R. James, Walter de la Mare, Algernon Blackwood, E.F. Benson, A.N.L. Munby, R.H. Malden, etc. Publishes a thrice-yearly journal, *All Hallows*, which includes new fiction in the genre and non-fiction of relevance to the genre.

Graham Greene Birthplace Trust

Rhenigidale, Ivy House Lane, Berkhamsted HP4 2PP
☎01442 865158
✉ secretary@grahamgreenebt.org
www.grahamgreenebt.org
Secretary *Ken Sherwood*
SUBSCRIPTION £8 (UK, £20 for 3 years);
£11 (Europe, £27); £15 (RoW, £40)

Founded on 2 October 1997, the 93rd anniversary of Graham Greene's birth, to promote the appreciation and study of his works. Publishes a quarterly newsletter, occasional papers, videos and compact discs. Organises the annual four-day Graham Greene Festival during the weekend nearest to the writer's birthday (2nd October) and administrates the Graham Greene Memorial Awards.

The Ivor Gurney Society

2 Turrall Street, Barbourne, Worcester
WR3 8AJ
☎01497 820541
✉ jp-hay@beeb.net
www.ivor.gurney.net
SUBSCRIPTION £12.50 (individual);
£5 (student); £12.50 (group/library)

To promote interest in Ivor Gurney and his context and to make his music and poetry available to a wider audience by way of performances, readings, conferences, recordings and publications. To enhance and promote informed scholarship on all aspects of his life and work through the publication of a regular newsletter and an annual journal, available to society members. To maintain and expand the Gurney archive at Gloucester Central Library.

Rider Haggard Society

27 Deneholm, Whitley Bay NE25 9AU
☎0191 252 4516   Fax 0191 252 4516
✉ RB27Allen@aol.com
www.riderhaggardsociety.org.uk
Contact *Roger Allen*
SUBSCRIPTION £9 p.a. (UK); £10 (overseas)

Founded 1985 to promote appreciation of the life and works of Sir Henry Rider Haggard, English novelist, 1856–1925. News/books exchange and meetings every 18 months.

James Hanley Network

Old School House, George Green Road,
George Green, Wexham SL3 6BJ
☎01753 578632
✉ gostick@london.com
www.jameshanley.mcmail.com/index.htm
Network Coordinator *Chris Gostick*

An informal international association founded in 1997 for all those interested in exploring and publicising the works and contribution to literature of the novelist and dramatist James Hanley (1901–1985). Publishes an annual newsletter. Occasional conferences are planned for the future. All enquiries welcome.

The Thomas Hardy Society

PO Box 1438, Dorchester DT1 1YH
☎01305 251501   Fax 01305 251501
✉ info@hardysociety.org
www.hardysociety.org
Honorary Secretary *Mike Nixon*
SUBSCRIPTION £18 (individual); £25
(corporate); £22.50 (individual, overseas);
£30 (corporate, overseas)

Founded 1967 to promote the reading and study of the works and life of Thomas Hardy. Thrice-yearly journal, events and a biennial conference. An international organisation.

The Henty Society

Hayfield, Bourne Fields, Twyford, Winchester
SO21 1NY
☎01962 713164
Honorary Secretary *Bruce Lees*
SUBSCRIPTION £13 p.a. (UK); £16 (overseas)

Founded 1977 to study the life and work of George Alfred Henty, and to publish research, bibliographical data and lesser-known works, namely short stories. Organises conferences and social gatherings in the UK and North America, and publishes bulletins to members. Published in 1996: *G.A. Henty (1832–1902) a Bibliographical Study* by Peter Newbolt.

James Hilton Society

49 Beckingthorpe Drive, Bottesford,
Nottingham NG13 0DN
www.jameshiltonsociety.co.uk
Honorary Secretary *J.R. Hammond*
SUBSCRIPTION £10 (UK/EU); £7 concession

Founded 2000 to promote interest in the life and work of novelist and scriptwriter James Hilton (1900–1954). Publishes *The Hiltonian* (annually) and *The James Hilton Newsletter* (quarterly) and organises meetings and conferences.

Sherlock Holmes Society (The Musgraves)

Hallas Lodge, Greenside Lane, Cullingworth,
Bradford BD13 5AP
☎01535 273468
✉ hallaslodge@btinternet.com
Contacts *John Hall, Anne Jordan*
SUBSCRIPTION £10 p.a. (UK)

Founded 1987 to promote enjoyment and study of Sir Arthur Conan Doyle's Sherlock Holmes through publications and meetings. One of the largest Sherlock Holmes societies in Great Britain. Honorary members include Bert Coules, Richard Lancelyn Green, Edward Hardwicke, Clive Merrison and Douglas Wilmer. Past honorary members: Dame Jean Conan Doyle, Peter Cushing, Jeremy Brett and Michael Williams. Open membership. Lectures, presentations and consultation on matters relating to Holmes and Conan Doyle available.

Sherlock Holmes

See **The Franco-Midland Hardware Company**

Hopkins Society
41 North Drive, Rhyl LL18 4SW
☎01745 354151
✉ bill&meljones@aol.com
www.hopkinsoc.freeserve.co.uk
Contact *Imelda Jones*
SUBSCRIPTION £7 p.a. (UK); £10 (overseas)

Founded 1990 to celebrate the life and work of Gerard Manley Hopkins; to inform members of any publications, courses or events about the poet. Holds an annual lecture on Hopkins in the spring; produces two newsletters a year; sponsors and organises educational projects based on Hopkins' life and works.

Housman Society
80 New Road, Bromsgrove B60 2LA
☎01527 874136
✉ info@housman-society.co.uk
www.housman-society.co.uk
Contact *Jim Page*
SUBSCRIPTION £10 (UK); £12.50 (overseas)

Founded 1973 to promote knowledge and appreciation of the lives and work of A.E. Housman and other members of his family, and to promote the cause of literature and poetry. Sponsors a lecture at the **Hay Festival** each year under the title of 'The Name and Nature of Poetry'. Publishes an annual journal and biannual newsletter.

W.W. Jacobs Appreciation Society
3 Roman Road, Southwick BN42 4TP
☎01273 871017   Fax 01273 871017
Contact *A.R. James*

Founded 1988 to encourage and promote the enjoyment of the works of W.W. Jacobs, and stimulate research into his life and works. No subscription charge. Material available for purchase includes *W.W. Jacobs*, a biography published in 1999, price £12, post paid, and *WWJ Book Hunter's Field Guide*, a narrative bibliography published in 2001, price £6, post paid.

Richard Jefferies Society
Eidsvoll, Bedwells Heath, Boars Hill, Oxford OX1 5JE
☎01865 735678
www.bath.ac.uk/~lissmc/rjeffs.htm
Honorary Secretary *Lady Phyllis Treitel*
Membership Secretary *Mrs Margaret Evans*
SUBSCRIPTION £7 p.a. (individual); £8 (joint); life membership for those over 50

Founded 1950 to promote understanding of the work of Richard Jefferies, nature/country writer, novelist and mystic (1848–87). Produces newsletters, reports and an annual journal; organises talks, discussions and readings. Library and archives. Assists in maintaining the museum in Jefferies' birthplace at Coate near Swindon. Membership applications should be sent to *Margaret Evans*, 23 Hardwell Close, Grove, Nr Wantage OX12 0BN.

Jerome K. Jerome Society
c/o Fraser Wood, Mayo and Pinson, 15/16 Lichfield Street, Walsall WS1 1TS
☎01922 629000   Fax 01922 721065
✉ tonygray@jkj.demon.co.uk
www.jeromekjerome.com
Honorary Secretary *Tony Gray*
SUBSCRIPTION £7.50 p.a. (ordinary);
    £25 (corporate); £3.75 (under 21/over 65)

Founded 1984 to stimulate interest in Jerome K. Jerome's life and works (1859–1927). One of the Society's principal activities is the support of a small museum in the author's birthplace, Walsall. Meetings, lectures, events and a newsletter, *Idle Thoughts*. Annual dinner in Walsall near Jerome's birth date (2nd May).

The Captain W.E. Johns Appreciation Society
221 Church Road, Northolt UB5 5BE
✉ brian@zhong-ding.com
Contact (Notts meeting) *Brian Woodruff* (at address above ☎07843 680048)
Contact (Twyford) *Joy Tilley* (☎01785 240299)

Society for the appreciation of W.E. Johns, creator of Biggles. Meets twice a year in Nottingham and Twyford, near Reading (see above for contacts). Biannual magazine, *Biggles Flies Again* (Editor, *Jennifer Schofield* ☎/fax 01243 671209).

Johnson Society
Johnson Birthplace Museum, Breadmarket Street, Lichfield WS13 6LG
☎01543 264972
✉ jdhsec@lichfieldrambler.co.uk
www.lichfieldrambler.co.uk
Hon. General Secretary *Mrs Norma Hooper*
SUBSCRIPTION £7.50 p.a.; £10 (joint)

Founded 1910 to encourage the study of the life, works and times of Samuel Johnson (1709–1784) and his contemporaries. The Society is committed to the preservation of the Johnson Birthplace Museum and Johnson memorials.

Johnson Society of London
255 Baring Road, Grove Park, London
SE12 0BQ
☎020 8851 0173
✉ JSL@nbbl.demon.co.uk
www.nbbl.demon.co.uk/index.html
President *Lord Harmsworth*
Honorary Secretary *Mrs Z.E. O'Donnell*
SUBSCRIPTION £12 p.a.; £15 (joint)

Founded 1928 to promote the knowledge and appreciation of Dr Samuel Johnson and his works. Publishes an annual journal, *New Rambler* and occasional newsletter. Regular meetings from October to April in the meeting room of Wesley's Chapel, City Road, London on the second Saturday of each month, and a commemoration ceremony around the anniversary of Johnson's death (December) held in Westminster Abbey.

The David Jones Society
48 Sylvan Way, Sketty, Swansea SA2 9JB
☎01792 206144   Fax 01792 205305
✉ anne.price-owen@sihe.ac.uk
www.sihe/ac/uk/davidjones
Contact *Anne Price-Owen*
SUBSCRIPTION £18 (individual);
   £30 (corporate)

Founded 1996, the Society aims to promote and encourage knowledge of the painter-poet David Jones. The Society hosts annual scholarly meetings. The annual subscription includes a copy of the *David Jones Journal*. Unsolicited material relating to David Jones, art, literarure or any of his philosophies may be sent for consideration for publication in the journal.

The Just William Society
Easter Badbea, Dundonnell IV23 2QX
✉ philandpaula@easter-badbea.co.uk
Secretary/Treasurer *Paula Cross*
SUBSCRIPTION £7 p.a. (UK); £10 (overseas);
   £5 (juvenile/student); £15 (family)

Founded 1994 to further knowledge of Richmal Crompton's *William* and *Jimmy* books. An annual 'William' meeting is held in April. The Honorary President of the Society is Richmal Crompton's niece, Richmal Ashbee.

The Keats–Shelley Memorial Association (Inc)
Registered office: 1 Satchwell Walk, Royal Priors, Leamington Spa CV32 4QE
☎01926 427400   Fax 01926 335133
Contact *Honorary Secretary*
SUBSCRIPTION £10 p.a.

Founded 1903 to promote appreciation of the works of Keats and Shelley, and their circle. One of the Society's main tasks is the preservation of 26 Piazza di Spagna in Rome as a memorial to the British Romantic poets in Italy, particularly Keats and Shelley. Publishes an annual review of Romantic Studies, the *Keats-Shelley Review*, promotes bursaries and competitive writing on Romantic Studies (see **Keats-Shelley Prize** under *Prizes*) and arranges events and lectures for Friends. The *Review* is edited by *Angus Graham-Campbell*, c/o Eton College, Windsor SL4 6EA.

The Kenny/Naughton Society
Aghamore, Ballyhaunis, Co. Mayo, Republic of Ireland
✉ paulwdrogers@hotmail.com
www.aghamoregaa.com/society/knsociety.htm
Chairman *Paul W.D. Rogers*
Patron *Mrs Erna Naughton*

Founded in 1993 to commemorate two writers who had links with Aghamore: P.D. Kenny (1862–1944), who wrote under the pseudonym 'Pat' and Bill Naughton (1910–1992), best known as the author of *Alfie*. Holds an annual school over the October bank holiday weekend which includes lectures, drama, debate and competition (**Bill Naughton Short Story Competition** – see entry under *Prizes*).

Kent & Sussex Poetry Society
39 Rockington Way, Crowborough TN6 2NJ
☎01892 662781
✉ joyce@kentandsussexpoetrysociety.org
www.kentandsussexpoetrysociety.org
Publicity Secretary *John Arnold*
SUBSCRIPTION £10 p.a. (full); £6 (concessionary; country members living farther afield, senior citizen, under-16, unemployed)

Founded 1946 to promote the enjoyment of poetry. Monthly meetings are held in Tunbridge Wells, including readings by major poets, a monthly workshop and an annual writing retreat week. Publishes an annual folio of members' work based on Members' Competition, adjudicated and commented upon by a major poet. Runs an annual **Open Poetry Competition** (see entry under *Prizes* and details on website) and Saturday workshops twice a year with leading poets.

The Kilvert Society
Sandalwood, North End Road, Steeple Claydon, Buckingham MK18 2PG
☎01296 730498

Secretary *Mr D. Elvins*
SUBSCRIPTION £12 p.a.; £15 (two persons at same address)

Founded 1948 to foster an interest in the Diary, the diarist and the countryside he loved. Publishes three journals each year; during the summer holds three weekends of walks, commemoration services and talks.

The Kipling Society

6 Clifton Road, London W9 1SS
☎020 7286 0194   Fax 020 7286 0194
✉ jane@keskar.fsworld.co.uk
www.kipling.org.uk
Honorary Secretary *Jane Keskar*
SUBSCRIPTION £22 p.a. (£20 p.a. by standing order)

Founded 1927. The Society's main activities are: maintaining a specialised library in London; answering enquiries from the public (schools, publishers, writers and the media); arranging a regular programme of lectures, especially in London and in Sussex, and an annual luncheon with guest speaker; maintaining a small museum and reference at The Grange, in Rottingdean near Brighton; issuing a quarterly journal. (For the Kipling mailbox discussion list, e-mail to Rudyard-Kipling@jiscmail.ac.uk) This is a literary society for all who enjoy the prose and verse of Rudyard Kipling (1865–1936) and are interested in his life and times. Please contact the Secretary by letter, telephone, fax or e-mail for further information.

The Kitley Trust

Woodstock, Litton Dale, Litton SK17 8QL
☎01298 871564
✉ stottie2@waitrose.com
Contact *Rosie Ford*

Founded 1990 by a teacher in Sheffield to promote the art of creative writing, in memory of her mother, Jessie Kitley. Activities include: biannual poetry competitions; a 'Get Poetry' day (distribution of children's poems in shopping malls); annual sponsorship of a writer for a school; campaigns; organising conferences for writers and teachers of writing. Funds are provided by donations and profits (if any) from competitions.

Lancashire Authors' Association

Heatherslade, 5 Quakerfields, Westhoughton, Bolton BL5 2BJ
☎01942 791390
✉ eholt@cwctv.net
General Secretary *Eric Holt*

SUBSCRIPTION £10 p.a.; £13 (joint); £1 (junior)

Founded 1909 for writers and lovers of Lancashire literature and history. Aims to foster and stimulate interest in Lancashire history and literature as well as in the preservation of the Lancashire dialect. Meets three times a year on Saturday at various locations. Publishes a quarterly journal called *The Record*, which is issued free to members, and holds eight annual competitions (open to members only) for both verse and prose. Comprehensive library with access for research to members.

The Landor Society of Warwick

11 Watersfield Gardens, Sydenham, Leamington Spa CV31 1NT
☎01926 337874
✉ portlandbooks@quicknetuk.com
Honorary Secretary *Mrs Jean Field*
SUBSCRIPTION £7 p.a. (UK/EU); £10 (joint); £12 (overseas)

Founded 2000 to promote interest in the life and works of the Warwick-born writer Walter Savage Landor (1775–1864). Holds a Landor Birthday Dinner each year, and reading and discussion meetings most months. Publishes newsletter twice a year.

The Philip Larkin Society

c/o Department of Humanities, The University of Hull, Hull HU6 7RX
☎01482 465640   Fax 01482 466107
✉ j.a.osborne@hull.ac.uk
www.philiplarkin.com
Contact *Dr John Osborne*
SUBSCRIPTION £18 (Full rate); £12 (unwaged/senior citizen); £4 (student)

Founded in 1995 to promote awareness of the life and work of Philip Larkin (1922–1985) and his literary contemporaries; to bring together all those who admire Larkin's work as a poet, writer and librarian; to bring about publications on all things Larkinesque. Organises a programme of events ranging from lectures to rambles exploring the countryside of Larkin's schooldays and publishes a biannual journal, *About Larkin*.

The D.H. Lawrence Society

24 Briarwood Avenue, Nottingham NG3 6JQ
☎0115 950 3008
Secretary *Ron Faulks*
SUBSCRIPTION £14; £12 (concession); £16 (European); £19 (RoW)

Founded 1974 to increase knowledge and the

appreciation of the life and works of D.H. Lawrence. Monthly meetings, addressed by guest speakers, are held in the library at Eastwood (birthplace of DHL). Organises visits to places of interest in the surrounding countryside, supports the activities of the D.H. Lawrence Centre at Nottingham University, and has close links with DHL Societies worldwide. Publishes two newsletters and one journal each year, free to members.

The T.E. Lawrence Society
PO Box 728, Oxford OX2 9ZJ
www.telsociety.org
Chairman *Philip Kerrigan*
Honorary Secretary *To be appointed*
SUBSCRIPTION £18 (UK); £23 (overseas)

Founded 1985 as a non-profit making, educational, registered charity to advance awareness of the life and work of Thomas Edward Lawrence and to promote research into his life and work. Publishes four newsletters and two journals per year. A biennial symposium is held, usually in Oxford, to bring members together to share both academic and social interests. The Society encourages the formation of regional groups of which, currently, there are seven: three in England (Northwest, London, Dorset), one in Europe (Netherlands), two in the USA (Eastern and Western States) and one in Japan.

The Leamington Literary Society
52 Newbold Terrace East, Leamington Spa CV32 4EZ
☎01926 425733
Honorary Secretary *Mrs Margaret Watkins*
SUBSCRIPTION £10 p.a.

Founded 1912 to promote the study and appreciation of literature and the arts. Holds regular meetings every second Tuesday of the month (from September to June) at the Royal Pump Rooms, Leamington Spa. Also smaller groups which meet regularly to study poetry and the modern novel. The Society has published various books of local interest.

Lewes Monday Literary Club
c/o 1c Prince Edward's Road, Lewes BN7 1BJ
☎01273 478512
✉ chris.lutrario@btinternet.com
Contact *Christopher Lutrario*
SUBSCRIPTION £20 p.a.; £5 (guest, per meeting)

Founded in 1948 for the promotion and enjoyment of literature. Seven meetings are held during the winter generally on the last Monday of each month (from October to April) at the White Hart Hotel in Lewes. The Club attracts speakers of the highest quality and a balance between all forms of literature is aimed for. Guests are welcome to attend meetings.

The George MacDonald Society
The Library, Kings College, Strand, London WC2R 2LS
☎01342 823859
✉ macdonald-society@britishlibrary.net
www.macdonaldsociety.org *linked with:*
www.george-macdonald.com
Contact *John Docherty*
SUBSCRIPTION £10 p.a. (individual);
£13 (joint); £7 (unwaged); £11 (overseas)

Founded 1981 to increase awareness of 'the uniqueness and importance of MacDonald's writings'. Notable among Victorian writers for his radical mixture of genres: MacDonald's fantasy works influenced H.G. Wells, C.S. Lewis and J.R.R. Tolkien, among many others, and his 'realistic' novels offered a fascinating glimpse into Victorian Scottish life. The Society organises conferences and workshops in Britain and abroad, often in association with other societies with related interests. Publishes an annual journal, *North Wind*, with contributions from most of the leading MacDonald scholars worldwide and a newsletter, *Orts*.

The Friends of Arthur Machen
78 Greenwich South Street, Greenwich, London SE10 8UN
☎020 8691 7836
✉ jrc@amarantus.ndo.co.uk
www.machensoc.demon.co.uk
Contact *Jeremy Cantwell*
SUBSCRIPTION £15 p.a. (UK); £18 (EU/overseas); $32 (US)

Founded 1998. (Formerly the Arthur Machen Society.) Promotes a wider readership of Arthur Machen and a greater understanding of his life and work. Members receive hardback journals (*Faunus*) and newsletters (*Machenalia*).

The Marlowe Society
9 Middlefield Gardens, Hurst Green Road, Halesowen B62 9QH
☎0121 421 1482   Fax 0121 421 1482
✉ marsocpt@aol.com
www.marlowe-society.org
Membership Secretary *Frieda Barker*
Treasurer *Bruce Young*
SUBSCRIPTION £12 p.a. (individual); £7 p.a.

(pensioner/student/unwaged); £15 p.a. (overseas); £200 (group); £100 (individual life membership)

Founded 1955. Holds meetings, lectures and discussions, stimulates research into Marlowe's life and works, encourages production of his plays and publishes a biannual newsletter. At a ceremony on 11th July 2002 the Society celebrated their success in establishing a memorial to the playwright and poet in Poets' Corner in Westminster Abbey.

The John Masefield Society

The Frith, Ledbury HR8 1LW
☎01531 631647 Fax 01531 631647
✉ pcarter2@wanadoo.fr
www.sas.ac.uk/ies/Full%20Text%20Archive/Masefield/Society/jmsws.htm

Chairman *Peter Carter*
SUBSCRIPTION £5 p.a. (individual); £8 (family, institution, library); £10 (overseas); £2.50 (junior, student)

Founded in 1992 to stimulate the appreciation of and interest in the life and works of John Masefield (Poet Laureate 1930–1967). The Society is based in Ledbury, the Herefordshire market town of his birth and holds various public events in addition to publishing a journal and occasional papers.

William Morris Society

Kelmscott House, 26 Upper Mall, Hammersmith, London W6 9TA
☎020 8741 3735 Fax 020 8748 5207
✉ william.morris@care4free.net
www.morrissociety.org

Contact *Helen Elletson*
SUBSCRIPTION £18 p.a.

Founded 1955 to promote interest in the life, work and ideas of William Morris (1834–1896), English poet and craftsman.

The Neil Munro Society

8 Briar Road, Kirkintilloch, Glasgow G66 3SA
☎0141 776 4280
✉ brian@bdosborne.fsnet.co.uk
www.neilmunro.co.uk

Secretary *Brian D. Osborne*
SUBSCRIPTION £12 (annual); £7 (unwaged); £15 (institutional)

Founded in 1996 to encourage interest in the works of Neil Munro (1863–1930), the Scottish novelist, short story writer, poet and journalist. An annual programme of meetings is held in Glasgow and Munro's home-town of Inveraray.

Publishes *ParaGraphs*, a twice-yearly magazine, sponsors reprints of Munro's work and is developing a Munro archive.

Bill Naughton

See **The Kenny/Naughton Society**

Violet Needham Society

c/o 19 Ashburnham Place, London SE10 8TZ
☎020 8692 4562
✉ richardcheffins@aol.com

Honorary Secretary *R.H.A. Cheffins*
SUBSCRIPTION £7.50 p.a. (UK & Europe); £11 (RoW)

Founded 1985 to celebrate the work of children's author Violet Needham and stimulate critical awareness of her work. Publishes thrice-yearly *Souvenir*, the Society journal with an accompanying newsletter; organises meetings and excursions to places associated with the author and her books. The journal includes articles about other children's writers of the 1940s and 1950s and on ruritanian fiction. Contributions welcome.

The Edith Nesbit Society

21 Churchfields, West Malling ME19 6RJ
www.the-railway-children.co.uk

Chairman *Margaret McCarthy*
SUBSCRIPTION £7 p.a.; £9 (joint); £80 (life)

Founded in 1996 to celebrate the life and work of Edith Nesbit (1858–1924), best known as the author of *The Railway Children*. The Society's activities include a regular newsletter, booklets, talks and visits to relevant places.

The Wilfred Owen Association

c/o 17 Belmont, Shrewsbury SY1 1TE
☎01743 460089
www.1914-19.co.uk/owen

Chairman *Michael Grayer*
SUBSCRIPTION Adults £6 (£10 overseas); £4 (senior citizen/student/unemployed); £15 (UK group/institution); £25 (overseas group/institution)

Founded 1989 to commemorate the life and works of Wilfred Owen by promoting readings, visits, talks and performances relating to Owen and his work. The Association offers practical support for students of literature and future poets through links with education, support for literary foundations and information on historical and literary background material. Membership is international with 700 members. Publishes a regular newsletter and annual journal. Speakers are available.

The Elsie Jeanette Oxenham Appreciation Society

32 Tadfield Road, Romsey SO51 5AJ
☎01794 517149
✉ abbey@bufobooks.demon.co.uk
www.bufobooks.demon.co.uk/abbeylnk.htm

Membership Secretary/Treasurer *Ms Ruth Allen*
SUBSCRIPTION £7.50 p.a.; enquire for
overseas rates

Founded 1989 to promote the works of Elsie J.
Oxenham. Publishes a newsletter for members,
The Abbey Chronicle, three times a year; Editor
Fiona Dyer (fionadyer@btopenworld.com). 500+
members.

Thomas Paine Society

43 Eugene Gardens, Nottingham NG2 3LF
☎0115 986 0010
President *The Rt. Hon. Michael Foot*
Honorary Secretary *R. W. Morrell, MBE* (at
address above)
Treasurer *Stuart Wright*
SUBSCRIPTION (minimum) £15 p.a. (UK); $35
(overseas); £5 (unwaged/pensioner/student)

Founded 1963 to promote the life and work of
Thomas Paine, and continues to expound his
ideals. Meetings, newsletters, lectures and research
assistance. The Society has members worldwide
and keeps in touch with American and French
Thomas Paine associations. Publishes magazine,
The Journal of Radical History, twice yearly (Editor,
R. W. Morrell) and a newsletter. Holds occasional
exhibitions and lectures, including the biannual
Thomas Paine Memorial Lecture and the annual
Eric Paine Memorial Lecture.

The John Polidori Literary Society

PO Box 6078, Nottingham NG16 4HX
Founder & President *Franklin Bishop*

Founded 1990 to encourage appreciation of the
life and works of John William Polidori MD
(1795–1821), novelist, poet, tragedian, philosopher, diarist, essayist, reviewer, traveller and one
of the youngest students to obtain a medical
degree (at the age of 19). He was one-time intimate of the leading figures in the Romantic
movement and travelling companion and private physician to Lord Byron. He was a pivotal
figure in the infamous Villa Diodati ghost story
sessions in which he assisted Mary Shelley in
the creation of her *Frankenstein* tale. Polidori
introduced into literature the enduring icon of
the vampire portrayed as an aristocratic, hand-

some seducer with his seminal work, *The
Vampyre – A Tale*, published in 1819. A Green
Plaque, erected by the City of Westminster,
celebrates the birthplace of Polidori at 38 Great
Pulteney Street, Westminster, London.

The Beatrix Potter Society

9 Broadfields, Harpenden AL5 2HJ
☎01582 769755
✉ beatrixpottersociety@tiscali.co.uk
www.beatrixpottersociety.org.uk
SUBSCRIPTION UK: £15 p.a. (individual);
£20 (institution); Overseas: £20
(individual); £25 (institution)

Founded 1980 to promote the study and appreciation of the life and works of Beatrix Potter
(1866–1943). Potter was not only the author of
The Tale of Peter Rabbit and other classics of children's literature; she was also a landscape and
natural history artist, diarist, farmer and con-
servationist, and was responsible for the preservation of large areas of the Lake District
through her gifts to the National Trust. The
Society upholds and protects the integrity of
the unique work of Potter, her aims and
bequests; holds regular talks and meetings in
London and elsewhere with visits to places
connected with Beatrix Potter. International
Study Conferences are held in the UK and the
USA. The Society has an active publishing programme. (UK Registered Charity No. 281198.)

Anthony Powell Society

76 Ennismore Avenue, Greenford UB6 0JW
☎020 8864 4095   Fax 020 8864 6109
✉ secretary@anthonypowell.org.uk
www.anthonypowell.org.uk
Patron *John M. A. Powell*
Honorary Secretary *Dr Keith C. Marshall*
SUBSCRIPTION £20 p.a. (individual);
£30 (joint/gold); £12 (student);
£100 (organisation)

Founded in June 2000 to advance education and
interest in the life and works of the English
author Anthony Powell (1905–2000). The
Society's major activity is a biennial Powell conference, the first two of which were at Eton
College (2001) and Balliol College, Oxford
(2003); with a Centenary Conference planned
for December 2005 in London. The Society
organises events for members, ranging from 'pub
meets' to talks and visits to places of Powell interest as well as publishing a quarterly *Newsletter*.
Member of the **Alliance of Literary Societies**.

The Powys Society

25 Mansfield Road, Taunton TA1 3NJ
☎01823 278177
✉ peter_lazare@hotmail.com
www.powys-society.org
Honorary Secretary *Peter Lazare*
SUBSCRIPTION £18.50 (UK); £22 (overseas); £10 (student)

The Society (with a membership of 300) aims to promote public education and recognition of the writings, thought and contribution to the arts of the Powys family; particularly of John Cowper, Theodore and Llewelyn, but also of the other members of the family and their close associates. The Society holds two major collections of Powys published works, letters, manuscripts and memorabilia. Publishes the *Powys Society Newsletter* in April, June and November and *The Powys Journal* in August. Organises an annual conference as well as lectures and meetings in Powys places.

The J.B. Priestley Society

Eldwick Crag Farm, High Eldwick, Bingley BD16 3BB
☎01274 563078
✉ reavill@globalnet.co.uk
www.jbpriestley-society.com
President *Tom Priestley*
Chairman *Dr Ken Smith*
Honorary Secretary *R.E.Y. Slater*
Membership Secretary *Tony Reavill*
SUBSCRIPTION £10 (individual); £5 (concession); £15 (group/family)

Founded 1997 to widen the knowledge and understanding of Priestley's works; promote the study of his life and his social, cultural and political influences; provide members of the Society with lectures, seminars, films, journals and stimulate education projects; promote public performances of his works and the distribution of material associated with him. For further information, contact the Membership Secretary at the address above.

The Barbara Pym Society

St Hilda's College, Oxford OX4 1DU
☎01865 276867   Fax 01865 276820
✉ eileen.roberts@st-hildas.oxford.ac.uk
www.pym.org
Chairman *Deirdre Bryan-Brown*
SUBSCRIPTION £15 p.a. (individual); £22 p.a. (household); £8 p.a. (concession)

Aims to promote interest in and scholarly research into the works of Barbara Pym; to bring together like-minded people to enjoy the exploration of all aspects of her novels and to continue to encourage publishers to keep her novels in print. Annual weekend conference at St. Hilda's College in September, focusing on a theme or a particular novel. Annual North American Conference at Harvard Law School. Annual one-day spring meeting in London, with speaker. Publishes a newsletter, *Green Leaves*, bi-annually. In addition to reports on conferences and society activities, the newsletter includes scholarly papers and various unpublished items from the Pym archives at the Bodleian Library (i.e. short stories).

The Queen's English Society

Honorary Secretary: The Clergy House, Hide Place, London SW1P 4NJ
☎020 7630 1819
✉ enquiries@queens-english-society.com
www.queens-english-society.com
Honorary Secretary *David Ellis*
SUBSCRIPTION £12 p.a. (ordinary); £15 (family/corporate)

Founded in 1972 to promote and uphold the use of good English and to encourage the enjoyment of the language. Holds regular meetings and conferences to which speakers are invited, an annual luncheon and publishes a quarterly journal, *Quest*, for which original articles are welcome.

Rainbow Poetry Recitals

14 Lewes Crescent, Brighton BN2 1FH
☎01424 444072
Administrators *Hugh Hellicar, Dorothy Steers*
SUBSCRIPTION £6 (individual); £10 (joint/family); £15 (school)

Founded 1994. Regular recitals of poetry and other literature are held in Sussex and London. Seminars and creative writing groups in some branches. Members' library in Sussex. Quarterly magazine.

The Arthur Ransome Society Ltd

Abbot Hall Art Gallery & Museum, Kendal LA9 5AL
☎01539 722464
✉ tarsinfo@arthur-ransome.org
www.arthur-ransome.org/ar
Trustee Chairman *Geraint Lewis*
Company Secretary *Mike Glover*
SUBSCRIPTION UK: £5 (junior); £10 (student); £15 (adult); £20 (family); £40 (corporate); Overseas: £5 (junior); £10 (student); £20 (adult); £25 (family) Payable in local currency in US, Canada, Australia, Japan and NZ

Founded in 1990 to celebrate the life and to promote the works and ideas of Arthur Ransome, author of *Swallows and Amazons* titles for children, biographer of Oscar Wilde, works on the Russian Revolution and extensive articles on fishing. TARS seeks to encourage children and adults to engage in adventurous pursuits, to educate the public about Ransome and his works, and to sponsor research into his literary works and life.

The Romany Society
10 Haslam Street, Bury BL9 6EQ
☎0161 764 7078
✉ philshelley@btopenworld.com
www.romanysociety.org.uk
Honorary Secretary *John Thorpe* (at address above)
Publications Officer *Phil Shelley*
SUBSCRIPTION £5 (individual); £9 (family); £10 (institution); £3.50 (student/unwaged)

Promotes the life, work and conservation message of the Rev. G. Bramwell Evens – 'Romany' – the first broadcasting naturalist who influenced generations of listeners to his *Out With Romany* radio programmes on the BBC during the 1930s and 1940s and with his series of natural history books. The Romany Society was established orignally following Evens' death at the age of 59 in 1943 and ran until 1965. Revived in 1996, the Society holds an annual members' weekend to areas of significance in the Romany story, erects memorial plaques where appropriate, encourages media coverage of Romany and supports young naturalists with the Romany Memorial Grant.

The Followers of Rupert
31 Whiteley, Windsor SL4 5PJ
☎01753 865562
✉ followersofrupert@hotmail.com
www.rupertthebear.org.uk
Membership Secretary *Mrs Shirley Reeves*
SUBSCRIPTION UK: £15; £17 (joint); Europe, airmail: £18 (individual); £20 (joint); RoW, airmail: £20 (individual); £22 (joint)

Founded in 1983. The Society caters for the growing interest in the Rupert Bear stories, past, present and future. Publishes the *Nutwood Newsletter* quarterly which gives up-to-date news of Rupert and information on Society activities. A national get-together of members – the Followers Annual – is held during the autumn.

The Ruskin Society of London
20 Parmoor Court, Summerfield, Oxford OX2 7XB
☎01865 310987   Fax 01865 240448

Honorary Secretary *Miss O.E. Forbes-Madden*
SUBSCRIPTION £15 p.a.

Founded 1986 to promote interest in John Ruskin (1819–1900) and his contemporaries. All aspects of Ruskinia are introduced. Functions are held in London. Publishes the annual *Ruskin Gazette*, a journal concerned with Ruskin's influence. Affiliated to other literary societies.

The Ruskin Society
49 Hallam Street, London W1W 6JP
☎020 7580 1894
✉ cgamble@britishlibrary.net
Honorary Secretary *Dr Cynthia. J. Gamble*
Honorary Treasurer *The Hon. Mrs Catherine Edwards*
SUBSCRIPTION £10 p.a. (payable on 1st Jan.)

Founded in 1997 to encourage a wider understanding of John Ruskin and his contemporaries. Organises lectures and events which seek not only to explain to the public at large the nature of Ruskin's theories but also to place these in a modern context.

The Malcolm Saville Society
78a Windmill Road, Mortimer RG7 3RL
✉ mystery@witchend.com
www.witchend.com
Chairman *Richard Griffiths*
SUBSCRIPTION £7.50 p.a. (UK/EU); £12 (overseas)

Founded in 1994 to remember and promote interest in the work of the popular children's author. Regular social activities, booksearch, library, contact directory and four magazines per year.

The Dorothy L. Sayers Society
Rose Cottage, Malthouse Lane, Hurstpierpoint BN6 9JY
☎01273 833444   Fax 01273 835988
www.sayers.org.uk
Contact *Christopher Dean*
SUBSCRIPTION £14 p.a. (UK); £16.50 (Europe); $34 (US)

Founded 1976 to promote the study of the life, works and thoughts of Dorothy Sayers; to encourage the performance of her plays and publication of her books and books about her; to preserve original material and provide assistance to researchers. Acts as a forum and information centre, providing material for study purposes which would otherwise be unavailable. Annual conventions, usually in August and other meetings. Co-founder of the Dorothy L.

Sayers Centre in Witham. Publishes bi-monthly bulletin, annual proceedings and other papers.

The Bernard Shaw Information & Research Service

27 Cavendish Avenue, South Ruislip HA4 6QJ
✉ dianeuttley@georgebernardshaw.com
www.georgebernardshaw.com
President *Diane S. Uttley*

Established in 1997 by writer and Shaw specialist Diane S. Uttley who was custodian of and lived in the writer's home, Shaw's Corner, from 1989 to 1997. The service is used by enthusiasts and academics; literary, theatrical and biographical.

The Shaw Society

51 Farmfield Road, Downham, Bromley
BR1 4NF
☎020 8697 3619   Fax 020 8697 3619
✉ anthnyellis@aol.com
Honorary Secretary *Ms Barbara Smoker*
SUBSCRIPTION £15 p.a. (individual); £22 (joint)

Founded 1941 to promote interest in the life and works of G. Bernard Shaw. Meetings are held on the last Friday of every month (except July, August and December) at Conway Hall, Red Lion Square, London WC1 (6.30 pm for 7.00 pm) at which speakers are invited to talk on some aspect of Shaw's life or works. Monthly playreadings are held on the first Friday of each month (except August). Over 40 years ago the Society began the annual open-air performance held at Shaw's Corner, Ayot St Lawrence in Hertfordshire, on the weekend nearest to Shaw's birthday (26th July). A celebrity lunch is to be held at RADA on 29 July 2006 to celebrate Shaw's 150th birthday. Publishes a quarterly newsletter and a biannual magazine, *The Shavian*. (No payment for contributors.)

The Robert Southey Society

1 Lewis Terrace, Abergarwed, Neath SA11 4DL
☎01639 711480
Contact *Robert King*
SUBSCRIPTION £10 p.a.

Founded 1990 to promote the work of Robert Southey. Publishes an annual newsletter and arranges talks on his life and work. Open membership.

The Laurence Sterne Trust

See **The Friends of Shandy Hall**

Robert Louis Stevenson Club

12 Dean Park, Longniddry EH32 0QR
☎01875 852976   Fax 01875 853328

✉ alan@amarchbank.freeserve.co.uk
Secretary *Alan Marchbank*
SUBSCRIPTION £20 p.a. (individual); £26 p.a. (overseas); £150 (10-year)

Founded in 1920 to foster interest in Robert Louis Stevenson's life and works. The Club organises an annual lunch and other events. Publishes *RLS Club News* twice a year.

The Bram Stoker Society

43 Castle Court, Killiney Hill Road, Killiney, Republic of Ireland
✉ gothicalbert@eircom.net
benecke.com/stoker.html *and*
benecke.com/vampire.html
Honorary Treasurer *Dr Albert Power*
SUBSCRIPTION £10 p.a. (UK); E10 (Europe); $20 (US/RoW)

Founded 1980. Aims to promote the study and appreciation of Bram Stoker's works, including his place in the Gothic horror tradition, and his influence on later writers in the areas of cinema, music and theatre. Publishes an occasional newsletter, an annual journal of scholarly articles and organises a regular programme of activities with its affiliated body, The Bram Stoker Club of Trinity College Dublin. These include screenings, annual memorial lectures and the annual summer school held in July. Subscription payments by cheque or postal order (made out to The Bram Stoker Society) should be sent to the Hon. Treasurer at the address above.

The R.S. Surtees Society

Manor Farm House, Nunney, Near Frome
BA11 4NJ
☎01373 836937   Fax 01373 836574
✉ rssurtees@fsmail.net
www.r.s.surteessociety.org
Contact *Orders and Membership Secretary*
SUBSCRIPTION £10

Founded 1979 to republish the works of R.S. Surtees and others.

The Tennyson Society

Central Library, Free School Lane, Lincoln
LN2 1EZ
☎01522 552862   Fax 01522 552858
✉ kathleenjefferson@lincolnshire.gov.uk
www.tennysonsociety.org.uk
Honorary Secretary *Miss K. Jefferson*
SUBSCRIPTION £10 p.a. (individual); £12 (family); £15 (corporate); £125 (life)

Founded 1960. An international society with

membership worldwide. Exists to promote the study and understanding of the life and work of Alfred, Lord Tennyson. The Society is concerned with the work of the Tennyson Research Centre, 'probably the most significant collection of mss, family papers and books in the world'. Publishes annually the *Tennyson Research Bulletin*, which contains articles and critical reviews; and organises lectures, visits and seminars. Annual memorial service at Somersby in Lincolnshire.

The Angela Thirkell Society

54 Belmont Park, London SE13 5BN
☎020 8244 9339
✉ penny.aldred@ntlworld.com
www.angelathirkellsociety.com
www.angelathirkell.org (N. American branch)
Honorary Secretary *Mrs. P. Aldred*
SUBSCRIPTION £10 p.a.

Founded in 1980 to honour the memory of Angela Thirkell as a writer and to make her works available to new generations. Publishes an annual journal, holds an AGM in the autumn and a spring meeting which usually takes the form of a visit to a location associated with Thirkell. Has a flourishing North American branch which has frequent contact with the UK parent society.

The Dylan Thomas Society of Great Britain

5 Church Park, Mumbles, Swansea SA3 4DE
☎01792 520080
Contact *Mrs Eryl Jenkins*
SUBSCRIPTION £5 (individual); £8 (two adults from same household)

Founded 1977 to foster an understanding of the work of Dylan Thomas and to extend members' awareness of other 20th century writers, especially Welsh writers in English. Meetings take place monthly, mainly in Swansea.

The Edward Thomas Fellowship

1 Carfax, Undercliff Drive, St Lawrence, Isle of Wight PO38 1XG
☎01983 853366
✉ colingthornton@btopenworld.com
Hon. Secretary *Colin G. Thornton*
SUBSCRIPTION £7 p.a. (single); £10 p.a. (joint)

Founded 1980 to perpetuate and promote the memory of Edward Thomas and to encourage an appreciation of his life and work. The Fellowship holds a commemorative birthday walk on the Sunday nearest the poet's birthday

(3rd March); issues newsletters and holds various events.

The Tolkien Society

65 Wentworth Crescent, Ash Vale GU12 5LF
Fax 0870 0525569
✉ membership@tolkiensociety.org
www.tolkiensociety.org
Membership Secretary *Trevor Reynolds*
SUBSCRIPTION £20 p.a. (UK); £22 (overseas)

An international organisation which aims to encourage and further interest in the life and works of the late Professor J.R.R. Tolkien, CBE, author of *The Hobbit* and *Lord of the Rings*. Current membership stands at 1200. Publishes *Mallorn* annually and *Amon Hen* bi-monthly.

The Trollope Society

Maritime House, Old Town, Clapham, London SW4 0JW
☎020 7720 6789   Fax 020 7627 2965
✉ trollsoc@barset.fsnet.co.uk
www.trollopesociety.org
Contacts *John Letts, Phyllis Eden*

Founded 1987 to study and promote Anthony Trollope's works. Publishes the complete works of Trollope's novels and travel books.

Wainwright Society

Kendal Museum, Station Road, Kendal LA9 6BT
☎01539 721374
✉ membership@wainwright.org.uk
www.wainwright.org.uk
Membership Secretary *Morag Clement*
SUBSCRIPTION £10 p.a. (per household – from 1st Jan.)

Founded in 2002 'to keep alive the things that Alfred Wainwright (1907–1991) promoted through his guidebooks (*Pictorial Guides to the Lakeland Fells*), started 50 years ago, and the many other publications which were the "labour of love" of a large portion of his life'. Produces a newsletter three times per year, organises walks, events, annual dinner and lecture.

Edgar Wallace Society

84 Ridgefield Road, Oxford OX4 3DA
www.edgarwallace.org
Organiser *Miss Penny Wyrd*
SUBSCRIPTION £15 p.a.; £10 (senior citizen/student); overseas: £20; £15 (senior citizen/student)

Founded in 1969 by Wallace's daughter,

Penelope, to bring together all who have an interest in Edgar Wallace. Members receive a brief biography of Edgar by Penelope Wallace, with a list of published book titles. A newsletter, *Crimson Circle*, is published three times a year.

The Walmsley Society

April Cottage, No 1 Brand Road, Hampden Park, Eastbourne BN22 9PX
☎01323 506447
✉ walmsley@haughshw.demon.co.uk
Honorary Secretary *Fred Lane*
SUBSCRIPTION £12 p.a.; £14 (family); £11 (student/senior citizen); £15 (overseas, £25 for 2 years)

Founded 1985 to promote interest in the writings of Leo Walmsley and to foster an appreciation of the work of his father, the artist Ulric Walmsley. Two annual meetings – one held in Robin Hood's Bay on the East Yorkshire coast, spiritual home of the author Leo Walmsley. Publishes a journal twice-yearly and newsletters, and is involved in other publications which benefit the aims of the Society. A biography of Leo Walmsley is now available.

Sylvia Townsend Warner Society

2 Vicarage Lane, Fordington, Dorchester DT1 1LH
☎01305 266028
✉ judith@bond.vispa.com
www.townsendwarner.com
Contact *Eileen Johnson*
SUBSCRIPTION £10 p.a.; $20 (overseas)

Founded in 2000 to promote a wider readership and better understanding of the writings of Sylvia Townsend Warner.

Mary Webb Society

8 The Knowe, Willaston, Neston CH64 1TA
☎0151 327 5843
✉ suehigginbotham@yahoo.co.uk
www.marywebb.VZE.com
Secretary *Sue Higginbotham*
SUBSCRIPTION UK: £10 p.a. (individual); £13 p.a. (joint); Overseas: £13 p.a. (individual); £15 p.a. (joint)

Founded 1972. Attracts members from the UK and overseas who are devotees of the literature of Mary Webb and of the beautiful Shropshire countryside of her novels. Publishes biannual journal, organises summer schools in various locations related to the authoress's life and works. Archives; lectures; tours arranged for individuals and groups.

H.G. Wells Society

51 Riseholme Road, Gainsborough DN21 1YT
hgwellsusa.50megs.com
Honorary Secretary *Dr S. McClean*
SUBSCRIPTION £16 (UK/EU); £19 (overseas); £20 (corporate); £10 (concessions)

Founded 1960 to promote an interest in and appreciation of the life, work and thought of Herbert George Wells. Publishes *The Wellsian* (annual) and *The H.G. Wells Newsletter* (three issues yearly). Organises meetings and conferences.

The Oscar Wilde Society

100 Peacock Street, Gravesend DA12 1EQ
✉ vanessasalome68@aol.com
Honorary Secretary *Vanessa Harris*

Founded 1990 to promote knowledge, appreciation and study of the life, personality and works of the writer and wit Oscar Wilde. Activities include meetings, lectures, readings and exhibitions, and visits to locations associated with Wilde. Members receive a journal, *The Wildean*, twice-yearly and a newsletter, *Intentions* (six per year).

The Charles Williams Society

35 Broomfield, Stacey Bushes, Milton Keynes MK12 6HA
✉ charles_wms_soc@yahoo.co.uk
www.geocities.com/charles_wms_soc
Contact *Honorary Secretary*

Founded 1975 to promote interest in, and provide a means for the exchange of views and information on the life and work of Charles Walter Stansby Williams (1886–1945).

The Henry Williamson Society

7 Monmouth Road, Dorchester DT1 2DE
☎01305 264092
✉ zseagull@aol.com
www.henrywilliamson.org
General Secretary *Mrs Sue Cumming*
Membership Secretary *Mrs Margaret Murphy* (16 Doran Drive, Redhill RH1 6AX
☎01737 763228;
✉ mm@misterman.freeserve.co.uk)
SUBSCRIPTION £12 p.a.; £15 (family); £5 (student)

Founded 1980 to encourage, by all appropriate means, a wider readership and deeper understanding of the literary heritage left by the

20th-century English writer Henry Williamson (1895–1977). Publishes annual journal.

The P.G. Wodehouse Society (UK)

26 Radcliffe Road, Croydon CR0 5QE
✉ christinehewitt@waitrose.com
www.pgwodehousesociety.org.uk
www.eclipse.co.uk/wodehouse
Membership Secretary *Christine Hewitt*
SUBSCRIPTION £15 p.a. (£20 Dec–March, for membership extended to May the following year)

Formed in 1997 to promote enjoyment of the works of P.G. Wodehouse, author, lyricist, playwright and journalist, creator of Lord Emsworth, Jeeves & Wooster and many more. Membership of 1000+. Publications include the quarterly journal, *Wooster Source* and regular *By The Way* papers. Meetings and events are held in London and around the country. The Society is allied to Wodehouse societies around the world.

The Parson Woodforde Society

22 Gaynor Close, Wymondham NR18 0EA
☎01953 604124
✉ mabrayne@supanet.com
www.parsonwoodforde.org.uk
Membership Secretary *Mrs Ann Elliott*
SUBSCRIPTION £12.50 (UK); £25 (overseas)

Founded 1968. Aims to extend and develop knowledge of James Woodforde's life and the society in which he lived and to provide the opportunity for fellow enthusiasts to meet together in places associated with the diarist. Publishes a quarterly journal and newsletter. The Society is producing a complete edition of the diary of James Woodforde. To date, fourteen volumes of diary material have been published covering the period 1759–1795.

The Virginia Woolf Society of Great Britain

Fairhaven, Charnleys Lane, Banks, Southport PR9 8HJ
✉ stuart.n.clarke@btinternet.com
www.virginiawoolfsociety.co.uk
Contact *Stuart N. Clarke*
SUBSCRIPTION £15 p.a.; £20 (overseas)

Founded 1998 to promote interest in the life and work of Virginia Woolf, author, essayist and diarist. The Society's activities include trips away, walks, reading groups and talks. Publishes a literary journal, *Virginia Woolf Bulletin*, three times a year.

The Wordsworth Trust

Dove Cottage, Grasmere LA22 9SH
☎01539 435544   Fax 01539 435748
✉ enquiries@wordsworth.org.uk
www.wordsworth.org.uk
Contacts *Natalie Tye, Allan King*

Founded in 1890, the Trust is a living memorial to the life and poetry of William Wordsworth and his contemporaries. As the centre for British Romanticism, the Trust, with its wealth of manuscripts, books, drawings and pictures, provides the full context for understanding and celebrating a major cultural moment in history in which Britain played a profound role. (Registered Charity No. 1066184.)

WW2 HMSO PPBKS Society

3 Roman Road, Southwick BN42 4TP
☎01273 871017   Fax 01273 871017
Contact *A.R. James*

Founded 1994 to encourage collectors and to promote research into HMSO's World War II series of paperbacks. Most of them were written by well-known authors, though in many cases anonymously. No subscription charge. Available for purchase: Collectors' Guide (£5); Bibliography (£3); Handbook, *Informing the People* (£10).

The Yeats Society Sligo

Yeats Memorial Building, Douglas Hyde Bridge, Sligo, Republic of Ireland
☎00 353 71 914 2693
Fax 00 353 71 914 2780
✉ info@yeats-sligo.com
www.yeats-sligo.com
President *Michael Keohane*
SUBSCRIPTION €25 (single); €40 (couple); €127 (corporate)

Founded in 1958 to promote the heritage of W.B. Yeats and the Yeats family. Attractions include continuous updated Yeats exhibitions for public viewing, annual Yeats International Summer School in August and Yeats Winter School in January. The Yeats Summer Festival is held each August and lectures are held in the winter and spring, sponsored by the Institute of Technology, Sligo. Poetry readings and workshops aimed at local writers are held on a regular basis in conjunction with Arts Officer, Sligo Co. Council.

Yorkshire Dialect Society

51 Stepney Avenue, Scarborough YO12 5BW
Secretary *Michael Park*
SUBSCRIPTION £10 p.a.

Founded 1897 to promote interest in and preserve a record of the Yorkshire dialect. Publishes dialect verse and prose writing. Two journals to members annually. Details of publications are available from YDS, 61 Moor Lane, Carnaby, Bridlington YO16 4UT.

Francis Brett Young Society

92 Gower Road, Halesowen B62 9BT
☎0121 422 8969
www.fbysociety.co.uk
Honorary Secretary *Mrs Jean Hadley*
SUBSCRIPTION £7 p.a. (individual); £10 (couple sharing a journal); £5 (student); £7 (organisation/overseas); £70 (life); £100 (joint, life)

Founded 1979. Aims to provide a forum for those interested in the life and works of English novelist Francis Brett Young and to collate research on him. Promotes lectures, exhibitions and readings; publishes a regular newsletter.

Arts Councils and Regional Offices

Arts Council England
14 Great Peter Street, London SW1P 3NQ
☎020 7333 0100 Textphone 020 7973 6564
Fax 020 7973 6590
✉ enquiries@artscouncil.org.uk
www.artscouncil.org.uk
Chairman *Professor Sir Christopher Frayling*
Chief Executive *Peter Hewitt*
Director of Literature *Gary McKeone*

Founded 1946. Arts Council England is the national development agency for the arts in England, distributing public money from government and the National Lottery to artists and arts organisations. Arts Council England works independently and at arm's length from government. Information about Arts Council England funding is available on the website, by e-mail or by contacting the enquiry line on 0845 300 6200.

Arts Council England has 9 regional offices:

Arts Council England, East
Eden House, 48–49 Bateman Street,
Cambridge CB2 1LR
☎0845 300 6200 Fax 0870 242 1271
Textphone 01223 306893

Arts Council England, East Midlands
St Nicholas Court, 25–27 Castle Gate,
Nottingham NG1 7AR
☎0845 300 6200 Fax 0115 950 2467

Arts Council England, London
2 Pear Tree Court, London EC1R 0DS
☎0845 300 6200 Fax 020 7608 4100
Textphone 020 7608 4101

Arts Council England, North East
Central Square, Forth Street, Newcastle upon
Tyne NE1 3PJ
☎0845 300 6200 Fax 0191 230 1020
Textphone 0191 255 8500

Arts Council England, North West
Manchester House, 22 Bridge Street,
Manchester M3 3AB
☎0845 300 6200 Fax 0161 834 6969
Textphone 0161 834 9131

Arts Council England, South East
Sovereign House, Church Street, Brighton
BN1 1RA
☎0845 300 6200 Fax 0870 242 1257
Textphone 01273 710659

Arts Council England, South West
Bradninch Place, Gandy Street, Exeter
EX4 3LS
☎0845 300 6200 Fax 01392 229229
Textphone 01392 433503

Arts Council England, West Midlands
82 Granville Street, Birmingham B1 2LH
☎0845 300 6200 Fax 0121 643 7239
Textphone 0121 643 2815

Arts Council England, Yorkshire
21 Bond Street, Dewsbury WF13 1AX
☎0845 300 6200 Fax 01924 466522
Textphone 01924 438585

The Arts Council/ An Chomhairle Ealaíon
70 Merrion Square, Dublin 2, Republic of
Ireland
☎00 353 1 618 0200   Fax 00 353 1 676 1302
✉ artistsservices@artscouncil.ie
www.artscouncil.ie
Director *Mary Cloake*
Literature Specialist (English language)
  Bronwen Williams
Literature Specialist (Irish language) *Róisín Ní
  Mhianáin*
Artists' Services Manager *Paul Johnson*

The development agency for the arts in Ireland. An autonomous statutory body, appointed by the Irish government to promote and assist the arts. Established by the Arts Act of 1951. In fulfilling its remit, the Council provides advice to the Irish government on artistic matters; advice, assistance and support to individuals, arts organisations and a wide range of governmental and non-governmental bodies; and financial assistance to individuals and organisations for artistic purposes. The Council also part funds the programmes of county and city arts officers throughout the country. It consists of 12 members and a chair appointed by the Minister for Arts, Sport and Tourism for a period of not more than five years. Its state grant in 2005 was €61 million.

Of particular interest to individual writers is

the Council's free booklet, *Support for Artists*, which describes bursaries, awards and schemes on offer and how to apply for them. Applicants to these awards must have been born in, or be resident in, the Republic of Ireland.

The Arts Council of Northern Ireland

MacNeice House, 77 Malone Road, Belfast BT9 6AQ
☎028 9038 5200   Fax 028 9066 1715
✉ dsmyth@artscouncil-ni.org
www.artscouncil-ni.org
Literature and Language Arts Officer *Damian Smyth*

Funds book production by established publishers, programmes of readings, literary festivals, writers-in-residence schemes and literary magazines and periodicals. Occasional schools programmes and anthologies of children's writing are produced. Annual awards and bursaries for writers are available. Holds information also on various groups associated with local arts, workshops and courses.

Scottish Arts Council

12 Manor Place, Edinburgh EH3 7DD
☎0131 226 6051   Fax 0131 225 9833
✉ help.desk@scottisharts.org.uk
www.scottisharts.org.uk

Director *Graham Berry*
Head of Literature *Gavin Wallace*
Literature Officers *Jenny Attala, Sophy Dale*
Literature Secretary *Catherine Allan*

Principal channel for government funding of the arts in Scotland. The Scottish Arts Council (SAC) is funded by the Scottish Executive. It aims to develop and improve the knowledge, understanding and practice of the arts, and to increase their accessibility throughout Scotland. It offers around 1300 grants a year to artists and arts organisations concerned with the visual arts, crafts, dance and mime, drama, literature, music, festivals and traditional, ethnic and community arts. It is also a distributor of National Lottery funds to the arts in Scotland. SAC's support for Scottish-based writers with a track record of publication includes bursaries, writing fellowships and book awards (see entries under **Bursaries, Fellowships and Grants** and **Prizes**). Information offered includes lists of literature awards, literary magazines, agents and publishers.

The Arts Council of Wales/ Cyngor Celfyddydau Cymru

9 Museum Place, Cardiff CF10 3NX
☎029 2037 6500   Fax 029 2022 1447
www.artswales.org.uk
www.celfcymru.org.uk

The Arts Council of Wales (ACW) is the development body for the arts in Wales. Specific responsibility for services to individual writers, including bursaries, mentoring, the critical writers services and writers in residence/on tour are provided by the **Welsh Academy** and **Ty Newydd Writers' Centre**. Responsibility for promoting the publishing and sales of books from Wales and funding literary magazines rests with the **Welsh Books Council**. ACW also provides other bursaries and grant schemes that might be of interest and benefit to writers.

UK Writers' Courses

ENGLAND

Berkshire

University of Reading
The School of Continuing Education, London Road, Reading RG1 5AQ
☎0118 378 8347
✉ Cont-Ed@reading.ac.uk
www.reading.ac.uk/ContEd
An expanding programme of creative writing courses, including *Life into Fiction*; *Poetry Workshop*; *Getting Started*; *Writing Fiction*; *Publishing Poetry*; *Scriptwriting*; *Playwriting, Travel Writing*; *Comedy Writing* and *Writing for Radio*. There is also a public lecture by a writer and a reading by students of their work, and various Saturday workshops. Tutors include novelist Leslie Wilson and poets Jane Draycott and Susan Utting, David Grubb and Paul Bavister. Fees vary depending on the length of course. Concessions available.

The Write Coach
2 Rowan Close, Wokingham RG41 4BH
☎0118 978 4904
✉ enquiries@thewritecoach.co.uk
www.thewritecoach.co.uk
Contact *Rebecca Hill*
Workshops and one-to-one coaching (both in person and by telephone) 'to assist both professional and aspiring writers to become more successful, break through their blocks, build confidence, increase motivation and expand creativity'. Free e-zine and free initial consultation available. See website for details.

Buckinghamshire

Missenden Abbey Adult Learning,
Great Missenden HP16 0BD
☎0845 045 4040   Fax 01753 783756
✉ adultlearningchil@buckscc.gov.uk
www.aredu.org.uk/missendenabbey
Residential and non-residential weekend workshops, Easter and summer school. Programmes have included *Writing Stories for Children*; *Short Story Writing*; *Poetry Workshop*; *Writing for TV and Film*; *Writing Comedy for Television*; *Life Writing*; *Travel Tales*.

National Film & Television School
Beaconsfield Studios, Station Road, Beaconsfield HP9 1LG
☎01494 731425   Fax 01494 674042
✉ info@nftsfilm-tv.ac.uk
www.nftsfilm-tv.ac.uk
www.nftsscreenwriting.org
Two-year programme covering all aspects of screenwriting from the development of ideas through to final production. Studying alongside other filmmaking students allows writers to have their work tested in workshops and productions. Unlike a Screenwriting MA set in an academic institution, this course is set in a working studio and the emphasises practical filmmaking and contact with industry personnel through seminars and pitching sessions. The course requires and encourages a high level of dedication and a prolific output. Year One deals with the basic principles of storytelling, the craft of screenwriting for film and television and the collaborative nature of production, and includes several short writing assignments. Year Two focuses on longer writing assignments, with students writing a feature script and TV project as well as their MA dissertation. Opportunities may be available to write short fiction or animation scripts for production. A five-week *Feature Development* course is also offered at intervals during the year – details available from the Screenwriting Department's website or the main School website. In partnership with **The Script Factory**, The NFTS also offers a two-year, part-time Diploma in *Script Development*.

Cambridgeshire

National Extension College
Michael Young Centre, Purbeck Road, Cambridge CB2 2HN
☎01223 400350   Fax 01223 400325
✉ info@nec.ac.uk
www.nec.ac.uk/courses/arts
Runs a number of home-study courses on wri-

ting which include: *Essential Editing*; *Creative Writing* (which leads to an OCN Level 2 Cert.); *Writing for Money*; *Essential Design*. Contact the NEC for a free copy of the *Guide to Courses* which includes details of fees and course enrolment. 'You can enrol at any time, study at home, work at your own pace and fit learning into your lives.' The NEC is accredited by the Open Distance Learning Quality Council.

University of Cambridge Institute of Continuing Education

Madingley Hall, Madingley, Cambridge
CB3 8AQ
☎01954 280399   Fax 01954 280200
www.cont-ed.cam.ac.uk

A wide range of weekend, five-day and week-long creative writing courses for adults is offered by the University at the Institute of Continuing Education's residential headquarters at Madingley Hall. Evening courses are also available in Cambridgeshire and surrounding areas. Details of all courses can be found on the website or phone for a brochure.

Cheshire

Burton Manor

Burton Village, Neston CH64 5SJ
☎0151 336 5172   Fax 0151 336 6586
✉ enquiry@burtonmanor.com
www.burtonmanor.com

Wide variety of short courses, residential and non-residential on writing and literature, including *Creative Writing Workshop* and *Press Workshop*. Full details in brochure.

Cornwall

University College Falmouth

Woodlane, Falmouth TR11 4RH
☎01326 211077
www.falmouth.ac.uk
www.bloc-online.com (magazine)

Contact *Admissions*

Postgraduate/MA professional writing pro-gramme. An intensive vocational writing pro-gramme developing skills in fiction, magazine journalism/features, screenwriting. Students work on an extended writing project and form links with other PgDips such as television pro-duction and broadcast journalism. The course website won a Guardian Media Award 1999.

Cumbria

Higham Hall College

Bassenthwaite Lake, Cockermouth CA13 9SH
☎01768 776276   Fax 01768 776013
✉ admin@highamhall.com
www.highamhall.com

Winter and summer residential courses. Programme includes *Creative Writing*; *Writing for Radio and TV*. Brochure available.

Derbyshire

Real Writers

PO Box 170, Chesterfield S40 1FE
☎01246 238492   Fax 01246 520934
✉ info@real-writers.com
www.real-writers.com

Correspondence service with personal tuition from working writers. Also runs an annual short story competition. Send s.a.e. for details.

Swanwick – The Writers' Summer School

The Hayes Conference Centre, Nr Alfreton
Derbyshire
✉ jean.sutton@lineone.net

Secretary *Jean Sutton*

Offers six-days of informal talks, discussion groups, interactive workshops and quizzes. Com-petitions and 'a lot of fun'. All levels welcome. Held mid-August from Saturday to Friday morning. Cost (2005) £285–420 per person, all inclusive. S.a.e. to the Secretary at 10 Stag Road, Lake, Sandown, Isle of Wight PO36 8PE (☎01983 406759/e-mail as above).

University of Derby

Admissions Office, Kedleston Road, Derby
DE22 1GB
☎01332 622236   Fax 01332 622754
✉ J.Bains@derby.ac.uk
www.derby.ac.uk

Contact *Carl Tighe*

With upwards of 300 students, this is one of the oldest *Creative Writing* operations at degree level in the UK. The subject offers a BA Hons *Creative Writing* with particular strengths in Short Stories, Writing and New Technologies and Storytelling. All teaching is done through practical workshops led by established and experienced writers. In the final year students produce an independent research project on a subject of their choice. The subject also con-tributes to the BA Hons Combined Studies.

Devon

Arvon Foundation (Devon)
See entry under **Greater London**

Dartington College of Arts
Totnes TQ9 6EJ
☎01803 862224   Fax 01803 861666
✉ registry@dartington.ac.uk
www.dartington.ac.uk

BA(Hons) *Writing* or *Writing (Contemporary Practices)* or *Writing (Scripted Media)*: exploratory approaches to writing as it relates to performance, visual arts, sound arts and contemporary culture. Encourages the interdisciplinary, with minor awards and electives in arts and cultural management, choreography, music, theatre, visual performance. Contact Director of Writing: see www.dartington.ac.uk/pw/

Exeter Phoenix
Bradninch Place, Gandy Street, Exeter EX4 3LS
☎01392 667080   Fax 01392 667599
www.exeterphoenix.org.uk

Regular literature events, focusing on readings by living poets and other writers, often linked to wider performance programmes including the annual tEXt festival in May. Tutors in a wide range of writing skills run classes and workshops, listed in the brochure of Phoenix activities. 'Uncut Poets' group holds monthly meetings.

Fire in the Head Creative Writing Programme
PO Box 17, Yelverton PL20 6YF
☎01822 841081
✉ roselle.angwin@internet-today.co.uk
www.fire-in-the-head.co.uk
Contact *Roselle Angwin*

Imaginative and comprehensive year-round writing programme in poetry, fiction (short and novel-writing), reflective writing and creative development. Roselle Angwin, director and tutor, is a poet and author whose courses have been featured in *The Guardian* and *The Sunday Times*. Also available is an editorial consultancy.

University of Exeter
Room 206, School of English, Queen's Building, Queen's Drive, Exeter EX4 4QH
☎01392 264352   Fax 01392 264594
✉ soe.pgoffice@ex.ac.uk
www.ex.ac.uk/english

Offers BA (Hons) in *English* with 2nd and 3rd-year options in creative writing, poetry, short fiction, screenwriting and creative non-fiction.

MA *English with Creative Writing*: poetry, novella, screenwriting, life writing and novel. PhD *Creative Writing*.

Dorset

Bournemouth University
Bournemouth Media School, Weymouth House, Talbot Campus, Fern Barrow, Poole BH12 5BB
☎01202 595553   Fax 01202 595530
Programme Administrator *Katrina King*

Three-year, full-time BA(Hons) course in *Scriptwriting for Film and Television*.

Essex

National Council for the Training of Journalists
Latton Bush Centre, Southern Way, Harlow CM18 7BL
☎01279 430009   Fax 01279 438008
✉ info@nctj.com
www.nctj.com

For details of journalism courses, both full-time and via distance learning, please write to the NCTJ enclosing a large s.a.e. or visit the website.

Writing Life
PO Box 4065, Braintree CM7 9RJ
☎01376 343759
✉ info@creativewritinglife.co.uk
www.creativewritinglife.co.uk
Contact *Mrs Bernie Ross*

Home study course. Postal and e-mail tuition in *Creative Writing*, from anywhere in the world. Fiction speciality: one-off critiques and on-going mentoring. Also: economy e-mail-only version: www.writing-in-a-nutshell.net

Gloucestershire

Chrysalis – The Poet In You
with Jay Ramsay, BA Hons (Oxon), PGDip, UKCP member
5 Oxford Terrace, Uplands, Stroud GL5 1TW
☎01453 759436/020 7794 8880
✉ jay@ramsay3892.fsnet.co.uk
www.lotusfoundation.org.uk

Offers postal courses, day and weekend workshops (including 'The Sacred Space of the Word'), an on-going poetry group based in London and Gloucestershire and individual therapy related to the participant's creative process. The Chrysalis course itself consists of Part 1, 'for those who feel drawn to reading more poetry as well as wanting to start to write their own', and Part 2, 'a more in-depth course designed for those who are already writing and who want to go more deeply into its process and technique, its background and cultural history'. Both courses combine course notes with in-depth individual correspondence and feedback. Editing and information about publication also provided. Brochure and workshop dates available from the address above.

Wye Valley Arts Centre
The Coach House, Mork, St Briavel's, Lydney GL15 6QH
☎01594 530214/01291 689463
Fax 01594 530321
✉ wyeart@cwcom.net
www.wyeart.cwc.net

Residential courses (Monday to Friday and weekends) – held at The Coach House, a country house near Tintern Abbey – include *Creative Writing* and *Fiction Workshop*. 'All styles and abilities. Companions and other guests not taking the courses are welcome to stay.'

Hampshire

Annual Writers' Conference, Bookfair & Workshops, Winchester
University College Winchester, Winchester SO22 4NR
☎01962 827056
✉ barbara.large@writers-conference.com *or* kate.harrison@winchester.ac.uk
www.winchester.ac.uk
www.awc-workshops.ndo.co.uk
Conference Director *Barbara Large, MBE, FRSA, FUCW*
Honorary Patron *Beryl Bainbridge*
23–30 July 2006. This Festival of Writing, now in its 26th year, attracts international authors, playwrights, poets, agents and editors who give workshops, mini courses, editor appointments, lectures and seminars to help writers harness their creativity and develop their writing, editing and marketing skills. Fifteen writing competitions are attached to the conference. All first-place winners are published in *The Best of* series annually. The Bookfair offers delegates a wide choice of exhibits including Internet author services, publishers, booksellers, printers and trade associations. See also **Pitstop**

Refuelling Writers' Weekend Workshops under *Writers' Circles and Workshops*.

Highbury College, Portsmouth
Dovercourt Road, Cosham, Portsmouth PO6 2SA
☎023 9238 3131   Fax 023 9237 8382
✉ media.journalism@highbury.ack.uk
www.highbury.ac.uk
Contact *Course Administrator* (☎023 9231 3287)

The 20-week fast-track courses include: *Pre-entry Magazine Journalism*; *Pre-entry Newspaper Journalism*; and Postgraduate Diploma in *Broadcasting Journalism*, run under the auspices of the Periodicals Training Council, the National Council for Training of Journalists and the Broadcast Journalism Training Council respectively.

Southampton Institute
East Park Terrace, Southampton SO14 0YN
☎023 8031 9000
✉ Richard.Hudson@Solent.ac.uk
www.solent.ac.uk
Contact *Rick Hudson* (☎023 8031 9097)

Courses offered: BA(Hons) *Media Writing*; BA (Hons) *Writing Fashion & Culture*; BA(Hons) *Journalism*. Writing may be taken as a specialism in MA *Media* or BA *Popular Fiction* and BA *Screenwriting*; BA *Magazine Journalism and Feature Writing*.

University College Winchester
Winchester SO22 4NR
☎01962 841515   Fax 01962 842280
www.winchester.ac.uk
Contact *Enquiries* (☎01962 827249)

Three-year degree course in *Journalism*, including practical modules in broadcasting, production, web design, news and feature writing.
   Three-year degree course in *Drama, Community Theatre and Media Creative Writing* (as part of joint honours), including *Writing for Devised Community Theatre* and *Writing for Television Documentary*.
   MA course in *Theatre for Development* – one year, full-time course with major project overseas or in the UK. MA course in *Writing for Children* available on either a one or two-year basis. Also MA in *Creative and Critical Writing*.

University of Portsmouth
School of Creative Arts, Film and Media, Portsmouth PO1 2DZ
☎023 9284 6132   Fax 023 9284 3082
✉ creative@port.ac.uk

Contact *School of Creative Arts, Film and Media*
Offers creative writing degrees across a wide
range of undergraduate programmes. Both MA
and PhD are available. The School is a partner
in a national AHRB Research training project
in Creative Writing. Staff include national and
international award-winning writers. Runs an
annual creative writing conference and regular
international events.

Hertfordshire

Liberato Breakaway Writing Courses
9 Bishop's Avenue, Bishop's Stortford
CM23 3EJ
☎01279 833690
✉ liberato@tesco.net
www.liberato.co.uk
Contact *Maureen Blundell*

Specialises in beginner fiction writers with day,
weekend and week-long courses. Emphasis on
individual writing with written ms critiques
and one-to-one sessions. Weekends held at
Polstead in Suffolk throughout the year. Greek
weeks in June on the Saronic island of Agistri –
fiction and songwriting courses. Four-day fic-
tion/poetry course at Leiston, near Aldeburgh
in Suffolk in September. Fiction and poetry
days in the Gibberd Garden, Old Harlow, Essex,
March to November. Also offers postal and e-
mail ms critiques on all fiction/autobiography.

Isle of Wight

Annual Writers' Weekend Conference
F ★ F Productions, 39 Ranelagh Road,
Sandown PO36 8NT
☎01983 407772   Fax 01983 407772
✉ felicity@writeplot.co.uk
www.writeplot.co.uk
Contact *Felicity Fair Thompson*

Kent

North West Kent College
Oakfield Lane, Dartford DA1 2JT
☎01322 629436/0800 074 1447 (Freephone
helpline)   Fax 01322 629468
www.nwkent.ac.uk
Contact *Neil Nixon*, Head of School, Media &
    Communications

Two-year, full-time course that explores writing

from a number of angles, teaching essential skills,
market and academic aspects of the subject.
Successful students progress to work or the University of Greenwich, the latter option allowing
them to gain a BA(Hons) in Humanities from a
further year of study. Staff include scriptwriters,
novelists and a book publisher. Students compile
a portfolio in the final year.

University of Kent
Information, Advice & Guidance Unit, APS,
The Registry, Canterbury CT2 7NZ
☎01227 827272
✉ information@kent.ac.uk
www.kent.ac.uk

Undergraduate certificate courses in *Practical
Writing* and *Imaginative Writing*. Also combined
studies – *English and Creative Writing*.

Lancashire

Alston Hall College
Alston Lane, Longridge, Preston PR3 3BP
☎01772 784661   Fax 01772 785835
✉ alston.hall@ed.lancscc.gov.uk
www.alstonhall.com

Holds regular day and residential *Creative
Writing* workshops. Full colour brochure available.

Edge Hill College of Higher Education
St Helen's Road, Ormskirk L39 4QP
☎01695 575171
✉ sheppard@edgehill.ac.uk
Contact *Dr R. Sheppard*

Offers a two-year, part-time MA in *Writing
Studies*. Combines advanced-level writers' workshops with closely related courses in the poetics
of writing and contemporary writing in English.
There is also provision for MPhil and PhD-level
research in writing and poetics. A full range of
creative writing courses is available at undergraduate level, in poetry and fiction writing
which may be taken as part of a modular BA.

Lancaster University
English & Creative Writing, Bowland College,
Bailrigg, Lancaster LA1 4YN
☎01524 594169   Fax 01524 594247
✉ l.kellett@lancaster.ac.uk
Contact *Lyn Kellett*

Offers practical graduate and undergraduate
courses in writing fiction, poetry and scripts. All
based on group workshops – students' work-in-

progress is circulated and discussed. Distance learning MA now available. Graduates include Andrew Miller, Justin Hill, Monique Roffey, Alison MacLeod, Jacob Polley.

Leicestershire

Leicester Adult Education College, Writing School

2 Wellington Street, Leicester LE1 6HL
☎0116 233 4343   Fax 0116 233 4344
✉ vm1@leicester-adult-ed.ac.uk
www.leicester-adult-ed.ac.uk

Contact *Valerie Moore*

Offers a wide range of part time creative writing and journalism courses throughout the year. The programme offers a mix of critical workshops, one-day and term-length courses, and short craft modules. Supports writers through to publication and has strong links with local media.

Greater London

Arvon Foundation

National Administration: 2nd Floor, 42A Buckingham Palace Road, London SW1W 0RE
☎020 7931 7611   Fax 020 7963 0961
www.arvonfoundation.org

Devon: Totleigh Barton, Sheepwash, Beaworthy EX21 5NS
☎01409 231338 Fax 01409 231144
Email t-barton@arvonfoundation.org

Yorkshire: Lumb Bank, Heptonstall, Hebden Bridge HX7 6DF
☎01422 843714   Fax 01422 843714
✉ l-bank@arvonfoundation.org

Inverness-shire: Moniack Mhor, Teavarran, Kiltarlity, Beauly IV4 7HT
☎01463 741675
✉ m-mhor@arvonfoundation.org

Shropshire: The Hurst, Clunton, Craven Arms SY7 0JA
☎01588 640658 Fax 01588 640509
✉ hurst@arvonfoundation.org

Joint Presidents *Terry Hands, Sir Robin Chichester-Clark*
Chairman *Prue Skene, CBE*
National Director *Stephanie Anderson*

Founded 1968. Offers people of any age (over 16) and any background the opportunity to live and work with professional writers. Four-and-a-half-day residential courses are held throughout

the year at Arvon's four centres, covering poetry, fiction, drama, writing for children, songwriting and the performing arts. Bursaries towards the cost of course fees are available for those on low incomes, the unemployed, students and pensioners. Runs a biennial poetry competition (see entry under *Prizes*).

Birkbeck College, University of London

School of English and Humanities, Malet Street, London WC1E 7HX
☎020 77079 0689
✉ A.Whiting@bbk.ac.uk
www.bbk.ac.uk/eh/eng

Contact *Anne Marie Whiting*

Taught by published writers, Birkbeck offers an MA course in *Fiction Writing*. The course will extend and cultivate existing writing skills, help develop writing to a professional level and is supported by masterclasses and readings from visiting professionals. All classes are held in the evening. Study part-time over two years or full-time over one year. Applications must be supported by a portfolio of creative writing. Download an application form from the website.

The Central School of Speech and Drama

Embassy Theatre, Eton Avenue, London NW3 3HY
☎020 7722 8183   Fax 020 7722 4132
✉ n.wood@cssd.ac.uk

Contact *Nick Wood*, Course Leader

MA in *Advanced Theatre Practice*. One-year, full-time course aimed at providing a grounding in principal areas of professional theatre practice – *Writing for Performance, Dramaturgy, Directing, Performance, Puppetry* and *Design*, with an emphasis on collaboration between the various strands. *Writing for Performance* students have the opportunity of working with companies to create new and innovative work for the theatre. Prospectus available. Nick Wood is also editor of the Dramaturgy Forum website www.dramforum.net

City Lit

Keeley Street, Covent Garden, London WC2B 4BA
☎020 7492 2652   Fax 020 7492 8256
✉ humanities@citylit.ac.uk

The Writing School offers a wide range of courses from *Ways Into Creative Writing* and *Writing for Children* to *Playwriting* and *Writing*

Short Stories. Various lengths of course available. The Department offers information and advice during term time.

City University

Education and Lifelong Learning, Northampton Square, London EC1V 0HB
☎020 7040 8268   Fax 020 7040 8256
✉ conted@city.ac.uk
www.city.ac.uk/conted/cfa/write

The Courses for Adults evening programme includes: *Certificate in Novel Writing* (three term course); *Novel Writing and Longer Works; Towards Publication; Writing Crime Fiction; Writing for Children; Writing Television Drama.*

The Complete Creative Writing Course at the Groucho Club

☎020 7249 3711   Fax 020 7683 8141
✉ maggie.h@blueyonder.co.uk
www.creative-writing.pwp.blueyonder.co.uk

Contact *Maggie Hamand*

Courses of ten two-hour sessions held at the Groucho Club in London's Soho, starting in January, April and September, Monday or Saturday afternoons, 2.30 pm – 4.30 pm. Beginners and advanced courses offered. Courses include stimulating exercises, discussion and weekly homework. The tutors are novelists Maggie Hamand and Henrietta Seredy. £195 for whole course.

The Drill Hall

16 Chenies Street, London WC1E 7EX
☎020 7307 5061   Fax 020 7307 5062
✉ admin@drillhall.co.uk
www.drillhall.co.uk

Holds a number of writing classes and workshops. Regular tutors include Carol Burns and Peter Carty.

London College of Communication

Elephant & Castle, London SE1 6SB
☎020 7514 6562
✉ info@lcc.arts.ac.uk
www.lcctraining.co.uk
www.lcc.arts.ac.uk

Intensive courses in journalism. Short courses, run by ARTSCOM at the Elephant & Castle address above, include: *News Writing; Feature Writing; Sub-editing; Scriptwriting for TV & Film.* Also offers five-day specialist journalism courses in newswriting, subediting, print journalism, radio journalism and online journalism plus a three-week course in broadcast TV journalism. In addition, *Effective Copywriting, Effective Writing Techniques for Public Relations.* For individuals and companies 'tailor-made training' services can be provided. Prospectus and information leaflets available; ☎020 7514 8193 or access the website.

London School of Journalism

126 Shirland Road, London W9 2BT
☎020 7289 7777   Fax 020 7432 8141
✉ info@lsjournalism.com
www.home-study.com

Contact *Student Administration Office*

Distance learning courses with an individual and personal approach. Students remain with the same tutor throughout the course. Options include: *Short Story Writing; Writing for Children; Poetry; Freelance Journalism; Media Law; Improve Your English; Cartooning; Thriller Writing.* Fees vary but range from £295 for *Enjoying English Literature* to £395 for *Journalism and Newswriting.* NUJ-recognised Postgraduate Diploma Courses taught in London (three month full-time, six month part-time, nine month evening classes). Online postgraduate diploma course also available.

Middlesex University

School of Humanities, White Hart Lane, London N17 8HR
☎020 8411 5000   Fax 020 8411 6652
✉ tmadmissions@mdx.ac.uk
www.mdx.ac.uk

The UK's longest established writing degree offers a Single or Joint Honours programme in *Creative and Media Writing* (full or part-time). This modular programme gives an opportunity to explore journalism, poetry, prose fiction and dramatic writing for a wide range of genres and audiences. Option for work experience in the media and publishing. Contact Admissions or *Maggie Butt,* Programme Leader (m.butt@mdx. ac.uk)

MA in *Writing* (full-time, part-time; day and evening classes) includes writing workshops; critical seminars; lectures and workshops from established writers; introduction to agents and publishers. Options available: Fiction, Poetry or Scriptwriting. Contact *Sue Gee* ☎020 8411 5941 (s.gee@mdx.ac.uk)

Also offer research degrees M.Phil/PhD in *Creative Writing.* The University has a thriving Writing Centre running an annual literary festival, weekly talks, community projects and writers in residence.

PMA Training
The PMA Centre for Media Excellence,
10 Cynthia Street, London N1 9JF
☎020 7278 0606
✉ training@pma-group.com
www.pma-group.com

One/two/three-day editorial, PR, design and publishing courses held in central London. High-powered, intensive courses run by Fleet Street journalists and magazine editors. Courses leading to a Gold Standard qualification include: *News-Writing*; *Feature Writing*; *Investigative Reporting*. Fees range from £360 to £780 plus VAT. Special rates for freelances.

Roehampton University
Roehampton Lane, London SW15 5PUH
☎020 8392 3232   Fax 020 8392 3131
www.roehampton.ac.uk

Three-year BA(Hons) programmes in *Drama, Theatre and Performance Studies*; *Television Studies*; *Film Studies and Screen Practice* include courses on writing for stage and screen, creative writing, cultural and news studies and journalism.

The Script Factory
Welbeck House, 66–67 Wells Street, London W1T 3PY
☎020 7323 1414
✉ general@scriptfactory.co.uk
www.scriptfactory.co.uk

Established in 1996, The Script Factory is a screenwriter and script developer organisation set up to bridge the gap between writers and the industry, and to promote excellence in screenwriting. Specialising in training, screenings, masterclasses and various services from its base in central London, The Script Factory operates throughout the UK and internationally. For the best source of information on upcoming activities, courses and latest news, and to join the free mailing list, check out the website

Soho Theatre Company
See entry under *Theatre Producers*

Travellers' Tales
92 Hillfield Road, London NW6 1QA
✉ info@travellers-tales.net
www.travellers-tales.net

Travellers' Tales is Britain's only training agency for first-time travel writers and photographers. Offers professional courses in inspiring locations with top experts. Tutors include award-winning authors William Dalrymple and Colin Thubron, and travel editors Hilary Bradt and Jonathan

Lorie. Weekend courses are held in London and week-long retreats on remote Cornish cliffs.

University of Westminster
School of Media, Arts and Design, Harrow Campus, Watford Road, Harrow HA1 3TP
☎020 7911 5903   Fax 020 7911 5955
✉ harrow-admissions@wmin.ac.uk
www.wmin.ac.uk

Courses include part-time MAs available in *Journalism Studies*; *Film and Television Studies*; *Screenwriting and Producing*; *Public Communication and Public Relations*; *Communication and Communication Policy*.

Greater Manchester

Manchester Metropolitan University – The Writing School
Department of English, Geoffrey Manton Building, Rosamond Street West, off Oxford Road, Manchester M15 6LL
☎0161 247 1732/1   Fax 0161 247 6345
✉ m.schmidt@mmu.ac.uk

Course Convenors *Michael Schmidt, Heather Beck* (online)

Closely associated with **Carcanet Press Ltd** and *PN Review*, The Writing School offers two 'routes' for students to follow: *Poetry* and *The Novel*. A key feature of the programme is regular readings, lectures, workshops and master-classes by writers, publishers, producers, booksellers, librarians and agents. Tutors include Simon Armitage, Carol Ann Duffy, Sophie Hannah, Jeffrey Wainwright, Heather Beck, Paul Magrs, Michael Symmons Roberts and Tiffany Murray. The course is available online as well as through the campus (contact *Heather Beck*, Online Convenor: h.beck@mmu.ac.uk).

University of Manchester
English & American Studies, School of Arts, Histories and Cultures, Humanities Lime Grove, Oxford Road, Manchester M13 9PL
☎0161 275 3144   Fax 0161 275 5987
✉ englishpg@manchester.ac.uk
www.art.man.ac.uk/english/pgdegree/ ma.htm#novel

Course Director *Suzannah Dunn*

Offers a one-year MA in *Novel Writing*.

University of Salford
Postgraduate Admissions, School of Media, Music & Performance, Adelphi Building, Peru Street, Salford M3 6EQ

☎0161 295 6027   Fax 0161 295 6023
✉ r.humphrey@salford.ac.uk
www.smmp.salford.ac.uk
MA in *Television and Radio Scriptwriting*. Two-year, part-time course taught by professional writers and producers. Also offers masterclasses with leading figures in the radio and television industry.

The Writers Bureau
Sevendale House, 7 Dale Street, Manchester
M1 1JB
☎0161 228 2362   Fax 0161 236 9440
✉ studentservices@writersbureau.com
www.writersbureau.com

Comprehensive home-study writing course with personal tuition service from professional writers. Fiction, non-fiction, articles, short stories, novels, TV, radio and drama all covered in detail. Trial period, guarantee and no time limits. Writing for children, using the Internet to sell your writing and biographies, memoirs and family history courses also available. ODLQC accredited. Quote Ref. EH06. Free enquiry line: 0800 856 2008.

The Writers Bureau College of Journalism
Address etc. as The Writers Bureau above

Home-study course covering all aspects of journalism. Real-life assignments assessed by qualified tutors with the emphasis on getting into print. Comprises 28 modules and three handbooks. Ref: EHJ06. Free enquiry line: 0800 298 7008.

The Writers College
Address etc. as The Writers Bureau above

The Art of Writing Poetry Course from The Writers Bureau sister college. A home-study course with a more 'recreational' emphasis. The 60,000-word course has 17 modules and lets you complete six written assignments for tutorial evaluation. Quote Ref. EHP06. Free enquiry line: 0800 856 2008.

Merseyside

University of Liverpool
Continuing Education, 126 Mount Pleasant,
Liverpool L69 3GR
☎0151 794 6900/6952 (24 hours)
Fax 0151 794 2544
✉ conted@liverpool.ac.uk
www.liv.ac.uk/conted
Course Organiser *Dr John Redmond*

Courses include: *An Introduction to Creative Writing; The Short Story and the Novel; Introduction to Writing Poetry; The Craft of Creative Writing; Writing Your Life Story; Science Fiction Writing; An Introduction to Journalism; Scriptwriting: Theatre Playwrights' Workshop and Situation Comedy*. Most courses take place on one evening or daytime meeting weekly, with some Saturdays and linked days. Courses offer university credits towards a Certificate in Higher Education in Creative Writing or for personal development purposes. For most courses no previous knowledge is required. There are fee concessions for those who are receiving certain benefits or are retired. Free prospectus on request or see the website.

Norfolk

University of East Anglia
School of Literature and Creative Writing,
Norwich NR4 7TJ
☎01603 593820   Fax 01603 593799
✉ pglit@uea.ac.uk
www.uea.ac.uk/eas
Contact *Kerry Durnford*, Postgraduate Admissions

UEA has a history of concern with contemporary literary culture. Among its programmes is the MA in *Creative Writing* (founded by Angus Wilson and Malcolm Bradbury in 1970/71). The course has three parallel entry points: Prose fiction, poetry and scriptwriting. A series of weekly workshops provide intensive examination of students' work, and also draw on aspects of teaching in nineteenth and twentieth century literature, literary theory and film and cultural studies.

Northamptonshire

Knuston Hall Residential College for Adult Education
Irchester, Wellingborough NN29 7EU
☎01933 312104   Fax 01933 357596
✉ enquiries@knustonhall.org.uk
www.knustonhall.org.uk

Writing courses being held in 2005 included: *Writing and Illustration for Children; Telling a Tale* and *Creative Writing*.

Northumberland

Community Creative Writing
'Sea Winds', 2 St Helens Terrace, Berwick-upon-Tweed TD15 1RJ
☎01289 305213

✉ mavismaureen@aol.com

Contact/Tutor *Maureen Raper, MBE*

The courses, which are held at the Community Centre College, Berwick-upon-Tweed as well as by distance learning for those unable to travel into class, include: *Creative Writing for Beginners*; *Writing for Children*; *Writing Comedy*; *Writing for Radio and Television*; *Writing Crime and Mystery*. All courses are verified by North East Open College Networks.

Nottinghamshire

The Nottingham Trent University

Humanities Faculty Office (Post Graduate Studies), Clifton Lane, Nottingham NG11 8NS
☎0115 848 6677   Fax 0115 848 6632
✉ hum.postgrad@ntu.ac.uk
www.human.ntu.ac.uk/writing

MA in *Creative Writing*. Hands-on and workshop-based, the course concentrates primarily on the practice and production of writing. A choice of options from *Fiction, Poetry, Creative Non-Fiction, New Media Writing, Children's Writing* and *Scriptwriting*. Assignments and a dissertation, but no formal exams. Staff are all established writers. Current visiting professors: Peter Porter and Jenny Diski. Also a full programme of visiting speakers. Study either full-time or part-time – all classes held in the evenings. Further details and application forms from the Faculty Office (details above).

Oxfordshire

University of Oxford Department for Continuing Education

Rewley House, 1 Wellington Square, Oxford OX1 2JA
☎01865 280356   Fax 01865 270309
✉ pp@conted.ox.ac.uk
www.conted.ox.ac.uk

Creative writing classes held during the autumn and spring terms. There are also one-week summer school courses, a two-year part-time Diploma and a two-year part-time MSt in *Creative Writing*. Early booking is advised.

Shropshire

Arvon Foundation (Shropshire)

See entry under **Greater London**

Somerset

Ammerdown Centre

The Ammerdown Conference and Retreat Centre, Radstock, Bath BA3 5SW
☎01761 433709   Fax 01761 433094
✉ centre@ammerdown.org
www.ammerdown.org

Courses include a five-day creative writing course. Residential facilities. Brochure available or full details on the website.

Bath Spa University College

Newton Park, Bath BA2 9BN
☎01225 875875   Fax 01225 875444
✉ enquiries@bathspa.ac.uk
www.bathspa.ac.uk

Contact *Admissions Officer* (☎01225 875821)

MA in *Creative Writing*. A course for creative writers wanting to develop their work. Teaching is by published writers in the novel, poetry, short stories and scriptwriting. In recent years, several students from this course have received contracts from publishers for novels, awards for poetry and short stories and have had work produced on BBC Radio. MA in *Writing for Young People*. A course for writers for children of all ages, from the picture-book age through to adolescent and 'crossover' writing, which aims at markets among adults as well as young people. An experienced teaching team helps and encourages students to create a significant body of writing, with practical plans for its place in the real world of publishing.

Dillington House

Ilminster TA19 9DT
☎01460 52427/Minicom: 01460 258640
Fax 01460 52433
✉ dillington@somerset.gov.uk
www.dillington.co.uk

Dillington House is one of the finest historic houses in Somerset. Provides short residential courses across a wide range of subjects, including writing and literary appreciation. Full details of the programme are available in the free brochure and on the website.

Institute of Copywriting

Honeycombe House, Bagley, Wedmore BS28 4TD
☎01934 713563   Fax 01934 713492
✉ copy@inst.org
www.institute.org/copy

Comprehensive copywriting home-study course, including advice on becoming a self-employed copywriter. Each student has a personal tutor who is an experienced copywriter and who provides detailed feedback on the student's assignments.

University of Bristol

Department of English, 3/5 Woodland Road, Bristol BS8 1TB
☎0117 954 6969
www.bris.ac.uk/english

Contact *Continuing Education Organiser*

A variety of short courses and day schools for both experienced writers and absolute beginners, including courses exploring reading and mental health and writing for therapeutic purposes. Also offers *Diploma in Creative Writing*. Detailed brochure available.

Staffordshire

Keele University

The Centre for Continuing and Professional Education, Keele University, (Freepost ST1666), Newcastle under Lyme ST5 5BR
☎01782 583436

Evening and weekend courses on literature and creative writing. The 2005/6 programme includes courses on novel writing, writers workshops and sessions on poetry writing.

Surrey

The Guildford Institute of the University of Surrey

Guildford Institute of the University of Surrey, Ward Street, Guildford GU1 4LH
☎01483 562142   Fax 01483 451034
✉ guildford-institute@surrey.ac.uk

The Guildford Institute is the venue for various creative writing courses. It also hosts Guildford Writers, a writers' circle meeting on alternate Tuesday evenings from 7.30 pm to 9.30 pm. Members of the group are writing short stories, poetry or novels, and bring their work to read aloud to the group for other members' advice, constructive criticism and general comments. New members are always welcome.

Royal Holloway

University of London, Department of Drama and Theatre, Egham Hill, Egham TW20 0EX
☎01784 443922   Fax 01784 431018
✉ drama@rhul.ac.uk

Contacts *Dan Rebellato, David Wiles*

Three-year BA courses in *Drama and Creative Writing* or *English and Creative Writing*, during which students progressively specialise in playwriting, poetry or fiction. Playwriting can be studied as part of the BA *Drama and Creative Writing* degree and poetic practice is an option in the *English* programme. Playwriting can be studied at postgraduate level in the MA in *Theatre* and there is an MA in *Poetic Practice*.

University of Surrey

Adult and Continuing Education, University of Surrey, Guildford GU2 7XH
☎01483 683151   Fax 01483 686191
✉ ace@surrey.ac.uk
www.surrey.ac.uk

The certificate programme includes several *Creative Writing* courses. For autumn 2005 these will be held at the **Guildford Institute**. The courses carry credits and can build to a university award. For details, contact *Jane Bradford*, Course Secretary on the number above.

Sussex

The Earnley Concourse

Earnley, Chichester PO20 7JL
☎01243 670392   Fax 01243 670832
✉ info@earnley.co.uk
www.earnley.co.uk

Offers a range of residential and non-residential courses throughout the year. Previous programme has included *Creative Writing: Getting Started*; *Secrets of a Professional Novelist*. Brochure available.

Lewes Live Literature

See entry under *Festivals*

University College Chichester

Bishop Otter Campus, College Lane, Chichester PO19 6PE
☎01243 816000   Fax 01243 816080
✉ S.Norgate@ucc.ac.uk

Contact *Stephanie Norgate*, Route Leader, MA in Creative Writing (01243 816296)

Postgraduate Certificate/Diploma/MA in, both full and part-time, in *Creative Writing*.

University of Sussex

Centre for Continuing Education, The Sussex Institute, Essex House, Brighton BN1 9QQ
☎01273 877888/877001
✉ cce@sussex.ac.uk
www.sussex.ac.uk/cce

Contact *Richard Crane*

MA in *Dramatic Writing*: the student is treated as a commissioned writer working in theatre, TV, radio or film with professional directors and actors. Includes workshops, masterclasses, a residential weekend and a showcase of new work. Two years, part-time. Convenor: *Richard Crane*. Certificate in *Creative Writing*: short fiction, novel and poetry for imaginative writers. Two-year, part-time. Convenors: *Richard Crane, Mark Slater*.

Tyne & Wear

University of Sunderland

Centre for Lifelong Learning, Joseph Cowen House, Newcastle upon Tyne NE1 7RU
☎0191 515 2800   Fax 0191 515 2890
www.sunderland.ac.uk/cll

Courses include: *Creative Writing: Feature Writing* and *Writing From the Inside Out*, a workshop for women. Contact the Secretary, Adult Education Programme.

West Midlands

Starz! – Film and Theatre Performing Arts

Christmas House, Chester Road, Castle Bromwich, Solihull B36 0ET
☎0121 749 7147

Creative Director *Gavin Prime*

Teaching disabled, disadvantaged and mainstream children. The only totally free theatre and film school of this type in England. Students range in age from eight to 23 and work in all ways connected to performing arts. This includes writing and showing them the structure of the business and how to try and get work accepted.

University of Birmingham

Centre for Lifelong Learning (CLL), Selly Oak, Birmingham B29 6LL
☎0121 414 3413   Fax 0121 414 5619
✉ e.m.braekkanpayne@bham.ac.uk

Certificate of Higher Education in *Creative Writing* – two years, part-time. Classes in theory and practice of writing in a wide range of literary genres. Course brochures are available from the address above. The course includes progression routes to Diploma and BA(Hons) Degree. Students who can demonstrate qualifications or writing skills equivalent to Certificate level may apply to join the Diploma of Creative Writing.

The University also offers an MPhil in *Playwriting Studies*. Contact *Sarah Woods*, Senior Tutor, at the Department of Drama and Theatre Arts (☎0121 414 5998).

University of Warwick

Open Studies, Centre for Lifelong Learning, Coventry CV4 7AL
☎024 7652 8286
✉ k.rainsley@warwick.ac.uk *or* l.downs@warwick.ac.uk

Creative writing courses held at the university or in regional centres. Subjects include: *Creative Writing*; *Lifestory Writing*; *Creative Writing for All*; *Writing Creatively*; *Writing for Pleasure*. One-year certificates in *Creative Writing* and *Journalism* available.

Wiltshire

Marlborough College Summer School

Marlborough SN8 1PA
☎01672 892388   Fax 01672 892476
✉ admin@mcsummerschool.org.uk
www.mcsummerschool.org.uk

Summer School with literature and creative writing included in its programme. Caters for residential and day students. Brochure available giving full details and prices.

Urchfont Manor College

Urchfont, Devizes SN10 4RG
☎01380 840495   Fax 01380 840005

Short courses – days, residential weeks and weekends – offered in a varied programme which includes literature and creative writing. 'Beautiful location; historic environment; delicious home cooking.' Send for a brochure.

Yorkshire

Arvon Foundation (Yorkshire)

See entry under **Greater London**

Leeds Metropolitan University

H505, City Site, Calverley Street, Leeds LS1 3HE
☎0113 283 2600 ext 3330
✉ r.hibbert@leedsmet.ac.uk
www.lmu.ac.uk

Administrator *Richard Hibbert*

Offers a Postgraduate Certificate/Diploma/MA in *Screenwriting (Fiction)*.

Open College of the Arts
Unit 1B, Redbrook Business Park, Wilthorpe Road, Barnsley S75 1JN
☎01226 730495   Fax 01226 730838
✉ open.arts@ukonline.co.uk
www.oca-uk.com

The OCA correspondence course, *Starting to Write*, offers help and stimulus from experienced writers/tutors. Emphasis is on personal development rather than commercial genre. Subsequent levels available include specialist poetry, fiction and autobiographical writing courses. OCA writing courses are accredited by the University of Glamorgan. Prospectus and Guide to Courses available on request.

Sheffield Hallam University
Faculy of Development & Society, Sheffield Hallam University, Collegiate Crescent, Sheffield S10 2BP
☎0114 225 2543   Fax 0114 225 2430
✉ fdsenquiries@shu.ac.uk
www.shu.ac.uk

Offers MA in *Creative Writing* (one-year, full-time; also part-time).

University of Hull
Scarborough Campus, Filey Road, Scarborough YO11 3AZ
☎01723 362392   Fax 01723 370815
✉ a.head@hull.ac.uk
www.hull.ac.uk

Director of Studies *Andrew Head*

BA Single Honours in *Theatre and Performance Studies* incorporates opportunities in writing and other media across each level of the programme. Works closely with the Stephen Joseph Theatre and its artistic director Alan Ayckbourn. The theatre sustains a policy for staging new writers (see entry under *Theatre Producers*). The campus hosts the annual National Student Drama Festival which includes the International Student Playscript Competition (details from The National Information Centre for Student Drama; nsdf@hull.ac.uk).

University of Leeds
The Lifelong Learning Centre, Leeds LS2 9JT
✉ sce@leeds.ac.uk

Contact *Rebecca O'Rourke*

In March 2005 The Lifelong Learning Centre replaced both the School of Continuing Education and Office for Part-Time Education. This follows closure of the Middlesbrough off-campus Centre and a significant reduction in the creative writing provision throughout Cleveland, North Yorkshire and West Yorkshire. Students on existing programmes of study – from Continuing Education Certificates in *Creative Writing* through to part-time degrees – will be able to continue their studies. These courses, to be held on the Leeds campus during the day and evening, will also be open to the general public. It is hoped that the Lifelong Learning Centre will be able to offer part-time study in *Creative Writing* in future.

University of Leeds, Bretton Hall Campus
School of Performance and Cultural Industries, Bretton Hall Campus, West Bretton, Wakefield WF4 4LG
☎0113 343 9022/9241
✉ g.f.lyons@leeds.ac.uk

Contact *Garry Lyons* or *Linda Smith*, Secretary (pculs@leeds.ac.uk)

Offers one-year full-time/two-year part-time MA course in *Creative Writing* designed for competent though not necessarily published writers. Also offers a three-year *Creative Writing* BA. Details from *Simon Ross* (s.j.ross@leeds.ac.uk).

University of Sheffield
Institute for Lifelong Learning, 196–198 West Street, Sheffield S1 4ET
☎0114 222 7000   Fax 0114 222 7001
www.shef.ac.uk/till

Certificate in *Creative Writing* (Degree Level 1) and a wide range of courses, from foundation level to specialist writing areas, open to all. Courses in poetry, prose, journalism, scriptwriting, comedy, travel writing, writing using ICT/Web, writing for children. Brochures and information available from the address above.

Yorkshire Art Circus
School Lane, Glasshoughton, Castleford WF10 4QH
☎01977 550401
✉ admin@artcircus.org.uk
www.artcircus.org.uk

Administrator *Angela Sibbit*

Offers an annual programme of courses in creative writing, poetry, self-publishing and book production. Mostly daytime courses. Brochure available. Yorkshire Art Circus is now offering a Writer Development Programme which will provide advanced support for writers wishing to extend their careers, and include a mentoring scheme, skills development in areas such as editing, proofreading and publicity, and the presentation and sale of mss. The scheme is aimed at serious writers who have already reached a certain level of ability. Participants will be expected to contribute their expertise to assist other writers.

IRELAND

Dingle Writing Courses Ltd
Ballintlea, Ventry Co. Kerry
☎00 353 66 915 9815
Fax 00 353 66 915 9815
✉ info@dinglewritingcourses.ie
www.dinglewritingcourses.ie
Directors *Abigail Joffe, Nicholas McLachlan*

An autumn programme of weekend residential courses for beginners and experienced writers alike. Tutored by professional writers the courses include poetry, fiction, starting to write and writing for theatre as well as special themed courses. Past tutors have included Michael Donaghy, Paul Durcan, Anne Enright, Nuala Ni Dhomhnaill, Carlo Gébler, Jennifer Johnston, Paula Meeham. Also organises tailor-made courses for schools, writers' groups or students on a *Creative Writing* programme.

Queen's University of Belfast
Institute of Lifelong Learning, Belfast
BT7 1NN
☎028 9097 3323   Fax 028 9097 1084
✉ ill@qub.ac.uk
www.qub.ac.uk/ill

Courses have included *Creative Writing*; *Writing for Profit and Pleasure* and *Scriptwriting*.

University of Dublin (Trinity College)
Graduate Studies Office, Arts Building, Trinity College, Dublin 2
☎00 353 1 608 1166   Fax 00 353 1 671 2821
✉ gradinfo@tcd.ie
www.tcd.ie/owc

Contact *Admissions*

Offers an MPhil *Creative Writing* course. A one-year, full-time course intended for students who are seriously committed to writing or prospective authors.

The Writer's Academy
Carrig-on-Bannow, Co. Wexford
☎00 353 51 561789
✉ thewritersacademy@eircom.net
www.thewritersacademy.net

Distance learning freelance article writing

course, critique service and marketing advice. Personal tuition plus expert information and support for writers of all abilities.

SCOTLAND

Arvon Foundation (Inverness-shire)
See entry under **Greater London**

Edinburgh University
Office of Lifelong Learning, 11 Buccleuch Place, Edinburgh EH8 9LW
☎0131 650 4400   Fax 0131 667 6097
✉ oll@ed.ac.uk
www.cce.ed.ac.uk
www.lifelong.ed.ac.uk

Several writing-orientated courses and summer schools. Course information online.

7:84 Summer School
See **7:84 Theatre Company Scotland** under *Theatre Producers*

University of Dundee
Continuing Education, Nethergate, Dundee DD1 4HN
☎01382 344809   Fax 01382 221057
✉ s.z.norrie@dundee.ac.uk
www.dundee.ac.uk/learning

Various creative writing courses held at the University and elsewhere in Dundee, Perth, Angus and Perthshire. Detailed course brochure available.

University of Glasgow
Department of Adult and Continuing Education, 11 Eldon Street, Glasgow G3 6NH
☎0141 330 1835/1829 (Enquiries/Brochure)
Fax 0141 330 1821
✉ enquiry@ace.gla.ac.uk
www.gla.ac.uk/adulteducation

Runs writers' workshops and courses at all levels; all friendly and informal. Daytime and evening meetings. Tutors are all experienced published writers.

University of St Andrews
School of English, The University, St Andrews KY16 9AL
☎01334 462666   Fax 01334 462655
✉ english@st-andrews.ac.uk
www.st-andrews.ac.uk

Offers postgraduate study in *Creative Writing*.

Modules in Writing Fiction and Writing Poetry. Students submit a dissertation of original writing – prose fiction of 15,000 words or a collection of around 30 short poems. Taught by Professor Douglas Dunn, John Burnside, Kathleen Jamie, A.L. Kennedy, Meaghan Delahunt and Don Paterson. Also offers PhD in *Creative Writing*.

WALES

Ty Newydd Writers' Centre

Llanystumdwy, Criccieth LL52 0LW
☎01766 522811   Fax 01766 523095
✉ post@tynewydd.org
www.tynewydd.org

Residential writers' centre set up by the Taliesin Trust with the support of the **Arts Council of Wales** to encourage and promote writing in both English and Welsh. Most courses run from Monday evening to Saturday morning. Each course has two tutors and a maximum of 16 participants. A wide range of courses for all levels of experience. Early booking essential. Fees from £350 inclusive. People on low incomes may be eligible for a grant or bursary. Course leaflet available. (See also *Organisations of Interest to Poets*.)

University of Glamorgan

Treforest, Pontypridd CF37 1DL
☎01443 483598
www.glam.ac.uk

Director, The National Centre for Writing
Professor Tony Curtis, FRSL

MPhil in *Writing*: a two-year part-time Masters degree for writers of fiction and poets. Established 1993. Contact *Professor Tony Curtis* at the School of Humanities, Law and Social Sciences.

MA in *Scriptwriting (Theatre, TV or Radio)*: a two-year part-time Masters degree for scriptwriters. Contact *Dr Richard J. Hand*.

BA in *Creative and Professional Writing*: a three-year course for undergraduates. Contact *Rob Middlehurst*.

University of Wales, Aberystwyth

Department of English, Hugh Owen Building, Aberystwyth SY23 3DY
☎01970 622534   Fax 01970 622530
www.aber.ac.uk/english

BA in *English and Creative Writing*, a three-year

course taught in part by practising writers: Director of Creative Writing, novelist and poet, Jem Poster and poets Tiffany Atkinson, Matthew Francis and Kelly Grovier. Also offers PhD and taught MA in *Writing* with modules in narratology and poetry, writing and publication.

University of Wales, Bangor

Department of English, College Road, Bangor LL57 2DG
☎01248 382102   Fax 01248 382102
✉ els029@bangor.ac.uk
www.bangor.ac.uk/ccpa

PhD *Creative and Critical Writing*; MA *Creative Studies (Creative Writing)*; BA *English Literature with Creative Writing*; BA *English Language with Creative Writing* and new BA *Creative Studies*. Also MA *Creative Studies (Film Practice)*; MA *Creative Studies (Drama Practice)*; MA *Creative Studies (Media Practice)*.

John Wilson's Writing Courses

Argoed Hall, Tregaron SY25 6JR
☎01974 298070
✉ john.wilson@virgin.net

Residential writing intensives ranging from basic skills to workshops in creative and business writing and journalism. For advanced writers an opportunity to understand and develop the creative process is provided. The courses normally run from Thursday evening to Sunday afternoon, with B&B accommodation and lunch at Argoed Hall, with evening meals (or full board) at nearby hotels. Phone or e-mail for details.

Writers' Holiday at Caerleon

School Bungalow, Church Road, Pontnewydd, Cwmbran NP44 1AT
☎01633 489438
✉ writersholiday@lineone.net
www.writersholiday.net

Contact *Anne Hobbs*

Annual six-day comprehensive conference including 12 courses for writers of all standards held in the summer at the University of Wales' Caerleon Campus. Courses, lectures, concert and excursion all included in the fee. Private, single and en-suite, full board accommodation. Courses have included *Writing for Publication*; *Writing Poetry*; *Writing Romantic Fiction* and *Writing for the Radio*.

Writers' Circles and Workshops

Directory of Writers' Circles, Courses and Workshops
39 Lincoln Way, Harlington LU5 6NG
☎01525 873197
✉ diana@writers-circles.com
www.writers-circles.com

Directory of UK writers' circles, courses and workshops, edited by Diana Hayden. Contains contact details and information about meetings in the UK and Republic of Ireland. Updated twice annually.

Writers' Circles Handbook
Oldacre, Horderns Park Road, Chapel-en-le-Frith SK23 9SY
☎01298 812305
✉ oldacre@btinternet.com
www.btinternet.com/~oldacre

Contact *Jill Dick*

Handbook for writers' circles, with invaluable information, articles and a comprehensive list of all known UK circles and groups meeting in the UK. Some overseas entries too. Free regular updates available after initial purchase (£5, post free).

Biscuit, Writers Conference 2006
Biscuit Publishing, PO Box 123, Washington, Newcastle upon Tyne NE37 2YW
☎0191 431 1263   Fax 0191 431 1263
✉ info@biscuitpublishing.com
www.biscuitpublishing.com

Contact *Brian Lister*

Second annual conference, to be held at the Lindisfarne Centre, University of Durham in April 2006. Residential weekend of masterclasses, exhibitions, seminars, debates and other fringe events. Open to all poets and prose writers.

Carmarthen Writers' Circle
Lower Carfan, Tavernspite, Whitland SA34 0NP
☎01994 240441

Contact *Jenny White*

Founded 1989. The Circle meets monthly on the second Monday of the month at the Indoor Bowls Centre, Carmarthen. All levels and genres welcome.

Caron Writers
Argoed Hall, Tregaron SY25 6JR
☎01974 298070
✉ john.wilson@virgin.net

Contact *John Wilson*

Founded in 2002, the group meets from 2.00 pm to 4.00 pm on the final Saturday of most months (not July or August). Each session comprises announcements, a key topic and a workshop based on it. Emphasis is on fun, discussion and achievement. 'Outstanding results have been achieved and members are gaining considerable success in creative writing competitions and independent publishing.' All genres welcome. No joining fee but £2.50 per session includes light refreshments. Phone or e-mail for details.

Chiltern Writers' Group
151 Chartridge Lane, Chesham HP5 2SE
☎01494 772308
✉ chilwriters@netscape.net
chilternwriters.netfirms.com

SUBSCRIPTION £15 p.a.; £10 (concessions); £3 (non-members meetings)

Guest speakers, workshops, manuscript critiques and monthly meetings. Regular newsletter and competitions.

The Cotswold Writers' Circle
Bliss's Cottage, Lower Chedworth, Cheltenham GL54 4AN
☎01285 720668
✉ elaine@pandelunt.co.uk

Patron *Elizabeth Webster*
Membership Secretary *Elaine Lunt*
Competition Secretary *Mrs Anne Brookes*

The Circle meets every Tuesday morning (except second Tuesday of the month) in Cirencester. Activities include workshops with well-known authors and an International Open Writing Competition; closing date 31 January annually (send s.a.e. for details). Winners published in the Circle's anthology, *Pen Ultimate*.

Creative Writers
See **Sunderland City Library and Arts Centre**

Cumbrian Literary Group
'Calgarth', The Brow, Flimby, Maryport
CA15 8TD
☎01900 813444
President *Glyn Matthews*
Secretary *Joyce E. Fisher*

Founded 1946 to provide a meeting place for readers and writers in Cumbria. The Group meets once a month (April to November) in Keswick. Invites speakers to meetings and holds annual competitions for poetry and prose. Publishes *Bookshelf* magazine. Further details from the Secretary at the address above.

'Sean Dorman' Manuscript Society
3 High Road, Britford, Salisbury SP5 4DS
Director *Jan Smith*

Founded 1957. Provides mutual help among writers and aspiring writers in England, Wales and Scotland. By means of circulating manuscript parcels, members receive constructive comment on their own work and read and comment on the work of others. Full details and application forms available on receipt of s.a.e.

East Anglian Writers
77 Marlborough Road, Norwich NR3 4PL
✉ benjamin.scott@ntlworld.com
Chair *Benjamin Scott*

A group of over 110 professional writers living in Norfolk, Suffolk, Essex, Cambridgeshire and Bedfordshire. Affiliated to the **Society of Authors**. Aims to help writers socialise and promote their work. Informal pub meetings, speakers' evenings and contact point for professional writers in the area.

Eastbourne's Anderida Writers
20 Vian Avenue, Eastbourne BN23 6EY
☎01323 737677
Secretary *Stella Freshney*

Creative workshops for Sussex authors. Talks and competitions.

Euroscript
Unit 1.07, 56 Shoreditch High Street, London
E1 6JJ
☎0780 336 9414
✉ scriptcounsel121@blueyonder.co.uk
www.euroscript.co.uk

Script development organisation offering creative and editorial input to professional writers and producers. Develops screenplays through an intensive modular programme, including residential script workshops; provides script reports and runs an annual film story competition. Open to writers of any nationality. Write or access the website for further information.

Gay Authors Workshop
BM Box 5700, London WC1N 3XX
Contact *Kathryn Byrd*

Established 1978 to encourage and support lesbian/gay writers. Regular meetings and a newsletter. GAW gave rise to **Paradise Press** (see entry under *Small Presses*).

Guildford Writers
See **The Guildford Institute of the University of Surrey** under *UK Writers' Courses*

Historical Novel Folio
17 Purbeck Heights, Mount Road, Parkstone, Poole BH14 0QP
☎01202 741897
Contact *Doris Myall-Harris*

An independent postal workshop – single folio dealing with any period before World War II. Send s.a.e. for details.

'How to Self-Publish Your Book' Workshops
'Chinook', Southdown Road, Winchester
SO21 2BY
☎01962 712307
✉ barbara.large@writers-conference.com *or*
kate.harrison@winchester.ac.uk
www.winchester.ac.uk
www.awc-workshops.ndo.co.uk
Contact *Barbara Large, MBE, FRSA, FUCW*

One-day workshops to inform writers who wish to self-publish their books about the digital and lithographic processes. Participants will learn the skills of researching, writing and revising their mss; the use of photographs, maps, diagrams, illustrations, desgn and formatting; types of paper, fonts, sizes, ISBN numbers and costs, and marketing their books.

Janus Writers
See **Sunderland City Library and Arts Centre**

Kops and Ryan Advanced Playwriting Workshops
41B Canfield Gardens, London NW6 3JL
☎020 7624 2940/7263 8740

Tutors *Bernard Kops, Tom Ryan*

Three ten-week terms per year from September. Small group writing and improvisation workshops. Instruction in film technique and private tutorials. Call for details.

Lewes Live Literature

See entry under *Festivals*

London Writers' Circle

54 Rokeby Gardens, Woodford Green IG8 9HR
☎020 8504 2506
✉ colleenmcmath@amserve.com
Membership Secretary *Colleen McMath*
SUBSCRIPTION £20 (London); £10 (Country); £6 (Overseas).

Founded 1924. Encourages writers of all grades in poetry, short story and feature writing. Monthly meetings, social events and quarterly magazine.

North West Playwrights (NWP)

18 Express Networks, 1 George Leigh Street, Manchester M4 5DL
☎0161 237 1978
www.newplaysnw.com

Founded 1982. Operates a script-reading service, classes and script development scheme and *The Lowdown* newsletter. Services available to writers in the region only.

Pier Playwrights

9 Jew Street, Brighton BN1 1UT
☎01273 735353
✉ admin@pierplaywrights.co.uk
www.pierplaywrights.co.uk
Contact *Chris Taylor*
SUBSCRIPTION £25 (individual); £15 (unwaged); £50 (company)

Run by playwrights for playwrights throughout the South East region. Workshops by visiting professionals, script reading, courses, residencies, etc. and a monthly newsletter.

Pitstop Refuelling Writers' Weekend Workshops

University College Winchester, Winchester SO22 4NR
☎01962 712307/827056
✉ barbara.large@writers-conference.com *or* kate.harrison@winchester.ac.uk
www.winchester.ac.uk
www.awc-workshops.ndo.co.uk
Director *Barbara Large, MBE, FRSA, FUCW*

Following on from the **Annual Writers'**

Conference in Winchester, these are small-group writing workshops under the guidance of professional writers. 2006 workshop dates are 17–19 March and 20–22 October.

Player-Playwrights

See entry under *Professional Associations*

Screenwriters' Workshop

c/o NPA, Unit 1.07, The Tea Building, 56 Shoreditch High Street, London E1 6JJ
☎020 7613 0440
✉ screenoffice@tiscali.co.uk
www.screenwritersworkshop.co.uk
SUBSCRIPTION £40 p.a.

Established 1983, this educational charity helps writers into the film and TV industries. Runs *Feedback* – a script-reading service. Full details on the website.

Scribo

1/31 Hamilton Road, Bournemouth BH1 4EQ
☎01202 302533
Contacts *K. & P. Sylvester*

Scribo (established over 20 years ago) is a postal workshop for novelists dealing with both manuscript folios (e.g. fantasy/sci-fi, mainstream, women's fiction, crime, literary) and forum folios (discussion, information exchange). No annual subscription. Send s.a.e. for further details.

Script Yorkshire

Membership: 9 Barker's Road, Sheffield S7 1SD
✉ members@scriptyorkshire.co.uk
www.scriptyorkshire.co.uk
Membership *Caroline Small*

Formerly known as Yorkshire Playwrights. Relaunched in 2005 as Script Yorkshire. A support and advocacy organisation for scriptwriters across performance and broadcast media which aims to empower Yorkshire's scriptwriters by giving them the skills and insights they need to develop their own careers. Open to professional or aspiring scriptwriters (theatre, radio, TV and film) who live or work in Yorkshire. Company membership also available. Visit the website for further information or write to the address above.

Short Story Writers' Folio/ Children's Novel Writers' Folio

5 Park Road, Brading, Sandown, Isle of Wight PO36 0HU
☎01983 407697
✉ nott.wortley-dawn@tiscali.co.uk
Contact *Mrs Dawn Wortley-Nott*

Postal workshops – members receive constructive criticism of their work and read and offer advice on fellow members' contributions. Send an s.a.e. for further details.

Society of Sussex Authors
Bookends, Lewes Road, Horsted Keynes, Haywards Heath RH17 7DP
☎01825 790755   Fax 01825 790755
✉ michael@bookends.claranet.com
Contact *Michael Legat*
Founded 1968. Six meetings per year, held in Lewes, plus social events. Membership restricted to Sussex-based writers only.

South Manchester Writer's Workshop
c/o Didsbury Methodist Church Hall, Sandhurst Road, Didsbury
✉ mail@manchester-writers.freeserve.co.uk
www.manchester-writers.freeserve.co.uk
Contact *Philip Caveney*
Weekly meetings, open to all, held every Tuesday. Phone or access the website for more details.

Southwest Scriptwriters
☎0117 909 5522
✉ info@southwest-scriptwriters.co.uk
www.southwest-scriptwriters.co.uk
Secretary *John Colborn*
Founded 1994 to offer support to regional writers for all media. The group meets at the Theatre Royal, Bristol.

Speakeasy – Milton Keynes Writers' Group
46 Wealdstone Place, Springfield, Milton Keynes MK6 3JG
☎01908 663860
✉ speakeasy@writerbrock.co.uk
www.mkweb.co.uk/speakeasy
Contact *Martin Brocklebank*
Monthly meetings on the first Friday of each month at 8.00 pm. Full and varied programme includes Local Writer Nights where work can be read and peformed and Guest Nights where writers, poets and journalists are invited to speak. Mini-workshops and information nights are also in the programme. Invites entries to Open Creative Writing Competitions. Phone, e-mail or send s.a.e. for details to address above.

Spread the Word
77 Lambeth Walk, London SE11 6DX
☎020 7735 3111   Fax 020 7735 2666
✉ info@spreadtheword.org.uk
www.spreadtheword.org.uk
Contact *General Manager*
Develops new writing and live literature through twice-yearly season of creative writing workshops, talks, reading groups, cross arts projects and one-to-one surgeries.

Sussex Playwrights' Club
2 Brunswick Mews, Hove BN3 1HD
☎01273 730106
www.newventure.org.uk
Secretary *Dennis Evans*
Founded 1935. Monthly readings of members' work by experienced actors. Membership open to all. Meetings held at New Venture Theatre, Bedford Place, Brighton.

Tooting & Balham Writers' Circle
☎07970 715080
✉ jasonyoung72@yahoo.com
www.writers-circles.com/tooting.html
Contact *Jason Young*
Founded 2003. A local version of the **London Writers' Circle**, currently homeless but negotiating space with the **British Film Institute** to facilitate Monday or Friday evening meetings on a monthly basis.

Ver Poets
15 Brampton Road, St Albans AL1 4PP
☎01727 864898
✉ daphne.schiller@virgin.net
Secretary *Daphne Schiller*
Founded 1966. Postal and local members. Meets in St Albans, runs evening meetings and daytime workshops and organises competitions.

Verulam Writers' Circle (St Albans)
46 Gadebridge Lane, Hemel Hempstead HP1 3HF
☎01442 217741
www.verulamwriterscircle.org.uk
Contact *Nick Cook*
Founded 1956. Offers constructive criticism, talks and workshops. Meetings are held fortnightly at St Michael's Church Hall, St Michael's Road, St Albans.

Walton Wordsmiths
27 Braycourt Avenue, Walton on Thames KT12 2AZ
☎01932 702874
✉ words@stickler.org.uk

www.cajunmoon.co.uk

Contact *Wendy Hughes*

Founded in 1999 by Wendy Hughes. Supports writers of all grades and capabilities by offering constructive criticism and advice.

Wordworks

See **Northamptonshire Libraries & Information Services** under *Library Services*

Workers' Educational Association

National Office: Quick House, 65 Clifton Street, London EC2A 4JE

☎020 7426 3450

✉ national@wea.org.uk

www.wea.org.uk

Founded in 1903, the WEA is a charitable provider of adult education with students drawn from all walks of life. It runs writing courses and workshops in many parts of the country which are open to everyone. Contact your local WEA office for details of courses in your region.

Eastern Botolph House, 17 Botolph Lane, Cambridge CB2 3RE

☎01223 350978 ✉ eastern@wea.org.uk

East Midlands 39 Mapperley Road, Mapperley Park, Nottingham NG3 5AQ

☎0115 962 8400 ✉ eastmidlands@wea.org.uk

London 4 Luke Street, London EC2A 4XW

☎020 7613 7550 email london@wea.org.uk

North East 1st Floor, Unit 6, Metro Riverside Business Park, Delta Bank Road, Gateshead NE11 9DJ

☎0191 461 8100 ✉ northeast@wea.org.uk

North West Suite 405, The Cotton Exchange, Old Hall Street, Liverpool L3 9JR

☎0151 243 5340 ✉ northwest@wea.org.uk

Southern 57 Riverside 2, Sir Thomas Longley Road, Rochester ME2 4DP

☎01634 730101 ✉ southern@wea.org.uk

South West Bradninch Court, Castle Street, Exeter EX4 3PL

☎01392 490970 ✉ southwest@wea.org.uk

West Midlands 78–80 Sherlock Street, Birmingham B5 6LT

☎0121 666 6101 ✉ westmidlands@wea.org.uk

Yorkshire and Humber 6 Woodhouse Square, Leeds LS3 1AD

☎0113 245 3304 ✉ yorkshumber@wea.org.uk

Scottish Association Riddle's Court, 322 Lawnmarket, Edinburgh EH1 2PG

☎0131 226 3456 ✉ hq@weascotland.org.uk

Writers in Oxford

✉ hampton.oxford@dial.pipex.com

www.writersinoxford.org

Membership Secretary *Julie Summers*

Chairman *Janie Hampton*

SUBSCRIPTION £20 p.a.

Founded 1992. Open to published authors, playwrights, poets and journalists. Literary seminars and social functions. Publishes *The Oxford Writer* newsletter.

Yorkshire Playwrights

See **Script Yorkshire**

Miscellany

AR&E

25 Barrow Street, New York, NY 10014, USA
☎001 212 924 9942   Fax 001 212 924 1864
✉ info@agentresearch.com
www.agentresearch.uk.net
Contact *Bill Martin*

Founded 1996. Provides authors, editors and other professionals with data on clients and sales made by literary agents in the USA, UK and Canada, i.e. who sells what to whom for how much. Information is culled from the trade and general press, and collection has been continuous since 1980. Individual reports on specific agents and various forms of ms-agent match-up services are available. See website for pricing or send s.a.e. Publishes *Talking Agents*, the AR&E newsletter (10 p.a.). The website offers a free service of agent verification: information on whether or not the database reflects that a given agent has created a public record of sales.

Arjay Research

20 Rookery View, Little Thurrock, Grays RM17 6AS
☎01375 372199   Fax 01375 372199
✉ RogWJ@aol.com
www.copy-editing.net
Contact *Roger W. Jordan*

All aspects of international merchant shipping and naval research undertaken by former shipping archivist and editor. Extensive maritime library and comprehensive databases on *inter alia* ships wrecked/lost and passenger and cruise ships. Terms by arrangement.

Combrógos

10 Heol Don, Whitchurch, Cardiff CF14 2AU
☎029 2062 3359
Contact *Professor Meic Stephens*

Founded 1990. Arts and media research, editorial services, specialising in books about Wales or by Welsh authors. 'Encyclopaedic knowledge of Welsh history, language, literature and culture.'

Jacqueline Edwards

104 Earlsdon Avenue South, Coventry CV5 6DQ
✉ twigsbranches@yahoo.co.uk
Contact *Jacqueline Edwards, MA, LLB(Hons)*

Historical research – family, local and 19th and 20th century legal history. Covers Warwickshire, Gloucestershire, Wiltshire, Worcestershire, Cambridgeshire and the National Archive, Kew, London.

Firefly Media

PO Box 3703, Trowbridge
☎01380 871331   Fax 01380 871331
✉ info@ffmedia.co.uk
www.ffmedia.co.uk
Contact *Julia McCutchen*

Following years working in-house as a director and publisher of non-fiction, Firefly Media was founded in 2001 by publishing consultant and creativity coach Julia McCutchen. A one-to-one service provides advice, feedback and information on any aspect of writing and the publishing process, tailored to suit individual requirements. Help is given on writing proposals and in-depth workshops cover the key stages to publication and explain how authors can prepare their work for presentation to the right people in the right way for the best chance of success. Self-publishing options also covered.

Impressions of Monmouth

Unit 3, The New Building, Ellwood Road, Milkwall, Coleford GL16 7LE
☎01594 839407   Fax 01594 839287
✉ books@impressionsmon.demon.co.uk
www.impressionsofmonmouth.com
Contact *David James*

Advice and technical assistance for those wishing to self-publish with full design, printing and binding services. Yearbooks, commemorative books, personal, family, local histories, etc. Print runs as low as 25 copies. Fixed prices.

The Indepublishing Agency

✉ enquiries@indepublishing.com
www.indepublishing.com
Contact *Jo Henry*

Founded 2003. Agent for authors of self-published titles (fiction, children's, fact-based, self-help, business) seeking advice, consultancy and representation. No scripts. Initial contact by

e-mail. Reading fee: £35 per 30,000 words.
COMMISSION 10% (for books taken on under
pre-agreed contract).

International Booksearch Service
☎020 7639 8900
✉ sarah.fordham@btinternet.com
www.scfordham.com
Contact *S.C. Fordham*

Founded 1992. International book search service for out-of-print books. A free service with
no obligation to buy the book when found.
Experienced in finding books for authors,
researchers, TV and film companies, newspapers, magazines, etc.

Caroline Landeau
8 Elystan Place, London SW3 3LF
☎07050 600420   Fax 07050 605641
✉ winmacweb@hotmail.com
Contact *Caroline Landeau*

Experienced research and production – films,
multimedia, books, magazines, exhibitions, animation, general interest, art, music, crime, travel,
food, film, theatre.

M-Y Books Ltd
The Seed Warehouse, Maidenhead Yard,
Hertford SG14 3AW
☎01992 586279
www.m-ybooks.co.uk
Contact *Jonathan Miller*

Offers promotional and marketing services to
the self-published author or small publisher.

Murder Files
Dommett Hill Farm, Hare Lane, Buckland
St. Mary, Chard TA20 3JS
☎01460 234065
✉ enquiry@murderfiles.com
www.murderfiles.com
Contact *Paul Williams*

Founded 1994. Crime writer and researcher specialising in British murders. Holds information
on thousands of well-known and less well-
known murders dating from 1400 to the present
day. Copies of press cuttings available from 1920
onwards. Details of executions, particularly at the
Tyburn and Newgate. Information on British
hangmen. Specialist in British police murders
since 1700. CD-ROM *The Ultimate Price – The
Unlawful Killing of British Police Officers*, Part 1
(1700–1899) & Part 2 (1900–2000) available.
Service available to general enquirers, writers,
researchers, TV, radio, video, etc.

Nielsen BookNet
3rd Floor, Midas House, 62 Goldsworth Road,
Woking GU21 6LQ
☎0870 777 8710   Fax 0870 777 8711
✉ info@nielsenbooknet.co.uk
www.nielsenbooknet.co.uk

Provides a range of e-commerce services that
allows all parts of the book industry to trade electronically, regardless of their size or location.
Services include BookNet Web for booksellers &
Publishers/distributors; TeleOrdering and EDI.

Nielsen BookScan
3rd Floor, Midas House, 62 Goldsworth Road,
Woking GU21 6LQ
☎01483 712222   Fax 01483 712220
✉ info@nielsenbookscan.co.uk
www.ielsenbookscan.co.uk

Nielsen BookScan collects transactional data at
the point of sale from tills and despatch systems
of all the major book retailers in the UK, Ireland
and South Africa. Each week data is coded and
analysed, producing complete market information for retailers, publishers, libraries, agents
and the media within 72 hours of the week ending Saturday.

Ormrod Research Services
Weeping Birch, Burwash TN19 7HG
☎01435 882541
✉ richardormrod@aol.com
Contact *Richard Ormrod*

Established 1982. Comprehensive research service: literary, historical, academic, biographical,
commercial. Verbal quotations available. Also editing, indexing, ghost-writing and critical reading.

Patent Research
Dachsteinstr. 12a, D–81825 Munich, Germany
☎00 49 89 430 7833
Contact *Gerhard Everwyn*

All world, historical patents for researchers,
authors, archives, museums and publishers. Rates
on application.

The United Kingdom Copyright Bureau
110 Trafalgar Road, Portslade BN41 1GS
☎01273 277333   Fax 01273 705451
✉ info@copyrightbureau.co.uk
www.copyrightbureau.co.uk
Contacts *Ralph de Straet von Kollman, Petra Ginman*

The UKCB provides a secure copyright service
at reasonable cost, enabling multiple copyrights

to be registered nominally when required. Prices are advertised on the website including the UKCB's solicitors, etc. Copyrights preferred on floppy disk or CD-ROM; mss are not accepted due to storage space.

Melanie Wilson

72 High Street, Syston LE7 1GQ
☎0116 260 4442   Fax 0116 260 1396
✉ MelanieWilson@dragonflight.co.uk

Contact *Melanie Wilson*

Comprehensive research service for books, magazines, newspapers, documentaries, films, radio, education, TV drama. Includes free world-wide booksearch service and groundwork for factual basis for all media presentations, particularly in historical research, costume and textiles, crafts, food and cooking, weapons and uniforms, traditional storytelling, past technology, living history displays and exhibitions.

Press Cuttings Agencies

Durrants
Discovery House, 28–42 Banner Street,
London EC1Y 8QE
☎020 7674 0200   Fax 020 7674 0222
✉ contact@durrants.co.uk
www.durrants.co.uk

Wide coverage of all print media sectors including foreign press plus Internet, newswire and broadcast monitoring. High speed, early morning press cuttings from the national press by web or e-mail. Overnight delivery via courier to most areas or first-class mail. Well presented, laser printed, A4 cuttings. Rates on application.

International Press-Cutting Bureau
224–236 Walworth Road, London SE17 1JE
☎020 7708 2113   Fax 020 7701 4489
✉ info@ipcb.co.uk
www.ipcb.co.uk

Contact *Robert Podro*

Covers national, provincial, trade, technical and magazine press. Cuttings are normally sent twice weekly by first-class post. Basic charges are £70 per month + £1 per cutting.

Romeike Ltd
Romeike House, 290–296 Green Lanes,
London N13 5TP
☎0800 289543   Fax 020 8882 6716
✉ info@romeike.com
www.romeike.com

Contact *Steve Young*

Monitors national and international dailies and Sundays, provincial papers, consumer magazines, trade and technical journals, teletext services as well as national radio and TV networks. Back research, advertising checking and Internet monitoring, plus analysis and editorial summary service available.

**We Find It
(Press Clippings)**
40 Galwally Avenue, Belfast BT8 7AJ
☎028 9064 6008   Fax 028 9064 6008

Contact *Avril Forsythe*

Specialises in Northern Ireland press and magazines, both national and provincial. Rates on application.

Bursaries, Fellowships and Grants

Arts Council Bursaries, Ireland
See **The Arts Council/An Chomhairle Ealaíon** under *Arts Councils and Regional Offices*

The Authors' Contingency Fund
The Society of Authors, 84 Drayton Gardens, London SW10 9SB
☎020 7373 6642   Fax 020 7373 5768
✉ info@societyofauthors.org
www.societyofauthors.org
This fund makes modest grants to published authors who find themselves in sudden financial difficulties. Contact the **Society of Authors** for an information sheet and application form.

The Authors' Foundation
The Society of Authors, 84 Drayton Gardens, London SW10 9SB
☎020 7373 6642   Fax 020 7373 5768
✉ info@societyofauthors.org
www.societyofauthors.org
Grants to writers whose publisher's advance is insufficient to cover the costs of research involved. Application by letter to The Authors' Foundation giving details, in confidence, of the advance and royalties, together with the reasons for needing additional funding. Grants are sometimes given even if there is no commitment by a publisher, so long as the applicant has had a book published and the new work will almost certainly be published. About £80,000 is distributed each year. Contact the **Society of Authors** for full entry details. Final entry dates: 30 April and 30 September.

The K. Blundell Trust
The Society of Authors, 84 Drayton Gardens, London SW10 9SB
☎020 7373 6642   Fax 020 7373 5768
✉ info@societyofauthors.org
www.societyofauthors.org
Grants to writers whose publisher's advance is insufficient to cover the costs of research. Author must be under 40, has to submit a copy of his/her previous book and the work must 'contribute to the greater understanding of existing social and economic organisation'. Application by letter. Contact the **Society of Authors** for full entry details. Final entry dates: 30 April and 30 September.

Alfred Bradley Bursary Award
c/o BBC Radio Drama, Room 2130, New Broadcasting House, Oxford Road, Manchester M60 1SJ
☎0161 244 4052   Fax 0161 244 4248
Contact *Coordinator*
Established 1992. Biennial award in commemoration of the life and work of the distinguished radio producer Alfred Bradley. Aims to encourage and develop new radio writing talent in the BBC North region. There is a change of focus for each award, e.g. previous years have targeted comedy drama, verse drama, etc. Entrants must live in the north of England. The award is given to help writers to pursue a career in writing for radio. Further information can be found on bbc.co.uk/writersroom Previous winners: Julia Copus, Michael Stewart, Ben Tagoe, Katie Douglas.
AWARD Up to £6000 over two years and a BBC Radio Drama commission, the opportunity to develop further ideas with Radio Drama.

British Academy Small Research Grants
10 Carlton House Terrace, London SW1Y 5AH
☎020 7969 5200   Fax 020 7969 5300
www.britac.ac.uk
Contact *Assistant Secretary, Research Grants*
Award to further original academic research at postdoctoral level in the humanities and social sciences. Entrants must be resident in the UK. See website for final entry dates.
AWARD £7500 (maximum).

Cholmondeley Awards
The Society of Authors, 84 Drayton Gardens, London SW10 9SB
☎020 7373 6642   Fax 020 7373 5768
✉ info@societyofauthors.org
www.societyofauthors.org
Founded 1965 by the late Dowager Marchioness of Cholmondeley. Annual honorary awards to

recognise the achievement and distinction of individual poets. 2004 winners: John Agard, Ruth Padel, Lawrence Sail, Eva Salzman.
AWARD £8000 (total).

Olive Cook Prize
See **Tom-Gallon Trust Award**

Tony Doyle New Writers' Bursary Award
BBC Northern Ireland Drama, Broadcasting House, Ormeau Avenue, Belfast BT2 8HQ
☎02890 338497   Fax 02890 338408
✉ tvdrama.ni@bbc.co.uk
www.bbc.co.uk/ni/drama
Contacts *Deirdre Cartmill, Stephen Wright*

A biannual award, the bursary is aimed at encouraging Irish writers to write for television – the medium in which Tony Doyle had his greatest successes. It also aims to inform writers of the opportunities that television affords and to nurture long-term creative links between all broadcasters and writers in Ireland. Writers must have an Irish background and must not have had a drama in English previously produced for television. Final entry date is usually 31 January each year (opens in October). Previous winners: Danny Stack (2004), Dominique Moloney (2003). The winner receives a cash prize of £2000. The finalists are invited to a residential seminar to introduce them to the world of television drama through a series of intensive sessions with the BBC Northern Ireland Drama Development Team and experienced practitioners. Two typed copies of a 60-minute script for an original television drama should be submitted. Only one entry accepted per person. Enties must be in English. Contact the department and ask for criteria as these may change annually.

The Economist/Richard Casement Internship
The Economist, 25 St James's Street, London SW1A 1HG
☎020 7830 7000
✉ geoffreycarr@economist.com
www.economist.com
Contact *Geoffrey Carr* Science Editor (re. Casement Internship)

For an aspiring journalist under 25 to spend three months in the summer writing for *The Economist* about science and technology. Applicants should write a letter of introduction along with an article of approximately 600 words suitable for inclusion in the Science and Technology Section. Competition details normally announced in the magazine late January or early February and 4–5 weeks allowed for application.

European Jewish Publication Society
PO Box 19948, London N3 3ZJ
Fax 020 8346 1776
✉ cs@ejps.org.uk
www.ejps.org.uk
Contact *Dr Colin Shindler*

Established in 1995 to help fund the publication of books of European Jewish interest which would otherwise remain unpublished. Helps with the marketing, distribution and promotion of such books. Publishers who may be interested in publishing works of Jewish interest should approach the Society with a proposal and manuscript in the first instance. Books which have been supported recently include: *The History of Zionism* Walter Laqueur; *Photographing the Holocaust* Janina Struk; *Isaac Rosenberg: Selected Poems and Letters* ed. Jean Liddiard; *Migrations* Gloria Gervitz; *The Arab-Israeli Cookbook* Robin Soans. Also supports the publication of poetry, and translations from and into other European languages.
GRANT £3000 (maximum).

Fulbright Awards
The Fulbright Commission, Fulbright House, 62 Doughty Street, London WC1N 2JZ
☎020 7404 6880   Fax 020 7404 6834
www.fulbright.co.uk
Contact *British Programme Manager*

The Fulbright Commission offers a number of scholarships given at postgraduate level and above, open to any field (science and the arts) of study/research to be undertaken in the USA. Length of award is typically an academic year. Application deadline for postgraduate awards is usually late October/early November of preceding year of study; and mid-March/early April for postdoctoral awards. Further details and application forms are available on the Commission's website. Alternatively, send A4 envelope with sufficient postage for 100g with a covering letter explaining which level of award is of interest.

Tony Godwin Memorial Trust
c/o 38 Lyttelton Court, Lyttelton Road, London N2 0EB
☎020 8209 1613
✉ info@tgmt.org.uk
www.tgmt.org.uk
Chairman *Iain Brown*

Biennial award established to commemorate the life of Tony Godwin, a prominent publisher in the 1960s/70s. Open to all young people (under 35 years old) who are UK nationals and working, or intending to work, in publishing. The award provides the recipient with the means to spend at least one month as the guest of an American publishing house in order to learn about international publishing. The recipient is expected to submit a report upon return to the UK. Next award: 2006; final entry date: 31 December 2005. Previous winners: George Lucas (Hodder), Clive Priddle (Fourth Estate), Richard Scrivener (Penguin), Lisa Shakespeare (Weidenfeld & Nicolson), Fiona Stewart (HarperCollins).

AWARD Bursary of approx. US$5000.

Eric Gregory Trust Fund

The Society of Authors, 84 Drayton Gardens, London SW10 9SB
☎020 7373 6642   Fax 020 7373 5768
✉ info@societyofauthors.org
www.societyofauthors.org

Annual awards of varying amounts are made for the encouragement of poets under the age of 30 on the basis of a submitted collection. Open only to British-born subjects resident in the UK. Final entry date: 31 October. Contact the **Society of Authors** for full entry details. 2004 winners: Nick Laird, Elizabeth Manuel, Abi Curtis, Sophie Levy, Saradha Soobrayen.

AWARD £24,000 (total).

The Guardian Research Fellowship

Nuffield College, Oxford OX1 1NF
☎01865 278542   Fax 01865 278666

Contact *The Administrative Officer*

One-year fellowship endowed by the Scott Trust, owner of *The Guardian*, to give someone working in the media the chance to put their experience into a new perspective, publish the outcome and give a *Guardian* lecture. Applications welcomed from journalists and management members, in newspapers, periodicals or broadcasting. Research or study proposals should be directly related to experience of working in the media. Accommodation and meals in college will be provided and a stipend. Advertised biennially in November.

Hawthornden Literary Institute

Hawthornden International Retreat for Writers, Lasswade EH18 1EG
☎0131 440 2180   Fax 0131 440 1989

Contact *The Administrator*

Established 1982 to provide a peaceful setting where published writers can work in silence. The Castle houses up to six writers at a time, who are known as Hawthornden Fellows. Writers from any part of the world may apply for the fellowships. No monetary assistance is given, nor any contribution to travelling expenses, but once arrived at Hawthornden, the writer is the guest of the Retreat. Applications on forms provided must be made by the end of November for the following calendar year. Previous winners include: Les Murray, Alasdair Gray, Helen Vendler, David Profumo, Hilary Spurling.

Francis Head Bequest

The Society of Authors, 84 Drayton Gardens, London SW10 9SB
☎020 7373 6642   Fax 020 7373 5768
✉ info@societyofauthors.org
www.societyofauthors.org

Provides grants to published British authors over the age of 35 who need financial help during a period of illness, disablement or temporary financial crisis. Contact the **Society of Authors** for an information sheet and application form.

Jerwood Awards

See **The Royal Society of Literature/Jerwood Awards**

Ralph Lewis Award

University of Sussex Library, Brighton BN1 9QL
☎01273 678158   Fax 01273 678441
✉ p.a.ringshaw@sussex.ac.uk

Established 1985. Occasional award set up by Ralph Lewis, a Brighton author and art collector who left money to fund awards for promising manuscripts which would not otherwise be published. The award is given in the form of a grant to a UK-based publisher in respect of a publication of literary works by new authors. No direct applications from writers. Previous winners: **Peterloo Poets**; **Serpent's Tail**; **Stride Publications**.

The Elizabeth Longford Grants

The Society of Authors, 84 Drayton Gardens, London SW10 9SB
☎020 7373 6642   Fax 020 7373 5768
✉ info@societyofauthors.org
www.societyofauthors.org

Biannual grant, sponsored by Flora Fraser and Peter Soros, to a historical biographer whose publisher's advance is insufficient to cover the costs of research involved. Contact the **Society**

of Authors for full details. Final entry dates: 30 April and 30 September.

GRANT £2500.

The John Masefield Memorial Trust

The Society of Authors, 84 Drayton Gardens, London SW10 9SB

☎020 7373 6642   Fax 020 7373 5768

✉ info@societyofauthors.org

www.societyofauthors.org

This trust makes occasional grants to professional poets (or their immediate dependants) who are faced with sudden financial problems. Contact the **Society of Authors** for an information sheet and application form.

Somerset Maugham Trust Fund

The Society of Authors, 84 Drayton Gardens, London SW10 9SB

☎020 7373 6642   Fax 020 7373 5768

✉ info@societyofauthors.org

www.societyofauthors.org

Annual awards designed to encourage writers under the age of 35 to travel. Given on the basis of a published work of fiction, non-fiction or poetry. Open only to British-born subjects resident in the UK. Final entry date: 20 December. 2004 winners: Charlotte Mendelson *Daughters of Jerusalem*; Mark Blayney *Two Kinds of Silence*; Robert Macfarlane *Mountains of the Mind*.

AWARDS £12,000 (total).

The Airey Neave Trust

PO Box 36800, 40 Bernard Street, London WC1N 1WJ

☎020 7833 4440

✉ hanthoc@aol.com

www,aireyneavetrust.org.uk

Contact *Hannah Scott*

Initiated 1989. Annual research fellowships for up to three years – towards a book or paper – for serious research connected with national and international law, and human freedom. Preferably attached to a particular university in Britain.

Newspaper Press Fund

See **NPF**

North East Literary Fellowship

Arts Council England, North East, Central Square, Forth Street, Newcastle upon Tyne NE1 3PJ

☎0191 255 8542   Fax 0191 230 1020

www.artscouncil.org.uk

Contact *Literature Officer*

A competitive fellowship in association with the Universities of Durham and Newcastle upon Tyne. Contact **Arts Council England, North East**, for details.

Northern Rock Foundation Writer's Award

New Writing North, 2 School Lane, Whickham, Newcastle upon Tyne NE16 4SL

☎0191 488 8580   Fax 0191 488 8576

✉ mail@newwritingnorth.com

www.nr-foundationwriters.com

Contact *Silvana Michelini*

Annual award established in 2002 with the aim of liberating established writers who live in the region from work other than writing. Applicants must have at least two books published by a recognised publisher and *must* live and work in Northumberland, Tyne and Wear, County Durham, Cumbria or Teesside. 2005 winner: poet Gillian Allnutt.

AWARD £60,000 (£20,000 a year for three years).

Northern Writers' Awards

See **New Writing North** under *Professional Associations and Societies*

NPF The Journalists' Charity

Dickens House, 35 Wathen Road, Dorking RH4 1JY

☎01306 887511   Fax 01306 888212

✉ enquiries@npf.org.uk

Director/Secretary *David Ilott*

Aims to relieve distress among journalists and their dependants. Continuous and/or occasional financial grants; also retirement homes for eligible beneficiaries. Further information and subscription details available from the Director.

PAWS (Public Awareness of Science) Drama Fund

The PAWS Office, OMNI Communications, Suite 37, Chancel House, Neasden Lane, London NW10 2TU

www.pawsdrama.com

Contacts *Barrie Whatley, Andrew Millington*

Established 1994. PAWS encourages and supports television drama drawing on science, engineering and technology. It offers a range of activities to bring science and technology to TV drama writers and producers in an easily accessible way.

Events: covering the latest science and technology topics and enabling writers to meet scientists and engineers (see website); Contacts &

Information Service: aims to put writers and producers in 'one-to-one' contact with specialists who can help them develop their TV drama ideas. Send requests with a contact phone number to info@pawsomni.globalnet.co.uk or write to the PAWS Office; New Funding Scheme: rolling funding support primarily intended to help writers and producers who have a recent track record of successful TV drama experience to bring their ideas closer to production. People with lesser experience are welcome to apply but no funding is reserved for this category. To discuss funding e-mail ideas05@pawsomni.globalnet.co.uk or write to the PAWS Office.

Pearson Playwrights' Scheme
80 Strand, London WC2R 0RL
www.pearson.com
Administrator *Jack Andrews, MBE*

Awards four bursaries to playwrights annually, each worth £6500. Applicants must be sponsored by a theatre which then submits the play for consideration by a panel. Each award allows the playwright a twelve-month attachment. Applications invited via theatres in October each year. For up-to-date information, e-mail *Jack Andrews*.

Charles Pick Fellowship
School of Literature and Creative Writing, University of East Anglia, University Plain, Norwich NR4 7TJ
☎01603 492810   Fax 01603 507728
✉ v.striker@uea.ac.uk
www.uea.ac.uk/eas/fellowships/pick.shtml
Contact *Val Striker*

An annual award, founded in 2001 by the Charles Pick Consultancy in memory of the publisher and literary agent who died in 2000, to support a new unpublished writer of fictional or non-fictional prose. Award of the Fellowship, which is residential from August to January, is judged on the quality of writing and reference from a literary agent, editor or accredited creative writing teacher. Previous winner: Alistair Daniel. Deadline for applications: 31 January each year.

AWARD £10,000 plus free campus accommodation.

Peggy Ramsay Foundation
Hanover House, 14 Hanover Square, London W1S 1HP
☎020 7667 5000   Fax 020 7667 5100
✉ laurence.harbottle@harbottle.com
www.peggyramsayfoundation.org
Contact *G. Laurence Harbottle*

Founded 1992 in accordance with the will of the late Peggy Ramsay, the well-known agent. Grants are made to writers for the stage who have some experience and who need time and resources to make writing possible. Grants are also made for writing projects by organisations connected with the theatre. The Foundation does not support production costs or any project that does not have a direct benefit to playwriting. Writers must have some record of successful writing for the stage.

GRANTS total £150,000 to £200,000 per year.

The Royal Literary Fund
3 Johnson's Court, off Fleet Street, London EC4A 3EA
☎020 7353 7150   Fax 020 7353 1350
✉ egunnrlf@globalnet.co.uk
www.rlf.org.uk
Secretary *Eileen Gunn*

Grants and pensions are awarded to published authors of several works in financial need, or to their dependants. Examples of author's works are needed for assessment by Committee. Contact the Secretary for further details and application form.

The Royal Society of Literature/Jerwood Awards
The Royal Society of Literature, Somerset House, Strand, London WC2R 1LA
☎020 7845 4676   Fax 020 7845 4679
✉ rsl&jerwood@billingplace.co.uk
www.rslit.org
Submissions *Paula Johnson*

The awards offer financial assistance to authors engaged in writing their first major commissioned works of non-fiction. Three awards: one of £10,000 and two of £5000 will be offered annually to writers working on substantial non-fiction projects. Open to UK and Irish writers and writers who have been resident in the UK for at least three years. Applications for the awards should be submitted by end August. Further details available on the website.

Scottish Arts Council Book Awards
Scottish Arts Council, 12 Manor Place, Edinburgh EH3 7DD
☎0131 226 6051   Fax 0131 225 9833
✉ sophy.dale@scottisharts.org.uk
www.scottisharts.org.uk
Contact *Sophy Dale*, Literature Officer

Awards are made annually and are given in recognition of high standards in fiction, poetry and literary non-fiction. Authors should be Scottish or resident in Scotland, but books of Scottish interest by other authors are eligible for consideration. Applications are made by publishers only, and the closing date is 31 January for books published in the previous calendar year.

AWARDS Three shortlisted adult and three shortlisted children's writers each receive an award of £2000. The Scottish Arts Council Book of Year Award is worth a total of £10,000 and the Children's Book of the Year is a total of £5000.

Scottish Arts Council Creative Scotland Awards

Scottish Arts Council, 12 Manor Place, Edinburgh EH3 7DD
☎0131 226 6051/ Help Desk: 0845 603 6000
Fax 0131 225 9833
✉ help.desk@scottisharts.org.uk
www.scottisharts.org.uk

The scheme offers awards of £30,000. Available to established artists based in Scotland working in any medium, including writing.

Scottish Arts Council New Writers' Bursaries

Scottish Arts Council, 12 Manor Place, Edinburgh EH3 7DD
☎0131 226 6051   Fax 0131 225 9833
✉ gavin.wallace@scottisharts.org.uk
www.scottisharts.org.uk

Contact *Gavin Wallace*, Head of Literature

Ten bursaries of £2000 awarded annually to enable previously unpublished writers of literary work more time to devote to their writing. Applicants should be based in Scotland.

Scottish Arts Council Writers' and Playwrights' Bursaries

Scottish Arts Council, 12 Manor Place, Edinburgh EH3 7DD
☎0131 226 6051   Fax 0131 225 9833
✉ gavin.wallace@scottisharts.org.uk
www.scottisharts.org.uk

Contact *Gavin Wallace*, Head of Literature

Bursaries to enable published writers of literary work and recognised playwrights to devote more time to their writing. Around 20 bursaries of up to £15,000 awarded annually; deadline for applications in July and January. Application open to writers based in Scotland.

Laurence Stern Fellowship

Department of Journalism, City University, Northampton Square, London EC1V 0HB
☎020 7040 4036   Fax 020 7040 8594
✉ a.r.mckane@city.ac.uk
www.city.ac.uk/journalism

Contact *Anna McKane*

Founded 1980. Awarded to a young journalist experienced enough to work on national stories. It gives them the chance to work on the national desk of the *Washington Post*. Benjamin Bradlee, the *Post's* Vice-President-at-Large, selects from a shortlist drawn up in March/April. 2004 winner: Mary Fitzgerald of the *Belfast Telegraph*. Full details available on the website.

Tom-Gallon Trust Award and the Olive Cook Prize

The Society of Authors, 84 Drayton Gardens, London SW10 9SB
☎020 7373 6642   Fax 020 7373 5768
✉ info@societyofauthors.org
www.societyofauthors.org

An award of £1000 is made on the basis of a submitted story to fiction writers of limited means who have had at least one short story accepted for publication. Both awards are biennial and are awarded in alternate years. Contact the **Society of Authors** for an entry form. Final entry date 31 October.

The Betty Trask Awards

The Society of Authors, 84 Drayton Gardens, London SW10 9SB
☎020 7373 6642   Fax 020 7373 5768
✉ info@societyofauthors.org
www.societyofauthors.org

These annual awards are for authors who are under 35 and Commonwealth citizens, awarded on the strength of a first novel (published or unpublished) of a traditional or romantic nature. The awards must be used for a period or periods of foreign travel. Final entry date: 31 January. Contact the **Society of Authors** for an entry form. 2004 winners: Louise Dean *Becoming Strangers*; Hannah MacDonald *The Sun Road*; Anthony Cartwright *The Afterglow*, Siddharth Dhanvant Shanghvi *The Last Song of Dusk*. AWARD £20,000 (total).

The Travelling Scholarships

The Society of Authors, 84 Drayton Gardens, London SW10 9SB
☎020 7373 6642   Fax 020 7373 5768
✉ info@societyofauthors.org

www.societyofauthors.org

Annual honorary grants to established British writers. No submissions. 2004 winners: Tim Binding, Colm Tóibín.

AWARD £6000 (total).

UEA Writing Fellowship

School of English and American Studies, University of East Anglia, University Plain, Norwich NR4 7TJ

☎01603 592734   Fax 01603 593522

www.uea.ac.uk/eas/fellowships/
writingfellow.shtml

Director of Personnel & Registry Services
J.R.L. Beck

Established 1971. Awarded to a writer of established reputation in prose fiction and poetry for a period of six months, January to end June. The duties of the Fellowship are discussed at an interview. It is assumed that one activity will be the pursuit of the Fellow's own writing. In addition the Fellow will be expected to teach an undergraduate creative writing workshop in the School of English and American Studies during the Spring semester, and to undertake a programme of events around the county in association with Arts Council England, East. Office space and some limited secretarial assistance will be provided. Applications for the Fellowship should be lodged with the Director of Personnel & Registry Services in the autumn; candidates should submit two examples of recent work. Previous winner: David Flusfeder.

AWARD £7500, plus accommodation as required.

David T.K. Wong Fellowship

School of Literature and Creative Writing, University of East Anglia, University Plain, Norwich NR4 7TJ

☎01603 592810   Fax 01603 507728

✉ v.striker@uea.ac.uk

www.uea.ac.uk/eas/fellowships/wong/
wong.shtml

Contact *Val Striker*

Founded 1998. An annual endowment to enable a writer of promise to spend a year at the University writing a work of fiction on some aspect of life in the Far East. Judged on the basis of submitted written work, the award is open to all nationalities. Final entry date: 31 October. 2004/5 winner: Rattawut Lapcharoensap.

AWARD £25,000

Prizes

Academi Book of the Year Awards

Academi, 3rd Floor, Mount Stuart House, Mount Stuart Square, Cardiff CF10 5FQ
☎029 2047 2266   Fax 029 2049 2930
✉ post@academi.org

Annual non-competitive prizes awarded for works of exceptional literary merit written by Welsh authors (by birth or residence), published in Welsh or English during the previous calendar year. There is one major prize in English, the Book of the Year Award, and one major prize in Welsh, Gwobr Llyfr y Flwyddyn.
PRIZES £7000 to each winner.

J.R. Ackerley Prize

English PEN, 6–8 Amwell Street, London EC1R 1UQ
☎020 7713 0023   Fax 020 7837 7838
✉ enquiries@englishpen.org
www.englishpen.org

Commemorating the novelist/autobiographer J.R. Ackerley, this prize is awarded for a literary autobiography, written in English and published in the year preceding the award. Entry restricted to nominations from the Ackerley Trustees only ('please do not submit books'). 2004 winner: Bryan Magee *Clouds of Glory*.
PRIZE £1000, plus silver pen.

Aldeburgh Poetry Festival Prize

See **Jerwood Aldeburgh First Collection Prize**

Alexander Prize

Royal Historical Society, University College London, Gower Street, London WC1E 6BT
☎020 7387 7532   Fax 020 7387 7532
✉ rhs.info@sas.ac.uk

Contact *Executive Secretary*

Awarded for a historical essay of not more than 8000 words. Competitors may choose their own subject for the essay. Closing date: 1 November.
PRIZE £250 or a silver medal.

ALPSP Awards/ALPSP/ Charlesworth Awards

ALPSP, 47 Vicarage Road, Old Moulsham, Chelmsford CM2 9BS
☎01245 260571   Fax 01245 260935
www.alpsp.org
Contact *Lesley Ogg*

Presented in recognition of significant achievement in the field of learned and professional publishing by the **Association of Learned and Professional Society Publishers** and the Charlesworth Group. The awards were originally for excellence in design and typography in journals but since 2001 they also recognise innovation, contribution to not-for-profit publishing, library-publisher relations and service to ALPSP. The awards are international and open to publishers, organisations and individuals. Details available on the Association's website.

Hans Christian Andersen Awards

IBBY, Nonnenweg 12, Postfach, CH-4003 Basel, Switzerland
☎00 41 61 272 2917   Fax 00 41 61 272 2757
✉ ibby@ibby.org
www.ibby.org

Administrative Director *Liz Page*

The highest international prizes for children's literature: The Hans Christian Andersen Award for Writing, established 1956; The Hans Christian Andersen Award for Illustration, established 1966. Candidates are nominated by National Sections of IBBY (The International Board on Books for Young People). Biennial prizes are awarded, in even-numbered years, to an author and an illustrator whose body of work has made a lasting contribution to children's literature. 2004 winners: Award for Writing: Martin Waddell (Ireland); Award for Illustration: Max Velthuijs (The Netherlands).
AWARD Gold medals.

Angus Book Award

Angus Council Cultural Services, County Buildings, Forfar DD8 3WF
☎01307 461460   Fax 01307 462590
✉ cultural.services@angus.gov.uk

Contact *Moyra Hood*, Educational Resources Librarian

Established 1995. Designed to try to help teenagers develop an interest in and enthusiasm for reading. Eligible books are read and voted on by third-year schoolchildren in all eight Angus secondary schools. 2004 winner: Alan

Gibbons *The Edge*.
PRIZE £250 cheque, plus trophy in the form of a replica Pictish stone.

Annual Theatre Book Prize
See **The Society for Theatre Research Annual Theatre Book Prize**

Artists' Choice Award for Art Instruction Book of the Year
PO Box 3, Huntingdon PE28 0QX
☎01832 710201   Fax 01832 710488
✉ award@acaward.com
www.acaward.com
Contact *Henry Malt*
Established 1995 by Artists' Choice Book Club to recognise the quality of books published in this specialised field. Books must have an element of art instruction and be first published in the UK. 2005 winner: *Botanical Illustration*, Siriol Sherlock.
    PRIZE Cheque presented to the author; trophy to the publisher.

Arts Council Children's Award
Arts Council England, 14 Great Peter Street, London SW1P 3NQ
☎020 7973 6480
✉ charles.hart@artscouncil.org.uk
www.artscouncil.org.uk
Contact *Theatre Writing Section*
Founded 2000. An annual award for playwrights who write for children up to the age of 12. The plays, which must have been produced professionally, should be suitable for children up to the age of 12 and be at least 45 minutes long. The playwright must be resident in the UK. Contact the Theatre Writing Section for full details and application form. 2005 winner: Abi Bown *Hey There Boy with the Bebop*.
    AWARD £6000.

Arvon Foundation International Poetry Competition
2nd Floor, 42a Buckingham Palace Road, London SW1W 0RE
☎020 7931 7611   Fax 020 7963 0961
✉ london@arvonfoundation.org
www.arvonfoundation.org
Contact *The London Office*
Established 1980. Biennial competition (next in 2006) for poems written in English and not previously broadcast or published. There are no restrictions on the number of lines, themes, age of entrants or nationality. No limit to the number of entries. Entry fee: £7 per poem. Previous win-

ners: Paul Farley *Laws of Gravity*; Don Paterson *A Private Bottling*.
    PRIZE (1st) £5000 and £5000 worth of other prizes sponsored by Duncan Lawrie Limited.

Authors' Club First Novel Award
Authors' Club, 40 Dover Street, London W1S 4NP
☎020 7499 8581   Fax 020 7409 0913
✉ secretary@authorsclub.co.uk
www.authorsclub.co.uk
Contact *Lucy Jane Tetlow*
Established 1954. This award is made for the most promising work published in Britain by a British author, and is presented at a dinner held at The Arts Club. Entries for the award are accepted from publishers from September of the year in question and must be full-length (short stories are not eligible). For further details/application form, contact *Lucy Jane Tetlow* or access the website. 2003 winner: Dan Rhodes *Timoleon Vieta Come Home*.
    AWARD £1000.

Aventis Prizes for Science Books
c/o The Royal Society, 6–9 Carlton House Terrace, London SW1Y 5AG
☎020 7451 2576   Fax 020 7930 2170
✉ aventisprizes@royalsoc.ac.uk
www.aventisprizes.com
Contact *Aosaf Afzal*
Annual prizes established in 1988 to celebrate the best in popular science writing. Awarded to books that make science more accessible to readers of all ages and backgrounds. Managed by the Royal Society and sponsored by the Aventis Foundation. All entries must be written in English and their first publication in the UK must have been between 1 January and 31 December; submission by publishers only. Educational textbooks published for professional or specialist audiences are not eligible. 2005 winners: Philip Ball *Critical Mass* (General Prize); Robert Winston *What Makes Me, Me?* (Junior Prize).
    PRIZES (total) £30,000: £10,000 to each winner; £1000 to each of the five shortlisted authors in each prize.

The BA/Nielson BookData Author of the Year Award
Booksellers Association Ltd, 272 Vauxhall Bridge Road, London SW1V 1BA
☎020 7802 0801   Fax 020 7802 0803
✉ anna.okane@booksellers.org.uk
www.booksellers.org.uk
Contact *Anna O'Kane*

Founded as part of the BA Annual Conference to involve authors more closely in the event. Authors must be British or Irish. Not an award open to entry but voted on by the BA's membership. 2005 winner: Alexander McCall Smith. AWARD £1000, plus trophy.

BAAL Book Prize

BAAL Publications Secretary, School of Education, University of Leeds, Leeds LS2 9JT
✉ a.g.white@education.leeds.ac.uk
www.baal.org.uk

Contact *Goodith White*

Annual award made by the British Association for Applied Linguistics to an outstanding book in the field of applied linguistics. Final entry at the end of October/November. Nominations from publishers only. 2004 winner: Ron Scollon and Suzie Wong Scollon *Discourses in Place: Language in the Material World*

Verity Bargate Award

Soho Theatre Company, 21 Dean Street, London W1D 3NE
☎ 020 7287 5060   Fax 020 7287 5061
✉ writers@sohotheatre.com
www.sohotheatre.com

Contact *Rachel Taylor*, Literary Assistant

The award was set up to commemorate the late Verity Bargate, co-founder and director of the **Soho Theatre Company**. This national award is presented biennially for a new and unperformed play (next in 2006). To go on the mailing list, please e-mail or send s.a.e. to *David Lane*. Previous winners include: Matt Charman, Shan Khan, Fraser Grace, Lyndon Morgans, Adrian Pagan, Diane Samuels, Judy Upton and Toby Whithouse.

BBC Wildlife Magazine Poet of the Year Awards

BBC Wildlife Magazine, Origin Publishing, 14th Floor, Tower House, FairFax Street, Bristol BS1 3BN
☎ 0117 927 9009   Fax 0117 933 8032

Annual award for a poem, the subject of which must be the natural world and/or our relationship with it. Entrants may submit one poem only of no more than 50 lines with the entry form which appears in the magazine. Closing date for entries varies from year to year. Contact the magazine for entry information.

PRIZES Poet of the Year: £500, publication in the magazine, plus reading of the poem on Radio 4's *Poetry Please*; runners-up: cash prizes, plus publication in the magazine; four young poets awards.

BBC Wildlife Magazine Travel Writing Award

BBC Wildlife Magazine, Origin Publishing, 14th Floor, Tower House, FairFax Street, Bristol BS1 3BN
☎ 0117 928 9009   Fax 0117 934 9008
✉ wildlifemagazine@originpublishing.co.uk
www.bbc.wildlifemagazine.com

Awarded to a travel essay that is a true account involving an intimate encounter with wildlife, either local or exotic. The essay should convey a strong impression of the environment and incorporate the idea of travel and discovery. Maximum 800 words. Contact the magazine for entry information.

PRIZE Publication in the magazine, plus 'holiday of a lifetime'.

The BBCFour Samuel Johnson Prize for Non-Fiction

Colman Getty PR, Middlesex House, 34–42 Cleveland Street, London W1T 4JE
☎ 020 7631 2666   Fax 020 7631 2699
✉ alice@colmangettypr.co.uk

Contact *Alice Kavanagh*

Established 1998. Annual prize sponsored by BBCFour. Eligible categories include the arts, autobiography, biography, business, commerce, current affairs, history, natural history, popular science, religion, sport and travel. Entries submitted by publishers only. 2004 winner: Anna Funder *Stasiland*.

PRIZE £30,000; £1000 to each shortlisted author.

David Berry Prize

Royal Historical Society, University College London, Gower Street, London WC1E 6BT
☎ 020 7387 7532   Fax 020 7387 7532
✉ rhs.info@sas.ac.uk

Contact *Executive Secretary*

Annual award for an essay of not more than 10,000 words on Scottish history. Closing date: 31 October.

PRIZE £250,

Besterman/McColvin Medal

42 Moors Lane, Winsford CW7 1JX
☎ 020 7255 0500   Fax 020 7255 0501
www.cilip.org.uk

Part of the ISG (CILIP)/Nielsen BookData Reference Awards. Annual award for an outstanding reference work first published in the UK during the preceding year. Consists of two categories: printed and electronic. Works eligible for consideration include: encyclopedias, general and special dictionaries; annuals, yearbooks and directories; handbooks and compendia of data; atlases. Nominations are invited from members of **CILIP**, publishers and others. 2003 winners: *Early Printed Books Catalogue 1478–1840: Catalogue of the British Architectural Library, Early Imprints Collection Vol 5* (printed); *xreferplus www.xrefer.com* published by xrefer ltd (electronic).

AWARD Medal and cash prize for each category.

The Biographers' Club Prize
17 Sutherland Street, London SW1V 4JU
☎020 7828 1274   Fax 020 7828 7608
✉ lownie@globalnet.co.uk
www.booktrust.org.uk

Contact *Andrew Lownie*

Established 1999 by literary agent, biographer and founder of the Biographers' Club, Andrew Lownie, to finance and encourage first-time writers researching a biography. Sponsored by the *Daily Mail*. Open to previously un-commissioned and unpublished writers producing a proposal of 15–20 pages, broken down by chapter with a note of author's credentials, the market for the book, sources used, competing/comparable books and ten-page sample chapter. 2004 winner: Linda Porter.

PRIZE £1000.

Birdwatch Bird Book of the Year
c/o Birdwatch Magazine, B403A The Chocolate Factory, 5 Clarendon Road, London N22 6XJ
☎020 8881 0550

Contact *Dominic Mitchell*

Established in 1992 to acknowledge excellence in ornithological publishing – an increasingly large market with a high turnover. Annual award. Entries, from publishers, must offer an original and comprehensive treatment of their particular ornithological subject matter and must have a broad appeal to British-based readers. 2004 winner: *Gulls of Europe, Asia and North America* Klaus Malling Olsen and Hans Larsson.

Biscuit International Short Fiction Prize
Biscuit Publishing, PO Box 123, Washington, Newcastle upon Tyne NE37 2YW
☎0191 431 1263   Fax 0191 431 1263
✉ info@biscuitpublishing.com

www.biscuitpublishing.com

Contacts *Brian Lister, Jacqui Lister*

Founded 2000. Annual award that aims to support new writers of short fiction. The 'Top Ten' winners are published in an anthology and recorded on audio CD. In addition, the winning author has separate publication. Closing date: 31 May. Previous winners: Tracey Fuller *The System Was Turned On*; Sue Vickerman *The Sensitively Thin Bill of the Shag*; Angela Readman *Almost Elvis*; Gillian Garnham *A Place Proper to Grow Wise In*.

PRIZES Publication and cash awards.

Bisto/CBI Book of the Year Awards
17 Lower Camden Street, Dublin 2, Republic of Ireland
☎00 353 1 475 0445   Fax 00 353 1 475 3716
✉ info@childrensbooksireland.com

Contact *Jenny Murray*

Founded 1990 as Bisto Book of the Decade Awards. This led to the establishment of an annual award made by the Irish Children's Book Trust, later to become Children's Books Ireland. Open to any author or illustrator of children's books born or resident in Ireland; open to English or Irish languages. Final entry date 31 January. 2004 winners: Audrey Flegg *Wings Over Delft*; Alan Titley *Amach*; Kate Thompson *Origins*; Anita Jeram *You Can Do It Sam*; Niamh Sharkey *The Ravenous Beast*.

PRIZES €3000 (Bisto Book of the Year); €1000 (Eilís Dillon Award); three merit awards of €1000 each.

James Tait Black Memorial Prizes
University of Edinburgh, David Hume Tower, George Square, Edinburgh EH8 9JX
☎0131 650 3619   Fax 0131 650 6898
www.englit.ed.ac.uk/jtbinf.htm

Contact *Department of English Literature*

Established 1918 in memory of a partner of the publishing firm of **A.&C. Black Ltd**. Two prizes, one for biography and one for fiction. Closing date for submissions: 30 September. Each prize is awarded for a book published in Britain in the previous twelve months. 2004 winners: David Peace *GB84* (fiction); Jonathan Bate *John Clare: A Biography* (biography).

PRIZES £3000 each.

Blue Peter Book Awards
c/o Awards Administrator, Fraser Ross Associates, 6 Wellington Place, Edinburgh EH6 7EQ

☎0131 553 2759   Fax 0131 657 4412
✉ lindsey.fraser@tiscali.co.uk
www.bbc.co.uk/bluepeter

Contacts *Lindsey Fraser, Kathryn Ross*

Established in 1999 to highlight paperback fiction, poetry and non-fiction for young people. The initial shortlist is selected by a panel of adults and the final decisions are taken by a panel of Blue Peter judges. Final entry date: mid-June. Previous winners: Nicky Singer *Feather Boy*; Philip Reeve *Mortal Engines*; Simon Bartram *Man on the Moon*.

AWARD Trophy.

Boardman Tasker Award
Pound House, Llangennith, Swansea SA3 1JQ
☎01792 386215   Fax 01792 386215
✉ margaretbody@lineone.net
www.boardmantasker.com

Contact *Maggie Body*, Honorary Secretary

Established 1983, this award is given for a work of fiction, non-fiction or poetry, whose central theme is concerned with the mountain environment and which can be said to have made an outstanding contribution to mountain literature. Authors of any nationality are eligible, but the book must have been published or distributed in the UK for the first time between 1 November 2004 and 31 October 2005. Entries from publishers only. 2004 winner: Trevor Braham *When the Alps Cast Their Spell*.

PRIZE £2000 (at Trustees' discretion).

Bollinger Everyman Wodehouse Prize
Everyman's Library, Northburgh House, 10 Northburgh Street, London EC1V 0AT
☎020 7566 6350   Fax 020 7490 3708
✉ dcampbell@randomhouse.co.uk *or* natalia@everyman.uk.com
www.everyman.uk.com

Contact *Natalia Rolleston*

Established in 2000 by Everyman's Library, Bollinger and the Hay Festival to celebrate comic writing in memory of P.G. Wodehouse. Books are nominated by readers of the *Sunday Times* and visitors to www.bol.com. 2005 winner: Marina Lewycka *A Short History of Tractors in Ukrainian*.

The Booker Prize for Fiction
See **The Man Booker Prize for Fiction**

Booktrust Early Years Awards
Booktrust, Book House, 45 East Hill, London SW18 2QZ
☎020 8516 2972   Fax 020 8516 2978
✉ tarryn@booktrust.org.uk
www.booktrust.org.uk

Contact *Tarryn McKay*

Formerly the Sainsbury's Baby Book Award, established in 1999. Annual awards with three categories: the Baby Book Award, the Best Book for Pre-School Children (up to the age of 5), and an award for the Best New Illustrator. Books to be submitted by publishers only; authors and illustrators must be of British nationality or other nationals who have been resident in the UK for at least five years.

PRIZE £2000 for each category; in addition the Best New Illustrator receives a specially commissioned award.

Booktrust Teenage Prize
Book House, 45 East Hill, London SW18 2QZ
☎020 8516 2986   Fax 020 8516 2978
✉ hannah@booktrust.org.uk
www.bookheads.org.uk

Contact *Hannah Rutland*

Established 1993. Annual prize that recognises and celebrates the best in teenage fiction. Funded and administered by Booktrust. Open to works of fiction for young adults in the UK, the books to be published between 1 July 2004 and 30 June 2005. Final entry date in March. 2004 winner: Anne Cassidy *Looking for JJ*.

PRIZE £1500.

Harry Bowling Prize
c/o Coseley House, Munslow, Craven Arms SY7 9ET
✉ dana@mbalit.co.uk
www.harrybowlingprize.net

Contact *Dana Arnott*

Established 2000 in honour of Harry Bowling, 'the king of Cockney sagas' (died 1999). Biennial award (next in 2006), sponsored by **Headline Book Publishing**, to encourage writers of adult fiction set in London. Open to anyone who has not been published previously. Final entry date: 31 March. Entry fee charged; forms from address above (enclose s.a.e.) or via the website. 2002 joint winners: Catherine Woodman *Waking Up*; Mark Lalbeharry *The Symian Curve*.

PRIZES Winner, £1000; two runners-up, £100 each.

The Branford Boase Award
8 Bolderwood Close, Bishopstoke, Eastleigh SO50 8PG
☎023 8060 0439
✉ anne@marleyhcl.freeserve.co.uk

www.henriettabranford.co.uk

Administrator *Anne Marley*

Established in 2000 in memory of children's novelist, Henrietta Branford and editor and publisher, Wendy Boase. To be awarded annually to encourage and celebrate the most promising novel by a new writer of children's books, while at the same time highlighting the importance of the editor in nurturing new talent. 2004 winner: Mal Peet *Keeper* (author); Paul Harrison **Walker Books** (editor).

AWARD Specially commissioned box, carved and inlaid in silver with the Branford Boase Award logo.

The Bridport Prize

Bridport Arts Centre, South Street, Bridport DT6 3NR
☎01308 485064   Fax 01308 485120
✉ frances@poorton.demon.co.uk
www.bridportprize.org.uk

Contact *Frances Everitt*, Administrator

Annual competition for poetry and short story writing. Unpublished work only, written in English. Winning stories are read by a literary agent, the winning poems are put forward to the **Forward Prize**, and an anthology of winning entries is published. Final entry date: 30 June. Send s.a.e. for entry forms.

PRIZES £3000, £1000 & £500 in each category, plus 10 supplementary prizes of £50 each.

Katharine Briggs Folklore Award

The Folklore Society, c/o The Warburg Institute, Woburn Square, London WC1H 0AB
☎020 7862 8564
✉ enquiries@folklore-society.com
www.folklore-society.com

Contact *The Convenor*

Established 1982. An annual award in November for the book, published in Britain and Ireland between 1 June in the previous calendar year and 30 May, which has made the most distinguished non-fiction contribution to folklore studies. Intended to encourage serious research in the field which Katharine Briggs did so much to establish. The term folklore studies is interpreted broadly to include all aspects of traditional and popular culture, narrative, belief, custom and folk arts. 2004 winner: Steve Roud *The Penguin Guide to the Superstitions of Britain and Ireland*.

PRIZE £50, plus engraved goblet.

British Book Awards

Publishing News, 7 John Street, London WC1N 2ES
☎0870 870 2345   Fax 0870 870 0385
✉ mailbox@publishingnews.co.uk
www.britishbookawards.com

Established 1988. Viewed by the book trade as the one to win, 'The Nibbies' are presented annually. The awards are made in various categories. Each winner receives the prestigious Nibbie and the awards are presented to those who have made the most impact in the book trade during the previous year. 2004 winners included: Lynne Truss, Monica Ali, Alexander McCall Smith, David Attenborough, Mark Haddon. For further information contact: Merric Davidson, 12 Priors Heath, Goudhurst, Cranbrook TN17 2RE (☎/Fax 01580 212041; email nibbies@mdla.co.uk).

British Czech & Slovak Association Prize

The BCSA Prize Administrator, 24 Ferndale, Tunbridge Wells TN2 3NS
☎01892 543206
✉ prize@bcsa.co.uk
www.bcsa.co.uk

Contact *Prize Administrator*

The British Czech & Slovak Association offers an annual prize for the best piece of original writing, in English, on the links between Britain and the Czech and Slovak Republics, or describing society in transition in those Republics since the Velvet Revolution in 1989. Entries can be fiction or factual, should not have been previously published and should be up to 2000 words in length. Submissions are invited from individuals of any age, nationality or educational background. Closing date: 30 June. Entry details for 2006 should be checked with the Prize Administrator. 2004 winner: Barbara Peacock *Romantic Gothic Castles in Britain and Bohemia*.

PRIZE £300, presented at the BCSA's annual dinner in London. Second prize, £100. The winning entry is published in the *British Czech & Slovak Review*.

British Fantasy Awards

201 Reddish Road, South Reddish, Stockport SK5 7HR
☎0161 476 5368 (after 6.00 pm)
✉ faliol@yahoo.com
www.britishfantasysociety.org.uk

Secretary *Robert Parkinson*

Awarded by the **British Fantasy Society** by members at its annual conference for Best Novel and Best Short Story categories, among others. Not an open competition. Previous winners include: Ramsey Campbell, Dan Simmons, Michael Marshall Smith, Thomas Ligotti.

British Press Awards
Press Gazette, Quantum House, 19 Scarbrook Road, Croydon CR9 1LX
☎020 8565 3056   Fax 020 8565 4395
✉ andreah@quantumbusinessmedia.com
www.britishpressawards.com
'The Oscars of British journalism.' Open to all British morning and Sunday newspapers sold nationally and news agencies. March event. Run by *Press Gazette*.

British Science Fiction Association Awards
59 Shirley Road, Croydon CR0 7ES
☎020 8656 0137
✉ awards@fishlifter.demon.co.uk
www.bsfa.co.uk
Awards Administrator *Claire Brialey*
Established 1970. Categories for novel, short fiction and artwork. The awards are announced and presented at the British National Science Fiction Convention every Easter. 2004 winners: Ian McDonald *River of Gods* (novel); Stephen Baxter *Mayflower II* (short fiction); Stephan Martinière, for the cover of *Newton's Wake* by Ken MacLeod.

British Sports Journalism Awards
See **Sports Writers' Association of Great Britain** under *Professional Associations*

The Browning Society Poetry Prize
84 Addison Gardens, London W14 0DR
☎020 7602 3094   Fax 020 7602 3771
✉ pamela@tvdox.com
www.browningsociety.org
Contact *Pamela Neville-Sington*
Established in 2004 to encourage interest in the Brownings' poetry among young people. Held annually, the competition focuses on two different Browning poems – one by Elizabeth and one by Robert; visit the website for details. Open to students between the ages of 9 and 19 who are citizens of or resident in the UK. Final entry date: 15 March.
PRIZE £100 for students aged 9–13; £200 for students 14–19.

The Caine Prize for African Writing
51a Southwark Street, London SE1 1RU
☎020 7378 6234   Fax 020 7378 6235
✉ info@caineprize
www.caineprize.com
Administrator *Nick Elam*
Secretary *Jan Hart*
Annual award founded in 1999 in memory of Sir Michael Caine, former chairman of Booker plc, to recognise the worth of African writing in English. Awarded for a short story by an African writer, published in English anywhere in the world. 'An African writer' is someone who was born in Africa, or who is a national of an African country, or whose parents are African, and whose work has reflected African sensibilities. Final entry date: 31 January; submissions by publishers only. 2004 winner: Brian Chikwava *Seventh Street Alchemy*.
PRIZE $15,000.

The Calouste Gulbenkian Prize
See **The Translators Association Awards**

James Cameron Award
City University, Department of Journalism, Northampton Square, London EC1V 0HB
☎020 7040 8221   Fax 020 7040 8594
Contact *The Administrator*
Annual award for journalism to a reporter of any nationality, working for the British media, whose work is judged to have contributed most during the year to the continuance of the Cameron tradition. 2004 winner: John Ware.

Canadian Poetry Association (Annual Poetry Contest)
Canadian Poetry Association, 331 Elmwood Dr., Suite 4-212, Moncton, New Brunswick E1A 1X6, Canada
www.canadianpoetryassoc.com
Annual contest open to members and non-members of the CPA worldwide. Submission fee: $5 per poem. See the website for entry details. All winning poems are published on the CPA website.
Six cash PRIZES and publication in *Poetmata*.

Cardiff International Poetry Competition
PO Box 438, Cardiff CF10 5YA
☎029 2047 2266   Fax 029 2049 2930
✉ post@academi.org
www.academi.org

Contact *Peter Finch*

Established 1986. An annual competition supported by Cardiff Council for unpublished poems in English of up to 50 lines. Closing date in January.
PRIZE £7000 (total).

Carey Award

Society of Indexers, Blades Enterprise Centre, John Street, Sheffield S2 4SU
☎0114 292 2350   Fax 0114 292 2351
✉ admin@indexers.org.uk
www.indexers.org.uk

Secretary *Ann Kingdom*

A private award made by the Society to a member who has given outstanding services to indexing. The recipient is selected by Council with no recommendations considered from elsewhere.

Carnegie Medal

See **CILIP: The Chartered Institute of Library and Information Professionals Carnegie Medal**

Sid Chaplin Short Story Competition

Shildon Town Council, Civic Centre Square, Shildon DL4 1AH
☎01388 772563   Fax 01388 775227

Contact *Mrs J.M. Stafford*

Established 1986. Annual short story competition. Maximum 3000 words; £2 entrance fee (juniors free). All stories must be unpublished and not broadcast and/or performed. Application forms available from March; closing date: May.
PRIZES £300 (1st); £150 (2nd); £75 (3rd); £50 (Junior).

Children's Book Circle Eleanor Farjeon Award

See **Eleanor Farjeon Award**

The Children's Laureate

Booktrust, Book House, 45 East Hill, London SW18 2QZ
☎020 8516 2976   Fax 020 8516 2978
✉ childrenslaureate@booktrust.org.uk
www.childrenslaureate.org

Contact *Nikki Marsh*

Established 1998. The Laureate is awarded biennially to an eminent British writer or illustrator of children's books both in celebration of a lifetime's achievement and to highlight the role of children's book creators in inspiring, informing and entertaining young readers. 2005 winner: Jacqueline Wilson.
AWARD Medal and £10,000.

CILIP: The Chartered Institute of Library and Information Professionals Carnegie Medal

7 Ridgmount Street, London WC1E 7AE
☎020 7255 0650   Fax 020 7255 0651
✉ ckg@cilip.org.uk
www.ckg.org.uk

Established 1936. Presented for an outstanding book for children written in English and first published in the UK during the preceding year. Fiction, non-fiction and poetry are all eligible. 2003 winner (presented in 2004): Jennifer Donnelly *A Gathering Light*.
AWARD Medal.

CILIP: The Chartered Institute of Library and Information Professionals Kate Greenaway Medal

7 Ridgmount Street, London WC1E 7AE
☎020 7255 0650   Fax 020 7255 0651
✉ ckg@cilip.org.uk
www.ckg.org.uk

Established 1955. Presented annually for the most distinguished work in the illustration of children's books first published in the UK during the preceding year. 2003 winner (presented in 2004): Shirley Hughes *Ella's Big Chance*.
AWARD Medal. The Colin Mears Award (£5000 cash) is given annually to the winner of the Kate Greenaway Medal.

Arthur C. Clarke Award for Science Fiction

60 Bournemouth Road, Folkestone CT19 5AZ
☎01303 252939
✉ arthurcclarkeaward@yahoo.com
www.clarkeaward.com

Administrator *Paul Kincaid*

Established 1986. The Arthur C. Clarke Award is given annually to the best science fiction novel with first UK publication in the previous calendar year. Both hardcover and paperback books qualify. Made possible by a generous donation from Arthur C. Clarke, this award is selected by a rotating panel of judges nominated by the **British Science Fiction Association**, the **Science Fiction Foundation** and the Science Museum. 2004 winner: Neal Stephenson *Quicksilver*.

AWARD £2005 (award increases by £1 per year), plus trophy.

David Cohen Prize for Literature

Arts Council England, 14 Great Peter Street, London SW1P 3NQ
☎020 7973 5325 Fax 020 7973 6983
✉ info.literature@artscouncil.org.uk
www.artscouncil.org.uk

Literature Director *Gary McKeone*
Literature Administrator *Jessica Ryan*

Established 1993 by the Arts Council and awarded biennially, the David Cohen Prize for Literature is one of the most distinguished literary prizes in Britain. It recognises writers who use the English language and who are citizens of the UK and the Republic of Ireland, encompassing dramatists as well as novelists, poets and essayists. The prize is for a lifetime's achievement and is donated by the David Cohen Family Charitable Trust. Set up in 1980 by David Cohen, general practitioner and son of a property developer, the Trust has helped composers, choreographers, dancers, poets, playwrights and actors. The Council is providing a futher £12,500 (The Clarissa Luard Award) to enable the winner to commission new work, with the dual aim of encouraging young writers and readers. Previous winners: William Trevor, Dame Muriel Spark, Harold Pinter, V.S. Naipaul, Doris Lessing, Beryl Bainbridge and Thom Gunn. 2005 winner: Michael Holroyd.

AWARD £40,000, plus £12,500 towards new work.

The Commonwealth Writers Prize

Cumberland Lodge, The Great Park, Windsor SL4 2HP
☎01784 497792
✉ ginnyfelton@cumberlandlodge.ac.uk
www.commonwealthwriters.com

Contact *Ginny Felton*

Established 1987. An annual award to reward and encourage the upsurge of new Commonwealth fiction. Any work of prose or fiction is eligible, i.e. a novel or collection of short stories. No drama or poetry. The work must be first written in English by a citizen of the Commonwealth and be first published in the year before its entry for the prize. Entries must be submitted by the publisher to the region of the writer's Commonwealth citizenship. The four regions are: Africa, Eurasia, S.E. Asia and South Pacific, Caribbean and Canada. 2005 winner: Andrea Levy *Small Island* (Best Book Award); Chimamanda Ngozi Adichie *Purple Hibiscus* (Best First Book Award).

PRIZES £10,000 for Best Book; £3000 for Best First Book; 8 prizes of £1000 for each best and first best book in four regions.

The Thomas Cook Travel Book Award

Thomas Cook Publishing, PO Box 227, Peterborough PE3 8XX
☎01733 417352

Established in 1980 by The Thomas Cook Group. Annual award given to the author of the book, published (in the English language) in the previous year, which most inspires the reader to want to travel. Submissions by publishers only. 2004 winner: Richard Grant *Ghost Riders*.

AWARD £10,000.

The Duff Cooper Prize

54 St Maur Road, London SW6 4DP
☎020 7736 3729 Fax 020 7731 7638

Contact *Artemis Cooper*

An annual award for a literary work of biography, history, politics or poetry, published by a recognised publisher (member of the **Publishers Association**) during the previous 12 months. The book must be submitted by the publisher, not the author. Financed by the interest from a trust fund commemorating Duff Cooper, first Viscount Norwich (1890–1954). 2004 winner: Anne Applebaum *Gulag: A History of the Soviet Camps*.

PRIZE £4000.

Rose Mary Crawshay Prize

The British Academy, 10 Carlton House Terrace, London SW1Y 5AH
☎020 7969 5200 Fax 020 7969 5300
www.britac.ac.uk

Contact *British Academy Secretary*

Established 1888 by Rose Mary Crawshay, this prize is given for a historical or critical work by a woman of any nationality on English literature, with particular preference for a work on Keats, Byron or Shelley. The work must have been published in the preceding three years.

PRIZES under review.

Crime Writers' Association (Cartier Diamond Dagger)

PO Box 273, Boreham Wood WD6 2XA
✉ secretary@thecwa.co.uk
www.thecwa.co.uk

Contact *The Secretary*

Established 1986. An annual award for a lifetime's outstanding contribution to the genre. 2005 winner: Ian Rankin.

Crime Writers' Association (The Gold Dagger for Non-Fiction)
PO Box 273, Boreham Wood WD6 2XA
✉ secretary@thecwa.co.uk
www.thecwa.co.uk
Contact *The Secretary*

Sponsored by the Mystery and Thriller Book Club. Annual award for the best non-fiction crime book published during the year. Nominations from publishers only. 2004 joint winners: John Dickie *Cosa Nostra* and Sarah Wise *The Italian Boy*.
AWARD Dagger, plus cheque (sum varies).

Crime Writers' Association (The CWA Ellis Peters Historical Dagger)
PO Box 273, Boreham Wood WD6 2XA
✉ secretary@thecwa.co.uk
www.thecwa.co.uk
Contact *The Secretary*

Sponsored by the Estate of Ellis Peters, Time Warner and **Headline**. Established 1999. Annual award for the best historical crime novel. Nominations from publishers only. 2004 winner: Barbara Cleverly *The Damascened Blade*.
AWARD Dagger, plus cheque.

Crime Writers' Association (The Gold and Silver Daggers for Fiction)
PO Box 273, Boreham Wood WD6 2XA
✉ secretary@thecwa.co.uk
www.thecwa.co.uk
Contact *The Secretary*

Sponsored by the Mystery and Thriller Book Club. Two annual awards for the best crime fiction published during the year. Nominations for Gold Dagger from publishers only. 2004 winners: Sara Paretsky *Blacklist* (Gold); John Harvey *Flesh and Blood* (Silver).
AWARD Dagger, plus cheque (sum varies).

Crime Writers' Association (The Ian Fleming Steel Dagger)
PO Box 273, Boreham Wood WD6 2XA
✉ secretary@thecwa.co.uk
www.thecwa.co.uk
Contact *The Secretary*

Founded 2002. Annual award for the best thriller, adventure or spy novel. Sponsored by Ian Fleming (Glidrose) Publications Ltd to celebrate the best of contemporary thriller writing. 2004 winner: Jeffery Deaver *Garden of Beasts*.
AWARD Dagger, plus cheque.

Crime Writers' Association (The Short Story Dagger)
PO Box 273, Boreham Wood WD6 2XA
✉ secretary@thecwa.co.uk
www.thecwa.co.uk
Contact *The Secretary*

Established 1993. Sponsored by the Mystery and Thriller Book Club. An award for a published crime story. Publishers should submit three copies of the story by 30 September. 2004 winner: Jeffery Deaver *The Weekender*.
PRIZE Dagger, plus cheque.

Crime Writers' Association (The Creasey Dagger for Best First Crime Novel)
PO Box 273, Boreham Wood WD6 2XA
✉ secretary@thecwa.co.uk
www.thecwa.co.uk
Contact *The Secretary*

Established in 1973 following the death of crime writer John Creasey, founder of the **Crime Writers' Association**. This award, sponsored by **BBC Audio Books**, is given annually for the best crime novel by an author who has not previously published a full-length work of fiction. Nominations from publishers only. 2004 winner: Mark Mills *Amagansett*.
AWARD Dagger, plus cheque.

Crime Writers' Association (The Dagger in the Library)
PO Box 273, Boreham Wood WD6 2XA
✉ secretary@thecwa.co.uk
www.thecwa.co.uk
Contact *The Secretary*

Reinstated 2002. Annual award (sponsored by **Random House**) to the author whose work has given most pleasure to readers. Nominated and judged by librarians. 2004 winner: Alexander McCall Smith.
AWARD Dagger, plus cheque.

Crime Writers' Association (The Debut Dagger)
New Writing Competition, P.O. Box 273, Boreham Wood WD6 2XA
✉ debut.dagger@thecwa.co.uk
www.thecwa.co.uk

Contact *The Secretary*

Annual competition (sponsored by **Orion**) for unpublished writers to submit the first 3000 words and 500 word outline of a crime novel (entry fee and form required). For full details see website or send s.a.e. to address above. 2004 winner: Ellen Grubb *The Doll Makers*.

AWARD Dagger, plus cheque.

Hunter Davies Prize
See **Lakeland Book of the Year Awards**

Felix Dennis Prize for Best First Collection
See **The Forward Prizes for Poetry**

Isaac & Tamara Deutscher Memorial Prize
Faculty of Law & Social Sciences, SOAS, University of London, Thornaugh Street, Russell Square, London WC1H 0XG
Contact *Dr Alfredo Filho*

An annual award in recognition of, and as an encouragement to, outstanding research in or about the Marxist tradition. Made to the author of a published book. Final entry date: 1 May.

AWARD £250.

George Devine Award
17A South Villas, London NW1 9BS
☎020 7267 9793 (evenings only)
Contact *Christine Smith*

Annual award for a promising new playwright writing for the stage in memory of George Devine, artistic director of the **Royal Court Theatre**, who died in 1965. The play, which can be of any length, does not need to have been produced. Send two copies of the script, plus outline of work, to *Christine Smith*. Closing date: 1 March 2006. Send s.a.e. for the script to be returned if required. Information leaflet available from January on receipt of s.a.e.

PRIZE £10,000.

Dingle Prize
British Society for the History of Science, 5 Woodcote Green, Fleet GU51 4EY
☎01252 641135
✉ execsec@bshs.org.uk
www.bshs.org.uk

Biennial award made by the BSHS to the best book in the history of science (broadly construed) which is accessible to a wide audience of non-specialists. Next award: 2005. Previous winners: Ken Alder, *The Measure of All Things*;

Deborah Cadbury *The Dinosaur Hunters*; Steven Shapin *The Scientific Revolution*.

PRIZE £300.

Michael Donaghy Prize
See **The Forward Prizes for Poetry**

Drama Association of Wales Playwriting Competition
The Old Library, Singleton Road, Splott, Cardiff CF24 2ET
☎029 2045 2200   Fax 029 2045 2277
✉ aled.daw@virgin.net
Contact *Teresa Hennessy*

Annual competition held to promote the writing of one-act plays in English and Welsh of between 20 and 50 minutes' playing time. Application forms from the address above.

The John Dryden Competition
British Comparative Literature Association/British Centre for Literary Translation, School of Literature and Creative Writing , University of East Anglia, Norwich NR4 7TJ
Fax 01603 250599
✉ transcomp@uea.ac.uk
www.bcla.org

Competition Organiser *Dr Jean Boase-Beier*

Established 1983. Annual competition open to unpublished literary translations from all languages. Maximum submission: 25 pages.

PRIZES £350 (1st); £200 (2nd); £100 (3rd); plus publication for all winning entries in the Association's annual journal. Other entries may receive commendations.

The Duke of Westminster's Medal for Military Literature
Royal United Services Institute for Defence and Security Studies, Whitehall, London SW1A 2ET
☎020 7930 2602   Fax 020 7321 0943
✉ sarahh@rusi.org
www.rusi.org

Contact *Sarah Haybittle*

Established 1997 this annual award is sponsored by the Duke of Westminster and aims to mark a notable and original contribution to the study of international or national security, or the military profession. Work must be in English, by a living author, and have been published as a book, rather than an article, in the preceding or next six months of the closing date for entries. 2004 winner: Professor Gerard de Groot.

PRIZE Silver medal, £1000. Winning author is invited to give lecture at RUSI and collect medal from the Duke of Westminster.

The Dundee Book Prize

City of Discovery Campaign, 3 City Square, Dundee DD1 3BA
☎01382 434275   Fax 01382 434096
✉ deborah.kennedy@dundeecity.gov.uk
www.dundeecity.gov.uk/bookprize
Contact *Deborah Kennedy*

Launched in 1996, this is a biennial award. Previous winners include Andrew Murray Scott for *Tumulus* and Claire-Marie Watson for *The Curewife*. Entry qualifications are detailed in the entry form. Launch date: April 2005. Final entry date: February 2006.
PRIZE £6000, plus publication of novel.

S.T. Dupont Golden PEN Award for Lifetime Distinguished Service to Literature

English PEN, 6–8 Amwell Street, London EC1R 1UQ
☎020 7713 0023   Fax 020 7837 7838
✉ enquiries@englishpen.org
www.englishpen.org

Awarded to a senior writer, with a distinguished body of work over many years, who has made a significant and constructive impact on fellow writers, the reading public and the literary world. Nominations by members of English PEN only. Previous winners include: Francis King, Harold Pinter, Doris Lessing, Michael Frayn. 2004 winner: Nina Bawden.
PRIZE A specially engraved trophy and gold pen donated by S.T. Dupont.

The Encore Award

The Society of Authors, 84 Drayton Gardens, London SW10 9SB
☎020 7373 6642   Fax 020 7373 5768
✉ info@societyofauthors.org
www.societyofauthors.org

Established 1990. Awarded for the best second published novel or novels of the year. Final entry date: 30 November. Details from the **Society of Authors**. 2004 winner: Michelle de Kretser *The Hamilton Case*.
PRIZE £10,000.

Envoi Poetry Competition

Envoi, 44 Rudyard Road, Biddulph Moor, Stoke on Trent ST8 7JN
☎01782 517892
Contact *Roger Elkin*

Run by *Envoi* poetry magazine. Competitions are featured regularly, with prizes of £300, plus three annual subscriptions to *Envoi*. Winning poems along with full adjudication report are published. Send s.a.e. to Competition Secretary at the address above.

Euroscript Film Story Competitions

See **Euroscript** under *Writers' Circles and Workshops*

Geoffrey Faber Memorial Prize

Faber & Faber Ltd, 3 Queen Square, London WC1N 3AU
☎020 7465 0045   Fax 020 7465 0034

Established 1963 as a memorial to the founder and first chairman of **Faber & Faber**, this prize is awarded in alternate years for the volume of verse and the volume of prose fiction published in the UK in the preceding two years, which is judged to be of greatest literary merit. Authors must be under 40 at the time of publication and citizens of the UK, Commonwealth, Republic of Ireland or South Africa. 2004 winner: Glyn Maxwell *The Nerve*.
PRIZE £1000.

The Alfred Fagon Award

The Royal Court Theatre, Sloane Square, London SW1W 8AS
www.talawa.com/afa/how.htm

Founded 1985. An annual award, in memory of playwright Alfred Fagon, which is open to any playwright of Caribbean descent, resident in the UK, for the best new stage play in English (television and radio plays and film scripts not eligible). Two copies of the script (plus s.a.e. for return), together with a brief history of the play and c.v. (including author's Caribbean connection), should be sent to the address above by the end of August. 2004 winner: Michael Abbensetts.
AWARD £5000.

Eleanor Farjeon Award

✉ childrensbookcircle@hotmail.co.uk
www.childrensbookcircle.org.uk

This award, named in memory of the much-loved children's writer, is for distinguished services to children's books either in this country or overseas, and may be given to a librarian, teacher, publisher, bookseller, author, artist, reviewer, television producer, etc. Nominations from members of the **Children's Book Circle**. 2004 winner: Jacqueline Wilson.
AWARD £750.

Fish Fiction Prizes

Fish Publishing, Durrus, Bantry, Republic of Ireland

☎00 353 27 55645

✉ info@fishpublishing.com

www.fishpublishing.com

Contact *Clem Cairns*

International Short Story Prize. Founded 1994. Annual award which aims to discover, encourage and publish exciting new literary talent. The best 15 stories are published in an anthology. Closing date: 30 November.

PRIZE €10,000 (1st).

One Page Story Prize (250 words): best 10 stories published in the *Fish Anthology*.

PRIZE FUND €2000.

Unpublished Novel Prize. Send first chapter and synopsis. Winning novel published, plus advance on royalties. Closing date: 30 September. Details of entry fees, further prizes and on-line entry form can be found on the website.

Sir Banister Fletcher Award

Authors' Club, 40 Dover Street, London W1S 4NP

☎020 7408 5092   Fax 020 7409 0913

✉ secretary@authorsclub.co.uk

www.authorsclub.co.uk

Contact *Lucy Jane Tetlow*

This award was created by Sir Banister Fletcher, President of the **Authors' Club** for many years, and is presented annually. The prize alternates between books on architecture and the fine arts. In 2004 the prize was awarded for the best book on art published during the previous two years. Submissions to *Lucy Jane Tetlow* at the Authors' Club.

The John Florio Prize

See **The Translators Association Awards**

The Paul Foot Award

National Union of Journalists, Headland House, 308–312 Gray's Inn Road, London WC1X 8DD

Contact *Ben Tisdall* (Midas PR ☎020 7584 7474)

Annual award, established in 2005 by *The Guardian* and *Private Eye* for campaigning journalism in memory of former contributor Paul Foot. Submissions can be made by individual journalists, teams of journalists or publications for work appearing between October 2004 and August 2005. Single pieces or entire campaigns are eligible. Final entry date: 12 September

2005. No broadcast material. 'Please do not send original material; entries will be acknowledged but no further correspondence can be entered into.'

AWARD £10,000.

The Forward Prizes for Poetry

Colman Getty PR, Middlesex House, 34–42 Cleveland Street, London W1T 4JE

☎020 7631 2666   Fax 020 7631 2699

✉ kate@colmangettypr.co.uk

Contact *Kate Wright-Morris*

Established 1992. Three awards: the Forward Prize for Best Collection, the Felix Dennis Prize for Best First Collection and the Michael Donaghy Prize for Best Single Poem which is not already part of an anthology or collection. All entries must be published in the UK or Republic of Ireland and submitted by poetry publishers (collections) or newspaper and magazine editors (single poems). Individual entries of poets' own works are not accepted. 2004 winners: Kathleen Jamie (best collection), Leontia Flyn (best first collection), Daljit Nagra (best single poem).

PRIZES £10,000 (best collection); £5000 (best first collection); £1000 (best single poem).

The FosterGrant Romantic Novel of the Year

57 Coniger Road, London SW6 3TB

☎020 7736 4968

Award Organiser *Mary de Laszio*

Established 1960. Annual award for the best romantic novel of the year, open to non-members as well as members of the **Romantic Novelists' Association**. Novels must be published in the UK between specified dates and authors must be based in the UK unless members of the RNA. 2005 winner: Katherine Davies *A Good Voyage*. Send s.a.e. to the organiser for entry form.

AWARD £10,000.

The Frogmore Poetry Prize

42 Morehall Avenue, Folkestone CT19 4EF

www.frogmorepress.co.uk

Contact *Jeremy Page*

Established 1987. Awarded annually and sponsored by the Frogmore Foundation. The winning poem, runners-up and short-listed entries are all published in the magazine. Previous winners: Bill Headdon, John Latham, Diane Brown, Tobias Hill, Mario Petrucci, Gina Wilson, Ross Cogan, Joan Benner, Ann Alexander, Gerald

Watts, Katy Darby, David Angel.
PRIZE The winner receives 200 guineas and a life subscription to the biannual literary magazine, *The Frogmore Papers*.

FT & Goldman Sachs Business Book of the Year Award

Financial Times, One Southwark Bridge, London SE1 9HL
☎020 7873 3000   Fax 020 7873 3072
✉ bookaward@ft.com
www.ft.com/bookaward

Contacts *Katy Hemmings, Lucy Ellison*

Established in 2005 to identify the book that provides the most compelling and enjoyable insight into modern business issues, including management, finance and economics. Titles must be published for the first time in the English language, or in English translation, between 31 October 2004 and 1 November 2005. Submissions by a publisher or *bona fide* imprint which holds English language rights in the book.
AWARD £30,000 (winner); shortlisted authors receive £5000 each.

Martha Gellhorn Trust Prize

Rutherfords, Herbert Road, Salcombe TQ8 8HN
Annual prize for journalism in honour of one of the twentieth century's greatest reporters. Open for journalism published in English, giving 'the view from the ground – a human story that penetrates the established version of events and illuminates an urgent issue buried by prevailing fashions of what makes news'. The subject matter can involve the UK or abroad. Six copies of each entry should be sent to the address above by 19 March 2006. Previous winners include: Robert Fisk, Jeremy Harding, Geoffrey Lean.
PRIZE £5000.

The Gladstone History Book Prize

Royal Historical Society, University College London, Gower Street, London WC1E 6BT
☎020 7387 7532   Fax 020 7387 7532
✉ rhs.info@sas.ac.uk

Contact *Executive Secretary*

Established 1998. Annual award for the best new work on any historical subject which is not primarily related to British history, published in the UK in the preceding calendar year. The book must be the author's first (solely written) history book and be an original and scholarly work of historical research. Closing date: 31 December.

2003 winner: Patrick Major *The Death of the KPD: Communism and Anti-Communism in West Germany 1945–1956*.
PRIZE £1000.

Glenfiddich Food & Drink Awards

c/o Wild Card PR, 299 Oxford Street, London W1C 2DZ
www.glenfiddich.com/foodanddrink

Known as the 'Cooker Bookers' or the 'Oscars' of the gastronomic world, the awards aim to recognise excellence in writing, publishing and broadcasting on the subjects of food and drink. There were 11 category winners in 2005 from work published or broadcast in the UK and the Republic of Ireland. 2005 winners: Food Book: *Shopped: The Shocking Power of British Supermarkets* Joanna Blythman; Drink Book: *Phylloxera* Christy Campbell; Food Writer: Christopher Hirst for work in *The Independent*; Cookery Writer: Matthew Fort for work in *The Guardian Weekend*; Drink/Bar Writer: Mike Chapple for work in the *Liverpool Daily Post*; Wine Writer: Anthony Rose for work in *The Independent Magazine*; Restaurant Critic: Terry Durack for work in *The Independent on Sunday Review*; Regional Writer: Robert Cockroft for work in the *Yorkshire Post Magazine*; Television Programme: *Beyond River Cottage* presented by Hugh Fearnley-Whittingstall, Keo Films for Channel 4; Radio Programme: *Made in Shetland* for BBC Radio 4; Photography: John Reardon for work in *Observer Food Monthly*; GQ/Glenfiddich Food & Drink Personality of the Year: Gordon Ramsay; Glenfiddich Independent Spirit Award: Jeanette Orrey and Jamie Oliver for Jamie's School Dinners and Feed Me Better Campaign; Glenfiddich Trophy: Hugh Fearnley-Whittingstall.
AWARD Overall winner (chosen from the category winners) £3000, plus the Glenfiddich Trophy (which is held for one year); category winners £1000 each, plus a case of Glenfiddich Single Malt Scotch Whisky.

The Phillip Good Memorial Prize

QWF Magazine, PO Box 1768, Rugby CV21 4ZA
✉ jo.good@ntlworld.com
www.qwfmagazine.co.uk

Contact *Competition Secretary*

Established in 1997, the competition is run by *QWF Magazine*. The prize commemorates the memory of Phillip Good (late husband of *QWF* editor, Jo Good) and is for short stories of less than 5000 words in any style or genre (except children's). Open entry. Entrants may request in-depth critique of their stories for an extra fee. For entry forms send s.a.e. to the address above. Closing date: 31 December.

PRIZES (total) at least £525, plus free subscription to *QWF Magazine*; also book prizes and publication for winning authors.

Gourmand World Cookbook Awards

Pintor Rosales 36, 28008 Madrid, Spain
☎00 34 91 541 6768   Fax 00 34 91 541 6821
✉ icr@virtualsw.es
www.cookbookfair.com
Contact *Edouard Cointreau*

Founded in 1995 by Edouard Cointreau to reward those who 'cook with words'. The only world competition for food and wine books in all languages. Annual event. In 2003 there were 53 local or regional competitions worldwide, with the winners competing for the 'Best Book in the World' award. Previous winner: *Family Food*, Heston Blumenthal.

Kate Greenaway Medal
See **CILIP: The Chartered Institute of Library and Information Professionals Kate Greenaway Medal**

The Griffin Poetry Prize
6610 Edwards Boulevard, Mississauga, Ontario, Canada L5T 2V6
☎001 905 565 5993   Fax 001 905 564 3645
✉ info@griffinpoetryprize.com
www.griffinpoetryprize.com
Contact *Ruth Smith*, Manager

Annual award established in 2000 by Toronto-based entrepreneur, Scott Griffin, for books of poetry written in or translated into English. Trustees include Margaret Atwood and Michael Ondaatje. Submissions from publishers only.

PRIZES A total of C$80,000, divided into two categories: International and Canadian.

The Guardian Children's Fiction Award
The Guardian, 119 Farringdon Road, London EC1R 3ER
☎020 7239 9694   Fax 020 7713 4366
Children's Book Editor *Julia Eccleshare*

Established 1967. Annual award for an outstanding work of fiction for children aged seven and over by a British or Commonwealth author, first published in the UK in the year of the award, excluding picture books. Final entry

date: 1 June. No application form necessary. 2004 winner: Meg Rosoff *How I Live Now*.
AWARD £1500.

The Guardian First Book Award
The Guardian, 119 Farringdon Road, London EC1R 3ER
☎020 7239 9694
Contact *Literary Editor*

Established 1999. Annual award for new authors published in English in the UK. All genres eligible, apart from academic, guidebooks, children's, educational, manuals, reprints and TV, radio and film tie-ins. 2004 winner: Armand Marie Leroi *Mutants*. Submissions are only received direct from publishers, not from individual authors. Self-published work is not eligible.

AWARD £10,000, plus *Guardian/Observer* advertising package.

Guild of Food Writers Awards
48 Crabtree Lane, London SW6 6LW
☎020 7610 1180   Fax 020 7610 0299
✉ awards@gfw.co.uk
www.gfw.co.uk
Contact *Christina Thomas*

Established 1985. Annual awards in recognition of outstanding achievement in all areas in which food writers work and have influence. Entry is not restricted to members of the Guild. Entry form available from the address above. 2004 winners: Derek Cooper Award: Felicity Lawrence for investigative articles in *The Guardian*; Michael Smith Award: 'Women's Institute', *The Food Programme*, presented by Sheila Dillon; Jeremy Round Award for Best First Book: Vicky Bhogal *Cooking like Mummiji*; Food Journalist of the Year: Bee Wilson for work in the *Sunday Telegraph Magazine*; Cookery Journalist of the Year: Angela Nilsen for work in 'The Ultimate' series in *BBC Good Food Magazine*; Food Book of the Year: Paul Richardson *Indulgence: Around the World in Search of Chocolate*; Cookery Book of the Year: Madhur Jaffrey *The Curry Bible*.

Gwobr Llyfr y Flwyddyn
See **Academi Book of the Year Awards**

James W. Hackett Award
See **The British Haiku Society** under *Organisations of Interest to Poets*

Hastings National Poetry Competition
See **Hastings International Poetry Festival First of All** under *Festivals*

Hellenic Foundation Prize
See **The Translators Association Awards**

Felicia Hemans Prize for Lyrical Poetry
University of Liverpool, PO Box 147,
Liverpool L69 7WZ
☎0151 794 2458   Fax 0151 794 2454
✉ wilderc@liv.ac.uk
Contact *The Sub-Dean, Faculty of Arts*
Established 1899. Annual award for published or unpublished verse. Open to past or present members and students of the University of Liverpool. One poem per entrant only. Closing date 1 May.
PRIZE £30.

The Hessell–Tiltman Prize for History
English PEN, 6–8 Amwell Street, London EC1R 1UQ
☎020 7713 0023   Fax 020 7837 7838
✉ enquiries@englishpen.org
www.englishpen.org
Founded 2002. Awarded for a history book, written in English (including translations) and aimed at a wide audience. Submissions by publishers only. 2004 winner: Tom Holland *Rubicon*.
PRIZE £3000 and Silver Dupont pen.

Heywood Hill Literary Prize
Prize suspended.

Hidden Brook Press International Poetry Anthology Contests
109 Bayshore Road, RR#4, Brighton,
Ontario, Canada K0K 1H0
☎001 613 475 2368   Fax 001 801 751 1837
✉ writers@hiddenbrookpress.com
www.HiddenBrookPress.com
International poetry competitions: No Love Lost Poetry Anthology Contest; The Open Window Poetry Anthology Contest and Seeds International Poetry Chapbook Anthology Contest. Electronic and hard copy submissions are required. Closing dates and full entry details can be found on the website.

William Hill Sports Book of the Year
Greenside House, Station Road, Wood Green,
London N22 7TP
☎020 8918 3731   Fax 020 8918 3728
✉ pressoffice@williamhill.co.uk

Contact *Graham Sharpe*
Established 1989. Annual award introduced by Graham Sharpe of bookmakers William Hill. Sponsored by William Hill and thus dubbed the 'Bookie' prize, it is the first, and only, Sports Book of the Year award. Final entry date: September. 2004 winner: Peter Oborne *Basil D'Oliveira*.
PRIZE (reviewed annually) £16,000 package including £15,000 cash, hand-bound copy, £1000 free bet. Runners-up prizes.

Calvin & Rose G. Hoffman Prize
King's School, Canterbury CT1 2ES
☎01227 595501
Contact *The Headmaster*
Annual award for distinguished publication on Christopher Marlowe, established by the late Calvin Hoffman, author of *The Man Who was Shakespeare* (1955) as a memorial to himself and his wife. For unpublished works of at least 5000 words written in English for their scholarly contribution to the study of Christopher Marlowe and his relationship to William Shakespeare. Final entry date: 1 September each year.

L. Ron Hubbard's Writers of the Future Contest
PO Box 218, East Grinstead RH19 4GH
Contest Administrator *Andrea Grant-Webb*
Established 1984 by L. Ron Hubbard to encourage new and amateur writers of science fiction, fantasy and horror. Quarterly awards with an annual grand prize. Entrants must submit a short story of up to 10,000 words, or a novelette less than 17,000 words, which must not have been published previously. The contest is open only to those who have not been published professionally. Previous winners: Roge Gregory, Malcolm Twigg, Tom Brennan, Alan Smale, Janet Barron. Send s.a.e. for entry form.
PRIZES £640 (1st), £480 (2nd) and £320 (3rd) each quarter; Annual Grand Prize: £2500. All winners are awarded a trip to the annual L. Ron Hubbard Achievement Awards which include a series of professional writers' workshops, and are published in the *L. Ron Hubbard Presents Writers of the Future* anthology.

The Richard Imison Memorial Award
The Society of Authors, 84 Drayton Gardens SW10 9SB
☎020 7373 6642   Fax 020 7373 5768
✉ info@societyofauthors.org

www.societyofauthors.org

Contact *The Secretary, The Broadcasting Committee*

Annual award established 'to perpetuate the memory of Richard Imison, to acknowledge the encouragement he gave to writers working in the medium of radio, and in memory of the support and friendship he invariably offered writers in general, and radio writers in particular'. Administered by the **Society of Authors** and generally sponsored by the **Peggy Ramsay Foundation**, the purpose is 'to encourage new talent and high standards in writing for radio by selecting the radio drama by a writer new to radio which, in the opinion of the judges, is the best of those submitted.' An adaptation for radio of a piece originally written for the stage, television or film is not eligible. Any radio drama first transmitted in the UK between 1 January and 31 December by a writer or writers new to radio, is eligible, provided the work is an original piece for radio and it is the first dramatic work by the writer(s) that has been broadcast. Submission may be made by any party to the production in the form of two copies of an audio cassette (not-returnable) accompanied by a nomination form. 2004 winner: Stephen Sharkey *All You On the Good Earth*.

PRIZE £1500.

The Independent Foreign Fiction Prize

c/o Literature Department, Arts Council England, 14 Great Peter Street, London SW1P 3NQ

☎020 7973 5325   Fax 020 7973 6983

✉ info.literature@artscouncil.org.uk

www.artscouncil.org.uk

Contact *Jessica Ryan*

Awarded for translated fiction by living authors first published in Britain in the year preceding the award. 2005 winner: *Windows on the World* by Frédéric Beigbeder, translated by Frank Wynne.

PRIZE £10,000 shared equally between author and translator.

The International IMPAC Dublin Literary Award

Dublin City Library & Archive, 138–144 Pearse Street, Dublin 2, Republic of Ireland

☎00 353 1 674 4802   Fax 00 353 1 674 4879

✉ literaryaward@dublincity.ie

www.impacdublinaward.ie

Established 1995. Sponsored by Dublin City Council and a US-based productivity improvement firm, IMPAC, this prize is awarded for a work of fiction written and published in the English language or written in a language other than English and published in English translation. Initial nominations are made by municipal public libraries in major and capital cities worldwide, each library putting forward up to three books to the international panel of judges in Dublin. 2004 winner: Tahar Ben Jelloun *This Blinding Absence of Light*.

PRIZE €100,000 (if the winning book is in English translation, the prize is shared €75,000 to the author and €25,000 to the translator).

International Reading Association Literacy Award

International Reading Association, 800 Barksdale Road, PO Box 8139, Newark, Delaware 19714–8139, USA

☎001 302 731 1600   Fax 001 302 731 1057

✉ pubinfo@reading.org

www.reading.org

Executive Director *Alan E. Farstrup*

The International Reading Association is a non-profit education organisation devoted to improving reading instruction and promoting literacy worldwide. In addition to the US $15,000 award presented by UNESCO each year on International Literacy Day (8 September), the organisation gives more than 25 awards in recognition of achievement in reading research, writing for children, media coverage of literacy and literacy instruction.

International Student Playscript Competition

See **University of Hull** under *UK Writers' Courses*

Jerwood Aldeburgh First Collection Prize

The Poetry Trust, The Cut, 9 New Cut, Halesworth IP19 8BY

☎01986 835950   Fax 01986 835959

✉ info@thepoetrytrust.org

www.thepoetrytrust.org

Contact *Naomi Jaffa*

Awarded to the author of what in the opinion of the panel of judges is the best first full collection of poetry published in Great Britain and Eire in the preceding twelve months. The prize was relaunched in 2003 with substantial new funding from the Jerwood Charity. The winner receives £2000 plus an invitation to read at the **Aldeburgh Poetry Festival** the following year. 2004/5 winner: Julia Casterton *The Doves of Finisterre*.

Jewish Quarterly Literary Prizes
PO Box 37645, London NW7 1WB
☎020 8343 4675
www.jewishquarterly.org
Administrator *Pam Lewis*

Formerly the H.H. Wingate Prize. Annual awards (one for fiction and one for non-fiction) for works which best stimulate an interest in and awareness of themes of Jewish interest. Books must have been published in the UK in the year of the award (written in English originally or in translation) by an author resident in Britain, the Commonwealth, Israel, Republic of Ireland or South Africa. 2005 winners: David Besmozgis *Natasha and Other Stories* (fiction); Amos Oz *A Tale of Love and Darkness* (non-fiction).
PRIZES £4000 each.

Samuel Johnson Prize for Non-Fiction
See **The BBCFour Samuel Johnson Prize for Non-Fiction**

Mary Vaughan Jones Award
Cyngor Llyfrau Cymru (Welsh Books Council), Castell Brychan, Aberystwyth SY23 2JB
☎01970 624151   Fax 01970 625385
✉ wbc.children@wbc.org.uk
www.wbc.org.uk
Contact *The Administrator*

Triennial award for distinguished services in the field of children's literature in Wales over a considerable period of time. 2003 winner: Elfyn Pritchard.
AWARD Silver trophy.

Keats–Shelley Prize
Keats–Shelley Memorial Association, 117 Cheyne Walk, London SW10 0ES
☎020 7352 2180   Fax 020 7352 6705
✉ harrietcullenuk@yahoo.com
www.keats-shelley.com
Contact *Harriet Cullen*

Established 1998. Annual award to promote the study and appreciation of Keats and Shelley, especially in the universities, and of creative writing inspired by the younger Romantic poets. Two

categories: essay and poem; open to all ages and nationalities. Previous winners: Jane Draycott, Joe Francis, Leonie Rushforth, Stephen Burley, Linda Rose Parkes, Olivia McCannon, David Olshansky, Isobel Lusted and Porscha Fermanis.
PRIZE £3000 distributed between the winners of the two categories.

The Petra Kenney Poetry Competition
PO Box 32, Filey YO14 9YG
✉ morgan@kenney.uk.net
www.petrapoetrycompetition.co.uk
Contact *Secretary*

Established 1995. Annual poetry award. Original, unpublished poems up to 80 lines on any theme. Closing date: 1 December. Entry fee: £3 per poem. Send s.a.e. for rules and entry form.
PRIZES £1000 (1st); £500 (2nd); £250 (3rd) plus inscribed Royal Brierley Crystal Vase; and three highly commended prizes of £125 each. New prizes for comic verse: £250 (1st); £124 (2nd) and Young Poets (14–18): £250 (1st); £125 (2nd).

Kent & Sussex Poetry Society Open Competition
13 Ruscombe Close, Southborough, Tunbridge Wells TN4 0SG
☎01892 543862
Chairman *Clive R. Eastwood*

Annual competition. Entry fee: £3 per poem, maximum 40 lines.
PRIZES £1000 (total).

Kiriyama Pacific Rim Book Prize
Kiriyama Institute, 650 Delancy St, Suite 101, San Francisco, CA 94107–2082, USA
☎001 415 777 1628   Fax 001 415 777 1646
✉ info@kiriyamaprize.org
www.kiriyamaprize.org
Contact *Jeannine Cuevas*, Prize Manager

Founded 1996 with the aim of promoting books that contribute to greater understanding and cooperation among the peoples and nations of the Pacific Rim and South Asia, this annual award takes its name from the Reverend Seiyu Kiriyama. Entry details may be obtained from the address above or from the website. 2005 winners: Nadeem Aslam *Maps for Lost Lovers* (fiction); Suketu Mehta *Maximum City: Bombay Lost and Found* (non-fiction).
PRIZES $30,000, divided between both winners.

Kraszna-Krausz Book Awards

122 Fawnbrake Avenue, London SE24 0BZ
☎020 7738 6701   Fax 020 7738 6701
✉ awards@k-k.org.uk
www.k-k.org.uk

Administrator *Andrea Livingstone*

Established 1985. Annual award to encourage and recognise oustanding achievements in the publishing and writing of books on the art, practice, history and technology of photography and the moving image (film, television, video and related screen media). Books in any language, published worldwide, are eligible. Entries must be submitted by publishers only. Prizes for books on still photography alternate annually with those for books on the moving image (2005: moving image). 2004 winners: Antonio Biasiucci *Res: Lo Stato delle Cose*; Mitch Epstein *Family Business*.

PRIZES £5000 in each of the main categories; £1000 special commendations.

Lakeland Book of the Year Awards

Cumbria Tourist Board, Ashleigh, Holly Road, Windermere LA23 2AQ
☎01539 444444   Fax 01539 444041
✉ slindsay@gocumbria.org
www.golakes.co.uk

Contact *Sheila Lindsay*

Established in 1984 by local author and broadcaster Hunter Davies in conjunction with the Cumbria Tourist Board, the books entered can be about any aspect of life in the county of Cumbria, from local history books and walking guides to novels and poetry. The contest attracts entries from both new and established authors. Since the establishment of the awards they have grown in importance and are now attracting in the region of 60 entries annually, all competing for the Hunter Davies Prize for the Lakeland Book of the Year.

In addition to the Hunter Davies Prize there are currently five categories including Award for Guides, Walks and Places; Award for People and Social History; Award for Arts and Culture; Award for Heritage and Tradition; and the Best Illustrated Book. Sponsors include Titus Wilson and Son Ltd, the Bill Rollinson Trust, the Cumberland Building Society and Barclays. Closing date for entries is mid-March. The awards are presented at a charity luncheon in early June.

AWARDS £100 for each category together with a framed certificate. Overall winner of the Hunter Davies Prize for the Lakeland Book of the Year also receives a cheque for £100 and a framed certificate.

Lancashire County Library Children's Book of the Year Award

Lancashire County Library Headquarters, County Hall, PO Box 61, Preston PR1 8RJ
☎01772 534751   Fax 01772 534880
✉ jacob.hope@lcl.lancscc.gov.uk

Award Coordinator *Jake Hope*

Established 1986. Annual award, presented in June for a work of original fiction suitable for 12–14-year-olds. The winner is chosen by 13–14-year-old secondary school pupils in Lancashire. Books must have been published between 1 September and 31 August in the previous year of the award and authors must be UK and Republic of Ireland residents. Final entry date: 1 September each year. 2004 winner: Chris Wooding *Poison*.

PRIZE £1000, plus engraved glass decanter.

Lannan Literary Award

Lannan Foundation, 313 Read Street, Santa Fe, New Mexico 87501, USA
☎001 505 986 8160
www.lannan.org

Established 1989. Annual awards given to writers of exceptional poetry, fiction and non-fiction who have made a significant contribution to English-language literature, as well as emerging writers of distinctive literary merit who have demonstrated potential for outstanding future work. On occasion, the Foundation recognises a writer for lifetime achievement. Candidates for the awards are recommended to the Foundation by a network of writers, literary scholars, publishers and editors. Applications for the awards are not accepted.

Legend Writing Award

39 Emmanuel Road, Hastings TN34 3LB
www.legendwritingaward.com

Contact *Legend Coordinator*

Established 2001. Annual award to encourage new fiction writers resident in the UK. The competition is for short stories of 2000 words maximum and there is no set theme. Closing date: 31 August. Entry fee: £5. Rules/entry form available from website or by sending s.a.e. to address above. The competition is organised by Hastings Writers' Group and prize-winning entries are selected by its patron, author, David Gemmell.

PRIZES £500 (1st); £250 (2nd); £100 (3rd); plus three runners-up prizes of £50.

The Library Association Awards
See CILIP: The Chartered Institute of Library and Information Professionals individual awards

The Astrid Lindgren Memorial Award for Literature (ALMA)
Swedish National Council for Cultural Affairs, PO Box 8743, SE-103 98 Stockholm, Sweden
☎00 46 8 519 264 00/08
Fax 00 46 8 519 264 99
✉ anna.cokorilo@alma.se
www.alma.se
Director *Anna Cokorilo*

Established 2002 by the Swedish government in memory of the children's author Astrid Lindgren. Administered by the Swedish National Council for Cultural Affairs, it is an international award for children's and young people's literature given annually to one or more recipients, irrespective of language or nationality. Writing, illustrating and storytelling, as well as reading promotion activities may be awarded. Selected organisations worldwide are invited to submit nominations once a year; jury members may also contribute nominations. 2005 winners: Philip Pullman (UK), Ryôji Arai (Japan).

AWARD SEK 5 million (approx. €500,000)

John Llewellyn Rhys Prize
Booktrust, Book House, 45 East Hill, London SW18 2QZ
☎020 8516 2972   Fax 020 8516 2978
✉ tarryn@booktrust.org.uk
www.booktrust.org.uk
Contact *Tarryn McKay*

Established 1942. An annual young writer's award for a memorable work of any kind. Entrants must be 35 or under at the time of publication; books must have been published in the UK in the year of the award (the award runs a year behind; the next prize will be 2004). The author must be a citizen of the UK or the Commonwealth, writing in English. 2003 winner: Charlotte Mendelson *Daughters of Jerusalem*.

PRIZE £5000 (1st); £500 for shortlisted entries.

The London Writers Competition
Room 224a, The Town Hall, Wandsworth High Street, London SW18 2PU
☎020 8871 8711   Fax 020 8871 7630
✉ arts@wandsworth.gov.uk

www.wandsworth.gov.uk
Contact *Wandsworth Arts Office*

Arranged by Wandsworth Borough Council in association with Roehampton, University of Surrey. An annual competition, open to all writers who live, work or study in the Greater London area. Work must not have been published previously. There are four sections: poetry, short story, play and fiction for children.

PRIZES £1000 for each section, with a first prize of £600. All winning entries are published.

The Elizabeth Longford Prize for Historical Biography
The Society of Authors, 84 Drayton Gardens, London SW10 9SB
☎020 7373 6642   Fax 020 7373 5768
✉ info@societyofauthors.org
www.societyofauthors.org

Established in 2003 in memory of Elizabeth Longford and sponsored by Flora Fraser and Peter Soros. Awarded annually for a historical biography published in the year preceding the prize. No unsolicited submissions. 2004 winner: Katie Whitaker *Mad Madge*.

PRIZE £3000.

Longman-History Today Book of the Year Award
c/o History Today, 20 Old Compton Street, London W1D 4TW
☎020 7534 8000
Contacts *Peter Furtado, Marion Soldan*

Established 1993. Annual award set up as joint initiative between the magazine *History Today* and the publisher Longman (**Pearson Education**) to mark the past links between the two organisations, to encourage new writers, and to promote a wider public understanding of, and enthusiasm for, the study and publication of history. Submissions are made by publishers only. 2005 joint winners: Nikolaus Wachsmann *Hitler's Prisons*; J.L. Laynesmith *The Last Medieval Queens*.

PRIZE £1000 (see *History Today* from July 2005).

The Clarissa Luard Award
See **David Cohen Prize for Literature**

Sir William Lyons Award
The Guild of Motoring Writers, 39 Beswick Avenue, Ensbury Park, Bournemouth BH10 4EY
☎01202 518808   Fax 01202 518808

✉ gensec@gomw.co.uk
www.guildofmotoringwriters.co.uk
Contact *Patricia Lodge*

An annual competitive award to encourage young people in automotive journalism and to foster interests into motoring and the motor industry. Entrance by two essays and interview with Awards Committee. Applicants must be British, aged 17–23 and resident in UK. Final entry date: 30 September.

McColvin Medal
See **Besterman/McColvin Medal**

W.J.M. Mackenzie Book Prize
Political Studies Association, Department of Politics, University of Newcastle, Newcastle upon Tyne NE1 7RU
☎0191 222 8021   Fax 0191 222 3499
✉ psa@ncl.ac.uk
www.psa.ac.uk

PSA Executive Director *Jack Arthurs*

Established 1987. Annual award to best work of political science published in the UK during the previous year. Submissions from publishers only. Final entry date: 31 October. Prizes are judged in the year following publication and awarded the year after that. 2003 winner: Andrew Gamble *Between Europe and America: The Future of British Politics.*

McKitterick Prize
Society of Authors, 84 Drayton Gardens, London SW10 9SB
☎020 7373 6642   Fax 020 7373 5768
✉ info@societyofauthors.org
www.societyofauthors.org

Contact *Awards Secretary*

Annual award for a full-length novel in the English language, first published in the UK or unpublished. Open to writers over 40 who have not had any novel published other than the one submitted (excluding works for children). Closing date: 20 December. 2004 winner: Mark Haddon *The Curious Incident of the Dog in the Night-time.*
PRIZE £4000.

Enid McLeod Prize
Franco-British Society, Room 227, Linen Hall, 162–168 Regent Street, London W1R 5TB
☎020 7734 0815   Fax 020 7734 0815

Executive Secretary *Kate Brayn*

Established 1982. Annual award to the author of the work of literature published in the UK which, in the opinion of the judges, has contributed most to Franco-British understanding. Any full-length work written in English by a citizen of the UK, Commonwealth, Republic of Ireland, Pakistan, Bangladesh and South Africa. No English translation of a book written originally in any other language will be considered. Nominations from publishers for books published between 1 January and 31 December of the year of the prize. Closing date: 31 December. 2004 winner: Antonia Fraser *Marie Antoinette.*
PRIZE Cheque.

Macmillan Prize for a Children's Picture Book Illustration
Macmillan Children's Books, 20 New Wharf Road, London N1 9RR
☎020 7014 6124   Fax 020 7014 6142
✉ d.pinner@macmillan.co.uk
www.panmacmillan.com

Contact *Dianne Pinner*, Macmillan Children's Books

Set up in order to stimulate new work from young illustrators in art schools, and to help them start their professional lives. Fiction or non-fiction. **Macmillan** have the option to publish any of the prize winners.
PRIZES £1000 (1st); £500 (2nd); £250 (3rd).

The Mail on Sunday Novel Competition
Postal box address changes each year (see below)

Annual award established 1983. Judges look for a story/character that springs to life in the 'tantalising opening 50–150 words of a novel'. Details of the competition, including the postal box address, are published in *The Mail on Sunday* in July/August. 2004 winner: Irene Barrall.

AWARDS £400 book tokens and a writing course at the **Arvon Foundation** (1st); £300 tokens (2nd); £200 tokens (3rd); three further prizes of £150 tokens each.

The Man Booker International Prize
Colman Getty PR, Middlesex House, 34–42 Cleveland Street, London W1T 4JE
☎020 7631 2666   Fax 0207631 2699
✉ pr@colmangettypr.co.uk
www.manbookerinternational.com

Established in 2004 to complement **The Man Booker Prize for Fiction** by recognising one writer's achievement in literature and their signif-

icant influence on writers and readers worldwide. Sponsored by the Man Group, this biennial award is given to a living author who has published fiction either originally in English or whose work is generally available in translation into the English language. Submissions for the prize are not invited. Where the winning author's work has been translated into English an additional prize of £15,000 is awarded to the translator. The winning author chooses who the translator's prize should go to and whether it is to be awarded to one translator or divided between several. Inaugural winner: Ismail Kadare.
PRIZE £60,000.

The Man Booker Prize for Fiction

Colman Getty PR, Middlesex House,
34–42 Cleveland Street, London W1T 4JE
☎020 7631 2666   Fax 0207631 2699
✉ pr@colmangettypr.co.uk
www.themanbookerprize.com

Contact *Alice Kavanagh* (Submissions)

The Booker Prize for Fiction was originally set up by Booker plc in 1968 to reward merit, raise the stature of the author in the eyes of the public and encourage an interest in contemporary fiction. In April 2002 it was announced that the Man Group had been chosen by the Booker Prize Foundation as the new sponsor of the Booker Prize. The sponsorship is due to run for five years during which time the prize will be known as the Man Booker Prize for Fiction. United Kingdom publishers may enter up to two full-length novels, with scheduled publication dates between 1 October 2005 and 30 September 2006. In addition, any title by an author who has previously won the Booker or Man Booker Prize and any title by an author who has been shortlisted in the last ten years may be submitted. 2004 winner: Alan Hollinghurst *The Line of Beauty*.
PRIZE The winner receives £50,000. The six shortlisted authors each receive £2500.

Marsh Award for Children's Literature in Translation

National Centre for Research in Children's Literature, Roehampton University, Froebel College, Roehampton Lane, London SW15 5PJ
☎020 8392 3008   Fax 020 8392 3819
✉ g.lathey@roehampton.ac.uk

Contact *Dr Gillian Lathey*

Established 1995 and sponsored by the Marsh

Christian Trust, the award aims to encourage translation of foreign children's books into English. It is a biennial award (next award: 2007), open to British translators of books for 4–16-year-olds, published in the UK by a British publisher. Any category will be considered with the exception of encyclopedias and reference books. No electronic books. 2005 winner: Sarah Adams for her translation of *Eye of the Wolf* by Daniel Pennac.
PRIZE £1000.

Marsh Biography Award

The English-Speaking Union, Dartmouth House, 37 Charles Street, London W1J 5ED
☎020 7529 1564   Fax 020 7495 6108
✉ katie_brock@esu.org
www.esu.org

Contact *Katie Brock*

A biennial award for the most significant biography published over a two-year period by a British publisher. Next award October 2005. 2003 winner: Brenda Maddox *Rosalind Franklin, The Dark Lady of DNA*.
AWARD Membership of the ESU and £4000, plus a silver trophy presented at a dinner.

Colin Mears Award

See **CILIP: The Chartered Institute of Library and Information Professionals Kate Greenaway Medal**

Medical Book Awards

The Society of Authors, 84 Drayton Gardens, London SW10 9SB
☎020 7373 6642   Fax 020 7373 5768
✉ info@society of authors.org
www.societyofauthors.org

Contact *Secretary, Medical Writers Group*

Annual awards sponsored by the Royal Society of Medicine. Nine categories for medical texts published in the twelve months preceding the deadline. Contact the **Society of Authors** for entry details. Closing date: 20 April.
PRIZES £6500 (total).

The Mercedes-Benz Award for the Montagu of Beaulieu Trophy

Guild of Motoring Writers, 39 Beswick Avenue, Ensbury Park, Bournemouth BH10 4EY
☎01202 518808   Fax 01202 518808
✉ gensec@gomw.co.uk
www.guildofmotoringwriters.co.uk

Contact *Patricia Lodge*

First presented by Lord Montagu on the occasion

of the opening of the National Motor Museum at Beaulieu in 1972. Awarded annually to a member of the **Guild of Motoring Writers** who, in the opinion of the nominated jury, has made the greatest contribution to recording in the English language the history of motoring or motor cycling in a published book or article, film, television or radio script, or research manuscript available to the public.

CASH PRIZE sponsored by Mercedes-Benz UK.

Mere Literary Festival Open Competition

'Lawrences', Old Hollow, Mere BA12 6EG
☎01747 860475
www.merewilts.org.uk

Contact *Mrs Adrienne Howell* (Events Organiser)

Annual open competition which alternates between short stories and poetry. The winners are announced at the **Mere Literary Festival** during the second week of October. The 2005 competition was for short stories. Closing date for entries: July. For further details, including entry fees and form, access the website or contact the address above from 1 March with s.a.e.

CASH PRIZES.

Meyer-Whitworth Award

Arts Council England, 14 Great Peter Street, London SW1P 3NQ
☎020 7973 6480
✉ charles.hart@artscouncil.org.uk
www.artscouncil.org.uk

Contact *Theatre Writing, Theatre Department*

This annual award is intended to help further the careers of UK playwrights who are not yet established, and to draw contemporary theatre writers to the public's attention. Nominations are made by directors of professional theatre companies. Plays must have been written in the English language and produced professionally in the UK during the past 12 months. Candidates will have had no more than two of their plays professionally produced. No writer who has won the award previously may re-apply and no play that has been submitted previously for the award is eligible. Further details and application form from the address above.

AWARD £8000.

MIND Book of the Year

Granta House, 15–19 Broadway E15 4BQ
☎020 8215 2305   Fax 020 8215 2269
✉ h.finch@mind.org.uk

www.mind.org.uk

Established 1981. Annual award, in memory of Sir Allen Lane, for the author of a book published in the current year (fiction or non-fiction), which furthers public understanding of mental health problems. 2004 winner: Hilary Mantel *Giving Up the Ghost.*

The Mitchell Prize for Art History/The Eric Mitchell Prize

c/o The Burlington Magazine, 14–16 Duke's Road, London WC1H 9SZ
☎020 7388 8157   Fax 020 7388 1230
✉ annette.bradshaw@burlington.org.uk

Executive Director *Caroline Elam*
Contact *Annette Bradshaw*

The Mitchell Prize is awarded for a book which has made an outstanding and original contribution to the understanding of the visual arts, and The Eric Mitchell Prize is awarded for the best exhibition catalogue. Both must be on western art, written in English and published in the previous two years. Nominations should be submitted by publishers before the end of April 2006. 2004 winners: Colin Bailey *Patriotic Taste: Collecting Modern Art in Pre-Revolutionary Paris* (The Mitchell Prize); Thomas Kren and Scot McKendrick *The Triumph of Flemish Manuscript Painting in Europe*, The J. Paul Getty Museum, Los Angeles and the Royal Academy of Arts, London (The Eric Mitchell Prize).

PRIZES $10,000 each.

Momaya Press Short Story Writing Competition

Momaya Press, Flat 1, 189 Balham High Road, London SW12 9BE
☎020 8673 9616
✉ infouk@momayapress.com
www.momayapress.com

Contact *Monisha Coruth*

Established 2004. Annual competition open to writers in the English language worldwide. Entries, which should not have been published previously, can be in any style and format and on any subject, 2500 words maximum. Entry fee: £6; final entry date: 30 May 2006. Submissions via entry form on the website.

PRIZES £130 (1st); £65 (2nd), plus 8 honourable mentions; all winners are published in the *Momaya Annual Review.*

Scott Moncrieff Prize

See **The Translators Association Awards**

The Oscar Moore Screenwriting Prize

The Oscar Moore Foundation, c/o Screen International, 33–39 Bowling Green Lane, London EC1R 0DA

☎020 7505 8080   Fax 020 7505 8087

✉ sade.sharp@emap.com

www.screendaily.com

Coordinator *Sade Sharp*

Established 1997. Annual prize in honour of Oscar Moore, former *Guardian* columnist and editor-in-chief of *Screen International*, who died in 1996. The genre for the competition changes each year (comedy for 2005), as does the closing date. Contact the Foundation to obtain an entry form. 2004 winner: Marcus Shepherd *A Killing in the Woods*.

AWARD £10,000 cash, plus week-long script development course courtesy of Arista, and performance of the winning script by **The Script Factory**.

Shiva Naipaul Memorial Prize

The Spectator, 56 Doughty Street, London WC1N 2LL

☎020 7405 1706   Fax 020 7242 0603

✉ lucy@spectator.co.uk

Contact *Lucy Vickery*

Established 1985. Annual prize given to an English language writer of any nationality under the age of 35 for an essay of not more than 3000 words describing a culture alien to the writer. Final entry date is 31 May.

PRIZE £3000.

NASEN Special Educational Needs Book Awards

NASEN House, 4–5 Amber Busisness Village, Amber Close, Amington, Tamworth B77 4RP

☎01827 311 500   Fax 01827 313 005

✉ welcome@nasen.org.uk

www.nasen.org.uk

Organised by the National Association for Special Educational Needs (NASEN) and the *Times Educational Supplement* (TES). Three awards: The Children's Book Award, for the book that most successfully provides a positive image of children with special educational needs; The Academic Book Award celebrates the work of authors and editors who have made an outstanding contribution to the theory and practice of special education; The Books for Teaching and Learning Award is presented for curriculum materials for pupils or teachers in early years, primary or secondary phases. Deadline: 21 June 2006. Eligibility: books must have been published in the UK within the year (Academic) preceding the award.

PRIZE £500 each category.

National Poetry Anthology

United Press, Admail 3735, London EC1B 1JB

☎0870 240 6190   Fax 0870 240 6191

www.unitedpress.co.uk

Contact *Julie Embury*

Free-to-enter annual poetry competition. Organisers United Press allow up to three poems (20 lines and 160 words maximum each) by annual closing date of 30 June. They select around 250 regional winners in the UK. These receive a free copy of the annual book, *The National Poetry Anthology* and vote for the overall winner who receives £1000 and a trophy to keep for life.

National Poetry Competition

The Poetry Society, 22 Betterton Street, London WC2H 9BX

☎020 7420 9895   Fax 020 7240 4818

✉ marketing@poetrysociety.org.uk

www.poetrysociety.org.uk

Contact *Competition Organiser (WH)*

One of Britain's major open poetry competitions. Closing date: 31 October. Poems on any theme, up to 40 lines. For rules and entry form send s.a.e. to the competition organiser at the address above or enter the competition via the website.

PRIZES £5000 (1st); £1000 (2nd); £500 (3rd); plus 10 commendations of £50.

National Sporting Club Sports Book Awards (in association with WHSmith)

NSC, Café Royal, 68 Regent Street, London W1B 5EL

☎020 7437 0144   Fax 020 7437 5441

✉ david@nationalsportingclub.co.uk

www.nationalsportingclub.co.uk

Chairman *David Willis*

Established 2003. Annual awards presented at a lunch at the Café Royal in London in May. In the inaugural year there were four categories of awards: autobiography, biography, best illustrator or best new writer. Books submitted must have been published in the previous calendar year. Final entry date: 15 December. 2004 winner: Gareth Southgate and Andy Woodman *Woody and Nord*.

Bill Naughton Short Story Competition

Box No. 2004, Aghamore, Ballyhaunis, Co. Mayo, Republic of Ireland
www.aghamoregaa.com/society/knschool.htm

Organised by the **Kenny/Naughton Society**. Stories may be on any topic and no more than 2500 words in length. All work must be unpublished; typed scripts only with no name or address appearing on the work. Entry fee: £5, €7 or US$8 per story; three stories may be submitted for the price of two. Closing date: 1 September each year. No entry form required.

PRIZES £150 €200) (1st); £100 €130) (2nd); £50 €65) (3rd). Best stories published in a collection entitled *Splinters*.

Nestlé Smarties Book Prize

Booktrust, Book House, 45 East Hill, London SW18 2QZ
☎020 8516 2986   Fax 020 8516 2978
✉ hannah@booktrust.org.uk
www.booktrusted.com

Contact *Hannah Rutland*

Established 1985 to encourage high standards and stimulate interest in books for children, this prize is given for a children's book (fiction or poetry), written in English by a citizen of the UK or an author resident in the UK, and published in the UK in the year ending 31 October. There are three age-group categories: 5 and under, 6–8 and 9–11. Uniquely, the shortlist for each age category is judged by classes of schoolchildren, who enter a competition to win a chance to be Young Judges. 50 classes from each age category judge the books, deciding who gets Gold, Silver and Bronze. The class projects entered for the judging process are then judged to see which classes will come to London for the prize presentation. 2004 Gold Award winners: Mini Grey *Biscuit Bear* (5 and under); Paul Stuart and Chris Riddell *Fergus Crane* (6–8 and Kids' Clubs Special Network Award); Sally Grindley *Spilled Water* (9–11).

PRIZES in each category: £2500 (gold); £1500 (silver); £500 (bronze).

The New Writer Prose & Poetry Prizes

The New Writer, PO Box 60, Cranbrook TN17 2ZR
☎01580 212626   Fax 01580 212041
✉ admin@thenewwriter.com
www.thenewwriter.com

Contact *Merric Davidson*

Established 1997. Annual award. Open to all poets writing in the English language for an original, previously unpublished poem or collection of six to ten poems. Also open to writers of short stories and novellas/serials, features, articles, essays and interviews. Final entry date: 30 November. Previous winners: Mark Granier, Ros Barber, Celia de Fréine, John Hilton.

PRIZES (total) £2000, plus publication in annual collection published by *The New Writer*.

New Writing Ventures

c/o Book Trust, Book House, 45 East Hill, London SW18 2QZ
☎020 8516 2972   Fax 020 8516 2978
✉ tarryn@booktrust.org.uk
www.booktrust.org.uk

Contact *Tarryn McKay*

Established in 2005 by The New Writing Partnership in association with Arts Council England, and administered by Booktrust, this annual award is aimed at emerging writers of adult fiction, non-fiction and poetry, written in English. Open only to unpublished writers who are resident in England. Final entry date: 1 July 2006.

PRIZES £5000 for each category

'The Nibbies'

See **British Book Awards**

Nielsen Gold & Platinum Book Awards

Nielsen BookScan, 3rd Floor, Midas House, 62 Goldsworth Road, Woking GU21 6LQ
☎01483 712222   Fax 01483 712220
✉
gold&platinumawards@nielsenbookscan.co.uk
www.nielsenbookscan.co.uk

Contact *Kim Crooke*

Established in 2000 to award actual consumer purchases of a title through UK bookshops. Awarded to any title, in all its editions, that sells more than 500,000 copies (Gold) or one million copies (Platinum) over a period of five consecutive years. 2004 winner: Paulo Coelho *The Alchemist* (Gold).

AWARDS Commemorative plaque issued by the publisher to the author.

No Love Lost Poetry Anthology Contest

See **Hidden Brook Press International Poetry Anthology Contest**

Nobel Prize

The Nobel Foundation, PO Box 5232,
102 45 Stockholm, Sweden
☎00 46 8 663 0920   Fax 00 46 8 660 3847
www.nobel.se

Contact *Information Section*

Awarded yearly for outstanding achievement in physics, chemistry, physiology or medicine, literature and peace. Founded by Alfred Nobel, a chemist who proved his creative ability by inventing dynamite. In general, individuals cannot nominate someone for a Nobel Prize. The rules vary from prize to prize but the following are eligible to do so for Literature: members of the Swedish Academy and of other academies, institutions and societies similar to it in constitution and purpose; professors of literature and of linguistics at universities or colleges; Nobel Laureates in Literature; presidents of authors' organisations which are representative of the literary production in their respective countries. British winners of the literature prize, first granted in 1901, include Rudyard Kipling, John Galsworthy and Winston Churchill. Winners since 1995: Seamus Heaney (Ireland); Wislawa Szymborska (Poland); Dario Fo (Italy); José Saramago (Portugal); Günter Grass (Germany); Gao Xingjian (France); V.S. Naipaul (Great Britain); Imre Kertész (Hungary), J.M. Coetzee (South Africa). Nobel Laureate in Literature 2005: Elfriede Jelinek (Austria).

The Noma Award for Publishing Africa

PO Box 128, Witney OX8 5XU
☎01993 775235   Fax 01993 709265
✉ maryljay@aol.com
www.nomaaward.org

Contact *Mary Jay*, Secretary to the Managing Committee

Established 1979. Annual award, founded by the late Shoichi Noma, President of Kodansha Ltd, Tokyo. The award is for an outstanding book, published in Africa by an African writer, in three categories: scholarly and academic; literature and creative writing; children's books. Entries, by publishers only, by 28 February for a title published in the previous year. Maximum number of three entries. Previous winners: Abosede Emanuel *Odun Ifa/Ifa Festival*; Hamdi Sakkut *The Arabic Novel: Bibliography and Critical Introduction 1865–1995*; Elinor Sisulu *Walter and Albertina Sisulu – In Our Lifetime*.

PRIZE US$10,000 and presentation plaque.

C.B. Oldman Prize

Special Libraries & Archives, University of Aberdeen, King's College, Aberdeen AB24 3SW
☎01224 274266   Fax 01224 273891
✉ r.turbet@abdn.ac.uk

Contact *Richard Turbet*

Established 1989 by the International Association of Music Libraries, UK & Ireland Branch. Annual award for best book of music bibliography, librarianship or reference published the year before last (i.e. books published in 2002 considered for the 2003 prize). Previous winners: Andrew Ashbee, Michael Talbot, Donald Clarke, John Parkinson, John Wagstaff, Stanley Sadie, William Waterhouse, Richard Turbet, John Gillaspie, David Fallows, Arthur Searle, Graham Johnson, Michael Twyman, David Wyn Jones.

PRIZE £200.

Ondaatje Prize

See **The Royal Society of Literature Ondaatje Prize**

Open Window Poetry Anthology Contest

See **Hidden Brook Press International Poetry Anthology Contests**

Orange Prize for Fiction/Orange Award for New Writers

Booktrust, 45 East Hill, London SW18 2QZ
☎020 8516 2972   Fax 020 8516 2978
✉ tarryn@booktrust.org.uk
www.orangeprize.co.uk

Contact *Tarryn McKay*

Established 1996. Annual award founded by a group of senior women in publishing to 'create the opportunity for more women to be rewarded for their work and to be better known by the reading public'. Awarded for a full-length novel written in English by a woman of any nationality, and published in the UK between 1 April and 31 March of the following year. 2005 winner: Lionel Shriver *We Need to Talk About Kevin*.

PRIZE £30,000 and a work of art (a limited edition bronze figurine known as 'The Bessie' in acknowledgement of anonymous prize endowment).

A new prize, the **Orange Prize for New Writers**, will be awarded for the first time in 2005. All first works of fiction, written by women of any age or nationality, published in the UK between 1 April 2004 and 31 March

2005, will be eligible (short story collections and novellas also eligible). Inaugural winner: Diana Evans *26a*

The Orwell Prize

Blackwell Publishing, 9600 Garsington Road, Oxford OX4 2DQ
☎01865 476264 Fax 01865 471264
✉ verity.warne@oxon.blackwellpublishing.com
Contact *Verity Warne*

Jointly established in 1993 by the George Orwell Memorial Fund and the *Political Quarterly* to encourage and reward writing in the spirit of Orwell's 'What I have most wanted to do ... is to make political writing into an art'. Two categories: book or pamphlet; newspaper and/or articles, features, columns, or sustained reportage on a theme in non-fiction or fiction. Submissions by editors, publishers or authors. 2004 winners (for work published in 2003): Robert Cooper *The Breaking of Nations*; special award by Reuters to the family of the late Hugo Young of *The Guardian* for *Supping with the Devils* and for his 'outstanding contribution to political journalism'.
PRIZES £1000 for each category.

Ottakar's and Faber National Poetry Competition

Ottakar's Plc, Brewery House, 36 Milford Street, Salisbury SP1 2AP
☎01722 428500 Fax 01722 428502
✉ enquiries@ottakars.co.uk
www.ottakars.co.uk
Contacts *Jon Howells, Jo James*

Established 1997. Annual competition in support of National Book Day and to promote poetry within Ottakar's bookshops and their local communities. Maximum 40 lines; only one poem per applicant. The poems, which must be previously unpublished, can be on any subject and in any style. 2004 winner: Jessika Hartleb.
PRIZE £500 (National winner) plus publication in a national newspaper.

The Wilfred Owen Award for Poetry

c/o 17 Belmont, Shrewsbury SY1 1TE
☎01743 460089
www.1914-18.co.uk/owen
Contact *Michael Grayer*

Established in 1988 by the **Wilfred Owen Association**. Given to a poet whose poetry reflects the spirit of Owen's work in its thinking, expression and inspiration. Applications are not sought; the decision is made by the Association's committee. Previous winner: Seamus Heaney.
AWARD A silver and gunmetal work of art, suitably decorated and engraved.

OWG Awards for Excellence

Outdoor Writers' Guild, PO Box 118, Twickenham TW1 2XB
☎020 8538 9468 Fax 020 8538 9468
✉ sec@owg.org.uk
www.owg.org.uk
Contact *Hazelle Jackson*, Secretary

Established 1980. Annual awards by the **Outdoor Writers' Guild** to raise the standard of outdoor writing, journalism, broadcasting and photography. Categories include guidebook, outdoor book, feature (one-off), feature (regular), photography. Open to OWG members only. Final entry date: June.

The Oxford Weidenfeld Translation Prize

St Anne's College, Oxford OX2 6HS
☎01865 274820 Fax 01865 274899
✉ patrick.mcguinness@st-annes.ox.ac.uk
Contact *The Fellows' Secretary*

Established in 1996 by publisher Lord Weidenfeld to encourage good translation into English. Annual award to the translator(s) of a work of fiction, poetry or drama written in any living European language. Translations must have been published in the previous year. Submissions from publishers only. For further information, contact *Dr Patrick McGuinness* at the address above.
PRIZE £1500.

PEN Awards

See **J.R. Ackerley Prize**; **S.T. Dupont Golden PEN Award for Lifetime Distinguished Service to Literature**; **The Hessell-Tiltman Prize for History**

Pendleton May First Novel Award

Guildford Book Festival, c/o Tourist Information Centre, 14 Tunsgate, Guildford GU1 4QT
☎01483 444334
✉ director@guildfordbookfestival.co.uk
www.guildfordbookfestival.co.uk
Contacts *Glenis Pycraft, Pamela Thomas*

Established in 1998 and sponsored by

Pendleton May Insurance Brokers & Financial Advisors and Guildford Arts, this annual award was originally to encourage local talent and new writers in the South East of England but in 2005 writers from the rest of England are eligible. Submissions must be from agents or publishers with accompanying letter (proofs accepted). Books to be published between one Guildford Book Festival and the next (October to October) and shortlisted authors must be prepared to attend the presentation. 2004 winner: Panos Karnezis *The Maze*.

PRIZE £2500 (presented during the Festival).

Samuel Pepys Award

Samuel Pepys Award Trust, Montreal House, Winson, Cirencester GL7 5EL
☎01285 740331

Contact *Jolyon Dromgoole, MA (Oxon), FRSA*

Established 2003. Biennial award (next in 2007) given by the Samuel Pepys Award Trust for a book that makes the greatest contribution to the understanding of Samuel Pepys, his times or his contemporaries. 2003 winner: Claire Tomalin *Samuel Pepys: The Unequalled Self*.

AWARD £2000, plus commemorative medal.

Peterloo Poets Open Poetry Competition

The Old Chapel, Sand Lane, Calstock PL18 9QX
☎01822 833473
✉ info@peterloopoets.com
www.peterloopoets.com

Contact *Harry Chambers*

Established 1986. Annual competition for unpublished English language poems of not more than 40 lines. Final entry date: 1 March. Send s.a.e. for rules and entry form. Previous winners: David Craig, Rodney Pybus, Debjani Chatterjee, Donald Atkinson, Romesh Gunesekera, Anna Crowe, Carol Ann Duffy, Mimi Khalvati, John Lyons, M.R. Peacocke, Alison Pryde, Carol Shergold, John Weston, Maureen Wilkinson, Chris Woods, Judy Gahagan, Carol Rumens.

PRIZES £1500 (1st); £1000 (2nd); £500 (3rd); £100 (4th); plus 10 prizes of £50; 15–19 age group: 5 prizes of £100.

Poetry Business Competition

The Studio, Byram Arcade, Westgate, Huddersfield HD1 1ND
☎01484 434840   Fax 01484 426566
✉ edit@poetrybusiness.co.uk
www.poetrybusiness.co.uk

Contact *The Competition Administrator*

Established 1986. Annual award which aims to discover and publish new writers. Entrants should submit a short manuscript of poems. Winners will have their work published by the **Poetry Business** under the Smith/Doorstop imprint. Final entry date: end of October. Contact for conditions of entry. Previous winners include: Pauline Stainer, Michael Laskey, Mimi Khalvati, David Morley, Moniza Alvi, Selima Hill, Catherine Smith, Daljit Nagra.

PRIZES Publication of full collection; runners-up have pamphlets; 20 complimentary copies. Also cash prize (£1000) to be shared equally between all winners.

The Poetry Society's National Poetry Competition

See **National Poetry Competition**

The Portico Prize

The Portico Library, 57 Mosley Street, Manchester M2 3HY
☎0161 236 6785   Fax 0161 236 6803
✉ librarian@theportico.org.uk
www.theportico.org.uk

Contact *Miss Emma Marigliano*

Established 1985. Administered by the Portico Library in Manchester. Biennial award for a work of fiction or non-fiction published between the two closing dates. Set wholly or mainly in the North West of England, including Cumbria and the High Peak District of Derbyshire. Next award: 2006 (the Library's bicentenary year). Previous winners include: Anthony Burgess *Any Old Iron*; Jenny Uglow *Elizabeth Gaskell: A Habit of Stories*. 2004 winner: Terry Wyke *Public Sculpture of Greater Manchester*.

PRIZE £3000.

The Dennis Potter Screenwriting Award

BBC Broadcasting House, Whiteladies Road, Bristol BS8 2LR
☎0117 974 7586

Contact *Jeremy Howe*, Executive Producer, Drama

Annual award established in 1995 in memory of the late television playwright to 'nurture and encourage the work of new writers of talent and personal vision'. Submissions should be made through a BBC TV drama producer or an independent production company (no start date confirmed; contact *Jeremy Howe* for further information).

The Premio Valle Inclán
See **The Translators Association Awards**

The Mathew Prichard Award for Short Story Writing
Competition Secretary, 3 Queen Anne Square, Cardiff CF10 3ED
www.samwaw.ik.com
Competition Organiser *South and Mid-Wales Association of Writers*
Competition Secretary *Rosemary Johnson* (at address above)

Established 1996 to provide sponsorship and promote Wales and its writers. Entry fee: £5; NB two copies of scripts required (non-returnable). Competition open to all writers in English; the final entry date is 28 February each year. Entry forms and information from the website.
PRIZES A total of £2000; £1000 (1st).

V.S. Pritchett Memorial Prize
The Royal Society of Literature, Somerset House, Strand, London WC2R 1LA
☎020 7845 4676   Fax 020 7845 4679
✉ info@rslit.org
www.rslit.org

Established 1999. Awarded for a previously unpublished short story of between 2000 and 5000 words. For entry forms, please contact the Secretary from 15 November onwards. Closing date: 31 January. Entrants must be a citizen and/or resident of the UK and the Republic of Ireland.
PRIZE £1000.

Pulitzer Prizes
The Pulitzer Prize Board, 709 Journalism Building, Columbia University, 2950 Broadway, New York, NY 10027, USA
☎001 212 854 3841   Fax 001 212 854 3342
✉ pulitzer@www.pulitzer.org
www.pulitzer.org

Awards for journalism in US newspapers, and for published literature, drama and music by American nationals. 2005 winners include: Marilynne Robinson *Gilead* (fiction); Steve Coll *Ghost Wars* (non-fiction).

Real Writers Short Story Awards
PO Box 170, Chesterfield S40 1FE
☎01246 520834
✉ info@real-writers.com
www.real-writers.com
Awards Coordinator *Lynne Patrick*

Established 1994. Annual award, open to anyone who writes in English. Maximum length: 5000 words; entry fee: £5. Optional full-page critique for additional fee. 2003 winner: Ginny Swart.
AWARDS £2500 (1st), plus section prizes. Prizewinners have the opportunity to pitch a novel to a leading publisher. Winning entries published in an anthology.

The Red House Children's Book Award
The Federation of Children's Book Groups, The Old Malt House, Aldbourne SN8 2DW
☎01672 540629   Fax 01672 541280
✉ marianneadey@aol.com
Coordinator *Marianne Adey*

Established 1980. Awarded annually for best book of fiction suitable for children. Unique in that it is judged by the children themselves. 2004 winner: Michael Morpurgo *Private Peaceful*.
AWARD Portfolio of letters, drawings and comments from the children who took part in the judging. Silver bowls and trophy.

Trevor Reese Memorial Prize
Institute of Commonwealth Studies, School of Advanced Studies, University of London, 28 Russell Square, London WC1B 5DS
☎020 7862 8844   Fax 020 7862 8820

Established in 1979 with the proceeds of contributions to a memorial fund to Dr Trevor Reese, Reader in Commonwealth Studies at the Institute and a distinguished scholar of Imperial History (d.1976). Biennial award (next award 2007 for works published 2005–06) for a scholarly work, usually by a single author, in the field of Imperial and Commonwealth History published in the preceding two academic years. All correspondence relating to the prize should be marked 'Trevor Reese Memorial Prize'.
PRIZE £1000.

Regional Press Awards
Press Gazette, Quantum House, 19 Scarbrook Road, Croydon CR9 1LX
☎020 8565 3056   Fax 020 8565 4395
✉ andreah@quantumbusinessmedia.com
www.regionalpressawards.co.uk

Comprehensive range of journalist and newspaper awards for the regional press. Five newspapers of the year, by circulation and frequency, and a full list of journalism categories. Open to all regional journalists, whether freelance or staff. July event. Run by the *Press Gazette*.

Renault UK Journalist of the Year Award

Guild of Motoring Writers, 39 Beswick Avenue, Ensbury Park, Bournemouth BH10 4EY
☎01202 518808   Fax 01202 518808
✉ gensec@gomw.co.uk
www.guildofmotoringwriters.co.uk

Contact *Patricia Lodge*

Originally the Pierre Dreyfus Award and established 1977. Awarded annually by Renault UK Ltd in honour of Pierre Dreyfus, president director general of Renault 1955–75, to the member of the **Guild of Motoring Writers** who is judged to have made the most outstanding journalistic effort in any medium during the year. Particular emphasis is placed on initiative and endeavour.

The Romantic Novel of the Year

See **The FosterGrant Romantic Novel of the Year**

Rooney Prize for Irish Literature

Rooney Prize, Strathin, Templecarrig, Delgany, Co. Wicklow, Republic of Ireland
☎00 353 1 287 4769/287 4376
Fax 00 353 1 287 2595
✉ rooneyprize@ireland.com

Contacts *Jim Sherwin, Thelma Cloake*

Established 1976. Annual award to encourage young Irish writing to develop and continue. Authors must be Irish, under 40 and published. A non-competitive award with no application procedure.
PRIZE €10,000.

Royal Economic Society Prize

The Economic Journal, Department of Economics, London Business School, Regent's Park, London NW1 4SA
☎020 7706 6777   Fax 020 7402 0718
✉ econjournal@london.edu

Contact *Andrew Scott*

Annual award for the best article published in *The Economic Journal*. Open to members of the Royal Economic Society only. Previous winners: Professors Kip Viscusi, Mark Armstrong, Jim Heckman, Jeffrey Smith, Richard Dickens and Casey Mulligan.
PRIZE £3000.

Royal Society of Literature Awards

The Royal Society of Literature Ondaatje Prize, V.S. Pritchett Memorial
Prize and (under *Bursaries, Fellowships and Grants*) **The Royal Society of Literature/Jerwood Awards**

The Royal Society of Literature Ondaatje Prize

The Royal Society of Literature, Somerset House, Strand, London WC2R 1LA
☎020 7845 4676   Fax 020 7845 4679
✉ paulaj@rslit.org
www.rslit.org

Submissions *Paula Johnson*

Administered by the **Royal Society of Literature** and endowed by Sir Christopher Ondaatje, the prize is awarded annually to a book of literary merit, fiction or non-fiction, best evoking the spirit of place. All entries must be published within the calendar year 2005 and should be submitted between 1 September and 1 December 2005. The writer must be a citizen of the UK, Commonwealth or Ireland. Further details available on the website. 2005 winner: Rory Stewart *The Places In Between*.
PRIZE £10,000.

Runciman Award

The Anglo-Hellenic League, c/o The Hellenic Centre, 16–18 Paddington Street, London W1U 5AS
☎020 7486 9410   Fax 020 7486 4254 (c/o Hellenic Centre)

Contact *The Administrator*

Established 1985. Annual award, sponsored by the National Bank of Greece. Founded by the Anglo-Hellenic League to promote Anglo-Greek understanding and friendship, for a work wholly or mainly about some aspect of Greece or the Hellenic scene, which has been published in its first English edition in the UK or in Greece during the previous year and listed in Whitaker's Books in Print. Named after the late Sir Steven Runciman, former chairman of the Anglo-Hellenic League. The Award may be given for a work of fiction, poetry, drama or non-fiction; concerned academically or non-academically with the history of any period; biography or autobiography, travel and topography; the arts, architecture, archaeology and the environment; the social and political sciences and current affairs; a guide book or a translation from the Greek of any period. Final entry date in late January; award presented in May/June. 2004 winner: Prof. Roderick Beaton *George Seferis – Waiting for the Angel – A Biography*.
AWARD £5000.

The Saga Award for Wit

c/o Colman Getty PR, Middlesex House,
34–42 Cleveland Street, London W1T 4JE
☎020 7631 2666   Fax 020 7631 2699
✉ pr@colmangettypr.co.uk
www.saga.co.uk

Contact *Award Administrator*

Established 2003. Annual award, dubbed 'The
Silver Booker', was created by *Saga Magazine* to
recognise and promote the gentle art of humorous writing. A work of fiction or non-fiction by
a British author aged 50 or over on publication.
Books must be submitted by the UK publisher
or nominated by the judges; no submissions by
authors. 2004 winner: Christopher Robbins *The
Empress of Ireland*.

AWARDS £20,000; £1000 for each shortlisted author.

Sagittarius Prize

Society of Authors, 84 Drayton Gardens,
London SW10 9SB
☎020 7373 6642   Fax 020 7373 5768
✉ info@societyofauthors.org
www.societyofauthors.org

Established 1990. For first published novel by
an author over the age of 60. Final entry date:
20 December. Full details available from the
Society of Authors. 2004 winner: William
Newton *The Two Pound Tram*.

PRIZE £4000.

Sainsbury's Baby Book Award

See **Booktrust Early Years Awards**

The David St John Thomas Charitable Trust Competitions and Awards

PO Box 6055, Nairn IV12 4YB
☎01667 453351
✉ dsjtcharitynairn@fsmail.net

Competition & Awards Manager *Lorna
Edwardson*

A large programme of writing competitions
and awards including annual ghost story and
love story competitions (each 1600–1800
words with £1000 first prize), and open poetry
competition (poems up to 32 lines, total prize
money £1000). Publication of winning entries
is guaranteed, usually in *Writers' News/Writing
Magazine* and/or annual anthology. The awards
are led by the annual Self-Publishing Award,
established in 1993, which is open to anyone
who has self-published a book during the preceding calendar year. There are four categories

each with a £250 prize; the overall winner is
declared self-publisher of the year with a total
award of £1000. For full details, send large s.a.e.
to the address above.

The Saltire Literary Awards

Saltire Society, 9 Fountain Close, 22 High
Street, Edinburgh EH1 1TF
☎0131 556 1836   Fax 0131 557 1675
✉ saltire@saltiresociety.org.uk
www.saltiresociety.org.uk

Administrator *Kathleen Munro*

Established 1982. Annual awards, one for Book of
the Year, the other for Best First Book by an
author publishing for the first time. Open to any
author of Scottish descent or living in Scotland,
or to anyone who has written a book which deals
with either the work and life of a Scot or with a
Scottish problem, event or situation. Nominations are invited from editors of leading newspapers, magazines and periodicals. 2004 winners:
The Faculty of Advocates/Saltire Society Scottish
Book of the Year: Andrew Greig *In Another Light*;
Royal Mail/Saltire Society Scottish First Book of
the Year: Peter Hill *Stargazing*. The National
Library of Scotland/Saltire Society Research
Book of the Year: J. Forbes Munro *Maritime
Enterprise and Empire* and Randall Stevenson *The
Last of England*.

PRIZES £5000 (Scottish Book); £1500 (First
Book); £1500 (Research Book).

Schlegel–Tieck Prize

See **The Translators Association Awards**

Science Writer Awards

The Daily Telegraph, 1 Canada Square, Canary
Wharf, London E14 5DT
☎020 7538 6478   Fax 020 7513 2512
✉ enquiries@science-writer.co.uk
www.science-writer.co.uk

Contact *Roger Highfield*

Established 1987, this award is designed to
bridge the gap between science and writing,
challenging the writer to come up with a piece
of no more than 700 words that is friendly,
informative and, above all, understandable.
Sponsored by BASF, the award is open to two
age groups: 16–19 and 20–28.

AWARD Winners and runners-up receive cash
prizes and have the opportunity to have their
pieces published on the science pages of *The
Daily Telegraph*. The winner in each category
also gets an all expenses paid trip to the USA
for the meeting of the American Association for
the Advancement of Science and an invitation

to meet Britain's most distinguished scientists at the British Association's Festival of Science. There is also a prize for schools and a prize for teachers. To check launch date, visit the website, telephone the hotline number or e-mail for further information.

The Scotsman & Orange Short Story Award

c/o The Scotsman, 108 Holyrood Road, Edinburgh EH8 8AS
www.scotsman.com

Contact *David Robinson*, Books Editor

An annual award, established in 2004, to encourage, support and reward short story-writing in Scotland. Open to people who were born or are living in Scotland, the competition is themed each year (subject to be announced with the launch of the next competition in October 2005). Inaugural winner: Rob Smith.

PRIZES £7500 (1st); £500 (five runners-up); 20 best entries selected for publication in annual book.

Scottish Book of the Year
See **The Saltire Literary Awards**

Scottish History Book of the Year
The Saltire Society, 9 Fountain Close, 22 High Street, Edinburgh EH1 1TF
☎0131 556 1836   Fax 0131 557 1675
✉ saltire@saltiresociety.org.uk
www.saltiresociety.org.uk

Administrator *Kathleen Munro*

Established 1965. Annual award in memory of the late Dr Agnes Mure Mackenzie for a published work of distinguished Scottish historical research of scholarly importance (including intellectual history and the history of science). Editions of texts are not eligible. Nominations are invited and should be sent to the Administrator. Previous winner: Marjory Harper *Adventurers and Exiles*.

PRIZE Bound and inscribed copy of the winning publication.

SEEDS International Poetry Chapbook Anthology Contest
See **Hidden Brook Press International Poetry Anthology Contests**

SES Book Prizes
University of Sunderland, School of Education & Lifelong Learning, Forster Building, Chester Road, Sunderland SR1 3SD

☎0191 515 2364   Fax 0191 515 2628
✉ gill.crozier@sunderland.ac.uk

Contact *Professor Gill Crozier*

Annual awards given by the Society for Educational Studies for the best books on education published during the preceding year. Nominations by publishers or by individual authors based in the UK.

PRIZES £2000, £1000 and £400.

Bernard Shaw Translation Prize
See **The Translators Association Awards**

André Simon Memorial Fund Book Awards
29a Great Pulteney Street, Bath BA2 4BU
☎01225 336305   Fax 01225 421862
✉ tessa@tantraweb.co.uk

Contact *Tessa Hayward*

Established 1978. Awards given annually for the best book on drink, best on food and special commendation in either. 2004 winners: Erik Millstone and Tim Lang *Atlas of Food*; Richard Mayson *The Wines and Vineyards of Portugal*. Special Commendation: Nigel Slater *Toast*.

AWARDS £2000 (best book); £1000 (special commendation); £200 to shortlisted books.

WHSmith Literary Award
WHSmith PLC, 3rd Floor, 180 Wardour Street, London W1F 8FY
☎01793 616161
✉ jennie.webb@whsmith.co.uk
www.whsmithplc.com

Contact *Jennie Webb*, Team Coordinator, Group Communication

The long-standing WHSmith Literary Award, now in its 46th year, is not put out to public vote but is decided by a panel led by the Professor of English Literature at Merton College, Oxford and Chief Book Reviewer for the *Sunday Times*, John Carey.

PRIZES Each winning author receives a trophy and £5000.

The Society for Theatre Research Annual Theatre Book Prize
c/o The Theatre Museum, 1e Tavistock Street, London WC2E 7PR
✉ e.cottis@btinternet.com
www.str.org.uk

Established 1997. Annual award for books, in English, of original research into any aspect of the history and technique of the British Theatre. Not restricted to authors of British nationality nor books solely from British publishers. Books must be first published in English (no translations) during the calendar year. Play texts and those treating drama as literature are not eligible. Publishers submit books directly to the independent judges and should contact the Book Prize Administrator for further details. 2004 winner: Meredith Daneman *Margot Fonteyn*.

AWARD £400.

Sony Radio Academy Awards
Alan Zafer & Associates, 47–48 Chagford Street, London NW1 6EB
☎020 7723 0106   Fax 020 7724 6163
✉ secretariat@radioawards.org
www.radioawards.org

Contact *The Secretariat*

Established 1982 in association with the **Society of Authors** and Sony UK. Presented in association with the **Radio Academy**. Annual awards to recognise excellence in radio broadcasting. Entries must have been broadcast in the UK between 1 January and 31 December in the year preceding the award. The categories for the awards are reviewed each year.

Southport Writers' Circle Poetry Competition
32 Dover Road, Southport PR8 4TB
Contact *Mrs Hilary Tinsley*

For previously unpublished work. Entry fee: £2 per poem. Any subject, any form; maximum 40 lines. Closing date: end April. Poems must be entered anonymously, accompanied by a sealed envelope marked with the title of poem, containing s.a.e. Entries must be typed on A4 paper and be accompanied by the appropriate fee payable to Southport Writers' Circle. No application form is required. Envelopes should be marked 'Poetry Competition'. Postal enquiries only. No calls.

PRIZES £200 (1st); £100 (2nd); £50 (3rd); additional £25 Humour Prize.

The Spoken Word Awards
The Audiobook Publishing Association, c/o 18 Green Lanes, Hatfield AL10 9JT
☎07971 280788
✉ charlotte.mccandlish@ntlworld.com

Contact *Charlotte McCandlish*

Hosted by the **Audiobook Publishing Association**, the Awards are for excellence in the spoken word industry and recognise the valuable work of all those involved with the production of audiobooks. There are 23 categories of award, consisting of 16 Consumer Awards (including Drama, Biography, Original Audio, Poetry, Children's and Comedy), four Trade Awards (including Best Retailer and Best Media Coverage) and three Performance Awards (Male and Female Performer of the Year and Spoken Word Audio of the Year).

PRIZES Glass trophy for the 'Gold' awards; certificates for 'Silver' and 'Bronze'.

Bram Stoker Awards for Superior Achievement
Horror Writers Association, PO Box 50577, Palo Alto, CA 94303, USA
✉ hwa@horror.org
www.horror.org

Contact *Nancy Etchemendy*

Founded 1988 and named in honour of Bram Stoker, author of *Dracula*. Presented annually by the **Horror Writers Association** (HWA) for works of horror first published in the English language. Works are eligible during their first year of publication. HWA members recommend works for consideration in eight categories: Novel, First Novel, Short Fiction, Long Fiction, Fiction Collection, Poetry Collection, Anthology and Non-fiction. In addition, Lifetime Achievement Stokers are occasionally presented to individuals whose entire body of work has substantially influenced horror.

Strokestown International Poetry Prize
Strokestown International Poetry Festival, Strokestown, Co. Roscommon, Republic of Ireland
☎00 353 8723 61794
✉ pat.compton@anpost.ie *or*
pbushe@eircom.net
www.strokestownpoetryprize.com

Contacts *Pat Compton, Paddy Bushe*

Annual poetry festival and competition now in its seventh year. Established to reward excellence in poetry. Festival takes place the first weekend in May. Readings and competitions over three days. A centrepiece of the festival is the Strokestown International Poetry prize.

PRIZES €4000 (£2500); runners–up prizes of €2000 (2nd) and €1000 (3rd) with €450 reading fee for seven other shortlisted poets. Also prizes totalling €2400 for winning poems in the Irish language. There is also €1000 for a political or topical satire in verse.

Sunday Times Writer of the Year Award

The Sunday Times, 1 Pennington Street, London E1 9XW
☎020 7782 5770   Fax 020 7782 5798
www.societyofauthors.org

Established 1987. Annual award to fiction and non-fiction writers. The panel consists of Sunday Times journalists and critics. Previous winners: Anthony Burgess, Seamus Heaney, Stephen Hawking, Ruth Rendell, Muriel Spark, William Trevor, Martin Amis, Margaret Atwood, Ted Hughes, Harold Pinter, Tom Wolfe, Robert Hughes. No applications; prize at the discretion of the Literary Editor.

Sunday Times Young Writer of the Year Award

The Society of Authors, 84 Drayton Gardens, London SW10 9SB
☎020 7373 6642   Fax 020 7373 5768
✉ info@societyofauthors.org

Contact *Awards Secretary*

Established 1991. Annual award given on the strength of the promise shown by a full-length published work of fiction, non-fiction, poetry or drama. Entrants must be British citizens, resident in Britain and under the age of 35. The panel consists of Sunday Times journalists and critics. Closing date: 31 October. The work must be by one author, in the English language, and published in Britain. Applications by publishers via the **Society of Authors**. 2004 winner: Robert Macfarlane *Mountains of the Mind*.

Reginald Taylor and Lord Fletcher Essay Prize

Journal of the British Archaeological Association, Institute of Archaeology, 36 Beaumont Street, Oxford OX1 2PG

Contact *Dr Martin Henig*

A biennial prize, in memory of the late E. Reginald Taylor and of Lord Fletcher, for the best unpublished scholarly essay, not exceeding 7500 words, on a subject of archaeological, art history or antiquarian interest within the period from the Roman era to AD 1830. The essay should show *original* research on its chosen subject, and the author will be invited to read the essay before the Association. The essay may be published in the journal of the Association if approved by the Editorial Committee. Closing date for entries is 30 April 2006. All enquiries by post, please. No phone calls. Send s.a.e. for details.
PRIZE £300 and a medal.

Theakston's Old Peculier Prize for the Crime Novel of the Year

1 Victoria Avenue, Harrogate HG1 1EQ
☎01423 562303   Fax 01423 521264
✉ crime@harrogatefestival.org.uk
www.harrogate-festival.org.uk/crime

Contact *Sharon Canavar*, Festival Manager

Established 2005. Sponsored by Theakston's Old Peculier in association with Ottakar's Bookshops, the award is open to full-length crime or mystery novels by British authors, published in the UK. It is the only crime fiction prize to be voted for by the general public following announcement of a long list in April. The winner of the inaugural prize was due to be announced on the opening night of the **Theakston's Old Peculier Harrogate Crime Festival** (see entry under *Festivals*).
PRIZE £3000 cash.

The Dylan Thomas Prize

The Dylan Thomas Centre, Somerset Place, Swansea SA1 1RR
☎01792 474051
✉ info@dylanthomasprize.com
www.dylanthomasprize.com

Contacts *Andrew Wood, Tim J. Prosser*

Founded 2004. A major biennial prize which rewards writing in the English language by authors under the age of 30 from anywhere in the world. Final entry date: 1 March 2006. The award will be presented at the Dylan Thomas Literary Festival in Swansea in autumn 2006. Further entry details can be found on the website.
PRIZE £60,000.

The Tir Na N-Og Award

Cyngor Llyfrau Cymru (Welsh Books Council), Castell Brychan, Aberystwyth SY23 2JB
☎01970 624151   Fax 01970 625385
✉ wbc.children@wbc.org.uk
www.wbc.org.uk

An annual award given to the best original book published for children in the year prior to the announcement. There are three categories: Best Welsh Fiction; Best Welsh Non-fiction; Best English Book with an authentic Welsh background.
AWARDS £1000 (each category).

TLS/Blackwells Poetry Competition

Times Literary Supplement, Admiral House, 66–68 East Smithfield, London E1W 1BX

☎020 7782 3000   Fax 020 7782 3300
www.the-tls.co.uk

Contacts *Mick Imlah* (Poetry Editor, *TLS*),
Sonia Allen

Established 1997. Annual open competition.
Entry details published in the *TLS*. 2003 winner: Stephen Knight.
PRIZES £2000; three runners-up £500 each.

The Translators Association Awards

The Translators Association, 84 Drayton
Gardens, London SW10 9SB
☎020 7373 6642   Fax 020 7373 5768
✉ info@societyofauthors.org
www.societyofauthors.org

Contact *Awards Secretary*

Various awards for published translations into
English from Dutch and Flemish (The Vondel
Translation Prize), French (Scott Moncrieff
Prize), German (Schlegel-Tieck Prize), Greek
(Hellenic Foundation Prize), Italian (The John
Florio Prize), Portuguese (The Calouste
Gulbenkian Prize), Spanish (The Premio Valle
Inclán) and Swedish (Bernard Shaw Translation
Prize). Contact the **Translators Association**
for full details.

The Betty Trask Awards

See entry under *Bursaries, Fellowships and
Grants*

The Trollope Society
Short Story Prize

Maritime House, Old Town, Clapham,
London SW4 0JW
☎020 7720 6789   Fax 020 7627 2965
✉ pamela@tvdox.com
www.trollopestoryprize.org

Contacts *Pamela Neville-Sington, John Williams*

Established in 2001 to encourage interest in
Trollope's novels among young people with the
emphasis on reading – and writing – for fun. The
competition, which is held annually, focuses on a
different Trollope book each year; visit the website for details. Open to students (aged 21 and
younger) of all countries. Final entry date: 15
January. The winning story will be published in
the Society's quarterly journal, *Trollopiana*.
PRIZE £1000.

Sir Peter Ustinov Television
Scriptwriting Award

The International Academy of Television Arts
& Science, 888 Seventh Avenue, 5th Floor,
New York, NY 10019, USA

☎001 212 489 6969   Fax 001 212 489 6557
✉ sebastien@iemmys.tv
www.iemmys.tv

Contact *Sebastien Auscher*

Established 1998. The late Sir Peter Ustinov gave
his name to the Academy's Television Scriptwriting Award. This annual competition is
designed to motivate novice writers worldwide.
The scriptwriter cannot be a United States citizen nor resident and must be below 30 years of
age. Final entry date: 1 September. 2002 winner:
Howard Hund (UK).

PRIZE The award winner will receive
US$5000 and the opportunity to work with an
established writer as mentor.

Ver Poets Open Competition

181 Sandridge Road, St Albans AL1 4AH
☎01727 762601

Contact *Gillian Knibbs*

Various competitions are organised by **Ver
Poets**, the main one being the annual Open for
unpublished poems of no more than 30 lines
written in English. Entry fee: £3 per poem.
Entry form available from address above. Two
copies of poems typed on A4 white paper. *Vision
On*, the anthology of winning and selected
poems, and the adjudicators' report are normally
available from mid-June. Final entry date: 30
April. Back numbers of the anthology are available for £4, post-free; one copy each free to those
included.

PRIZES £500 (1st); £300 (2nd); £100 (3rd).

Also runs High Lights, an open competition
for younger poets (aged 15–19). Entry fee: £2
per poem; closing date: 31 October.

PRIZES £150 (1st); £100 (2nd); £50 (3rd);
£50 (St Albans Schools Prize).

Vogue Talent Contest

Vogue, Vogue House, Hanover Square, London
W1S 1JU
☎020 7152 3003   Fax 020 7408 0559

Contact *Frances Bentley*

Established 1951. Annual award for young writers and journalists (under 25 on 1 January in the
year of the contest). Final entry date is in April.
Entrants must write three pieces of journalism
on given subjects.

PRIZES £1000, plus a month's paid work
experience with *Vogue*; £500 (2nd).

The Vondel Translation Prize

See **The Translators Association Awards**

Wadsworth Prize
for Business History

Business Archives Council, c/o Ms Fiona
Maccoll, Records Manager, Rio Tinto plc,
6 St James Square, London SW1Y4LD
☎020 7753 2123   Fax 020 7753 2211
✉ fiona.macoll@riotinto.com

Contact *Fiona Maccoll*

Established 1978. Annual award for the best
book published on British business history. 2004
winner: Professor J. Forbes Munro *Maritime
Enterprise and Empire: Sir William Mackinnon and
his Business Network – 1823–1893.*
PRIZE £500.

Walford Award

42 Moors Lane, Winsford CW7 1JX
☎020 7255 0500   Fax 020 7255 0501
www.cilip.org.uk

Part of the ISG (CILIP)/Nielsen BookData
Reference Awards. Awarded to an individual
who has made a sustained and continual contribution to British bibliography over a period of
years. The nominee need not be resident in the
UK. The award is named after Dr A.J. Walford,
a bibliographer of international repute. 2003
winner: Paul W. Nash.

AWARD Cash prize and certificate.

The David Watt Prize

Rio Tinto plc, 6 St James's Square, London
SW1Y 4LD
☎020 7753 2316   Fax 020 7930 3249
✉ davidwattprize@riotinto.com

Contact *The Administrator*

Initiated in 1988 to commemorate the life and
work of David Watt. Annual award, open to
writers currently engaged in writing for
English language newspapers and journals, on
international and national affairs. The winners
are judged as having made 'outstanding contributions towards the greater understanding of
national, international or global issues'. Entries
must have been published during the year preceding the award. Final entry date 31 March.
2003 winner: David Gardner *Democracy is Just a
Mirage.*
PRIZE £7500.

The Harri Webb Prize

10 Heol Don, Whitchurch, Cardiff CF14 2AU
☎029 2062 3359

Contact *Professor Meic Stephens*

Established 1995. Annual award to commemorate the Welsh poet, Harri Webb (1920–94), for

a single poem in any of the categories in which
he wrote: ballad, satire, song, polemic or a first
collection of poems. The poems are chosen by
three adjudicators; no submissions. Previous
winner: Grahame Davies.
PRIZES £100/£200.

Whitbread Book Awards

The Booksellers Association, Minster House,
272 Vauxhall Bridge Road, London
SW1V 1BA
☎020 7802 0802   Fax 020 7802 0803
✉ anna.okane@booksellers.org.uk
www.whitbread-bookawards.co.uk

Contact *Nicola Tarling*

Established 1971. The awards celebrate and promote the best contemporary British writing.
They are judged in two stages and offer a total of
£50,000 prize money. The awards are open to
novel, first novel, biography, poetry and children's
book, each judged by a panel of three judges,
with two young judges joining the panel for the
Whitbread Children's Book Award. The winner
of each award receives £5000. The Whitbread
Book of the Year (£25,000) is chosen from the
category winners. Writers must have lived in
Britain and Ireland for three or more years.
Submissions received from publishers only.
Closing date: early July. Sponsored by Whitbread
PLC. 2004 winners: Geraldine McCaughrean
Not the End of the World (children's); Andrea Levy
Small Island (novel & overall winner); Susan
Fletcher *Eve Green* (first novel); John Guy *My
Heart is My Own: The Life of Mary Queen of Scots*
(biography); Michael Symmons Roberts *Corpus*
(poetry)

Whitfield Prize

Royal Historical Society, University College
London, Gower Street, London WC1E 6BT
☎020 7387 7532   Fax 020 7387 7532
✉ rhs.info@sas.ac.uk

Contact *Executive Secretary*

Established 1977. An annual award for the best
new work within a field of British history, published in the UK in the preceding calendar year.
The book must be the author's first (solely
written) history book and be an original and
scholarly work of historical research. Final entry
date: 31 December. Previous winners: John
Goodall *God's House at Ewelme: Life, Devotion
and Architecture in a Fifteenth-Century Almshouse*;
Frank Salmon *Building on Ruins: The Rediscovery
of Rome and English Architecture.*
PRIZE £1000.

John Whiting Award

Arts Council England, 14 Great Peter Street, London SW1P 3NQ
☎020 7973 6480
✉ charles.hart@artscouncil.org.uk
www.artscouncil.org.uk

Contact *Theatre Writing, Theatre Department*

Founded 1965. Annual award to commemorate the life and work of the playwright John Whiting (*The Devils, A Penny for a Song*). Open to any writer who has received an award during the previous two years from **Arts Council England** or a commission or production by a theatre in receipt of Arts Council subsidy. Awarded to the writer whose play most nearly satisfies the following criteria: a play in which the writing is of special quality; a play of relevance and importance to contemporary life; a play of potential value to the British theatre. No writer who has won the award previously may reapply and no play that has been submitted for the award previously is eligible. Contact the theatre writing section for full details and application form.

PRIZE £6000.

Wilkins Memorial Poetry Prize

Birmingham & Midland Institute, 9 Margaret Street, Birmingham B3 3BS
☎0121 236 3591   Fax 0121 212 4577
www.bmi.org.uk

Administrator *Mr P.A. Fisher*

The Birmingham & Midland Institute, as organiser of the competition, is seeking new young talent and to this end has changed the structure of the competition. Class 1 – Open Class: for anyone whose 16th birthday fell on or before 2 July 2006 (entry fee: £3); Class 2 – Student Class: open to those whose 18th birthday fell on or before 20 July 2006 or whose 22nd birthday fell on or after that date (entry fee: £1 per poem); Class 3 – Sixth-form Class: for those registered in a sixth form on 20 July 2006 (entry fee: £1 per poem). Enquire for closing dates.

PRIZES Class 1: £400 (1st), £200 (2nd), £100 (3rd); Class 2: £200; Class 3: £100.

H.H. Wingate Prize

See **Jewish Quarterly Literary Prizes**

Wolfson History Prizes

Wolfson Foundation, 8 Queen Anne Street, London W1G 9LD
☎020 7323 5730   Fax 020 7323 3241

Contact *Executive Secretary*

The Wolfson History Prizes, established in 1972, are awarded annually to promote and encourage standards of excellence in the writing of history for the general reading public. 2003 winners (awarded in 2004): Diarmaid MacCulloch *Reformation: Europe's House Divided 1490–1700*; Frances Harris *Transformations of Love: The Friendship of John Evelyn and Margaret Godolphin*; Julian Jackson *The Fall of France: The Nazi Invasion of 1940*.

The David T.K. Wong Prize for Short Fiction

International PEN, 9/10 Charterhouse Buildings, Goswell Road, London EC1M 7AT
☎020 7253 4308   Fax 020 7253 5711
✉ gvincent@dircon.co.uk
www.internatpen.org

Contact *Gilly Vincent*

Established 2000, this international prize is presented every other year to promote literary excellence in the form of the short story written in English. Unpublished stories of between 2500 words to 6000 words are welcome from writers worldwide, but entries must incorporate one or more of International PEN's ideals as set out in its Charter. *Entries should not be sent direct to International PEN but should be submitted via the entrant's local PEN Centre.* Details of closing date should be obtained from individual Centres. In those few countries without a PEN Centre, entrants can be directed to the nearest appropriate centre by International PEN. Copies of PEN's Charter, in English, French and Spanish and addresses of PEN Centres can be found on the website. 2002/3 winner: Chimamanda Ngozi Adichie *Half of a Yellow Sun*.

PRIZE £7500 (1st).

The World Fantasy Awards

UK Administrator: 24 Pearl Road, London E17 4QZ
☎020 8521 3034
✉ fletcherove@hotmail.com
www.worldfantasy.org/awards

UK Administrator *Jo Fletcher*

Annual awards, founded in 1975 by Kirby McCauley and other professionals working in fantasy and horror to recognise and award excellence in the field. The shortlist is selected by popular vote by members of the World Fantasy Conventions with judges selecting the winners. Categories: Life Achievement, Novel, Novella, Short Fiction, Anthology, Collection,

Artist, Special Award – Professional, Special Award – Non-Professional. Final entry date: May.

WRITE
See **Royal Exchange Theatre Company**

The Writers Bureau Poetry and Short Story Competition
The Writers Bureau, Sevendale House, 7 Dale Street, Manchester M1 1JB
☎0161 228 2362   Fax 0161 228 3533
✉ studentservices@writersbureau.com
www.writersbureau.com/competition
Competition Secretary *Angela Cox*

Established 1994. Annual award. Poems should be no longer than 40 lines and short stories no more than 2000 words. £5 entry fee. Closing date: 31 July 2005.

PRIZES in each category: £1000 (1st); £400 (2nd); £200 (3rd); £100 (4th); £50 (x 6).

Yorkshire Post Book Awards
Yorkshire Post Newspapers Ltd, PO Box 168, Wellington Street, Leeds LS1 1RF

Contact *Duncan Hamilton*, Deputy Editor

Annual awards: **Yorkshire Post Novel of the Year Award; Yorkshire Post Non-Fiction Book of the Year Award; Best Title With a Yorkshire Theme.** Awarded to the book which, in the opinion of the judges, is the best work published in the preceding year.

PRIZE £1200 (Novel of the Year); £1200 (Non-Fiction Book of the Year); £500 (Best Title with a Yorkshire Theme) .

YoungMinds Book Award
Youngminds, 102–108 Clerkenwell Road, London EC1M 5SA
☎020 7336 8445   Fax 020 7336 8446
✉ bookaward@youngminds.org.uk
www.youngminds.org.uk/bookaward
Contacts *Richard Meier, Tarryn Hawley*

Established 2003. This award is given to a published work of literature that throws fresh light on the ways a child takes in and makes sense of the world he or she is growing into – novels, memoirs, diaries, poetry collections which portray something of the unique subtlety of a child's experience. 2004 winner: Miriam Toews *A Complicated Kindness*.

PRIZE £3000.

Library Services

Aberdeen Central Library

Rosemount Viaduct, Aberdeen AB25 1GW
☎01224 652500   Fax 01224 641985
✉ centlib@aberdeencity.gov.uk
www.aberdeencity.gov.uk

OPEN 9.00 am to 7.00 pm Monday to
Thursday; 9.00 am to 5.00 pm Friday
(Reference & Local Studies/Business &
Technical: 9.00 am to 8.00 pm); 9.00 am to
5.00 pm Saturday. Branch library opening
times vary

OPEN ACCESS
General reference and loans. Books, pamphlets,
periodicals and newspapers; videos, CDs, DVDs;
arts equipment lending service; Internet and
Learning Centre for public access; photographs of
the Aberdeen area; census records, maps, newspapers; online databases, patents and standards.
The library offers special services to housebound
readers. Non-resident administrative fee.

Armitt Gallery, Museum & Library

Rydal Road, Ambleside LA22 9BL
☎015394 31212   Fax 015394 31313
✉ info@armitt.com
www.armitt.com

OPEN 10.00 am to 4.30 pm Monday to Friday
FREE ACCESS (To view original material please
give prior notice)
A small but unique reference library of rare
books, manuscripts, pictures, antiquarian prints,
maps and museum items, mainly about the Lake
District. It includes early guidebooks and topographical works, books and papers relating to
Ruskin, H. Martineau, Charlotte Mason and others; fine art including work by W. Green, J.B.
Pyne, John Harden, K. Schwitters, and Victorian
photographs by Herbert Bell; also a major collection of Beatrix Potter's scientific watercolour
drawings and microscope studies. Museum and
Exhibition open seven days per week from 10.00
am to 5.00 pm. Entry charge for museum.

The Athenaeum, Liverpool

Church Alley, Liverpool L1 3DD
☎0151 709 7770   Fax 0151 709 0418
✉ info@theathenaeum.org.uk

www.theathenaeum.org.uk

OPEN 9.00 am to 4.00 pm Monday and
Tuesday; 9.00 am to 9.00 pm Wednesday to
Friday

ACCESS To club members; researchers by application only
General collection, with books dating from
the 15th century, now concentrated mainly on
local history with a long run of Liverpool
directories and guides. SPECIAL COLLECTIONS
Liverpool playbills; William Roscoe; Blanco
White; Robert Gladstone; 18th-century plays;
19th-century economic pamphlets; the Norris
books; Bibles; Yorkshire and other genealogy.
Some original drawings, portraits, topographical material and local maps.

Bank of England Information Centre

Threadneedle Street, London EC2R 8AH
☎020 7601 4715   Fax 020 7601 4356
✉ informationcentre@bankofengland.co.uk
www.bankofengland.co.uk

OPEN 9.00 am to 5.30 pm Monday to Friday

ACCESS For research workers by prior arrangement only, when material is not readily available elsewhere
50,000 volumes of books and periodicals.
2000 periodicals taken. UK and overseas coverage of banking, finance and economics. *Special
collections* Central bank reports; UK 17th–19th-
century economic tracts; government reports in
the field of banking.

Barbican Library

Barbican Centre, London EC2Y 8DS
☎020 7638 0569/7638 0568 (24-hr renewals)
Fax 020 7638 2249
✉ barbicanlib@corpoflondon.gov.uk
www.cityoflondon.gov.uk/libraries

OPEN 9.30 am to 5.30 pm Monday and
Wednesday; 9.30 am to 7.30 pm Tuesday
and Thursday; 9.30 am to 2.00 pm Friday;
9.30 am to 4.00 pm Saturday

OPEN ACCESS
Situated on Level 2 of the Barbican Centre,
this is the Corporation of London's largest lend-

ing library. Study facilities are available plus free Internet access. In addition to a large general lending department, the library seeks to reflect the Centre's emphasis on the arts and includes strong collections (including DVDs, videos and CD-ROMs), on painting, sculpture, theatre, cinema and ballet, as well as a large music library with books, scores and CDs (sound recording loans available at a small charge). Also houses the City's main children's library and has special collections on finance, natural resources, conservation, socialism and the history of London. Service available for housebound readers. A literature events programme is organised by the Library which supplements and provides cross-arts planning opportunities with the Barbican Centre artistic programme. Reading groups meet in the library on the first Tuesday and Thursday of every month.

Barnsley Public Library

Central Library, Shambles Street, Barnsley S70 2JF
☎01226 773930   Fax 01226 773955
✉ barnsleylibraryenquiries@barnsley.gov.uk
www.barnsley.gov.uk/service/libraries/index.asp

OPEN Lending & Reference: 9.30 am to 7.00 pm Monday and Wednesday; 9.30 am to 5.30 pm Tuesday and Friday; 9.30 am to 4.00 pm Saturday. Telephone to check hours of other departments and other branch libraries.

OPEN ACCESS
General library, lending and reference. Archive collection of family history and local firms; local studies: coal mining, local authors, Yorkshire and Barnsley; large junior library. (Specialist departments are closed on certain weekday evenings and Saturday afternoons.)

BBC Written Archives Centre

Peppard Road, Caversham Park, Reading RG4 8TZ
☎0118 948 6281   Fax 0118 946 1145
✉ heritage@bbc.co.uk
www.bbc.co.uk/heritage
Contact *Jacqueline Kavanagh*

OPEN 9.30 am to 5.30 pm Monday to Friday
ACCESS For reference, by appointment only, Wednesday to Friday
Holds the written records of the BBC, including internal papers from 1922 to 1979 and published material to date. 20th century biography, social history, popular culture and broadcasting. Charges for certain services.

Bedford Central Library

Harpur Street, Bedford MK40 1PG
☎01234 350931/270102 (Reference Library)
Fax 01234 342163
www.bedfordshire.gov.uk

OPEN 9.30 am to 7.00 pm Monday and Wednesday; 9.30 am to 5.30 pm Tuesday, Thursday, Friday; 9.30 am to 5.00 pm Saturday
OPEN ACCESS
Lending library with a wide range of stock, including books, music, audiobooks, DVDs and videos; reference and information library, children's library, local history library and Internet facilities.

Belfast Public Libraries: Central Library

Royal Avenue, Belfast BT1 1EA
☎028 9050 9150   Fax 028 9033 2819
✉ info.belb@ni-libraries.net
www.belb.org.uk
www.ni-libraries.net

OPEN 9.00 am to 8.00 pm Monday and Thursday; 9.00 am to 5.30 pm Tuesday, Wednesday, Friday; 9.00 am to 1.00 pm Saturday
OPEN ACCESS To lending libraries; reference libraries by application only
Over two million volumes for lending and reference. SPECIAL COLLECTIONS United Nations depository; complete British Patent Collection; Northern Ireland Newspaper Library; British and Irish government publications. The Central Library provides the following Reference Departments: General Reference; Belfast, Ulster and Irish Studies; Music. A Learning Gateway includes public Internet facilities and a Learndirect Centre. The Lending Library is one of over 20 branches along with a range of outreach services to hospitals, care homes and housebound readers.

BFI National Library

21 Stephen Street, London W1T 1LN
☎020 7255 1444   Fax 020 7436 2338
✉ library@bfi.org.uk
www.bfi.org.uk

OPEN 10.30 am to 5.30 pm Monday and Friday; 10.30 am to 8.00 pm Tuesday and Thursday; 1.00 pm to 8.00 pm Wednesday; Telephone Enquiry Service operates from 10.00 am to 5.00 pm (Closed 1.00 pm to 2.00 pm)
ACCESS For reference only; annual, 5-day and limited day membership available

The world's largest collection of information on film and television including periodicals, cuttings, scripts, related documentation, personal papers. Main library catalogue available via website.

Birmingham and Midland Institute

9 Margaret Street, Birmingham B3 3BS
☎0121 236 3591   Fax 0121 212 4577
www.bmi.org.uk

Administrator & General Secretary *Philip Fisher*

ACCESS Members only

Established 1854. Later merged with the Birmingham Library which was founded in 1779. The Library specialises in the humanities, with approximately 100,000 volumes in stock. Founder member of the **Association of Independent Libraries**. Meeting-place of many affiliated societies devoted to poetry and literature.

Birmingham Library Services

Central Library, Chamberlain Square, Birmingham B3 3HQ
☎0121 303 4511
✉ central.library@birmingham.gov.uk
www.birmingham.gov.uk/libraries

OPEN 9.00 am to 8.00 pm Monday to Friday; 9.00 am to 5.00 pm Saturday

Over a million volumes. *Research collections* include the Shakespeare Library; War Poetry Collection; Parker Collection of Children's Books and Games; Johnson Collection; Milton Collection; Cervantes Collections; Early and Fine Printing Collection (including the William Ridler Collection of Fine Printing); Joseph Priestley Collection; Loudon Collection; Railway Collection; Wingate Bett Transport Ticket Collection; Labour, Trade Union and Co-operative Collections. *Photographic archives:* Sir John Benjamin Stone; Francis Bedford; Francis Frith; Warwickshire Photographic Survey; Boulton and Watt Archive. Also, Charles Parker Archive; Birmingham Repertory Theatre Archive and Sir Barry Jackson Library; Local Studies (Birmingham); Patents Collection; Song Sheets Collection; Oberammergau Festival Collection.

Booktrust Children's Reference Library

Book House, 45 East Hill, London SW18 2QZ
☎020 8516 2985   Fax 020 8516 2978
✉ ed@booktrust.org.uk
www.booktrust.org.uk
www.booktrusted.com

Contact *Mr E. Zaghini*

OPEN 9.00 am to 5.00 pm Monday to Friday (by appointment only)

ACCESS For reference only

A comprehensive collection of children's literature, related books and periodicals. Aims to hold most of all children's titles published within the last two years. An information service covers all aspects of children's literature, including profiles of authors and illustrators. Reading room facilities.

Bournemouth Library

22 The Triangle, Bournemouth BH2 5RQ
☎01202 454848   Fax 01202 454840

OPEN 10.00 am to 7.00 pm Monday; 9.30 am to 7.00 pm Tuesday, Thursday, Friday; 9.30 am to 5.00 pm Wednesday; 10.00 am to 2.00 pm Saturday

OPEN ACCESS

Main library for Bournemouth with lending, reference and music departments, plus the Heritage Zone – local and family history.

Bradford Central Library

Princes Way, Bradford BD1 1NN
☎01274 433600   Fax 01274 395108
✉ public.libraries@bradford.gov.uk

OPEN 9.00 am to 7.30 pm Monday to Friday; 9.00 am to 5.00 pm Saturday

OPEN ACCESS

Wide range of books and media loan services. Comprehensive reference and information services, including major local history collections and specialised business information service.

Brighton Jubilee Library

Jubilee Street, Brighton BN1 1GE
☎01273 290800
www.citylibraries.info/libraries/jubilee.asp

OPEN 10.00 am to 7.00 pm Monday and Tuesday; 10.00 am to 2.00 pm Wednesday and Friday; 10.00 am to 8.00 pm Thursday; 10.00 am to 4.00 pm Saturday

ACCESS Limited stock on open access; material for reference use and lending

Specialisations include art and antiques, history of Brighton, local illustrations, Hebrew and Oriental literature, natural history, children's books, World War Two and large bequests of rare and historical books.

Bristol Central Library

College Green, Bristol BS1 5TL
☎0117 903 7200   Fax 0117 922 1081

www.bristol-city.gov.uk
www.digitalbristol.org
OPEN 9.30 am to 7.30 pm Monday, Tuesday
and Thursday; 10.00 am to 5.00 pm
Wednesday; 9.30 am to 5.00 pm Friday and
Saturday; 1.00 pm to 5.00 pm Sunday
OPEN ACCESS
Lending, reference, art, music, business and
local studies are particularly strong. DVD, video
and CD collections on site. Facilities available:
PCs (large screen with Jaws and Zoomtext),
Internet, printing; videophone on site; black &
white and colour photocopiers.

British Architectural Library
Royal Institute of British Architects, 66
Portland Place, London W1B 1AD
☎020 7580 5533   Fax 020 7631 1802
✉ info@inst.riba.org
www.architecture.com
RIBA British Architectural Library Drawings
& Archives Collections: ☎020 7307 3708
Members' Information Line: ☎020 7307 3600
(membership number required); Public Infor-
mation Line (50p per min.): ☎0906 302 0400
OPEN 10.00 am to 8.00 pm Tuesday; 10.00 am
to 5.00 pm Wednesday to Friday; 10.00 am
to 1.30 pm Saturday; Closed Sunday,
Monday and any Saturday preceding a Bank
Holiday; full details on the website
ACCESS Free to RIBA members; non-members
must buy a day ticket (£14/£7 concessions,
but on Tuesdays between 5.00 pm–8.00 pm and
Saturdays £7/£3.50); subscriber membership
available (write for details); loans available to
RIBA and library members only
Collection of books, drawings, manuscripts,
photographs and periodicals. All aspects of architecture, current and historical. Material both
technical and aesthetic, covering related fields
including: interior design, landscape architecture,
topography, the construction industry and
applied arts. Brochure available; queries by telephone, letter, e-mail or in person. Charge for
research (min. charge £40 + VAT).

The British Library
Admission to St Pancras Reading Rooms –
British Library Readers' Passes

Everyone is welcome to visit the British Library
exhibition galleries or to tour the building.
However, to use the reading rooms you will need
to apply for a reader's pass, for which identification is required. The British Library issues passes
to those who need to use its collections –

researchers, innovators and entrepreneurs across
all fields of study, and in academic, commerce or
private research – whether or not they are affiliated to a research institution. Proof of home
address is required: e.g. a utility bill, bank statement or driving licence; and proof of signature,
i.e. a bank or credit card, passport, driving licence
or national identity card.
Admissions staff discuss with applicants their
need to use the collections (it is helpful to take
with you anything which supports your application, e.g. a business card, professional membership card or details of the items you wish to
see).
For further information, visit the website at
www.bl.uk or contact the Reader Admissions
Office, The British Library, 96 Euston Road,
London NW1 2DB ☎020 7412 7677 Fax 020
7412 7794 Email reader-admissions@bl.uk

British Library Asia, Pacific and Africa Collections
96 Euston Road, London NW1 2DB
☎020 7412 7873   Fax 020 7412 7641
✉ oioc-enquiries@bl.uk
www.bl.uk
OPEN 10.00 am to 5.00 pm Monday; 9.30 am
to 5.00 pm Tuesday to Saturday; closed for
public holidays
ACCESS By British Library reader's pass
A comprehensive collection of printed volumes and manuscripts in the languages of North
Africa, the Near and Middle East and all of Asia,
plus records of the East India Company and
British government in India until 1947. Also
prints, drawings and paintings by British artists of
India.
For information on British Library collections and services, visit the website.

British Library Business Collections
96 Euston Road, London NW1 2DB
☎020 7412 7454 (free enquiry service)
Fax 020 7412 7453 (free enquiry service)
✉ business-information@bl.uk
www.bl.uk/bis
OPEN 10.00 am to 8.00 pm Monday; 9.30 am
to 8.00 pm Tuesday to Thursday; 9.30 am to
5.00 pm Friday and Saturday; closed for
public holidays
ACCESS By British Library reader's pass
The BL holds the most comprehensive collection of business information literature in the
UK. This includes market research reports and

journals, directories, company annual reports, trade and business journals, house journals, trade literature and electronic services.

British Library Early Printed Collections/Rare Books and Music Reading Room

96 Euston Road, London NW1 2DB
☎020 7412 7676   Fax 020 7412 7577
✉ rare-books@bl.uk
www.bl.uk

General enquiries about reader services & advance reservations: ☎020 7412 7676
Fax 020 7412 7609
✉ reader-services-enquiries@bl.uk

OPEN 10.00 am to 8.00 pm Monday; 9.30 am to 8.00 pm Tuesday to Thursday; 9.30 am to 5.00 pm Friday and Saturday; closed for public holidays

ACCESS By British Library reader's pass

Early Printed Collections, which is an integral part of British Library Scholarship and Collections, selects, acquires, researches and provides access to material printed in the British Isles to 1914 and in Western European languages before 1851. The collections are available in the Rare Books and Music Reading Room at St Pancras which also functions as the focus for the British Library's extensive collection of humanities microforms.

Further information about Early Printed Collections can be found at the British Library website.

British Library Humanities Reading Room

96 Euston Road, London NW1 2DB
☎020 7412 7676   Fax 020 7412 7789
✉ reader-services-enquiries@bl.uk
www.bl.uk/resources/humanities

Open 10.00 am to 8.00 pm Monday; 9.30 am to 8.00 pm Tuesday, Wednesday, Thursday; 9.30 am to 5.00 pm Friday and Saturday; closed for public holidays

ACCESS By British Library reader's pass

This reading room is the focus for the Library's modern collections service in the humanities. It is on two levels, Humanities 1 and Humanities 2 and provides access to the Library's comprehensive collections of books and periodicals in all subjects in the humanities and social sciences and in all languages apart from Oriental. These collections are not available for browsing at the shelf. Material is held in closed access storage and needs to be identified and ordered from store using an online catalogue. A selective open access collection on most humanities subjects can be found in Humanities 1 whilst in Humanities 2 there are open access reference works relating to periodicals and theses, to recorded sound and to librarianship and information science.

To access British Library catalogues, go to the website.

British Library Manuscript Collections

96 Euston Road, London NW1 2DB
☎020 7412 7513   Fax 020 7412 7745
✉ mss@bl.uk
www.bl.uk

OPEN 10.00 am to 5.00 pm Monday; 9.30 am to 5.00 pm Tuesday to Saturday; closed for public holidays

ACCESS Reading facilities only, by British Library reader's pass; a written letter of recommendation and advance notice is required for certain categories of material

Two useful publications, Index of Manuscripts in the British Library, Cambridge 1984–6, 10 vols, and The British Library: Guide to the Catalogues and Indexes of the Department of Manuscripts by M.A.E. Nickson, help to guide the researcher through this vast collection of manuscripts dating from Ancient Greece to the present day. Approximately 300,000 mss, charters, papyri and seals are housed here.

For information on British Library collections and services and to access British Library catalogues, including the Manuscripts online catalogue, visit the website.

British Library Map Collections

96 Euston Road, London NW1 2DB
☎020 7412 7702   Fax 020 7412 7780
✉ maps@bl.uk
www.bl.uk/collections/maps

OPEN 10.00 am to 5.00 pm Monday; 9.30 am to 5.00 pm Tuesday to Saturday; closed for public holidays

ACCESS By British Library reader's pass

A collection of about 4.5 million maps, charts and globes, manuscript, printed and, increasingly, digital, with particular reference to the history of British cartography. Maps for all parts of the world in a wide range of scales, formats and dates, including the most comprehensive collection of Ordnance Survey maps and plans. SPECIAL COLLECTIONS King George III Topographical Collection and Maritime Collection, the Crace Collection of maps and plans of London and the cartographic archive of the Ministry of Defence (i.e. GSGS).

For information on British Library collections and services, visit the website.

To access main British Library catalogues, go to the website at catalogue.bl.uk

British Library Music Collections

96 Euston Road, London NW1 2DB
☎020 7412 7772   Fax 020 7412 7751
✉ music-collections@bl.uk
www.bl.uk

OPEN 10.00 am to 8.00 pm Monday; 9.30 am to 8.00 pm Tuesday to Thursday; 9.30 am to 5.00 pm Friday and Saturday; closed for public holidays

ACCESS By British Library reader's pass

SPECIAL COLLECTIONS The Royal Music Library (containing almost all Handel's surviving autograph scores), The Zweig Collection of Music & Literary Mss, The Royal Philharmonic Society Archive and the Paul Hirsch Music Library. Also a large collection (about one and a quarter million items) of printed music (UK via legal deposit) and about 100,000 items of manuscript music, both British and foreign.

The British Library website contains details of collections and services, and provides access to the catalogues.

British Library Newspapers

Colindale Avenue, London NW9 5HE
☎020 7412 7353   Fax 020 7412 7379
✉ newspaper@bl.uk
www.bl.uk/collections/newspapers.html

OPEN 10.00 am to 5.00 pm Monday to Saturday (last newspaper issue 4.15 pm); closed for public holidays

ACCESS By British Library reader's pass or Newspaper Library pass (available from and valid only for Colindale)

Major collections of English provincial, Scottish, Welsh, Irish, Commonwealth and selected overseas foreign newspapers from c.1700 are housed here. Some earlier holdings are also available. London newspapers from 1801 and many weekly and fortnightly periodicals are also in stock. (London newspapers pre-dating 1801 are housed at the new library building in St Pancras (96 Euston Road, NW1) though many are available at Colindale Avenue on microfilm.) Readers are advised to check availability of material in advance.

For information on British Library Newspapers collections and services, visit the website.

British Library Science, Technology and Medicine Information

96 Euston Road, London NW1 2DB
☎020 7412 7676 (General Enquiries)
Fax 020 7412 7495
✉ scitech@bl.uk
www.bl.uk

Patent enquiries: ☎020 7412 7903 Fax 020 7412 7480 ✉ patents-information@bl.uk
www.bl.uk/patents

Business enquiries: ☎020 7412 7454 (Business quick enquiry line available 9.00 am to 5.00 pm Monday to Friday)

OPEN 10.00 am to 8.00 pm Monday; 9.30 am to 8.00 pm Tuesday to Thursday; 9.30 am to 5.00 pm Friday and Saturday; closed for public holidays

Engineering, business information on companies, markets and products, physical science and technologies. British, European and Patent Co-operation Treaty patents and trade marks.

For information on British Library collections and services, visit the website.

To access British Library catalogues go to the website at catalogue.bl.uk

British Library Social Sciences & Official Publications

96 Euston Road, London NW1 2DB
☎020 7412 7676   Fax 020 7412 7761
✉ social-sciences@bl.uk
www.bl.uk/collections/social/social.html

OPEN Reading Room: 10.00 am to 8.00 pm Monday; 9.30 am to 8.00 pm Tuesday to Thursday; 9.30 am to 5.00 pm Friday and Saturday; closed for public holidays

ACCESS By British Library reader's pass

Provides an information service on the social sciences, law, public administration, and current and international affairs, and access to current and historical official publications from all countries and intergovernmental bodies. Maerial available in the reading room includes House of Commons sessional papers, UK legislation, UK electoral registers, up-to-date reference books on official publications and on the social sciences, a major collection of statistics and a browsing collection of recent social science books and periodicals; other collections are kept in closed stores and items have to be ordered for delivery to the reading room.

To access British Library catalogues, go to the website at catalogue.bl.uk

British Library Sound Archive

96 Euston Road, London NW1 2DB
☎020 7412 7676   Fax 020 7412 7441
✉ sound-archive@bl.uk
www.bl.uk/soundarchive

OPEN 10.00 am to 8.00 pm Monday; 9.30 am to 8.00 pm Tuesday to Thursday; 9.30 am to 5.00 pm Friday and Saturday; closed for public holidays
Listening service (by appointment)
Northern Listening Service British Library Document Supply Centre, Boston Spa: 9.15 am to 4.30 pm Monday to Friday

OPEN ACCESS
An archive of over 1,000,000 discs and more than 200,000 hours of tape recordings, including all types of music, oral history, drama, literature, poetry, wildlife, selected BBC broadcasts and BBC Sound Archive material. Produces a twice-yearly newsletter, *Playback*.

For information on British Library Sound Archive collections and services, visit the website.

British Psychological Society Library

c/o Psychology Library, Senate House Library, Senate House, Malet Street, London WC1E 7HU
☎020 7862 8451/8461   Fax 020 7862 8480
✉ enquiries@shl.lon.ac.uk
www.shl.lon.ac.uk

OPEN Term-time: 9.00 am to 9.00 pm Monday to Thursday; 9.00 am to 6.30 pm Friday; 9.30 am to 5.30 pm Saturday (Holidays: 9.00 am to 6.00 pm Monday to Friday; 9.30 am to 5.30 pm Saturday)

ACCESS Members only; Non-members £5 day ticket

Reference library, containing the British Psychological Society collection of periodicals – over 140 current titles housed alongside the University of London's collection of books and journals. Largely for academic research. General queries referred to **Swiss Cottage Library** in London which has a good psychology collection.

Bromley Central Library

London Borough of Bromley – Directorate of Education & Libraries, High Street, Bromley BR1 1EX
☎020 8460 9955   Fax 020 8313 9975
✉ reference.library@bromley.gov.uk
www.bromley.gov.uk

OPEN 9.30 am to 6.00 pm Monday,
Wednesday, Friday; 9.30 am to 8.00 pm Tuesday and Thursday; 9.30 am to 5.00 pm Saturday

OPEN ACCESS
A large selection of fiction and non-fiction books for loan, both adult and children's. Also DVDs, videos, CDs, cassettes, language courses, open learning packs, CD-ROM and Playstation games for hire. Other facilities include CD-ROMs, computer hire, People's Network Internet, local studies library, 'Upfront' teenage section, large reference library with photocopying, fax, microfiche and film facilities, 'Bromley Knowledge' – online community information, reading groups and Local Links (access to council services). SPECIALIST COLLECTIONS include: H.G. Wells, Walter de la Mare, Crystal Palace, The Harlow Bequest, and the history and geography of Asia, America, Australasia and the Polar regions.

Bromley House Library

Angel Row, Nottingham NG1 6HL
☎0115 947 3134
✉ nfl@bromho.freeserve.co.uk
Librarian *Carol Allison*

OPEN 9.30 am to 5.00 pm Monday to Friday; also first Saturday of each month from 10.00 am to 12.30 pm

ACCESS For members only
Founded 1816 as the Nottingham Subscription Library. Collection of 30,000 books including local history, topography, biography, travel and fiction.

CAA Library and Information Centre

Aviation House, Gatwick Airport RH6 0YR
☎01293 573725   Fax 01293 573181
www.caa.co.uk

OPEN 9.30 am to 4.30 pm Monday to Friday

OPEN ACCESS
A collection of books, reports, directories, statistics and periodicals on most aspects of civil aviation and related subjects.

Cambridge Central Library (Reference Library & Information Service)

7 Lion Yard, Cambridge CB2 3QD
☎0845 045 5225   Fax 01223 712036
✉ cambridge.central.library@cambridgeshire.gov.uk
www.cambridgeshire.govuk/library

OPEN 9.00 am to 7.00 pm Monday to Friday; 9.00 am to 5.30 pm Saturday

OPEN ACCESS Large stock of books, periodicals, newspapers, maps, plus comprehensive collection of directories and annuals covering UK, Europe and the world. Microfilm and fiche reading and printing services. Online access to news and business databases. News databases on CD-ROM; Internet access. Monochrome photocopiers.

Camomile Street Library
12–20 Camomile Street, London EC3A 7EX
☎020 7247 8895
✉ camomile@corpoflondon.gov.uk
www.cityoflondon.gov.uk/camomilestlibrary
OPEN 9.30 am to 5.30 pm Monday to Friday

OPEN ACCESS Corporation of London lending library. Wide range of fiction and non-fiction books and language courses on cassette, foreign fiction, paperbacks, maps and guides for travel at home and abroad, children's books, a selection of large print, and collections of DVDs, videos and music CDs, books in Bengali. Spoken word recordings on cassette and CD. Free Internet access.

Cardiff Central Library
Frederick Street, St David's Link, Cardiff CF10 2DU
☎029 2038 2116   Fax 029 2087 1599
✉ robboddy@hotmail.com
www.libraries.cardiff.gov.uk
OPEN 9.00 am to 6.00 pm Monday, Tuesday, Wednesday, Friday; 9.00 am to 7.00 pm Thursday; 9.00 am to 5.30 pm Saturday
General lending library with the following departments: leisure, music, children's, local studies, information, science and humanities.

Carmarthen Public Library
St Peter's Street, Carmarthen SA31 1LN
☎01267 224824   Fax 01267 221839
✉ wtphillips@carmarthenshire.gov.uk
OPEN 9.30 am to 7.00 pm Monday, Tuesday, Wednesday, Friday; 9.30 am to 5.00 pm Thursday and Saturday

OPEN ACCESS Comprehensive range of fiction, non-fiction, children's books and reference works in English and in Welsh. Large local history library. Free Internet access and CD-ROM facilities. Large Print books, books on tape, CDs, CD-ROMs, cassettes, DVDs and videos available for loan.

Catholic Central Library
St Michaels Abbey, Farnborough Road, Farnborough GU14 7NQ
✉ librarian@catholic-library.org.uk
www.catholic-library.org.uk
OPEN ACCESS For reference (non-members must sign in; loans restricted to members)
Contains books, many not readily available elsewhere, on theology, religions worldwide, scripture and the history of churches of all denominations.

The Centre for the Study of Cartoons and Caricature
See entry under *Picture Libraries*

City Business Library
1 Brewers' Hall Garden, off Aldermanbury Square, London EC2V 5BX
☎020 7332 1812/(3803 textphone)
Fax 020 7332 1847
✉ cbl@corpoflondon.gov.uk
www.cityoflondon.gov.uk/libraries
OPEN 9.30 am to 5.00 pm Monday to Friday (except public holidays)

OPEN ACCESS Local authority free public reference library run by the Corporation of London. Books, directories, periodicals, newspapers and electronic databases of current business interest. Provided for anyone with a business informatin enquiry and is one of the leading public resource centres in Britain in its field. Large directory collection for both the UK and overseas, plus companies information, market research reports, management, banking, insurance, investment and statistics. Free public Internet access. No academic journals or textbooks.

Commonwealth Secretariat Library
Marlborough House, Pall Mall, London SW1Y 5HX
☎020 7747 6164   Fax 020 7747 6168
✉ library@commonwealth.int
www.thecommonwealth.org
Librarian *David Blake*
Open 10.00 am to 4.45 pm Monday to Friday

ACCESS For reference only, by appointment
Extensive reference source concerned with economy, development, trade, production and industry of Commonwealth countries; also human resources including women, youth, health, management and education. Includes the archives of the Secretariat.

Corporation of London Libraries

See **Barbican Library**; **Camomile Street Library**; **City Business Library**; **Guildhall Library**

Coventry Central Library

Smithford Way, Coventry CV1 1FY
☎024 7683 2314/2395 (Minicom)
Fax 024 7683 2440
✉ central.library@coventry.gov.uk
www.coventry.gov.uk

OPEN 9.00 am to 8.00 pm Monday to Friday; 9.00 am to 4.30 pm Saturday; 12.00 am to 4.00 pm Sunday

OPEN ACCESS

Located in the middle of the city's main shopping centre. Approximately 120,000 items (books, cassettes, CDs and DVDs) for loan; plus reference collection of business information and local history. SPECIAL COLLECTIONS Cycling and motor industries; George Eliot; Angela Brazil; Tom Mann Collection (trade union and labour studies); local newspapers on microfilm from 1740 onwards. Over 300 periodicals taken. 'Peoplelink' community information database available.

Department for Environment, Food and Rural Affairs

Nobel House, 17 Smith Square, London SW1P 3JR
☎020 7238 3000   Fax 020 7238 6591

DEFRA Helpline 08459 335577 (local call rate) − general contact point which can provide information on the work of DEFRA, either directly or by referring callers to appropriate contacts. Available 9.00 am to 5.00 pm Monday to Friday (excluding Bank Holidays)

OPEN 9.30 am to 5.00 pm Monday to Friday

ACCESS For reference (but at least 24 hours notice must be given for intended visits)

Large stock of volumes on temperate agriculture.

Derby Central Library

Wardwick, Derby DE1 1HS
☎01332 255398   Fax 01332 369570
www.derby.gov.uk/libraries

OPEN 9.30 am to 7.00 pm Monday, Tuesday, Thursday, Friday; 9.30 am to 1.00 pm Wednesday; 9.30 am to 4.00 pm Saturday

Local Studies Library
25B Irongate, Derby DE1 3GL
☎01332 255393 Fax 01332 255381

OPEN 9.30 am to 7.00 pm Monday and Tuesday; 9.30 am to 5.00 pm Wednesday, Thursday, Friday; 9.30 am to 4.00 pm Saturday

OPEN ACCESS

General library for lending, information and Children's Services. The Central Library also houses specialist private libraries: Derbyshire Archaeological Society; Derby Philatelic Society. The Local Studies Library houses the largest multimedia collection of resources in existence relating to Derby and Derbyshire. The collection includes mss deeds, family papers, business records including the Derby Canal Company, Derby Board of Guardians and the Derby China Factory. Both libraries offer free Internet access.

Devon & Exeter Institution Library

7 Cathedral Close, Exeter EX1 1EZ
☎01392 251017
✉ J.P.Gardner@exeter.ac.uk
www.devonandexeterinstitution.org.uk

OPEN 9.00 am to 5.00 pm Monday to Friday

ACCESS Members only (temporary membership available)

Founded 1813. Under the administration of Exeter University Library. Contains over 36,000 volumes, including long runs of 19th-century journals, theology, history, topography, early science, biography and literature. A large and growing collection of books, journals, newspapers, prints and maps relating to the South West.

Doncaster Library and Information Services

Central Library, Waterdale, Doncaster DN1 3JE
☎01302 734305   Fax 01302 369749
✉ Reference.Library@doncaster.gov.uk
library.doncaster.gov.uk

OPEN 9.00 am to 6.00 pm Monday; 8.30 am to 6.00 pm Tuesday and Friday; 8.30 am to 8.00 pm Wednesday and Thursday; 9.00 am to 5.00 pm Saturday

OPEN ACCESS

Books, spoken word cassettes/CDs, DVDs, videos. Reading aids unit for people with visual impairment; activities for children during school holidays, including visits by authors, readers' groups, etc. Also reference library and Local Studies library.

Dorchester Library (part of Dorset County Library)

Colliton Park, Dorchester DT1 1XJ
☎01305 224440 (lending)/224448 (reference)

Fax 01305 266120

✉ Dorchesterreflibrary@dorset-cc.gov.uk

OPEN 10.00 am to 7.00 pm Monday; 9.30 am
to 7.00 pm Tuesday, Wednesday, Friday;
9.30 am to 5.00 pm Thursday; 9.00 am to
4.00 pm Saturday

OPEN ACCESS
General lending and reference library, including special collections on Thomas Hardy, the
Powys Family and William Barnes. Periodicals,
children's library, CD-ROMs, free Internet
access. Video lending service.

Dundee Central Library
The Wellgate, Dundee DD1 1DB
☎01382 431500   Fax 01382 431558
✉ central.library@dundeecity.gov.uk
www.dundeecity.gov.uk

OPEN Lending & Local Studies Departments
and General Reference: 9.30 am to 6.00 pm
Monday, Tuesday, Friday; 10.00 am to 6.00
pm Wednesday; 9.30 am to 8.00 pm
Thursday; 9.30 am to 5.00 pm Saturday.
Commerce & Technology: 9.30 am to 9.00
pm Monday, Tuesday, Thursday, Friday;
10.00 am to 9.00 pm Wednesday; 9.30 am
to 5.00 pm Saturday.

ACCESS Reference services available to all; lending services to those who live, work, study or
were educated within Dundee City

Adult lending, reference and children's serv-
ices. Art, music, audio, video and DVD lending
services. Internet access. Schools service
(Agency). Housebound and mobile services.
SPECIAL COLLECTIONS The Wighton Collection
of National Music; The Wighton Heritage
Centre; The Wilson Photographic Collection;
The Lamb Collection.

Durning-Lawrence Library
See **Senate House Library**

English Nature
Northminster House, Peterborough PE1 1UA
☎01733 455000   Fax 01733 568834
✉ enquiries@english-nature.org.uk
www.english-nature.org.uk

OPEN 8.30 am to 5.00 pm Monday to
Thursday; 8.30 am to 4.30 pm Friday

ACCESS *Bona fide* students only. Telephone
library for appointment on 01733 455094

Information on nature conservation, nature
reserves, SSSIs, planning, legislation, etc. English
Nature is the government-funded body whose

purpose is to promote the conservation of
England's wildlife and natural features.

Equal Opportunities Commission
Arndale House, Arndale Centre, Manchester
M4 3EQ
☎0845 601 5901   Fax 0161 838 8303
✉ info@eoc.org.uk
www.eoc.org.uk

The EOC is open to the public via the
Helpline (0845 601 5901) 9.00 am to 5.00
pm Mondays to Fridays.

Essex County Council Libraries
Goldlay Gardens, Chelmsford CM2 0EW
☎01245 284981   Fax 01245 492780
✉ essexlib@essexcc.gov.uk
www.essexcc.gov.uk

Essex County Council Libraries has 73 static
libraries throughout Essex as well as 13 mobile
libraries and three special-needs mobiles.
Services to the public include books, newspapers, periodicals, CDs, cassettes, videos, pictures,
CD-ROMs and Internet access as well as postal
cassettes for the blind and subtitled videos.
Specialist subjects and collections are listed
below at the relevant library.

Chelmsford Library
PO Box 882, Market Road, Chelmsford
CM1 1LH
☎01245 492758 Fax 01245 492536
✉ chelmford.library@essexcc.gov.uk

OPEN 8.30 am to 7.00 pm Monday to Friday;
8.30 am to 5.30 pm Saturday; 12.30 pm to
4.30 pm Sunday

Colchester Library
Trinity Square, Colchester CO1 1JB
☎01206 245900 Fax 01206 245901
✉ colchester.library@essexcc.gov.uk

OPEN 8.30 am to 7.30 pm Monday, Tuesday,
Wednesday and Friday; 8.30 am to 5.00 pm
Thursday and Saturday; 12.30 pm to
4.30 pm Sunday

Local studies, music scores; Castle collection
(18th-century subscription library); Cunning-
ton collection; Margaret Lazell collection; Taylor
collection.

Harlow Library
The High, Harlow CM20 1HA
☎01279 413772 Fax 01279 424612
✉ harlow.library@essexcc.gov.uk

OPEN 9.00 am to 7.00 pm Monday to Friday;

9.00 am to 5.00 pm Saturday; 1.00 pm to 4.00 pm Sunday

Sir John Newson Memorial collection; Maurice Hughes Memorial collection.

Loughton Library

Traps Hill, Loughton IG10 1HD
☎020 8502 0181 Fax 020 8508 5041
✉ loughton.library@essexcc.gov.uk

OPEN 9.00 am to 7.00 pm Monday, Tuesday, Wednesday and Friday; 9.00 am to 1.00 pm Thursday; 9.30 am to 5.30 pm Saturday; 11.00 am to 3.00 pm Sunday

National Jazz Foundation Archive.

Saffron Walden Library

2 King Street, Saffron Walden CB10 1ES
☎01799 523178 Fax 01799 513642

OPEN 9.00 am to 7.00 pm Monday, Tuesday, Thursday, Friday; 9.00 am to 5.00 pm Saturday; 1.00 pm to 4.00 pm Sunday (closed Wednesday)

Victorian studies collection.

Witham Library

18 Newland Street, Witham CM8 2AQ
☎01376 519625 Fax 01376 501913

OPEN 9.00 am to 7.00 pm Monday, Tuesday, Thursday, Friday; 9.00 am to 5.00 pm Saturday (closed Wednesday); 1.00 pm to 4.00 pm Sunday

Drama. Dorothy L. Sayers and Maskell collections.

Family Records Centre

1 Myddleton Street, London EC1R 1UW
☎020 8392 5200   Fax 020 8487 9214
✉ frc@nationalarchives.gov.uk
www.familyrecords.gov.uk/frc

OPEN 9.00 am to 5.00 pm Monday, Wednesday, Friday; 10.00 am to 7.00 pm Tuesday; 9.00 am to 7.00 pm Thursday; 9.30 am to 5.00 pm Saturday (closed public holidays)

ACCESS for reference; no i.d. required

The Centre provides a family history service to visitors, advising on how to use the wealth of genealogical records available, including births, marriages and deaths and census returns. Part of the **National Archives** (see entry).

The Fawcett Library

See **The Women's Library**

Foreign and Commonwealth Office Library

King Charles Street, London SW1A 2AH
☎020 7008 3925   Fax 020 7008 3270
✉ library-enquiries@fco.gov.uk
www.fco.gov.uk

ACCESS By appointment only

An extensive stock of books, pamphlets and other reference material on all aspects of historical, socio-economic and political subjects relating to countries covered by the Foreign and Commonwealth Office. Particularly strong on colonial history, early works on travel, and photograph collections, mainly of Commonwealth countries and former colonies, c. 1850s–1960s.

Forestry Commission Library

Forest Research Station, Alice Holt Lodge, Wrecclesham, Farnham GU10 4LH
☎01420 22255   Fax 01420 23653
✉ library@forestry.gsi.gov.uk
www.forestry.gov.uk
www.forestresearch.gov.uk

OPEN 9.00 am to 5.00 pm Monday to Thursday; 9.00 am to 4.30 pm Friday

ACCESS By appointment for personal visits

Approximately 20,000 books on forestry and arboriculture, plus 500 current journals. CD-ROMS include TREECD (1939 onwards). Offers a Research Advisory Service for advice and enquiries on forestry (☎01420 23000) with a charge for consultations and diagnosis of tree problems exceeding ten minutes.

French Institute Library

Institut français, 17 Queensberry Place, London SW7 2DT
☎020 7073 1350   Fax 020 7073 1363
✉ library@ambafrance.org.uk
www.institut-francais.org.uk

OPEN 12 noon to 7.00 pm Tuesday to Friday; 12 noon to 6.00 pm Saturday; Children's Library: 12 noon to 6.00 pm Tuesday to Saturday; closed in August; closed for one week at Christmas

OPEN ACCESS For reference and consultation (loans restricted to members)

A collection of over 55,000 volumes mainly centred on French cultural interests with special emphasis on language, literature and history. Books in French and English. Collection of videos, periodicals, CDs (French music), CD-ROMs; special collections: 'France Libre'. Denis Saurat MSS, recordings of lectures, press-cuttings on French current affairs. Inter-library loans; quick information service; Internet access to members. Group visits on request. Children's library (8000 documents).

John Frost Newspapers

22b Rosemary Avenue, Enfield EN2 0SS
☎020 8366 1392/0946   Fax 020 8366 1379
✉ andrew@johnfrostnewspapers.com
www.johnfrostnewspapers.co.uk

Contacts *Andrew Frost, John Frost*

A collection of 80,000 original newspapers (1630 to the present day) and 200,000 press cuttings available, on loan, for research and rostrum/stills work (TV documentaries, book and magazine publishers and audiovisual presentations). Historic events, politics, sports, royalty, crime, wars, personalities, etc., plus many in-depth files.

Gloucestershire County Council Libraries & Information

Quayside House, Shire Hall, Gloucester GL1 2HY
☎08452 305420   Fax 01452 425042
✉ libraryhelp@gloucestershire.gov.uk
www.gloucestershire.gov.uk
Head of Libraries & Information *David Paynter*

OPEN ACCESS

The service includes 39 local libraries and six mobile libraries. The website (GlosNet) includes library opening hours, mobile library route schedules; the library catalogue; and a book renewal/reservations facility.

Goethe-Institut Library

50 Princes Gate, Exhibition Road, London SW7 2PH
☎020 7596 4040   Fax 020 7594 0230
✉ library@london.goethe.org
www.goethe.de/london
Librarian *Gerlinde Buck*

OPEN 1.00 pm to 8.00 pm Monday to Thursday; 1.00 pm to 5.00 pm Saturday

Library specialising in German literature and books/audiovisual material on German culture and history: 20,000 books (4000 of them in English), 120 periodicals, 13 newspapers, 3700 audiovisual media (including 1200 videos/DVDs), selected press clippings on German affairs from the German and UK press, information service, photocopier, video facility. Also German language teaching material for teachers and students of German.

Goldsmiths' Library
See **Senate House Library**

Greater London Record Office
See **London Metropolitan Archives Library Services**

Guildford Institute of the University of Surrey Library

Ward Street, Guildford GU1 4LH
☎01483 562142   Fax 01483 451034
✉ c.miles@surrey.ac.uk
Librarian *Clare Miles*

OPEN 10.00 am to 3.00 pm Tuesday to Friday

OPEN ACCESS To members only but open to enquirers for research purposes

Founded 1834. Some 14,000 volumes of which 7500 were printed before the First World War. The remaining stock consists of recently published works of fiction and non-fiction. Newspapers and periodicals also available. SPECIAL COLLECTIONS include an almost complete run of the *Illustrated London News* from 1843–1906, a collection of Victorian and early 20th century local history ephemera albums, and about 400 photos and other pictures relating to the Institute's history and the town of Guildford. Publishes Library newsletter twice-yearly.

Guildhall Library

Aldermanbury, London EC2P 2EJ
☎See below   Fax 020 7600 3384
www.cityoflondon.gov.uk/guildhalllibrary

ACCESS For reference (but much of the material is kept in storage areas and is supplied to readers on request; proof of identity is required for consultation of certain categories of stock). Free, *limited* enquiry service available.

Also a fee-based service for in-depth research:
☎020 7332 1854 Fax 020 7600 3384
✉ search.guildhall@corpoflondon.gov.uk
www.cityoflondon.gov.uk/search_guildhall

Part of the Corporation of London libraries. Seeks to provide a basic general reference service but its major strength, acknowledged worldwide, is in its historical collections. The library is divided into three sections, each with its own catalogues and enquiry desks. These are: Printed Books; Manuscripts; the Print & Maps Room.

PRINTED BOOKS
☎020 7332 1868/1870
✉ printed books.guildhall@corpoflondon.gov.uk

OPEN 9.30 am to 5 pm Monday to Saturday; NB closes on Saturdays preceding Bank Holidays; check for details

Strong on all aspects of London history, with wide holdings of English history, topography and genealogy, including local directories, poll books and parish register transcripts. Also good collections of English statutes, law reports, parliamentary debates and journals, and House of Commons papers. Home of several important collections deposited by London institutions: the Marine collection of the Corporation of Lloyd's, the Stock Exchange's historical files of reports and prospectuses, the Clockmakers' Company library and museum, the Gardeners' Company, Fletchers' Company, the Institute of Masters of Wine, International Wine and Food Society and Gresham College.

MANUSCRIPTS
☎020 7332 1862/3
✉ manuscripts.guildhall@corpoflondon.gov.uk
www.history.ac.uk/gh/
OPEN 9.30 am to 4.45 pm Monday to Saturday (no requests for records after 4.30 pm; no manuscripts can be produced between 12 noon and 2 pm on Saturdays); NB closes on Saturdays preceding Bank Holidays; check for details

The official repository for historical records relating to the City of London (except those of the Corporation of London itself, which are housed at the Corporation Records Office). Records date from the 11th century to the present day. They include archives of most of the City's parishes, wards and livery companies, and of many individuals, families, estates, schools, societies and other institutions, notably the Diocese of London and St Paul's Cathedral, as well as the largest collection of business archives in any public repository in the UK. Although mainly of City interest, holdings include material for the London area as a whole and beyond.

PRINTS & MAPS ROOM
☎020 7332 1839
✉ prints&maps@corpoflondon.gov.uk
OPEN 9.30 am to 5.00 pm Monday to Friday

An unrivalled collection of prints and drawings relating to London and the adjacent counties. The emphasis is on topography, but there are strong collections of portraits and satirical prints. The map collection includes maps of the capital from the mid-16th century to the present day and various classes of Ordnance Survey maps. Other material includes photographs, theatre bills and programmes, trade cards, book plates and playing cards as well as a sizeable collection of Old Master prints. Over 30,000 items

have been digitally imaged on Collage, including topographical prints, some maps, a small number of photographs and all the Guildhall Art Gallery collection. Collage website: collage.cityoflondon.gov.uk

Guille–Alles Library
Market Street, St Peter Port, Guernsey GY1 1HB
☎01481 720392   Fax 01481 712425
✉ ga@library.gg
www.library.gg
OPEN 9.00 am to 5.00 pm Monday, Thursday, Friday, Saturday; 10.00 am to 5.00 pm Tuesday; 9.00 am to 8.00 pm Wednesday
OPEN ACCESS For residents; payment of returnable deposit by visitors. Music CD collection: £10 for two-year subscription
Lending, reference and information services. Public Internet service.

Herefordshire Libraries and Information Service
Shirehall, Hereford HR1 2HY
☎01432 359830   Fax 01432 260744
www.libraries.herefordshire.gov.uk
OPEN Opening hours vary in the libraries across the county
ACCESS Information and reference services open to anyone; loans to members only (membership criteria: resident, being educated, working, or an elector in the county or neighbouring authorities; temporary membership to visitors. Proof of identity and address required)

Information service, reference and lending libraries. Non-fiction and fiction for all age groups, including normal and large print, spoken word cassettes, and CDs, music CDs, videos, DVDs, playstation2. Hereford Library houses the largest reference section and the county local history collection, although some reference material and local history is available at all libraries. Internet access at all libraries. *Special collections* Cidermaking; Beekeeping; Alfred Watkins; John Masefield; Pilley.

University of Hertfordshire Library
College Lane, Hatfield AL10 9AB
☎01707 284678   Fax 01707 284666
www.herts.ac.uk/lis
OPEN See website for term-time and vacation opening hours
ACCESS For reference use of printed collec-

tions. Appropriate ID required for Visitor's pass. For further information please refer to the website.

Highgate Literary and Scientific Institution Library

11 South Grove, London N6 6BS
☎020 8340 3343   Fax 020 8340 5632
✉ librarian@hlsi.net

OPEN 10.00 am to 5.00 pm Tuesday to Friday; 10.00 am to 4.00 pm Saturday (closed Sunday and Monday)

ANNUAL MEMBERSHIP £50 (individual); £80 (household)

25,000 volumes of general fiction and non-fiction, with a children's section and extensive local archives. SPECIAL COLLECTIONS on local history, London, and local poets Samuel Taylor Coleridge and John Betjeman.

Highland Libraries, The Highland Council, Education, Culture and Sport Service

Library Support Unit, 31a Harbour Road, Inverness IV1 1UA
☎01463 235713   Fax 01463 236986
✉ libraries@highland.gov.uk
www.highland.gov.uk

OPEN Library opening hours vary to suit local needs. Contact administration and support services for details (8.00 am to 6.00 pm Monday to Friday)

OPEN ACCESS
Comprehensive range of lending and reference stock: books, pamphlets, periodicals, newspapers, compact discs, audio and video cassettes, maps, census records, genealogical records, photographs, educational materials, etc. Free access to the Internet in all libraries. Highland Libraries provides the public library service throughout the Highlands with a network of 43 static and 12 mobile libraries.

Holborn Library

32–38 Theobalds Road, London WC1X 8PA
☎020 7974 6345

OPEN 10.00 am to 7.00 pm Monday and Thursday; 10.00 am to 6.00 pm Tuesday, Wednesday and Friday; 10.00 am to 5.00 pm Saturday

OPEN ACCESS
London Borough of Camden public library. Includes the London Borough of Camden Local Studies and Archive Centre.

Sherlock Holmes Collection (Westminster)

Marylebone Library, Marylebone Road, London NW1 5PS
☎020 7641 1206   Fax 020 7641 1019
✉ ccooke@westminster.gov.uk
www.westminster.gov.uk/libraries/special/sherlock.cfm

OPEN 9.30 am to 8.00 pm Monday, Tuesday, Thursday, Friday; 10.00 am to 8.00 pm Wednesday; Closed Saturday and Sunday (unless by prior arrangement)

ACCESS By appointment only
Located in Westminster's Marylebone Library. An extensive collection of material from all over the world, covering Sherlock Holmes and Sir Arthur Conan Doyle. Books, pamphlets, journals, newspaper cuttings and photos, much of which is otherwise unavailable in this country. Some background material.

IHR Library

See **The Institute of Historical Research Library**

Imperial College Central Library

See **Science Museum Library**

Imperial War Museum

Department of Printed Books, Lambeth Road, London SE1 6HZ
☎020 7416 5342   Fax 020 7416 5246
✉ books@iwm.org.uk
www.iwm.org.uk

OPEN 10.00 am to 5.00 pm Monday to Saturday (restricted service Saturday; closed on Bank Holiday Saturdays and two weeks during the year for annual stock check)

ACCESS For reference (but at least 24 hours' notice must be given for intended visits)
A large collection of material on British and Commonwealth 20th-century life with detailed coverage of the two world wars and other conflicts. Books, pamphlets and periodicals, including many produced for short periods in unlikely wartime settings; also maps, biographies and privately printed memoirs, and foreign language material. Additional research material available in the following departments: Art, Documents, Exhibits and Firearms, Film, Sound Records, Photographs. Active publishing programme based on reprints of rare books held in library. Catalogue available.

The Institute of Historical Research

Senate House, Malet Street, London
WC1E 7HU
☎020 7862 8760   Fax 020 7862 8762
✉ IHR.Library@sas.ac.uk
lib.sas.ac.uk

OPEN 9.00 am to 8.45 pm Monday to Friday;
9.00 am to 4.45 pm Saturday and some
public holidays

ACCESS For reference only. Non-members are
advised to telephone to check availability of
items before visiting.

Reference collection of printed primary
sources, bibliographies, guides to archives, periodicals and works covering the history of
Western Europe from the fall of the Roman
Empire. Holds a substantial microform collection of mainly British material from repositories outside London.

Instituto Cervantes

102 Eaton Square, London SW1W 9AN
☎020 7201 0757   Fax 020 7235 0329
✉ biblon@cervantes.es
www.cervantes.es

OPEN 12 noon to 6.30 pm Monday to Friday;
9.30 am to 2.00 pm Saturday

OPEN ACCESS For reference and lending
Spanish language and literature, history, art,
philosophy. The library houses a collection of
books, periodicals, videos, DVDs, slides, tapes,
CDs, cassettes, CD-ROMs specialising entirely
in Spain and Latin America.

Italian Institute Library

39 Belgrave Square, London SW1X 8NX
☎020 7396 4425   Fax 020 7235 4618
www.italcultur.org.uk

OPEN 10.00 am to 1.30 pm and 2.30 pm to
5.00 pm Monday to Friday; 2.30 pm to
8.00 pm Wednesday (during term time only)

OPEN ACCESS For reference
A collection of over 21,000 volumes relating
to all aspects of Italian culture, including DVDs
and CDs relating to Italian cinema. Texts are
mostly in Italian, with some in English.

Jersey Library

Halkett Place, St Helier, Jersey JE2 4WH
☎01534 759991 (lending)/759992 (reference)
Fax 01534 769444
✉ library@jsylib.gov.je
www.jsylib.gov.je

OPEN 9.30 am to 5.30 pm Monday, Wednesday,
Thursday, Friday; 9.30 am to 7.30 pm
Tuesday; 9.30 am to 4.00 pm Saturday

OPEN ACCESS
Books, periodicals, newspapers, CDs, DVDs
and language packs, cassettes, videos, microfilm,
specialised local studies collection, public
Internet access. Branch Library at Les
Quennevais School, St Brelade. Mobile library
and homes services. Open Learning Centre.

Kent County Central Library

Kent Libraries and Archives, Springfield,
Maidstone ME14 2LH
☎01622 696511   Fax 01622 696494
www.kent.gov.uk/libs

OPEN 9.30 am to 5.30 pm Monday,
Wednesday, Friday; 9.30 am to 6.00 pm
Tuesday; 9.30 am to 7.00 pm Thursday;
10.00 am to 5.00 pm Saturday

OPEN ACCESS
50,000 volumes available on the floor of the
library plus 250,000 volumes of non-fiction,
mostly academic, available on request to staff.
English literature, poetry, classical literature,
drama (including play sets), music (including
music sets). Strong, too, in sociology, art history,
business information and government publications. Loans to all who live or work in Kent;
those who do not may consult stock for reference or arrange loans via their own local library
service.

Leeds Central Library

Calverley Street, Leeds LS1 3AB
☎0113 247 8911   Fax 0113 247 8426
www.leeds.gov.uk/libraries

OPEN 9.00 am to 8.00 pm Monday, Tuesday,
Wednesday; 9.30 am to 5.30 pm Thursday;
9.00 pm to 5.00 pm Friday; 10.00 am to
5.00 pm Saturday; 12.00 am to 4.00 pm
Sunday

OPEN ACCESS to lending libraries; reference
material on request. Free public Internet access.

Lending Library
☎0113 247 8270
✉centrallending@leedslearning.net

Music Library
☎0113 247 8273
✉ musiclibrary@leedslearning.net
Scores, books, video and audio.

Business & Research Library
☎0113 247 8282
✉ information.for.business@leeds. gov.uk *and*
businessandresearch@ leedslearning.net

Company information, market research, statistics, directories, journals and computer-based information. Extensive files of newspapers and periodicals plus all government publications since 1960. SPECIAL COLLECTIONS include military history, Judaic, early gardening books.

Art Library
☎0113 247 8247
✉ artlibrary@leedslearning.net
Major collection of material on fine and applied arts.

Local Studies Library
☎0113 247 8290
✉ localstudies@leedslearning.net
Extensive collection on Leeds and Yorkshire, including maps, books, pamphlets, local newspapers, illustrations and playbills. Census returns for the whole of Yorkshire also available. International Genealogical Index and parish registers.

Leeds City Libraries has an extensive network of 65 branch and mobile libraries.

Leeds Library
18 Commercial Street, Leeds LS1 6AL
☎0113 245 3071   Fax 0113 245 1191
OPEN 9.00 am to 5.00 pm Monday to Friday
ACCESS To members; research use upon application to the librarian
Founded 1768. Contains over 125,000 books and periodicals from the 15th century to the present day. SPECIAL COLLECTIONS include Reformation pamphlets, Civil War tracts, Victorian and Edwardian children's books and fiction, European language material, spiritualism and psychical research, plus local material.

Library of the Religious Society of Friends
Friends House, 173 Euston Road, London NW1 2BJ
☎020 7663 1135   Fax 020 7663 1001
✉ library@quaker.org.uk
www.quaker.org.uk
OPEN 1.00 pm to 5.00 pm Monday, Tuesday, Thursday, Friday; 10.00 am to 5.00 pm Wednesday
OPEN ACCESS A letter of introduction from a college, employer, publisher or Friends meeting is required for researchers who are not members of the Society (it is advisable to make an appointment before visiting)
Quaker history, thought and activities from the 17th century onwards. Supporting collec-

tions on peace, anti-slavery and other subjects in which Quakers have maintained long-standing interest. Also archives and manuscripts relating to the Society of Friends.

Lincoln Central Library
Free School Lane, Lincoln LN2 1EZ
☎01522 510800   Fax 01522 535882
✉ lincoln.library@lincolnshire.gov.uk
www.lincolnshire.gov.uk
OPEN 9.30 am to 7.00 pm Monday to Friday; 9.30 am to 4.00 pm Saturday
OPEN ACCESS to the library; appointment required for the Tennyson Research Centre
Lending and reference library. Special collections include Lincolnshire local history (printed and published material, photographs, maps, directories and census data) and the Tennyson Research Centre (contact *Grace Timmins* Email grace.timmins@lincolnshire.gov.uk).

Linen Hall Library
17 Donegall Square North, Belfast BT1 5GB
☎028 9032 1707   Fax 028 9043 8586
✉ info@linenhall.com
www.linenhall.com
Librarian *John Gray*
OPEN 9.30 am to 5.30 pm Monday to Friday; 9.30 am to 4.00 pm Saturday
OPEN ACCESS For reference (loans restricted to members)
Founded 1788. Contains about 200,000 books. Major Irish and local studies collections, including the Northern Ireland Political Collection relating to the current troubles (c. 250,000 items).

Literary & Philosophical Society of Newcastle upon Tyne
23 Westgate Road, Newcastle upon Tyne NE1 1SE
☎0191 232 0192   Fax 0191 261 4494
✉ library@litandphil.org.uk
www.litandphil.org.uk
Librarian *Kay Easson*
OPEN 9.30 am to 7.00 pm Monday, Wednesday, Thursday; 9.30 am to 8.00 pm Tuesday; 9.30 am to 5.00 pm Friday; 9.30 am to 1.00 pm Saturday
ACCESS Members; research facilities for *bona fide* scholars on application to the Librarian
200-year-old library of 140,000 volumes, periodicals (including 130 current titles), classical music on vinyl recordings and CD, plus a collection of scores. Free public lectures, events

and recitals. Recent publications include: *The Reverend William Turner: Dissent and Reform in Georgian Newcastle upon Tyne* Stephen Harbottle; *History of the Literary and Philosophical Society of Newcastle upon Tyne, Vol. 2 (1896–1989)* Charles Parish; *Bicentenary Lectures 1993* ed. John Philipson.

Liverpool Libraries and Information Services

William Brown Street, Liverpool L3 8EW
☎0151 233 5829   Fax 0151 233 5886
✉ refbt.central.library@liverpool.gov.uk
www.liverpool.gov.uk
OPEN 9.00 am to 8.00 pm Monday to Thursday; 9.00 am to 7.00 pm Friday; 9.00 am to 5.00 pm Saturday; 12 noon to 4.00 pm Sunday

OPEN ACCESS
Humanities Reference Library A total stock in excess of 120,000 volumes and 24,000 maps, plus book plates, prints and autographed letters. SPECIAL COLLECTIONS Walter Crane and Edward Lear illustrations, Kelmscott Press, Audubon.

Business and Technology Reference Library Extensive stock dealing with all aspects of science, commerce and technology, including British and European standards and patents and trade directories.

Audio Visual Library Extensive stock relating to all aspects of music. Includes 128,000 volumes and music scores, over 3000 CDs, 2000 videos and 800 DVDs.

Record Office and Local History Department Material relating to Liverpool, Merseyside, Lancashire and Cheshire, together with archive material mainly on Liverpool. Proof of name and address required to obtain reader's ticket.

University of the Arts London – London College of Communication

Library and Learning Resources, Elephant and Castle, London SE1 6SB
☎020 7514 6527   Fax 020 7514 6597
www.lcc.arts.ac.uk

ACCESS Appointment required
Library and Learning Resources provides books, periodicals, slides, CD-ROMs, videos and computer software on all aspects of the art of the book, printing, management, film/photography, graphic arts, plus retailing. SPECIAL COLLECTIONS history and development of published and unpublished scripts and the art of the western book.

The London Library

14 St James's Square, London SW1Y 4LG
☎020 7930 7705   Fax 020 7766 4766
✉ membership@londonlibrary.co.uk
www.londonlibrary.co.uk
Librarian *Miss Inez Lynn*
OPEN 9.30 am to 5.30 pm Monday, Friday, Saturday; 9.30 am to 7.30 pm Tuesday, Wednesday, Thursday
ACCESS For members only (£180 p.a., 2005)

With over a million books and 8000 members, The London Library 'is the most distinguished private library in the world; probably the largest, certainly the best loved'. Founded in 1841, it is a registered charity and wholly independent of public funding. Its permanent collection embraces most European languages as well as English. Its subject range is predominantly within the humanities, with emphasis on literature, history, fine and applied art, architecture, bibliography, philosophy, religion, and topography and travel. Some 8000–9000 titles are added yearly. Most of the stock is on open shelves to which members have free access. Members may take out up to 10 volumes; 15 if they live more than 20 miles from the Library. The comfortable Reading Room has an annexe for users of personal computers. There are photocopiers, CD-ROM workstations, free access to the Internet, and the Library also offers a postal loans service.

Membership is open to all: prospective members are required to submit a refereed application form in advance of admission, but there is at present no waiting list for membership. The London Library Trust may make grants to those who are unable to afford the full annual fee; details on application.

London Metropolitan Archives Library Services

History Library: 40 Northampton Road, London EC1R 0HB
☎020 7332 3820/7278 8703 (Minicom)
Fax 020 7833 9136
✉ ask.lma@corpoflondon.gov.uk
www.cityoflondon.gov.uk/lma
Contact *The Enquiry Team*
ACCESS For reference only
This 100,000 volume library covers all aspects of the life and development of London, with strong holdings on the history and organisation of London local government. As the former Greater London Council History Library, the collection covers all subjects of London life,

from architecture and biography to theatres and transport. The collection includes London directories from 1677 to the present, Acts of Parliament, statistical returns, several hundred periodical titles and public reports.

Lord Louis Library
Orchard Street, Newport, Isle of Wight
PO30 1LL
☎01983 527655/823800 (Reference Library)
Fax 01983 825972
✉ reflib@postmaster.co.uk
OPEN 9.00 am to 5.30 pm Monday to
Wednesday and Friday; 10.00 am to 8.00
pm Thursday; 9.00 am to 5.00 pm Saturday;
10.00 am to 4.00 pm Sunday

OPEN ACCESS
General adult and junior fiction and non-fiction collections; local history collection. Free Internet access in all branches of the library on the Isle of Wight Also the county's main reference library.

Manchester Central Library
St Peters Square, Manchester M2 5PD
☎0161 234 1900   Fax 0161 234 1963
✉ mclib@libraries.manchester.gov.uk
www.manchester.gov.uk/libraries
OPEN 10.00 am to 8.00 pm Monday to
Thursday; 10.00 am to 5.00 pm Friday and
Saturday; Commercial and European Units:
10.00 am to 6.00 pm Monday to Thursday;
10.00 am to 5.00 pm Friday and Saturday

OPEN ACCESS
One of the country's leading reference libraries with extensive collections covering all subjects. Departments include: Commercial, European, Technical, Social Sciences, Arts, Music, Local Studies, Chinese, General Readers, Language & Literature. Large lending stock and VIP (visually impaired) service available. Free Internet access.

Marylebone Library (Westminster)
See **Sherlock Holmes Collection**

The Mitchell Library
North Street, Glasgow G3 7DN
☎0141 287 2999   Fax 0141 287 2815
www.glasgowlibraries.org
OPEN 9.00 am to 8.00 pm Monday to
Thursday; 9.00 am to 5.00 pm Friday and
Saturday

OPEN ACCESS
One of Europe's largest public reference libraries with stock of over 1,200,000 volumes.

It subscribes to 48 newspapers and more than 1200 periodicals. There are collections in microform, records, tapes and videos, as well as CD-ROMs, electronic databases, illustrations, photographs, postcards, etc.

The library contains a number of special collections, e.g. the Robert Burns Collection (5000 vols), the Scottish Poetry Collection (12,000 items) and the Scottish Drama Collection (1650 items).

Morrab Library
Morrab House, Morrab Gardens, Penzance
TR18 4DA
☎01736 364474
Librarian *Annabelle Read*
OPEN 10.00 am to 4.00 pm Tuesday to Friday;
10.00 am to 1.00 pm Saturday

ACCESS Non-members may use the library for a small daily fee but may not borrow books

Formerly known as the Penzance Library. An independent subscription lending library of over 40,000 volumes covering virtually all subjects except modern science and technology, with large collections on history, literature and religion. There is a comprehensive Cornish collection of books, newspapers and manuscripts including the Borlase letters; a West Cornwall photographic archive; many runs of 18th- and 19th-century periodicals; a collection of over 2000 books published before 1800.

The National Archives
Kew, Richmond TW9 4DU
☎020 8876 3444   Fax 020 8487 1974
✉ enquiry@nationalarchives.gov.uk
www.nationalarchives.gov.uk
OPEN 9.00 am to 5.00 pm Monday,
Wednesday, Friday; 10.00 am to 7.00 pm
Tuesday; 9.00 am to 7.00 pm Thursday;
9.30 am to 5.00 pm Saturday (closed public
holidays and 29 November to 4 December
for annual stocktaking)

ACCESS for reference, by reader's ticket, available free of charge on production of proof of identity (UK citizens: banker's card or driving licence; non-UK: passport or national identity card. Telephone for further information)

Over 168 kilometres of shelving house the national repository of records of central government in the UK and law courts of England and Wales, which extend in time from the 11th to the 20th century. Medieval records and the records of the State Paper Office from the early 16th to late 18th century, plus the records of the Privy Council Office and the Lord Chamberlain's and

Lord Steward's departments. Modern government department records, together with those of the Copyright Office dating mostly from the late 18th century. Under the Public Records Act, records are normally only open to inspection when they are 30 years old.

National Library of Ireland
Kildare Street, Dublin 2, Republic of Ireland
☎00 353 1 603 0200   Fax 00 353 1 676 6690
✉ info@nli.ie
www.nli.ie

OPEN 10.00 am to 9.00 pm Monday to Wednesday; 10.00 am to 5.00 pm Thursday and Friday; 10.00 am to 1.00 pm Saturday

ACCESS Passes are issued for genealogical research or to consult newspapers; Readers Ticket required for access to other material.

Collections include books, manuscripts, prints and drawings, maps, photographs, newspapers, music, ephemera and genealogical materials.

National Library of Scotland
George IV Bridge, Edinburgh EH1 1EW
☎0131 226 4531   Fax 0131 622 4803
✉ enquiries@nls.uk
www.nls.uk

OPEN Main Reading Room: 9.30 am to 8.30 pm Monday, Tuesday, Thursday, Friday; 10.00 am to 8.30 pm Wednesday; 9.30 am to 1.00 pm Saturday. Map Library: 9.30 am to 5.00 pm Monday, Tuesday, Thursday, Friday; 10.00 am to 5.00 pm Wednesday; 9.30 am to 1.00 pm Saturday

ACCESS to all reading rooms, for research not easily done elsewhere, by reader's ticket

Collection of over seven million volumes. The library receives all British and Irish publications. Large stock of newspapers and periodicals. Many special collections, including early Scottish books, theology, polar studies, baking, phrenology and liturgies. Also large collections of maps, music and manuscripts including personal archives of notable Scottish persons.

National Library of Wales
Aberystwyth SY23 3BU
☎01970 632800   Fax 01970 615709
www.llgc.org.uk

OPEN 9.30 am to 6.00 pm Monday to Friday; 9.30 am to 5.00 pm Saturday (closed Bank Holidays and the week after Christmas)

ACCESS to reading rooms by reader's ticket, available on application. Open access to a wide-ranging exhibition programme

Collection of over four million books and including large collections of periodicals, maps, manuscripts and audiovisual material. Particular emphasis on humanities in printed foreign material, and on Wales and other Celtic areas in all collections.

National Meteorological Library and Archive
FitzRoy Road, Exeter EX1 3PB
☎01392 884841   Fax 0870 900 5050
✉ metlib@metoffice.gov.uk
www.metoffice.gov.uk

OPEN Library: 8.30 am to 4.30 pm Monday to Friday; Archive: 10.00 am to 6.00 pm

ACCESS By Visitor's Pass available from the reception desk; advance notice of a planned visit is appreciated

The major repository of most of the important literature on the subjects of meteorology, climatology and related sciences from the 16th century to the present day. The Library houses a collection of books, journals, articles and scientific papers, plus published climatological data from many parts of the world. The Technical Archive (National Meteorological Archive, Great Moore House, Sowton Industrial Estate, Bittern Road, Exeter EX2 7XZ ☎01392 360987, Fax 0870 900 5050; email metarc@metoffice.gov.org.uk) holds the document collection of meteorological data and charts from England, Wales and British overseas bases, including ships' weather logs. Records from Scotland are stored in Edinburgh and those from Northern Ireland in Belfast.

The Natural History Museum Library
Cromwell Road, London SW7 5BD
☎020 7942 5460   Fax 020 7942 5559
✉ library@nhm.ac.uk
www.nhm.ac.uk/library/index.html

OPEN 10.00 am to 4.30 pm Monday to Friday

ACCESS To *bona fide* researchers, by reader's ticket on presentation of identification (telephone first to make an appointment)

The library is in five sections: general; botany; zoology; entomology; earth sciences. The sub-department of ornithology is housed at the Zoological Museum, Akeman Street, Tring HP23 6AP (☎01442 834181). Resources available include books, journals, maps, manuscripts, drawings and photographs covering all aspects of natural history, including palaeontology and mineralogy, from the 14th century to the present day. Also archives and historical collection on the museum itself.

Newcastle upon Tyne City Library

Princess Square, Newcastle upon Tyne
NE99 1DX
☎0191 277 4100   Fax 0191 277 4137
✉ city.information@newcastle.gov.uk *or*
information@newcastle.gov.uk
www.newcastle.gov.uk/libraries

LOCAL STUDIES
✉ local.studies@newcastle.gov.uk

OPEN 9.00 am to 8.00 pm Monday to
Thursday; 9.00 am to 5.00 pm Friday and
Saturday; 12 noon to 4.00 pm Sunday

Extensive local studies collection, including
newspapers, illustrations and genealogy. Also
business, science, humanities and arts.

Norfolk Library & Information Service

Norfolk and Norwich Millennium Library,
The Forum, Millennium Plain, Norwich
NR2 1AW
www.norfolk.gov.uk/council/departments/lis/
libhome.htm

OPEN Lending Library, Reference and
Information Service and Norfolk Studies:
9.00 am to 8.00 pm Monday, Wednesday,
Thursday, Friday; 10.00 am to 8.00 pm
Tuesday; 9.00 am to 5.00 pm Saturday.
EXPRESS: 9.00 am to 9.30 pm Monday to
Friday; 9.00 am to 8.30 pm Saturday; 10.30
am to 4.30 pm Sunday

OPEN ACCESS
Reference lending library (stock merged
together) with wide range, including books,
recorded music, music scores, plays and videos.
Houses the 2nd Air Division Memorial Library
and has a strong Norfolk Heritage Library.
Extensive range of reference stock including
business information. Online database and CD-
ROM services. Public fax and colour photocopying, free access to the Internet. EXPRESS
(fiction, sound & vision library within a library)
– selection of popular fiction, videos, CDs and
DVDs available, with extended opening hours.

Northamptonshire Libraries & Information Service

Library HQ, PO Box 216, John Dryden House,
8–10 The Lakes, Northampton NN4 7DD
☎01604 237959   Fax 01604 237937
✉ nlis@northamptonshire.gov.uk

Since 1991, the Libraries and Information
Service has offered its 'Wordworks' diary of literature events. The rolling programme now
attracts exciting literary names as well as new
and locally-based writers. Writers have an
opportunity to read at a variety of venues
around the country. Literature workshops,
activities and other events are supported.
Regular book displays and dedicated notice
boards in libraries support the programme
across the county.

Northumberland Central Library

The Willows, Morpeth NE61 1TA
☎01670 534518/534514   Fax 01670 534513
✉ libraries@northumberland.gov.uk
www.northumberlandlibraries.com

Open 10.00 am to 8.00 pm Monday, Tuesday,
Wednesday, Friday; 9.30 am to 12.30 pm
Saturday (closed Thursday)

OPEN ACCESS
Books, periodicals, newspapers, story cassettes,
CD-ROMs, DVDs, CDs, videos, Free Internet
access, word processing facilities, prints, microforms, vocal scores, playsets, community resource
equipment. SPECIAL COLLECTIONS Northern
Poetry Library: 15,000 volumes of modern
poetry (see entry under *Organisations of Interest
to Poets*); Cinema: comprehensive collection of
about 5000 volumes covering all aspects of the
cinema; Family History.

Nottingham Central Library

Angel Row, Nottingham NG1 6HP
☎0115 915 2828   Fax 0115 915 2840
✉ enquiryline@nottinghamcity.gov.uk
www.nottinghamcity.gov.uk

OPEN 9.30 am to 7.00 pm Monday to Friday;
9.00 am to 1.00 pm Saturday

OPEN ACCESS
General public lending library: business
information, online information, the arts, local
studies, religion, community languages, literature. Videos, DVDs, periodicals, spoken
word, recorded music, CD-ROM service – textual information on CD-ROM on public
access machines. People's Network Internet,
providing free public access. SPECIAL COLLEC-
TION on D.H. Lawrence. Extensive back-up
reserve stocks. Drama and music sets for loan to
groups. Art gallery – contemporary exhibitions;
coffee shop.

Nottingham Subscription Library Ltd

See **Bromley House Library**

Office for National Statistics, National Statistics Information and Library Service
1 Drummond Gate, London SW1V 2QQ
☎0845 601 3034/01633 812399 (Minicom)
Fax 01633 652747
✉ info@statistics.gov.uk
www.statistics.gov.uk
OPEN 9.00 am to 5.00 pm; appointment required; visitors must supply some form of identification
Also: National Statistics Information and Library Service, Government Buildings, Cardiff Road, Newport NP9 1XG
OPEN as above
Wide range of government statistical publications and access to government Internet-based data. Census statistical data from 1801; population and health data from 1837; government social survey reports from 1941; recent international statistical data (UN, Eurostat, etc.); monograph and periodical collections of statistical methodology. The library in south Wales holds a wide range of government economic and statistical publications.

Orkney Library and Archive
44 Junction Road, Kirkwall KW15 1AG
☎01856 873166   Fax 01856 875260
✉ general.enquiries@orkney.gov.uk *and*
archives@orkneylibrary.org.uk
www.orkneylibrary.org.uk
OPEN 9.00 am to 8.00 pm Monday to Thursday; 9.00 am to 6.00 pm Friday; 9.00 am to 5.00 pm Saturday. Archives: 9.00 am to 4.45 pm Monday, Wednesday, Friday; 9.00 am to 7.45 pm Thursday; 9.00 am to 1.00 pm and 2.00 pm to 5.00 pm Saturday
OPEN ACCESS
Local studies collection. Archive includes sound and photographic departments.

Oxford Central Library
Westgate, Oxford OX1 1DJ
☎01865 815549   Fax 01865 721694
✉ oxfordcentral.library@oxfordshire.gov.uk
www.oxfordshire.gov.uk
OPEN Call 01865 815509 for details
General lending and reference library including the Centre for Oxfordshire Studies. Also periodicals, audio visual materials, music library, children's library and Business Information Point.

PA News Centre
Central Park, New Lane, Leeds LS11 5DZ
☎0870 830 6824   Fax 0870 830 6801
✉ palibrary@pa.press.net
www.pa.press.net
OPEN 8.00 am to 6.00 pm Monday to Friday; 10.00 am to 6.00 pm Saturday; 8.00 am to 4.00 pm Sunday
OPEN ACCESS
PA News, the 24-hour national news and information group, offers the PA Digital Library which holds Press Association stories. Personal callers welcome or research undertaken by in-house staff.

Penzance Library
See **Morrab Library**

City of Plymouth Library and Information Services
Central Library, Drake Circus, Plymouth PL4 8AL
www.plymouthlibraries.info
OPEN ACCESS
CENTRAL LIBRARY LENDING DEPARTMENTS
Lending ☎01752 305912
✉ lendlib@plymouth.gov.uk
Children's Department ☎01752 305916
✉ childrens.library@plymouth.gov.uk
Music & Drama Department
☎01752 305914 ✉ music@plymouth.gov.uk
OPEN 9.00 am to 7.00 pm Monday and Friday; 9.00 am to 5.30 pm Tuesday, Wednesday, Thursday; 9.00 am to 5.00 pm Saturday
The Lending departments offer books on all subjects; language courses on cassette and foreign language books; the Holcenberg Jewish Collection; books on music and musicians, drama and theatre; music parts and sets of music parts; play sets; DVDs, videos; song index; cassettes and CDs; public Internet access.
CENTRAL LIBRARY REFERENCE DEPARTMENTS
Reference ☎01752 305907
✉ ref@plymouth.gov.uk
Business Information ☎01752 305908
✉ keyinfo@plymouth.gov.uk
Local Studies & Naval History Department ☎01752 305909
✉ localstudies@plymouth.gov.uk
OPEN 9.00 am to 7.00 pm Monday to Friday; 9.00 am to 5.00 pm Saturday

The Reference departments include an extensive collection of Ordnance Survey maps and town guides; community and census information; marketing and statistical information; Patents; books on every aspect of Plymouth; naval history; Mormon Index on microfilm; Baring Gould manuscript of 'Folk Songs of the West'; public Internet access.

Plymouth Proprietary Library
Alton Terrace, 111 North Hill, Plymouth
PL4 8JY
☎01752 660515
Librarian *John R. Smith*
OPEN Monday to Saturday from 9.30 am (closing time varies)
ACCESS To members; visitors by appointment only
Founded 1810. The library contains approximately 17,000 volumes of mainly 20th-century work. Member of the **Association of Independent Libraries**.

The Poetry Library
See entry under *Organisations of Interest to Poets*

Polish Library
238–246 King Street, London W6 0RF
☎020 8741 0474   Fax 020 8741 7724
✉ bibliotekapolska@posklibrary.fsnet.co.uk *or* polish.library@posk.org
Librarian *Mrs Jadwiga Szmidt*
OPEN 10.00 am to 8.00 pm Monday and Wednesday; 10.00 am to 5.00 pm Friday; 10.00 am to 1.00 pm Saturday (library closed Tuesday and Thursday)
ACCESS For reference to all interested in Polish affairs; limited loans to members and *bona fide* scholars only through inter-library loans
Books, pamphlets, periodicals, maps, music, photographs on all aspects of Polish history and culture. SPECIAL COLLECTIONS Emigré publications; Joseph Conrad and related works; Polish underground publications; bookplates.

Poole Central Library
Dolphin Centre, Poole BH15 1QE
☎01202 262424   Fax 01202 262442
✉ poolelibrary@poole.gov.uk
OPEN 8.00 am to 7.00 pm Monday; 8.30 am to 6.30 pm Tuesday, Wednesday, Thursday; 8.00 am to 7.00 pm Friday; 9.00 am to 5.00 pm Saturday
OPEN ACCESS

General lending and reference library, including Healthpoint health information centre, business information, children's library, periodicals and newspapers, cafe, IT suite and meeting room.

Press Association Library
See **PA News Centre**

Public Record Office
See **The National Archives**

Reading Central Library
Abbey Square, Reading RG1 3BQ
☎0118 901 5950   Fax 0118 901 5954
✉ info@readinglibraries.org.uk
www.readinglibraries.org.uk
OPEN 9.30 am to 5.30 pm Monday and Friday; 9.30 am to 7.00 pm Tuesday and Thursday; 9.30 am to 5.00 pm Wednesday and Saturday
OPEN ACCESS
Ground Floor: Fiction, audio-visual material, children's library; First Floor: Newspapers, nonfiction – biography, business, careers, cookery, DIY, engineering, gardening, health, languages, law, mind, body & spirit, pets, science, social studies, sport, transport, travel; Second Floor: LearnDirect, non-fiction – art, music, literature, plays, computing; Third floor: Non-fiction – world history, national history, local history. Magazines and periodicals and Internet access on all floors.

Richmond Central Reference Library
Old Town Hall, Whittaker Avenue, Richmond TW9 1TP
☎020 8940 5529   Fax 020 8940 6899
✉ reference.services@richmond.gov.uk
www.richmond.gov.uk
OPEN 9.30 am to 6.00 pm Monday, Thursday, Friday (Tuesday until 1.00 pm; Wednesday, 8.00 pm and Saturday, 5.00 pm)
OPEN ACCESS
General reference library serving the needs of local residents and organisations. Internet access and online databases for public use.

Royal Geographical Society (with the Institute of British Geographers)
1 Kensington Gore, London SW7 2AR
☎020 7591 3000   Fax 020 7591 3001
www.rgs.org

See website for details. For information on the Picture Library see entry under *Picture Libraries*.

Royal Institute of Philosophy
See **Senate House Library, University of London**

Royal Society Library
6–9 Carlton House Terrace, London SW1Y 5AG
☎020 7451 2606   Fax 020 7930 2170
✉ library@royalsoc.ac.uk
www.royalsoc.ac.uk
OPEN 10.00 am to 5.00 pm Monday to Friday

ACCESS Open to all researchers with an interest in the history of science, the Fellowship of the Royal Society and science policy. Researchers are advised to contact the Library in advance of their first visit.

History of science, scientists' biographies, science policy reports, and publications of international scientific unions and national academies from all over the world.

RSA (Royal Society for the Encouragement of Arts, Manufactures & Commerce)
8 John Adam Street, London WC2N 6EZ
☎020 7930 5115   Fax 020 7839 5805
www.theRSA.org
OPEN Library: 8.30 am to 8.00 pm every weekday. Archive material by appointment

ACCESS to Fellows of RSA; by application and appointment to non-Fellows (Contact Librarian, ☎020 7451 6874 or ✉ library@rsa.org.uk)

Archives of the Society since 1754. A collection of approximately 10,000 volumes; international exhibition material.

Royal Society of Medicine Library
1 Wimpole Street, London W1G 0AE
☎020 7290 2940   Fax 020 7290 2939
✉ library@rsm.ac.uk
www.rsm.ac.uk
Director of Information Services *Ian Snowley*
OPEN 9.00 am to 8.30 pm Monday to Thursday; 9.00 am to 5.30 pm Friday

ACCESS For reference only, on introduction by Fellow of the Society or temporary membership is available to non-members; £12 per day; £35 per week; £90 per month. Identification required.

Books, periodicals, databases on postgraduate biomedical information. Extensive historical collection dating from the fifteenth century and medical portrait collection.

Eric Frank Russell Archive
See **Science Fiction Foundation Research Library**

St Bride Printing Library
Bride Lane, London EC4Y 8EE
☎020 7353 4660   Fax 020 7583 7073
✉ library@stbrideinstitute.org
www.stbride.org
OPEN 12 noon to 5.30 pm Tuesday and Thursday; 12 noon to 9.00 pm Wednesday

OPEN ACCESS
A public reference library maintained by the St Bride Foundation. Appointments advisable for consultation of special collections. Every aspect of printing and related matters: publishing and bookselling, newspapers and magazines, graphic design, calligraphy and type, papermaking and bookbinding. One of the world's largest specialist collections in its field, with over 50,000 volumes, over 3000 periodicals (200 current titles), and extensive collection of drawings, manuscripts, prospectuses, patents and materials for printing and typefounding. Noted for its comprehensive holdings of historical and early technical literature.

Science Fiction Foundation Research Library
Liverpool University Library, PO Box 123, Liverpool L69 3DA
☎0151 794 3142   Fax 0151 794 3142
✉ asawyer@liverpool.ac.uk
www.liv.ac.uk/~asawyer/sffchome.html
Contact *Andy Sawyer*

ACCESS For research, by appointment only (telephone first)

This is the largest collection outside the US of science fiction and related material – including autobiographies and critical works. SPECIAL COLLECTION Runs of 'pulp' magazines dating back to the 1920s. Foreign-language material (including a large Russian collection), and the papers of the Flat Earth Society. The collection also features a growing range of archive and manuscript material, including the Eric Frank Russell archive. The University of Liverpool also holds the Olaf Stapledon and John Wyndham archives.

Science Museum Library
Imperial College Road, London SW7 5NH
☎020 7942 4242   Fax 020 7942 4243
✉ smlinfo@nmsi.ac.uk

www.nmsi.ac.uk/library

OPEN 9.30 am to 9.00 pm Monday to Friday (closes 5.30 pm outside academic terms); 9.30 am to 5.30 pm Saturday

OPEN ACCESS Reference only; no loans
National reference library for the history and public understanding of science and technology, with a large collection of source material. Operates jointly with Imperial College Central Library.

Scottish Poetry Library

See entry under *Organisations of Interest to Poets*

Senate House Library, University of London

Senate House, Malet Street, London WC1E 7HU
☎020 7862 8461/62 (Information Centre)
Fax 020 7862 8480
✉ enquiries@shl.lon.ac.uk (Information Centre)
www.shl.lon.ac.uk
MEMBERSHIP DESK: ☎020 7862 8439/40
✉ userservices@shl.lon.ac.uk

OPEN Term-time: 9.00 am to 9.00 pm Monday to Thursday; 9.00 am to 6.30 pm Friday; 9.30 am to 5.30 pm Saturday. Vacation: 9.00 am to 6.00 pm Monday to Friday; 9.30 am to 5.30 pm Saturday (closed on Sundays and at certain periods during Bank Holidays)

The Senate House Library is a major academic research library predominantly based across the Humanities and Social Sciences. Housed within its 16 floors are some two million titles including 5500 current periodicals and a wide range of electronic resources. It contains a number of outstanding research collections which, as well as supporting the scholarly activities of the University, attract researchers from throughout the United Kingdom and internationally. These include: English (e.g. the Durning-Lawrence Library and Sterling Collection of first editions); Economic and Social History (the Goldsmiths' Library, containing 70,000 items ranging from 15th to early 19th century); Modern Languages (primarily Romance and Germanic); Palaeography (acclaimed as being the best open access collection in its field in Europe); History (complementary to the Institute of Historical Research); Music, Philosophy (acts as the Library of the Royal Institute of Philosophy); Psychology (includes the BPS library); Major area studies

collections (Latin-American, including Caribbean; United States and Commonwealth Studies, British Government Publications and maps). The Library has a wide range of Special Collections holdings. Check the website for full details of collections and current access arrangements.

Sheffield Libraries, Archives and Information

Central Library, Surrey Street, Sheffield S1 1XZ
☎0114 273 4712   Fax 0114 273 5009
✉ libraries@sheffield.gov.uk
www.sheffield.gov.uk (click on 'In your area')

Central Lending Library

☎0114 273 4727 (enquiries)/4729 (book renewals)

OPEN 10.00 am to 8.00 pm Monday; 9.30 am to 5.30 pm Tuesday, Thursday and Friday; 9.30 am to 8.00 pm Wednesday; 9.30 am to 5.30 pm Saturday

Books, talking books, large print, language courses, European fiction, books in cultural languages, play sets. Free Internet access. Writers' Resource Centre, Wednesday evenings, 5.00 pm to 7.00 pm. Proof of signature and a separate proof of address required to join.

Sheffield Archives

52 Shoreham Street, Sheffield S1 4SP
☎0114 203 9395 Fax 0114 203 9398
✉ archives@sheffield.gov.uk

OPEN 9.30 am to 5.30 pm Tuesday to Thursday; 9.30 am to 1.00 pm and 2.00 pm to 5.00 pm Saturday (documents should be ordered by 5.00 pm Thursday for Saturday); closed Monday and Friday

ACCESS By reader's pass
Holds documents relating to Sheffield and South Yorkshire, dating from the 12th century to the present day, including records of the City Council, churches, businesses, landed estates, families and individuals, institutions and societies. Free Internet access.

Arts and Social Sciences and Sports Reference Service

☎0114 273 4747/8

OPEN 10.00 am to 8.00 pm Monday; 9.30 am to 5.30 pm Tuesday, Thursday, Friday; 9.30 am to 8.00 pm Wednesday; 9.30 am to 5.30 pm Saturday

ACCESS For reference only
A comprehensive collection of books, periodicals and newspapers covering all aspects of arts

(excluding music), sports, social sciences and free Internet access.

Music and Video Service

☎0114 273 4733V

✉ music&video.library@sheffield.gov.uk

OPEN as for Central Lending Library above

ACCESS For reference and lending

An extensive range of books, CDs, cassettes, scores, etc. related to music. Also a video cassette and DVD loan service. Free Internet access.

Local Studies Service

☎0114 273 4753

✉ local.studies@dial.pipex.com

OPEN as for Arts & Social Sciences above (except Wednesday 9.30 am to 5.30 pm)

ACCESS For reference

Extensive material covering all aspects of Sheffield and its population, including maps, photos and videos. Free Internet access. Photograph collection available: www.pictureSheffield. com

Business, Science and Technology Reference Services

☎0114 273 4736/7 or 273 4742

✉ cbt.library@sheffield.gov.uk

OPEN as for Arts & Social Sciences above

ACCESS For reference only

Extensive coverage of science and technology as well as commerce and commercial law. British patents and British and European standards with emphasis on metals. Hosts the World Metal Index. The business section holds a large stock of business and trade directories, and reference works with business emphasis. Free Internet access.

Sheffield Information Service

☎0114 273 4712 Fax 0114 275 7111

✉ sis@britishlibrary.net

www.sheffieldhelpyourself.org.uk

OPEN 10.00 am to 5.30 pm Monday; 9.30 am to 5.30 pm Tuesday to Saturday

Full local information service covering all aspects of the Sheffield community. Free Internet access.

Children's and Young People's Library Service

☎0114 273 4734

✉ cyp.library@sheffield.gov.uk

OPEN 10.30 am to 5.00 pm Monday and Friday; 1.00 pm to 5.00 pm Tuesday, Wednesday, Thursday; 9.30 am to 5.30 pm Saturday

Books, spoken word sets, videos; under-five play area; teenage reference section; readings and promotions; storytime sessions. Free Internet access.

Shetland Library

Lower Hillhead, Lerwick ZE1 0EL

☎01595 693868   Fax 01595 694430

✉ shetlandlibrary@sic.shetland.gov.uk

www.shetland-library.gov.uk

OPEN 10.00 am to 7.00 pm Monday, Wednesday, Thursday; 10.00 am to 5.00 pm Tuesday, Friday, Saturday

General lending and reference library; extensive local interest collection including complete set of *The Shetland Times, The Shetland News* and other local newspapers on microfilm and many old and rare books; audio collection including talking books/newspapers. Junior room for children. Disabled access and Housebound Readers Service (delivery to reader's home). Mobile library services to rural areas. Open Learning Service. Same day photocopying service. Publishing programme of books in dialect, history, literature. Learning centre providing access to learning opportunities including Internet.

Shoe Lane Library

Hill House, Little New Street, London EC4A 3JR

☎020 7583 7178   Fax 020 7353 0884

✉ shoelane@corpoflondon.gov.uk

www.corpoflondon.gov.uk

OPEN 9.00 am to 5.30 pm Monday, Wednesday, Thursday, Friday; 9.00 am to 6.30 pm Tuesday

OPEN ACCESS

Corporation of London general lending library, with a comprehensive stock of 50,000 volumes, most of which are on display.

Shrewsbury Library and Reference & Information Service

Castlegates, Shrewsbury SY1 2AS

☎01743 255300   Fax 01743 255309

✉ shrewsbury.library@shropshire-cc.gov.uk

www.shropshire-cc.gov.uk/library.nsf

OPEN 9.30 am to 5.00 pm Monday, Wednesday, Friday; 9.30 am to 8.00 pm Tuesday and Thursday; 9.00 am to 5.00 pm Saturday; 1.00 pm to 4.00 pm Sunday

OPEN ACCESS

The largest public library in Shropshire. Books, cassettes, CDs, talking books, DVDs, videos, language courses. Open Learning and study centre with public use computers for word processing and Internet access. Music, literature and art book collection for lending and reference. The West Midlands Literary Heritage Collection is housed at Shrewsbury Library.

Spanish Institute Library
See **Instituto Cervantes**

Sterling Collection
See **Senate House Library**

Suffolk County Council Libraries & Heritage
Endeavour House, Russell Road, Ipswich
IP1 2BX
☎01473 265086   Fax 01473 216847
✉ asksuffolk@libher.suffolkcc.gov.uk
www.suffolkcc.gov.uk/libdirect

OPEN See website for details of individual libraries or contact Endeavour House as above. Major libraries open seven days a week; all libraries open Sunday

ACCESS A single library card gives access to the lending service of 43 libraries and resource centres across the county. Loans can be collected and/or returned at any service point. Details on website

Full range of lending and reference services, free public access to the Internet. Wide range of online services for registered library users through the Suffolk Libraries Direct pages, e.g. self-service reservations, renewals, free access to subscription services. Suffolk InfoLink Plus database gives details of local organisations throughout the county. SPECIAL COLLECTIONS include Suffolk Archives and Local History Collection; Benjamin Britten Collection; Edward Fitzgerald Collection; Seckford Collection and Racing Collection (Newmarket). The Suffolk Infolink service gives details of local groups and societies and is available in libraries throughout the county and on the website.

Sunderland City Library and Arts Centre
28–30 Fawcett Street, Sunderland SR1 1RE
☎0191 514 1235   Fax 0191 514 8444
✉ enquiry.desk@sunderland.gov.uk
www.sunderland.gov.uk/libraries

OPEN 9.30 am to 7.30 pm Monday and Wednesday; 9.30 am to 5.00 pm Tuesday, Thursday, Friday; 9.30 am to 4.00 pm Saturday

The city's main library for lending and reference services. Local studies and children's sections, plus Sound and Vision department (CDs, DVDs, cassettes, videos, CD-ROMs, talking books). The City of Sunderland also maintains community libraries of varying size, offering a range of services, plus mobile libraries. Free Internet access is available in all libraries across the city. A Books on Wheels service is available to housebound readers; the Schools Library Service serves teachers and schools. Two writers' groups meet at the City Library and Arts Centre: Janus Writers, every Wednesday, 1.30 pm to 3.30 pm. Creative Writers, every Tuesday, 6.30 pm to 8.30 pm.

Swansea Central Reference Library
Alexandra Road, Swansea SA1 5DX
☎01792 516753/516757
Fax 01792 516759
✉ central.library@swansea.gov.uk
www.swansea.gov.uk/index.cfm?articleid=397

OPEN 9.00 am to 7.00 pm Monday, Tuesday, Wednesday, Friday; 9.00 am to 5.00 pm Thursday and Saturday. The Library has a lending service but hours tend to be shorter – check in advance (☎01792 516750/1)

ACCESS For reference only (Local Studies closed access: items must be requested on forms provided)

General reference material; also Welsh Assembly information, statutes, company information, maps, European Community information. Local studies: comprehensive collections on Wales; Swansea & Gower; Dylan Thomas. Local maps, periodicals, illustrations, local newspapers from 1804. B&w and colour photocopying and fax facilities, free computer and Internet access available (library membership required and pre-booking recommended) and microfilm/microfiche copying facility.

Swiss Cottage Central Library
88 Avenue Road, London NW3 3HA
☎020 7974 6522   Fax 020 7974 6532

OPEN 10.00 am to 7.00 pm Monday and Thursday; 10.00 am to 6.00 pm Tuesday, Wednesday, Friday; 10.00 am to 5.00 pm Saturday

OPEN ACCESS
Over 300,000 volumes in the lending and reference libraries. Home of the London Borough of Camden Information and Reference Services.

Theatre Museum Library & Archive
1e Tavistock Street, London WC2E 7PR
☎020 7943 4727   Fax 020 7943 4777
✉ tmenquiries@vam.ac.uk

www.theatremuseum.org.uk

OPEN 10.30 am to 4.30 pm Wednesday to Friday

ACCESS By appointment only

The Theatre Museum was founded as a separate department of the Victoria & Albert Museum in 1974 and moved to its own building in Covent Garden in 1987. The museum (open Tuesday to Sunday 10.00 am to 6.00 pm) houses permanent displays, temporary exhibitions, a studio theatre, and organises a programme of special events, performances, lectures, guided visits and workshops. The library houses the UK's largest performing arts research collections, including books, photographs, designs, engravings, programmes, press cuttings, etc. All the performing arts are covered but strengths are in the areas of theatre, dance, musical theatre and stage design. A large store in west London houses the Museum's special collections of archives. The reading room is relocating to Blythe House at the west London premises in 2005 – see website for schedule.

Thurrock Communities, Libraries & Cultural Services

Grays Library, Orsett Road, Grays RM17 5DX

☎01375 383611   Fax 01375 370806

✉ grays.library@thurrock.gov.uk

OPEN 9.00 am to 7.00 pm Monday, Tuesday, Thursday; 9.00 am to 5.00 pm Wednesday, Friday, Saturday; branch library opening times vary

OPEN ACCESS

General library lending and reference through ten libraries and a mobile library. Services include books, magazines, newspapers, audiocassettes, CDs, videos and language courses. Large collection of Thurrock materials. Internet and Microsoft Office.

Truro Library

Union Place, Truro TR1 1EP

☎01872 279205 (lending)/272702 (reference)

✉ truro.library@cornwall.gov.uk

www.cornwall.gov.uk/library

OPEN 8.30 am to 6.00 pm Monday to Friday; 9.00 am to 4.00 pm Saturday

Books, cassettes, CDs, videos and DVDs for loan through branch or mobile networks. Study centre and IT suite. Reference collection. SPECIAL COLLECTIONS on local studies.

Western Isles Libraries

Public Library, 19 Cromwell Street, Stornoway HS1 2DA

☎01851 708631   Fax 001851 708676

www.cne-siar.gov.uk

OPEN 10.00 am to 5.00 pm Monday to Wednesday; 10.00 am to 6.00 pm Thursday and Friday; 10.00am to 5.00.pm Saturday

OPEN ACCESS

General public library stock plus local history and Gaelic collections, including maps, videos, printed music, cassettes and CDs; also census records and Council minutes, and a music collection. Branch libraries on the isles of barra, Benbecula, Harris and Lewis.

City of Westminster Archives Centre

10 St Ann's Street, London SW1P 2DE

☎020 7641 5180/4879 (Minicom)

Fax 020 7641 5179

✉ archives@westminster.gov.uk

www.westminster.gov.uk/archives

OPEN 10.00 am to 7.00 pm Tuesday Wednesday, Thursday, 10.00 am to 5.00 pm Friday and Saturday (closed Monday)

ACCESS For reference

Comprehensive coverage of the history of Westminster and selective coverage of general London history. 22,000 books, together with a large stock of maps, prints, photographs, local newspapers, theatre programmes and archives.

Westminster Music Library

Victoria Library, 160 Buckingham Palace Road, London SW1W 9UD

☎020 7641 1300   Fax 020 7641 4281

✉ musiclibrary@westminster.gov.uk

www.westminster.gov.uk/libraries/special/music

OPEN 11.00 am to 7.00 pm Monday to Friday; 10 am to 5.00 pm Saturday

OPEN ACCESS

Located at Victoria Library, this is the largest public music library in the South of England, with extensive coverage of all aspects of music, including books, periodicals and printed scores. No recorded material, notated only. Lending library includes a small collection of CDs and videos.

Westminster Reference Library

35 St Martin's Street, London WC2H 7HP

☎020 7641 1300   Fax 020 7641 4606

✉ referencelibrarywc2@westminster.gov.uk

www.westminster.gov.uk/libraries

OPEN Main Library: 10.00 am to 8.00 pm

Monday to Friday; Art & Design: 1.00 pm to 8.00 pm Monday to Friday; 10.00 am to 5.00 pm Saturday

ACCESS For reference only

A general reference library with emphasis on the following: Art & Design – fine and decorative arts, architecture, graphics and design; Performing Arts – theatre, cinema, radio, television and dance; Official Publications – major collection of HMSO publications from 1947, plus parliamentary papers dating back to 1906; Business – UK directories, trade directories, company and market data; Official EU Depository Library – carries official EU material; Periodicals – long files of many titles. One working day's notice is required for some government documents and most older periodicals. Extensive picture resource library.

The Wiener Library

4 Devonshire Street, London W1W 5BH
☎020 7636 7247   Fax 020 7436 6428
✉ info@wienerlibrary.co.uk
wienerlibrary.co.uk
Director *Ben Barkow*
Education and Outreach Coordinator
Katherine Klinger

OPEN 10.00 am to 5.30 pm Monday to Friday

ACCESS By letter of introduction (readers needing to use the Library for any length of time should become members)

Private library – one of the leading research centres on European history since the First World War, with special reference to the era of totalitarianism and to Jewish affairs. Founded by Dr Alfred Wiener in Amsterdam in 1933, it holds material that is not available elsewhere. Books, periodicals, press archives, documents, pamphlets, leaflets, photo archive, audiovisual material, brochures.

Vaughan Williams Memorial Library

English Folk Dance and Song Society, Cecil Sharp House, 2 Regent's Park Road, London NW1 7AY
☎020 7485 2206 ext. 18/19
Fax 020 7284 0523
✉ library@efdss.org
www.efdss.org
Contact *Malcolm Taylor*

OPEN 9.30 am to 5.30 pm Tuesday to Friday; 10.00 am to 4.00 pm 1st & 3rd Saturday (sometimes closed between 1.00 pm and 2.00 pm)

ACCESS For reference to the general public, on payment of a daily fee; members may borrow books and use the library free of charge

A multimedia collection: books, periodicals, manuscripts, tapes, records, CDs, films, videos. Mostly British traditional culture and how this has developed around the world. Some foreign language material, and some books in English about foreign cultures. Also, the history of the English Folk Dance and Song Society.

Dr Williams's Library

14 Gordon Square, London WC1H 0AR
☎020 7387 3727
✉ enquiries@dwlib.co.uk

OPEN 10.00 am to 5.00 pm Monday, Wednesday, Friday; 10.00 am to 6.30 pm Tuesday and Thursday

OPEN ACCESS to reading room (loans restricted to subscribers). Visitors required to supply identification. Annual subscription £10; ministers of religion and certain students £5

Primarily a library of theology, religion and ecclesiastical history. Also philosophy, history (English and Byzantine). Particularly important for the study of English Nonconformity. Trustees of Dr Williams's Library manage the Congregational Library on behalf of the Memorial Hall Trustees.

Wolverhampton Central Library

Snow Hill, Wolverhampton WV1 3AX
☎01902 552025 (lending)/552026 (reference)
Fax 01902 552024
✉ wolverhampton.libraries@dial.pipex.com
www.wolverhampton.gov.uk

OPEN 9.00 am to 7.00 pm Monday to Thursday; 9.00 am to 5.00 pm Friday and Saturday

Archives & Local Studies Collection

42–50 Snow Hill, Wolverhampton
WV2 4AB
☎01902 552480

OPEN 10.00 am to 5.00 pm Monday, Tuesday, Friday, 1st and 3rd Saturday of each month; 10.00 am to 7.00 pm Wednesday; closed Thursday

General lending and reference libraries, plus children's library and audiovisual library holding cassettes, CDs, videos and music scores. Internet access.

The Women's Library

London Metropolitan University, Old Castle Street, London E1 7NT

☎020 7320 2222   Fax 020 7320 2333
✉ moreinfo@thewomenslibrary.ac.uk
www.thewomenslibrary.ac.uk
Director *Antonia Byatt*
OPEN Reading Room: 9.30 am to 5.00 pm
Tuesday to Friday (8.00 pm Thursday);
10.00 am to 4.00 pm Saturday
OPEN ACCESS Exhibition: 9.30 am to 5.30 pm
Monday to Friday (8.00 pm Thursday); 10.00
am to 4.00 pm Saturday

The Women's Library, national research library for women's history, is the UK's oldest and most comprehensive research library on all aspects of women in society, with both historical and contemporary coverage. The Library includes materials on feminism, work, education, health, the family, law, arts, sciences, technology, language, sexuality, fashion and the home. The main emphasis is on Britain but many other countries are represented, especially the Commonwealth and developing countries. Established in 1926 as the library of the London Society of Women's Service (formerly Suffrage), a non-militant organisation led by Millicent Fawcett. In 1953 the Society was renamed after her and the library became the Fawcett Library.

COLLECTIONS include: women's suffrage, work, education, women and the church, the law, sport, art, music, abortion, prostitution. Mostly British materials but some American, Commonwealth and European works. Books, journals, pamphlets, archives, photographs, posters, postcards, audiovisual materials, artefacts, scrapbooks, albums and press cuttings dating mainly from the 19th century although some materials date from the 17th century.

The Library's new building, which opened in 2002, includes a reading room, exhibition space, café, education areas and a conference room, and is the cultural and research centre for anyone interested in women's lives and achievements.

Worcestershire Libraries and Information Service

Cultural Services, Worcestershire County Council, County Hall, Spetchley Road, Worcester WR5 2NP
☎01905 766231   Fax 01905 766244
✉ libraries@worcestershire.gov.uk
www.worcestershire.gov.uk/libraries

OPEN Opening hours vary in the 22 libraries, the History Centre and mobile libraries covering the county; all full-time libraries open at least one evening a week until 7.00 pm or 8.00 pm, and on Saturday until

4.00 pm; part-time libraries vary

ACCESS Information and reference services open to anyone; loans to members only (membership criteria: resident, being educated, working, or an elector in the county or neighbouring authorities; temporary membership to visitors. Proof of identity and address required. No charge for membership or for borrowing books.)

Information service, and reference and lending libraries. Non-fiction and fiction for all age groups, including normal and large print, spoken word cassettes, sound recordings (CD, cassette), videos, maps, local history, CD-ROMs for reference at main libraries, free public Internet access in all libraries. Joint Libraries Service/County Record Office History Centre with resources for local and family history. SPECIAL COLLECTIONS Carpets and Textiles; Needles & Needlemaking; Stuart Period; A.E. Housman.

John Wyndham Archive
See **Science Fiction Foundation Research Library**

York Central Library
Museum Street, York YO1 7DS
☎01904 655631   Fax 01904 611025
✉ reference.library@york.gov.uk

Lending Library
OPEN 9.30 am to 8.00 pm Monday, Tuesday, Friday; 9.30 am to 5.30 pm Wednesday and Thursday; 9.30 am to 4.00 pm Saturday

General lending library including videos, CDs, DVDs, CD-ROMs, music cassettes, audio books, children's storytapes language courses and printed music. Large print books. Photocopying, Internet and fax facilities.

Reference Library
OPEN 9.00 am to 8.00 pm Monday, Tuesday, Wednesday, Friday; 9.00 am to 5.30 pm Thursday; 9.00 am to 4.00 pm Saturday

General reference library; periodicals, newspapers, local newspaper index, EU information, organisations database; local studies library for York and surrounding area; business information service; microfilm/fiche readers for national and local newspapers; census returns and family history resource; general reference collection. Maintains strong links with other local history resource centres, namely the Borthwick Institute, York City Archive and York Minster Library. CD-ROM and Internet facilities. Room 18: IT resource centre available to the public. In addition, 14 branch libraries and one mobile, serving the City of York Council area.

Zoological Society Library

Regent's Park, London NW1 4RY
☎020 7449 6293   Fax 020 7586 5743
✉ library@zsl.org
www.zsl.org

OPEN 9.30 am to 5.30 pm Monday to Friday

ACCESS To members and staff; non-members by application

160,000 volumes on zoology including 5000 journals (1300 current) and a wide range of books on animals and particular habitats. Slide collection available and many historic zoological prints.

Picture Libraries

Acme
See **Popperfoto.com**

actionplus sports images
54–58 Tanner Street, London SE1 3PH
☎020 7403 1558   Fax 020 7403 1526
✉ pictures@actionplus.co.uk
www.actionplus.co.uk

Founded 1986. Specialist sports and action library providing complete and creative international coverage of over 300 varieties of professional and amateur sport. Elite, junior, professional, amateur, extreme, disabled, minority, offbeat, major and minor events, adults, children, high and low, fast and slow. Millions of images covering over 30 years of sport.

Lesley & Roy Adkins Picture Library
Ten Acre Wood, Whitestone, Exeter EX4 2HW
☎01392 811357   Fax 01392 811435
✉ mail@adkinsarchaeology.com
www.adkinsarchaeology.com

Colour coverage of archaeology, antiquity, heritage and related subjects in the UK, Europe, Egypt and Turkey. Subjects include towns, villages, housing, landscape and countryside, churches, temples, castles, monasteries, art and architecture, gravestones and tombs, inscriptions and antiquarian views. No service charge if pictures are used.

The Advertising Archive Limited
45 Lyndale Avenue, London NW2 2QB
☎020 7435 6540   Fax 020 7794 6584
✉ suzanne@advertisingarchives.co.uk
www.advertisingarchives.co.uk

Contacts *Suzanne Viner, Larry Viner*

With over one million images, the largest collection of British and American press ads, TV commercial stills and magazine cover illustrations in Europe. Material spans the period from 1850 to the present day. Expert in-house research; rapid service, competitive rates. On-line database and digital delivery available. Visitors by appointment.

akg-images Ltd, The Arts and History Picture Library
5 Melbray Mews, 158 Hurlingham Road, London SW6 3NS
☎020 7610 6103   Fax 020 7610 6125
✉ enquiries@akg-images.co.uk
www.akg-images.co.uk

Contact *Julia Engelhardt*

Collection of 250,000 images with direct access to ten million (more than 200,000 available as high resolution scans) kept in the Berlin AKG Library. Specialises in art, archaeology, history, topography, music, personalities and film.

Bryan & Cherry Alexander Photography
Higher Cottage, Manston, Sturminster Newton DT10 1EZ
☎01258 473006   Fax 01258 473333
✉ alexander@arcticphoto.co.uk
www.arcticphoto.co.uk

Contact *Cherry Alexander*

Arctic and Antarctic specialists; indigenous peoples, wildlife and science in polar regions; Norway, Iceland, Siberia and Alaska.

Alpine Garden Society
AGS Centre, Avon Bank, Pershore WR10 3JP
☎01386 554790   Fax 01386 554801
✉ ags@alpinegardensociety.org
www.alpinegardensociety.org

Contact *Peter Sheasby*

Over 24,000 colour transparencies (35mm) covering plants in the wild from many parts of the world; particularly strong in plants from mountain and sub-alpine regions, and from Mediterranean climates; South Africa, Australia, Patagonia, California and the Mediterranean. Extensive coverage of show alpines in pots and in gardens and of European orchids. Full slide list available.

Alvey & Towers
The Springboard Centre, Mantle Lane, Coalville LE67 3DW
☎01530 450011   Fax 01530 450011
✉ alveytower@aol.com

www.alveyandtowers.com

Contact *Emma Rowen*

Houses one of the country's most comprehensive collections of transport images depicting not only actual transport systems but their surrounding industries as well. Also specialist modern railway image collection.

Andes Press Agency
26 Padbury Court, London E2 7EH
☎020 7613 5417   Fax 020 7739 3159
✉ apa@andespressagency.com
www.andespressagency.com

Contacts *Val Baker, Carlos Reyes*

80,000 colour transparencies and 300,000 b&w, specialising in social documentary, world religions, Latin America and Britain.

Heather Angel/Natural Visions
Highways, 6 Vicarage Hill, Farnham GU9 8HJ
☎01252 716700   Fax 01252 727464
✉ hangel@naturalvisions.co.uk
www.naturalvisions.co.uk

Contact *Valerie West*

Constantly expanding worldwide natural history, wildlife and landscapes: polar regions, tropical rainforest flora and fauna, all species of plants and animals in natural habitats from Africa, Asia (notably China and Malaysia), Australasia, South America and USA, urban wildlife, pollution, biodiversity, global warming. Also worldwide gardens and cultivated flowers. Can send a digital lightbox to authors with an e-mail. The library then supplies high resolution digital files direct to the publisher.

Aquarius Library
PO Box 5, Hastings TN34 1HR
☎01424 721196   Fax 01424 717704
✉ aquarius.lib@clara.net
www.aquariuscollection.com

Contact *David Corkill*

A unique collection of film stills, star portraits and candids covering the entire history of the cinema to the present day. Available as high resolution downloads from the Aquarius Library website containing thousands of film and TV titles and over 100,000 high quality stills. Postal deliveries and free searches also available.

Architectural Association Photo Library
36 Bedford Square, London WC1B 3ES
☎020 7887 4066   Fax 020 7414 0782
✉ valerie@aaschool.ac.uk

www.aaschool.ac.uk

Contacts *Valerie Bennett, Sarah Franklin, Henderson Downing*

100,000 35mm transparencies on architecture, historical and contemporary. Archive of large-format b&w negatives from the 1920s and 1930s.

ArenaPAL
Lambert House, 55 Southwark Street, London SE1 1RU
☎020 7403 8542   Fax 020 7403 8561
✉ enquiries@arenapal.com
www.arenapal.com

'All the entertainment pictures you'll ever need.' Continually updated specialist performing arts image collection covering classical music, opera, theatre, musicals, film, pop, rock, jazz, instruments, festivals, venues, circus, ballet and contemporary dance, props and personalities. Over two million images from late 19th century onwards. Please phone, fax or e-mail to make a selection.

ArkReligion.com
57 Burdon Lane, Cheam SM2 7BY
☎020 8642 3593   Fax 020 8395 7230
✉ images@artdirectors.co.uk
www.arkreligion.com

Contacts *Helene Rogers, Bob Turner*

Extensive coverage of all religions.

Art Directors & Trip Photo Library
57 Burdon Lane, Cheam SM2 7BY
☎020 8642 3593   Fax 020 8395 7230
✉ images@artdirectors.co.uk
www.artdirectors.co.uk

Contacts *Helene Rogers, Bob Turner*

Extensive coverage, with over 750,000 images, of all countries, lifestyles, peoples, etc. with detailed coverage of all religions. Backgrounds a speciality.

Aspect Picture Library Ltd
40 Rostrevor Road, London SW6 5AD
☎020 7736 1998/7731 7362
Fax 020 7731 7362
✉ Aspect.Ldn@btinternet.com
www.aspect-picture-library.co.uk

Colour and b&w worldwide coverage of countries, events, industry and travel, with large files on art, namely paintings, space, China, the

Middle East, French villages, English villages and Ireland.

Australia Pictures

28 Sheen Common Drive, Richmond
TW10 5BN
☎020 7602 1989   Fax 020 7602 1989
✉ equilibrium.films@virgin.net

Contact *John Miles*

Collection of 4000 transparencies covering all aspects of Australia: Aboriginal people, paintings, Ayers Rock, Kakadu, Tasmania, underwater, reefs, Arnhem Land, Sydney. Also Africa, Middle East and Asia.

Aviation Picture Library

116 The Avenue, St Stephens, West Ealing, London W13 8JX
☎020 8566 7712/07860 670073 (mobile)
Fax 020 8566 7714
✉ avpix@aol.com
www.aviationpictures.com

Contact *Austin John Brown*

Specialists in the aviation field but also a general library which includes travel, architecture, transport, landscapes and skyscapes. SPECIAL COLLECTIONS aircraft and all aspects of the aviation industry, including the archival collection of John Stroud; aerial obliques of Europe, USA, Caribbean and West Africa; architectural and town planning. Photographers for *Flyer* magazine in the UK. Commissions undertaken on the ground and in the air.

aviation–images.com

42B Queens Road, London SW19 8LR
☎020 8944 5225   Fax 020 8944 5335
✉ pictures@aviation-images.com
www.aviation-images.com

Contacts *Mark Wagner, Mark Steele*

500,000+ aviation images, civil and military, archive and modern, from the world's best aviation photographers. Member of **BAPLA** and RAeS.

Axel Poignant Archive

115 Bedford Court Mansions, Bedford Avenue, London WC1B 3AG
☎020 7636 2555   Fax 020 7636 2555
✉ Rpoignant@aol.com

Contact *Roslyn Poignant*

Anthropological and ethnographic subjects, especially Australia and the South Pacific. Also Scandinavia (early history and mythology), Sicily and England.

Barnardo's Photographic and Film Archive

Barnardo's House, Tanners Lane, Barkingside, Ilford IG6 1QG
☎020 8498 7345   Fax 020 8498 7090
✉ stephen.pover@barnardos.org.uk
www.barnardos.org.uk

Image Librarian *Stephen Pover*

The Barnardo's image archive is a unique resource of images of social history from 1872 to 1905. Images can be sent either by post, ISDN or e-mail. Office hours: Monday to Friday, 9.30 am to 4.30 pm.

Colin Baxter Photography Limited

Woodlands Industrial Estate, Grantown-on-Spey PH26 3NA
☎01479 873999   Fax 01479 873888
✉ sales@colinbaxter.co.uk
www.colinbaxter.co.uk

Contacts *Colin B. Kirkwood* (Marketing), *Mike Rensner* (Editorial)

Over 50,000 images specialising in Scotland. Also the Lake District, Yorkshire, France, Iceland and a special collection on Charles Rennie Mackintosh's work. Publishes guidebooks plus books, calendars, postcards and greetings cards on landscape, cityscape and natural history containing images which are primarily, but not exclusively, Colin Baxter's. Also publishers of the *Worldlife Library* of natural history books, and a range of books and stationery based on reproductons of the designs of Charles Rennie Mackintosh.

BBC Natural History Unit Picture Library

See **Nature Picture Library**

The Photographic Library Beamish, The North of England Open Air Museum

The North of England Open Air Museum, Beamish DH9 0RG
☎0191 370 4000   Fax 0191 370 4001
✉ museum@beamish.org.uk
www.beamish.org.uk

Comprehensive collection; images relate to the North East of England and cover agricultural, industrial, topography, advertising and shop scenes, people at work and play. Also on laser disk for rapid searching. Visitors by appointment weekdays.

Francis Bedford

See **Birmingham Library Services** under *Library Services*

Ivan J. Belcher
Colour Picture Library

57 Gibson Close, Abingdon OX14 1XS
☎01235 521524   Fax 01235 521524

Extensive colour picture library specialising in top-quality medium-format transparencies depicting the British scene. Particular emphasis on tourist, holiday and heritage locations, including famous cities, towns, picturesque harbours, rivers, canals, castles, cottages, rural scenes and traditions photographed throughout the seasons. Mainly of recent origin and constantly updated.

Andrew Besley PhotoLibrary

'Trenerth Barton', Fraddam, Near Hayle TR27 5EP
☎01736 850086   Fax 01736 850086
✉ bes.pix@btinternet.com
www.andrewbesley-photolibrary.co.uk

Contact *Andrew Besley*

Specialist library of 20,000 images of West Country faces, places and moods.

bfi Stills, Posters and Designs

British Film Institute, 21 Stephen Street, London W1T 1LN
☎020 7957 4797   Fax 020 7323 9260
✉ stills.films@bfi.org.uk
ww.bfi.org.uk/collections/stills/index.html

'*bfi* Stills, Posters and Designs is the world's most comprehensive collection of film and television images.' The collection captures on and off screen moments, portraits of the world's most famous stars – and those behind the camera who made them famous – as well as publicity posters, set designs, images of studios, cinemas, special events and early film and TV technologies. Rapid access to these images can be provided by photographic or digital reproduction. Visits by appointment only.

Blackwoods Picture Library

See **Geoslides Photography**

Anthony Blake Photo Library

20 Blades Court, Deodar Road, Putney, London SW15 2NU
☎020 8877 1123   Fax 020 8877 9787
✉ info@abpl.co.uk
www.abpl.co.uk

'Europe's premier source' of food and wine related images. From the farm and the vineyard to the plate and the bottle. Cooking and kitchens, top chefs and restaurants, country trades and markets, worldwide travel with an extensive Italian section. Many recipes available to accompany transparencies. Free brochure available.

Peter Boardman Collection

See **Chris Bonington Picture Library**

Boating Images Photo Library

7 Elstree Close, Meole Brace, Shrewsbury SY3 9QF
☎05511 400187
✉ phil@boating-images.com
www.boating-images.com

Contact *Phil Pickin*

Comprehensive online boating image library. For marine, lifestyle, maritime heritage and inland waterways – worldwide. New images weekly. Search available.

Chris Bonington Picture Library

Badger Hill, Nether Row, Hesket Newmarket, Wigton CA7 8LA
☎016974 78286   Fax 016974 78238
✉ frances@bonington.com
www.bonington.com

Contact *Frances Daltrey*

Based on the personal collection of climber and author Chris Bonington and his extensive travels and mountaineering achievements; also work by Doug Scott and other climbers, including the Peter Boardman and Joe Tasker Collections. Full coverage of the world's mountains, from British hills to Everest, depicting expedition planning and management stages, the approach march showing inhabitants of the area, flora and fauna, local architecture and climbing action shots on some of the world's highest mountains.

Boulton and Watt Archive

See **Birmingham Library Services** under *Library Services*

The Bridgeman Art Library

17–19 Garway Road, London W2 4PH
☎020 7727 4065   Fax 020 7792 8509
✉ london@bridgeman.co.uk
www.bridgemanart.co.uk

Head of Picture Research *Jenny Page*

Fine art photo archive acting as an agent to more than 1000 museums, galleries and picture owners around the world. Large-format colour transparencies of private collections, artists, paintings, sculptures, prints, manuscripts, antiquities and the decorative arts. The Library is currently expanding at the rate of 500 new images each week and has offices in Paris, New York and Berlin. Collections represented by the library include the British Library, the National Galleries of Scotland, the National Library of Australia, and the National Gallery of South Africa. Fully searchable catalogue online.

British Library Picture Library and Images Online/ Reproductions

British Library, 96 Euston Road, London NW1 2DB

Images Online ☎020 7412 7614
Fax 020 7412 7771 ✉ imagesonline@bl.uk
www.bl.uk/imagesonline

Reproductions ☎01937 546060
Fax 01937 546333
✉ reproductions-customer-services@bl.uk
www.bl.uk/reproductions

The Picture Library holds a growing number of images from the British Library's collections of manuscripts, books, maps, music and philately. Transparencies or prints are available for hire and printouts are supplied free for selection purposes.

The fully searchable website, Images Online, includes images scanned from the Library's existing transparencies. High-resolution images are available on CD-ROM; smaller JPEGs can be purchased online and downloaded instantly.

Reproductions offers high quality paper copying, microfilming, photographic and digital services to customers who require copies from the following collection areas: Maps, Music, Printed Books, Manuscripts and the Asia, Pacific and Africa Collections. Copying service available; see Reproductions website for details.

Brooklands Museum Picture Library

Brooklands Museum, Brooklands Road, Weybridge KT13 0QN
☎01932 857381 Fax 01932 855465
✉ info@brooklandsmuseum.com
www.brooklandsmuseum.com

Contacts *John Pulford* (Curator of Collections), *Julian Temple* (Curator of Aviation)

About 40,000 b&w and colour prints and slides. Subjects include: Brooklands Motor Racing 1907–1939; British aviation and aerospace, 1908 to the present day, particularly BAC, Hawker, Sopwith and Vickers aircraft built at Brooklands.

Hamish Brown MBE, D.Litt, FRSGS Scottish Photographic

26 Kirkcaldy Road, Burntisland KY3 9HQ
☎01592 873546 Fax 01592 873546

Contact *Hamish Brown*

Coverage of most topics and areas of Scotland (sites, historic, buildings, landscape, mountains), also travel, mountains, general (50,000 items) and Morocco. Commissions undertaken.

Capital Pictures

85 Randolph Avenue, London W9 1DL
☎020 7286 2212 Fax 020 7286 1218
✉ sales@capitalpictures.com
www.capitalpictures.com

Contact *Phil Loftus*

Specialises in photographs of famous people from the worlds of showbusiness, rock and pop, television, politics, royalty and film stills.

The Centre for the Study of Cartoons and Caricature

The Templeman Library, University of Kent at Canterbury, Canterbury CT2 7NU
☎01227 823127 Fax 01227 823127
✉ N.P.Hiley@kent.ac.uk *or*
J.M.Newton@kent.ac.uk
library.kent.ac.uk/cartoons/

Contacts *Dr Nicholas Hiley, Jane Newton*

A national research archive of over 90,000 original cartoons and caricatures, supported by a library of books, papers, journals, catalogues and assorted ephemera. A computer database of 110,000 cartoons provides quick and easy catalogued access via the Web. A source for exhibitions and displays as well as a picture library service. Specialises in historical, political and social cartoons from British newspapers.

Cephas Picture Library

Hurst House, 157 Walton Road, East Molesey KT8 0DX
☎020 8979 8647 Fax 020 8224 8095
✉ pictures@cephas.co.uk
www.cephas.com

The wine industry and vineyards of the world is the subject on which Cephas has made its reputation. 100,000 images make this one of the most comprehensive and up-to-date archives in Britain. Almost all wine-producing countries and all aspects of the industry are covered in depth. Spirits, beer and cider also included. A major food and drink collection now also exists, through preparation and cooking, to eating and drinking.

Giles Chapman Library

13A The Drive, Sevenoaks TN13 3AB
☎01732 452547
✉ chapman.media@virgin.net
Contact *Giles Chapman*

Around 125,000 colour and b&w images of cars and motoring, from 1945 to the present day. No research fees.

Christian Aid Photo Section

PO Box 100, London SE1 7RT
☎020 7523 2232/5   Fax 020 7620 0719
✉ photos@christian-aid.org
Contacts *J. Cabon, B. Nicholson, C. Lands*

Pictures are mainly from Africa, Asia and Latin America, relating to small-scale, community-based programmes. Mostly development themes: health, agriculture, education, urban and rural life.

Christie's Images Ltd

1 Langley Lane, London SW8 1TJ
☎020 7582 1282   Fax 020 7582 5632
✉ imageslondon@christies.com
www.christiesimages.com
Contact *Mark Lynch*

The collection spans 80 categories representing every culture, from the distant past to the present day. An unrivalled collection from Old Masters to Impressionists and Twentieth Century master-pieces. Antiquities, Art Nouveau and Decorative Art, Books and Manuscripts, Contemporary Art and Furniture, Music and Movie Memorabilia, Textiles, Toys. Experienced researchers will search for specific requests.

Chrysalis Images

The Chrysalis Building, Bramley Road, London W10 6SP
☎020 7314 1400   Fax 020 7314 1583
✉ permissions@chrysalisbooks.co.uk
Contacts *Sarah Stewart-Richardson, Kirsty Symons*

One million photographs and illustrations, colour and b&w, on military, history, transport, cookery, crafts, natural history, space and travel.

The Cinema Museum

The Master's House, Old Lambeth Workhouse, off Renfrew Road, London SE11 4TH
☎020 7840 2200   Fax 020 7840 2299
✉ martin@cinemamuseum.org.uk

Colour and b&w coverage (including stills) of the motion picture industry throughout its history, including the Ronald Grant Archive. Smaller collections on theatre, variety, television and popular music.

John Cleare/Mountain Camera

Hill Cottage, Fonthill Gifford, Salisbury SP3 6QW
☎01747 820320   Fax 01747 820320
✉ cleare@btinternet.com
www.mountaincamera.com

Colour and b&w coverage of mountains and wild places, climbing, ski-touring, trekking, expeditions, wilderness travel, landscapes, people and geographical features from all continents. Specialises in the Himalaya, Andes, Antarctic, Alps and the British countryside, and a range of topics from reindeer in Lapland to camels in Australia, from whitewater rafting in Utah to ski-mountaineering in China. Commissions and consultancy work undertaken. Researchers welcome by appointment. Member of **BAPLA** and the **OWG**.

Michael Cole Camerawork

The Coach House, 27 The Avenue, Beckenham BR3 5DP
☎020 8658 6120   Fax 020 8658 6120
✉ mikecole@dircon.co.uk
Contacts *Michael Cole, Derrick Bentley*

Probably the largest and most comprehensive collection of tennis pictures in the world. Over 50 years' coverage of the Wimbledon Championships. M.C.C. incorporates the tennis archives of Le Roye Productions, established in 1945.

Collections

13 Woodberry Crescent, London N10 1PJ
☎020 8883 0083   Fax 020 8883 9215
✉ collections@btinternet.com
www.collectionspicturelibrary.com
www.collectionspicturelibrary.co.uk
Contact *Brian Shuel*

Extensive coverage of the British and Ireland, from the Shetlands to the Channel Islands and Connemara to East Anglia, including people, traditional customs, workers, religions and pastimes, as well as places both well known and obscure, and an extensive collection of 'things'. Includes the landscapes of Fay Godwin. Visitors are welcome but please make an appointment.

Corbis Images

111 Salusbury Road, London NW6 6RG
☎020 7644 7644   Fax 020 7644 7645
✉ sales.uk@corbis.com
www.corbis.com

A unique and comprehensive resource containing more than 65 million images, with over 2.1 million of them available online. The images come from professional photographers, museums, cultural institutions and public and private collections worldwide. Subjects include history, travel, celebrities, events, science, world art and cultures.

Sylvia Cordaiy Photo Library

45 Rotherstone, Devizes SN10 2DD
☎01380 728327   Fax 01380 728328
✉ info@sylvia-cordaiy.com
www.sylvia-cordaiy.com

Over 170 countries on file from the obscure to main stock images – Africa, North, Central and South America, Asia, Atlantic, Indian and Pacific Ocean islands, Australasia, Europe, polar regions. Covers travel, architecture, ancient civilisations, world heritage sites, people worldwide, environment, wildlife, natural history, Antarctica, domestic pets, livestock, marine biology, veterinary treatment, equestrian, ornithology, flowers. UK files cover cities, towns villages, coastal and rural scenes, London collection. Transport, railways, shipping and aircraft (military and civilian). Aerial photography. Backgrounds and abstracts. Also the Paul Kaye B/W archive.

Country Images Picture Library

27 Camwood, Bamber Bridge, Preston
PR5 8LA
☎01772 321243   Fax 0870 137 8888
✉ terrymarsh@wpu.org.uk
www.countryimages.info

Contact *Terry Marsh*

35mm and medium format colour coverage of landscapes and countryside features generally throughout the UK (Cumbria, North Yorkshire, Lancashire, southern Scotland, Isle of Skye, St Kilda and Scottish islands, Wales, Cornwall), France (Alps, Pyrenees, Provence, Charente-Maritime, Hérault, Aube-en-Champagne, Loire valley, Somme) and Australia. Commissions undertaken.

Country Life Picture Library

King's Reach Tower, Stamford Street, London
SE1 9LS
☎020 7261 6337   Fax 020 7261 6216
✉ camilla_costello@ipcmedia.com
www.clpicturelibrary.co.uk

Contact *Camilla Costello*

Over 150,000 b&w negatives dating back to 1897, and 80,000 colour transparencies. Country houses, stately homes, churches and town houses in Britain and abroad, interiors of architectural interest (ceilings, fireplaces, furniture, paintings, sculpture), and exteriors show-ing many landscaped gardens, sporting and social events, crafts, people and animals. Visitors by appointment. Open Tuesday to Friday.

Philip Craven Worldwide Photo-Library

Surrey Studios, 21 Nork Way, Nork, Banstead
SM7 1PB
☎0870 220 2121
www.philipcraven.com

Contact *Philip Craven*

Extensive coverage of British scenes, cities, villages, English countryside, gardens, historic buildings and wildlife. Worldwide travel and wildlife subjects on medium and large-format transparencies.

Sue Cunningham Photographic

56 Chatham Road, Kingston upon Thames
KT1 3AA
☎020 8541 3024   Fax 020 8541 5388
✉ pictures@scphotographic.com
www.scphotographic.com

Extensive coverage of many geographical areas: South America (especially Brazil), Eastern Europe from the Baltic to the Balkans, various African countries, Western Europe including the UK. Colour and b&w. Member of **BAPLA**.

Dale Concannon Collection
See **Phil Sheldon Golf Picture Library**

Dalton–Watson Collection
See **The Ludvigsen Library**

The Defence Picture Library

8 Creykes Court, Craigie Drive, The Millfields, Plymouth PL1 3JB
☎01752 401800/01752 312061
Fax 01752 402800
✉ picdesk@defencepictures.com
www.defencepictures.com

Contacts *David Reynolds, Jessica Kelly, James Rowlands, Andrew Chittock*

Leading source of military photography covering all areas of the UK Armed Forces, supported by a research agency of facts and figures. More than one million images. Visitors welcome by appointment.

Douglas Dickins Photo Library

2 Wessex Gardens, Golders Green, London
NW11 9RT
☎020 8455 6221

Sole Proprietor *Douglas Dickins; FRPS*

Worldwide colour and b&w coverage, specialising in Asia, particularly India, Indonesia and Japan. *In Grandpa's Footsteps*, highly illustrated book of world travel published by The Book Guild in 2000.

Dominic Photography

4B Moore Park Road, London SW6 2JT
☎020 7381 0007   Fax 020 7381 0008

Contacts *Zoë Dominic, Catherine Ashmore*

Colour and b&w coverage of the entertainment world from 1957 onwards: dance, opera, theatre, ballet, musicals and personalities.

E&E Picture Library – Ecclesiastical and Eccentricities

Beggars Roost, Woolpack Hill, Brabourne Lees, Ashford TN25 6RR
☎01303 812608   Fax 01303 812608
✉ isobel@picture-library.freeserve.co.uk
www.picture-library.freeserve.co.uk

Contact *Isobel Sinden*

Specialises in world religions, manuscripts, buildings, artifacts, clothes, festivals, clergy, arts, culture, history, pilgrimages, ancient stones, Bible lands, symbols, carvings, death and burial worldwide, ancient to modern. Curiosities such as follies, mazes, towers, bridges, clocks, knights, royalty, signs, lighthouses, schools, magic. Also wind, water, transport and nature.

Patrick Eagar Photography

1 Queensberry Place, Richmond TW9 1NW
☎020 8940 9269   Fax 020 8332 1229
✉ patrick@patrickeagar.com
www.patrickeagar.com

The cricket library consists of Patrick Eagar's work over the last 30 years with coverage of over 270 Test matches worldwide, unique coverage of all eight World Cups, countless one-day internationals and player action portraits of over 2000 cricketers. The wine library consists of vineyards, grapes and festivals from Argentina to New Zealand. France and Australia are specialist areas. Photographs can be supplied by e-mail, on CD, prints and transparencies.

Ecoscene

Empire Farm, Throop Road, Templecombe BA8 0HR
☎01963 371700
✉ sally@ecoscene.com
www.ecoscene.com

Contact *Sally Morgan*

Expanding colour library of over 80,000 transparencies specialising in all aspects of the environment: pollution, conservation, recycling, restoration, wildlife (especially underwater), habitats, education, landscapes, industry and agriculture. All parts of the globe are covered with specialist collections covering Antarctica, Australia, North America. Sally Morgan, who runs the library, is a professional ecologist and expert source of information on all environmental topics. Photographic and writing commissions undertaken. Images delivered by e-mail or available for download.

Edifice

Cutterne Mill, Evercreech BA4 6LY
☎01749 831400
✉ info@edificephoto.com
www.edificephoto.com

Contacts *Philippa Lewis, Gillian Darley*

Colour coverage of architecture, buildings of all possible descriptions, gardens, urban and rural landscape. Specialises in details of ornament, period style and material. British Isles, USA, Africa, Europe and Japan all covered. Detailed list available, visits by appointment. Website is searchable on line.

Education Photos

April Cottage, Warners Lane, Albury Heath, Guildford GU5 9DE
☎01483 203846
✉ johnwalmsley@educationphotos.co.uk
www.educationphotos.co.uk

Formerly the John Walmsley Photo Library. Specialist library of learning/training/working subjects. Comprehensive coverage of learning environments such as playgroups, schools, colleges and universities. Images reflect a multiracial Britain. Commissions undertaken.

English Heritage Photo Library

23 Savile Row, London W1S 2ET
☎020 7973 3338/9   Fax 020 7973 3027
✉ photo.library@english-heritage.org.uk
www.english-heritage.org.uk

Contact *Celia Sterne*

Images of English castles, abbeys, houses, gardens, Roman remains, ancient monuments, battlefields, industrial and post-war buildings, interiors, paintings, artifacts, architectural details, conservation, archaeology, scenic views, landscapes.

Mary Evans Picture Library

59 Tranquil Vale, Blackheath, London SE3 0BS
☎020 8318 0034   Fax 020 8852 7211

✉ pictures@maryevans.com
www.maryevans.com

Historical archive of illustrations, photographs, prints and ephemera documenting all aspects of the past, from ancient times to the later decades of the 20th century. Subject areas: social and political history, portraits, events, transport, costume, trade and industry, places worldwide and natural history plus specialist material on folklore and paranormal phenomena. Notable collections include the Weimar Archive documenting the Third Reich, Barnaby's Library covering social scenes and events from the 1930s to the 1970s; and the Thomas Fall Collection of historic dog photographs. MEPL's own material is complemented by many contributors such as Sigmund Freud Copyrights, the **Women's Library** (women's rights) and the Meledin Collection of 20th century Russian history. Over 150,000 images searchable online with 60,000 scanned in high-resolution for immediate download. Brochure on request. Founder member of **BAPLA**. Compilers of the *Picture Researcher's Handbook* by Pira International.

Exile Images

1 Mill Row, Brighton BN1 3SU
☎01273 208741   Fax 01273 382782
✉ pics@exileimages.co.uk
www.exileimages.co.uk

Contact *Howard Davies*

Online photo library with over 8000 pictures of refugees, conflict, asylum seekers, UK protests and Third World issues. Picture editors can search and download high resolution photographs online.

Eye Ubiquitous

65 Brighton Road, Shoreham BN43 6RE
☎01273 440113   Fax 01273 440116
✉ library@eyeubiquitous.com
www.eyeubiquitous.com

General stock specialising in social documentary worldwide, and an extensive travel related collection.

Faces and Places

☎020 7602 1989/07930 622964 (mobile)
✉ equilibrium.films@virgin.net *or*
john@facesandplacespix.com
www.facesandplacespix.com

Extensive worldwide library built up over 20 years which covers 40,000 photographs focusing mainly on travel, tourism, unusual locations, indigenous peoples, scenery and underwater photography; Australia, Tibet, Mali, Yemen and Iran.

Thomas Fall Collection

See **Mary Evans Picture Library**

Famous Pictures & Features Agency

13 Harwood Road, London SW6 4QP
☎020 7731 9333   Fax 020 7731 9330
✉ info@famous.uk.com
www.famous.uk.com

Celebrity features agency with a growing library of high quality celebrity interviews and digital images to accompany text. The library is supplied by a team of freelance celebrity journalists and photographers from the UK, US and around the world, keeping it up-to-date with a variety of the hottest features on a daily basis. 'We are always looking out for new writers who specialise in material dealing with *famous* people.'

ffotograff

10 Kyveilog Street, Pontcanna, Cardiff CF11 9JA
☎029 2023 6879
✉ ffotograff@easynet.co.uk
www.ffotograff.com

Contact *Patricia Aithie*

Library and agency specialising in travel, exploration, the arts, architecture, traditional culture, archaeology and landscape. Based in Wales but specialising in the Middle and Far East; Africa, Central and South America; Yemen and Wales are strong aspects of the library. Churches and cathedrals of Britain and Crusader castles.

Financial Times Pictures

One Southwark Bridge, London SE1 9HL
☎020 7873 3671   Fax 020 7873 4606
✉ photosynd@ft.com

Photographs from around the world ranging from personalities in business, politics and the arts, people at work and other human interests and activities. '*FT* Graphics are outstanding in their ability to make complex issues comprehensible.' Delivery via ISDN or e-mail.

Fine Art Photographic Library Ltd

2A Milner Street, London SW3 2PU
☎020 7589 3127   Fax 020 7584 1944
✉ info@fineartphotolibrary.com
www.fineartphotolibrary.com

Over 30,000 large-format transparencies, with a specialist collection of 19th and 20th century paintings. CD-ROM available.

Firepix International
68 Arkles Lane, Anfield, Liverpool L4 2SP
☎0151 260 0111/0777 5930419 (mobile)
Fax 0151 260 0111
✉ info@firepix.com
www.firepix.com
Contact *Tony Myers*

The UK's only fire photo library. 23,000 images of fire-related subjects, firefighters, fire equipment manufacturers. Website contains 15 categories from industrial fire, domestic, digital images and abstract flame. Member of **BAPLA**.

Fogden Wildlife Photographs
16 Locheport, North Uist, Western Isles HS6 5EU
☎01876 580245   Fax 01876 580777
✉ susan.fogden@virgin.net
www.fogdenphotos.com
Contact *Susan Fogden*

Natural history collection, with special reference to rain forests and deserts. Emphasis on quality rather than quantity; growing collection of around 15,000 images.

Food Features
Farnham Forge, 5 Upper Church Lane, Farnham GU9 7PW
☎01252 735240   Fax 01252 735242
✉ frontdesk@foodpix.co.uk
www.foodpix.co.uk
Contacts *Steve Moss, Alex Barker*

Specialised high-quality food and drink photography, features and tested recipes. Clients' specific requirements can be incorporated into regular shooting schedules.

Christine Foord
Colour Picture Library
155B City Way, Rochester ME1 2BE
☎01634 847348   Fax 01634 847348

Specialist library with over 1000 species of British and European wild flowers, plus garden flowers, trees, indoor plants, pests and diseases, mosses, lichen, cacti and the majority of larger British insects.

Forestry Commission
Picture Library
231 Corstorphine Road, Edinburgh EH12 7AT
☎0131 314 6411

✉ neill.campbell@forestry.gsi.gov.uk
www.forestry.gov.uk/pictures
Contacts *Douglas Green, Neill Campbell*

The official image bank of the Forestry Commission, the library provides a single source for all aspects of forest and woodland management. The comprehensive subject list includes tree species, scenic landscapes, employment, wildlife, flora and fauna, conservation, sport and leisure.

Werner Forman Archive Ltd
36 Camden Square, London NW1 9XA
☎020 7267 1034   Fax 020 7267 6026
✉ wfa@btinternet.com
www.werner-forman-archive.com

Colour and b&w coverage of ancient civilisations, oriental and primitive societies around the world. A number of rare collections. Searchable website.

Formula One Pictures
2013 Pomaz, Buzavirag U.6. Hungary
☎00 36 26 322 826/07905 819 555 (mobile)
✉ jt@f1pictures.com
www.f1pictures.com
Contact *John Townsend*

500,000 35mm colour slides, b&w and colour negatives and digital images of all aspects of Formula One Grand Prix racing including driver profiles and portraits.

Robert Forsythe Picture Library
16 Lime Grove, Prudhoe NE42 6PR
☎01661 834511   Fax 01661 834511
✉ robert@forsythe.demon.co.uk
www.forsythe.demon.co.uk
Contacts *Robert Forsythe, Fiona Forsythe*

25,000 transparencies of industrial and transport heritage; plus a unique collection of 70,000 items of related publicity ephemera from 1945. Image finding service available. Robert Forsythe is a transport/industrial heritage historian and consultant. Nationwide coverage, particularly strong on northern Britain. A bibliography of published material is available.

Fortean Picture Library
Henblas, Mwrog Street, Ruthin LL15 1LG
☎01824 707278   Fax 01824 705324
✉ janet.bord@forteanpix.demon.co.uk
www.forteanpix.demon.co.uk
Contact *Janet Bord*

30,000 colour and 45,000 b&w images: mysteries and strange phenomena worldwide, including ghosts, UFOs, witchcraft and monsters; also antiquities, folklore and mythology. Subject list available.

The Fotomas Index (UK)
12 Pickhurst Rise, West Wickham BR4 0AL
☎020 8776 2772   Fax 020 8776 2236
✉ fotomasindex@btconnect.com
Contact *John Freeman*

General historical collection, mostly pre-1900. Subjects include London, topography, art, satirical, social and political history. Large portrait section.

The Francis Frith Collection
Frith's Barn, Teffont, Salisbury SP3 5QP
☎01722 716376   Fax 01722 716881
✉ julia_skinner@francisfrith.co.uk
www.francisfrith.co.uk

Contact *Julia Skinner*, Managing Editor
Publishers of *Frith's Photographic Memories* series of illustrated local books, all featuring nostalgic photographs from the archive, founded by Frith in 1860. The archive contains over 360,000 images of 7000 British towns.

John Frost Newspapers
See entry under *Library Services*

Andrew N. Gagg's Photo Flora
Town House Two, Fordbank Court, Henwick Road, Worcester WR2 5PF
☎01905 748515
✉ andrew.n.gagg@ntlworld.com
homepage.ntlworld.com/a.n.gagg/photo/phot oflora.html

Specialist in British and European wild plants, flowers, ferns, grasses, trees, shrubs, etc. with colour coverage of most British and many European species (rare and common) and habitats; also travel in India, Sri Lanka, Nepal, Egypt, China, Mexico, Thailand, Tibet, Vietnam and Cambodia.

Galaxy Picture Library
34 Fennels Way, Flackwell Heath, High Wycombe HP10 9BY
☎01628 521338   Fax 01628 520132
✉ robin@galaxypix.com
www.galaxypix.com
Contact *Robin Scagell*

Specialises in astronomy, space, telescopes, observatories, the sky, clouds and sunsets. Composites of foregrounds, stars, moon and planets prepared to commission. Editorial service available.

Garden and Wildlife Matters Photo Library
'Marlham', Henley's Down, Battle TN33 9BN
☎01424 830566   Fax 01424 830224
✉ gardens@gmpix.com
www.gardenmatters.uk.com
www.gmpix.com
Contact *Dr John Feltwell*

Collection of 110,000 6×4" and 35mm images. General gardening techniques and design; cottage gardens and USA designer gardens. 9000 species of garden plants and over 1000 species of trees. Flowers, wild and house plants, trees and crops. Environmental, ecological and conservation pictures, including sea, air, noise and freshwater pollution, SE Asian and Central and South American rainforests; Eastern Europe, Mediterranean. Recycling, agriculture, forestry, horticulture and oblique aerial habitat shots from Europe and USA. 24/7 service. Digital images supplied worldwide.

Garden Picture Library
Unit 12, Ransome's Dock, 35 Parkgate Road, London SW11 4NP
☎020 7228 4332   Fax 020 7924 3267
✉ info@gardenpicture.com
www.gardenpicture.com
Picture Research Manager *Lorraine Shill*

'Our inspirational images of gardens, plants and gardening lifestyle offer plenty of scope for writers looking for original ideas to write about.' The collection covers all garden related subjects; everything from plant portraits to floral graphics and garden design details to whole landscapes. Brings together the work of over 100 professional photographers from across the gardening globe. Holds approximately 400,000 fully captioned images of which around 15,000 are available digitally. In-house picture research can be undertaken on request or searches can be made online via keyword or subject category to create lightboxes which can be e-mailed or downloaded. Visitors to the library are welcome by appointment and copies of promotional literature are available on request.

Ed Geldard Photo Collection
9 Sunderland Bridge Village, Durham DH6 5HB
☎0191 378 2592
✉ ed@camera-one.freeserve.co.uk
Contact *Ed Geldard*

Approximately 25,000 colour transparencies and b&w negs, all by Ed Geldard, specialising in mountain landscapes: particularly the mountain regions of the Lake District, and the Yorkshire limestone areas, from valley to summit. Commissions undertaken. Books published: *Wainwright's Tour of the Lake District*; *Wainwright in the Limestone Dales*; *The Lake District*.

Genesis Space Photo Library
20 Goodwood Park Road, Bideford EX39 2RR
☎01237 477883
✉ tim@spaceport.co.uk
www.spaceport.co.uk
Contact *Tim Furniss*

Contemporary and historical colour and b&w spaceflight collection including rockets, spacecraft, spacemen, Earth, moon and planets. Catalogue of 775 images on website.

Geo Aerial Photography
4 Christian Fields, London SW16 3JZ
☎020 8764 6292/0115 981 9418
Fax 020 8764 6292/0115 981 9418
✉ geo.aerial@geo-group.co.uk
www.geo-group.co.uk
Contact *Kelly White*

Established 1990 and now a growing collection of aerial oblique photographs from the UK, Scandinavia, Asia and Africa – landscapes, buildings, industrial sites, etc. Commissions undertaken.

GeoScience Features
6 Orchard Drive, Wye TN25 5AU
☎01233 812707   Fax 01233 812707
✉ gsf@geoscience.demon.co.uk
www.geoscience.demon.co.uk
Fully computerised and comprehensive library containing the world's principal source of volcanic phenomena. Extensive collections, providing scientific detail with technical quality, of rocks, minerals, fossils, microsections of botanical and animal tissues, animals, biology, birds, botany, chemistry, earth science, ecology, environment, geology, geography, habitats, landscapes, macro/microbiology, peoples, sky, weather, wildlife and zoology. Over 300,000 original colour transparencies in medium and 35mm-format. Subject lists and CD-ROM catalogue available. Incorporates the RIDA photolibrary.

Geoslides Photography
4 Christian Fields, London SW16 3JZ
☎020 8764 6292/0115 981 9418
Fax 020 8764 6292/0115 981 9418
✉ geoslides@geo-group.co.uk

www.geo-group.co.uk
Contact *John Douglas*

Established in 1968. Landscape and human interest subjects from the Arctic, Antarctica, Scandinavia, UK, Africa (south of Sahara), Middle East, Asia (south and southeast); also Australia, via Blackwoods Picture Library. Also specialist collections of images from British India (the Raj) and Boer War.

Getty Images
101 Bayham Street, London NW1 0AG
☎0800 376 7981   Fax 020 7544 3334
✉ sales@gettyimages.com
www.gettyimages.com
Contact *Sales Department*

'Getty Images is the world's leading imagery company, creating and providing the largest collection of still and moving images to communication professionals around the globe. From sports and news photography to archival and contemporary imagery, Getty Images' products are found each day in newspapers, magazines, advertising, films, television, books and websites.' For those who wish to commission photographers to fulfil specific needs, the company maintains a full-service department for custom-shot images.

Martin and Dorothy Grace
40 Clipstone Avenue, Mapperley, Nottingham NG3 5JZ
☎0115 920 8248
✉ graces@lineone.net
Colour coverage of Britain's natural history, specialising in trees, shrubs and wild flowers. Also ferns, birds and butterflies, habitats, landscapes, ecology.

Ronald Grant Archive
See **The Cinema Museum**

Sally and Richard Greenhill
357 Liverpool Road, London N1 1NL
☎020 7607 8549   Fax 020 7607 7151
✉ sr.greenhill@virgin.net
www.srgreenhill.co.uk
Photo Librarian *Denise Lalonde*

Social documentary photography in colour and b&w of working lives: pregnancy and birth, child development, education, work, old people, medical, urban. Also Modern China, 1971 to the present; most London statues. Some material from Borneo, USA, India, Israel, Philippines and Sri Lanka.

V.K. Guy Ltd

Silver Birches, Troutbeck, Windermere
LA23 1PN
☎015394 33519   Fax 015394 32971
✉ vic@vk.guy.co.uk
www.vkguy.co.uk

Contacts *Vic Guy, Mike Guy, Paul Guy,
Nicola Simon*

25,000 5×4" UK and Ireland scenic transparencies from Shetland in the north to the Channel Isles in the south, suitable for tourism brochures, calendars, etc. Can be supplied digitally and browsed through via the online database. Colour catalogue also available.

Angela Hampton 'Family Life Picture Library'

Holly Tree House, The Street, Walberton,
Arundel BN18 0PH
☎01243 555952   Fax 01243 555952
✉ enquiries@familylifepictures.co.uk
www.familylifepictures.co.uk

Contact *Angela Hampton*

Specialist library of over 50,000 images on all aspects of contemporary lifestyle, including pregnancy, childbirth, babies, children, parenting, behaviour, education, medical, holidays, pets, family life, relationships, teenagers, women and men's health, over-50s and retirement. Also domestic and farm animal life. Environmental and travel. Commissions undertaken. Offers fully illustrated text packages on most subjects and welcomes ideas for collaboration from writers with proven, successful background.

Tom Hanley

41 Harefield, Esher KT10 9TG
☎020 8972 9165   Fax 020 8972 9164
✉ Tomhanley31@hotmail.com

Colour and b&w coverage of London, England, Europe, Canada, India, the Philippines, Brazil, China, Japan, Korea, Taiwan, the Seychelles, Cayman Islands, USA. Also pop artists of the 1960s, First World War trenches, removal of London Bridge to America, and much more. Current preoccupation with Greece, Turkey, Spain and Egypt, ancient and modern.

Robert Harding Picture Library

58–59 Great Marlborough Street, London
W1F 7JY
☎020 7478 4000   Fax 020 7478 4161
✉ info@robertharding.com
www.robertharding.com

A leading source of stock photography with over two million colour images covering a wide range of subjects – worldwide travel and culture, geography and landscapes, people and lifestyle, architecture, business and industry, medicine, sports, food and drink. Rights protected and royalty-free images. Can supply images as transparencies, on CD or ISDN. Visitors welcome; telephone or visit the website.

Dennis Hardley Photography, Scottish Photo Library

Rosslynn, Benderloch, Oban PA37 1ST
☎01631 720434   Fax 01631 720434
✉ dennis.hardley@btinternet.com *and*
info@scotphoto.com
www.scotphoto.com

Contacts *Dennis Hardley, Tony Hardley*

Established 1974. About 30,000 images (6×7", 6×9" format colour transparencies) of Scotland: castles, historic, scenic landscapes, islands, transport, etc. Also English views – Liverpool, Chester, Bath, Weston Super Mare, Sussex, Somerset and Cambridge.

Jim Henderson Photographer & Publisher

Crooktree, Kincardine O'Neil, Aboyne
AB34 4JD
☎01339 882149   Fax 01339 882149
✉ JHende7868@aol.com
www.jimhendersonphotography.com

Contact *Jim Henderson, AMPA, ARPS*

Scenic and general activity coverage of the north east Scotland/Grampian region and Highlands for tourist, holiday and activity illustration. Specialist collection of over 300 Aurora Borealis displays from 1989–2004 in Grampian and co-author of *The Aurora* (pub. 1997). Author and photographer for *Aberdeen* and *Aberdeen & Royal Deeside* titles for Aberdeen Journals. Large collection of recent images of Egypt: Cairo through to Abu-Simbel. Commissions undertaken.

Heritage and Natural History Photographic Library

37 Plainwood Close, Summersdale, Chichester
PO195YB
☎01243 533822   Fax 01243 533822
Contact *Dr John B. Free*

Specialises in insects (particularly bees and beekeeping), tropical and temperate agriculture and crops, archaeology and history worldwide.

John Heseltine Archive
Mill Studio, Frogmarsh Mill, South
Woodchester GL5 5ET
☎01453 873792
✉ john@heseltine.co.uk
www.heseltine.co.uk

Contact *John Heseltine*

Over 200,000 colour transparencies and digital
files of landscapes, architecture, food and travel
with particular emphasis on Italy and the UK.

Christopher Hill Photographic
17 Clarence Street, Belfast BT2 8DY
☎028 9024 5038   Fax 028 9023 1942
✉ sales@scenicireland.com
www.scenicireland.com

Contact *Christopher Hill*

A comprehensive collection of scenic landscapes of Ireland. Every aspect of Irish life is
shown, concentrating on the positive. Also large
miscellaneous section. The website contains
over 6000 images available to buy online.

Hobbs Golf Collection
5 Winston Way, New Ridley, Stocksfield
NE43 7RF
☎01661 842933   Fax 01661 842933
✉ info@hobbsgolfcollection.com
www.hobbsgolfcollection.com

Contact *Margaret Hobbs*

Specialist golf collection: players, courses, art,
memorabilia and historical topics (1300–present). 40,000+ images, mainly 35mm colour
transparencies and b&w prints. Commissions
undertaken. Author of 30 golf books.

David Hoffman Photo Library
c/o BAPLA, 18 Vine Hill, London
EC1R 5DZ
☎020 8981 5041   Fax 020 8980 2041
✉ info@hoffmanphotos.com
www.hoffmanphotos.com

Contact *David Hoffman*

Commissioned photography and stock library
with a strong emphasis on social issues built up
from 35mm journalistic and documentary
work dating from the late 1970s. Files on drugs
and drug use, policing, disorder, riots, youth,
prostitution, protest, homelessness, housing,
environmental demonstrations and events,
waste disposal, alternative energy, industry and
pollution. Wide range of images especially from
UK and Europe but also USA, Canada,
Venezuela, Mexico and Thailand. General files
on topical issues and current affairs plus specialist files from leisure cycling to local authority
services. Many photographs available for online
delivery from www.alamy.com

Holt Studios International Ltd
Coxes Farm, Branscombe, Seaton EX12 3BJ
☎01297 680569   Fax 01297 680478
✉ library@holt-studios.co.uk
www.holt-studios.co.uk

Specialist photo library covering world agriculture, horticulture, gardens and gardening from
pictorial and technical aspects. Worldwide
assignments undertaken.

Houghton's Horses/
Kit Houghton Photography
Radlet Cottage, Spaxton, Bridgwater TA5 1DE
☎01278 671362   Fax 01278 671739
✉ kit@enterprise.net
www.houghtonshorses.com

Contacts *Kit Houghton, Debbie Cook*

Specialist equestrian library of over 300,000
transparencies on all aspects of the horse world,
with images ranging from the romantic to the
practical, step-by-step instructional and competition pictures in all equestrian disciplines
worldwide. Online picture delivery.

Chris Howes/Wild Places
Photography
PO Box 100, Abergavenny NP7 9WY
☎01873 737707   Fax 01873 737707
✉ photos@wildplaces.co.uk

Contacts *Chris Howes, Judith Calford*

Expanding collection of over 50,000 colour
transparencies and b&w prints covering travel,
topography and natural history worldwide, plus
action sports such as climbing. SPECIALIST AREAS
include caves, caving and mines (with historical
coverage using engravings and early photographs), wildlife, landscapes and the environment, including pollution and conservation.
Europe (including Britain), USA, Africa and
Australia are all well represented within the collection. Commissions undertaken.

Huntley Film Archive
191 Wardour Street, London W1F 8ZE
☎020 7287 8000   Fax 020 7287 8001
✉ films@huntleyarchives.com
www.huntleyarchives.com

Contact *Amanda Huntley*

Originally a private collection, the library is
now a comprehensive archive of rare and vintage documentary film dating from 1895.

50,000 films on all subjects of a documentary nature. Online catalogue available.

Jacqui Hurst

66 Richford Street, Hammersmith, London W6 7HP
☎020 8743 2315/07970 781336 (mobile)
✉ jacquih@dircon.co.uk
www.jacquihurstphotography.co.uk
Contact *Jacqui Hurst*

A specialist library of traditional and contemporary applied arts, regional food producers and markets. The photos form illustrated essays of how something is made and finish with a still life of the completed object. The collection is always being extended and a list is available on request. Commissions undertaken.

Hutchison Picture Library

65 Brighton Road, Shoreham-by-Sea BN43 6RE
✉ library@hutchisonpictures.co.uk
www.hutchisonpictures.co.uk

Worldwide contemporary images from the straight-forward to the esoteric and quirky. Over half a million documentary colour photographs on file, covering people, places, customs and faiths, agriculture, industry and transport. SPECIAL COLLECTIONS include the environment and climate, family life (including pregnancy and birth), ethnic minorities worldwide (including Disappearing World archive), conventional and alternative medicine, and music around the world. Search service available.

Illustrated London News Picture Library

20 Upper Ground, London SE1 9PF
☎020 7805 5585   Fax 020 7805 5905
✉ research@ilnpictures.co.uk
www.ilnpictures.co.uk

Engravings, photographs and illustrations from 1842 to the present day, taken from magazines published by Illustrated Newspapers: *Illustrated London News*; *Graphic*; *Sphere*; *Tatler*; *Sketch*; *Illustrated Sporting and Dramatic News*; *Illustrated War News 1914–18*; *Bystander*; *Britannia & Eve*. Social history, London, Industrial Revolution, wars, travel. Visitors by appointment.

Images of Africa Photobank

11 The Windings, Lichfield WS13 7EX
☎01543 262898   Fax 01543 417154
✉ info@imagesofafrica.co.uk
www.imagesofafrica.co.uk

Contact *David Keith Jones, FRPS*

Over 135,000 images covering Botswana, Chad, Egypt, Ethiopia, Kenya, Lesotho, Madagasca, Malawi, Morocco, Namibia, Rwanda, South Africa, Swaziland, Tanzania, Uganda, Zaire, Zambia, Zanzibar and Zimbabwe. 'Probably the best collection of photographs of Kenya in Europe.' A wide range of topics are covered. Strong on African wildlife with over 80 species of mammals including many sequences showing action and behaviour. Popular animals like lions and elephants are covered in encyclopædic detail. More than 100 species of birds and many reptiles are included. Other strengths include National Parks and reserves, natural beauty, tourism facilities, traditional and modern people. Most work is by David Keith Jones, FRPS; several other photographers are represented. An attractive colour brochure is available. The Library offers next day delivery by post or same day by e-mail when requested.

Imperial War Museum Photograph Archive

All Saints Annexe, Austral Street, London SE11 4SJ
☎020 7416 5333   Fax 020 7416 5355
✉ photos@iwm.org.uk
www.iwm.org.uk

A national archive of over eight million photographs illustrating all aspects of 20th century conflict. Emphasis on the two world wars but includes material from other conflicts involving Britain and the Commonwealth. Majority of material is b&w, although holdings of colour material increases with more recent conflicts. Visitors welcome by appointment, Monday to Friday, 10.00 am. to 5.00 pm.

Infoterra Ltd

Atlas House, Wembley Road, Leicester LE3 1UT
☎0116 273 2314   Fax 0116 273 2400
✉ david.reed@infoterra-global.com
www.infoterra-global.com
Contact *David Reed*

Leading supplier of earth observation data, including satellite imagery, aerial photography and airborne remote sensing.

International Photobank

Unit D1, Roman Hill Business Park, Broadmayne DT2 8LY
☎01305 854145   Fax 01305 853065
✉ peter@internationalphotobank.co.uk

www.internationalphotobank.co.uk
Over 450,000 transparencies, partly medium-format. Colour coverage of travel subjects: places, people, folklore, events. Assignments undertaken for guide books. ISDN digital service available for newspapers, magazines and other users.

Robbie Jack Photography

45 Church Road, Hanwell, London W7 3BD
☎020 8567 9616   Fax 020 8567 9616
✉ robbie@robbiejack.com
www.robbiejack.com

Contact *Robbie Jack*

Built up over the last 22 years, the library contains over 400,000 colour images of the performing arts – theatre, dance, opera and music. Includes West End shows, the RSC and Royal National Theatre productions, English National Opera and Royal Opera. The dance section contains images of the Royal Ballet, English National Ballet, the Rambert Dance Company, plus many foreign companies. Also holds the largest selection of colour material from the Edinburgh International Festival. Researchers are welcome to visit by appointment. From 2001 began offering colour transparencies as digital images which are being added to on a daily basis.

David King Collection

90 St Pauls Road, London N1 2QP
☎020 7226 0149   Fax 020 7354 8264
✉ davidkingcollection@btopenworld.com
www.davidkingcollection.com

Contact *David King*

250,000 b&w original and copy photographs and colour transparencies of historical and present-day images. Russian history and the Soviet Union from 1900 to the fall of Khrushchev; the lives of Lenin, Trotsky and Stalin; the Tzars, Russo-Japanese War, 1917 Revolution, World War I, Red Army, the Great Purges, Great Patriotic War, etc. SPECIAL COLLECTIONS on China, Eastern Europe, the Weimar Republic, John Heartfield, American labour struggles, Spanish Civil War. Open to qualified researchers by appointment, Monday to Friday, 10.00 am to 6.00 pm. Staff will undertake research; negotiable fee for long projects. David King's latest photographic books: *The Commissar Vanishes*, documenting the falsification of photographs and art in Stalin's Russia, and *Ordinary Citizens*, mugshots of victims shot without trial from the archives of Stalin's secret police. Soviet posters from the David King Collection are on display throughout 2006 at Tate Modern, London.

The Kobal Collection

2 The Quadrant, 135 Salusbury Road, London NW6 6RJ
☎020 7624 3300   Fax 020 7624 3311
✉ info@picture-desk.com
www.picture-desk.com

Colour and b&w coverage of Hollywood films: portraits, stills, publicity shots, posters, ephemera. Visitors by appointment.

Kos Picture Source Ltd

7 Spice Court, Ivory Square, Plantation Wharf, London SW11 3UE
☎020 7801 0044   Fax 020 7801 0055
✉ images@kospictures.com
www.kospictures.com

Specialists in water-related images including international yacht racing and cruising, classic boats and superyachts, and extensive range of watersports. Also worldwide travel including seascapes, beach scenes, underwater photography and the weather.

Ed Lacey Collection

See **Phil Sheldon Golf Picture Library**

Frank Lane Picture Agency Ltd

Pages Green House, Wetheringsett, Stowmarket IP14 5QA
☎01728 860789   Fax 01728 860222
✉ pictures@flpa-images.co.uk
www.flpa-images.co.uk

Colour coverage of natural history, environment, pets and weather. Represents Sunset from France, Foto Natura from Holland, Minden Pictures from the US and works closely with Eric and David Hosking, plus 270 freelance photographers. Website with 60,000 images.

Last Resort Picture Library

Manvers Studios, 12 Ollerton Road, Tuxford, Newark NG22 0LF
☎01777 870166   Fax 01777 871739
✉ LRPL@dmimaging.co.uk
www.dmimaging.co.uk

Contact *Jo Makin*

Subject areas include agriculture, architecture, computing, education, food, industry, landscape, people at work, skiing, trees, flowers. Images cover a wide variety of topics rather than specialising, ranging from the everyday to the obscure. 'Bespoke service available through our linked photographic studio. Contact us for details.'

LAT Photographic

Somerset House, Somerset Road, Teddington
TW11 8RU
☎020 8251 3000   Fax 020 8251 3001
✉ lat.photo@haynet.com
www.latphoto.co.uk

Motor sport collection of over nine million images dating from 1895 to the present day.

André Laubier Picture Library

Flat 2, 1 Bishops Road, London N6 4HP
☎020 8341 2947

An extensive library of photographs from 1935 to the present day in 35mm and medium-format. Main subjects are: archaeology and architecture, art and artists (wood carving, sculptures, contemporary glass), botany, historical buildings, sites and events, landscapes, nature, leisure sports, events, experimental artwork and photography, people and travel. Substantial stock of many other subjects including: birds, buildings and cities, folklore, food and drink, gardens, transport. SPECIAL COLLECTION Images d'Europe (Austria, Britain, France, Greece, S.W. Ireland, Italy, Spain, Turkey, Egypt – from Cairo to Abu Simbel, Norway and former Yugoslavia). Africa and Kenyan safari. PRIVATE COLLECTION World War II to D-Day. List available on request. Correspondence welcome in English, French or German.

Lebrecht Music and Arts

58b Carlton Hill, London NW8 0ES
☎020 7625 5341/7372 8233
Fax 020 7625 5341
✉ pictures@lebrecht.co.uk
www.lebrecht.co.uk

Contact *Elbie Lebrecht*

Classical music, opera, jazz, rock, musicians, instruments, performers, writers, artists, architects, sculptors, historical personalities, politicians, society and glamourous showbusiness personalities.

The Erich Lessing Archive of Fine Art & Culture

c/o ak-images Ltd, The Arts and History Picture Library, 5 Melbray Mews, 158 Hurlingham Road, London SW6 3NS
☎020 7610 6103   Fax 020 7610 6125
✉ enquiries@akg-images.co.uk
www.akg-images.co.uk

Archive of large-format transparencies and high resolution scans depicting the contents of many of the world's finest art galleries as well as ancient archaeological and biblical sites. Represented by **akg-images Ltd**.

Life File Photos Ltd

26 Ambleside Drive, Oxford OX3 0AQ
☎01865 422002   Fax 01865 422002
✉ lifefile@ntlworld.com
www.lifefilephotos.com

Contact *Caroline Birch*

300,000 images of people and places, lifestyles, industry, environmental issues, natural history and customs, from Afghanistan to Zimbabwe. Stocks most of the major tourist destinations throughout the world, including the UK.

Lindley Library, Royal Horticultural Society

80 Vincent Square, London SW1P 2PE
☎020 7821 3051   Fax 020 7821 3022

Contact *Picture Librarian*

22,000 original drawings and approx. 8000 books with hand-coloured plates of botanical illustrations. Appointments are necessary to visit the collection; all photography is carried out by their own photographer.

Link Picture Library

33 Greyhound Road, London W6 8NH
☎020 7381 2261/2433   Fax 020 7385 6244
✉ lib@linkpicturelibrary.com
www.linkpicturelibrary.com

Contact *Orde Eliason*

100,000 images of South Africa, India, China, Vietnam and Israel. A more general collection of colour transparencies from 100 countries worldwide. Link Picture Library has an international network and can source material not in its file from Japan, Scandinavia, India and South Africa. Original photographic commissions undertaken.

London Aerial Photo Library

Studio D1, Fairoaks Airport, Chobham, Woking GU24 8HU
☎01276 855997   Fax 01276 855455
✉ info@londonaerial.co.uk
www.londonaerial.co.uk

Contact *Amanda Campbell*

250,000 colour negatives of aerial photographs covering most of Britain, with particular emphasis on London and surrounding counties. Includes large library of digital images. No search fee. E-mailed library prints are supplied free of charge to enquirers. Welcomes enquiries in respect of either general subjects or specific sites and buildings.

London Metropolitan Archives

40 Northampton Road, London EC1R 0HB
☎020 7332 3820/7278 8703 (Minicom)
Fax 020 7833 9136
✉ ask.lma@corpoflondon.gov.uk
www.cityoflondon.gov.uk/lma

Contact *The Enquiry Team*

London Metropolitan Archives (LMA) is the largest local authority record office in the UK. Holds over 32 miles of archives – an enormous amount of information about the capital and its people. These include records of London government, hospitals, charities, businesses and parish churches. Types of record range from books and manuscript documents to photographs, maps and drawings. 'Nearly 900 years of London history can be brought to life at LMA.' There is also a 100,000 volume reference library specialising in London history. See entry under *Library Services*.

London's Transport Museum Photographic Library

39 Wellington Street, London WC2E 7BB
☎020 7379 6344   Fax 020 7565 7252
www.ltmuseum.co.uk

Contacts *Hugh Robertson, Simon Murphy, Samantha Ratcliffe*

Around 100,000 b&w images from the 1860s and 20,000 colour images from c.1975. SPECIALIST COLLECTIONS Poster archive, Underground construction, corporate design and architecture, street scenes, London Transport during the war. Collection available for viewing by appointment on Monday and Tuesday. No loans system but prints and transparences can be purchased. Digital images available on CD-ROM.

Lonely Planet Images

See **Lonely Planet Publications** under *UK Publishers*

Ludvigsen Library

Scoles Gate, Hawkedon, Bury St Edmunds IP29 4AU
☎01284 789246   Fax 01284 789246
✉ library@ludvigsen.com
www.ludvigsen.com

Contact *Karl Ludvigsen*

Extensive information research facilities for writers and publishers. Approx. 400,000 images (both b&w and many colour transparencies) of auto-mobiles and motorsport, from 1890s through 1980s. Glass plate negatives from the early 1900s; Formula One, Le Mans, motor car shows, vintage, antique and classic cars from all countries. Includes the Dalton-Watson Collection and the work of noted photographers such as John Dugdale, Edward Eves, Peter Keen, Max le Grand, Karl Ludvigsen, Rodolfo Mailander, Ove Nielsen, Stanley Rosenthall and others.

MacQuitty International Photographic Collection

7 Elm Lodge, River Gardens, Stevenage Road, London SW6 6NZ
☎020 7385 5606   Fax 020 7385 5606
✉ miranda.macquitty@btinternet.com

Contact *Dr Miranda MacQuitty*

Colour and b&w collection on aspects of life in over 70 countries: dancing, music, religion, death, archaeology, buildings, transport, food, drink, nature. Visitors by appointment.

Magnum Photos Ltd

Ground Floor, 63 Gee Street, London EC1V 3RS
☎020 7490 1771   Fax 020 7608 0020
✉ magnum@magnumphotos.co.uk
www.magnumphotos.com

Head of Library *Hamish Crooks*

Founded 1947 by Cartier Bresson, George Rodger, Robert Capa and David 'Chim' Seymour. Represents over 50 of the world's leading photo-journalists. Coverage of all major world events from the Spanish Civil War to present day. Also a large collection of personalities.

The Raymond Mander & Joe Mitchenson Theatre Collection

Jerwood Library of the Performing Arts, Trinity College of Music, King Charles Court, Old Royal Naval College, London SE10 9JF
☎020 8305 4426   Fax 020 8305 9426
✉ rmangan@tcm.ac.uk
www.mander-and-mitchenson.co.uk

Contact *Richard Mangan*

Enormous collection covering all aspects of the theatre: plays, actors, dramatists, music hall, theatres, singers, composers, etc. Visitors welcome by appointment.

The Roger Mann Collection

Wensley Court, 48 Barton Road, Torquay TQ1 4DW
☎01803 323868   Fax 01803 616448
✉ rogermann48bart@aol.com

www.therogermanncollection.co.uk

Contact *R.F. Mann*

Comprehensive collection of cricket photographs covering the period 1750–1945. The photographs feature most of the first-class players, teams, Test match action and overseas tours of the period. This collection includes almost 2000 original match scorecards, cartoons, images, prints, postcards, cigarette cards, letters and the personal memorabilia of many of the best-known players of the time. Also some coverage of the period 1946–1970.

S&O Mathews Photography

Little Pitt Place, Brighstone, Isle of Wight PO30 4DZ

☎01983 741098   Fax 01983 740592

✉ oliver@mathews-photography.com

www.mathews-photography.com

Specialist stock library of fine photographs of botanical and horticultural subjects, plants, plant portraits and plant associations, as well as gardens, including views, details and features.

Institution of Mechanical Engineers

1 Birdcage Walk, London SW1H 9JJ

☎020 7973 1265   Fax 020 7222 8762

✉ library@imeche.org.uk

www.imeche.org.uk

Historical images and archives on mechanical engineering. Open 9.15 am to 5.30 pm, Monday to Friday. Telephone for appointment.

Meledin Collection

See **Mary Evans Picture Library**

The MerseySlides Collection

c/o Tropix Photo Library, 44 Woodbines Avenue, Kingston-upon-Thames KT1 2AY

☎020 8546 0823/0151 625 4576

Fax 0870 706 1317

✉ images@tropix.co.uk

www.tropix.co.uk

Contact *Veronica Birley*

The MerseySlides Collection comes from **Tropix Photo Library** and contains powerful images of Liverpool, Merseyside, Wirral, Cheshire and much of North West England. Also North Wales, Scotland, other parts of England, Ireland and some Europe. Assignment and studio photography are regularly undertaken for a wide range of clients, both commercial and editorial. Photography is available in all formats including digital and panoramic.

Lee Miller Archives

Farley Farm House, Chiddingly, Near Lewes BN8 6HW

☎01825 872691   Fax 01825 872733

✉ archives@leemiller.co.uk

www.leemiller.co.uk

The work of Lee Miller (1907–77). As a photojournalist she covered the war in Europe from early in 1941 to VE Day with further reporting from the Balkans. Collection includes photographic portraits of prominent Surrealist artists: Ernst, Eluard, Miró, Picasso, Penrose, Carrington, Tanning, and others. Surrealist and contemporary art, poets and writers, fashion, the Middle East, Egypt, the Balkans in the 1930s, London during the Blitz, war in Europe and the liberation of Dachau and Buchenwald.

Mirrorpix

21 Bruton Street, London W1J 6QD

☎020 7293 3700   Fax 020 7293 2712

✉ desk@mirrorpix.com

www.mirrorpix.com

Commercial Director *John Churchill*

Contact *Lisa Rayman*

For the past 100 years the photographers of the *Daily Mirror* and its sister titles have recorded both the light and dark sides of British life in startling detail. The people, places, events and movements that have shaped modern Britain can be found in the comprehensive catalogue.

Monitor Picture Library

The Forge, Roydon, Harlow CM19 5HH

☎01279 792700   Fax 01279 792600

✉ info@monitorpicturelibrary.com

www.monitorpicturelibrary.com

Colour and b&w coverage of 1960s, '70s and '80s personalities and celebrities from: music, entertainment, sport, politics, royals, judicial, commerce etc. Specialist files on Lotus cars. Syndication to international, national and local media.

Moroccan Scapes

Seend Park, Seend SN12 6NZ

☎01380 828533   Fax 01380 828630

✉ chris@realmorocco.com

www.realmorocco.com

Contact *Chris Lawrence*

Specialist collection of Moroccan material: scenery, towns, people, markets and places, plus the Atlas Mountains. Over 18,000 images.

Motoring Picture Library

National Motor Museum, Beaulieu
SO42 7ZN
☎01590 614656   Fax 01590 612655
✉ motoring.pictures@beaulieu.co.uk
www.motoringpicturelibrary.com

Contact *Jonathan Day*

Three-quarters of a million b&w images, plus
100,000 colour images covering all forms of
motoring history from the 1880s to the present
day. Commissions undertaken. Own studio.

Mountain Camera

See **John Cleare**

Moving Image Communications

The Maidstone Studios, Vinters Park,
Maidstone ME14 5NZ
☎01622 684569   Fax 01622 687444
✉ mail@milibrary.com
www.milibrary.com

Contact *Nathalie Banaigs*

Over 16,000 hours of quality archive and con-
temporary footage, including: Channel X; TVAM
Archive 1983–92; British Tourist Authority –
BTA (1930 to present day); Drummer Films
(travel classics, 1950–70); The Freud Archive
(1930–39); Film Finders (early cinema); Adrian
Brunel Films; Cuban Archives; Stockshots (time-
lapse, cityscapes, land and seascapes, chroma-key);
Space Exploration (NASA); Wild Islands; Flying
Pictures; National Trust.

Museum of Antiquities
Picture Library

University and Society of Antiquaries of
Newcastle upon Tyne, Newcastle upon Tyne
NE1 7RU
☎0191 222 7846   Fax 0191 222 8561
✉ m.o.antiquities@ncl.ac.uk
www.ncl.ac.uk/antiquities

Contact *Lindsay Allason-Jones*

25,000 images, mostly b&w, of special collections including: Hadrian's Wall Archive (b&ws
taken over the last 100 years); Gertrude Bell
Archive (during her travels in the Near East,
1900–26); and aerial photographs of archaeological sites in the North of England. Visitors
welcome by appointment.

Museum of London
Picture Library

150 London Wall, London EC2Y 5HN
☎020 7814 5604   Fax 020 7600 1058
✉ picturelib@museumoflondon.org.uk

The Museum of London Picture Library tells the
story of London from its earliest settlers to the
present day. Suffragettes: photographs and memorabilia; Museum Objects: gallery and reserve
collections – Prehistoric, Roman, Saxon,
Medieval, Tudor, Stuart, Georgian, Victorian,
London Now; Photographs: social history of the
capital – working life, East End, inter-war years,
the Blitz, post-war; Prints and Caricatures: political and social satire, architecture; Paintings: dating
from the 17th century, portraits, landscapes,
cityscapes.

The National Archives

Ruskin Avenue, Kew, Richmond TW9 4DU
☎020 8392 5225   Fax 020 8487 1974
✉ image-library@nationalarchives.gov.uk

Contacts *Paul Johnson, Hugh Alexander*

British and colonial history from the Domesday
Book to the 1970s, shown in photography, maps,
illuminations, posters, advertisements, textiles
and original manuscripts. Approximately 30,000
5"x4" and 35mm colour transparencies and b&w
negatives. Open: 9.00 am to 5.00 pm, Monday to
Friday.

National Galleries of Scotland
Picture Library

The Dean Gallery, Belford Road, Edinburgh
EH4 3DS
☎0131 624 6258/6260   Fax 0131 623 7135
✉ picture.library@nationalgalleries.org

Contact *Deborah Hunter*

Over 80,000 b&w and several thousand images
in colour of works of art from the Renaissance
to present day. SPECIALIST SUBJECTS cover fine
art (painting, sculpture, drawing), portraits,
Scottish, historical, still life, photography and
landscape. Colour leaflet and CD-ROM guide
available on request.

National Maritime Museum
Picture Library

Greenwich, London SE10 9NF
☎020 8312 6631/6704   Fax 020 8312 6533
✉ picturelibrary@nmm.ac.uk
www.nmm.ac.uk/picturelibrary

Contacts *David Taylor, Doug McCarthy*

Over 400,000 maritime-related images, including
oil paintings from the 16th century to present
day, prints and drawings, historic photographs,
plans of ships built in the UK since the beginning
of the 18th century, models, rare maps and charts,
globes, manuscripts, navigation and scientific
instruments, etc. Over 80,000 items within the

collection are now photographed and with the Historic Photographs Collection form the basis of the picture library's stock.

National Meteorological Library and Archive

See entry under **Library Services**

National Monuments Record

National Monuments Record Centre, Kemble Drive, Great Western Village, Swindon SN2 2GZ
☎01793 414600   Fax 01793 414606
✉ nmrinfo@english-heritage.org.uk
www.english-heritage.org.uk

The National Monuments Record is the first stop for photographs and information on England's heritage. Over 10 million photographs, documents and drawings are held. English architecture from the first days of photography to the present, air photographs covering every inch of England from the first days of flying to the present, and archaeological sites. The Record is the public archive of English Heritage (see **English Heritage Photo Library**).

National Museum of Photography, Film & Television

See **Science & Society Picture Library**

National Portrait Gallery Picture Library

St Martin's Place, London WC2H 0HE
☎020 7312 2474/5/6   Fax 020 7312 2464
✉ picturelibrary@npg.org.uk
www.npg.org.uk

Contact *Tom Morgan*

Pictures of brilliant, daring and influential characters who have made British history are available for publication. Images can be searched, viewed and ordered on the website. Copyright clearance is arranged for all images supplied.

National Railway Museum Research Centre

Leeman Road, York YO26 4XJ
☎01904 686235   Fax 01904 611112
✉ nrm.researchcentre@nmsi.ac.uk
www.nrm.org.uk

Part of the **Science & Society Picture Library**. 1.5 million images, mainly b&w, covering every aspect of railways from 1850s to the present day. Open Monday to Friday, 10.00 am to 5.00 pm. Visitors by prior (telephone) appointment.

The National Trust Photo Library

36 Queen Anne's Gate, London SW1H 9AS
☎020 7447 6788/9   Fax 020 7447 6767
✉ photo.library@nationaltrust.org.uk
www.ntpl.org.uk

Contact *Chris Lacey*

Collection of mixed-format transparencies covering landscape and coastline throughout England, Wales and Northern Ireland; also architecture, interiors, gardens, paintings and conservation, plus a new collection of wildlife photographs. Award-winning brochure available on request. Profits from the picture library are reinvested in continuing the work of the Trust.

Natural History Museum Picture Library

Cromwell Road, London SW7 5BD
☎020 7942 5401/5324   Fax 020 7942 5212
✉ nhmpl@nhm.ac.uk
www.nhm.ac.uk/piclib

Contacts *Rupert Calvocoressi, Jamie Owen*

Pictures from the Museum's collections, including dinosaurs, man's evolution, extinct species and fossil remains. Also pictures of gems, minerals, birds and animals, plants and insect specimens, plus historical artworks depicting the natural world.

Nature Photographers Ltd

West Wit, New Road, Little London, Tadley RG26 5EU
☎01256 850661
✉ info@naturephotographers.co.uk
www.naturephotographers.co.uk

Contact *Dr Paul Sterry*

Over 150,000 images on worldwide natural history and environmental subjects. The library is run by a trained biologist and experienced author on his subject.

Nature Picture Library

BBC Broadcasting House, Whiteladies Road, Bristol BS8 2LR
☎0117 974 6720   Fax 0117 923 8166
✉ info@naturepl.com
www.naturepl.com

Contact *Helen Gilks*

A collection of 150,000 nature photos from around the world, including strong coverage of animal portraits and behaviour. Other subjects covered include plants, pets, landscapes and travel, environmental issues and wildlife film-makers at work. Thousands of images can be viewed online and downloaded direct for reproduction.

Peter Newark's Picture Library

3 Barton Buildings, Queen Square, Bath
BA1 2JR
☎01225 334213   Fax 01225 480554

Over one million images covering world history from ancient times to the present day. Includes an extensive military collection of photographs, paintings and illustrations. Also a special collection on American history covering Colonial times, exploration, social, political and the Wild West and Native-Americans in particular. Subject list available. Telephone, fax or write for further information.

NHPA Ltd

Little Tye, 57 High Street, Ardingly RH17 6TB
☎01444 892514   Fax 01444 892168
✉ nhpa@nhpa.co.uk
www.nhpa.co.uk

Library Manager *Tim Harris*

Extensive coverage on all aspects of natural history – animals, plants, landscapes, environmental issues, gardens and pets. Over 150 photographers worldwide provide a steady input of high-quality images. SPECIALIST FILES include the unique high-speed photography of Stephen Dalton, extensive coverage of African and American wildlife, also rainforests, marine life and the polar regions. UK agents for the ANT collection of Australasian material. Pictures are generally supplied direct to publishers; individual writers must request material via their publisher. See the website to view over 29,000 pictures available at high resolution.

Odhams Periodicals Library

See **Popperfoto.com**

Offshoot

See **Skishoot**

Only Horses Picture Agency

27 Greenway Gardens, Greenford UB6 9TU
☎020 8578 9047   Fax 020 8575 7244
✉ onlyhorsespics@aol.com
www.onlyhorsespictures.com

Colour and b&w coverage of all aspects of the horse. Foaling, retirement, racing, show jumping, eventing, veterinary, polo, breeds, personalities.

Oxford Picture Library

15 Curtis Yard, North Hinksey Lane, Oxford
OX2 0LX
☎01865 723404   Fax 01865 725294
✉ opl@cap-ox.com

www.cap-ox.co.uk

Contacts *Chris Andrews, Annabel Matthews*

Specialist collection on Oxford: the city, university and colleges, events, people, spires and shires. Also, the Cotswolds, architecture and landscape from Stratford-upon-Avon to Bath; the Thames and Chilterns, including Henley on Thames and Windsor; Channel Islands, especially Guernsey and Sark. Aerial views of all areas specified above. General collection includes wildlife, trees, plants, clouds, sun, sky, water and teddy bears. Commissions undertaken.

Oxford Scientific (OSF)

Ground Floor, Network House, Station Yard,
Thame OX9 3UH
☎01844 262370   Fax 01844 262380
✉ enquiries@osf.co.uk
www.osf.co.uk

Account Executives *Rebecca Marsden* (stills),
    Sandra Berry (footage)

Collection of 350,000 colour transparencies and digital files of wildlife and natural science images supplied by over 300 photographers worldwide, covering all aspects of wildlife plus landscapes, weather, seasons, plants, pets, environment, anthropology, habitats, science and industry, space, creative textures and backgrounds, and geology. Macro and micro photography. UK agents for Animals Animals, USA, Okapia, Germany and Dinodia, India. Research by experienced researchers for specialist and creative briefs. Visits welcome, by appointment.

Hugh Palmer

21 Walton Crescent, Oxford OX1 2JG
✉ hugh@hughpalmer.com
www.hughpalmer.com

Extensive collection of landscapes, rural life and architecture from Britain and Europe, as featured in *The Most Beautiful Villages* series of books published by Thames & Hudson.

Panos Pictures

1 Honduras Street, London EC1Y 0TH
☎07814 791830
✉ pics@panos.co.uk
www.panos.co.uk

Documentary colour and b&w library specialising in Third World and Eastern Europe, with emphasis on environment and development issues. Leaflet available. Fifty per cent of all profits from this library go to the Panos Institute to further its work in international sustainable development.

Charles Parker Archive
See **Birmingham Library Services** under
Library Services

Ann & Bury Peerless Picture Library
St David's, 22 King's Avenue, Minnis Bay,
Birchington-on-Sea CT7 9QL
☎01843 841428   Fax 01843 848321
www.peerlessimages.com

Contacts *Ann Peerless, Bury Peerless*

Specialist collection on world religions: Hinduism, Buddhism, Confucianism, Taoism, Jainism, Christianity, Islam, Sikhism, Zoroastrianism (Parsees of India). Geographical areas covered: India, Afghanistan (Bamiyan Valley of the Buddhas), Pakistan, Bangladesh, Sri Lanka, Cambodia (Angkor), Java (Borobudur), Bali, Thailand, Russia, Republic of China, Spain, Poland, Uzbekistan (Samarkand and Bukhara), Vietnam. Basis of collection (35mm colour transparencies), historical, cultural, extensive coverage of art (sculpture and miniature paintings), architecture including Pharaonic Egypt.

Photofusion
17A Electric Lane, London SW9 8LA
☎020 7733 3500   Fax 020 7738 5509
✉ library@photofusion.org
www.photofusion.org

Contact *Liz Somerville*

Colour and b&w coverage of contemporary social and environmental UK issues including babies and children, disability, education, the elderly, environment, family, health, housing, homelessness, people and work. Brochure available.

The Photolibrary Wales
2 Bro-nant, Church Road, Pentyrch, Cardiff CF15 9QG
☎029 2089 0311   Fax 029 2089 0311
✉ info@photolibrarywales.com
www.photolibrarywales.com

Contacts *Steve Benbow, Kate Benbow*

Over 100,000 colour transparences covering all areas and subjects of Wales. Represents the work of 140 photographers, living and working in Wales.

Photos Horticultural
PO Box 105, Ipswich IP1 4PR
☎01473 257329   Fax 01473 233974
✉ library@photos-horticultural.com
www.photos-horticultural.com

Wide selection of horticultural subjects, gardens, practical, plants cultivated and wild from around the world. Now available online via the website. Commissions for photography and illustrated features undertaken.

PictureBank Photo Library Ltd
Parman House, 30–36 Fife Road, Kingston upon Thames KT1 1SY
☎020 8547 2344   Fax 020 8974 5652
✉ info@picturebank.co.uk
www.picturebank.co.uk

Over 400,000 colour transparencies covering people (girls, couples, families, children), travel and scenic (UK and world), moods (sunsets, seascapes, deserts, etc.), industry and technology, environments and general. Commissions undertaken. Visitors welcome. Member of **BAPLA**. New material on medium/large format welcome.

Pictures Colour Library
10 James Whatman Court, Turkey Mill, Ashford Road, Maidstone ME14 5SS
☎01622 609809   Fax 01622 609806
✉ Researcher@PicturesColourLibrary.co.uk
www.picturescolourlibrary.co.uk

Travel and travel-related images depicting lifestyles and cultures, people and places, attitudes and environments from around the world, including a comprehensive section on Great Britain.

H.G. Ponting
See **Popperfoto.com**

Popperfoto.com
The Old Mill, Overstone Farm, Overstone, Northampton NN6 0AB
☎01604 670670   Fax 01604 670635
✉ inquiries@popperfoto.com
www.popperfoto.com

Home to over 14 million images, covering 150 years of photographic history. Renowned for its archival material, a world-famous sports library and stock photography. Popperfoto's credit line includes Bob Thomas Sports Photography, UPI, Acme, INP, Planet, Paul Popper, Exclusive News Agency, Victory Archive, Odhams Periodicals Library, Illustrated, Harris Picture Agency, and H.G. Ponting. Colour from 1940, b&w from 1870 to the present. Major subjects covered worldwide include events, personalities, wars, royalty, sport, politics, transport, crime, history and social conditions. Material available on the same day to clients throughout the world. Nearly

200,000 high-resolution images online available by direct download, e-mail, ISDN, FTP and CD. Researchers welcome by appointment.

PPL (Photo Agency) Ltd
Bookers Yard, The Street, Walberton, Arundel BN18 0PF
☎01243 555561　Fax 01243 555562
✉ ppl@mistral.co.uk
www.pplmedia.com

Contacts *Barry Pickthall, Emma Brenton*

Two million pictures covering watersports, sub-aqua, business and commerce, travel and tourism; pictures of yesteryear and a fast growing archive on Sussex and the home counties. Pictures available in high resolution directly from website.

Premaphotos Wildlife
Amberstone, 1 Kirland Road, Bodmin PL30 5JQ
☎01208 78258　Fax 01208 72302
✉ authors@premaphotos.co.uk
www.premaphotos.com

Contact *Jean Preston-Mafham*, Library Manager
Natural history worldwide. Subjects include flowering and non-flowering plants, fungi, slime moulds, fruits and seeds, galls, leaf mines, seashore life, mammals, birds, reptiles, amphibians, insects, spiders, habitats, scenery and cultivated cacti. Commissions undertaken. Visitors welcome. 'Make sure your name is on our mailing list to receive regular, colourful mailers.'

Professional Sport UK Ltd
18–19 Shaftesbury Quay, Hertford SG14 1SF
☎01992 505000　Fax 01992 505020
✉ pictures@prosport.co.uk
www.professionalsport.com

Photographic coverage of tennis, soccer, athletics, golf, cricket, rugby, winter sports and many minor sports. Major international events including the Olympic Games, World Cup soccer and all Grand Slam tennis events. Also news and feature material supplied worldwide. Online photo archive; photo transmission services available for editorial and advertising.

Public Record Office Image Library
See **The National Archives**

Punch Cartoon Library
87–135 Brompton Road, London SW1X 8XL
☎020 7225 6710　Fax 020 7225 6712
✉ punch.library@harrods.com
www.punch.co.uk

Owner *Punch Limited*
Gives access to the 500,000 cartoons published in *Punch* magazine between 1841–1992. The library has a 500+ subject listing and can search on any topic. Social history, politics, fashion, fads, famous people and more by the world's most famous cartoonists, including Tenniel, du Maurier, Pont, Fougasse, E.H. Shepard and Emmett.

PWA International Ltd
4 Brightfield Road, Lee, London SE12 8QF
☎020 8297 3434　Fax 020 8297 0617
✉ pwaint@dircon.co.uk
www.pwainternational.com

Contact *Terry Allen*

Leading comprehensive library of story illustrations comprising work by some of the UK's best-known illustrators, including book covers and magazines.

Railfotos
Millbrook House Ltd., Unit 1, Oldbury Business Centre, Pound Road, Oldbury B68 8NA
☎0121 544 2970　Fax 0121 253 6836 (quote Millbrook House)

One of the largest specialist libraries dealing with railway subjects worldwide. Colour and b&w dating from the turn of the century to present day. Up-to-date material on UK, South America and Far East. Visitors by appointment.

Redferns Music Picture Library
7 Bramley Road, London W10 6SZ
☎020 7792 9914　Fax 020 7792 0921
✉ info@redferns.com
www.redferns.com

Picture library covering every aspect of music, from 18th century classical to present day pop. Over one million archived artists and other subjects including musical instruments, recording studios, crowd scenes, festivals, etc. Brochure available. Over 150,000 images available on the website.

Retna Pictures Ltd
Stills Road, Pinewood Studios, Pinewood Road, Iver Heath SL0 0NH
☎01753 785450　Fax 01753 785 451
✉ ukinfo@retna.co.uk
www.retna.co.uk

Established 1978, Retna Pictures Ltd is a leading picture agency with two libraries: celebrity/music and lifestyle. The former specialises in images of international and national celebrities, early and contemporary music, films and personalities. The lifestyle library specialises in people, family life, work, leisure and food. Both libraries are constantly receiving new material from established and up and coming photographers.

Rex Features Ltd
18 Vine Hill, London EC1R 5DZ
☎020 7278 7294   Fax 020 7696 0974
✉ library@rexfeatures.com
www.rexfeatures.com
Contact *Glen Marks*, Sales Manager
Extensive picture library established in the 1950s. Daily coverage of news, politics, personalities, showbusiness, glamour, humour, art, medicine, science, landscapes, royalty, etc.

Royal Air Force Museum
Grahame Park Way, Hendon, London NW9 5LL
☎020 8205 2266   Fax 020 8200 1751
✉ photographic@rafmuseum.org
About a quarter of a million images, mostly b&w, with around 1500 colour in all formats, on the history of aviation. Particularly strong on the activities of the Royal Air Force from the 1870s to 1970s. Researchers are requested to enquire in writing only.

The Royal Collection, Photographic Services
Windsor Castle, Windsor SL4 1NJ
☎01753 868286   Fax 01753 620046
✉ photoservices@royalcollection.org.uk
Contact *Shruti Patel*
Photographic material of items in the Royal Collection, particularly oil paintings, drawings and watercolours, works of art, and interiors and exteriors of royal residences. 35,000 colour transparencies, plus 25,000 b&w negatives.

Royal Geographical Society Picture Library
1 Kensington Gore, London SW7 2AR
☎020 7591 3060   Fax 020 7591 3061
✉ pictures@rgs.org
www.rgs.org/picturelibrary
Contact *Justin Hobson*
A strong source of geographical and historical images, both archival and modern, showing the world through the eyes of photographers and explorers dating from the 1830s to the present day. The RGS Contempory Collection provides up-to-date transparencies from around the

world, highlighting aspects of cultural activity, environmental phenomena, anthropology, architectural design, travel, mountaineering and exploration. Offers a professional and comprehensive service for both commercial and academic use.

RSPB Images
PO Box 7515, Billericay CM11 1WR
☎01268 711471   Fax 01268 710353
✉ rspb@thatsgood.biz
www.rspb-images.com
Contact *Wendy Hollis*
Colour images of birds, butterflies, moths, mammals, reptiles and their habitats. Also colour images of all RSPB reserves. Growing selection of various habitats. Online search facility of over 30,000 digitised images.

RSPCA Photolibrary
RSPCA Trading Limited, Wilberforce Way, Southwater, Horsham RH13 9RS
☎0870 754 0150   Fax 0870 753 0150
✉ pictures@rspcaphotolibrary.com
www.rspcaphotolibrary.com
Photolibrary Manager *Andrew Forsyth*
Over 100,000 colour transparencies and over 5000 b&w/colour prints. A comprehensive collection of natural history images whose subjects include mammals, birds, domestic and farm animals, amphibians, insects and the environment, as well as a unique photographic record of the RSPCA's work. Also includes the Wild Images collections. Catalogue available. No search fees.

Russia and Eastern Images
'Sonning', Cheapside Lane, Denham, Uxbridge UB9 5AE
☎01895 833508
✉ easteuropix@btinternet.com
www.easteuropix.com
Architecture, cities, landscapes, people and travel images of Russia and the former Soviet Union. Considerable background knowledge available and Russian language spoken.

Peter Sanders Photography Ltd
24 Meades Lane, Chesham HP5 1ND
☎01494 773674/771372   Fax 01494 773674
✉ photos@petersanders.com
www.petersanders.com
Contacts *Peter Sanders, Hafsa Garwatuk*
Specialises in the world of Islam in all its aspects from culture, arts, industry, lifestyles, celebrations, etc. Areas included are north, east and

west Africa, the Middle East (including Saudi Arabia), China, Asia, Europe and USA. A continually expanding library.

ScenicIreland.com
See **Christopher Hill Photographic**

Science & Society Picture Library
Science Museum, Exhibition Road, London SW7 2DD
☎020 7942 4400   Fax 020 7942 4401
✉ piclib@nmsi.ac.uk
www.nmsi.ac.uk/piclib/
Contact *David Thompson*

'The Science & Society Picture Library has one of the widest ranges of photographs, paintings, prints, posters and objects in the world.' The images come from the Science Museum, the **National Railway Museum** and the National Museum of Photography, Film & Television which now includes the Royal Photographic Society collection. Images are available as high or low resolution files via e-mail, FTP or direct from the website.

Science Museum
See **Science & Society Picture Library**

Science Photo Library
327–329 Harrow Road, London W9 3RB
☎020 7432 1100   Fax 020 7286 8668
✉ info@sciencephoto.com
www.sciencephoto.com

Subjects covered include the human body, health and medicine, research, genetics, technology and industry, space exploration and astronomy, earth science, satellite imagery, environment, flowers, plants and gardens, nature and wildlife and the history of science. The whole collection, more than 150,000 images, is available online.

Seaco Picture Library
Sea Containers House, 20 Upper Ground, London SE1 9PF
☎020 7805 5831   Fax 020 7805 5905
✉ seaco.pictures@seacontainers.com
Contact *Luci Gosling*

Approx. 250,000 images of containerisation, shipping, fast ferries, manufacturing, fruit farming, ports, hotels and leisure.

Mick Sharp Photography
Eithinog, Waun, Penisarwaun, Caernarfon LL55 3PW
☎01286 872425   Fax 01286 872425
✉ mick.jean@virgin.net

Contacts *Mick Sharp, Jean Williamson*

Archaeology, ancient monuments, buildings, churches, countryside, environment, history, landscape, past cultures and topography. Emphasis on British Isles but material also from other countries. Features the photos of both Mick Sharp and Jean Williamson. Access to other specialist collections on related subjects. Commissions undertaken. Medium format and 35mm colour transparencies plus b&w prints from 5×4 negatives.

Phil Sheldon Golf Picture Library
40 Manor Road, Barnet EN5 2JQ
☎020 8440 1986   Fax 020 8440 9348
✉ gill@philsheldongolfpics.co.uk *or*
phil@philsheldongolfpics.co.uk
www.philsheldongolfpics.co.uk

An expanding collection of over 600,000 quality images of the 'world of golf'. In-depth worldwide tournament coverage including every Major championship and Ryder Cup since 1976. Instruction, portraits, trophies and over 400 golf courses from around the world. Also the Dale Concannon collection covering the period 1870 to 1940, the classic 1960s collection by photographer Sidney Harris and the Ed Lacey Collection.

Skishoot–Offshoot
Hall Place, Upper Woodcott, Whitchurch RG28 7PY
☎01635 255527   Fax 01635 255528
✉ skishootsnow@aol.com
www.skishoot.co.uk
Contacts *Kate Parker, Jo Crossley*

Skishoot ski and snowboarding picture library has 400,000 images. Offshoot travel library specialises in France.

The Skyscan Photolibrary
Oak House, Toddington, Cheltenham GL54 5BY
☎01242 621357   Fax 01242 621343
✉ info@skyscan.co.uk
www.skyscan.co.uk

As well as the Skyscan Photolibrary collection of unique balloon's-eye views of Britain, the library now includes the work of photographers from across the aviation spectrum; air to ground, aviation, aerial sports – 'in fact, anything aerial!' Links have been built with photographers across the world; photographs can be handled on an agency basis and held in house, or as a brokerage where the collection stays with the photographer; terms 50/50 for both. Commissioned photography arranged. Enquiries welcome.

Snookerimages (Eric Whitehead Photography)
25 Oak Street, Windermere LA23 1EN
☎015394 48894
✉ snooker@snookerimages.co.uk
www.snookerimages.co.uk
Over 30,000 images of snooker from 1982 to the present day.

Solo Syndication Ltd
17–18 Haywards Place, Clerkenwell, London EC1R 0EQ
☎020 7566 0360   Fax 020 7566 0388

Syndication Director *Trevor York*
Sales *Danny Howell, Nick York*
Online transmissions *Geoff Malyon*
(☎020 7566 0370)
Three million images from the archives of the *Daily Mail, Mail on Sunday, Evening Standard* and *Evening News*. Hard prints or Mac-to-Mac delivery. 24-hour service.

Sotheby's Picture Library
34-35 New Bond Street, London W1A 2AA
☎020 7293 5383   Fax 020 7293 5062
✉ piclib.london@sothebys.com

Contacts *Joanna Ling, Sue Daly*

The library consists of over 200,000 selected transparencies of pictures sold at Sotheby's. Images from the 15th to the 20th century. Oils, drawings, watercolours, prints and decorative items. 'Happy to do searches or, alternatively, visitors are welcome by appointment.'

South American Pictures
48 Station Road, Woodbridge IP12 4AT
☎01394 383963   Fax 01394 380176
✉ morrison@southamericanpictures.com
www.southamericanpictures.com
Specialist site: www.nonesuchinfo.info

Contact *Marion Morrison*

Colour and b&w images of South/Central America, Cuba, Mexico, New Mexico (USA), Dominican Republic and Haiti, including archaeology and the Amazon. There is an archival section, with pictures and documents from most countries. Now with 40 contributing photographers. All images are supplied digitally.

The Special Photographers Library
236 Westbourne Park Road, London W11 1EL
☎020 7221 3489   Fax 020 7792 9112
✉ info@specialphotographers.com
www.specialphotographers.com

Represents over 100 contemporary fine art photographers who are unusual in style, technique or subject matter.

Still Digital
8 Saxe Coburg Place, Edinburgh EH3 5BR
☎0131 332 3874
✉ info@stilldigital.co.uk
www.stilldigital.co.uk

Contact *John Hutchinson*

Fully searchable and downloadable service for thousands of Scottish images.

Still Pictures' Whole Earth Photolibrary
199 Shooters Hill Road, London SE3 8UL
☎020 8858 8307   Fax 020 8858 2049
✉ info@stillpictures.com
www.stillpictures.com

Contacts *Kate Watson, Mark Edwards*

Founded 1970. High profile photo library specialising in environment, the Third World, social issues and nature. Represents 10 leading European and US agencies and over 400 photographers as well as the United Nations Environment Programme (UNEP) archive, the Christian Aid collection (see entry) and a growing selection of images from Woodfall Wild Images (see entry). The website has nearly 100,000 images online, ready for instant download.

Stockfile
5 High Street, Sunningdale SL5 0LX
☎01344 872249   Fax 01344 872263
✉ info@stockfile.co.uk
www.stockfile.co.uk

Contacts *Jill Behr, Steven Behr*

Specialist cycling collection with emphasis on mountain biking. Expanding adventure sports section covering snow, land, air and water activities.

Stockscotland.com
Croft Studio, Croft Roy, Crammond Brae, Tain IV19 1JG
☎01862 892298   Fax 01862 892298
✉ info@stockscotland.com
www.stockscotland.com

Contact *Hugh Webster*

150,000 Scottish images with 10,000 currently available online.

Sir John Benjamin Stone
See **Birmingham Library Services** under *Library Services*

Jessica Strang Photo Library
504 Brody House, Strype Street, London
E1 7LQ
☎020 7247 8982   Fax 020 7247 8982
✉ jessica@jessicastrang.plus.com

Contact *Jessica Strang*

Approximately 60,000 transparencies covering architecture, interiors (contemporary), gardens, 'obsessive and not just small but tiny, or from almost no space at all', men, women, couples and animals in architecture, and vanishing London details. Recycled ideas for the home.

Joe Tasker Collection
See **Chris Bonington Picture Library**

Tate Enterprises Picture Library
Top Floor, The Lodge, Tate Britain, Millbank, London SW1P 4RG
☎020 7887 8871   Fax 020 7887 8805
✉ picture.library@tate.org.uk
www.tate.org.uk

Contact *Alison Miles*

Approximately 8000 images of British art from the 16th century; international 20th century painting and sculpture. Artists include William Blake, William Hogarth, J.M.W. Turner, Dante Gabriel Rossetti, Barbara Hepworth, Henry Moore, Stanley Spencer, Pablo Picasso, Mark Rothko, Salvador Dali, Lucien Freud and David Hockney. Colour transparencies of more than half the works in the main collection are available for hire. For a fee, new photography is available depending on the location and condition of the art work. B&w prints of nearly all the works in the collection can be purchased. Colour slides and prints can be made on request providing a colour transparency exists. A digital service for picture buyers is under development and a specific site, accessible on the Tate homepage, will be available in 2006.

Bob Thomas Sports Photography
See **Popperfoto.com**

Thoroughbred Photography Ltd
The Hornbeams, 2 The Street, Worlington
IP28 8RU
☎01638 713944
✉ mail@thoroughbredphoto.com
www.thoroughbredphoto.com

Contacts *Trevor Jones, Gill Jones, Laura Green*

Extensive library of high-quality colour images depicting all aspects of thoroughbred horseracing dating from 1987. Major group races, English Classics, studs, stallions, mares and foals, early morning scenes, personalities, jockeys, trainers and prominent owners. Also international work: USA Breeders' Cup, Arc de Triomphe, French Classics, Irish Derby, Dubai racing scenes, Japan Cup and Hokkaido stud farms; and more unusual scenes such as racing on the sands at low tide, Ireland, and on the frozen lake at St Moritz. Visitors by appointment.

Rick Tomlinson Marine Photo Library
St George's Bay House, Bay View Road, Port St Mary, Isle of Man
☎01624 834272   Fax 01624 835363
✉ ricktom@compuserve.com
www.rick-tomlinson.com

Contacts *Rick Tomlinson*

Established 1985. Specialises in marine subjects. 100,000 35mm transparencies of yachting, racing, cruising, Whitbread Round the World Race, Volvo Ocean Race, Americas Cup, Tall Ships, RNLI Lifeboats, Antarctica, wildlife and locations.

TopFoto
PO Box 33, Edenbridge TN8 5PB
☎01732 863939   Fax 01732 860215
✉ admin@topfoto.co.uk
www.topfoto.co.uk

Contact *Alan Smith*

International editorial distributor with over one million pictures available online to download and 12 million in hard copy, representing 40 leading suppliers.

B.M. Totterdell photography
Constable Cottage, Burlings Lane, Knockholt
TN14 7PE
☎01959 532001   Fax 01959 532001
✉ btrial@btinternet.com

Contact *Barbara Totterdell*

Specialist volleyball library covering all aspects of the sport.

Tessa Traeger Picture Library
7 Rossetti Studios, 72 Flood Street, London
SW3 5TF
☎020 7352 3641   Fax 020 7352 4846
✉ info@tessatraeger.com
www.tessatraeger.com

Food, gardens, travel and artists.

Travel Ink Photo & Feature Library

The Old Coach House, 14 High Street, Goring on Thames, Nr Reading RG8 9AR
☎01491 873011   Fax 01491 875558
✉ info@travel-ink.co.uk
www.travel-ink.co.uk

Contact *Amanda Greenwood*

A collection of over 120,000 travel, tourism and lifestyle images, carefully edited and constantly updated, from countries worldwide. SPECIALIST COLLECTIONS from the UK, Greece, France, Hong Kong, Far East, Canada, USA and Caribbean. The website offers a fully captioned and searchable selection of over 20,000 images and is ideal for picture researchers.

Peter Trenchard's Image Store Ltd

The Studio, West Hill, St Helier, Jersey JE2 3HB
☎01534 769933   Fax 01534 789191
✉ peter-trenchard@jerseymail.co.uk
www.peter-trenchard.com

Contact *Peter Trenchard, FBIPP, AMPA, PPA*

Slide library of the Channel Islands – mainly tourist and financial-related. Commissions undertaken.

Tropix Photo Library

44 Woodbines Avenue, Kingston upon Thames KT1 2AY
☎020 8546 0823/0151 625 4576
Fax 0870 706 1317
✉ images@tropix.co.uk
www.tropix.co.uk

Contact *Veronica Birley*

Specialises in images of developing nations: travel and editorial pictures emphasising the attractive and progressive, not just the problems. Evocative photos concerning the economies, environment, culture and society of 100+ countries across Africa, Central and South America, Caribbean, Eastern Europe, Middle East, Indian sub-continent, South East Asia, CIS and Far East; also Antarctica. Also incorporating **MerseySlides Collection** (see entry). Assignment photography available worldwide. All photos supplied with detailed captions. Rapid response with one-hour digital delivery available. Established 1982. **BAPLA** member.

True North Picture Source

26 New Road, Hebden Bridge HX7 8EF
☎01422 845532
✉ john@trunorth.demon.co.uk

Contact *John Morrison*

30,000 transparencies on 35mm and 6×4.5cm format on the life and landscape of the north of England, photographed by John Morrison.

Ulster Museum Picture Library

Botanic Gardens, Belfast BT9 5AB
☎028 9038 3000 ext 3113
Fax 028 9038 3103
✉ patricia.mclean.um@nics.gov.uk
www.ulstermuseum.org.uk

Contact *Mrs Pat McLean*

SPECIALIST SUBJECTS art (fine and decorative, late 17th–20th century), particularly Irish art, archaeology, ethnography, treasures from the Armada shipwrecks, geology, botany, zoology, local history and industrial archaeology. Commissions welcome for objects not already photographed.

United Nations Environment Programme (UNEP)

See **Still Pictures' Whole Earth Photolibrary**

Universal Pictorial Press & Agency Ltd

29–31 Saffron Hill, London EC1N 8SW
☎020 7421 6000
✉ contact@uppa.co.uk
www.uppa.co.uk

News Editor *Peter Dare*

Photo archive dates back to 1944 and contains approximately four million pictures. Colour and b&w coverage of news, royalty, politics, sport, arts, and many other subjects. Commissions undertaken for press and public relations. Fully interactive digital photo archive accessible via ISDN or modem. Full digital scanning, retouching and transmission facilities.

UPI

See **Popperfoto.com**

V&A Images

Victoria and Albert Museum, Cromwell Road, South Kensington, London SW7 2RL
☎020 7942 2966   Fax 020 7942 2482
✉ vanda.images@vam.ac.uk
www.vandaimages.com

A vast collection of photographs from the world's largest museum of decorative and applied arts, reflecting culture and lifestyle spanning over 1000 years of history to the present time. Digital delivery of large format transparencies of contemporary and historical textiles, costumes and fashions, ceramics, furniture, metalwork, glass, sculpture, toys, and games, design and photographs from around the world. Unique photographs include 1960s fashion by John French, Harry Hammond's behind the scenes pop idols, Houston Rogers theatrical world of the 1930s to 1970s, images of royalty by Lafayette, Cecil Beaton, and the 19th century pioneer photographers. Images from the National Art Library and Library of Art & Design, and from the Theatre Museum and Museum of Childhood are readily available.

Valley Green

Barn Ley, Valley Lane, Buxhall, Stowmarket IP14 3EB
☎01449 736090   Fax 01449 736090
✉ pics@valleygreen.co.uk

Contacts *Joseph Barrere, Colette Barrere*

'Profusion of perennials – all correctly labelled.' Over 10,000 hardy plant transparencies in stock, plus watercolours and line drawings available. Commissions undertaken as well as creative copywriting.

Victory Archive

See **Popperfoto.com**

Vin Mag Archive Ltd

84–90 Digby Road, London E9 6HX
☎020 8533 7588   Fax 020 8533 7283
✉ piclib@vinmag.com
www.vinmagarchive.com

Formerly the Vintage Magazine Company. A collection of half a million movie, TV, celebrity and sports images available online. Contact Angela for code and password.

John Walmsley Photo Library

See **Education Photos**

Warwickshire Photographic Survey

See **Birmingham Library Services** under *Library Services*

Waterways Photo Library

39 Manor Court Road, Hanwell, London W7 3EJ
☎020 8840 1659   Fax 020 8567 0605
✉ watphot39@aol.com
www.waterwaysphotolibrary.com

Contact *Derek Pratt*

A specialist photo library on all aspects of Britain's inland waterways. Top-quality 35mm and medium-format colour transparencies, plus a large collection of b&w. Rivers and canals, bridges, locks, aqueducts, tunnels and waterside

buildings. Town and countryside scenes, canal art, waterway holidays, boating, fishing, windmills, watermills, watersports and wildlife.

Philip Way Photography

2 Green Moor Link, Winchmore Hill, London N21 2ND
☎020 8360 3034
✉ pwphotography1@btinternet.com

Contact *Philip Way*

Over 10,000 images of St Paul's Cathedral: historical exteriors, interiors and events (1686–2004).

Weimar Archive

See **Mary Evans Picture Library**

The Wellcome Trust Medical Photographic Library

210 Euston Road, London NW1 2BE
☎020 7611 8348   Fax 020 7611 8577
✉ medphoto@wellcome.ac.uk
medphoto.wellcome.ac.uk

Contact *Clive Coward*

Approximately 180,000 images on the history of medicine and human culture worldwide, including religion, astronomy, botany, genetics, landscape and cell biology.

Eric Whitehead Photography

25 Oak Street, Windermere LA23 1EN
☎015394 48894
✉ snooker@snookerimages.co.uk
www.snookerimages.co.uk

The agency covers local news events, PR and commercial material, also leading library of snooker images (see **Snookerimages**).

Wild Images

See **RSPCA Photolibrary**

Wild Places Photography

See **Chris Howes**

David Williams Picture Library

50 Burlington Avenue, Glasgow G12 0LH
☎0141 339 7823   Fax 0141 337 3031
✉ david@scotland-guide.co.uk

Specialises in travel photography with wide coverage of Scotland, Iceland and Spain. Many other European countries also included plus smaller collections of Western USA and Canada. The main subjects in each country are: cities, towns, villages, 'tourist haunts', buildings of architectural or historical interest, landscapes and natural features. The Scotland and Iceland collections include many pictures depicting physical geography and geology. Photographic commissions and illustrated travel articles undertaken. Catalogue available.

The Neil Williams Classical Collection

22 Avon, Hockley, Tamworth B77 5QA
☎01827 286086   Fax 01827 286086
✉ neil@classicalcollection.co.uk
Contact *Neil Williams, PGDip(Mus), BA(Hons)Hum*

Archive specialising in classical music ephemera, particularly portraits of composers, musicians, conductors and opera singers, comprising of old and sometimes very rare photographs, postcards, antique prints, cigarette cards, stamps, First Day Covers, concert programmes, Victorian newspapers, etc. Also modern photos of composer references such as museums, statues, busts, paintings, monuments, memorials, graves. Other subjects include ballet, musical instruments, concert halls, opera houses, 'music in art', manuscripts, opera scenes, music-caricatures, bands, orchestras and other music groups. Also writer of concert programme notes and CD inserts for classical music, as well as being a commissionable composer.

Vaughan Williams Memorial Library

English Folk Dance and Song Society, Cecil Sharp House, 2 Regent's Park Road, London NW1 7AY
☎020 7485 2206 ext. 18/19
Fax 020 7284 0523
✉ library@efdss.org
www.efdss.org

Mainly b&w coverage of traditional/folk music, dance and customs worldwide, focusing on Britain and other English-speaking nations. Photographs date from the late 19th century to the present day.

The Wilson Photographic Collection

See **Dundee Central Library** under **Library Services**

Windrush Photos, Wildlife Agency

99 Noah's Ark, Kemsing, Sevenoaks TN15 6PD
☎01732 763486   Fax 01732 763285
✉ dt@windrushphotos.demon.co.uk
www.windrushphotos.com
Contact *David Tipling*

Specialists in birds (worldwide) and British wildlife. Photographic and features commissions are regularly undertaken for publications in the UK and overseas. The agency acts as ornithological consultants for all aspects of the media. **BAPLA** member.

Woodfall Wild Images

17 Bull Lane, Denbigh LL16 3SN
☎01745 815903   Fax 01745 814581
✉ wwimages@woodfall.com
www.woodfall.com
Contacts *David Woodfall*

A comprehensive and specialist collection of wildlife, landscape and environmental photographs from both the UK and the rest of the world. Award winning photography by the world's more imaginative photographers. All formats, 35mm to panoramic. 'Personal and friendly service.' Subjects include: birds, animals, insects and marine life, trees and forests, wildflowers, all habitats worldwide and canals. Environmental issues such as pollution, conservation and habitat destruction, the weather and climate, landscapes and scenics. Suitable for advertising, editorial, calendars and design purposes.

World Pictures

43–44 Berners Street, London W1T 3ND
☎020 7580 1845/7436 0440
Fax 020 7580 4146
✉ worldpictures@btinternet.com
www.worldpictures.co.uk
Contact *David Brenes*

600,000 colour transparencies of travel and emotive material.

Yemen Pictures

28 Sheen Common Drive, Richmond TW10 5BN
☎020 7602 1989   Fax 020 7602 1989
www.facesandplaces.pix.com

Large collection (4000 transparencies) covering all aspects of Yemen – culture, people, architecture, dance, qat, music. Also Africa, Australia, Middle East, and Asia.

York Archaeological Trust Picture Library

Cromwell House, 13 Ogleforth, York YO1 7FG
☎01904 663051   Fax 01904 663024
✉ ckyriacou@yorkarchaeology.co.uk
www.yorkarchaeology.co.uk

Specialist library of rediscovered artifacts, historic buildings and excavations, presented by the creators of the highly acclaimed Jorvik Viking Centre. The main emphasis is on the Roman, Anglo-Saxon and Viking periods.

The John Robert Young Collection
61 De Montfort Road, Lewes BN7 1SS
☎01273 475216   Fax 01273 475216

✉ johnrobert@pxvobiscum.fsnet.co.uk

Contact *Jennifer Barrett*

50,000 transparencies and monochrome prints on religion, travel and military subjects. Major portfolios: religious communities; the French Foreign Legion; the Spanish Legion; the Royal Marines; the People's Liberation Army (China).

Settling Accounts

Ian Spring takes an expert look at the latest Budget
and explains how writers can be tax wise

'No man in the country is under the smallest obligation, moral or other, to arrange his affairs as to enable the Inland Revenue to put the largest possible shovel in his stores.

The Inland Revenue is not slow, and quite rightly, to take every advantage which is open to it ... for the purpose of depleting the taxpayer's pockets. And the taxpayer is, in like manner, entitled to be astute to prevent as far as he honestly can the depletion of his means by the Inland Revenue.'
Lord Clyde, Ayrshire Pullman v Inland Revenue Commissioners, 1929

Income Tax

What is a professional writer for tax purposes?

Writers are professionals while they are writing regularly with the intention of making a profit; or while they are gathering material, researching or otherwise preparing a publication.

A professional freelance writer is taxed under section 5 Income Tax (Trading and Other Income) Act 2005. The taxable income is the amount receivable, either directly or by an agent, on his behalf, less expenses wholly and exclusively laid out for the purpose of the profession. If expenses exceed income, the loss can either be set against other income of the same or preceding years or carried forward and set against future income from writing. If tax has been paid on that other income, a repayment can be obtained, or the sum can be offset against other tax liabilities. Special loss relief can apply in the opening years of the profession. Losses made in the first four years can be set against income of up to three earlier years.

Where a writer receives very occasional payments for isolated articles, it may not be possible to establish that these are profits arising from carrying on a continuing profession. In such circumstances these 'isolated transactions' may be assessed under section 687 Income Tax (Trading and Other Income) Act 2005. Again, expenses may be deducted in arriving at the taxable income but, if expenses exceed income, the loss can only be set against the profits from future isolated transactions, or other income assessable under section 687.

In the tax year 1996/97 a new tax system came into effect called Self Assessment. Under Self Assessment the onus is on the individual to declare income and expenses correctly. Each writer therefore has to decide whether profits arise from a professional or occasional activity. The consequences of getting it wrong can be expensive by way of interest, penalties and surcharges on additional tax subsequently found to be due. If in any doubt the writer should seek professional advice.

Income

A writer's income includes fees, advances, royalties, commissions, sale of copyrights, reimbursed expenses, etc., from any source anywhere in the world whether or not brought to the UK (non UK resident or domiciled writers should seek professional advice).

Agents

It should be borne in mind that the agent stands in the shoes of the principal. It is not always realised that when the agent receives royalties, fees, advances, etc. on behalf of the author those receipts became the property of the author on the date of their receipt by the agent. This applies for Income Tax and Value Added Tax purposes.

Expenses

A writer can normally claim the following expenses:

(a) Secretarial, typing, proof-reading, research. Where payment for these is made to the author's wife or husband they should be recorded and entered in the spouse's tax return as earned income which is subject to the usual personal allowances. If payments reach relevant levels, PAYE should be operated.

(b) Telephone, faxes, Internet costs, computer software, postage, stationery, printing, equipment maintenance, insurance, dictation tapes, batteries, any equipment or office requisites used for the profession.

(c) Periodicals, books (including presentation copies and reference books) and other publications necessary for the profession, but amounts received from the sale of books should be deducted.

(d) Hotels, fares, car running expenses (including repairs, petrol, oil, garaging, parking, cleaning, insurance, road fund tax, depreciation), hire of cars or taxis in connection with:

(i) business discussions with agents, publishers, co-authors, collaborators, researchers, illustrators, etc.

(ii) travel at home and abroad to collect background material.

As an alternative to keeping details of full car running costs, a mileage rate can be claimed for business use. This rate depends on the engine size and varies from year to year. This is known as the Fixed Profit Car Scheme and is available to writers whose turnover does not exceed the VAT registration limit, currently £60,000.

(e) Publishing and advertising expenses, including costs of proof corrections, indexing, photographs, etc.

(f) Subscriptions to societies and associations, press cutting agencies, libraries, etc., incurred wholly for the purpose of the profession.

(g) Rent, council tax and water rates, etc., the proportion being determined by the ratio of the number of rooms used exclusively for the profession, to the total number of rooms in the residence. But see note on Capital Gains Tax below.

(h) Lighting, heating and cleaning. A carefully calculated figure of the business use of these costs can be claimed as a proportion of the total.

(i) Agent's commission, accountancy charges and legal charges incurred wholly in the course of the profession including cost of defending libel actions, damages in so far as they are not covered by insurance, and libel insurance premiums. However, where in a libel case damages are awarded to punish the author for having acted maliciously the action becomes quasi-criminal and costs and damages may not be allowed.

(j) TV and video rental (which may be apportioned for private use), and cinema or theatre tickets, if wholly for the purpose of the profession.

(k) Capital allowances:

(i) On motor cars the allowance is 25% in the first year and 25% of the reducing balance in each successive year limited to £3000 each year.

(ii) For all other business equipment, e.g. TV, radio, hi-fi sets, tape and video recorders, Dictaphones, office furniture, photographic equipment, etc. there was a First Year Allowance of 40% until 31 March 2004. For small businesses (which most authors will be), for two years from 1 April 2004 the First Year Allowance is increased to 50%. After the first year there is an annual Writing Down Allowance of 25% of the reducing balance.

The allowances for both categories mentioned above will be reduced to exclude personal (non-professional) use where necessary.

(l) Lease rent. The cost of lease rent of equipment is allowable; also on cars, subject to restrictions for private use, and for expensive cars.

(m) Other expenses incurred wholly and exclusively for professional purposes. (Entertaining expenses are not allowable in any circumstances.)

NB It essential to keep detailed records. Diary entries of appointments, notes of fares and receipted bills are much more convincing to the Inland Revenue who are very reluctant to accept estimates.

The Self Assessment regime makes it a legal requirement for proper accounting records to be kept. These records must be sufficient to support the figures declared in the tax return.

In addition to the above, tax relief is available on:

(a) Premiums to pension schemes such as the Society of Authors Retirement Benefits Scheme. Depending on age, up to 40% of net earned income can be paid into a personal pension plan. New rules for allowing pension premiums come into effect on 6th April 2006. Anyone one with an existing pension scheme would be well advised to have their arrangements reviewed before that date to see if they need take any action.

(b) Gift Aid payments to charities. Any amount.

Capital Gains Tax

The exemption from Capital Gains Tax which applies to an individual's main residence does not apply to any part of that residence which is used exclusively for business purposes. The appropriate proportion of any increase in value of the residence, since purchase or 31 March 1982 if later, can be taxed when the residence is sold, subject to adjustment for inflation to March 1998 and subsequent length of ownership, at the individual's highest rate of tax.

Writers who own their houses should bear this in mind before claiming expenses for the use of a room for writing purposes. Arguments in favour of making such claims are that they afford some relief now, while Capital Gains Tax in its present form may not stay for ever. Also, where a new house is bought in place of an old one, the gain made on the sale of the first study may be set off against the cost of the study in the new house, thus postponing the tax payment until the final sale. For this relief to apply, each house must have a study and the author must continue his profession throughout. On death there is an exemption of the total Capital Gains of the estate.

Alternatively, writers can claim that their use is non-exclusive and restrict their claim to the cost of extra lighting, heating and cleaning to avoid any Capital Gains Tax liability.

Can a writer average out his income
over a number of years for tax purposes?

The Budget in March 2001 introduced measures which will enable writers to average their profits (made wholly or mainly from creative works) over two or more consecutive years. If the profits of the lower year are less than 70% of the profits of the higher year or the profits of one year (but not both) are nil, the author will be able to claim to have the profits averaged. Where the profits of the lower year are more than 70% but less than 75% of the profits of the higher year a pro-rata adjustment is made to both years to reduce the difference between them.

The first years that can be averaged are 2000/1 and 2001/2.

It is also possible to average out income within the terms of publishers' contracts, but professional advice should be taken before signature. Where a husband and wife collaborate as writers, advice should be taken as to whether a formal partnership agreement should be made or whether the publishing agreement should be in joint names.

Is a lump sum paid for an outright sale of the
copyright or part of the copyright exempt from tax?

No. All the money received from the marketing of literary work, by whatever means, is taxable. Some writers, in spite of clear judicial decisions to the contrary, still seem to think that an outright sale of, for instance, the film rights in a book is not subject to tax. The averaging relief described above should be considered.

Remaindering
To avoid remaindering authors can usually purchase copies of their own books from the publishers. Monies received from sales are subject to income tax but the cost of books sold should be deducted because tax is only payable on the profit made.

Is there any relief where old copyrights are sold?
No. There was relief available until April 2001 but was then withdrawn. The averaging relief described above should be considered.

Are royalties payable on publication of a book abroad subject to both foreign tax as well as UK tax?
Where there is a Double Taxation Agreement between the country concerned and the UK, then on the completion of certain formalities no tax is deductible at source by the foreign payer, but such income is taxable in the UK in the ordinary way. When there is no Double Taxation Agreement, credit will be given against UK tax for overseas tax paid. A complete list of countries with which the UK has conventions for the avoidance of double taxation may be obtained from The Centre for Non-Residents, Inland Revenue, St John's House, Merton Road, Bootle, Merseyside L69 9BB, or a local tax office.

Residence abroad
Writers residing abroad will, of course, be subject to the tax laws ruling in their country of residence, and as a general rule royalty income paid from the United Kingdom can be exempted from deduction of UK tax at source, providing the author is carrying on his profession abroad. A writer who is intending to go and live abroad should make early application for future royalties to be paid without deduction of tax to The Centre for Non-Residents, address as above. In certain circumstances writers resident in the Irish Republic are exempt from Irish Income Tax on their authorship earnings.

Are grants or prizes taxable?
The law is uncertain. Some Arts Council grants are now deemed to be taxable, whereas most prizes and awards are not, though it depends on the conditions in each case. When submitting the Self Assessment annual returns, such items should be excluded, but reference made to them in the 'Additional Information' box on the self-employment (or partnership) pages.

What is the item 'Class 4 N.I.C.' which appears on my Self Assessment return?
All taxpayers who are self-employed pay an additional national insurance contribution if their earned income exceeds a figure which varies each year. This contri-

bution is described as Class 4 and is calculated when preparing the return. It is additional to the self-employed Class 2 contribution but confers no additional benefits and is a form of levy. It applies to men aged under 65 and women under 60.

Should an author use a limited company?

Changes in the tax regime have made the incorporation of businesses more and more attractive and there are advantages in so doing for businesses with relatively low levels of profit although these advantages were reduced in the 2004 Budget. However, there are disadvantages in all cases and particular considerations for authors. The advice of an accountant, knowledgeable about the affairs of authors, should be sought if incorporation is contemplated.

Value Added Tax

Value Added Tax (VAT) is a tax currently levied at 17.5% on:

(a) the total value of taxable goods and services supplied to consumers,
(b) the importation of goods into the UK,
(c) certain services or goods from abroad if a taxable person receives them in the UK for the purpose of their business.

Who is taxable?

A writer resident in the UK whose turnover from writing and any other business, craft or art on a self-employed basis is greater than £60,000 annually, before deducting agent's commission, must register with HM Revenue & Customs as a taxable person. Turnover includes fees, royalties, advances, commissions, sale of copyright, reimbursed expenses, etc. A business is required to register:

- at the end of any month if the value of taxable supplies in the past twelve months has exceeded the annual threshold; or
- if there are reasonable grounds for believing that the value of taxable supplies in the next twelve months will exceed the annual threshold.

Penalties will be claimed in the case of late registration. A writer whose turnover is below these limits is exempt from the requirements to register for VAT but may apply for voluntary registration and this will be allowed at the discretion of HM Revenue & Customs.

A taxable person collects VAT on outputs (turnover) and deducts VAT paid on inputs (taxable expenses) and where VAT collected exceeds VAT paid, must remit the difference to HM Revenue & Customs. In the event that input exceeds output, the difference will be refunded by HM Revenue & Customs.

Outputs (Turnover)

A writer's outputs are taxable services supplied to publishers, broadcasting organisations, theatre managements, film companies, educational institutions, etc. A tax-

Inputs (Expenses)

Taxable at the standard rate if supplier is registered	Taxable at the zero or special rate	Not liable to VAT
Rent of certain commercial premises	Books (zero)	Rent of non-commercial premises
Advertisements in newspapers, magazines, journals and periodicals	Coach, rail and air travel (zero)	Postage
Agent's commission (unless it relates to monies from overseas)	Agent's commission (on monies from overseas)	Services supplied by unregistered persons
Accountant's and solicitor's fees for business matters	Domestic gas and electricity (5%)	Subscriptions to the Society of Authors, PEN, NUJ, etc.
Agency services (typing, copying, etc.)		Insurance
Word processors, type-writers and stationery		
Artists' materials		
Photographic equipment		
Tape recorders and tapes		
Hotel accommodation		Outside the scope of VAT
Taxi fares		
Motorcar expenses		PLR (Public Lending Right)
Telephone		Profit shares
Theatres and concerts		Investment income
NB This list is not exhaustive		

able writer must invoice, i.e. collect from, all the persons (either individuals or organisations) in the UK for whom supplies have been made, for fees, royalties or other considerations plus VAT. An unregistered writer cannot and must not invoice for VAT. A taxable writer is not obliged to collect VAT on royalties or other fees paid by publishers or others overseas. In practice, agents usually collect VAT for the registered author.

Remit to Customs
The taxable writer adds up the VAT which has been paid on taxable inputs, deducts it from the VAT received and remits the balance to Customs. Business with HM Customs is conducted through the local VAT offices of HM Revenue & Customs which are listed in local telephone directories, except for VAT returns which are sent direct to the HM Revenue & Customs, VAT Central Unit, Alexander House, 21 Victoria Avenue, Southend on Sea, Essex SS99 1AA.

Accounting

A taxable writer is obliged to account to HM Revenue & Customs at quarterly intervals. Returns must be completed and sent to VAT Central Unit by the dates shown on the return. Penalties can be charged if the returns are late.

It is possible to account for the VAT liability under the Cash Accounting Scheme (leaflet 731), whereby the author accounts for the output tax when the invoice is paid or royalties, etc., are received. The same applies to the input tax, but as most purchases are probably on a 'cash basis', this will not make a considerable difference to the author's input tax. This scheme is only applicable to those with a taxable turnover of less than £660,000 and, therefore, is available to the majority of authors. The advantage of this scheme is that the author does not have to account for VAT before receiving payments, thereby relieving the author of a cash flow problem.

If turnover is less than £660,000 it is also possible to pay VAT by nine estimated direct debits, with a final balance at the end of the year (see leaflet 732). This annual accounting method also means that only one VAT return is submitted.

Flat Rate Scheme

Small businesses can elect to pay VAT under a flat rate scheme (FRS). This is open to businesses with business income up to £150,000 a year (this figure may be subject to change in the second 2005 Finance Act. Under the normal VAT accounting rules, each item of turnover and every claimed expense must be recorded and supported by evidence, e.g. invoices, receipts, etc. Under the FRS, detailed records of sales and purchases do not have to be kept. A record of gross income (including zero rated and exempt income) is maintained and a flat rate percentage is applied to the total. This percentage is then paid over to HM Revenue & Customs. The percentage varies from one profession or business to another but for authors is 11%. In the first year of registration this percentage is reduced by 1%.

The aim of the scheme is to reduce the amount of time and money spent in complying with VAT regulations and this is to be welcomed. However, there are disadvantages:

- The detailed records of income and expenses are still going to be required for taxation purposes.
- Invoices on sales are issued in the normal way.
- The percentage is applied to all business income. So 11% VAT will effectively be paid on income from abroad, zero rated under the normal basis, and PLR, otherwise exempt.

For many authors, normal VAT accounting has imposed a good, timely discipline for dealing with accounting and taxation matters.

Registration

A writer will be given a VAT registration number which must be quoted on all VAT correspondence. It is the responsibility of those registered to inform those to whom they make supplies of their registration number. The taxable turnover limit which determines whether a person who is registered for VAT may apply for cancellation of registration is £58,000.

Voluntary registration

A writer whose turnover is below the limits may apply to register. If the writer is paying a relatively large amount of VAT on taxable inputs – agent's commission, accountant's fees, equipment, materials, or agency services, etc. – it may make a significant improvement in the net income to be able to offset the VAT on these inputs. A writer who pays relatively little VAT may find it easier, and no more expensive, to remain unregistered.

Fees and royalties

A taxable writer must notify those to whom he makes supplies of the VAT Registration Number at the first opportunity. One method of accounting for and paying VAT on fees and royalties is the use of multiple stationery for 'self-billing', one copy of the royalty statement being used by the author as the VAT invoice. A second method is for the recipient of taxable outputs to pay fees, including authors' royalties, without VAT. The taxable writer then renders a tax invoice for the VAT element and a second payment, of the VAT element, will be made. This scheme is cumbersome but will involve only taxable authors. Fees and royalties from abroad will count as payments for exported services and will accordingly be zero-rated.

Agents and accountants

A writer is responsible to HM Revenue & Customs for making VAT returns and payments. Neither an agent nor an accountant nor a solicitor can remove the responsibility, although they can be helpful in preparing and keeping VAT returns and accounts. Their professional fees or commission will, except in rare cases where the adviser or agent is himself unregistered, be taxable at the standard rate and will represent some of a writer's taxable inputs.

Income Tax

An unregistered writer can claim some of the VAT paid on taxable inputs as a business expense allowable against income tax. However, certain taxable inputs fall into categories which cannot be claimed under the income tax regulations. A taxable writer, who has already claimed VAT on inputs, cannot charge it as a business expense for the purposes of income tax.

Certain services from abroad

A taxable author who resides in the United Kingdom and who receives certain services from abroad must account for VAT on those services at the appropriate tax rate on the sum paid for them. Examples of the type of services concerned include: services of lawyers, accountants, consultants, provision of information and copyright permissions.

Inheritance Tax

Inheritance Tax was introduced in 1984 to replace Capital Transfer Tax, which had in turn replaced Estate Duty, the first of the death taxes of recent times. Paradoxically, Inheritance Tax has reintroduced a number of principles present under the old Estate Duty.

The general principle now is that all assets owned at death are chargeable to tax (currently 40%) except the first £275,000 of the estate and any assets passed to a surviving spouse or a charity. Gifts made more than seven years before death are exempt, but those made within this period may be taxed on a sliding scale. No tax is payable at the time of making the gift.

In addition, each individual may currently make gifts of up to £3000 in any year and these will be considered to be exempt. A further exemption covers any number of annual gifts not exceeding £250 to any one person.

If the £3000 is not fully utilised in one year, any unused balance can be carried forward to the following year (but no later). Gifts out of income, which do not reduce one's living standards, are also exempt if they are part of normal expenditure.

At death all assets are valued; they will include any property, investments, life policies, furniture and personal possessions, bank balances and, in the case of authors, the value of copyrights. All, with the sole exception of copyrights, are capable (as assets) of accurate valuation and, if necessary, can be turned into cash. The valuation of copyright is, of course, complicated and frequently gives rise to difficulty. Except where they are bequeathed to the owner's husband or wife, very real problems can be left behind by the author.

Experience has shown that a figure based on two to three years' past royalties may be proposed by the Inland Revenue in their valuation of copyright. However, this may not be reasonable and may require negotiation. If a book is running out of print or if, as in the case of educational books, it may need re-vision at the next reprint, these factors must be taken into account. In many cases the fact that the author is no longer alive and able to make personal appearances, or provide publicity, or write further works, will result in lower or slower sales. Obviously, this is an area in which help can be given by the publishers, and in particular one needs to know what their future intentions are, what stocks of the books remain, and what likelihood there will be of reprinting.

There is a further relief available to authors who have established that they have been carrying on a business, normally assessable under Case II of Schedule D, for at least two years prior to death. It has been possible to establish that copy-rights are treated as business property and in these circumstances, Inheritance Tax 'business property relief' is available. This relief at present is 100% so that the tax saving can be quite substantial. The Inland Revenue may wish to be assured that the business is continuing and consideration should therefore be given to the appointment, in the author's will, of a literary executor who should be a quali-fied business person or, in certain circumstances, the formation of partnership between the author and spouse, or other relative, to ensure that it is established the business is continuing after the author's death.

If the author has sufficient income, consideration should be given to building up a fund to cover future Inheritance Tax liabilities. One of a number of ways would be to take out a whole life assurance policy which is assigned to the children, or other beneficiaries, the premiums on which are within the annual exemption of £3000. The capital sum payable on the death of the assured is exempt from inheritance tax.

Tax credits

Working authors may also be eligible to claim Child Tax Credit and Working Tax Credit.

Child tax credit is the main way that families receive money for their younger children and for 16–18 year olds in education. A claim is based on your income and you can claim whether or not you are working. All families (with children) with an income up to £58,000 a year (or up to £66,000 a year if your child is under one year old) can claim. To qualify, you must be aged 16 or over, usually live in the UK and if single, (or separated) claim based on your individual circumstances. If you are married or a man and woman living together (or a same sex couple from December 2005) you must claim together based on joint circumstances and income.

Working tax credit is a payment to top up earnings of the lower paid (whether employed or self employed including those who do not have children). To qualify, you must be aged 16 or over and you or your partner responsible for a child and you must work at least 16 hours a week. If you are part of a couple with children, greater amounts may be claimed if you jointly work at least 30 hours a week provided one of you works for at least 16 hours. Childless couples cannot add their hours together to qualify for the 30 hour element. If you do not have children and you do not have a disability, you must be aged 25 or over and work at least 30 hours a week. It is also possible that your working tax credit will be increased to assist with the cost of registered or approved childcare

Anyone wondering how best to order his affairs for tax purposes should consult an accountant with specialised knowledge in this field. Experience shows that a good accountant is well worth his fee which, incidentally, so far as it relates to professional matters, is an allowable expense.

The information contained in this section has been prepared by Ian Spring of Moore Stephens, Chartered Accountants, who will be pleased to answer questions on tax problems. Please write to Ian Spring, c/o The Writer's Handbook, 34 Ufton Road, London N1 5BX.

Company Index

Subject Index